The Eleanor Roosevelt Papers: Vol. I
The Human Rights Years,
1945–1948

The Eleanor Roosevelt Papers: Vol. I
The Human Rights Years,
1945–1948

Allida Black, *Editor*
John F. Sears and Mary Jo Binker, *Associate Editors*
Craig Daigle and Michael Weeks, *Assistant Editors*
Christopher Alhambra, *Electronic Editor*

with

Christopher Brick, Kristen Gwinn, Bryan Peery, and Sarah Wilkes,
Editorial Fellows

The George Washington University
Washington, DC

CHARLES SCRIBNER'S SONS
An imprint of Thomson Gale, a part of The Thomson Corporation

THOMSON
GALE

Detroit • New York • San Francisco • New Haven, Conn. • Waterville, Maine • London

THOMSON
★
™
GALE

The Eleanor Roosevelt Papers, Vol. 1:
The Human Rights Years, 1945–1948
Allida M. Black, Editor

For permission to use material from this product, submit your request via Web at http://www.gale-edit.com/permissions, or you may download our Permissions Request form and submit your request by fax or mail to:

Permissions Department
Thomson Gale
27500 Drake Rd.
Farmington Hills, MI 48331-3535
Permissions Hotline:
248-699-8006 or 800-877-4253 ext. 8006
Fax: 248-699-8074 or 800-762-4058

Since this page cannot legibly accommodate all copyright notices, the credits constitute a extension of the copyright notice.

While every effort has been made to ensure the reliability of the information presented in this publication, Thomson Gale does not guarantee the accuracy of the date contained herein. Thomson Gale accepts no payment for listing; and inclusion in the publication of an organization, agency, institution, publication service, or individual does not imply endorsement of the editors or publisher. Errors brought to the attention of the publisher and verified to the satisfaction of the publisher will be corrected in future editions.

Cover photo © Bettmann/CORBIS

LIBRARY OF CONGRESS CATALOGING-IN-PUBLICATION DATA

Roosevelt, Eleanor, 1884-1962.
   [Selections. 2006]
   The Eleanor Roosevelt papers / Allida M. Black, editor in chief ; foreword by Hillary Rodham Clinton.
      Includes bibliographical references and index.
      Contents: p. 1. The human rights years, 1945-1948 --
      ISBN-13 978-0-684-31475-4 (v. 1 : alk. paper)
      ISBN-10 0-684-31475-4 (v. 1 : alk. paper)
      1. Roosevelt, Eleanor, 1884-1962--Archives. 2. Presidents' spouses--United States--Archives. 3. United States--Politics and government--1945-1953--Sources. 4. United States--Politics and government--1953-1961--Sources. 5. United States--Politics and government--1961-1963--Sources. I. Black, Allida M. (Allida Mae), 1952- II. Title.

   E807.1.R48A42 2006
   973.917--dc22

                                                                              2006020946

This title is also available as an e-book.
ISBN-13 978-0-684-31548-5, ISBN-10 0-684-31548-3
Contact your Thomson Gale representative for ordering information.
Printed in the United States of America

10 9 8 7 6 5 4 3 2 1

With respect, affection, and gratitude,

The Eleanor Roosevelt Papers dedicates this volume to:

Curtis Roosevelt

Maureen Corr

and

Beth Newburger Schwartz

Contents

1945: April–December

CONTENTS

CONTENTS

CONTENTS

CONTENTS

CONTENTS

1946: June–December

CONTENTS

CONTENTS

1947: January–June

CONTENTS

1947: July–December

CONTENTS

CONTENTS

CONTENTS

CONTENTS

1948: July–December

CONTENTS

CONTENTS

Acknowledgments

For the past six years, the Eleanor Roosevelt Papers Project benefited from a vast, dedicated, kind, and generous network of scholars, editors, teachers, students, human rights workers, citizen activists, elected officials, and foundations. United (and not a little awed) by the fierce commitment Eleanor Roosevelt displayed to the issues she championed, these disparate individuals shared their expertise, worked their Rolodexes, and opened their wallets to ensure that ER's voice would be preserved for the ages. Those who love ER, as well as those who use this edition, owe them heartfelt thanks and respect. The Eleanor Roosevelt Papers Project could not have produced this volume without them.

The Roosevelt family, especially Curtis Roosevelt, Anna Eleanor Roosevelt, Nancy Roosevelt Ireland, and Eleanor Roosevelt Seagraves, immediately embraced our proposal and not only helped secure financial support but waived all permission fees associated with the reprinting of ER's copyrighted work. Curtis and Anna opened their homes to us, shared documents with us, and offered invaluable insight into their life with ER.

The Franklin and Eleanor Roosevelt Institute, led by the indefatigable William J. vanden Heuvel, not only shared its office space with our editorial team when we often bivouacked at the Franklin D. Roosevelt Presidential Library and Museum, but also offered the essential financial support necessary to craft the proposal, conduct the initial document search, and shepherd the proposal through the National Historical Publications and Records Commission and the National Endowment for the Humanities.

Dr. Cynthia Koch, director of the Franklin D. Roosevelt Library and Museum, immediately embraced the project and made the library our most valued partner. Her expert archival staff, Karen Anson, Bob Parks, Virginia Lewick, and Mark Renovitch; their supervisors Bob Clark and Ray Teichman; curator Herman Eberhardt; and deputy director Lynn Bassanesse provided so much assistance (with unfailing good humor) that they all should be considered part of the ER Papers editorial team.

Claudine Bacher and Carol Hillman of Save America's Treasures Honoring Eleanor Roosevelt: Saving Val-Kill Cottage Project personify generosity and camaraderie. Our projects started at the same time and often approached the same donors. Yet rather than engage in a turf war for ER-related funds, their immediate response was to ask how they could help and to suggest ways that we could work collaboratively. Together, we built document-based education programs that took ER into primary and secondary classrooms and raised critical funds for one another's projects.

The George Washington University embraced the project, offered essential financial support, and folded it into the life of the university. The editor would particularly like to thank President Stephen Joel Trachtenberg, Vice President Don Lehman, and Associate Vice President Carol Segilman for the special interest they have taken in our work as well as history department chairs Ed Berkowitz, Muriel Atkin, and Tyler Anbinder; Columbia College of Arts and Sciences deans Lester Lefton, Jean Folkerts, William Frawley, Diana Lipscomb, and Nina Mikhalevsky Perry; and Helen Spencer, Mary Milbauer, Veronica Terrell, and Carol Crane of the Office of Sponsored Research. A particular thanks goes to vice-presidents Betsy Curtler and Gene Finn for the patience they displayed in teaching this historian the skills she needed to become the venture capitalist the project demanded.

We also benefited from the wise counsel of extraordinary documentary editors. Charlene Bickford and Helen Veit of the First Federal Congress Project, Roger Bruns and Michael Meier of the National Historical Publications and Records Commission (NHPRC), David Chesnutt of the Henry Laurens Papers, Candace Falk of the Emma Goldman Papers, Esther Katz and Cathy Moran Hajo of the Margaret Sanger Papers, Barbara Oberg of the Thomas Jefferson Papers, and Bob Rosenberg of the Thomas Edison Papers helped us craft the methods necessary to address the challenges ER and the Eleanor Roosevelt Papers Project posed to editorial form and convention. Sharon Stevens of the George Marshall Papers kindly combed the Marshall Archives for us to verify a damaged document. Judy Beck applied her encyclopedic knowledge of the *Chicago Manual of Style* in marathon proofreading sessions.

The editor would also like to thank Piers Brendon and Allen Packwood, the keepers of the Winston Churchill Papers, for their uncommon generosity during her visits to Churchill College, Cambridge.

Scholarship is by definition a solitary endeavor. However, James MacGregor Burns, Blanche Wiesen Cook, Susan Dunn, Mary Ann Glendon, William Leuchtenburg, Brigid O'Farrell, Leo Ribuffo, Arthur Schlesinger, Jr., Geoffrey Ward, and Susan Ware displayed such consistent support for our efforts that when the editorial team consulted their work, we often felt as though they were in the room with us as we interrogated the documents. Master teachers Paul Benson, Hank Bitten, Linda Bouchey, Dennis Dennenberg, Sally Gilbert, Kathy Schollenberger, Al Vinck, and Rick Walters showed us how to envision a volume that would introduce the work and world of ER to a whole new audience and generation, proving once again the indivisible link between scholarship and teaching.

Scribner's had never published a documentary edition when Karen Day asked Frank Menchaca to meet with the editor in the summer of 2003. Yet Menchaca believed in the project so much, he agreed to risk his standing within the Thomson Corporation to publish it even though the manuscript was still only an amorphous image in our minds. We are grateful for his commitment as well as the painstaking skill of his dedicated editorial staff: Carol Schwartz, Kristin Hart, Melissa McDade, John Fitzpatrick, and Jay Flynn.

We also thank Mea Rhee and Kathryn de Boer for designing the book. Breffni Whelan provided invaluable assistance as we assembled our index.

As the editorial team began collecting, accessioning, selecting, transcribing, and proofreading the material from which this volume emerged, we knew that we faced daily financial and staffing challenges. Never did we imagine, however, that we would be the beneficiary of the boundless dedication of undergraduate students, whose interest in the project and close relationships with the editorial staff not only inspired them to embrace historical methods but also to make the project their home base. Their commitment was total and the respect the editorial team has for them is immense. Not only did they become historians, they incorporated ER's vision and energy into their own world, often modeling their career choices on the actions and in the arenas the volume recounts.

Thus, the editorial team would like to recognize the contributions Charlotta Åsell, Brittany Baron, Tiffany Basdekis, Libby Blossom, Cristina Brooks, Paula Butera, Dan Buzzuto, Diana Caley, Camille Camacho, Jill Caruso, Caitlin Coast, Claire Connors, Stephanie Cooke, Jamie DeBottis, Wendy Doernberg, Rupal Doshi, Anna Dundulk, Stephanie Eisenman, Victoria Emanuelson, Kristyn Feldner, Julia Fletcher, Ericka Galegher, Erin Gamble, Tammy Gasan-Dzhalalova, Acquania Gibbs, James Gilbreath, Valkyrie Hanson, Jennifer Hebst, Scott Heerman, Gale Hemmann, Elizabeth Hill, Sophia Hong, Rebekah Hutman, Jenilee Keefe, Melissa Kimball, Adrienne Kohart, Soo Lee, Robert Lintott, Bianca Lott, Jessica Lynd, Nicholas Manzaris, David

Nolte, Andrew Novak, Tripti Oka, John Osterholt, Sarah Peacock, Beth Pellettieri, Jessica Poznick, Yeugeniya (Jane) Rabinovich, Alena Reisman, Sarah Robbins-Pennimun, Morgan Robinson, Robert Rogers, Glen Roscoe, Diana Sands, Naomi Schneidmill, Allison Schultz, Ben Schuman-Stoler, Izabella Shuvayev, Sunny Sims, Todd Spivak, Catie Stremlau, Jolan Turkington, Swathi Veeravalli, Krysta Vollbrecht, Megan Warther, Daphnie Watkins, Tiffani Wesley, Elizabeth Wilson, Jessica Wormwald, Catherine Wrisley, Liesl Yamaguchi, and Cecilia Zhou made to this volume.

When we began the project, the editorial team relied on doctoral students to work alongside us as protégés and colleagues. As we huddled in collaboration, the inquisitiveness and thoroughness of these young scholars made the editors better historians. The editorial team is indebted to them in ways that words cannot convey. Thus, we salute Margaret Bauman, Sara Berndt, Laura Blumenthal, Christopher Brick, John Emrich, Thomas Faith, Victoria Grieve, Eugenia Gusev, Kristen Gwinn, Katherine Kelly, Stacy Lowe, Bryan Peery, Jennifer Weck, and Sarah Wilkes for their research and writing skills, intellectual curiosity, patience, good humor, and dedication. If readers could see the number of email suggestions, questions, and edits this extraordinary team sent in the wee pre-dawn hours, they could get but a taste of the commitment these young historians brought to the project.

Securing funding necessary to produce documentary editions is challenging in the best of times. In a post–9/11 world it is daunting. The Eleanor Roosevelt Papers could not operate without the endorsement and support of the National Historical Publications and Records Commission (NHPRC), the National Endowment for the Humanities (NEH), and the Institute for Museum and Library Services (IMLS). The editorial team takes special pleasure in thanking Roger Bruns, Max Evans, Michael Meier, and Ann Newhall of the NHPRC; Elizabeth Arndt, Margot Backus, and Michael Hall of the NEH; and Allen Weinstein, Archivist of the United States, for their support and counsel.

Any views, findings, conclusions, or recommendations expressed in this volume do not necessarily represent those of the NEH, the NHPRC, or the IMLS.

As critical as this federal support is, however, the Eleanor Roosevelt Papers is increasingly dependent upon private funds for timely completion of its work. In particular, the editors would like to thank Agnes Varis of Agvar Chemicals, the American Express Foundation, the Gladys Kreible Delmas Foundation, Judith Hope and the Eleanor Roosevelt Conference Committee, Inc., the Franklin and Eleanor Roosevelt Institute, Carol Hillman and Claudine Bacher of Honoring Eleanor Roosevelt: Saving Her Val-Kill Home, the Horace Goldsmith Foundation, Peter Kovler and the Blum Kovler Foundation, Jack Rosenthal and the New York Times Company Foundation, Kristie Miller and the Ruth McCormick Tankersley Trust, and the 21st Century ILGWU Heritage Fund for their longstanding support.

We also offer our sincere appreciation to the following foundations and organizations: Capstone Research, Inc., the Fannie and Stephen Kahn Charitable Foundation, the General Electric Foundation, Guild of Professional Tour Guides of Washington, DC, the Hackensack High School Student Association, the Horace W. Goldsmith Foundation, the Daniel M. Neidich and Brooke G. Neidich Foundation, the David and Susan Bershad Foundation, the George J. and Theresa L. Cotsirilos Family Foundation, the If Hummingbird Foundation, the JKW Foundation, the Kovler Fund, the Louise Gartner Philanthropic Fund, the Melinda and William J. vanden Heuvel Foundation, Inc., the Model Editions Partnership, the National Park Foundation, the New York Community Trust–Pilot House Fund, the New York Community Trust–Wallace Reader's Digest Special Projects Fund, the Northern Virginia Hebrew Congregation, the Polio Society, Ramapo College of New Jersey, Ramapo Indian Hills Regional High School District, Ridgewood High School Association, the Ruth Jameson Trust, the Ruth McCormick Tankersley Charitable Trust, the Sam and Sooky Goldman Foundation, Second Thursday Networking Women, the Susan Bacher Fund, Teachers-Teachers.com, the L. J. and Mary C. Skaggs Foundation, the Waldwick Board of Education, Washington International School, the Western Carolina Women's Coalition,

ACKNOWLEDGMENTS

the William H. Donner Foundation, the Windom Fund, and the Women's National Democratic Club Educational Foundation.

The staff would like to thank the following persons whose individual contributions helped match the challenges our federal funders required:

Linda L. Aaker, Linda Koch Adelson, Adele Logan Alexander, Margo Alexander, Beth Arthur, Claudine Bacher, Martha Baker, Celia Goldwag Barenholtz, Cecile C. Bartman, Thomas Bartman (Norma Bartman Foundation), Maurine Hoffman Beasley, William H. Becker, Susan Beckerman, Patricia Bell-Scott, Denise Benmosche, Charlene Bickford, George E. Blancett, Margaret G. Bonner, Hyman Bookbinder, John Brademas, Christopher Breiseth, Mary Kim Brewster, Joan M. Brierton, Robert Brink, Carolyn Buck-Luce, Robert and Salli M. Buzzell, Jr., Angela Cabrera, George Casey, Katherine Cerullo, Mary P. Champenois, Forrest Church, K. G. Clarke, Ida Cole, Blanche Weisen Cook, Jean Marshall Crawford, Fred P. Crouch, The Revs. Frank Crumbaugh and Gretchen Zimmerman, Elizabeth Curtler, Milly Hawk Daniel, Karen Darner, Nancy Daunton, Paul De Morgan, Catherine J. Denial, Lucy Denney, Debra S. Elston, William R. Everdell, Elinor K. Farquhar, Justin Feldman, Ruth Jameson Fine, Gene Finn, Nancy M. Folger, Estelle B. Freedman, Allen B. Freeman, Catherine Freideman, Catherine Fuerst, Ahuva Genack, Robin M. Gerber, Joanne G. Gloege, Fredrica Goodman, Paul Greenberg, Roberta W. Greene, Catherine Gretta, Kompa Guide, Karoly S. Gutman, Cynthia Harrison, Margaret K. Hatton, Mary Lou Heissenbuttel, Vicki Heller, Sylvia Ann Hewlett, Carol B. Hillman, Judith Hope, Robert Hopkins, Margo Horner, Janet F. Imerman, Nancy Roosevelt Ireland, Jill Iscoe, Dr. Barbara Jackson, Christie Jacobs, Leslie Jacobson, Rosalie Jenkins, Carolyn W. Johnson, Herschel and Ruth Kanter, Erin Kaufman, Katherine Moser Kelly, Cynthia Koch, Peter Kovler, Liz Krueger, Janet Ruth Lambertz, Linda H. Lamel, Deborah E. Lans, Marsha Laufer, Judy Leon, Carol B. Levin, Ann F. Lewis, Janine Lindquist, Chandler Roosevelt Lindsley, Roberta Lisker, Renee M. Lohman, Carmen Lomellin, Peg Lorenz, and Joel K. Lovelace.

Roanne L. Mann, Mercedes M. Marquez, Linda G. Maryanov, Elizabeth Matheson, Edith P. Mayo, Edward McCord, Elizabeth McDaniel, Lissa K. McLean, Frank Menchaca, Michelle Mew, Sally A. S. Michael, Nina Mikhalevsky Perry, Kristie Miller, Shirley B. Miller, Sondra Miller, Carol Murray, Sondra Myers, Gaylord Neely, Beth W. Newburger, Joanne Woodward Newman, Kathleen G. Noonan, Michael O'Connor, Darlene Smith Osterholt, Ellen Overton, Christine Owens, Ruth Oyen, Rose S. Parish, James F. Passikoff, Susan and Alan Patricof, E. J. Pinuel, Mavis E. Presler, Susan Prokop, Brenda Rezah, Bonnie N. Risse, Maria Holleran Rivera, Anita and Larry Roberts, Anna Eleanor Roosevelt, Christopher duPont Roosevelt, Curtis Roosevelt, David A. Roosevelt, David B. Roosevelt, Eleanor Roosevelt, James Roosevelt, Laura D. Roosevelt, Mrs. Mary Roosevelt, Philippa B. Roosevelt, William D. Roosevelt, Franklin Roosevelt III, Elliott Roosevelt, Jr., Edith S. Sands, Mildred L. Savacool, Rita Saverino, Susan Scanlon, Frances Schenkkan, Betty Schlein, Stephen C. Schlesinger, Daniel Schorr, Richard Schwartz, Gary Thomas Scott, Eleanor R. Seagraves, Elayne Seaman, Sondra Seba, Marsha Seeman, Ruth E. Shinn, Laura Sillerman, Carol Esther Smith, Tom Spence, Brett Spodak and Amy Highstein, Brian Steffan, Jamie Stern, John J. Sweeney, Selma Sweetbaum, Frances Taft, Deborah F. Tannen, John G. Tarleton, Jannie G. Taylor, Dr. Julianne Thomas, Eugene F. Tighe, III, Judith Tuller, Jo S. Uehara, Ann Schwartz Unitas, Katrina vanden Heuvel, Susan W. Ware, Cecille Wasserman, Joy Watson, Robert P. Watson, Michael W. Weeks, Charles Weiss, Mary Margaret Whipple, Debbie Whitfill, Kate Roosevelt Whitney, Rivington R. Winant, Judy Summer Winick, Robert V. Witeck, Marc R. Wittlif, Joanne Witty, Lisa C. Wohl, Penelope Wolff, Michael Worch, and Carol Zaslow.

Clearly this volume is a collaborative endeavor. The depth and variety of these acknowledgments celebrate collegiality, scholarship, and financial support.

At the same time, we owe a particular debt to Senator Hillary Rodham Clinton, Ann F. Lewis, Congressman Jim Moran, Curtis Roosevelt, Maureen Corr, and Beth Newburger.

While First Lady, Hillary Rodham Clinton asked Ann Lewis and Beth Newburger to convene the President's Commission on Women in American History. Once the commission heard our proposal for a documentary edition of ER's papers, it gave us our first imprimatur, enabling us to raise the seed money necessary to begin the project. Mrs. Clinton's keen interest carried over into the Senate. Indeed, Senator Clinton's support has been so strong that one of the first decisions she made after entering the Senate was to chair our honorary advisory board. For five years, she has been our most steadfast supporter—tracking our progress, attending our fundraisers, publicizing our work, encouraging us when we succumbed to fatigue- and financed-induced despair, celebrating the discovery of new documents, and even agreeing immediately to write the foreword, despite a work schedule that rivals ER's. In the process, she became more than our chair, she became our friend and our senator.

Congressman Jim Moran defended the humanities during consecutive budget crises. A stalwart defender of the NHPRC and the NEH, he lent his strong voice to appropriations battles and supported our request to the IMLS.

Finally, this book is dedicated to Curtis Roosevelt, Maureen Corr, and Beth Newburger, each of whom in their own terse, honest, and honorable manner, give daily evidence of ER's courage, dignity, commitment, and compassion.

Foreword

I am pleased to participate in the publication of *The Eleanor Roosevelt Papers, Volume I: The Human Rights Years, 1945–1948*. I have been a strong supporter of this project, both as First Lady and as Senator, and I am thrilled that we, and future generations, will have the opportunity to know more about this extraordinary woman and leader.

I would like to thank Dr. Allida Black, Executive Director of The Eleanor Roosevelt & Human Rights Project at George Washington University. Her determination and single-minded efforts honor Eleanor Roosevelt's memory and help keep her legacy alive. She has been on a mission to find every piece of paper that Mrs. Roosevelt ever sent to anyone or was sent to her, every article she ever wrote and every speech she ever made. Dr. Black has found relevant documents from all over the world, in places as far-flung as South Africa and Vietnam. Mrs. Roosevelt went anywhere and everywhere she thought her presence would make a difference, and as I learned from my own personal experience as First Lady, no matter how far away my travels took me, Eleanor Roosevelt preceded me.

This ambitious compendium deals with Mrs. Roosevelt's post–White House years, the part of her life that has received the least attention from biographers and students of history, but which, in many ways, is the time when she wielded influence we are only now beginning to understand. It begins with President Roosevelt's death in April of 1945 and ends with the adoption of the Universal Declaration of Human Rights in December of 1948. It contains 410 documents selected from more than 90,000 documents the *Papers* staff has collected from 263 archives in fifty states and nine nations. They have been selected because they most accurately reflect Eleanor Roosevelt's voice and the actions she took both at home and within the United Nations to help the world recover from the horrors of World War II and the Great Depression. *Volume I* addresses three major points: 1) what drove Eleanor Roosevelt to work so hard for the betterment of humankind and why; 2) the issues she addressed and why they are so relevant today; and 3) what she actually accomplished.

When one ponders the why and wherefore of what drove Mrs. Roosevelt, one must look at her intense sense of compassion and duty, qualities for which I admire her the most. This sense of obligation was intensified by the horrors of World War II, the Holocaust, and the sacrifice of our soldiers. During the war she carried a prayer in her wallet that read: "Dear Lord, lest I continue in my complacent ways, help me to remember that someone died for me today. And, if there be war, help me to remember to ask and to answer, am I worth dying for?"

Mrs. Roosevelt wrote about and acted upon issues foreign and domestic. Many of the foreign policy questions she addressed have stunning relevance today: human rights; the creation and role of the United Nations; the crucial importance of foreign aid; immigration and refugees; the atomic bomb and the regulation of atomic energy; the volatility of the Balkan states; U.S. dependence on oil and its impact on our policy in the Middle East; and support for a Jewish state.

On the domestic front, Mrs. Roosevelt worked for civil rights, equal employment opportunities, and the appointment of more women to government posts. She spoke out about the scourge of anti-Semitism, the dangers of loyalty oaths and excessive government investigations, and the rights of labor. She promoted public education and national health insurance. Of national health insurance she wrote: "Without health no nation can successfully defend itself against the aggression of other nations, either in the military or the economic fields. If we want to retain our leadership in the world we must see that our people are healthy and vigorous. The spirit of adventure and the power to show initiative will die out if we do not preserve the health of the nation. I can see objections to almost any plan that is attempted, but like so many things, I believe it is better to begin and make the changes as we learn from experience. We need to make the attempt to improve the general health of the people of our country." Amen.

When FDR died, Mrs. Roosevelt immediately knew that she wanted to continue her journalism career. She wrote her nationally syndicated column, *My Day*, in order to educate Americans about policy and politics, and in so doing, goad them into action. She produced 8,000 columns and was the third most syndicated columnist of her time. A select group of columns appears in these papers and reflects not only the broad range of issues about which Mrs. Roosevelt cared so deeply, but the persuasiveness with which she expounded upon them. The *My Day* columns were the model for my own column as First Lady, *Talking It Over*.

From her Hyde Park home, Val-Kill Cottage, a place I have visited on more than one occasion and whose preservation efforts I have supported over many years, ER corresponded with the seminal political and diplomatic figures of the day on such pressing issues as the establishment of the World Bank and the International Monetary Fund (Bernard Baruch and Edward Stettinius), the creation of the United Nations International Children's Emergency Fund (Harry Truman), the military's increasing influence in diplomatic policy (George Marshall), and the urgent need for government response to racial and religious violence (Walter White and Attorney General Tom Clark). Regularly, she opened her doors to supporters and critics alike, inviting them to come to the cottage to continue the conversations, trusting that a personal conversation would accomplish more than a prolonged and posturing correspondence.

In Eleanor Roosevelt's words, we can see how she embodied the struggles of the early part of the twentieth century; how she took what she experienced in her own life and translated it into work on behalf of others. As one reads these papers, I believe one will be struck by the breadth of Mrs. Roosevelt's interests and concerns, and also by the passion, eloquence, and honesty with which she wrote. Of the Holocaust she penned: "When will our consciences grow so tender that we will act to prevent human misery rather than avenge it?"

Eleanor Roosevelt once asked, "Where do human rights begin? In small places, close to home, so close and so small that they cannot be seen on any maps of the world. Such are the places where every man, woman, and child seeks equal justice, equal opportunity, equal dignity without discrimination." As the Chair of the United Nations commission drafting the Universal Declaration of Human Rights, Eleanor Roosevelt worked tirelessly from 1946 to 1948. The Declaration was adopted as a common standard for human dignity and makes clear that "All human beings are born free and equal in dignity and rights." It states: "The advent of a world in which human beings shall enjoy freedom of speech and belief and freedom from fear and want has been proclaimed as the highest aspirations of the common people." These were the overarching constructs of her political philosophy, these were her highest aspirations for the world's citizens.

Throughout history, and even today, we have witnessed a cold dark region of the human soul that permits one group to de-humanize another. It was that all-too-human characteristic that the Declaration and Eleanor Roosevelt wanted to help resist.

Eleanor Roosevelt's legacy as a person, as a leader, as an inspiration, can help today to guide us in protecting the human rights of all people and, in particular, of children. Through *Volume I* of the Eleanor Roosevelt Papers, we honor her work, her legacy, her timeless values and ideals, and her commitment to imagining a better future for all people. As you read through this volume, I hope her words will be a call to action.

Senator Hillary Rodham Clinton
Washington, DC

Introduction

ONCE SHE FOUND HER VOICE, Eleanor Roosevelt changed the world.

A complex, multifaceted woman who became one of, if not the, most important women of the twentieth century, ER worked in a variety of venues to promote a society respectful of political and civil liberties and a government supportive of economic security and social justice. As social reformer, party activist, journalist and author, First Lady, diplomat, and humanitarian, ER challenged Americans "to foster democracy and not to fall a prey to fear."[1] Yet she realized that democracy alone could not solve problems or eradicate fear. "In dealing with the new nations of the world," she wrote as she lay dying:

> we must relearn the meaning of that noble word *respect*. That is the only sound and enduring basis for any relationship among peoples, as it is among individuals. We must learn to respect the various methods of development of the new nations, so long as they grant to the individual certain basic rights. We cannot say to them "If you will accept our way of life we will help you." If we are going to build a strong and peaceful world, we must be intelligent enough to help new nations in terms of their needs and not of our personal theories.[2]

BORN OCTOBER 11, 1884, into a family defined by wealth, privilege, and social lineage, ER had, by the time she left the White House on April 20, 1945, to a remarkable degree, transcended the trappings of noblesse oblige. In the process, she had helped not only to redefine citizens' responsibilities to one another but also their responsibilities to their government and their government's responsibilities to them.

However, as ER and her biographers recount, this transition was neither smooth nor painless. The traumas of her early life—her mother's disapproval and sudden death, her father's adoration and fatal battle with morphine and alcohol, her intense self-doubt and loneliness—are so well known as to be part of American consciousness. Her intense relationships with Allenswood Academy headmistress Marie Souvestre and her "Auntie Bye," Theodore Roosevelt's sister Anna Roosevelt Cowles, provided both buffers against criticism and models for independent thought and action. As ER strove to meet the social obligations her family expected of her and to discover what other options life held in store for her, she fell in love with Franklin Delano Roosevelt, her fifth cousin once removed. FDR wooed her for three years, against the dramatic landscape of New York City progressive reform, her "Uncle Teddy's" presidency, and Sara Delano Roosevelt's outspoken disapproval of their relationship. Even the date of their wedding, March 17, 1905, was set so that the President, who would be in town to lead the Saint Patrick's Day Parade, could give his favorite niece away. Soon ER and Sara would often disagree over the best way to raise the Roosevelt children while FDR would focus his energies on his political career.

Eight years later, Woodrow Wilson appointed FDR assistant secretary of the navy, and ER moved the children to Washington, D.C. Over the course of the Wilson administration, ER ventured into the political arena, developed what would become lifelong relationships with labor activists, found independence, experienced the horrors of war, confronted FDR's infidelity, and worked to redefine their marriage—in the process abandoning several traditional social conventions official Washington demanded of her. In 1920, FDR, then the Democratic nominee for vice president, invited ER, for the first time, to accompany him on the campaign trail. Although FDR urged her to travel with him, she expected the experience to be different and more intimate. They spent time together only when he spoke in public as FDR preferred to spend the evenings playing cards with his political team. ER spent most of her time reading, clipping articles about the campaign, reviewing speeches, or sitting alone in her railcar. When Louis Howe, FDR's political advisor and confidante, noticed the increased time she spent alone, he reached out. As he tutored her on campaign strategy and press coverage, a remarkable bond developed. Howe saw the political figure ER could become and she found in Howe a kindred spirit, someone who, while devoted to FDR, recognized his weaknesses but saw the leader FDR could become.

The Coolidge landslide dashed FDR's hopes of staying in Washington and prodded ER to plan a new, more fulfilling life in New York. Dreading "a winter of four days in New York with nothing but teas and luncheons and dinners to take up my time," ER "mapped out a schedule" in which she spent Monday through Thursday in New York City and the weekend in Hyde Park.[3] While FDR conferred with Howe to plan his next political move, ER caucused with leading women reformers, took an active role in organizations committed to policy rather than charity, learned to evaluate legislation, and began to develop her own political network. In the process, she defended the League of Nations and the World Court, critiqued the first Red Scare, and began to write for political newsletters.

In 1921, polio would force both Roosevelts to reconstruct and reinvent their lives. ER and FDR increasingly spent time apart. They were, however, vacationing together on Campobello Island when infantile paralysis struck FDR. ER rarely left his side, providing round-the-clock care, as a completely immobilized FDR battled to regain even the smallest measure of movement. They developed a new trust and respect for one another. Determined to reinforce her husband's desire to lead a full life, ER battled his mother, who thought her son should remain under her care, and worked to keep FDR up to date with issues and in contact with friends and the political world. In 1923, when FDR decided to recuperate spending time fishing with close colleagues on a Florida houseboat and at his retreat in Warm Springs, Georgia, ER re-entered politics as both her husband's stand-in and as party organizer and social reformer. She merged the networks she had built before polio with the newly formed Women's Division of the State Democratic Committee and the organizations Howe and FDR asked her to address.

ER soon became known as a leading political leader in her own right. She helped direct the Women's City Club, the National Consumers League, the Women's Division of the Democratic State Committee, and the New York chapters of the League of Women Voters and the Women's Trade Union League. Repeatedly she goaded women's and other reform groups to set realistic goals, prioritize their tasks, and delegate assignments. As Democratic Women's Committee vice president and finance chair, ER wrote articles discussing campaign strategies for the *Women's Democratic News*, defining issues and party positions for one of its most active sectors. As chair of the Civic League's City Planning Department, she coordinated its responses on housing and transportation issues, chaired its legislation committee, pushed through a reorganization plan, arbitrated disputes over child labor laws, promoted workmen's compensation, and, in a move that made banner headlines across New York State, strongly urged adoption of an amendment to the Penal Law legalizing the distribution of birth control information among married couples. In 1924, she chaired both the Bok Peace Prize Committee and the women's delegation to the platform committee of the Democratic National Convention and served as then governor Al Smith's liaison to women voters.

Increasingly comfortable speaking in public, ER testified before the New York State Assembly in support of protective labor legislation for women and children, convinced the state Democratic Party to appoint equal numbers of men and women to party committees, and represented various reform organizations before the state and national party platform committees. In 1925, she turned to radio to address audiences the *News* could not reach, engaged in debates across the state, and began the first of her thirty-six annual national lecture tours. A staunch supporter of Robert Wagner's 1926 campaign for the US Senate, ER traveled New York as one of Wagner's leading advocates. The next year, she began writing for the popular press and hosted a conference of 400 women in Hyde Park to organize a woman's peace movement. Her pragmatism attracted attention within the party and women's political organizations. Soon the major media began to cover her activities, culminating in an April 1928 feature article for the *New York Times Magazine*, which described ER as "a woman [of influence] who speaks her political mind."[4]

The 1928 gubernatorial election presented a new challenge to both Roosevelts. Their relationship moved more toward a professional collaboration between peers.

As first lady of New York, she struggled to balance her commitment to political reform with her husband's political agenda. ER's private loyalty was to the Democratic Women's Committee, whose newsletter she continued to edit covertly. Although she refrained from delivering "political speeches," she continued to travel the remote upstate regions with committee organizer Molly Dewson. When post-election polls showed a 20 percent increase in the upstate Democratic vote, James Farley credited the victory to ER's "real sense of politics." Aware of how difficult it was for a politician and his staff to face unpopular decisions, ER urged the appointment of individuals who had the nerve to disagree openly with FDR. She lobbied successfully for Frances Perkins's appointment as secretary of labor and for Nell Schwartz to fill the vacancy Perkins's appointment left on the State Industrial Commission. ER strongly objected to FDR retaining any of Smith's cabinet. In particular, she opposed Belle Moskowitz's reappointment as personal secretary to the governor and Robert Moses's reappointment as secretary of state.

Perhaps most important, ER began to apply political finesse to resolve disagreements within FDR's inner circle. She regularly facilitated conflicts between FDR intimates Howe and Farley and acted as a political stand-in when FDR could not or chose not to participate in the discussion. Certainly there is no clearer indication of ER's prominence within the Howe-FDR-Farley triangle than its decision to send her to issue the administration's rebuke of Tammany Mayor Jimmy Walker's conduct.

The move to the White House presented ER a more complicated dilemma.

Although she told the press throughout the campaign that she "would be very much at home in Washington" if FDR were elected, she confided her dread to reporters she trusted. Riding in a day coach to Albany with Lorena Hickok on November 9, 1932, ER unburdened her thoughts for the record. "I never wanted it even though some people have said that my ambition for myself drove him on … I never wanted to be a President's wife." Fearful that her support for her husband be misunderstood, she clarified her stance. "For him, of course, I'm glad—sincerely. I could not have wanted it any other way. After all I'm a Democrat, too." However, "now I shall have to work out my own salvation. I'm afraid it may be a little difficult. I know what Washington is like. I've lived there."[5]

Aware of the criticism she would receive when she continued her activities, ER refused to abandon the expertise she had achieved. She argued that she had no choice but to continue. "I'll just have to go on being myself, as much as I can. I'm just not the sort of person who would be any good at [any] job. I dare say I shall be criticized, whatever I do." ER's aversion to any other role was so strong that in the week before the inauguration, she impetuously wrote Marion Dickerman and Nancy Cook that she was contemplating divorcing FDR.

Thus, when ER entered the White House in March 1933, she did so reluctantly and with mixed feelings. FDR insisted that she stop her political activities and refused her offers to help with his mail, act as his unofficial ambassador, or serve as administrative assistant. Trapped by convention, she recognized that "the work [was his] work and the pattern his pattern" and that she "was one of those who served his purposes."[6] She turned to Howe and Hickok for guidance. Hickok suggested that ER capitalize on the good relations she developed with women journalists during the 1932 campaign by holding her own press conferences. Howe, respectful of her political acuity and supportive of her desire to reject the confines of the White House, wanted her to continue to speak out and frequently advocated ER's positions before FDR. Howe also advised ER to reach out to Americans ravaged by the Depression. By October 1933, she had traveled more than 40,000 miles examining social and economic conditions in all regions of the nation. Her observations and those of her correspondents only reinforced the impressions she had formed during the final days of the campaign. She returned to Washington convinced that relief programs alone could not counteract the Depression and that basic economic reforms were essential. The favorable press she received for her travels (as well as the popularity of her own press conferences) convinced FDR that he erred in curtailing her activity.

In August 1933, ER resumed writing for the popular press, beginning the monthly Mrs. Roosevelt's Page for *Pictorial Review*. Announcing that she would donate her monthly thousand-dollar fee to charity, ER then proceeded to ask her readers to help her establish "a clearinghouse, a discussion room" for "the particular problems which puzzle you or sadden you" and to share "how you are adjusting yourself to new conditions in this amazing changing world." Entitling the article "I Want You to Write to Me," ER reinforced the request throughout the piece. "Do not hesitate," she wrote, "to write to me even if your views clash with what you believe to be my views." Only a free exchange of ideas and discussion of problems would help her "learn of experiences which may be helpful to others."[7] By December, she had responded to 300,000 letters she received from "forgotten Americans."

Her constituency expanded, and ER began to promote her own version of the New Deal. Worried that supporters of FDR rivals Huey Long and Charles Coughlin felt neglected by the New Deal, she wanted to make herself available to them. Also concerned that the Federal Emergency Relief Administration (FERA) programs did not meet enough of people's needs, she pressured FERA administrator Harry Hopkins to hire Hickok to tour different parts of the nation, observe FERA programs, and report to him on the programs' effectiveness. Hickok sent copies of these honest, harsh field reports to ER, daily confirming the many obstacles those seeking relief encountered.

ER made her concerns public. "The unemployed are not a strange race. They are like we would be if we had not had a fortunate chance at life," she wrote in 1933.[8] The distress they encountered, not their socio-economic status, should be the focus of relief.

Determined to make the New Deal as much reform as relief, ER pressured Interior Secretary Harold Ickes and FERA Administrator Hopkins to address those most marginalized by FDR's policies. She criticized the Economy Act for penalizing married federally employed women; urged the Civil Works Administration to hire unemployed women; carefully monitored the construction of the Arthurdale subsistence homestead at Morgantown, West Virginia; facilitated the creation of the National Youth Administration; and spurred the development of the Federal One Programs for writers, artists, dancers, and actors. Disappointed that Social Security did not cover the majority of Americans and include health coverage, she reinvigorated her call for a living wage, the right to organize, national health insurance, and safe working conditions.

Like FDR, ER thought fear the greatest threat to democracy. Unlike FDR, however, she paid close attention to democracy's most vocal critics, especially African Americans and student activists. She coordinated the 1934 meeting between FDR and NAACP leader Walter White to discuss anti-lynching legislation; prodded Henry Wallace, Aubrey Williams, and Hopkins to resist Jim Crow relief practices; acted as Mary McLeod Bethune's White House ombudsman; and spoke out strongly against racial violence. Her 1938 defiance of Birmingham segregation laws at the Southern Conference for Human Welfare drew national attention to Jim Crow months before her resignation from the DAR in support of Marian Anderson. From 1936 to 1940, ER lent the same support to the American Youth Congress, despite the strong opposition of FDR's aides, and worked with Farley, head of the Democratic National Committee, and Dewson, head of the Women's Division of the DNC, to discuss the role of women in political elections.

ER's skillful use of the media helped offset criticism her activism provoked. In December 1935, she began her daily syndicated column My Day which, by 1940, had a circulation equal to that of Walter Lippmann and Dorothy Thompson. She continued to devote four weeks to a nation-wide lecture tour. She expanded her reading audience, launching a monthly question and answer magazine column, If You Ask Me; writing more than 100 articles for magazines, newsletters, and policy journals; and releasing the first installment of her autobiography (*This Is My Story*) and two small books on foreign policy (*This Troubled World*) and democratic values (*The Moral Basis of Democracy*). She also returned to radio. Thus, as FDR's second term came to an end, the adminis-tration's supporters and its critics recognized ER as a political force in her own right.

When FDR decided to seek an unprecedented third term as president, both Roosevelts con-fronted soul-searching questions as to how best to combat fascism and Axis violence. ER struggled to reconcile an intense abhorrence of war with a realpolitik commitment to containment. This was not an easy position to maintain and caused ER to weigh deeply held but often conflicting beliefs. However, by late 1939 Hitler's aggression forced her to recognize that America would eventually have to take military action to defeat fascism.

Refusing to abandon the New Deal to "Dr. Win the War," ER insisted that winning the war was only half the battle. To secure lasting victory, to have its "rendezvous with destiny," America must also win the peace. She thought the bombing of Pearl Harbor, the ferocious language of Aryan propaganda, and the dramatic appeal of US propaganda could unite the nation only for so long before social fissures would threaten Americans' resolve. Thus, as FDR prepared for war by wooing manufacturers and a reluctant Congress to the benefits of defense production, ER prepared for war by arguing that wartime policy must balance military preparedness with democratic social and eco-nomic policies. World War I, she insisted, showed what happened when nations focused on win-ning the war, but refused to plan for winning the peace.

ER grew more outspoken about race, linking Aryanism with Jim Crow practices. She cham-pioned the creation of the Fair Employment Practices Commission, reporting to FDR that he must recognize that the NAACP and the March on Washington movement could turn out at least twice as many demonstrators in search of jobs than those activists and fans who had traveled to Washington the year before to hear Marion Anderson sing at the Lincoln Memorial. She support-ed an integrated military and played a key role in securing the Tuskegee Airmen's combat assign-ments. She grew so vocal in her call for housing for African American defense workers that both the New York and Mississippi press blamed her for the 1943 Detroit race riot. Her outspokenness goaded FBI Director J. Edgar Hoover to become convinced she had "colored" blood and to instruct his agents to increase the bureau's monitoring of her activities.

She did not limit her remarks to African Americans.

After Kristallnacht, she worked with the Emergency Rescue Committee, the US Committee for the Care of European Children, and the Children's Crusade for Children. She also offered crit-ical support to Varian Fry's rescue operations. Indeed, her support for refugee work was so public that she received hundreds of petitions from people trying to enter the United States, some of whom she was able to assist. She lobbied in vain for the Child Refugee Bill, which would have allowed 10,000 Jewish children a year for two years to enter the United States above the usual German quota. When the United States entered the war, she continued to advocate a more open policy and to assist individual refugees to gain admittance to the country. She spoke out forcefully against the restrictive visa policies of FDR's longtime friend Breckinridge Long and worked with Assistant Secretary of State Sumner Welles to issue more entrance visas.

She lent her public support and private counsel to those opposing FDR's plans for internment (only to acquiesce to FDR's probable demand for silence). She praised Mexican immigrants who came to California to work as agricultural workers and condemned those who attacked them in the Los Angeles Zoot Suit riot. She urged women to enlist in military service and to work in the defense industries. She pressed for equal pay. When women could not find child care, leaving their children unattended or locked in cars while they worked, ER lobbied to secure day care facilities on their job sites.

This activism did not distract ER from paying intense attention to soldiers' sacrifices. She corresponded with hundreds of enlisted men who wrote her and she used her column to report their concerns and to argue that the best way to honor their courage was to make democracy work at home. She pressed FDR to let her visit the troops in the Pacific, only to have him reject her plea until the summer of 1943, when he found it politically expedient to get her out of the country. Over five weeks, she visited thousands of American troops stationed over twenty-three islands. Haunted by their sacrifice, she began to carry a prayer in her wallet that read: "Dear Lord, Lest I continue my complacent way, help me to remember that somewhere, somehow out there, a man died for me today. As long as there be war, I then must ask and answer am I worth dying for?"[9]

As the war drew to a close, ER rejoiced in FDR's 1944 State of the Union address in which he called for an "economic bill of rights." Sharing his hopes for the United Nations, she paid close attention to the organizational plans his staff circulated in early 1945 and looked forward to attending the opening ceremony with him. FDR died April 12, 1945, thirteen days before fifty nations assembled in San Francisco to ratify his plan for the United Nations.

NOW THAT SHE WAS NO LONGER FIRST LADY, ER grew anxious to leave the White House. "I never did like to be where I no longer belonged," she confided to Joe Lash a few days after FDR's death. The emptiness of the White House made her feel "desolate" and "without purpose" and, although she was "weary," she could not "rest."[10]

The pressures started immediately. As they returned from FDR's funeral, Henry Morgenthau, Jr., asked her to settle FDR's estate as soon as possible so she "could speak out to the world as Eleanor Roosevelt," arguing that "it [is] most important that [your] voice be heard." Hickok consoled and prodded. After encouraging ER to "take a few days off this Spring and Summer to rest," she then reminded her that "you are going to be more your own agent, freer than you've ever been before." ER must be prepared, Hickok concluded, for the "very active and important place" awaiting her. The Associated Press agreed, succinctly summarizing the pressures facing ER with a front page headline: "Mrs. Roosevelt Will Continue Column; Seeks No Office *Now*."[11]

ER had her own expectations about the future; but, unlike her friends and the media, she was undecided about what actions she should take to achieve them. Although she did not want to be viewed solely as a former First Lady, ER feared that without the "ear of the president" she would lose the influence she had struggled to attain. At times she succumbed to these anxieties only to encounter jocular criticism from those closest to her. When ER lapsed into a moment of despondence and informed young friends that she merely wanted to write, visit her family, and live "a peaceful life," Trude Lash teasingly suggested that they all go buy ER a lace cap as a retirement gift.[12]

Recalling the anxiety of these transition months, ER noted in *On My Own* that she was sure of only three things when she returned to Hyde Park: she wanted to continue her columns, simplify her lifestyle, and "not feel old . . . [or] useless." She knew her keen interest in the world around her, her eagerness to confront "every challenge and opportunity to learn more," and her "great energy and self-discipline" were tremendous assets. She understood how much weight her support carried but worried that her influence might tip the political scales in ways that she could not control. Consequently, while she was now free of the "certain restrictions FDR demanded," ER faced 1945 impatient with slow-paced domestic reform and uncomfortable with her undefined future. "Of one thing I am sure," she wrote in early May, "in order to be useful we must stand for the things we feel are right, and we must work for those things wherever we find ourselves. It does very little good to believe something unless you tell your friends and associates of your beliefs." Vowing that she would not become "a workless worker in a world of work," she struggled to define the parameters of a new life in politics.[13]

Yet these new boundaries did not mean a new political agenda. ER did not want to forsake the New Deal. In fact, she planned to do the exact opposite. If FDR had replaced "Dr. New Deal" to become "Dr. Win the War" and resented her wartime insistence on domestic reform, ER anticipated that his successor would be even less likely to pursue the controversial programs FDR had abandoned when conservatives seized control of Congress. She thought that if the New Deal was to re-enter the political arena, she would have to assist in orchestrating its return. Whether she did this by promoting candidates or policy was up to her. What was important was that she select a mode of operation that allowed her the greatest leeway in pursuing her own goals while protecting her husband's legacy.

Although she took a few deliberate steps to rebuild her life after FDR—turning the Roosevelt family home over to the government, moving into Val-Kill Cottage, and pursuing a career as a political columnist—most of ER's plans for the future remained vague. She did believe that "the story is over." After all, FDR had died; and although their relationship had grown more profession-al than personal, ER did grieve. What took time for her to recognize was that FDR's death expand-ed, rather than limited, her sphere of influence. No longer just FDR's "Missus," she could now choose to speak out and act as either his widow or as herself.

The challenge facing ER in mid-1945 was how to balance these two identities.

The challenges Harry Truman faced were more complex: how to inherit the presidency, how to bring the war to a conclusion, and how to govern under the shadow of two Roosevelts.

THE 410 DOCUMENTS reproduced in this volume (and the 499 excerpted in annotation) recount ER's efforts to make her voice heard in the period between FDR's death and the adoption of the Universal Declaration of Human Rights. As discussed in the following section on Editorial Principles and Practices, the editors selected documents that most accurately reflect ER's voice and the voices she heard while addressing the issues she thought paramount. These documents contain detailed discussions of American politics, diplomacy, and policy, as well as countless examples of individual responses to the challenges depression, war, containment, and the struggle for human rights presented to the average American as well as to citizens the world over. They not only tell the tale of Eleanor Roosevelt's development as a political force and the impact she had on American politics and the United Nations, but also the serious treatment she received from those in power. They depict her vision and her prejudices, her convictions and her doubts, her patience and her anger, her prescience and her miscalculations. Most of all, they reflect the actions she took (and did not take) to promote human rights at home and abroad.

Eleanor Roosevelt refused to seek elective office, preferring instead to speak for herself rather than her party. In her correspondence, columns, speeches, endorsements, and negotiations, she played a pivotal role in defining liberalism and its critics on both the left and the right.

Yet as her criticism of Truman, Wallace, John L. Lewis, and W. E. B. Du Bois illustrates, her liberalism was tempered by pragmatism, position, and a desire for progress. On the other hand, her strong opposition to loyalty oaths coupled with her personal loyalty to Alger Hiss and Lauchlin Currie drove her to discount testimony from those she disdained.

ER did not create or negotiate the United Nations Partition Plan for Palestine, but her pres-sure on the Truman administration and Secretary of State George Marshall showed in unmistak-able terms the consequences the administration would face should they change course. At the same time, she bemoaned how oil dominated US Middle East policy while she refused to address Wadad Dabbagh's examples of "what injustice" the plan "caus[ed] to us the Arabs."[14] It would take her a decade to do so.

ER, who had long championed protective labor legislation, did not support the Equal Rights Amendment. However, she pressed Truman to appoint women throughout his administration, called for equal pay for equal work, and supported proposals to insure that the Universal Declaration of Human Rights specifically included issues of concern to women. She recognized that her efforts helped "women inch forward" but thought she was "too old to be carrying on the fight."[15] It would take a decade for ER to drop her opposition to the amendment.

ER's commitment to an international organization dedicated to preventing war and mitigating combat dated to the creation of the League of Nations. The carnage, sacrifice, and xenophobia World War II made rampant forced her to reconsider her own role in preserving peace and what role an international organization could or should play in mediating world conflict. She entered the United Nations hopeful that the world could work together and that the United States could find a way to work with the Soviet Union. Her experience with refugees and the Soviet position on refugees changed that. Nevertheless, she continued talking with Soviet delegates and searching for common ground.

Soon human rights dominated her agenda. As this volume indicates, she dedicated most of her energies to the creation of a declaration and the preparation of covenants on human rights. In the process, she moved to embrace social and economic rights and legally binding agreements, and to press the State Department to move beyond thinking only of political and civil rights and to recognize the need for human rights covenants. While she succeeded in the first, it would take decades for the second. Although she failed to convince the Soviet bloc nations to change their conduct, she did mitigate their opposition enough to prevent their veto of key human rights provisions. As chair of the drafting committee, she worked closely with John Humphrey, Charles Malik, René Cassin, and Peng-chun Chang to craft a proposal to present to the Human Rights Commission and then shepherded countless drafts through dozens of committee debates. Without her stewardship it is doubtful the Declaration would have ever made it through the drafting and adoption process.

This first of five volumes presents a representative selection of the actions ER took to define, implement, and promote human rights and the impact her work had at home and abroad. Readers will disagree over various decisions she made, language that she used, or the priorities she established. Yet her impact is unquestioned.

Eleanor Roosevelt played a critical role in defining one of the most critical issues of our time—human rights.

Allida Black
Washington, DC

---

1. ER, "Keepers of Democracy," in A. Black, *What I Hope*, 67.

2. ER, *Tomorrow Is Now*, 45.

3. ER quoted in A. Black, *Casting*, 10.

4. S. J. Woolf, "A Woman Speaks Her Political Mind: Mrs. Franklin D. Roosevelt Points Out that in Spite of Equal Suffrage the Men Still Run the Parties," *NYT*, 8 April 1928, SM2.

5. ER quoted in A. Black, *Casting*, 21.

6. *TIR*, 76.

7. ER, "I Want You to Write to Me," in A. Black, *What I Hope*, 13–17.

8. ER quoted in A. Black, *Casting*, 29.

9. A. Black, *Casting*, 92.

10. See Document 1, ER to Lorena Hickok, 19 April 1945, and Joseph Lash to ER, 19 April 1945, AERP.

11. A. Black, *Casting*, 52; Lorena Hickok to ER, 13 April 1945, LAHP; "Mrs. Roosevelt Will Continue Column; Seeks No Office Now," *The (Washington) Evening Star*, 19 April 1945, A1.

12. Trude Lash quoted in A. Black, *Casting*, 53.

13. *OMO*, 2, 4, 12; Lash, *Years*, 38; *MD*, 8 May 1945; A. Black, *Casting*.

14. See header, Document 347, ER to Wadad Dabbagh, 13 May 1947.

15. See Document 92, ER to Joseph Lash, 13 February 1946.

Editorial Principles and Practices

The Documentary Record

Eleanor Roosevelt left a voluminous legacy in a wide variety of media, including print, radio, film, and television. Between 1921 and 1962, ER wrote twenty-seven books, more than 8,000 columns, and approximately 580 articles. She generated an average of 45,000 letters a year (and received an average of 175,000 letters a year) while she served as First Lady. Although no official estimates of her post–White House correspondence exist, documents collected by the Eleanor Roosevelt Papers suggest that she received an average of 50,000 letters and generated an average of 21,000 letters annually from April 12, 1945, to November 7, 1962. Furthermore, she delivered more than seventy-five speeches a year. From 1945 through 1948, radios around the world carried more than thirty of her speeches and interviews. From 1948 through 1961, she hosted more than 326 radio broadcasts featuring interviews with many of the world's major leaders and commentary on the most pressing issues of the day and appeared as a guest on more than seventy news programs. From 1959 until early fall 1962, Education Television broadcast her monthly television show *Prospects of Mankind*, a roundtable discussion with prominent politicians, artists, activists, and intellectuals.

The Eleanor Roosevelt Papers Project found this material in more than 600 collections scattered among 263 archives in all fifty states and nine nations. Roughly one half of the documents are housed in 4,842 archival boxes at the Franklin D. Roosevelt Presidential Library and Museum (FDRL) in Hyde Park, New York. Thousands of other documents are distributed throughout the nation in more than 500 collections. The United Nations Archives, the US Mission to the United Nations, and Record Groups 59 and 84 of the National Archives house more than 3,000 documents related to ER's tenure as a member of the American delegation to the United Nations. While her radio and televisions shows, as well as copies of a few of the national and international shows on which she appeared, are housed in FDRL, others are preserved in the Library of Congress, the National Archives, the WGBH Archives, and local historical societies and news stations. Taped and written transcripts of speeches, interviews, and press conferences ER gave while abroad are housed in archives in Britain, France, Germany, India, Russia, Japan, and Israel.

These records contain detailed discussions of American politics, diplomacy, and policy as well as countless examples of individual responses to the challenges depression, war, containment, and the struggle for human rights presented to the average American as well as citizens the world over. They not only tell the tale of Eleanor Roosevelt's development as a political force in her own right and the impact she had on American politics and the United Nations, but also the serious treatment she received from those in power. They disclose the inner workings of four presidential administrations, the United Nations, and the major social and political movements of the postwar world. They reveal the intense struggles her correspondents and advisors had confronting a war-scarred world, the conflicting advice they gave her, and the material she reviewed and the people ER consulted while determining her own course of action.

EDITORIAL PRINCIPLES AND PRACTICES

Selection

Time and financial constraints prevent the creation of a comprehensive documentary edition. As discussed in more detail in the Introduction, the editor, with the strong concurrence of the National Historical Publications and Records Commission (NHPRC) and other Roosevelt scholars, decided to produce a highly selective edition designed to present an authoritative resource on Eleanor Roosevelt's political and human rights record and to encourage further research on her life and the issues she addressed. As the editorial team searched manuscript collections, it excluded from consideration any document that did not reflect or discuss the actions and positions ER took as political leader, diplomat, and stateswoman. In short, it weeded out any material that did not discuss politics, policy, world events, philosophy, faith, social justice, or government.

In the process, the project collected more than 130,000 documents of which approximately 15,000 fall within the period the volume covers, 1945–1948. Thus, the most daunting challenge the editorial team confronted was choosing which documents to include in this volume. The editors then decided to build the volume around ER's human rights work, as she considered that her most important life's work, and to define human rights the way ER did, as both domestic and international in scope, and including both political and civil rights and social and economic rights.

As the editors initiated the process of selecting documents for publication, they gave priority to material that illustrated ER's multiple and intertwined roles as political commentator, activist, advice columnist, and moralist; expressed ER's views on the full range of human rights issues with which she was concerned, including both civil and political rights and social and economic rights; demonstrated her use of the wide range of media available to her; displayed the range of emotional styles or tones with which she addressed issues; and reflected ER's extraordinary impact on the lives of ordinary people who wrote to her asking for help, advice, or her opinion on contemporary issues.

As the editorial team finalized selection, it evaluated documents based on four criteria. First, did the document illustrate one of the seminal events, themes, or issues of ER's public life? Second, did it reveal ER's distinctive voice, offer strong insight into her decision making, and reflect the various tones and approaches she adopted to make herself heard? Third, did it have significant impact on politics, policy, and public opinion? Fourth, did it disclose critical information she used to reach a position?

ER left a paper trail as diverse as the arenas in which she operated. The editors wanted to create an edition mirroring the various ways ER made her voice heard; therefore, they decided to include a variety of document types to illustrate the multiple ways ER spoke, wrote, worked, and organized.

Material selected for this volume falls into five categories: correspondence from and to ER; the diary she kept during the first session of the General Assembly; material she wrote for publication (My Day and If You Ask Me columns as well as articles for national magazines and organizational newsletters); public statements (speeches, press conference transcripts, and radio broadcasts); and government and UN documents.

Correspondence predominates the 410 annotated documents. Of the 2,685 letters by ER we collected for this period, editors selected 169 for inclusion in their entirety and excerpted key passages from an additional 108 in headers and endnotes. This selection represents approximately 11 percent of the correspondence ER generated.

Editors also decided to include correspondence she received to illustrate sustained discussions she had with political leaders, colleagues, activists, and the general public, at home and abroad. Editors collected 4,193 letters written to ER during this same period and reproduced 91 and excerpted an additional 138 in annotation, representing approximately 6 percent of all the correspondence she received.

ER did not keep a diary; however, to satisfy her family and close friends interest in her activities in the first session of the United Nations, she kept notes detailing her activities during the first session of the General Assembly and her responses to the events of the day, typed them up and mailed them to her secretary Malvina "Tommy" Thompson to distribute among ER's trusted circle. The editors included seven entries and excerpted two more from the twenty-seven entries ER made, representing 52 percent of the diary entries.

The first career decision ER made after learning of FDR's death is that she wanted to continue her journalism career. Indeed, she valued her column so much that she repeatedly rejected offers to seek elected office by saying she could make her voice heard more fully in her published writings than in an elected or other political position. Thus, the editors decided to include a good sampling of her six-day-a-week nationally syndicated column My Day, a smaller excerpted sampling of her monthly question and answer column If You Ask Me, and samples of articles she wrote for major magazines such as *Look* and the *Saturday Evening Review* as well as organizational newsletters. When selecting My Days for inclusion in their entirety, the editorial team decided to select from only those columns that were devoted to one subject rather than to a cross-section of world events and national politics. Of the 1,265 My Day columns ER wrote during this period, sixty-eight My Days are reprinted in their entirety and another 106 are excerpted, representing a sample of 13 percent. As If You Ask Me was a question and answer column, the editors selected specific entries to include rather than the entire column. Of the 166 entries that composed If You Ask Me from May 1945 through December 1948, the editors reprinted twelve and excerpted another five, representing approximately 15 percent of the answers ER dispensed.

Once she and son James settled FDR's estate, she resumed both her lecture tour and her travels on behalf of political and social organizations. As ER most often spoke extemporaneously, the only extant record of her remarks appear in local press coverage of her visits. Using My Day and correspondence to track her travels, the editors then examined local newspaper accounts of her visits. Of the sixty-two speeches the team retrieved, fifteen are reprinted in their entirety and another sixteen excerpted, representing approximately 50 percent of the remarks the editorial team could locate. Remarks ER made during her speaking appearances often generated more attention than the speech she delivered. Moreover, as a UN delegate, her formal press conferences, and the statements she released to the press offer unique insight into ER's struggle to speak independently while also serving as a representative of the State Department. Editors reproduced eleven of her press conferences and statements to the press and excerpted an additional eleven, representing 44 percent of the transcripts it could locate. Readers will also find three transcripts of, and another two excerpts from, radio shows upon which ER appeared, representing 19 percent of extant transcripts.

As a member of the US delegation to the United Nations, ER participated in public hearings, committee meetings, and departmental briefings. While searching the UN Archives, Record Groups 59 and 84, as well as the Charles Malik Papers and other relevant collections, the editors located both verbatim transcripts of UN committee meetings in which ER either participated as chair or as ranking US delegate, memoranda of conversation detailing the author's conversation with ER in detail for official state department files, material ER reviewed to prepare for the sessions, and correspondence between key officials discussing their separate conversations with ER on US foreign policy. In all, the editorial team located 1,054 documents, of which 13 are printed in their entirety, 8 are printed as excerpts, and another 113 are excerpted in annotation, representing approximately 13 percent of the retrieved material.

Establishing Text

Approximately half of the material in this volume is unique, including all of ER's outgoing correspondence. In My Day, the editors transcribed the final wire service copy ER sent to the syndicate for publication. If You Ask Me excerpts are taken from the published column. Other published works are transcribed from and verified against the most public source that could be located. If there are several copies of a particular letter, the recipient's copy is reproduced.

On a few occasions ER dictated a note to her secretary who would then jot ER's comments down on a note pad, type them onto stationary without making a carbon copy, file the note pad page, and mail the letter. In those instances, the text of the secretarial note is the only extant copy of the correspondence. It is then transcribed and a date suggested.

ER regularly corresponded with individuals who did not preserve their papers. Thus, often no recipient's copy could be located. In those instances, the file copy is transcribed, noted as such, and reproduced without a signature. If the file copy is undated and the editorial team is unable to verify a date from other documents, a range of dates is supplied.

As ER preferred to speak extemporaneously, her papers contain few prepared remarks. The public remarks reproduced in this volume came from two sources: transcriptions of tape recorded remarks and press coverage. In cases where several press covered the speech, editors compared the coverage, selected the most detailed record illustrating the points ER made, and referenced the other coverage in the annotation. If no additional press coverage could be found, then the remarks quoted in that article are compared to other remarks ER made on similar topics in the same time period.

The United Nations transcripts and summary records are the body's official records.

Organization of the Volume

The volume is divided into seven chronological sections, each of which is arranged by the recorded or publication date. Documents dated only by month appear at the beginning of each month. Undated correspondence is noted by [?] and placed where corroborating evidence recommends. Each section contains documents that stand alone and groups of related documents. Within the set of related documents, the placement order is determined by the date of the first document in the series. To facilitate readers' access to related documents (e.g., a My Day column and the response it generated, letters ER exchanged with a specific correspondent) and to see how ER's arguments changed or hardened throughout the exchange, the editors placed the related documents together as one group.

Each section is introduced by a short essay describing the documents in that section and the issues ER and her peers addressed.

Each document is numbered. Any reference to that document included elsewhere in the annotation contains the document number. Each document is followed by a location note indicating the document type and repository.

Transcription

The editors strove to reproduce the document as accurately as possible while at the same time creating a document that is convenient for the reader to use. As the vast majority of material included in this volume was typed or printed, editors could easily validate transcription. Handwritten material was transcribed blind by two assistant editors, the text compared, and then verified by the editor. In the one case in which the editor had reservations about a certain transcription, she took the original text to a colleague of ER's who had great familiarity with her handwriting for her assessment of the word in question and the transcription in general.

Paragraph structure, misspellings, grammar, abbreviations, capitalization, initials, underlinings, salutations, closings, and signatures are reproduced as they appear in the document. The correct spelling of proper names is referenced in the endnotes. Missing words supplied by the editors are inserted inside brackets []. Text the author inserted is silently placed where the author's notes position it and is identified as author-inserted text in the endnotes. Marginalia written by someone other than the author or recipient was not reproduced unless it had direct bearing on the document and the author could be determined. That information is included in the annotation. Handwritten postscripts are transcribed at the end of the document and then described in the annotation as handwritten. In two cases, this information is also included in the headnote to the document.

To ensure a more readable text, the editors silently corrected obvious typos ("tow" people to "two" people), replaced ampersands with "and," and standardized the placement of dates, the indentation of paragraphs, and the spacing between words. The editors did not reproduce personal or governmental letterhead; however, if ER wrote a letter on an organization's letterhead, that information is recorded in the endnote.

The place of authorship, publication, or discussion is noted next to the document date in brackets. In My Day, the dateline appears as it did in the original manuscript ER telegraphed to the syndicate. In instances where the author or the document did not identify the place in which it was written, editors turned to other primary sources to confirm place. For ER-authored documents, My Day helped pinpoint her location. For non–ER authored material, editors checked other material written on the same day, national newspapers, and government records (memoranda, calendars, *Congressional Record*) to determine place.

Annotation and Editorial Aids

Annotation serves two purposes in this volume: to include excerpts from other documents related to ER's human rights work and to assist a non-specialist in understanding the documents and, therefore, ER's life and times.

The annotation comes in four forms: headnotes, endnotes, biographical portraits, and a chronology. Headnotes introduce the document, often by excerpting other primary documents to set the stage for the document reproduced in its entirety. To facilitate use by students, teachers, the general public, and those scholars not familiar with the range of issues ER addressed, the editors created endnotes identifying not only the obscure people and policy discussed in the documents, but also the major leaders, political events, policies, legislation, and ideologies non-scholars might find useful to understand the document's import. Endnotes also allowed editors to include snippets of documents that relate to the main document but would be extraneous to the information excerpted in the header. Readers should be aware that while extensive, the information contained in the annotation is not exhaustive. To encourage users to continue digging into the material used for annotation, the editors included full bibliographic information, including page numbers, of the primary and secondary sources from which the annotation is derived.

A collection of biographical portraits follows the last document. Readers should know that when they first encounter a name in a document and there is no endnote associated to that person, the reader is to refer to the biographical portrait in the back of the book. Each entry not only summarizes a person's career but also links that person to the specific issues this volume covers.

The editors also prepared a chronology of the major events discussed in the volume.

The editors, with the strong, generous support of Scribner's, selected nearly 100 photographs to help to illuminate the text for the reader. Each photograph captures an event, personality, or political slant discussed in the documents. When possible, editors crafted annotation linking the illustrations to a particular document.

Editors designed a comprehensive, multilevel index to reflect not only the events, names, legislation, and organizations discussed in the document but also that direct readers to the wide range of concepts, ideas, and policies represented in the documents.

Chronology

1945

April 12	ER reviews trusteeship strategy with Charles Taussig. FDR dies of a cerebral hemorrhage in Warm Springs, GA. ER informs Harry Truman of FDR's death. Truman sworn in as president.
April 19	ER announces she will not seek and does not want a political position. House Labor Committee refuses to send Fair Employment Practices bill to floor. Chairwoman Mary Norton accuses committee of "unfairness."
April 20	ER leaves Washington, making Val-Kill Cottage in Hyde Park, NY, her home.
April 22	Eight members of Congress and seventeen journalists, invited by Eisenhower, tour recently liberated German concentration camps.
April 25–June 26	United Nations Conference on International Organization convenes in San Francisco.
May 7	German forces surrender to Eisenhower in Reims, France.
May 26	ER rejects Harold Ickes's request that she run for the US Senate.
June 26	Truman addresses the United Nations Conference in San Francisco, then, with leaders of fifty nations, signs the United Nations Charter.
June 27	Truman appoints James Byrnes secretary of state, replacing Edward Stettinius.
July 17–August 2	Truman, Winston Churchill, and Josef Stalin meet at Potsdam; Churchill defeated in election and is replaced by Clement Attlee July 29.
July 27	ER rejects offer to chair the National Citizens Political Action Committee (NCPAC).
July 28	US Senate ratifies UN Charter by a vote of 89–2.
August 6	US drops atomic bomb on Hiroshima, Japan.
August 9	US drops atomic bomb on Nagasaki, Japan.
August 15	Truman holds 7 PM press conference announcing Japan's surrender.
August 18	Truman issues executive order removing price, wage, production, and other wartime controls.
August 31	Truman asks Attlee to admit 100,000 Jewish refugees into Palestine.
September 2	Japan officially surrenders to General Douglas MacArthur.

September 6	Truman addresses Congress, presenting a twenty-one part legislative package calling for full employment, unemployment compensation, an increase in the minimum wage, housing construction, permanent farm price supports, increased public works projects, and a permanent Fair Employment Practices Commission (FEPC).
October 23	Truman asks Congress to adopt a peace-time universal military training program.
October 31	ER begins a New England tour for the National Citizens Political Action Committee (NCPAC).
November 15	Truman, Attlee, and Mackenzie King call for a UN Atomic Energy Commission.
November 19	Truman proposes compulsory national health insurance.
November 21	The United Auto Workers (UAW) begins striking against ninety-five General Motors plants. The strike will last until March 13, 1946.
December 14	Truman phones ER, requesting she join the US delegation to the United Nations.
December 19	ER announces she will chair the American Committee for Yugoslav Relief and that she would accept appointment to the US delegation, if the Senate confirmed her. Senate votes 99–1 in her favor, with Senator Theodore Bilbo the lone dissenter.
December 20	The US, United Kingdom, USSR, and France sign Control Council Law No. 10, creating a tribunal to prosecute war criminals.
December 31	The US delegation, including ER, depart for the General Assembly.

1946

January 3	ER holds press conference aboard the *Queen Elizabeth*, telling reporters in an off-the-record remark, "For the first time in my life I can say just what I want. For your information it is wonderful to feel free."
January 10–February 14	First session of the United Nations General Assembly convenes in London. ER appointed US delegate to the Third Committee (Humanitarian, Social and Cultural Affairs).
January 17	UN Security Council holds its first meeting. ER delivers her first major address as a UN delegate at London's Royal Albert Hall.
January 18–February 9	Southern Democrats in Senate filibuster Fair Employment Practices Commission bill. On February 9, vote for closure fails and Senate foregoes further discussion of FEPC in current session.
January 25	Third Committee votes to establish the Human Rights Commission under the Economic and Social Council.
February 4	ER addresses the Pilgrim Society in London, the first woman to do so.
February 5	Women delegates to UN General Assembly issue an appeal calling on the women of the world to participate in national and international affairs.
February 12	ER and Andrei Vyshinsky debate UN's responsibility in handling European refugees before the General Assembly.

February 13–16	ER visits displaced persons camps in Germany.
February 15	Harold Ickes resigns from Interior to protest Truman's proposed appointment of Edwin Pauley as undersecretary of the navy.
February 20	Truman signs Employment Act of 1946, mandating federal responsibility to maximize employment and establishing the Council of Economic Advisors.
February 21	Truman appoints Chester Bowles to lead the re-instituted Office of Economic Stabilization to control escalating prices.
February 24	Juan Perón elected president of Argentina.
Februay 25–26	Tennessee Highway Patrol arrests more than 100 African Americans in town of Columbia after overnight "race riot." Two days later, two of those arrested are killed in scuffle with guards.
February 27	ER meets with Truman at White House to discuss the UN's first session.
February 28	Fair Employment Practices Commission Day in New York. ER addresses crowd of 15,000 at Madison Square Garden urging Congress to pass the FEPC bill.
March 5	Churchill delivers "iron curtain" speech at Westminster College in Fulton, MO.
April 1	United Mine Workers begin two-month strike.
April 29–May 20	Nuclear Commission on Human Rights convenes at Hunter College in New York City. ER elected chair by acclamation.
April 30	Anglo-American Commission of Inquiry on Palestine releases report recommending the admission of 100,000 Jewish refugees into Palestine.
May 23–25	Railroad workers strike and return to work forty-eight hours later when Truman deems their action a threat to national security and threatens to draft them into the military.
May 28	ER presents Human Rights Commission report to the UN Economic and Social Council (ECOSOC).
June 4	Truman accepts Edward Stettinius's resignation as US delegate to the UN Security Council.
June 11	Truman issues Executive Order 9735 establishing the Cabinet Committee on Palestine to aid in the immigration of 100,000 Jews to Palestine.
June 12	Ernest Bevin rejects Anglo-American Committee of Inquiry's recommendation to admit 100,000 Jews to Palestine in a speech before the Labour Party Convention.
June 14	Bernard Baruch presents plan for international control of atomic energy to UN's Commission on Atomic Energy. Grand Jury in Columbia, TN, finds no evidence of civil rights violations in Highway Patrol's handling of "race riots."
July 9	ER's article "Why I Do Not Choose To Run" appears in *Look*.
July 25	Truman re-establishes Office of Price Administration.

September 3	ER delivers keynote speech at New York State Democratic Convention.
September 6	Secretary of State Byrnes delivers speech in Stuttgart calling for the immediate unification of Germany.
September 12	Secretary of Commerce Henry Wallace criticizes Truman administration's foreign policy at Madison Square Garden rally.
September 19	Churchill delivers "United States of Europe" speech in Zurich calling for a unified Germany and France.
September 20	Truman demands Wallace's resignation two days after the secretary released a confidential letter to the president in which he criticized Truman's foreign policy.
October 1	Elliott Roosevelt's observations on FDR, *As He Saw It*, published by Duell, Sloan and Pearce.
October 11–20	ER and Lady Stella Reading join women from fifty-three nations at the International Assembly of Women in South Kortright, NY. ER delivers the closing address.
October 23– December 15	Second part of first session of UN General Assembly convenes in Flushing, NY. UN relocates to Lake Success during this session.
November 7	Republicans gain control of Senate (51–45) and House (246–188) in mid-term election.
December 3	German Pastor Martin Niemöller arrives in New York to begin month-long speaking tour of US.
December 11	General Assembly establishes United Nations Children's International Emergency Fund.
December 12	General Assembly adopts resolution condemning Francisco Franco and urging UN member nations to withdraw ambassadors from Madrid.
December 15	In a speech before the General Assembly, ER calls for the creation of the International Refugee Organization (IRO). General Assembly adopts draft constitution of IRO and establishes preparatory commission to begin the organization's work.
December 28	Independent Citizens Committee of the Arts, Sciences and Professions (ICCASP) and National Citizens Political Action Committee (NCPAC) merge to form the Progressive Citizens of America (PCA).
December 29	ER urges PCA national political director C. B. Baldwin to remove Communists from its membership.

1947

January 3	ER and other anti-Communist liberals assemble in New York City to found Americans United for Democratic Action (ADA).
January 6	Truman delivers a State of the Union address, in which he calls for increased immigration quotas for displaced persons, including Jewish refugees.
January 21	General George Marshall replaces James Byrnes as secretary of state.

January 27–February 10	The eighteen-nation UN Human Rights Commission (HRC), charged with drafting an international bill of human rights, holds its first session. The group unanimously elects ER chair.
February 7	The British government announces that it will terminate its Mandate for Palestine in May 1948.
March 1	Attacks on British military posts throughout Palestine by Jewish insurgents lead the British Mandate government to declare martial law.
March 9–April 24	The Moscow Conference of the Council of Foreign Ministers brings together the "Big Four"—the US, the USSR, Great Britain, and France—to discuss the political and economic future of Germany.
March 12	Truman addresses Congress, requesting $400 million appropriation to provide direct military and economic aid to Greece and Turkey in an effort to contain Communist expansionism (Truman Doctrine).
March 21	Truman issues Executive Order 9835 establishing a federal employee loyalty program to find and remove Communists and Communist sympathizers from government service.
May 13	The UN General Assembly appoints an eleven-nation Special Committee on Palestine (UNSCOP) to study the Palestine problem and make recommendations for action by September 1947.
May 22	Congress authorizes $400 million aid package to Greece and Turkey.
May 24	ER delivers the Founder's Day Address at Roosevelt College in Chicago.
June 4	Representative William Stratton introduces bill to admit 400,000 displaced persons into the United States over the next four years.
June 5	James Roosevelt, chair of the California Democratic Committee, issues a report critical of Truman's foreign policy. DNC chair Gael Sullivan, who with ER is scheduled to address the Jackson Day Dinner, arrives in Los Angeles and cancels his scheduled appearance. ER delivers the keynote address. In a commencement speech at Harvard University, Secretary of State George Marshall outlines a plan for economic recovery in Europe (Marshall Plan).
June 6	Congress passes the Labor-Management Relations Act of 1947, known as the Taft-Hartley Act.
June 9–25	The eight-member drafting committee of the Commission on Human Rights, chaired by ER, begins work in Lake Success, NY, on a declaration of human rights.
June 20	Truman vetoes Taft-Hartley Act. Congress overrides his veto June 23.
July 11–August 2	The *Exodus*, a ship containing 4,500 Jewish refugees from Europe, departs France for Palestine. Upon its arrival, British troops deny the refugees entry and re-route the ship back to France.
September 2–October 23	The NAACP pressures ER to accept the petition detailing the violation of African American rights it will present to the UN Commission on Human Rights. ER refuses, telling Walter White, "It isn't as though everyone did not know where I stand. It is just a matter of proper procedure."

CHRONOLOGY

September 16– November 29	The UN General Assembly convenes in Lake Success, NY, for its second session.
October 20	The House Un-American Activities Committee begins public hearings to investigate Communism in the entertainment industry.
October 21	The UN General Assembly passes Resolution 109, calling for the monitoring of "threats to the political independence and territorial integrity of Greece" by its northern Balkan neighbors.
October 29	The President's Committee on Civil Rights issues its report, *To Secure These Rights*, recommending the enactment of federal anti-lynching and anti-segregation legislation.
November 13	ER writes Truman opposing his loyalty program, saying, "I feel we have capitulated to our fear of Communism."
November 29	The UN General Assembly approves Resolution 181, endorsing UNSCOP's recommendation to partition Palestine into separate Arab and Jewish states.
December 2–17	The Commission on Human Rights meets in Geneva, Switzerland, to vote on a draft of the declaration of human rights for distribution to all UN member nations for review and comment.
December 29	Henry Wallace calls for "a new political alignment in America," announces his candidacy for president, and declares there is no difference between "a Truman and a Republican."
December 31	ER opposes Wallace's candidacy, telling her readers, "He will merely destroy the very things he wishes to achieve. I am sorry that he has listened to people as inept politically as he is himself."

1948

February 2	Truman sends Congress a ten-point program based on the report of the President's Committee on Civil Rights.
March 19	Warren Austin, as head of the US delegation to the UN, proposes a temporary trusteeship for Palestine under the UN Trusteeship Council, in place of the partition plan approved by the UN.
March 22	ER tells Marshall and Truman she will publicly oppose the US reversal of policy on Palestine and offers her resignation from the UN Human Rights Commission. Marshall refuses to accept her resignation.
March 27	ER departs on a month-long trip to Europe. Her itinerary includes speeches at the dedication of a statue of FDR in Grosvenor Square in London, to the Pilgrim Society in London, and at the University of Utrecht in the Netherlands.
April 3	Truman signs the Foreign Assistance Act of 1948 (European Recovery Program, or Marshall Plan) into law.
May 10	Truman orders the army to operate railroads to prevent a nationwide rail strike.
May 14	British Mandate in Palestine expires and Israel declares itself a state. Truman immediately grants *de facto* recognition.

May 19	House of Representatives passes Mundt-Nixon Bill requiring the Communist Party and "Communist-front" organizations to register with the Attorney General.
May 24	Third session of Human Rights Commission opens at Lake Success, NY, and begins revising the draft human rights declaration and covenant.
May 26	In South Africa, the National Party and its ally, the Afrikaner Party, win the majority of seats in the Parliament; apartheid formalized soon after.
June	The *Christian Register* publishes "Liberals In This Year of Decision," ER's rebuttal to Wallace.
June 21–25	Republican Party nominates Thomas Dewey for president and Earl Warren for vice-president.
June 24	USSR begins blockade of Berlin.
June 26	Truman orders airlift of supplies to Berlin; airlift continues until 30 September 1949.
July 12–15	Democratic Party nominates Truman for president and Kentucky Senator Alben Barkley for vice-president. Southern Democrats walk out of the Democratic convention and later nominate Strom Thurmond for president on the States Rights (Dixiecrat) ticket.
July 24–26	Progressive Party nominates Henry Wallace for president and Glen Taylor for vice president.
August 3	Whittaker Chambers testifies before House Committee on Un-American Activities, and accuses former State Department employee Alger Hiss and FDR's former assistant Lauchlin Currie of spying for the Soviet Union. Hiss denies charges. ER publicly defends Hiss and Currie.
August 18	At Truman's request, ER travels to Washington to confer with the president and Secretary Marshall on how best to handle the upcoming General Assembly Session. She agrees to give a major address on human rights.
September 28	ER delivers speech, "The Struggle for Human Rights," at the Sorbonne in Paris.
September 28–December 7	Third Committee of the UN General Assembly reviews the draft human rights declaration prepared by the Human Rights Commission, and debates amendments.
October 4	ER endorses Truman for president.
October 23–24	ER speaks to German women in Stuttgart, Germany, and visits Jewish and Ukrainian displaced persons camps.
October 31	In a radio broadcast from Paris, ER's only speech of the 1948 election campaign, she urges Americans to vote for Truman.
November 2	Truman is re-elected as president, defeating Dewey, Wallace, and Thurmond.
November 8	ER launches joint radio program with her daughter Anna Roosevelt Boettiger on ABC.

December 9–10	The UN General Assembly adopts the Universal Declaration of Human Rights by a vote of 48 to 0 with 8 abstentions. In her address to the delegates, ER urges them to remember that as they evaluate "a declaration of basic principles of human rights and freedoms" they should be aware that "we stand today at the threshold of a great event both in the life of the United Nations and in the life of mankind." The delegates give her a standing ovation for the leadership she displayed in its creation and adoption.
December 20	Laurence Duggan, who had been targeted by Mundt and Nixon, dies after falling from his office window.
December 21	ER requests a meeting with Truman to review the last session of the General Assembly.
December 22	ER uses her radio broadcast to attack the Ku Klux Klan, telling her audience, "Intolerance now bears a new mask—the mask of brotherhood. Bigotry has been streamlined."
December 28	ER prepares a memorandum Truman requested in preparation for their meeting in early January, writing, "The thing above all others which I would like to bring to your attention is that we are now engaged in a situation which is as complicated as fighting the war."

Abbreviations

Repositories and Manuscript Collections

AzU	University of Arizona Library	
	LWDP	Lewis W. Douglas Papers
CStMLK	Martin Luther King, Jr. Papers, Stanford University, Stanford, California	
	DGP	David Garrow Papers
CtY	Sterling Memorial Library, Yale University, New Haven, Connecticut	
	MLP	Max Lerner Papers
	FWP	Florence Willert Papers
DCU	Catholic University, Washington, DC	
	PMP	Philip Murray Papers
DcWaMMB	Mary McLeod Bethune Council House National Historical Site, National Archives for Black Women's History, Washington, DC	
	MMBP	Mary McLeod Bethune Papers
DDEL	Dwight David Eisenhower Presidential Library, Abilene, Texas	
	DDEP	Dwight David Eisenhower Papers
DGU	Lauinger Library, Special Collections, Georgetown University, Washington, DC	
	HLHP	Harry Lloyd Hopkins Papers
DLC	Library of Congress, Washington, DC	
	APRP	A Phillip Randolph Papers
	BPO	*Boston Post*
	BSCPR	Brotherhood of Sleeping Car Porter Records
	FJHH	Florence Jaffray (Hurst) Harriman Papers
	NAWSAP	National American Woman Suffrage Association Records
	NAACP	National Association for the Advancement of Colored People Records
	CHM	Charles Habib Malik Papers

ABBREVIATIONS

FDRL	Franklin Delano Roosevelt Presidential Library, Hyde Park, New York	
	AERP	Anna Eleanor Roosevelt Papers
	ARHP	Anna Roosevelt Halstead Papers
	CPTP	Charles Taussig Papers
	EJFP	Edward J. Flynn Papers
	FDRJrP	Franklin Delano Roosevelt, Jr. Papers
	DGC	David Gurewitsch Collection
	JRP	James Roosevelt Papers
	JPHP	E & James Hendrick Collection
	JPLP	Joseph P. Lash Papers
	LAHP	Lorena A. Hickok Papers
	SWP	Sumner Welles Papers
HSTL	Harry S. Truman Presidential Library, Independence, Missouri	
	HSTOF	Harry S. Truman Papers, Official Files
	HSTPF	Harry S. Truman Papers, Permanent Files
	HSTSF	Harry S. Truman Papers, President's Secretary's Files
	HSTWHCF	Harry S. Truman Papers, White House Central Files
	JPHP	James P. Hendrick Papers
	SIRP	Samuel I. Rosenman Papers
	PPF	Harry S. Truman Papers, President's Personal File
	TCP	Tom Clark Papers
IaU-LI	University of Iowa Libraries, Special Collections, Iowa City, Iowa	
	CBBP	Calvin Benham Baldwin Papers
	HAWP	Henry A. Wallace Papers
ICRC	Roosevelt University Library, Chicago, Illinois	
	RUA	Roosevelt University Archives
MCR-S	The Arthur and Elizabeth Schlesinger Library on the History of Women in America, Radcliffe College, Cambridge, Massachusetts	
	FLCKP	Florence Ledyard Cross Kitchett Papers
NARA II	National Archive and Records Administration, College Park, Maryland	
	RG59	Record Group 59: Central Files of the Department of State, 1778–1963

	RG84	Record Group 84: Records of the United States Mission to the United Nations and its Predecessors 1945-66
MiDW-AL		Walter P. Reuther Library, Archive of Labor History and Urban Affairs, Wayne State University, Detroit, Michigan
	UAWPOWR	International Union, United Automobile, Aerospace, and Agricultural Implement Workers of America President's Office: Walter P. Reuther Collection, 1933–1970
MU		W. E. B. Du Bois Library, University of Massachusetts, Amherst, Massachusetts
	WEBDP	W. E. B. (William Edward Burghardt) Du Bois Papers
MWelC		Wellesley College, Wellesley, Massachusetts
	UNORGA	Official Records, General Assembly, United Nations
	UNOR ECOSOC	Official Records, Economic and Social Council, United Nations
	RM:UND	Readex Microfiche: United Nations Documents
NCC-RB		The Herbert H. Lehman Suite and Papers, Columbia University, New York, New York
	JGMP	James G. McDonald Papers
NjP-SC		Princeton University Library, Special Collections and Manuscript Division, Princeton, New Jersey [Seely G. Mudd Library]
	AESP	Adlai E. Stevenson Papers
	BBP	Bernard Baruch Papers
	JFDP	John Foster Dulles Papers
PU-Ar		University of Pennsylvania Archives, Philadelphia, Pennsylvania
	LMP	Lewis Mumford Papers
StEdNL-M		National Library of Scotland, Edinburgh, Scotland
	PACM	Papers of Arthur Cecil Murray
ViLxM		George C. Marshall Research Foundation, Lexington, Virginia
	GCMP	George Catlett Marshall Papers
ViLxV		Virginia Military Institute, Lexington, Virginia
	GCMP	George Catlett Marshall Papers
WHi		State Historical Society of Wisconsin, Madison, Wisconsin
	ADAR	American for Democratic Action Records
	HGDP	Helen Gahagan Douglas Papers

ABBREVIATIONS

Standard References and Journals

ANB	*American National Biography*
ANBO	*American National Biography Online*
APSR	*American Political Science Review*
BI	*Biography Index*
BLD	*Black's Law Dictionary, Fifth Edition*
BRDS	*Biographic Register of the Department of State*
BDUSC	*Biographical Directory of the United States Congress*
CB	*Current Biography*
CBE	*Cambridge Biographical Encyclopedia, Second Edition*
CDAB	*Concise Dictionary of American Biography*
CE	*The Columbia Encyclopedia, Sixth Edition*
DAB	*Dictionary of American Biography*
DNB	*Dictionary of National Biography*
DPB	*Dictionary of Political Biography*
EAACH	*Encyclopedia of African-American Culture and History*
ELAACL	*Encyclopedia of Latin American and Caribbean Literature 1900-2003*
ELAH	*Encyclopedia of Latin American History*
EMME	*Encyclopedia of the Modern Middle East*
ENYC	*Encyclopedia of New York City*
EAI	*Encyclopedia American, International Edition*
EJH	*Encyclopedia of Jewish History*
EJW	*Encyclopedia of Jewish Women*
ERE	*Eleanor Roosevelt Encyclopedia*
EUN	*Encyclopedia of the United Nations and International Agreements*
FDRE	*Franklin D. Roosevelt Encyclopedia*
HDP	*Historical Dictionary of Poland, 1945-96*
HSTE	*Harry S. Truman Encyclopedia*
IWW	*Index to Women of the World from Ancient to Modern Times; Biographies and Portraits*
JWIA	*Jewish Women in America*
NAW	*Notable American Women*
NAWCTC	*Notable American Women: Completing the Twentieth Century*
NAWMP	*Notable American Women: The Modern Period*

NEB	New Encyclopedia Britannica
OCAMH	Oxford Companion to American Military History
OCP	Oxford Companion to Philosophy
OCPW	Oxford Companion to the Politics of the World
OCWWII	Oxford Companion to World War II
OEWH	Oxford Encyclopedia of World History
OMO	On My Own
OTCWH	Oxford Dictionary of Twentieth Century World History
OWW	Oxford Who's Who
OWWTC	Oxford Who's Who in the Twentieth Century
POFD	Pocket Oxford-Hachette French Dictionary
RCAH	The Readers Companion to American History
WH	Women Humanitarians: A Biographical Dictionary of British Women Active Between 1900 and 1950
WWSCE	Who's Who in the Socialist Countries of Europe
WWUN	Who's Who in the United Nations
WWWA	Who Was Who in America

Official Records: The United States and The United Nations

FRUS	Foreign Relations of the United States
RDS	Register of the Department of State
SDB	State Department Bulletin
UNOR ECOSOC	United Nations Official Records Economic and Social Council
UNORGA	United Nations Official Records General Assembly
YUN	Yearbook of the United Nations

Newspapers and Periodicals

IYAM	If You Ask Me
LHJ	Ladies Home Journal
MD	My Day
Newsweek	Newsweek Magazine
NYHT	New York Herald Tribune
NYT	New York Times
NYWT	New York World Tribune
PM	PM

ABBREVIATIONS

TL	*The Times of London*
Time	*Time Magazine*
WP	*Washington Post*

1945

"We have to start again under our own momentum
and wonder what we can achieve."

Eleanor Roosevelt did not anticipate leaving the White House in 1945. Yet less than four months after Franklin Roosevelt's fourth inauguration, she faced personal, professional, and political crises. As she confided to Lorena Hickok, "Franklin's death ended a period in history and now in its wake for lots of us who lived in his shadow periods come and we have to start again under our own momentum and wonder what we can achieve."[1] That same day, in order to quell speculation as to what new career she would pursue, she told her reading public that because she "was the wife of the President, certain restrictions were imposed upon me. Now I am on my own, and I hope to write as a newspaper woman."[2]

Although undecided about what path her career should take, ER knew that it must include her daily column and the political and policy work to which she had devoted her life. She resisted pressures to run for office, however, telling Secretary of the Interior Harold Ickes that her children should have that option and that she felt "very strongly" she could be more useful in other ways. The moment she accepted a party position she "would have to follow the party line pretty consistently" and while she wanted "to continue to work with the Democrats and for them," she thought the public "knowledge that I will be free of any obligation may at times be healthy." Reassuring Ickes that "my voice will not be silent," ER then promised that she would "help the liberals in this country."[3] In short, the issue was not what actions ER would take, but what forum (both public and private) she would use to make herself heard.

The following seventy-three documents recount the ways ER used her political voice and managed her new political position. They demonstrate the various vehicles—My Day and If You Ask Me columns, correspondence with world leaders and average citizens, speeches and the question and answer sessions that followed, petitions, and private conversations—ER used to address the issues she thought most critical to securing a just peace at home and around the world. Equal parts policy and politics, the documents also reflect ER's intense party loyalty and the political strategies she thought essential to Democratic victories in 1946 and 1948.

ER initially made My Day the centerpiece of her communications strategy. This nationally syndicated column allowed ER to speak to the American public from her home in Hyde Park, New York, while she helped settle FDR's estate and oversaw the transfer of the president's family home to the government. She used the column in a variety of ways—to support specific legislation, to tutor the American public on the nation's role in the postwar world, to advise (and goad) Congress and the president, to explain the economic underpinnings of international agreements like the Bretton Woods accords, and to rally support for the politics and social action she thought essential to securing prosperity and peace.

In the process, she told her readers why she thought full and fair employment so essential to democracy, why she thought the United Nations crucial to postwar stability, why she feared the atomic bomb, why she did not "fear" American Communists, why she held German citizens accountable for Hitler and the Holocaust, why she had little patience with political squabbles, and why she accepted appointment to the United Nations. Twice, the *New York Times* found these columns so important that it reprinted them on its front page, despite having to pay a competitor to do so. Yet, as her correspondence with David Dubinsky, Ben Rose, and Harry Truman illustrates, not everyone agreed with her positions—and in those circumstances, the column often spurred extended conversation with colleagues and strangers.

The correspondence included in this section reflects ER's attempt to define a new role for herself while continuing both to influence Truman's legislative and diplomatic policies and shape the Democratic agenda. Although a few letters present a deferential tone, ER's correspondence reflects a sharp political acumen she rarely displayed in public. Whether advising Truman on how best to handle Churchill and manage legislative relationships with Congress, or questioning Sidney Hillman and C. B. Baldwin on how they planned to raise the funds necessary to keep the liberal National Citizens Political Action Committee afloat, or challenging Walter Winchell's coverage of her remarks, ER went straight, but politely, to the point. Moreover, when critiquing the performance of party leaders such as Robert Hannegan, she could be quite blunt. As she wrote Ed Flynn, "Mr. Dewey is capable of playing a clever political game and we will not only have to be good politicians but really make our party honest, standing for the things which most of us as individuals know are right."[4]

By fall, with her duties to FDR's estate almost completed, ER resumed public speaking in a variety of settings. Although she adjusted her tone to each audience she addressed, she devoted her considerable energies to telling her listeners that American domestic policies have huge international implications. In Boston, she argued that "we are in an important moment in history. What happens here in the United States will either give courage to people in the other parts of the world, or on the other hand, will sap their courage."[5] In Newark, she urged her audience to cast out fear: "We must have confidence in one another and must avoid a situation where everybody approaches everyone else with suspicion."[6] In Chicago, she confessed that "it takes just as much determination to work for peace as it does to win a war" and she wondered "if we're going to have the courage and the strength to sustain our effort to win the peace."[7]

Thus by late December, when ER agreed to Truman's request that she join the US delegation to the United Nations, she had reasserted her voice, made her positions clear, and decided on a new political path. She did so, she told her readers, because "I feel a great responsibility to the youth who fought the war … Everyone of us has a deep and solemn obligation to them which we should fulfill by giving all that we are capable of giving to the making of peace so they can feel that the maximum good has come from their sacrifice."[8]

---

1. See Document 1, ER to Lorena Hickok, 19 April 1945.

2. See Document 2, My Day, 19 April 1945.

3. See Document 11, ER to Harold Ickes, 26 May 1945.

4. See Document 17, ER to Ed Flynn, 8 June 1945.

5. See Document 55, "Mrs. Roosevelt in PAC Talk Here," 1 November 1945.

6. See Document 47, "Suspicion as Peace Bar Feared by Mrs. Roosevelt," 2 October 1945.

7. See Document 59, Founder's Day Dinner Address, Roosevelt College, 10 November 1945.

8. See Document 69, My Day, 22 December 1945.

Thousands of grieving Americans lined the streets of Washington, DC, as FDR's funeral cortege passed April 14, 1945. As the nation struggled with the shock of his death, ER admitted her own sense of "melancholy and uncertainty." See Document 1. AP IMAGES.

Truman, who had attended FDR's funeral, returned to Hyde Park the following year to pay his respects. After visiting Truman in June 1945, ER told a friend she found him "the loneliest man I ever saw ... I am so sorry for him and he tries so hard." See Document 17. © CORBIS.

An SS guard works in a mass grave at Bergen-Belsen shortly after British troops liberated the concentration camp. "The horror-filled pictures and stories … make one shudder," ER wrote, as she wondered how "highly educated and civilized" people could become "sadists who enjoy seeing other human beings suffer." See Document 4. AP IMAGES.

Malvina "Tommy" Thompson and ER worked together for more than forty years. Confidante, secretary, gatekeeper, and editor, Tommy managed ER's correspondence, typed ER's dictated columns, and distributed ER's London diary. She also pressed ER to join the US delegation to the UN. See Documents 1, 3, and 68. © CORBIS.

Although ER respected and worked well with Democratic leaders Edward Flynn and James Farley (first and fourth men seated in the row), she challenged other party "bosses," especially Edward Kelly (third in the row), for corrupting the political process. See Documents 15–17. LISA LARSEN/TIME LIFE PICTURES/ GETTY IMAGES.

As she monitored the San Francisco Conference, ER wrote Secretary Stettinius expressing particular concern about Argentina's admission to the UN. By 1947, as the US increased its cooperation with Juan Perón's government, she asked Sumner Welles why we should cooperate with a nation where Germany is "the predominant influence?" See Documents 22 and 201. THOMAS D. MCAVOY/TIME LIFE PICTURES/ GETTY IMAGES.

ER thought Stettinius "brought the San Francisco Conference to a very successful conclusion." When Truman flew out to witness the signing ceremony, he replaced Stettinius with Byrnes. ER disapproved: "I hate Jimmy Byrnes going in because with all his ability, I think he is primarily interested in Jimmy Byrnes." See Document 22. GEORGE SKADDING/TIME LIFE PICTURES/GETTY IMAGES.

ER worked closely with Mayor Fiorello La Guardia and labor leader Sidney Hillman. In 1945, however, ER refused to endorse La Guardia's self-appointed successor and Hillman's request that she chair the National Citizens Political Action Committee because "it would alienate the Democratic Party." See Documents 25 and 31–34. © BETTMANN/CORBIS.

After the bombing of Hiroshima, ER wrote, "This new discovery cannot be ignored … If we desire our civilization to survive, then we must accept the responsibility of constructive work and of the wise use of a knowledge greater than any ever achieved by man before." See Document 35. © BETTMANN/CORBIS.

Bevin, Molotov, and Byrnes reconvened in Moscow in late 1945. ER had told an audience "the failure of the [first] meeting was … a foregone conclusion. When three men knew each other's background and temperament as little" as they did, she was not surprised "they could not reach agreement." See Document 48. AP IMAGES.

NAACP pickets the Daughters of the American Revolution in 1945 over its refusal to allow pianist Hazel Scott Powell to use Constitution Hall. "Discrimination," ER wrote, "sears the souls of human beings whose only fault is that God, who made us all, gave their skin a darker color." See Document 51. AP IMAGES.

In February 1945, FDR discussed Palestine with Ibn Saud and later assured the Saudi king that he "would take no action ... hostile to the Arab people." When Arab leaders accused Truman of neglecting FDR's pledge, Jewish leaders grew so concerned that Rabbi Wise asked ER to address the controversy. See Document 54. FOX PHOTOS/HULTON ARCHIVES/GETTY IMAGES.

ER and UAW president Walter Reuther, seen here in 1954, worked closely together for more than twenty years. In the fall of 1945, ER endorsed the Reuther-led UAW strike, praised its members' willingness to "risk their very livelihoods," and raised money for its strike fund. See Document 65.

© BETTMANN/CORBIS.

As the UAW strike escalated, ER resisted calls to resign from her own union. She replied "I believe that the prosperity of the people is tied up with the success of big and little business, but I see no way for business to prosper unless the people prosper." See Document 64. © BETTMANN/CORBIS.

ER arranged for W. E. B. Du Bois, Mary McLeod Bethune, and Walter White to serve as consultants to the US delegation to the San Francisco Conference. In December, she sought their advice before leaving for the General Assembly. See Document 71. NATIONAL PARK SERVICE, MARY MCLEOD BETHUNE COUNCIL HOUSE NATIONAL HISTORIC SITE, NATIONAL COUNCIL OF NEGRO WOMEN RECORDS. CATALOG NUMBER: MAMC 000073, IMAGE NUMBER MAMC-073-0474. PHOTOGRAPHER UNKNOWN.

LEAVING THE WHITE HOUSE

April 12, 1945, Eleanor Roosevelt held a press conference, discussed Russian war relief with Nina Magidoff and fair employment practices with Malcolm Ross, reviewed FDR's trusteeship plans with Charles Taussig,[1] and addressed a fund-raiser for a local charity. At 4:30 PM, FDR's press secretary Steve Early summoned her back to the White House. FDR had died of a cerebral hemorrhage in Warm Springs, Georgia. She telegraphed her sons, "HE DID HIS JOB TO THE END AS HE WOULD WANT YOU TO DO" and, with her daughter Anna, sat in her study, waiting to tell Truman that the president had died. After offering her support to the new president, she then left to claim her husband's body in Warm Springs. A little before midnight, after traveling five hours by plane and car, she reached the Little White House, retrieved his casket, and boarded the train for a twelve-hour return trip to Washington.[2]

After the president was laid to rest in Hyde Park, ER reached out to those whom she and her husband held in high regard. She confided to Harry Hopkins and Trude Lash, as they traveled back to the White House, that she had met with Truman after the service "to offer her help—as far as personalities are concerned, and that [the president] gratefully accepted the offer [or] at least he said he would ask for help." April 15, she wrote General George Marshall relaying how her husband "always spoke of his trust in you and his affection for you" and thanking the general for his "kindness and thoughtfulness in all the arrangements made." April 16, she confessed to Elinor Morgenthau that "readjusting is not so hard physically but mentally. I realize I counted much on Franklin's greater wisdom and it leaves one without much sense of backing." The following day, she wrote Henry Wallace, even though she hoped to see him before she left Washington, to make sure that he knew "that I feel that you are peculiarly fitted to carry out the ideals which were closest to my husband's heart …"[3]

ER spent her last day in the White House trying to balance "a great sense of relief" she felt after completing her various tasks against the concerns she had for the future. As she later wrote:

> I rode down in the old cagelike White House elevator that April morning with a feeling of melancholy and something of uncertainty, because I was saying good-by to an unforgettable era and I had given little thought to the fact that from this day forward I would be on my own.[4]

Yet as she admitted to her trusted confidante Lorena Hickok, she had already begun to consider what she could accomplish in her own right.

1

Eleanor Roosevelt to Lorena Hickok
19 April 1945 [Washington, DC]

Hick dearest,

The Trumans have just been to lunch and nearly all that I can do is done.[5] The upstairs looks desolate and I will be glad to leave tomorrow. It is empty and without purpose to be here now.

I've asked Helen[6] and Mary Norton[7] to come in on their way to Congress and say goodbye tomorrow and the Cabinet comes at 11. At 3 the top secretaries Steve,[8] Dr. Mac.[9] etc. At 3:30 office forces, at 4:30 household garage etc., at 5:30 I leave for the 6 p.m. train and so endeth a period.

Franklin's death ended a period in history and now in its wake for lots of us who lived in his shadow periods come and we have to start again under our own momentum and wonder what we can achieve. I hope you and I will be working together but as I don't intend to take on anything new till all the business of the Estate is over, you may be at new work before I am.[10]

I may be a bit weary when we get home tomorrow but I'm so glad you will be at the apartment.[11] Tommy[12] will probably be more weary than I am!

Much love dear,
E.R.

ALS LHP, FDRL

---

1. See Document 37.

2. ER to James, Franklin, Jr., Elliott, and John Roosevelt, 12 April 1945, AERP; Truman, vol. 1, 5; Lash, *Eleanor*, 720–22.

3. Trude Lash to Joe Lash, 15 April 1945, JPLP, FDRL; ER to George Marshall, 15 April 1945, CGMPUI; Lash, *World*, 186; ER to Henry Wallace, 17 April 1945, HAWP, IaU-LI.

4. ER to Joe Lash, 19 April 1945, JPLP, FDRL; Roosevelt, *OMO*, 1.

5. Although the Trumans had offered to live in Blair House to give ER time to move out of the White House, she declined their offer, wanting to vacate the mansion as soon as possible. The morning of April 19, she finished her personal packing as well as overseeing the removal of her husband's possessions and said goodbye to the press assigned to cover her throughout FDR's presidency (A. Black, *Casting*, 52).

6. Rep. Helen Gahagan Douglas (D-CA).

7. Rep. Mary Norton (D-NJ).

8. Stephen Tyree Early served as FDR's press secretary from 1933 to 1945 (*FDRE*).

9. Ross T. McIntire served as FDR's personal physician from 1935 to 1945 (*FDRE*).

10. Hickok, battling severe diabetes, resigned her position as executive secretary of the Women's Division of the Democratic National Committee and left Washington in March 1945. ER, who had helped secure that position for Hickok and who remained concerned about her precarious financial and physical health, had encouraged Hickok since FDR's 1944 victory to line up another, less taxing position to offset the loss in income she knew her friend would confront. When Hickok could not secure a full-time position, ER and Congresswoman Norton hired her to be their part-time research assistant for fall 1945. Hickok did not find permanent employment until 1947, when she joined the staff of the Women's Division of the State Democratic Committee of New York (*NAW*).

11. ER returned to her apartment, 29 Washington Square West, New York City.

12. Malvina ("Tommy") Thompson.

ON STARTING OVER

The morning of April 19, ER held a farewell tea for the sixty women reporters who had covered her throughout the Roosevelt administration. She then made two announcements. First, that she would continue writing her daily column, and that when they met again as competitors, she hoped she would also "often meet them as friends in many places." Responding to questions, she also announced that she would not attend the conference charged with organizing the United Nations. As Bess Furman reported:

> In a voice unusually low, Mrs. Roosevelt told her plans and requested that she not be directly quoted. Aside from continuing her writing, she said, she will not decide on anything until after she finishes the job that has to be done, helping to follow her husband's own wishes as to his effects.[1]

She also released the column below, hoping to stem the tide of speculation as to what position her future offered. The column did not end press inquiries. That evening, the *Washington Star* reported that "Mrs. Roosevelt Will Continue Column: Seeks No Office Now" and at 10 PM that evening, as ER exited the cab which brought her from Penn Station to her New York City apartment, she again faced a crowd of reporters questioning her about her plans, all of whom remained unconvinced by her declaration that "the story is over."[2]

2

My Day
19 April 1945

WASHINGTON, Wednesday—One has to live in Washington to know what a city of rumors it is. Sometimes the rumors are based on fact, sometimes they are just based on what somebody said to somebody else!

Yesterday I was interested to hear a number of such rumors.[3] First, that I wanted to be a special delegate to the San Francisco Conference.[4] I had to tell Congresswoman Norton that I could not possibly go, and beg her not to make a speech about it.[5]

Then, I heard a rumor that I was going to run for a Federal elective position and, finally, that I was a candidate for Secretary of Labor![6] I had to tell several people quite forcibly that nothing would induce me to run for public office or to accept an appointment to any office at the present time.

I have two jobs that I consider myself obligated to do and that I want to do. My daily column I have always looked upon as a job which I wanted to have considered on its merits. Because I was the wife of the President, certain restrictions were imposed upon me. Now I am on my own, and I hope to write as a newspaper woman. I certainly should have background to bring to the job, and if I have not developed powers of observation and correct reporting in the past years, that will soon be discovered.

My magazine page is also a contract that I wish to fulfill as well as I possibly can.[7] Outside of these two occupations, I hope I shall be able to do an occasional article on subjects which are of interest to me and to others.

For the next few months, however, there is a great deal of business which I feel it is an obligation to attend to both because of my husband and my children. My husband was a collector, with a great interest in history. This means that the children and I have many things which we must go over and which we cannot consider from the purely personal point of view, since, in acquiring them, my husband thought of their historic interest to the public and their value to future generations rather than of their value to us as a family.[8]

The sad news has just come to us that Ernie Pyle has been killed at the front with our boys on Okinawa. To thousands and thousands of people all over the world, his column has brought the best understanding of the human side of our fighting men.

Mr. Pyle wanted above everything else to see them and to be with them in the Pacific. I am glad he had the opportunity but, like many others, I shall miss his column, with its gracious understanding of human beings. I shall never forget how much I enjoyed meeting him here in the White House last year and how much I admired this frail and modest man who could endure hardships because he loved his job and our men.[9]

TMs AERP, FDRL

---

1. Bess Furman, "Mrs. Roosevelt Bids Press Adieu," *NYT*, 20 April 1945, 20.

2. "Roosevelt Family Leaves the White House," *NYT*, 21 April 1945, 21.

3. The source of the rumor is unknown.

4. Fifty nations, allied in the war against Germany and Japan, agreed to attend the United Nations Conference on International Organization (UNCIO) scheduled to convene in San Francisco April 25, 1945, to approve the goals and framework under which the new organization would operate. Before arriving, member nations had endorsed the Atlantic Charter and the Tehran Declaration and reviewed the proposals generated at the Dumbarton Oaks conference and the Yalta summit. While all understood the necessity of an international organization committed to peace and collective security, several nations had serious reservations about the Dumbarton Oaks and Yalta agreements. Their delegates arrived in San Francisco instructed to ensure that the charter of the new organization would contain the clarifications they thought essential both to their individual needs and the organization's success. After two months of debate, the delegates adopted the UN Charter and set October 24, 1945, as the date upon which it would take effect.

The San Francisco conference, largely the vision of FDR, increasingly occupied his time before his death. Anne O'Hare McCormick, the last journalist to interview FDR, left the president convinced that he saw UNCIO "as the crowning act of his career." As she later reported, even though the war daily drew closer to conclusion, the president "fixed" all his thoughts "on the meeting at the Golden Gate" where, he hoped, "the forge of war was still hot enough to fuse the nations together."

Indeed, FDR paid such detailed attention to conference planning that he took control of conference logistics away from the State Department, and spent the day before his death planning the seating chart, coordinating the delegates' arrival schedules, and tracing the train route he and ER would take to San Francisco (Schlesinger, *Creation*, 1–72; Anne O'Hare McCormick, "His 'Unfinished Business'—And Ours," *NYT*, 22 April 1945, SM3). See also *n*4 Document 3.

5. ER looked forward to accompanying FDR to the conference, telling him that "having the first UN meeting in San Francisco is a stroke of genius," and worked with Democratic National Committee leader Gladys Tillett to get more women appointed to the US delegation. ER had announced April 2 that she would accompany FDR to San Francisco for the conference; indeed, she had discussed the mechanics and timing of the conference with such fervor that Martha Strayer of the *Washington Daily News* noted in her transcript of the press conference that "Mrs. Roosevelt was interested in the organization of the United Nations more keenly than she had been in anything since the early days of the New Deal." April 12, in what would be her final press conference

as First Lady, ER again reiterated her strong support for the five women's organizations scheduled to attend the meeting.

Representative Norton, who knew of ER's commitment to UNCIO, called her four days after FDR's death to urge ER to attend, arguing that she could make both symbolic and substantive contributions. ER, though very interested, resisted her friend's arguments, citing protocol and estate matters (Beasley, *Press Conferences*, 331, 334; Lash, *Years*, 719; Mary Norton to Lorena Hickok, 18 April 1945, LAHP, FDRL).

6. Upon hearing of FDR's death, Secretary of Labor Frances Perkins offered her resignation to Truman, effective July 1. Truman, who thought her "a grand lady—but no politician," accepted her offer, confided to his close aides that "he really didn't want a woman in the cabinet anyway," asked her to resign earlier than she had planned, and replaced her with his close friend Lewis Schwellenbach (Hamby, *Man*, 306–7).

7. In June 1941, ER began If You Ask Me, a monthly question and answer column *Ladies' Home Journal* (*LHJ*) carried until June 1949, when ER signed with *McCall's*, which published the column until ER's death in 1962. Already a veteran columnist before signing with *LHJ*, ER had edited *Babies, Just Babies* (October 1932–June 1933), and written monthly columns for the *Women's Democratic News* (April 1930–December 1935), *Woman's Home Companion* (August 1933–July 1935), and *Democratic Digest* (August 1937–1941) (Edens, viii).

8. FDR's will provided that ER would receive the income from his estate during her lifetime. He also left Springwood, the Roosevelt family home in Hyde Park, to the National Park Service with the proviso that ER and the children could continue to live there during their lifetimes, if they chose to do so. ER and the children agreed among themselves that they did not wish to exercise this right. All the rest of the property, including ER's Val-Kill Cottage, remained the property of the estate. After debating whether she could afford to purchase it, ER decided to buy 842 acres of land, including Val-Kill and Top Cottage, the retreat FDR built on Dutchess Hill in 1938, from the estate and go into partnership with her son Elliott, who wished to manage the property as a farm.

After FDR's death, ER spent a great deal of her time packing, unpacking, and making decisions about how to dispose of furniture, china, books, and other personal property that had to be removed from Springwood before the government took possession on June 15 (Lash, *Years*, 24–26, 58; "Roosevelt Estate Put at $1,943,888," *NYT*, 7 June 1947, 15).

9. Ernie Pyle (1900–1945), widely admired war correspondent who recorded in his nationally syndicated column the daily existence of ordinary soldiers at war, was killed by Japanese machine gun fire on the island of Ie near Okinawa on April 18, 1945. ER, who admired Pyle, lobbied him over tea November 3, 1943, telling him of the sense of neglect the soldiers conveyed to her during her five-week tour of bases and hospitals in the Pacific Theatre, and asking him "to do for the boys in the South Pacific what you had done for those in Africa" ("Ernie Pyle Is Killed on Ie Island; Foe Fired When All Seemed Safe," and "Ernie Pyle," *NYT*, 19 April 1945, 1 and 26; Tobin, 128–30).

On FDR and the Founding of
the United Nations

Although ER devoted the bulk of her time to settling FDR's estate, she used My Day to remind her readers of the opening of the San Francisco conference and to urge them to follow its proceedings closely.

3

My Day
25 April 1945

HYDE PARK, Tuesday—Last night my feet ached, because all day long I had stood saying to people: "Yes, that trunk goes in such and such a room … Those things go into the library … Those things go into the dining room … Those can stay in the hall." In the meantime Miss Thompson did the same thing at the cottage[1] until, she said, her back ached. Both of us ran up and downstairs many times during the day and called each other on the telephone trying to decide where different things went.

Tomorrow the San Francisco conference will open. My husband and I had looked forward to traveling leisurely across the country and spending that day in San Francisco. He had talked over his speech; he had even looked over a first draft.[2] But when I asked him why he really wanted to go all that distance for one day, he said: "I am going to pray over the delegates."[3]

I think that is the way we are all approaching this important conference. For a long time we have been building points of contact where the United Nations could work on some specific thing in unison. The organization of food for the world, the organization of rehabilitation and relief, world labor problems, world educational problems—all these have been stepping stones. Delegates from many nations have discussed these problems one at a time.[4] Early meetings of the leaders of the great nations laid a greater stress on plans for winning the war, but lately they have begun to envision the broad lines of peace on which all the nations might work together.[5]

Now, at last, we come to the San Francisco meeting, the purpose of which is not to write in detail all the plans for the future. Rather, it is merely to set up an organization before which, at a later time, these problems of peace will come up for discussion. The setting up of this machinery is not an end in itself, but it is an essential step on the way. Without the machinery, future generations could never build a peaceful world.

Someone said to me the other day that in the past we relied so completely as a nation upon my husband in international matters, that perhaps more of us would now recognize our duty to carry some of the burden ourselves. Instead of being satisfied just to follow, we would take a more active interest. I know that President Truman and our Secretary of State, Mr. Stettinius, together with the other members of our delegation,[6] will do all they possibly can to bring about a cooperative spirit among the delegates and to set up a framework within which we can work in the future.

Our job is to build an atmosphere in the country as a whole that will reassure the other peoples of the world as to our firm intention to live in a peaceful and democratic world. Above everything else, we should let our delegates know that we are keenly following every move at this historic meeting.

TMs AERP, FDRL

---

1. Two buildings sat adjacent to Fal-Kill Creek on the Roosevelt property. In 1925, FDR commissioned Harry Toombs to design a simple structure to serve as both a home for Marion Dickerman

and Nancy Cook, ER's close friends and political colleagues, and as a Roosevelt family retreat. In 1926, ER and the two women built a larger structure adjacent to the cottage in which they established Val-Kill Industries, a pilot program to train unemployed agricultural workers to become furniture makers and craftsmen. In 1936, the three partners could no longer sustain the losses the project generated and a rift (that would eventually derail it) appeared in the women's friendship, prompting ER to remodel the building as a residence in 1937. The rambling stucco structure, made up of about twenty rooms of various sizes, provided living quarters for herself and her secretary, Malvina ("Tommy") Thompson, and guest rooms for the many children, grandchildren, friends, and colleagues who would visit her there during the years that followed. For additional information on ER's purchase of Val-Kill Cottage from the Roosevelt estate, see *n*5 Document 2. For information on the dissolution of the Val-Kill partnership see Cook, vol. 2, 525–37.

2. FDR had instructed Archibald MacLeish to draft remarks for him to deliver at the opening session of UNCIO. The draft FDR reviewed described the conference as "perhaps the most important new beginning in the history of mankind." It conveyed the president's hopefulness, that despite the collapse of the League of Nations, the UN would succeed, because "never before in the history of the relations to each other of the peoples of the world have nations worked together as we worked together" to win the war and create the United Nations. Urging the delegates to look past the differences that may arise, the draft then urged the delegates to recognize the importance of the charter they would develop:

> No one expects—no one who has studied the history of human law expects—that the charter which this Conference produces will answer all the questions or resolve all the problems. No charter, no constitution, no basic document was ever drafted which did not have its flaws. We shall deceive ourselves if we do not acknowledge at the outset that later generations may wish to change our work, to enlarge its scope, to alter its applications. But we shall do worse than deceive ourselves if we do not realize also the existence of a charter of world organizations is more important than the details of its terms. What is important in a new beginning is to begin.

FDR would then conclude his remarks:

> Let us make the proposed organization as perfect as we can before wc approve it. But let us not sacrifice approval to perfection in the final choice. Let us rather make a beginning now than wait to build a perfect world thereafter. Let us rather take action now "in full faith and confidence" that our work will be improved with time, than refuse to act because our work is not what every one of us could wish (Draft, Address to be Delivered by the President at the Opening of the San Francisco Conference, AMP, LOC; Sherwood, 841).

3. See *n*1 Document 2.

4. Although the International Agricultural Institute, the first international organization created to address food and agriculture policy, began operations in 1905, most of the international organizations with which ER worked grew out of the League of Nations' postwar work. In 1919, the League established the International Labour Organization (ILO) to create guidelines supporting compassionate labor policy, adequate living conditions, and legally binding arbitration procedures. In 1923, the League convened its Food Commission to propose remedies to the increasing problems world hunger posed to international security and, in 1939, forty-four nations agreed to create the United Nations Relief and Rehabilitation Administration (UNRRA) to "provide humanitarian aid and assistance in ways that none of them could provide alone" to the "suffering peoples" of Asia and Europe. In 1943, the United Nations (those nations united in the war against Germany and Japan) met in Hot Springs, Arkansas, adopted the Hot Springs Food Declaration announcing that the lack of food can be "justified neither by ignorance nor by harshness of nature," and called for the establishment of the Food and Agricultural Organization (FAO) to address the problems of

hunger and poverty. The international campaign for education, however, took a different path, pre-ferring instead to work through independent groups, such as the Women's League for Peace and Freedom, and individual petitions to the Permanent Court of International Justice (Palmowski, 289–90; *EUN*, 269–70, 368–71; Lauren, 116, 157).

5. See *n*1 Document 2. The idea of the United Nations, largely the vision of FDR, evolved over the course of the war beginning at the Atlantic Charter Conference in August 1941, the first sum-mit meeting between FDR and Churchill. Representatives of the United States, Great Britain, China, and the Soviet Union began drafting detailed plans for the international organization at a conference at Dumbarton Oaks in Washington in the fall of 1944 and the structure and powers of the United Nations became important topics of discussion among FDR, Churchill, and Stalin at the Yalta conference in January 1945 (Schlesinger, 33–73).

6. February 14, FDR appointed Sen. Tom Connally (D-TX) and Sen. Arthur Vandenberg (R-MI), chair and ranking member of the Senate Foreign Relations Committee; Rep. Sol Bloom (D-NY) and Rep. Charles Eaton (R-NJ), chair and ranking member of the House Foreign Affairs Committee; Harold Stassen, the former Republican governor of Minnesota; and Virginia Gildersleeve, dean of Barnard College to the US delegation. Secretary of State Edward Stettinius served as its chair ("Stassen Appointed a Delegate To United Nations Conference," *NYT*, 14 February 1945, 1).

On Germans and the Holocaust

At the request of General Dwight D. Eisenhower, congressmen and journalists visited the Nazi concentration camps in Germany in late April 1945. As the Allies liberated the camps, photographs and detailed reports on the atrocities committed there received wide publicity. The horrors of the camps raised painful questions about complicity and citizen inaction, which ER addressed in the following column.

4

My Day
28 April 1945

NEW YORK, Friday—The Congressional committee now visiting concentration camps in Germany are viewing things which we at home find it difficult to take in. The horror-filled pictures and stories which we have been getting day by day in our various newspapers make one shudder.[1] The sufferings inflicted on war victims is cruel enough. But one also wonders what must have been done to a people who are willing to inflict such suffering. Something must have happened that we know nothing about to turn people who were highly educated and civilized into sadists who enjoy seeing other human beings suffer.

I read that one of our men, who had been a prisoner of the Germans and who is now back in this country, laughed when it was suggested that the townspeople near one of these camps did not know what was going on. He pointed out that there was constant communication between the camp and the town, and that it would have been impossible for the people of the town to be oblivious of what was happening. It is therefore not just a question of soldiers obeying orders. It is a question of civilians reaching such a state of servitude that they accepted without protest whatever happened to other human beings.

No wonder we are concerned about what kind of government and education shall be carried on during the occupation period. None of us can achieve much that is worthwhile unless we understand what happened to these people; and I am frank to say that, for me, it is still a complete mystery. I went to school with German girls, I have known German men and women.[2] The military caste always seemed to me obnoxious, both as travel companions and as passers-by on the street. But the average human beings in Germany seemed just like other people.

The Nazi regime, the SS and the Gestapo are, of course, an obvious explanation. But how could they have become entrenched without the people being aware of what was happening? That is the really terrifying question. One wonders if other people could be fooled in the same way, and one longs to know how to prevent its happening anywhere to any people ever again.

Our men who have been prisoners of war, and who have seen these horrors which we read about, will have lost some of that confidence in their fellow human beings which is part of the heritage of every American citizen. It will take time to make them believe again that predominately people have good intentions, and I don't think they will be patient with talk which does not materialize into action.

TMs, AERP, FDRL

1. See, for example, William S. White, "Congress, Press to View Horrors," *NYT*, 22 April 1945, 13; "Congressmen and Army Chiefs Get a Firsthand View of Nazi Horror Camps," *NYT*, 27 April 1945, 3; William S. White, "War Crime Report Horrifies Capital," *NYT*, 16 May 1945, 10.

2. ER also traveled in Germany with her parents as a child and with FDR on her honeymoon. Some of her classmates at Allenswood school for girls in England, which she attended from 1899 until 1902, were German. Carola von Passavant (von Schaeffer-Bernstein after her marriage) became a good friend until she supported Hitler's government. She and ER had stayed in touch until World War I, and then corresponded again in the 1930s when ER was baffled that Carola, a devout Christian, could support Hitler. After Hitler's defeat, the two women met again in Frankfurt, when ER asked American army personnel to help her locate her classmate. Their encounter was painful. When ER asked her classmate how she could be "so devoted to the principles of the church yet not protest the mistreatment of the Jews," von Schaeffer-Bernstein replied "sometimes it is wiser not to look over the hill." ER responded while it was good to see her again, "there is a sadness … which I am afraid it is hard to get away from" (Lash, *Eleanor*, 75–76, 149, 203, 561, 567, 574–75, 582; *Years*, 116; Carola von Schaeffer-Bernstein to ER, 14 March 1949, and ER to Carola von Schaeffer-Bernstein, 11 April 1949, AERP).

On the Dangers of Racial Superiority

By 1939, ER had begun to equate American racism with Aryanism, when she asked audiences around the nation "why curse Hitler and support Jim Crow?" When A. Philip Randolph and other leaders formed the March on Washington coalition in 1940 to pressure FDR into outlawing segregation in defense industry employment, ER sided with coalition leaders, with whom FDR asked her to meet, and argued in favor of their stance. FDR then created the Fair Employment Practices Commission (FEPC) to monitor hiring practices.[1]

As war production decreased and unemployment in defense industries increased, Congress could not agree on how (or if) the agency's funding should be continued. Two competing bills dominated congressional debate. One decreased the agency's budget and extended the FEPC's mandate only until the end of the war. The other, Representative Norton's proposal for a permanent FEPC, languished in the House Rules Committee, whose members refused to allow it to come to the floor for a vote.[2]

ER, as the following column illustrated, lent her vocal support to Norton's proposal.

5

My Day
30 April 1945

NEW YORK, Sunday—Representative Mary Norton of New Jersey is making a magnificent fight for the passage of the Fair Employment Practices bill. This bill would give us a permanent group in the government whose function it would be to see that, as far as employment goes throughout this country, there is complete equality of opportunity and treatment for all.

Many people have come to think of this bill as being of value only to certain minority groups. I think it is important for the public in general to understand clearly that the bill, while it may be of value to these groups, is equally vital to each and every one of us who are citizens of the United States. If we do not see that equal opportunity, equal justice and equal treatment are meted out to every citizen, the very basis on which this country can hope to survive with liberty and justice for all will be wiped away.

Are we learning nothing from the horrible pictures of the concentration camps which have been appearing in our papers day after day?[3] Are our memories so short that we do not recall how in Germany this unparalleled barbarism started by discrimination directed against the Jewish people? It has ended in brutality and cruelty meted out to all people, even to our own boys who have been taken prisoner. This bestiality could not exist if the Germans had not allowed themselves to believe in a master race which could do anything it wished to all other human beings not of their particular racial strain.

There is nothing, given certain kinds of leadership, which could prevent our falling a prey to this same kind of insanity, much as it shocks us now. The idea of superiority of one race over another must not continue within our own country, nor must it grow up in our dealings with the rest of the world. It is self-evident that there are people in certain parts of the world who, because of different opportunities and environment, have not progressed as far as other people in what we call civilization. That does not mean, however, that they will forever be inferior in our type of civilization. Given the same kind of opportunities, they may do better than we have done.

Looking at the war-torn world of today, we cannot say that our civilization has been perfect. We can only say that we have created greater material comfort for human beings and that we are struggling to find a way of living together peacefully and cooperatively in the future.

That is a great step forward, and we are taking it internationally; but we must also take it within our own borders. We cannot complain that the Germans starved and maltreated our boys if we at home do not take every step—both through our government and as individuals—to see not only that fairness exists in all employment practices, but that throughout our nation all people are equal citizens. Where the theory of a master race is accepted, there is danger to all progress in civilization.

TMs AERP, FDRL

---

1. A. Black, "Champion."

2. June 25, 1941, FDR signed Executive Order 8802, which outlawed discrimination in defense and government agencies on the basis of "race, creed, color, or national origin" and created the Fair Employment Practices Commission (FEPC), a temporary agency charged with monitoring employment practices to promote "full and equitable participation of all workers in the defense industries." More symbolic than effective, the FEPC nevertheless proved to be a lightning rod for liberals and conservatives (Kennedy, *Freedom*, 767; Hamby, *Beyond*, 61).

See also *n*2 Document 12 for ER's further discussions of FEPC congressional debates.

3. See *n*1 Document 4. In a letter to Winston Churchill on April 30, 1945, ER wrote: "The news that we get day by day of the shocking behavior of the Germans, makes one realize the depths of degradation to which fanaticism plunges a whole people. We must pledge ourselves, with God's help, to prevent any recurrence of what we are witnessing today" (ER to Winston Churchill, 30 April 1945, AERP).

6

If You Ask Me [excerpt]
Ladies' Home Journal May 1945

What is the difference between Russia grabbing a slice of Poland and Germany doing it? How can we condone one, and condemn the other?[1]

It is against the conscience of the American people to take any land from a sovereign state, but I think there are some differences in the situation which you state.

We must remember that Poland for two hundred years in the past invaded parts of Russia, that her boundaries have been changed over and over again,[2] and that when Germany invaded Poland she knew that Great Britain had concluded an alliance with Poland which bound her to come to Poland's aid.[3]

In the course of the war Russia's alliances have changed. She first had a defensive alliance with Germany, hoping to prevent the invasion of her own country until she was ready to defend herself.[4] When the invasion by Germany came, Russia had already gone into a part of Poland where a great many of the people were Slavs.[5] Her great objective in the future is not the acquisition of more territory, since she has as much land as anyone could want, but she does want to make her boundaries as secure as possible. If she can achieve this even by taking some land from the conquered and giving it to a country like Poland, from which she is taking some land, but with whom she hopes to establish friendly relationships, we may not condone it, but we cannot look upon it in the same light as we would the outright conquest of a nation by a power that planned to make the people completely subservient to their wishes, as Germany did.

TMsex LHJ, DLC

———

1. At the Yalta conference, FDR, British prime minister Winston Churchill, and Marshall Josef Stalin, chair of the Soviet Council of Peoples Commissars and the State Defense Committee, agreed that Russia would receive the eastern third of Poland. (Germany, whose attack on Poland on September 1, 1939 had precipitated World War II, was to compensate Poland for the territorial loss with some of its land.) As the war ended, the Allies disagreed as to where the Polish border should be set with the British and Americans preferring the River Oder and the Soviets preferring the River Neisse (*HSTE*; Ralph et al., 589).

2. In the sixteenth and seventeenth centuries, Poland existed as an independent nation whose borders stretched from the Baltic to the Black Sea. However, the weakness of the Polish government and the corruption of its nobility undercut the independent government and increased its vulnerability to foreign incursion. In 1772, Poland lost its realm as Russia, Austria, and Prussia carved up its territory. As internal tensions increased, Russia intervened in 1795 and governed the kingdom of Poland as a Russian protectorate. Despite concessions made at the Congress of Vienna, Poland did not regain independence until 1918, and even then Lithuania and Soviet Russia continued to dispute its boundaries, especially after the Treaty of Versailles treated Poland as a buffer state for the Soviet Union (*OEWH*, 531–32; Ralph et al., 576).

3. The British signed a formal treaty with Poland on August 25, 1939.

4. The Germans and the Russians signed two agreements on August 23, 1939, a nonaggression pact and a secret protocol dividing Eastern Europe into German and Russian spheres of influence (Dziewanowski, 242).

5. Hitler's forces invaded Soviet Russia on June 21, 1941. At that point, the Soviets had already occupied Eastern Poland, including those parts of the Ukraine and Byelorussia ceded to the Poles in 1921 (Dziewanowski, 243).

On Churchill, Stalin, and
the German Surrender

When Truman announced the end of the war in Europe on May 8, ER, who had listened to his radio address, wrote to say that she had been "deeply moved" and that she hoped the end of the war in Europe "will in some small way lighten your burdens for which we are all grateful." Knowing that May 8 was also the president's birthday, she closed her note offering her "best wishes that your future birthdays will be happier ones."[1]

Truman's eight-page handwritten reply, however, focused more on her May 10 column than it did her congratulations. Concerned to read in My Day that although ER "listened to many of the broadcasts" throughout the day, she could not stop "wondering why the Russians withheld their announcement of the end of the war until 6 in the evening," Truman decided to "explain the situation" to her.[2]

7

Harry Truman to Eleanor Roosevelt
10 May 1945 [The White House]

Dear Mrs. Roosevelt:

Your note of the 8th is most highly appreciated. The whole family were touched by your thoughtfulness.

I noticed in your good column today you expressed some surprise at the Russian attitude on the close of the European War.[3]

I think I should explain the situation to you. On Wednesday April 25th our Minister to Sweden sent a message to me saying that Himmler wanted to surrender to Gen. Eisenhower all their troops facing the Western Front and that the Germans would continue to fight the Russians. Before our State Department could get the message deciphered the Prime Minister called me from London and read the message to me.[4] That was the great mystery of the trip to the Pentagon Bldg.[5]

The matter was discussed with our Staff and the offer was very promptly refused. The Russians were notified of our joint action. Prince Bernadotte of Sweden informed our Minister that Hitler had had a brain blowup of some sort and would be dead in twenty four hours—so Himmler had informed him. The P.M. and I decided that when the Gestapo Butcher said a man would be dead in twenty four hours he usually made good on the promise.[6]

Negotiations went on for two more days—we, always insisting on complete unconditional surrender on all fronts. The German idea, of course, was to split the three great powers and perhaps make things easier for themselves. Our Headquarters kept me informed all the time by almost hourly messages. We were nearly at an agreement and the famous Connolly statement came out and completely upset the apple cart.[7] Himmler was displaced by Admiral Doenitz[8] and a new start was made.

Germans delayed and delayed trying all the time to quit only on the Western Front. They finally offered Norway, Denmark, Holland and the French Ports they still held but wanted to keep resisting the Russians. Our Commanding General finally told them that he would turn loose all we had and drive them into the Russians. They finally signed at Rheims the terms of unconditional surrender effective at 12:01 midnight of May 8-9.[9]

In the meantime Churchill, Stalin and I had agreed on a simultaneous release at 9A.M. Washington time, 3 P.M. London and 4 P.M. Moscow time. Then the Associated Press broke faith with Gen. Eisenhower.[10] The Germans kept fighting the Russians and Stalin informed me that he had grave doubts of the Germans carrying out the terms. There was fighting on the Eastern front right up to the last hour.

In the meantime Churchill was trying to force me to break faith with the Russians and release on the 7th, noon Washington time, 6 P.M. London, 7 P.M. Moscow. I wired Stalin and he said the Germans were still firing. I refused Churchill's request and informed Stalin of conditions here and in England and that unless I heard from him to the contrary I would release at 9 A.M. May 8th. I didn't hear so the release was made, but fighting was still in progress against the Russians. The Germans were finally informed that if they didn't cease firing as agreed they would not be treated as fighting men but as traitors and would be hanged as caught. They then ceased firing and Stalin made his announcement the 9th.

He had sent me a message stating the situation at 1 A.M. May 8th and asking postponement until May 9th. I did not get the message until 10 A.M. May 8, too late, of course, to do anything.

I have been trying very carefully to keep all of my engagements with the Russians because they are touchy and suspicious of us. The difficulties with Churchill are very nearly as exasperating as they are with the Russians. But patience I think must be our watch word if we are to have World Peace. To have it we must have the whole hearted support of Russia, Great Britain and the United States.

I hope this won't bore you too much—but I thought you'd like to know the facts. Please keep it confidential until it can be officially released.

Please accept my thanks again for your good message.

Most sincerely,
Harry S. Truman

ALS AERP, FDRL

> In her reply, ER reported concerns that she did not discuss in My Day, offered blunt advice on the best way to handle Churchill, and warned the president to be on the alert for aides, who, for their own political reasons, might delay passing information up the chain of command. She knew "those little things had been done" to FDR "now and then," and she thought she should warn the president to watch his military aides closely. Concerned also that Truman would need as much help dealing with Stalin as he did with Churchill, ER recommended that he speak with her son Elliott, whose advice she thought would be as candid as the advice she had just dispensed.

8
———

Eleanor Roosevelt to Harry Truman
14 May 1945 [Hyde Park]

Dear Mr. President:

I was very much touched to have you take the trouble to write me that long letter in longhand about the Russian situation. Please, if you write again, do have it typed because I feel guilty to take any of your time.

I am typing this because I know my husband always preferred to have things typed so he could read them more quickly and my handwriting is anything but legible.

Your experience with Mr. Churchill is not at all surprising. He is suspicious of the Russians and they know it. If you will remember, he said some pretty rough things about them years ago and they do not forget.[11]

Of course, we will have to be patient, and any lasting peace will have to have the Three Great Powers behind it. I think, however, if you can get on a personal basis with Mr. Churchill, you will find it easier. If you talk to him about books and let him quote to you from his marvelous memory everything on earth from Barbara Fritche to the Nonsense Rhymes and Greek tragedy, you will find him easier to deal with on political subjects.[12] He is a gentleman to whom the personal element means a great deal.

Mr. Churchill does not have the same kind of sense of humor that the Russians have. In some ways the Russians are more like us. They enjoy a practical joke, rough-house play and they will joke about things which Mr. Churchill thinks are sacred. He takes them dead seriously and argues about them when what he ought to do is to laugh. That was where Franklin usually won out because if you know where to laugh and when to look upon things as too absurd to take seriously, the other person is ashamed to carry through even if he was serious about it.

You are quite right in believing that the Russians will watch with great care to see how we keep our commitments.

A rumor has reached me that that message from Mr. Stalin to you was really received in plenty of time to have changed the hour but it was held back from you.[13] Those little things were done to my husband now and then. I tell you of this rumor simply because while you may have known about it and decided that it was wise just not to receive it in time, you told me in your letter that you did not receive it and I have known of things which just did not reach my husband in time. That is one of the things which your Military and Naval aides ought to watch very carefully.

Sometime when you have time, since my son, Elliott, is in Washington now and then, you might like to let him tell you about what he learned of the Russians when he was there. He was in Russia quite a good deal and helped establish our airforce there and he has an old friend who is the only American who has flown with the Russians from the very beginning. Elliott gets on well with them and understands the peculiar combination that can look upon human life rather cheaply at times and yet strive for an ideal of future well-being for the people and make the people believe in it. He has an understanding of their enjoyment of drama and music and the arts in general and he realizes what few people seem to understand—namely that when you telescope into a few years a development in civilization which has taken hundreds of years for the people around you to achieve, the development is very uneven.[14]

I will, of course, keep confidential anything which comes to me in any letter from you and I will never mention it, and I would not use a private letter in any public way at any time.

I would not presume to write you this letter only you did say you would like me to give you some little personal impressions of these people, gathered from my husband's contacts, before you went to meet them and as I realize that may happen soon, I thought perhaps you would like this letter now.

If you or any of your family ever feel like getting away from formality and spending a few days with me in this very simple cottage, I should love to have you and I am quite accustomed to the necessary Secret Service protection.

With much gratitude for the trouble which you took, and with my kind regards to Mrs. Truman and your daughter, believe me,

Very cordially yours,
Eleanor Roosevelt

TLS AERP, FDRL

---

1. ER to HST, 8 May 1945, PPF, HSTL.

2. *MD*, 10 May 1945.

3. In her column of May 10, 1945, ER wrote that although she had listened to most of the coverage during the day, she still wondered "why the Russians withheld their announcement of the end of the war until 6 in the evening. In any case, now it has been announced by the Big Three and there must be great rejoicing in Russia, which has suffered so much."

4. As Truman recorded in his memoirs, although Herschel V. Johnson, the American minister to Sweden, had relayed Reichsfuhrer Heinrich Himmler's proposal to the White House, when Prime Minister Churchill phoned Truman to discuss it, the president had not yet seen the offer, only "a short message saying that there was such a message in existence" and that he had "no other information except" that which Churchill now relayed. The prime minister then summarized the British ambassador's report on Himmler's request to meet with Count Folke Bernadotte, a nephew of King Gustav V of Sweden, who often traveled to wartime Germany on humanitarian missions as vice-chairman of the Swedish Red Cross. Himmler, after informing Bernadotte that Hitler had suffered a fatal brain hemorrhage that placed Himmler "in a position of full authority," proposed that Bernadotte ask the Swedish government "to make arrangements ... for him to meet General Eisenhower in order to capitulate on the whole Western Front." Bernadotte responded that "Himmler could simply order his troops to surrender." When Himmler suggested that Norway and Denmark might also be included in this capitulation, Bernadotte conceded "there might be some point in a meeting because special technical arrangements might have to be made with Eisenhower and de Gaulle if the Germans were to lay down their arms in those two countries." Himmler then made it clear that German troops would only "surrender to either British, American or Swedish troops" and that he hoped "to continue resistance on the Eastern Front at least for a time." Bernadotte replied that such a situation "was hardly possible, in fact, that it would not be acceptable to the Allies" and that Himmler's stance "may mean a lot of unnecessary suffering and loss of human life." The Swedes, however, agreed to pass this message to British and American officials "who were, as far as the Swedish Government were concerned, at complete liberty to transmit it to the Soviet Government" to insure "that the Swedish Government would in no way be, or propose to be, an instrument in promoting any attempt to sow discord between the Allies."

Churchill, assuming Truman had seen Johnson's summary of the meeting, telegraphed the president: "There can be no question that as far as His Majesty's Government is concerned, arranging thus an unconditional surrender simultaneously to the three major powers." Frustrated after waiting two hours for Truman's reply, Churchill then called the president to determine his response to Himmler's proposal, only to learn that Truman had not yet seen his cable. Churchill then told Truman what he had wired Soviet Premier Josef Stalin:

> There can be no question as far as state history is concerned about anything else but unconditional surrender simultaneously to the three major powers. We consider Himmler should be told that German folk either as individuals or in units should everywhere surrender themselves to the Allied troops or representatives on the spot. Until this happens, the attack of the Allies upon them on all sides and in all theaters where resistance continues will be prosecuted with the utmost vigor!

Truman concurred and agreed to send his own wire stating:

> I am informed by the American Minister to Sweden that Himmler, speaking for the German government in the absence of Hitler due to incapacity, approached the Swedish government with an offer to surrender all the German forces on the western front including Holland, Denmark and Norway. In keeping with our agreement with the British and Soviet governments it is the view of the United States government that the only acceptable terms of surrender are unconditional surrender at all fronts to the Soviet Union, Great Britian and the United States (Truman, vol. 1, 89–94; "Himmler's Offer Sent Via Sweden," *NYT*, 29 April 1945, 3).

5. On April 25 Truman made an unexpected visit to the Pentagon to meet with Secretary of War Henry Stimson, Acting Secretary of State Joseph C. Grew, and the chiefs of staff of the armed services. The *New York Times* reported that the meeting took place and "caused excitement in the War Department building and an air of mystery throughout the national capital," but neither the White House nor the Pentagon provided an explanation at the time. When pressed later in the day, Truman's staff tried to characterize the meeting as an inspection of the Pentagon (Bertram D. Hulen, "President Visits Pentagon Offices," *NYT*, 26 April 1945, 6).

6. As Reichsfuhrer-SS, Himmler directed the Gestapo and the Waffen-SS. In 1943, Hitler also made him minister of the interior. In that position he assumed responsibility for the mass murder of Jews and other populations the Nazis targeted for destruction (*OWWTC*).

7. On April 28 reporters asked Senator Tom Connally (D-TX), chair of the Senate Foreign Relations Committee and vice-chair of the American delegation to the UNCIO, to comment on Truman's prompt dismissal of rumors of German capitulation. The senator contradicted the president and, citing an unnamed, "authoritative" source, announced that he believed Germany would announce its unconditional surrender "momentarily" ("Nazis' End Near," *NYT*, 29 April 1945, 1).

8. Grand Admiral Karl Doenitz (1891–1980). When Hitler learned of Himmler's attempt to negotiate a peace with the United States and Britain, the Fuhrer replaced Himmler with Doenitz, his second in command. Doenitz succeeded Hitler as German head of state after Hitler committed suicide on April 30, 1945 (*OCAMH*, 296; Kershaw, *Hitler*, 183–84).

9. Field Marshal Alfred Jodl formally surrendered German forces to General Dwight D. Eisenhower, supreme commander of the Allied forces in Europe (SHAEF), on May 7, 1945, at Eisenhower's headquarters at Reims, France (*OCAMH*, 296).

10. Brigadier General Frank Allen, Jr., the public relations officer for SHAEF, accompanied the sixteen wire service reporters selected to observe the "top secret" German surrender. He instructed each correspondent that "this story is off the record until the respective heads of the Allied Governments announce the fact to the world" and "pledge[d] each and every one of you on your honor not to communicate the result of this conference or the fact of its existence until it is released by SHAEF." Edward Kennedy of the Associated Press filed his story on the German surrender before the release time set by SHAEF, thus violating the agreement and prompting a bitter, public debate among the press ("Bitter Controversy Over Ethics," *NYT*, 9 May 1945, 1).

11. ER's specific reference is unknown, but Churchill had delivered two major addresses widely reported in the United States, attacking the character and ethics of Soviet Russia. In an October 17, 1938, radio broadcast, Churchill compared the Soviets to the Nazis:

> like the Communists, the Nazis tolerate no opinion but their own. Like the Communists, they must seek from time to time, and always, mark you, at shorter intervals, a new prize, a new victim. The dictator in all his pride is held in the grip of his party regime. He can go forward; he cannot go back. He must blood his hounds and show them sport or else be destroyed by them ... As Byron wrote one hundred years ago, "These pagan things of sabre sway, with fronts of brass and feet of clay."

He continued this theme January 20, 1940, after the Soviets invaded Finland, telling his listeners that only the "magnificent" resistance of Finland to the "Nazi and Bolshevik threats" shows:

> what free men can do. There, exposed for all the world to see, is the military incapability of the Red Army and of the Red Air Force. Many illusions about Soviet Russia have been dispelled in these few and fierce weeks of fighting in the Arctic Circle. Every one can see how communism robs the soul of a nation, how it makes it abject and hungry in peace and proves it base and abominable in war.

On January 24, *Pravda* responded to Churchill's "slanderous allegations against the Soviet Union," arguing that "naturally, Churchill misses no occasion to slander the Soviet Union … But this sounds unconvincing. The English Minister has said too much" ("Text of Address by Winston Churchill Replying to Chancellor Hitler," *NYT*, 17 October 1938, 5; "Text of Churchill's Speech on War Prospects," *NYT*, 21 January 1940, 30; "Churchill 'Nervous,' Soviet Press States," *NYT*, 26 January 1940, 4).

12. ER later described FDR and Churchill's working style in an article published posthumously.

> My husband was not given to sitting up late at night after dinner, as a rule, but during Mr. Churchill's visit he stayed up, and I am sure he was deeply interested at all times, for they seemed from the very first not only to have a good understanding of each other but to enjoy each other's company. They both loved history, both loved the navy, and while I think Mr. Churchill had a more catholic interest in literature, they had some particular literary interests in common. For instance, on one occasion I drove down in the car with them to Shangri-La. This was a retreat which had been set up for my husband for weekends in warm weather when he could not go far away. We drove through the town of Frederick, Maryland, and Franklin pointed to a window and said it was the window from which Barbara Fritchie had hung the Union colors. Mr. Churchill then recited the whole of the Barbara Fritchie poem. My husband and I looked at each other, for each of us could have quoted a few lines, but the whole of the Barbara Fritchie poem was quite beyond us! Franklin happened to be fond of Edward Lear's Nonsense Rhymes, and I can remember Mr. Churchill capping every rhyme my husband quoted. How long they could go on, I don't know, but fortunately a turn in the road brought an end to this particular amusement.

John Greenleaf Whittier's popular poem, "Barbara Fritchie" (1864), praises the woman who allegedly defied Confederate troops under Stonewall Jackson as they marched through Frederick, Maryland, by flying the Stars and Stripes from the attic room of her house (Roosevelt, "Churchill at the White House;" Lounsbury, *Yale*, 163).

13. The source of the rumor that the message had, in fact, arrived in plenty of time, is unknown.

14. ER thought her son, Elliott Roosevelt, who had accompanied FDR to the Atlantic, Casablanca, and Tehran conferences, and who had earned the rank of air force brigadier general for his service in the North African and Mediterranean air campaigns and for photo reconnaissance essential to D-Day planning, could offer valuable observations to the homebound president. Furthermore, Elliott had traveled to Russia twice during the war. In May 1944, he joined Eighth Air Force officers charged with assessing the Soviet airfields the Allied air forces would use in the shuttle bombing of Germany. During his week-long stay, especially during his visit to Poltava field, he "learned to respect the vigor with which [the Soviets] overcame obstacles" and "the forthright way in which the Red Army solved the question of supply and transport." He "carried away the impression that the Russians were almost childishly eager to get along with us, cooperate with us." Truman did as ER suggested and found his meeting with Elliott "very pleasant" and the exchange of "vital information" useful (Elliott Roosevelt, *As He Saw It*, 217–18; Harry S. Truman to ER, 18 May 1945, AERP).

On the Bretton Woods Accords

ER often used My Day to call her readers to action. As this discussion of the Bretton Woods accords demonstrates, when Congress prepared to debate a proposal ER strongly supported, she used her column to explain the plan to her readers and to encourage them to tell their elected officials how they "feel about this."

9
_____

My Day
21 May 1945

HYDE PARK, Sunday—Some of my friends are very much exercised because they fear that the Bretton Woods plan will not go through.[1] This financial plan frightens many people purely because it is a financial plan and they think they cannot understand it.

Two hundred financial experts, representing 44 nations, met together at Bretton Woods in New Hampshire last summer for several weeks and agreed on this plan after much discussion and, naturally, some compromise. The main feature is the stabilization of currencies all over the world for the benefit of international trade.

How is this done? Through a world bank and a monetary fund. The bank will have a capital of $9,100,000,000, to which every nation contributes in proportion to its wealth. Our share is $3,175,000,000. Voting power and control correspond to contributions. The bank will approve and guarantee loans for reconstruction and development of countries ruined by the war.

Some foolish people will ask: Why do we have to concern ourselves with the development and reconstruction of the ruined countries? The answer is simple. We are the greatest producing country in the world. We need markets not only at home, but abroad, and we cannot have them unless people can start up their industries and national economy again and buy from us. If Europe or Asia falls apart because of starvation or lack of work for their people, chaos will result and World War III will be in the making. In that event, we know that we will have to be a part of it.

Why do we need a monetary fund? This fund is an international stabilization pool of $8,800,000,000, to which we contribute $2,750,000,000. Members may borrow from it, to the extent of 25 per cent of their own contributions in any one year, in order to stabilize their currency.

We need to stabilize currencies throughout the world because in the past there has been much speculative trading in currencies. Economic warfare results, and in time this brings us to shooting warfare.[2] The simple way to look at it is this: If you want to sell goods in Holland, and their currency is depressed between the day that they agree to buy and the day they actually pay for what they buy, they are unable to buy because it costs them too much. The outcome is either that we lose our markets, or we are paid the amount we bargained for in money that does not have the value we expected it to have—which is a loss to us as individual merchants or traders. Consequently, we need both the bank and the fund for our own security, as well as for that of the rest of the world.

You can write your Senators and Representatives and tell them how you feel about this. Whether you are a farmer or a merchant, whether your business is big or little, you are personally affected by it. Even if you don't sell directly to a foreign country, you are indirectly affected—for the prosperity of the country means your prosperity, and we cannot prosper without trade with our neighbors in the world of tomorrow.

TMs AERP, FDRL

----

1. Although Bernard Baruch told ER he thought the agreements inadequate because they did not ensure American access to British markets, there is no written record between ER and friends who feared the plan's defeat. The following month, the House passed the bill by a vote of 345 to 18. The United States became the first nation to ratify the plan when the Senate voted 61 to 16 in favor, July 19, 1945 (John H. Crider, "Senate Votes 61–16 to Adopt Bretton Act," *NYT*, 29 July 1945, 1).

2. After World War I many nations, including the United States, abandoned the gold standard, a move that benefited them individually but left the world without a workable way to pay international debts. Believing that the resulting economic instability was one of the principal causes of World War II, many postwar American leaders, including Harry Truman, Dean Acheson, and Cordell Hull, saw free trade and stable currencies as critical components of a lasting peace (Chace, 102–3; Boyd, 114; *HTSE*).

On ER's Political Future

Major party leaders, especially those in New York State determined to weaken Governor Thomas Dewey's presidential aspirations, refused to take ER's professed hiatus from politics seriously. Henry Morgenthau, Jr., and others continued to press her to replace Frances Perkins as secretary of labor. Democratic National Committeeman Ed Flynn encouraged her to run for governor, and Harold and Jane Ickes lobbied her to run for the Senate.[1]

10

Harold Ickes to Eleanor Roosevelt
21 May 1945 [Washington, DC]

My dear Mrs. Roosevelt:

Jane tells me that she had an opportunity to discuss briefly with you, when we had the pleasure of being your guests at Hyde Park, the possibility of your running for public office.[2]

I hope that you will bear with me if I suggest that I do not agree with your thought that you would be able to do more in behalf of your views if you did not hold public office. I believe that you would have much more influence if you should speak and write from the background of public office than otherwise.

I do not profess to have any expert views with respect to the political situation of New York State but my conviction is that you could be elected to any office in that State next year. I should doubt whether you would be even remotely interested in the mayoralty. That job is too exacting and too saturated with petty and personal details. I think that it is terribly important that Governor Dewey should be defeated if he is a candidate for reelection and in my opinion you could defeat him. However, it seems to me that the United States Senate would offer you your best opportunity, both as a forum and as a field for the work that you are particularly qualified to do. While there is no doubt of the influence that you can exert as a private citizen, it has been my experience that the man who holds a public office of dignity and distinction has a sounding board that no private citizen can have.

I hope that you will be a candidate for Senator next year. In any event, I hope that you will take no position for some time at least that would preclude such a possibility. After all, you can always say "no" and it cannot be predicted that you might not want to be in a position to become a candidate in certain contingencies that cannot now be foreseen.

It may have been the last time that I had a talk with the late President Roosevelt that I brought up the question of New York in 1946. I expressed the fervent hope that nothing would be left undone to defeat Governor Dewey. If he should run and fail of election next year, he would be effectively disposed of as a possible candidate for President in 1948 and I regard him as an unsafe and dangerous man even although he is trying in many ways to prove how liberal he now is. The President agreed with me.[3] He told me that he had in mind as a possible Democratic ticket General O'Dwyer[4] for Mayor, Senator Mead[5] for Governor and Fiorello LaGuardia[6] for United States Senator.

I like LaGuardia. I think that he has made a great Mayor although I recognize that he has lost a great deal of his popularity and strength during the last few years.[7] However, with President Roosevelt gone it would seem to me that there would be little chance either of nominating or electing LaGuardia as Senator. So if I could wave a magic wand, I would choose the ticket suggested by President Roosevelt, except that I would substitute you for LaGuardia as United States

Senator. It is my judgement that you would be unbeatable and you would help greatly to defeat Governor Dewey. In my view, this would be better than running for Governor, although I believe that you could be elected to that office. If I had my way, I would not choose for you an office that would mean hampering administrative details that would not leave you as much time as you would need for leadership on the social and political issues that will confront this country during the next few years.

And so I venture the hope that you will not now or in the near future foreclose any possibility of becoming a candidate for United States Senator.

John and Anna and little Johnny[8] are spending the week end with us and we are all enjoying it. Little Johnny seemed to be perfectly at home right from the beginning and he and our two little children[9] are hitting it off perfectly.

I would like to take advantage of this opportunity to tell you that Jane and I thoroughly enjoyed our visit to Hyde Park last week end. We thank you for your gracious hospitality. I am very glad indeed that I had a chance to see the house and get some comprehension of the problems that will confront the National Park Service. I hope that the bill that I have sent to Congress will be passed in due course and that we will be granted an appropriation that will make it possible for us to do what we ought to do and want to do along the line of our general discussion.[10]

With personal regards,

Sincerely yours,
Harold L. Ickes

TLS AERP, FDRL

11

Eleanor Roosevelt to Harold Ickes
26 May 1945 [Hyde Park]

Dear Mr. Secretary:

I very much appreciate your letter of the 21st.

I feel very strongly that running for office is not the way in which I can be most useful. My children have labored for many years under the very baffling necessity of considering their business of living as it affected their Father's position and I want them to feel in the future that any running for public office will be done by them.[11]

That does not mean, however, that I do not feel my responsibility as a citizen, but the minute I accept a position from the party and am a new hand, I would have to be willing to follow the party line pretty consistently. I hope to continue to work with the Democrats and for them but I think the knowledge that I will be free of any obligation may at times be very healthy.

I agree with you that it is important what happens in 1946 and 1948 and I feel strongly that the Democrats should remain in power if we can free ourselves to the extent of at least controlling our reactionary Southerners, but I do not think my running for any office would be useful.

I am not going to do anything for the summer months but in the autumn I shall begin to do speaking[12] and perhaps start on some job again by the first of the year when I think what is needed of me for settling the estate will be pretty well accomplished. I may go on a trip for the Red Cross[13] or for the syndicate.[14]

I should be able to help the liberals in the country and if I can write interesting columns and do an article now and then my voice would not be silent.[15]

I am deeply grateful to you and Jane for your interest. I am not going to make any decisions as to what I will do or what I won't do and no doors are permanently closed, but I feel I ought to tell you that I have no intention of running for public office.

Very cordially yours,

TLc AERP, FDRL

---

1. Blum, *Diaries*, 424; Lorena Hickok to ER, 13 April 1945, AERP.

2. Ickes married Jane Dahlman in 1938, three years after his first wife, State Representative Anna Wilmarth Ickes, died in an automobile accident. Jane Dahlman Ickes, a close friend of Anna Roosevelt Boettiger, also felt close enough to ER to seek ER's advice on how she could continue working for "controversial" social causes "without jeopardizing her husband's position." As she grew more at ease in cabinet circles, she became more outspoken in support of conservation, civil rights, and planned parenthood. When Secretary and Mrs. Ickes visited Hyde Park May 14 to discuss the Department of the Interior's impending ownership of Springwood, the Roosevelt ancestral home, Jane Ickes "pressed" ER to run for the US Senate ("Mrs Ickes Dies in Crash of Auto Near Santa Fe," *NYT*, 1 September 1935, 1; Lash, *Eleanor*, 456–57; Lash, *Years*, 27; *MD*, 14 May 1945).

3. In the 1944 campaign, Dewey often attacked FDR by saying "let's get this straight, the man who wants to be President of the United States for sixteen years is, indeed, indispensable. He is indispensable to Harry Hopkins, to Madame Perkins, to Harold Ickes … to Sidney Hillman and the Political Action Committee … to Earl Browder, the ex-convict and pardoned Communist leader … Shall we … accommodate this motley crew?" Ickes responded by sending the press his "letter of resignation" in which he charged that should Dewey become "our Never-Never President [he] will be besieged by favors from the hordes of hungry politicians" supporting him: Gerald L. K. Smith, Hamilton Fish, publisher Cissy Patterson, and isolationists Stephen Day and Werner Schroeder. In October 1944, Ickes told radio audiences in Newark that he was "glad" that Dewey, who would speak after him, would discuss "'Honesty in Government.' This will be a double adventure into the unknown by Mr. Dewey. He knows little if anything about the Government and, judging by his campaign speeches, he is totally unfamiliar with honesty." FDR, aware of how important Ickes's contributions were to his reelection, wrote his secretary "a personal note" November 27 "to send his compliments to The Curmudgeon on this greatest performance of his career. There is, I understand, some complaint from pieces of Republicans that I have a buzz saw for the Secretary of the Interior. I can't say I blame them and I must say I like it" (Watkins, 813–17).

4. William O'Dwyer.

5. FDR called James Michael Mead (1885–1964), the two-term state assemblyman from Buffalo who became a ten-term congressman and would serve eight years in the US Senate, one of the "best vote getters" in the history of New York. A New Deal Democrat, Mead decided not to seek reelection to the Senate so that he could challenge Dewey in the gubernatorial election of 1946 (Smith, 459–63).

6. Fiorello La Guardia.

7. La Guardia wanted to leave the mayor's office and on May 7 made what the *New York Times* called his "not quite entirely unexpected announcement" that he would not seek a fourth term as mayor. Much of his agenda had been accomplished, and his last term had been less productive than his previous two, partly because he squandered much good will early in World War II when he ran for a third term while directing the federal Office of Civilian Defense. At the same time, his consistent lack of support for Republican candidates at the state and national level also alienated many

state party leaders, who did not want to back him for another term. FDR's untimely death also robbed him of an important ally. However, he gave different reasons to the press: that he believed "in the principle of rotation in office," his age, and that he had "had practically no vacation or rest in twelve years" (*FDRE*, 232; "Mr. La Guardia's Withdrawal," *NYT*, 7 May 1945, 16; "New York's Next Mayor" and "Way Now Seems Open for Democratic Mayor," *NYT*, 13 May 1945, E2 and E10).

8. John and Anna Roosevelt Boettiger and their son, John.

9. When Ickes married Dahlman, Ickes brought his biological son Raymond, his adopted son Robert, his stepson Wilmarth, and his adopted stepdaughter Frances Bryant to their family. Jane and Harold Ickes then had two children of their own, Harold McEwan and Jane Elizabeth (Watkins, 605, 654–56, 713).

10. See *n*4, Document 2. Anna Roosevelt Boettiger forwarded ER an Interior Department memorandum prepared for Ickes that outlined the supplemental budget necessary both to secure the transfer of the land FDR left to the government and to establish, maintain, and interpret the estate as the Franklin D. Roosevelt National Historic Site. ER wanted to secure the continued employment of those Roosevelt staffers already working on the project, and Ickes wanted her to provide the detailed information requested by the interpretative staff. After each agreed to the other's stipulations, they reached arrangements "very satisfactory" to both parties (A. E. Demaray to Harold Ickes, 21 May 1945; ER to Ickes, 27 May 1945, AERP).

11. At this point, ER's four sons were finishing their wartime service and making postwar plans. When they returned home in 1945, James and Franklin, Jr., quickly began solidifying their political connections. James returned to California as an executive vice president of Roosevelt and Sargeant, an insurance firm, and began planning his successful 1946 campaign to become chair of the California State Democratic Committee. Franklin, Jr., acted much faster than his older brother. Immediately after his October 1945 discharge from the navy, he served as housing chair of the American Veterans Committee. In 1947, he would help organize Americans for Democratic Action. Elliott contracted to edit an edition of his father's correspondence and published his own memoir of his time with his father at the Casablanca and Cairo conferences, *As He Saw It*, in which he argued for a nonmilitarized, international organization for global peace. John, whose service in the Pacific fleet earned him the rank of lieutenant commander, had little interest in politics and devoted his time to finance and business operations. Anna continued her publishing career by securing, with ER's help, a weekly newspaper in Phoenix, Arizona (*FDRE*; Asbell, 201, 216, 223).

12. Beginning in 1936, ER did two lecture tours a year until FDR's death; however, she limited her speaking engagements in 1945. Not only did she want to settle FDR's estate as quickly as possible, she also told Anna that she did not want to go "on any speaking trips that required a reservation till the war is over." In October, she resumed her travels lecturing in Illinois, Massachusetts, and New Jersey to raise funds for organizations she supported. (See Document 55, Document 59, Document 63.) In November, she began a series of lectures for the Downtown Community School program at St. Mark's Episcopal Church in New York City. She resumed her lecture tour in late 1946 following her return from the UN General Assembly meeting in London (Lash, *Eleanor*, 421–24; Lash, *World*, 226).

13. ER had served World War I soldiers at the Red Cross canteen in Union Station. At the outset of World War II she tried to go to Europe under the group's auspices but Red Cross President Norman Davis and Secretary of State Cordell Hull feared she would be captured. She did visit many Red Cross facilities during her 1942 trip to Great Britain and finally, in summer 1943, she traveled to seventeen Pacific islands, New Zealand, and Australia as the organization's "Special Delegate" (Lash, *Eleanor*, 690; Roosevelt, *Autobiography*, 242–43, 254–55).

14. United Features Syndicate, which distributed My Day.

15. ER will make the same argument publicly in June 1946. See Document 137.

ON THE IMPORTANCE OF UNIONS

_12_

My Day
26 May 1945

HYDE PARK, Friday—I was amused the other day to be sent an editorial from a paper published in the southwestern part of the country,[1] which claimed that there was no more reason for backing the fair employment of people regardless of race, color or religion than there would be to back a bill insisting that people be employed regardless of whether they were union members or not.[2]

It seems to me that this is a very peculiar attitude. It shows a lack of understanding of the reasons why we have unions and of why it is possible to insist that people in certain industries shall join a union before they are employed. Unions were established for the protection of the workers. Like all other organizations composed of human beings, unions sometimes go wrong; but the objective for which unions exist still stands. Agreements under which certain employers employ only union members are entered into after negotiation between the union and the employer.

I know that in certain unions the fees demanded are too high, and practices sometimes arise which are harmful to the union members. But the remedy lies in their own hands. Under a democratic form of government you have to use your franchise, and use it fearlessly, to be free and to have the kind of government that you desire. The same holds good in a union organization.

I have always felt that the closed shop was debatable, but I have never felt that the desirability of joining a union was debatable.[3] There are plenty of associations of employers. Evidently they feel there is something valuable to be derived from group associations. Since that is the case, it seems to me quite plain that there are advantages to be derived for the worker in forming associations.

The last part of the editorial sent to me suggests that there is something un-American in employing anyone who is not a native-born citizen, and that a native-born American citizen should get a job ahead of any foreign-born person, regardless of qualifications and without being a union member. Apparently, this editorial writer would have us ignore the fact that an industry may happen to have an agreement with a union requiring that a worker shall be a member of the union. In war work, besides, it is very rare for anyone who is not an American citizen to be employed. If he is, it must be because he is really needed and has been carefully checked. Yet I think this question, in any event, was simply raised as a red herring to confuse people about the real issue of whether unions are valuable to the workers or not.

TMs AERP, FDRL

---

1. ER did not keep a copy of this editorial for her records. A search of ER's papers revealed that she also did not discuss this editorial with close friends and relatives in the southwest. Therefore, its content remains unknown.

2. See Document 5. The editorial addressed the current congressional debate over appropriations for the Fair Employment Practices Commission (FEPC). Since its inception, the FEPC's operational funds had come from the president's emergency fund. In February 1944, the Budget Bureau approved the FEPC's request, which was then forwarded to FDR for his approval. As FDR prepared to sign it, Georgia Democrat Richard Russell, chair of the Senate Appropriations Committee and one of the committee's fiercest critics, attempted to strip the FEPC allocation from the president's domain (and thus abolish it) by introducing legislation to the Subcommittee on Education

and Labor mandating that no funds could be allocated to any agency established by executive order "if Congress has not appropriated any money specifically for such an agency … or specifically authorized the expenditure of funds by it." The subcommittee quickly concurred. May 26, Congress adopted Russell's proposal, thus requiring congressional, rather than presidential, approval of the FEPC budget. The House then voted 141 to 103 against continued support for the agency. The Southern press rejoiced, declaring along with the Montgomery, Alabama, *Advertiser* that death of "the meddlesome committee" meant that "Eleanor Roosevelt and others" could not "force their ideas of racial equality on the people of the South." The House, however, voted to continue funding, albeit a smaller appropriation than the committee requested. Despite Russell's repeated efforts to kill the committee in conference, the FEPC survived. FDR then campaigned for a permanent committee.

As the 1945 appropriations debates began, Congress weighed two pieces of FEPC-related legislation in spring 1945. One dealt solely with appropriations for the coming fiscal year and limited the committee's authority to gathering and analyzing data and making recommendations to the president. The other, supported by ER's close friend Congresswoman Mary Norton, would have made the FEPC a permanent investigative body that could prosecute offenders in federal court. Congress was in the process of cutting the first bill while Southern conservatives were refusing to allow the second out of the House Rules Committee (Reed, 156–59; Hamby, *Man*, 61).

3. ER joined the Newspaper Guild in 1936 and remained a loyal member until her death in 1962. While she opposed the closed shop, in 1941 she told striking electrical workers that she had "always been interested in organizations for labor" and that she had "always felt that it was important that everyone who was a worker join a labor organization, because the ideals of the organized labor movement are high ideals" (Roosevelt, "Workers Should Join Trade Unions").

ON STETTINIUS AND
THE SAN FRANCISCO CONFERENCE

Although ER refused appointment as a special delegate to the San Francisco conference, she followed the deliberations there with great care. Often she turned to Secretary of State Edward Stettinius for his assessment of the proceedings and for clarification on positions proposed by the American delegation. Of particular concern to ER was the contentious debate over the admission of Polish and Argentine delegates. Stettinius, who admired both Roosevelts and shared their commitment to building the United Nations, valued ER's expression of support, took care to keep her up to date, and responded to her inquiries "in detail."

As the conference drew to a close, the secretary addressed the nation to report on the progress the United Nations had made to date and announced five major goals by which America would govern its foreign policy. He then wrote ER to "clarify our policy" supporting the seating of Argentina and opposing that of Poland, and enclosed "for your convenience, a marked copy of my speech, for I am anxious that you should not feel that we have deviated from the policies of President Roosevelt." Although ER listened to the broadcast, she appreciated the gesture and made the first of several invitations for the secretary to visit her in New York. "I shall be very anxious to see you after you get back," she wrote, "and hear in detail about the conference. I am in New York fairly frequently and perhaps it would be more convenient for you to see me there."

Still worried that the contention over Poland and Argentina would undermine American confidence in the United Nations, she dedicated two columns to Stettinius's remarks. The columns pleased the secretary and, as he wrote ER June 11, he "keenly looked forward" to seeing her "after the Conference is successfully concluded." [1]

13

My Day
31 May 1945

HYDE PARK, Wednesday—I listened to Secretary Stettinius' speech on Monday evening and read it the next day, and in addition I have read many of the editorials and comments upon it.[2]

It was fitting, I think, for our Secretary of State, the head of our United States delegation, to report to this nation and to the men in the armed services during the fifth week of the conference. The objective for which we all live and fight today is ultimately to have a peaceful world. This conference is one of many early steps in the direction of world unity. It is the most important one so far, because without the organization which we hope it will establish no further steps could be taken.

I liked the way in which Secretary Stettinius gave the background for his speech.[3] When we think that representatives of almost 50 nations are gathered in San Francisco, and stop to realize for a minute what our internal differences are when we try to agree on some specific policy, we get a better conception of the gigantic task of making all those nations agree on a charter and on the framework of an organization which will bring them together in the future and give them an opportunity to build for peace.

Two things stand out in my mind as I think of this report. I would like to speak of one point today.

Our Secretary of State did not shirk the unpleasant task of talking to us about Argentina[4] and Poland,[5] and that showed courage. Many of us—and I am among the many—wondered whether the decision reached in Mexico City to grant Argentina the opportunity to join in the conference, if she fulfilled certain conditions, was a wise one. We know that there are many people in Argentina who are neither Fascists nor in sympathy with the Fascists. But we also know that the policy of the government has been controlled by people who either were in sympathy with the Fascists or had made up their minds that it was to Argentina's economic and political advantage to continue close ties with the fascist nations.[6] Today, with Germany decisively defeated, it is quite evident that that was a bad guess.

The people who could think that way, however—who could ignore the rights and wrongs of the world situation, and believe in fascist doctrines—are certainly no more to be trusted in the democratic family of nations than they were before it became evident to them that their bread would be better buttered by joining with the democracies.

Secretary Stettinius minced no words, however, in speaking of what would be expected in the future.[7] We evidently thought it wise to handle a difficult situation in this way, and as long as the people of our country are aware of exactly what the situation is and why we have done certain things, I think we are safe.

TMs AERP, FDRL

14

My Day
1 June 1945

HYDE PARK, Thursday—Yesterday I wrote about one of the points raised in Secretary of State Stettinius' recent speech, and today I would like to continue with a discussion of the Polish issue.

It is evident that the Yalta agreement, as far as Poland is concerned, became difficult to carry out and the much-to-be-desired creation of a new government was not accomplished. Poland has a right to freedom. But it is evident, too, that Russia, in return for her valiant fighting, has a right to feel that her European doorway is safe. That being the case, the type of government which exists in Poland and the boundaries which are finally agreed upon will be of greater concern to Russia than to any of the other Allies. Some compromise will have to be reached. It is not yet clear what can or should be done, but I think it is good that Secretary Stettinius spoke out and did not treat these subjects as something which the people of this country were not concerned with.[8]

All thoughtful people agree that Russia, Great Britain and ourselves must cooperate in peace as we have cooperated in war, if the world is to have peace.[9] Therefore, I like very much the plain speaking on the part of our Secretary of State, which emphasized for all of us the fact that machinery cannot make peace. Only the good will of peoples and their leaders can develop understanding and create an atmosphere in which peace can exist.[10]

We might as well frankly face the fact that in this country there are many people who do not like the British empire. Sometimes this feeling may be a carry-over from old world backgrounds; sometimes it is still our Revolutionary War; sometimes it is a sense of inferiority, which makes us insist on our superiority and look down on anything which differs from our own habits and customs.[11]

Fundamentally, however, I think it is most often the type of dislike which exists in families now and then. The various members will call each other names, but they do not like it when outsiders do it. I do not think there is any real fear in this country of war between the English-speaking nations of the world.[12]

Our feeling toward Russia, however, is different. She is an unknown quantity. Her strength is not yet measured. The fact that she has done in some 25 years what the rest of Europe has taken several hundred years to do gives many a sense of insecurity. We know how rapidly her people have become literate. We know their fanaticism in defense of their form of government and of the leaders who have turned medieval conditions into a modern industrial civilization. We often do not understand that such rapid development means uneven development. I am told that throughout Russia you often hear the phrase, "It will be better." That is a sign that they know their full accomplishment is not yet achieved. Something great has happened, nevertheless. We, in this country, do not quite understand it as yet, and there lies one of the reasons for our uncertainty.

With both Great Britain and Russia, however, we must decide that peace is worth the effort we must make in order to understand and like each other, and that effort must extend to all other countries as well.

TMs AERP, FDRL

---

1. Edward Stettinius to ER, 29 May 1945; ER to Edward Stettinius, 5 June 1945; Edward Stettinius to ER, 11 June 1945, AERP.

2. Secretary Stettinius delivered his nationwide radio address May 27, 1945. The *New York Times* reprinted the speech in its entirety and in a lead editorial declared that the "report tells the story of steady progress toward realistic goals, pitfalls avoided and much accomplished." Its editors concluded "the record supports Mr. Stettinius when he expresses the belief that the Charter now nearing completion is a better, more liberal and more hopeful plan than the draft which was agreed upon last autumn in the preliminary meeting at Dumbarton Oaks" ("Text of Stettinius' Speech Projecting a Five-Point Foreign Policy for This Country" and "Report from San Francisco," *NYT*, 29 May 1945, 8 and 14).

3. Stettinius began his speech by predicting "a strong and democratic charter solidly based on the Dumbarton Oaks proposals." He then summarized the agreements reached at the Yalta and Dumbarton Oaks conferences; recapped the debates regarding the seating of Byelorussian, Ukranian, Argentine, and Polish delegates; and cited specific examples of Allied-Soviet cooperation. The secretary then detailed the actions he thought most essential to the creation of an effective international organization: a security council bestowed with "power to settle a dispute in its early stages and to stop preparations for war before war actually begins;" the inclusion of an "effective trusteeship system" in the UN Charter; and the creation of the Economic and Social Council (ECOSOC). Arguing that human rights and economic freedoms were crucial components of peace, Stettinius concluded, "we must realize that our most important task in the next decade is not likely the enforcement of peace, but to prepare the social and economic basis for peace. If the work of the Economic and Social Council is well done, we will have gone far toward eliminating in advance the causes of another world war a generation hence." If America fully participated in ECOSOC, Stettinius concluded, she "will have [her] greatest opportunity once and for all to break the vicious cycle of isolationism, depression, and war" ("Text of Stettinius' Speech Projecting a Five-Point Foreign Policy for This Country," *NYT*, 29 May 1945, 8).

4. Although the Argentine government under President Ramón S. Castillo publicly maintained a neutral position during the war, Castillo remained sympathetic to the Axis powers, whom he believed would defeat the Allies. US relations with Castillo's government cooled when it refused to ally with the nine Latin American states who entered the war on the Allied side after the attack on Pearl Harbor. The tensions continued when General Edelmiro Farrell replaced Castillo. The United States recalled its ambassador in February 1944. The issue escalated after Yalta, when the Allied powers agreed that only nations who had agreed to fight the Axis powers would be allowed entry into the United Nations. Secretary of State Cordell Hull feared that a Latin American delegation that did not include Argentina would undermine the San Francisco conference and devised a plan to settle the "Argentine Question" during the Chapultepec meeting of Latin American countries in

Mexico City. After extensive pressure by the State Department and its Latin American allies, the "new Argentina" agreed March 27, 1945, to endorse the Chapultepec resolutions declaring war on Japan and Germany, endorsing the Dumbarton Oaks proposal, and agreeing to "stifle aggression within the Western Hemisphere" (Blanksten, 400–414).

5. At Yalta, the Allies agreed that the Communist-dominated Polish Provisional government established at Lublin in 1944 would be reorganized to include Polish democratic leaders from the London-based Polish government in exile. To ensure continued control, the Lublinites and the Soviets wanted a veto over the composition of the new government. FDR opposed this demand and the situation remained deadlocked. Frustrated with Soviet intransigence over the issue, Truman sent FDR's wartime envoy, Harry Hopkins, to the USSR in late May to negotiate an agreement with Josef Stalin. Believing continued Allied wartime unity was more important than a coalition government and free elections in Poland, Hopkins compromised and allowed the Soviets to retain control of the Polish government. In return, Stalin agreed to back the US proposal that the Great Powers' veto at the UN extend only to substantive matters. Stalin's support ended the stalemate that had developed in San Francisco and ensured the UN Charter's adoption.

The question of whether or not to admit Communist Poland and former German ally Argentina to the UN quickly became one of the most vexing problems confronting the San Francisco conference. The Soviets linked the two issues to one another and to the admission of two of its client states, Byelorussia and the Ukraine. The Soviets, while supporting Poland's admission, opposed the admission of Argentina, arguing that it implied a double standard—if the Argentine pro-Nazi government was admitted even though its government was considered unrepresentative, then the Polish government should be admitted on the same basis (Donovan, 54–57; Schlesinger, 96–98; 135–38, 193–218).

6. In March 1944, nationalists with Fascist sympathies, enraged by President Ramirez's severing of diplomatic ties with the Axis powers, overthrew his government and installed minister of defense General Edelmiro Farrell (1887–1980) and his deputy Colonel Juan Perón (1895–1975) as president and vice president and minister of defense (Newton, 285).

7. Stettinius told his audience that the "paramount" US wartime aim "in this hemisphere has been to eliminate Axis penetration and to unite all the Americas in the struggle against the evil forces" of Fascism. He then argued that "by voting to admit Argentina … the United States … had by no means changed its position that Argentina is expected to carry out effectively all of her commitments under the Mexico City declaration. On the contrary, we consider that her admission to the San Francisco Conference increases her obligation to do so. We expect the Argentine nation to see that this obligation is fulfilled." As for Poland, the secretary conceded that the "negotiations for reorganization of the Warsaw Provisional Government have been disappointing." Nevertheless, he continued, "it is the intention of the United States to exert all its influence, in collaboration with the Soviet Union and Great Britain toward fulfillment of the Yalta agreement on Poland" ("Text of Stettinius' Speech Projecting a Five-Point Foreign Policy for This Country," *NYT*, 29 May 1945, 8).

8. After Stettinius addressed the controversy surrounding the seating of the Argentine delegation, he turned his attention to the seating of the Polish Provisional Government. "It is a matter of deep regret to the United States that the people of Poland who have suffered so terribly and fought so bravely during the war are not represented in our deliberations. Poland is a United Nation and should be here. But there are two Polish Governments—the London Government and the Warsaw Provisional Government." The secretary then argued that the Soviets had undermined the Yalta accords and that the "negotiations for reorganization of the Warsaw Provisional Government have been disappointing." After asserting that the United States intended to "exert all its influence" to secure the British and Soviet adherence to the accords, he concluded that he wished "to make it absolutely clear that the primary objective" of American foreign policy "is to continue and strengthen in the period of peace that wartime solidarity" and "to broaden the scope of our agreement and to reach common understanding where it does not yet exist." He concluded, "we have the right to

expect the same spirit and the same approach of our great allies" ("Text of Stettinius' Speech Projecting a Five-Point Foreign Policy for This Country," *NYT*, 29 May 1945, 8).

9. To assure British Prime Minister Winston Churchill that the United States and the USSR were not excluding Great Britain from any postwar deliberations, Truman sent former US Ambassador to Moscow Joseph E. Davies to London (Donovan, 55–56; Hamby, *Man*, 320).

10. When assessing the chances of the charter's success, Stettinius told his audience that he had "no doubt that the charter prepared here will offer great hope for peace;" however, he could not "speak so surely if" he tried "to answer the question: Will it work? Will it keep the peace?" That, he concluded, depends on "the will to peace which the nations of the world support" and the extent to which they apply that will "to build strength into the charter and the world organization. We can do no more at San Francisco than to establish the constitutional basis upon which the world can live without war—if it will" ("Text of Stettinius' Speech Projecting a Five-Point Foreign Policy for This Country," *NYT*, 29 May 1945, 8).

11. Opposition to British colonialism within the Roosevelt administration first arose during the debates over the free trade provisions of the Atlantic Charter and hardened after the invasion of the Philippines and the fall of Singapore. Although Elliott Roosevelt, who was preparing a book on his father's world views for publication later in 1945, would argue that FDR's opposition to empire was so strong that he used the charter as a means to dismantle it, ER knew his conversion to anti-colonialism took a few more months.

December 28, 1941, FDR gave his "solemn pledge" to all Filipinos that "their freedom will be redeemed and their independence established and protected." In February he approved Assistant Secretary of State Sumner Welles's Memorial Day address in which he proclaimed "our victory must bring in its train the liberation of all peoples … The principles of the Atlantic Charter must be guaranteed to the world as a whole—in all oceans and in all continents … The age of imperialism is over." FDR broached this directly when Churchill visited the White House in March, arguing, to his guest's outrage, that "the lessons of American Independence could be applied to India."

Pundits began to make this argument as well. For example, February 15, 1942, Walter Lippman used his column to argue that when the British could not hold Singapore, the Allies had to accept "what hitherto they lacked the will and imagination to do: they must identify their cause with the freedom and the security of the peoples of the East, putting away the 'white man's burden' and purging themselves of the taint of an obsolete and obviously unworkable white man's imperialism." Indeed, ER often made the same argument in her wartime writings, as when she told readers of the *American Magazine* that "what Kipling calls 'the White Man's Burden' is one of those things we can not have any longer" (Louis, *Imperialism*, 121–47; Roosevelt, "What Are We Fighting For?").

12. ER knew quite well the extent of the disagreements that FDR and Churchill had on this issue, as she too had the same arguments with the prime minister and his staff (Meacham, 197–201, 314–15, 361; Lash, *Eleanor*, 664).

ELEANOR ROOSEVELT AND
DEMOCRATIC PARTY POLITICS

ER's "patent distaste" for political bosses made her exceedingly wary of Truman's reliance on Robert Hannegan, who chaired the Democratic National Committee. In the midst of the 1944 vice-presidential contest, ER had written Lorena Hickok: "Mr. Hannegan came to see F. at the Chicago station and I gathered after he left that a conservative would be the next V.P. I'm sorry because I think it is bad politics …" Perhaps Hickok reinforced ER's suspicions when she declared that "I'm convinced the only way to keep Mr. Hannegan under control is to get tough with him now." FDR's election did not cool either Hickok's emotions or ER's concerns. "I'm awfully tired of Mr. Hannegan and Mr. Pauley," Hickok wrote November 20, 1944, "and anyway, I think we are now witnessing the twilight of the Democratic Party."[1]

After FDR's death, Truman's close association with Hannegan remained a source of concern. April 15, as they returned to Washington after FDR's funeral, ER told Trude Lash she "would tell Truman what she thinks of people (like Hannegan, Pauley, etc.) but that she will tell him only once,—after that the responsibility will be his." June 2, ER again confided to Trude "that there is much in the political field that worries me but I doubt that I could be much help." She continued this theme the following day when she told Trude that even though she was "glad Truman came out for the FEPC—I wrote Hannegan a letter and sent the President a copy on general observations of policy and if I get any answer I'll let you know."[2]

15

Eleanor Roosevelt to Harry Truman
3 June 1945 [Hyde Park]

Dear Mr. President:

I am enclosing a copy of a letter which I have just sent to Mr. Hannegan, as I have been doing a lot of thinking along these lines since I have been back in New York State. I feel I have an obligation to send this to you as well to Mr. Hannegan.

You will know, I am sure, that I have written out of genuine interest in the Administration and in the Party, and above everything else, out of interest in the country.

I have no idea whether you agree with me or not, but all I can do is to send you the results of my observations and my conversations with people in the last few weeks.[3]

I should also like to bring to your attention, in case you missed it, a broadcast which came from overseas in Germany the morning of June 2nd, shortly after midnight. I listened because I know Bill Chaplin, the AP reporter who was one of the speakers. I know he is an honest and reliable reporter. This was the last apparently of three reports from Germany but it was the first I heard and it horrified me.[4] I think it would be worth your while to get it and read it. It came over WEAF in New York City.[5] If such conditions actually exist in Germany I think the people of this country have a right to feel outraged and I gather from letters I received from boys now in Germany that these conditions are not exaggerated by this reporter.[6] I am quite sure that both the Secretary of War and General Marshall as well as you yourself should read these broadcasts.

Please do not bother to answer this letter. I simply felt that I had an obligation to write to you.

Very cordially yours,
Eleanor Roosevelt

TLS HSTOF, HSTL

16

Eleanor Roosevelt to Robert Hannegan
3 June 1945 [Hyde Park]

Dear Mr. Hannegan:

I have been thinking a good deal about the political situation as I view it from New York State. I know that my husband felt very strongly that we have to carry the Congressional election in 1946 in order to win in 1948. If Governor Dewey is not defeated the chances are that we will be defeated in 1948, so what happens to him is vitally important.

I notice a number of things. Governor Dewey certainly learned from the last campaign that he could not ignore the colored vote and, at the expense of some of his most conservative support, he is now playing up very strongly to the minority groups in this State and also to the liberals.[7]

On the other hand, the impression is spreading that the Democratic Party as far as President Truman is concerned, is doing a good job from the liberal point of view in most of the things which he has done, but that in Congress, particularly in the Senate, we are still going to have a strong fight by the conservative southern Democratic Senators on our hands. If they filibuster on the FEPC[8] and on the Poll Tax,[9] I think we will have a big group of people feeling that there is a chance even though there is a conservative monied power in the Republic[an] Party, that the Republican Party may be more liberal from the point of view of racial and religious questions and we may lose a certain number of people to that party who would ordinarily be Democrats, but who want to serve notice that there is one issue on which they will vote with the party which they consider is doing the right thing on that issue.

You may find others who will feel that neither party with the conservative elements can be trusted and that both parties are controlled by these elements, and the time has come to form a third party. That third party, of course, will not win, but on the other hand it will defeat the Democratic Party because we know the Democratic Party can not win unless it has the liberal vote and some liberal Republican elements voting with it.

I know that you feel strongly, and I know that Mr. Fitzpatrick[10] in New York feels strongly, that we must build up the Democratic Party organization throughout the country. I am entirely in agreement with this because we have to have people to put on campaigns and to do the work not only of the campaigns, but the in-between campaign work. However, the day when an organization such as Tammany[11] in New York and Prendegast[12] in Kansas City could really swing elections has gone by. The people want to know what the things are for which the party stands, and they want to be convinced that those are going to be put through. Mr. Kelly[13] in Chicago has a good organization, but if Mr. Kelly had not played fair with a great many people he would not hold his organization. That holds good of practically all of your Democratic Party groups today. So while these organizations are vitally important to the Party, I think you have to add something which has often been neglected, namely, a program which meets the needs and wins the approval of the rank and file of the voters.

At the present time, that would include many things concerning veterans, health, social security, education, and above all, the sense that we are moving forward in our foreign policy to a peaceful world and in our economic policy to a realization of responsibility for economic situations throughout the world which would affect our own in the long run.

I know, of course, it is rather presumptuous of me to talk to you about the general political situation which you and the others must have considered already, probably in much more detail and with far better powers of observation than I can possibly bring to it at the present time.

There is one phase of the whole picture with which I think I am more familiar and more closely connected than many of the people whom you know well, namely, the situation of the women who are not the regular party workers, but who are the women you have to have with you to win in campaigns. Many of them are feeling that while Miss Perkins was not particularly popular during the last few years as Secretary of Labor, still she was a woman in the Cabinet.[14] There will be no woman in the Cabinet and there has been no suggestion so far of any woman or women in comparably important positions. Most of the women whom you have to have with you to win elections, do not expect positions, but they like to feel that some women are in the policy making positions and I think that they must feel that this is not just for a brief time but permanently.

I know many men are made a little uncomfortable by having women in these positions, but I think the time has come to face the fact that you have to win as many women's votes as you do men's votes and that the Democratic Party probably has more strength among women if it stands as the liberal party and the party of human rights than it has among the men.

From the point of view of doing something for our biggest minority group—the colored people—I think you will have to make some good appointments to commissions where you choose a man because he is a good man and has ability, and it just happens he is colored which you forget about in the work which he does.

I think the administration will have to try to get the FEPC and the Poll Tax vote out on the floor of the Senate and not allow it to be killed by a filibuster. If you can get a vote on these two issues, it is one step forward and the men who vote against them are known and their position is out in the open. A fight can be made on them on their record in voting. If these two issues are killed without a record vote and then there is discrimination in employment and the economic situation becomes unfair to racial and religious groups, I think we will be in danger of creating a lack of unity in the nation as a whole which will affect the Democratic Party more than it will affect the Republican Party.

I will be interested to know what you think of these points because, of course, I am interested in the success of the Democratic Party, and I am equally interested in the progress of our nation which transcends party lines.

Very sincerely yours,

TLc AERP, FDRL

ER met with Truman when she traveled to Washington June 8. Although pleased that he did speak with Hannegan, ER expressed her continued concerns about Truman's abilities to govern. June 11 she told Hickok that while her White House lunch with Truman did not make her "feel queer in the house it all seemed so different," she left worried about the president, whom she thought "very unhappy":

> His family is gone, the house is bare and stiff and he's the loneliest man I ever saw. He's not accustomed to night work or reading and contemplation and he doesn't like it. He's not at ease and no one else is. I am so sorry for him and he tries so hard.

The following day she elaborated on this in a letter to Trude Lash. "I think Truman is trying to follow FDR's policies and yet win more friends in Congress and among

Republican leaders. He may succeed and if he does more power to him. He is shrewd but when he has to formulate policies it will be hard."[15]

Her report to Bronx Democratic Committee Chair Ed Flynn focused more on the political than the personal.

17

Eleanor Roosevelt to Edward Flynn

8 June 1945 [Washington, DC]

My dear Ed:

I had lunch today with President Truman. He is very much worried by the democratic situation in New York City and frankly, I am worried about it too.[16]

I hardly think that the ticket even with Mr. O'Dwyer to head it, can stand up against the Republican ticket.[17] I do not vote in New York City so I suppose it is no concern of mine, except I feel that every democratic defeat helps Dewey in the State.

I rather think your having been ill means that they haven't had the benefit of your advice and I do not know whether they can do anything about the two nominations, by what has been said about them, I should think they were exceptionally weak, and Mr. O'Dwyer not strong enough to carry them against what looks to be a fairly strong Republican ticket.[18]

I think Mr. Fitzpatrick will have every opportunity now to build up the democratic organization in the State,[19] but even the best of democratic organizations will not win unless we have the completely unattached liberals and many of the liberal Republicans, with us and we definitely have to show the farming part of the State that we are serving their interests in Washington and through Washington, in the State.

In addition, we definitely have to hold the colored vote and show that the gestures made by Mr. Dewey were not honest-to-goodness interest.[20] This is not going to be easy and we better be planning our program now for the city and the state. Mr. Dewey is capable of playing a clever political game and we will not only have to be good politicians but really make our party honest, standing for the things which most of us as individuals know are right.

I meant to talk to you about all this when you came to lunch, but seeing President Truman made me conscious of the fact that he is really troubled.

Very cordially yours,

TLc AERP, FDRL

---

1. Lash, *World*, 130; ER to Lorena Hickok, 16 July 1944, LAHP, FDRL; Lorena Hickok to ER, n.d.; Lorena Hickok to ER, 20 November 1944, AERP.

2. Trude Lash, notes, 15 April 1945, JPLP, FDRL; ER to Trude Lash 2 and 4 June 1945, JPLP, FDRL.

3. Over the course of her first month outside the White House, ER met with Secretary of the Interior Harold Ickes, his wife Jane, Secretary of the Navy James Forrestal, FDR's former assistant Jonathan Daniels, Postmaster General and former Democratic Party Chair Frank Walker, and

FDR's former law partner Harry Hooker. See also Document 10 and Document 11 (*HSTE*; *MD*, 1 May and 2 June 1945; "Henry S. Hooker, Lawyer, 84, Dies," *NYT*, 19 May 1964, 37).

4. ER refers to an NBC radio broadcast from Paris by W. W. (Bill) Chaplin (1895–1978), the Paris-based radio correspondent for the Associated Press, the International News Service, and the National Broadcasting Company, who provided live reports on conditions in southern Germany and Austria. She may have heard his Memorial Day report on civilian wartime behavior in the neighborhood of the Dachau concentration camp. Following his visit to the liberated camp, Chaplin called for a stern justice in occupied Germany and railed against the "propaganda" about "good Germans" who claimed not to have known about the camps. Or she may have heard his June 1 report, in which he reported that German soldiers rather than Allied troops were still policing the Austrian Tyrol region and argued that the Americans occupying Germany should take a page from the Russian playbook, stop being soft, and act more like "conquerors." Chaplin's partner in these reports on Germany, Roy Porter, told of ongoing sabotage perpetrated against Allied troops, Germans who continued to act as though their country had not lost the war, and the incompetence of some American personnel supervising the occupation. A New York City native and president of the Overseas Press Club, Chaplin had reported extensively on World War II and spent sixteen years with NBC. In addition, his reporting career included stints with Associated Press and the International News Service (Library of Congress Recorded Sound Reference Center, radio broadcast tape "[NBC] News Report from Paris," RWB 522 B1, 27 May 1945 and an abbreviated version of this story on radio broadcast tape RWB 520 A1, 30 May 1945; radio broadcast tape, "[NBC] News," RWB 556 A1, 1 June 1945; "NBC Reporter W.W. Chaplin," *WP*, 22 August 1978, C11).

5. The major NBC affiliate in New York City.

6. For examples of correspondence ER received from soldiers from 1942 through 1945 see boxes 827–842, Children Named After Eleanor Roosevelt and Letters from Servicemen and Women, Section 100.1 of AERP.

7. In November 1944, after a particularly vicious campaign, FDR received his smallest margin of victory, 25.6 million to 22 million votes for Dewey. Dewey's advisors knew that the CIO PAC's get-out-the-vote campaign played a decisive role in FDR's victory; however, they took heart from an analysis that showed that a shift of less than 300,000 votes in a few key states would have sent Dewey to the White House. In a postelection strategy session, RNC chair Herbert Brownell urged Dewey to adopt a domestic agenda that included support for the FEPC, anti-poll tax legislation, extension of Social Security to 20 million uncovered workers, and an equal rights amendment for women as a way to bring working class and minority voters into the Republican camp (R. Smith, 438–41; Kennedy, 792–93).

8. See *n*1 Document 5 and *n*2 Document 11.

9. Seven southern states levied taxes on voters, a policy designed to disenfranchise black voters who, as low-paid tenant farmers and sharecroppers, rarely had money to spend for any purpose. Although two states had repealed the tax by June 1945, five still collected it. The House had three roll call votes on measures to abolish the tax in 1945. A Senate filibuster blocked consideration of the measure (Key, 578–618).

10. Paul E. Fitzpatrick (1897–1977), son of the Democratic Party leader in Erie, businessman from Buffalo, and strong party advocate for FDR, replaced New York State Democratic chair James Farley when Farley refused to endorse FDR's fourth reelection campaign. Fitzpatrick chaired the state party from 1944 to 1953 and, with Ed Flynn, helped muster critical support for Truman's renomination in 1948 ("Paul E. Fitzpatrick Is Dead at 79," *NYT*, 2 July 1977, 13).

11. Tammany Hall was the home of the New York City Democratic machine, whose relationship with FDR remained frayed after Governor Roosevelt forced the resignation of Mayor James Walker, September 1, 1932. Torn by internal disputes and La Guardia's successful multi-party coalition,

Tammany sold its headquarters in 1943, moved into the offices of the New York State Democratic Committee, and remained ineffective throughout the 1940s, only to revive briefly in the late '40s and '50s under the leadership of Carmine De Sapio (Freidel, 75–76; Allen, passim).

12. ER meant the political machine controlled by Kansas City boss Tom Pendergast. Once the most powerful machine in the nation, it collapsed in 1939 after Pendergast was imprisoned for income tax evasion (Hamby, *Man*, 233).

13. Chicago Mayor Edward Kelly's machine worked to support FDR, Democratic governors, and the national party thereby securing the support of party leaders. As Harold Ickes recalled in his diary, when Attorney General Frank Murphy wanted to "clean up Chicago because it was the worst mess in the country," Murphy "hoped 'they' would let him go ahead. I found out," Ickes noted, "that it was surmised that the President would not permit Murphy to go ahead with the investigation on account of Ed Kelly." Murphy then told Ickes that he knew he was waiting "for the green light that probably will not flash." Weakened by a series of scandals, the machine splintered in 1945 (Wilson, 69–71).

14. In 1937, Perkins refused to deport Harry Bridges, one of the organizers of the 1934 longshoreman's strike, when evidence later surfaced that he might be a Communist. Although Bridges's deportation hearing had been scheduled for April 25, on April 6 the Fifth Circuit Court of Appeals ruled in *Kessler v. Strecker* that it was illegal to assume that membership in the Communist Party implies the desire to "overthrow by force and violence the government of the United States." Perkins decided to postpone the Bridges hearing until the Supreme Court ruled on *Kessler*. Rep. Martin Dies, Jr. (D-TX), then accused her of concealing evidence, and Rep. J. Parnell Thomas introduced a resolution demanding her impeachment. Although the Judiciary Committee rejected the resolution, the Republican minority reported that Perkins had been "lenient and indulgent" and that she deserved the "official and public disapproval of this Committee." ER supported her throughout the controversy. For Truman's assessment of Perkins, see *n*6 Document 2 (G. Martin, 406–19; ER to Anne Choate, 9 February 1939, AERP).

15. ER to Hickok, 11 June 1945, LPHP, FDRL; ER to Trude Lash, 12 June 1945, JPHP, FDRL.

16. Mayor Fiorello La Guardia's announcement in May 1945 that he would not seek reelection caught political party leaders by surprise and set off a scramble for viable candidates. See also Document 31–34.

17. See *n*3, Document 10. The New York City mayoral race had three credible, well-supported candidates: O'Dwyer, the mayoral candidate endorsed by both the Democratic and American Labor Parties; Judge Jonah J. Goldstein, the Republican-Liberal-Fusion Party candidate; and La Guardia's anointed heir, City Council President Newbold Morris, who ran under the No Deal Party banner. Socialist Party candidate Joseph G. Glass, Workers Party nominee Max Schactman, and Industrial Government Party candidate Eric Hass also competed for the mayoralty ("6 in Mayor Race Discuss Housing," *NYT*, 22 October 1945, 30).

18. ER was not the only Democrat concerned about O'Dwyer's vulnerability. Goldstein had been elected to the general sessions bench as a Democrat. After Goldstein's rival for the Liberal Party nomination announced that he would seek reelection as city comptroller rather than challenge Goldstein, O'Dwyer worried that an unchallenged Goldstein could undermine party support for his election. He immediately telegraphed party leaders to call a conference "to substitute more outstanding candidates as his running mates" for city comptroller and city council president. Goldstein then attacked O'Dwyer, hinting that an O'Dwyer administration could not control either the Tammany machine or the Communists who sought to infiltrate city hall. O'Dwyer's supporters then countered that his victory would seriously undercut Dewey's chances for reelection as governor and another future run as Republican presidential candidate.

November 6, the voters proved ER's and O'Dwyer's fears misguided as they gave O'Dwyer a landslide victory, elected his entire slate, allowing Goldstein only one district victory, the traditional Republican Ninth in Manhattan (Ibid; James A. Hagerty, "Record Plurality," *NYT*, 7 November 1945, 1).

19. See *n*10, Document 16.

20. Dewey worked hard to make inroads into the African American vote. In December 1944, after losing to FDR, he urged the Republican National Committee to adopt a twelve-point charter that included strong public commitment to anti-poll tax legislation, extension of social security payments to categories omitted by the New Deal, and a Fair Employment Practices Commission. Three months later, Dewey had also proclaimed the week of February 12–18 as "Negro History Week" and, two days before ER wrote this letter, appointed Elmer A. Carter, the African American editor of the National Urban League's magazine, to the five-member State Commission Against Discrimination charged with enforcing a new law against employment bias (Smith, *Dewey*, 439–40; "Negro History Hailed," *NYT*, 11 February 1945, 34; "Dewey Picks Anti-Bias Board of 5 to Bar All Job Discriminations," *NYT*, 7 June 1945, 21).

ON EARL BROWDER AND
THE COMMUNIST PARTY OF THE UNITED STATES

Eleanor Roosevelt often intended her column to spur public debate. In this case, as her close friend Joseph Lash argued, she intended that her response to Moscow's demotion of Earl Browder, whose leadership of the Communist Party of the United States (CPUSA) helped launch support for a Popular Front politics, be read in Moscow. Yet the column also shaped American press coverage of the actions taken by the CPUSA. For example, the *New York Times*, which did not carry My Day, found this column so important that it requested permission from the *New York World Telegram* to print the column in its entirety the day following its release. The *Times* introduced the column by saying ER "expressed her belief yesterday that issues involved in the future peace and friendly relations between the United States and Russia would be solved only when the whole situation of Communists outside the Soviet Union is cleared up 'authoritatively.'"[1]

18

My Day
9 June 1945

WASHINGTON, Friday—At the moment, certain actions of American Communists in this country have added fuel to the general fear of Communism as an international force.

Earl Browder has been reprimanded for an attitude which many of us believed had represented the attitude of the Soviet government.[2]

We, in this country, feel that any nation has a right within its own borders to the kind of government it feels best meets the needs of the people. It is only when those beliefs begin to encroach on other nations and on other people, and to endanger their free beliefs and actions by attempting to propagandize them, either openly or secretly, that fear is awakened. The next step, we have learned through the rise of Fascism, is to try by force to push upon the rest of the world the beliefs which your particular nation holds. That is what we, including the Soviet Union, have had to fight, and the war has been a long, cruel war.

It frightens us to see any group in our midst proposing to propagandize instead of cooperating where possible and letting people think and act for themselves. This might lead to war at home and abroad. Therefore, the French Communist leader and the American Communists who encourage a policy of world revolution have done the peace of the world harm.

The American Communist party had been cooperative where they could be. But now, as we understand it, they are out to force Communism on our democracy. That we will not tolerate.

I am not afraid of the Communists in the United States. They are a very small group, and my feeling has always been that as long as the needs of our people are met by our own form of government, democracy need have no fear of the growth of other ideas, either in the field of economics or of government.

As a people, we are not afraid of the Soviet Union. We feel kindly toward the Soviet people. Our soldiers admire them, and so do our people generally, for the way they have fought in the war. We do not understand them very well, nor do we understand their problems or their real feelings about things which affect us deeply. That understanding can only come gradually, as we get to know each other better, and we cannot know each other unless we live in a peaceful world.

The sooner we clear up authoritatively this whole situation of the Communist party outside of the Soviet Union, the better chance we will have for peace in the future. The Russian people should know this, and so should the people of the United States. If they both demand a clarification of a situation which may grow until it endangers peace in the world, responsible people will have to listen. Light may break on what now seems a situation through which all the people who want to make trouble between the United States and the Soviet Union can do so.

TMs AERP, FDRL

The column generated the attention ER hoped it would; however, when readers used ER's words to justify actions she opposed, she wrote another column to clarify her position.

19

My Day
22 June 1945

HYDE PARK, Thursday—I have been sent, by the Communist Political Association, a statement of the resolution which they are considering and will vote on as an expression of the American Communist point of view and as their guide for action.[3] As a document, it is excellent; but I think I should clarify, for two groups in this country, the column which I wrote a short time ago.

On the one hand, the Communist Political Association felt that I had not been entirely fair with them.[4] On the other hand, I have been sent words of praise by some people who, whenever they differ with anyone, decide that that person should be labeled a Communist, and who are also afraid of our association with the USSR.

I want to make it absolutely clear that my whole desire in writing that column on the American Communists was to show how it is possible to work with the USSR and the people of that great country, and why we need have no fear of them. Those of us who take the trouble to understand it know what Communism in Russia is. We also know that any leader, no matter how powerful, has to listen to the people with whom he works. While for obvious reasons the people of Russia are still largely dictated to by their leaders, they have objectives and opportunities for growth in freedom, just as we had when we wrote our Constitution.

We have not quite attained the objectives which we wrote into our Constitution, but they are there as standards by which we measure our success. No one has any doubt of what our government is. No one need have any doubt as to what the government of the USSR is today, nor as to the hopes and aims of its people. We may not agree with those aims or methods, but we need not fear what we know.

I, for one, think democracy better than Communism if the people exercise their power. Nevertheless, I feel we can cooperate with the USSR and its people, just as we do with other nations.

I hope the Communist Political Association will forgive me if I am frank with them. What I object to in the American Communists is not their open membership, nor even their published objectives. For years, in this country, they taught the philosophy of the lie. They taught that allegiance to the party, and acceptance of orders from party heads whose interests were not just those of the United States, were paramount.

I happen to believe that anyone has a right to be a Communist, to advocate his beliefs peacefully and accept the consequences. A Communist here will be—quite rightly, it seems to me—under certain disadvantages. He will not be put into positions of leadership. I do not believe that he should be prevented from holding his views and earning a livelihood.

But because I have experienced the deception of the American Communists, I will not trust them.[5] That is what I meant when I said that I did not think the people of this country would tolerate the type of American Communists who say one thing and do another.

TMs, AERP, FDRL

---

1. Lash, *Years*, 31; "Mrs. Roosevelt Criticizes Reds' New Line; Sees It Endangering Amity with Russia," *NYT*, 10 June 1945, 7.

2. No American was more closely associated with the Communist activity within the United States than Earl Browder (1891–1973). As long-standing general secretary of the Communist Party of the United States, its presidential candidate in the 1936 and 1940 elections, and head of the Communist Political Association (CPA), Browder vigorously promoted a Popular Front politics. However, soon after Stalin signed the nonaggression pact with Germany, police suspicious of Communists arrested Browder for a passport violation he committed in the 1920s. Quickly tried and convicted, Browder began a four-year jail term (which FDR commuted to time served in May 1942). The year following his release, Browder praised the Tehran conference and argued that "an identity of interests existed between American capitalism with its increased productive capacity and the progress of the war-torn and underdeveloped world in need of capital and goods." Such public support for wartime labor-management cooperation angered CPA Chair William Z. Foster who worked to undercut Browder. By April 1945, tensions flared and Jacques Duclos (1896–1975), second-in-command of the French Communist Party (PCF), published an article in the French party's paper criticizing Browder for his collaborationist position and for fostering harmony between labor and capital. The *Daily Worker*, clearly reflecting Soviet disapproval of Browder's moderate stance, then reprinted Duclos's article in English. The next month, bowing to Soviet pressure, Browder indicated the CPA would rededicate itself to a policy of political activity based on class struggle rather than collaboration; however, he voted against the motions supporting this direction. When the CPA decided to reconstitute the Communist Party, it ousted Browder from his position as general secretary in 1945 and expelled him from the party the following year (*EAL*, 111–13; *DAB*, vol. 1, 147; James A. Hagerty, "Browder Shift Seen Aiding Flynn," *NYT*, 26 May 1945, 1; "Reds Here Reverse Browder Policies," *NYT*, 5 June 1945, 21).

3. A search of ER's 1945 correspondence did not produce this statement. For more on the Communist Political Association see *n*2 Document 18.

4. See Document 18.

5. The CPUSA's attempts in the 1930s to take control of the American Youth Congress, an organization in which ER took special interest, contributed to her view, as did attempts by Josephine Truslow Adams, an activist in left and Communist causes, to exaggerate the closeness of her relationship with ER and FDR (Lash, *Eleanor*, 585–612; A. Black, *Casting*, 152; Isserman, *Which Side*, 131, 146–47).

20

"Tolerance Is an Ugly Word"[1]
Coronet July 1945

I do not like the word tolerance. If you tolerate something, you do not like it very much.

I believe that what we have to do in this country is to stop disliking things and like them.

In the future the world is going to be tied together by airplanes and radio, and we are going to be near many people whom we have not had to know in the past. It is not going to be possible just to tolerate our neighbors. We are going to like them or they are not going to like us. Our neighbors are going to include people whose skins are yellow, brown, red, black and white. Their religions will be more varied than the color of their skins and our liking must come from understanding. Regardless of race or religion, human beings have certain things in common and we must discover that quickly.

We, in this country, are a highly mechanized people. We have inventive genius where machinery is concerned, and mechanical skills. Some of the things that we have accomplished seem nothing short of miracles to other people.

Other people understand things, however, which we know little about. Our boys who have been in India are coming back to tell us about snake charmers and the people who make flowers grow before your eyes. These are powers we know nothing about.

So we have things to learn from other people just as they have things to learn from us, but we are not going to learn if we just "tolerate" each other.

I have an idea that we are going to find some fundamental traits, such as kindness and integrity and love of children, are present in many human beings.

If we can do away with fear, we will begin to love. If we are not afraid of aggression among nations, either in the military sense or the economic sense, we may have peace. If we are not afraid of being dominated by those who are stronger than ourselves, then we will learn to like people and to cooperate with them.

First we must cease to be afraid of our neighbors at home and take the word "tolerance" out of our vocabulary and substitute for it the precept, live and let live, cooperate in work and play and like our neighbors. If we do this, we will soon find that our basic needs and desires are the same, and that given the same opportunities for development, we develop in much the same way.

The problem is not to learn tolerance of your neighbors, but to see that all alike have hope and opportunity and that the community as a whole moves forward.

Eleanor Roosevelt

Coronet 18 (July 1945): 118

---

1. An abbreviated version of this article appeared in *Negro Digest* 3 (October 1945), 7–8.

On Being a Correspondent in Russia

In late April, United Features Syndicate expanded its distribution of My Day to include a few major international newspapers.[1] Once the war in Europe ended, the syndicate urged ER to go to Russia to report on conditions there. ER then turned to Harry Hopkins for advice, asking if spring 1946 would be a good time as she thought "flying [during the winter] might not be too good and the weather there a little difficult." Hopkins replied June 26:

> I don't know if you would consider going to the Soviet Union in September of this year, but if you could do it early in the fall I think it would be better than waiting until next May, altho, of course, that would be all right. Averell[2] has a very good plane which he can bring from Paris to Russia which I am sure you could use with a first rate crew, and I have no doubt they would let you see everything you wanted to see everywhere in the country.

ER replied four days later that "if it is important" she could make the trip in September. "However," she added, "when I do go I shall go as a correspondent for the . . . Syndicate and use whatever transportation the other correspondents use." Thus, she "did not want to use Averell's private plane." She closed by stating that she "would not want to do a lot of parties, etc., except of course, for calling on Marshall Stalin" and asking Hopkins what he thought "of my going purely as a correspondent and not as Franklin's widow."[3]

Before responding to United Features, she wrote Truman to seek his approval.

21

Eleanor Roosevelt to Harry Truman
2 July 1945 [Hyde Park]

Dear Mr. President:

It has been suggested to me by the United Feature Syndicate for which I write a column, that they would be glad to have me go to Russia. I wrote and asked Harry Hopkins and I have talked with Mr. Edward Flynn, and both of them feel that I should go in September rather than wait until next spring which was my first intention.[4]

I haven't spoken to the Syndicate about going at any immediate time because I wanted first to make sure that it would meet with your approval to have me go to Russia, either now or in the spring.

I would not want in any way to complicate anything that you may be doing or contemplate doing.

I would want to go as a correspondent in the usual way, but I realize that being my husband's widow, there would have to be a little more of the formal paying of respects and possibly even of entertainment. I would do my best to keep this down to a minimum, but I naturally do not want to be rude or to offend the Russian government and the Russian people. I would primarily be gathering information on the situation and interests of women and children from every angle and I would hope that the whole trip could be undertaken and finished in the space of four to six weeks.

Please be entirely frank in your own feelings in the matter because it is far more important that you be not hampered or bothered by anything anyone else does, and I know that your path at the present time must be anything but smooth.[5]

With all good wishes to you in the fight for the quick ratification of the Charter,[6] believe me,

Very cordially yours,
Eleanor Roosevelt

TLS SIRL, HSTL

---

1. ER to Joe Lash, 19 April 1945, JPLP, FDRL; ER to Anna Boettiger, 27 August, 1945, ARBHP, FDRL.

2. Averell Harriman, who had helped FDR implement Lend-Lease, also served as his emissary to Russia and attended all major wartime conferences. Harriman, who had a "close personal relationship" with Stalin, then served as the US ambassador to the Soviet Union (*HSTE*).

3. ER to Harry Hopkins, 24 June 1945, HHP, GULLSC; Harry Hopkins to ER, 26 June 1945, AERP; ER to Hopkins, 30 June 1945, AERP.

4. However, her appointment to the United Nations in December 1945 and her subsequent responsibilities as the US representative to its Committee on Humanitarian, Social and Cultural Affairs precluded any extensive travel. After leaving the United Nations, ER twice attempted to visit Russia. She tried to go as a reporter for *Look* in 1954 only to have her visit derailed when the visa for the Russian-speaking reporter she hoped would accompany her did not arrive before her scheduled departure date. Ironically, her 1957 visit to Russia, during which she conducted her historic interview with Nikita Khrushchev, occurred only after the State Department refused to issue her a visa so that she might visit the People's Republic of China for the *New York Post*. ER then arranged to go to the USSR, with her secretary Maureen Corr and close friend (and fluent Russian speaker) David Gurewitsch. She also returned to Russia for a second trip the following year (ER to Harry Truman, 5 July 1945, AERP; Rosenman to ER, 9 July 1945, AERP; ER to Hopkins, 30 June 1945 and Harry Hopkins to ER, 26 June 1945, AERP; Roosevelt, *Autobiography*, 369–98; and Lash, *Years*, 32–33, 267–71).

5. Truman did not object to ER's requests to travel to Russia, even after her appointment to the United Nations, writing her December 17 that she could "go if she wished." He noted the times she could travel as he reviewed her request, scrawling across the bottom of her letter "First UNO meeting in January for 30 days and next meeting not until last of April" (marginalia in Truman's hand on ER to Harry Truman, 31 December 1945, HSTSF, HSTL).

6. That morning, Truman made a historic trip to Congress, where he presented the UN Charter to members of the Senate and addressed a chamber filled with senators, their staffs, reporters, and those fortunate enough to get seats in the gallery. Notable as much for its rarity (it was only the sixth time since 1789 when a president himself presented a treaty before the Senate) as it was for its content, Truman capitalized on his bold move to remind the members that their 1943 resolutions calling for an international security organization gave them a "hand in shaping" the charter and urged them to adopt it quickly. "The choice before the Senate is now clear … The choice is between this Charter and no charter at all."

Truman, like ER, knew the importance of prompt adoption. Although the public welcomed the San Francisco conference, the sixteen weeks it took to approve the charter no doubt dulled some Americans' interest. Morever, polls showed that while Americans welcomed the concept of the United Nations, fewer than half believed it could reduce the possibility of war. Of perhaps even more concern to ER was Truman's decision at the end of the San Francisco conference to replace the secretary of state with James Byrnes, whom ER did not trust.

The Senate Foreign Relations Committee opened hearings July 9 and the full Senate ratified the charter August 8, 1945 (Schlesinger, 268–70; Lash, *Years*, 31; A. Black, *Casting*, 56–57; ER to James Roosevelt, 27 June 1945, FDRL; "Truman to Report to People Tonight on Big 3 and War," *NYT*, 9 August 1945, 1).

ON ARGENTINA, POLAND, AND THE UNITED NATIONS

July 6, ER wrote to offer her support for Stettinius when she learned of his dismissal by Truman. She again invited him to visit her in New York.

The president, who thought Stettinius pompous and not suspicious enough of the Soviets, wanted to make his loyal friend, Jimmy Byrnes, secretary of state. Neither Truman nor his envoy George Allen, the party operative with whom the president regularly played poker, handled Stettinius with the respect the secretary and his friends thought he deserved. Ironically, Allen fired Stettinius the day the San Francisco conference approved the UN Charter, the event often seen as his greatest accomplishment, and did so in ways that Stettinius later described as "a kick in the pants." When others heard that the secretary would be replaced and how he was removed from office, anger quickly surfaced. Arthur Vandenberg called it "a presidential decapitation" and journalist Arthur Krock called the secretary to say that Bernard Baruch and Senator Harry Byrd wanted to have "a showdown" with Truman over this. When, on June 27, Truman announced that Stettinius would join the American delegation to the United Nations and that Byrnes would succeed him as secretary of state, ER was dismayed but pragmatic, writing her son James that she thought Stettinius:

> brought the San Francisco Conference to a very successful conclusion. I suppose now Jimmy Byrnes will become Secretary of State and Mr. Stettinius will go to London and Heaven knows what will happen to [Ambassador to Great Britain John] Winant. I have heard it rumored that he might be sent to Paris which might or might not be good. I hate Jimmy Byrnes going in because with all of his ability, I think he is primarily interested in Jimmy Byrnes but after all, Father used him and I imagine that President Truman will feel that his past association will make working together easier.[1]

22

Edward Stettinius to Eleanor Roosevelt
10 July 1945 [The White House]

Dear Mrs. Roosevelt,

I deeply appreciate the sentiments contained in your note of July 6.

The memories of your husband were an inspiration to me throughout the San Francisco Conference.[2]

I opened the hearings before the Senate Foreign Relations Committee yesterday and the atmosphere was excellent. I am confident we will get the Charter ratified by the Senate within three or four weeks.[3]

I am sending to you, under separate cover, a copy of my statement yesterday which gives an overall review of the Charter and its implications.[4] I am also having prepared for you a special memorandum on Argentina and Poland since you say you are still mystified about them, and I feel confident that after you understand the facts you will agree that nothing else could have been done under the circumstances. Of course, no action was taken in these matters without the unanimous approval of the United States Delegation, as well as the approval of President Truman.

I have no plans to be in New York any time soon but I do hope that I will have a chance to see you before long.

With best wishes always,

Sincerely yours,
Edward Stettinius, Jr.

TLS, AERP, FDRL

ER read Stettinius's testimony carefully and found his "overall view of the Charter and its implications" informative. Yet she made it very clear that not only would she be "most interested to have the memorandum on Argentina and Poland" but that she would also welcome time to discuss these issues with him face to face. Stettinius replied that although he could "think of nothing that would give Mrs. Stettinius and myself more pleasure than a quiet weekend at Hyde Park," their visit would have to wait until the Senate ratified the Charter and his travels associated with its adoption were over. Yet he wanted ER to know that he "shall regret all [his] life that it was not possible for Mr. Roosevelt to participate in our success in San Francisco and to actually preside over the first meeting of the United Nations." The next week, he sent ER the following memo on the Poland and Argentina credentials battle.[5]

"I am more than grateful to you for the time and trouble you took to explain the Argentina question to me," ER replied August 3. "I never seemed to be able to gather from the newspapers just what the situation was. Argentina, however, does not seem to be behaving as well as one might wish." Determined to meet with him to discuss these issues, she concluded by enclosing her contact information in New York City.[6]

23

Edward Stettinius to Eleanor Roosevelt
26 July 1945 [The White House]

Personal and Confidential

Dear Mrs. Roosevelt,

I promised to explain to you how it came about that Argentina was admitted to the San Francisco Conference and Poland was refused admission.

At the Mexico City Conference, the matter of the recognition of the Argentine Government by the United States, as well as the other American Republics, and its adherence to the United Nations declaration, as well as the possibility of its being invited to participate at UNCIO, were discussed at length. The Mexico City Conference unanimously declared its hope that Argentina would "implement a policy of co-operative action with the other American nations so as to identify herself with the common policy which these nations are following and so as to orient her own policy so that she may achieve her incorporation into the United Nations as a signatory to the joint declaration entered into by them."[7] In the middle of March an agreement was reached between the United States and the other Latin American countries attending the Mexico City Conference that when Argentina declared the existence of a state of war with Germany and Japan, expressed conformity with the principles and declarations of the final Act of Mexico City, and complied with such principles and declarations, it would be permitted to sign the final Act of Mexico City, would then be recognized by the Governments of the American nations, and the United States as the depository State would then request that Argentina be invited to sign the joint declaration of the United Nations.[8] A memorandum embodying this agreement was approved and initialed by President Roosevelt. It was clearly understood that, if Argentina were admitted to the ranks of the United Nations, she could not be refused the right to participate in UNCIO.

On March 22, 1945, Argentina declared War on Germany and Japan, expressed adherence to the Mexico City declaration, and took steps to implement this decision. On April 4, she was permitted to sign the final Act of Mexico City. On April 9, the American Republics re-established relations with her. On April 16, Argentina officially requested permission to sign the United Nations declaration and pressed, with considerable support from other Latin American countries, for admission to UNCIO. I postponed a decision on this request until after the Conference met.

You will recall that early in the Conference, the Soviet Union took the position that the Ukraine and White Russia must not only be admitted to the Organization, which was unanimously agreed to at one of the first meetings of the Steering Committee, but that they should also be admitted forthwith to the Conference itself. The Russians were adamant on this matter and refused to agree to the organization of the Conference for business until this was done. The Latin American countries, in their turn, felt strongly that Argentina should be admitted to the ranks of the United Nations and to the Conference, and refused flatly to agree to the admission to the Conference of the Ukraine and White Russia unless Argentina were also seated. It was hoped that an agreement would be reached between the Russians and Latin Americans. This, however, proved impossible as Molotov[9] would not agree to seat Argentina unless the so-called Polish Lublin Government were also seated immediately, to which, of course, we could not agree. After careful consideration, the delegation decided that the only way to meet this situation was to vote for the admission of both Argentina and the Soviet Republics. It was of the utmost importance that the Conference should get down to its business of writing the Charter, and this seemed the only way to avoid a deadlock.

As far as the question of admitting Poland is concerned, it was of course at that time entirely out of the question for the United States to agree to the seating of the Polish Lublin Government;[10] to have done so would have meant sacrificing any chance of getting the Soviet Government to live up to the Yalta decision on Poland. If we had given in on this point I am certain that Harry Hopkins could never have worked out the satisfactory arrangement which has now led to our recognition of the Provisional Government of Poland in which all of the old parties are represented.[11]

I hope this letter will set at rest some of the questions which have bothered you. Unfortunately, for various reasons which you will understand, it has not been possible to explain publicly the details of what took place.

I may try to go off for a short rest, soon, and I hope I shall have a chance to see you before very much longer.

With best wishes, always,

Sincerely yours,
Edward R. Stettinius, Jr.

TLS AERP, FDRL

---

1. Thomas P. Campbell and George C. Herring, *The Diaries of Edward R. Stettinius, Jr., 1943–1946*, 399–404; Schlesinger, 248; ER to James Roosevelt, 27 June 1945, JRP, FDRL.

2. On the San Francisco conference, see *n*1 Document 2.

3. The Senate Foreign Relations Committee opened hearings on the UN Charter July 9, 1945, with Stettinius and Byrnes as the first two witnesses. President Truman and Senator Tom Connally, chairman of the committee, pushed for prompt ratification. On July 14, the committee unanimously recommended ratification and the Senate approved it July 28 by an 89-to-2 vote. France, the Soviet Union, and Great Britain all ratified the charter in the following month and it came into force as "part of the law of nations" on October 24, with the deposit of the twenty-ninth country's ratification (James B. Reston, "Charter Hearings Begun by Senators; Passage Is Likely," *NYT*, 10 July 1945, 1; "Roll Call Re-echoes in Silence of Galleries," *WP*, 29 July 1945, M1; Bertram D. Hulen, "Charter Becomes 'Law of Nations,' 29 Ratifying It," *NYT*, 25 October 1945, 1).

4. In his remarks, the secretary described the UN Charter as "both a binding agreement to preserve peace and to advance human progress and a constitutional document creating the international machinery by which nations can cooperate to realize these purposes in fact." The United Nations will work for "the maintenance of international peace and security; the development of friendly relations among nations based on respect for the equal rights and self-determination of peoples; co-operation in solving international problems of an economic, social, cultural and humanitarian character, and in promoting respect for human rights and fundamental freedoms for all."

"The Charter," he concluded, "of course, is not a perfect instrument." He was "sure it will be improved with time as the United Nations gain experience in its application;" however, he believed "it offers to the United States and to the world a truly effective instrument for lasting peace." The charter set a course "within the capacity of the nations at this period of world history to follow" and established "a direction of our highest aspirations for human advancement in a world at peace." Indeed, "the five major Nations proved at San Francisco beyond the shadow of any doubt that they can work successfully and in unity with each other and with the other United Nations under this Charter ... No country has a greater stake than ours in a speedy beginning upon the task of realizing in fact the promise which the United Nations Charter offers to the world." For complete text of Stettinius's remarks see "Text of the Statement by Stettinius to Senate Hearing on the Charter of the United Nations," *NYT*, 10 July 1945, 6.

5. ER to Edward Stettinius, 13 July 1945, AERP.

6. ER to Edward Stettinius, 3 August 1945, AERP.

7. Twenty nations, including the United States, attended the Inter-American Conference on Problems of War and Peace held in Mexico City where they passed the Act of Chapultepec, requiring joint action in repelling aggression against an American state. Stettinius played a key role in these deliberations, which were in part aimed at Argentina, its military build-up, and a desire to bring a democratic Argentina "back into the family of American nations" and, thus allow its admission into the United Nations Conference on International Organization (the San Francisco conference on the founding of the United Nations). See *n*4 Document 13.

A version of this "Political and Military Defense" resolution appeared in "Excerpts Highlighting Accomplishments of Inter-American Parley in Mexico City," *NYT*, 9 March 1945, 12.

8. See *n*4 Document 13.

9. Vyacheslav Molotov.

10. Here Stettinius references the seating of the Lublin (provisional) government as the representative of Poland at the United Nations.

11. See *n*5 Document 13.

ELEANOR ROOSEVELT AND THE NATIONAL CITIZENS POLITICAL ACTION COMMITTEE

ER's public refusal of political positions did not dissuade her supporters from trying to secure her commitment to their organizations. Ironically, she had tried to persuade Vice President Henry Wallace, once FDR acceded to the pressures of Democratic conservatives and removed him from the 1944 ticket, to accept the job Sidney Hillman, Calvin Baldwin, and the new National Citizens Political Action Committee (NCPAC) now offered her—the position of national chair. As Wallace recalled in his diary November 10:

> She felt that Sidney Hillman was not suitable for heading up such a broad liberal organization. She said furthermore that even though I had a position in the government, she thought I could go in on such an organization ... Later in the day I called her up and told her the first thing that occurred to me was that whatever was done should have the complete and enthusiastic blessing of Sidney Hillman. Second, I told her that I felt the only way any liberalism could express itself on a national basis was through the Democratic Party and I felt it would be damaging to the Democratic Party and to the liberalism boys if I should take the position she suggested ...[1]

Now in the summer of 1945, Sidney Hillman came to ER to offer her the leadership position of the organization he had created. Hillman's Congress of Industrial Organizations Political Action Committee played a decisive role in the hotly contested 1944 election and he planned to create an organization targeted to an audience beyond labor. This offer intrigued her enough to discuss it several times with Joe and Trude Lash. Both ER and her friends knew of Communist activity within NCPAC and while not dissuaded by the Communist presence, the Lashes encouraged her to investigate the offer further and, especially, to determine "precise" lines of authority.

ER met with Hillman, Baldwin, and the NCPAC board the night of July 18. She reported to Joe Lash that the discussion:

> left me torn in my mind. I don't know how useful I will be to them. I have an aversion to taking on responsibility except individually and this is a big one. On the other hand, it seems the one group that has organized nationally and can sway political parties and they need to be swayed.[2]

24

Eleanor Roosevelt to C. B. Baldwin
19 July 1945 [Hyde Park]

Dear Mr. Baldwin:

There is one point which I forgot to bring up on Tuesday night and that is the question of finances.

I can not participate in any money raising and think I would be more of a drawback than a help in that direction.

I would therefore, like to know how you plan to raise your budget, how you have done so in the past, and just what your plans are for financing the work which is planned.

Very sincerely yours,
Eleanor Roosevelt

In a handwritten note across the bottom, she added "The more I think about it, the N.C.P.A.C. needs a young man as full time chairman!"

TLS CBBP, IaU–LI

> Baldwin replied that NCPAC raised all its revenues through solicitation of wealthy liberals and progressives; fund-raising events, such as dinners and lunches, at which progressive political leaders spoke; and direct mail solicitations. He assured ER that she would not be asked to solicit funds or sign any fund-raising letters.[3] ER continued deliberating NCPAC's offer until she reached the conclusion that she "did not feel [she] could control the committee's policies."[4] On July 27, she informed Hillman that she would not accept his proposal.

25

Eleanor Roosevelt to Sidney Hillman
27 July 1945 [Hyde Park]

Dear Mr. Hillman:

I have given long and serious consideration to the very kind offer which you and the Board made to me.

Needless to say I am deeply interested in the possibilities of NCPAC, and in the program of work which I feel would not achieve its maximum influence if I became its chairman. I would bring additional difficulties and no great strength. As you went out the other night, I told you the things which I felt needed to be considered.

I think that if I speak for you and I am available for consultation unofficially at any time, when any of your workers feel I can be of use, I will be doing you more service than if I actually undertake to give you part of my time as your chairman. I have decided that if I became chairman instead of being helpful with the Democratic Party, it would alienate the Democratic Party and I think it is important to keep the Democratic Party close to both the CIO-PAC and the NC-PAC.

I shall not take the chairmanship or the presidency of any organization at present. I shall do what writing and radio work I can to forward the general ideas which seem to me to be emerging as the important ideas of this period when we hope to begin building peace.

I think I may do a considerable amount of traveling which is a further reason for not feeling it right at the present time to affiliate in any responsible administrative capacity with any organization.

With the deepest appreciation of the confidence which you and your board have shown me, and the hope that I may be of real value to you in the future, even though I am foregoing the honor of being your chairman, I am,

Very sincerely yours,

TLc AERP, FDRL

———————————

1. Blum, ed., *The Price of Vision*, 390–91.

2. ER to Joe Lash, 20 July 1945, JPLP, FDRL; Lash, *World*, 201.

3. C. B. Baldwin to ER, 24 July 1945, AERP.

4. Lash, *World*, 208.

<hr />
26
<hr />

"From the Melting Pot—An American Race"

Liberty 14 July 1945

Some of you may remember my column long ago about the cemetery at Guadalcanal.[1] I have thought about that cemetery many times here at home when I have heard people say "Perhaps Hitler was not so far wrong in his attitude toward the Jews. They are shysters; they do not take their full part in the war"; or "Gee, when this war is over we will not have any more wops coming into this country." The "wops" referred to may be Italians, Russians, or people from any one of the Balkan countries. "You know the Negroes can't fight; all they can do is drive a truck," is another comment; or, "All the Catholics, the Irish Catholics especially, think they run this country." You may also hear someone say, "The Japanese-Americans are making a good record in Italy, but you can never trust these guys—you can't know what they are thinking about. They have Oriental minds."

Invariably such remarks bring that Guadalcanal cemetery before my eyes. The chapel there was built by the natives and given to the men of the United States. The altar, the cross, and the altar ornaments were carved by the natives. From the rafters hang the symbols they have preserved in their own religion—the fish and the birds which represent life to them. The flag of the United States flies in front of the chapel, and outside, row on row, are the graves of the men who were killed that all the people of the United States might be free.

As I walked along the rows of crosses, I saw adjoining graves of a man of the Jewish faith, a Catholic boy, and a Protestant. On each grave hangs the little tin dish, once part of his mess kit and now decorated by his comrades—the only sign of their affection they could leave. Some of them had scratched doves or candles with their knives, along with a religious verse, but all the dishes bear such tributes as: "A grand guy," "A great pal." The names of his pals are all signed for everyone to see.

Those names show plainly the origin of these U.S. soldiers. They came from Russia, Germany, the Balkan states, France, the Scandinavian countries, Great Britain, from every race in the world. Every religion is represented—a silent testimony to the fact that American boys fought side by side, and lie side by side in death. The place of their origin and their religion make them no less martyrs who kept their country free. All of them deserve equal honor from us, and all of them rise up to chide us when we mouth the utterances that breed disunity in our homeland.

In this country we have meant to be the great melting pot of the world. Wave after wave of immigration came to our shores. All of us, either ourselves or our ancestors, came from foreign lands. The only people who "belong" here are the Indians.

The variety of our backgrounds has been one of our great strengths. We owe our continued vigor over a long period of years to the adventurous blood which has been pumped into our veins. People who stay at home, too dispirited to get out and seek something better than they have known before, do not come to new worlds. For many generations we kept on adding pioneer strength and character that enriched our original stock.

Even the Negro slaves who came here against their will brought us a strong and adventurous spirit. It took not only health but character and a will to live to survive the conditions under which they were brought to this country, and their years of hardship and bondage. To find people of the Negro race emerging from slavery with the ability to adapt and improve themselves quickly is a sign that their ancestors who came originally were strong and vigorous, with latent powers far beyond what we might have expected.

It is estimated that the immigration from 1776 to 1820 did not exceed 250,000, but by 1840 it was nearly 100,000 for a single year. By 1850 it was just short of 400,000.

Between 1900 and the outbreak of the first World War, immigration soared to unheard-of figures, reaching an all-time high of nearly 1,300,000 in 1907. During the war period, immigration dropped to a little over 100,000 in 1918, but quickly recovered to 800,000 in 1920, and about 700,000 in 1924. Then it was cut sharply by law.[2]

But our melting pot has not melted too successfully. Instead of all being welded together into one American race, we find, despite occasional intermarriage, settlements which retain the characteristics of the mother country: Little Italys; Little Polands or Irelands; districts where primarily Jewish people or Negro people are found; German cities; Norwegian and Danish settlements in rural areas. All these make us conscious of our differences; there is not that complete flowing together and obliteration of old lines of difference which we should like to see.

The most optimistic among us will have to agree that there are barriers which keep us from integrating and intermarrying as rapidly as possible.

Let us consider what these barriers are.

Perhaps by far the greatest is that of language. Children born here of foreign parents go to public school and learn English; sometimes this erects a greater barrier between them and their parents than the one which separates them from youngsters of different backgrounds.

But there is one thing which they do not acquire in schools. That is the foreign names to which they are born and which they take to school and on into life. These names often segregate people as much as does color or religion, and keep them tied to their particular backgrounds and the homelands from which they came.

This question of a name is not just one of identification with a background or group, as Polish-Americans or German-Americans or Italian-Americans, for many men are proud of their origin and do not want to lose identity with it, but it has an economic facet as well. A boy may have graduated from the best college in the country, but when he goes looking for a job, he will find a foreign and unpronounceable name a handicap. The boy with the easy name, given approximately the same qualifications, gets the job.

Perhaps this is one of the very first things that we ought to consider in our effort to become actually one people.

Perhaps when a baby is born on our soil or when an individual becomes naturalized, he ought to be given the opportunity, if he desires it, to change his foreign name to its American equivalent. Nowadays, however, anyone doing this is liable to find himself accused of trying to hide his background and origin. What is wrong about changing Lowenstein to Livingston, Rabinowitz to Robinson, or any of these comparatively foreign names to a simpler version? Unkind things are said about people who change their names, yet we should welcome and honor people willing to take this step toward complete Americanization. It may prove to be a most important factor in bringing about a more unified American people.

Many and many a time in this country a romance has been disrupted when one or the other was reluctant to bring the new friend home to the family circle because of his foreign name. His looks were not against him, but his name awoke distrust. Obviously he belonged to a foreign group and therefore he might not be welcome in the girl's family group. If the name had not kept these young people apart, they might have come to know each other better and understood their respective backgrounds. Thus the way to romance might have been open.

This is a little thing, but it has its effect on marriage and keeps different groups from integrating. Of course love can conquer obstacles, but I want to point out that a foreign name unnecessarily hampers the beginnings of friendship.

Some might prefer to retain their own names under all circumstances. For them the way is clear. But to others it may seem obvious common sense to adopt an Americanized name as soon as possible. Having once Americanized our names, we can count, I think, on our schools and our communities doing much toward building a uniform pattern of living.

The second obstacle to amalgamation in the United States lies, of course, in the customs and habits in the home. School friendships will wipe out some of these differences or help the family to fit its habits, arts, and skills into its new life. Its foreign customs will become Americanized as they fit into the new pattern.

The American Christmas, for instance, is a curious mixture of habits and customs brought here from all over the world. People have often kept their Old World customs, but have adapted them to the American situation.

Probably the most difficult of barriers is the difference in religious beliefs. Our Constitution was based on the concept that we should all practice our religious faiths in complete freedom. So it is peculiarly American to insist that even if people of different faiths marry, all of them shall have a right to practice their religion in the way they consider fitting.

This theory is so deeply ingrained in most Americans that even people wholly ignorant of certain religious tenets are still willing to concede others a right to religious freedom. I think the only real danger of our curtailing religious rights lies in the possibility that some of our church groups might come to wield too much influence in the nation's political and economic life.[3] I think that would provoke very serious opposition because of the strong feeling in this country that the church should confine itself to spiritual matters, leaving affairs of government and economy entirely free from church influence or domination.

Looking at the factors which seem to be barring us from making one nation out of our curiously variegated background, I think we will find our real obstacles are few indeed.

Liberty 22 (14 July 1945): 17, 89.

---

1. ER visited the cemetery on Guadalcanal on September 16, 1943, during her wartime tour of American bases and hospitals in the South Pacific. September 23, she told readers of My Day:

> The natives of Guadalcanal completed a week ago the chapel which stands near the graves and it is a labor of love. The design of the matting on the sides and roof is intricate and beautiful. They have made candlesticks for the altar from young bamboo stalks, the cross carved of wood inlaid with mother of pearl is reversible, in order to be useable for Protestants or Catholics, since all faiths use this chapel. Many Jewish boys lie side by side with those of other faiths. As you read what their buddies have written, it brings home forcibly that the important thing is neither your nationality nor the religion you professed, but how your faith translated itself in your life.
>
> A flag waves over the cemetery. Someday grass will grow, palms will wave in the breeze and cast their shade over the white crosses and it will be peaceful here. I think, however, the real memorial to show the love we bore for those who lie here, must be built where we live by the way in which we make our lives count. We must build up the kind of world for which these men died. They may never have put it into words, but I think they wanted a world where no one is hungry or in want for the necessities of life as they saw them.
>
> I am sure they wanted freedom and opportunity, but I question whether for many of them the results of opportunity would have been measured only by the success in acquiring this world's goods. Too many soldiers have discovered that the things which bring them happiness cannot always be bought with money. Long ago a man told me the big thing men got out of a war was the sense of shared comradeship and loyalty to each other. Perhaps that is what we must develop at home to build the world for which our men are dying (*MD*, 23 September 1943).

2. The Johnson-Reed Act of 1924 restricted immigration and imposed annual quotas that greatly favored northern Europeans over those seeking to immigrate from southern and eastern Europe. The act allotted no quota to the Japanese. The Chinese Exclusion Act of 1882 already denied admission to the Chinese (*RCAH*, 361, 536, 781).

3. ER particularly feared the political and economic influence of the Roman Catholic Church. In July 1949 her strong stand against federal aid to private and parochial schools provoked a major public confrontation with New York Cardinal Francis Joseph Spellman (Lash, *Years*, 156–67).

ON MARTIN NIEMÖLLER, PART 1

ER had admired Pastor Martin Niemöller, whose 1937 detention for criticizing Hitler's interference with the Confessing Church made him a symbol of anti-Nazi heroism. She had helped to publicize his story in the 1940 anti-Nazi film, *Pastor Hall*, which her son James distributed in the United States.[1] Yet her opinion of him changed dramatically after the June 5, 1945, press conference in Naples, Italy, where he admitted that he had volunteered to serve the German navy "in any capacity," declared that "the greatest short-coming of the Weimar Republic was that it never could impose authority on the German People, who longed for such authority," and, after stating that as "a churchman he was not interested in politics," refused to denounce Nazi policies.

When Niemöller and his fellow detainees argued that "Germany is unsuited to any form of democratic government so far tried in western countries," he became a litmus test for the reconstruction of Germany.[2] His many admirers saw him as a martyr who had suffered for speaking out against Hitler, while his detractors never forgot his early collaboration with the National Socialists and viewed his calls for forgiveness as nothing more than asking the world to forget the crimes of the Germans.

When ER chose to make her opposition public in My Day, she received stinging criticism from his supporters.

27

My Day
7 August 1945

NEW YORK, Monday—I was surprised to see the other day that Pastor Martin Niemoeller was being considered by some of our American officials to head the first post-war German government,[3] and I was glad to see, under a later date, the report that the United States Army authorities had cancelled a speech by the same Rev. Niemoeller, which one of the Protestant chaplains had asked him to make.[4]

Pastor Niemoeller won great fame because of his opposition to the rise of the Nazis. A movie was made about him and he was heralded in this country as a hero for his resistance.[5] We saw him portrayed as an example of what a Protestant minister of great courage could endure for the cause of freedom. He spent eight years in a concentration camp until he was liberated by the Allied forces.

After being freed, however, he made a statement which must have shocked many people in this country. In part, he said: "The German people like to be governed, not to mingle in politics. The greatest shortcoming of the Weimar Republic[6] was that it never could impose authority on the German people, which longed for such authority."[7]

That statement sounds almost like a speech from Mr. Hitler. Later, also, Pastor Niemoeller admitted that from his concentration camp he had offered his services "in any capacity to the German Navy when the war began." He did not claim any political opposition to the Nazis. He said that as a churchman he was not interested in politics, but that he was unable to accept any authority which claimed the right to override that of the church. Pastor Niemoeller sounds to me like a gentleman who believes in the German doctrine of the superiority of race.

It is easy to understand devotion to one's country when attacked from without, but Niemoeller's expressed ideas make him unfit to establish any kind of government which would train the German people in democracy. The object of the Allies' occupation of Germany is to eradicate Naziism and the beliefs which the Nazis held, and to make it impossible for them to build a new generation ready to go to war.

One can understand the difficulties faced by our military authorities in finding Germans suited to take office in the country, but I should think they would hesitate to accept Niemoeller.

I have heard people who interviewed Niemoeller in an American camp, immediately after his liberation, say something like this: "Niemoeller is a trouble maker of the first order. He claimed our camp was worse than a concentration camp, and told us that we should not dare write: 'Niemoeller is liberated.' He is a dangerous pan-German,[8] preaching adherence to God and His greatness in forgiving, looking down at us Americans as if he wanted to say: 'Why don't you people forget what has been, as our Lord tends to forgive, and let's live together under a new Heaven, on a new earth with nothing but love and understanding.'"[9]

What a millenium that would be for the guilty Germans!

TMs AERP, FDRL

Not all Americans or American military personnel reacted as ER did to Niemöller's interview. For example, Ben Lacy Rose, a Presbyterian minister from Fayetteville, North Carolina, stationed in Germany as chaplain to the army's 113th Calvary (Mechanized Group), wrote to express his dismay over this column. Rose, who had interviewed Niemöller for the *Christian Century*, asked the theologian to respond to ER's accusations. He then forwarded a transcript of the interview for ER's response.[10]

28

Ben L. Rose to Eleanor Roosevelt
4 September 1945 [Germany]

Dear Mrs. Roosevelt:

My heart was saddened by your attack on Pastor Martin Niemoeller in your column, "My Day", of August 8, 1945. It was a surprise to me that you, whose eyes are usually so clear of prejudice, were this time so blinded by it.

On several occasions recently I have had [the] opportunity to talk with Pastor Martin Niemoeller. A more humble Christian man one will hardly find. He and I disagree on several subjects, such as: separation of Church and State, but one cannot but be impressed by his sincere love of Jesus Christ. Let that never be doubted.

In your column you quoted one of Pastor Niemoeller's statements to the effect, "The German people like to be governed, not to mingle in politics, etc. etc.". If you do not agree with that statement you simply do not know the German people today. A more true statement of the German attitude today could hardly be worded. I have shown the statement to any number of my fellow officers (and we have been in Germany since September of last year, long enough to know a little about the German people) and they agree that it is absolutely true. I have shown the statement to a number of my Dutch friends (who lived under the German rule of their country, and who, by the way, hate with consuming passion anything that is German) and even they agree that the statement is absolutely true. How often Germans have said to me when I accused them of allowing Hitler to come to power, "Well, we must have a leader". Whether Pastor Niemoeller's statement sounds like Hitler or not, the statement is still true. Should one refrain from speaking the truth simply because it sounds like Hitler?

To answer the opinions expressed in your article which I think do Pastor Niemoeller great injustice, I am enclosing a copy of an interview which I had with him a few days ago. One or two of my questions were prompted by your article.[11]

It is a rule in our country that a man is not condemned without first being given a hearing. I feel that you have condemned and done great hurt to the name of a great Christian without first giving him a hearing.

Sincerely,
Ben L. Rose

TLS AERP, FDRL

ER remained unswayed by Rose's argument.

___29___

Eleanor Roosevelt to Ben L. Rose
20 September 1945 [Hyde Park]

My dear Chaplain Rose:

I was interested in your letter about Pastor Martin Niemoeller and thank you for writing me as you did.

I certainly do not think that a man should be condemned without a hearing, and I did not write my article about Pastor Niemoeller until after I had read his own statement. I was shocked by it, and wrote with only that in mind as previous to reading his statement I had greatly admired him. Pastor Niemoeller is not condemned for speaking the truth and sounding like Hitler.[12]

All of us who know Germans are aware that they like to be governed, but this attitude should not be encouraged. They should be made to realize that they are responsible for their leaders and for their form of government.

Very sincerely yours,

TLc AERP, FDRL

Yet ER remained concerned enough about her correspondence with Rose to seek Trude Lash's assessment of the debate. Trude responded bluntly.

___30___

Trude Lash to Eleanor Roosevelt
1 October 1945 [New York City]

Dearest Mrs. Roosevelt:

I am returning Capt. Rose's letter and the report of his interview with Pastor Niemoeller. Your letter, it seems to me, answers his questions though I am not sure he will understand after having misunderstood so completely your column. His interview proves nothing as you did not question Pastor Niemoeller as a Christian or even a Church leader—but only as a political leader, and there is not a single sentence in Capt. Rose's interview which proves that Pastor Niemoeller is <u>not</u> a pan-

Germanist and does <u>not</u> want a soft peace for Germany. I do think professional Christians are very easily fooled.

My love to you,
Trude

TLS AERP, FDRL

———————————

1. "James Roosevelt Gets British Film," *NYT*, 16 July 1940, 21; "Mrs. Roosevelt Filmed for Anti-Nazi Picture," *NYT*, 18 July 1940, 26; "The Screen in Review," *NYT*, 21 September 1940, 20.

2. Niemöller, with five other recently released prisoners of war, addressed a news conference in Naples June 5 in which he made several statements reprinted in papers nationwide. The first dealt with the German attitude toward citizenship, in which he declared that "the German people like to be governed, not to mingle in politics," that his countrymen were "incapable" of American-style democracy, that "every country has a different kind of democracy," and that the key challenge was to "find the kind of democracy which would be useful for Germany."

The second series of statements dealt with his own outlook. As Sam Pope Brewer reported, Niemöller, a naval commander during the First World War, acknowledged that when World War II began, even though he was imprisoned in Dachau, he volunteered for Hitler's navy. He justified this action as a decision made by "a German father whose sons had been drafted into the fighting line." Rather than renounce fascism or Hitler's government, Niemöller stated that he opposed the Fuhrer because "he was unable to accept any authority that claimed a right to override that of the church."

His final comments dealt with horrors of the concentration camps. He responded to reporters' questions about his own detention by saying that he "did not receive ill treatment" and that he, like most Germans, was "shocked and shattered" by the photographs depicting life in the death camps (Sam Pope Brewer, "Niemoeller Asks Iron Rule of Reich," *NYT*, 5 June 1945, 11; "Topics of the Town," *NYT*, 8 June 1945, 18).

3. Although the statement to which ER refers is unknown, the popular *New York Times* "Abouts" column asked readers on May 13, 1945, if there were "no independent-minded Germans left to take over the leadership of their country?" It then answered its own question: "Well, there's Pastor Martin Niemoeller. He said from the start: 'God is my Fuehrer,' and he stuck to it" (*NYT*, 13 May 1945, SM2).

4. Niemöller had been scheduled to speak on July 31, 1945, at the Protestant chapel at the headquarters of the United States Forces, European Theatre (USFET), about "the responsibilities and opportunities of the Christian church." The Associated Press reported that although USFET gave no reason for canceling the speech, "it is understood from an authoritative source" that "the pastor's recent observations on his desire to serve as a U-boat commander in World War II, as he did in World War I, and the political character of some of his recent remarks" made him an "unacceptable speaker" ("Niemoeller Talk Canceled by U.S. Occupation Force," *NYT*, 1 August 1945, 7).

5. In 1940, a British film company turned *Pastor Hall*, a dramatic account of Niemöller's life written by the Jewish exile Ernst Toller, into a widely distributed film. James Roosevelt handled its American distribution and ER appeared in its prologue. Four years later, in Paramount's *The Hitler Gang*, the docudrama the *New York Times* called "a reasonably absorbing chronicle of Hitler's rise to power," Ivan Triesault's portrayal of Niemöller depicts the pastor as the personification of the heroism necessary to outlast Hitler's tactics and to assist the "Allied counterattack" ("James Roosevelt Gets British Film," *NYT*, 16 July 1940, 21; "Mrs. Roosevelt Filmed for Anti-Nazi

Picture," *NYT*, 18 July 1940, 26; "The Screen in Review," *NYT*, 21 September 1940, 20; "The Screen," *NYT*, 8 May 1944, 15).

6. Established in Germany after its defeat in World War I, the Weimar Republic (1919–33) struggled to cope with the consequences of the harsh and unpopular Versailles Peace Settlement. Weakened by pressure from Hitler's Nazi party, and unable to deal effectively with the inflation, unemployment, and rebellion that followed in the wake of the treaty, the Weimar Republic finally collapsed. Following his 1932 reelection, President Paul von Hindenburg appointed Hitler chancellor. After a fire destroyed the German Reichstag (parliament) building, Hitler declared a national emergency and, when Hindenburg died in 1934, he named himself president and founded the Third Reich (*OEWH*).

7. See *n*2.

8. Pan-Germanists, who believed in the superiority of the Nordic or German "race," favored the political unification of all German-speaking peoples and the domination of central and eastern Europe by Germany (*NEB*, vol. 9).

9. ER's files do not identify those with whom she spoke.

10. Ben Lacy Rose, "As Niemoeller Sees Germany's Future," *The Christian Century*, vol. 62, 10 October 1945, 1155–57.

11. Rose interviewed Niemöller in Frankfurt, Germany, on September 3, 1945. The four-page, typed transcript Rose forwarded ER included twenty-four questions and responses, including the following exchanges.

When Rose asked Niemöller if the Confessing Church, which he led, "spoke out against concentration camps, persecution of the Jews, etc.," Niemöller replied, "Yes, it spoke against them to Hitler himself in no uncertain terms."

When Rose asked, "On exactly what points did you openly oppose the Nazis?" Niemöller said:

I spoke of the forgeries in the church elections, of the lies of the Goebbels propaganda, of the plan for the destruction of the Churches and of the Christian way of life, of the persecution of the Jews, of the education of party-members and leaders to enmity against the Bible and the Christian faith, and I showed by my sermons how these things must lead to the ruin of our whole nation and people.

When Rose asked the pastor why, after he was imprisoned in Dachau, he offered to serve in the German navy, Niemöller replied:

It was certainly not for the reason that I wanted to fight Hitler's war for him, and most assuredly not with any idea of trying to redeem myself with the Nazis. I was thinking only of my people and my country. At that time I saw three possibilities ahead for Germany: 1. total defeat, which would be bitter for Germany, 2. total victory for the Nazis, which would be even bitterer for Germany, and 3. to fight on in the hope that the Nazis might be thrown out of government and a negotiated peace reached. It was on the latter that I pinned my hopes. If the latter occurred, and I had good hopes that it might, I did not want to be in prison but wished to be free in order that I might do my part for the future of my country …

When Rose asked if he had told reporters after being freed, "Do not dare say that Niemoeller is liberated," Niemöller said, "No, I had no reason to say that and never did."

When asked if "the German people are responsible for the War and Nazism," Niemöller argued that "inasmuch as they allowed Hitler to come to power with his party" they were; however, "the nation was too worn out to oppose [Hitler] with strength."

When Rose followed up by asking "Should the German people be punished in any way for the war," Niemöller responded:

The German people have been punished already by God; its young people, and the old ones as well, have died at the front and at home; its cities and towns have been destroyed with all their contents; the people are starving, how much so the next winter will show; and the hopes and ideals of the whole nation have been shattered.

When asked "Should the world just say to Germany, 'We forgive you', and then start again? Are not punitive and corrective measures necessary?" Niemöller replied:

'The world' will not be able to say, 'We forgive you', but the Christians in the world should say so, and they should just start anew with us. Punitive measures against the nation will not help. The Christian people of Germany and many who begin once more to believe in God know that no man can punish them more than God has done. The others would only be made to say, 'Hitler was not the worst, after all'. So they would turn to radicalism and underground propaganda of all kinds. But corrective measures are necessary and wholesome, beginning with a new way of youth education and a slow re-education to public responsibility. I think the way in this direction will be open" (Ben L. Rose, "An Interview with Pastor Martin Niemoeller," Frankfurt on Main, Germany, 3 September 1945, AERP).

12. In December 1946, when Niemöller arrived in the United States to make a speaking tour at the invitation of the Federal Council of Churches of Christ in America, ER again protested (*MD*, 4 December 1946). See Document 164 and Document 165.

On the New York City Mayoral Race

ER followed the New York City municipal elections and the political rivalries in labor with increasing concern. Not only had La Guardia's sudden announcement that he would not seek re-election startled her, but labor, the Democrats' most stalwart ally, seemed to be preoccupied in an internal political battle that could weaken the Democrats' chance to recapture the mayoralty. In 1944, David Dubinsky and Alex Rose, key leaders in the garment industry unions, thought Communists had secured too much influence in Sidney Hillman's American Labor Party, and instructed their followers to leave the ALP and help them create the Liberal Party.[1] Both parties had supported FDR, but FDR's death accentuated the Hillman-Dubinsky rivalry[2] and ER feared that Dubinsky's automatic rejection of William O'Dwyer, the Labor Party candidate, would create a wedge in voter turnout that could cost the Democrats the election.[3] Furthermore, La Guardia had just announced his sponsorship of an independent No Deal Party and pledged August 8 in a fifteen-minute radio address a "real, hard, open fight against the Tammany combination as well as against the other political machine tickets" to insure that the city would "not be turned over to the political bosses, to big-shot racketeers, to the 'home breakers and judge-makers'" who would "return to the old time of political control with patronage, privilege, pap, perquisites and pilfer."[4]

The night of La Guardia's broadcast, ER's close friend, National Women's Trade Union League President Rose Schneiderman,[5] called to express concern over ER's rejection of the NCPAC position,[6] and to discuss the campaign. ER then wrote Dubinsky August 9 that she "ought to tell" him she thought the Liberal Party shortsighted "in backing Judge Goldstein[7] who is Governor Dewey's candidate, just because you never really want to agree with the American Labor Party. ... This fight in New York City may have an effect on the state and the nation and I am not at all sure that the Liberal Party has taken the long view." She offered her help in resolving the differences between the two organizations and urged Dubinsky not to "hesitate to ask" for her help. He need not worry about any fallout she might receive by entering this fray because she was "not worried about being involved too deeply on either side of this slight difficulty which exists between your warring factions."[8]

Just as La Guardia used the radio to make his position known, ER used her August 9 column to express her concerns about an election she predicted would be viewed by many as "the opening gun" in a series of critical state and national elections. The *New York Times* found her position so noteworthy that it reprinted the column August 10 under the headline "Democrat Backed by Mrs. Roosevelt."[9]

31

My Day
9 August 1945

New York, Wednesday—New York City politics seems more confused this year than usual. First, the Republican party nominates for Mayor a one-time Democrat, and Governor Dewey backs him in spite of a few things said by the candidate in a past campaign which must now be buried in oblivion![10] Then, the Democrats nominate a really good man, General O'Dwyer. To be sure, they, too, cannot get away without a little confusion and a few changes in running mates. But the ultimate product is good.

And now Mayor La Guardia, who has done much for New York City, backs another good man, Newbold Morris, who is a regular Republican but who does not have Governor Dewey's backing and does not seem to want it. He is to run on a "No Deal" ticket—whatever that may mean, since no politicians get away without some deals. The only important thing to know is whether they are good or bad deals, because "deals" is really another word for "plans," and one must plan. It is the way one plans that matters, and whether the plans leave one freedom of action for the future.[11]

Well, there is the picture, and ordinarily, as a voter of upstate New York, I would be only remotely concerned about a mayoralty election in the City of New York. This year, however, it looks to me as though not only the citizens of New York City are concerned. This election is of importance to the state and the nation. It is the opening gun in a campaign which is already being waged—under cover, to be sure, but nevertheless with skill and tenacity—by certain groups in the country, represented largely in the Republican party. These groups will nominate a Judge Goldstein because they can use him, and because they think by so doing they can carry certain elements with them that have been with the Democrats in the past.[12]

These groups hope that the people may be fooled, but I have great confidence in the people. We, the people, are growing in wisdom politically; we have learned to study the candidates and weigh them as men and as public servants; we weigh their backing and what that backing means.

Newbold Morris is a good man but he cannot be elected, and I think the voters of this city are wise enough to know that if General O'Dwyer could fight for the things that he considered right against such strong forces in Brooklyn, he will fight for these things in City Hall.

The Mayor of New York in the next few years will meet great problems, problems that touch both business and labor, since their interests are closely allied. He will need an understanding of the wider horizons that reach out from this great port to the far ends of the world. General O'Dwyer has had the opportunity to learn and to see the distant scene in the last few years. I think New York City voters, in electing him, will give themselves a "Good Deal" and help in the fight for control by the people as against control by certain powerful groups.

TMs, AERP, FDRL

Dubinsky liked neither ER's letter to him nor her column.

_____ 32 _____

David Dubinsky to Eleanor Roosevelt
24 August 1945 [New York City]

Dear Mrs. Roosevelt:

Thank you for your letter of August 9th. I intended to write to you sooner, but frequent absences from the city during the past two weeks prevented me from doing so.

As you know, I am very keenly interested in New York City politics. In view of the remarks concerning this year's mayoralty election contained in your letter, which coincide with the views expressed in your column of the same day in the New York World-Telegram,[13] I am taking the liberty of commenting upon several salient points which, in my judgment, should be made clear.

1. It is a fact that from January until May, the Liberal Party worked for an understanding with the Democrats on a good government candidate. We pointed out to them that the Democratic Party established for itself an enviable record in State and national politics and that it was time that the Democrats rehabilitated their unsavory reputation in municipal politics.[14] It was also agreed with Messrs Flynn and Kelly[15] that our joint candidate was not to accept the designation of the

American Labor Party.[16] This plan failed because O'Dwyer[17]—emboldened by the Mike Quill,[18] Marcantonio[19] support, plus the support of some of the worst elements in the local political machines including the underworld—threatened Mr. Kelly with a primary fight.[20] I can personally testify to the fact that Mr. Flynn was dismayed at these developments—and very much regretted the failure of the plan. Mr. Flynn has refused to make common cause with the American Labor Party in his own county.

2. Judge Goldstein[21] and Joseph McGoldrick[22] are not, in the first instance, Republican Party candidates. They were the original selections of the Liberal Party. While Mr. McGoldrick was our first choice for the nomination, it was he who urged us to unite around Judge Goldstein. As a matter of fact, on May 10, the New York Times headlined the news that Judge Goldstein was the choice of the Liberal Party for the mayoralty nomination. Several weeks later, he was nominated by the Republican Party.[23]

3. The Citizens' Union,[24] the Fusion Party,[25] the Citizens' Non-Partisan Committee—the same good government forces which broke several years ago the grip of Tammany[26] misrule and plunder in New York City—are all solid in their support of this ticket. Good government in New York City depends upon the unity of these forces. Irrespective of State or national politics, the record shows that in every fusion movement here the Republican Party always supported good government. You, no doubt, know that without Republican support, LaGuardia could never have been elected mayor of New York City.

4. In your column you say: "These groups will nominate a Judge Goldstein because they can use him." This is most unfair to Judge Goldstein, and, so far as I know, there is nothing substantial on which this unfriendly judgement may be based. Judge Goldstein, if elected, will be less under Republican influence than LaGuardia has been. LaGuardia was a Republican whereas Judge Goldstein has always been an independent Democrat. Those of us who have consistently fought for the cause of good government have confidence in Judge Goldstein's liberal and progressive outlook. The New York Post editorial of August 20 gives a true picture of the O'Dwyer candidacy and the forces back of it when it states: "The election of O'Dwyer would greatly strengthen the Clarence Neal-Marcantonio[27] forces led by gangster Frank Costello[28] and the Communists controlling the American Labor Party. O'Dwyer would be forced to consult these evil groups in making his major appointments and in forming his basic policies."

5. Do you really see nothing more in our effort to develop an honest, liberal movement in New York State than a "war among factions"? In your article and statements you have affirmed that democratic liberals cannot make common cause with those who practice the "philosophy of deception and the lie." Why then are you critical of us when we seek to organize a political party which refuses to make a united front with the Communists? The stubborn facts of experience have led the Labor Parties of Britain, of New Zealand, and Australia to the same position, and the Cooperative Commonwealth Federation of Canada[29] has also steadfastly refused to combine with the Communists. This is no minor issue; it reaches to the roots of the whole democratic cause. It also touches fundamental issues in the field of public affairs and morals. As we struggle to develop this kind of an honest progressive political movement in this city and State, we had every reason to hope for your sympathetic understanding, now that you have changed your decision about participating in this year's municipal campaign.

6. Let me assure you, Mrs. Roosevelt, that the Liberal-Fusion-Republican coalition in the 1945 municipal campaign carries no implications whatsoever about 1946 or 1948, just as our joint efforts with the Republicans in 1937 and 1941 in support of LaGuardia had no bearing on our attitude in the elections of 1940, 1942 or 1944.[30] It is hardly necessary to point out the fact that the Dewey support of LaGuardia in those years did not necessarily throw LaGuardia into the Dewey ranks. In this year's campaign, we are not fighting the battles of 1944, 1946 or 1948; nor should we be charged with the sordid purpose of attempting to "fool the people." We are fighting to prevent any possible comeback of the corrupt Tammany machine which is being aided and abetted by the Communists and their ilk.

This sums up our position in this municipal campaign. And, Mrs. Roosevelt, may I say further that your remark that "… this slight difficulty which exists between your warring factions" involves not a mere whim and is therefore not slight but is a matter of principles. And whether we win or lose is less important than the principles we are fighting for.

I also wish to take the opportunity to state here that your decision not to assume the chairmanship referred to in your letter will, in my opinion, prove a service to the cause of liberalism in the future.[31]

With kind personal regards, I am

Sincerely yours,
David Dubinsky

TLS AERP, FDRL

33

Eleanor Roosevelt to David Dubinsky
27 August 1945 [New York City]

Dear Mr. Dubinsky:

Many thanks for your letter of August 24th.

I think Judge Goldstein's weakness is that he is not the Republican Party candidate and yet he has accepted to run as a candidate of the Republican Party.[32] Whether the Liberal Party nominated him first is of little consequence because being nominated by the Liberal Party would not mean election for anybody.[33]

I would agree with you that Mayor LaGuardia could not have been elected had he not been a candidate of a fusion movement, but Mayor LaGuardia is quite a different proposition from Judge Goldstein. The two are not synonymous. I am sure you are not naive enough to think that because Judge Goldstein was not a Republican that he will not have to be beholden to them if elected. He will have to be beholden to them to a greater extent than Mayor LaGuardia who was a Republican.

I know quite well that there are forces in New York City back of General O'Dwyer which are not good forces.[34] I do not think they are any worse than the Republican forces. Neither party has a corner on gangsters or corrupt politicians.

The American Labor Party in New York City undoubtedly has some communists in it but that does not mean it is controlled by communists. However, I know very little about it, but I do not think that General O'Dwyer will be controlled by either the communists element in the Labor Party or the Tammany Hall-Costello group.[35] I do think that Judge Goldstein will find it very hard to be ungrateful to the Republican Party and hold his allegiance only to the Liberal Party.

I have told you, Dear Mr. Dubinsky, all along that I felt the split among labor people was bad for the labor movement. I feel it is bad politically in New York City.

I know you are fighting the communists, but I think you would fight them far more satisfactorily if you and Mr. Hillman were together in the same organization and not weakening each other by being separated.

You told me that what you did in this campaign did not in any way mean that the Liberal Party or you individually would follow along the same lines in 1946 and 1948, but I differ with you in believing that what happens in New York City is going to give strength one way or the other to what will happen in '46 and '48. Of course, I think you should fight corruption and control by the communists but if you did it together instead of as two separate groups, I think you would get much better results.

Very cordially yours,

TLc AERP, FDRL

Dubinsky continued to insist that his reading of the election's potential impact was correct. September 20 he sent ER a copy of FDR's 1941 endorsement of La Guardia "in which [the president] made it clear that municipal elections have no bearing on either state or national elections." Dubinsky "thought it might be of interest to recall it" since "many of us have forgotten it."[36] ER did not change her mind.

34

Eleanor Roosevelt to David Dubinsky
24 September 1945 [Hyde Park]

Dear Mr. Dubinsky:

I was amused by your sending me my husband's statement in 1941.[37] It is, of course, entirely true that mayoralty elections were held in off years so that the interests of the city could be separated from the interests of the state and nation, but no one can presume to say that the circumstances which my husband faced at the time he made that statement, are duplicated today. You know as well as I do that they are not.

Mayor LaGuardia was not beholden to any Republican Governor who was the titular head of his party.[38] Judge Goldstein has changed his party politics in order to get this nomination and he will be beholden to a Republican Governor, whom you acknowledge you do not consider a liberal and whom you do not desire to strengthen.[39]

A mayor of New York City can build up considerable strength and you know that in a gubernatorial election, a Republican must be beaten in New York City.

I think General O'Dwyer's record shows that he has stood in the past for what was right even when he had some pretty tough people to buck.[40] I think he will do that again.

I may be wrong and you may be wrong, since you believe that Judge Goldstein will be beholden to you and therefore a good Mayor. We will have to wait for time to prove which one of us is guessing right.

Very sincerely yours,

TLc AERP, FDRL

1. As leader of the ILGWU, Dubinsky worked to increase the political power of labor by founding the American Labor Party (ALP) following the Supreme Court's 1935 decision to overturn the National Industrial Recovery Act. Formed as the New York division of the National Labor Non-Partisans League, the ALP ran Franklin Roosevelt as their presidential candidate in 1936, 1940, and 1944 as well as their own candidates at the local level (Bone, 278–80).

2. As presidents of rival unions in rival associations, Hillman and his CIO-affiliated Amalgamated Clothing Union and Dubinsky's AFL-affiliated International Ladies Garment Workers Union (ILGWU) competed for members and standing within the labor movement.

3. Hillman, who had left the AFL in 1942 to support the Democratic candidate for governor, returned to the AFL the following year, bringing with him the CIO Political Action Committee he founded. When Earl Browder convinced the CPUSA to rename itself the Communist Political Association (CPA) and agree to work within a two-party system for economic change, Hillman agreed to work with the CPA to support reform. Dubinsky thought this alliance would alienate the moderate voters, refused to work with the AFL and Hillman, and formed the Liberal Party (Bone, 278–80).

4. Clayton Knowles, "La Guardia Urges Election of Morris to Foil City Bosses," *NYT*, 8 August 1945, 1.

5. Rose Schneiderman (1882–1972), whose friendship with ER dated back to the 1919 meeting of the International Congress of Working Women, played a key role in shaping both Roosevelts' attitudes toward organized labor and, in particular, the issues working women faced regarding wages, working conditions, and access to education, recreational facilities, and political networks run by career women. ER respected her political abilities so much that she asked FDR, who quickly agreed, to appoint Schneiderman to the National Labor Relations Board. As the NLRB's only woman member, she devoted her time to writing codes for industries with predominantly female workforces. Her service there led to her appointment in 1937 as secretary of labor for New York State, a post she resigned in 1943 to devote her full attention to the National Woman's Trade Union League and the labor movement in general. What Schneiderman and ER discussed that night is unknown (*NAWMP*, 631–33; *JWIA*, 1209–11; Lash, *Eleanor*, 280–81, 310; Cook, vol. 2, 77).

6. See Document 24 and Document 25.

7. For information on Goldstein see *n*17 Document 17.

8. ER to David Dubinsky, 9 August 1945, AERP.

9. "Democrat Backed by Mrs. Roosevelt," *NYT*, 10 August 1945, 11.

10. For information on Goldstein see *n*17 Document 17.

11. When City Council President Morris announced his candidacy, he said it would be contingent upon obtaining 25,000 signatures by August 15 endorsing the following declaration in support of the No Deal position:

> We have no political party. We do not intend to form a political party. We have made no deals with any party or group or person. We present this opportunity to the people of the City of New York if they desire to continue a non-political, non-partisan, efficient city government administered by experienced officials. We have made no pledge or promise of any kind to any party, group or person, expect this one pledge to the City of New York to give an efficient, honest administration of its affairs during the next four years (James Hagerty, "Morris Announces Entry for Mayor on No Deal Ticket," *NYT*, 5 August 1945, 1).

12. Journalists such as Roy Roberts in Syracuse also speculated that Dewey supported Goldstein to make inroads in the Jewish vote deemed critical for his reelection in 1946 (Beyer, 215).

13. The *New York World-Telegram* carried My Day.

14. The Liberal Party, whose appeal rested on its image as an independent reform organization dedicated to eliminating bossism in New York City, objected to Tammany Hall's influence within the Democratic Party as strongly as it objected to the Communist influence within the ALP. La Guardia's election sidelined Tammany Hall from mayoral politics. His sudden withdrawal from the mayoral race gave Tammany the chance to reexert its influence. While Hillman's ALP interpreted

this election in terms of its impact on national and state elections, Dubinsky and his Liberal Party allies saw this election solely in local terms and refused to ally with any candidate who did not share their strong anti-Tammany convictions. County Democratic leaders Ed Flynn (the Bronx) and Frank Kelly (Brooklyn) shared Dubinsky's concerns and had pledged not to support a candidate with ties to Tammany. However, Dubinsky did not share the ALP's and ER's dislike of Dewey, because Dewey refused to restore home work, the reinstatement of which had been the ILGWU's "most troublesome issue." Thus, removing Communists from the union movement remained more important to Dubinsky than defeating Dewey (Bone, 272–82).

15. Frank Kelly (1880–1946), who began chairing the Kings County Democratic Organization (Brooklyn) in 1928, helped secure large pluralities for FDR's presidential elections, plan national party conventions, and secure Truman's nomination as vice president. Although unable to defeat La Guardia, Kelly navigated several Democratic victories in county, borough, and judicial races. Known throughout the party for keeping his promises, Kelly remained a highly influential leader in party circles for two decades ("Frank Kelly Dies," *NYT*, 6 July 1946, 10).

16. See *n*2 above.

17. See *n*3 Document 10 and *n*16–17 Document 17.

18. Michael Quill (1905–1966), an Irish-immigrant transit worker who joined forces with the CPUSA to organize the 30,000-member Transport Workers Union, quickly developed a reputation as an effective, charismatic organizer. Elected TWU president in 1935, he promptly became one of New York's most powerful labor leaders and one of Dubinsky's most powerful rivals. Elected to the New York City Council with the support of the American Labor Party in 1937, he lost his seat in 1939 after quipping that he "would rather be called a Red by the rats than a rat by the Reds," only to regain it in 1943. He served on the council until 1949. *New York Times* reporter James Hagerty believed that Dubinsky's "real objection" to O'Dwyer's election was his friendship with the "communistic" Quill (*ANBO*; James Hagerty, "Way Now Seems Open for Democratic Mayor," *NYT*, 13 May 1945, E10).

19. Vito Marcantonio (1902–1954) learned to cross party lines as a young man by organizing the La Guardia Political Club and running La Guardia's Washington congressional office until voters caught in the Roosevelt sweep sent La Guardia back to New York City. When La Guardia regrouped to win the 1934 mayoral contest, Marcantonio organized his own successful Republican-City Fusion Party congressional campaign in 1934. As a congressman, he supported the New Deal, although he worked hard to push it to the left. Defeated in the anti-Republican sweep of 1936, Marcantonio revitalized his career by allying with the AFL, whose backing helped secure his reelection in 1938. In Congress, he argued the money the administration allocated for defense should be spent on the unemployed, demanded American support for the Republicans in the Spanish Civil War, and defended the Nazi-Soviet Pact until Germany invaded Russia. When World War II began, he supported FDR's defense initiatives and called for strong civil rights legislation at home. Although a leader of the American Labor Party who often sided with the Communists, his strong ties with his constituents, labor, and Tammany Hall helped secure him the nominations of the Republican and Democratic Parties, as well as the American Labor Party, in 1942 and 1944 (*ANB*).

20. If Kelly and Flynn backed another candidate for mayor, O'Dwyer's supporters, under the leadership of Queens party leader James Roe, planned to pursue the struggle in the Democratic primary. This inter-party wrangle drew intense press coverage, even though O'Dwyer had not yet announced his candidacy and had declared his intent to work with State Party Chair Paul Fitzpatrick to reach "an agreement satisfactory to all groups" ("O'Dwyer Backers Prepare for Fight," *NYT*, 28 May 1945, 21).

21. See *n*17 Document 17.

22. Joseph D. McGoldrick (1901–1978), a Columbia professor turned reform politician, served as New York City comptroller in 1934 and again from 1938 to 1945. In early May, McGoldrick broke with La Guardia by siding with the five borough presidents to defer acquisition of lands for Idlewild Airport. His vote spurred speculation, which he encouraged, that he would challenge La Guardia, only to have the mayor's withdrawal from the race undercut his prospects. By June 8, he threw his support to Goldstein ("Liberals Discuss 3 for Mayoralty: McGoldrick, Pecora and Goldstein," *NYT*, 10 May 1945, 38; Joseph P. Treaster, "Joseph McGoldrick, LaGuardia Aide," *NYT*, 6 April 1978, B10; James Hagerty, "Goldstein to Head Tri-Party Ticket in Mayoralty Race," *NYT*, 8 June 1945, 1).

23. In fact, the *New York Times*' headline on May 10 read, "Liberals Discuss 3 for Mayoralty: McGoldrick, Pecora and Goldstein." The Liberal Party did not offer the nomination to Goldstein until June 7 after the Liberal, Republican, and City Fusion parties all agreed to run Goldstein as their candidate ("Liberals Discuss 3 for Mayoralty: McGoldrick, Pecora and Goldstein," *NYT*, 10 May 1945, 38; James A. Hagerty, "Goldstein to Head Tri-Party Ticket in Mayoralty Race," *NYT*, 8 June 1945, 1).

24. Elihu Root and other New York City leaders founded the Citizens' Union in 1897 to run candidates against Tammany Hall in the municipal election of that year. After 1908 it operated as a nonpartisan civic association, seeking to nurture clean elections and good government (*ENYC*).

25. More of a coalition than a party, the Fusion or City Fusion Party drew support from good government Republicans, anti-Tammany Democrats, labor, new immigrants, and others seeking to elect a New York City government that would put an end to the corrupt practices of Tammany Hall. In 1933, the Fusionists selected La Guardia to run for mayor along with a slate of other reform candidates. During his administration, however, La Guardia's lack of support for Fusionist candidates coupled with his refusal to grant them any patronage antagonized Fusionist leaders and, by 1937, crippled the nascent party. Nevertheless the Fusionists continued to function as an anti-Tammany coalition into the postwar years (Kessner, 239–45, 396–97, 570–73).

26. See *n*11 Document 16.

27. Clarence Neal (1889–1957), as chair of Tammany Hall's Committee on Organization and Elections, exerted strong influence on decisions made by Tammany leader Edward Loughlin. He also served as Tammany's intermediary with racketeer Frank Costello. Tammany and Marcantonio's American Labor Party both backed O'Dwyer ("C.H. Neal Jr., 68, Aided Tammany," *NYT*, 17 January 1957, 29).

28. Frank Costello (1891–1973), an underworld boss with close ties to Tammany, used the wealth and power he gained from racketeering to buy political influence (*ANB*).

29. The Cooperative Commonwealth Federation of Canada, a Socialist political party formed in 1932, sought to eradicate capitalism, implement socialized planning, and transform Canada into a "cooperative commonwealth" through the democratic process. In 1944, the Saskatchewan CCF formed North America's "first socialist government" and instituted the universal healthcare system that would serve as the model for Canadian national policy (*NEB*).

30. The Liberal Party supported Democratic congressional and presidential candidates in those elections.

31. Dubinsky supported ER's decision not to lead NCPAC. Dubinsky, who once described NCPAC founder Hillman as a "front man for the Communists," feared that any organization associated with Hillman would be susceptible to Communist infiltration (Fraser, 522). See Document 24 and Document 25.

32. See *n*17 Document 17.

33. See *n*17 Document 17 and *n*23 above.

34. See *n*27 and *n*28 above.

35. See *n*28 above.

36. David Dubinsky to ER, 20 September 1945, AERP.

37. Dubinsky enclosed FDR's radio address in which he proclaimed:

> Mayor LaGuardia and his administration have given the city the most honest, and I believe, the most efficient municipal government of any within my recollection. The fact that the city's election has no relationship to national politics but is confined to civic policies, is attested by the fact that the constitution of the State provides for the municipal election in off years when neither a Governor, nor a President, nor a member of the House or Senate of the United States are to be chosen (Typed transcript "President Roosevelt's Address," *NYT*, 25 October 1941, attached to David Dubinsky to ER, 20 September 1945).

38. La Guardia's multiparty coalition and strong relationship with FDR helped the mayor seek election without relying on Dewey's Republican coattails. Furthermore, "a cool contempt" permeated the La Guardia-Dewey relationship (Heckscher, 243).

39. See *n*17 Document 17.

40. As Brooklyn district attorney in the early 1940s, O'Dwyer successfully prosecuted a number of professional killers associated with Murder, Inc. His campaign against organized crime resulted in seven convictions and executions. His failure to convict syndicate leaders Frank Costello and Albert Anastasia, however, and missing evidence and the death of a key witness while in police custody raised questions about O'Dwyer's seriousness when it came to indicting the bosses. He continued to make a name for himself as a crime fighter by using his wartime service in the US Army Air Corps to uncover and prosecute those engaged in fraudulent activities. Yet when he returned home and ran for mayor, he accepted fund-raising support from Costello (*ANB*; Kessner, 571).

ON THE ATOMIC BOMB

The day after the United States dropped the atomic bomb on Hiroshima, ER told readers of My Day:

> The only safe counter weapon to this new power is the firm decision of mankind that it shall be used for constructive purposes only. This discovery must spell the end of war ... In the past we have given lip service to the desire for peace. Now we meet the test of really working to achieve something basically new in the world. Religious groups have been telling us for a long time that peace could be achieved only by a basic change in the nature of man. I am inclined to think that this is true. But if we give human beings sufficient incentive, they may find good reasons for reshaping their characteristics ... This new discovery cannot be ignored. We have only two alternative choices: destruction and death—or construction and life! If we desire our civilization to survive, then we must accept the responsibility of constructive work and of the wise use of a knowledge greater than any ever achieved by man before.[1]

After Truman ordered a second bomb dropped on Nagasaki August 9, she devoted her next My Day to urging Japan's surrender and arguing against using the atomic bomb as a weapon in US-Soviet diplomacy.

35

My Day
11 August 1945

NEW YORK, Friday—I could not help feeling a little sad, yesterday, when the news came that we had had to use our second atomic bomb. I had hoped that after the first bomb, which was followed by Russia's declaration of war and their prompt entry into Manchuria, the Japanese would decide to accept unconditional surrender and the loss of life could come to an end. I still hope that may happen; and it is also the hope of a great many other people, for all news agencies seem to be aware that a momentous decision must be made by Japan within the next few days. The Japanese will either capitulate or face complete destruction.[2]

In the rapid succession of world events, I am interested to see how short are people's memories! Once upon a time the Americans and the British were being urged at every turn to start a second front in Europe. At that time, the Soviet Union was carrying a very heavy burden in the war against Germany. She thought us over-cautious in our preparations and a long time coming to her aid. People in this country were quite indignant at this. They wondered if Russia did not understand that an ocean lay between us and Europe, and that problems of supply and transportation were overwhelming.

Now the boot is on the other foot. If it had not been for the atomic bomb, we would have heard a continual wail because the Soviet Union was so slow in coming to our aid. She is reciprocating by wondering whether we have no understanding of the fact that an army had to be transported practically across a continent! I can hear some people say: "Oh, but the Russian army needs no supplies. They can live off the country." Perhaps—but guns and ammunition and all the other mechanized equipment must get from Germany to the borders of Manchuria, and it is probably a tremendous feat that the Soviet Union has been able to join us so soon.

Somehow we must try to get over some of the attitudes we have held, not only as regards the Soviet Union but as regards other people. For instance, I heard someone say the other day: "Well, perhaps we will be fighting the Soviet Union." In the light of the late developments, that now means annihilation. There is only one answer to these fears, and that is a belief that the Soviet Union and the United States, as well as the United Nations as a whole, can live peacefully together—and a determination on the part of their people to do so.

Some irresponsible people even say that the Soviet Union purposely waited until the last minute, when the war was almost won, so they could be included in the benefits when peace came, but would not have to carry a heavy burden in the Pacific war. I can only remark that those who say this have no understanding of the Russian character and no knowledge of the facts. As far as military commitments are concerned, I have never heard it said that the Soviet Union had shirked any of them or had ever broken her word.

TMs AERP, FDRL

———————

1. *MD*, 8 August 1945.

2. In a statement broadcast on V-J Day (August 14), ER urged her listening audience to recognize the "tremendous challenge" atomic energy presented.

> … Peace has not come, however, as the result of the kind of power which we have known in the past, but as the result of a new discovery which as yet is not fully understood, nor even developed. There is a certain awe and fear coupled with our rejoicing today, because we know that there are new forces in the world, partly understood but not as yet completely developed and controlled. This new force is a tremendous challenge to the wisdom of men, and for that reason I know that most of us feel that it must be subject to their collective wisdom. Just as it was discovered by the pooling of knowledge from men of many races and religions, so it must be ruled in its development.
>
> We should not think only of its destructive power for this new discovery may hold within it the germs of the greatest good that man has ever known. But that good can only be achieved through man's wisdom in developing and controlling it.
>
> Today we have a mixture of emotions, joy that our men are freed of constant danger, hope that those whom we love will soon be home among us, awe at what man's intelligence can compass, and a realization that that intelligence uncontrolled by great spiritual forces, can be man's destruction instead of his salvation … ("V-J Day, Columbia Broadcasting Company," AERP).

See *n*5 Document 47 and *MD*, 10 and 21 August, 1945.

ON THE JAPANESE SURRENDER

At 7:00 PM, August 14, Truman read a statement to reporters crowded into his office announcing he had received "this afternoon a message from the Japanese government" that he considered "full acceptance of the Potsdam Declaration which specifies the unconditional surrender of Japan." Later that evening, ER delivered remarks over CBS radio[1] and received a call from Truman.

Yet, as she wrote Lorena Hickok and the president the following evening, grave concerns about the future tempered her joy. "Isn't it wonderful to be in a world where peace has come?" she asked. "I find that many are worried however. President Truman called me last night and spoke almost at once of the dreadful problem abroad—I hope he speaks with confidence however, for the people need it in spite of their rejoicing."[2]

36

Eleanor Roosevelt to Harry Truman
15 August 1945 [New York City]

Dear Mr President:

I greatly appreciated your calling me last night. It is a weight off one's heart to have the war over. For you, however, I appreciate only too well what the new problems are. I feel that our safety lies in attacking with as much breadth of vision and imagination these problems as we did the war problems. The government must keep control till we are on an even keel from the economic standpoint.[3] You will have pressures from every side but I am sure your own wisdom and experience and faith in God will guide you aright.

My best wishes to Mrs. Truman. These are great days in which we live. God bless you both.

Sincerely yours,
Eleanor Roosevelt

ALS AERP, FDRL

---

1. See *n*2 Document 35.

2. ER to Lorena Hickok, 15 August 1945, LPHP, FDRL.

3. Fearing inflation and massive unemployment, ER favored maintaining wartime restrictions during the transition to a peacetime economy and, then, only easing them gradually. The next two days she used My Day to address her concerns.

> There seems to be an increasing interest in the removal of all war restrictions, as indicated by articles that I have read lately in the press. I feel, however, that we should give some of these restrictions very careful consideration. Of necessity, for quite some time to come, there is going to be very little to buy. If we remove such restrictions as, for instance, price ceilings and rationing, the people who have money will pay high prices for what they want. Those who have little money will first spend all their savings and then be unable to buy their fair share of the necessities of life.

It seems to me much fairer to continue our war restrictions on the things that are really necessary, like food and clothing and household utensils, so that we may all share alike in the supply that does exist. In the matter of machinery, it seems to me again advisable to have restrictions that will direct: 1– The making of machinery, first, for the manufacture of those things which are most essential to getting people back to work; 2– The conversion at once of factories needed for the greater production of farm machinery. That machinery should be obtained as soon as possible, in our own interests and in the interests of the rest of the world. As things become more plentiful, finally, the OPA [Office of Price Administration] could reduce ration points until eventually they are eliminated (*MD*, 17 August 1945. See also *MD*, 16 August 1945).

Eleanor Roosevelt and
Trusteeship Politics

When ER met with trusted advisors, she could be quite blunt in her assessment of politics and personalities, especially when the discussion focused on issues she thought of vital importance. Charles Taussig, an original member of FDR's "Brains Trust," had also worked closely with ER for a decade, beginning with their efforts to convince FDR to create an educational program for unemployed youth. ER then secured Taussig's appointment as chair of the National Youth Administration National Advisory Board.[1]

The memorandum below is a continuation of a conversation that began when Taussig visited ER in the White House the afternoon of April 12, 1945, which occurred, unbeknownst to both parties, as FDR lay dying in Warm Springs. Taussig, whom FDR had appointed to lead the Anglo-American Caribbean Commission, went to ER to get her help in securing a "definite directive for action" from FDR on how the president wished to handle trusteeship issues at the San Francisco conference.

The Departments of State, War, and Navy had proposed conflicting guidelines as to how areas designated as trusteeships should be governed. Early that year the Yalta accords established a "trusteeship formula" that included not only those areas then considered mandates under the League of Nations but also territory stripped from defeated enemy nations and "any other territory that may voluntarily be placed under trusteeship."[2] The Navy and War Departments insisted that the Japanese islands and "certain strategic areas in the Pacific" remain in "the complete control" of the US government and that "the matter of international trusteeship not be discussed at the San Francisco conference, or at least not discussed until there is a firm agreement as to the United States jurisdiction over the Japanese mandated islands."[3] The State Department countered that if "these areas, with adequate safeguards" were not included "within the trusteeship system, we shall prejudice all possibility of international trusteeship and that it would appear to large sections of the public to violate our expressed statements against annexation of territory as a result of war."[4]

Taussig, who had worked more closely with FDR on this issue than any other advisor, wanted the president to support the State Department's proposal that one, "the mandated territories and territories which may be separated from the enemy ... be placed under the trusteeship system, with only such safeguards as may be demonstrably necessary for security purposes," and two, that the government undertake "a vigorous effort to obtain acceptance of that policy at the San Francisco Conference."[5] FDR had cabled Taussig from Warm Springs, "Your message on International Trusteeship is approved in principle" and added that he would meet with representatives of the three departments within the next two weeks.[6]

Taussig then requested a meeting with ER "to consult her about the current controversy ... regarding the trusteeship problem to come up in San Francisco." As they began their conversation in the Red Room, ER told him that she "was more or less conversant with the controversy" and that she had read Marquis Child's column on trusteeships that morning.[7] Taussig, as he recorded in an internal memorandum later that evening,[8] asked ER:

> to read, which she did, the draft of the Yalta Agreement on trusteeships,[9] the Secretary of State's telegram to the President which had been sent to Warm Springs (dated April 9, 1945). I outlined the President's reply which came over the teletype[10]... I also let her read the memorandum of my conversation with the President of March 15 which she read slowly and carefully.[11] I told Mrs. Roosevelt that the position taken in the Department on the President's reply

was one of vacillation and hesitancy as to the meaning of the President's reply. I said I thought that it was a definite directive for action.[12] She said, "Of course. Franklin has given the green light to go on with the Five-Power Conference and to keep trusteeship on the agenda for San Francisco." I said that that was my interpretation. I told her that Stettinius seemed unwilling to make a decision; that Pasvolsky, who favored keeping trusteeship on the agenda, was obtuse in his presentation of the case[13] and that Jimmy Dunn definitely opposed it.[14]

I told Mrs. Roosevelt that I was worried about the situation; that all of the work the President had done with Churchill over the last few years on this subject and the plans that the President had made might well be nullified if we did not handle this situation properly now. I said even at this stage, we had materially weakened our diplomatic position. I referred to the various editorials that had been appearing in the press during the last few weeks on this subject and also Admiral King's speech with which she was cognizant.

She said, of course that Jimmy Dunn would oppose it; "he is a Fascist". She said the trouble in this country is that we are always looking for Communists but completely ignore the Fascists.

I said that in view of the circumstances and the great importance of the subject at San Francisco and the necessity of living up to the Yalta Agreement, that the Secretary of State ought immediately to get a clarifying telegram from the President. She said she would telephone the President; that there might be a slight delay in her getting him but she would try to get an answer at least by the following day and telephone me. I suggested to her that the President's telegram might read along these lines, "Proceed with the Five-Power Conference immediately using State Department as basis, reserving right to make minor technical changes at San Francisco". Mrs. Roosevelt said that she would take care of the matter and advise me.

We walked out of the Red Room and she walked rapidly to the elevator when I called her back. I asked her if I could arrange through her to make any emergency contacts with the President when we were in San Francisco. She said that she and the President were going out by train and then returning by train, … but that I could contact her in Washington and she would arrange immediately to get any messages I might have for the President to him.[15]

Although FDR's sudden death undercut Taussig's stature in the interdepartmental debate, he remained optimistic about the adoption of the president's trusteeship plan.

April 20, as he traveled to the United Nations conference, Taussig wrote ER that "it appears that now we will have a united delegation at San Francisco to press for the fulfillment of the President's ideals" and that he would continue to "fight for the objectives to which the President dedicated himself." He concluded his condolences by offering his support: "I know that you will continue to give your leadership to forward-looking social and political action, and I hope that you will call on me to be of whatever assistance I can."[16]

By the time the train carrying Taussig and the other delegates reached San Francisco, Stettinius, bowing to pressure from Truman and the military, secured adoption of an eleven-point memorandum more aligned with Stimson than FDR. Trusteeships would occur only "by the subsequent agreement" of the nations currently governing them and the strategic territories requested by the War Department were to remain under US rather than UN control. An angry Taussig argued that this was not what FDR wanted and recited their last conversation on this point. FDR, he said, believed that "to deny the objective of independence … would sow the seeds of the next world war" and that America must "take the leadership and indicate … that we do not back the imperial role of the handful of non-Asiatics."[17]

ER had followed the debates over Allied interdependence, colonial independence, and United Nations trusteeship policies with the same interest she paid to the Poland-Argentina question. Just as she turned to Stettinius for inside information regarding the compromise reached to seat the Polish and Argentine delegations, she turned to Taussig to brief her on the American delegation's internal deliberations over trusteeship at San Francisco. As the memorandum below indicates, she realized how little FDR's image swayed Truman's team and what concerted effort the public would need to exert to call attention back to the Rooseveltian vision for a new postwar order.

After her appointment to the United Nations, ER also reached out to political and civic leaders as she prepared her own internal briefing book on the subject.[18]

37

Charles Taussig Conversation with Eleanor Roosevelt

27 August 1945 [New York City]

Mrs. Roosevelt was interested to hear the inside story of the Trusteeship fight at San Francisco; I told her the story.[19] She was surprised at Bowman's performance[20] also Dean Gildersleeve—her vote against independence—said that she would see to it that the Dean was not appointed to other Commissions.[21] She had her usual say re Jimmy Dunn;[22] She was surprisingly bitter re Byrnes; said he was a double crosser and could not be trusted.[23]

I said the public needed education on trusteeship. She said if I would prepare a memo for her she would use it in her column which she said had a larger circulation now [than] when she was in the White House. She said she would write it whenever I thought the time was right.[24]

I told her how little influence the memory of FDR had with the US Delegation but had much influence with the delegations of the smaller countries.[25] She said that did not surprise her; She said that she would probably take on two radio programs in addition to her column; She did not seem pleased with Potsdam but did not go into particulars.[26] Said that FDR had had considerable success with Stalin at Yalta and had said that Stalin would play ball if approached right.[27]

CWT

TMem AERP, FDRL

---

1. Charles W. Taussig (1896–1952), special advisor to the secretary of state on Caribbean affairs and chair of the Anglo-American Caribbean Commission, had a longstanding relationship with both FDR and ER. In addition to joining the "Brains Trust" in 1933, the young president of the American Molasses Corporation also advised American delegates to the World Economic Conference. He shared many of ER's commitments to social reform, including a restructured national health system and humanitarian outreach. Under his leadership, the Anglo-American Caribbean Commission developed what the *NYT* called "the first instance, pre-Marshall Plan, of successful international cooperation in economic and social aid." He, more than any of FDR's advisors, knew the president's plans for trusteeships and the San Francisco conference and, with his knack for practical implementation of controversial projects, became FDR's point man in the

trusteeship planning meetings (A. Black, *Casting*, 31–32; "C. W. Taussig Dead," *NYT*, 11 May 1948; Louis, 484, 538).

2. Top Secret, Supplement to Message for the President from the Secretary of State, International Trusteeships, CWTP, Caribbean Commission: 1945, FDRL.

3. Harold Ickes, Memorandum for the President, 5 April 1945, CWTP, Caribbean Commission: July to December inclusive, FDRL.

4. Message for the President from the Secretary of State, International Trusteeships, CWTP, Caribbean Commission: 1945, FDRL.

5. Ickes, Memorandum for the President, 5 April 1945.

6. Quoted in Louis, 492.

7. Childs's column discussed the debate within the administration and amongst its allies over "the military and industrial disarmament of Germany" (Marquis Childs, "Washington Calling," *WP*, 12 April 1945, 6).

8. Charles Taussig, Conversation at the White House with Mrs. Roosevelt, 3 pm to 3:30 pm in the Red Room, 12 April 1945, Caribbean Commission: 1945, CWTP, FDRL.

9. See *n*2.

10. See *n*6.

11. Taussig met with FDR March 15 and discussed in depth the military's desire for control over strategic territories. Roosevelt told Taussig that he disagreed with the navy's interpretation of "strategic trust territories," that he preferred two categories of open and closed territories, and that the open territories "should be subject to international agreements." Security concerns need not dominate the debates, the president continued, because "if the military wanted at a later date due to change in strategy to make all or part of the open area a closed area, it should be provided that this could be done with the approval of the Security Council." When FDR asked if the navy was "trying to grab everything," Taussig replied that he thought "the military had no confidence in the United Nations" and asked the president if he had heard Admiral Russell Willson call the trustee-ship team "the international welfare boys." FDR then stated his position clearly: "Neither the Army nor the Navy had any business administering the civilian government territories; that they had no competence to do this." As the conversation turned to the future of Asia, they discussed the position France would have in Indo-China and New Caledonia. Taussig reported that FDR, after hesitation, decided that "if we can get the proper pledge from France to assume for herself the obligations of a trustee," then he "would agree to France retaining these colonies with the proviso that independence was the ultimate goal." When Taussig asked Roosevelt if "he would settle for self government," the president "said no. I asked him if he would settle for dominion status. He said no—it must be independence. He said that this is to be the policy and you can quote me in the State Department" (Memorandum of Conversation with the President, 15 March 1945, CWTP, FDRL. See also Louis, 484–86).

12. Stettinius respected Stimson, who worked to undermine Stettinius's support for FDR's views. Stimson told the secretary of state that America fought the war "to throw out an aggressor and restore peace and freedom ... and the bases (in the Pacific) had been stolen by the aggressor who had used them to attack us and destroy our power;" thus, the bases should remain under American control to prevent future attacks. Stettinius then sided with Stimson, only to back away a few days later when he learned of a State Department memorandum sent to FDR supporting the president's position. The secretary tried to remain neutral, going so far as to tell Stimson April 6 that he did not want to be a part of a military proposal. When he learned that Stimson was submitting the proposal anyway and that he would be caught between defending his department and alienating Stimson, Stettinius called Forrestal to ask him to explain to Stimson "that he had disassociated him-

self" from the State Department memorandum by claiming that he "was out of town when it was written" (Louis, 490–93).

13. Leo Pasvolsky (1894–1953), an economist who served as special assistant to the secretary of state, led the drafting of the Declaration of National Independence, served as the department's point person on trusteeship and coordinated planning on the issue for the United Nations. He also served as the American liaison to the British on trusteeship issues and chaired the interdepartmental Committee on Dependent Areas, on which Taussig served. He would serve as an advisor to the American delegation to San Francisco, where he helped negotiate the compromise over veto power accepted by the Big Five nations (Louis, 360–61, 444–47; "Dr. Leo Pasvolsky of U.N. Fame Dead," *NYT*, 7 May 1953, 31).

14. When Stettinius replaced Cordell Hull as secretary of state, he appointed James (Jimmy) Clement Dunn (1890–1979), "a wealthy croquet-playing" foreign service officer, as assistant secretary for European affairs. When ER learned of the appointment, she phoned and then wrote FDR to express deep concern over such a stalwart conservative in such an influential position.

> I am quite sure that Jimmy Dunne is clever enough to tell you that he will do what you want and to allow his subordinates to accomplish things which will get by and which will pretty well come up in the long time results to what he actually wants to do. The reason that I feel we cannot trust Dunne is that we know he backed Franco and his regime in Spain. We know that now he is arguing [with] Mr. Winant and the War Department in favor of using German industrialists to rehabilitate Germany because he belongs to the group which Will Clayton [who had once belonged to the Liberty League] represents, plus others, who believe we must have business going in Germany for the sake of business here. I suppose I should trust blindly when I can't know and be neither worried or scared and yet I am both and when Harry Hopkins tells me he is for Clayton, etc. I'm even more worried. I hate to irritate you and I won't speak of this again but I wouldn't feel honest if I didn't tell you now.

ER also knew of Dunn's close working relationship with Breckenridge Long on limiting visas to European Jews (Goodwin, 173, 525; ER to FDR, 4 December 1944, Roosevelt Family Papers, FDRL; Louis, 41).

15. The day after FDR's funeral, Stettinius called Taussig to say that he was "heart-sick" when he heard about the meetings and asked Taussig for "his word" that he "would not do anything without consulting him in San Francisco" (Taussig, untitled memorandum, 16 April 1945, CWTP, FDRL).

16. Charles Taussig to ER, 20 April 1945, CWTP, FDRL.

17. Schlesinger, 234–35; Campbell and Herring, 319–22; Louis, 538.

18. See Document 71, Document 72, and Document 79.

19. What consensus there was in the American delegation over trusteeship unraveled May 12, 1945, when the Russian and Chinese delegations proposed that "independence" be included as a stated goal in the UN Charter. The colonial powers, especially France and Great Britain, immediately objected, arguing against interference in the internal affairs of member states and "Russia's newfound interest in colonial affairs." Harold Stassen then added a third dimension—interdependence—and cited the United States, "whose strength is not based on their complete independence as separate entities, but on their unity and interdependence" as the model. An outraged Taussig retorted: "(1) Independence as a goal for all peoples who aspire to and are capable of it has been the traditional and sacred policy of this Government. It has been exemplified in our policy in the Philippines, and it has been reiterated on numerous occasions by President Roosevelt ... and Cordell Hull, (2) An excellent opportunity is afforded to make a profitable gesture on behalf of the peoples of the Orient as well as those in Africa and the Caribbean, (3) The Russians and especial-

ly the Chinese will be able to capitalize on their stand for 'independence' against the opposition of the non-Asiatic peoples of the West unless we take a strong position." Taussig did not sway the delegation (Louis, 537).

20. Isaiah Bowman (1878–1950), the renowned geographer, university president, and advisor to Woodrow Wilson during the Paris Peace Conference of 1919, chaired the State Department's advisory committee on territorial concerns and advised FDR on issues related to Palestine. He served as a member of the American delegation to San Francisco and for most of the debates over trusteeship, remained an articulate spokesperson for colonial independence and international trusteeships. Taussig and ER considered him a strong supporter of FDR's trusteeship plans. However, after fellow delegate Harold Stassen's argument that the United States should not side with Russia and China in support of independence lest it give the two nations cover for their own ambitions while it found itself "committed to the breaking up of the British Empire," Bowman broke away from Taussig. Bowman now focused on Russia rather than the colonial areas. He responded to Taussig's position, arguing that "when perhaps the inevitable struggle came between Russia and ourselves the question would be who were our friends. Would we have as our friends those whom we had weakened in the struggle or those who had been strengthened?" He finally decided to reject FDR's vision of gradual independence because "he ultimately thought British friendship was worth more than the abstract ideal of independence" (Louis, 54, 537–39).

21. FDR had appointed Barnard College Dean Virginia C. Gildersleeve (1877–1965), founder and president of the International Federation of University Women, as the only woman member of the US delegation to the San Francisco conference. As a delegate she helped draft the preamble to the UN Charter and played a key role in the creation of UNESCO. However, she did not support FDR's trusteeship goals. Rather, she supported Stassen's claim that trusteeship policies designed to create independent states played into Russian desires for territory and told Taussig that while the delegation did not "intend to grab" territory, it did "intend to hold what is necessary for our security." When Truman did not appoint Gildersleeve to the London delegation, she accepted a request from General Douglas MacArthur to help rebuild the Japanese education system. Ironically, as angry as ER was with her over her trusteeship stance, she had to serve with Gildersleeve briefly in London when Truman appointed her as an alternate delegate to ECOSOC. ER, however, did work to prevent the dean's future appointments; and Gildersleeve resigned from ECOSOC after one year's service (Schlesinger, 237; Agnes Meyer, "Dean Gildersleeve Popular Choice," *WP*, 11 March 1945, B1; "Virginia Gildersleeve, Educator, Dead at 87," *WP*, 9 July 1965, C8).

22. See *n*14.

23. Two months earlier she wrote her son James, "I hate Jimmy Byrnes going in [the delegation] because with all his ability, I think he is primarily interested in Jimmy Byrnes ..." (ER to James Roosevelt, 27 June 1945, JRP, FDRL).

24. Taussig did not submit a memorandum to ER. After her appointment to the United Nations, ER supported the independence position. However, as she was not appointed to the Trusteeship Council, protocol demanded that she refer questions on this matter to those who sat on the council. See Document 71, Document 72, and Document 79.

25. See *n*11 and *n*14.

26. Truman, Stalin, and Churchill, until he was replaced by Attlee July 28, held the last of the Allied war conferences at a former Hohenzollern palace in Potsdam, Germany, not far from Berlin. From July 17 to August 2, 1945, representatives of the Big Three issued a declaration demanding "unconditional surrender" from Japan; agreed that Germany, under a central Allied Control Council, must be reorganized in ways to prevent the return of military dictatorships; supported the prosecution of war criminals; settled on the management of war reparations; and convinced the Soviet Union to enter the war against Japan in mid-August. Although the conference did not

address Stalin's request to redefine the German-Polish border, it did agree to his proposal to transfer German land east of the Oder and Neisse Rivers to Poland (*RCAH*).

ER later told Joe Lash and Sam Rosenman she "understood why Truman did not want to meet with Stalin, that he did not have the confidence that he could deal with him," and that she did not disagree with Rosenman when he said that Jimmy Byrnes "had been a very bad and evil influence and practically acted as president at Potsdam." She also told her cousin, journalist Joe Alsop, that she did "not believe that anyone had talked 'turkey' with Mr. Stalin" since Harry Hopkins (Lash, *World*, 404–5; ER to Joe Alsop, 26 April 1945, in Lash, *Years*, 86).

27. See *n*2 Document 14.

ELEANOR ROOSEVELT AND UNITED FEATURE
SYNDICATE'S RUSSIAN ASSIGNMENT

Before Truman, who was preparing to leave for Potsdam, could respond to her letter of July 2,[1] ER sent another letter July 5 to say that a journalist recently returned from Russia told her that April would be just as good a time to go and, because of other obligations, she would prefer to go then. Samuel Rosenman (1896–1973), FDR's speech writer and now counsel to Truman, telephoned ER July 9 to say that the president had delegated her travel requests to him, with instructions "to see that arrangements are made for you any time you wish to go." He then agreed to consult with Hopkins as to which would be the most effective time for her visit.[2]

Once ER decided that spring 1946 would be the best time for her visit, she then wrote the secretary of state to ask if she could include China in this trip as well.

38

Eleanor Roosevelt to James Byrnes
30 August 1945 [Hyde Park]

Dear Mr. Secretary:

The United Feature Syndicate for which I write a column, would like to have me go to Russia next Spring. I have also been asked by Madame Chaing to come to China in the early Spring.[3] I have not asked the syndicate whether they would like me to take the trip to China as well.

Before I make any positive arrangements I wanted to ask you about it. I did ask President Truman about going to Russia and he sent me word through Judge Rosenman[4] he would be glad to have me make any trip I wanted to make and that he wanted it facilitated in any way possible.

This, however, is not exactly the ordinary kind of a trip. I am going as a newspaper writer, but I realize that I can not shed the fact that I am my husband's widow. I would like to make the trip useful in as many ways as possible and to do that I must ask your advice. First, would you be willing to ascertain if the powers-that-be in Russia really would like me to come and will give me the usual writers' freedom and facilities for moving about and seeing things? My object, of course, would be to see what they plan to do for women and children in the social field and that would include education, hospitals, etc. I realize that they can not be actually accomplishing a great deal but what they plan should be of great interest to us.

Also, if I have to stop anywhere on the way, do you have any preference as to where I go and where I stop? Would you have to notify anyone of my passing through?

Please understand that I am not asking for any special privileges. I am only asking to be helpful and to do what you think would be helpful. I do not want to travel any differently from any other correspondent. If I have to attend any type of receptions I should hope you would arrange to have them kept at a minimum. On the other hand I do not want to hurt anyone's feelings.

Madame Chaing assured me that I would be given no surveillance and every facility to see and to travel if I would come to China but I do not even want to mention this to the syndicate until I get your advice, as that trip might have implications that you would like to consider.[5]

Very sincerely yours,
Eleanor Roosevelt

TLS CFDF, NARA II

Byrnes then delegated the request to Undersecretary of State Dean Acheson, who, at Hopkins and ER's suggestion, contacted Averell Harriman, the US ambassador to the Soviet Union, for his assessment. Acheson then reported back to ER.

_39_

Dean Acheson to Eleanor Roosevelt
14 September 1945 [Washington, DC]

<u>Personal</u>

Dear Mrs. Roosevelt:

As I expected I have received a very prompt and enthusiastic reply from Ambassador Harriman about your prospective visit to Russia.

He reports that when he spoke to Vyshinski, the Russian Vice Commissar for Foreign Affairs and explained in detail the purpose of your visit, the latter stated spontaneously that the Russian people and the Soviet Government would welcome you enthusiastically in whatever capacity you might chose to visit the Soviet Union. He added that "she comes to us, however, as Mrs. Eleanor Roosevelt, the wife of the revered President and a woman we admire and highly respect." Vyshinski emphasized that the Russian people would be honored by and much interested in your presence. He made it quite clear that the Soviet Government would be only too happy to have you visit Russia and would offer you every facility to see and do what you wished.[6]

Ambassador Harriman on his own behalf expressed the sincere hope that you would go to Russia and added that he felt your visit, not only because of your presence in Russia but also because of your writing about your trip, would be of very real importance.

He suggested that you reconcile yourself to the role of a most honored guest. However, he pointed out that it would not handicap you in obtaining material but would take part of your time, and offered his assistance in keeping the time consumed to the minimum.

Ambassador Harriman not only expressed the hope but also recommended that you stay at Spaso House and stressed the fact that he and his daughter, Kathleen, would both greatly enjoy having you with them. Aside from the personal pleasure it would give them, he pointed out that other visitors, including writers, had found that they had greater freedom as well as greater comfort at Spaso House than at the hotels. In the light of the above he said he recommended that you stay with them even if the Soviet Government should offer you its guest house.

In connection with the possibility of your visit to China I can see no reason at the present time why you should not accept Madame Chiang's invitation if you wish to do so.

Your questions about stops along the way will, I believe, be answered in part by the transportation facilities available when you make your journey. After we know when you are going and the route you expect to follow we shall, of course, let our diplomatic or consular officers know your plans and your wishes so that they may help you carry them out. You will, of course, need a passport and visas for the countries you intend to visit and it will require a little time to take care of all the details so it would be helpful if you could let us know two or three weeks before your departure what your itinerary will be.

When I telegraphed Ambassador Harriman about your desire to go to Russia I told him that no decision had been reached and cautioned him to treat the matter as confidential. Nevertheless, I understand that the Soviet Consul General in New York has been authorized by his Government to state to you, and probably publicly also, that you have a standing invitation from the Society of

Cultural Relations with Foreign Countries to visit Russia and that he is prepared to issue a visa to you at any time. I hope that he will not make any statement that might disclose your plans before you wished to make them public but in any event I thought you would wish to know that such a possibility existed.

    With kindest personal regards,

Sincerely yours,

Dean Acheson

Tlcst, CFDF, NARA II

---

1. For ER to Harry Truman, 2 July 1945, see Document 21.

2. Sam Rosenman to ER, 9 July 1945, AERP.

3. Soong Mei-ling Chiang Kai-shek (1898–2003), the wife of Nationalist Chinese President Chiang Kai-shek, who made the first of several visits to the United States in 1943 to secure American support for Nationalist China in its war against Japan, had returned to China the night before, August 29, after receiving an urgent message from her husband. A skillful, powerful political force in her own right, Madame Chiang received national acclaim after her stirring address to Congress in support of the Nationalist cause generated billions of dollars in aid, and she often visited the Roosevelts in the White House. While there is no written record of the request ER mentions above, as Madame Chiang had made New York City her American home, one can assume that she had either seen ER recently or phoned her before her departure ("Mrs. Chiang Kai-Shek at the White House," *NYT*, 30 August 1945, 4; Seth Faison, "Madame Chiang, 105, Chinese Leader's Widow, Dies," *NYT*, 24 October 2003, C10).

4. See *n*3 Document 21.

5. ER would not go to Russia until 1957 and would never visit China (James Byrnes to ER, 14 September 1945, AERP; Roosevelt, *Autobiography*, 369; Lash, *Years*, 267).

6. Andrei Vyshinsky then served as deputy minister of foreign affairs for the USSR.

ON FULL EMPLOYMENT

_____40_____

My Day
30 August 1945

HYDE PARK, Wednesday—The committee in Washington has been holding hearings on what is known as the Full Employment Bill,[1] and in reading the papers I gather that there was a great volume of support for the passage of this bill. However, I have also read a considerable number of articles where the authors seem to feel that while full employment is a desirable objective, this bill will do no good. In fact, they say, it is pernicious, because all that we need is to remove all restrictions on private industry and private industry will do the job.[2]

These people, it seems to me, are unrealistic and have short memories. There were no restrictions on private industry during the depression; and we cannot afford another depression. It therefore seems to me that we should back and fight for a bill which faces the realities of the situation.

Private industry should do all that it possibly can, and it should be given every opportunity to do it. One little practice which existed in the past, however, should not be revived. An oversupply of labor, ready to accept low wages in preference to starvation, should never again be allowed to exist to increase the profits of employers and investors. To prevent this, the government has to see that the conditions under which men work and the returns which they receive for their work are adequate, and that all men who want to work have an opportunity to work, so that they are not held in a forced pool of unemployment for the benefit of employers.

This may mean that investors and the management side of business can claim only a reasonable return on their investments and on their part of the work of industry. That is one of the things which we have to accept if the world is to be a better world for the average man and woman in the future.

If, with these restrictions, industry can do the whole job, then let us be grateful and let them do it. If at any time they can not do it, however, then the government must have in reserve new things to develop for the good of the whole country—things that will provide more opportunities in the future for industry to use more labor.

Some people seem to feel that of necessity this must constantly increase our national debt.[3] But that is not a necessity. Many government investments have paid out in the past, and will pay out many times over in the future. The thing for us to remember is that the men who fought this war on the various fronts throughout the world, and in the shops at home, have fought it to obtain a better way of life. They want more security, less fear, greater happiness. This is not communism. This is what democracy must make possible. Otherwise, it will not survive this period of world change.

TMs AERP, FDRL

_____

1. The Senate Banking and Commerce Committee began its hearing on the Keynesian-based Full Employment Bill, introduced by Senator Robert Wagner (D-NY) and seven of his colleagues and supported by 116 members of the House. The legislation required the federal government to commit to "enough compensatory spending to wipe out unemployment." A national coalition of liberal organizations led by the National Farmers Union and the Union for Democratic Action organized to support its passage and Truman called it one of his "must" pieces of legislation. Yet by late

August, controversy surrounded the bill and Truman's leadership as liberals worried that the administration had not devised a strategy to secure its passage. The bill stalled in Congress, where the House stripped its right to employment provisions. The bill emerged in final form as the Employment Act of 1946 which, rather than assuring full employment, mandated that the government work to ensure "maximum employment" and established the Joint Economic Committee in Congress and the president's Council of Economic Advisors (Hamby, *Beyond*, 61–69).

2. For examples of articles appearing in newspapers ER regularly read see "Full Employment Endorsed by Ruml," *NYT*, 6 June 1945, 26; C. P. Trussell, "House Move Seeks to Prolong Recess," *NYT*, 22 August 1945, 24; "Full Employment World Peace Need, Byrnes Declares," *NYT*, 22 August 1945, 1; Frederick Barkley, "'Right to Work' Is Debated," *NYT*, 26 August 1945, E10; Clarence D. Long, "America's Full Employment: Its Effect on Price Stability," *WP*, 26 August 1945, B4.

3. At the end of 1945, the national debt was $252.7 billion (*HSUS*, 664).

41

If You Ask Me [excerpt]

Ladies' Home Journal September 1945

Will you kindly tell us in what sense we are born equal?

I suppose what is meant when people say we are born free and equal, is that we have equal opportunity to make of ourselves whatever our abilities will allow us to become. It is true that heredity and environment play a part in everybody's development. When you see people, however, with the same heredity and the same surroundings, who differ, you realize that there is something inherent in an individual which makes him take advantage of his opportunities and do better, perhaps, than someone else. It is that equality of opportunity for an individual to strive for himself which is meant when people talk about being born equal.

Why should we acknowledge a party named Communist? I thought ours was supposed to be a two-party government.

As far as I know, under the law we are not obligated to have any particular number of political parties. There are rules governing how a party can get its name on the ballot. You have to have a certain number of voters and signers of a petition, and if you comply with the law, any party can get on the ballot. It happens that we have had two major parties in this country so that we ordinarily function as though there were only two which were important in an election, but frequently the minor groups get together and make a difference in the outcome of an election.

TMsex, DLC

ER had long championed a comprehensive national health insurance program, even lob-bying FDR to include it in his original social security proposals.[1] When Senators Robert Wagner (D-NY) and James Murray (D-MT) and Representative John D. Dingell (D-MI) introduced legislation calling for national health insurance as part of the federal provi-sions for social security in 1943, she lent her public, enthusiastic support even though Congress defeated the bill then and again in 1944. When the trio reintroduced a revised version May 12, 1945, she told readers of My Day, "the health bill seems to me to give us more hope than we have ever had for health in our communities throughout the nation."[2] When Truman later announced that he would send a similar proposal to Congress, she wrote him to express her support for his efforts on this issue.[3] She sent the following endorsement to the Writer's War Board, a group of noted authors, poets, and playwrights committed to encouraging citizen engagement in home front issues, for pub-lication in September 1945.

_42_

Public Health
September 1945

In the last Presidential campaign, both the Republican and the Democratic Parties acknowl-edged the fact that something must be done to make available to the whole population of our nation, adequate medical care from pre-natal days to old age.[4]

The Democratic Administration, of course, has accepted the responsibility for putting its promises in the form of a Bill which will start the ball rolling toward better public health. This Bill is known as the Wagner-Murray-Dingle Bill.[5] But now we are beginning to see the same old game develop as we saw it at the end of the last war. We learned the same lessons then, namely, that our people are not the healthiest people in the world and need not only better medical care, but better food and more knowledge on the subject of health. But we quarreled as to how we would achieve our objectives and did nothing. We are headed that way again.

The way to begin is to begin. This Bill may not be perfect, but it is a step in the awakening of interest in the question of health for everyone, not for those alone who can afford to pay for it.

Let us tell our representatives in Congress that this is one of the things we want to do and keep on doing, so that twenty-five years from now our young people will be far healthier than they were found to be during this last draft.

Without health no nation can successfully defend itself against the aggression of other nations, either in the military or the economic fields. If we want to retain our leadership in the world we must see that our people are healthy and vigorous. The spirit of adventure and the power to show initiative will die out if we do not preserve the health of the nation. I can see objections to almost any plan that is attempted, but like so many things, I believe it is better to begin and make the changes as we learn from experience. We need to make the attempt to improve the general health of the people of our country.

TMsd AERP, FDRL

---

1. Lash, *Eleanor*, 465–67; Cook, vol. 2, 62–63, 416–18.

2. *MD*, 7 September 1945.

3. See Document 45.

4. In his January 11, 1944, annual address to Congress, the "Economic Bill of Rights" speech, FDR called for "a Second Bill of Rights under which a new basis of security and prosperity can be established for all—regardless of station, race or creed," which included "the right to adequate medical care and the opportunity to achieve and enjoy good health" (Zevin, 396).

5. The Wagner-Murray-Dingell bill proposed using funds collected from employees and employers to create a social insurance trust fund (with government contributions beginning within the next fifteen years) to finance a dramatic expansion of social security coverage. Not only would it add an additional 15,000,000 domestics, farm workers, small businesspeople, and employees of nonprofit institutions to the social security rolls, it would also cover workers and their families. The social insurance system would include prepaid health, unemployment, and disability insurance, as well as provide more generous retirement and survivors benefits. States would receive federal grants to enlarge hospitals and expand existing health coverage for pregnant women, infants, and children (C. P. Trussell, "Congress Gets Security Bill Adapting Beveridge Plan," *NYT*, 4 June 1943, 1; "Expanding Social Security," *NYT*, 26 May 1945, 14).

ER misspelled "Dingle."

ON THE PEARL HARBOR COMMISSION
AND CONGRESS

The surprise attack on Pearl Harbor produced immediate congressional cries for investigation. In January 1942, FDR appointed Associate Justice Owen Roberts to chair a special inquiry into the attack. Roberts's commission placed the blame at the feet of navy and army commanders at Pearl Harbor, Admiral Husband E. Kimmell and Major General Walter C. Short, faulting them for inadequate preparation and communication and "too lightly heed[ing]" the warnings from Washington. FDR refused to make the committee report public, arguing that doing so in wartime would put military personnel at risk. Congress thus passed resolutions extending the statute of limitations for the commanders' courts-martial until the war's end.

By 1944, election politics ignited more speculation, especially after *Colliers* published an article by Senator (and vice-presidential nominee) Harry Truman in its August issue indicting Kimmell and Short for their lack of cooperation. Kimmell, whom the navy had just placed on inactive duty, denied Truman's allegations and declared the Roberts report did "not contain the basic truths about the … catastrophe." The following December, Secretaries Stimson and Forrestal announced that separate boards of inquiry conducted by the army and navy found that while some unidentified army officers "lacked skill and judgement" the evidence investigated by both panels "does not warrant and will not support" court-martial proceedings.

Congress waited until Japan surrendered August 15 to press for hearings. August 17, Senator David Walsh (D-MA), chair of the Senate Naval Affairs Committee, asked Forrestal to deliver the "complete file of the navy's investigation" to the committee and make recommendations for how its content should be released to the public. August 23, Truman summoned Roberts to the White House. August 29, the Pearl Harbor Army and Navy Boards of Inquiry released their reports to the press. The army blamed Short for his "failure … to adequately alert his command for war"; Secretary of State Cordell Hull for delivering a series of demands to the Japanese November 26, 1941, which the Japanese construed as an ultimatum "to withdraw from the Asiatic mainland"; and General George Marshall for his "failure to advise his deputy chiefs of staff" about "the critical situation in the Pacific," as well as his "failure to keep General Short fully informed on the international situation and the probable outbreak of war." The navy report, while citing inadequate communication procedures, held no officer accountable.[1]

ER wrote the following column August 30, the day after the president released the reports from the military boards of inquiry.

43

My Day
1 September 1945

HYDE PARK, Friday—I have just been reading the Army and Navy reports on Pearl Harbor, as well as the innumerable newspaper comments. It all seems to me rather futile. Perhaps the simplest thing for us all to do would be to say that, in varying degrees, every one of us has been to blame. Our joint feelings, beliefs and actions had an effect on some of those in places of authority, and the division of blame is an extremely difficult thing to assess.

How often, for instance, was Congress asked for more appropriations to fortify Wake and Guam? Do we blame Congress for not listening to these requests? They were deaf because they did not think their constituents would consider that money wisely spent.

Are we going to censure General Marshall today even if he didn't send explicit enough directions to General Short in Pearl Harbor in 1941, and forget the magnificent record which he has made during the past four years? Are we going to take away the credit for the achievements of General Gerow and Admiral Stark even if they did fall short in some specific way in the Pearl Harbor situation?

If we had been clamoring for preparedness as a nation, we would not have allowed certain writers and papers and radio speakers to hurl the epithet of "warmonger" at the many people who warned us in the years before Pearl Harbor that war might be coming. Secretary Stimson's diary shows that President Roosevelt warned that the Japanese might attack on a certain day. Yet that wasn't the first warning he had given that we should prepare for war—and some of you may remember what certain newspapers in this country said about those warnings.

Is Secretary Hull, after his years of patient, wise leadership, now to be censured because he decided the time had come to take certain diplomatic steps as regards Japan? He was exercising his best judgment, and it would be well if we remembered how easy it is to be wise when you look back after events have occurred and how extremely difficult it sometimes is to gauge what those events will be.

It is very human to do little straight thinking about our own shortcomings. We want to accuse and punish our good and loyal public servants who have worked themselves to the point of ill health, and some of them even to death. Instead of marveling at the few mistakes they made, we harp upon those mistakes and give scant praise for all the years where they worked successfully and well. Yet we do not turn on our real enemies—the propagandists, writers and speakers who kept us unaware of danger, who tried to divide us and weaken us, and who are in our midst today, untouched and as dangerous to our peace efforts as they were to our war efforts.

Recriminations will not bring back our dead. Instead of recriminations, it would be safer and wiser if we determined in the future never again to be a flabby and ill-prepared people.

TMs AERP, FDRL

Truman responded to the column as soon as he read it.

44

Harry Truman to Eleanor Roosevelt
1 September 1945 [The White House]

Dear Mrs. Roosevelt:

I have just returned to the White House study from the executive office. The first thing I always do is look at the Scripps-Howard News and read the editorial page and your column. Today you've really "hit the jackpot"—if I may say that to the First Lady.

I am asking one of my good Senatorial friends to put it in the Congressional Record on Tuesday for the sake of history.[2] I only turned the reports loose because I was very reliably informed that the sabotage press had paid a very large price for them in order to release them on V.J. Day.[3] It is my opinion that they'll be a nine days cause for conversation and be forgotten in victory.

I see red every time this same press starts a ghoulish attack on the President, (I never think of anyone as the President but Mr. Roosevelt).

My very best regards and greatest respect I am

Sincerely
Harry S. Truman

ALS AERP, FDRL

Rather than continue discussing the Pearl Harbor reports, ER's reply to the president focused on his September 6 message to Congress, where he laid out his goals for reconversion and his twenty-one point legislative agenda. With Sam Rosenman's assistance, Truman created a comprehensive legislative package he considered "a combination of a first inaugural and a first State of the Union message." This 16,000-word "domestic message," which Truman acknowledged as "one of the lengthiest messages that a President had ever sent to Congress," was "designed to be as liberal and as far-reaching" as the pledges FDR made in the 1940 and 1944 elections. Trying to silence those who feared him too conservative to continue the New Deal, Truman declared his commitment to tax reduction; full employment; a permanent FEPC; an increase in the minimum wage; increased funding for unemployment insurance, public works programs, and housing construction; and the establishment of the National Science Foundation and universal military training. He also promised that he would soon send Congress his plans for national health insurance, federal aid to education, and an expanded social security system.[4]

45

Eleanor Roosevelt to Harry Truman
7 September 1945 [Hyde Park]

Dear Mr. President,

I am glad you liked my column and very much flattered that you read it.

May I say how much I admire your courage as shown in your message? You may be defeated, but you have stated your position clearly and I am sure Congress must uphold you if you make one or two clear talks to the people. I find the man in the street is backing you and gaining confidence in you just as his confidence and support built up for my husband.

Please remember me to Mrs. Truman. I wish you could all spend a weekend with me in Hyde Park this autumn.

With thanks and good wishes in your peace time–home front battles.

Cordially yours,
Eleanor Roosevelt

ALS HSTSF, HSTL

---

1. "Pearl Harbor," *NYT*, 23 August 1945, 8; James B. Reston, "Army Lays Attack to Foreign Policy," *NYT*, 30 August 1945, 1; "Walsh Asks Files on Pearl Harbor," *NYT*, 18 August 1945, 4; "Pearl Harbor Summary," *NYT*, 30 August 1945, 1.

2. There is no record of whom Truman contacted or the identity of the "sabotage press."

3. Although the Allies announced the surrender of Japanese forces on August 14, 1945 (Victory over Japan Day), the formal surrender was scheduled to occur September 2, 1945 (*OTCWH*).

4. Truman, vol. 1, 484–85. For press coverage see "The President's Message," *NYT*, 7 September 1945, 22; C. P. Trussell, "Congress Reacts: Members Seem Agreed Message Is Guide to Post-War Action; Partisanship Rises," *NYT*, 7 September 1945, 1; and Felix Belair, Jr., "Covers Wide Field," *NYT*, 7 September 1945, 1.

On the UAW Strike Against
General Motors

When the war ended, military spending decreased, overtime pay ended, and unemployment increased. As Congress debated full employment legislation, organized labor acted to keep its members' wages equal to what they had made in a wartime economy. July 19, the United Auto Workers, the largest union in the Congress of Industrial Organizations, announced that once the Allies secured victory over Japan, the UAW would authorize strikes "in every plant where a present grievance continues to exist." The union had no recourse, its president, R. J. Thomas, argued, because "employers in the automobile industry simply haven't accepted the union." September 14, union leadership announced its call for an industry-wide, 30 percent wage increase. It also promised to "crack down hard on all unauthorized strikes" and to only strike one company at a time.[1]

Although the UAW targeted General Motors, the following day Ford Motor Company, the last of the major automobile manufacturers to recognize collective bargaining, which also had a history of violent wartime clashes with its workers, reacted to the UAW announcement by firing 50,000 workers:

> In the face of crippling and unauthorized strikes against many of our suppliers, the Ford Motor Company is being forced to halt virtually all of its production operations late today.
>
> We have considered all angles of the situation. We wanted to keep men at work ... Instead we are telling 50,000 of our employees to stay off their jobs indefinitely.

Ford then appealed to "the country as a whole to [recognize] the seriousness of the situation. There can be no return to peacetime production so long as this condition exists. Every day without a full day's work delays the industrial comeback of this nation." The company concluded its announcement criticizing labor's insistence "on selfish policies when everyone's economic future is at stake."[2]

The UAW disagreed with Ford's decision to halt production, arguing that the UAW-CIO Executive Committee had taken control of the local affiliated with the Kelsey-Hayes Wheel Company (whose 4,500 workers walked off the job three weeks earlier after management fired four of its members). UAW leadership countered that it was taking "all steps possible" to settle the wildcat strike "as rapidly as possible." By September 15, 300,000–350,000 defense workers in Detroit had lost their jobs.[3]

As a member of the CIO-affiliated Newspaper Guild, ER quickly became a lightening rod for the CIO's critics. The *New York Times* once again thought My Day so newsworthy that it purchased the following column from the *New York World-Telegram* and published it September 20 under the headline "Mrs. Roosevelt Upholds Labor Union Right to Ask Pay Rises as Industry Reconverts."[4]

46

My Day
19 September 1945

HYDE PARK, Tuesday—I was urged by someone the other day to resign from the CIO as a patriotic gesture because of the strikes in the Ford plant.[5] I was told that it was terrible for the workers to strike when the industrialists were trying so hard to give jobs.

If this is a sample of the thinking which is going on, I believe the time has come for some of us to state clearly what we really feel and know about the economic situation which faces us in the reconversion period.

First of all, unions are not perfect. They are made up of human beings. But neither are employers perfect; they also are human beings. I happen to have been told by a number of people that a few of our biggest employers—not all of them, but a few of them—think quite honestly that this is the time to break the power of labor through destroying their unions if they can. These industrial leaders believe quite honestly that it would be better for the country to return to what to them seems normal—to a situation in which the costs are largely saved in whatever you manufacture by the cutting down of the number of jobs and of the wages of the workers.

Let us examine this theory. As long as there are other jobs being created into which people can go, the creation of labor-saving devices which benefit only the employer make very little difference. But we have reached a point today where labor-saving devices are good only when they do not throw the worker out of his job. It is fine to produce more things than ever before, but in doing so we must benefit the employee as well as the employer. We must make it possible for him to work fewer hours, and at the same time permit him to have the things which he makes at lower cost and to continue to have the wages which make it possible for him to be a consumer. His wages are the part of our wealth which is most constantly in circulation, just as what the farmer makes is important to us because that also is immediately spent.

The circulation of money is a necessity to prevent depressions. Therefore, if too much money goes into the hands of people who can save it and not put it back into circulation, we will have a depression. When we live on invested money, instead of on the fruits of our own labor, of necessity that money must bring in less. The stockholder or investor must expect less return than the original worker.

I do not know whether the demands of Mr. Ford's workers should all be granted.[6] But I think there should have been set up, long ago, labor-management committees where questions such as this one could be threshed out. Men should not have to strike for something which probably must be accepted in the future—the right to work fewer hours and yet receive the same wages. It should be a question for sensible men to settle in conference. We need a big national income with money kept in circulation if we are not to go through another depression in which both employer and employee will suffer.

E.R.

TMs AERP, FDRL

---

1. "UAW Plans Demand for 30 Percent Rise," *NYT*, 15 September 1945, 2; "Labor Crisis," *NYT*, 16 September 1945, E1.

2. "CIO Auto Head to Call Strikes After Victory," *WP*, 20 July 1945, 7; James B. Reston, "Company in Blunt Attack," *NYT*, 15 September 1945, 1–2.

3. "Ford Ends all Production, Blames Crippling Strikes; All Auto Industry Menaced," *NYT*, 15 September 1945, 1; "Union Picks Giant GMC As Its First Strike Target," *WP*, 16 September 1945, M1; "Outside Strikes Halt Ford Plants," *NYT*, 6 September 1945, 15.

4. "Mrs. Roosevelt Upholds Labor Union Right to Ask Pay Rises as Industry Reconverts," *NYT*, 20 September 1945, 20.

5. ER did not save the material she used to write this column; therefore, there is no way to determine who asked her to leave the union.

6. October 5, Ford announced that it would begin rehiring workers as the wildcat strike at Kelsey-Hayes Wheel Company drew to a close. By October 12, more than 35,000 workers returned, with another 5,000 due back in the next week. The remaining strikers would press for significant wage increases. February 27, Ford announced that it would increase wages an average of eighteen cents an hour, a 14.8 percent wage increase. While this was less than half the increase sought by the UAW, it set the highest wages for any automobile manufacturer. The UAW strike against General Motors ended the following month, securing a 17 percent wage increase for workers in GM facilities. For ER's assessment of GM-UAW negotiations, see Document 64 (Associated Press, "Ford Plants to Resume Next Week with Kelsey Wheel Strike Ending," *NYT*, 6 October 1945, 1; "Full Work Monday Is Ordered by Ford," *NYT*, 13 October 1945, 2; Walter Ruch, "Deadlock Is Ended," *NYT*, 27 February 1946, 1; Lichtenstein, 220–47).

September 29, 500 students in East Harlem's Benjamin Franklin High School and James Otis Junior High School engaged in day-long street violence, attacking each other with knives, bottles, homemade pistols, stones, and bricks. Allegedly angry over the pay their coaches received, groups of black and white students fought each other so intensely that they repelled the 200 police called in to calm the disturbance and trampled a woman and her baby carriage. School officials disputed the salary pretext for the fight and argued that the riot instead stemmed from the students' and their parents' dissatisfaction with integrated schools. The *New York Times* reported that the police found a different motive: "A dispute over a basketball game between a Negro and a white team on Thursday, in friction over dominance of the school's activities between the student bodies of each race, and in reports which had a Negro teacher striking a white pupil."[1] Mayor La Guardia ordered police commissioners to establish units prepared to confront school violence and the placement of uniformed and plain clothes officers in the schools. He then devoted his weekly radio address to the riot, blaming the disgruntled coaches for inciting students already on the edge. "Children on strike! Children demonstrating! Children protesting and challenging school authorities! I don't blame the parents," the mayor declared, "I am sure that the parents feel most unhappy about it, but I do say 'shame, shame, shame' to those on the city payroll who provoked these children. What is to happen to democracy if children in high schools feel that government can be defied?"[2]

Three days later, ER traveled to Newark, New Jersey, to join La Guardia and Channing Tobias for the Freedom Rally organized by the American Federation of Negro College Students. As she wrote in My Day:

> The Mayor was there and the auditorium was crowded, and I was glad to see that it really was a joint meeting of many people of different national origins and of varied religions. After the Mayor's greeting, Dr. Channing Tobias spoke, and both young and old seemed to feel the significance at the present moment of a meeting to emphasize the unity of the American people.[3]

ER rarely spoke from prepared text, preferring instead to speak either extemporaneously or from notes jotted while en route to the speech. Like most of her public remarks, the only extant text is the press coverage she received. The *Newark Evening News* captured ER's remarks that night, which offer a clear example of how she wove domestic and international issues, issues of local concern and national policy, into her speeches. Echoing the mayor, she asked what is to happen to democracy if government leaders cannot be trusted to act as mature leaders.

47

"Suspicion as Peace Bar Feared by Mrs. Roosevelt"

Newark Evening News 2 October 1945

Anxiety that suspicions and lack of mutual confidence will hamper peace was expressed last night by Mrs. Franklin D. Roosevelt before 1,000 in the auditorium of South Side High School at a postwar freedom rally sponsored by the American Federation of Negro College Students.[4]

"I look with great anxiety on the meetings of our representatives which don't settle questions," Mrs. Roosevelt said. "We must have confidence in one another and must avoid a situation where everybody approaches everybody else with suspicions. I am very much afraid that's what's happening in the seats of the mighty."

The former first lady said that individuals must have the integrity and determination "to do what's right. We can't be represented unless we have within us the thing we want represented," she said. "It's what you do personally that counts."

Attired in deep mourning, Mrs. Roosevelt discussed the atomic bomb, saying scientists who had worked on its development in this country told her we "delude ourselves by thinking we hold a secret we could keep." She described the discovery of the release of atomic power as a "race with other scientists which we won but perhaps by a very narrow margin. Its principles," she said, "are known wherever in the world men think and the secret will not long remain."

The real problem, she declared, is not who holds the secret "even if we trust ourselves so completely as to believe we wouldn't use it except in a righteous cause." Pointing out that atomic bomb scientists declare it possible for a small aggressor nation to destroy the rest of the world with it overnight, Mrs. Roosevelt stated it evolved into a question of "who decided to use it first."

"If we really want peace," she said, "it has to begin in every human heart. There has to be a strong desire for it in the hearts of men, women and young people."[5]

She questioned whether so-called strikes among metropolitan high school students originates in the schools and said she believes they begin outside, through the influence of the students' elders, possibly in the home.[6]

The problem of settling these differences cannot be put off from one generation to another, she declared, "but in view of atomic power this generation has got to face its problems and solve questions. If we want peace we've got to do the job and do it now, not leave it to the boys who come home or the boys and girls in school. They will carry on, but we have to do the beginning.

"Each of us has to make sure that freedom really exists, that in our hearts we have the spirit that really wants freedom not just for ourselves but for the other fellow too. We must want the kind of freedom in which people discipline themselves sufficiently so that every one has rights."

"The four freedoms really hang together," she asserted. "We can't have freedom from fear without freedom from want and equality of opportunity; that is, getting a job you are able to do, in government, in meeting other people who make up your community and feeling that together you can achieve freedom and peace. If we don't achieve it in this country where we have a miniature league of nations," she said, "how in the world do you think we are going to achieve it in the world as a whole?"

Pnews, DLC

---

1. Alexander Feinberg, "Student 'Strikes' Flare into Riots in Harlem Schools," *NYT*, 29 September 1945, 1.

2. "Athletic Coaches Scored by Mayor," *NYT*, 1 October 1945, 11.

3. *MD*, 3 October 1945.

4. ER's My Day of October 3, 1945, also described the assembly at which Newark Mayor Vincent Murphy and Dr. Tobias spoke.

5. ER elaborated on this point a week earlier, as the Council of Foreign Ministers first convened in London to draft the peace treaty agreements for Europe. She then told her readers:

I have been somewhat disturbed lately to read statements in the public press by members of Congress and military officers which seem to assume that the atomic bomb is a secret that can be kept by this nation, if we so desire. The scientists who worked on the discovery, and who should know more about it than anyone else, insist that it is no secret. No scientific discovery can long remain secret when the fundamental principles involved are so widely known; and in this particular case, the fundamental principles of atomic energy and its release were widely known even before the particular developments for this project were undertaken. The technical and engineering details will soon be discovered by other scientists in other lands.

It seems to me that this discovery has made imperative an educational undertaking in every country in the world. Every man, every woman—everywhere—must grow up knowing that since this discovery of how to use atomic energy for destruction, annihilation faces them unless they learn to live in a peaceful world and to allow the policing of the world to be done by an international security agency.

The sovereignty which each nation will have to renounce is not too high a price to pay for the continuation of our civilization. Almost every country in the world has the needed raw materials for the manufacture of these bombs, and the little countries can do it as well as the big ones. All that is needed, to destroy, is to act first. Are we going to live in constant dread of all our neighbors? Except for the completely happy-go-lucky person, able to wipe out all thought of the future, no one could go to bed at night with any sense of security. Once a weapon is discovered, it will always be used by those who are in desperate straits.

The day we found the secret of the atomic bomb, we closed one phase of civilization and entered upon another (*MD*, 25 September 1945).

See *n*1 Document 35.

6. The following day she made similar points in My Day:

I think Mayor La Guardia was right to be horrified when he heard of the rumored high school riots here, and of the actual ones in Chicago and in Gary, Indiana. It seems to me, however, that while on the surface we can blame certain organizations and leaders who may [have] been impressing on these young minds the differences among people rather than their likenesses, we elders cannot escape from the main responsibility. Parents at home must know when their children are rioting, or developing the ideas which lead to riots. If they do not know, it shows a lack of family communication and mutual interest which is sad indeed (*MD*, 3 October 1945).

REBUTTING WALTER WINCHELL

October 9, ER traveled to New Haven, Connecticut, as *Time* magazine later reported, to break "her silence on what she thinks" of Truman's policies. Her comments on the president's "thinking about the atomic bomb"[1] and her insinuation that James Byrnes "used inept tactics at the Council of Foreign Ministers" meeting[2] not only were reprinted in the New Haven press, but also published in *Time* under the banner "Mrs. Roosevelt Speaks Out." Radio coverage was more pronounced after Walter Winchell told his audience that ER "had sharply attacked Secretary of State Byrnes."[3] When "several people" told ER about his October 14 broadcast, she wrote Winchell, enclosing a copy of the *New Haven Evening Register* coverage of her speech, to say that she "had no intention of criticizing Secretary Byrnes" and that she was "sorry that someone gave you incorrect information."[4]

48

"Mrs. Roosevelt Says U.S. Must Forget Fears"
New Haven Evening Register 10 October 1945

Another great war cannot be avoided unless the United States as a world leader forgets her fears of other nations and learns to understand their problems, Mrs. Eleanor Roosevelt said yesterday. She spoke before an overflow audience of nearly 700 men and women at a luncheon meeting of the Connecticut Federation of Democratic Women's Clubs at the Hotel Taft.

The secret of the atomic bomb cannot be kept by this country as long as men think in other parts of the world, Mrs. Roosevelt said. If there is a next war, "it will be easier for nomadic Arabs and the cowboy in the West to escape bombs than it will be for New York or New Haven. We have to have peace or gradually all people and all highly concentrated centers of civilization will be destroyed."

Many Americans are afraid of Russia or Great Britain, Mrs. Roosevelt said. "With such fear we can never arrive at an understanding or at real co-operation. We must not let ourselves indulge in suspicion of other peoples or judge them without taking into consideration the conditions they face."

Although Americans had many inconveniences during the war, "quite honestly, we never did wonder when the enemy was going to land on our shores. The end of the war left us much less tired than the other peoples of the world. We have initiative, strength, and courage and a tremendous sense of confidence in ourselves. I hope it is justified."

The United States must be an example to other nations, Mrs. Roosevelt said. Other nations will say, "if the United States cannot solve its economic problems, how can we; if they cannot learn to live with others, how can we?" America has the most wealth and strength now; other nations will be envious and wary of her intentions.

America's leadership is the responsibility of the people of the nation. "We are the Government of this country and we assume responsibility for the actions of our representatives. We cannot shovel off this responsibility on anyone else. We must make many fundamental changes in our thinking although many of us are a little disconcerted about this change, about the necessity of beginning peace in a stranger and newer world than we had expected."

Mrs. Roosevelt warned the audience against sinking back into the apathy that characterized the end of the last war. "If we do, we may wake up some morning to find that scientists have been thinking in some other part of the world. There will be no more declared wars; the only advantage in the next war will be—who acts first."

"We should not be discouraged," Mrs. Roosevelt said, "by the results of the failure of the Foreign Ministers to reach an understanding. The failure of the meeting as almost a foregone conclusion. When three men knew each other's background and temperament as little as did Mr. Byrnes, Mr.

Bevin[5] and Mr. Molotoff, they could not reach agreement. We must learn to have great patience and to view world problems through the eyes of other nations. But we should not be discouraged by one failure. If we really mean business, we will have peace in this world where peace is imperative."

PNews AERP, FDRL

> Winchell, while professing his support for ER, continued to address the controversy, telling his radio audience October 21 that although ER had written him to object to his "inaccurate" reporting and to state for the record that she "had no intention of criticizing Secretary Byrnes," as much as he would be "glad" to retract his report, "page 22 of the current issue of *Time*, that's 'Time Magazine,' ... practically confirms what I reported Sunday night. *Time*'s report calls Mrs. Roosevelt's speech 'an outspoken blast.'"[6]

49

"Mrs. Roosevelt Speaks Out" [excerpt]
Time 22 October 1945

...To a large bipartisan audience of women (and a few men) at New Haven, Conn., Mrs. Roosevelt delivered an outspoken blast at the President's policy of keeping U.S. detailed knowledge of the atomic bomb a secret. Her conclusion: this was an implication that the U.S. could not trust its former allies. But would the secret hold? Said she: "Even those most hopeful that we can hold this secret expect others to trust us when we, apparently, do not trust anyone else... I wonder if President Truman is not forgetting that the atomic bomb became important to us only when we realized that an enemy nation was trying to develop it?"

She added: "We let ourselves indulge in suspicion of the motives of other peoples of the world. With fear you never arrive at an understanding or real cooperation. If we trust others, we may come out with a compromise, and that will be a step forward. I hope that we ... are going to make fundamental changes in our thinking and acting, which alone can bring about peace."

Mrs. Roosevelt was asked if she was discouraged by the failure of the London Conference. Her reply: "No. I don't think it surprising that men who knew each other so little as they did could not arrive at the answers to all the questions they considered. Mr. Bevin and Mr. Byrnes were entirely new, and we should have known from his background that Mr. Bevin would be difficult. Mr. Byrnes was put in the position of mediator and he was not prepared."

PMag, DLC

> After listening to Winchell's broadcast, ER wrote the following retort.

50

Eleanor Roosevelt to Walter Winchell
22 October 1945 [Hyde Park]

Dear Mr. Winchell:

I listened to your broadcast last night and I was distressed that you felt you had to say I had written you. I had not meant to put you in that position. I just wanted you to know that I had not attacked Secretary Byrnes.

Perhaps I should have explained what really happened. Someone asked me whether I was disappointed by the failure of the Ministers' meeting and I explained that I was not disappointed because I felt a meeting of that kind required more preparation that had been possible for this one. Mr. Molotov is an old hand and had attended other meetings but Secretary Byrnes and Mr. Bevin were new, and in order to discuss controversial international questions, one had to build up among the men themselves personal confidence and liking. That had not been possible in such a short time.

Mr. Bevin had an age old quarrel with everything that Mr. Molotov stood for and had fought the British communists in his own unions.[7] Therefore Secretary Byrnes started out with the necessity of being an arbiter between the two and I am not even sure that he knew this was the case.

Secretary Byrnes had very little time to establish the kind of relationship with the other two men which would make it possible for him to do the job effectively. It seemed to me therefore that after they had time to get to know each other better and to establish confidence by the way they treated each other, there was every hope that in the future they might be able to accomplish more at their meetings.

I am not writing this because I want you to speak on the radio. I only hate you not to know the exact truth of any situation. You do such a magnificent job of defending the things my husband stood for and believed and for which all of us try to be useful and to continue his work.

Very sincerely yours,

TLc AERP, FDRL

---

1. By late October, Truman had not yet announced his position on allied access to matters related to the atomic bomb. At the September 21 cabinet meeting, the president "indicated considerable sympathy" for Secretary of War Henry Stimson's proposal that America and Great Britain make "a direct and forthright approach" to Russia to develop an atomic energy program, dedicated to disarmament and the commercial and humanitarian use of atomic energy. Yet no one discussed the "deliberately sketchy" details about the inevitable sharing of scientific information with the Soviets. The president would not endorse the Baruch Plan for the international control of atomic energy until 1946 (Donovan, 129–33).

2. Adhering to the agreements reached at Potsdam, the three leaders agreed that the foreign ministers of the United States, Great Britain, and the Soviet Union (Byrnes, Bevin, and Molotov) should form a council to determine the terms of the peace treaty—including the fate of those nations who had allied with Germany. Byrnes and Bevin refused to negotiate settlement terms until the Soviet army adhered to the agreements reached at Yalta. Molotov responded by chiding the Allies on their refusal to include France and Nationalist China in the discussions and by repeatedly referencing American control of the atomic bomb. Discussions deadlocked when Molotov insisted that the Italian colonies in North Africa be designated UN trusteeships and placed under Soviet control. Fearing Soviet control of the Mediterranean naval and air space, the meeting dissolved in acrimony (*HSTE*; Hamby, *Man*, 330–342).

3. Living up to his slogan, "Winchell...HE SEES ALL...HE KNOWS ALL," Walter Winchell wrote a syndicated gossip column and carried his colorful prose to the airwaves for four decades. A product of working-class America, he felt an obligation to reveal the private lives of entertainers and politicians to the masses. At the height of his popularity, two-thirds of the nation followed his running commentary, and few politicians could ignore his ability to sway public opinion. Although his support of Franklin D. Roosevelt led many liberals to look to Winchell as an ally in the press, personal animosity towards President Truman ensured Winchell no longer provided the Democrats with favorable publicity. By the early 1950s, Winchell joined forces with J. Edgar

Hoover and Sen. Joseph McCarthy (R-WI) in their attacks on liberals as "soft" on Communism (Gabler, xi–xvi, 345–46).

4. ER to Walter Winchell, 18 October 1945, AERP.

5. Ernest Bevin.

6. Winchell's papers at the New York Public Library do not contain an audio transcript of this broadcast; however, William Hassett saved a typed transcript of this portion of the broadcast in his papers housed at FDRL.

7. Before he became a member of Parliament and foreign secretary, Bevin, a stalwart anti-Communist, served as general secretary of the Workers and Transport Union (1921–40) and in 1937, chaired the Trades Union Conference (*OWW*).

On Hazel Scott, the Daughters
of the American Revolution,
and Constitution Hall

In 1939, in a controversy that received world-wide attention, ER resigned from the Daughters of the American Revolution (DAR) over its refusal to allow Marian Anderson to sing in its Constitution Hall. ER and Harold Ickes then joined forces to secure permission for Anderson to deliver a free concert at the Lincoln Memorial, where she performed on Easter Sunday, April 9, 1939, before a crowd of 75,000. October 13, 1945, the DAR reignited the debate surrounding its segregation policy by refusing to rent the hall to Hazel Scott, a popular African American pianist, singer, and actress, who had performed with the Count Basie Orchestra and starred in both Broadway and Hollywood productions. Press coverage immediately compared Scott to Anderson and referenced ER's resignation.[1] Scott's husband, Representative Adam Clayton Powell, Jr. (D-NY), and his colleague, Representative Claire Booth Luce (R-CT), condemned the DAR's position, with Luce asking her local DAR affiliate to protest the organization's action, concluding her request with a warning that "if no such resolution can be drafted by our chapter I shall, of course, be forced to resign from the DAR."[2]

Two days later ER devoted My Day to discrimination in the nation's capital.

51

My Day
15 October 1945

HYDE PARK, Sunday—This is Sunday, and I think that on this day, above all others, most of us think of what we can do to bring the people of our nation to an understanding that peace, democracy and real unity among the peoples of the world depend on our willingness to accept the fact that all of us, regardless of race or creed or color, belong to one human family.

Some of us may feel that we have developed beyond others, due to circumstances of birth or native ability. This is not incompatible with a belief that we must have equality of opportunity throughout the world, and that when people achieve a high level of success they must be given recognition for that success, regardless of their background, racial origin or religion.

In this recent controversy centering, again, around the granting of the use of the hall owned in the District of Columbia by the Daughters of the American Revolution for a concert by the gifted pianist, Mrs. Hazel Scott Powell, I do not think one can hold the Daughters of the American Revolution alone responsible. There is an agreement among all theatre owners in the District of Columbia as to how their theatres shall be used.[3] Only the public can make the theatre owners change that agreement.

It is sad that in our nation's capital, where the eyes of the world are upon us, we should allow discrimination which impedes the progress and sears the souls of human beings whose only fault is that God, who made us all, gave their skin a darker color.

One might hope that an organization such as the Daughters of the American Revolution would have the courage to stand alone, if need be, and break this agreement which, though it may be unwritten, is nevertheless binding. They should be very sure of their own position and their own background, and they must be conscious of their Revolutionary ancestry, who came as immigrants to this country to escape discrimination in other lands.

It would be a rather glorious crusade for this organization to lead. To advocate human rights and insist that those who attain the highest artistic standards are to be judged as artists, and not discriminated against because of race or creed or color, would be in keeping with our Revolutionary traditions. They could so easily lead, and leaders are sorely needed today. Only those who are secure and who have convictions such as our forefathers had—that men have a right to stand on their achievements—could make this fight and give heart to others to join with them. Who could do it better than the daughters of Revolutionary great-grandfathers?

TMs AERP, FDRL

---

1. See *MD*, February 27, 1939, for ER's discussion of her decision to resign from the DAR. For a full description of ER's actions see A. Black, "Champion."

2. *EAACH*; "A. C. Powell Jr. Wed with Difficulties," *NYT*, 2 August 1945, 21; "ALP Inquiry in Capital on D.A.R.," *NYT*, 14 October 1945, 46; "Trumans Condemn D.A.R. Ban," *NYT*, 13 October 1945, 16.

3. ER later participated in a challenge to this agreement.

ELEANOR ROOSEVELT AND
THE UNITED AUTO WORKERS STRIKE

_____ 52 _____

Walter Reuther to Eleanor Roosevelt
15 October 1945 [Detroit?]

My dear Mrs. Roosevelt:

On September 24 in the New York Times, Mr. Henry Hazlitt,[1] Financial Editor, had the following to say in his column:

"Last week Mrs. Eleanor Roosevelt, in a column that probably set a record for the number of antique economic fallacies packed into that many lines of type, proved to her own satisfaction that we can realize our fondest dreams if only we stop technical progress, have everybody work fewer hours but get the same wages and spend them immediately.[2] She was encouraged to make these pronouncements by the letter a few days before of Walter P. Reuther, vice president of the UAW-CIO, who insisted that the automobile workers could easily get a 30 percent hourly wage increase without adding a penny to the price of a car."[3]

Since Mr. Hazlitt accuses me of being responsible for the fallacies in your economic thinking, I thought you might be interested in having a copy of a pamphlet which we recently prepared on the question of "How to Raise Wages without Increasing Prices."[4] We are preparing further material based upon government figures and corporation financial reports, which will prove that our economic contention is sound. If you would like copies of this material when it is completed, I shall be most happy to forward it to you.

With kind personal regards,

Sincerely yours,

TLc UAWPOWR, MiDW-AL

_____ 53 _____

Eleanor Roosevelt to Walter Reuther
25 October 1945 [Washington, DC]

My dear Mr. Reuther:

Many thanks for sending me the quotation from Mr. Hazlitt's column, and also for the pamphlet. I was interested in both of them, but suggest that rather than send any further material to me, you send it to Mr. Hazlitt!

Very sincerely yours,
Eleanor Roosevelt

TLS UAWPOWR, MiDW-AL

———————

1. Henry Hazlitt (1894–1993), a proponent of free markets who opposed collective bargaining and minimum wage laws, worked as an editorial writer for the *New York Times* from 1934 until 1946

(Louis Uchitelle, "Henry Hazlitt, 98, a Journalist Who Concentrated on Economics," *NYT*, 10 July 1993, 27).

2. In her September 19 column, reprinted in its entirety as Document 46, ER wrote:

> As long as there are other jobs being created into which people can go, the creation of labor-saving devices which benefit only the employer make very little difference. But we have reached a point today where labor-saving devices are good only when they do not throw the worker out of his job. It is fine to produce more things than ever before, but in doing so we must benefit the employee as well as the employer. We must make it possible for him to work fewer hours, and at the same time permit him to have the things which he makes at lower cost and to continue to have the wages which make it possible for him to be a consumer. His wages are the part of our wealth which is most constantly in circulation, just as what the farmer makes is important to us because that also is immediately spent.
>
> The circulation of money is a necessity to prevent depressions. Therefore, if too much money goes into the hands of people who can save it and not put it back into circulation, we will have a depression. When we live on invested money, instead of on the fruits of our own labor, of necessity that money must bring us in less. The stockholder or investor must expect less return than the original worker (*MD*, 19 September 1945).

3. Reuther and his United Automobile Workers made their demands for a 30 percent increase in wages in a letter from Reuther to C. E. Wilson, president of General Motors, dated August 18 and published in the *New York Times* on September 16. Reuther argued that the wage freeze during the war, the return to a forty-hour work week after the war that resulted in a 30 percent decrease in take-home pay, and rising living costs made the increase necessary, and that GM's high profits would make it unnecessary to raise prices in order to absorb the increased labor costs. To secure their demands, Reuther and the UAW threatened a strike by 300,000 workers at General Motors, followed by strikes at Ford and Chrysler. In making his case to the War Labor Board on June 30, 1945, Reuther argued: "Wages can be increased without increasing prices. Increased production must be supported by increased consumption, and increased consumption will be possible only through increased wages" ("Reuther Puts Case for GM Wage Rise," *NYT*, 16 September 1945, 4; Louis Stark, "Auto Leaders Seek Washington Action in the Labor Crisis," *NYT*, 18 September 1945, 1; Lichtenstein, 222).

4. The pamphlet, missing from both Reuther's and ER's papers, was apparently based on a memorandum of the same title sent by Reuther to William H. Davis, director of the Office of Economic Stabilization, on June 30, 1945 (Lichtenstein, 493 *n9*).

On FDR, King Ibn Saud, and
a Jewish State in Palestine

October 5, alarmed by reports that FDR had changed his mind about Palestine after the Yalta conference and had promised Saudi Arabian King Ibn Saud that he would not support the Jews in Palestine, Rabbi Stephen Wise, ER's close friend and co-chairman of the American Zionist Emergency Council, wrote her suggesting that she might need to correct the record.[1] Wise, who discussed the establishment of a Jewish state in Palestine with FDR in March after the president returned from Yalta, remained convinced of FDR's continued support for a Jewish state. As the rabbi told the press upon leaving FDR, the president had authorized him to tell the media that FDR reaffirmed the commitment he had made in October 1944 to Wise regarding the administration's support for the establishment of a Jewish state in Palestine "as soon as practicable."[2]

The controversy about FDR's position on Palestine began August 20, 1945, when Abdel Rehman Azzam Bey, secretary general of the Arab League, criticized Truman's statement that the United States favored allowing as many Jewish refugees into Palestine as possible. Bey countered, "We would like to remind him of one of the last promises made by President Roosevelt, when he put his hand in the hand of King Ibn Saud and promised him that he would not support the Jews in Palestine."[3] On August 28, the American Zionist Emergency Council challenged Bey's assertion that FDR had made such a promise.[4] Truman also rejected Bey's pronouncement telling a reporter attending his September 26 press conference that no record of FDR making such a pledge existed.[5] Angered by Truman's denial, King Saud threatened to publish the letters he and FDR had exchanged after their meeting.[6]

Anticipating this disclosure, Secretary of State James F. Byrnes released the letters himself October 18. In his letter to Ibn Saud, FDR wrote to communicate:

> to you the attitude of the American Government toward Palestine and make clear our desire that no decision be taken with respect to the basic situation in that country without full consultation with both Arabs and Jews.
>
> Your Majesty will also doubtless recall that during our recent conversation I assured you that I would take no action, in my capacity as Chief of the Executive Branch of this Government, which might prove hostile to the Arab people.

In a statement issued along with the letters, Byrnes reassured the Arabs that the United States would not come to any final decisions about proposals regarding Palestine without "full consultation with Jewish and Arab leaders."[7]

From Rabbi Wise and others ER knew of the anguish that news of FDR's assurances to King Saud caused in the Jewish community. October 22, Leon Forem, a journalist who had written a biography of FDR in Yiddish, wrote ER that the publication of the FDR–Ibn Saud letters created "a depressed feeling amongst Jews throughout this country"; that "some ... even say that the President has, in a way, betrayed them (for they loved and trusted him so much)"; and that "a few articles in the Yiddish press" expressed this as well. ER responded that while FDR "meant the Jewish people no harm," he also "dreaded war between them and the more numerous Arabs and hoped a more amicable agreement could be reached," and "felt that he had not succeeded with Ibn Saud."[8]

Three days after she received Forem's letter, she published the following column, which Wise suggested she write when he first informed her of the controversy.

54

My Day

25 October 1945

WASHINGTON, D. C., Wednesday—Since the Secretary of State released the letter written by my husband to King Ibn Saud, in which he gave assurance that the United States would take no action without consultation with both the Jewish leaders and the Arab leaders, I think the rumors surrounding this subject are clarified.

There have been so many assertions both abroad and at home of what had been said in conversations, that I think many people felt somewhat confused. I had heard my husband, on a number of occasions after his return from Yalta, give an account of the visit paid him by King Ibn Saud. My husband stated that he felt his conversations with the Arab king had been a failure, since the king had told him that as long as he lived he did not wish any change. An influx into Palestine of Jewish people from the big cities of the world—like London, Paris, Berlin, New York—would meet resistance because it tended to change the way of life of the whole land. The Arabs, said King Ibn Saud, are of the same Semitic race as the Jews, and got on well when their backgrounds were similar. My husband said that King Ibn Saud asserted that he had been a warrior all of his life; he was not interested either in farming or forestry; his people were herdsmen and nomads, and he wished no change.

My husband felt that a later generation might feel differently, but at present there was very little hope of a changed attitude on the part of the Arabs where Palestine was concerned.

It has always seemed to me very unwise to quote people after they are dead. Their written documents, of course, can be considered in the light of the circumstances and the period in which they were written. They are factual and represent at least what the man himself put down at that period.

Even that, I think, is sometimes misleading, because all intelligent people change their minds in view of changed circumstances and conditions. Only stupid people remain rigid and inflexible in their opinions and ideas. Therefore you can really never tell what a man who has been a thinker and a leader, in either public or private life, would think or do if he were alive and facing new circumstances. You can take what he has written and what he said and what you know of his character and principles, and it may influence you in your thinking. But it should never be considered as the attitude of the man in the new situation. A new decision should always be the result of new thinking.

There is one other consideration in quoting the dead. They can no longer speak for themselves. They can neither explain why they did or said certain things, nor give the reasons which influenced them at the time. Therefore it seems to me that using past utterances to influence new decisions is not only unfair but very unwise. People who may themselves have had some special axe to grind, and who quite easily may have understood a conversation in the light of their own desires instead of those of the speaker, are never reliable reporters.

TMs AERP, FDRL

---

1. Wise to ER, 5 October 1945, AERP.

2. Penkower, 314, 334–35.

3. "Arab League Aide Quotes Roosevelt," *NYT*, 20 August 1945, 17.

4. "Zionists Challenge Roosevelt Story," *NYT*, 28 August 1945, 15.

5. "Palestine 'Pledge' Denied by Truman," *NYT*, 27 September 1945, 14.

6. Clifton Daniel, "Arab Press Hails Roosevelt Letter," *NYT*, 20 October 1945, 5.

7. "Text of Letters Exchanged by Ibn Saud and Roosevelt," *NYT*, 19 October 1945, 4; "U.S. Bars Decision on Palestine Without Consulting Jews, Arabs," *NYT*, 19 October 1945, 1.

8. Forem to ER, 22 October 1945, AERP; ER to Leon Forem, 12 November 1945, AERP.

CAMPAIGNING FOR THE NATIONAL CITIZENS POLITICAL ACTION COMMITTEE

Although ER rejected the chairmanship of NCPAC, she spoke on its behalf when she traveled, often headlining its major fund-raising events. For example, when she traveled to Framingham, Massachusetts, October 30 to visit the State Reformatory for Women, she spent the next day raising money for NCPAC, its Massachusetts affiliate, and the Massachusetts Independent Voters Association. She would make the same remarks in similar appearances in Newark, New Jersey, the following week. Again the only extant copy of her remarks is the coverage the event received in the local newspapers.[1]

55

"Mrs. Roosevelt in PAC Talk Here"
The Boston Post 1 November 1945

Delay in action by Congress in putting through Pres. Truman's domestic program[2] may be due to the fact that the legislators "are wondering if we care about the President's program," Mrs. Eleanor Roosevelt, widow of Pres. Roosevelt, told 1200 last night at a dinner of the Massachusetts Political Action Committee in the Copley-Plaza Hotel.[3]

Mrs. Roosevelt followed another speaker[4] who had accused Congress bluntly of being "on a sit-down strike"[5] and urged that Mr. Truman should be impressed of the necessity of getting "beyond the stage of taking Congress out to lunch." She referred to this with the statement that she agreed that "Congress has not been overactive in putting through the President's domestic program—but Congress may be wondering if we, the people, care about the President's program.

"The people should tell Congress what they want—what they are willing to pay for—what they are willing to stand behind. I am sure that our representatives in Congress want to know," she said as she urged action on the part of voters.

"We are in an important moment of history. What happens here in the United States will either give courage to people in the other parts of the world, or on the other hand, will sap their courage.

"People must use their imaginations to understand what our real responsibility is in the world today," Mrs. Roosevelt declared, after asserting that people all over the world are looking at us and saying that we have not suffered as they have suffered, that we have no devastated regions, and that we are far better fed than any other nation involved in the war.

"For the second time in their lifetimes many of these people are coming back to homes that are nothing but piles of rubble. When Princess Juliana went back to Holland and then returned here to get her children, she couldn't keep the tears from her eyes as she told me of the sufferings of the children of the Netherlands. Little boys, from 8 to 12 years of age, carried all of the responsibility of bringing food to families because the older children were not allowed out—they were in danger of being taken for use as slave labor.[6] In one part of France, I am told that 50 percent of the children have tuberculosis. We would be worried if that happened in any part of our country. It is natural that those people should look to us."

The President's widow told of her observations during the depression in this country, declaring that it took the economic sufferers here sometimes three years or more to get back their initiative. She likened them to the people of the other nations.

"They will hear that we didn't vote quickly on funds to keep UNRRA (United Nations Relief and Rehabilitation Administration) going, and upon relief to other people.[7]

"It is very necessary that in order that we may have a peaceful world, we must use our imagination, so that we really can extend the hand of good will. There will be no peace unless in our lives and as individuals we want to do things to bring peace. We must look upon people of the world as fellow human beings—worthy of our help. We must recognize that they will have to be back on their feet before they can buy the goods of our production. We must have these markets at home and abroad.

"When my husband returned from Africa,[8] he told me that if we could do something to lift up the other peoples just one peg, they would buy from the United States more things than we ever dreamed of. For these people abroad to have the right spirit they must have food. Much of our future depends on a realization of our leadership and what it means. We will have to whether we want to or not. It is not the job of the government, not the job of our leaders. It is the job of everyone of us," she said.

At the close of another address made earlier at a tea of the Massachusetts Independent Voters' Association in the Hotel Puritan by Mrs. Roosevelt, Mrs. J. Anton deHaas, a member of the general council of the Massachusetts Independent Voters' Association, urged that the appointment of Mrs. Roosevelt as a delegate from the United States to the United Nations Organization be sought by independent voters throughout the country.[9]

More than 800 members and friends of the Independent Voters' Association jammed into the Crystal Room of the Puritan to hear the former First Lady outline the steps she thinks the United States must take to lead the world into peace.

"We must recognize the fact that we face a new era. We have a new power this nation can use to bring about great benefit or great harm. It is no longer enough to desire peace or to hope for peace. We must say we intend to have peace and then determine the steps to be taken to get it.

"We must be a strong nation, but we must change our concepts of progress and national strength. We have gained the opportunity again to try to build that better world our soldiers dreamed about when they were fighting. Our victory was made possible by the soldiers, by the workers, by the housewives, by the businessmen, by the bankers and by members of all walks of life. They are the people who must now work just as sincerely and effectively for peace.

"The government is the least important in this picture, because the government only reflects the views and desires of the people. I am amazed at how little we have accomplished in the weeks since the war in comparison with how much we accomplished during the war.

"The program which the President recommended to Congress has not been acted upon with one exception, a program which was defeated.[10] Legislation such as full employment will be passed by Congress or not passed, depending upon the expression of the will of the people."

During the introduction of another speaker, J. Caswell Smith, Jr., reference had been made to the fact that the Red Cross in taking blood donations had put the blood of colored people into containers separate from those which contained the donations of the whites.[11]

Digressing from her planned speech at her opening in the Copley-Plaza, Mrs. Roosevelt declared "the story is only partially true." She said she had become interested in what she called "the curious contention of the Red Cross about the blood banks."

"I went to the Red Cross and they told me, 'We are not responsible—the army is responsible for that.' The army then told me that it was not responsible, 'because if we did do it that way, we would have riots among our patients in the hospitals.'

"The army did not have the courage to take a stand because it didn't know what the people wanted. The Red Cross did not have the courage because it did not know.

"People don't speak out and that is used as a reason or an excuse by the people at the top."

Gov. Tobin,[12] who spoke briefly at the dinner, highly praised Mrs. Roosevelt for her courage in carrying her views to the people at a time when she is still bearing the grief of the loss of her husband.

Sen. Charles W. Tobey,[13] Republican of New Hampshire, in his speech before the big gathering, declared in talking about the atom bomb, "We are in a very dangerous position. We are looked upon by other nations as an aggressor nation, and this is indicated by Molotov's statement at the London conference to the effect that all Sec. Byrnes had to do was to wave the atomic bomb at other nations and they would have to capitulate.[14] This shows what is in the back of the minds of other nations. If we allow the atomic race to develop a third world war is in the making.

PNews BPO, DLC

---

1. "Aid in Launching New Election Campaign," *Newark Evening News*, 9 November 1945, AERP; "Mrs. F.D.R. Heard Here," *Newark Star Ledger*, 9 November 1945, AERP.

2. See Document 45.

3. ER, who addressed New Jersey NCPAC events the following week, thought these dinners worth her time, writing in My Day: "If these dinners bring about as much political action as they seem to create enthusiasm at the dinners themselves, I think we are awakening a sense of participation in government which should be extremely valuable" (*MD*, 2 November 1945).

4. Other event speakers included Sen. Charles W. Tobey (R-NH) (1880–1953); Massachusetts Governor Maurice J. Tobin (1901–1953); Unitarian minister Stephen H. Fritchman (1902–1981), who edited the denomination's journal, the *Christian Register*; J. Caswell Smith, Jr., executive secretary of the Urban League of Boston; and historian Howard Mumford Jones (1892–1980) ("Mrs. Roosevelt Speaks Tonight," *Boston Herald*, 31 October 1945, LOCPC; "Mrs. F.D. Here, Would Like to Attend Peace Parley," *Boston Globe*, 1 November 1945, LOCPC).

5. ER made much the same point in My Day writing that:

> now we are in the curious position of having forgotten to safeguard the people who worked loyally through the war and who kept their promise to see us through the crises. It isn't just the soldiers who are bewildered and who wonder whether the war was worth fighting. There must be great groups of other people in this country who begin to wonder whether we don't sometimes have sitdown strikes on the part of capital and on the part of government (*MD*, 27 October 1945).

6. ER first met Juliana von Orange Nassau (1909–2004), Dutch crown princess and future queen of the Netherlands, January 17, 1941, when Juliana and her family came for an extended stay in the White House. Juliana, who with her parents fled the Netherlands May 10, 1940, to avoid capture by the Germans, often visited ER both in Washington and in Hyde Park. Their friendship would intensify after the war's end when they collaborated on international relief efforts and in development projects that required international cooperation. In July 1945, Juliana traveled from Ottawa to Hyde Park to pay tribute to FDR. It was an emotional reunion, prompting Juliana to write ER a letter of "apology to you for not having myself more in hand when I was with you. I struggled so hard, but I failed and I could have slapped myself for I can't think of anything to do I hate more in a situation like this" (Lash, *Love*, 399; Lash, *World*, 79–81,140; Juliana to ER, 15 July 1945, AERP).

7. On November 9, 1943, forty-four nations agreed to found the United Nations Relief and Rehabilitation Administration (UNRRA) to provide critically needed food, medicine, housing, and clothing to Allied nations in Europe and Asia. "The first and in some ways the most fruitful of broadly based international organizations" created in response to World War II, UNRRA distributed tons of food and medical supplies, erected hundreds of hospitals, restored dozens of transportation systems, and tended to roughly one million refugees. UNRRA also pledged never to use relief and rehabilitation "as a political weapon" and to refrain from using race, class, gender, creed,

and political belief as a basis for distributing supplies. To engage in such behavior, it declared, would impede delivery of basic food and supplies "necessary to sustain life" and thus violate basic human rights. At the time of this speech, Congress had not yet authorized its 1945 allocation to UNRRA (Lauren, 157).

See Document 66 for a full discussion of the funding debate.

8. No evidence exists as to which of FDR's African journeys ER references here. In 1943, FDR traveled twice to Northern Africa. In January he conferred with Churchill in Casablanca and in November, while in route to the Tehran conference, he stopped in Cairo to confer with Churchill and Nationalist Chinese president Chiang Kai-shek. Churchill and FDR then returned to Cairo after the Tehran conference to conclude their discussions (*FDRE*).

9. The *Boston Globe* quoted ER as saying that "of course" she would "like to be a delegate to an international peace conference" and, after noting the shift from her comment the previous April that "she believed herself 'too old' to sit in a peace conference," described her comment as "an exercise of the feminine privilege of changing her mind" ("Mrs. F.D. Here, Would Like to Attend Peace Parley," *Boston Globe*, 1 November 1945, LOCPC).

For a discussion of ER's earlier position see Document 2.

10. September 25, the House Ways and Means Committee voted 14 to 10 (with 4 Democrats joining 10 Republicans) to "indefinitely postpone" consideration of a modified version of Truman's Unemployment Compensation Bill, even though the Senate had voted in favor of a stronger bill earlier that session (C. P. Trussell, "House Group Votes, 14 to 10, to Shelve Jobless Pay Bill," *NYT*, 16 September 1945, 1).

11. November 5, 1941, the army and navy surgeons general sent a confidential memo to the American Red Cross stating the War Department's "desire" to use only blood collected from white donors in its treatment of wounded personnel, a policy they contended honored the wishes of the majority of those in uniform. When the NAACP objected, the Red Cross offered contradictory statements: a December 28 press release ridiculing the policy and an official response to former federal district judge William Henry Hastie's protest acknowledging the procedure and insisting that "the differences of opinions on this subject are such that they cannot be reconciled by the Red Cross." By late January 1942, the Red Cross announced that it would collect blood from both white Americans and African Americans; however, the blood would be labeled, processed, and disbursed to American soldiers on a racial basis. This second decision further angered the African American community, particularly the African American press, who, with Hastie's help, tried to get the policy changed. Despite the negative publicity, the Red Cross insisted that it had "no alternative but to recognize the existence of the point of view which, if disregarded, would militate against the effective use of plasma." The Red Cross continued the practice until 1950 when both military and Red Cross leadership agreed to remove racial categories from donor registration cards ("No Bar to Negroes as Blood Donors," *NYT*, 18 January 1942, 16; McGuire, 73–77).

12. See Document 45. Tobin, who as governor supported a state FEPC bill and described racial discrimination as a "hideous evil" and a critical threat to world peace, introduced ER as "one of the greatest ladies the world has ever known." Tobin, whose 1937 unexpected defeat of Boston mayor James Curley inspired John O'Connor's *The Last Hurrah*, lost his Senate reelection campaign. When his gubernatorial term ended, he joined the Truman administration as secretary of labor, a position he held throughout the second term. ER later wrote that he "brought a thoughtful and serious greeting to the gathering; and he was most kind to me, which I deeply appreciated" (*ANB*; "Maurice J. Tobin, Truman Aide, Dies," *NYT*, 20 July 1953, 17; *MD*, 2 November 1945).

13. See Document 45. An outspoken, independent Republican, Tobey entered the US Senate in 1938, after serving as both governor of New Hampshire and a two-term congressman, and served until his death in 1953. A member of the Senate Committee on Banking and Currency as well as

the Committee on Interstate and Foreign Commerce, Tobey reversed his prewar isolationism to become an enthusiastic member of the American delegation to the Bretton Woods conference ("Senator Charles Tobey Dies at 73," *NYT*, 25 July 1953, 1).

14. The conference ended in early October after three weeks of increasingly acrimonious meetings between the representatives of the United States, Great Britain, France, China, and the USSR. Soviet Foreign Minister Molotov adopted a new policy of "open ridicule" toward American possession of the atomic bomb. Upon meeting Byrnes at the outset of the conference, he asked the secretary of state if he had "brought the bomb" in his pocket. Shortly thereafter, he toasted Byrnes at a banquet saying, "Of course, we all have to pay great attention to what Mr. Byrnes says because the United States are the only people who are making the atomic bomb." For more on the conference, see Document 47 and Document 50 (C. L. Sulzberger, "London Peace Parley Ends with No Accord on Issues," *NYT*, 3 October 1945, 1; Hamby, *Man*, 339).

PUSHING FOR FULL EMPLOYMENT

ER grew "very anxious" as she watched Congress dismantle the twenty-one point program Truman proposed September 6. By the end of September, the Senate Finance Committee had struck down his proposal for a $25 weekly unemployment compensation, and the House Ways and Means Committee expressed its opposition to a watered-down unemployment bill. Congress had rejected Truman's budget, voting to repeal the excise tax and reduce taxes by $9,000,000 more than the White House proposed. Truman's decision to lift the wartime regulation of construction materials had backfired, sending housing prices soaring, and encouraging the construction of more profitable entertainment establishments rather than moderately priced houses for returning veterans. Strikes, both authorized and wildcat, increasingly occupied his time. Many liberals, concerned by his promotion of John Snyder[1] to director of Office of War Mobilization and Reconversion, worried that Truman could not manage the situation and foresaw "rough sledding ahead."[2]

ER had watched FDR reorganize the presidency and the White House staff to assume many legislative functions traditionally associated with Congress. From working with its staff, she knew how effective presidential aides could be in securing congressional support for embattled legislation[3] and, in the letter below, encouraged Truman to act as Roosevelt did when he became embattled.

——— 56 ———

Eleanor Roosevelt to Harry Truman

1 November 1945 [New York City]

My dear Mr. President:

I am very anxious that the Administration do all it possibly can in providing full employment.[4] It seems to me if a group of people, such as those who worked for instance for special legislation in the past, might be formed within Mr. Snyder's office.[5] They might do some very good work both for the people and with Congress to uphold your program.[6]

I know that Mr. Allen[7] works on legislation but I feel that no one man can possibly do all the work that needs to be done.

Very sincerely yours,
Eleanor Roosevelt

TLS HSTOF, HSTL

Truman assured ER that he was doing "all I can privately to get the bill out of the Committee" and wondered whether she had "anyone particular ... in mind" that could help pass his full employment proposals. Despite his protestations, Truman could not get his bill out of committee. December 5, the committee recommended its own bill, which excluded both the right to work and the federal compensatory spending necessary to achieve full employment.

_57_

Harry Truman to Eleanor Roosevelt
6 November 1945 [The White House]

Dear Mrs. Roosevelt:

Thank you for your letter of November first.

I am very hopeful that we can get the Congress to pass the major parts of the program announced in my Message to the Congress of September 6, 1945.[8] I am particularly hopeful that the Full Employment legislation will be passed, and am bending every effort to that end.[9] You probably read my public statement about it in the Wage-Price Policy speech of October 30, 1945.[10] I am doing all I can privately to get the bill out of the Committee.

I have a small group of people working on different parts of the program both in Mr. Snyder's office and out of it.[11] As you probably have learned long ago, it is not easy to get the right kind of people with the correct social point of view who have influence with those Congressmen who are blocking the program.

I wonder whether there is anyone in particular that you have in mind.

I am most anxious to get the program adopted, and would be very thankful to you for any further suggestions you can make.

I certainly hope you will continue to write me your views frankly from time to time.

With kindest regards,

Very sincerely,
Harry S. Truman

TLS AERP, FDRL

---

1. John W. Snyder (1895–1985), a conservative St. Louis banker with whom ER had clashed when he served as Jesse Jones's deputy at the Reconstruction Finance Corporation, returned to Washington when his old friend Harry Truman appointed him director of the Office of War Mobilization and Reconversion. Opposed to any extension of New Deal policies, Snyder "vehemently" clashed with other Truman appointees who favored liberal policies, advising the president that any "extension of the New Deal would be disastrous for the country and politically harmful to Truman" (Donovan, 109, 111).

2. Donovan, 118–22.

3. FDR believed that the president must initiate policy rather than merely react to congressional initiatives. In the early days of the New Deal, FDR sent Jim Farley, Tommy Corcoran, and "a host of aides" to lobby Congress so often that congressional Democrats complained of the practice's unseemliness to Vice President John Garner only to have him reject their characterization. "Now look here," he told disgruntled party members, "it doesn't matter what kind of fool you think he is; he's your fool as long as he's President and leader of your party." As he encountered more opposition, FDR decided to reorganize his team into "a more compact organization." In 1939, Executive Order 8248 created the Executive Office of the President, gave the president six administrative assistants who possessed "a passion for anonymity," and placed six key agencies, such as the Bureau of the Budget and the White House Office, under his control. This reorganization, while helpful to the president's lobbying efforts, did not consolidate all of his congressional team into one office.

For example, Tommy Corcoran and Benjamin Cohen continued to operate out of their respective agencies (Patterson, *Conservatism*, 40; Leuchtenburg, *New Deal*, 327, 340–41).

4. See *n*1 Document 40 for discussion of Truman's original proposal. By November, the Senate, after extensive hearings and floor debate, passed S.280, a bill that required the government to promote, but not ensure, full employment, by a 70–21 vote. Sen. Glen Taylor (D-ID), one of the bill's original sponsors, saw this as a bitter defeat, saying the amendment "waters [the government's budgetary commitment to full employment] down until it would say, 'We will see that you have a job if something does not interfere.'" The House Committee on Expenditures began hearings on three full employment bills September 25. Truman, Snyder, and other presidential aides knew the House would support a bill more conservative than the amended bill the Senate sent to it for consideration. The House hearings ended a week after ER sent this letter (Bailey, 115–25, 153–54).

5. In addition to directing the reconversion office, Snyder coordinated, at Truman's request, the four-person cabinet lobbying team (Treasury Secretary Fred Vinson, Commerce Secretary Henry Wallace, Labor Secretary Lewis Schwellenbach, and Agriculture Secretary Clinton Anderson) assigned to secure passage of the president's full employment proposal. However, as Steven Bailey observed, Snyder's "hostility to the principles of a liberal bill was a major breach in the phalanx of Executive pressure" (Bailey, 162).

6. See *n*1 Document 40.

7. George E. Allen (1896–1973), the DNC secretary whose friendship with Truman began when FDR asked him "to keep an eye on" Truman during the 1944 campaign, had a reputation among Democrats as a crass, "back-slapping fixer." He first joined the Truman administration as an unpaid advisor charged with assessing various plans for terminating war-related agencies. His penchant for self-promotion and unsavory business practices undercut his effectiveness with Congress. Aware of the difficulties Allen presented, Truman kept working with him, out of his deep affection for Allen's mentor, Pat Harriman. In the winter of 1946, Truman removed Allen from his informal position on the president's staff by appointing him to the Reconstruction Finance Commission (Hamby, *Man*, 305; Donovan, 177).

8. Truman already knew that the original bill would not pass. Two weeks earlier, on October 25, he met with committee members Carter Manasco (D-AL) and William Whittington (D-MS) and agreed not to insist upon the principle, or inclusion, of the phrase "full employment." The president agreed to their concessions on the advice of Secretary Vinson, who warned that any bill with this phrase would die in committee and the administration's best chance at strengthening the bill lay with the conference committee (Bailey, 161–62).

9. That week Budget Bureau director Harold Smith and Secretaries Schwellenbach, Vinson, Wallace, and Anderson appeared before the committee declaring their support for the administration's original full employment legislation. Snyder, who also testified that week, wilted under the committee's questioning to the extent that *Collier's* coverage of his testimony concluded "Snyder came to testify in favor of the government's Full Employment Bill and was maneuvered into a position where he was talking *against* it" (Bailey, 162–63).

10. Stressing the necessity that Congress "speedily adopt some effective legislation which embodies the principles underlying full employment," Truman denounced the congressional delay:

> The American people are entitled to know now that this Government stands for prosperity and jobs—not depression and relief. Passage of a full employment bill will give the American people this assurance.
>
> The responsibility for the damaging delay in enacting this legislation is definitely at the door of the Committee on Expenditures in the Executive Departments of the House of Representatives ("President Truman's Broadcast Address Explaining His New Policy on Wages and Prices," *NYT*, 31 October 1945, 14).

11. See *n*5. Vinson's special assistant, Ansel Luxford, Snyder's special assistant, Creekmore Fath, and Thomas Emerson, general counsel to the Office of War Mobilization and Reconversion, often acted as the administration's chief lobbyists on full employment (Bailey, 162).

Interceding for Refugee Aid

ER often acted as an intermediary, either carrying or seconding requests from organizational leaders to administration officials. In this case, ER's friend, the philanthropist Adele Rosenwald Levy (1892–1960),[1] asked ER to help her get permission to travel to Europe to investigate conditions facing Jewish refugees. ER wrote the State Department to underscore her support for Levy and her work. The State Department approved the trip and Levy traveled to Europe, returning to New York at the end of January, 1946, and then commenced the fund-raising campaign for the United Jewish Appeal. In November of 1946, Levy again successfully sought ER's assistance with the State and War Departments for another trip to Europe to follow up on the conditions of Jewish refugees.[2]

58

Eleanor Roosevelt to Dean Acheson
15 November 1945 [New York City]

Dear Mr. Acheson:

Mrs. David Levy, who was Adele Rosenwald, is extremely anxious to go for The Joint Distribution Committee,[3] to Europe to see at first hand the conditions of Jewish people, and return in order to help in their fund raising campaign.

It will be an extremely valuable service if she can go because we are going to need all of the private aid possible if there is not to be death and pestilance rampant throughout Europe this winter. The Jewish people are the hardest hit of them all.[4]

Mrs. Levy has tried to get the assurance of a priority on her return trip, and so far has been unsuccessful.

If you think it as important as I do, could you talk to the War Department and arrange it? She would have to go soon in order to be able to see what she must see and get back by the time the fund raising campaign starts in early February.

Very cordially yours,

TLc AERP, FDRL

---

1. Levy devoted the majority of her postwar efforts to raising funds to assist displaced persons through the United Jewish Appeal, the Citizens Committee on Displaced Persons, and the Jewish Joint Distribution Committee, organizations in which she held executive posts and which ER supported. In addition to their professional working relationship, including their support of the Wiltwyck School for Boys, Levy and ER maintained a close, personal friendship until Levy's death (*EJW*; Lash, *Love*, 349, 351; "Mrs. David M. Levy Dead at 67; Civic and Social Service Leader," *NYT*, 13 March 1960, 86).

2. ER to Dean Acheson, 15 and 26 November 1946, AERP; Dean Acheson to ER, 19 November 1946, AERP; ER to Robert Patterson, 15 November 1946, AERP; Robert Patterson to ER, 27 November 1946, AERP; "Child Care Abroad Still at Low Ebb," *NYT*, 31 January 1946, 10.

3. The American Jewish Joint Distribution Committee, founded in 1914 to aid Palestinian Jews, assisted more than 700,000 Jews, mostly in displaced persons (DP) camps, following World War

II. The organization helped Jewish refugees by providing direct aid as well as helping to reunite families, establishing job training programs, and promoting Jewish religious and cultural traditions within the DP camps. In June of 1945, the committee joined with the United Palestine Appeal and the National Refugee Service under the umbrella group United Jewish Appeal for Refugees Overseas Needs and Palestine in their efforts to raise $75,000,000 to aid Jewish refugees and displaced persons in Europe ("3 Jewish Groups Settle Dispute," *NYT*, 4 June 1945, 32; "3 Jewish Agencies Back United Appeal," *NYT*, 11 June 1945, 18; "Jewish Children Out of Nazi Camps," *NYT*, 24 August 1945, 6; American Jewish Joint Distribution Committee, http://www.jdc.org/who_history.html, accessed 22 September 2005).

4. Approximately six million Jews perished in the Holocaust, and following the liberation of the last concentration camps in May of 1945, Jews continued to struggle in Europe. In addition to continued violence against their communities, European Jews needed both direct relief aid and assistance finding their family members. Many of the survivors, particularly from eastern Europe, remained in displaced persons camps, and as winter approached, many worried how the needs of the displaced persons population would be met, given uncertain food and fuel supplies. See *n2* Document 74 (Gilbert, 318–22, 329–30).

On Winning the Peace

In mid-November 1945, ER traveled to Chicago to celebrate the founding of Roosevelt College,[1] an institution born out of its faculty's opposition to racial and ethnic discrimination.

In November 1944, the governing board of Central YMCA College instructed its president, Edward J. Sparling, to impose religious, ethnic, and racial quotas on its student body and to prohibit the classroom discussion of "controversial subjects." Sparling, who earlier battled the YMCA's practice of maintaining an all-white swimming complex, refused to conduct the surveys necessary to establish the demographics the board requested. After the board told him his "qualifications" did not meet presidential standards, he resigned under protest April 17, 1945. An angry faculty, after voting no confidence in the board, then voted 62 to 1 to sever ties with the college and follow Sparling to a not-yet-operational college. That afternoon, Sparling and his colleagues founded Roosevelt College "even though they had no student body in place, no building or equipment, no library, no accreditation, and no endowment."

From its outset, the college committed itself to being open to all students, declaring in its charter that its mission was "to provide educational opportunities to persons of both sexes and of various races on equal terms." It admitted African American, Jewish, and Japanese students at a time when law and custom excluded them from other institutions, and it welcomed many children of working-class immigrants from Eastern Europe. Its faculty included African Americans, Asians, and European emigres.[2] ER, who saw this as a "living memorial" to FDR,[3] joined author Thomas Mann, CIO president Philip Murray, and philanthropist Marshall Field on the college board and helped recruit other board members.[4]

59

Founders' Day Dinner Address, Roosevelt College
16 November 1945 [Chicago]

Honorable Mayor, distinguished guests, ladies and gentlemen:

It is a great pleasure to be here tonight and to dedicate Roosevelt College. I had a most interesting time this afternoon going to the College and seeing education which is being carried on in a really democratic way—a faculty and students working together and equally enthusiastic about democracy in education.[5]

I could not help thinking that it would have been a most interesting experience to my husband. He used to say that he would like to start a school; and I think that it would have had some things in common with Roosevelt College, as it was evident that they really loved the things that they were doing. And after all, education is at its best when everyone is so enthusiastic about the work that they're doing; that instead of being work, it's pleasure. That was the way you felt, not only the students, but the faculty felt, about their work at the College.

I like to think that when you live democracy, as they are living it there, that you are probably setting a pattern and doing the best kind of teaching because you're showing your city and your state and your nation that actually democracy in education can be a fact. Here it's working; the very things that people tell you won't work do work, and the people who make them work are enjoying it.

One of the boys who introduced me this afternoon was a little nervous, I think, but did a very good job. He had such pride in what his school was doing. And when you get that sense of pride, you know that real democracy is at work. And I think in this country that the best thing we can do today is to show the world that we here can really have in action the ideal that we have talked about and written about and sometimes forgotten, but that we can really have it work. And it can be done by young and old together.

Democracy is something which we have always talked a great deal about. But we've always known that we didn't really have a true democracy in all the things that we believed democracy should represent. But we knew that we had an ideal and that when we were ready, we would work to achieve it. Well, nothing made us hurry.

But now, we have to hurry, because the world has changed. The war has changed the whole world; and from now on we who talked about democracy have got to live it, because we know that unless we prove by our example to the world that democracy is not just words, it's something that through education you can achieve, then the world will have no proof that democracy is a possibility and that the things which make us live in peace together are possible, not only in the United States but in the world as a whole.

Here in this great city you have many, many races, many religions; and in Roosevelt College those races and those religions will meet. They will work together, and it will be an example of what can be achieved by cooperation.

I'm tempted sometimes to think that though we have been strong in the military way, and we have to be strong in the economic way, we also have to be strong, I think, in a spiritual way; because we have to lead the world and we know that we've built up here the strongest production center of the whole world. We know that we have today the greatest military power in the world. But sometimes I think we're a little appalled at the fact that we have to have the spiritual strength to lead the world, that we have to prove here that the world can live in peace. We are the proving ground. If we can do it, then perhaps the world can do it.

And that is something which is going to require education in many, many ways. It's not going to be enough in the future to have people who know how to make war. We're going to have to have people, too, who know how to cultivate an atmosphere in the world which leads to peace; because peace, as we all know, is just as hard to attain as victory in a war. We had to give the best that was in us to win the war.

Sometimes I wonder if we're going to have the courage and the strength to sustain our effort to win the peace. It takes just as much determination to work for peace as it does to win a war. And now we have before us that long-time struggle of teaching our people and teaching the world how we can live together and exemplify the great democratic principles.

I was asked a question the other day in a forum in Walter Reed Hospital,[6] and I've talked about it several times since because I can't get it out of my own mind. A wounded boy looked up at me and said: "My wounds are hardly healed, and yet on every hand I hear it said that we will have to go to war again, that one of our allies is likely to be our next enemy. And here at home we men who fought for what we hoped to find, a better world to live in, are seeing nothing but dissension, people quarelling with each other over how they will do this and that. I sometimes wonder, Mrs. Roosevelt, whether it was worth fighting the war."

That's a pretty tough question to have a boy ask you. And all that I could think of was, "You fought and you won the war, so that we and you together might have the opportunity to work to build the better world that you dreamed of as you fought the war." But I think we have to do a little more than just talk about it. I think we have to do some very realistic education. And one of the first things, perhaps, is to face the fact of our own strength. Why should we be afraid of any other nation in the world? Why should we swallow a tale that perhaps we may have to fight one of our allies? Can't we remember that it was our planes and our tanks and our guns and our ammunition that helped all of our allies to stop the Germans, to stop the Japanese?[7]

We have, it seems to me, very short memories. If anyone should be afraid, it is of us they might well be afraid, for we have proved our strength in war. Now we have to prove that we can work together with all the peoples of the world where they have good will that we can build for peace, that we can educate our young people and that our old people can face a period which required immediate action, can face that period unafraid, can prepare to help the rest of the world and do it without fear, do it with good will; and they sense that our own strength and our own example can give the rest of the world the hope that will lead us all to peace.

TSp RUA, ICRC

------

1. Roosevelt College merged with the Chicago School of Music in 1954, reorganizing itself as Roosevelt University. Five years later, the university rededicated the institution to honor both Franklin and Eleanor Roosevelt (Lynn Weiner, "Roosevelt University," *Encyclopedia of Chicago*, http://www.encyclopedia.chicagohistory.org/pages/1093.html, accessed 22 September 2005).

2. Gross, *Roosevelt University*, 4.

3. "Mrs. Roosevelt to Dedicate New College," *Roosevelt College News*, 15 November 1945, vol. 1, 1, Roosevelt College Archives, RUA, ICRC.

4. ER's friends Marian Anderson, Pearl Buck, Ralph Bunche, Albert Einstein, Gunnar Myrdal, and Albert Schweitzer also served as early members of the Board of Directors ("History of Roosevelt University," http://www.roosevelt.edu, accessed 25 May 2005).

5. The college pioneered democratic decision making within its various governing bodies. Faculty, students, and alumni held voting positions on the University Senate and the Board of Trustees; faculty elected deans and the president. Not only did it admit anyone who applied and maintained academic standing, it also modeled its class meeting times around the work schedules of its students by holding small classes from early morning to late evening hours as well as on weekends. Refusing to build classes around lectures, the college preferred to use experimental learning practices and Socratic discussion models ("History of Roosevelt University," http://www.roosevelt.edu, accessed 25 May 2005).

6. October 23, ER attended an open forum with wounded army veterans at Walter Reed Hospital, the military's premier medical facility, in Washington, DC (*MD*, 26 October 1945).

7. During World War II, the Lend-Lease program supplied arms and munitions to Great Britain and the Soviet Union who fought as allies against Nazi Germany (*OCAMH*).

Assessing the Truman Administration

By late November, in addition to widespread labor unrest and consumer dissatisfaction with rising housing and rent prices, Truman, who received conflicting advice on price controls from OPA director Chester Bowles and OWMR director John Snyder on how best to manage prices and ration supplies, now had to manage conflicting demands on American farm products while deciding how best to administer foreign aid. Should price controls remain on farm staples? If not, how would the public, many of whom resented controls on their wages, react when they had to pay more for food? Furthermore, if rationing continued, how could America respond to the cries for humanitarian aid from Europe, where deprivation bordered on starvation, when the public questioned whether or not there was an adequate food supply for the United States? Lastly, how much debt should the United States assume as it lent funds to Great Britain, France, Yugoslavia? In short, the problems confronting Truman clearly showed "the difficulties of satisfying domestic consumers while meeting larger national obligations and moral imperatives" and the difficulties of questioning "liberal efforts at economic management that generally had served the country well in depression and war."[1]

November 4, ER's good friend Bernard Baruch released his letter to Representative Albert Gore (D-TN), who had requested the financier's advice on how best to evaluate the conflicting demands on the American economy. Baruch argued that the only way to "win the race between price and living costs" occurring at home and abroad was "to get an over-all picture of the balance sheet of the country—a kind of inventory that would show" the national debt and monies committed to Bretton Woods and UNRAA agreements, estimate the nation's productive capabilities, and "survey all our mineral, agricultural and other natural resources." Once this survey was completed, the nation could best decide how to manage wage, price, and production controls and the increasing international demand for American financial aid.[2]

ER thought this recommendation so vital that she devoted much of her November 14 column to Baruch's "very sensible suggestion" that "before we make loans to other nations, we should know exactly what our own resources for the future are going to be." A survey of this kind seems to me important," she wrote, "but it is difficult to estimate what you can do in the future, since the work of our engineers and scientists is one of the unpredictable elements in the picture. None of us knows what might be worked out by cooperation with other nations." She thought "the suggestion … that a world conference be held, at which world resources would be considered and future plans made" a smart one because it could lead to "better production in many lands and better trade facilities … planned to increase the prosperity of many nations. That is almost like world pioneering," she concluded, "and ought to appeal to the adventurous spirit in our own county."[3]

The following week she made the same suggestion to President Truman.

_____ 60 _____

Eleanor Roosevelt to Harry Truman

20 November 1945 [New York City]

Dear Mr. President:

I hope you will forgive my writing you this letter, but I, like a great many other citizens, have been deeply concerned about the situation as it seems to be developing both at home and abroad. I have a deep sense that we have an obligation, first of all, to solve our own problems at home, because our failure must of necessity, take away hope from the other nations of the world who have so much more to contend with than we have.

It seems to me, therefore, that we must get to work.

The suggestion that was made the other day that a survey of our resources be made, on which we base not only our national economy, but what we lend to other nations, would seem to me sound, if the person making the investigation had sufficient standing to be accepted by management and labor as well.

In situations of this kind, my husband some times turned to Mr. Bernard M. Baruch, because of his wealth of experience and his standing with the industrialists of the country. At the same time, I think that even the young labor leaders, like Walter Reuther and James Carey,[4] believe in his integrity. If it could be possible to get the Detroit situation started up by giving both management and labor something so they would at least agree to go to work until, let us say, next October on condition that Mr. Baruch was asked to gather a staff of experts, I feel he would consult with both sides as he always has in the past.[5]

If there was a limit for the time of the report, I think labor would not feel that it was being taken for a ride.

When it comes to lending money, it seems to me that we should lend other nations equally. If we lend only to Great Britain, we enter into an economic alliance against other nations, and our hope for the future lies in joint cooperation.[6] We should only lend in small amounts at present. Until we get into production we can not sell any of these countries in great quantities and there is no value in their having the money unless they can use it. They would also profit by this type of survey and we would be making no promises which we could not carry out.

If you talk to Mr. Baruch, I think you must do so only if you yourself, feel confidence in him, because once you accept him you will find, as my husband did, that many of those around you will at once, cast doubts upon whatever he does,[7] but that would be true even if the job were given to the Angel Gabriel.

I think Mr. Baruch has proved in the past, his ability to see things on a large scale, and where financial matters are concerned, he certainly knows the world picture which is what we need at the present time.

I am very much distressed that Great Britain has made us take a share in another investigation of the few Jews remaining in Europe. If they are not to be allowed to enter Palestine, then certainly they could have been apportioned among the different United Nations and we would not have to continue to have on our consciences, the death of at least fifty of these poor creatures daily.[8]

The question between Palestine and the Arabs, of course, has always been complicated by the oil deposits,[9] and I suppose it always will. I do not happen to be a Zionist, and I know what a difference there is among such Jews as consider themselves nationals of other countries and not a separate nationality.

Great Britain is always anxious to have some one pull her chestnuts out of the fire, and though I am very fond of the British individually and like a great many of them, I object very much to being used by them. I am enclosing a copy of a letter bearing on the subject.[10]

Lastly, I am deeply troubled about China. Unless we can stop the civil war there by moral pressure and not by the use of military force, and insist that Generalissimo Chiang give wider representation to all Chinese groups, which will allow the middle of the road Democratic League to grow, I am very much afraid that continued war there may lead us to general war again.[11]

Being a strong nation and having the greatest physical, mental and spiritual strength today, gives us a tremendous responsibility. We can not use our strength to coerce, but if we are big enough, I think we can lead. It will require, however, great vision and understanding on our part. The first and foremost thing, it seems to me, is the setting of our own house in order, and so I have made the suggestion contained in the first part of this letter. I shall quite understand, however, if with the broader knowledge which is yours, you decide against it, but I would not have a quiet conscience unless I wrote you what I feel in these difficult days.

    With every good wish, I am,

Very cordially yours,
Eleanor Roosevelt

TLS HSTOF, HSTL

Truman responded to each point ER raised.

61

Harry Truman to Eleanor Roosevelt

26 November 1945 [The White House]

Dear Mrs. Roosevelt:

    Thanks very much for your letter of the twentieth, to which I have given much thought.

    I have particularly had under consideration for some time the suggestion about a study of our national resources with a view to what we can afford to do. I think that it is a very good suggestion, and expect to take some action on it.[12]

    I doubt very much whether that kind of a study, however, would have much to do with the immediate situation in Detroit, although it is barely possible that it might influence the ultimate conclusion in a great many labor situations.

    With respect to our foreign loans, I am sure that you have a deep appreciation of the reasons for our policy. We feel that it is necessary not only for the welfare of Great Britain but for our own welfare and for the welfare of the entire world that the British economy be not allowed to disintegrate. Equally important is the necessity of reestablishing world trade by helping the British expand their own trade instead of taking refuge in a tightened sterling bloc.

    What we hope to do for Great Britain we also hope to do eventually for Russia and our other Allies, for it will be impossible to continue a stable world economy if a large part of the world has a disordered economy which would result in bitter trade rivalries and impassable barriers.

    I am very hopeful that we really shall be able to work out something in Palestine which will be of lasting benefit. At the same time we expect to continue to do what we can to get as many Jews as possible into Palestine as quickly as possible, pending any final settlement.

    In China, as you know, a definite commitment was made by the three major powers to support the Central Government in disarming and removing the Japanese troops now in China. I know you realize how important to the future peace in the Far East and throughout the world is this objective. All of us want to see a Chinese Government eventually installed and maintained by free elections—one which will include all democratic elements. I do not see how we can do that unless we first help clear the land of the Japanese aggressors.[13]

    All of these things take a great deal of time as you know from personal experience. I am sure that it was the late President's experience, as it is mine, that we are very apt to meet criticism in the press and often in the Congress from those who are unfamiliar with the facts and to whom the facts cannot be disclosed. He often talked to me about how difficult that part of the Presidency was. However, I feel proud that our objectives are the same as those which actuated your late husband. Indeed I have no aim other than to carry them out.

I want you to know how much I appreciate your writing to me from time to time, and hope you will continue to do so.

With kindest regards,

Very sincerely,
Harry S. Truman

TLS AERP, FDRL

————————

1. Hamby, *Man*, 369–71.

2. Bernard Baruch to Albert Gore, reprinted in "Baruch Advocates We Take New Inventory Before New Loans," *NYT*, 5 November 1945, 1.

3. *MD*, 14 November 1945.

4. James B. Carey (1911–1973), secretary-treasurer of the Congress of Industrial Organizations, 1938–1955, also served as one of labor's representatives to Roosevelt's Office of Production Management, the National War Mediation Board, and the National War Labor Board. Beginning in 1946, Truman appointed Carey to several high-profile positions: the Presidential Commission on Civil Rights, the Presidential Non-Partisan Commission on Foreign Aid, and the Labor Advisory Committee to the Office of Defense Mobilization. See Biographical Portraits for Walter Reuther ("James B. Carey Is Dead," *NYT*, 12 September 1973, 50).

5. Tensions between GM and UAW intensified in the three weeks after Truman committed himself to "free and fair collective bargaining" in an October 30 radio address. October 21, UAW vice president Walter Reuther wrote GM president C. E. Wilson asking him to "personally enter into negotiations with us in accordance with the President's mandate." Wilson responded by offering a much smaller increase than the 30 percent the UAW demanded and by refusing to open the GM books to arbitrators or promise that it would not raise prices to meet the wage increase. Truman then announced a National Labor Management Conference would be held at the White House November 5. Truman, after lecturing the attendees on the need to avert strikes, turned the meeting over to commerce secretary Henry Wallace and labor secretary Lewis Schwellenbach and left. By November 20, the largest strike in world history seemed imminent. UAW set a twenty-four-hour deadline for GM to say whether or not the company would agree to arbitration and prepared its 350,000 members in 102 plants in 20 states to prepare for the strike. The strike began the next day and continued for another 112 days.

Baruch, who directed the War Industries Board in the First World War and who rejected FDR's offer to head the Office of Economic Stabilization, held no formal position in Roosevelt's administration, preferring instead to act as a sounding board on wartime economic proposals presented to the president (Louis Stark, "Labor, Industry Back Truman on Bargaining," *NYT*, 4 November 1945, 1; Lichtenstein, 232; Walter Ruch, "Showdown Close in Auto Pay Fight," *NYT*, 17 November 1945, 12; Walter Ruch, "Union Demands G.M. Arbitrate," *NYT*, 20 November, 1945, 1).

6. After World War II ended, the Lend-Lease program, which provided loans to Great Britain and the USSR expired, and in its wake, both Great Britain and the USSR turned to the United States for financial aid. Truman sent Undersecretary of State William Clayton to London to investigate conditions there. Byrnes immediately rejected Hopkins's proposed $10 billion loan to the Soviets and argued against any aid going to Russia. France also requested aid. By fall, Truman had decided to lend money to Britain only and worried that Congress would reject any aid linked in any way to Russia. American and British economic experts entered into negotiations September 1945, and

reached agreement on a $3.75 billion loan at 2 percent interest in early December. Although the Soviets received assurance that they would receive a billion dollar loan from the Export-Import Bank in Washington, the loan never materialized (Hamby, *Man*, 352; "Experts Discuss British Loan Need," *NYT*, 11 September 1945, 13; Brooks Atkinson, "Soviet Loan Proposal Poses Big Problem," *NYT*, 21 September 1945, 6; John Crider, "British Get 55-Year 2% Loan," *NYT*, 7 December 1945, 1; John Crider, "Fund Established," *NYT*, 28 December 1945, 1).

7. Baruch, who had not supported FDR in 1932 and who had a gift for self-promotion, remained a controversial figure within FDR's circle, despite his placement of key aides Hugh Johnson and George Peek in high-level positions. For example, when FDR asked him to direct the War Production Board in 1943, Donald Nelson objected and secured the appointment for himself (*FDRE*; Freidel, *Rendevous*, 421).

8. At Potsdam, Truman prepared proposals for Churchill asking him to lift Great Britian's immigration quota and permit 100,000 Jewish refugees to enter Palestine. Clement Attlee, who replaced Churchill during the conference, requested time to study the proposal. When Truman returned home, he announced that the United States favored the admission of "as many Jews as possible into Palestine," thus prompting the public discussion of FDR's correspondence with Saudi Arabian King Ibn Saud. (See Document 54.) In September, Truman sent Attlee a letter hand carried by Byrnes recommending the granting of 100,000 immigration visas. Attlee responded saying that any such action "would probably cause serious disturbances throughout the Middle East, involving a large military contingent, and would arouse widespread anxiety in India." He then suggested a bi-national study of the immigration issue. On November 13, President Truman announced that the United States would accept British foreign secretary Ernest Bevin's offer to form the Anglo-American Committee of Inquiry to examine the problem of Jewish refugees in Europe and the situation in Palestine. The outcry from prominent Democrats, rabbis, and New Yorkers was immediate and furious (John H. Crider, "Truman Discloses U.S. Palestine Role," *NYT*, 14 November 1945, 13; Donovan, 312–15).

9. Although geologists speculated that crude oil deposits might be present in undrilled areas around the Dead Sea, Palestine's central link to concerns about oil was its strategic location on the Mediterranean Sea. In 1945, American and British oil companies began plans for two oil pipelines through Palestine—one line from Saudi Arabia and another from Iraq (Julian Louis Meltzer, "Palestine's Fate Is Linked to Oil," *NYT*, 3 May 1944, 10; "Iraq to Get Big Pipe Line," *NYT*, 13 June 1945, 4; "Palestine Oil Line to Be Approved," *WP*, 24 October 1945, 10; "Ibn Saud Won't Use Oil Rights to Force Action Against Jews," *WP*, 2 December 1945, B2).

10. A notation on the document reveals that the "letter never made it to the file"; thus its author and contents are unknown.

11. Although a truce was reached by Chiang Kai-shek, leader of the Chinese Nationalists, and Mao Zedong, the Communist leader, in order to defend China against the Japanese, the relationship between the parties was tenuous during World War II. Following the end of the war, the two parties planned talks that would include the Democratic League, a coalition of smaller political parties within China, but these plans were abandoned when open conflict erupted between Nationalists and Communists over control of northern China ("Agreement in China," *NYT*, 7 October 1945, E2; Ralph, et al., 733–36).

12. Truman did not have the resources study conducted.

13. The Allies, including the USSR who signed a treaty with him in August 1945, officially recognized Chiang Kai-shek as the leader of China. By fall 1945, Japanese troops controlled most of northeastern and eastern China, from Manchuria to Canton, while Mao's Communist troops held the other northern regions. Americans then transported Chiang's Nationalist troops into Communist-controlled northern China, in order to coordinate the surrender of the remaining Japanese troops in the area. Although American policy was to stay out of the internal affairs of

China, Mao's Communists charged that by facilitating the relocation of Nationalist troops into northern cities, the United States was interfering in China's domestic politics (Brooks Atkinson, "Chungking Makes Deal with Russia," *NYT*, 19 August 1945, E5; Reynolds, 42; "China Reds Charge Meddling by U.S.," *NYT*, 20 October 1945, 6; "Chiang Said to Get Manchuria Permit," *NYT*, 14 November 1945, 1).

ON TRUMAN'S NATIONAL
HEALTH INSURANCE PROPOSAL

November 19, Truman sent Congress a detailed message outlining his plan for compulsory national health insurance. Refuting Republican claims that this plan meant "socialized medicine," the president argued that while all workers would be required to contribute to the common fund, patients and physicians would continue to have the freedom of choice they had prior to his proposal. The response to his proposal was swift, passionate, and, primarily a "partisan row." ER once again lent her support to the proposal, this time using My Day and a full-page *New York Times* advertisement to encourage citizen advocacy on its behalf.[1]

62

My Day [excerpt]
24 November 1945

HYDE PARK, Friday—I have signed today an endorsement of President Truman's health message.[2] There is only one point that seems to me not quite to coincide with our practice in other things. For instance, you do not pay school taxes only up to a certain percentage of your income. You pay taxes according to the size of your income. Furthermore, no matter what your income may be, you can send your children to public school, and it seems to me that the same should apply in the case of these new health services. The proposed tax is to be four per cent on incomes up to $3600 a year. No matter how much income we have, only that amount, apparently, is taxed for this plan; and only people with that income, or less, are expected to make use of it.

Unless the health needs of the people as a whole can be met by this tax on a portion of the national income, it would seem to me entirely fair to expect to be taxed in proportion to our income, just as we are taxed for education. In some places the school tax may be based on real estate instead of income, but at least everyone pays the same ratio to his possessions. It seems to me that those of us who have more income or more land, whichever the basis of the tax, should pay regardless of whether we use the health plan or not—on the theory that all citizens are entitled to take advantage of any plan which is for the good of the citizens in general. If they do not take advantage of it, that is their choice.

This does not seem to me to have anything whatever to do with socialized medicine;[3] and I am particularly glad that the proposed plan recognizes the need for giving help to our medical schools, since research and education are essential to keeping up the standards of medical care. This may make it possible for young doctors to work in rural communities, where medical care has been very inadequate in the past.

Medical practice is so varied in a rural community that it probably would give invaluable experience to any young man who was willing to put in up to five years in doing this kind of work. It is probably the most exacting kind of work that can be done, and yet it might reach for the first time sections of our country which, from the health point of view, have been almost totally neglected in the past.[4]

TMsex AERP, FDRL

---

1. "Text of the President's Health Message Calling for Compulsory Medical Insurance," *NYT*, 20 November 1945, 13; Edward T. Follard, "Truman Plan for Health Insurance Starts a Row," *NYT*, 30 November 1945, 1; see Document 42.

Following this message Senator Wagner (D-NY) and Representative Dingell (D-MI) introduced bills outlining the president's message. See also the Wagner-Murray-Dingell Bill in *n*5 Document 42 (Felix Belair, Jr., "Truman Asks Law to Force Insuring of Nation's Health," *NYT*, 20 November 1945, 1).

2. The petition declared that "President Truman's Health Plan would increase productivity, reduce disease, save lives. We have read his message to Congress. We endorse it ... We urge Congress to prompt action." It then discussed the need for "a national health plan," why it should "be administered locally," why federal aid should go "through" the states, and why the plan was "not 'socialized' medicine." More than 100 individuals signed (and financed the publication of) the petition. Those joining ER in supporting the petition included the presidents of Sears and Roebuck, RCA, Mount Holyoke College, the National Farmers Union, and the American Civil Liberties Union; Mayor La Guardia and Mayor-elect O'Dwyer; noted academics from Harvard, Columbia, Fisk, and University of Chicago; as well as philanthropists, actors, doctors, and writers. For the full text of the petition and its supporters, see page 17 of the December 10, 1945, *New York Times*.

3. Although Truman's health insurance plan enjoyed much support, it was consistently met with the outcry that such legislation was in essence socialized medicine. Most notably, the American Medical Association interpreted compulsory health insurance as such, warning that it was a step toward totalitarianism ("191 Leaders Back Health Program," *NYT*, 1 December 1945, 24; Hamby, *Man*, 497).

4. The final paragraph of this column discussed the Salvation Army's 80th anniversary celebration in Kansas City. ER concluded her brief discussion of its activities by saying, "I think the thing I like about them above all else is that there is no one whom they look upon as unredeemble!"

As the following front-page article by Lester Allen illustrates, the comments ER made during question and answer sessions often received more attention than the speech she delivered.

63

"Mrs. Roosevelt Hits Mme. Chiang
Says She Could Talk About Democracy but
Didn't Know How to Live It
Cites Hotel Incidents"

The Boston Post 5 December 1945

FORT DEVENS, Dec. 4—Declaring that Mme. Chiang Kai-shek,[1] wife of the generalissimo,[2] a guest at the White House during her American visit, could talk very convincingly of democracy but did not know how to live it, Mrs. Eleanor Roosevelt, widow of the President, told wounded GIs at Lovell General Hospital, Fort Devens,[3] today, that wherever she went Mme. Chiang was in fear of her life and was flanked by a retinue of 40 persons.

Talking to a recreation hall filled with wounded veterans of the Pacific and European theatres, Mrs. Roosevelt gave her astonishingly frank criticism of Mme. Chiang during a question period when a veteran asked her how the civil war in China differed from the civil war in Spain.[4]

"China has never been a united nation," Mrs. Roosevelt said. "The Chinese people have still to learn how to live with one another as a unified people. I noticed this particularly in my talks with Mme. Chiang. She is two different people. She could talk very convincingly about democracy and its aims and ideals and be perfectly charming, but she hasn't any idea how to live it."

Mrs. Roosevelt whose visit to Lovell General Hospital was for the purpose of talking and meeting wounded GIs, declared that wherever Mme. Chiang went she traveled with a retinue of 40 people. "She couldn't understand how I dared to travel around with only my secretary as a companion. She wanted to know who answered the telephone for us, who packed our bags and who bought our tickets and was amazed when I told her that we did those things for ourselves. I visited her once in a hospital in New York and when she learned I had traveled to the hospital by subway she said, 'How do you dare do that? You are the President's wife.' I told her that I was just a private citizen and that no one would harm me or molest me."

She also described how Mme. Chiang had hotel lobbies cleared before she would pass through because she feared harm. "She told me that communists were very dangerous people, and she couldn't comprehend how I dared to go around unattended when there were communists in this country. It old her that communists here are a very small minority and that there is not the slightest danger from them so long as a democratic form of government meets the needs of the people."

Mentioned as a possible candidate for the United States Senate from New York, Mrs. Roosevelt declared that she has no desire to enter political life, and said, "I had heard that story, and I have no intention of entering politics."[5]

In behalf of the wounded GIs Mrs. Roosevelt was greeted by PFC Hong O. Wong of 158 Huntington ave., Boston, who was seriously wounded by a mortar shell on Okinawa with the 96th Division, and PFC Vincent F. Noe of 39 Wall st., West End, who was seriously wounded in the Saar Basin, where he was captured by the Germans while fighting with the 94th Division. Wong, born in Canton, China, and Noe, born in Syracuse, Sicily, told Mrs. Roosevelt of their birthplace and she said, "Well, you are both fine American boys."

The wounded men, many of whom had to be assisted to the recreation hall to see Mrs. Roosevelt, put some pointed questions to her when she invited questions from the floor. One GI asked her if the United States need fear the Soviet Union as a future aggressor.

"Has it ever occurred to you," said Mrs. Roosevelt, "that Russia might reasonably be afraid of us? She has never started a war, but has always gone to war to defend herself from invasion. Actually, Russia is at the same period of economic development that we passed through 100 years ago, and the Russians want to have peace in which to develop their nation and obtain the good things of life which we now have."

After talking to the wounded men at the recreation hall, Mrs. Roosevelt visited a ward where seriously injured men are immobilized in traction splints and casts, and talked with each man.

PNews BPO, LOC

———————————

1. See *n*2, Document 38.

2. Chiang Kai-shek. See *n*13 Document 61.

3. Beginning in 1941, Lovell General Hospital provided "general hospital care for troops stationed in New England, Northern New York, and patients evacuated by the Port of Boston or by air transport" at its newly constructed facilities, near the northwest border of Fort Devens in Shirley, Massachusetts (C. David Gordon, "Fort Devens hospital named for Army's first surgeon general," http://www.devenshistoricalmuseum.org/first_surgeon_general.html, accessed 22 September 2005).

4. Spain, unlike China, united under one government from 1931 to 1936, after the Second Republic deposed the monarchy. From 1936 to mid-1939, a civil war raged in Spain between those loyal to the newly established republican government (the Republicans) and those who favored a conservative, militaristic system (the Nationalists). Efforts for a negotiated peace failed in early 1939, and on April 1, 1939, General Francisco Franco's victorious Nationalists entered the final Republican stronghold of Madrid where he received the unconditional surrender of the Republican army (*OTCWH*).

5. See Document 2, Document 10, and Document 11.

1945

On the United Auto Workers Strike

After the White House labor-management conference deadlocked and the UAW strike entered its third week, Truman, without consulting either labor or management, asked Congress to apply the Railway Labor Act to the automobile industry, appointed a fact-finding commission, and imposed a mandatory thirty-day "cooling-off" period. December 6, the day following Truman's actions, GM and UAW agreed to return to the negotiation table. Negotiations crumbled, however, when GM made no concessions and insisted on its prestrike offer of a 10 percent wage increase with no guarantee against price increases.[1]

ER tried to remain optimistic that the negotiations would succeed. In the following column, ER lent her support to the UAW proposal and to embattled OPA director Chester Bowles.

64

My Day

8 December 1945

NEW YORK, Friday—The General Motors management and the United Automobile Workers' leaders have renewed their negotiations. If the threat of legislation which neither side wants, brought about a willingness on the part of management to renew a serious effort at collective bargaining, then it is doing a service.

If, however, it is only the promise that prices may be raised, because we have recognized that there is an increase in living costs, and that therefore wages should be raised, then I think we may be doing the public, and that includes both management and labor, a great disservice.

Any of us who remember the First World War, realize that a rise in prices now will start inflation that may give us a boom at first. But it inevitably will give us a depression afterwards, and it is the "little" people who suffer in a depression. The "big" people suffer, too, but not as a rule actual hunger and cold and lack of shelter.

Mr. Chester Bowles of the OPA, has been like a voice in the wilderness on the question of sticking to price ceilings,[2] and I surmise that the pressure on him from business groups must be tremendous. I am quite sure that the public is not sitting in his outer office, but I doubt if we ever could find a time when representatives of some large business could not be found on his calendar of visitors.

If we do not hold our rent and price ceilings, we can look forward to a repetition of conditions as they were in the early 1930's. This may seem hard to business, because it does limit their ability to earn greater profits at a time when the demand for goods is great. It means that apparently they will have to bear a greater cost for labor and get no compensation by higher prices from the public.

I have faith, however, in the ingenuity and ability of our business people on the management level. I am quite sure that if faced with this fact, once they accept it, they will set themselves to work to find ways of cheapening the cost of manufacture of their products without really impairing the quality.

Mr. Ford taught us many years ago that greater profits can be made out of increased output,[3] and I do not think that our industrialists, as a whole, will ignore that lesson. This will mean that our people, the average you and me, will be able to have more things that we really want because our wages will be higher and the cost of the things we desire will remain stable.

THE ELEANOR ROOSEVELT PAPERS: VOLUME 1 1945–1948

149

I want to see business prosper. I believe that the prosperity of the people is tied up with the success of big and little business, but I see no way for business to prosper unless the people prosper. We must have prosperity in this country before we can give a lift to the other nations of the world who are going to find prosperity much harder to attain than we. In the future their prosperity will mean more than it does now to us. Today there are savings in this country and needs to be filled far above our average requirements. Later we will need greater markets in other nations and that is why their prosperity is linked to ours.

TMs AERP, FDRL

> When negotiations between the UAW and GE collapsed, ER joined with Reuther to raise funds to help strikers purchase Christmas presents for their children and authorized him to use her name to encourage others to do the same. ER gave financial support as well, sending a check to the fund December 2. December 14, Reuther further capitalized on ER's strong support by sending the following wire to notable clergy, scientists, civic leaders, and philanthropists asking them to join with ER in establishing a national committee to support the strikers. By January, the committee would reorganize as the National Committee to Aid the Families of Striking GM Workers, and ER would join its Board of Directors.[4]

65

Walter Reuther to Eleanor Roosevelt
14 December 1945 [Detroit]

MRS ELEANOR ROOSEVELT:

THE FOLLOWING WIRE:

"200,000 GM WORKERS THEIR WIVES AND THEIR CHILDREN ARE FACED WITH THE PROSPECT OF A BITTERLY COLD AND CHEERLESS CHRISTMAS AS A RESULT OF THE ARROGANT REFUSAL FOR THE GIANT GENERAL MOTORS CORPORATION TO NEGOTIATE, CONCILIATE, OR ARBITRATE THE PROPOSAL OF THE UAW-CIO FOR MAINTENANCE OF WARTIME TAKE-HOME PAY.[5] THEY HAVE REJECTED OUR PROPOSAL OF PUBLIC NEGOTIATIONS, CONDEMNED OUR UNWILLINGNESS TO ROB THE CONSUMER BY ACCEPTING WAGE ADJUSTMENTS TIED TO PRICE INCREASES, AND ATTACKED OUR SUGGESTION THAT THE DISPUTE BE RESOLVED BY REFERENCE TO THE ARITHMETIC IN THE CORPORATION BOOKS RATHER THAN BY RESORT TO ECONOMIC POWER. THE GM WORKERS HAVE STAKED THEIR SLENDER RESOURCES, THEIR WILLINGNESS TO WALK THE FREEZING PICKET LINES, THEIR VERY LIVELIHOODS IN THIS FIGHT, AND THEY WILL NOT WAVER. THIS [IS] THE FIGHT OF ALL AMERICANS FOR AN ECONOMY OF ABUNDANCE. MRS ELEANOR ROOSEVELT, BISHOP WILLIAM SCARLETT,[6] AND BISHOP BERNARD J SHEIL[7] HAVE CONSENTED TO JOIN IN SPONSORING FORMATION OF A COMMITTEE OF 100 DISTINGUISHED AMERICANS TO RAISE FUNDS FOR A WHITE CHRISTMAS FOR EVERY CHILD OF A GM WORKER.[8] WE ARE REQUESTING YOU TO JOIN WITH THEM IN SERVING AS SPONSORS FOR THIS COMMITTEE. MAY WE HAVE YOUR IMMEDIATE REPLY TO THIS URGENT REQUEST?"

HAS BEEN SENT TO ARTHUR COMPTON,[9] JAMES B CONANT,[10] JOSEPHUS DANIELS,[11] MARSHALL FIELD,[12] HARRY EMERSON FOSDICK,[13] HELEN HAYES,[14] HENRY J MORGANTHAU,[15] BISHOP G BROMLEY OXNAM,[16] HAROLD UREY,[17] WALTER WHITE AND RABBI STEPHEN S WISE.

WE SHALL INFORM YOU IMMEDIATELY AS TO THE REPLIES RECEIVED FROM THESE PEOPLE.
MANY THANKS FOR YOUR COOPERATION.

WALTER P REUTHER

Tel AERP, FDRL

---

1. Donovan, 120–21; Walter Ruch, "Renewed GM Offer of 10% Sharply Rejected by Union; Thomas Holds Out for 30%," *NYT*, 7 December 1945, 1.

2. As director of the Office of Price Administration, Bowles administered the agency charged with managing price, wage, and rent controls and directing rationing programs from 1941 to 1946. In the immediate aftermath of the war, Bowles battled Treasury Secretaries Fred Vinson and John Snyder over how gradually to ease wage, price, and production controls. Bowles insisted that corporate profits could handle wage increases without dramatic increases in prices. Convinced that rapid deregulation would fan inflation, he argued that there must be a systematic, gradual easing of controls and rationing in order to maintain a stable balance between wages and prices. Snyder thought this impractical and counterproductive. Bowles also battled Agriculture Secretary Clinton Anderson when Bowles recommended that Truman cut rations of meat, fats, and oils by 10 percent so that more stock could be sent to war-ravaged Europe. Truman sided with Anderson. The Office of Price Administration set price and rent controls and directed rationing in the United States from 1941 through 1946 (*HSTE*).

3. In 1901, Henry Ford, Sr., opened the Ford Motor Company's plant in Highland Park, Michigan, where he hoped to design a rapid assembly system for his Model T. By 1913, motors, bodies, and transmissions traveled on conveyer belts as workers stationed along the belt assembled the automobile (*ANB*).

4. ER to Walter Reuther, 21 December 1945, UAWPOWR, MiDW-AL; Lichtenstein, 237.

5. See *n*6 Document 46, and *n*5 Document 60.

6. William Scarlett (1883–1973), then the bishop of the Protestant Episcopal Diocese of Missouri, had first sided with labor as a parish priest in Phoenix, where he quickly became known as "the one clergyman who did not fear the power of the copper mining companies." As dean of Christ Church in St. Louis, Scarlett established the Social Justice Commission and helped mediate disagreements over milk prices, a threatened strike by streetcar workers, and the dispute between the Progressive Mine Workers and their employers. A strong advocate of the social gospel, Scarlett became known as "the conscience of the church" and would work with ER on labor, human rights, and civil rights issues (*ANB*).

7. Bernard J. Sheil (1886–1969), the Roman Catholic auxiliary bishop for Chicago, had close ties to FDR and to labor. A good friend of Thomas ("Tommy the Cork") Corcoran, Sheil's stature in the Roosevelt administration grew when he attacked Father Charles Coughlin's anti-Roosevelt broadsides. In 1937, Sheil's strong public support of the CIO campaign to organize Chicago meat packers and his enthusiastic endorsement of John L. Lewis earned him a national reputation as a friend of labor. An outspoken critic of segregation and anti-Semitism, Sheil gave eloquent voice to his position that for democracy to work, all citizens must be included in its various endeavors (*ANB*).

8. This group became the National Committee to Aid the Families of GM Strikers (Lichtenstein, 237).

9. Arthur H. Compton (1892–1962), a Nobel laureate in physics and the chancellor of Washington University, also had close ties to the Roosevelt administration. In 1941, at FDR's

request, Compton chaired the scientific committee charged with determining whether a nuclear weapon could be produced and, then again at FDR's request, left academe to direct the Manhattan Project's Metallurgical Laboratory. After V-J Day, Compton returned to St. Louis and his duties at Washington University (*ANB*).

10. James B. Conant (1893–1978), the Nobel laureate in chemistry who became president of Harvard, spent the years 1939 to 1946 in the Office of Scientific Research and Development, where he helped coordinate the development of the atomic bomb and other war-specific scientific projects. As president of Harvard, his views on education became more progressive and he gradually began "to see education as a social instrument to preserve the society rather than merely as an instrument to train the most academically able" (*ANB*).

11. Josephus Daniels (1862–1948), a well-known North Carolina progressive and publisher, served as Woodrow Wilson's secretary of the navy which made him then Assistant-Secretary Franklin Roosevelt's immediate superior. In 1933, Daniels joined his former assistant's administration as ambassador to Mexico, where he remained committed to the Good Neighbor Policy. He returned to the *Raleigh News and Observer* in 1943, where his editorials championed public education and the Good Health Program (*ANB*).

12. Marshall Field, III (1893–1956), heir to the Chicago department store fortune, publisher, and philanthropist, was a good friend of ER's. A stalwart New Dealer, he founded the liberal, advertising-free newspaper *PM* and created the *Chicago Sun* to offer an alternative to Robert McCormick's conservative *Chicago Tribune*. As chief officer of the Field Foundation, he gave generous financial support to many of the organizations ER held dear—the NAACP, Roosevelt University, and Americans for Democratic Action (*ANB*).

13. Harry Emerson Fosdick (1878–1969), the Social Gospel theologian for whom New York City's Riverside Presbyterian was built, became the nation's most famous liberal Protestant pastor and its most public pacifist. A popular author, professor, commanding preacher, and the voice of radio's National Vespers Hour, Fosdick, despite his close friendship with John D. Rockefeller, Jr., gave voice to mainstream liberal concerns. His daughter Dorothy would later work with ER at the first session of the United Nations in January 1946. See *n*19, Document 75 (*ANB*).

14. Helen Hayes (1900–1993), whose award-winning performances on stage and in film earned her the title first lady of American Theater, remained an outspoken philanthropist throughout her long life. The mother of a young woman with polio, Hayes served as the national spokesperson for the March of Dimes and was credited by Jonas Salk as one of the major contributors to his effort to combat the disease (*ANB*).

15. Henry Morgenthau (1856–1946), the successful real estate lawyer, diplomat, and philanthropist, chaired the Democratic National Committee's finance committee in 1912 and joined Wilson's administration as his ambassador to Turkey, where he handled the requests for evacuation and refugee aid with such skill that the Turks offered him a cabinet post and the British and French awarded him decorations for valiant service. In 1920, he chaired the League of Nations Refugee Board where he helped 1.25 million Greeks who had been expelled from Turkey. His ties to labor began in 1908 with his service on the tenement reform Committee on Congestion of Population and reached new levels of intensity with his appointment to the Committee of Safety, which organized in response to the Triangle Shirtwaist Factory fire. Like ER, he also volunteered at Rivington Street Settlement House (*ANB*).

16. Garfield Bromley Oxnam (1891–1963), a Methodist bishop who then served as president of both the Federal Council of Churches and DePauw University, also worked closely with John Foster Dulles on the council's Commission on a Just and Durable Peace. In 1945, Oxnam went to Europe at the military's request to meet with army and navy chaplains and again at the end of the year to serve as chaplain to a commission charged with investigating relief and refugee matters in Germany. Beginning with his defense of the 1923 Los Angeles longshoremen's strike, Oxnam

remained a strong advocate of labor, often addressing labor conventions and testifying on labor's behalf before various congressional committees (*ANB*). See also Document 164.

17. Harold Urey (1893–1981), a Nobel Prize–winning chemist and University of Chicago professor, also worked on the Manhattan Project; however, unlike his colleagues above, Urey became "deeply involved in efforts to control atomic energy." He protested the bombing of Hiroshima and Nagasaki, argued against an American monopoly of atomic weapons, and championed an international ban on nuclear arms and the stockpiling of atomic weapons (*ANB*).

On Funding the United Nations Relief
and Rehabilitation Administration

———— 66 ————

My Day
18 December 1945

NEW YORK, Monday—According to the newspapers yesterday the Emergency Appropriation Bill of $2,400,000,000 which carried $750,000,000 as a contribution for the United States to the work of the United Nations Relief and Rehabilitation Administration, was passed on December 15[1].

However, this Bill has to go back to the Conference Committee to smooth out any differences between the Senate and House Bills. Even then according to the accounts, "the appropriation for UNRRA does not become effective until Congressional action is completed on the additional scheduled appropriation of $1,350,000,000 which will cover our contribution for next year."[2]

We must not allow ourselves to be lulled into complacency, therefore, and to think that since our $750,000,000 has been passed, UNRRA can go ahead and make its plans. It now seems vital that, before Congress goes home on the 20th, they pass next year's appropriation.[3]

Otherwise no money will be actually on hand, according to the above item, with which UNRRA can carry through its plans. It would seem impossible for the members of Congress to go home and enjoy their Christmas vacations with the weight of the suffering of the world constantly before them, and no action yet taken to alleviate it.

It would, I think, be for all of us a sadder Christmas. Our representatives in Congress must be conscious of this, and yet I am sometimes a little bit confused by[4] their apparently inconsistent reactions to this suffering.

For instance, as far as I have been able to find out, there has been comparatively little protest over the fact that the Germans—Jews, Protestants and Catholics—who have spent years of the war in concentration camps, and therefore should be regarded as our Allies who fought from within Germany, are treated similarly to the Germans who fought the war against us, whether as soldiers or civilians.

I see also that thirty-four Congressmen, Democrats and Republicans, have petitioned that our army be instructed immediately to increase the rations for the German people.[5] I do not want German people to starve, but the returning soldiers all speak of the fact that German children are well-fed and well-clothed. It is obvious that they would be, since for five years the wealth of all the conquered countries has been siphoned off into Germany.

There is no question, according to the reports of the men coming home, that the German people are better able to withstand this winter than our Allies, in spite of the fact that coal will be lacking and they will have less food than they had as a conquering nation.[6]

I feel very strongly, as I think all fair-minded people feel, that the ration given the German people this year should be limited to the bare necessities of life and that whatever we can give in excess of what is now being shipped to our Allies should go to them and not to Germany.

It is our Allies who for five years have been on a starvation diet. They are the people whose houses are cold, whose clothing is scant and they are the ones who fought with us to end the war.

TMs AERP, FDRL

1. Although thirty members of UNRRA contributed to the relief effort, the United States provided 73 percent of the funding for operations. This appropriation bill referred to the first half of the US installment for the second year, which totaled $1,350,000,000. For further information on UNRRA see *n7* Document 55 ("47 Countries Pledge UNRRA $3,611,942,710," *NYT*, 12 January 1946, 28; *HSTE*; Woodbridge, 105–8).

2. The account of the conference committee ER quoted is cited in "UNRRA $750,000,000 Passed by Senate," *NYT*, 16 December 1945, 21.

3. Congress approved the $750,000,000 appropriation December 19 ("$750,000,000 Fund Voted for UNRRA," *NYT*, 20 December 1945, 2).

4. The editors removed the typographical error "of" from this point of the sentence, as it was removed when the syndicate copyedited the submission.

5. November 28, Truman released the report he had received from Byron Price, whom he had asked to assess Allied policy regarding occupied Germany. Price's self-described "blunt" report criticized De Gaulle's insistence upon "the economic dismemberment of Germany" and implied that the American ration of 1,500 calories a day would lead to starvation and an outbreak of epidemics. He concluded, "the approved medical ration to prevent starvation is 2,000 calories, and there is no likelihood that such a ration would permit the bombed-out, freezing pedestrian Germans to live anything like as well as the European average" (W. H. Lawrence, "Price Criticizes Policy in Germany," *NYT*, 29 November 1945, 1).

December 15 the following Senators wrote Truman demanding an immediate response to "the appalling famine in Germany and Austria": Howard Smith (R-NJ); James Eastland (D-MS), Harlan Bushfield (R-SD), Albert Hawkes (R-NJ), Henrik Shipstead (R-MN), Milton Young (R-ND), Raymond Willis (R-IN), Edward Moore (R-OK), Edwin Johnson (D-CO), Allen Ellender (D-LA), Alexander Wiley (R-WI), Bourke Hickenlooper (R-IA), Clayton Buck (R-DE), James Murray (D-MT), William Stanfill (R-KY), Orrice Murdock (D-UT), William Langer (R-ND), Robert La Follette, Jr. (R-WI), Sheridan Downey (D-CA), Leverett Saltonstall (R-MA), Homer Capehart (R-IN), Arthur Capper (R-KS), Hugh Butler (D-NE), Burton Wheeler (D-MT), Kenneth Wherry (R-NE), Clyde Hoey (D-NC), David Walsh (D-MA), Edward Carville (D-NV), Charles Tobey (R-NH), Joseph O'Mahoney (D-WY), Glen Taylor (D-ID), Joseph Guffey (D-PA), George Radcliffe (D-MD), and Henry Bridges (R-NH) ("34 Senators Urge Food for Germans," *NYT*, 16 December 1945, 14).

6. For an example of correspondence ER received from servicemen, see First Lieutenant Roger Ernst to ER, 19 December 1945, AERP.

On Discrimination against
Japanese Americans

In early December, a former War Relocation Authority officer wrote ER to recount discriminatory practices against Japanese Americans living in Northern California. His letter reported a resolution passed by county supervisors denying indigent aid to all Japanese Americans unless they volunteered for military service, the refusal of stores and restaurants to serve any Japanese Americans (including military personnel), the systematic application of escheat to violate the Alien Land Act, the unanimous refusal of insurance agencies to insure Japanese American property, and the exclusion of Japanese Americans who died in combat from county honor rolls. December 18, ER redacted the name and address of her correspondent and forwarded his letter to Truman, saying that she "thought the facts he gives should be brought to your attention."[1]

As Truman's response indicates, he forwarded the material to Tom Clark, with instructions to address "this disgraceful conduct."

67

Harry Truman to Eleanor Roosevelt
21 December 1945 [The White House]

My dear Mrs. Roosevelt:

I read the letter about the treatment of American-Japanese in the west with a lot of interest and have forwarded the letter to the Attorney General with a memorandum asking him to try to find a solution for it.[2]

This disgraceful conduct almost makes you believe that a lot of our Americans have a streak of Nazi in them.

Sincerely yours,
Harry S. Truman

TLS AERP, FDRL

---

1. The letter ER forwarded to Truman that he then forwarded to Clark could not be located in either the Roosevelt or Truman libraries; however, ER also forwarded the same letter to California governor Earl Warren who then sent a copy to California Attorney General Robert W. Kenny, whose copy we cite in this note. The editors are grateful to Professor Greg Robinson of Quebec University, who kindly shared this document with us (Earl Warren to Robert Kenny, n.d., Robert Kenny Papers, Bancroft Library; ER to Harry Truman, 18 December 1945, HSTL).

2. Truman sent both documents to Tom C. Clark on December 21 asking, "isn't there some way we can shame these people into doing the right thing by these loyal American-Japanese[?]" On January 10, 1946, Clark replied that while the Justice Department was concerned about "the complaints of violence and deliberate discrimination" it had no power to act. Citing wartime precedent, he advised Truman to issue a directive empowering the department to investigate all such incidents and act if federal jurisdiction was found. The order also directed the department to share the results of any such investigation with state officials and aid any subsequent state actions including prose-

cution. Clark also noted that he had asked for an investigation into the charges mentioned in ER's letter. Truman signed the directive on January 17, 1946 (Harry Truman to Tom Clark, 21 December 1945; Memorandum for the President, 10 January 1946; Sam Rosenman to Harry Truman, 17 January 1946; Harry Truman to Tom Clark, 17 January 1946, HSTL).

ELEANOR ROOSEVELT ACCEPTS APPOINTMENT
TO THE UNITED NATIONS

Truman realized that, despite ER's increasing private and public frustration with his leadership, a public formal relationship with her could shore up his popularity. As Byrnes later recalled, Truman told him:

> in the fall of 1945 … there were two persons he had to have on his political team, Secretary Wallace and Mrs. Eleanor Roosevelt—Mr. Wallace because of his influence with labor and Mrs. Roosevelt because of her influence with the Negro voters. He said he could "take care of Henry," but he wanted me to find an appointment for Mrs. Roosevelt in the field of foreign affairs. The following week, in recommending a list of delegates to the first meeting of the United Nations Assembly in London, I placed Mrs. Roosevelt's name at the top of the list, expressing the belief that because of her husband's deep interest in the success of the United Nations she might accept. Truman telephoned to her immediately, while I was still in the office, and she did agree to serve.[1] To the surprise of some of the other members, she proved to be a good team worker, rendering outstanding service, and was warmly congratulated by other delegates.[2]

After ER telephoned Truman to say that she accepted the appointment, he sent her the following letter detailing her duties.

68

Harry Truman to Eleanor Roosevelt
21 December 1945 [The White House]

My dear Mrs. Roosevelt:

I am pleased to inform you that I have appointed you one of the representatives of the United States to the first part of the first session of the General Assembly of the United Nations to be held in London early in January 1946. A complete list of this Government's Delegation is enclosed herewith.[3]

The United States representation at the first meeting of the General Assembly will be headed by the Secretary of State as Senior Representative or in his absence by The Honorable Edward R. Stettinius, Jr.[4]

In so far as the General Assembly will deal with matters covered by the report of the Preparatory Commission,[5] the representatives of the United States will be expected to support the recommendations made therein unless the position of the United States on a particular recommendation is reserved, in which case the representatives will be guided by my special instructions. I am, however, authorizing the Senior Representative, after consultation with the other representatives, to agree to modifications of the Preparatory Commission's recommendations which in his opinion may be wise and necessary.

In so far as matters may arise which are not covered by the report of the Preparatory Commission, I shall transmit through the Senior Representative any further instructions as to the position which should be taken by the representatives of the United States.

I have instructed the Senior Representative to act as the principal spokesman for the United States in the General Assembly.

You, as a representative of the United States, will bear the grave responsibility of demonstrating the wholehearted support which this Government is pledged to give to the United Nations organization, to the end that the organization can become the means of preserving the international peace and of creating conditions of mutual trust and economic and social well-being among all peoples of the world. I am confident that you will do your best to assist the United States to accomplish these purposes in the first meeting of the General Assembly.

Sincerely yours,
Harry S. Truman

TLS AERP, FDRL

69

My Day
22 December 1945

NEW YORK, Friday—Now that I have been confirmed by the Senate,[6] I can say how deeply honored I feel that President Truman has named me one of the delegates to the General Assembly of the United Nations Organization.[7] It is an honor, but also a very great responsibility. I know it has come to me largely because my husband laid the foundation for this Organization through which we all hope to build world peace.

In many ways I am sure I will find much to learn; but all of life is a constant education. Some things I can take to this first meeting—a sincere desire to understand the problems of the rest of the world and our relationship to them; a real good-will for all peoples throughout the world; a hope that I shall be able to build a sense of personal trust and friendship with my co-workers, for without that type of understanding our work would be doubly difficult.

This first meeting, I imagine, will be largely concerned with organization and the choice of a site within this country as a permanent home.

Being the only woman delegate from this country, I feel a great responsibility, also, to the women of my own country. In other lands women have gone with their men into the fighting forces.[8] Here we have more nearly followed the traditional pattern of working and waiting at home.

To be sure, some of our work was done outside the home in places which the mothers and wives of earlier days never would have dreamed could be a woman's working sphere.[9] But fundamentally we were doing what we could to help our men win the war. We were striving to give them, when they returned, the kind of country and the kind of home they had dreamed of and sometimes gave even their lives to preserve.

I feel a great responsibility to the youth who fought the war. When they were not called upon to make the supreme sacrifice, they gave years of their lives which most of them would rather have spent in building up their personal futures. Some of them will carry handicaps incurred in fighting the war, throughout the rest of their lives. Every one of us has a deep and solemn obligation to them which we should fulfill by giving all that we are capable of giving to the making of the peace so they can feel that the maximum good has come from their sacrifice.

Willy-nilly, everyone of us cares more for his own country than for any other. That is human nature. We love the bit of land where we have grown to maturity and known the joys and sorrows of life. The time has come however when we must recognize that our mutual devotion to our own land must never blind us to the good of all lands and of all peoples.

In the end, as Wendell Willkie said, we are "One World"[10] and that which injures any one of us, injures all of us. Only by remembering this will we finally have a chance to build a lasting peace.

I am sure in President Truman's heart, as in that of everyone of our delegates, is the prayer that in this coming year, we may make measurable strides towards good-will and peace on earth.

TMs AERP, FDRL

Immediately after her Senate confirmation, ER reached out to several dozen colleagues and activists, seeking their "most expeditious" briefings on decisions the United Nations had made to date and the issues they hoped she would bring before the General Assembly.[11]

The following three letters, written by individuals with whom ER had worked for a decade, illustrate the candor with which staff treated her and the expectations activists placed upon her.

70

Archibald MacLeish[12] to Eleanor Roosevelt
27 December 1945 [New York City]

Dear Mrs. Roosevelt:

I think the quickest and most expeditious way to brief you on the history of UNO down to your first London meeting would be through a combination of one document and one man. The document is the Report to the President on the San Francisco Conference which is the basic Bible of the whole operation. The Letter of Transmittal to the President from the Secretary of State, which I wrote, contains a summary in relatively brief form.[13] The remainder of the volume treats the functional sections of the Charter in detail. You undoubtedly have a copy, but I am asking the State Department to send you one today.

The human side of the job would be best done by Adlai Stevenson in London. Adlai has acted as head of the United States Delegation since Ed Stettinius left and did most of the ground work before that. He was my associate at San Francisco and in the Department, working on the press problem in its various aspects. He is extremely intelligent, and he is also an accurate reporter. An hour or two of Adlai would be worth many days of document reading. Please don't let Adlai's modesty and self-deprecation throw you off: he is one of the principal experts on the whole subject.[14]

The matters weighing on my own mind are, first, the vital necessity of staffing UNO and other United Nations Organizations with new, vigorous, imaginative and effective people and not with the tired hacks of diplomacy whom the various Foreign Offices will want to get rid of, or with the rather moth-eaten relics of Geneva.[15] Some of the Geneva people are, of course, excellent. A lot are not.

Second, I am worried about the Department's attitude toward the United Nations Educational, Scientific and Cultural Organization, the Constitution of which was drafted at our London meeting in November.[16] The Department is traditionally scornful of that whole side of foreign relations—a side which is increasingly important from day to day.[17] I am still in doubt as to whether the Moscow agreement on the Atomic Energy Commission with its provision for the exchange of scientific information is going to include or exclude UNESCO. If UNESCO is excluded, either on the ground that the Russians are not members or on any other ground, it would be a serious blow to the new and very promising Organization and a blow also to the forty-three nations which took part in the London meeting.[18]

May I say in closing what I know you realize—that millions of your fellow citizens are profoundly thankful to Almighty God that you are a member of the Delegation.

> Yours faithfully,
> Archie MacLeish

TLS AERP, FDRL

ER had arranged for the three-person NAACP delegation—Walter White, W. E. B. Du Bois, and Mary McLeod Bethune—to receive the accreditation necessary to attend the San Francisco conference as a nongovernmental organization.[19] Before she sailed for London, she asked her good friend NAACP Executive Secretary Walter White for his input on what actions he thought the NAACP would want the United Nations to take. White then contacted his fellow delegates and forwarded their concerns to ER.

71

Walter White to Eleanor Roosevelt
28 December 1945 [New York City]

Dear Mrs. Roosevelt:

In response to your request for information on the desires of American Negroes for your guidance as a member of the American delegation to the U.N.O. I telegraphed Mrs. Bethune and had hoped that I would have her reply to include in this letter, but it has not yet come. Since you are leaving tomorrow I am therefore sending on this letter which is a combination of the ideas of Dr. DuBois—who with Mrs. Bethune served as Associate Consultant at San Francisco—and my own.

The following are matters which might be stressed in the assembly of the U.N.O.:

(1) The placing of all colonies mandated after World War I under U.N.O. trusteeship[20] and the development of immediate means of preparing these colonies for self-government and independence.[21]

(2) A world-wide and sincere campaign to abolish the entire colonial system as one of the chief causes of war, poverty and disease.

(3) A world campaign of education for the uneducated colonial and other peoples.

(4) A world campaign to utilize all the resources of science, government and philanthropy to abolish poverty for all people in our time.

(5) Denial to the Union of South Africa to annex former German Southwest Africa because the South African treatment of native peoples is undemocratic and uncivilized.[22]

(6) The restoration of Eritrea[23] and Somaliland[24] to Ethiopia and the withdrawal of British troops.

(7) Freedom and independence for Indonesia,[25] India,[26] Burma,[27] Indo-China[28] and Siam.[29]

(8) Democracy for China.[30]

(9) Withdrawal of recognition of Franco's Spain.[31]

> Ever sincerely
> Walter White

TLS AERP, FDRL

_72_

Walter White to Eleanor Roosevelt

28 December 1945 [New York City]

Dear Mrs. Roosevelt:

Just a few minutes after I had sent you a Special Delivery letter containing Dr. DuBois' and my suggestions, the following telegram came from Mrs. Bethune containing several excellent additional ideas:

"My suggestions for inclusion in letter follow:

First, Careful review concerning the establishment of the trusteeship system;[32]

Second, One of the basic qualifications for employment on the UNO permanent Secretariat should be sympathetic attitude toward and technical experience with the problems of racial minorities;

Third, Elimination of laws imposing race restrictions on migration and citizenship by several Latin American countries;[33]

Fourth, Recommend to United Nations Educational and Cultural Organizations[34] that Negroes be included among exchange students from Europe and other nations to be invited to attend Southern schools such as Fisk, Talladega, Atlanta University, etc."[35]

> Ever sincerely
> Walter White

TLS AERP, FDRL

---

1. ER did not immediately accept Truman's offer. Franklin, Jr., was lunching with his mother when the president called, and overheard ER telling Truman that she could not possibly accept because she had "no foreign policy experience … and did not know parliamentary procedure." Returning to the lunch table, he pressed his mother to reconsider, and Tommy Thompson seconded his argument. ER later recalled that her immediate reaction was:

> "Oh, no! It would be impossible … How could I be a delegate to help organize the United Nations when I have no background or experience in international meetings."

> Miss Thompson urged me not to decline without giving the idea careful thought. I knew in a general way what had been done about organizing the United Nations. After the San Francisco meeting in 1945, when the Charter was written, it had been accepted by the various nations, including our own, through their constitutional procedures. I knew, too, that we had a group of people … working with representatives of other member nations in London to prepare for the formal organizing meeting. I believed the United Nations to be the one hope for a peaceful world. I knew that my husband had placed great importance on the establishment of this world organization.

> At last I accepted in fear and trembling. But I might not have done so if I had known at that time that President Truman could only nominate me as a delegate and that the nomination would have to be approved by the United States Senate, where certain senators would disapprove of me because of my attitude toward social problems and more especially youth problems (ER, *Autobiography*, 299).

2. Byrnes, 373. For expressions of a delegate's change of heart about ER see Document 92.

3. In addition to ER, the members of the American delegation were Secretary of State James Byrnes, former Secretary of State Edward Stettinius (as US representative to the Security Council), Senate Foreign Relations Committee Chair Tom Connally (D-TX), and ranking member of the Senate Foreign Relations Committee Arthur Vandenberg (R-MI). The alternates included Representatives Sol Bloom (D-NY) and Charles Eaton (R-NJ), the chair and ranking member of the House Foreign Affairs Committee; former postmaster general and DNC chair Frank Walker; former senator and RNC chair John Townsend, Jr.; and John Foster Dulles, who advised Thomas Dewey on foreign policy (Lash, *Years*, 39).

4. James F. Byrnes replaced Stettinius as secretary of state in July.

5. The United Nations Preparatory Commission met in London from November 24 to December 23, 1945, to establish the basic operating procedures governing the UN and to prepare an agenda for the first meeting of the General Assembly scheduled to convene January 10, 1946. Once the parties agreed that discussions related to the atomic bomb would be postponed until the General Assembly convened, the commissioners established procedures governing decisions related to the permanent location of the UN, the composition of the Steering Committee for the General Assembly, the establishment of the Temporary Trusteeship Committee, the observation of the Security Council by member states not on the council, and how organizations established by the League of Nations would be brought into the UN ("Initial UNO Group Postpones Parley," *NYT*, 20 November 1945, 7; Sydney Gruson, "UNO Body Winds Up Preparatory Job," *NYT*, 24 December 1945, 6).

6. Majority Leader Alben Barkley polled the Senate, at Truman's request, to see if the Senate would confirm ER. He found some opposition (some Republicans reported John Foster Dulles's opposition to her liberalism and William Fulbright (D-AR) thought her so inexperienced that her appointment could signal disrespect for the UN); however, only Theodore Bilbo (D-MS), who objected to her civil rights positions, voted against her confirmation (Lash, *Years*, 320).

7. See Document 68.

8. The Soviet Union, for example, formed three all-women air regiments that fought the Germans on the Eastern Front. In Great Britain, men and women served together in antiaircraft artillery units on British soil. In France, many women joined the Resistance (Myles, 6–7, 21; Treadwell, 301; Leckie, 741).

9. America's female work force grew from 14.6 million in 1941 to 19.4 million in 1944. Two million women, encouraged by the Rosie the Riveter campaign, worked in defense plants building aircraft and destroyers and manufacturing weapons and a wide variety of military necessities. By 1943, half of the workers at Boeing's Seattle plant were women. In addition, approximately 350,000 American women volunteered for military service (Woloch, 460; Boyer, 24).

10. Wendell Willkie (1892–1944), though defeated by FDR in 1940, accepted FDR's 1942 request to fly around the world to show that American political opponents were united in their determination to defeat Fascism. Willkie visited battle zones in Africa, the Soviet Union, and China and described his goodwill journey in *One World*. Published in 1943, it quickly became an influential plea for postwar international cooperation (*FDRE*; Boyer, 5).

11. For example, see Chester S. Williams to ER, 28 December 1945, AERP.

12. For examples of MacLeish's work on the UN see *n*2 Document 3. See also Biographical Portraits.

13. In the eleven-page Summary Letter for the President MacLeish described the rationale for and the organization of the United Nations. He began with the San Francisco conference, which "had one purpose and one purpose only: to draft the charter of an international organization through

which the nations of the world might work together in their common hope for peace." After recapping the focus and "the demonstrated capacity of its members to work together," MacLeish then summarized the "moral and idealistic" and the "realistic and practical" functions of the UN, as defined in its charter:

> As a declaration, the Charter commits the United Nations to the maintenance of "international peace and security", to the development of "friendly relations among nations based on the principle of equal rights and self determination of peoples", and to "international cooperation in the solution of international problems", together with "the promotion and encouragement of respect for human rights and fundamental freedoms". More precisely, the United Nations agree to promote ("with a view to the creation of conditions necessary for peaceful and friendly relations among nations") "higher standards of living, full employment, and conditions of economic and social progress and development; solutions of international economic, social, health, and other related problems; international cultural and educational cooperation; and universal respect for and observance of human rights and fundamental freedoms for all without distinction as to race, language, religion or sex".

> Further, in its capacity as a declaration, the Charter states the "principles" (although they are, for the most part, rules of conduct rather than principles) which its members accept as binding. "Sovereign equality of the member states" is declared to be the foundation of their association with each other. Members are to "settle their international disputes by peaceful means" and in such manner as not to endanger international peace, security and justice. Members are to "refrain in their international relations from the threat or use of force against the territorial integrity or political independence of any member or state or in any manner inconsistent with the purposes of the organization". At the same time members bind themselves to give "every assistance to the organization in any action taken by it" in accordance with the Charter, and to refrain from giving assistance to any state against which the Organization is taking preventive or enforcement action.

The Summary concluded with a review of the four major UN bodies: the Security Council, the General Assembly, the Economic and Social Council, and the International Court of Justice. MacLeish ended his summary with an appeal for strong US commitment:

> If we are earnestly determined, as I believe we are, that the unnumerable dead of two great holocausts shall not have died in vain, we must act in concert with the other nations of the world to bring about the peace for which these dead gave up their lives. The Charter of the United Nations is the product of such concerted action. Its purpose is the maintenance of peace. It offers means for the achievement of that purpose. If the means are inadequate to the task they must perform, time will reveal their inadequacy as time will provide, also, the opportunity to amend them. But whatever its present imperfections, the Charter of the United Nations, as it was written by the Conference of San Francisco, offers the world an instrument by which a real beginning may be made upon the work of peace. I most respectfully submit that neither we nor any other people can or should refuse participation in the common task (Summary Letter to the President from Edward R. Stettinius, Jr., 23 June 1945, AMP, DLC).

14. Adlai E. Stevenson II (1900–1965), the Chicago attorney whose grandfather served as Grover Cleveland's vice president, had rejoined the Roosevelt administration in 1942 as special assistant to Secretary of the Navy Frank Knox. Stevenson had just returned home in 1944 after Knox's death, disappointed that he did not receive a higher post within the Navy Department, when his good friend MacLeish pressured him to serve as his deputy in the State Department. Stevenson agreed, after Stettinius also offered him the position of his special assistant to the San Francisco conference, where, in addition to being the delegation's official "leaker," he drafted Security Council-related

proposals for both Stettinius and John Foster Dulles and helped MacLeish secure the inclusion of freedom of speech and communication in the UN Charter. Although Stevenson had returned to Chicago once the conference ended, he lobbied to continue working with the delegation. Stettinius tapped him to serve as his deputy to the London Preparatory Commission charged with "bridging the gap" between the adoption of the charter and the convening of the first General Assembly. There he focused primarily on the organizational issues confronting the General Assembly, argued for the UN to be permanently located in the United States, and worked closely with other delegation leaders, especially Andrei Gromyko, J. P. Noel-Baker, and Paul-Henri Spaak. In November, Stevenson replaced Stettinius, whose sudden illness forced his early departure, as chair of the American delegation. Stevenson hoped to serve on the American delegation and, when Truman did not select him, appealed to Illinois leaders to urge his appointment, at least, as an alternate. Disappointed, he nevertheless agreed to Acheson's request that he serve as "one of the senior advisors" accompanying the delegation to London (J. Martin, 220–34).

15. A reference to the League of Nations headquarters in Geneva, Switzerland.

16. While meeting in London in 1945, representatives of forty-four nations endorsed the United Nations Educational, Scientific and Cultural Organization (UNESCO), an advisory body authorized by its constitution "to contribute to peace and security by promoting collaboration among the nations through education, science and culture, in order to further universal respect for justice, the rule of law and for the human rights and fundamental freedoms which are affirmed for the peoples of the world, without distinction of race, sex, language, or religion, by the Charter of the United Nations." As detailed in Article I, its main function is "to collaborate in the work of advancing the mutual knowledge and understandings of peoples through all means of mass communication and to that end recommend such international agreements as may be necessary to promote the free flow of ideas by word and image (Boyd, 124–25; Archibald MacLeish to Dean Acheson, 30 December 1945, in Winnick, 337–38).

MacLeish, who led the American delegation to the UNESCO meeting, viewed the organization as "the intellectual steel for the UN itself." Because it moved beyond the academe "to the level of the child," MacLeish thought UNESCO's commitment to using international media to promote mutual understanding essential to the preservation of peace (Donaldson, 393).

17. Three days after MacLeish wrote ER, he wrote Dean Acheson, then undersecretary of state, "If the Department, having sent a Delegation to London to set up UNESCO, is now in doubt as to whether UNESCO should be entrusted with two of its most important functions [overseeing exchanges of scientific information and monitoring the international activities of the mass media] it would seem to follow that the Department's confidence, or, at any rate, interest, in UNESCO was fairly slight" (Archibald MacLeish to Dean Acheson, 30 December 1945, in Winnick, 337–38; Donaldson, 393).

18. Byrnes, who had flown to Moscow to meet with Stalin, secured Stalin's endorsement of a UN commission on atomic energy. Stalin agreed, with the provision that the commission report to the UN Security Council where the United States and the USSR had vetoes. UNESCO did not come up in the discussions. The Soviets, who did not participate in the UNESCO organizing conference, did not join the agency until 1954 (Chace, 123–24).

19. Lewis, 505.

20. After World War I the victorious European allies reallocated the German colonies in Africa and many of the lands that made up the Ottoman Empire, which had allied itself with Germany. At the same time, the Japanese wanted to take over the German concessions in China. The League of Nations ultimately sanctioned all these arrangements.

The territories under consideration for UN trusteeship status included: the African territories of East and West Togoland, North and South Cameroons, Tanganyika, Ruanda-Urandi, South-West Africa, Libya, Eritrea, Italian Somaliland, British Somaliland, and Ogaden; the Far East territories of North-East New Guinea, the Solomon Islands, New Britain, New Ireland, Nauru, Western Samoa, the Mariana, Caroline and Marshall Islands, the Kurile Island, and Korea; and in the Middle East, Palestine (MacMillan, 98–106, 381–409, 423–25; Boyd, 94–96).

21. See *n2* Document 37. At the San Francisco conference, the NAACP and the State Department's highest-ranking African American, Ralph Bunche (1903–1967), tried to pressure Stettinius and the American delegation to support a trusteeship plan that would promote independence for all colonial people through quiet diplomacy and a public relations campaign. Their efforts failed. Balancing the United States' preference for independence with the need to maintain good relations with Great Britain and France, both of whom had large colonial empires, Edward Stettinius worked out a series of compromises in the UN Charter that called for both self-government and independence for colonial peoples. The NAACP did not support these compromises because they left the colonial system intact while providing no outlet for colonial people to submit their grievances. The NAACP also wanted the Trusteeship Council to have jurisdiction over all colonies, not just those that had been League of Nations mandates or those the Allies acquired as a result of World War II. For ER on the trusteeship issue, see Document 37 (Anderson, 50–51, 53–54, 57; S. Schlesinger, 232–36; Hoopes and Brinkley, 204).

22. After World War I, South Africa accepted the League of Nations mandate for German South-West Africa (modern-day Namibia), which it had captured during the war. In 1946, the UN ended the mandate after refusing South Africa's request to annex the territory and made it a trusteeship territory under South African administration (*OEWH*; *EUN*, 532–33).

23. Originally an Italian colony, Eritrea came under British military rule in 1941 (*OEWH*).

24. In the 1880s, Britain, Italy, Ethiopia, and France divided up Somaliland to prevent any other country from taking over the territory. Despite internal resistance, the British Protectorate endured until 1940, when it fell to the invading Italians. British and South African troops recovered the area in 1941, and a British military protectorate governed the land until 1948 when British civilian administration took control (World History at KML History of Somalia http://www.zum.de/whkmla/region/eastafrica/xsomaliland.html, accessed 22 September 2005).

25. Indonesia, a Dutch colony, had also been occupied by the Japanese during World War II (*OEWH*).

26. India, the largest British colony, had been agitating for its independence since the end of the nineteenth century (*OEWH*; Ralph et al., 638–48).

27. Britain annexed Burma (Myanmar) in 1886, and made it part of British India (*OEWH*).

28. France governed Indo-China (present day Cambodia, Vietnam, and Laos) until the Japanese seized control in 1943. In December 1945, the French demanded that the territory be returned to them and prepared to evict the Japanese from Vietnam (*OEWH*, 111–12, 381, 706).

29. Siam, also known as Thailand, remained an independent nation while maintaining strong ties to France (*OEWH*).

30. See *n*11 Document 60.

31. Francisco Franco Bahamonde. At the Potsdam conference, Truman, Atlee, and Stalin agreed not to support Spain's admission to the UN because of its government's ties to the Axis Powers before and during World War II. Following World War II, the Allies regarded Spain as the last stronghold of Fascism, and in 1946 the UN prohibited Spanish membership until Franco was deposed. As Cold War tensions increased in the late 1940s, Truman resumed relations with Spain as a buttress against Communist encroachment in Europe. The UN admitted Spain in 1955. Franco ruled until his death, when a constitutional monarchy was restored. Also see Document 161 and Document 172 regarding ER on Franco (EWH, 242; *DPB*,173, 174; *EUN*, 771).

32. State Department advisor and NAACP ally Ralph Bunche continued to strengthen the Trusteeship Council's provisions regarding colonial people at the meetings of the UN Preliminary Commission's Executive Committee in London in the early fall of 1945 and at the first two sessions of the UN General Assembly in 1946. At critical points in these meetings, he was able to put in place processes that ensured the concerns of colonial people would be heard and acted upon. The Trusteeship Council, established in December of 1946, met for the first time in March 1947; by then Bunche directed the UN's Trusteeship Division (Urquhart 126–27; 131–36).

33. During the last half of the nineteenth century many Latin American countries, among them Brazil, Argentina, Cuba, and Uruguay, encouraged the immigration of white Europeans to "whiten" their societies and meet labor shortages in their expanding economies. When European migration failed to provide the necessary workers, Latin American countries imported nonwhite workers from Asia and the Caribbean including hundreds of thousands of black workers from the French and British West Indies who arrived between 1900 and 1930. Many of these people worked for large American agricultural concerns such as United Fruit or the burgeoning sugar and oil industries. By the 1930s the employment bubble for both whites and blacks burst causing economic dislocation, heightening racial and political tensions, and contributing to the growth of Fascist-like, right-wing groups. Some countries including Argentina, Brazil, Cuba, and Uruguay tightened their immigration laws in an effort to keep their own citizens employed and minimize internal turmoil. For example, in 1926 the Panamanian legislature made it illegal for non-Spanish speaking blacks to settle there and specified that 75 percent of the workforce in local businesses be native born. Brazil and Cuba also passed similar workforce legislation in the 1930s (Andrews, 135–40; 153–54).

34. United Nations Educational, Scientific and Cultural Organization (UNESCO). See *n*16 above.

35. The leading African American universities, established by the Freedmen's Bureau in the aftermath of the Civil War.

ON THE AMERICAN COMMITTEE FOR
YUGOSLAV RELIEF

Throughout the summer, ER used her column to raise funds for war relief. She paid particular attention to Yugoslavia, whose citizens rose up against their German-allied government to lead a brutal guerrilla war against the German army. Her appointment to the United Nations did not curtail her support. December 24, she reported to readers of My Day that the previous Thursday she met with the American Committee for Yugoslav Relief and agreed to serve as its honorary chairman because she had been "particularly touched by the stories of the want and suffering among the children of that country." "This rather small population," she continued, "became a unit in the Allied war against Fascism. Women and children were included as part of the fighting forces. Now there are many children without parents, and the casualties among them from privation and starvation are somewhere around 80 percent."

Hoping to gain her readers' attention, she recounted how two children "brought me samples of the kind of food which we hope will be sent" to Yugoslav children:

> One of them, a little boy who might have been six years old, looked at me with solemn and sad eyes, so I asked him where he came from. Without a smile, he answered: 'I am a Filipino guerilla.' I imagine there are many similar sad-eyed and solemn children in Yugoslavia, Greece, Poland, Czechoslovakia, Russia and many other countries where the horrors of war have born[1] as heavily on the children as upon their elders.[2]

As the letter below illustrates, the day before ER sailed to London, she also appealed to major individual donors to support the relief effort. Here she approaches Orson Welles, who had lent very public support to FDR, to support the committee. The following day, the committee announced that Welles would be the master of ceremonies at its New Year's Day concert in Town Hall.[3]

73

Eleanor Roosevelt to Orson Welles[4]
30 December 1945 [New York City]

Dear Mr. Welles:

It seems to be the fate of the Yugoslav people to fight with odds massed against them. In war, they held back twenty Axis divisions with captured weapons and with bare hands.[5] In peace, they are forced to fight hunger, disease and cold without even the barest essentials of food, medicine and clothing.

During the four years of their Resistance, we were unable to supply them with a single gun, a single tank. Today they need our help more. You can conquer an enemy with bare hands. But can you feed a child with empty hands?

It was with such thoughts that I recently accepted the honorary chairmanship of the American Committee for Yugoslav Relief, an organization that is doing a vital job well.[6] I would like, before leaving tomorrow for UNO conference in London,[7] to do some one thing that will enable the committee to work even more effectively.

I am convinced that it is people who are the ultimate explanation of achievements in any field. Therefore, I am inviting a few distinguished fellow-Americans to join our Board of Trustees and I would welcome your association with us in this worthy work.[8]

I know you are engaged in many other admirable activities,[9] but I hope you will nevertheless accept since so much can be done in exchange for so very little of your time.

If you would write me in care of the Committee (235 East 11th Street, New York City) while I am in Europe, your answer will reach me promptly.

Best wishes for the New Year—

Eleanor Roosevelt

TLS WELL, IULL

---

1. Spelling error in the original.

2. *MD*, 24 December 1945. For a sample of ER's previous statements on Yugoslavia see *MD*, 11 September 1945.

3. "Welles to Head Jazz Concert," *NYT*, 31 December 1945, 12; "Program of Jazz Traces Its History," *NYT*, 2 January 1945, 28.

4. Orson Welles (1915–1985), the actor, co-writer, and director of the landmark American film *Citizen Kane* and the star of the radio play "The War of the Worlds," which convinced thousands of Americans that Martians had successfully invaded New Jersey, first met FDR through his work with the Federal Theatre Project. Welles lent his directorial skills to the administration by editing some of FDR's speeches, serving as script consultant to the Treasury Department, and promoting the fifth War Loan drive. Recognizing Welles's unique ability to attract voters, FDR asked him to broadcast a nationwide address for the Democratic National Committee the night before the 1944 election (Leaming, 185–86, 280–84, 291–94).

5. In the spring of 1941, the German invasion of Russia stalled when the Yugoslavs refused to honor the agreement their government signed making Yugoslavia a satellite of Nazi Germany. Following an internal coup and a subsequent German invasion in April, the Nazis divided Yugoslavia among their allies (Italy, Bulgaria, and Romania). However, a Yugoslav Communist, Josip Broz ("Tito") (1892–1980) organized a joint Serbo-Croatian resistance movement that with Western aid waged a remorseless guerrilla war that led to the liberation of Yugoslavia—and the destruction of Tito's enemies—in 1944. In 1945 Tito established a Communist government in the country with Soviet help (*OEWH*, 739; Dziewanowski, 251, 288; Leckie, 225–26, 724–26; "Tito: The Fighter-Survivor Who Unified a Country," *NYT*, 5 May 1980, A13).

6. The committee began its work May 10, 1941, when twelve Yugoslav fraternal groups joined forces to raise money to send relief supplies to Yugoslavia in the immediate aftermath of what FDR termed the "barbaric invasion" of their homeland. By the time ER joined the organization, Zlatko Balokovic served as president. In addition to collecting supplies and raising monies, the committee also urged UNRRA to address the Yugoslav crisis. By summer 1946, Welles and several other of ER's associates had joined the board: Jo Davidson, Melvyn Douglas, Fiorello La Guardia, Philip Murray, Mary McLeod Bethune, Mrs. Marshall Field, Channing Tobias, and Miriam van Kleeck (Michael N. Nisselson to ER, 25 September 1945, AERP).

7. The first session of the UN General Assembly, which opened on January 10, 1946 (Meisler, 358).

8. Early in January 1946 Welles spoke on behalf of the committee in New York (Higham, 227).

9. Welles harbored his own political ambitions. In October 1943, he published the first in a series of articles for *Free World*, a political journal "devoted to democracy and world affairs." He then began an unsuccessful stint as a daily political columnist for the *New York Post* (which had ended

in November 1945) and was preparing to put his political views on the air with a nationally syndicated weekly radio broadcast. His fame led to much speculation, ranging from *Free World* publisher Louis Olivet's suggestion that he should be secretary-general of the United Nations to several rumors that he would seek to represent California or Wisconsin in the US Senate (Leaming, 299–304, 306–9, 316–17).

January–May

1 9 4 6

"When will our consciences grow so tender that we will act to prevent human misery rather than avenge it?"

Eleanor Roosevelt joined her fellow delegates to the United Nations December 31,

1945, as they sailed to London for the first meeting of the General Assembly. When reporters traveling with the delegation asked what she wanted to accomplish, ER replied: "I have one main interest—that we do set up an organization that can function," adding that given "the kind of background I have, my interest is in things that contribute—which are the causes of war." She deflected speculation about a more political career. She wanted to do as much writing and organizing as she could and that she expected "to continue doing what I have done."[1] As the excerpts from her London diary indicate, she kept as packed a schedule as she did in the White House, often beginning before breakfast and ending after midnight.

When her male colleagues chose ER to represent the United States on the Third Committee (Social, Humanitarian, and Cultural Affairs), she, to the surprise of all involved, soon had to grapple directly with issues in which she had long taken a keen interest: refugees, relief and rehabilitation, and human rights. Ironically, refugees emerged as the most prominent issue before the General Assembly, as the Communist and non-Communist delegates clashed over the management of the displaced persons camps in Europe and plans for a new agency to take over the refugee functions of UNRRA. The Soviet Union and its allies contended that displaced persons should be required to return to their nations of origin, but the United States and other Western nations argued that refugees should have the right to resettle elsewhere if they chose to do so. ER first debated this issue with the Communist representatives in the Third Committee, then "fought it out" in the General Assembly with Andrei Vyshinsky, the Soviet delegate. As ER told Joe Lash, "when Mr. Dulles said goodbye to me this morning, he said 'I feel I must tell you that when you were appointed I thought it was terrible and now I think your work has been fine!' So—against the odds, the women inch forward but I'm rather old to be carrying on the fight!"[2]

ER's journey abroad also deepened her understanding of the plight of refugees. At the close of the General Assembly, she flew to occupied Germany to tour displaced persons camps for Jews, Poles, and people from the Baltic. She heard the stories of the survivors of the Nazi concentration camps and the pleas of Jewish survivors to emigrate to Palestine. While still there, she used her My Day column to try to communicate to her readers the impact the camps had on her. She described conditions with "an aching heart." She then asked, "When will our consciences grow so tender that we will act to prevent human misery rather than avenge it."[3]

ER's experience in London and Germany defined many of the challenges she would confront and discuss over the next two years: how to make the UN strong, how to deal with the Russians, how to arouse Americans to shoulder their international responsibilities, how to create effective agencies to meet the needs of displaced persons, how to resettle thousands of refugees scattered among dozens of displaced persons camps throughout Europe, and how to reach an international agreement on the principles of human rights to forestall future abuses. The documents in this section reflect these themes.

Convinced that America had been "spared for a purpose" from the destruction that other nations endured during the war, ER used all avenues at her disposal—columns, speeches, articles, private conversation, correspondence—to urge Americans recognize what they had at stake and assume both the responsibility and the financial cost of world leadership. Less that twenty-four hours after returning from Europe, ER addressed a United Jewish Appeal rally, telling the audience, in graphic detail, what she saw and heard in the camps. In a March 1 meeting with Truman, ER summarized the delegation's work and her visit to the camps. She then followed up with a detailed memo highlighting her major concerns. Two weeks later she returned to Washington to address the Women's Joint Congressional Committee, insisting Americans must learn that "you cannot live for yourselves alone. You depend on the rest of the world and the rest of the world depends on you."[4]

The correspondence in this section also addresses many of the themes that emerged in London and Germany. For example, she recounted her concerns over Argentina's admission to the UN to Joe Lash. She shared her dismay that the US-British alliance proposed by Winston Churchill in his

March 5 "Iron Curtain Speech" would sharpen differences with the Soviet Union and weaken the UN with Arthur Murray. When the Anglo-American Commission of Inquiry, on which James McDonald served, recommended the admission of 100,000 refugees into Palestine, ER expressed her approval to McDonald and told him, "I think we should have the courage to tell the Arabs that we intend to protect Palestine."[5] Later that spring, Carrie Chapman Catt wrote asking for ER's help with the proposed Subcommission on the Status of Women.

Documents in this section also reflect the human rights issues ER addressed at home, including horrific racial violence, discrimination in housing, fears of inter-racial marriage, workers' rights to organize, and labor's right to strike. Her correspondence with Walter White and others documents ER's response to the "racial pogrom" in Columbia, Tennessee and her work with the National Committee for Defense of Columbia, Tennessee Riot Victims. When Allen Smith wrote to report that "the white people in my part of Virginia" think "you have done the Negro far more harm than you have done good,"[6] ER used her short retort to reframe the debate. Furthermore, as the material on the railroad strike illustrates, ER used a variety of venues to explain volatile political actions while carving out her own unique stance.

In March, ER accepted an assignment that enabled her to further develop the role of international human rights leader she assumed in London. After the conclusion of the General Assembly meeting in February, the UN Economic and Social Council appointed her to the "nuclear" commission on human rights and when the commission met for the first time in May 1946, its members unanimously elected ER chairman. The excerpt from the fourth meeting of the nuclear commission included in this section shows ER urging her colleagues to think of themselves as "representatives of the peoples of the world," not just their own governments and, when necessary, "to advocate something that it may be difficult for one's own government to carry through."[7]

---

1. See Document 74, Memorandum of Press Conference, 3 January 1946.

2. See Document 92, ER to Joseph Lash, 13 February 1946.

3. See Document 93, My Day, 16 February 1946.

4. See Document 99, Address by Eleanor Roosevelt to the Women's Joint Congressional Committee, 14 March 1946.

5. See Document 101, ER to Arthur Murray, 13 April 1946.

6. See header Document 108, ER to Allen Smith, 24 April 1946.

7. See Document 110, Commission on Human Rights of the Social and Economic Council Summary Record, Fourth Meeting [excerpt], 2 May 1946.

Senator Vandenberg, ER, Edward Stettinius, and Senator Connally traveled to London aboard the Queen Elizabeth. As they drove through the city en route to the General Assembly, ER told friends Connally "kept repeating: 'Where is all this destruction I've heard so much about, things look all right to me.'" See Document 75. © BETTMANN/CORBIS.

January 8, ER addressed 1,000 British women wed or engaged to US servicemen at the Rainbow Corner, a Red Cross recreation center for American soldiers in London. The women were struggling to obtain passports and transportation necessary for them to join their loved ones in America. See Documents 75 and 77. MILES/EXPRESS/HULTON ARCHIVES/GETTY IMAGES.

Byrnes's performance at the General Assembly did not impress ER. "I watch our delegation with great concern. Secy. Byrnes seems to me to be afraid to decide on what he thinks is right and stand on it … We could lead but we don't." See Document 80. © BETTMAN/CORBIS.

ER, A. Philip Randolph, and La Guardia pressed FDR to create the FEPC. When Congress debated its future, Randolph organized a rally to urge its continuation. He wrote ER "The filibuster now going on in Congress makes public awareness urgent and your attendance at the rally imperative." ER agreed. See Document 85. © BETTMANN/CORBIS.

The UN's first session achieved "real accomplishments." Member states' collaboration "really proved that the organization has life" and gave it "a great strength which was lacking in the League." Thus, "we have learned the lesson that becoming involved in war does not lie entirely in any one nation's hands." See Document 87. DAVID E. SCHERMAN/TIME LIFE PICTURES/GETTY IMAGES.

ER described the Zeilsheim displaced persons camp: "There is a feeling of desperation and sorrow … beyond expression. An old woman knelt on the ground, grasping my knees. I lifted her up, but could not speak. What could one say at the end of a life which had brought her such complete despair?" See Document 93. PHOTO BY MAXINE RUDE, COLLECTION OF CENTER FOR HOLOCAUST GENOCIDE STUDIES, UNIVERSITY OF MINNESOTA.

"They wanted me to go up to the stone monument that they themselves had built and the plaque that they had engraved to the 6,000,000 Jews who had been killed. They wanted me to hear ... what they wanted, what they had hoped for ... you wondered how they could hope for anything." See Document 95. UNITED STATES HOLOCAUST MEMORIAL MUSEUM. THE VIEWS OR OPINIONS EXPRESSED IN THIS BOOK, AND THE CONTEXT IN WHICH THE IMAGES ARE USED, DO NOT NECESSARILY REFLECT THE VIEWS OR POLICY OF, NOR IMPLY APPROVAL OR ENDORSEMENT BY, THE UNITED STATES HOLOCAUST MEMORIAL MUSEUM.

ER and Truman met at the end of each UN session to assess the US delegation's work. In a memo recapping their first discussion, she wrote "the whole social structure of Europe is crumbling and we might as well face the fact that leadership must come from us or it will inevitably come from Russia." See Document 97. © BETTMANN/CORBIS.

In March 1946, Churchill told a Fulton, Missouri, audience that "an iron curtain had descended across the Continent" and that the English-speaking nations must create an alliance to contain Communist nations. ER disagreed, calling the speech a "very unwise" provocation that would spur the creation of hostile alliances and cartels. See Documents 100–101. AP IMAGES.

Displaced Polish Jews confined in Berlin jostle to receive their daily bread ration. ER told friends that "a new type of political refugee is appearing—people who … if they stay at home or go home will probably be killed." The issue soon dominated the General Assembly's first session. See Documents 77–78. KEYSTONE/HULTON ARCHIVES/GETTY IMAGES.

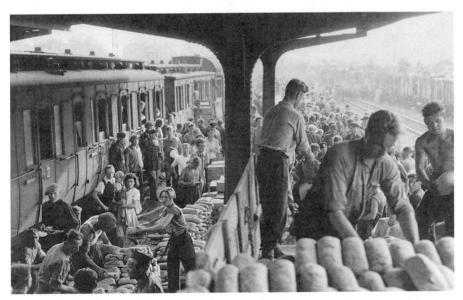

The UN Relief and Rehabilitation Administration carried "the burden of actually seeing that people do not starve," running its camps "as well as possible." ER urged ECOSOC, in designing UNRRA's replacement, to give "careful consideration" to all "complex and controversial" problems refugees confronted: "political, economic, social and humanitarian." See Documents 111 and 95. HAACKER/HULTON ARCHIVES/GETTY IMAGES.

ER empathized with coal miners and once visited an Ohio mine to underscore her support. She did not, however, respect their UMW president. "I wonder whether, with all his vaunted wisdom and foresight, John L. Lewis knew, when he started the coal-strike ball rolling, where it would come to rest." See Document 115. © BETTMANN/CORBIS.

May 25, Truman told Congress he would request "temporary legislative authority" to draft striking railroad workers into the army. While ER praised his leadership, she hoped he realized "that there must not be any slip, because of the difficulties of our peace-time situation, into a military way of thinking." See Document 115. AP IMAGES.

When police attacked the African American section of Columbia, Tennessee, ER decried the "lynch threats," the "armed invasion of the Negro district," and the flagrant disregard for the law. She then raised funds and pressed the Justice Department "to assure them the justice denied them by sworn officers of the law in Tennessee." See Document 118. FOX PHOTOS/GETTY IMAGES.

"I Can Say Just What I Want"

> ER held her first press conference after her appointment to the American delegation to the United Nations aboard the London-bound *Queen Elizabeth*, the luxury sea liner turned troop ship carrying the delegation, its staff, and the reporters assigned to the first meeting of the UN General Assembly in London, England.[1] The text below is the only extant coverage of her remarks. Although ER thought this transcript "incorrect," she retained it for her files and distributed it to friends at home. The questions she fielded reflect the continued interest in her political career, the system she developed to handle her mail, and the expectations she held for the General Assembly's first session. Of particular note is her off-the-record comment that "for the first time in my life I can say just what I want" and how "wonderful" it was "to feel free."

74

Memorandum of Press Conference Held by Mrs. Eleanor Roosevelt

3 January 1946 RMS Queen Elizabeth

Q. There is actually a great anxiety over anti-Semitism all over Europe.[2]

MRS. ROOSEVELT: Not only that. I mean granted that you can't eliminate everything else, you still—I heard someone tell about a man who came directly from there and gave a story of one man who had been at Belsen who had gone through from the very beginning to come out alive, although every member of his family were either killed or had died. He had managed to give such a dramatic story that the person who spoke to me said he would never get over the feeling of guilt that he hadn't done more here to help that situation.[3] Now you have to know we are not easily moved because we haven't seen very much. And you have to be told a story, a very compelling story, to make one of us, a pretty comfortable people, feel that our own sense of guilt was tremendous in this situation.

I have talked and seen quite a lot of people who have been in concentration camps and been in Dachau and places like that,[4] and I recognize the fact that as for us we cannot imagine something we have never seen.

Q. What is your suggestion as to how you might get this across to the people at home?

A. That is a terrible problem. You can write and talk all you like about it. I have done my best,[5] but to people who have never seen or heard anything similar to it it is practically impossible to get it across. Nothing makes it live.

Q. I have even talked to people who have seen horror pictures and talked about it afterwards as if it were a theory or fiction of some kind on the screen.

A. They don't want to believe it. It is a defense mechanism and you push it away and close your mind to its implications because you don't want to know.

Q. Do you have any specific problems or proposals for dealing with refugees? I notice the Agenda has been changed under the Order of Business.[6]

A. I think they really do not mean refugees but displaced persons generally, and I have no specific remedy. I would like very much to hear what is said. I was very glad when the President announced that we would, up to our quota, our limit, take people who are displaced persons[7]—because I don't see how we can ask the rest of the world to do something if we don't take some part in it ourselves; and for that reason we must accept some responsibility. I do not think you can be indifferent to the misery that exists in a tremendous area and just think of people dying without doing something about it. I think it does something to the people who are indifferent just as well as to the people who died.

Q. Do you think something should be done—can be done—at this first meeting?

A. If there is any opportunity it should be done—the sooner the better because according to all reports people are dying at the rate of 50 a day in Germany. Supposedly we are feeding them.[8]

Q. I was wondering if something could be done.

A. I think something could be done even on a temporary basis to start a movement for such people. I don't mean by that that we could take up any permanent solution—such as the Palestine question[9]—but something could be done to start moving people in different directions.

Q. Do you have any feeling about the competency of the small group of people coming over here who have very little knowledge of this country and who will look for a site for the permanent home?[10]

A. I really don't know who the people are because we don't have any vote in that. I don't know the names of the people who are coming. But I should think that if they know what the requirements are they should be able to judge whether any place was capable of fulfilling the requirements. I don't know what the requirements are. They have been working on it and must know.

Q. There has been quite a lot of discussion about the possibility of putting it at Hyde Park.

A. I don't own Hyde Park. The Government owns Hyde Park and I would have nothing to say about that.[11]

Q. What is your particular interest, Mrs. Roosevelt, as a member of the Delegation? I noticed last night you raised various questions about the specialized agencies and the social and humanitarian problems.[12]

A. I have one main interest—that we do set up an organization that can function. I think that is the main interest of everybody on the Delegation—that we set up machinery and begin to go to work; because no one is going to set up a perfect—51 nations are not going to set up a final and perfect organization but are going to set up something which can start to give us a chance to build for peace. I think this is the main objective of everybody on our Delegation. Naturally by having the kind of background I have, my interest is in the things that contribute—which are the causes of war.

One of the things that contributed to the League's failure was the fact that although many of the Committees did quite remarkable work, they were always referring controversial questions to special committees. The work of those committees never got back to where it was brought out into the open and discussed.[13] It is quite important to be able to enforce what a group decides. But the permanent job that has to be done is to eliminate the causes that bring them to war. Naturally with the kind of background that I have I am interested in that as compared to the background to match the rest of the world.

Q. That is really the job in a lot of little ways.

A. All of the different things come into that. That is one of the reasons I asked about the specialized things—Food and Agriculture, world labor conditions.[14] All of those things ... into the understanding and solution of the of the causes of war ... from my point of view they are the important part ... should think about.[15]

And I don't think the general public is well enough aware of any aspect of the United Nations work. I have been interested for a long time. I have sat in and listened to all these people who are here talk, and I have heard things that have been said.[16]

I remember the League and all the discussions that came before that. I was pretty close to all of that. I came home on the trip when President Wilson brought the Covenant home;[17] and yet I can sit here and be told things about the details every day, so how can we expect that the general public is really going to have a very good understanding of the details. I think there is a very wide appreciation of the need to prevent war. I think that if the atomic bomb did nothing more it scared people to the point where they realized that either they do something about it or chances were there would be a morning when they would not wake up. So, I think that for the first time there is a real general interest which you can discern.

I find it and I think you would find greater interest among your soldiers coming home from this war than those who came home from the last war. I have been talking to hospital people, and the questions they ask are so much more aware of the need for certain things than the questions you would get at the end of the last war. That, I think, is very encouraging. The younger generation, the people who fought the war and the people who worked during the war are very much more aware of what might happen in the world than they were at the end of the last war.

Q. Do you think that the people in Europe, in Russia for example, would have the same feeling?

A. I haven't any way of knowing. I was in England in the autumn of 1942 when most of our soldiers were just arriving and went from there to Casablanca while I was still in England, so I only have as real comparison talking with the British people at that time.[18] Now I have had no real contact with the peoples of the countries in Europe. I have had letters from some of the French people and some Italians but most of those letters, except in few cases of people that I know, are begging letters.

From letters from the people that I know in France, I am sorry to say, I get a sense of hopelessness which I hope is not indicative of a lasting feeling, but which is probably indicative of the years of depleted physical condition. I am interested in letters that I have had the last year from women in England because up to that time I thought that morale was really extraordinary.[19] This last year I can detect a great change in the acceptance of minor (major for us) discomforts there when bombs were dropping on their heads but they became harder and harder to bear.[20] I know of one officer who has been on a carrier. He said his wife runs a home for the children in Liverpool. She was ready to give up but while the war was on she was never ready to give up, which is understandable, utterly and completely.

If you and I had to stand up for five years against the type of thing I saw in England for three weeks, I know I would be ready to give up and it would be completely understandable. But I think it is something we should be aware of because it does put a greater responsibility on us. It means that we have the courage and stamina and have to give it in some way to other people.

Q. What type of writing do you plan for your column; are you going to write about the meeting?

A. Only in so far as it is open to all the press. If at any time the press is admitted to everything, and I imagine the press will be, I might mention what has happened at that time. I plan to deal with such things that are outside. I would like very much if I can to draw some comparisons, not that I hope to get a real picture across but I would love to get as much as I can across of the drabness of life—by telling little things.[21]

My husband had a cousin who lived in London and she was bombed out of two apartment houses. Right in the middle of the war she decided to buy a house. It was cheaper than before and it was a better buy so she bought it. Then two bombs came along and her door was blown completely off and the windows were smashed. The windows were covered up again but the door could not be taken care of so it was put back and leaned up and stayed in that way and that is where it still is.[22] You get mad because someone can't come and mend the door for two weeks, but she has been nearly 9 months with a door that couldn't close. I think those little things might possibly be good things to tell and that is what I rather hope to be able to do. That is purely an effort to bring a little more awareness of different conditions in life and I don't know whether I can make it interesting or whether I can make it worthwhile.

But I also think that I will write of anything in a purely social way that might interest people at home, because you would have the opportunity of knowing that you did it or you might have some interest in writing certain reactions.

Q. Are you planning to stay right with the Delegation?

A. Yes.

Q. You are staying at the Claridge?[23]

A. Yes. I plan to try to do a job.

Q. What other plans do you have, Mrs. Roosevelt, to carry out your interest? Through what machinery do you plan to operate beyond the conference? People who know at home have speculated about your future. Can you say anything about that?

A. I shall go on doing what I have done. Do as much writing as I can; work with such organizations that I can; I expect to continue doing what I have done. OFF THE RECORD. For the first time in my life I can say just what I want. For your information it is wonderful to feel free.

Q. There has been speculation whether you might run for Senator of New York.

A. I do not intend to run for office or to accept a party position of any kind. I don't mean by that that I wouldn't take this sort of thing because I think I could be useful here and I feel that I had enough background and equipment to be of some use here but I don't intend to do anything which I feel I haven't really the background for.

Q. I was in New York in November and I was told that you would carry New York State like nobody's business if you intend to run.

A. I don't intend to run. No, I think that when you get to be 61 you might better be helping younger people do the job. After all they have a job to work at for a good many more years than you have and it is much better to help younger people that you think have real interest and convictions than it is for you yourself to stay in harness.[24]

Q. Going back to one minor point. I am curious what you do about these begging letters that you get from abroad.

A. The letters from foreign countries which are purely begging letters, if they seem to me to be sincere I sent them on. For example the Italian letters were sent on to Myron Taylor who sent them to people who could investigate them. He started the organization over there for relief.[25] I learned a long while ago that there was no use in doing things for individuals unless you can investigate the people.

People who beg by letter frequently do not want help but they may lead you to real conditions and you start investigations.

(Spoke of the woman who asked for replacement of rare coins, and young girl who asked for shoes and dress for graduation)

I made the grave mistake, on leaving the White House, of thinking I would have no mail. But I have never had less than 100 a day and frequently 300 and 400 a day. It is just a perfectly terrible job and I keep hoping it is going to disappear but so far it hasn't.[26]

Q. Are most of them begging letters?

A. No, strangely enough, when the war came a great deal of the character changed. Of course in the White House it was mostly dealing with those that hoped to get in the Government. The year after my husband went into the White House, I got 300,000 letters. We built up a system that the obvious letters went to the different departments and anything that nobody wanted was always left for me to answer—between 50 and 60 letters every night.[27] In a way it was the best education in this country I had ever had. It was an education in the USA during the depression. The whole character changed in the war. Most letters were regarding soldiers—can you find out where my boy is; my boy is in camp and his father is dying; and, can you find out what is happening to my boy. The reply to these letters was that the information was governed by military rules. But nevertheless that in itself seemed to be something which seemed to have a strengthening substance. I can't tell you why but it did. It is a mystery. Of course, at first it was largely things that they felt the President had done and that now they can't quite understand it. The President used to tell us, what does this mean—why doesn't this happen or why doesn't that happen. Also there were some concrete things, such as, could you tell us how one would go about getting certain things.

On the average, I could have given away $20,000 a day.[28]

Q. You spoke of this feeling of a greater awareness on the part of the returning veterans. What is your own feeling about what kind of a spiritual reaction we are going to have as a result of the war? Do you expect a let down of the general moral standards as in the last war?

A. I think that depends so tremendously upon the men. You will get it among the women because they haven't felt the war except for anxiety and losing their men; but none, except the few who have been abroad for the Red Cross or WACS[29]—except for that very small percentage practically no woman in America has actually wondered when she left in the morning whether she would have a home at night.

Having that experience, I think, is an incentive to fight for peace, for this type of organization which we haven't got. That worries me terribly, because it is going to depend a lot upon the women if the will to do it is going to live. And I am afraid that the women who know it are going to be sapped of strength, and perhaps the women who have the strength will not know enough to put in the strength. The theory is they desire them but lack putting the pay into it. You don't get anything unless you pay for it. (It all depends on) what you are willing to give up in order to have a chance for peace and whether you are willing to have some hardship, and that is hard to do.

(Told story of Dutch publisher who had spent 4 years in concentration camp and who, in his travels through the Middle West had listened to some of his friends complaining of all the hardships in traveling at home. He said he could not tell that back in Holland because his people would not understand the feeling.)[30]

The men have to tell their stories and make their people understand or else how are we going to fulfill our obligations?

Q. What do you think about the pessimistic talk about having to go to war with Russia?

A. I don't think we have to go to war with Russia. I don't think we have to go to war with anybody, but it depends a good deal upon our willingness to think about people as people. Why should the Russian people want war any more than we do? Why shouldn't they be as much at present, or a little more, afraid of us than we are of them, and why shouldn't we try to build a little confidence?

There is no surer way of going to war than being afraid of what other people are going to do to you. I think we need to build our own confidence, and through having confidence in ourselves, the confidence of the rest of the world. I don't see why we can't start thinking of the Russians as individual people rather than as we get a picture of them as a great big bear.

TMem AERP, FDRL

---

1. The General Assembly convened in London, January 10, 1946. For more on ER and the delegation's duties see Document 68 (Lash, *Years*, 39; "UNO May Throw Light Upon Moscow Meeting," *NYT*, 23 December 1945, E3).

2. Reports of anti-Semitism in postwar Europe began appearing in the American press in the summer of 1945. In October anti-Jewish attacks and riots occurred in Poland and Slovakia as repatriated Jewish refugees sought the return of their homes and property, causing approximately 200 Polish Jews per day to cross the border into the American and British zones in Austria. According to a report ER received in November from former USO entertainer Helen Waren, who aided Jewish refugees in Germany, much of the hostility came from possible former Nazi collaborators who feared Soviet retribution. In France, opposition to the return of Nazi-confiscated Jewish property in French hands was weaker but still present, while in Austria, the hostility of low-level officials delayed the restoration of housing and jobs to returning Jewish refugees ("Jews in U.S. Zone of Reich Find Conditions Improving," *NYT*, 26 August 1945, 1; "Anti-Semitism Rife in Central Europe," *NYT*, 9 September 1945, 22; "Polish Jews Flee into Austria Daily," *NYT*, 7 October 1945, 15; "Refuge for Jews," *NYT*, 14 October 1945, E2; "Flight of Few Jews Left Is in View as Polish Anti-Semitism Strikes," *NYT*, 27 October 1945, 6; Helen Waren to ER, November 1945, GCMP, ViLxM).

3. The identities of the person who told the story and the person who was imprisoned at Bergen-Belsen are unknown. Nearly 50,000 Jews and non-Jews died at Bergen-Belsen, a Nazi concentration camp in northwestern Germany. After the war more than 112,000 displaced persons lived there making it the largest Jewish displaced persons camp in the British occupation zone (Rebecca Weiner, "Bergen-Belsen," The American-Israeli Cooperative Enterprise, http://www.jewishvirtuallibrary.

org/jsource/Holocaust/Belsen.html, accessed 18 January 2005; United States Holocaust Memorial Museum, "Bergen-Belsen," http://www.ushmm.org/wlc/article.php?lang=en&ModuleId=10005224, accessed 12 July 2005).

4. ER did not reveal the identities of those with whom she discussed Dachau, the Nazi camp that during its twelve-year existence imprisoned more than 188,000 people from thirty-four nations, an estimated 53,000 of whom died from the treatment they received while incarcerated there (United States Holocaust Memorial Museum, "Dachau," *Holocaust Encyclopedia*, http://www.ushmm.org/wlc/article.php?lang=en&ModuleId=10005214, accessed 18 January 2005).

5. For examples of ER's initial efforts to publicize the horrors of the Nazi death camps, see Document 4. The Holocaust continued to preoccupy ER. In her May 2 column she used the example of the concentration camps to buttress her contention that the Fascists were more dangerous than the Communists because the former's ideology affected "the nature and the souls of all human beings who fall under their domination." September 24 she drew attention to that because of

> a legalism which sets down how we shall treat German nationals, both civilians and prisoners of war, our authorities feel bound to make no distinction in their treatment of German nationals whom they found in concentration camps in Germany.

> We have not even removed many of these people from places where filth and disease are rampant. These prisoners of the Nazis were largely Jewish, though among them may be found political prisoners of other religious beliefs and national origin who were opposed to the Nazis. They have been interned, many of them for years, under horrible conditions. They have lacked food and clothing; cleanliness has been impossible, and they have been under constant fear of torture and maltreatment. We prolong these years of horror because, legally, they are German nationals.

> This seems to me unthinkable. I am sure that the people of our country, if they were aware of this particular situation, would feel as strongly as I do that those who have suffered under the Nazis—no matter what their nationality or religion—are not our enemies or the enemies of the Allied nations, and should not be treated as such.

> These are the things which happen because general directives have to govern situations which cover large areas of territory, and at first it is hard to foresee the exceptions which have to be made in almost every situation. I hope, however, that these terrible conditions, which affect so many thousands of human beings, will be corrected as soon as possible (*MD*, 2 May and 24 September 1945).

6. Because of its size, scope, and urgency, the United Nations Preparatory Commission (see *n*5, Document 68) added the refugee question to the assembly's agenda even though they originally intended the first session of the General Assembly to focus primarily on organizational issues. In early 1946, approximately 1.5 to 2 million refugees who refused repatriation for political reasons or who wished to immigrate to Palestine or the United States remained in camps in the Allied zones of occupation (ER London Diary, 2 January 1946, AERP; United States Delegation to the General Assembly First Delegation Meeting, 2 January 1946, RG84, NARA II; "Opening Session To-Day," *TL*, 10 January 1946, 14; Refugees, UN: Publications 1945–46, AERP; "Repatriation Task Will End in Fall," *NYT*, 6 July 1945; Boyd, 110; United States Holocaust Memorial Museum, "Holocaust Encyclopedia, Postwar Refugee Crisis and the Establishment of the State of Israel," http://www1.ushmm.org/wlc/article.php?lang=en&ModuleId=10005459, accessed 27 January 2005).

7. On December 22, 1945, President Truman announced that he had directed several governmental agencies to expedite admission into the United States of 39,000 displaced persons within the quota system established by the Immigration Act of 1924. Because the Immigration Act set quotas at 2 percent of each nationality residing in the United States in 1890, and limited total immigration to 165,000 annually, the directive could only have a minimal impact on solving the Jewish refugee crisis in Europe. But the president believed that by taking this step, he could set an exam-

ple to the other countries of the world which were able to receive some of these "war sufferers." "I feel that it is essential that we do this ourselves to show our good faith in requesting other nations to open their doors for this purpose," said Truman. "Common decency and the fundamental comradeship of all human beings require us to do what lies within our power to see that our established immigration quotas are used in order to reduce human suffering" ("Truman Statement on Displaced Persons," *NYT*, 23 December 1945, 6; Kolsky, 125).

8. ER also used the figure of fifty fatalities a day in her November 7, 1945, column but provided no source for this information in either document. She implied in the column that she may have heard it rather than read it. The daily caloric ration for Jewish refugees in the American zone of occupied Germany in late May 1945 ranged from 2,000 to 3,100 calories a day depending on whether the displaced persons lived independently (less food) or in camps (more food). In December, a group of US army generals toured a Jewish displaced persons camp in Landsberg, Germany, in the American Occupied Zone that was reportedly short of food. They found the meals there "adequate though monotonous and too starchy" (*MD*, 7 November 1945; "Jews in U.S. Zone of Reich Find Conditions Improving," *NYT*, 26 August 1945, 1; "Displaced Jews in Worse Plight," *NYT*, 20 November 1945, 6; "Army Finds Camp of Jews Crowded," *NYT*, 7 December 1945, 5).

9. For more on the status of the Palestine question, see Document 54, *n*8 and *n*9 Document 60, Document 61.

10. The United Nations Preparatory Commission designated a seven-member subcommittee under the chairmanship of Dr. Stoyan Gavrilovitch of Yugoslavia to determine a site for the organization's permanent home in the eastern United States. Other members of the committee were Dr. Shu Hsi-hsu of China, vice chairman; François Brière, France; Awny el-Khalidi, Iraq; Major Kenneth A. Younger, Great Britain; Dr. Julio A. Lacarte, Uruguay; and George Saksin, USSR. The group arrived in the United States on January 5, 1946 ("Peace Site Group Flies to U.S. Today," *NYT*, 4 January 1946, 11; "UNO Group in Washington," *NYT*, 7 January 1946, 3).

11. As of January 1, 1946, Hyde Park remained on the list of potential sites for the UN's permanent home along with sites in New York, Connecticut, Massachusetts, and New Jersey. Publicly ER expressed no preference, although she wrote her aunt, Maude Gray, that "the Republicans are so opposed [to Hyde Park], they are afraid it might perpetuate FDR's name!" However, on September 11, 1945, she did write Truman about the possibility of using FDR's home and the nearby Rogers estate as the UN headquarters. "There is great interest in the Village [of Hyde Park] in having all or some of the property … selected as the permanent headquarters … You will get the local petition eventually but I thought I'd pass the idea on now." Three days later Truman replied: "Your suggestion is an excellent one but I don't know what the program will be with regard to the location … Sometime when you are in Washington I will be glad to discuss the whole thing with you." See also *n*7 Document 140 ("UNO Will Choose Two Places in U.S." *NYT*, 1 January 1946, 16; "UNO Group in Washington," *NYT*, 7 January 1946, 3; "Interim UN Site Here Is Discussed," *NYT*, 9 January 1946, 10; "UNO Body Inspects Hyde Park Estates," *NYT*, 11 January 1946, 2; ER to Maude Gray, 22 January 1945, AERP; ER to Harry Truman, 11 September 1945; Harry Truman to ER, 14 September 1945, HSTL).

12. In her travel diary for this trip, ER says of this meeting "now I've spent an hour and a half with the press getting a repetition of much that we've had this morning from [Alger] Hiss and [Leo] Pa[s]volsky." However, ER's papers contain no record of any questions she asked or the issues she raised (ER's London Diary, 2 January 1946, AERP).

13. For example, delegates to the first League of Nations disarmament conference in Geneva (1932–34) organized committees on such technical issues as arms traffic, air disarmament, and security; however, these groups only met intermittently and their reports were tabled (Whittaker, 106).

14. See *n*12 above. At this point the specialized agencies included the United Nations Educational, Scientific and Cultural Organization (UNESCO), the Food and Agriculture Organization (FAO),

the International Monetary Fund, and a provisional version of the International Civil Aviation Organization (ICAO). The International Labor Organization (ILO), founded in 1919 under the auspices of the League of Nations, became a UN agency in December 1946 ("A Short History of FAO" http://www.fao.org/UNFAO/about/history_en.html, accessed 17 January 2005); International Civil Aviation Organization (ICAO), "Foundation of the International Civil Aviation Organization" (ICAO) http://www.icao.int/icao/en/ro/eurnat/history02.htm, accessed 17 January 2005; http://www.un.org/aboutun/chart.html, accessed 17 January 2005).

15. The stenographer's carbon folded over onto itself and thus this part of the text was not captured.

16. See *n*12 above. ER's diary discusses her formal and informal meetings with members of the delegation and State Department staff on such issues as trusteeship, the agenda for the first session of the General Assembly, and the development of an international health organization. ER also attended reporters' shipboard interview with State Department officials (ER's London Diary, 31 December 1945, 2 January and 4 January 1946, AERP; Lash, *Years*, 40; James B. Reston, "Her UNO Task Set by Mrs. Roosevelt," *NYT*, 6 January 1946, 17).

17. Early in January 1919, ER accompanied FDR, then assistant secretary of the navy, to Europe where he supervised the liquidation of naval property. They returned in February on the same ship carrying President Woodrow Wilson and his wife, Edith. The president had just completed negotiations securing the support of Allied ministers for the Treaty of Versailles (and, therefore, the League of Nations Covenant). Aboard ship, the Roosevelts attended a Washington's Birthday luncheon at which Wilson said, "The United States must go in [to the League of Nations] or it will break the heart of the world for she is the only nation that all feel is disinterested and all trust." Both Roosevelts supported the League during and after the ratification fight, and FDR made US entry into the League the centerpiece of his losing vice-presidential campaign in 1920. Twelve years later, FDR, then a contender for the 1932 Democratic presidential nomination, abandoned his support for the League in part to appease publisher William Randolph Hearst, a leading isolationist. His disavowal of the League created tension with ER whose support for the league never wavered (Lash, *Eleanor*, 229–34, 346–48; Dallek, 18–19; Graff, 384–85; Schlesinger, 26).

18. In October 1942, ER visited Great Britain for three weeks to observe the war effort on the British home front and see American troops stationed there who were preparing for the invasion of North Africa the following month. For more on ER's travels to the European and Pacific theatres during World War II, see *n*13 Document 11 (Lash, *Eleanor*, 657–68; Leckie, 483–84).

19. During World War II, ER closely followed the work of British social worker Lady Stella Reading (1894–1971), head of England's Women's Voluntary Services for Civil Defense (WVSCD), which used women's defense work as a way to attack "class distinctions." (ER and Reading had known each other since 1918 when Reading's husband served as British ambassador to the United States.) ER considered WVSCD a model for American civil defense efforts and toured many of its installations with Reading during her wartime trip to Great Britain (see *n*18 above).

In September 1945, ER published part of a letter from Reading, who continued to lead WVSCD after the war, to publicize the difficult conditions in postwar Britain and the British attitude toward their hardships. According to Reading, "the one predominating worry" then was housing. "Alongside of that we are … full of apprehension of the difficulties we are going to have to meet this coming winter in food, clothing and fuel. In fact, it looks as if one's worries will not let up for quite a little while. But undoubtedly the fact that we need no longer worry in regards to people facing death does make a very great difference." Not everyone was as optimistic. Anthony Stephens, a newly demobilized British soldier and the son of one of ER's Allenswood classmates, Lottie Simpson, wrote that "the future looks rather depressing, with so much misunderstanding and hatred in the world which the Press seems to foster instead of smooth away" (Lash, *Eleanor*, 638–39, 644–45, 666; Cook, vol. 2, 375; *MD*, 11 September 1945; Anthony Stephens to ER, 8 January 1946, AERP).

For a sample of the information ER received on postwar conditions in France see, ER to Frances Willert, 31 August 1945, AERP.

20. Civilian casualties in Great Britain during World War II totaled 146,777 (60,595 killed and 86,182 wounded), more than half of which occurred in London ("Civilian Casualties," http://www.grolier.com/wwii/wwii_16.html, accessed February 20, 2005).

21. For example, February 9 ER wrote that she hoped Americans would "realize how much normal life in Britain has changed and what it means when an English family today gives a guest from overseas a dinner … frequently, this one meal takes a whole week's ration of every member of the family, particularly where meat or fats of any kind are concerned" (*MD*, 9 February 1946).

22. Possibly ER refers to Muriel Delano Robbins Price-Collier Martineau, daughter of FDR's maternal aunt, Katherine Delano Robbins Price-Collier. Martineau lived in England (Sara Delano Roosevelt Diaries, 1910, FDRL).

23. The Claridge is a hotel in the Mayfair section of London where the US delegation stayed during the first session of the UN General Assembly (Lash, *Years*, 41).

24. For more on ER's refusal to run for office and her post-White House career plans, see Document 10 and Document 11. A *New York Times* article in November 1945 reported "a good deal of support" for ER if she chose to run for the Senate in 1946 in the event that the incumbent, Sen. James M. Mead (D-NY), decided to challenge Republican governor Thomas Dewey for the governorship (James A. Hagerty, "Dewey's Prestige Lowered by GOP Defeat in the City," *NYT*, 11 November 1945, 70; Smith, R. 466).

25. Myron C. Taylor (1874–1959), personal representative of the US President to Pope Pius XII from 1939 to 1950, helped organize American Aid for Italy, Inc., a relief organization composed of Catholics, Quakers, labor unions, the YMCA, the Salvation Army, and other organizations, which sent clothing, milk, vitamins, and medicine to liberated Italy beginning in December 1944. A close friend of FDR's, Taylor served as chairman of the board of the US Steel Corporation (1932–1938) and chairman of the Evian Conference for relief of political refugees (1938) and vice chairman of the Intergovernmental Commission on Political Refugees (1938–1944) ("Myron Taylor Dies; Ex-Envoy to Vatican," *NYT*, 7 May 1959, 1; Clare Boothe Luce, Letter to the Editor, *NYT*, 29 May 1945, 14; Papers of Myron C. Taylor, HSTL; "Intergovernmental Committee on Refugees, Appointment of Earl G. Harrison as United States Representative," *State Department Bulletin*, 18 March 1945, 452).

26. Immediately after FDR's death, ER received large quantities of mail—as many as 25,000 letters in the first week alone. Malvina "Tommy" Thompson, ER's secretary, answered much of the routine correspondence with the help of temporary or part-time secretaries who also drafted letters. ER also used My Day on several occasions in 1945 and early 1946 to issue a blanket acknowledgment or to thank those who remembered her at Christmas, on V-E Day, and at the start of her trip to Europe for the UN General Assembly meeting. While ER was in Europe, Thompson handled all the important mail and much of the routine correspondence. She wrote her "Precious Person":

> I have been answering all of the important mail and keeping what I think is important. I doubt that you will have to read much of it. Hick told me you suggested my sending her things to read, but very little has come in. So many of the letters are requests for jobs at the UNO and Dorothy Dow found out from the State Dept. how to answer them so they are easily handled. You still get letters from women wanting their men back and those are easily handled, and the same goes for veterans who aren't satisfied with their pensions, etc. Several others want you to find apartments for them, etc. A good many letters asking you to speak all over the country—to which I replied that you could make no commitments, and probably would be busy during February after you get back.

(*MD*, 18, 24, and 26 April 1945; 12 May 1945; 13 June 1945; 24 December 1945; and 3 January 1946; Frances M. Seeber, "I Want You to Write to Me: The Papers of Anna Eleanor Roosevelt," *Prologue* 2 Summer 1987, 95–105; Malvina Thompson to ER, (5 letters) n.d., AERP).

27. Within six months of the publication of her 1933 article "I Want You to Write to Me," in *Woman's Home Companion*, ER received more than 300,000 letters, many of them seeking help, intervention, or advice. To handle these letters and the thousands of others she subsequently received as first lady, ER devised a system whereby she sent many of the letters to the relevant government agencies. Often she followed up on these queries writing to agency heads and members of the cabinet. She and "Tommy" Thompson drafted replies to others. Thompson and Edith Helm, White House social secretary, drafted replies for routine correspondence. Anything else that remained, ER dealt with herself personally, drafting and signing the replies (Cook, vol. 2, 115; A. Black, *Casting*, 26; and Seeber).

28. Although ER supported numerous organizations, such as the the American Friends Service Committee, the NAACP, and the Bryn Mawr summer school for working women, she also received hundreds of individual requests for financial assistance daily from Americans struggling to cope with the economic consequences of the depression or war. For examples of appeals during the Great Depression, see MacElvaine and Seeber. (Cook, vol. 2, 3, 26, 115, 141, 201–2, 356).

29. The US Women's Army Corps.

30. ER's papers do not contain the name of the Dutch publisher. ER mentioned this publisher and his American wife and a similar encounter with a representative of the Norwegian press (all unnamed) in a December 1945 column to publicize the postwar suffering of America's Allies and encourage US support for the reconstruction of Europe's economy (*MD*, 14 December 1945).

ELEANOR ROOSEVELT'S LONDON DIARY

From December 31, 1945, when the American delegation left New York, until February 11, just before the conclusion of the General Assembly, ER kept an almost daily diary. Its twenty-seven entries, composed as a series of letters to her secretary "Tommy" Thompson, records her daily activities, the people she met, and her observations on a range of topics. As Tommy received these dispatches, she distributed them to various members of the family and a few friends, such as Trude W. Lash and Lorena Hickok.[1] Although a few of the entries overlap somewhat with My Day, if ER covered a topic in her column, she might refer to her discussion of that event in her column rather than repeating her observations in the diary. The editors chose seven of ER's London diary entries to include here.

75

London Diary
6 January 1946

The columns describe the landing and drive to London and our luxury here,[2] so I will only say that Sen. Connolly[3] kept repeating: "Where is all this destruction I've heard so much about, things look all right to me". I started to point out bombed spots but soon found he just wasn't interested. They all went out to lunch today with Lady Astor[4] and Adlai Stevenson[5] went with them and he told me the Senators made much the same remarks to him. Cliveden probably did nothing to change their point of view.[6] Lady Reading is really grieved that you are not here.[7] She came in for a moment and then the Noel Bakers.[8] They were chiefly concerned to impress on me that in my speech at Albert Hall I must not say the League had failed, since it had really laid the groundwork for all that was being done today, etc.[9] He was a great League man and they tell me feels called upon to defend it at every turn. John Winant came in and was sweet. It is hard to believe that whatever his financial troubles are that there is any lack [of] integrity involved.[10] The tears came to his eyes in talking of Franklin. The rest of the evening was recorded in the column.[11] At nine-thirty this morning Miss Cuddy came and she stayed until nearly one.[12] We did two columns and I dictated some notes and listened to her phone some messages in order to judge what she would do. I think she will do all right, though she is not as good as the one who will be at the office, slower and not as accurate.

I talked to Maude on the telephone and I think they will come over soon,[13] as I told her I will be busier every day. She too was sad that you were not here. She will have to share my room and David will go to a friend's flat.[14] The hotels are filled to capacity all the time.

Marty Gellhorn left for Batavia the day before I arrived, so I shall not see her as she will be gone six weeks.[15] I'm very sorry. I saw Mary Hornaday on the boat, and after the press conference tomorrow afternoon I'll ask her to tea.[16] I went out to lunch with Louise Morley,[17] then investigated my office and had the LaRue Browns to tea.[18] Dined and stayed late with Mr. Stevenson. Miss Fosdick was there so I won't have to see her separately for business reasons, but I like her and will try to see her now and then.[19] Four of the state department people dropped in and we talked late, now I must go to bed for I begin tomorrow breakfast at eight. Miss Cuddy at nine and I have to be at a full delegation meeting at the office at eleven.

TDi AERP, FDRL

76

London Diary
7 January 1946

Two letters from you today.[20]

Breakfast here is eatable (Claridges). I take tea and toast in the morning. For the rest if I am not going to a friend, I eat at the Embassy canteen which is a four block walk. I have now from nine to ten to do all personal work, columns, notes, telephones, and beginning next Monday I will have to do personal stuff from eight to nine as we have a delegation meeting at the office every morning at nine-fifteen. It is a five minute brisk walk from the hotel but we meet on the seventh floor and the lift runs more slowly, and far less reliably than the one in our old apartment house here. Therefore, I must leave at nine sharp. At ten-thirty we must be at the general meeting place in a church house near Westminister Abbey, nearly a fifteen minute drive. Committee meetings will be there and we do not get back till late. This morning I began work at nine here. At eleven we met at 20 Grosvenor Square, which is our office building, for our first delegation meeting to decide on press policy. Senator Vandenburg is difficult. I was worried about independent action but he doesn't want to even listen to anyone else. On the boat he circulated a secret memo giving his objections to the working of the Moscow resolution. He gave it to the press in confidence but says, tonight it is on the front pages of New York and London papers. The Times man sent it in and says everyone knew about it.[21] Ten minutes before a scheduled press conference at five-thirty, Mr. Dulles told Mr. Stettinius that he and Mr. V. could not go to a press conference where they could not answer questions, this had been agreed to this morning because Secy. Byrnes arrives tomorrow night and this should be discussed with him. After we had gone up, Sen. V. walked in and took some of the remaining press people up to his room. It seemed to me pretty shoddy behavior though I was in sympathy with parts of his memo. I think he is right that language should be clear. Mr. S. seemed to show up well, calm and no apparent anger.

To go back to my diary, our meeting ended at twelve-thirty. I went to my office and went over what had come in there, and at one-fifteen John Winant came to take me with him to lunch at the Churchills. They were charming, the only other guests were the First Lord of the Admiralty and Lady Cunningham. He was at Quebec.[22]

I am on the "Humanitarian and Cultural Committee" and Senator Townsend is put on with me[23]. At three in my office we met the technical advisers, got our home work, a weighty sheaf of several pages, which I still must read tonight. Arranged to meet at ten-thirty tomorrow morning.

At four I talked to both United Press people here for an hour. At five I gave a tea party for Mesdames Connelly, Vandenburg, Dulles. Lady Reading came, Dorothy Brown brought the Marchesa Roselli and Lady Salter rang up so I asked her.[24] Ben Welles and his fiancee came in,[25] and also Mrs. Blaisdell who is working for UNRRA, and I think I accomplished what I hoped and these ladies will see something of what the war has meant to England and they won't leave thinking this hotel is the way everyone is living.[26] They will have to tell their husbands since together I fear they only dine in good society and visit the Clivedens which still exist.[27]

At five thirty I was sent for to go to Mr. Stettinius's room and hear the bad news about Vandenburg and Dulles. Then we went to the press conference where all went well till the inevitably question came: "Where are the two Republican members of the delegation? Does their absence indicate a split in the delegation?" Mr. S. said: "Certainly not, you men who were on the boat know that is not so. I think Sen. Vandenburg is probably at a committee meeting." Then we left quickly.[28]

My tea party was still going on so they seemed to have a good time. At seven I joined Frank Walker and his daughter, we met Louise Morley and as I wanted the two young people to meet, I asked her to come along to the canteen with us and we had a pleasant dinner.[29] I saw Josephine

Roche there and to my surprise she greeted me warmly. She is over here on coal and has visited many of the mines.[30] Many people come up to speak and seem glad that I go to the canteen so I guess my hunch was right and it was a good thing to do, besides the fact that the food is better. Since my return at eight-thirty I've written several long hand notes. One of the Queen who sent me today a sweet note of welcome. I am sending home by slow mail carbons of all columns, letters that we should keep or you might like to see. Everything is ready for tomorrow morning and I must go to bed and read. It is 12:30.

TDi, ARHP2, FDRL

___77___

London Diary
9 January 1946

I didn't write last night because it was too late after I got back from Mrs. LaRue Brown's[31] where I went for dinner and got things tidied up so I could go to work this morning. Miss Cuddy comes at 8:30 and apologizes for being late, when I just barely manage to drink my tea and get it taken away!

Yesterday morning I worked with Miss Cuddy till 10:30 and from then till one I attended a meeting in Mr. Stettinius' room, going over the people the delegation was to back for the various positions with the reasons for the choices. They now want Spaak of Belgium for President of this session of the Assembly.[32] The Big Five are not asking for any of the elective positions so as to avoid being thought to want too much domination![33] The British and ourselves would like Pearson of Canada for Sec. Gen., but that will take Canada off the Security Council.[34] This type of choosing runs through all the positions but all may change at a moment's notice so I won't tell you any more.

I went to a Red Cross ceremony which I described in my column, all except the fact that I had to make an extra speech to the British staff to tell them how much we appreciated their work.[35] I got home barely in time to go to the Browns. Mr. Brown came to get me and we walked as it was only three blocks and the rain was just the usual drizzle. I got home about ten and worked till 12:30.

Secy. Byrnes got in on time yesterday and Mrs. B. came with him. Mr. Bevin called on him in the evening and he saw the Senators and Mr. Stettinius and all seems to be serene on the atomic bomb statement which stirred up such a rumpus with Sen. V.[36] I am not sure the gentleman does not like a little newspaper publicity. The mail is heavy on every conceivable subject as it was last time, so I keep both secretaries busy though their has been no work for the conference yet for Miss Norton to do.[37]

I went at eleven-thirty today to the delegates and alternates meeting here in the hotel with the Secy. He talked pleasantly to us till one and then we had a picture taken and I lunched with the Dulles. At three I was at the office, signed mail, dictated all she had and the first draft of my Albert Hall speech,[38] was home at 4:15 for a photograph for the paper which will carry my column,[39] got rid of them and of Miss C.[40] and at five Mr. Van Kleffens of the Netherlands came to tea. You will remember him as the Minister for Foreign Affairs but he is now not very popular with the new government and has had a breakdown which sent him to Switzerland for a month and apparently eliminated his name from consideration as Sec. Gen.[41] Louise Morley,[42] Frank Walker's daughter,[43] a Lt. Woodlock,[44] a friend of Mrs. Woodward,[45] Miss Fosdick and Mary Hornaday[46] came in too and I think every one had a pleasant time. Mary Hornaday has been to Yugoslavia and Greece and is deeply stirred by what she has seen. I had dinner alone tonight, read a long memo on the refugee question which we must try to put off till the next part of this session, and still be prepared on if Great Britain insists on having it taken up. A new type of political refugee is appearing—people who have been against the present governments and if they stay at home or go home will probably be killed. Britain is supporting most of them and would like the expense shared—the budget for the job might run to double what is contemplated for the whole of UNO.[47] I have a few more things to read tonight.

If the second part of this session isn't till May, the Russian trip may be possible this April. Otherwise it will have to wait till towards the end of the summer as I want to be home this summer. The session may keep us away sometime anyway. All of our people want this session to end in three weeks and if that happens then even if I went to Germany I'd be home if they can arrange for me to fly, by the 18th or 8th.

TDi AERP, FDRL

---

1. Lash, *World*, 209–11.

2. ER recorded her impressions of the British countryside in My Day:

> It is a moving thing to return to a country which you have seen in time of war and take stock of what the intervening years of continued war have done not only to material things, but to the people themselves.
>
> As we drove through Southampton and then through the countryside and the little villages, I marveled at the work which had been done to clear up destruction in the towns. Anyone who has known the British countryside in the past cannot help but see great changes—fences, walls, hedges, which then would have been in 'apple-pie' order, now very often resemble our rather haphazard ways in the United States. A traveler coming from the United States for the first time might not realize that spaces between houses in towns and villages are usually the work of a bomb and not the result of never having been used.
>
> Nature has a way of covering up very quickly the scars made by man in the woods and fields, but if you look carefully you will see where exploding bombs have left their marks in regions far from military objectives. What strikes the experienced eye is the neglect which has come about because people could not afford to keep up their houses or grounds. The actual cutting down of woods, necessitated by the need for increased agricultural production, must have been a great sacrifice to many landowners. In the United States to see a bit of fence knocked down and not immediately replaced is nothing very unusual, but here in the days before the war it would have been very quickly repaired (*MD*, 8 January 1946).

As she traveled to London, she noticed "that while the shops put on a rather brave display in their windows, there is really little to buy and the rationing system is still in full force." The delegation, however, stayed in relative luxury:

> We are staying at Claridge's where we are spared the rigors of a private home or a less luxurious hotel. Having been warned that we would be cold, I suffered from the heat on arrival and had to turn off the little electric heaters which I am sure had been turned on to keep the American guests happy. I am glad that when I was here before in 1942 I stayed in a number of British homes. Otherwise I am afraid that this visit would give me little conception of what the life of the average individual family has been and still is in this embattled island (*MD*, 9 January 1946).

3. Senator Tom Connally (D-TX).

4. Lady Astor (1879–1964), born Nancy Langhorne in Virginia, married Waldorf Astor in England and became the first woman member of the British Parliament. She held her seat for twenty-five

years. After the Munich agreement, the press wrongfully charged Lord and Lady Astor and their friends with being Hitler sympathizers and labeled them "the Cliveden Set," referring to the Astors' country home. FDR referred to the supposedly pro-Nazi "Cliveden Set" in a press conference and when Lady Astor complained, ER wrote to apologize. ER attended a luncheon with women members of Parliament arranged by Lady Astor when she visited Great Britain in 1942 (Fox, 422–23; Lash, *Eleanor*, 664; "Lady Astor Dies; Sat in Commons," *NYT*, 3 May 1964, 1).

5. For Adlai Stevenson, see *n*14 Document 70.

6. Lady Astor entertained the delegation at Cliveden, the Astor family mansion in Buckinghamshire (see *n*4, above).

7. ER reported on her reunion with Lady Stella Reading in her column:

> I can hardly tell you how heartwarming it was to have Lady Reading, who has been head of the Women's Voluntary Services all through the war, knock at my door almost before I had taken off my coat after arriving. She was leaving the hotel, because the rooms were needed for our party, and going to the country for the weekend. Her own little house, into which she is just moving, would not have the water turned on until Monday. Just to see her for a few minutes made me feel welcome (*MD*, 9 January 1946).

8. Philip Noel-Baker and his wife. See *n*15 Document 78.

9. For the Albert Hall speech, see Document 81.

10. John Winant (1889–1947) had held the position of American ambassador to Great Britain since 1940. Prior to his appointment as ambassador, Winant, a progressive Republican and FDR's close friend, served as assistant director (1935 and 1937) and director of the International Labor Organization (1937–1940) where his integrity and commitment to labor issues won him many friends. As US ambassador to Great Britain during World War II, Winant's sincerity and practical assistance earned him affection and respect. ER liked Winant, who had helped arrange her 1942 trip to Great Britain. Financial difficulties plagued Winant throughout his career. Poorly managed investments in Texas oil fields in the 1920s, ill-advised stock purchases before the 1929 stock market crash, an unwillingness to cut household staff and expenses, and unrestrained philanthropic giving left him bankrupt by 1935. By 1946, he owed creditors about three-quarters of a million dollars. Despair over his indebtedness contributed to his suicide in 1947 (Bellush, 81–85, 92, 121, 134, 227).

11. After Ambassador Winant's visit, Dorsey Fisher, an American embassy staff member who had accompanied ER in her travels in Great Britain when she visited in 1942, and Louise Morley (see *n*17 below) stopped by and the three of them went to eat at the American Embassy Canteen: "I think we all feel better because we know the food is American Army food so we are not taking away from the scant provisions of Great Britain." Before unpacking, ER talked with Henry Tosti Russell who represented United Features, the distributor of My Day in London (*MD*, 9 January 1946).

12. Mildred Cuddy was ER's secretary in London for her columns and personal correspondence. The secretarial work for ER's UN-related duties was performed by Agnes Norton, who had been assigned to ER by the State Department (ER's London Diary, 4 January 1946, AERP).

13. Maude Livingston Hall Gray was ER's aunt, confidante, and regular correspondent. See also Document 74 (Lash, *Eleanor*, 180–81).

14. David Gray (1870–1968), Maude's husband, served as the American minister to Ireland from 1940 to 1947 ("David Gray Dies; Former Envoy, 97," *NYT*, 13 April 1968, 25).

15. ER's friendship with Martha Gellhorn (1908–1998), a journalist and war correspondent, extended back to the early years of the New Deal when Gellhorn wrote field reports for the Federal

Emergency Relief Administration (FERA). Lorena Hickok brought Gellhorn's work to ER's attention, and ER introduced Gellhorn to FDR so that he could hear her observations firsthand (*NAWCTC*).

16. Mary J. Hornaday (1906–1982), a reporter for the *Christian Science Monitor,* also chaired ER's first White House press conferences ("Mary Hornaday Dies, Former Monitor Writer," *NYT,* 22 April 1982, D23).

17. Louise Morley Cochrane (1918–?) worked for the American Red Cross in Great Britain. ER accepted Morley's invitation to speak to almost 1,000 British women wed or engaged to US servicemen who found it difficult to obtain passports and transportation necessary for them to join their husbands or fiancés in America. Later during her stay in London, ER spoke to 700 officers and enlisted men, also at Morley's request ("GI Brides in Britain Demonstrate Again," *NYT,* 14 October 1945, 19; Lash, *Years,* 47).

18. Herman LaRue Brown (1890–1969), one of FDR's Harvard classmates and an attorney, supported him politically in Massachusetts. His wife, Dorothy Kirchwey Brown (?–1981), had worked with ER in the 1920s building the League of Women Voters (Lash, *World,* 211n; Finding Aid, Herman LaRue Brown Papers, Harvard Law School).

19. Dorothy Fosdick (1914?–1997) served as State Department advisor to the US delegation to the General Assembly. Fosdick, who participated in American planning for an international organization beginning in 1942, worked on the creation of the United Nations at the Dumbarton Oaks and San Francisco conferences, and advised the American delegation during the first sessions of the new organization ("Dorothy Fosdick, 83, Adviser on International Policy, Dies," *NYT,* 10 February 1997, B9). See also Document 99.

20. Malvina Thompson did not date most of the letters she sent to ER in London and not all the letters may have survived. One of the letters ER refers to here contains news of various friends and family members and of Tommy's work. In one paragraph, Tommy refers to some of the frequent topics of ER's daily mail during this period: "In all the mail that has come in there is nothing very fundamental in the way of suggestions, and no letters from anyone with any weight. I know we all should have weight, but most people just want peace, a free Palestine, a world language, world currency, a new calendar, etc." (Thompson to ER, n.d., JRP, FDRL).

21. Senator Vandenberg strongly objected to the wording of the agreement on atomic energy that Secretary of State Byrnes had signed in Moscow in December because Vandenberg feared it would lead to a giveaway of American atomic secrets. On December 28, before leaving for London, he met with President Truman to voice his objections and together they drafted a press release stating that the United States would not share secrets about the making of atomic weapons without putting an adequate international inspection system in place first. Vandenberg, however, wished to make sure that the Russians and the British agreed with the American interpretation of the agreement. He leaked his concerns about what he regarded as Byrnes's soft attitude toward the Russians to the press, which printed reports about a split in the American delegation over the atomic issue. In response to pressure from Vandenberg, Connally, and Truman, Byrnes announced on January 6, before leaving for London, that the United States would seek a revision or clarification of the agreement with the Soviet Union and Britain on atomic energy in order to insure that the United States would not be asked to share atomic weapons secrets. "Four days before the opening of the first United Nations Assembly meeting here [in London]," the *New York Times* reported, "Secretary of State James F. Byrnes faced the embarrassing task of advising Moscow and London that the agreement he signed in Moscow to create the United Nations Commission on Atomic Energy was not acceptable to the United States Senate." On January 8, the *Times* reported that Byrnes carried with him to London a new formulation of American policy on atomic energy aimed at reassuring Vandenberg and healing the split in the American delegation over the issue. Byrnes denied having receiving a letter from Vandenberg, although reports from London indicated that Vandenberg had sent him "a communication worded in rather sharp language" (Hamby, *Man,* 342–46; James B.

Reston, "Senators Demand Atom Pact Change to Insure Secrecy," *NYT*, 7 January 1946, 1; W. H. Lawrence, "Byrnes Declares Congress Has Veto on UNO Atom Plan," *NYT*, 8 January 1946, 1).

22. Andrew Browne Cunningham, Viscount Cunningham of Hyndhope (1883–1963), who held the post of first sea lord, and Lady Nona Cunningham. ER and Cunningham were both at the second Quebec conference between FDR and Churchill in September 1944 (*DNB*; Woolner, 31, 160; *MD*, 13 September 1944).

23. Senator John G. Townsend, Jr. (1871–1964), a Republican senator from Delaware from 1929 to 1940, served as an alternate delegate to the first meeting of the UN General Assembly. ER "liked" Townsend whom she thought "honest, plain, … but not very brilliant" ("Americans Sailing for UNO Assembly," *NYT*, 30 December 1945, 5; "John G. Townsend Jr., 92, Is Dead," *NYT*, 11 April 1964, 25; Lash, *World*, 214).

24. For Dorothy Brown, see *n*18. "The Marchessa Roselli" was possibly Signor Piero Roselli (?–1960), an Italian lawyer with many British clients. Lady Salter was the wife of Sir Arthur Salter, who directed the requisitioning of ships for the British during World War I, headed the economic and financial division of the League of Nations secretariat in the 1920s, and later became a professor at Oxford ("Signor Piero Roselli," *TL*, 8 July 1960, 15; *DNB*).

25. Benjamin Welles (1916–2002) was the son of ER's old friend Sumner Welles ("Benjamin Welles, Biographer and Journalist, is Dead at 85," *NYT*, 4 January 2002, C10).

26. ER never provided a more thorough identification for "Mrs. Blaisdell." Based on State Department and newspaper records, she most likely was either the wife of Thomas C. Blaisdell (1895–1988), chief of mission for economic affairs in London; or the wife of Donald C. Blaisdell (1899–1988), an advisor of the US delegation to the Preparatory Commission of United Nations in London at the time (Jesus Rangel, "Thomas Blaisdell Jr., Who Helped Frame Aid Plan, Dies at 93," *NYT*, 31 December 1988, 8; *RDS 1946*, 143–44; "Donald Blaisdell, 88, City College Professor," *NYT*, 13 July 1988, B4).

27. For Cliveden, see *n*4.

28. *New York Times* reporter James Reston noted Vandenberg and Dulles's absence when the American delegation met the press:

> They stayed away, it appears, for two reasons—first, they undertook to come here and carry out the instructions of the Truman Administration and those instructions have not yet arrived; and, second, there is excellent reason for believing that they did not want to be questioned about America's policy on atomic energy until they could see Mr. Byrnes here tomorrow and find out whether they can agree with what he proposes.

Reston concluded however that what appeared to be a significant split in the American delegation was "one of procedure rather than of substance" (James B. Reston, "Our UNO Delegates Divided Over Plans," *NYT*, 8 January 1946, 1).

29. Frank Comerford Walker (1886–1959), a friend of ER's, served as an alternate representative on the American delegation. His daughter Laura Hallie Walker accompanied him to London. Walker, one of FDR's chief political advisors, served as postmaster general from 1940 to 1945 and chairman of the Democratic National Committee between 1943 and 1944 ("Walker One of Farley's Best Friends," *WP*, 1 September 1940, 2; "Frank Walker, Ex-Postal Chief," *WP*, 14 September 1959, B2). For Louise Morley, see *n*17.

30. Josephine Roche (1886–1976), a leading reformer in the coal industry, invited the United Mine Workers to organize the workers at her company, Rocky Mountain Fuel. FDR appointed her assistant secretary of the treasury and she helped shape welfare and health policy during the New Deal. When ER and her friend Esther Lape pressured FDR to initiate policies to improve medical care for the poor, he asked the Interdepartmental Committee to Coordinate Health and Welfare

Activities, which Roche chaired, to prepare recommendations. The 1938 Roche Report and a conference that followed resulted in the drafting of the Wagner Health Act of 1939, but the American Medical Association opposed the bill and it died in committee. From 1939 to 1944 Roche worked as president of the National Consumers' League (*NAWCTC*; Lash, *Eleanor*, 465–66).

31. For Mrs. LaRue (Dorothy) Brown, see *n*18.

32. The American delegation initially encouraged Trygve Lie (1896–1968), Socialist foreign minister of Norway, to run for president of the General Assembly, but, when the Russians supported him, the United States failed to speak on his behalf. Paul Henri Spaak (1899–1972), Socialist foreign minister of Belgium, won by a few votes. ER thought the American delegation had handled the election badly (*OEWH*; Lash, *Years*, 45; *CBE*).

33. As the permanent members of the UN Security Council, each of which could prevent it from acting by exercising a veto, the Big Five (the United States, the Soviet Union, Great Britain, France, and China) possessed much greater power in the UN than the other member nations (*OEWH*).

34. The Russians objected to Lester B. Pearson (1897–1972), the leader of the Canadian delegation to the UN, because he was from North America and the UN headquarters would be there. They suggested instead either the Yugoslavian ambassador to Washington, Stanoje Simitch, or the Polish foreign minister, Wincenty Rzymowski. The two sides compromised by choosing Trygve Lie of Norway, whom the Russians apparently preferred all along (*CBE*; Lash, *Years*, 51). See also *n*23 Document 84.

35. ER did not describe the Red Cross ceremony in her My Day column, but she mentioned the role of the American Red Cross in assisting the wives and fiancées of American servicemen (*MD*, 10 January 1946). She also spoke to a group of these women. See *n*15 Document 94.

36. For the controversy stirred up by Senator Vandenberg, see *n*21. Byrnes's public assurances that the United States would not share any information on the making of atomic weapons without the establishment of an effective international inspection system mollified Senator Vandenberg and reunified the American delegation on the issue (James B. Reston, "Byrnes Unifies Delegation: Senators in Accord on Bomb," *NYT*, 9 January 1946, 1).

37. For Miss Norton, ER's secretary for her UN work, see *n*12.

38. For the Albert Hall speech, see Document 81.

39. As United Features Syndicate distributed My Day (and the photograph that its members could use to illustrate the column) in the United States and Europe, ER probably meant the photographer with the syndicate rather than one sent by a specific paper.

40. Her secretary, Mildred Cuddy.

41. Dr. Eelco Van Kleffens (1894–1983), foreign minister of the Netherlands, who during WWII worked with the exiled government in London. After his return from the San Francisco conference, the Dutch press, most notably *Waarfeid*, attacked "his leadership of the smaller nations" at the conference, declaring that it disturbed "the good relations" between the Netherlands, Britain, and Russia ("Dutch Election Asked," *NYT*, 27 June 1945, 5).

42. For Louise Morley, see *n*17.

43. For Frank Walker's daughter, see *n*29.

44. The editors have been unable to identify Lt. Woodlock.

45. Possibly Ellen Sullivan Woodward, ER's good friend, who had run the women's divisions of various agencies, beginning with the Civil Works Administration (*NAWMP*; A. Black, *Casting*, 35).

46. For Mary Hornaday, see *n*16.

47. The issue of refugees and whether they should be forced to return to their countries of origin became the hottest issue at the first session of the General Assembly. ER may have been reading the memo on the refugee question ("Refugees," USGA/Ia/SCHCom/Del Min/3) in preparation for the meeting with her advisors on the refugee issue the following day. The British initially favored the establishment of an agency within the UN to deal with refugees; the Americans sought the creation an independent agency (see *n*12 Document 78 and header to Document 86).

DRAFTING THE US POSITION ON REFUGEES

On the day the General Assembly convened for the first time, ER met with her alternate, former Senator John Townsend (R-DE),[1] and a group of American advisors to determine the American position and strategy regarding the urgent problem of postwar refugees. This issue would later dominate the agenda of the Third Committee (Social, Humanitarian and Cultural Affairs) on which ER represented the United States.[2] The group discussed a tentative draft State Department position paper entitled "Refugees," which outlined the role the UN should play in handling the refugee crisis in Europe. It proposed that the UN take general responsibility for refugee matters, but called for the creation of "a specialized international agency" to deal directly with the refugees. The General Assembly would first establish an ad hoc committee to report on existing inter-governmental refugee agencies and make "recommendations as to the form and scope of action of the specialized agency." The General Assembly would then draw up an agreement for the establishment of the new agency and determine its relationship to the UN. An alternative plan presented in the position paper established the same agency, but retained it as "a subsidiary organ" of the United Nations with a separate budget line. The United States believed that Britain would push in the General Assembly for creating a refugee organization as a subsidiary of the UN and for including the cost in the regular UN budget. The position paper raised "serious objections" to such a course of action.[3]

78

Minutes of Meeting of Committee 3 Group[4]
10 January 1946

<u>Present</u>: Mrs. Roosevelt, Mr. Feller,[5] Mr. Townsend, Mr. Mulliken,[6] Miss Miller,[7] Mr. Fowler,[8] Mr. Taylor,[9] Mr. Hyde,[10] Mr. Sandifer, and Mr. Burnett[11]

<u>Refugees</u>

A general discussion took place of the document entitled "Refugees" (USGA/Ia/SHCom/3) January 9, 1946. Mr. Fowler traced a little of the background of the refugee problem as it had arisen in the Preparatory Commission.[12] The British proposal in the Preparatory Commission had been opposed by the United States. The Australians had then suggested an organ under Article 22[13] and this had been supported by New Zealand. Mr. Fowler declared that he thought it possible that the British might now follow this new line of approach.

The discussion turned to the numbers and types of refugees and in this Mr. Feller presented approximate figures to indicate the dimensions of the problem. In this connection the document "Refugees: Additional Material on the Scope and Nature of the Problem", (USGA/Ia/SHCom/3/Supplement) January 9, 1946, was presented and its figures (page 4) were examined.[14] Mrs. Roosevelt said that it seemed clear to her that there would be great difficulty at the present time in getting a numerically accurate picture of the situation that an immediate decision ought to be avoided, and that some kind of fact-finding procedure would be necessary.

Mr. Feller pointed out that two principles had constantly lain behind the United States position in regard to the "dissident" refugees: (1) to encourage them to return to their own countries by every means possible but (2) not to force their repatriation.

Mrs. Roosevelt said that she was chiefly interested in finding out what our position was to be and what the procedure should be in developing that position. Mr. Feller said that the British position had stiffened noticeably following an instruction by Mr. Noel-Baker. Mr. Noel-Baker was eager that the United Nations should undertake operating functions and that he saw in the refugee problem an opportunity for the Organization to develop its strength in this way.[15]

Mrs. Roosevelt said it was her understanding that the United Nations was not to have operating functions but was simply to make recommendations on policy to the member governments. Mr. Feller thought that this whole problem would have to be carefully considered. Should we stand, he asked, on the constitutional position that we have heretofore maintained, or should we begin to alter our position somewhat in the direction desired by the British? Mr. Feller said that he thought developments would have to take place along three lines: (1) the formulation of an American position on the refugee question; (2) direct conversations with the British at a high level; (3) the formulation of an American position on the constitutional question.

Mrs. Roosevelt said that the constitutional question had certainly better be settled. She had understood that the American position was quite opposed to the undertaking of actual operations by the Organization. Mr. Sandifer thought that this question ought to be more fully explored. Following a discussion, it seemed to be agreed that the United Nations should not operate in this particular field even if the constitutional question were resolved in favor of it doing so. It was also argued that the constitutional question ought not to be presented so sharply as to encourage a decision against operations that might debar the United States for a long time from espousing any operating policies at all. There appeared to be a consensus that it would be unfortunate to get at this time a definite decision that the Organization should not engage in operations. It would be better to keep away from the theoretical aspects of the matter and to base our decision on the practical aspects of the question.

It was pointed out that, if a specialized agency were set up to handle the refugee question, it could adopt whatever quota system of contributions would best express the relative interests of the participating states in the refugee question—something which would aid the British very much by relieving them of the large proportion of the total contribution which they now carry.

Mr. Feller said that it was generally supposed, particularly by the Congressional members of the U. S. Delegation, that UNRRA would have ceased its operations very soon after January 1, 1947. It was important therefore, he argued, that a specialized agency should be ready to function in the refugee field by that time.[16] Miss Miller asked whether the dates of April 1 and July 1, as set forth in the draft memorandum entitled "Refugees" would be feasible dates to meet. Mr. Sandifer said that those dates had been simply presented for discussion, and urged that this paper be now examined for its concrete proposals. Mr. Mulliken said that he agreed with the assumption of this paper; that the United States position could not be limited to a proposal merely to study the refugee problem. Mr. Fowler commented that this was correct, and that the American position in the Preparatory Commission had indicated American recognition of (1) the urgency of the problem, and (2) of the fact that existing agencies were inadequate.

Discussion took place on point 3 of the proposed United States position.[17] After some discussion, it was agreed to omit all reference to the specific committees of the General Assembly from which the ad hoc committee should be drawn. Mr. Feller declared that the idea of an ad hoc committee was essentially a good one, but that he cautioned lest an ad hoc committee be composed of a higher proportion of representatives from the countries of Eastern Europe than would be the case if the committee were constituted by the Economic and Social Council.

A considerable discussion took place on point 4.[18] Mr. Fowler said that the convening authority should be the countries members of the ad hoc committee. Mr. Mulliken suggested that the Economic and Social Council should convene the conference. Mr. Burnett argued that it would be better not to set up special combinations of states to accomplish what was provided for in an orderly way in the Charter. Mrs. Roosevelt said that she too thought it was better to use regular channels whenever possible. Mr. Fowler emphasized the political issues involved in the refugee question and thought that this was a justification for having the conference called by a special procedure. Mr. Mulliken argued that the Economic and Social Council would have the administrative mechanism by which to call a conference. Mrs. Roosevelt inquired why the next Assembly could not call the conference. Mr. Mulliken said that the next Assembly, it was now thought, might not meet until July 1st. Mr. Sandifer said that that was why he had proposed in point 3 that the Committee should report directly to the members of the United Nations, that is, in order to avoid delay. Mrs. Roosevelt thought that the conference should not be called by the states, that it would be better to have it called by the Assembly. Mr. Fowler agreed, that especially with a view to meeting the British position so far as possible, it would be better to have the conference called by the Assembly, but, he said, he was concerned about the possibility of delay. Mr. Mulliken pointed out that the Assembly could provide at the present session for a conference to meet on a definite date, prior to the first of July. Mr. Sandifer agreed that this would be possible and said that he would attempt to re-draft his paper along this line.

Mr. Fowler inquired whether we should wait for a British proposal to be made in the General Assembly. Mrs. Roosevelt thought that it was generally better to take the initiative when that was possible. Mr. Fowler said that we could have a draft resolution ready to present. Senator Townsend inquired whether the British would present any proposal on this question since they knew that would encounter heavy opposition. Mr. Fowler believed that the British would offer their proposal again but in a somewhat modified form.[19]

The meeting adjourned at 12:45 p.m.

TD, AERP, FDRL

---

1. For Senator John G. Townsend, Jr., see *n*23 Document 76.

2. The UN General Assembly divided its work into seven committees. The Third Committee handled a range of educational, cultural, health, and humanitarian projects, including human rights questions. The other six committees dealt with civil and political affairs, economic/financial affairs, trusteeship issues, administrative and budgetary policies, legal issues, and special political details (Boyd, 53–55).

3. Third Committee, Refugees, Tentative Draft, 10 January 1946 (USGA/Ia/SHCom/Del Min/3), AERP.

4. Third Committee, Refugees, Tentative Draft, 10 January 1946 (USGA/Ia/SHCom/3 Rev. 1), AERP.

5. A close friend and advisor to Secretary-General Lie, Abraham H. Feller (1904–1952) served as general counsel to the United Nations and as head of its legal department from 1946 until 1952 ("Feller Leaves UNRRA," *NYT*, 7 November 1945, 15; Russell Porter, "A. H. Feller, Ill 2 Weeks, Eludes Wife's Effort to Prevent Suicide," *NYT*, 14 November 1952, 1).

6. Otis E. Mulliken (1907–1972) served as the delegation's advisor on technical problems at the meetings and by the end of the year became chief of the State Department's Division of International Labor, Social and Health Affairs ("Stresses Social Aims in U.S. Foreign Policy," *NYT*, 23 November 1946, 9).

7. An active member of the International Labour Organization, Frieda S. Miller (1889–1973) devoted her life to labor reform. In 1944, she succeeded Mary Anderson as the director of the Women's Bureau in the Labor Department (*NAW*).

8. William Fowler (1903–1981), foreign trade specialist, advised the US delegation in this capacity (*RDS 1948*, 217).

9. Economist William H. Taylor (1906–?) served as an advisor to the United Nations from the Treasury Department. For eight years he remained under suspicion for espionage activities and in

1955, Elizabeth Bentley accused him of Communist affiliation and espionage. He successfully challenged the accusation and thus the credibility of the Loyalty Board's reliance upon secret and unsubstantiated sources (Anthony Lewis, "The Taylor Decision: A Security Case History," *NYT*, 15 January 1956, E8).

10. Louis K. Hyde, Jr. (1901–?), a State Department advisor on technical problems, joined the federal government in 1942 and began working with the US delegation to the United Nations in July of 1945 (*RDS 1948*, 278–79).

11. Philip M. Burnett (1908–?), an employee of the State Department since 1942, assisted the US delegation in his capacity as a specialist on international organization affairs (*RDS 1948*, 143).

12. On the Preparatory Commission, see *n*5, Document 68. At this meeting, the British proposed the creation of a new commission under ECOSOC to handle the refugee situation. Following debate they withdrew the proposal for a commission and agreed that any UN body organized to address the refugee problem—even an agency with limited powers—would be better than none (USGA/Ia/SHCom/3 Rev. 1 Tentative Draft, AERP; "Limited UNO Board on Refugees Seen," *NYT*, 15 January 1946, 8).

13. Article 22 of the United Nations Charter reads, "The General Assembly may establish such subsidiary organs as it deems necessary for the performance of its functions" ("Charter of the United Nations," http://www.un.org/aboutun/charter).

14. The supplement estimated that by mid-1946 the following groups of "non-repatriable refugees" would remain in Europe: "500,000 Poles, Estonians, Latvians, Lithuanians, and Yugoslavs in the three western zones of Germany and Austria; 200,000 Spanish Republicans, in France; 100,000 German and Austrian Jews, in Sweden, Italy, Belgium, Netherlands, France, and Shanghai; 300,000 'Nansen' refugees, chiefly in France, who as a result of the events of World War II, have been again uprooted; 250,000 members of the Polish Army, in Italy and Northwestern Europe; and 50,000 wives and children of the above, in Middle East and East Africa." The estimated total of "non-repatriables for whose permanent establishment some long-term concerted international effort will presumably have to be made" totaled between 1,250,000 and 1,500,000 (USGA/Ia/SHCom 3/Supplement, 9 January 1946).

15. Philip Noel-Baker (1889–1982), a British Labour politician, Quaker, disarmament proponent, and League of Nations advocate, became involved with United Nations work in 1944. At this first meeting, Noel-Baker, in his capacity as minister of state, headed the British delegation. A long-serving British Labour Party MP, Noel-Baker also held a variety of posts in Attlee's postwar government, including a position as a minister of state in the Foreign Office. In 1959, he would receive the Nobel Peace Prize ("Lord Noel-Baker Dies at 92; Winner of Nobel Peace Prize," *NYT*, 9 October 1982, 30; *DNB*).

16. In fact, UNRRA (United Nations Relief and Rehabilitation Administration), an international agency devoted to providing relief aid to World War II victims in Europe and Asia, closed down its European operations in 1947, transferring them to other international organizations. The congressional members of the US delegation to the first General Assembly included Senator Tom Connally (D-TX); Senator Arthur H. Vandenberg (R-MI); Representative Sol Bloom (D-NY); and Representative Charles A. Eaton (R-NJ). For more on UNRRA, see *n*7 Document 55 (Camille Cianfarra, "750,000 DP's Face Crisis in 80 Days," *NYT*, 9 April 1947, 12; Lash, *Years*, 39; Kathleen Teltsch, "UNRRA's End Tonight Finds Many Nations Still in Need," *NYT*, 30 June 1947, 1).

17. The third point of the proposed US position in the discussed document reads: "An ad hoc committee of the General Assembly should be charged with a.) examining the existing intergovernmental agencies dealing with refugees; b.) making a report to the members of the United Nations not later than April 1, 1946, with recommendations as to the form and scope of action of the specialized agency envisaged under paragraph 2" (USGA/Ia/SHCom/3 Rev. 1 Tentative Draft, AERP).

18. The fourth point states, "A conference of the members of the United Nations should be convened under the auspices of the General Assembly not later than June 1, 1946 to consider the report of the ad hoc committee and to prepare an agreement for the establishment of the agency contemplated in paragraph 2. The Secretary General of the United Nations should issue the invitations and make the necessary preparations for the conference" (USGA/Ia/SHCom/3 Rev. 1 Tentative Draft, AERP).

19. For the disposition of the British proposal on refugees, see Document 86 and its header.

FIELDING QUESTIONS ON THE UNITED NATIONS

Nine days after arriving in London, ER held her first press conference at the American Embassy. M. J. McDermott, the delegation's liaison to the press, accompanied her and prepared this transcript.

_79_

Memorandum of Press Conference
15 January 1946 [Grosvenor Square]

MRS. ROOSEVELT: How do you do everybody? Those of you who are far away will have to ask questions quite loud; otherwise I won't be able to hear you. Will you go right ahead?

Q. What do you think of Hyde Park for UNO?

A. I haven't any thoughts. It doesn't belong to me. I would like UNO to be wherever its requirements can be most adequately met because I feel that it is so important that the home of UNO become a most important center, that what goes on there be known by the people—not only all the people of the United States but people all over the world.[1]

Q. There is a report from Washington that there is a split in the American Delegation over the question of trusteeship.[2]

A. I would not be one to answer that, not being on the Trusteeship Committee, but I know of no split in the American Delegation. I have heard of no difficulties whatsoever and I have been to every meeting of the Delegation.[3]

Q. What are your own views as to what should be done with the specific problems—

A. My own views. That, of course is a question which as a citizen I really have no opinion on until I know more of what the decisions are as to trusteeships and as to what we as a government think necessary for the people of the world in the future.

Q. Would you tell us, Mrs. Roosevelt, what is your opinion of the suggestion that Mr. Churchill should be the Secretary of the UNO?[4]

A. Be Secretary of the UNO? I hardly think Mr. Churchill would like that suggestion.

Q. There is a report in the press that you might be going on to Russia after the Assembly.[5] Could you tell us if that is so, and if on your way you would be visiting any other European country?

A. I don't expect to go to Russia or anywhere else now. I expect to go home. I have wanted to go to Russia and for some time it has been suggested that I might go for United Features to do some writing, but no definite date has ever been set and it is more indefinite than ever in view of the fact that I don't know when the next part of this session takes place; it might have some influence on my plans here in the next few months.[6]

MCDERMOTT: Any more questions?

Q. Mrs. Roosevelt, what is likely to be one of the first or major questions brought before the Social Committee of the General Assembly?[7]

A. We have only had one meeting and that was to elect Peter Fraser[8] as Chairman, so I have no idea what will come up later on. I hope I shall know a little more about it, but at the present time we have had nothing brought before us as yet. We have had no other meeting but the first one.

Q. Will the Trusteeship Committee deal with the question of Palestine and if they do will it be in conjunction with the Anglo-American Committee?[9]

A. I don't know. I have not heard it said and I should think that if it was a question that dealt with the question of Palestine that the Anglo-American Committee might very easily be asked to appear before them, but I have not heard whether that is to come up or not.

Q. I have heard that the Arab Delegation to the UNO have requested an interview with the Anglo-American Committee.

A. Well, I should think that would be perfectly natural.

Q. What kind of a world organization do you envisage to deal with refugees, Mrs. Roosevelt? What do you think would be necessary? Would it be of a permanent nature or a non-permanent nature?

A. I would think that the question of refugees would probably come up in Committee III. It might not. It might come up in one of the others, but I should think it would come up there. I should think that eventually either it would be a question that would be settled at this part of the session— this session being largely devoted to organization—or either it would come up in the second part. I don't know but I should think eventually it would find itself before the Economic and Social Council and perhaps referred by them to the General Assembly or settled in some way.

Q. Do you personally feel that there should be a permanent committee for refugees?

A. I don't know why we should add to committees. I never believe in new committees when committees are set up to deal with questions and certainly the Economic and Social Council ought to be able to deal with it.

Q. There are still troops in Persia, Syria and Lebanon. The governments of these states are asking for withdrawal of the troops.[10] Will the Security Council take that up?

A. Whether it will in this part, I don't know, because this is largely devoted to organization. I don't know whether it can come up on the agenda of this session, but if it is on the agenda it might quite easily come up under the Security Council of the General Assembly direct.

Q. Mrs. Roosevelt, an effort was made by the Russian Delegation today at a meeting of the General Committee[11] to secure appearance of the World Trade Federation[12] either before a subcommittee or a committee, and possibly the Assembly itself. There was considerable debate about what should be the relationship between such organization as a world trade organization and the Assembly—presumably through the Economic and Social Council. I wonder if you have any views of your own.[13]

A. I would have to give you my own views. I know nothing of what the Delegation views are. As I understand the set up, all the specialized organizations which are governmental and those which are non-governmental are expected to negotiate with the ESC their particular kind of agreement with the UNO, and they will not, many of them, deal with governments too; but my understanding is that both governmental and non-governmental organizations are expected to come into association with the organization through negotiations conducted with the ESC. I should think that organization would conform to the general pattern of all other international organizations outside of the governmental group, since the same machinery is provided for both governmental and non-governmental organizations.

Q. Could you say, Mrs. Roosevelt which subject in the activities of the Assembly you are most interested in?

A. There are a great many things, but I would say my main objective is to see an organization set up which can attempt to build a way in which nations can cooperate together when their individual efforts fail to find solutions to problems which otherwise lead to war. Now in doing that they must, of course, do things within the organization, to try to eliminate before they come to the point where people are ready to go to war the things which in the past have led nations to war. Therefore, those are the things that interest me the most.

Q. Mrs. Roosevelt, among the very few women delegates and advisers I have heard some suggestion of the resumption of the old status of a women's committee or of some such body.[14]

A. I don't know because I haven't heard much discussion on that. I was not in San Francisco and haven't had an opportunity to meet many of the women who are here. I hope to meet some of them this afternoon. It has been suggested that we all meet together in this room this afternoon, but I have not heard any direct suggestion of a specific committee. I should think that if we could bring any question under an existing committee it would be a good idea. I do not like the multiplication of committees as long as some committees are prepared to take up the questions. I don't mean that if there isn't a committee to take it up you shouldn't set up one.[15]

Q. Is this a closed meeting you are going to have here this afternoon?

A. It is not for the press. We are just meeting each other and having a chance to talk to each other for the first time.

Q. How many women will be here?

A. I really don't know, but I have looked around the Hall for the women delegates, assistant delegates and advisers and have not seen more than twenty. There may be more but I haven't seen them.[16]

Q. Do you feel that women are inadequately represented at the conference, Mrs. Roosevelt?

A. I would like to see more women, because I think the more women feel they are involved in the success of something the more interest they take, and I think it is important that women as well as men take a deep interest in the success of this organization.[17] The best organization in the world can't function really well unless the peoples back of the organizations really are keenly interested all the time. Mr. Byrnes said that in his speech yesterday, and I think it is absolutely true that the real hope of making any organization successful is that all over the world the peoples really feel that the organization is theirs and they are responsible for what their leaders do.[18]

Q. Would you consider letting a few women journalists attend this afternoon?

A. No, this is purely an informal meeting of women delegates.

Q. When do you think the members of the satellite countries, like the Italians, should be admitted to the UNO?[19]

A. Just as soon as their country is qualified to come into the UNO.[20]

MRS. ROOSEVELT: Is that all?

CORRESPONDENTS: Thank you, Mrs. Roosevelt.

M. J. McDermott

TMem, AERP, FDRL

---

1. See *n*11, Document 74. In a letter to Truman concerning the possible selection of Hyde Park as UN headquarters, ER wrote:

> I have told those who came to me that a decision of this kind would have to be made by a majority of the nations and that our government could make no such decision alone. The idea seems to me good, however and I wondered if our house and the Vanderbilt Mansion couldn't all be used at times of meeting and make a very acceptable center? (ER to Truman, 11 September 1945, HSTSF, HSTL).

2. Early January 1946, the *Washington Post* and the *New York Times* reported disagreement within the American delegation over what should be done with the Marshall, Caroline, and Marianas Islands, all mandated territories taken by the United States from Japan during World War II. The reports described indecision and division among the delegates and State Department officials, with some in the American delegation favoring UN trusteeship for the islands, others remaining undecided, and special military advisor, General George C. Kenney, pushing for total US control. In November, the United States proposed the UN place the islands under a trusteeship system with the United States as administering authority. The UN Security Council approved the plan April 2, 1947, and the following July Congress passed the joint trusteeship resolution ("U.S. Inaction Clouds Up Trusteeship Set-Up," *NYT*, 15 January 1946, 1; Edward T. Folliard, "Majority of Others to Be Placed under Joint Trusteeship," *WP*, 16 January 1946, 1; "Text of the United States Proposal on Trusteeship in the Pacific," *NYT*, 7 November 1946, 24; "U.S. Assumes Rule of Isles in Pacific," *NYT*, 20 July 1947, 35).

3. On the Trusteeship Committee, see *n*11 Document 37 and Document 71.

4. Prior to the election of Trygve Lie as UN secretary-general in February 1946, some British Conservatives proposed nominating Winston Churchill for the position ("UNO Opened; Attlee Asks World Unity," *NYT*, 11 January 1946, 1).

5. The *New York Times* printed an Associated Press report January 15 that ER planned "to visit Russia some time after the United Nations General Assembly adjourned, but she declared she was undecided as to the exact time of her departure" ("Mrs. Roosevelt to Visit Russia after UNO Session," *NYT*, 15 January 1946, 9).

6. ER still planned to visit Russia in either the spring or summer. See Document 21, header and *n*5 Document 38, and Document 39.

7. When the Third Committee on Social, Humanitarian and Cultural Affairs commenced work, the question of what to do with war refugees currently living in displaced persons camps became one of the first issues debated. ER spoke for the American delegation on this issue, arguing that displaced persons must be allowed to decide themselves whether or not to return to their home-lands. See also Document 86 (Glendon, 27–30).

8. Born in Scotland, Peter Fraser (1884–1950) emigrated to New Zealand, where he was active in union and Socialist politics. Fraser became a prominent Labour Party politician, serving as prime minister of New Zealand from 1940 to 1949. In addition, he attended the UN founding confer-ence in San Francisco, chaired the committee that drafted the UN Charter's trusteeship chapter, and worked to limit dominance of the organization by the big powers. ER described him as "fair to the utmost" ("Peter Fraser Dies in New Zealand, 66," *NYT*, 12 December 1950, 33; ER's London Diary, 6 February 1946, AERP).

9. Organized in November 1945, the Anglo-American Committee of Inquiry on Palestine studied the problem of Jews remaining in Europe and the question of Jewish immigration to Palestine. The committee issued its report in late April 1946, recommending admission of 100,000 Jewish refugees in Europe to Palestine, but rejecting arguments for a Jewish state. The itinerary of the Anglo-American Committee attached to its official report does not list a meeting between the com-mittee and the Trusteeship Council (*HSTE*; "Texts of Statements by Bevin and Truman on Jews and Palestine," *NYT*, 14 November 1945, 12; Felix Belair, Jr., "Joint Palestine Body Bars a Jewish State, But Urges Entry of 100,000 Refugees," *NYT*, 1 May 1946, 1. See *n*8 Document 60).

10. The presence of Soviet, British, and French troops in Iran, Syria, and Lebanon after the end of World War II raised the question of postwar sovereignty before the UN Security Council in February 1946. The council decided unanimously that the troops must be removed, though mem-bers stood divided on when the withdrawal should occur. The prolonged presence of Soviet troops in Iran after the war precipitated a US-Soviet stand-off in 1946 and the Soviets eventually with-drew in May 1946. British and French troops finally withdrew from Syria in April 1946 and Lebanon in December (James B. Reston, "Council Is Divided on UNO Authority in Levant Policing," *NYT*, 16 February 1946, 1; *HSTE*; "British Out of Syria," *NYT*, 18 April 1946, 6; British-French Exit from Syria Settled," *NYT*, 5 March 1946, 3; "French Out of Lebanon," *NYT*, 1 January 1947, 18).

11. The Steering Committee of the General Assembly ("Labor Role in UNO Pressed by Soviet," *NYT*, 16 January 1946, 4).

12. The reporter apparently meant the World Federation of Trade Unions, which sought consulta-tive representation in the General Assembly and voting representation in the Economic and Social Council of the UN. See "Labor Role," ibid.

13. In January 1946, the General Assembly appointed a special subcommittee to consider the rela-tionship between the World Federation of Trade Unions (WFTU) and the Economic and Social Council. In February, the General Assembly's Political and Security Committee voted to grant the WFTU "consultative affiliation" with the Economic and Social Council (James B. Reston, "Britain Offers UNO Trusteeships Over Three Mandates in Africa," *NYT*, 18 January 1946, 1; "UNO Committee Votes to Admit AFL and World Union Federation," *NYT*, 13 February 1946, 18).

14. Prior to World War II, various international women's rights organizations pushed the League of Nations to initiate an inquiry into the status of women. The League responded in 1938 by appointing a seven-member Committee of Experts on the Status of Women, made up of four women and three men. The committee's work, which continued until the outbreak of the war, brought it into contact with women's groups who assisted in the examination of women's legal status (Rupp, 220; Stienstra, 76). See also Document 112.

15. For ER's views on establishing a UN commission on the status of women, see Document 83, Document 112, and Document 120.

16. ER responded by inviting the women on the other delegations to tea and "about sixteen" of them accepted her first invitation, including the unidentified Russian woman. There were some twenty-five women in total attendance at the first General Assembly, nineteen of whom, including ER, represented eleven member states as delegates, alternates, and advisors. The remaining women worked as secretaries to the delegations (ER, *Autobiography*, 305; "Mrs. Roosevelt Affirms Women's Value to UNO," *NYT*, 28 January 1946, 3; Pidgeon, 109).

17. Women joined new internationalist groups that emerged during the war to work for promotion of a new, permanent world body committed to long-term peace. These included such groups as the Women's Action Committee for Victory and Lasting Peace (successor to the National Committee on the Cause and Cure of War) and the Association for the United Nations (later renamed the United Nations Association), which cultivated grassroots support for the UN in the United States and elsewhere and built on a network developed by the League of Nations Association (Stienstra, 75–79).

18. In his January 14 speech before the General Assembly, Secretary Byrnes stated:

> If the United Nations becomes a working institution with broad popular support, devoted to the development of peace, security and human well-being, whatever defects there may be in its lettered provisions will not be beyond practical remedy. Institutions that come to live in the minds and the hearts of the people somehow manage to meet every crisis ("Secretary Byrnes' Address before the UNO General Assembly," *NYT*, 15 January 1946, 6).

19. The satellite countries to which the reporter refers are those nations that entered an alliance with Nazi Germany during World War II; such as Japan, Italy, Bulgaria, Hungary, Romania, and Finland. The UN admitted most of the so-called satellite countries in the mid 1950s (Keegan, 130, 150, 505; "List of Member States," http://www.un.org.overview/html, accessed 1 March 2005).

20. Article 4 of the UN Charter concerning membership states:

> 1. Membership in the United Nations is open to all other peace-loving states which accept the obligations contained in the present Charter and, in the judgment of the Organization, are able and willing to carry out these obligations.

> 2. The admission of any such state to membership in the United Nations will be effected by a decision of the General Assembly upon the recommendation of the Security Council ("Charter of the United Nations," http://www.un.org/aboutun/charter, accessed 1 March 2005).

ELEANOR ROOSEVELT'S LONDON DIARY

80

London Diary
16 January 1946

Your nice long letter came this morning after what seemed like a long silence and I was beginning to worry.[1] How long my letters were in reaching you!

I heard today that the Army does want me in Germany and now I shall plan to go to Ireland the day after the conference ends, spend one night,[2] come back here and leave for Germany at once.[3] The army will deliver me in New York. I am glad to be flying back but I'll probably send my big bag by boat with one of the others.

I am doing my column now from 8:30 to 9:30 every morning and if I don't finish I dash back and dictate while I drink my soup for lunch. The dinner last night was interesting as a sight, and I like Peter Fraser[4] who sat one side of me but the old Belgian Ambassador[5] sat on my other side and I never liked him when he was in Washington. I'm telling all about this dinner in my column.[6]

Today I lunched with the Noel Bakers who live in Lord Robert Cecil's old London house and he was there. He is very deaf but has transferred his allegiance from the League to UNO. He went to the first session but no one recognized him and he could hear nothing so he goes no more.[7] Old age is pathetic. Noel Baker is for the English what Mr. Stettinius has been for us.[8] I watch our delegation with great concern. Secy. Byrnes seems to me to be afraid to decide on what he thinks is right and stand on it. I am going to try to tell him tactfully that everyone has to get the things they need from us and that is our ace in the hole. We could lead but we don't. We shift to conciliate and trail either Gr. Britain or Russia and at times I am sure a feeling that we had convictions and would fight for them would be reassuring to them. Secy. Byrnes is afraid of his own delegation. He has held very few meetings and now we begin to need them and yet we have to ask to see him in separate groups. It isn't that he is leaving me out, for the others complain to me.[9]

I spoke to the agencies having representatives here tonight from six to seven. Saw the Associated Country Women of the World[10] for ten minutes and then Molly Flynn of UNRRA[11] came in and we went to the Embassy canteen for dinner. She told me much about the refugee question which I needed to know, but I didn't get to my desk as early as I should. Now I must go to bed.

The men are all so anxious to go home that I think we may finish by the 3rd, and then I'd be home a week later. I'd like to go west about two weeks after I get home and do four lectures.[12] If the next part of this is in the spring then I'd like to wait a month before going west because Russia will be out till late summer.[13]

TDi AERP, FDRL

---

1. As Tommy (Malvina Thompson) dated only a few of her letters to ER, some of which are missing from the files, and ER makes no references to its content, it is not possible to determine which of Tommy's letters ER refers to here. See *n*20 Document 76.

2. Maude and David Gray, ER's aunt and uncle, lived in Ireland. She visited them at the end of her trip, before returning to the United States (ER's London Diary, 11 February 1946, AERP). See *n*13 and *n*14 Document 75.

3. ER went to Germany in mid-February for several days, where she toured Frankfurt am Main, several displaced persons camps, and Berlin (*MD*, 15, 16, and 18 February 1946).

4. For Peter Fraser, see *n*8 Document 79.

5. Emile, Baron de Cartier de Marchienne (1871–1946), who died four months later ("Baron de Cartier, Belgian Envoy, 74," *NYT*, 11 May 1946, 23).

6. *MD*, 19 January 1946.

7. Lord Robert Cecil (Edgar Algernon Robert Gascoyne, Viscount Cecil of Chelwood) (1864–1958) was a British lawyer, parliamentarian, diplomat, and cabinet minister. Shocked by the devastation of World War I, he came to believe that civilization could only be preserved through the creation of an effective international organization for the maintenance of peace. As the British representative at the Paris Peace Conference in charge of negotiations to form the League of Nations, he became one of its architects. After 1927, unhappy with the policies of the British government toward the League of Nations, he devoted himself to organizing public support for the organization. He served as president of the British League of Nations Union from 1923 to 1945. In 1937 he received the Nobel Peace Prize. At the final meeting of the League in Geneva in 1946, he said, "The League is dead; long live the United Nations!" (*DNB*).

8. Like Stettinius, Philip Noel-Baker helped to draft the United Nations Charter (Nobel Peace Prize 1959, http://nobelprize.org/peace/laureates/1959/index.html, accessed 18 January 2005). See also *n*15 Document 78.

9. Byrnes had reason to fear his delegation. Both Senators Tom Connally and Arthur Vandenberg believed he had been far too conciliatory with the Russians during recent negotiations in Moscow and leaked their fears to the press (see *n*21 Document 76). ER herself had developed a deep distrust of Byrnes well before joining the delegation (see *n*23 Document 37). In October 1945, Walter Winchell reported that she had publicly attacked Byrnes. Although she denied it, she did express concerns about his inexperience in foreign affairs and failure to grasp the role he needed to play (see Document 50). Byrnes's manner of managing his role did not instill confidence in others, as well. George F. Kennan, then counselor in the US embassy in Moscow, after observing Byrnes during the negotiations with the Russians, complained in his diary on December 19, 1945, about Byrnes's lack of a deliberate method or clear goals: "He plays his negotiations by ear, going into them with no clear or fixed plan, with no definite set objectives or limitations. He relies entirely on his own agility and presence of mind and hopes to take advantage of tactical openings … [H]is main purpose is to achieve some sort of an agreement, he doesn't much care what." Truman himself was beginning to lose patience with Byrnes's failure to communicate with him (Hamby, *Man*, 342–43, 346).

On January 21, following ER's instructions, Malvina Thompson excerpted the passage on Byrnes from ER's January 16 diary, beginning with "I watch our delegation with great concern," and sent it to Bernard Baruch.

10. Associated Country Women of the World, an international group offering support for rural women, constituted formally as an association between the world wars ("About ACWW," ACWW, http://www.acww.org.uk/NEWpages/aboutacww.html, accessed 12 January 2005).

11. Molly Flynn (1896?–1961) was an experienced welfare administrator who had worked with ER during the war planning programs for the Volunteer Participation Division of the Office of Civilian Defense (OCD) when ER served briefly as the office's assistant director. Beginning in 1944, Flynn worked for UNRRA's displaced persons division (Lash, *Eleanor*, 646; "Miss Molly Flynn, Ex-Official at U.N.," *NYT*, 13 June 1961, 35). See *n*7 Document 55.

12. ER toured the western United States in March 1946, visiting her grandchildren (John Roosevelt's children, while John and his wife Anne were in New York) and giving lectures in Phoenix, Tucson, San Diego, Los Angeles, and Omaha. Her March 23 lecture at the Shrine

Auditorium in Los Angeles concerned the UN's "actual machinery" and "how it functions," according to her March 25 My Day column (Letter from ER to Florence Willert, 30 March 1946, FWP, CtY; *MD*, 23 and 25 March 1946).

13. "Out," i.e., "out of the question," possibly due to ER's schedule and Russian weather conditions. ER still hoped to make the visit to Russia that she began contemplating in the summer of 1945, but she did not go until 1957. See *n*4 Document 21 and *n*6 Document 79.

ON HOPES FOR THE UNITED NATIONS

ER and the other United Nations delegates received a formal welcome from the British United Nations Association[1] at the Royal Albert Hall on January 17. In addition to Field Marshal Sir Harold Alexander, the speakers included Sir Walter Citrine, Lady Megan Lloyd-George, the Archbishop of Canterbury Geoffrey Francis Fisher,[2] and ER. She described the scene a few days later:

> On Thursday I attended a reception held in Albert Hall as welcome to the UNO delegates. The hall was filled to the very top gallery, and Field Marshal Sir Harold Alexander presided. Besides the speeches, the choir of the Welsh Temple of Peace sang and there was a fine organ recital. The little incident I enjoyed more than anything else was the whispered remark from Lord Robert Cecil, who sat beside me. Looking up at the Field Marshal in the chair and listening to the choir singing some truly martial songs, he said: "We go about peace in a very belligerent way, don't we!" I think the evening must have been a great satisfaction to him, however. So much of his life has been given to trying to make the old League a successful instrument to keep peace in the world, that it must be good to feel again the same spirit of hope stirring. This time the backing is stronger and broader, and therefore there is greater hope of success.[3]

The following is a draft of the speech ER delivered, her first major public address on her new responsibilities as a UN delegate. Although ER prepared no final version of her remarks, her notes on the typed draft reflect the sentiments she wished to convey to the more than 200 people assembled in the audience.[4]

81

Albert Hall Speech
17 January 1946 [London]

Draft Second

(Information as to appropriate beginning ... who is to be mentioned ... will be furnished by W.W. Chaplin.)

I need hardly say that as one of the Delegates to this first United Nations Assembly meeting I am deeply moved by the welcome which the British United Nations Association has extended to us. This Association has a history. It did much to acquaint its people with the work of the League of Nations and arouse their interest in it, and it will continue its work for the United Nations.

{The United States has always wanted peace. It wants peace today and as a people we will work for the success of the United Nations Organization.}

Wodrow Wilson, who believed so whole-heartedly that an association of nations could be successfully formed and could keep the peace of the world, is being vindicated today since we are meeting again to carry on his idea. We have as a background the knowledge which we gained through the work done by the League of Nations. I hope we shall profit by the successes and failures of the League but that now we will not concentrate on looking backwards but will look forward and attempt to build an organization which truly shall represent the United Nations of the World.{[5]} My husband often said that first the war must be won but when _that_ was done _then_ all our efforts must be centered on building an organization through which all men could work for peace.

This first meeting is setting up the machinery. It has chosen the people who shall serve as representatives of their nations in the Assembly and the Security Council. Eighteen individuals representing the economic and social interests of the world have been elected to serve in the Economic and Social Council. They will all in the future take up the problems that must arise between nations and try to find solutions before they reach a point where the use of force is necessary. We must not forget that everyone who represents the people of one nation also represents the people of all nations for we now know that what happens to people in <u>any</u> part of the world is of concern to people in <u>every</u> part of the world.

The Secretary-General and the permanent secretariat will be taking a new organization ... a new idea in fact ... and making it a living, vital, functioning body which will grow from year to year and reflect their vigor, their imagination and their foresight. No organization, however, no matter how active its staff may be, even though its representatives come from every nation in the world, can accomplish anything unless the peoples make it their instrument. They must know their representatives and follow their activities with understanding and with constant interest. It is important that this organization and its representatives be a part of the consciousness of every citizen, and that every citizen feel a personal responsibility to face the problems which face his representatives. By his interest he will bring strength to his representative's actions. It is sometimes hard to arrive at the collective thought of any people but today we have more methods for spreading information and for keeping in touch with people than we have ever had before. All these methods of communication, I think, should be used to arouse <u>and keep aroused</u> the feeling among the people of the world that our problems <u>must</u> find peaceful solutions. The great destructive forces which man has now discovered make it imperative for the sake of the future of mankind that we grow in moral consciousness and in social understanding as rapidly as we have grown in scientific, industrial and mechanical knowledge.

In the hearts of men and women all over the world I am sure there are prayers, daily, that the war which we have just been through may be the last war which any young generation will have to engage in. On Memorial Day 1945 in this great city of London the Rev. A.C. Don preached at St. Margaret's Westminster.[6] He said of those who died in this Second World War: "They died that we might live; may we so live that they shall not have died in vain. Let us then go forward into the unknown future with far-seeing vision and in the fear of God. So shall we keep faith with the gallant dead."

The King, in his address to the Chief Delegates, stressed the great opportunity before us.[7] We, as delegates here, can look back upon a long line of men who have tried to bring peace on earth; who have labored singly and together for the brotherhood of man. I believe that if we keep before us and before our peoples the main objective which is that there <u>shall</u> be built an organization whose aims shall be to keep the peace of the world, we <u>can</u> succeed. As Delegates we shall have to remember that often our own special interests may have to be subordinated to the interests of the world as a whole. Human nature is sometimes greedy; sometimes selfish; but always, <u>somewhere</u>, there is a spark of the divine intelligence, and we may do well all of us to remember the injunction that "Whosoever will save his life shall lose it but whosoever will lose his life for my sake the same shall save it."[8] Those are the words of one of the world's great teachers. We must be willing to learn the lesson that cooperation may imply compromise, but if it brings a world advance it is a gain for each individual nation. There will be those who doubt the ability of human beings to rise to these new heights but the alternative is not possible to contemplate. We must build faith in the hearts of those who doubt, we must re-kindle faith in ourselves when it grows dim, and find some kind of divine courage within us that will make us keep on till on Earth we have Peace and Good Will among Men.

TSpd AERP, FDRL

---

1. The British United Nations Association, like its American counterpart, the American Association for the United Nations, was a successor to an organization that had been formed to promote pub-

lic understanding of and support for the League of Nations. The earlier organization (the British League of Nations Union) had been headed by Lord Robert Cecil from 1923 to 1945 (*DNB*). See also *n*7 Document 80.

2. Field Marshal Sir Harold Alexander (1891–1969) was deputy commander-in-chief to General Eisenhower of the Allied Forces in the Mediterranean theater in World War II, and led the Allies to many decisive victories. After the war, he was appointed governor-general of Canada. Sir Walter Citrine (1887–1983) was general secretary of the British Trades Union Congress. Lady Megan Lloyd-George (1902–1966), the daughter of former Prime Minister David Lloyd-George, was a Liberal Party member of the House of Commons. Lord Fisher of Lambeth (1887–1972) was archbishop of Canterbury from 1945 to 1961 ("Lord Citrine," *TL*, 26 January 1983, 14; "Lady Megan Lloyd-George: A Fiery Particle of Radicalism," *TL*, 16 May 1966, 12; "Lord Fisher of Lambeth: Former Archbishop of Canterbury," *TL*, 16 September 1972, 14).

3. *MD*, 21 January 1946.

4. ER preferred, when possible, to speak extemporaneously. Minutes of the first meeting of the US delegation record that:

> Mrs. Roosevelt inquired regarding the clearance necessary for Representatives who were asked to make addresses before groups in London. She said that she had been asked to address a meeting in Albert Hall. Mr. Stettinius suggested that it would be wise to adopt the procedure followed at San Francisco whereby any member of the Delegation who was asked to speak would clear arrangements with Mr. McDermott and furnish Mr. McDermott a copy of the speech. This would insure that several Delegates were not speaking repetitiously on the same subjects. Mr. Vandenberg said that that would also make sure that the Delegation did not differ publicly. Mr. Connally said that the procedure was necessary to see that the Representatives did not take positions contrary to those of the Delegation. Mrs. Roosevelt asked for guidance on whether she must write out such short welcoming speeches as she expected to be called upon to give. She said she did not intend to speak regarding policy. She pointed out that there would be a great waste of time involved if all the speeches had to be written out in advance. Senator Connally thought it would be necessary to have advance written copies only as a matter of policy were involved. Mr. Stettinius said that he did not think it was necessary to write out all brief addresses, and said that the Delegation had full confidence in Mrs. Roosevelt's good discretion ("British Welcome to UNO: Delegates at the Albert Hall," *TL*, 18 January 1946, 2; United States Delegation to the General Assembly, First Delegation Meeting, USGA/Ia/Del. Min./1 (Chr), 2 January 1946, US Mission File, NARA II).

5. ER's notes indicate that she wanted the { } paragraph moved to this point in the text.

6. The Very Reverend Alan Campbell Don, dean of Westminster (1885–1966) ("Dr. Alan Don: Former Dean of Westminster," *TL*, 4 May 1966, 14).

7. George VI (1895–1952) reigned as king of England from 1936 until his death. On January 9 he hosted a banquet for the chief delegates at St. James's Palace. In his speech before the group, the king emphasized that the work of all three executive bodies of the UN, while difficult and challenging, remained the direct route to sustaining world peace (*DNB*; "The King's Welcome," *TL*, 10 January 1946, 5).

8. ER is quoting Jesus Christ speaking to his disciples, Luke 9:24 (King James Version).

On Jews, Relocation, and Palestine

ER told the press after the Senate confirmed her appointment to the US delegation, that she hoped she would "hear from people … about the various things which come up. It is important for the American delegation to realize the true feelings of the people at home." January 13, Aline May Lewis Goldstone responded to ER's request, objecting to her depiction of Jews as "only miserable, wretched human beings about whom something must be done." Calling her description a "discriminatory and prejudicial policy," she urged ER to move beyond seeing Jews in Europe as "objects of pity and charity" to seeing them as human beings with the rights of self-determination, "specific, ethno-political identity," and "their national territory, Palestine." "Regardless of how noble and important charity is," she concluded, "it has never solved any great problem in the history of mankind."[1]

82

Eleanor Roosevelt to Mrs. Lafayette A. Goldstone

18 January 1946 [London]

Dear Mrs. Goletstone:[2]

I fully appreciate your feeling but I think it is necessary to realize that the Jews of Central Europe are in this position, namely, that while they must be treated as human beings and the equals of any other people on earth, they are in dire need of food and clothing and shelter. Nobody questions their right to self-determination.

Unfortunately there are certain rather serious questions that arise as regards their return to Palestine, which many of them ardently desire. The Arabs claim possession and while they are willing to have the Jews that are already established there, they do not want a large influx of new settlers nor do they want it set up as a Jewish state.[3] Unless the British and the Americans are ready to protect the Jews by force from the Arabs it would seem like suicide to allow them to go back.[4]

I will grant you that there are only two things that can be done. First, allow them to go back and decide to defend them. They are not strong enough to defend themselves. It is not established that the land can support this new addition. Some reports are agreed that it can, others disagree.[5] The only other thing that can be done is to offer them citizenship in the various countries of the world and apportion them according to population. They would have the choice of countries that they wished to become nationals of up to the quota that each country assumes.[6] There are a number of Jews who want to be nationals of Palestine, and on the other hand, there are a number of Jews in our own country who much prefer to be nationals of the United States. They are on the same basis that a great many other people are who have come to us from other parts of the world, except that they have usually come from some European country or from Russia.

This is not a simple question—as some people would have us believe. Having appointed a new committee of inquiry we will have to await its report.[7] In the meantime, I think it is essential that material aid go to the Jewish people no matter where they are in Europe since they have a great contribution to make to the world and should not be allowed to die.

Very sincerely,

TLc AERP, FDRL

1. Aline May Lewis Goldstone (1878–1976), a founder of the American League for a Free Palestine and a published poet, was married to the architect Lafayette A. Goldstone ("Aline L. Goldstone," *NYT*, 6 May 1976, 40; Aline Goldstone to ER, 13 January 1946, AERP).

2. ER misread Goldstone's signature on her letter of 13 January as "Goletstone."

3. In early 1946, delegates from the Arab states told the Anglo-American Committee of Inquiry on Palestine that Arabs had occupied Palestine for more than a thousand years, and, therefore, their claim superseded any recent historical claim European Jews made to the land. The Arabs also testified they considered the Balfour Declaration and the British Mandate over Palestine a violation of their right to self-determination, declaring that it forced "upon them an immigration which they do not desire and will not tolerate." Lastly, the Arabs, objecting strongly to being burdened with world guilt regarding Hitler's persecution of the Jews, attached the "highest importance" to the fulfillment of the promises made by the British government in the White Paper of 1939, which limited Jewish immigration to Palestine to 75,000 over the next five years (Cohen, *Truman*, 122–46).

For more on the Anglo-American Committee of Inquiry, see *n*9 Document 79 and *n*2 Document 123. For ER's interpretation of Arab views on Jewish settlement in Palestine and a Jewish state, as well as the controversy over FDR's views on these issues, see Document 54. For controversies within the State Department and the Truman administration over Jewish immigration to Palestine and Zionism, see *n*5 below and Document 124.

4. A 1945 study conducted by the War Department determined that the American military had little desire to fight for a Jewish state. At least 400,000 troops, of which as many as 300,000 would have to come from the United States, the War Department report concluded, would be needed to keep order in Palestine in the face of large-scale Jewish immigration (Brands, 171).

5. In August of 1945, the head of the State Department's Bureau of Near Eastern and African Affairs, Loy Henderson, sent a report to Secretary of State Byrnes arguing that Palestine did not possess adequate housing to sustain a massive influx of Jewish immigrants from Europe. In fact, Henderson argued, Palestine lacked accommodations for the nearly 200,000 people already there. The same report also concluded that although Jews owned 90 percent of industry in Palestine, they could never provide enough jobs for all the immigrants. Henderson's report mirrored the conclusions of the 1939 British White Paper, which argued that, owing to the natural growth of the Arab population in Palestine, as well as the steady sale of Arab land to Jews, there was "no room for further transfers of Arab land, whilst in some other areas such transfers of land must be restricted if Arab cultivators are to maintain their existing standard of life and a considerable landless Arab population is not soon to be created." Not everyone, however, agreed with these conclusions. A 1937 royal commission of inquiry, headed by Lord Robert Peel, determined that Jewish immigration was not detrimental to the financial well-being of the Arab population, and argued that the issue of Jewish immigration to Palestine could be resolved by the creation there of a Jewish state (Brands, 170; Cohen, *Truman*, 122–46; Sachar, *Israel*, 222–23).

6. On December 22, 1945, Truman issued a directive to "expedite" the admission of "displaced persons and refugees," particularly orphaned children, to America up to the authorized limit in the US immigration laws "as an example to the world in relieving human misery." See *n*7 Document 74.

7. For the origins of the Anglo-American Committee of Inquiry, which began its work on January 4, 1946, see *n*8 Document 60 and *n*2 and *n*6 Document 123. For the committee's report, which was issued in April 1946 and recommended the immigration of 100,000 European Jews to Palestine and argued against the establishment of a Jewish state, see *n*9 Document 79. For Arab reaction to the report, see *n*3 Document 123.

ELEANOR ROOSEVELT'S LONDON DIARY

83

London Diary
23 January 1946

They now say the second part of this session will not be until early September,[1] so we will probably go to Russia in early May and return the end of June and stay at Hyde Park except for a motor trip to Campobello.[2] Tell George Bye I will start the autobiography when I go west.[3]

Today has been rather a long one. Meetings at 10:30 to 1:00. Mostly unnecessary speeches! Lunch with the Atlees,[4] pleasant. Came back with the Ambassador and he took me to dinner.[5] I stopped at his home and saw our old maid (girl who took care of us in 1942 when we had Winant's apartment)

We've just had an unpleasant time with Noel Baker who agreed with me to put in a certain kind of resolution on refugees this morning and this evening told Winant (who did not know what he was talking about) that he'd changed his mind and wouldn't go along.[6] Tomorrow a.m. I'll have a talk with the Secy[7] and then I hope he'll agree to my talking to Mr. Baker. Everyone says it is the way he often behaves. I think I remember similar things said about him in the past.[8]

The afternoon session was cancelled so I stopped at the office and then worked here and at five had Col. Meyers[9] and the two other crew officers to tea, a corporal, nephew of Governor Lehman who is going to London University and Louise Morley.[10] At 6:30 Lady Pethwick Lawrence (nice old lady)[11] and Mrs. Gram Swing (very high powered)[12] came to persuade me to back a woman's group in UNO with special privileges and I was non-committal as I don't think it should be done but I must, of course, look into it.[13] 7:30 I went to dine with Mr. and Mrs. George Catlin (Vera Brittain).[14] A pleasant dinner, usual three courses and a very cold house. Lots of people in afterwards.

Now I must go to bed.

TDi AERP, FDRL

84

London Diary
27 January 1946

Yesterday was busy and I didn't write. We met at 20 Grosvenor Square for a delegates meeting at 9:30, so I had to finish the column before leaving.[15] Sen. Vandenburg is funny about his committee, says they won't agree to anything and he doesn't know how long he'll be here, but I think he does it to be important.[16]

I didn't go to the plenary session. Our committee report as far as we've gone went in, but there was nothing controversial so I went to speak to the Army officers and men in this area at a movie theatre.[17] I spent an hour with them and it went well, I think. Had a call at the office from Sir Campbell Stewart who came for Lord Derby to ask me to a dinner the Pilgrims wanted to give for me. I said the 4th was the only safe date as I hope I can leave the 5th for Germany and so they are having it that night.[18] The Larue Browns[19] brought a Dr. Berman (democratic Argentina) to lunch. He came with the committee who brought the trophy to the apartment and that reminds me that I'd never sent it on. Will you attend to it?[20] He is here I gather hoping they will expel the present

Argentine government delegation but I just told him the case would have to go to the committee on Human Rights when the Economic and Social Council sets it up.[21]

At 2:30 Mr. Sidney Hillman came and seemed hopeful labor would come out well from the present struggle. He's gone to Germany.[22] At 3, Mr. Stettinius called a surprise meeting to go over again our position on Secretary General. Vandenburg's position is funny and I am interested in the way all the legislators react.[23] I think not having strong convictions they doubt their ability to defend a position which they may take so they can not decide on any position and go on arguing pros and cons endlessly.

At 3:30 I gave my vote[24] and left for a trip to see some new housing down near the docks[25] and I got the Mrs. Connelly, Vandenburg and Dulles to go and left them there when I had to come back to have Frances Archer-Shee (who flies home next week)[26] Helen Gifford (an old school mate)[27] and a Dr. Nusbaum, for tea. The latter is interested in freedom of religion and says the charter is too broad but I again said "Go to the Committee on Human Rights" not to me.[28] They left at 6:15 and I dined with Arthur Murray. He read me a chapter in a book he is about to publish. It is about FDR and very nice. Then he told me how he saw the world scene and I was interested. He was active in Washington with Grey and Tyrrel (during the first World War) and has been in Parliament and in business and more or less in touch right through the years. His opinion of Winston except for the period after Dunkirk is none too high.[29]

I got home at 11, but I had so much mail to sign and go through that I wrote no letters. This a.m., Sunday, I didn't breakfast till 9 and I left at 10 for Oxford. Bad fog for nearly half way then it cleared and was lovely. The country side is not so badly damaged and Oxford itself has few signs of harm, and is serene and beautiful. The Willerts' house is small and comfortable and Wanda (Willert grandchild and Mrs. R.'s Godchild)[30] came home from school to lunch and is a nice child. Arthur Willert gave me his views after lunch. He thinks much better of Winston though he too is a liberal.[31] Arthur Murray and he agree in their views on Russia and I think they agree fairly well with mine though I have a reservation. I'm not so convinced that Great Britain and ourselves must line up to keep the Russians in hand. I think we must be fair and stand for what we believe is right and let them, either or both, side with us. We have had that leadership and we must recapture it.[32]

I got home in time to dress and go up to Frank Walker's for sherry to meet Lady Gowen's daughter-in-law.[33] Then Jay Crane came in with Louise Morley[34] for dinner and Mr. Sandifer, my chief adviser. Jay Crane's picture of the refugee situation was helpful (he had been in Germany) to both of us for reasons he did not know, since one phase that he pictures strengthens the Russia position.[35] The whole question I'll tell you about, any of you who are interested, but it is too long to write.

After they left Ben Cohen came in and he and Mr. Sandifer and I talked for sometime. I said many things which I hope go back to the Secretary and the President.[36]

TDi AERP, FDRL

---

1. The General Assembly reconvened for its second session in late October 1946 (Lash, *Years*, 59). For ER's proposed Russian trip see *n*13 Document 80.

2. In a letter to "Tommy" Thompson on 13 January 1946, ER wrote, "I want to do some lectures and go to the west coast soon … I will go to Russia in the early or late summer, which ever fits in best with Elliott's summer plans, as I do want to go to Campo [Campobello] with them and be at Hyde Park when the children are there." As it turned out, she did not go to Russia in 1946, but began work that summer on her autobiography. Her life with family and friends was hectic. At this time, her son Elliott was writing *As He Saw It*, a book about his experiences as a wartime advisor to FDR, and, with his family, lived next door to ER at Hyde Park. To her daughter Anna she wrote, "It has been hectic since I got back. Everyone wants to see me, the mail is enormous and all the boys

are in and out." ER did travel to Campobello Island, New Brunswick, where the Roosevelts had a vacation home. For more on Elliot, see *n*17 Document 233 (Lash, *World*, 213, 227, 217, 222).

3. George Bye (1887?–1957), ER's literary agent, urged her to begin work on the second volume of her autobiography, which would cover the White House years and be published as *This I Remember* in 1949 ("George T. Bye, 70, Literary Agent," *NYT*, 25 November 1957, 31; Lash, *Years*, 58).

4. Clement Attlee (1883–1967), British prime minister, and his wife, Violet Helen (*DNB*).

5. Ambassador John Winant. See *n*10 Document 75.

6. For Philip Noel-Baker, see *n*15 Document 78. The next day, ER wrote in her diary: "I finally discovered Noel Baker wasn't making trouble for me but for Bloom on the UNO resolution." When the debate on the refugee question began in the Third Committee, the United Kingdom introduced a resolution proposing that the refugee question be referred to ECOSOC and ER spoke in support of it. See Document 86. (ER's London Diary, 24 January 1946, AERP).

7. Secretary of State James Byrnes.

8. It is unclear what ER meant by this remark, but Noel-Baker's biographer notes that he "made no secret of his impatience and dissatisfaction with some of the activities of the United Nations," and that he often did not cooperate well with his colleagues in the UN (Whittaker, 248, 335).

9. Apparently Major Myers, whom ER identifies in her diary as the pilot during her tour of American bases in the Caribbean in March 1944 (ER's London Diary, 21 January 1946, AERP; Lash, *Eleanor*, 696).

10. The identity of Lehman's nephew could not be determined. For Louise Morley see *n*17 Document 74.

11. A child of privilege, Lady Emmeline Pethwick-Lawrence (1867–1954) began her career volunteering for the West London Mission and continued to agitate for the interest of working class women. Although her primary political focus was Labour-related, she became a passionate suffragist and a key ally of Christabel Pankhurst, serving as treasurer for the Women's Social and Political Union and publisher of its "Votes for Women." She left the WSPU for the United Suffragists when the WSPU advocated increasingly militant tactics (property damage, etc.) to secure the vote for British women. World War I encouraged her to join the women's peace movement, and by 1926, she was elected president of the Women's Freedom League. Lady Pethwick-Lawrence wrote to ER welcoming her to London and asking if she and her house guest, Mrs. Gram Swing, could come speak with her about equality for women and the UN (*WH*; Lady Pethwick-Lawrence to ER, 17 January 1946, AERP).

12. Betty Gram Swing (1893?–1969), a leader in the American women's suffrage movement and wife of radio journalist Raymond Gram Swing, worked for the cause of equal rights both in the United States and England. As an observer at the first meeting of the General Assembly, she campaigned for the establishment of the Commission on the Status of Women ("Betty Gram Swing Dead at 76; Women's Rights Leader in 20's," *NYT*, 4 September 1969, 47).

13. ER commented on this proposal in her January 25 My Day column:

> On Wednesday afternoon, Lady Pethwick-Lawrence and Mrs. Raymond Gram Swing came to call on me.
>
> They evidently want to prevail on the Economic and Social Council to set up a special commission composed of women which would not be considered as a specialized agency but would have a closer relationship to the Council. I have not studied the question as yet, but it seems to me that any such non-governmental group, no matter how

strong numerically, should still be considered, under the provisions already laid down, only in a consultative capacity.

I can quite see that a commission representing many women's organizations throughout the world might speak for a very great number of women, but I think they should be treated on the same basis as other specialized agencies. Otherwise, an infinite number of similar groups would be demanding special recognition and special privileges in their relationship to the United Nations—a situation which would result in chaos. I think we should make a very great effort to live up to the sections in the Charter which provide for complete equality. I am sorry that Governments in all parts of the world have not seen fit to send more women as delegates, alternates or advisers to the Assembly, and I think it is in these positions that the women of every nation should work to see that equality exists.

I feel also that a variety of interests should be represented in every delegation. Business, labor and the professions have a great contribution to make to the questions that will come up before the Assembly. In every field today there are competent women who could be chosen as individuals outstanding in their field and not merely as women.

A few days later, she again addressed the issue in her column:

As so often happens, I think a difference of opinion is developing among the various groups of women as to the exact representation or affiliation they desire to have with the UNO. I myself believe the important thing is to stress the attitude taken in the very beginning of the UNO Charter, which reaffirms "faith in fundamental human rights, in the dignity and worth of the human person, in the equal rights of men and women and of nations large and small." This really means, I think, that women should come in on an equal basis—not even as specialized groups, unless they are representing some particular objective. Their influence should be felt as delegates, alternates and advisers.

Among the women now here are economists, lawyers and social workers, all leaders and experts in their various fields. With this type of representation, I believe, women really achieve what they want, which is to have on all important subjects the point of view of both men and women who are working together to frame the policies of the organization.

In June 1946, ECOSOC established the Commission on the Status of Women, in addition to the Commission on Human Rights, making it an integral part of the UN rather than a specialized agency (*MD*, 25 and 28 January 1946; Glendon, 32). See also Documents 112 and 120.

14. George Catlin (1896–1979), a British professor of political philosophy, taught politics at Cornell University from 1924 to 1935 and wrote about Anglo-American relations and the values Americans and the British share. His wife, Vera Brittain (1893–1970), a journalist, novelist, autobiographer, and speaker, gained prominence as an advocate of feminism and pacifism. She was an active member of the League of Nations Union ("Sir George Catlin," *TL*, 17 December 1979, 16; "Miss Vera Brittain," *TL*, 30 March 1970, 8).

15. Probably ER's My Day column published January 28, 1946, in which she describes her lunch on January 25 with British foreign minister Ernest Bevin in the House of Commons (*MD*, 28 January 1946).

16. Senator Vandenberg represented the United States on Committee Five (Administrative and Budgetary) ("Assignments of Delegates and Advisers by Committees," USSEC/9a, 10 January 1946, UNP, AERP).

17. ER means she did not go to the plenary session of the General Assembly because there was nothing controversial in the interim report of Committee Three, on which she served.

18. ER spoke at the Pilgrims Society dinner on February 4, 1946, the first woman in the history of the organization to do so. The Pilgrims Society, whose membership included representatives of the British elite, promoted Anglo-American friendship. Edward Stanley, Lord Derby (1865–1948), was the president of the Pilgrims Society. Sir Campbell Stuart (1885–1972), who later succeed Lord Derby as president of the society, was the treasurer of the fund to erect a statue of FDR in Grosvenor Square (*DNB*, "Mrs. Roosevelt at Pilgrims' Dinner," *TL*, 5 February 1946, 2). ER spoke again at the Pilgrims Society on April 12, 1948. See Document 336. See also Document 87.

19. Herman LaRue Brown and his wife Dorothy Browning Kirchwey Brown. See *n*18 Document 75.

20. Mr. Berman is probably Dr. Gregorio Berman, a "distinguished Argentine liberal and representative of the Argentine League of Rights of Man," whom Roger Baldwin, chairman of the International League of Rights of Man, and Francis G. Grant, chairman of the Latin American Committee, asked ER to see (Roger Baldwin and Francis G. Grant to ER, telegram, 18 January 1946, UNGC, AERP).

21. The Economic and Social Council established a nuclear commission on human rights after the conclusion of the London meetings in February and the permanent Human Rights Commission during its June meetings (Glendon, 30–32).

22. At the beginning of 1946, as the United States proceeded with reconversion from a wartime to a peacetime economy, workers demanded the wage increases they had foregone during the war and management pushed for price increases while resisting labor's demands. The conflict led to a series of strikes by automobile, electrical, packinghouse, and communication workers. Automobile workers had been on strike since November 21; steel workers struck on January 21. On January 22, United Press reported that labor disputes had put 1,650,000 workers out of work.

Hillman, chair of the CIO PAC, had left the United States January 24 as part of the World Federation of Trade Unions team charged with investigating living and working conditions in the four Allied occupied zones in Germany. Before he boarded his flight to London, he told the press that labor remained supportive of Truman's fact-finding investigations and that he was "very happy that labor has got a sense of responsibility to the needs of the nation at this time" (Donovan, *Conflict*, 162–66; "Hillman Departs for German Tour," *NYT*, 24 January 1946, 13).

23. When the Security Council chose Trygve Lie as Secretary-General, ER wrote in her diary: "It was well done I think and we took the lead though our first choice was Pearson of Canada. When we found the Russians wouldn't consent but would compromise, we proposed Lie." Vandenberg may have expressed concern that Russia might exert undue pressure on Lie because it shared a border with Norway, Lie's home country. ER noted in her diary, "I think [Lie] resents being considered a tool of Russia's. I think some of our men are wrong for I believe we can wield as much influence on Russia as she can on Norway." The other legislators included Senator Connally, Congressmen Bloom and Eaton, and ex-Senator Townsend (ER's London Diary, 25 and 29 January 1946, AERP; Lash, *Years*, 51). See also *n*32 Document 77.

24. ER voted in Committee Three on January 25. The committee unanimously adopted a report to the General Assembly approving the recommendations of the Preparatory Commission, which had proposed that ECOSOC establish a Commission on Human Rights, a Temporary Social Commission, a Commission on Narcotic Drugs, and a Demographic Commission (General Assembly, First Session, Summary Record (A/C.3/8, A/17), UNORGA, MWelC).

25. In the January 31 My Day column, ER wrote:

> I've had an opportunity, under the auspices of the Women's Volunteer Services, to see some of the new housing being put up in the badly blitzed London dock area. Along the wharves here, acres and acres of houses were destroyed.
>
> The housing program was planned in three parts. First, there were erected fairly primitive dwellings, consisting of two bedrooms, a living room, and a kitchen with run-

ning cold water. These furnished immediate shelter. The next step was prefabricated houses, which are expected to last ten years and are a little more comfortable.

Final step is well-built two-story houses which, in part, are also prefabricated. The heating units and plumbing all come ready for connection. These houses have a bathroom, hot and cold running water, and a heat duct going up from the first floor to the second. The little living room has a tiny fireplace, without which, I imagine, no British householder would feel really at home. There are three bedrooms as a rule.

These houses rent for about one pound a week. They are in the old slum areas, of course, and it is expected that all of them will be subsidized to some extent, since it is freely acknowledged here that it is not possible for private industry to provide decent housing for low-paid workers without a subsidy. The two-year and ten-year temporary houses are owned by the city government, so there is no danger of their being left standing to form new slums (*MD*, 31 January 1946).

26. In her January 16 My Day, ER mentions inviting Lady Archer-Shee, "an old family friend," to tea. This was possibly a member of the same Archer-Shee family whom ER visited at Campobello in the summer of 1950. Also, James Roosevelt courted a Lucy Archer-Shee while he was in college at Harvard (*MD*, 16 January 1946; Lash, *Eleanor*, 299; ER to Anna Roosevelt, 21 August 1950, AERP).

27. ER became friends with Helen Gifford when they both attended Allenswood. Gifford and her sister, Leonie, later founded their own school (Lash, *Eleanor*, 76).

28. Probably Dr. Jean Nussbaum, whom ER met for the first time during this opening session of the UN. Nussbaum, a French Seventh Day Adventist, represented small religious groups, such as the one he belonged to, in efforts to protect their religious freedom. He corresponded regularly with ER to report on issues of religious freedom in Yugoslavia and elsewhere. See *n*3 Document 272 (*MD*, 24 May 1954; M. Jean Nussbaum to ER, 19 June 1946, AERP; ER to John Foster Dulles, 29 July 1948, JFDP, NjP-SC).

29. Arthur Cecil Murray (1879–1962), Lord Elibank, one of ER's closest British friends, who served as one of her primary informants about the British perspective on foreign affairs and the situation in Europe. Murray befriended FDR and ER when he was serving as assistant military attaché at the British embassy in Washington at the end of World War I and FDR was assistant secretary of the navy. Murray had spent many years as a participant and observer of British politics, having served as a Liberal member of parliament from 1908 to 1923 and as private secretary to Sir Edward Grey (1862–1933), the British secretary of state for foreign affairs, from 1910 to 1914. In his letter to ER in March, 1946 deploring Churchill's "Iron Curtain" speech, Murray refers back to their conversation about Russia on the evening ER describes here. See Document 100. Grey and his former private secretary, Sir William Tyrrell (1866–1947), came to Washington in 1919 on a diplomatic mission and FDR and ER entertained them for dinner at that time (C. Black, 482–83; "Viscount Elibank, Ex-House Member," *NYT*, 6 December 1962, 43; *DNB*; Ward, 482).

30. This parenthetical identification appears to have been inserted by Tommy in typing the diaries.

31. Sir Arthur Willert (1882–1973), a British diplomat and journalist, and Lady Florence Willert maintained a long friendship with ER and FDR. Arthur Willert served as the London *Times* Washington correspondent from 1910 through 1920 and also as secretary of the British War Mission and representative of the Ministry of Information (1917 through 1918), overlapping with FDR's tenure as assistant secretary of the navy. FDR became an important contact for Willert and ER and Florence Willert corresponded regularly over the years. Willert became an expert on Anglo-American relations, helping to explain the views of the two nations to each other. He wrote frequently about international affairs and lectured in the United States from 1936 to 1939 ("Sir Arthur Willert," *TL*, 13 March 1973, 16; Lash, *Roosevelt and Churchill*, 24).

32. For Arthur Murray's views on Russia, see Document 100 and its header. No record of the conversation between ER and Murray alluded to here has been found, but the later document makes Murray's general point of view on Russia apparent.

33. For Frank Walker, see *n*29 Document 76. The identity of Lady Gowen's daughter-in-law is unknown.

34. For Louise Morley, see *n*17 Document 75.

35. Jay B. Krane (1923–1961) worked for the United Nations Relief and Rehabilitation Administration (UNRRA) during World War II where he became chief of the Reports and Statistics Division of the UNRRA Displaced Persons Programme in Europe ("Scope and Contents," Krane Collection, Reuther Library, Wayne State University, http://www.reuther.wayne.edu/collections/hefa_614.htm, accessed 28 July 2005).

36. Benjamin V. Cohen (1894–1983) served as one of the senior advisors to the American delegation and general counsel of the State Department. Cohen played a key role in the New Deal and ER knew him well. ER's views might have been communicated by Cohen to the president either through Byrnes or directly (*FDRE*).

THE MADISON SQUARE GARDEN RALLY
FOR THE FEPC

> While in the White House, ER worked closely with A. Philip Randolph[1] to help publicize the discrimination share croppers confronted, to secure a place for Marian Anderson to perform after the Daughters of the American Revolution refused her access to Constitution Hall, and to pressure FDR, albeit unsuccessfully, to stay Odell Waller's execution. In 1940, FDR turned to ER and La Guardia to help dissuade Randolph's March on Washington movement from pressing for nondiscriminatory clauses in federal contracts. ER sided with Randolph and urged FDR to sign Executive Order 8802. Six years later, Randolph sought her help in extending the program they helped create.[2]

85

A. Philip Randolph to Eleanor Roosevelt
28 January 1946 [New York City]

Dear Mrs. Roosevelt:

I am extremely grateful to know of your acceptance of Honorary Chairman for the FEPC rally being held at Madison Square Garden on February 26th.[3] The filibuster now going on in Congress makes public awareness urgent and your attendance at the rally imperative.[4] More important still would you consent to speak at the rally. Your message is invaluable to the cause.

Would it be possible for you to mention your Chairmanship in your Column?[5]

Very sincerely yours,
A. Philip Randolph

TLc BSCPR-APRP, DLC

---

1. Asa Philip Randolph (1889–1979), labor organizer and president of the Brotherhood of Sleeping Car Porters from 1925 to 1968. In early 1940, he assumed a leading role in organizing a coalition demanding both the government and private industries end discriminatory hiring practices in the defense industry. Under pressure from Randolph's March on Washington movement, FDR created a temporary Fair Employment Practices Committee (FEPC) by executive order in June 1941; Randolph continued to lobby for a permanent FEPC as co-chairman of the National Council for a Permanent FEPC (*FDRE; HSTE*).

2. J. Anderson, 241–61; A. Black, *Casting*, 93, 94, 122.

3. For a discussion of the Fair Employment Practices Committee, see *n*2 Document 12. On February 28, ER left a fund-raising dinner for the Union for Democratic Action to address the crowd of more than 15,000 who rallied at Madison Square Garden in support of a permanent Fair Employment Practices Act. Although no formal text of her remarks exists, the *Times* reported: "Mrs. Roosevelt said that at the recent UNO sessions, representatives of fifty-one nations had pledged themselves to a program of equality without discrimination, and declared that we could not exercise the leadership in the world that is ours by right and obligation if we failed to eliminate discrimination at home" ("Fight by Truman for FEPC Pledged," *NYT*, 1 March 1946, 23).

4. Truman supported statutory continuation of the committee beyond the beginning of 1946, but southern Democrats in Congress succeeded in blocking FEPC legislation through the first half of 1946. At the opening of the debate on legislation to renew FEPC funding, Senator John Overton of Louisiana (1875–1948) began a filibuster that southern Democrats sustained for 23 days, to delay voting on the bill. New York City Mayor William O'Dwyer (1890–1964) had designated February 28 as "Fair Employment Practice Committee Day" and the rally held at Madison Square Garden was used to attract public support for the FEPC bill stalled in Congress. Several other fair employment committees were established by executive order [after 1941], but they only received full legislative legitimacy in 1964 through the Civil Rights Act (Hamby, *Man*, 365; *HSTE*; C. P. Trussell, "Senate Is Thrown into Furor as FEPC Bill Is Called Up," *NYT*, 18 January 1946, 1; "Filibuster on FEPC Balks the Senate," *NYT*, 19 January 1946, 3; "Proclaims FEPC Day," *NYT*, 27 January 1946, 9; "Closure Defeated, FEPC Sidetracked; Filibuster Ended," *NYT*, 10 February 1946, 1; "Fight by Truman for FEPC Pledged," *NYT*, 1 March 1946, 23; "FEPC Bill Balked Again in House," *NYT*, 23 May 1946, 15).

5. Although ER used My Day to support the FEPC, she did not mention the rally in her column.

OPPOSING REFUGEE REPATRIATION

One of the most contentious issues debated at the first meeting of the UN General Assembly involved the question of what to do with displaced persons and other individuals who fled their countries after the war and refused repatriation for fear of political reprisals or death in their home countries. As she wrote to friends, "The battle is on about the refugee resolution."[1]

On January 26, Yugoslavia proposed halting assistance to those individuals who refused to return to their homelands, a resolution which many nations, among them the United States and Britain, considered a policy of forced repatriation.[2] Explaining the Yugoslav delegate's position in My Day, ER wrote: "Any who did not wish to return to their own country, from his point of view, were either war criminals or people who were out of sympathy with the form of government in their country and would, therefore, form pockets of resistance to the whole democratic movement in the world." Yugoslavia's resolution declared that "the problem of displaced persons has ceased to be one of the important international questions," and asked that the General Assembly refrain from establishing any body, permanent or temporary, to handle the refugee problem.

The General Assembly referred the proposal to the Social, Humanitarian and Cultural Affairs Committee (the Third Committee) where debate began on January 28. British minister of state Philip Noel-Baker opened the debate with a proposal that the refugee problem be referred to ECOSOC, where the United Kingdom hoped open discussion would lead to the creation of a new UN body—"under the direct authority of the Assembly"—whose sole responsibility would be to aid refugees. Britain had taken a leading role in the refugee debate for reasons that ER summarized in her diary on January 9:

> A new type of political refugee is appearing—people who have been against the present governments and if they stay at home or go home will probably be killed. Britain is supporting most of them and would like the expense shared— the budget for the job might run to double what is contemplated for the whole of UNO.

Thus, although ER also empathized with the Yugoslav delegate and wrote that she could "quite see his point that no democratic government wishes to support groups of their citizens who are working to overthrow that form of government," she believed that the refugee problem was one that the UN could not ignore and delivered the following speech in support of the British position.[3]

She dictated the final version of the statement while getting her hair and nails done.[4]

86

Problem of Refugees: Speech Delivered by the Representative of the United States of America at the Fourth Meeting of the Third Committee[5]
28 January 1946 [London]

MRS. ROOSEVELT (United States of America): I want to congratulate Mr. Noel-Baker on the very excellent statement he has made for the United Kingdom delegation on the refugee problem and its background.[6] Our delegation of the United States is happy to support the proposal of the United Kingdom that the question of refugees shall be referred to the Economic and Social Council for thorough examination in all its details under item 10 of the agenda for the first session of the Council and for report to the second part of the first session of the General Assembly.[7]

We in the United States delegation know well that the problem of refugees is an urgent problem and we know that ways must be found, in the interest of humanity and social stability, to return these thousands of people who have been uprooted from their homes and their countries to a settled way of life. Everyone at this table is familiar with the problem and must realize that it is important to find a way of dealing with it so as to remove it as a source of disturbance in the relationships of the nations now affected by it.

The people of the United States and their Government are deeply concerned for the refugees who, because of the war or of danger to their lives or liberty on account of their race, religion or political beliefs, have become victims of oppression and misery. In the summary contained in the United Kingdom proposal (annex 1, page 37) it is shown that the establishment of the Inter-governmental Committee on Refugees in March 1938 was largely due to the initiative taken by the United States. Half of the operational expenses of the Inter-governmental Committee have been borne by the United States since 1943 and the other half by the United Kingdom. Our Government took a leading part in the creation and organization of UNRRA. This organization in recent months has done much for the relief of persons made refugees by the war. I feel certain that our Government stands ready to continue to bear its fair share of the burden for such activities.[8]

We in the United States delegation, however, feel that the United Nations could not move on this problem without careful consideration and review of all the elements entering into it—political, economic, social and humanitarian. That is why we feel the need to recommend it to the Economic and Social Council for study and report. This seems to us a sound procedure since the Council is able to make a thorough and impartial examination and, on its findings, the interested Governments can determine the best future course for dealing with these complex and controversial problems.

Our support for the reference of the matter to the Economic and Social Council for a complete survey does not mean, however, that we are not conscious that speed in handling this matter is an important factor. According to present plans UNRRA will terminate its work in Europe at the end of 1946. The Inter-governmental Committee has done good work within its terms of reference and with the resources at its disposal, but it is quite evident, as the United Kingdom delegation has pointed out, that this Committee has not sufficient resources nor a sufficiently large and authoritative organization to handle the entire problem. When the League of Nations arrangements with the United Nations have been completed some disposition will have to be made of the work now performed by the High Commissioner for Refugees. This knowledge makes it plain that, upon the completion of the study by the Economic and Social Council, there must be prompt action to determine the manner in which the interested Governments shall deal with the refugee problem. The Government of the United States will be prepared, in cooperation with these Governments, to take prompt initiative in carrying out the necessary action.[9]

Pending the outcome of the proposed study and report, the United States delegation urges that existing inter-governmental agencies maintain their activities for the benefit of the refugees.

Tsptr UN ECOSOC, MWelC

––––––––––––

1. ER's London Diary, 9 January 1946, AERP.

2. Sydney Gruson, "UNO Urged to Push Refugees' Return," *NYT*, 27 January 1946, 14; "UNO Group Debates Issue of Refugees," *NYT*, 29 January 1946, 3; "Limited UNO Board on Refugees Seen," *NYT*, 15 January 1946, 8; Holborn, 31.

3. *MD*, 30 January 1946.

4. She dictated the final version of the statement; however, working with her State Department advisors, she had prepared at least two earlier versions of the speech (Draft Statement by Mrs. Roosevelt in Committee 3 Concerning the United Kingdom Proposal on Refugees, 25 January 1946 and untitled, undated draft, AERP).

5. Third Committee, First Session, Fourth Meeting, 28 January 1946 (USGA/Ia/SHCom/32/ USES/19), 56–57, UNORGA, MWelC).

6. In making the British proposal, Noel-Baker reviewed the history of the international response to refugees from just after World War I to 1946 and argued that the mechanisms in place, including the Inter-governmental Committee on Refugees established in 1938 and UNRRA, were inadequate to meet the current crisis. He pointed out that nearly all of the operational and financial responsibility for refugees had fallen on the governments of the United Kingdom and the United States. Given the situation, the United Kingdom proposed that the Third Committee refer the matter to ECOSOC for study and the preparation of recommendations to be acted upon at the next meeting of the committee (Committee Three Delegation of the United Kingdom Proposal Concerning Refugees (A/C.3/5) 23 January 1946, 37–43, UNORGA, MWelC).

7. Item 10 of the agenda for the Economic and Social Council read: "Discussion of the problem of refugees and other urgent matters in economic, social, cultural, educational, health, and related fields, as may be referred to the Council by the General Assembly or which the Council may find desirable to put on its agenda." When the US delegation to the Third Committee met on January 10, members remained unsure as to the stance Britain would adopt in the committee. See also Document 78 (ECOSOC, First Year, First–Third Session 1946, Agenda, X, UNOR ECOSOC, MWelC).

8. The British proposal on refugees included a history of the two organizations currently attempting to handle the refugee problem, the Inter-governmental Committee on Refugees (IGCR) and the United Nations Relief and Rehabilitation Administration (UNRRA). In March 1938, President Roosevelt called an international conference that he hoped would aid in relocating Jewish refugees from Germany and Austria. With Roosevelt's assurance that "no country would be expected or asked to receive a greater number of emigrants than is permitted by existing legislation," more than thirty nations met at Evian-les-Bains, France, in July 1938 and established the IGCR. Conceding that "all members of the I.G.C. contributed in fixed proportion to the *administrative* costs of the Committee," the British proposal asserted that "the United Kingdom accepted equal responsibility with the United States government, on a fifty-fifty basis, for underwriting, and in effect meeting the *operational* costs of the Inter-governmental Committee in the tasks of actually caring for refugees." In November 1945, when the committee approved a budget of $12,000,000 for 1946, the United States and Britain bore the brunt of the operational costs while receiving minimal contributions from only two nations, France and Norway. The United States also played a leading role in UNRRA: the State Department drafted the international agreement that established UNRRA, and former New York governor Herbert Lehman served as the organization's director general. Although UNRRA worked with the IGCR to provide temporary aid to refugees (those individuals who did not wish to return to their home countries), UNRRA's stated purpose was to make "preparations and arrangement … for the return of prisoners and exiles to their homes." The British proposal pointed out that caring for "persons displaced as a result of the war" until repatriation could be arranged marked the extent of UNRRA's authority. UNRRA was "not authorized under its present constitution to deal, except for a short period, with persons who, for any reason, definitely cannot return to their homes." The British delegation asked the Third Committee delegates to recommend to the General Assembly that ECOSOC investigate the refugee question with the possibility of establishing an organization to handle the situation (Committee 3 Delegation of the United Kingdom Proposal Concerning Refugees (A/C.3/5) 23 January 1946, UNORGA, MWelC; Dallek, 167; "12,000,000 Voted By Refugee Board," *NYT*, 22 November 1945, 22; Bertram D. Hulen, "U.S. Offers Plan for World Relief," *NYT*, 11 June 1943, 1; Holborn, 17; Vernant, 30-33). For more on UNRRA, See *n*7 Document 55.

9. Just as the British proposal underscored how the IGCR's lack of resources impeded its ability to handle the refugee crisis, ER lent her voice to publicizing UNRAA's funding crisis. (See Document 66). As an international organization established by an agreement between more than forty nations, UNRRA relied on appropriations from the governments of each of its member nations on an annual basis. The prolonged debates in Congress at the end of 1945 over the American contribution to UNRRA revealed the precarious existence of such an organization. Furthermore, since UNRRA's first meeting in November 1943, its General Council had been embroiled in the debate over whether or not individuals who did not wish to repatriate fell within its jurisdiction. It then decided that the organization would care for these individuals for a "reasonable period" until they could be placed in the care of the IGCR. At its third session in late 1945, UNRRA defined "reasonable period" as no longer than six months, and the organization's General Council announced its intentions to complete operations in Europe by the end of the year.

In addition to UNRRA and the IGCR, the only other machinery in place for dealing with refugees was the League of Nations high commissioner on refugees who provided legal protection to refugees through the issuance of passports and other civil documents that a refugee could not obtain otherwise. As League representatives were to begin negotiating the transfer of the League's assets to the UN in February 1946 with its scheduled dissolution in April, no one believed the high commissioner would continue his work for very long. In December 1946 the Office of the League of Nations High Commissioner closed. Sir Herbert Emerson (1881–1969), who served concurrently as the League's high commissioner and the IGCR director, transferred all of the League's functions in the area of aiding refugees to the IGCR.

The individuals who attempted to handle the refugee crisis within these organizations supported the British proposal to consolidate the responsibilities of the three agencies. The IGCR, at its November 1945 meeting in Paris, passed a resolution that allowed its executive committee to enter into negotiations with the General Assembly in the hopes that a new organization might be created within ECOSOC to relieve the IGCR of its responsibilities. Following the General Assembly's passing of a resolution which called upon ECOSOC to create a committee to investigate the refugee situation, UNRRA's General Council adopted a resolution declaring that "its members shall seek to do all in their power to expedite the early creation of a United Nations body capable of dealing in an effective manner with the problem" (Holborn, 22, 25, 30; Vernant, 26, 32; "Refugee Committee Asks UNO to Do Job," *NYT*, 23 November 1945, 11; Resolutions Adopted by the General Assembly During Its First Session, Resolutions 6(I) and 8(I), http://www.un.org/documents/ga/res/1/ares1.htm, accessed 1 November 2005).

For the continuation of the refugee debate in the General Assembly see Document 90 and Document 91.

ON ARGENTINA AND OTHER MATTERS

Joe Lash wrote ER in late January to ask her to "speak 'off the record'" at a dinner he and Trude were organizing in support of the Union for Democratic Action.[1] After recounting tales of his son, and ER's godson, Jonathan, he closed by telling ER that he had just finished "reading a long statement multigraphed by the *Nation* on why Argentina's membership in the UNO should be suspended. A convincing case is made out, but I expect that so long as England and all of Europe desperately needs Argentine beef nothing will happen."[2]

87

Eleanor Roosevelt to Joseph Lash
3 February 1946 [London]

Dearest Joe,

Your letter of the 27th was a joy and would have been answered sooner only work does pile up and the stream of people is endless! For the last two days I had no voice, no cold, so I think I must be weary. It is better today and I hope by tomorrow I'll be recovered since I may have to talk in committee meeting in the morning[3] and I'm speaking at a big dinner given by the "Pilgrims" in the evening. They tell me it is important and the first woman they've had in 40 yrs. so perhaps its fright has removed my voice![4]

I've got the 27th down and I hope I can do well for you and that this coming meeting will be as good as your first. Of course any arrangements you make are right with me.

I saw by the N.Y. Times that Mrs. Levy was home.[5] I hope I get in by the 20th. I will unless I am held up by weather.

Has Jonathan[6] got a tooth? I can't believe it and shall want to see him at once!

From over here the home strike situation tends to look more and more ominous since you view it with world needs constantly in the forefront.[7] The British and American papers are so very thorough, because so many of our troubles are similar!

I'm so happy about your article in the New Republic.[8] You will be interested to hear that I have found considerable interest in your idea for an exhibition here. Will you find out if your friend is back from the Philippines and get me the plans? Stettinius thinks the War and Navy Departments and State Department might do the war show and put it wherever UNO is as a permanent exhibit and each nation could have an economic, cultural show of its own and we have one like theirs with our economy and culture. Small scale models would then be shipped by UNO over the country. What do you think of this idea? I'm going to try to take it up as soon as I get back and go to Washington.[9]

Eventually the Security Council will have Argentina[10] brought before them but they seem to have enough to keep them busy for the moment. That Vishinsky and Bevin came thro' the first session on Greece and spoke their minds so plainly was good I think. Much is out in the open but Stettinius dined alone with me tonight and left at nine to see Bevin. Some way must be devised whereby neither will lose face and Greece will hold a free election or as free as possible. The Greeks want the British to keep order because they fear the Russians <u>within</u> Greece would cause civil war before the elections. Then they want the British out but they want Russian armies out of Bulgaria and Yugoslavia and the standing armies of those countries reduced.[11] We send food and clothing to Yugoslavia but they have an army of 300,000 men, so the peaceful pursuits are not getting much attention. They (the Yugoslavs) say if the armies outside their borders were free to return as peasants and the officers were all declared war criminals or just became exiles then they wouldn't need so many soldiers at home.[12] There you have just one simple little European problem. The Philippine delegate came to see me today and I feel very sorry for them and I think they are our direct economic responsibility.

I felt sad over Harry Hopkins death and people here felt they had lost a real friend. Today I see in the Times from N.Y. that McDuffie died on the 30th, Franklin's birthday. Even tho I did dismiss him for drinking I was fond of him and I'm sorry for poor old Lizzie.[13]

We are having a little trouble with drink in the military part of our delegation but now they are getting down to work. I hope it will straighten out.

Jay Krane[14] lunched with Senator Townsend[15] and me today and went to the service at St. Paul's Cathedral for the delegates. It was impressive but I wondered how the delegate from Saudi Arabia who sat in front of me with his flowing robes felt about it. Mr. Atlee read the lesson, he's not a very impressive man but he read very well.[16] The choir sang Spring-Rice's poem[17] which I like and so I enclose it, thinking you and Trude might be interested to see it. I enclose also 2 little medals which were sent me and I thought might interest the kids.

They expect to close Saturday. Monday morning I'll go to Germany, back I think the 14th to Ireland and from there fly home. I'll cable Tommy as I actually leave and write her when plans are definite.

I must go to bed. My thoughts are often with you. All my love is yours always.

Devotedly
E.R.

ALI LASH, FDRL

---

1. Founded December 10, 1941, by Freda Kirchwey, James Loeb, Frank Porter Graham, and Mark Stark, all of whom disagreed with Norman Thomas and the Socialist Party's isolationist sentiments, the UDA (whose membership never exceeded 10,000) dedicated itself to "fighting a two-front war for democracy" by "protecting democracy at home from reactionaries who desire to destroy social gains under the cover of the defense effort and by insisting that democratic terms of peace be made a part of the fight." Unlike its larger counterparts the CIOPAC, NCPAC and ICCASP, the UDA opposed Popular Front politics, "specifically excluded" the Communist Party from membership, and refused to participate in any Communist-supported events. Its platform committed the organization to the war against Fascism, "the socialization of great banks and industries, the formulation of a national planning board," steep graduated income taxes, and "government control of credit and investments" (Brock, 49; Gillon, 6).

2. In a letter to ER on January 27, Lash said that the UDA, for which he worked, planned to hold a fund-raising dinner in ER's honor in New York on February 27 and that ER would be asked to speak briefly off-the-record at that event and then at a mass meeting at Hunter College to be held after the dinner (Joseph Lash to ER, 27 January 1946, AERP; "Plea for UNO Made by Mrs. Roosevelt," *NYT*, 28 February 1946, 4).

3. ER was about to introduce a resolution in Committee Three on the refugee issue ("Delegation Meeting," 5 February 1946, USGA/Ia/Del Mins/Exec/12 (Chr), RG84, NARA II).

4. For the Pilgrims Society dinner, see *n*18 Document 84.

5. For Adele Rosenwald Levy (1892–1960), see Document 58, including notes. Levy was appointed head of the Women's Division of the United Jewish Appeal in late December of 1945, and trav-

eled to Europe for about one month "to survey conditions among displaced Jews," according to the *New York Times*. The *New York Times* covered her report when she returned in late January:

> Many of the 150,000 European Jewish children who survived the war still are receiving care that could not meet minimum standards here, Mrs. David M. Levy, national women's chairman of the United Jewish Appeal, asserted yesterday. Only one in ten escaped the Nazis and perhaps half of these youngsters now are orphans, Mrs. Levy declared in an interview on her return from a month abroad ("Heads Women's Division of United Jewish Appeal," *NYT*, 26 December 1945, 12; "Child Care Abroad Still at Low Ebb," *NYT*, 31 January 1946, 10).

6. Jonathan Lash, Joseph and Trude Lash's son (Lash, *World*, 202).

7. For ER's attitude towards organized labor, see especially Document 12 and Document 46. On the UAW strike in 1945, see Document 46, Document 52, Document 53, Document 64, and Document 65. By February 1946, more than 2 million workers were on strike in the United States. The largest group belonged to the United Steelworkers of America, but the mining and railroad industries were also affected. In the months before ER wrote this letter, meatpackers, telegraph workers, electrical workers, automobile workers, tug boat workers, longshoremen, and rubber workers had threatened or instituted strikes. The *Times* (London) covered the strikes in the United States fairly frequently, writing that the end of 1945 "finds the physical conversion of American industry to its customary peace-time activities far advanced in many lines, even complete in some … However, there are reasons to believe that this condition will not continue indefinitely … The principal break on production is labour troubles—labour troubles more numerous and more extensive than the country has known for many years" ("Reconversion in America," *TL*, 31 December 1945, 7; *HSTE*).

8. Lash wrote to ER on January 27: "The New Republic is using my article. It will not be signed which pleases me just as well, for it would not have made Trude's life any easier. I'm very happy that it will be used." Lash did not retain a copy of this article or correspondence related to it in his papers; thus, its title could not be determined (Joseph Lash to ER, 27 January 1946, AERP).

9. In a letter to Secretary of Commerce Wallace on April 27, ER said that she had spoken with Secretary of the Navy James Forrestal, Secretary of War Robert Patterson, Assistant Secretary of State Dean Acheson, and Undersecretary of the Interior Oscar Chapman about the idea for an exhibition at the UN that she had also discussed with him, but had not heard from any of them. She realized that since the UN did not have a permanent home, the exhibition could not be done right away, but she thought that if the UN was going to be at its temporary location for several years, it might be organized there first (ER to Henry Wallace, 27 April 1946, HSTL). On May 23, Dean Acheson, to whom Truman had referred ER's letter to Wallace, replied in a memo to Truman:

> With reference to the letter of April 27 which Mrs. Roosevelt wrote to Secretary Wallace and which you referred to me on May 4 concerning an exhibit in connection with the permanent headquarters of the United Nations, an officer of the Department has recently, at my request, discussed this matter with Mrs. Roosevelt in New York.
>
> The idea which a group of young air force officers suggested to Mrs. Roosevelt some time ago would be to have a rather elaborate exhibit in the form of dioramas, and the like, which would show the various places in the world where American troops have been in service during the recent war. This exhibit would be established in connection with whatever building might be erected by the United States Delegation to the United Nations at its permanent headquarters. Veterans would be expected to bring their families to visit the exhibit and in this way, as a matter of public information and education, the importance of world cooperation through the United Nations would be emphasized. I am asking Assistant Secretary Benton to explore this matter further with a view to determining its feasibility.

Nothing apparently came of this proposal (Dean Acheson to Harry Truman, 23 May 1946, HSTL; see also John C. Ross, Department of State, Memo of Conversation, 14 May 1946, RG84, NARA II).

10. Because of Argentina's collaboration with the German Nazis during and after the war and its totalitarian government under Juan Perón, some, including the Nation Associates, publisher of the *Nation*, called at this time for the suspension of Argentina from the UN ("UNO Move to Suspend Argentina Is Urged," *NYT*, 24 January 1946, 6; Joseph Lash to ER, 27 January 1946, AERP). See also Document 13.

11. The Soviet Union supported EAM/ELAS, the Communist-dominated organization that rose up in December 1945 and January 1946 against the British-backed Greek government. The leftists boycotted the Greek elections held on March 31, 1946, but the United States, which had urged that the elections be held, asserted that they were as fair as could be expected (*HSTE; NEB*).

12. Yugoslavia supported the Greek Communist insurgents, maintained a large army, and vehemently opposed US positions at the UN, but also received a great deal of aid from UNRRA, whose funds came largely from the United States (*HSTE*).

13. Harry Hopkins (1890–1946) died in New York on January 29. Irvin H. McDuffie (1882–1946) was FDR's valet; his wife, Lizzie, also worked for the Roosevelts ("Hopkins, 55, Dies in Hospital Here," *NYT*, 30 January 1946, 1; "Irvin M'Duffie, 63, Roosevelt's Valet," *NYT*, 31 January 1946, 20; James MacGregor Burns, "F.D.R., Ever the Happy Warrior," *NYT*, 12 April 1995, A1).

14. For Krane see *n*35 Document 84.

15. For Senator John G. Townsend, Jr., see *n*23 Document 76.

16. Clement Attlee (1883–1967) served as prime minister of Great Britain from 1945 to 1951. (*HSTE*).

17. In her diary for February 3, ER wrote: "It was a nice service and to my surprise they sang Cecil Spring-Rice's hymn which I think lovely … " (ER's London Diary, 3 February 1946, AERP). Sir Cecil Spring-Rice (1859–1918), the British ambassador to Washington from 1913 to 1918, wrote his famous hymn, "I Vow to Thee, My Country," in 1918. It is set to music from Gustav Holst's (1874–1934) *The Planets* suite (the hymn from "Jupiter") (*DNB*, suppl. 1912–21; "I Vow to Thee, My Country," http://geocities.com/cott1388/candle.html, accessed 12 October 2004).

ELEANOR ROOSEVELT'S LONDON DIARY

88

London Diary
6 February 1946

Your letter of the 29th came yesterday after your letter of the 1st by a whole day, but it was very welcome as it told me so many things I wanted to know.[1]

I will write my column each day from Germany and this Sunday I am writing three extra, short, home ones to cover journey home. If I am in Ireland, I'll file from there.[2]

There is delay here. We may not get done till Sunday or Monday. That delays Germany. I will cable when I leave for Germany and when I leave Ireland for US. You will then have to keep in touch with air lines for news. When you know when I get in make a hair appointment and a dentist appointment for the next day.

I will make no engagements except Washington on way to Phoenix if I go down for day, with the Women's Press club if Bess Furman wants me for lunch or dinner.[3] No other engagements until I get back from the west.

I am sorry I couldn't get a letter off yesterday so here is the diary for Tuesday and Wednesday. Column 8:30. Delegates meeting 9:30, reported on refugee troubles[4] and left for 10 a.m. committee meeting leaving Sen. Townsend with the boys in the delegation meeting which he loves. He joined me about 11.[5] Committee meeting was one long wrangle. Finally at one I asked for a vote, the Russians who always play for delay asked for a sub committee to try to get a resolution we could agree on. It is hopeless as there are fundamental disagreements but Peter Fraser is fair to the utmost.[6] He asked if I would withdraw my motion and then appointed a committee. I was a half hour late for lunch with the Anthony Edens[7] in the House of Commons. At 2:30 I opened a doll show. At 3:10 we sat down in the sub-committee at Church House and we got up at 6 having agreed on 25 lines! Then I went to the ceremony of the Women's Appeal which I hope got some play in the U.S.[8] Was home at 7 and dined with the Grenfells[9] at 8. At 10:45 when I was back and working, the advisers came down to show me a compromise paragraph they hope we might get agreement on. I finished the mail at 12:30 and was too weary to write.

At 8 a.m. we started on the column while I ate breakfast. No delegates meeting because the boys couldn't agree up to 11 last night in the Security Council[10] and so they couldn't have a meeting at 9:30 thank goodness!

At ten we went to work in the sub committee again and at 12:45 the Russians and Yugoslavs on one side, the British, Netherlands and U.S. had agreed to disagree on all new points brought up! Lunch with Miss Bernadine for women delegates and some others.[11] Plenary session at 3, election of judges and I was not needed.[12] Left at four. Lady Cripps and her International Youth Group came just six in the group.[13] Gave me a memorial resolution to FDR and we talked till 5:10.

Dictated tomorrow's column till 5:30, was called for and went to staff meeting of UNRRA office in London. Talk and question till 7.[14] Dressed, dined at 8 with Winant who has had bad flu and was up for first time.[15] We had a nice time alone and I left at 9:45 and have now finished mail and am going to bed.

Tomorrow we are trying to meet with an even smaller group before the sub committee meets but I think we cannot agree. I will tell any of you who are interested what I have learned in these meetings. It is a liberal education in backgrounds and personalities but one thing stands out. Since the Civil War we have had no political or religious refugees fleeing our country and we forget to take it into account.[16] No European or South American forgets it for a minute. Next it seems to take years of stability to make you look beyond your own situation and consider that there are human rights that operate for those who think in a way that you think wrong!

My voice is back and fine!

TDi AERP, FDRL

---

1. In her letter of January 29 (one of those that she dated), Tommy sent news of Truman appointments and rumored appointments, as well as reports on ER's son Elliott's comings and goings, ER's Val-Kill staff, and her dog Fala. She also reported that she and the new secretary she had hired "get about thirty to fifty letters a day. I won't have much for you to look at—just the things in which I think you are interested—such as a letter from Charles Taft asking for your frank for a club at Yale. I gave Hick all the publications which have come in, so she will have them digested for you" (Malvina Thompson to ER, 29 January 1946, JRP, FDRL).

2. After visiting Germany, ER stopped in Ireland on her way back to New York to visit her aunt and uncle, Maude and David Gray (*MD*, 15, 16, 19, and 21 February, 1946).

3. On March 14, before going to Phoenix and the West Coast, ER spoke before the Women's Joint Congressional Committee in Washington, but not at the National Women's Press Club (see Document 99). Bess Furman (1894–1969), Washington correspondent for the *New York Times*, covered ER's press conferences, travels, and other activities as an AP reporter during the White House years (*NAWMP*).

4. At the meeting of the US delegation, ER reported on the ongoing debate in Committee Three about how to resolve the refugee situation in Europe ("Delegation Meeting," 5 February 1946, USGA/Ia/Del Min/Exec/12 (Chr), RG84, NARA II). See header Document 86.

5. Senator Townsend (R-DE) served on Committee Three with ER. See *n*23 Document 76.

6. Committee Three remained deadlocked on drafting a resolution on establishing a new international agency to deal with European refugees. After Fraser appointed a subcommittee to try to resolve the issue, ER reported to the US delegation that "she was still struggling in a subcommittee to draft a resolution on refugees to which all could agree. A subcommittee had met for six hours and drafted 25 lines. The previous day they had met for three hours and had only agreed to disagree. She said that the United States would make one more effort in the subcommittee without Mr. Fraser because he was unpopular with the Russians and Yugoslavs for his attitude on this question" ("Delegation Meeting," 6 February 1946 (USGA/Ia/Del Min/Exec/13 [Chr]), 10, RG84, NARA II). For Peter Fraser, see *n*8 Document 79.

7. Anthony Eden (1897–1977) and his first wife Beatrice. Now a member of the opposition in Parliament, Eden served as British foreign secretary under Churchill during World War II.

8. ER wrote in My Day:

> The women working in the United Nations Organization met the other day to sign an appeal addressed to the women of every country in the world and to their Governments as well. We think it is very important, and so I am quoting from it here:
>
> > "This first Assembly of the United Nations marks the second attempt of the peoples of the world to live peaceably in a democratic world community. This new chance for peace was won through the joint efforts of men and women working for common ideals of human freedom at a time when the need for united effort broke down barriers of race, creed and sex. In view of the variety of tasks which women performed so notably and valiantly during the war, we are gratified that 18 women del-

egates and advisers are representatives from 11 of the member states taking part in the beginning of this new phase of international effort. We hope their participation in the work of the United Nations Organization may grow and may increase in insight and skill. To this end, we call on the Governments of the world to encourage women everywhere to take a more conscious part in national and international affairs, and on women to come forward and share in the work of peace and reconstruction as they did in the war and resistance. We recognize that women in various parts of the world are at different stages of participation in the life of their communities, that some of them are prevented by law from assuming the full rights of citizenship, and that they may therefore see their immediate problems somewhat differently. Finding ourselves in agreement on these points, we wish as a group to advise the women of all our countries of our strong belief that an important opportunity and responsibility confronts the women of the United Nations:—

1—To recognize the progress women made during the war and to participate actively in an effort to improve their standard of life in their countries, and participate in the work of reconstruction so that there will be qualified women ready to accept responsibility when new opportunities arise.

2—To train their children, boys and girls alike, to understand world problems and the need for international cooperation …

3—Not to permit themselves to be misled by anti-democratic movements now or in the future.

4—To recognize that the goal of full participation in the life and responsibilities of their countries and of the world community is a common objective toward which the women of the world should assist one another" (*MD*, 8 February 1946).

9. Possibly Vera Grenfell, lady-in-waiting to Princess Alice of Great Britain, whom ER met in Washington in the spring of 1945 (*MD*, 24 March 1945).

10. The Security Council remained deadlocked because the Soviet Union refused to agree to a motion clearing Great Britain of charges made by the Soviet Union that British behavior in Greece had threatened international peace ("Deadlock in Security Council," *TL*, 6 February 1946, 4).

11. Probably Minerva Bernardino (1907–1998), a delegate from the Dominican Republic. One of the few other women delegates at the first meeting of the General Assembly, Bernardino pressed the issue of women's rights at the United Nations and led the effort to establish the UN Commission on the Status of Women (Barbara Crossette, "Minerva Bernadino, 91, Dominican Feminist," *NYT*, 4 September 1998, A20).

12. On February 6, the General Assembly and the Security Council elected fifteen judges to the World Court (Sydney Gruson, "15 Judges Elected for World Court," *NYT*, 7 February 1946, 8).

13. Possibly Lady Isobel Cripps (1891–1979) who headed the British United Aid to China Fund (*DNB*).

14. ER reported in My Day:

I had an interesting meeting with the London staff of UNRRA the other day. Most of the staff are British, but there is a sprinkling of other nationalities. I talked for a little while and then they asked me questions, largely about the work of the UNO. UNRRA, of course, has had very wide experience in working with various nationalities, and I was interested to find that they had many of the same difficulties that we Assembly delegates have because of different languages and the different points of view that result from varying backgrounds. At the end of our meeting, one of the Russian members told me that he was impressed by my remark that working together was the very best medium for gaining mutual understanding (*MD*, 9 February 1946).

15. John Winant.

16. ER makes the same observation at the opening of her speech on the refugee question in the General Assembly on February 12. See the second to last paragraph of ER's response to Vyshinsky, Document 91.

RECAPPING THE UN'S FIRST SESSION

Four days before the scheduled end of the first session of the General Assembly, ER helped readers of My Day "evaluate some of its real accomplishments."[1]

<hr>

89

My Day
11 February 1946

LONDON—Since we are very near the end of this first session of the UNO conference, perhaps it would be well to evaluate some of its real accomplishments. The greatest, I think, is that at the end we still are a group of 51 nations working together. When I was originally asked to come over, I thought that all we would accomplish would be the organization of machinery and the election of a Secretary General. I felt that then it would be only wise to let a little time elapse for the Secretariat to be chosen and learn to work together and for the Secretary General to familiarize himself with his permanent home in the United States, even though it might be in temporary quarters there.[2] It would also be necessary for him to get to know the various people chosen to work for their governments on councils and commissions, since those bodies continue their work even when the Assemblies are not in session.

That is not, however, all that has happened. To be sure, the organizing was done, but what really proved that the organization has life and strength is what happened beyond that stage. The first important thing, I think, is that the Charter stood the test of the implementation period and proved that it is an adequate instrument under which machinery could be set up. Next, most of us were balancing the potential strength of the UNO against the first effort made through the League of Nations. Many of the European countries which had worked in that body, particularly those men who put their whole hearts into it, were hopeful of the success of this new organization but, perhaps because of their experience, a little skeptical.[3] The peoples of their countries in many cases could hardly be aroused to enthusiasm now for anything except where the next loaf of bread is coming from. It would have to be proved to them that this organization affected their daily lives or there would be no glimmer of interest.

It seems to me that the most encouraging thing at the start is the fact that the five great powers who fought and won the war[4] are here together to work out the machinery whereby we will try to create in the world an atmosphere in which a peaceful world might develop. In one very important way, this organization differs from the League of Nations. When the League was suggested the U. S., through its President, was deeply involved.[5] But under our kind of government it requires not only the interest of the Executive but the cooperation of both major political parties in our legislative bodies. They were not present at the framing of the League and took no part in its formation. When it came to be presented to Congress, it was possible for the Republican party to prevent the U. S. from becoming part of the organization.[6] The people of our country were indifferent. War is never popular in the U. S. and, never having had it actually on our own soil since the days of the Civil War, we were always obliged to send our men out of the country, which makes the whole proceeding much remoter from the civilian population. When the losses had been accepted and the men were home again, our great desire in the past has been to forget that war ever existed.

This time, however, I think we have learned the lesson that becoming involved in war does not lie entirely in any one nation's hands and that therefore we must concern ourselves in the affairs of the world, particularly in working for peaceful solutions of world difficulties. Otherwise, no matter how hard we try to keep aloof, we will wake up some morning to find ourselves involved. Fortunately this time, we now have on the U. S. delegation, and we had in San Francisco when the Charter was written, representatives of our Foreign Affairs Committee in both Senate and House.

Both our major political parties are represented and therefore they go back to report to their co-workers and their constituents throughout the nation, and support of the country on a non-political basis is assured.[7] For this reason, I feel that in the organization of the UNO there is a great strength which was lacking in the League, for no machinery to help build peace could be of any value unless the five great powers were involved and had to come to an agreement on whatever measures came before them.

With the end of this session in sight, everyone is anxious to get through now and go home. Since the Security Council is getting on with its work and the other committees seem also to be moving to a conclusion, I think it quite natural we should all have the urge to get back to our occupations at home which we have neglected for so long. My letters from home are becoming very urgent. I broke a great many engagements when I came over here and, quite aside from the fact that the part of my family which lives near me thinks I have been away quite a long time, some of the people who counted on me for various engagements during this current month are beginning to be a little worried as to whether I will really arrive or not![8]

TMs AERP, FDRL

---

1. She will make similar points in more detail in her March 29 article for *The Summary.* See Document 107.

2. The General Assembly of the United Nations elected its first secretary-general, Trygve Halvdan Lie (1896–1968) of Norway, on February 1, 1946. Lie was stationed at the temporary UN headquarters at Lake Success (Long Island, New York) until the permanent facility in New York City was established in 1949.

3. ER worried when League of Nations advocates such as Philip Noel-Baker and Lord Robert Cecil of England, as well as Gustavo Guerrero of El Salvador, expressed some doubts about the new United Nations. In her January 21 My Day column, ER noted that Guerrero "spoke of having taken part in the work of the first Assembly of the League of Nations, and he reminded his hearers of some of the pitfalls that lie ahead of this present organization." February 13, she wrote of her concern that Philip Noel-Baker's "old association with and devotion to the League of Nations [made] him, I think, extremely anxious for this new organization to succeed but, nevertheless, somewhat jealous for the accomplishments of the League and perhaps, at times, a little too much influenced by the past." For more on Noel-Baker, Lord Cecil, and the League of Nations–UN transition, see *n*15 Document 78, *n*7 Document 80, and Document 81 (*MD*, 21 January and 13 February 1946).

4. Great Britain, France, China, the United States, and the Union of Soviet Socialist Republics (*OEWH*).

5. At the end of the First World War, President Woodrow Wilson participated in the Paris peace negotiations that produced the Covenant of the League of Nations, part of the Treaty of Versailles. He then championed the covenant in the United States (*RCAH*).

6. Wilson encountered great difficulty in trying to obtain the Senate's ratification of the Covenant of the League of Nations. Concerned by the ambiguity of the League's purpose and powers as outlined in the covenant, the Republican-controlled Senate led by Henry Cabot Lodge agreed to ratification with several conditions. Wilson refused, deadlock ensued, and on November 19, 1919, the Senate voted against ratification, and thus, against US participation in the League of Nations (*RCAH*).

7. Unlike Wilson's 1919 staff at Versailles, which included only one Republican, Henry White, the five-member US delegation to the 1946 UNO meeting in London was bipartisan. For more on the members of the 1946 delegation, see *n*3 Document 68 (Lash, *Years*, 39; *RCAH*).

8. See *n*2 Document 83.

Debating Vyshinsky and United Nations Refugee Policy, Part 1

The debate on the displaced persons camps and the issue of repatriation, which had been carried on at length in the Third Committee,[1] was repeated in the General Assembly when the Third Committee submitted its report on the refugee question. The report recommended that the General Assembly pass a resolution directing the Economic and Social Council to create a special committee to study the issue of refugees and make recommendations to the council, which, in turn, would report back to the next session of the General Assembly.[2] The resolution included a number of principles that ECOSOC was to follow in preparing its recommendations. These principles included that no displaced persons should be forcibly required to return to their homeland. The Soviet Union and its ally, Yugoslavia, remained dissatisfied with the resolution drafted by the Third Committee, and, in the following speech, Andrei Vyshinsky, the Soviet delegate, reintroduced the amendments proposed by the Soviet Union that had been defeated during the committee's deliberations.[3]

90

Andrei Vyshinsky's Speech before UN General Assembly 29th Plenary Session

12 February 1946 [London]

MR. VYSHINSKY (Union of Soviet Socialist Republics) (*Translation from the Russian*): The Soviet delegation supports the draft resolution submitted to the General Assembly and prepared by the Third Committee, but it considers that the Assembly should insert in the resolution three additions.

The first addition raises a question of exceptional importance. If this question is not settled, it may nullify the whole resolution.

Point (*c*) (ii) of the Third Committee's draft resolution states that no refugees or displaced persons who have finally and definitely and, after receiving full knowledge of the facts, including adequate information from the Governments of their countries of origin, expressed valid objections to returning to their countries of origin, shall be compelled to return to their country of origin, provided they do not come under the provisions of point (*d*) below.[4]

The people who refuse to return to their country are not forced to do so. The man who is unwilling to serve his country is not obliged to return. But we should be logical, and having said that it depends upon the personal wish of the individual concerned whether he returns, we should give him the right to decide that question himself. He must not become the victim of fascist or semi-fascist propaganda directed against every principle that is obligatory for all of us. We cannot allow this fascist or semi-fascist propagandizing of refugees, which is not infrequently carried on in these camps and, indeed, in the most brazen manner. We cannot allow this propagandizing to turn these men into fascist agents and enemies working against the interests of the United Nations.

Today we read in the *Daily Herald* that the Third United States Army has frustrated the attempts of Yugoslav refugees in Germany to reconstruct a Royal Yugoslav army and to make another effort to plunge their country into a military adventure.[5] We have information of similar facts regarding Polish adventurers who are exploiting the refugee camps for their own purposes. Such facts are possible precisely because there is carried on in the camps fascist propaganda, which is inseparably linked with fascist crimes and which serves to prepare for them.

We cannot allow propaganda of this type. We therefore proposed the insertion of the following paragraph in point (*c*):

"(iv) No propaganda shall be permitted in refugee and displaced persons camps against the interests of the United Nations Organization or its individual Members, nor propaganda against returning to their native countries."

The Committee did not accept this addition. We consider that this refusal to include our addition is the result of an obvious misunderstanding, as its opponents saw in it a proposal to restrict freedom of speech in the camps. But this is not so. What we refer to is not freedom of speech. It is the abuse of freedom of speech. It is an appeal to commit treason. It is an incitement to engage in hostile activities. Propaganda that involves treason must not be allowed. That is why we ask again that this amendment be included in the report.

I now come to the second addition which we have suggested. Among the administrative staff of the camps there are people who are highly suspect and obviously criminal. How can we allow Germans to be among the administrative staff, and even at the head of the refugee camps, whereas the administration dealing with these persons should be recruited from among those who fought against the Germans?

There are camps where Germans are taking part in the management. We cannot tolerate such a state of affairs. Therefore we propose the following addition to the draft resolution:

"(v) The administrative personnel of refugee and displaced persons camps should be comprised primarily of representatives of the States concerned, whose citizens are the refugees."

What can be more logical than this? If in a camp there are Russian, Yugoslav, Ukrainian, Byelorussian refugees, why not recruit the administrative personnel of these camps from the fellow-citizens of the refugees? This would be justified, because who better than their fellow-citizens can help these people, give them assistance, care for them and inform them of the real state of affairs in their countries? This would be natural and just. I fail to see why this addition should not be accepted.

Finally, I come to the third addition proposed by the Soviet delegation. You will see that it is connected with point (*d*), which states that no action taken as a result of this resolution shall be of such a character as to interfere in any way with the surrender and punishment of war criminals, quislings and traitors, in conformity with present or future international arrangements or agreements.

This, of course, is absolutely right and should be fully supported, but we think this paragraph does not go far enough. The whole resolution deals with assistance to refugees, but it must not be thought that the traitors and quislings mentioned in this paragraph may avail themselves of this assistance. It is necessary, therefore, to state clearly in the resolution that no help and no assistance shall be given to quislings, traitors and war criminals, that these gentlemen shall be handed over to their respective Governments for trial and punishment and that they shall be sent back to their countries to undergo hard labour, whereby they might make amends for their crimes, which inflicted so much suffering upon the peoples of the United Nations. We suggest therefore our third addition, which reads:

"Quislings, traitors, and war-criminals, as persons who discredited themselves by collaboration in any form with the enemies of the United Nations, should not be regarded as refugees who are entitled to the protection of the United Nations. Quislings, traitors and war criminals who are still hiding themselves under the guise of refugees shall be returned to their countries immediately."

We maintain that this addition would be justified. These criminals, these traitors are not refugees. Those who still pass themselves off as refugees, should be sent back forthwith to their respective countries for trial and for the just appeasement of the public conscience, which has been deeply stirred by the fascist aggression perpetrated with the participation of these criminals. We think, therefore, that the additions proposed by the Soviet delegation should be included in the report, especially as this paragraph is merely the continuation of the idea by which the authors of point (c) were guided, and shows how to act and how to deal with these traitors. On behalf of the Soviet delegation, I press for the additions proposed by us.

Tsptr ORGAUN, MWelC

When Andrei Vyshinsky, the Soviet delegation's most skillful debater, made it clear that he was going to challenge the Third Committee's report in the General Assembly, the American delegation was caught off guard. "The question threw our delegation into a dither," ER reported in her autobiography. "There was a hurried and rather uncomfortable consultation among the male members and when the huddle broke up John Foster Dulles approached me rather uncertainly. 'Mrs. Roosevelt,' he began lamely, 'the United States must speak in the debate. Since you are the one who has carried on the controversy in the committee, do you think you could say a few words in the Assembly? Nobody else is really familiar with the subject.'" ER discussed what she was going to say with Durward Sandifer, her State Department advisor for the Third Committee, but spoke extemporaneously. Sandifer later called it "the most important speech ever given by an American delegate without a prepared text." The debate did not end on February 12 despite the defeat of the amendments proposed by Vyshinsky, however. The Russians and Yugoslavs continued to press their position in the committee appointed by ECOSOC and ER would again confront them on the same issues in the fall of 1946 during the debates in the Third Committee and General Assembly on the constitution of the International Refugee Organization.[6]

91

Eleanor Roosevelt's Speech before UN General Assembly 30th Plenary Session
12 February 1946 [London]

MRS. ROOSEVELT (United States of America): I am extremely sorry that we have to take up your time to go again into a discussion which has been thoroughly covered for two weeks in our Committee.

We agreed in part, we compromised, and I am extremely sorry that I have to oppose the speakers who have already spoken this evening.[7] I realize that we speak from different points of view, and I understand why to them this problem seems different from what it does to me.

I cannot recall that a political or a religious refugee has ever been sent out of my country since the Civil War.[8] I do remember that at that time one of my own relatives, because he came to this country and built a ship that ran contraband to the South, was not included in the amnesty.[9] But, otherwise, this has not been a question that has entered into my thinking.

Europe has had a succession of wars and changes in population, as well as changes in ownership of land. Therefore, it is natural that we approach the question from a different point of view;

but we here in the United Nations are trying to develop ideas which will be broader in outlook, which will consider first the rights of man, which will consider what makes man more free: not Governments, but man.

I think we have to recall a little of what happened in the Committee. We can agree on certain things. After a good deal of discussion paragraph (*c*) (ii) was accepted. Our friends who opposed the acceptance of the report as a whole and wished their amendments to be included took some persuading before they agreed to paragraph (*c*) (ii), but they did agree and they also agreed to paragraph (*d*). Now paragraph (*d*), it seems to me, fully covers their third paragraph, though it does not say that quislings, traitors and war criminals who are still hiding themselves under the guise of refugees should be returned to their countries immediately.[10]

None of us disagrees that those who had actively taken part against their countries should be returned and punished, but there are differences. Some people fought against the enemies of their country, but are still unwilling to go back because they do not agree with the present government in their countries. That, I think, is something we have to take into consideration; so that I do not think those words should be included. I think that all that we really should say is said in paragraph (*d*) of the report, which reads:

"Considers that no action taken as a result of this resolution shall be of such a character as to interfere in any way with the surrender and punishment of war criminals, quislings and traitors in conformity with present or future international arrangements or agreements."

I think that covers all that we need to safeguard: the return of the people who should be returned.

Now, let us take the paragraphs that it is proposed to add to this report. The first one is that:

"No propaganda should be permitted in refugee and displaced persons camps against the interests of the Organization of the United Nations or its Members, nor propaganda against returning to their native countries."

The second one, which must be read with the first, says:

"The personnel of refugee and displaced persons camps should, first of all, be comprised of representatives of States concerned, whose citizens are the refugees."

Now I never heard in the Committee the argument that Germans had been found in positions of authority in some of the refugee and displaced persons camps. That is a new argument. Naturally, no German should be allowed to be in that position, but it is fairly easy to find an occasional German in a refugee or displaced persons camp. These camps are, after all, places of refuge for people of many nationalities. They would not be there if they were ready to go back to their countries of origin. Therefore, I think it is fair to suppose that they are not in complete sympathy with the governments that are now in power in their countries of origin.

You must look at things from a wider point of view than the particular point of view that affects you as an individual at the moment. Suppose we turned this argument around, and suppose we said that any Spanish Republicans found in refugee camps should be sent back at once to their country of origin or that they should be put in camps where the personnel was of the present fascist government? Well, it is obvious this is ridiculous, because it is a fascist government. You would not do that.[11]

But there are other things less easy to get over. I happen to come from the United States. I used in the Committee an example. I am going to use it again; it is purely hypothetical. We happen to have an island in the Caribbean called Puerto Rico. Now in Puerto Rico there are several factions. One faction would like to become a State. Another faction would like to be entirely free. Another faction would like to stay just the way they are in their relation to the United States.[12]

Suppose, just for the sake of supposing, that we had a refugee camp. We belong to the United States, but are we going to say that the Puerto Ricans who happen to want to be free from the United States shall receive no letters from home, none of their home papers, no letters perhaps from people who have gone to live in other places, or information from other places? I think that we can stand up under having them free to get whatever information comes their way and make up their own minds. They are free human beings.

I think we have shown in the last few days that we do not intend to have refugee camps used as places for political agitation. We will prevent that whenever we discover it. But no propaganda, that is going pretty far.

What is propaganda? Are we so weak in the United Nations, are we as individual nations so weak, that we are going to forbid human beings to say what they think and to fear whatever their friends with their particular type of mind happen to believe in? Surely we can tell them, their own governments can tell them, all we want to tell them. We are not preventing them from hearing what each country wants them to hear, but we are saying, for instance, that in the United States we have people who have come there from war-torn Europe. They are in two different camps. They will write their relatives when they hear they are in different camps in Europe and they may not always say things that are exactly polite or in agreement with the United Nations. They may even say things against the United States, but I still think it is their right to say them and it is the right of men and women in refugee camps to hear them and to make their own decision.

I object to "no propaganda against the United Nations or any Member of the United Nations." It is like saying you are always sure you are going to be right. I am not always sure my Government or my nation will be right. I hope it will be and I shall do my very best to keep it as right as I can keep it and so, I am sure, will every other nation. But there are people who are going to disagree, and I think we aim to reach a point where we, on the whole, are so right that the majority of our people will be with us. We can always stand having amongst us the people who do not agree, because we are sure that the right is so carefully guarded, and the freedom of people is so carefully guarded, that we shall always have the majority with us.

For that reason I oppose including these amendments in a report which we have to accept, as I consider them to be restrictive of human rights and human freedom.

TSpex UNORGA, MWelC

92

Eleanor Roosevelt to Joseph Lash
13 February 1946 [London]

Joe dearest,

Your letter of the 3rd is here in fact it came soon after one from Trude and now I have another one from her which I will answer if I'm lucky enough to see George in Frankfurt.[13] I wrote him and have sent him word thro' channels to come and see me and I'm taking the nice suitcase John Golden sent to the steamer with things which I've collected for him to take to his mother.[14]

Yesterday we fought the whole battle over again in the Assembly on refugees which we had fought in committee and we won again hands down.[15] This time Mr. Vishinsky and I fought it out, evidently they, the Russians, don't let any but delegates speak in Assembly! The Russians are tenacious fighters but when we finally finished talking at 1 a.m. last night I shook hands and said I admired their fighting qualities and hoped some day on that kind of a question we would be on the same side and they were cordiality itself! Also you will be amused that when Mr. Dulles said goodbye to me this morning he said "I feel I must tell you that when you were appointed I thought it terrible and now I think your work here has been fine"! So—against odds, the women inch forward, but I'm rather old to be carrying on the fight.

All my responsibilities being over, I'm glad it is clearing and I've just got word that we will leave at 11 an hour later than we planned.

Certainly at home things sound bad. Some foolish walkouts but since then the tug boat strike seems to threaten all heat for you.[16] When will everyone settle down to business and realize that we live in "one world" and have obligations to others![17]

I dread this trip to the Continent. Everyone is so discouraged about conditions over there. I must stop and get a line off to Tommy but I have much to talk to you and Trude about. Mr. Bloom[18] and his wife came in yesterday and we had a long talk. Refreshing in many ways.

My love to Jonathan.[19] I have managed to find a little remembrance for him but there is just nothing to buy in England. Give Trude a hug for me and much, much love to you dear boy.

Devotedly
E.R.

ALI ARHP, FDRL

---

1. See Document 86.

2. "Question of Refugees: Report of the Third Committee to the General Assembly," 29th Plenary Meeting, 2/12/1946, A/45, Annex 17, 601, UNORGA, MWelC.

3. "Resolutions Adopted on the Reports of the Third Committee," "2. Question of Refugees," 30th Plenary Meeting, 12 February 1946, Resolutions 1946, 12, UNORGA, MWelC.

4. Paragraph (c)(ii) of the resolution submitted by the Third Committee to the General Assembly for approval, which Vyshinsky paraphrases, reads in full:

> No refugees or displaced persons who have finally and definitively, in complete freedom, and after receiving full knowledge of the facts including adequate information from the governments of their countries of origin, expressed valid objections to returning to their countries of origin and who do not come within the provisions of paragraph (d) below, shall be compelled to return to their country of origin. The future of such refugees or displaced persons shall become the concern of whatever international body may be recognized or established as a result of the report referred to in paragraph (a) and (b) above, except in cases where the government of the country where they are established has made an arrangement with this body to assume the complete cost of their maintenance and the responsibility for their protection ("Question of Refugees: Report of the Third Committee to the General Assembly," 29th Plenary Meeting, 12 February 1946, A/45, Annex 17, 601, UNORGA, MWelC).

ER quotes paragraph (d) in full in her response to Vyshinsky. The language of the resolution as adopted by the General Assembly is identical (Resolutions Adopted on the Reports of the Third Committee, 2. Question of Refugees, Thirtieth Plenary Meeting, 12 February 1946, Resolutions 1946, 12, UNORGA, MWelC).

5. The *New York Herald Tribune* reported that the US Army raided a Yugoslav displaced persons camp in Munich on February 11 where they removed a large quantity of documents and found small arms. A search revealed that many of the DPs had membership cards in the "Royal Yugoslavian Army of Bavaria," which had been organized for the purpose of overthrowing

President Tito and restoring the monarchy to Yugoslavia ("G.I.s Stage Raid on Polish and Yugoslav D.P.s.," *NYHT*, 12 February 1946, 12).

6. See Document 152 and Document 168 (Roosevelt, *Autobiography*, 308; Lash, *Years*, 52–53; Lash, Interview with Sandifer, 5 May 1970, JPLR, FDRL).

7. Andrei Vyshinsky and Ales Bebler (1907–1981), deputy foreign minister of Yugoslavia, spoke before ER.

8. ER made this point at greater length in her London Diary for February 6, 1946. See Document 88.

9. ER is referring to Captain James Bulloch who traveled to England on behalf of the Confederacy during the Civil War and secretly built the *Alabama*, which raided Union shipping until it was torpedoed. Bulloch and his brother Irvine, who served on the *Alabama*, were half-brothers of ER's grandmother, Martha Bulloch, who was married to Theodore Roosevelt, Sr. Because of their connection to the *Alabama*, neither of them received a pardon at the end of the Civil War and they went to live in Liverpool (Cook, vol. 1, 29; McCullough, *Mornings*, 64).

10. For the text of paragraph (c)(ii), see *n*4 above.

11. It would have been contrary to recent history for the Russians or Yugoslavs to support the forcible repatriation of Spanish Republican refugees to Fascist Spain. During the Spanish Civil War (1936–39), the Soviet Union provided military assistance to the Spanish Republicans, some of whom were Communists. When General Francisco Franco and his Nationalists won the war, thousands of Spanish Republican refugees fled the country. Franco's Fascist government remained in power after World War II, and many Spanish Republicans remained in exile. Ales Bebler, the Yugoslavian diplomat who spoke immediately before ER, had fought as a volunteer on the Republican side during the Spanish conflict, although ER may not have known that (*OEWH;* "Ales Bebler Dies at 74," *NYT*, 13 August 1981, D21).

12. Puerto Rico became an American possession in 1898 during the Spanish-American War. In 1917 an act of Congress declared Puerto Ricans to be American citizens, but the island's relationship to the United States remained unsettled and the population divided on the issue of statehood, independence, or maintaining the status quo (*OEWH*).

13. In his February 3, 1946, letter to ER, Lash discussed the future site of the United Nations, the Vyshinsky-Bevin interchange on Greece in London, and the Harry Hopkins funeral. He also expressed his concerns about the future of a Jewish state in Palestine, telling ER that "I'm for large scale Jewish emigration into Palestine especially in the present emergency, but I cannot see how one can establish it as a Jewish national state without riding roughshod over the Arabs … I would like to see a bi-national state guaranteed by the UNO." While in her letters Trude Lash emphasized that she remained skeptical about the intentions of the Russians, she also indicated her pleasure that President Truman had decided to allocate more funds for Europe, and that many people in the United States "actually believe that world government now is possible" (Joseph Lash to ER, 3 February 1946; Trude Lash to ER, 28 January and 6 February 1946, JPLP, FDRL).

14. When ER sailed for London, John Golden (1874–1955), a theatrical producer and old family friend, sent her away with gifts to keep her from being lonely. ER wished to pass this box of gifts along to Trude's mother, who still lived in Germany, through George Wenzel, Trude's brother (Lash, *Years*, 33, 40, 184, 241; "John Golden Dies at Bayside Home," *NYT*, 18 June 1955, 17).

15. See Document 86 and Document 91.

16. At 12:01 AM February 4, 3,500 New York City tugboat workers walked off the job to honor a work stoppage initiated by Local 333 of the International Longshoreman's Association after employers rejected their request for a forty-hour work week and an hourly wage increase. Mayor O'Dwyer anticipated that the strike would affect 80 percent of the city's fuel supplies and almost

50 percent of its food supply ("Tug Strike Begins, Threatens City's Food, Fuel Supply," *NYT*, 4 February 1946, 1).

17. Wendell Willkie gave the term "one world" currency in his 1943 best-selling work, *One World*, in which he articulated his hopes for world peace that would be realized through the establishment of a global organization with international authority over all nations. For more on Wilkie see *n*10 Document 69.

18. Sol Bloom, Democratic congressman from New York.

19. See header and *n*6 Document 87.

ON REFUGEES AND POSTWAR GERMANY

ER, at Stettinius's strong urging, traveled to Germany February 13–16 to investigate conditions displaced persons confronted there. Downplaying the diplomatic and investigative nature of her visit, she told *New York Times* reporter Kathleen McLaughlin the trip was her "own suggestion … tactfully put so [the Army] wouldn't have me if they didn't want me to visit our men before I go home …" ER, however, privately dreaded the tour, telling friends that she feared a journey to postwar Germany would be "a haunting horror."[1]

The following two columns and ER's speech for the United Jewish Appeal demonstrate the formidable observation skills ER honed throughout her political career.

93

My Day
16 February 1946

BERLIN, Friday—My visit to Frankfort was packed so full of emotions, it is hard to give you an adequate idea of what I saw and how I felt. Yesterday morning, we visited the Zeilsheim Jewish displaced-persons camp. It is one of the best, since the people are living in houses previously occupied by Germans.[2]

In these houses, each little family has a room to itself. Often a family must cross a room occupied by another in order to enter or leave the house, but there are doors and walls to separate them. If they like, they may bring food from the camp kitchen to their rooms and eat in what they call "home."

They made me a speech at a monument they have erected to the six million dead Jewish people. I answered from an aching heart. When will our consciences grow so tender that we will act to prevent human misery rather than avenge it?[3]

Someone asked a man, who looked old but couldn't have been really old, about his family. This was his answer: "They were made into soap." They had been burned to death in a concentration camp.

Outside the school, the children greeted me. They told me a little boy of ten was the camp singer. He looked six. He had wandered into camp one day with his brother, all alone, so he was the head of his family. He sang for me—a song of his people—a song of freedom. Your heart cried out that there was no freedom—and where was hope, without which human beings cannot live?[4]

There is a feeling of desperation and sorrow in this camp which seems beyond expression. An old woman knelt on the ground, grasping my knees. I lifted her up, but could not speak. What could one say at the end of a life which had brought her such complete despair?

From there we went to Wiesbaden and visited a displaced persons camp for Poles and Balts. These are refugees who, because of political differences with their present Governments, cannot see their way to return to their own countries, and yet they fought against the Nazis and many of them spent long years in concentration or forced-labor camps.[5]

Here they live in barracks, and the camp is run by a wonderful French UNRRA team. My admiration for these French people is unbounded. They have given the refugees work to do, and have repaired and made buildings habitable. To be sure, the buildings are only barracks and three families—seven people in all—were living in one bedroom, their quarters separated only by curtains. Privacy is hardly a thing you could achieve in these quarters, yet many of the families eat in these makeshift rooms because it is "home."

The food in this camp is supervised by a very capable woman, and they have a variety of diet for different ages, but soup and bread was the main meal. The soup for older people had beans in it; the soup for children had vegetables in it, with a little piece of meat.

The spirit here was far better than in the other camp—there were far more children and young people and more families who had stayed together. I noticed one little boy on crutches who had lost a leg. I was told he was one of eight children. The eldest girl, 18, takes care of all her brothers and sisters.

I went away from this camp more hopeful, but still with a sense of depression weighing upon me. What's the ultimate answer? We in UNO asked the Economic and Social Council to create a commission to study this refugee problem, but I cannot say I envy them their work. It will tear at their hearts. And the problem is so complicated, it will take people with great wisdom to write the recommendations that have to be presented to UNO at its next meeting in September.[6]

Late in the afternoon, back in Frankfort, I met a group of German newspaper correspondents. When they asked me whether I thought the whole German nation was responsible for the war, I answered what to me seems obvious. All the people of Germany have to accept responsibility for having tolerated a leadership which first brought such misery to groups of people within their own nation and later created world chaos.[7]

TMs AERP, FDRL

ER, despite feeling "saturated with ruins," paid the same close attention to the living conditions of the residents of Berlin (which the Allies had divided into four zones) as she did to the conditions refugees endured. Reflecting on the trip later, she recalled that "the whole journey ... had been a good one for me. I believed I had grown and matured and gained confidence."[8]

94

My Day
18 February 1946

LONDON, Sunday—I was driven around Berlin during my stay there, and I think I may say that I am saturated with ruins. The city seems completely destroyed, except in certain outlying sections. I doubt if anyone would recognize the Tiergarten or Unter Den Linden, and the Grunewald has been almost entirely cut down for firewood.[9] About 3,000,000 people still live in Berlin, but civilian Germans have no coal. They have to cut their own wood, which is rationed, and each person has enough coupons for one fire to cook meals and to boil a little water for washing during the day. In addition, one fairly big hall in town is heated so that the people can come there to get warmed up on very cold days.

Again looking at the people as carefully as possible, I found that the children appeared fairly healthy. There is hunger, but no starvation. There are people hauling little carts with wood who probably never hauled carts before in their lives. There are women working in groups to clear away the debris—far more women than men. Only civilians doing essential work can use a car. Automobiles are appearing which were hidden away before, and the little Hitler three-wheel cars with truck bodies are much in evidence.[10] There are many bicycles, but walking is still the main means of getting about. The Germans are being treated justly, but they should learn that they have lost a war—though only rarely do they seem willing as yet to accept the blame.[11]

We stopped in the Russian zone to see the building where Hitler lived and the shelter where he took refuge through the bombings. The great hall through which you walk to his office, and the office in which he worked, are all in varying degrees of destruction. I haven't quite thought of what it all meant to me, but I believe my most vivid impression was one of the utter smallness of a human being who needed so much outward grandeur to build up his sense of importance. The man himself is gone and the pomp and ceremony are no more. For some strange reason, verses from the Bible kept running through my mind. Humility and the strength which the humble man draws from outside himself when he is called upon to do tasks that are apparently beyond his human power—these are the qualities which make great men. That spirit is absent here. This nation has not known that spirit, but it will have to acquire something akin to it before it can face the colossal task of reconstruction.

I visited the "Bunker," an old air raid shelter used as an overnight station for German refugees ousted from other countries and now in search of new homes within their own borders. The room was crowded when I went in—largely women and children, with a few men. Disease has been kept down, although that seems a miracle. What is perhaps most revealing is the statement that the public health doctor of the district murmured in my ear: "The mothers are often indifferent"—that is, they let their children wander, they've lost so many. As we went out two children, a little boy of ten and his younger sister, sat on a bench stolidly waiting for someone to come and get them and give them shelter. Their mother had gone away and left them behind. But they didn't cry as children ordinarily would—they just sat motionless, and your heart went out to these innocent victims of a system which that great room of Hitler's represented.[12]

We stayed with General Clay in Berlin,[13] and Ambassador Murphy[14] came to dinner. Between them I think I learned of a few of the questions that can't be answered yet. You can measure the extent of physical damage done to cities, you can restore water supplies, gas and electricity, and you can rebuild the buildings needed to establish a military government. But how to gauge what has happened to human beings—that is incalculable. How soon will an economy which is being completely changed be reestablished, and what effect will the new situation have on the rest of the world? These are questions that cannot be answered now and may not be answered for a long time to come. The real answer will depend on the wisdom of the leaders of various nations and their ability to make their people understand the world conditions that we face today.

The men and girls in the various services have a feeling of the problem and the misery which exists all around them. At a soldiers club in Berlin, they smiled when I said I wondered how we were going to like eating dark bread at home. The boy next to me at table said: "I'd like to tell them what the people have over here." And, later, another soldier said to me: "I can't think why they had to fight each other. The language is a bar; but while our customs are different, all over we seem to have a lot of things that are just the same." That's really a great discovery—"all over we have a lot of things that are just the same." Those are the things we have to find and build on, and those, I imagine, are the only things that can give us hope.[15]

TMs AERP, FDRL

My Day's space limitations did not allow ER to discuss her visits to the refugee camps at length. Speeches, however, did, and, ER used her lectures to describe the conditions she had observed in great detail. The day after she returned from London, she addressed an audience of more than 2,000 attending the kick-off rally for the local campaign of the United Jewish Appeal at New York City's Waldorf Astoria Hotel.[16] She used her remarks not only to report on the suffering she witnessed, but also to argue that America had a special leadership role to play in abating the horrors confronting the postwar world:

> Europe, as it is today, gave me the most completely miserable sense of what people can suffer and how the suffering can numb them and how it can sap their strength. It gave me something else which I would like to pass on to you. It gave me the feeling that we have been saved for a reason. That reason must be that

we were expected to give leadership—spiritual leadership, moral leadership, physical leadership. If this is so, and if we fail, what is our punishment to be?

95

Speech before Women's Division of the United Jewish Appeal of Greater New York[17]
20 February 1946 [New York City]

As you know, I have just come home and I have not really had time to think through the most effective way of presenting to you the experiences which I have had. Therefore, I am going to try only to give you some of the impressions which are most vivid in my mind, since they are the things which I did after leaving the United Nations Conference.[18]

I went to Germany and spent only two-and-a-half days there, but in those two-and-a-half days I think I became more conscious than ever of what complete human misery there is in the world. When I came home yesterday and walked into my apartment and realized that there were no destroyed houses around me, it seemed very queer. (Where I had been, there was destruction wherever you looked.) And the house was warm, and nobody seemed to worry about whether we were going to have anything to eat. And I can only tell you that, for two-and-a-half days in Germany, those were the things that beat upon one every minute.

I went to four displaced persons camps.[19] I am going to tell you about the Jewish camp, which was run by UNRRA.[20] It was one of the very best camps; it was run as well as possible. But the thing that I feel is not only the physical aspect, but something that I can only describe in this way: What would happen to us if suddenly we had no real right to appeal to a government of our own?

I felt that all the time in the displaced persons camps—a kind of spiritual uprooting, a kind of being lost.

Even in the worst days of the depression, when I went down into the mining areas,[21] at least the people came to one and said, "We want our government to know." And they had the feeling that they had a right to tell their government.

Nobody has that right in a displaced persons camp. There just is nothing to hold onto.

As I have said, the camp I am talking about was one of the very best. The people were living in houses—houses that had been taken over from the German community. The kitchens were in barracks which had been built. The displaced persons there have 2,300 calories a day, as against 1,500 which the German people are allowed. But 2,300 calories a day gives you, I think, about the most uninteresting food and never really lets you be without hunger.

The thing which does vary their food a little bit in some places is that, since the Prisoner of War camps are closing, some of the surplus Red Cross packages have apparently been allowed to seep in. However, that is just a drop in the bucket.

Let me tell you about the breakfasts that they have, for children and everyone else. There is coffee with canned milk and some sugar—very little sugar—and a piece of bread. By the way, they have three meals a day in the Displaced Persons camps. For the main meal, you get soup, the basis of which is potatoes; now and then, you have some other vegetables; occasionally, they told me—but very rarely—they had a little piece of meat; and again, a hunk of dark bread. Sometimes, the bread is cut in slices, with margarine on it. Occasionally, you have some dried fruits, stewed fruits.

For supper, you again have tea or coffee—which is pretty bad coffee—and now and then the children can have a little bit of dried milk, particularly if they are not well. But the whole thing, of course, is based on a piece of bread that goes with whatever you have [to] drink.[22]

On the day that I was in the Jewish camp, the main meal was some powdered eggs—scrambled eggs. The people have such a longing to create a sense of home that they would take the powdered eggs from the kitchen and take them back to the one little room that they might have. By the way, in this particular camp they did have rooms—each family did have a room—but sometimes another family would have to go through their room to reach their own room.

You feel a kind of desperation about the dignity of the individual, the right to some privacy. They have done such pathetic things. The remnants of the families try so hard to make a home. I looked at these powdered eggs that were going to be carried back, and I thought, "Oh, Heavens, how horrible—the eggs will be cold when they get them back to their rooms." And yet, they would take them back, simply because—even though you ate and you slept and you sat in the same little place—that little place was home.

There is a building in this camp where children are kept who have wandered in off the road and have no older people with them. One little boy sang for me; he sang a Jewish song.[23] Of course, these children are much smaller than they should be for their age. This little, tiny, curly-haired thing was ten years old, but he didn't look much more than six or seven. The director told me that this little boy had just wandered in with a younger brother one day, and they had been at the camp ever since. He said that this little boy always sang for them. They called him their "singer" in the camp. But he had all the appearance of a worried, old man, because the care of his younger brother and himself weighed on his shoulders.

What those children have gone through is just indescribable.

I am not going to tell you some of the things, because you probably know them. I can only tell you that I came away with a sense of so much human misery and a sense of surprise that there was anything left which made it possible for them to be interested. They were interested in my coming there, but I couldn't [see] why they should care who came or why they should want anyone to come. But they did.

They wanted me to go up to the stone monument that they themselves had built and the plaque that they had engraved to the 6,000,000 Jews who had been killed. They wanted me to hear from the leader of the camp what they wanted, what they had hoped for.[24] There, again, you wondered how they could hope for anything.

There was one old woman there whom I don't think I will ever forget, because you looked at her and you felt that this was the end of life, and that life must have been so terrible to bring one at the end to what this poor old thing faced.

It is true they want to go back to Palestine.[25] They want to go back because that represents to them some roots. I don't know what the committee will recommend—and, as you know, the United Nations Organization, through the Economic and Social Council, is to set up a committee to go into the whole question of refugees, with a view to making recommendations as to what should happen when UNRRA does come to an end. The committee is going to be charged with an investigation of the whole problem, of which the Jewish problem is only one part. They are going to look into this whole problem and screen the different types of refugees. We don't have any realization of the difficulty of finding out about the different types of people.[26]

The camp that I went to, the Jewish camp near Frankfurt, had mostly Polish Jews—a few Germans, but mostly Polish. Another camp was almost entirely filled with what they called Balts, who are refugees from Lithuania, Estonia and Latvia.[27]

The committee will have to investigate that whole question of displaced people or uprooted people and try to find some answer as to whether there are any existing international agencies that can be strengthened and made capable of dealing with the whole problem.

We had a very interesting time in discussing the appointment of that Commission, because some people feel very strongly that, unless people are willing to go back to their own country, they must be against their country.[28] Well, of course, that isn't so. Many of these people did fight against the Fascist Regime, against the Nazis, but they are out of sympathy with existing regimes in their countries. Rightly, or wrongly, they are out sympathy with those regimes. I couldn't judge, you couldn't judge, without the study which I hope is going to be made.

However, that it is an international problem is evident to anyone who looks into it at all. It seems to me that in the next few months UNRRA will carry the burden of actually seeing that people do not starve in those places where UNRRA is functioning.

It is a mistake to think that the displaced persons camps in Germany are any worse than the displaced persons camps in other places, or that the standards of food are worse than those that they have in the other countries. In many cases, the condition is made worse in the other countries because of the fact that, for a long period, they were under Nazi occupation. Therefore, their strength has been sapped over a longer period. In Holland, for instance, under the occupation, a baby was allowed only 350 calories a day. Of course, babies just starved to death—just died.

I came home with the feeling that, every day, every one of us should say "Thank God that my roof is intact, that my room is warm" (and I think we had better learn not to be quite so warm; I think it would do us a great deal of good), "and thank God that we have enough to eat, so that we are not hungry."

The whole of Europe is hungry. But, worse than that, the whole of Europe is without any social structure. You see, the Nazis went through first and wiped out all the people who were doing the job of administering a town or a village or a city. They were simply wiped out. Then the Allies came along, and to a very large extent we had to root out whatever the Nazis had had there. The people who were administering those places were efficient, but they were Nazis, and they had to be removed. That is why, with those two currents having passed through, the leadership is gone.

I have the feeling that we let our consciences realize too late the need of standing up against something that we knew was wrong. We have therefore had to avenge it—but we did nothing to prevent it. I hope that in the future, we are going to remember that there can be no compromise at any point with the things that we know are wrong. We should remember that in connection with all the things that we do here, or in connection with anything at all in the world.

We cannot live in an island of prosperity in a sea of human misery. It just can't be done.

We may enjoy today all the things that I think we should be thankful for, but we cannot hold them when all around us there is a condition such as I am trying to make you feel. I don't think I am succeeding very well, because I cannot really tell you the things that pull one's heartstrings. However, I can assure you that you could not be in any one of the displaced persons camps without feeling that you could hardly bear it, that you could just hardly bear what human beings had endured.

I realize, and you would realize, that there comes a point at which a numbness must set in. If that did not happen, I think these people would all be out of their minds. When you talk to them, you realize that there is this numbness from which all of them are suffering. For instance, as I walked into one place, two children were being taken out with typhus. I told this story in my column, but I think that I will repeat it here because it is really the epitome of what you find there. It was an old shelter, and children were wandering in the underground corridors.

I said, "But the mothers will lose these children!" And the public health doctor who was with me said, "That is the sad part of it; the mothers are indifferent—they have lost so many children."

That shelter was only a transient shelter. It was not run by UNRRA, but run by the Army. The people came in and were supposed to go right out again, but sometimes they didn't go right out. They had only two meals a day there. The way they lived, the dirt, was horrible. They all had to be sprayed with DDT before they could even be allowed to register.

I went to the place where they were serving the second meal of the day—at four p.m.—a meal which consisted of soup and a piece of bread. I saw a woman with a little boy who was not eating anything. I stopped and said, "What is the matter? He doesn't seem to be eating."

She said, "Oh, he has fever. His sister has fever, too. She is too sick to sit up today, but the doctor came to see her. The boy will be sick, too."

She had no feeling that she could do anything about it. There was a complete acceptance, there was a numbness.

As I went out, two small children sat on a bench, with all their little belongings gathered around them. The public health doctor of that area said to me, "The mother left this morning when the group was called, and she must have forgotten the children, because she left them behind."

Well, you know and I know that most children left behind in such circumstances would have been in tears. But I went over and spoke to the little boy—he was nearly ten, and I suppose his sister was four or five—and I said, "I hope your mother comes back soon."

He said to me, "I am sad." And that was all he said. There were no tears. The little girl didn't move. They just sat there until someone would come and take them somewhere.

Those children epitomized the feeling that one gets. There wasn't any use in crying, you see. You never knew what would happen; you just accepted what fate brought to you.

I want to stress the point that it is not just the physical condition that is bad, horrible as it is—horrible as it is to live without privacy, to live (as some of them do) with even less privacy than there was at the Jewish camp which I visited, which at least had houses and room.

There was one camp that I saw which had a wonderful French UNRRA team running it.[29] I cannot say enough for the way those people had worked, particularly the doctor. A little corner of the room—no larger than the distance from the end of this table across the stage to the curtain— was divided into three parts by blankets hung up on strings at the height of a man's head. Three families—seven people in all—lived in those three divisions.

But it is not just that. It is the feeling that there has been a crumbling of the thing that gives most of us a sense of security, the feeling that we have roots, and that—as bad as the situation may be—we have a government to which we can appeal, we have people who are representing us and who can speak for us.

Charity is a wonderful thing, but it does not give one that sense of security. What is important is rehabilitation. The sooner the study is made, and the sooner those people can be taken where they can become citizens and feel that they are actually building a new life, the better it will be for the whole world.

Europe, as it is today, gave me the most completely miserable sense of what people can suffer and how the suffering can numb them and how it can sap their strength. It gave me something else which I should like to pass on to you. It gave me the feeling that we have been saved untold misery, and that we must have been saved for a reason. That reason must be that we were expected to give leadership—spiritual leadership, moral leadership, physical leadership. If that is so, and if we fail, what is our punishment going to be?

Of course, you cannot understand the languages that some of those people speak. But you just have to look at their faces and into their eyes to know that whatever leadership is coming has to come from us. It is especially the younger generation that is going to look to us, because we have the capacity to make the things that they need and to see that they get them, and we still have the strength to be leaders. If we don't give that leadership now, I don't know where in the world it is going to come from.

That is the thing I should like to leave with you. I think the most important thing for us to realize is the great responsibility that lies upon our shoulders and the fact that we must give something beyond what we have ever given before in the world—something that is no longer for ourselves at all, but for humanity as a whole.

TSp AERP, FDRL

1. Roosevelt, *OMO*, 54; ER to Kathleen McLaughlin, 17 January 1946; ER's London Diary, 16 January and 11 February 1946, AERP; "Mrs. Roosevelt Visits Refugees," *NYT*, 15 February 1946, 4.

2. The Zeilsheim Jewish displaced persons camp, located about twelve miles outside of Frankfurt in the US occupation zone, was the first camp ER visited in Germany. She arrived at the camp of approximately 3,200 displaced Jews on the morning of February 14 ("Displaced Persons Don't Eat Very Well, Says Mrs. Roosevelt," *WP*, 15 February 1946, 5).

3. ER spoke to the crowd, answered their questions, and promised to "tell as many people as possible of the human side of the problem." Afterwards she walked around the camp and talked with many people there about their situation. Press reports stated that she was followed by a crowd of about 400 Jews pleading, "send us back to Palestine," and holding bilingual signs with such messages as "We want to go, we have to go, we must go, we will go to Palestine" and "We Jewish children will no more stay on this bloody ground where our parents were destroyed. We will go home to Palestine." For more on ER's visit to Zeilsheim, see Document 95 ("Displaced Persons Don't Eat Very Well, Says Mrs. Roosevelt," *WP*, 15 February 1946, 5).

4. In a speech to over 3,000 people at the opening of the 1946 fund-raising campaign organized by the Hartford Jewish Federation, ER said of this boy: "I was told he sang, and I asked to hear him. He sang a song I had never heard. It was like a marching song, and I was told it was the Jewish song of freedom … He sang this song of freedom where there was no freedom and practically everyone around him was a slave" ("American Aid to Save Lost People of the World Asked by Mrs. Roosevelt," *Hartford Times*, 11 April 1946, 3; Mary Lou Wright, "Plight Told of Refugees in Europe," *Hartford Daily Courant*, 11 April 1946, 1).

5. The Wiesbaden (sometimes referred to as Gersdorff) displaced persons camp contained an estimated 6,500 Poles and Balts when ER visited there on the afternoon of February 14. For more on ER's visit to Wiesbaden, see Document 95 ("Displaced Persons Don't Eat Very Well," Says Mrs. Roosevelt," *WP*, 15 February 1946, 5).

6. Upon the recommendation of the UN General Assembly, the Economic and Social Council (ECOSOC) named a twenty-nation committee to study the problem of refugees and displaced persons on February 18. The members of the committee were Brazil, Canada, China, Belgium, the Dominican Republic, France, Lebanon, the Netherlands, New Zealand, Peru, Poland, Great Britain, the Soviet Union, the United States, Yugoslavia, Ukraine, White Russia, Australia, Columbia, and Czechoslovakia. For more on the development of the UN's refugee policy, see Document 78 and Document 86 ("UNO Economic Body Sets Up 5 Groups," *NYT*, 19 February 1946, 4).

7. ER met with a group of female German reporters in Frankfort where she "soberly" answered questions about "the possibility of Germany's ultimate restoration to the family of nations and their own responsibilities" in that process ("Mrs Roosevelt Visits Refugees," *NYT*, 15 February 1946, 4).

8. Roosevelt, *OMO*, 59.

9. The Tiergarten (a large park near the center of the city), Unter Den Linden (a famous boulevard), and the Grunewald (a forest within the city) embodied the beauty of prewar Berlin (*NEB* vol. 14).

10. ER seems to be referring to the Borgward Goliath F200, which was produced from 1933 to 1938. Borgward, the fourth largest auto manufacturer in Germany after Mercedes, Audi, and Opel, was converted to war manufacturing in 1936, and produced mainly personnel trucks and half-tracks for the Nazi war effort.

11. For more on ER's views on German responsibility for World War II, see Document 93.

12. For more on this encounter, see Document 95.

13. General Lucius Clay (1897–1978) served as General Dwight D. Eisenhower's deputy in charge of civil-military affairs in the American zone of occupied Germany. His responsibilities included: refugees, food, housing, health, industry, denazification, and the reestablishment of German self-governance. In 1947 he became the American military governor in Germany and commander of US forces in Europe. Clay, who considered ER "a great lady" and agreed with her about the need for increased immigration of European Jews, noted that her columns "were very much in support of what we were trying to do in Germany" (*ANBO*; J. Smith, 291, 339).

14. Ambassador Robert D. Murphy (1894–1978) served as Eisenhower's chief political advisor on Germany beginning in the fall of 1944 and in the American military government in Germany after Germany's defeat. Later he became the political advisor to General Clay and stayed on in Germany with the title of ambassador until 1949 (*ANB*).

15. ER spoke to more than 200 soldiers and WACs at a "jam-packed" Berlin Red Cross Club. Besides discussing the situation in postwar Europe she also gave her audience a four-point program for "getting along with the Russians": "Have convictions; be friendly; stick to your beliefs as they stick to theirs; work as hard as they do." ("Russians Weighed by Mrs. Roosevelt," *NYT*, 16 February 1946, 6; "Mrs. Roosevelt Tells GIs How To Like Reds," *WP*, 16 February 1946, 9).

16. The chapter's goal—$35 million of a $100 million national goal—was then "the largest sum ever sought by a single voluntary agency in New York's history." Other speakers at this event included Edith Altschul Lehman, spouse of Herbert Lehman, then UNRRA director general, and Rabbi Milton Steinberg of the Park Avenue Synagogue and author of "A Partisan Guide to the Jewish Problem" ("Leadership By U.S. Urged for Europe," *NYT*, 21 February 1946, 15).

17. The full title of this document is Address by Mrs. Franklin D. Roosevelt at the Opening Campaign Rally of the Women's Division of the United Jewish Appeal of Greater New York, at the Hotel Waldorf Astoria. Wednesday, February 20, 1946.

United Jewish Appeal (UJA), the major fund-raising agency for American Jews, collected funds for Jewish refugees in Europe, for Jews in Palestine, and for Jewish communities in the United States. Henry Morgenthau, Jr., after being forced to resign as secretary of the treasury soon after FDR's death, began raising funds for the UJA and became its general chairman in January 1947. He made it the central and passionate focus of his life. Morgenthau and his wife Elinor were among ER's oldest and closest friends. As part of her commitment to aid the thousands of Jews left homeless after the war in Europe, ER became a dedicated supporter of the UJA and of Morgenthau's efforts, speaking often at UJA events, signing fund-raising letters, and using her My Day column to publicly promote some of their initiatives.

In the June 11, 1946, My Day, she noted the broad support behind the UJA's drive in New York City and urged other communities to organize similar campaigns:

> I wonder how many of my readers know of the Community Committee of New York on behalf of the United Jewish Appeal ... I bring this to the attention of my readers because I feel strongly that every city, small or large, in this country would help to increase the feeling of brotherhood throughout the world if a similar committee was organized in their midst. The purpose is to help the survivors of the Jewish group in Europe who were the greatest sufferers under Hitler's fascist rise to power (*MD*, 11 June 1946).

Privately ER worked to make sure funding of the UJA was secured. After returning from Europe she wrote to Leonard Bernstein that she was:

> deeply concerned with the problem of the people for whom the United Jewish Appeal must raise a minimum of $100,000,000 ... Seeing how these people must live today gave me the feeling that we Americans have been saved from untold misery, and that we must

have been saved for a reason. That reason must be that we were expected to give leadership … We have the capacity to see that they get the things they need. We can help them get to Palestine—this uprooted people who have no other home to return to; and we have the added responsibility of helping some of them find a home here among us (ER to Leonard Bernstein, 22 July 1946, AERP).

Over a year later, in another appeal, she admitted: "The memory of what I saw in Europe since the war is still so deeply etched in my mind that I consider it my duty to do everything I can to help the stricken Jewish survivors of war and persecution. This is the principal reason I have taken an active part in advancing the cause of the United Jewish Appeal" (ER to Dr. Nemir, 11 November 1947, AERP; Morgenthau, 411; *EJH*).

18. ER would later describe her visit to Germany as "the most horrible 2 1/2 days I have ever spent" (Genevieve Reynolds, "Wishing Won't Buy Peace, Must Work for It, Says Mrs. Roosevelt," *WP*, 15 March 1946, C1).

19. During a two-and-a-half day visit to Germany, ER visited four displaced persons camps: Zeilsheim, Wiesbaden (also referred to as Gersdorff) both near Frankfurt, and two that she did not identify. She possibly could have visited Wittenau and Dueppel as they were located in Berlin. For more on these visits, see Document 93 and Document 94.

20. For more on ER's visit to Zeilsheim, see Document 93. For information on the United Nations Relief and Rehabilitation Administration, see *n*7 Document 55.

21. On August 18, 1933, ER, at the urging of Lorena Hickok and American Friends Service Committee secretary Clarence Pickett (1884–1965), visited the West Virginia coal mines to see the conditions confronting miners and their families. She encountered some of, if not the, worst living conditions the Great Depression inflicted on American citizens. ER, with FDR's support, devoted a great deal of energy to the region, taking personal interest in the Subsistence Homestead projects in the region—especially the community known as Arthurdale. She also lobbied within and without the White House for better working and living conditions for miners and their families. Nor did she limit her concern to West Virginia mines. In early July 1934, she visited the Ford mines and the nearby AFSC camp near Pikeville, Kentucky. May 22, 1935, she went down into the Willow Grove coal mine of the Hanna Coal Company in Bellaire, Ohio, studied the local conditions, and then delivered the commencement address at the People's University. Several media ridiculed her interest, to which ER responded by writing "In Defense of Curiosity" (Cook, vol. 2, 130–38; "Mrs. Roosevelt Goes into Kentucky Hills," *NYT*, 4 July 1934, 19; "Mine Studied by First Lady, 2 Miles Down," *WP*, 22 May 1935, 1). For ER's reaction upon returning from her first trip to West Virginia see her column in *Women's Democratic News*, September 1933, 6; and Roosevelt, *TIR*, 126–33.

22. While in Germany ER told troops stationed there that the food in the camps was as "about as appetizing as sawdust" ("Mrs. Roosevelt Visits Refugees," *NYT*, 15 February 1946, 4).

23. For more on this incident, see *n*4 above.

24. See Document 93 for ER's reaction to this incident.

25. See *n*3 above.

26. For the debate within the Third Committee on refugee relief, see Document 86, Document 90, and Document 91.

27. For more on ER's visit to Zeilsheim and Wiesbaden, see Document 93.

28. This was the position of the Soviet Union and its allies. See Eleanor Roosevelt, "Human Rights and Human Freedoms," *New York Times Magazine*, 26 March 1946, 21.

29. Wiesbaden displaced persons camp.

96

If You Ask Me [excerpt]
Ladies' Home Journal March 1946

As a delegate to the UNO, will you be guided under any circumstances by your individual judgement of what is right, or under certain possible circumstances by the principle, "My country: may it ever be right; but right or wrong, my country"?

I will, of course, as a delegate to the UNO have to abide by whatever rules are set up within our delegation to govern procedures. Where decisions of policy are made within the delegation, I will try to represent the people. I know, of course, that my feeling of what should be done or of what people want may be wrong, but I would certainly try to work for what I thought represented the major good of the world as a whole. I will try to think at all times of ultimate objectives rather than of the narrower and more immediate aspects of any question that comes up as it affects my own or any other individual country.

I will do this because I believe so firmly that the good of all people in the future must be paramount in order to make it possible for any one of us to live and be free and happy on this globe.

"My country: may it ever be right; but my country, right or wrong" is a very good precept for men in our military services, since they are under the orders of Congress and their Commander-in-Chief and really have very little opportunity to form the policies of the nation. They are practically obligated, once a decision is made, to carry it out. For the rest of us, however, who have an obligation to take part in the forming of policies, I think we should make every possible effort to fight for the things which we believe are right, making it clear to the people why we hold our beliefs, thus creating public opinion. The majority must rule, but minorities sometimes become majorities, and full knowledge for the people is the only way that we, in a democracy, can be truly representative of the will of the people.

Do you think it a sound principle of justice to try the so-called "war criminals" for acts that were not technically illegal under either German or Japanese or international law at the time they were committed?[1]

Yes, I think it is a sound principle of justice to try people for acts they committed, whether they were technically illegal or not at the time. I realize that this is not the procedure usually adhered to by the courts, but I have always felt that that was one of the unfortunate ways in which justice sometimes miscarries even in domestic issues.

TMsex DLC

---

1. Before World War II, military conduct during war was governed by the Geneva Convention of 1864 (which protected wounded soldiers); agreements reached at the 1899 and 1907 Hague Peace Conferences (which prohibited specific types of weaponry); and the Geneva Conventions of 1906 and 1929 (which applied specific rules of warfare to civilians, prisoners of war, and injured and ill soldiers). In 1943, in response to atrocities committed by Nazi Germany, the Allies signed the Declaration of Moscow, obligating each of them to prosecute individuals indicted for barbarous crimes committed during wartime. In August 1944, the Allies approved the London Agreement, mandating the creation of an International Military Tribunal, which would hear cases against those accused of both war crimes as well as "waging aggressive war and committing crimes against peace

and humanity." The Tribunal, made up of representatives from the United States, USSR, Great Britain, and France, then tried twenty-four Nazi leaders at Nuremberg from November 1945 to October 1946. Meanwhile, General Douglas MacArthur, the supreme commander of the Allied Powers, adhered to the Potsdam agreement and established an International Military Tribunal for the Far East, which met in Tokyo from May 1946 to November 1948, to decide the fate of twenty-eight Japanese leaders.

In both cases, the defendants argued that the tribunals were *ex post facto*, meaning that when the defendants' actions were committed there were no international laws in place to prohibit them. The tribunals not only rejected that argument but ruled that individuals, and not just the state, were responsible for their conduct and thus also rejected the defendants' argument that they were just following orders. Lastly, the Tribunals ruled that even if specific laws were not in place, the deeds had been considered crimes since before World War II, and the Weimar Republic's trying of German leaders for their roles in World War I served as precedent (*OCAMH*).

ON POSTWAR EUROPE, SOVIET POSTURING, AND PRESIDENTIAL CRONYISM

February 27, ER met with Truman at the White House to report on the recent session of the General Assembly. During their conversation, the president requested that ER send him a memorandum recapping their meeting. March 1, ER sent him the following memorandum reviewing "a few of the things I talked to you about," with a cover note expressing her hope "that you can find the time to read this horribly long screed …"[1]

97

Memorandum for the President
1 March 1946 [New York City]

First—the economic situation in Europe.

I feel very strongly that it can not be handled piecemeal. For the safety of the world, we have decided to change the center of European economy from Germany. Much of the coal and heavy industry emanated from Germany in the past. Now, as far as possible, Germany will be an agricultural nation. Unfortunately in giving Poland some of Germany's best land, we have complicated the industrial situation somewhat because she will have to have not only enough industry to meet her own internal needs, but enough industry to keep her people on a reasonable living basis which will mean a revival, at least, of the old toy industry and other light industries. When we made this decision, we also made the decision that Europe had to have in Great Britain, France, Holland and other countries, the things which Germany had once provided.[2]

Owing to the fact that this Second World War has done more than destroy material things, bad as that situation is in all these countries, a much greater responsibility is going to devolve on us not only materially but for leadership.

Great Britain is better off than the rest of Europe, but even in Great Britain our help in the provision of goods is going to be necessary.[3] In Europe it will not only be the provision of goods without which loans would be merely a farce, since you can not start a factory with money alone— you have to have machinery. We will also have to provide skilled administrators and skilled technicians. This will be necessary because Germany in over-running Europe wiped out one group of administrative officials, those who ran the towns and villages and cities, and those who ran the factories and businesses, etc. The Germans put in people whom they felt they could trust and they were usually efficient in large part. When we came and reconquered Europe we had to liquidate this second group and now there is no one left to take the leadership.

The young people returning from concentration camps and forced labor camps will nearly all of them spend some time in sanitariums, but they will not only have to rebuild their bodies. The suffering they have been through will have left a mark on their personalities.

I happen to remember the effect of unemployment and poverty in some of our mining areas in the depth of the depression. It took several years for people to regain self confidence and initiative, and that was not comparable to what these people in Europe have been through. That takes a large group out of the leadership area.

Amongst the resistance groups, you have young people who have missed out on five or six years of education which they must either now try to get or they must get something else which will make it possible for them to earn a living. Even more serious is the handicap that the virtues of life in the resistance during the invasion period, have now become far from virtues in a peaceful civilization. Lying, cheating, stealing and even killing was what they had to do. Now these are criminal offenses!

The whole social structure of Europe is crumbling[4] and we might as well face the fact that leadership must come from us or it will inevitably come from Russia. The economic problem is not one we can handle with a loan to Great Britain, a loan to France, a loan to Russia. It must be looked on as a whole. When we make the loans we must be prepared to send goods. This will mean very careful allocation over here so that our people will obtain only essentials and everything else, during the next couple of years, will go where it is needed even more.[5]

The economic problem is tied up with the problem of food. You can not rehabilitate people and expect them to work unless they are getting an adequate diet. At present that is not possible anywhere in Europe and the Far East and shortly we are going to have a real famine in India, and Burma, I am told.[6]

We are going to have to learn to stretch as we have never stretched before as far as food is concerned. I think we should begin an intensive campaign over the radio and in the newspapers to tell our people how to do this and to awaken in them a realization of the consequences, not perhaps this year or next, but five years hence if these people in Europe and Asia starve to death, or are not able to rehabilitate themselves and therefore are not able to buy some of our goods when our own savings have been spent. Even more serious is the threat of epidemics to world health, since starvation saps resistence to disease and there are no real boundaries today which will protect us if epidemics get started.[7]

Second—Russia.

I do not feel that there is any mystery about Russia as Senator Vandenburg in his speech, indicated. I liked his speech as a whole very much, but these unanswered questions I think, may lead to the flaming of uncertainty in this country which I think is one of the things we do not wish to do.[8]

In a great country like the USSR where her soldiers for the first time have discovered what other people have in the way of consumer goods, it must be realized that in one way or another, all people being human beings, they are going to demand the satisfying of the normal desires of people for better living. For that reason I think that intelligent people at the head of their government are anxious to establish economic conditions which will allow them to import and export without difficulty. Hence the agitation in Iran, the Dardanelles, etc. They are going to ask for political control to safeguard economic agreements but it is security in the economic situation that they seek. They must have it to secure political security at home but I do not think the political controls abroad are their first considerations.[9]

Along the European border of the USSR, however, she is chiefly concerned with her military security. That is why she will try to control the governments of the nations in all those areas and why she dreads seeing Germany built up as an industrial power against her. She will liquidate or allow governments under her control to liquidate any of the displaced people now outside her borders if they show signs of dissatisfaction or unrest against her control in these countries. She has not enough real security and stability to live with an opposition at home and this is difficult for us to understand. We have had no political refugees in our country since the days of the Civil War. The opposition is always in our midst and frequent changes occur, but we do it through the ballot and peacefully. They do it through revolution and the use of force. This is largely a question of maturity and of course, trust in the people themselves and not such great dependence on the absolute control of the head of the government.

It will take some time for Russia to achieve this, but there is no reason why we should not explain this to her. It will have to be stressed for her that the vast majority of displaced people in Europe today who long to go back to the countries of their origin, must be able to go back in safety and have enough freedom within their countries to feel that they control their national government internally, and their association with the Soviets is exclusively a real protection for the future.[10]

This holds good for what we call the Balts who are people from Estonia, Latvia, Lithuania and also for many Ukrainians outside of Ukraine today.

Poland has several factions and people going back, if they are not shot by one faction are afraid of being shot by the other. I suppose this holds good and will hold good for some of the other countries. Czechoslovakia seems to have worked out under Dr. Benes, a fairly satisfactory kind of government for everyone concerned. She does not, however, seem to feel free to differ with the Soviets judging by the way Mazaryk voted and that is because the Soviets haven't really been strong enough to explain that they are willing to have people do what they think is right and they will not attribute to them any less fundamental agreement amongst themselves.[11]

I think we should get a very much better understanding of the displaced persons situation but perhaps that can wait until the committee on refugees makes its report to the UNO. It might be well to prepare our people for the report, however, and also to make clear why certain things have to be said to Russia.[12]

Third—Mr. Winant

If Mr. John G. Winant could be made our permanent member on the Economic and Security Council, I think he could make the most valuable contribution of any one I know because of his long association with the Europeans on the ILO, and as Ambassador to London. He is really liked and trusted. I know that there are some stories circulated about him, but I am quite sure that he is fundamentally a loyal and honest person. I should like you to give him a chance to tell his side of any stories if they should be brought up as a reason for not appointing him.[13]

Fourth—Food

I wonder if in your food production program, we could not enlist the cooperation of South America and possibly increase their production by allotting to them some agricultural machinery?[14]

Fifth—Mr. David Gray

Mr. David Gray, our Minister to Ireland, asked me to give you his regards and to tell you we were going on leading the fight to have the Irish turn over the German diplomatic people to the courts as has been requested. Ireland is a curious country and even the Catholic Church situation is different from anywhere else in the world. I hope if Mr. Gray does get permission to return for a time this spring that you will allow him an opportunity to tell you about their very peculiar politics.[15]

ER appended a separate note reiterating her concerns about Truman's relationship with Edwin Pauley.

I must say something to you which I hate to say because I think you have so many troubles and I am conscious of them.

I know that in naming Mr. Pauley you were doing what Mr. Hannegan quite naturally asked you to do. I remember very well the pressure under which my own husband was placed and his agreement to name Mr. Pauley as Assistant Secretary of the Navy, and then we had a long discussion about it because I was very much opposed to having Mr. Pauley in any position where oil could be involved. Franklin assured me that if he put Mr. Pauley in as Assistant Secretary of the Navy, he would have nothing to do with oil because Mr. Forrestal would be over him and he would never be secretary.

I have seen in the papers both that Franklin had agreed to appointing him as Assistant Secretary and that he was to succeed Mr. Forrestal. I have been thanking my lucky stars that nobody asked me how I felt on this, as I would hate to have to say that I was opposed to his appointment, but I feel it only honest to tell you how very strong my opposition is. I know Mr. Pauley did a remarkable job in raising money for the Democratic National Committee, but he was in a position to do that job legitimately, and I am not sure that it was always done with the strictest of ethical considerations in the forefront.[16]

Any President frequently suffers from his friends as much as from his enemies, and it is the sense of loyalty and gratitude which often gets men in public life into the greatest of trouble. In this case, I think you would be bringing on yourself unnecessary anxiety and trouble if Mr. Pauley should by chance, get through. He may not want an Ambassadorship, but that would be considerably safer if he was not sent to a country that dealt with oil.

TMem HSTOF, HSTL

<hr>

98

Harry Truman to Eleanor Roosevelt
7 March 1946 [The White House]

Dear Mrs. Roosevelt:

Thanks a lot for all your trouble in sending me the memorandum of your visit to London. I read it with a lot of interest and it will be helpful to me.

I am sorry about the Pauley matter but I merely thought I was carrying out the Program. Personally I think very highly of Pauley and I think he is an honest man.[17]

I sincerely hope we can get this United Nations program implemented so it will work, and I know we can do it if we make up our minds to do it.[18] Your suggestion on the financing and rehabilitation of Europe is most interesting. It certainly was a pleasure to me to have an opportunity to discuss the situation with you the other day.

Sincerely yours,
Harry S. Truman

TLS AERP, FDRL

<hr>

1. ER to Harry Truman, 1 March 1946, HSTSF, HSTL.

2. At this point, the United States, Great Britain, and the Soviet Union were attempting to implement their Potsdam decision to de-industrialize Nazi Germany. Under this plan the Germans would retain enough industrial capacity to pay reparations to the European Allies and the Soviets, and maintain a standard of living no greater than that of their European neighbors. However, France's desire to replace Germany as the economic engine of Europe and preserve its own security by claiming the Saar coalfields, internationalizing ownership of the Ruhr coal and steel industries, and calling for the detachment of the Rhineland from German control, threatened these plans. ER, who favored reducing Germany's industrial and war-making capacity and increasing its dependence on agriculture, continued to have concerns about the Allies' plans for the economic rehabilitation of Germany. "Enough industry must be allowed in Germany so that she will not have to count on subsidies from other countries to live," she wrote in a May 1946 My Day. "The heavily industrial Ruhr area must function—and function quickly and effectively—but in the interests of the whole of Europe, not in the interests of Germany alone …" For more on ER's views on the demilitarization and reconstruction of Germany's economy see *n*3 Document 121. Much of Germany's best agricultural land was located east of the Oder and Neisse Rivers in what became the Soviet zone. The Soviet Union and Poland divided up this territory after the war. For more on

the transfer of German land to Poland, see *n*1 Document 6 (Gaddis, 325–28; Hogan, 29–32; Offner, 157–58; J. Smith, 357; Lash, *Eleanor*, 710; *MD*, 24 May 1946).

3. The British government estimated that World War II cost Great Britain a quarter of its economy. At the other end of the spectrum, the Poles estimated damage to their economy at two-fifths of its capacity, making Poland one of the poorest nations in Europe. For more on ER's views on the restoration of Europe's industrial and political cultures, see Document 95 (*HSTE*; Lukowski and Zawadzki, 250).

4. As ER told the United Jewish Appeal:

> The whole of Europe is hungry. But worse than that, the whole of Europe is without any social structure. You see, the Nazis went through first and wiped out all the people who were doing the job of administering a town or a village or a city. They were simply wiped out. Then the Allies came along, and to a very large extent we had to root out whatever the Nazis had had there. The people who were administering those places were efficient, but they were Nazis, and they had to be removed. That is why, with those two currents having passed through, the leadership is gone.

For a fuller discussion, see Document 95.

5. In early 1946, the United States negotiated a $3.75 billion loan for Great Britain, which Congress passed that summer. The French received a $550 million loan from the Import-Export Bank in December 1945 and would negotiate another $650 million loan with the United States in May 1946 along with the promise of a $500 million World Bank credit to modernize their economy. None of these transactions involved the shipment of goods. The Soviets asked the United States for a $6 billion reconstruction loan in 1945 and later applied for a $1 billion loan through the Import-Export Bank but neither loan materialized because Soviet-American relations worsened after the war (Hamby, *Man*, 352; *HSTE*; Paterson et al., 446–47).

6. ER's source for the information on the potential famine in India and Burma is unknown. However, in February 1946, the Emergency Economic Committee for Europe forecast that 240 million people in western and central Europe (excluding Albania, Ireland, Turkey, and the Soviet Union) faced severe food shortages due to the war and below average wheat crops. In early March, the *New York Times* reported that in India, where one million people starved in the famine of 1943, the rice crop was down 15 percent due to war and drought. Rice production in Burma also dropped significantly. See also *n*5 Document 66 ("140 Million in Europe to Get Only 2,000 Calories a Day," *NYT*, 7 February 1946, 1; "Food for India Asked to Avert New Famine; Delegation Arrives, Head Stresses Gravity," *NYT*, 1 March 1946, 9; "Asks We Eat Less," *NYT*, 8 February 1946, 1; Truman, vol. 1, 467).

7. Three weeks before ER wrote this memo, Truman announced a nine-point emergency program to curtail US consumption of wheat and fats and increase the shipments of these items abroad. On March 1, he met with his newly formed Famine Emergency Committee and its honorary chairman, former President Herbert Hoover, who had been the federal government's food administrator during and after World War I, to plan a campaign to generate public support for a voluntary program to reduce food consumption in the United States. In the latter part of February, ER used My Day to publicize the world food crisis and its link to epidemics. Writing from London in her February 14 column, she noted, "While it is reported that there is not actual starvation throughout Europe, there is hunger practically everywhere. That means people with less energy for work and less resistance to disease." Back in the United States on February 25, she wrote, "The thing one dreads ... is epidemics. These are more apt to occur where the people have been on low and undesirable diets for a long time and ... have had their resistance undermined (Truman, vol. 1, 467–72; "New Famine 'Board' Asks U.S. Cut Wheat Use by 25%, *NYT*, 2 March 1946. 1; *MD*, 14 February and 25 February 1946).

8. In his February 27 Senate speech, Senator Vandenberg described the question "What is Russia up to now?" as "the supreme conundrum of our time." He then went on to ask what Russia was up to in Eastern Europe, Manchuria, Iran, and other global hot spots as well as in the United States. In what observers described as a criticism of Secretary Byrnes's apparent appeasement of the Soviets at the first session of the UN General Assembly, Vandenberg called on the United States to take a harder line with the Russians and assume the moral leadership of the world. "The United States has no ulterior designs against any of its neighbors anywhere on earth. We can speak with the extraordinary power inherent in this unselfishness. We need but one rule. What is right? Where is justice? There let America take her stand" ("Text of Senator Vandenberg's Address on the United Nations Meeting in London," *NYT*, 28 February 1946, 4; "Senator Backs UNO, *NYT*, 28 February 1946, 1; "Vandenberg Urges State Dept. to Speak Out as Russia Does," *WP*, 28 February 1946, 1; Donovan, 189; Offner, 134).

9. The Soviet Union wanted an oil concession in Iran. In pursuit of this goal, the Soviets refused to remove their troops stationed there since World War II in violation of its agreement with the United States and Great Britain and also supported a separatist movement in Azerbaijan in northern Iran (site of the Baku oil fields). At this point, the United States had given the Soviet Union a March 2 deadline for the removal of its troops. As for the Dardanelles, even before the war ended, the Soviets pushed for military control of the straits separating Europe from Turkey, which Turkey had controlled since 1936. Truman, long suspicious of Soviet intentions toward the Dardanelles, believed Soviet activity in Iran presaged a possible attack on Turkey. For more on the situation in Iran, see *n*10 Document 79 (Chace, 141–43; Offner, 84–85, 112–14; Donovan, 189–90).

10. See also Document 152, Document 168, and Document 90.

11. Although the Communists controlled the Polish government at this point, their hold on power was fragile. The Socialists and the Peasant Parties also had their adherents as did many anti-Communist guerilla groups, who continued to exist in Poland until 1947. For more on Poland, see *n*5 Document 13 and *n*8 Document 14. President Edvard Beneš (1884–1948), a founder of modern-day Czechoslovakia, who served as president of the Czech government in exile during World War II, presided over a freely elected postwar coalition government made up of Communists and non-Communists. However Communists held many of the most important positions including the prime ministership and the Ministries of Interior (police) and Information. Conscious of their country's precarious position internally and externally, Beneš and Jan Masaryk (see gazetter) attempted to maintain good relations with both the United States and the USSR. ER met with Masaryk and Beneš during her 1942 visit to London, and she and Masaryk made a joint broadcast during the first meeting of the General Assembly. ER also commented on Masaryk's "very moving" speech on the work of UNRAA during the first session of the General Assembly.

At the first session of the UN General Assembly, the Russians and the Czechs voted alike most of the time. On those few occasions where they diverged, one country would vote and the other would abstain. For example, Czechoslovakia voted to place Southwest Africa under the international trusteeship system, while the USSR abstained. See also Document 166 (Lukowski and Zawadski, 251–54; *OEWH*; *HSTE*; *NEB*; Lash, *Eleanor*, 665; Statement by Mrs. Eleanor Roosevelt made in broadcast given at Columbia Studios, January 10, 1946, jointly with Mr. Jan Masaryk, AERP; *MD*, 4 February 1946; Schopen et al., 1, 7, 8, 352).

12. Following the debate between ER and Andrei Vyshinsky in the General Assembly on February 12, 1946, the General Assembly passed a resolution calling upon the Economic and Social Council to establish a Special Committee on Refugees and Displaced Persons. That committee, comprised of representatives of twenty countries, was scheduled to meet in April 1946 (Holborn, 34). See also Document 86, Document 90, and Document 91.

13. The stories she alludes to probably had to do with Winant's extreme financial indebtedness, see *n*10, Document 75. Truman appointed him permanent US representative on the United Nations

Economic and Social Council in March 1946 (Bellush, 85, 133, 136–39, 217; Lash, *Eleanor*, 658–59).

14. Instead of sending machinery, Truman sent Herbert Hoover on an eleven-nation visit to Latin America in May and June to seek food supplies for Europe and Asia. Hoover returned with commitments totaling approximately two million tons of cereals and beans for a four-month period (June–September) (R. Smith, *Uncommon*, 358–59; "More Food Stocks Found by Hoover," *NYT*, 20 June 1946, 1).

15. ER stopped in Ireland on her way home from Europe in February. For more information on David Gray, see *n*14 Document 75. A neutral country during World War II, Ireland initially refused postwar Allied requests to hand over German diplomats and agents because the Irish government wanted to uphold the right of asylum and preserve Irish neutrality. In 1947, the Irish government under increasing Allied pressure due to the start of the war crimes trials reversed its position and repatriated the agents. (The German ambassador who had been granted asylum in 1945 remained in Ireland.) Although the Irish constitution provided for the separation of church and state, the historic connection between Irish nationalism and the Roman Catholic Church made church-state relations unusually close in Ireland, and the Catholic ethos pervaded the country's political, social, educational, and cultural spheres. For example, divorce was forbidden under Irish law as were abortion and contraception. At the same time, the Irish government felt free to disregard the Catholic Church's views as it did during the Spanish Civil War when the Irish government refused to withdraw its recognition of the Spanish Republican government (*MD*, 21 February 1946; "Reports Neutrals Balk on Germans," *NYT*, 12 January 1946, 7; *OCWWII*; Hollis, 142, 158–59; Duggan, 245; Dwyer, 201, 209–10; Townshend, 125, 149).

16. On January 18, 1946, Truman nominated Edwin Pauley, Sr. (1903–1981), former finance chairman of the Democratic National Committee and a millionaire California oil man who then served as the US representative to the Allied Reparations Commission, to become undersecretary of the navy, at Secretary of the Navy Forrestal's suggestion. Pauley's conservative political views and his interest in offshore oil leases, including those areas where the navy owned oil reserves, troubled Secretary of the Interior Harold Ickes, who like ER, thought Pauley's appointment would lead to conflicts of interest. For more on Pauley, see the Biographical Portraits and *n*17 below. For more on Hannegan, see Document 15 and Document 16 (*HSTE*; Donovan, 178–83; Hamby, *Man*, 308).

17. Despite ER's concerns, Truman continued to support Pauley, who remained an "unofficial member" of the president's "kitchen cabinet." In 1947, Truman once again tried to find an official position for his friend, this time as a special assistant to the secretary of the army; however, after the Commodity Exchange Commission revealed that Pauley was a major oil speculator, Pauley resigned (*HSTE*; Lash, *Years*, 123).

18. The president refers to the proposed United National Food Collection Drive, a UNRAA-administered plan to collect food in the United States to be distributed overseas. ER had written Truman the day before to underscore the need to get the program working quickly (ER to Truman, 6 March 1946, HSTL).

"The Heavy Cost of Peace"

The evening of March 14, the Women's Joint Congressional Committee, representing more than ten million women, honored Eleanor Roosevelt for her position as the first woman delegate to the United Nations at the Mayflower Hotel.[1] Before ER took the podium, Senator Tom Connally told the audience that not only did ER work to increase the presence of women in the United Nations, she also performed "outstanding" work in whatever task she was assigned.

> She did not shirk responsibility. She toiled tirelessly on the committees to which she was assigned with splendid tact, with her great ability, and with force and persuasion she took part in debates, both in the committees and on the floor of the Assembly, where she received a tremendous ovation.[2]

ER then used the occasion to challenge Churchill's worldview and to spur support for increased foreign aid and humanitarian relief.

99

Address by Eleanor Roosevelt to the Women's Joint Congressional Committee

14 March 1946 [Washington D.C]

Madam Chairman,[3] Senator Connally, distinguished guests, Mrs. Wilson,[4] ladies and gentlemen, I am deeply touched by the honor which the organizations represented here have paid to me tonight and I am deeply touched by the Senator's introduction. I think that what really was accomplished in London was accomplished by our delegation working together. None of us did any better work than all the members of the delegation. We met and talked our problems over. We were given information by our advisers. I am glad that Miss Fosdick[5] is here this evening and I hope she will take back to the numerous people from the State Department, who worked with us my feeling of gratitude for the wonderful help which was given to all of us who were delegates, or alternates, and who needed help to do a good job.

I like the feeling that everyone of us went to London with; we had just one main objective: We wanted to set in motion an organization for which the Charter had been written, but which as yet was not actually functioning, and we wanted to set it in motion so that the world might hope for world peace in the future. We knew that setting up the organization wasn't going to give us world peace, but we knew that it was the machinery through which we could or would have world peace in the future.

I never forgot in those days in London the gratitude which we owe to President Woodrow Wilson and the people who had worked with him to set up the League of Nations because over and over again the work which had been done made it possible to do what we hope will prove to be more effective work this time. However, it cannot be more effective unless the peoples of the world state that it shall be effective.

I sometimes wonder if we in this country realize what our responsibility is. I have had people say to me in the course of the last few days, "Well, why should we give up food? Why should we be uncomfortable? Europe brought this situation on herself. What difference does it make to us?"[6] Sometimes, as I look at our domestic scene, I wonder if that is a widespread idea, if really we are thinking throughout this country that our domestic affairs can be isolated from world affairs. If we still think that, then I am afraid the future is a very, very dark future and I am afraid that our vision is a very narrow vision, because during the war we have developed in this country the greatest production capacity in the world. Now, if you produce very successfully, you produce for a purpose. You produce so that others may have what you produce, and they must be in a position so that they can have desires and the wherewithal to achieve their desires. Therefore, if we are chiefly concerned today with what happens to us in the next year or two and forget, because of that concern, what is happening to the rest of the world, then we are endangering the rest of the world surely, but ourselves just as surely in the course of the next few years. That is one of the lessons which I hope we are going to face and to learn fairly quickly. If we don't do it, I don't know just what is going to bring us to a realization of what another war would mean.

We are such a fortunate Nation. No bombs have dropped on us; no bombs have destroyed our homes and our factories. We have lost loved ones, but they fought in far away places and in many cases we cannot even imagine what they went through. We have been spared a good deal and I don't think we were spared because of some particular value in us as human beings which sets us apart from other human beings in the world. I think we were spared for a purpose which we can justify or we can find that there is nothing in us that arises to the challenge of the opportunity that is offered us. And if we cannot rise to that challenge, then perhaps we will not be spared again.

Several people have said to me in the course of the last few days, "Well, things look very bad." One young reporter said to me in New York the other night, "I wonder whether you share our pessimism. We on the newspapers think that the United Nations is going to have its last meeting. We don't see any real hope of success."

That can only happen if the peoples of the world abdicate actually saying what they feel. I don't believe our people or the people of Russia or the people of Great Britain want another war, but I do believe that we have to say how we feel. We have to say that force has been used for a long time in the world and it does not seem as though one could do away with it immediately; therefore, one must build collective force, which can be used by all the nations, or one cannot cut down on individual force. You have to build a strong United Nations and gradually you have to build the confidence of people in each other and in the ability to work together in order to hope for world peace.

When I went to London I thought that I really knew what war was like and that I knew why I never wanted to see my country subjected to war upon its own doorstep, but I don't think I ever realized what war today, without the atomic bomb, could actually accomplish, perhaps because I am a very old lady. I look back over a long period on Europe and Great Britain. I can remember Europe very well because some 47 years ago I went to school in England[7] and I lived with families in many of the countries where war has been on their doorstep, and I knew those cities and those countrysides before two World Wars had been fought.[8] Then at the end of the last war, within the six weeks after the armistice, I went over the front where we had fought,[9] and 10 years later I went back and saw how quickly nature helps us to forget.[10] I realize, however, that there were many things that even nature couldn't wipe out.

Then, in the Assembly, my first real thought that covered those periods was brought very sharply before me when we were looking for candidates for Secretary-General. The Senator will remember that we wanted candidates who had had experience in their own countries, who had made some name as executives and statesmen, but we wanted them to be fairly young, and as we talked something suddenly clicked in my mind. I remembered in '28 motoring through little villages in England, stopping in the evening and looking at the monument in the middle of the town, with its sides covered with names, and saying to the boys, "Those are the names of men who went from this little village, all of whom were killed in the war."[11] And then going to the little church. In nearly all those towns there is an old family tradition which prompts some member of each generation to go into politics in Great Britain. There were always these monuments. I remember one in particular on which were recorded the names of every young member of a certain family, the last of that family, all of whom had been killed, perhaps in the retreat from the Marne.[12]

Then we drove over the battlefield and suddenly the older of my boys[13] said to me, "This is a funny country, Mommy. Out of the fields there are only coming boys our age and old men. Where are the men in between whom we have coming out of the fields at home?" Dead, crippled, hospitalized! So, a whole generation practically was taken out of the leadership of Europe. That is something to remember.

We looked and we didn't find very many people in that age bracket, and that was a loss, a great loss to the whole of European civilization.

After I was through with my part of the work in London I went over for 2 ½ days only to our zone in Germany.[14] It is foolish to talk of really getting much information in 2 ½ days, but if you have a background of knowing a countryside and a country well—different countries well—and you have talked with many people, I think you may gain impressions even in 2 ½ days. If I needed an added reason for knowing why I wanted world peace and why I didn't want war on our doorstep, I gained it in 2 ½ days in our zone in Germany.

I wish everyone in this country could know what was accomplished without the atomic bomb in destruction. Remember that I saw destruction within 6 weeks at the end of the last war. So, I know what we did in the last war, too. However, the comparison is rather terrific. Berlin is a city of 5,000,000 or so inhabitants. Today they told me some 3,500,000 people still live there. The streets don't seem to have that number of people around. A good many of them, I don't believe, feel much like moving around, but those who are cold have to go and get their wood. They are on a ration; it is like this. You only get enough to cook your soup, which is your main meal for the day—and it is potato soup, with which you get a hunk of bread. That is your main meal. 1,500 calories are not a very great amount of food and you have none of the other foods to compensate. So you get a cup of coffee with a little teaspoon of sugar and a little condensed milk in it and a hunk of bread for breakfast and the same for supper, or a little leftover soup. That is not a very satisfactory diet. It will keep you alive, but you don't have much energy. You only do the things that you have to do.

The curious thing about war is that it is no respecter of persons. General Clay[15] lives in the one house which just happened to be spared in an area where everything else went. The windows were all out but they could be replaced, and it was a very comfortable house. A German industrialist lived in it who thought that he could be safe regardless of what happened to other people and although Berlin had by that time begun to be hungry, he was not hungry. He had barrels of food stored. When General Clay went in he found them. You see, in the end the industrialist who thought he could be selfish had exactly the same fate that all the other people have when war takes its toll on your doorstep.

Today the people of Berlin live in cellars or, if they can find a room which is watertight, they may live in that room.

The people of many other places in Europe have lived for many years not only in devastated cities but under the heel of a conqueror, and the result is a very terrifying thing in its effect on people. You may ask me why I think in 2 ½ days I can sense what happened to people. Well, it is a curious thing, but there is a feeling that spreads over a land and I don't think any one of you could spend time anywhere on the continent of Europe or talk long to any people who had been through the last 5 or 6 years and not get the feel of a civilization that of itself is going to have a very hard time coming back.

They require goods from us. There is not much use in giving them loans if we don't give them things to build up their country, machinery, to modernize their various necessary activities. They must have that from us because nobody else in the world can provide it today. They must have food because no one can starve and rehabilitate a country. They must have leadership, people who know how to do things and who have the energy to do them.

I kept trying to compare the people I was seeing with our people in the worst period that I remember in this country, the days of the depression in '33, in the worst sections that I could remember in this country. You may have forgotten, but I remember that it took some of our people 3 to 5 years, while they were out of work for that length of time, to get back their initiative and their confidence in themselves. Well, remember that those people, many of them young people, have been in concentration camps and labor camps for 4 or 5 years. One French woman said to me something that I felt and thought about as I went into Germany. She had said to me in London, "Aye, Madam, it is not just the physical rehabilitation that people go through. When people have suffered so much, they either go crazy or they die or something happens to their personality so that they cannot feel any more. When they come back now and go to a sanatorium, physically they may come back, but it varies how that sense of numbness goes. Sometimes it takes a long time; sometimes it never goes."

While that is happening that person does not provide leadership, that person is almost like a living dead person. Europe has many of those people.

There is another thing that we must remember. There were young people in the resistance movements all over Europe. They were brave, and for 4, 5, or 6 years they fought in the resistance movements. I think I should add this: That sometimes, we forget the range of age in the resistance movements. There were little children engaged in this dangerous work, and it went right up to the older people. The people we need today first of all are the young people from 15 to 25. Well, that age would ordinarily have been in school learning their skills, learning to earn a living, learning whatever they wished to do in life. They have not been to that kind of school; they have been to another kind, though, which matures one very rapidly. That is the school where every time you open a door death may wait just outside. That is a maturing school, but, you see, the things that were virtues in the resistance—lying, cheating, stealing, killing—are no longer virtues after the resistance is over. Now you say to your people, "Go back to school and learn how to live in a peaceful society. Go and keep your house, young ladies; it is time you were making a home. The things which you have done in the last few years are now criminal offenses, so don't do them any more."

That is rather a rapid change, isn't it? That is something hard to learn overnight. If you had to live with death as a possibility day in and day out, you were certain of a lot of excitement. It is not quite so easy to go back and keep your house and get an education and start out on peaceful living.

That is what I want you to think of when you say, as I hope you will every day of your lives, "We want to build for world peace. We want to use this machinery. We in this country are willing to pay the price for world peace."

It is a heavy price. It means education of a nation that has always been isolationist at heart. We love our own country. We have felt that our salvation lay in living within ourselves. Now suddenly we say to our people, "You cannot live for yourselves alone. You depend on the rest of the world and the rest of the world depends on you." That is a very hard lesson to learn. You haven't had any of these things happen to you that I have been telling you about. Yet interdependence is what we have to learn if we are going to be willing to pay the price for peace. We are today the strongest nation on earth, even though we have disarmed to an extent; that is to say, we have a smaller army and our people don't want to go to war, and we don't want to stay prepared for war, and we don't want to think of production as a world need. Nevertheless, the United States and Russia are the two nations, which, being the youngest, have the greatest vitality. I am not minimizing Great Britain's strength. I am not minimizing what Great Britain did for us when she stood alone for a whole year. We can never forget what Mr. Churchill's leadership meant in winning the war, but we should not have our vision clouded by thinking that the English-speaking people of the world, despite their strength, can get along without the far greater number of people that are not English-speaking.[16]

It is going to take much patience for us to learn about other people. We haven't been interested very much, and we have a lot to learn. They have a lot to learn about us. I know only too well some of the things that I consider fundamental that other nations don't consider quite so fundamental. There is one thing that I think we have to realize, however, and that is that we have taken for granted too much the fact that saying, "We are a republic and our way of life is democratic" does not teach people what we mean, nor is it telling them what the things are that we believe in and are willing to die for. It is much easier if you can just tell people a few things that they must believe and put it in very simple words and have them repeat it parrot fashion. Unfortunately, you cannot do that with democracy. Democracy is something you really have to understand and live. It is a little hard for people in other parts of the world not to find us at times a little inconsistent in our democracy.[17] They sometimes wonder whether some of the things which we say are really things we believe in, or whether they are just words that sound pretty.

Someone said to me in the Press Club,[18] "Well, we are not living up to the Atlantic Charter."[19] No, perhaps not; neither do we live up to everything in our Constitution,[20] but I think it is good for us to have the Constitution and the Bill of Rights[21] and I think it is a good thing for us to have the Atlantic Charter. I think it is a good thing to realize that 51 nations agreed to the Atlantic Charter. There will be things that all of us don't live up to right along and it would be well for us to remember that there are nations that have a great deal to learn and that are still young and are growing nations.

We have to have our own convictions and our faith so clear that we can state them and live by them and prove that what we say we actually mean, so we can say quite plainly that "we are not afraid of your beliefs; we can live in the same world with you, though you differ from us, because we can meet the needs of our people; and 20 years from now our people will have more of what they want than your people will have, and therein lies the proof that our beliefs are the best beliefs in the world." Just saying that you don't believe in certain things is all right, but you have to be able to prove what you say and the proof is the real achievement, over the years, of happiness for your people. No happiness can come to any people if we allow another world war.

I cannot tell you what destruction is. No one can. I think I will tell you one story which filled me with horror. In Great Britain today they have a little more than they have in Holland. Actually they have a great deal more, although we wouldn't think it much. Holland is hard hit. So, Great Britain takes several hundred children and keeps them 3 or 4 months and they go back much better in body than when they came. These children had to be outfitted in England. I suppose you wonder why it was necessary to outfit them there; the reason is you cannot buy anything in Holland today. You cannot buy a sheet of paper or a pen or a pencil. There are no consumer goods. You cannot buy anything in Russia. You cannot buy anything in any of these countries.

The children come over and they are given a set of clothes and a pair of shoes. The women who were doing the outfitting in England found that the children required shoes that were two sizes larger than the clothes they wore. That seemed odd. They pass two medical examinations, one in Holland and one in England. The medical examiners are careful because when people have been hungry (and some of them under the German occupation have starved because the calories were between 800 and 1,000) their resistance becomes pretty badly depleted and they are therefore prone to carry diseases and start them. So they have two examinations; yet no one had any explanation as to why they take shoes that are two sizes larger than the clothes they need and why they wear them out twice as quickly as the British children do. So, an orthopedic surgeon and an X-ray machine were brought to the camp where they were and they X-rayed the feet of those children and watched them walk. The feet spread out, heels going down first and then the toes and a shuffle. The X-rays showed that there were no bones in their feet; there was just gristle. That was the result of lack of food, of hunger. They were given calcium and they went back much better, but that is just one more tragic thing that war brings in its wake. There are many, many more stories I could tell. I could go on for a long time trying to tell you what this means to people, physically, mentally, and spiritually.

Somehow we have to understand, because unless we do, the leadership that we can take will slip out of our hands and the results will not just be bad for Europe, they will be equally bad for us in 2 or 3 or 5 years. We are a great production nation and we need people to buy from us. Economic questions are tied up with political questions the world over today. Don't ever look at anything that happens anywhere without trying to see it from all sides.

The fear of war (because most of these people know what war is and fear it) the fear of not being secure, of being invaded and the fear of the economic situation affects the political situation also. We have to understand things that we have never understood or really cared about before, things that we were glad to turn our backs on, things that we hoped profoundly would never be our business. Today it is our business, if we don't want war.

Everyone of us hopes in our hearts that if war comes again it will not be in our country any more than it was this time. I wonder how many of you read Goering's testimony today, that he had asked before the war in Germany came for the building of planes that would carry destruction to our production cities and get back to Germany, and he had asked for that before the war started.[22]

Don't let's fool ourselves that another war will see us come away scot free again. Let us know what has happened to the nations where war has been on their doorstep. Let's face what has happened to people and let's make up our minds whether we are ready to pay the price of peace. If we are, we are not going to be afraid to stand up for the things that we believe in in the world; oh, no, but we are going to examine what we do believe in and why, and we are going to look at the rest of the world, at least we are going to try to look at what other people need and what they believe in and what their fears and desires are, and see whether 51 nations meeting together can face those problems and deal with them collectively.

Let's stop counting entirely on individual strength and try to build up collective strength, not just collective military strength but collective moral and spiritual and economic strength, so that the world may be able to live in the future. Hunger, lack of opportunity, poverty, unhappy people—they make war; they make revolutions, and there are no more unreachable places. An epidemic today can reach us just as easily from Europe or from the Far East as if it started right in our midst.

Every morning remember that the thing we should pray for first is: God, give us understanding of what we have been spared and make us truly grateful, but in addition give us the strength to see that the sacrifices of those we loved have not been made in vain and to remember day in and day out that there is a price for peace, that we work for it just as we work in war, and that only through our work together can the world have hope in the future.

PSp HSTOF, HSTL

---

1. The Women's Joint Congressional Committee formed in 1920 after the achievement of women's suffrage. It consisted of twenty-two national women's organizations, with a combined total of more than ten million women members, working to lobby Congress on behalf of women. The twenty-two members included the American Association of University Women, the American Dietetic Association, the American Home Economics Association, the American Medical Women's Association, the American Nurses' Association, the American Psychotherapy Association, the Association for Childhood Education, the General Federation of Women's Clubs, the Girls' Friendly Society of the USA, the National Association of Nursery Education, the National Board of the Young Women's Christian Association, the National Congress of Parents and Teachers, the National Consumers' League, the National Council of Jewish Women, the National Education Association, the National Federation of Business and Professional Women's Clubs, the National Women's Trade Union League of America, the Service Star Legion, the United Council of Church Women, and the Women's National Homeopathic Medical Fraternity ("Proceedings at Dinner in Honor of Mrs. Franklin D. Roosevelt," 14 March 1946, 3, HSTOF, HSTL).

2. Remarks, Senator Tom Connally, "Proceedings at Dinner in Honor of Mrs. Franklin D. Roosevelt," 14 March 1946, 8, HSTOF, HSTL.

3. Mrs. Louis Ottenberg, vice chairman of the Women's Joint Congressional Committee, representing the National Council of Jewish Women ("Proceedings at Dinner in Honor of Mrs. Franklin D. Roosevelt," 14 March 1946, 5, HSTOF, HSTL).

4. Edith Bolling Galt (Mrs. Woodrow) Wilson ("Proceedings at Dinner in Honor of Mrs. Franklin D. Roosevelt," 14 March 1946, 7, HSTOF, HSTL).

5. Dorothy Fosdick, State Department advisor to the US Delegation to the General Assembly of the United Nations. See *n*19 Document 75.

6. Calling the food crisis in Europe "the worst hunger crisis in human history," Truman announced February 6 a 25 percent reduction in the amount of grain, meat, dairy products, fats, and oil available to the United States so that the United States might increase its food contribution to the UNRRA campaign against hunger in Europe. Reaction to the proposal was swift and decidedly mixed. That afternoon, leading US food producers criticized the sudden announcement, arguing that the proposal would reinstate food rationing and lower the profits the producers could receive. As criticism escalated, Truman asked former president Hoover, who served as food administrator during World War I, to coordinate the food collection effort (Felix Blair, "Asks We Eat Less," *NYT*, 8 February 1946, 1; "Food Men Upset by Truman Order," *NYT*, 8 February 1946, 8; "Hoover Urges U.S. to Heed Food Plea," *NYT*, 9 February, 5).

7. ER attended the Allenswood School in England from 1899 to 1902 (Cook, vol. 1, 101, 120).

8. ER went to Europe for the first time when she was six, visiting Germany, Austria, Italy, and France with her parents. During her years at Allenswood, she visited France and Italy, this time with Marie Souvestre, the director of the school. On their honeymoon, ER and FDR visited England, France, Italy, and Switzerland. On all of these trips, ER sometimes visited or stayed in the homes of people native to those countries (Lash, *Eleanor*, 34–37, 84–85, 147–50).

9. In January 1919, just after the end of World War I, ER visited the devastated battlefields of France with FDR, then assistant secretary of the navy (Lash, *Eleanor*, 231–32).

10. In 1929, ER motored through Ireland, England, Belgium, Germany, and France, and visited the World War I battlefields with Nancy Cook, Marion Dickerman, and two of her sons, John and Franklin Jr. (Lash, *Eleanor*, 32–33; Cook, vol. 1, 412–14).

11. ER is actually referring to her trip of 1929 (see *n*10 above). She spent most of 1928 working on Al Smith's campaign for the presidency. Between July and September 1929 she toured Europe with Franklin, Jr., John, Marion Dickerman, and Nancy Cook. The portion of the tour in England included visits to the Lake District, Stratford-on-Avon, Stonehenge, Salisbury, Winchester, Oxford, Hampton Court, and London. In her autobiography, ER again compared her feelings about Europe after each of the World Wars; she experienced the overwhelming "sense of the loss of a generation" (Davis, 94; Lash, *Eleanor*, 309–33; ER, *TIR*, 60).

12. The French retreated from the River Marne in 1914 after the first battle they fought there with the Germans during World War I (*OEWH*).

13. Franklin Roosevelt, Jr.

14. After its defeat in World War II, the Allies divided Germany into four zones of occupation: American, British, Russian, and French. The American forces controlled Bavaria, Wurttemberg, and Thuringia, as well as a supply corridor through Bremen, which remained under British control (*OEWH*; "Zones in Reich Listed," *NYT*, 13 May 1945, 10).

15. General Lucius Clay (1897-1978) served as General Dwight D. Eisenhower's deputy in charge of civil-military affairs in the American zone of occupied Germany. See *n*13 Document 94.

16. The transcript indicates that "prolonged applause" interrupted ER's remarks ("Proceedings at Dinner in Honor of Mrs. Franklin D. Roosevelt," 14 March 1946, 12, HSTOF, HSTL).

17. The audience received ER's remark with "laughter" ("Proceedings at Dinner in Honor of Mrs. Franklin D. Roosevelt," 14 March 1946, 12, HSTOF, HSTL).

18. The Women's Press Club of London bestowed an honorary membership upon ER on February 4. On this occasion she spoke about the first meetings of the United Nations and referred explicitly to tensions between Soviet and British delegates, believing it better to discuss disagreements rather than allow issues to "boil under the surface until they explode." See also ER's references to her press club speech in her diary entries and Document 88 ("London Roosevelt Memorial Pilgrims' Aim; Society Breaks Custom in Dinner to Widow," *NYT*, 5 February 1946, 5).

19. FDR and Churchill issued the Atlantic Charter after their first wartime conference in August 1941 as a statement of principles intended to shape the postwar world. Among the principles included were: the right of people to self-determination, the renunciation of territorial claims, the protection of nations against forced changes in territory, free trade, and freedom from want and fear. After the United States entered the war in December 1941, these principles became the war aims of the Allies and were later incorporated into the charter of the United Nations (*OEWH*).

20. "Laughter" again interrupted ER's sentence ("Proceedings at Dinner in Honor of Mrs. Franklin D. Roosevelt," 14 March 1946, 12, HSTOF, HSTL).

21. The transcript shows that "applause" disrupted ER mid-sentence ("Proceedings at Dinner in Honor of Mrs. Franklin D. Roosevelt," 14 March 1946, 12, HSTOF, HSTL).

22. Beginning on March 13, 1946, Hermann Wilhelm Göring (1893–1946) testified at his Nuremberg trial on German preparations for and conduct during World War II, defending Nazi policies and his own role in them. Göring, who had been commander of the Nazi paramilitary "Brownshirts" during the 1920s, became head of the German air force in 1934 and leader of the German rearmament program. He directed the Gestapo, which he created, until 1936 when Hitler put him in charge of managing the German economy. In 1943, after Göring had become addicted to drugs, Hitler ordered his immediate arrest and execution, fearing that Göring was attempting to make peace with the Allies and take over power from Hitler. During his testimony, however, Göring denied any disloyalty to Hitler and regretted that in the Fuhrer's last will and testament that he indicated his belief that Göring secretly negotiated with the enemy (Raymond Daniel, "Goering Defends Nazi Suppression from Witness Stand in Nuremberg," *NYT*, 14 March 1946, 1; "Göring in the Box," *TL*, 14 March 1946, 4; "Göring Denies Betrayal," *TL*, 19 March 1946, 4; *OEWH*).

For discussion of Göring's plan to derail American attempts to send military forces to support European allies, see Raymond Daniel, "Goering Cites Plan to Neutralize U.S.," *NYT*, 16 March 1946, 8.

On Winston Churchill

On March 5, 1946, Winston Churchill, now a private citizen, gave a speech at Westminster College in Fulton, Missouri, in which he applied the term "iron curtain" to the division between those countries in Eastern Europe that had come under Soviet domination after World War II and the non-Communist countries of Western Europe: "From Stettin in the Baltic to Trieste in the Adriatic," he declared, "an iron curtain has descended across the Continent." With President Truman in the audience, Churchill urged a strong alliance between Great Britain and the United States to curtail "the expansive and proselytizing tendencies" of the Soviet Union, an alliance that he felt was better equipped than the United Nations to protect democracy, keep the peace, and handle matters as vital as atomic secrets.[1]

Two days later, ER argued in My Day that "the situation does not seem to me to differ very greatly from the old balance of power politics that have been going on in Europe for hundreds of years." She then assessed Churchill's thesis:

> I think the time has come for us as a nation, perhaps for various nations, throughout the world to decide what really offers us the best chances for peace in the future. Mr. Churchill's speech in Missouri indicates his belief as a private individual that the future peace of the world can best be guaranteed by a military alliance between Great Britain and the United States. He believes that the people of both our countries want peace, but for some reason he is not equally sure apparently that this is the case where the peoples of other nations are concerned. I think he pays the English speaking people of the world a very high compliment. I hope that we could be trusted to have no selfish desires, not to think of our own interests first and therefore never to take advantage of our strength at the expense of other peoples. We must, however, it seems to me face the fact that were such an alliance formed other nations in the world would certainly feel that they must form independent alliances too. What is sauce for the goose must also be sauce for the gander.
>
> … Instead of running an armament race against each other and building up trade cartels and political alliances, we the nations of the world should join together each contributing a certain amount of military strength to be used only against an aggressor. We would use the forum of the United Nations to discuss our difficulties and our grievances using our diplomatic machinery to adjust such things as we could among ourselves, but bringing questions that individual governments disagreed on before the bar of the United Nations as a whole … I do not wonder that the elderly statesmen think this a new and revolutionary move in the international situation. I will grant that there are two possibilities here, the old way and the new way. We have seen the results of the old way, however, in war and destruction and we may still see starvation and pestilence stalk the earth as a result of the old way. Might it be wise to try the new way?[2]

ER's close friend, Arthur Murray, Lord Elibank, expressed similar concerns about Churchill's speech in the following letter. In it he refers to an evening he and ER spent in London during the first session of the General Assembly discussing the world situation.[3]

100

Arthur Murray to Eleanor Roosevelt

19 March 1946 [Edinburgh]

My dear Eleanor,

These are just a few lines—which do not expect or require an answer—to hope that, since your arrival home, you have been able to take some kind of a rest after your very hard, but fruitful work, when you were over here.[4]

You will soon be in the midst of U.N.O. activities again, and no doubt some of the same atmosphere which circulated through the meetings in London, will prevail again! This time, however, the atmosphere will have had some heat added to it by what I, and all my friends over here, consider to be the unnecessarily mischievous tone of certain passages in the speech made by Churchill at Fulton. I think you should be left in no doubt as to the feeling generally expressed by men of all parties in this country that the utterance was one of great unwisdom, and a source of embarrassment, as we know, to Bevin, the British Foreign Secretary; and as we feel, to your Secretary of State.[5] You know—because I outlined them to you during that evening (to which I look back with so much pleasure) when you dined with me at Carrington House—what my views have been on the subject of Russian imperialistic expansion.[6] On the other hand, there was one way and one way only to deal with any expansionist sentiments or actions on the part of Russia and that was through and by U.N.O., thus helping U.N.O., in immeasurable degree at the outset of its rough and difficult journey, to gather strength and purpose for its task of solving international differences and quarrels on a peaceful and not a warlike basis. Into this arena with all its difficulties and troubles, plunges, like a bull in a china shop, Winston Churchill. We will leave it at that.

The weather has been bitterly cold since you left but it is now more spring-like.

With every good wish.

Always yours very sincerely,
Arthur Murray

TLS AERP, FDRL

101

Eleanor Roosevelt to Arthur Murray

13 April 1946 [Hyde Park]

My dear Arthur:

I enjoyed your note very much.

Mr. Churchill thought it wise to make amends in his second speech, but the first one was very unwise.[7] There are some things which should be taken for granted. Certainly the United Nations will have all of the problems that one could think of at the present time.

With every good wish, I am,

Very cordially yours,
Eleanor Roosevelt

TLS PACM, StEdNL-M

1. Hamby, *Man*, 348; Harold B. Hinton, "Briton Speaks Out," *NYT*, 6 March 1946, 1.

2. *MD*, 7 March 1946. ER continued to criticize the speech in her remarks before the Women's Joint Congressional Committee (see Document 99) and in her March 27, 1946, column.

3. For Arthur Murray and ER's account of the evening in London with him, see *n*29 Document 84.

4. From December 31, 1945, to February 19, 1946, ER attended the first session of the United Nations General Assembly in London (January 10–February 15, 1946) and toured refugee camps in Germany (Meisler, 358; *MD*, 31 December 1945, and 16, 18, and 19 February 1946; James B. Reston, "Assembly of UNO Adjourns; Organization Survives Test," *NYT*, 15 February 1946, 1).

5. The British Labour government resisted demands from its left wing to repudiate Churchill's speech, but it tried to disassociate itself from his remarks by saying that he spoke as a private citizen. Undersecretary Hector McNeil, speaking on behalf of Foreign Secretary Ernest Bevin, said that "the question of an Anglo-United States military alliance has not arisen" and that Britain intended to continue to pursue its foreign policy goals through the United Nations (Ramsden, 156, 168; Herbert L. Matthews, "Britain Is Shaken by Russia's Moves," *NYT*, 12 March 1946, 1).

6. In her London diary of January 27, ER does not say what Murray said to her, but does mention that she disagreed with him on one point: "I'm not so convinced that Great Britain and ourselves must line up to keep the Russians in hand. I think we must be fair and stand for what we believe is right and let them either or both, side with us." See Document 84.

7. Churchill's "Iron Curtain Speech" generated both strong support and a storm of criticism from Stalin and the British and American left. Ten days later, speaking in New York City, Churchill said, "I do not wish to withdraw or modify a single word," but took a more conciliatory stance. "It's my earnest desire that Russia should be safe and prosperous." He then admitted that he favored a cooperative relationship between Britain and the United States rather than a military alliance, conceded that the Russians did not currently want to go to war, recognized the great losses they suffered during the war, and praised them for all their contributions to defeating the Nazis. "There is deep and widespread sympathy throughout, if I may be permitted to use the expression, the English-speaking world for the people of Russia, and an absolute readiness to work with them on fair and even terms to repair the ruin of war in every country." However, he warned, "If the Soviet Government does not take advantage of this sentiment, if on the contrary they discourage it, or chill it, the responsibility will be entirely theirs" (Ramsden, 160–61; "Text of Speech by Churchill at Dinner Given in His Honor by City," *NYT*, 16 March 1946, 2).

ELEANOR ROOSEVELT
AND THE COLUMBIA, TENNESSEE, RIOT

What began as a conflict between two African Americans and a white radio repairman on the morning of February 25, 1946, erupted into a situation that the national press described as a "race riot" in the small town of Columbia, Tennessee. That morning, unsatisfied with the repair work performed by William Fleming, Gladys Stephenson took her son James, recently returned from overseas service in the navy, to demand a refund. Heated words turned into a physical conflict between Fleming and James Stephenson. When the sheriff arrived on the scene, he arrested the Stephensons. News of Stephenson's physical confrontation with Fleming attracted a large crowd of armed whites to the town square who demanded that the sheriff turn over James Stephenson. Unbeknownst to the crowd gathered in the square, the sheriff released the Stephensons after leaders of the black community posted bond for the mother and son.

As they watched the crowd of whites increase in size, members of the black community took up arms to protect themselves from what seemed an imminent raid on their section of town. Their fear was not ungrounded: whites in Columbia had, on two separate occasions in the last two decades, lynched African Americans. Meanwhile, "a big bunch" of fifty beer-drinking whites tried to kick in the side door of the jail to kidnap the Stephensons. After the sheriff repelled their attack, two other whites, armed with revolvers and a shotgun, took a gallon of gasoline to burn down the Bottom, the African American business district. As the two arsonists entered the alley, both were wounded by shots fired from nearby buildings. Recognizing that the situation had escalated to the point where he could no longer control the townspeople, the sheriff called in the governor, who ordered the Tennessee State Guard and Highway Patrol to intervene.

The Highway Patrol raided the Bottom early in the morning of February 26. At least one member of the black community opened fire during the initial attack of the patrolmen. The troopers responded by emptying 125 rounds of ammunition into the building from which the shot was fired. They then proceeded to storm through the Bottom, destroying black property and beating the community's men, who, frightened by the troopers' quickness to open fire, now offered little resistance. In all, the troopers arrested more than 100 African Americans and detained them in the Columbia jailhouse. Two days later, after one prisoner seized a weapon and took aim at an officer, troopers released several rounds, killing two men and seriously wounding another. These two deaths, the first casualties during the series of events in Columbia, attracted the attention of the national press.[1]

The press tended to accept the view that the African Americans of Columbia were to blame. Both the *New York Times* and *Washington Post* ran the Associated Press article that included only the testimony of whites involved. The AP reporter included the sheriff's interpretation of events, which "attributed the disturbance to high feeling engendered by an altercation yesterday in which a Negro woman and her son pushed a white radio repairman through a window and the subsequent wounding of four policemen."[2]

NAACP leaders, fearing both a recurrence of racial violence and racially skewed prosecution strategy, immediately began preparing for the defense of those African Americans whose fate an all-white grand jury would soon decide. On March 14, the NAACP invited several organizations to its New York office and established the National Committee for Justice for Columbia, Tennessee. Having worked with ER in similar circumstances and knowing of ER's relationship with those whom he had asked to join the committee, Walter White then wired ER asking if she would serve as its co-chair.[3]

102

Walter White to Eleanor Roosevelt
19 March 1946

WOULD YOU BE WILLING TO SERVE AS CO-CHAIRMAN WITH DR. CHANNING H. TOBIAS OF A NATION-
AL COMMITTEE TO PUBLICIZE THE TRUTH AND PROVIDE DEFENSE FOR THE VICTIMS OF THE COLUM-
BIA, TENNESSEE RIOT. AS NEARLY AS WE CAN ASCERTAIN FROM THE AUTHORITIES MORE THAN 100
NEGROES ARE HELD ON VARIOUS CHARGES. LAST THURSDAY A MEETING OF 25 NATIONAL ORGANIZA-
TIONS CALLED BY NAACP AGREED TO ACT JOINTLY NOT ONLY IN DEFENDING INNOCENT VICTIMS AND
BRINGING GUILTY TO JUSTICE BUT TO STIR AND EDUCATE PUBLIC OPINION SO AS TO PREVENT REPE-
TITION OF SUCH OUTBREAKS. PLEASE WIRE COLLECT IF YOU WILL DO US THE HONOR OF SERVING.

Walter White

Tel NAACP, DLC

103

Eleanor Roosevelt to Walter White
22 March 1946 [en route to Los Angeles]

Mr. Walter White

HAPPY TO SERVE WITH DR. TOBIAS BUT FEAR UNABLE TO DO ANY WORK.

Mrs. Roosevelt

Tel NAACP, DLC

> On March 13, the day before the NAACP met with several groups in New York City, the
> Southern Conference of Human Welfare (SCHW)[4] sponsored the National Emergency
> Conference to Stop Lynch Terror in Columbia in Washington, DC. The sixty organiza-
> tions in attendance formed the United Committee Against Police Terror in Columbia,
> Tennessee,[5] and appointed SCHW President Clark Foreman[6] chairman and Mary
> McLeod Bethune vice-chairman.
>
> Bethune quickly realized that the two groups would be more effective if they com-
> bined their effort, and she voiced her position to ER in the following letter, which she
> copied to Foreman and the NAACP's Walter White and Channing Tobias.

104

Mary McLeod Bethune to Eleanor Roosevelt
23 March 1946 [Washington, DC]

My dear Mrs. Roosevelt:

We are most deeply concerned about the Columbia Tennessee police terror. It is most timely, in my opinion, for the most efficient, united effort that can be welded together, to give all that

we have in suppressing this situation, in order that it may not become a pattern for the entire country.

I am delighted that you have accepted the co-chairmanship with Dr. Tobias. You probably know that sixty odd organizations met in Washington to form a committee against this police terror in Columbia. This group formed a steering committee which chose Clark Foreman, as chairman and me as Vice-Chairman. Both Clark Foreman and I feel that you and Dr. Tobias can give the best and most influential direction to this drive, and we are prepared to subordinate our efforts to your leadership and to bring with us the sixty organizations which are already mobilizing their strength throughout the country.

We think it would be very unwise to have two organizations acting separately at the same time for the same purpose. We are all in agreement that the NAACP is the proper agency to handle the legal defense of the indicted Negroes. We however feel that the fight for democracy and decency, including the prosecution of the guilty state officials, cannot be the province of any one organization exclusively. In that fight we need the help of any existing organizations working with us.

In my judgement, we need an organization, in which all groups can unite for action and money raising, with you and Dr. Tobias the over-all chairmen. I hope, Mrs. Roosevelt, that you see that my main object is to prevent friction among the groups that must mobilize to make this an effective finished task.

Sincerely yours,
Mary McLeod Bethune

TLS NAACP, DLC

105

Walter White to Eleanor Roosevelt
25 March 1946

Dear Mrs. Roosevelt:

Mrs. Bethune has been good enough to send me a copy of her letter to you of March 23rd also sending copy to Mr. Clark Foreman.[7] At your earliest convenience I would like to talk this over with you and to give you the facts in greater detail than I can in a letter.

Mrs. Bethune is quite right that there should be no friction among the groups working on the Columbia case. The facts briefly are these:

When we heard, early on the morning of February 26th, of the so-called "riot" at Columbia, we communicated by long distance telephone with Tennessee and dispatched Maurice Weaver, an able and courageous young white lawyer of Chattanooga to Columbia to make an investigation for us in conjunction with Z. Alexander Looby, a member of our National Legal Committee who practices at Nashville.[8] A few days later, I flew to Nashville to help organize the preparations for defense of those victims who were innocent of any wrong doing. All of the defendants requested the NAACP in writing to defend them and we agreed to do so.

Our objectives are:

(1) to provide the maximum defense to those unjustly accused

(2) to utilize all possible means of seeing that the real culprits were brought to justice

(3) to take whatever steps are possible and necessary to secure restitution to those who suffered vandalism or violence and

(4) to mobilize public opinion so that the public will understand the real nature of the case.

We felt that if this pattern of violence could be checked by the above steps it would deter other mobs both in the South and in the North from attempting similar action; that if the pattern were established it might touch off similar explosions all over the country.

On my return to New York I was telephoned by George Marshall of the National Federation for Constitutional Liberties,[9] asking if I would attend, as a representative of the NAACP, a conference his organization, The Southern Conference for Human Welfare, and the United Mine, Mill and Smelter Workers Union were calling in Washington on March 13th. The purpose of the meeting he stated was to organize the defense for the victims of the Columbia riot. I informed Mr. Marshall that I could not be present because the NAACP had invited some 25 organizations to meet here at the Wendell Willkie Building on Thursday, March 14th for the same purpose. Inasmuch as the defendants have asked the NAACP to represent them, we felt that it was preferable that we work out a unified defense and presentation of the case to the country since we were, at the request of the defendants, charged with the responsibility of representing them.

The Washington group, however, went ahead with its plans and held a second meeting on March 18th at which time they voted, according to a letter to me from Clark Foreman, that they are "seeking an underwriting of $20,000 to cover the cost of field organization work and a money-raising campaign". He also informed me that a committee of 3 had been appointed to discuss working with the committee which was formed by the NAACP.

Here is a list of the organizations which met in Washington:[10]

Among them you will note the Communist Party. You and I recognize that the Communists have just as much a right to be active in this and any other case as anyone else. It is to their credit that they want to help. But practically and realistically their active participation in this case would create very heavy additional burdens on the defense and in the achievement of the objective of bringing the guilty to justice and awakening the country to the home-grown fascism and bigotry which lies back of this case. The guilty officials of Maury County and the State of Tennessee and the members of the mob who attempted to lynch Mrs. Gladys Stephenson and her son would welcome with glee the news that the Negro victims were being backed by the Communists. It is a tragic but true circumstance that the state of public opinion in Tennessee and in Maury County in particular is such that the mobbists could ask for no greater assurance of acquittal than to be able to say that this is a "communistic plot." The McKellar-Crump political machine would undoubtedly use this with joy and success in the coming political campaign where the decent people of the state are trying to break the Crump machine and elect a more decent person to the Senate.[11] We are most anxious to avoid anything that would either play into the hands of the would-be lynchers or to jeopardize the welfare of the defendants. What do you advise us to do in this case? Dr. Tobias has agreed to serve as co-chairman with you. Mayor LaGuardia has agreed to serve on the committee along with a number of others but he asked that we select "someone whose name would mean more in that capacity (treasurer)."

Ever sincerely,

TLc NAACP, DLC

> ER agreed that a joint organization would prove more effective than either organization working independently. Despite her original concern that she would be "unable to do any work," ER accepted White's request to chair a meeting of the NAACP and the Washington group's representatives. The groups met for the first time on April 4. Out of this meeting arose a new committee, which thereafter became known as the National Committee for Justice in Columbia, Tennessee (NCJCT).[12]

_106_

Minutes of Meeting of National Committee for Defense of Columbia, Tennessee "Riot" Victims

4 April 1946

Present: Co-Chairmen—Mrs. Roosevelt and Dr. Channing Tobias, group from Washington— Clark Foreman, Milton Kemnitz, Sidney Rodnam; Abraham Unger, National Lawyers Guild;[13] Palmer Weber,[14] CIO-PAC; Mary McLeod Bethune; Arthur B. Spingarn;[15] Justin Feldman, American Veterans Committee;[16] George Marshall, National Federation for Constitutional Liberties;[17] Dr. George Haynes,[18] Federal Council of Churches; Ollie Harrington[19] and Mr. White.

Mr. Foreman pointed out that despite the fact that the "riot" occurred in Tennessee it could have happened anywhere because there is a decided trend to "put the returning Negro veteran in his place" and that Tennessee is only the beginning. Mr. Foreman said that this is such a grave menace to democracy itself that everyone as individuals and organizations must mobilize to meet it.

Mr. Feldman pointed out that not only the question of raising money was important but also some sort of educational program which would be directed to the people of the nation which would indicate what the nature of the incident was and just how they can possibly guard against such violence recurring. Also the question of defending the victims of the attack, punishment of the officers guilty of the crime and whatever legal efforts are possible to get property damage restitution.

There was lengthy discussion concerning the inclusion of the Communist Party in the group working in coordination with the NAACP. Mrs. Roosevelt pointed out that should the Communist Party be part of that group there would be furnished the background for a statement by those who are really guilty and others in the South that the whole defense is a "communist plot". Mrs. Roosevelt expressed the opinion that it would endanger the success of our fight to include the Communist Party. Following further discussion, it was decided to turn to other business and work out this problem at a later date, being pointed out that the really important issue was that there was open action on the part of the authorities to try to prevent democracy in the South.

Mr. Weber stated that all important was

(1) that the NAACP have sufficient funds to carry on legal defense

(2) that there be a national educational drive on the question of race relations

(3) political work in the South and developing the vote of the Negro there

(4) the forming of a policy-steering committee that the people have confidence in and would also have support of all organizations.

Dr. Tobias expressed the opinion that in an emergency situation like the Columbia, Tennessee case people immediately begin to think in terms of organizations. This, he pointed out, can be harmful, as it has been in the past. He said that the rank and file, and particularly colored people, have turned to the NAACP because of its history in the winning of legal battles. He felt that since the NAACP has commanded the confidence of the people of the country, it was only logical that the legal defense be handled by the NAACP.

Mrs. Bethune stated that she was fully in accord with Dr. Tobias' statement.

Dr. Haynes agreed also and pointed out that in defending the victims of the "riot" there must be an example set for the entire world. He felt that the proposed steering committee be not more that 10 persons. He felt that the NAACP should choose such a committee since it had the responsibility of defending the victims. There was further discussion as to the process of setting up such a committee.

Mrs. Roosevelt summarized the suggestions—that the NAACP should appoint a small steering committee chosen from both groups and that that steering committee should formulate policy and make reports to the groups that are willing to take part in the three-fold program and not in any way interfere with the defense of the people but raise money for their defense, promote educational work and try to prevent the recurrence of such violence.

Dr. Haynes suggested that power be given the steering committee to outline the basic guiding basis of inclusion of groups, what they are to do and responsibility the group is to share.

Mr. White was of the opinion that the Association not choose the steering committee but that the co-chairmen select that group.

Mr. Spingarn made a motion that the co-chairmen be authorized to select that steering committee. The motion was seconded by Mrs. Bethune. An amendment was made by Mr. Foreman that the steering committee have power to raise money and to integrate whatever individuals and organizations it sees fit to.

It was suggested that a list of names be submitted to the co-chairmen from which would be selected a steering committee. Mr. Spingarn disagreed on the basis that members might overlook some capable persons. The co-chairmen requested that names be submitted to them and in the event that they thought of additional names such names would be circulated. The steering committee was given power to select its own chairman and that the co-chairmen of the National Committee be officers ex-oficio. There being no further business, the meeting was adjourned.

TMins NAACP, DLC

––––––––––––––

1. O'Brien, 7–40, quote 16–17; A. Black, *Casting*, 97–98.

2. "Disorders Halted in Tennessee City," *NYT*, 27 February 1946, 29; "Tenn. Rioting Ends; Troops Seize Weapons," *WP*, 27 February 1946, 5; "Sit-Down Staged by 568 Convicts," *NYT*, 1 March 1946, 2.

3. ER had close ties with four of the organizations attending the NAACP planning meeting—the Southern Conference on Human Welfare, the CIO-PAC, the Chicago Civil Liberties Committee, and the National Federation of Civil Liberties. ER had also worked closely with White on the NAACP's anti-lynching campaign and its defense of the imprisoned sharecropper Odell Waller, and had helped the NAACP secure the financial support critical to its legal efforts (A. Black, *Casting*, 37–41, 94, 137).

4. Founded in 1938 with both FDR and ER's strong support, the Southern Conference on Human Welfare brought together non-Communist Southern liberals dedicated to addressing the stark economic and racial conditions confronting states south of the Mason-Dixon Line. Led by the CIO-organizer Joseph Gelders, SCHW targeted southern employment practices (specifically the South's violent anti-union sentiments and its reliance on sharecropping and tenant farmers) and its strong support of the poll tax. Its board included ER, University of North Carolina President Frank Pert Graham, Lucy Randolph Mason, Clark Foreman, and Mary McLeod Bethune (Sitkoff, 128–32).

5. A. Black, *Casting*, 98; O'Brien, 34. For a list of the organizations involved in this committee, see *n*10 below.

6. Clark H. Foreman (1902–1977), a white, Harvard-educated Georgian who dedicated his career to civil rights action after witnessing a lynching, had impressed ER with his dedication to promoting civil rights prior to his taking action on the Columbia case. In 1942, ER defended Foreman when, as the director of defense housing for the Federal Works Agency, he provoked public criticism by using federal funds to construct the Sojourner Truth housing project in Detroit in an attempt to offer low-income housing to African Americans. Foreman, delighted at the prospect of working with

ER once again, wrote her on March 25 to add his "full concurrence" with this letter from Bethune (Werner Bamberger, "Clark H. Foreman, 75," *NYT*, 16 June 1977, 47; A. Black, *Casting*, 91; O'Brien, 34; Clark Foreman to ER, 25 March 1946, MMBP, DeWaMMB).

7. For Clark Foreman see *n*6 above.

8. Z. Alexander Looby (1899–1972), a graduate of Howard University, New York University, and Columbia Law School, was, until 1950, the sole African American attorney in Nashville. In 1951, he became the first African American elected to the Nashville City Council; and he represented Nashville students suing to implement *Brown v. Board of Education of Topeka et al.* Six years later, white critics of his defense of students engaged in sit-ins bombed his home. The bombing did not dissuade Looby (Untitled Article, *WP*, 26 March 1972, D10).

9. George Marshall (1904–2000), an economist, lawyer, and political activist, served as chairman of the National Federation for Constitutional Liberties (NFCL), an organization which merged with the International Labor Defense in April 1946 to form the Civil Rights Congress (CRC). Like its predecessors, the CRC fought to end the persecution of African Americans and Communist Party members alike, making the anti-Communist leaders of the NAACP uneasy. The CRC disbanded in 1956, following the House Committee on Un-American Activities' nine-year attack on the CRC. During the investigation, Marshall, who refused to turn over records to the committee, served a three-month prison term for contempt of Congress ("George Marshall," Obituaries, *Columbia College Today*, May 2001, http://www.college.columbia.edu/cct/may01/may01_obituaries.html, accessed March 1, 2006; "Civil Rights Group Called Red 'Front,'" *NYT*, 31 August 1947, 2; "Civil Rights Congress Votes for Dissolution," *NYT*, 10 January 1956, 25; C. Anderson, 60, 168–70).

10. White included the following list of organizations in the body of his letter: Southern Conference for Human Welfare; National Federation for Constitutional Liberties; International Union of Mine, Mill and Smelter Workers; National Association for the Advancement of Colored People, Houston, Texas, and Arlington, Virginia; National Negro Congress; American Veterans Committee; Congress of Industrial Organizations; Independent Citizens Committee; Interracial Fellowship League; African Methodist Episcopal Church, Chicago, Illinois; National Maritime Union; National Council of Negro Women; Metropolitan Community Church, Chicago, Illinois; League of Women Shoppers; National Lawyers Guild; Institute of Applied Religion; Communist Party; Amalgamated Clothing Workers; Chicago Civil Liberties Committee; National Council for Permanent Fair Employment Practices Committee; Methodist Federation for Social Service; Civil Rights Federation; Hudson County CIO Council; United Federal Workers; Cafeteria Workers, CIO; Methodist Church; United Office & Professional Workers of America; Fur and Leather Workers; United Steel Workers of America; International Longshoreman Warehouseman's Union; United People's Action Committee, Philadelphia, Pennsylvania; State, County and Municipal Workers of America; Congress for Civil Rights; American Youth for Democracy; Chicago Action Council; Farm Equipment Workers; Veterans-Citizens Committee to Oust Bilbo; American League Post 87, Chicago; International Workers Order; Federation of Colored Women; Delta Sigma Theta; Chicago Council of Negro Organizations; United Automobile Workers; United Packinghouse Workers; American Legion FDR Post; American Committee for Spanish Freedom; American Communications Association; N.C. Federation of Women's Clubs (colored); North Carolina Committee for Human Welfare; Washington Independent Union Council; Alpha Kappa Alpha Non-Partisan Council; Congress of Women's Auxiliaries; Hotel and Club Employees Union; the United Electrical, Radio and Machine Workers of America; as well as numerous local organizations, clergymen, professors, and other public-spirited individuals.

11. Memphis mayor and investment banker Edward Hull Crump (1876–1954) ran a political machine that controlled the Democratic Party in Tennessee for over twenty years. As a political boss, Crump opposed the Ku Klux Klan and supported FDR; however, he insisted that organized labor had no place in politics. When progressive groups such as the Congress of Industrial Organizations began to challenge his authority in the late 1930s, Crump denounced them as

Communists to discredit their efforts. Crump's power was not restricted to party politics. As long as his machine remained in power, he also controlled the state police and highway patrol, and he hired men who exerted force (both physical and political) in ways less "benevolent" than the Crump machine's "benevolent dictatorship." In 1946, Edward W. Carmack, backed by the CIO, challenged Crump's grip on state politics by running against Sen. Kenneth D. McKellar (D-TN), chairman of the Senate Appropriations Committee and Crump's strongest ally. On election day, demonstrations against the Crump machine grew so intense that when veterans protested in Athens, Tennessee, a deputy sheriff died trying to disperse the crowd. McKellar won the primary by a 75,000 vote margin (Harold B. Hinton, "Crump of Tennessee: Portrait of a Boss," *NYT*, 29 September 1946, 120; "He Liked to Run Things," *NYT*, 18 October 1954, 24; Virginius Dabney, "The Upper South: McKellar's Rival Plans 80 Tennessee Speeches," *NYT*, 26 May 1946, E8; *DAB*).

12. A. Black, *Casting*, 98. Quote taken from Document 103.

13. Abraham Unger (1899–1975) established himself as an attorney committed to the defense of civil rights and civil liberties by representing the African Americans accused of rape in the Scottsboro case in the 1930s and members of the Communist Party indicted under the Smith Act in the 1940s. Unger represented the National Lawyers Guild, an organization of legal professionals "who seek actively to eliminate racism; who work to maintain and protect our civil rights and liberties in the face of persistent attacks upon them; and who look upon the law as an instrument for the protection of the people rather than for their repression" ("Abraham Unger Is Dead at 76," *NYT*, 17 July 1975, 32; National Lawyers Guild, "About Us: Mission and History," http://www.nlg.org/about/aboutus.htm, accessed 1 March 2006).

14. Frederick Palmer Weber (1914–1975), a former teacher of philosophy and economics at the University of Virginia where he received his Ph.D., worked as research director of the Political Action Committee of the CIO, a position he had held since 1944 ("F. Palmer Weber, 72, Is Dead," *NYT*, 24 August 1986, 36).

15. Arthur Barnett Spingarn (1878–1971), an attorney committed to using the courts to fight for civil rights, served concurrently as president of the NAACP (1940–1966) and the NAACP Legal Defense and Education Fund (1940–1957) (*DAB*; Farnsworth Fowle, "Arthur Spingarn of the NAACP Is Dead," *NYT*, 2 December 1971, 1).

16. Justin N. Feldman served as director of veterans affairs of the American Veterans Committee, a racially integrated group of veterans formed as an alternative to the conservative American Legion and the Veterans of Foreign Wars. The American Veterans' Committee mission statement—as printed on its official letterhead—read, "To achieve a more democratic and prosperous America and a more stable world" (Egerton, 328; Justin Feldman to ER, 9 January 1947, AERP).

17. See *n*9 above.

18. George Edmund Haynes (1880–1960), a sociologist who received his Ph.D. from Columbia University (the first African American to earn a doctorate from that institution), studied race relations in the urban setting and actively worked to improve those relations by organizing conferences and clinics, first as the founder and executive secretary of the National Urban League (1910–1917) and then as the executive secretary of the Department of Race Relations of the Federal Council of Churches (1922–1946) (*DAB*; "George E. Haynes, Sociologist, Dies," *NYT*, 10 January 1960, 87).

19. Oliver Wendell Harrington (1912–1995), cartoonist and journalist, illustrated "Bootsie," a comic strip that satirized race relations in the United States, for over thirty-five years. Working as a wartime correspondent for the *Pittsburgh Courier* in Italy, Harrington met Walter White who, after the war ended, hired him to head the NAACP's public relations department. Harrington authored the NAACP's pamphlet describing the events in Columbia, entitled "Terror in Tennessee" (*ANBO*; Eric Pace, "Oliver Harrington, Cartoonist Who Created 'Bootsie,' Dies at 84," *NYT*, 7 November 1995, D22; O'Brien, 35). For the controversy surrounding "Terror in Tennessee," see header, Document 118.

CREATING A MACHINERY FOR PEACE

ER promoted the United Nations whenever and wherever she could. On February 19, 1946, Chester D. Owens, director of education at the progressive Elmira (New York) Reformatory, wrote ER to ask if she would contribute a guest column for *The Summary*, an eight-page weekly publication produced by the Elmira inmates and then circulated among prisoners across the country. ER's article, entitled "Mrs. Roosevelt Speaks," appeared in the March 29 issue.[1]

107

"Mrs. Roosevelt Speaks"
The Summary 29 March 1946

I have just come back from nine weeks in London where I attended the meeting which was attended by delegates of fifty-one countries. These delegates set up the machinery for an organization which we hope will help to preserve the peace of the world. We had thought that if we set up the organization and the members were appointed to the various permanent committees such as the Security Council[2] and the Economic and Social Council[3] and the judges were elected to the International Court[4] and a Secretary General[5] with his assistants[6] was also elected, that nothing further could be done until this latter gentleman had time to organize a secretariat.

Instead of this, a number of very difficult questions were at once handed to the Security Council[7] and while this has been considered by many people a drawback, I think it had good results. It is true that none of these questions were finally decided, but they were discussed and methods by which they could be considered were decided on.[8] Some people felt that because some rather heated language was used,[9] it would be more difficult to arrive at some kind of solution. I personally feel that it was a very good thing to have the discussion and to let everything come out in the open. My reason for feeling this way is not just that the actual members of governments, who exchanged points of view, let off steam and perhaps felt more kindly toward each other afterwards. I felt in addition, that the peoples of the different nations belonging to UNO learned a great deal by the mere fact that such plain language was exchanged and the peoples were obliged to think about what were the rights and wrongs in certain cases. Iran seemed very far away perhaps to most of the nations in the Assembly, but when people became so heated about it, I think a good many people got out their geographies and looked up where Iran was and perhaps began to wonder why Russia and Great Britain were so interested in preserving their influence in that far away and rather arid country.[10]

The first thing everyone thinks of in the case of Iran, is that there is oil there and to Great Britain the pipe line which comes out in the Persian Gulf is important, but to Russia the oil is probably of secondary interest. She has all the oil she needs in other areas,[11] but the outlet on the Persian Gulf and the control of traffic on the railroad is probably of great importance to Russia. It is an outlet for her goods if she has any to send out, and it is the place where imports can come from the Far East and even from the west coast of the United States. Russia is hungry for consumer goods just as we have been, but with her now it is a real need, for her people probably have a great desire to begin to see some results in better living in view of the long period that they have accepted sacrifices in order to prepare to fight a war.

It is somewhat difficult for us to understand nations with entirely different backgrounds and experiences from our own. Nevertheless, if we have any hope of finding peaceful solutions to problems as they arise, we can only do so by learning to have confidence in each other's intentions and integrity. At the present time there is more suspicion than good will in the world, and yet anyone who spent as I did, even a few days in an area where the last war was actually fought,[12] would feel that there is very little choice before us. Either we are going to have peace in the world, or we are going to have complete chaos if we drift into another war. We dropped no atom bombs on Europe and yet we succeeded in destroying the big cities in Germany so thoroughly[13] that when I was asked if Germany should rebuild Berlin, I could not help wondering how one could rebuild a complete ruin.

The material ruins, however, are not the most important. It is the deterioration of people. They have suffered so much in many cases, they are numb, and it will take a long while before they can accept responsibility and show initiative in facing the almost insoluable problems which lie all around them.

One might well say in this country—why bother about Europe, we can get along without her. Unfortunately we might get on well for the next couple of years if we filled our national needs. Unless, however, we began to have people buy from us in other countries, and pay for what they buy, we will not have outlets for the great production capacity which we built up during the war, and which we need if our people are to have employment. This means that we, in the United States, must begin to think not only of our domestic situation, but of ourselves as leaders in a world which needs what we can give. We were spared from destruction and therefore have the strength and power to influence the world situation and can only fulfill our destiny, I believe, by doing so.

TMs AERP, FDRL

---

1. Chester D. Owens to ER, 19 February 1946, AERP; Edens, 44.

2. See Document 89. The UN Security Council comprised five permanent members—the United States, the USSR, Great Britain, France, and China—and six temporary members who served one- or two-year terms. At its first session, the General Assembly elected Brazil, Poland, and Australia to two-year terms and Mexico, Egypt, and the Netherlands to one-year terms ("World News Summarized," *NYT*, 13 January 1946, 1).

3. The UN General Assembly elected China, France, Chile, Canada, Belgium, and Peru for three-year terms and the Soviet Union, United Kingdom, India, Norway, Cuba, and Czechoslovakia for two-year terms, while the United States, Ukraine, Greece, Lebanon, Colombia, and Yugoslavia were elected for one-year terms (Lie, 28; Boyd, 98).

4. On February 6, the UN General Assembly and the Security Council elected fifteen jurists to the International Court of Justice, one of the principal organs of the international organization. They included Judge Green H. Hackworth, legal advisor to Secretary of State James F. Byrnes (United States); Dr. Hsu Mo (China); Charles de Visscher (Belgium); Prof. Jules Basdevant (France); Jose Gustavo Guerrero (El Salvador); Sir Arnold D. McNair (Great Britain); Prof. Sergei Borisovitch Krylov (USSR); Fabela Alfaro (Mexico); Alejandro Alvarez (Chile); J. Philadelpho de Barros Azevedo (Brazil); Abdel Hamid Badawi Pasha (Egypt); John M. Read (Canada); Milovan Zoricitch (Yugoslavia); Helge Klaestad (Norway); Bohdan Winiarski (Poland) (Sydney Gruson, "15 Judges Elected for World Court," *NYT*, 7 February 1946, 8).

5. The UN General Assembly elected Norwegian foreign minister Trygve Lie, the organization's first secretary-general on February 1 (Lie, 17).

6. The earliest staff appointments included Adrian Pelt (the Netherlands) as assistant secretary-general in charge of UN conferences, Arkady Sobolev (USSR) as assistant secretary-general for Security Council affairs, David K. Owen (Great Britain) as executive assistant to the secretary-general, and A. H. Feller (United States) as general council to the secretary-general (Sydney Gruson, "Hollander, Russian in UNO Secretariat," *NYT*, 18 February 1946, 4).

7. Between January 19 and 21, the Security Council received reports on three disputes. Iran complained about the continuing presence of Soviet troops in its territory and Soviet interference in the

province of Azerbaijan. See *n*3 Document 144. In retaliation, the Soviets brought two complaints. Both dealt with the presence of British troops in two separate countries: Greece and Indonesia. On February 4, Syria and Lebanon complained about the presence of British and French troops on their territory in violation of a previous agreement (Chamberlin et al., 12–13; Lie, 30).

8. The Iranian situation ended after the USSR and Great Britain agreed to negotiate directly with one another. After some backstage maneuvering that resulted in a compromise between the two countries (the Soviets agreed to drop their charge that the presence of British troops in Greece constituted a threat to world peace while the British retracted their demand that the Security Council acquit them of the charge), the Greek debate ended with a statement from the Security Council president Norman Makin noting that the views of the Soviet Union and Great Britain and the other members of the Security Council had been heard and that the matter was closed. See *n*9 below. No resolution was passed on Indonesia. In the case of Syria and Lebanon, France and Great Britain complied with the council's vote to open immediate negotiations for the withdrawal of their troops, which took place shortly thereafter (James B. Reston, "UNO Settles Clash," *NYT*, 7 February 1946, 1; Lie, 28–34).

9. The exchanges between Soviet Deputy Minister of Foreign Affairs Andrei Vyshinsky and British Foreign Secretary Ernest Bevin over the situation in Greece were particularly harsh. Vyshinsky described the Greek leadership as "fascist scum" who ruled with British support and said that "such a situation constitutes a grave danger to the maintenance of peace and security." In response, Bevin said, "Have I or my Government ... been endangering the peace of the world? If this is true, you ought to tell me to leave this table, because you are established to maintain world peace, and I am branded, at the first meeting, as being the one person in the world disturbing and endangering world peace" (Lie, 31–32).

10. See *n*3 Document 144. After years of competition against each other for control of Iran, Russia and Great Britain signed a convention in 1907 that gave each country a sphere of influence in the country. Russia's sphere was in the north, while Great Britain dominated the south (*NEB*; Lie, 29).

11. The Soviet Union's oil fields were located in the Caucasus and Belarus. (Then-undeveloped oil fields also existed in Siberia.) After World War II, the Soviet Union acquired Gallicia with its oil fields at Lvov (MacMillan, 225; *OEWH*).

12. See Document 94 and Document 95.

13. By the end of the war in Europe, American and British flying forces, operating under the Casablanca Directive code-named Pointblank, had destroyed most major industrial cities in Germany—Schweinfurt, Kassel, Hamburg, Wurzburg, Darmstadt, Heilbronn, Wuppertal, Weser, Cologne, Magdeburg, Dresden, and the capital city of Berlin (Keegan, 415–36).

REBUTTING JIM CROW

In its March issue, *Ebony* featured a photographic essay on Eleanor Roosevelt's collegial relationships with African Americans, praising her as the "best White friend, patron and champion of Negro America," "a woman who practices what she preaches," and "the spiritual pinup girl of Negro Americans." Pages of photographs of ER entertaining the young boys from the Wiltwyck School and the entertainer Josh White and his family surrounded the text. "The party," the editor concluded, "was no stiff-lipped, formal shindig with lots of talk about interracial amity. Instead everyone just went about practicing interracialism by forgetting about color."[1]

April 12, Allen C. Smith of Kansas City, Missouri, who summered in Tidewater, Virginia, wrote ER to express his disapproval and to ask what she expected "to accomplish for the Negro race by these actions." After stating his thorough "belief that the Negro is entitled to the rights and privileges that a white man is entitled to … and a chance to better and improve his condition," he declared that an African American man "is not a social equal of the white man—and never will be." Furthermore,

> the consensus of opinion among the white people in my part of Virginia is that you have done the Negro far more harm than you have done good. In fact, the consensus of opinion everywhere seems to be that instead of helping the condition of the Negro, you and your late husband have set them back. You have caused racial enmity that did not exist before. And the greater the racial enmity is, the greater the Negro is going to suffer.

Smith concluded by arguing the need for African American professionals was "limited" and that "the Negro should be taught that there is no disgrace in the domestic occupations." He then asked ER to "impress upon them that they are entitled to all the rights and privileges of any other citizen, but that there is no occasion or necessity of, that they should even have a desire for social equality with the white man."[2]

108

Eleanor Roosevelt to Allen Smith
24 April 1946 [Hyde Park]

My dear Mr. Smith:

I have never preached nor advocated "social" equality. I do not believe in segregation in public places or conveyances. I think a person's behavior should be the only criterion.

I am glad you believe negroes are entitled to the fundamental rights guaranteed to all citizens.

There was mingling of the races and "mixed" children long before I was born. That is something you can't legislate apparently.

It doesn't do much good to urge negroes to be proud of their heritage when they are denied the right to be proud.

Many of us who never belonged to a minority group find it difficult to understand what it means to be barred from places because of race or religion especially in a country which boasts of our freedom.

Perhaps if we had made domestic work more pleasant and paid higher wages, we would not find people so unwilling now to enter it.[3]

Very sincerely yours,

TLc AERP, FDRL

―――――――――

1. "Hyde Park Party," *Ebony* 1, no. 5 (March 1946), 2.

2. Allen C. Smith to ER, 12 April 1946, AERP.

3. Rumors that ER encouraged African American domestics to form Eleanor Clubs, loose organizations of African American women organized to oppose exploitative working conditions, swirled around the South with such consistency that the media treated them as fact, prodding ER to ask the FBI to investigate whether such organizations existed. Here she makes the same point she was accused of making when she (according to rumor) encouraged African American domestics to confront the families that employed them (A. Black, *Courage*, 87).

ON IMMIGRATION TO PALESTINE

James G. McDonald served as one of ER's most knowledgeable informants about refugee matters.[1] In November 1945, Truman appointed McDonald, who was sympathetic to the Zionist cause, to the Anglo-American Committee of Inquiry. The committee's April 1946 report recommended that Great Britain admit 100,000 European Jews to Palestine as soon as possible (a figure Truman had proposed to Attlee in August 1945),[2] but failed to make a recommendation on the future government of Palestine.[3] Although the report was unanimous, deep and bitter divisions between the six British and six American members existed within the committee, and Truman remained uncertain. McDonald, worried that increased Zionist criticism would derail Truman's support for the immigration proposal, found himself having to lobby Ben-Gurion and other Zionist leaders not to push for a larger immigration quota—hence ER's reference below to the "terrible time" McDonald was having.[4]

109

Eleanor Roosevelt to James McDonald
28 April 1946 [Hyde Park]

Dear Mr. McDonald:

I can well imagine what a terrible time you are having. I see you have recommended that 100,000 be allowed to go to Palestine at once and I am glad of that.

I think we should have the courage to tell the Arabs that we intend to protect Palestine, but I suppose that is asking too much of us at the present time, though it would only take a small air-force and it would seem to me to keep them in order.[5]

I shall be very glad to see you and have a chance to talk to you when you get back.

Very sincerely yours,
Eleanor Roosevelt

TLS JGMP, NCC-RB

---

1. Beginning in 1933, James G. McDonald (1886–1964) served as high commissioner for refugees (Jewish and other) coming from Germany for the League of Nations but resigned in 1935, calling on the League and its member states to confront Germany about its increasingly hostile policies toward its Jewish and other "non-Aryan" populations. He visited the White House in May 1933, providing FDR and ER with a firsthand report on the situation in Germany, and stayed in regular contact with ER thereafter. They worked together to try to expedite the emigration of refugees from Europe, ER serving as a conduit between McDonald and the president. When communication broke down between the president's Advisory Committee on Political Refugees and the State and Justice Departments in 1940, ER arranged a meeting between McDonald, then committee chair, and FDR to resolve the problem ("Letter of Resignation of James G. McDonald," 27 December 1935, AUL; James McDonald to ER, 10 October 1940, JGMP, NCC-RB).

2. See Document 54.

3. Sydney Gruson, "Palestine Visas for 100,000 Urged by Anglo-U.S. Board," *NYT*, 23 April 1946, 1.

4. Most of the British members of the committee remained unhappy with the final result and the British government blocked implementation of the recommendations made in the report (Dinnerstein, 91, 93–95). See Document 60 for ER's views on the Anglo-American Committee. See Cohen, 127–30, for McDonald's efforts to secure Truman's commitment.

5. While the US government supported transporting Jewish refugees from Europe to Palestine, it opposed providing US troops to enforce the recommendations of the committee and protect the Jews in Palestine (Dinnerstein, 95).

INSTRUCTING THE NUCLEAR COMMISSION ON HUMAN RIGHTS

When the San Francisco conference approved the UN Charter, it mandated that the General Assembly "set up commissions in economic and social fields and for the promotion of human rights." [1] In 1946, following the opening session of the General Assembly, the United Nations Economic and Social Council (ECOSOC) established a nine-member "nuclear" commission on human rights to recommend a structure and mission for the permanent Human Rights Commission (HRC).[2] Unlike other commissions, however, the delegates appointed to this nuclear body would be chosen for their individual merits rather than their national affiliation.

When ER returned from London, she received a telegram from Secretary-General Lie asking if she would serve on the Human Rights Commission. After she accepted, ER then wrote Secretary Byrnes, "I have cabled Mr. Lie that I would accept. The cable stated that we would meet here in New York City and the meeting would last three weeks and my compensation would be $15 a day and traveling expenses." She then requested that the department supply secretarial help and a policy advisor.[3]

April 29 at New York's Hunter College, Henri Laugier, the assistant secretary-general for social affairs, called the first session of the nuclear commission to order. Laugier hoped the delegates would remember that "the free peoples" and "all of the people liberated from slavery, put in you their confidence and their hope, so that everywhere the authority of these rights, respect of which is the essential condition of the dignity of the person, be respected." After they elected their chair and agreed upon a structure for the full commission, they, with their other colleagues, "would start [the UN] on the road which the Charter set for it." He concluded his remarks:

> You are the seed out of which great and beautiful harvests come. You will have before you the difficult but essential problem to define the violation of human rights within a nation, which would constitute a menace to the security and peace of the world and the existence of which is sufficient to put in movement the mechanism of the United Nations for peace and security. You will have to suggest the establishment of machinery of observation which will find and denounce the violations of the rights of man all over the world. Let us remember that if this machinery had existed a few years ago … the human community would have been able to stop those who started the war at the moment when they were still weak and the world catastrophe would have been avoided.

As soon as Laugier finished his remarks, Dr. C. L. Hsia from China nominated ER as the commission's chair. All the delegates endorsed the nomination. ER, who did not anticipate this appointment, thanked her colleagues, stating:

> I shall do my best, although my knowledge of parliamentary law is somewhat limited. I know that we are all conscious of the great responsibility which rests upon us. I know we are all confident that we shall be able to do much to help the United Nations achieve its primary objective of keeping the peace of the world by helping human beings to live together happily and contentedly.[4]

110

Commission on Human Rights of the Social and Economic Council Summary Record, Fourth Meeting [excerpt]

2 May 1946 [Hunter College, New York City][5]

Chairman: Mrs. Franklin D. Roosevelt

THE CHAIRMAN: "I feel very strongly, judging by the letters that I am getting, that this Commission means a great deal to a great many people in the world, and I wanted to remind each one of you that while in the future people may be serving on the full Commission, either in the capacity of representatives of their governments or in the capacity of individuals, we who are here were chosen by the Economic and Social Council with the consent of course, of our governments, because we wouldn't be here unless our governments had acquiesced that they wanted us here. Nevertheless, to the peoples of the world, we here have a very grave responsibility, because they look upon us, regardless of the governments that we spring from, as their representatives, the representatives of the peoples of the world, and for that reason, I hope that every one of us is going to feel, in the consideration of the question of how we constitute the full Commission and of how we recommend that the work shall be undertaken, a grave personal responsibility as well as, naturally, a responsibility to represent what our governments believe is right.

But I think even beyond that, that sometimes points arise where one has to advocate something that it may be difficult for one's own government to carry through, and yet, if one believes it is right, I think one should advocate it, hoping that if it would be good for the world, it would therefore, in the end, be good for one's own government and one's own people too. For that reason, I just wanted to say this before we started our meeting this morning".

THE CHAIRMAN then explained that a memorandum had been prepared by the Secretariat, embodying references to the definitive composition of commissions in the Report of the Preparatory Commission[6] and in the United Kingdom Delegation document (E/Commissions/2),[7] as well as the informal and preliminary agreements reached by the Commission itself during previous meetings. She especially pointed to the advisability of selecting the membership of the full Commission on Human Rights from amongst all the Member Nations of the United Nations and the necessity of having at all times an equitable geographic distribution and a membership of highly qualified persons.

THE CHAIRMAN explained for the benefit of M. Cassin,[8] who had been unable to be present at former meetings, that three types of membership had been discussed:

1. all governmental representatives

2. all individual experts

3. mixed representation

She stated that the majority of members of the Commission had reached an informal agreement with all members of the Commission on Human Rights should be re-eligible, that they should be chosen from among all the United Nations, and not only from among members of the Economic and Social Council, and that a membership of eighteen would be satisfactory provided, however, that it should be possible to call in individual experts for sub-commissions or for their advice on specific problems.

M. Cassin agreed with the preliminary recommendations arrived by the majority of the Commission, that members of the full Commission should be re-eligible, that they should not be chosen exclusively from among the members of the Economic and Social Council, and that the number of eighteen would form a satisfactory basis for the full Commission. He also recommended a term of three years.

M. Laugier, Assistant Secretary-General,[9] suggested that eighteen might not be the best number, as a tie would be possible if THE CHAIRMAN should decide to vote; an odd figure divisible by three—twenty-one, for instance—might be preferable.

At the suggestion of THE CHAIRMAN, the members then agreed to vote on any item of the agenda on which general preliminary agreement had already been reached, as for instance, re-eligibility.

Mr. Neogy[10] raised the question of re-eligibility of governmental representative: will the governments be re-eligible or the individuals representing them?

THE CHAIRMAN suggested that the Economic and Social Council alone would be responsible for re-appointments. If a government refused to re-nominate a representative, another person could be nominated. She suggested that as there still seemed to be questions about re-eligibility, it might be better not to decide that point until agreement had been reached on other questions.

Type of Membership

THE CHAIRMAN asked for discussion on whether a majority of the members of the full Commission should be government representatives or individual experts, or whether the Commission should be evenly divided if it was decided to have mixed representation.

Mr. Neogy felt that as the Economic and Social Council was elected by the governments represented in the General Assembly, and as the members of the Economic and Social Council, in their turn, represented governments, the Commission On Human Rights, set up by the Economic and Social Council as demanded by the Assembly, should not again consist of representatives of governments. The Economic and Social Council should have the right to name any individual who could best help it in the discharge of its duty "to promote human rights". While the nuclear Commission should recommend that governments be allowed to make recommendations, the authority of appointment should lie entirely with the Economic and Social Council.

M. Cassin agreed completely with Mr. Neogy's suggestions and then recalled the historical developments in the fight for human rights. He pointed out that the first legally established world community was founded in the League of Nations. Instead of furthering justice in the individual nations, however, the course of justice and human rights regressed, as individual nations no longer felt compelled to intervene, but felt that the responsibility rested with the League of Nations. Nor did the League intervene, due to skillful and evasive interpretation of the Covenant.

Now as the United Nations are again establishing an instrument to defend and promote human rights, we must have collective action by the Economic and Social Council and it is this Council which must be responsible for the appointment of members of the Commission on Human Rights.

There are, M. Cassin pointed out disadvantages to non-governmental membership, in the past, Commissions consisting of individuals often reached lofty conclusions which were never observed, while commissions consisting of governmental representatives came to less ambitious but more effective conclusions. It might therefore be argued that our Commission would reach better results, if composed of governmental representatives. However, as Mr. Neogy pointed out, the Council has complete authority, and the Council is composed of governmental representatives.

It should, therefore, be possible to devise a method of selection whereby nominations could be made by governments, but appointments only by the Economic and Social Council.

M. Cassin explained that precedents of appointments in individual capacity have been established in three fields: (1) The League of Nations organ for intellectual co-operation consisting entirely of well-known individual experts; (2) The League of Nations' Mandate Commission; and (3) The Hague Court of Justice.

A method should, therefore, be devised to take into account proposals made by governments, but to give authority to appoint solely to the Economic and Social Council. Mixed membership, according to M. Cassin, would not provide a good method.

THE CHAIRMAN read Page 6 (1 and 2) of the United Kingdom Delegation document (E/Commissions/2) dealing with type of membership.

Dr. Hsia[11] agreed with M. Cassin that a commission consisting of mixed representatives would probably be unworkable, and supported the suggestion of the United Kingdom document Page 6, Section 2 on non-governmental representatives.

Mr. Brkish and Mr. Kriukov[12] agreed, with the views expressed by M. Cassin and the Chairman then summarized the consensus of opinion that all governments of the United Nations should have the right to make as many as two nominations and that the Economic and Social Council would appoint individuals as members of the Commission on Human Rights, with due consideration to the ability and experience of the nominees in the field of human rights.

Answering a question by Mr. Neogy, THE CHAIRMAN stated her opinion that the Economic and Social Council should choose members of the Commission on Human Rights solely from the nominations submitted by the United Nations governments, but asked for discussion on this point. No objections were offered, and THE CHAIRMAN repeated that it was the understanding of the nuclear Commission, that the Economic and Social Council should appoint the members of the full Commission solely from the nominations submitted by the governments of the United Nations.

M. Cassin raised the question of whether governments should nominate only their own nationals or might nominate nationals of other countries as is the practice with nominations to the Hague Court.

The Commission agreed that member governments of the United Nations should have the right to nominate nationals of another nation.

Dr. Hsia asked whether, in that case, it might not occur that two nationals of the same nation might at the same time hold membership on the Commission, but THE CHAIRMAN felt that this would be very unlikely and might happen only under very extraordinary circumstances.

The Commission agreed that no formal vote should be taken on any separate point (of Item 9 of the Agenda), but that the text of the informal agreement reached on each point should be circulated among the members of the Commission and the vote on the definitive composition of the full Commission should be taken on all points together, with any disagreements that might exist, duly recorded.

Point 2, Item 9

Number of Members

M. Cassin pointed out that twenty-one would be an advisable number, but that the most important factor in deciding the number of members was the kind of membership. If we had decided that the members are to be governmental representatives, substitutions could be made by the governments if members are unable to attend. As we have, however, decided on individual experts the number of absentees would have to be reckoned with, and we might have four substitutes who would be called in in case of illness.

THE CHAIRMAN pointed out that United Kingdom Delegation document (E/Commissions/2) suggests that no alternates (except in special cases) should be allowed for non-governmental representatives. She suggested that it might be possible to name out of the list of nominations submitted by the governments, in addition to the twenty-one members, four observers who would replace absent members in case of need. Dr. Hsia suggested that they might be called "reserve members" instead of observers.

Mr. Brkish expressed his preference for twenty-one members, four reserve members or alternates, the first group of members to be appointed in three categories (one year, two years, three years).

Dr. Hsia stated that two categories of members might not be advisable, and it might be better to name twenty-four or twenty-five members to provide for absences.

Mr. Neogy suggested eighteen, following the example of the Economic and Social Council, but offered to support the number twenty-one if the majority decided on twenty-one.[13]

THE CHAIRMAN suggested that the discussion be continued at the next meeting.

The meeting was adjourned at 12:20 P.M.

TSumex AERP, FDRL

———————

1. The Charter of the United Nations, Article 68 (www.un.org/aboutun/charter).

2. The UN applied the term nuclear to refer to a commission which acts as a precursor (of the nucleus of) of the full commission. The nuclear HRC planned the design and scope of the full eighteen-member Human Rights Commission. The members of the nuclear HRC included M. Paul Berg (Norway), René Cassin (France), Fernand Dehousse (Belgium), Victor Raul de la Torre (Peru), C. L. Hsia (China), K. C. Neogi (India), Dusan Brkish (Yugoslavia), and Nicolai Kiukov (USSR) (Members of the Commission of Human Rights, AERP).

3. ER to James Byrnes, 8 March 1946, RG59, NARA II.

4. HRC, Nuclear Commission, 1st Meeting, Summary Record, 29 April 1946, (E/HR/6/1 May 1946), 1–3, AERP.

5. HRC, Fourth Meeting, Summary Record, 6 May 1946 (E/HR/10), AERP.

6. The Preparatory Commission met on June 27, 1945, following the San Francisco conference (see n4 Document 2), and again on November 25, prior to the first session of the UN General Assembly. In addition to discussing essential matters of procedure and organization, the November 25 meeting also touched upon the topic of atomic energy regulation (Herbert L. Matthers, "Assembly Atom Rule Hinted as UNO Body Opens Session," *NYT*, 25 November 1945, 1).

7. The United Kingdom delegation issued several preliminary suggestions for determining membership in the HRC. Among these suggestions were that the commission be composed of twenty-five members, "the majority of whom might be non-governmental members," and that commissions be allowed "to call in non-governmental experts as required," subject to approval of the president of ECOSOC in consultation with the secretary general (Points to be Considered in Connection with the Definitive Composition of the Commission on Human Rights, Including Suggestions by the United Kingdom Delegation to the United Nations, E/Commissions/2, n.d., AERP).

8. René Cassin. See Biographical Portraits.

9. Henri Laugier. See Document 200 header.

10. K. C. Neogi, delegate to the HRC from India.

11. Dr. C. L. Hsia, delegate from China.

12. Dusan Brkish, delegate from Yugoslavia; and Nicolai Kiukov, delegate from the USSR.

13. Although the nuclear HRC recommended in its final report that the members of the permanent HRC be selected by the UN on their individual merits rather than by their governments, ECOSOC rejected this recommendation. In the end, the full Human Rights Commission includ-

ed representatives of eighteen UN member states, five from the major powers (the United States, the Soviet Union, the United Kingdom, France, and China); the remaining (who served staggered three-year terms), from the other member states. ECOSOC chose the other member states to be represented on the HRC; then the governments of those states nominated their own representatives. ECOSOC had to confirm the nominees, but, in practice, this was a formality (Glendon, 31–32).

On Preventing World War III

When the columnist Walter Lippmann returned from interviewing European leaders attending the Paris Peace Conference,[1] he published a blunt assessment of postwar diplomacy. "The most important conclusion," he reported May 4, was that "all European governments, all parties, and all leading men are acting as if there would be another war. There are some who dread it, some who want it, some who think it inevitable, some who think it can be averted." Thus, he argued, "the business of making peace has not even begun." Lippmann expressed particular concern over the British and Soviet rivalry regarding Germany. He found this dispute "so demonstrably dangerous, so utterly reckless, so certainly self-defeating" that America must remain "clear and resolute" to prevent another conflict.[2]

ER found his argument so compelling that she devoted a column to it.

My Day
7 May 1946

NEW YORK, Monday—I took up the paper one day last week and, after reading it through, decided that something is the matter with us as a people, for our Representatives in Congress are becoming temporizers. They are unable to make up their minds about anything because the American people are not clear and determined in their own minds where they stand and where they are going. A day later I read Mr. Walter Lippmann's column: "A Report on Europe".

His column will frighten a good many people, but I am very glad that he wrote it, because I am one of the people who believe that the sooner we face facts the better. No great power should gain any territory whatsoever out of this past war.

The great trouble internationally today is that we have built no confidence in each other. We think in the same old terms of individual strength and control through our own power. We forget that if that is the way we are going to think and act, we might just as well not have set up the United Nations. We might just as well never have ended the last war, for we are surely preparing for the next. Those who set up the United Nations believed in building collective power. Thus we could protect the rights of smaller nations of the world. The greater nations needed no more territory. In fact, in many cases some of their territory should become virtually self-governing and independent.

Great Britain and Russia and even the United States, where their military authorities are concerned, have all grown away, apparently, from this concept. But I hope that the United States can most easily recall it, and I think it is absolutely essential that the United States do so at once. Either we make peace and restore the world to a peaceful basis, or we prepare ourselves for the end of our civilization. If we are going to make peace, I think we are quite right in seeing to it that Central Europe is made impotent to start another war. I think we should aim, as far as possible, to make the small nations really free from military and political control on the part of the great nations. Therefore, we must build up in the United Nations a strong force, moral as well as military, that may be used against anyone who attempts to coerce any other peoples throughout the world.

We must become one world, and we realize today that we are far from being one world. There is only one way and that is by working together. Gradually we will come to see each other's point of view and modify our own. We will come to trust each other. Someday there must be one world or there can not be peace and the only machinery we have to achieve that end is the United Nations. It is not strong today, but it can become strong if we are determined to make it so.

TMs AERP, FDRL

1. From January 18 to July 12, the Council of Foreign Ministers convened a series of meetings in London and Paris to prepare drafts of treaties they proposed the Allies make with Italy, Rumania and Finland (*FRUS*, 1970, xix–xx).

2. Lippmann based his assessment upon his conversations with "responsible and representative men" who all concluded that another war was imminent. British-Soviet tensions flared over Russia's plan to create a sphere of influence in the Balkans and a trusteeship in the Mediterranean region, land largely dominated by the British (Walter Lippmann, "Today and Tomorrow: A Report on Europe," *WP*, 4 May 1946, 7; Lansing Warren, "Paris Conference Drops 'Peace' Tag," *NYT*, 31 March 1946, 9; Anne O'Hare McCormick, "Abroad: The Second Meeting of the Council of Foreign Ministers," *NYT*, 10 April 1946, 24; Marshall Andrews, "President Does Not Consider Paris Meeting of Ministers a Failure," *WP*, 10 May 1946, 1).

ON THE PROPOSED UN SUBCOMMISSION ON
THE STATUS OF WOMEN

President of the World Woman's Party for Equal Rights Lady Emmeline Petwick Lawrence (1867–1954) and American equal rights activist Betty Gram Swing (1893?–1969) met with ER during the opening session of the General Assembly to lobby for a separate UN commission, composed entirely of women, that would work to secure women's rights.[1] At their January meeting, ER promised to study the issue, but then publicly expressed skepticism about the proposal, noting in her January 25 column that women's organizations would be better served if utilized in a "consultative capacity" and therefore "treated on the same basis as other specialized agencies." Otherwise, she feared that numerous groups would demand similar status within the UN, which "would result in chaos."[2]

ER disagreed with some of the leaders of the women's movement about the best strategy for securing women's rights and achieving an equal voice in national and world affairs. A federal constitutional amendment would, ER believed, "make it possible to wipe out much of the legislation which has been enacted in many States for the protection of women in industry." She favored instead working on a state-by-state basis to end discriminatory legislation while still protecting the needs of women's industrial labor.[3] In the case of the commission, she differed on strategy, thinking it would be more effective to pressure governments to send more women delegates to the UN so that women would be represented fully in all the deliberations of the world body. Those campaigning for a separated commission succeeded, however, and ECOSOC created a Subcommission on the Status of Women, as a subsidiary of the Human Rights Commission.[4]

Carrie Chapman Catt (1859–1947), in addition to spearheading the woman suffrage movement in the United States and being a force behind the founding of the League of Women Voters and the National Committee on the Cause and Cure of War, was the woman whom ER most admired.[5] In the following letter, Catt reported on the controversy among women's rights activists over the nature and composition of the Subcommission on the Status of Women and strongly recommended the appointment of Dorothy Kenyon, an American lawyer, to the subcommission.[6]

Although there is no extant record of ER's response, Truman did appoint Kenyon to the the UN Commission on the Status of Women November 6.[7]

112

Carrie Chapman Catt to Eleanor Roosevelt
7 May 1946 [New Rochelle, NY]

My dear Mrs. Roosevelt:

A long time ago I had a birthday, and there was brought to me a box of beautiful flowers with your card in it. You, however had gone to England, and I concluded a letter sent you there, even though I should catch you, would only be a boresome additional item in your overfull program. So I waited until you came home. When you did I prepared to thank you for those flowers, but how you did buzz around, going here, there, and everywhere with such important things to do, and making speeches everywhere! I thought some day you would find a calm moment when you might pause and remember that you never had had a thank you for those flowers! Now there is something else to say, so I will combine the two duties.

I was greatly honored by the arrival of those flowers, and very much surprised that you should remember old lady Catt in the midst of your busy busy program. I have thought of them every day since, and always with renewed gratitude for all you have done for me.

I am so very glad that you are among the leaders of the new Anti-War Organization.[8] Women should know what war means, and I believe that if the men all fall down you will be able to lead on, nevertheless. I am a firm believer that the League of Nations did a great deal of good in its brief life and created a large number of anti-war citizens of the world, but we had to have another war it seems, and I am not so sure that we will not get a third, and perhaps still others too, but the movement is on the forward trend, and sometime war will end.

We are all very glad that you are chairman of the Commission on Human Rights. I am informed that a partly organized committee on the Status of Women is under the general Committee of Human Rights. There has been quite a disturbance among women over this committee. Originally there was such a Committee in the League of Nations, and they were going along with considerable vigor.[9] They had a good many meetings, and were going to accomplish something, but that came to an end, and the new "set-up" apparently did not wish to use the machinery formerly operating under the League of Nations. It seems that an appeal was made at San Francisco to adopt the same form of committee in order that the work might be continued, and it was to be formed of men and women. There came to that Conference two women who did not know each other—Bertha Lutz of Brazil[10] who was a regular delegate and Mrs. Street of Australia,[11] who had ideals. They put their heads together and proposed a committee on the status of women, to be comprised of women only. There was quite a row inside of the San Francisco Conference over the latter.[12]

I am informed that there is no English speaking woman on this minor committee,[13] and some of the women here who appealed to the San Francisco Conference to readopt the League of Nations Committee have never lost sight of the proposal, and are now very anxious that there should be an American woman appointed to that Committee who would be familiar with the evolution of the rights of women in the English speaking countries, and they all want Dorothy Kenyon, who is a lawyer, and who has now I think in her hands a complete report of the work of the old committee so far as it had gone.[14] I have talked with Miss Kenyon, and I have reason to believe that she would be very pleased to find herself on that committee and go forward with it.[15] I am also informed that there might be an objection to two American women, each with a vote, but the women suggested that the two women might only have one vote between them. I do not know about this, but at any rate I suggest that if possible you get Dorothy Kenyon on that Committee.[16] She is a fine woman as you know, and is amply prepared to serve there, whereas all the women seem to have their doubts about the qualifications of women from India, Lebanon, San Domingo, France, and Russia as suitable to make a platform of the status of women that would be satisfactory to the English speaking people. They did not have the long campaign for woman's rights that preceded the movement for Woman Suffrage. I should say from what I hear that the whole situation is quite a mess, but I may be wrong. If there is any way in which Dorothy Kenyon may be put to work at it, I think she might make order out of tangle.[17]

Please pardon this long letter.

Lovingly yours,
Carrie Chapman Catt

TLS AERP, FDRL

---

1. "Betty Gram Swing Dead at 76; Women's Rights Leader in 20's," *NYT*, 4 September 1969, 47; *WH*, 172–73; see also *n*11 and *n*12 Document 83.

2. *MD*, 25 January 1946.

3. For example, see Document 120 and Document 138.

4. For discussion of ER's public and private disagreements regarding the status the women's body would ultimately have within the UN, see Document 120.

5. *NYT*, 10 March 1947, 21; *NAWMP*; A. Black, *Casting*, 137–88; Cook, vol. 2, 128, 238, 364, 488.

6. Dorothy Kenyon (1888–1972), lawyer, judge, and women's rights activist, served as the US representative to the League of Nations' Committee to Study the Legal Status of Women Throughout the World (*NAW*).

7. See *n*15. If ER responded to this letter, neither ER, Catt, nor the National Committee on the Cause and Cure of War retained a copy.

8. She means the United Nations. Catt herself had become honorary chair of a new women's peace initiative, the Women's Action Committee for Victory and a Lasting Peace, which formed in March 1943, as the successor organization to the National Committee on the Cause and Cure of War ("New Anti-War Unit is Launched Here," *NYT*, 18 March 1943, 6; "Cure-of-War Group Dissolved at Meeting," *NYT*, 9 April 1943, 16).

9. For the League of Nations Committee of Experts on the Status of Women, see *n*14 Document. 79.

10. A Chapman Catt protégé, Bertha Lutz of Brazil (1894–1976) was a botanist, naturalist, long-term activist for women's rights, and a member of her country's Chamber of Deputies in 1936 and 1937. A leader in the fight for women suffrage in Brazil, she became a Brazilian delegate to the UN's charter conference in San Francisco and later served on the UN Commission on the Status of Women (Hahner, "Lutz," 474–75; "Brazilian Woman Hailed," *NYT*, 28 June 1946, 12; Rupp, *Worlds*, 222; *Yearbook of the United Nations, 1946–47*).

11. Jessie Street (1889–1970), an Australian Labour (and later Independent Labour) politician, served as the only female member of the Australian delegation to the San Francisco founding conference of the UN. She visited both Chapman Catt and ER in New York after the San Francisco meeting. Once appointed to the UN, the Commission on the Status of Women members elected her their first vice president. The Labour government under Ben Chifley did not appoint her for another term. Street had also actively lobbied the League of Nations on women's issues and attended meetings of the League's assembly in 1930 and 1938 (http://www.uncommonlives.naa.gov.au/, accessed, 4 August 2005; Street, *Truth or Repose?*, 266, 294–96; Radi, ed., *Jessie*, 2–4).

12. Apart from the question of making such a body "women only," not all organized women's rights advocates wanted women's issues to be discussed separately from general human rights issues at the United Nations. See Rupp, *Worlds*, 223–24.

13. She means full members of the subcommission. As an ex-officio member, ER did not vote ("Women's Equality Asked by U.N. Unit," *NYT*, 2 May 1946, 6).

14. On May 1, 1946, at a meeting of the UN Subcommission on the Status of Women in which ER also participated, Kenyon reported on the accomplishments of that committee. The subcommission's subsequent report to ECOSOC included a recommendation for a new survey of laws related to women's status.

Kenyon also wrote to ER about the controversy surrounding the Subcommission on the Status of Women, reporting on her conversation with Gabriela Mistral, a leading woman activist from Chile, who resigned from the subcommission on May 3 partly because it had no North American member, and to express her dismay that the subcommission neglected the needs of nonpolitical women (Radi, ed., *Jessie Street*, 188; "Women's Equality Asked by U.N. Unit," *NYT*, 2 May 1946, 6; Lucy Greenbaum, "World Goal Fixed in Women's Rights," *NYT*, 14 May 1946, 10; Dorothy Kenyon to ER, 3 May 1946, AERP).

15. Kenyon already belonged to a group, the American Association for the United Nations, that was lobbying ER in her capacity as chair of the Human Rights Commission to create further subcommissions on rights and install mechanisms for implementing antidiscrimination principles (American Association for the United Nations, Inc. to ER, 2 May 1946, NAACP papers, II, DLC).

16. The State Department also recommended that Truman consider Dorothy Kenyon, along with Frieda Miller and Frances Perkins, for appointment to the full commission. On November 6, 1946, the president appointed Kenyon as the first US representative to the Commission on the Status of Women; she served for a term of three years ("Truman Appoints U.N. Representatives," *NYT*, 7 November 1946, 14; "Comments and Recommendations on Report of Sub-Commission on Status of Women," 22 May 1946, SD/E/HR/ST/1, RG84, NARA II).

17. Kenyon used her new position to promote greater representation of women in UN agencies and improvements in women's political status and rights across the globe. She also repeatedly crossed swords with the commission's Soviet member at meetings over a broad range of issues encompassing political access, civil liberties, and economic opportunity. After Kenyon's three-year term ended, Truman selected Olive Remington Goldman to replace her ("Judge Dorothy Kenyon Is Dead," *NYT*, 14 February 1972, 32; "Special Rights Aim Again Loses in U.N.," *NYT*, 20 February 1947, 11; Albion Ross, "U.S., Soviet Women Clash on Rights of Wives of Foreigners Under Russian Restrictions," *NYT*, 26 March 1949, 5; *MD*, 11 March 1950).

ON INTERMARRIAGE

In her My Day column of March 7, 1946, ER published excerpts from a letter she received from an American man married to a Chinese woman. The husband acknowledged that when they wed, "they were entirely conscious" of the "general social reaction in the United States, most particularly in the west, against mixed marriage." Indeed, they married in Washington to avoid the California statute against miscegenation. However, the couple returned to Berkeley (where both had completed their doctoral work) so that he, a physicist, could work for the Donner Laboratory of Medical Physics. When the physicist rented an apartment, he did not tell the manager his wife was Chinese. A month later the manager confronted the wife, insulted her nationality, and told her that had he known, they would "not have been accepted as tenants." He then closed his letter to ER:

> I am writing for my Oriental friends, whom I know through my marriage and through residence at the Berkeley International House where I met my wife, for my Negro friends, for my Filipino and Mexican friends, and for the host of all these races whom I can only know as they are symbolized in my friends.

ER, who began her column by telling her readers that this "sad letter" illustrated "one of the the big problems" confronting the American people, closed it by saying this discrimination illustrated:

> that we deny the spirit of the religions to which we belong, for all religions recognize the equality of the human being before God. We deny the spirit of our own Constitution and Government which our forefathers fought to establish in this land, we make future good will and peace an impossibility for no United Nations organization can succeed when peoples of one race approach those of other races in a spirit of contempt.[1]

Although the column did not explicitly endorse intermarriage, ER often received harsh criticism for implying her approval of such relationships, as exemplified in this letter from one of her readers.

113

James Evans to Eleanor Roosevelt

7 May 1946 [Haverford, PA]

Dear Mrs. Roosevelt:

Your reply of April 18th to my letter of March 28th looks a good deal like an evasive "brush off".[2] Whether you think my letter sounded very Christian or not has little to do with the case discussed. But since you question the Christianity of my motive it might be well to remember that Christ never dodged an issue.

I naturally supposed that as a Columnist you would be prepared unequivocally to defend your published opinions. As the opinions you expressed in "My Day" of March 7th, seemed to warrant certain inferences which were not clearly expressed although they seemed fairly deductable and which are definitely related to a question which you yourself characterized as one of primary importance to the people of the United States, I felt at liberty to suggest to you a clarification of your meaning and an explicit declaration as to where you stand on the problem of interracial marriage in this country—particularly as between Negroes and Whites. Instead of frankly replying to this question you preferred curtly to question the sincerity and morality of my purpose in asking it.

That the problem is acute is amply evinced by the incidents frequently publicized in the daily press of which the enclosed clipping is an illuminating instance.[3]

If you wish to avoid an explanation of your position on this acute problem to the public whom you venture to criticize so harshly and whom you so confidently presume to instruct in your widely published utterances, that of course is your own affair.

Very truly yours,
James D. Evans

TLS AERP, FDRL

ER replied six days later, in a letter she dictated, to make it clear to Evans that she "had made the declaration before in two articles at least."[4]

114

Eleanor Roosevelt to James Evans

13 May 1946 [New York City]

My dear Mr. Evans:

I did not intend my letter as a "brush-off" and I was not dodging the issue. I thought you had probably read an article which I wrote in which I answered the very question which you now ask.[5]

I said that when people decided to marry, it was usually very difficult for anyone to do anything about it.

If a child of mine were to marry the decision that he or she wished to marry some one of another race—Negro, Asiatic, Oriental, I would feel that it was my duty to point out all the difficulties which life would hold in our civilization as it is at present, and I would not feel happy because I would know how much suffering lay ahead.

Nevertheless strong races usually swallow up less strong ones, and it is done through inter-marriage. I do not know whether it is much worse to have it done through inter-marriage than to have it done in the way it has been done in the south in the past, outside of wedlock.

However, I would like to state un-equivocally, that I do not consider the question of marriage of paramount importance. Marriages for a long time to come will be comparatively few. The important thing, in order that all citizens of the United States may live peacefully and happily, is equality of economic opportunity, equality of education, equality before the law and equality of opportunity to participate in government through the ballot.

Neither colored people, nor white people on any great scale are going to face the question of inter-marriage for many years to come.

Very sincerely yours,

TLc AERP, FDRL

---

1. *MD*, 7 March 1946.

2. ER did not keep his letter or a copy of her outgoing correspondence to him.

3. The enclosed article described how the Reverend Frank White of Norfolk, Virginia, faced legal discrimination from the state of Virginia and eventually lost his position in the church because of his marriage to an African American woman ("Wedding of Former Norfolk Minister to Negress Blocked," 31 January 1946, Associated Press).

4. ER scrawled this across the bottom of Evans's letter to her (James Evans to ER, 7 May 1946, AERP).

5. ER publicly disclosed her opinion on intermarriage in several publications. In December 1946, for example, she answered a question on the subject in her "If You Ask Me" column, stating:

> At the present time I think that intermarriage between Negroes and whites may bring to both of the people involved great unhappiness, because of the social pattern in which we happen to live. If, of course, two people, with full realization of what they are facing, decide they still want to marry, that is their right and no one else can interfere, but it takes very strong characters to face the kind of situation in which they will find themselves in almost any part of the world. For those I love, I should dread the suffering which must almost certainly lie ahead (*IYAM*, *LHJ*, December 1946, DL).

ON THE RAILROAD STRIKE AND THE
CHILDREN'S BUREAU

As coal and railroad strikes seized the nation's attention and the White House entered the negotiations after labor and management reached an impasse, ER devoted three My Day columns to the crisis.[1] May 20, she wrote:

> In this dispute, I cannot find it in my heart to blame the railroad men, because I know that life has been none too easy for them during the years of the war. They stood by when trains were crowded, when old equipment was being used and people were worried and tired. The cost of living has gone up, the hours of engineers and trainmen and conductors have been longer, not shorter; and when the war came to an end, there was no longer the patriotic reason to carry on. The men feel naturally enough that it is time for someone to think about them, instead of their having to think about the people.[2]

However, after labor struck against the federal government, which had just taken control of the rails while the White House arbitrated the dispute, ER wrote the following My Day, in which she continued to support labor, while bemoaning the absence of leadership in both management and labor—most especially the "vaunted wisdom and insight" of John L. Lewis.

My Day
25 May 1946

NEW YORK, Friday—Yesterday afternoon the railroad strike did actually start.[3] No postponement this time. And all over the country, one thing after another will slow down and stop. People will be made uncomfortable, raw materials will not come in, finished materials will not go out, jobs will close down. And if I am not mistaken, labor and management are going to find that all this is going to lead to some rather drastic results.

As I pointed out before, I do not blame labor itself, but the leadership in industry and, to some extent, in labor has been shortsighted. No one has managed to bring legitimate grievances to an end, and yet it is easy enough to realize that conditions which men endured during the war could not continue indefinitely afterward.

Management is chiefly concerned, I imagine, with replacing rolling stock and with the physical difficulties they have had to face as a result of the war, but the human problems eventually reach the boiling point. However, a whole nation's well-being should not be jeopardized by any group, whether they be miners or railroad or utility men.

Someone was telling me, not long ago, about a plan for labor courts where each difficulty, as it arose, would be brought in and analyzed on a fact-finding basis, and judges would render opinions as they do in any other court of law. That may be a possible solution. Great Britain, after the general strike there, set up the most complicated mechanism which, from that time on, seems to have obviated strikes on any big scale.[4] I have a feeling that that, or something similar to it, is what is going to come out of our present situation.

The public—and the workers themselves are included in the public—will not long accept any situation in which everybody suffers. I wonder whether, with all his vaunted wisdom and foresight, John L. Lewis knew, when he started the coal-strike ball rolling,[5] where it would come to rest.

In the past, there have been many people in the business world who have wanted to control government, and have controlled it to a great extent. In recent years, I think that same ambition has been in the minds of some of our labor leaders.

The leaders of industry sought control for a privileged few, but always I am sure that they would have added that, while a small group might hold power, it was for the benefit of the great mass of people. The well-being would flow down from the top. The leaders of labor who desire power today undoubtedly believe that they too desire it only for the benefit of the people as a whole, and they would say that what benefits the masses will flow up to the top and benefit the industrial leaders as well!

As a matter of fact, we are all tied together and depend upon each other, and what is really essential is that we find a method whereby all groups will be controlled for the benefit of the whole. That, I am afraid, means some kind of compulsory machinery, since voluntarily we don't seem to get together very well!

TMs AERP, FDRL

May 24 Truman used the radio to address the nation about "the railroad strike which threatens to paralyze all our industrial, agricultural, commercial and social life." As he told Congress the following day, he "tried to point out … the bleak picture which we faced at home and abroad if the strike is permitted to continue. The disaster will spare no one." Arguing that if the returning strikers did not return to the railroads, the president declared he had no choice but to request "temporary emergency legislation" authorizing "the President to draft into the armed forces of the United States all workers who are on strike against their Government." Moments after this announcement (and while he continued his address), the president deviated from his remarks to announce that the strike had been settled on the terms he proposed.[6]

In her May 28 My Day, ER praised the president for acting "in the interests of the public as a whole" in response to the strike, but expressed her hope that he and Congress would not pass legislative provisions for drafting strikers: "In time of war, it seems to me, men both in management and in industry should be liable to a draft wherever they can be of use. In time of peace, the use of this weapon against strikes does interfere with men's fundamental liberty to work or not to work."[7]

She then wrote the president directly to express her concerns about this precedent as well as his proposed reorganization of the Children's Bureau.

116

Eleanor Roosevelt to Harry Truman
27 May 1946 [New York City]

Dear Mr. President:

I was immensely impressed by your speech before the Congress, and I realize what very great burdens these last few weeks have put upon you. My admiration is great for the way in which you have acted in the public interest and ignored the political considerations.

You will forgive me, I hope, if I say that I hope you realize that there must not be any slip, because of the difficulties of our peace-time situation, into a military way of thinking, which is not natural to us as a people. I have seen my husband receive much advice from his military advisers and succumb to it every now and then, but the people as a whole do not like it even in war time, and in peace time military domination goes against the grain. I hope now that your anxiety is somewhat lessened, you will not insist upon a peace time draft into the army of strikers. That seems to me a dangerous precedent.[8]

I am also a little bit troubled over the re-organization of the Labor Department which will divide some of the functions of the Childrens Bureau.[9] Many of us who worked for the establishment of the Childrens Bureau are deeply concerned that in this re-organization it should at least become more efficient and not less efficient.

I know the various arguments because in previous plans for reorganization, Mr. Smith of the Budget Bureau,[10] my husband and various others, discussed these questions at length. I think it is logical to move it under Social Security and I hope that it will remain with Miss Lenroot[11] who has shown her capacity and ability to run it successfully, intact enough so that the main operations go on and perhaps only such things as deal directly with labor are taken away. I hope you have talked the whole thing over with Miss Lenroot and with some of the other people in her department who have worked for a long while on these questions.

The Children's Bureau is close to the hearts of many of the women in organized groups throughout the nation and they will be deeply interested in the outcome of whatever you do.[12]

Politically you are going to need the women if you decide to run in 1948 and if you decide not to run, whoever is nominated, will go down to defeat unless the great mass of women, both Republican and Democrat, back him in the next campaign.

With my congratulations on your courage and all good wishes, I am,

Very cordially yours,
Eleanor Roosevelt

TLS PPF, HSTL

117

Harry Truman to Eleanor Roosevelt
10 June 1946 [The White House]

Dear Mrs. Roosevelt:

I hope you will pardon my delay in answering your letter of May twenty-seventh, but as you can well imagine I have been quite busy.

It is very heartening to get your kind expressions with reference to some of the recent events in Washington. I have tried to carry out what I think is the best interests of the nation as a whole. I am sure that I have succeeded in wiping from my own mind any thought of the political considerations involved.

The dangers to our whole economic system stemming from the stagnation of the railroads were so great that there was no room for any politics. I am afraid, however, that in some quarters the old criterion of politics was still quite important.

As you know, the Senate has removed from the bill the provision for drafting strikers against the Government. I assure you that it was not easy for me to recommend such legislation. I tried to hedge it around with as many safeguards as possible. Among these safeguards was a limitation of its provisions to a handful of national industries in which a stoppage of work would affect our entire economy. There was also the limitation that its provisions could be made applicable only to those industries which already had been taken over by the Government.[13]

I am afraid that the Senate has taken all of the teeth out of the proposed emergency legislation.[14]

It is difficult to understand how the Congress can expect the President adequately to cope with emergencies such as faced this country ten days ago when the railroads were stalled, when the coal mines were in great danger of being closed down, and when a general shipping strike was imminent.[15]

I am glad you approve of moving the Children's Bureau over to the Federal Security Agency.[16] I too have been much impressed by the work of the Children's Bureau. I certainly do not think its activities should be curtailed in any way. I expect to talk to Miss Lenroot about the situation.

I welcome your advice and suggestions, and hope you will continue to write to me.

With kindest personal regards,

Sincerely yours,
Harry S. Truman

TLS AERP, FDRL

---

1. For other columns on the rail strike see *MD*, 14, 20, and 27 May 1946.

2. *MD*, 20 May 1946.

3. The railroad strike had initially been set for May 18, the date at which the federal government was set to take control of the railroads. However, an hour before the deadline Truman set to seize the railroads, he called Brotherhood of Locomotive Engineers president Alvaney Johnson and Brotherhood of Railroad Trainmen president Alexander Whitney, implied that a better offer was being prepared, and asked them to postpone the strike until May 23. Johnson and Whitney agreed to postpone and return to Washington to resume talks with the White House and management (Donovan, 208–10).

4. In May 1926, after British mine owners announced that when their government subsidy expired they would require their employees to work longer hours for less pay, the Miners' Federation struck. The General Council of the Trades Union Congress then called out a general strike across Britain May 3 to support the coal miners. The general strike ended ten days later; however, the miners continued striking for another six months, returning to work when they could no longer feed their families. The following year, the Trade Disputes and Trade Unions bill prohibited all general strikes. However, July 18, 1940, Minister of Labour Ernest Bevin utilized the special authority granted him in wartime to issue Order 1305, the Conditions of Employment and National Arbitration Order which outlawed strikes and lock-outs that had not first reported their grievances to the Ministry of Labour—and only then, if the minister had taken longer than three weeks "to refer the matter to settlement." The National Arbitration Council helped decrease work stoppages. It encouraged labor and management to negotiate and thus resolved more than half of their wartime disagreements and more than 2,000 claims presented to the ministry within the three-week time frame (Wigley, 14, http://www.catalogue.nationalarchives.gov.uk).

5. President of the United Mine Workers John L. Lewis called coal strikes in 1943, in April and November 1946, and again in 1948 and 1949. ER repeatedly took him to task in her column for being arrogant and irresponsible. The fifty-nine-day UMW strike, initiated on April 1, 1946, so severely curtailed production in many industries that Truman ordered his secretary of the interior to seize the mines. The miners called off the strike when Lewis secured an agreement for a "welfare and retirement fund," supported by a levy on each ton of coal mined, to be managed by a board composed of management and labor, a wage increase, vacation pay, an agreement to enforce a

revised Federal Mine Safety Code, and management's acceptance of NLRB decisions ("Labor Puzzle," *NYT*, 2 June 1946, E1). For ER's My Day postwar discussions of Lewis, see *MD*, 8, 9, and 29 May 1946 and 25 September 1946.

FDR and Lewis had an especially bitter relationship after the "Little Steel" strike in 1937. When FDR, who had supported the CIO sit-down strike in 1936, issued a "plague on both your houses" response to the steel strike, Lewis attacked the president in his Labor Day radio address. By 1940, Lewis refused to support FDR's reelection, telling his listeners in an October 25, 1940, radio address that "I think the reelection of President Roosevelt for a third term would be a national evil of the first magnitude" (Alinsky, 329–30; Dulles and Dubofsky, 308–11).

6. May 17, Truman met with union leaders Alvaney Johnson and Alexander Whitney, who informed him that their negotiations with management were deadlocked. The president then, while the leaders were still in his office, signed an executive order authorizing the Office of Defense Transportation to take over railroad operations at 4:00 the following afternoon (Donovan, 210; "Text of the President's Plea to Congress for Strike Action," *NYT*, 26 May 1946, 23; "President Scores Personal Triumph in His Grim Speech to Congress," *NYT*, 26 May 1946, 1).

7. *MD*, 28 May 1946.

8. See *MD*, 28 May 1946.

9. Under the reorganization plan several social welfare and social security agencies moved to the Federal Security Agency on July 16, 1946, including most of the Children's Bureau programs. The bureau's child labor unit remained under the Labor Department. Organized labor and other long-time advocates of the bureau feared that the reorganization would strip Katharine Lenroot of her authority to promote programs for children and set standards for child welfare ("Child Aid Lag Seen in Transfer Plan," *NYT*, 22 May 1946, 25; "Children's Bureau Backed by AFL-CIO," *NYT*, 24 May 1946, 16; "President Assures Children's Bureau," *NYT*, 11 June 1946, 23; John W. Edelman (CIO), "Letters to the Editor," *WP*, 15 June 1946, 6; "Senate Kills Permanent NHA, 45–31," *NYT*, 16 July 1946, 1; "Security Group Gets Children's Bureau," *NYT*, 17 July 1946, 20).

10. Harold D. Smith (1898–1947) served as director of the US Bureau of the Budget from 1939 to 1946, when he left to become vice president of the International Bank of Reconstruction and Development, also known as the World Bank (Felix Belair, Jr., "Smith Quits Budget Post To Take World Bank Job," *NYT*, 20 June 1946, 1; finding aid, Harold D. Smith Papers, HSTL).

11. Dr. Katharine F. Lenroot (1891–1982) first joined the US Children's Bureau as a special investigator in 1915, eventually serving as its head from 1934 to 1951. ER shared many of Lenroot's concerns about child welfare, worked alongside her as Lenroot drafted sections of the initial Social Security proposal and the Fair Labor Standards Act, worked with Lenroot to convene a White House Conference on Child Welfare, and frequently publicized her work in her My Day column (Ware, *Suffrage*, 97, 103; "Katharine Lenroot Dies," *WP*, 13 February 1982, B4; *MD*, 6 October 1944, 14 December 1944, and 2 April 1945).

12. The US Children's Bureau, established in 1912, represented one of the few federal agencies where professional women had a strong presence. Under its first director, Hull House veteran Julia Lathrop, the bureau promoted protective legislation for children's hours and wages, and brought attention to the issues of juvenile justice and imprisonment. By 1946, it led the legislative campaigns to "reduce infant and maternal mortality, improve child health, abolish child labor laws, identify the causes of illegitimacy, advocate care for children with 'special needs,' and—perhaps its greatest achievement—make federal aid to dependent children a noncontroversial part of the nation's duty" (Carp).

13. In response to President Truman's request for emergency legislation to deal with what the president called the "the obstinate arrogance" of rail-union leader Alexander Whitney, the House of Representatives passed a bill providing for the induction of strikers into the armed services and for

the transfer of all profits of strike-bound plants under government control to the Treasury Department. The measure also authorized the use of injunctions against those encouraging strikes and the loss of seniority rights by workers remaining on strike after government control had been assumed. For more on Truman's speech to Congress requesting emergency legislation see header and *n3* above (Samuel A. Tower, "House Votes Curbs, 303–13; "Senate Passes Own Bill First," *NYT*, 26 May 1946, 1; Hamby, *Man*, 378–79).

14. The following day Truman vetoed the Case labor disputes bill, arguing that its measures were counterproductive and did not deal with the underlying causes of industrial disputes. The House was unable to garner to enough votes to override his veto (C. P. Trussell, "President Vetoes Case Bill; Denies It Would End Strife; House Fails To Repass It," *NYT*, 12 June 1946, 1; "Mr. Truman and the Case Bill," *NYT*, 6 June 1946, 17).

15. A strike in the shipping industry was temporarily averted in mid-June (Louis Stark, "Ship Settlement at Deadline Accepted to Defer the Strike," *NYT*, 15 June 1946, 1).

16. For more on the creation of the Federal Security Agency see *n9* above. ER expressed her reservations about the reorganization of the Labor Department, which divided the functions of the Children's Bureau, in a letter to Truman on May 27 (Document 116).

ON THE NATIONAL COMMITTEE FOR JUSTICE IN COLUMBIA, TENNESSEE

Just as ER lent her name to a telegram soliciting organizational support for the National Committee for Justice in Columbia, Tennessee, she also lent her name to this letter, typed on NCJCT letterhead, which endorsed the committee's controversial report "Terror in Tennessee" and solicited contributions to continue its work. NCJCT distributed the letter to mailing lists provided by the CIO, the ACLU, the NAACP, Americans United, and other supportive organizations, ensuring that the letter reached more than 32,500 people.[1]

118

Fund-raising Letter for National Committee for Justice in Columbia, Tennessee
29 May 1946 [New York City]

Dear Friend:

Thirty-one Negro citizens of Columbia, Tennessee are under arrest, charged with crimes ranging from attempted murder in the first degree to carrying concealed weapons. Two other Negro prisoners have been killed, shot down in the Columbia jail by officers of the law.

These men, more than half of their number recently discharged servicemen, have been the innocent victims of race hatred and violence. The events which took place in Columbia on February 25th and 26th rose out of a dispute between a white shopkeeper and a Negro customer. They culminated in lynch threats, an armed invasion of the Negro district, wanton destruction of Negro property and wholesale arrests and beatings of Negro citizens. The enclosed pamphlet, "Terror in Tennessee," adequately describes this series of outrages.[2]

Our Committee was formed to provide every possible safeguard to those Negroes unjustly charged with crimes and to assure them the justice denied them by sworn officers of the law in Tennessee. We shall work with the legal staff of the National Association for the Advancement of Colored People in providing adequate legal defense to the victims. We will work to assure that those responsible for this bloodshed and mockery of the law be tried for the real crimes committed. We shall attempt, so far as it lies within our power, to provide reparations for the damage occasioned Negro businessmen and householders by brutal mob action. Finally and above all, we will tell the people this story of injustice and race hatred at Columbia so that Americans may take measures to guard against a repetition of this tragic situation in their own communities.

Please help us to win these objectives through your generous contribution. Every dollar you give will help to assure simple justice to humble men who today stand charged with crime while the real criminals are free. We want an America where every man, Negro or white, may stand on the same footing before the law. Help us to achieve that.

Sincerely yours,
Eleanor Roosevelt   Channing H. Tobias

P.S. This Committee represents a joint effort on the part of all organizations and individuals working to secure justice for the defendants in Columbia. If you have received and responded to a previous appeal in connection with this case, please pass this letter on to a friend.

TLS AERP, FDRL

1. Memo on Fund Raising, NAACP, DL. For information on the formation of the NCJCT, see *n*1 and *n*4 Document 105 and Document 102.

2. The NAACP published "Terror in Tennessee" as a response to press accounts placing the blame solely on African Americans. The pamphlet's dramatic depiction of events provoked immediate controversy. For example, countering the image of armed African Americans sniping from roof tops as white troops tried to restore order common in most coverage, "Terror in Tennessee" describes the Highway Patrol's entrance into Bottom as follows:

> Zero hour was at dawn on Tuesday morning. State patrolmen and guardsmen in full battle dress, armed with tommy-guns, automatic rifles and machine-guns, lay down a barrage, battle fashion. After a few minutes during which volley after volley crashed into the pitiful, wooden walls of the beleaguered houses, the small army began to advance into the smoke-filled area. Machine-gun bullets whipped into the windows and doors of the silent buildings. Walls disintegrated in the face of the hot machine-gun blasts. Inside their homes Negro citizens—men, women and children—lay flattened against their quivering floors" ("Terror in Tennessee," MMBP, DcWaMMD).

On April 29, 1946, Judge Elmer Davies, presiding over the federal grand jury responsible for investigating civil rights violations in Columbia, adjourned the jury and asked the FBI to investigate the publishers of "false-hoods and half-truths," referring to pamphlets circulated by a variety of organizations including the NAACP and the Communist Party. The grand jury's report of June 14 attributed "malicious intent and desire to incite racial discord" to those who circulated pamphlets. The report also reveals the jury's "regret" that "the mailing of such pamphlets does not constitute a violation of any Federal Statute" (O'Brien, 38–39; Report of Grand Jury in the Matter of the Racial Disturbance at Columbia, Tennessee, AERP).

While refusing to distance itself from the pamphlet's contents, at its July meeting, the National Committee for Justice in Columbia, Tennessee considered reprinting two *Washington Post* articles written by Agnes Meyer for inclusion with future fund-raising letters in place of "Terror in Tennessee" (Memo on Fund Raising, NAACP, DLC).

1946

"In our haste to get back to the business of normal living, have we forgotten to be the great people that we were expected to be?"

© CORBIS.

Eleanor Roosevelt played many roles in addition to serving as a delegate to the UN and often pursued the same objective through more than one channel. As tensions rose both at home and abroad, she increasingly expressed her concerns and lobbied those officials most capable of influencing policy. For example, she advised Truman that one must "always talk things out absolutely sincerely" with the Russians before taking action[1] and urged him to persuade Edward Stettinius to reconsider his resignation as US representative on the UN Security Council. She lobbied Secretary of State Byrnes to implement the recommendations of the Anglo-American Committee of Inquiry on Jewish settlements in Palestine and suggested to both the president and Attorney General Tom Clark that they release those conscientious objectors still in prison. She arranged a meeting between Bernard Baruch, then US representative to the UN Atomic Energy Commission, and Secretary of Commerce Henry Wallace after Baruch strongly objected to Wallace's public remarks about the atomic bomb and Wallace refused to see him. She also acted as an intermediary between Attorney General Clark and the NAACP leaders Walter White and Thurgood Marshall when, as co-chair of the National Committee for Justice in Columbia, Tennessee, she pressed their concern regarding the failure of the federal grand jury investigation to bring any of those responsible for the violence against African Americans and the destruction of their property to trial.

ER addressed issues of discrimination on a number of other fronts as well. In her essay, "The Minorities Question," she acknowledged that "racial and religious tensions in this country are becoming more acute." The "basic thing we must do is to stop generalizing," she suggested. "When we look at each individual without thinking of him as a Jew or as a Negro ... he stands on his own feet as an individual and we stand with him on an equal basis."[2] In correspondence included in this section she responded to one writer who characterized Jews as "unscrupulous" and "cunning" and another who asked her for her solution to the Jewish "problem."[3]

In the area of women's equality, ER pressed Truman to appoint more women to positions within his administration, just as she had urged governments to appoint more women to represent them at the UN. She did not support, however, efforts to establish a separate UN Commission on the Status of Women because she thought it more effective to have women represented in all discussions where they could work with men "in definite positions within the government and within their parties." Yet once the commission was established, she dropped her objections.[4] She continued to object to the Equal Rights Amendment on "purely practical grounds," explaining her reasoning in both private correspondence with Florence Kitchelt and Nora Stanton Barney and in My Day.

The documents in this section also illustrate ER's continuing engagement in liberal politics. Although ER used *Look* magazine to reiterate that she would not run for public office, she remained active in the Democratic Party, serving as temporary chair and keynote speaker at the New York State Democratic Convention. In the aftermath of the decisive Republican victory in the 1946 election, many liberals, including ER, concluded that allowing Communists to hold positions in unions and progressive political organizations hurt those organizations and the liberal cause. Although ER continued to believe that Americans should have the right to join the Communist Party, in December, she joined others in urging the Independent Citizens Committee of the Arts, Sciences and Professions (ICCASP) and the National Citizens Political Action Committee (NCPAC), which were about to merge into the Progressive Citizens of America (PCA), to "make up their minds to remove from their membership all people affiliated with, or supposed to have communist leanings to the American Communist Party."[5]

ER also continued to object to the intense support American clergy offered Martin Niemöller. When the German pastor ultimately arrived in the US for his lecture tour, ER once again questioned his beliefs as well as his conduct. When Bishop G. Bromley Oxnam, with whom she had worked on other social justice issues, objected to what he thought her bigoted stance, she replied that "bringing this gentleman here" is "stupid beyond words" because it might "lull" Americans into forgetting that "the German people are to blame, that they committed horrible crimes."[6]

The documents also detail how ER pressed for action on UN-related issues—such as the international control of atomic energy, providing adequate relief supplies for Europe, the repatriation or resettlement of refugees, and the escalating crisis in Palestine—even when the organization was not in session. For example, when British Foreign Secretary Ernest Bevin alleged that Americans favored the admission of Jewish refugees to Palestine because "we do not want them in New York," ER urged Americans to do their part, pointing out that it would be "quite possible to absorb far more than our share of the displaced people in Europe," but insisting that the "particular point at issue ... is that there are 100,000 Jews in Europe who must find homes immediately and they want to go to Palestine."[7]

When the shooting down of two American planes by Yugoslavia threatened to end American aid to Yugoslavia, ER wrote in My Day: "I do not want food and medical supplies confused with military supplies" and hoped "that we will always distinguish between the people and their governments in countries which are not our type of democracies." She then wondered if the American people themselves were partly responsible for some nations ceasing to trust and respect the United States: "In our haste to get back to the business of normal living, have we forgotten to be the great people that we were expected to be?"[8]

After the UN reconvened that fall, ER played a role in the founding of the International Refugee Organization (IRO) and the United Nations International Children's Fund (UNICEF). When, during the UN debates, the Soviets and their allies objected to the provision in the IRO constitution that permitted refugees to choose not to return to their countries of origin, ER again rose to counter their objection. As soon as the UN adopted the IRO constitution and established UNICEF, she used her column and personal contacts to promote US participation in the new agencies and to secure the public and private funding the agencies needed to begin operations. Tensions over Spain at the UN led Freda Kirchwey, who objected to US recognition of Franco's Spain, to hope that ER would use her "enormous" influence to persuade the Truman administration to take a tougher stance on the issue.[9] Although ER "as an individual" supported the recognition of the government in exile, she told Kirchwey that as a delegate she did "not feel actually conversant enough ... to set my opinion up against those of the Department of State. On the other hand, I do recognize that to just tell them to have a free election, and to do nothing about obtaining one, is a futile gesture which has worried me from the beginning."[10]

––––––––––

1. See Document 121, ER to Harry Truman, 1 June 1946.

2. See Document 151, "The Minorities Question," November 1946.

3. See Document 127, ER to Peggie Wingard, 14 June 1946 and Document 144, ER to George Van Horn Moseley, 5 September 1946.

4. See Document 159, ER to Louise Grant Smith, 3 December 1946.

5. See Document 173, ER to Calvin B. Baldwin, 29 December 1946.

6. See Document 165, ER to G. Bromley Oxnam, 21 December 1946.

7. See Document 129, My Day, 22 June 1946.

8. See Document 140, My Day, 23 August 1946.

9. See Document 160, Freda Kirchwey to ER, 3 December 1946.

10. See Document 161, ER to Freda Kirchwey, 4 December 1946.

Bernard Baruch told the UN Atomic Energy Commission that "behind the black portent of the new atomic age lies a hope which seized upon with faith, can work our salvation. If we fail," he concluded, "then we have damned every man to be the slave of fear." See Document 128. KEYSTONE/HULTON ARCHIVES/

GETTY IMAGES.

ER, unlike the religious leaders picketing the White House, found it "hard" to suppress "the feeling" that conscientious objectors exercised the "freedom to live up to their religious beliefs at the expense of some other boy's sacrifice." Yet after the war, she thought "the time has come to free these men." See Documents 132–34. MARIE HANSEN/TIME LIFE PICTURES/GETTY IMAGES.

[PN: END OF ART]

Although ER had refused offers to run for office or direct national political organizations, she conferred regularly with Democratic Party leaders and aspiring candidates. Here she talks with first-term congressman John F. Kennedy. They would soon disagree over what direction the party should take. See Documents 137 and 143. AP IMAGES.

"I can not bear to think of the Jews of Europe who have spent so many years in concentration camps, behind wire again on Cypress. It seems to me that the 100,000 Jews should be let into Palestine and that some real agreement should be reached with the Arabs." See Document 141. AP IMAGES.

[PN: END OF ART]

ER admired German pastor Martin Niemöller until he argued that Germans "like to be governed" and "longed for such authority." ER labeled his approach dangerous, arguing people "should be made to realize that they are responsible for their leaders." Her criticism drew stinging rebuttals. See Documents 28–30 and 164–65. © BETTMAN/CORBIS.

ER traveled to Washington to help found Americans for Democratic Action. She challenged those "other progressives, many of whom are far younger and more active than I am, and far more influential" to embrace "the job of awakening a sleeping people to the sense of responsibility" they must "accept." See Document 177. AMERICANS FOR DEMOCRATIC ACTION (ADA).

119

If You Ask Me [excerpt]

Ladies' Home Journal June 1946

Someone told me that you said recently in your column that the American people do not know how to govern themselves and need to be told. What exactly did you say?

I have absolutely no idea what I could have said in my column which gave such a peculiar impression. The only thing that I have said at various times is that, when the American people become apathetic and do not keep the control of their government in their own hands, it is bound to slip into the hands of those who make politics a profession. Therefore, because of their indifference, the American people may sometimes find themselves slaves to representatives who do not really represent them.

Don't you feel that the American people were misled in accepting the Four Freedoms[1] as ideals to fight for, and don't you think our boys who died for them died in vain?

No, I do not think the American people were misled any more than they were misled by our forefathers who wrote the Constitution and the Bill of Rights. We haven't yet achieved everything that was set down in the Constitution as our ultimate objective, but it did not hurt us any to have it set down, and it gives us something to strive for, and many people have died for these aims. Every time that we get a step nearer to the great conception that our forefathers had, we justify the faith of those who died, and this is true of a belief in the Four Freedoms and in the hope of their ultimate realization.

TMs DLC

----

1. In his January 6, 1941 State of the Union address, FDR told Congress that America "should look forward to a world founded upon four essential human freedoms," which he defined as Freedom of Speech and Expression, Freedom of Worship, Freedom from Want, and Freedom from Fear. The president and ER then continued to reference these principles throughout the war. Norman Rockwell's depictions of the Four Freedoms, which appeared in the *Saturday Evening Post* and were then turned into posters to sell war bonds, helped make these freedoms the ideals Americans felt they defended as they fought World War II (Zevin, "Four Freedoms Speech," 258–67; Murray and McCabe, 3–7, 61–62, 69–72).

ON WOMEN, EQUAL RIGHTS, AND
THE UNITED NATIONS

The Human Rights Commission and the UN Subcommission on the Status of Women disagreed over what the subcommission's final report should cover.[1] As the following column reports, ER, Cassin, and a few other human rights commissioners "felt that the report, because it was the work of a nuclear subcommission operating under very definite terms of reference, had perhaps covered too much ground and gone into too much detail, much of which might have been left for consideration by the full subcommission when it is appointed."

When the Subcommission on the Status of Women submitted its report to the Human Rights Commission on May 14, the commission, following suggestions made by ER and René Cassin, reduced, at least temporarily, the scope of the subcommission's future work by tabling the section of the report which outlined an ambitious political, social, and economic agenda.[2]

On May 15, Bodil Begtrup,[3] the chair of the Subcommission on the Status of Women, and four other members of the subcommission held a news conference at which they defended the scope of their report. Begtrup, the *New York Times* reported, "explained that the subcommission felt it necessary to cover a great deal of material in its report because women expected it … 'They want us to do something. We felt this responsibility rather heavily. We think our report is not detailed enough. As the field of discrimination is so vast our report has to be comprehensive, and it's not comprehensive enough.'"[4]

ER also foresaw a negative reaction from women in the United States who backed Alice Paul's National Woman's Party in its campaign to grant women full equality through the passage of an Equal Rights Amendment to the US Constitution. ER anticipated that her opposition to the proposed federal legislation might lead advocates of the amendment to think she would oppose the report of the Subcommission on the Status of Women.[5] As she makes clear here, that was not the case.

_____120_____

My Day
1 June 1946

HYDE PARK, Friday—As I was leaving the United Nations meeting last Tuesday, a newspaper woman stopped me to ask if there was a cleavage in the Human Rights Commission on the subject of the report made by the Subcommission on the Status of Women. I was glad to be able to tell her that there has been no disagreement that I know of on the part of any member of the commission.[6]

Some of us felt that the report, because it was the work of a nuclear subcommission operating under very definite terms of reference, had perhaps covered too much ground and gone into too much detail, much of which might have been left for consideration by the full subcommission when it is appointed. However, except for this one criticism, which certainly meant no fundamental cleavage in thinking, I heard no criticism of any of the recommendations made.

It is known that I have opposed a group of women in this country who have been in favor of an equal-rights amendment to our Constitution.[7] As some of them have been active in working on the outskirts, so to speak, of this subcommission, I suppose they felt that I would be in opposition to the report. That, of course, is not true.[8]

I believe that, if the ladies who are so anxious to have a Federal amendment for equal rights would devote as much energy toward changing the State laws which really interfere with the rights of our women, they would soon find they had little of which to complain. I am still opposed to an equal-rights amendment, which would make it possible to wipe out much of the legislation which has been enacted in many States for the protection of women in industry. This, however, has nothing to do with the report in question.

We cannot change the fact that women are different from men. It's true that some women can do more than men, and some can do men's jobs better than men can do them. But the fact that they are different cannot be changed, and it is fortunate for us that this is the case. The best results are always obtained when men and women work together, with the recognition that their abilities and contributions may differ but that, in every field, they supplement each other.

The report of the Subcommission on the Status of Women frankly recognized this difference and the need for special considerations where women are concerned.[9] I do not know whether the group I mentioned are opposed to this section of the report or not, but I am quite sure that, as this is an international report, they will have comparatively little influence on the thinking of the Economic and Social Council in its consideration of the report as a whole.

This report was undertaken with great seriousness, and I think the women who worked on it deserve great praise, especially the chairman, Mrs. Bodil Begtrup, who gave so much of her time and thought to having the report truly represent the thinking of the whole subcommission.

TMs AERP, FDRL

---

1. Although ER served as an ex-officio member of the UN Subcommission on the Status of Women and did not attend all its meetings, she supported its work and sometimes took an active role in its deliberations. According to a State Department report on the work of the subcommission, ER's "comments and warnings were disregarded. Full advantage was taken by the Sub-Commission of the fact that she had no vote and it can be said that she exercised little or no influence on the Sub-Commission's policy" ("Comments and Recommendations on Report of Sub-Commission on Status of Women," (SD/E/HR/ST/1), RG84, NARA II.

2. Instead of sending this part of the report on to ECOSOC, it asserted that it merited further study by the full subcommission once it was appointed.

3. Bodil Begtrup (1903–1987), active in the Danish National Council of Women since 1930, became a member of Denmark's delegation to the League of Nations Assembly in 1938 and chief film censor of Denmark during the Nazi occupation. After the war, Begtrup attended the first UN Assembly meetings in London as one of Denmark's delegates and chaired the Commission on the Status of Women until 1948. The following year, she was appointed Danish minister to Iceland ("Actively Resisted Nazis," *WP*, 6 March 1949, S11; "Bodil Begtrup," *CB 1946*; Hobbins, ed., *Edge of Greatness*, vol. 1, *n*49).

4. Begtrup quoted in Lucy Greenbaum, "U.N. Women Blunt on Full Equality," *NYT*, 16 May 1946, 10. The struggle continued when Begtrup requested and received permission to present her report in person before the Economic and Social Council rather than leaving this responsibility to ER. When she did so, Begtrup made a recommendation that the subcommission had not included in its report to the Human Rights Commission: that the Subcommission on the Status of Women be made a full commission. ECOSOC adopted this recommendation June 21, empowering the commission to examine women's "political, economic, civil, social, and educational" rights and to prepare recommendations the council could take to improve women's standing in these specific areas ("For the Digest," *Democratic Digest*, June 1946, AERP, FDRL; Glendon, 32;

"Commission on the Status of Women," http://www.un.org/womenwatch/daw/csw/, accessed 1 November 2005).

5. Although ER articulated her belief in the political equality of women, she feared that a constitutional amendment would negate state laws protecting women workers, particularly industrial workers (Lash, *World*, 107). See also Document 138, Document 155, and Document 156.

6. She may have meant Lucy Greenbaum (later known as Lucy Freeman [1916-2005]) of the *New York Times*, who had covered women's issues including ER, the United Nations, and the Subcommission on the Status of Women. Her colleague at the paper, Nancy MacLennan (later Lady Enniskillen), a former US foreign service officer, also covered United Nations news in these years (Lucy Greenbaum, "World Goal Fixed in Women's Rights," *NYT*, 14 May 1946, 10; "L.S. Greenbaum, Lawyer, 62, Dies," *NYT*, 29 August 1951, 25; "Lucy Freeman a Bride," *NYT*, 25 December 1952, 24; Lucy Freeman, 88, a Pioneer in Reporting on Mental Health," *NYT*, 3 January 2005, B6; cornell-magazine.cornell.edu/Archive/Nov1998/NovObits.html, accessed 4 August 2005).

7. Such groups included the National Woman's Party and the World Party for Equal Rights for Women (also known as the World Woman's Party), which Alice Paul had founded in 1938. Paul actively lobbied both the League of Nations and organizers of the United Nations to introduce the equal rights principle into their policies and statements of purpose. By 1946, groups such as the Federation of Business and Professional Women, the General Federation of Women's Clubs, and the National Association of Women Lawyers backed a version of the equal rights amendment. First introduced in 1923, the language of the proposed amendment changed over time, so that by 1946, it read: "Equality of rights under the law shall not be denied or abridged by the United States or by any State on account of sex" ("Women Hail Motion on World Equality," *NYT*, 12 December 1946, 3; Bess Furman, "Equal Rights Fail to Get Two-Thirds in Vote in Senate," *NYT*, 20 July 1946, 1; "'Equal Rights' Amendment," *NYT*, 20 July 1946, 12; Cott, 125, 324–25 *n*13; Rupp and Taylor, 59; Rowbotham, 253–54, 680 *n*85).

8. For more on ER's position on the Equal Rights Amendment in the United States, see Document 138.

9. The report recommended that, "while no disability should be attached to woman on the ground of her sex, in regard to the enjoyment of full equality in the exercise of social and labor rights and in the assumption of social and labor duties, special consideration may be given to woman on grounds of health and motherhood" (Lucy Greenbaum, "World Goal Fixed in Women's Rights," *NYT*, 14 May 1946, 10).

ON STETTINIUS'S RESIGNATION

Edward Stettinius, whom ER thought "more courageous and honest" than his successor Secretary of State James Byrnes, resigned from the American delegation to the United Nations because he objected to the administration's management of the delegation. As Stettinius recorded in his diary, when he discussed his resignation with Byrnes, "I pointed out the extremely inefficient and ineffective manner whereby no one person was responsible for the United Nations affairs … I did not feel that I was on the inner circle …" In his subsequent meeting with Truman, he told the president "With atomic work being handled by one group and social and economic and trusteeship work by another, and the State Department determining policy on Security Council affairs, I am just not needed."

While ER recognized Stettinius's limitations, she continued to value his counsel and wrote Truman, urging him to pressure Stettinius to rescind his resignation.[1]

121

Eleanor Roosevelt to Harry Truman
1 June 1946 [Hyde Park]

Dear Mr. President:

I read in the papers this morning that Mr. Stettinius's resignation has really come in and that you and Secretary Byrnes hope he will reconsider.

I am wondering just what his reasons are, but in any case, I feel there is no one who has had his long experience, nor been as devoted to the ideal of the United Nations, and if it is possible for you and Secretary Byrnes to get him to continue, I think it will keep a great many of us from feeling that the cause is a lost cause.

I can not help feeling that we need to be firm but we haven't always been firm in the right way in our foreign policy because one can only be successfully firm, if the people one is firm with, particularly the Russians, have complete confidence in one's integrity and I am not sure that our attitude on questions like Spain and the Argentine[2] and even in Germany itself, has been conducive to creating a feeling that we would always keep our word and that we would always talk things out absolutely sincerely before we took action.[3] We are bound to differ, of course, because we have fundamental differences, but I think these should be made clear. If at the top there was a complete sense of confidence and security and the policies at the top were really carried on at every level things might go better.

Very cordially yours,
Eleanor Roosevelt

TLS AERP, FDRL

Truman responded to ER's letter on June 4.[4] On the same day ER expressed her disappointment over Stettinius's resignation publicly, telling her readers that:

I was deeply grieved by the news that Edward R. Stettinius, Jr., our permanent member on the Security Council, had handed in his resignation, and I hope very much that the President and Secretary of State Byrnes can prevail upon him to remain. It seems to me that someone who has been so intimately connected with every step in the organization of the United Nations is very badly needed during these first years.

I realize that doing this work is a very great sacrifice and that there are few compensations for a man as young as Mr. Stettinius. I know he has done it from the beginning simply because he realized that our hope of future peace lay in the success of the United Nations idea. If his resignation means that he has come to the conclusion that the work cannot be accomplished and that we are not on the right path, then I think a great many of us will feel deeply discouraged.

122

Harry Truman to Eleanor Roosevelt

4 June 1946 [The White House]

Dear Mrs. Roosevelt:

I appreciated very much your good letter of the first and nobody was more surprised than I when I received the letter from Mr. Stettinius that he wanted to quit as representative of the United Nations Security Council. I urged him to stay but he was very anxious to quit, saying that he felt his job with the United Nations had been completed. I don't think it has but there is no way I can force a man to stay on the job if he doesn't want to stay.[5]

I am truly sorry that you are not pleased with the attitude of the United States toward Spain, Argentine, and Germany. Certainly we are trying to be consistent in these matters and are making every effort possible to get the United Nations on its feet as an active organization. I think that is the most important thing we have ahead of us. Naturally we expected to have difficulty with the Russians, French and British but none of the difficulties are insurmountable and I have every reason to believe that most of them will work out in a satisfactory manner. The conditions with which we are faced are not new as the result of the conflict—they are only greater in magnitude than they have been in the past because they are world-wide.

I do appreciate most sincerely your interest and your kindness in writing me. I'll be glad to hear from you on any subject at any time.

Sincerely yours,
Harry S. Truman

TLS, AERP, FDRL

---

1. As ER wrote her close friend Elinor Morgenthau: "Byrnes is much too small for the job and when all is said and done Stettinius is more courageous and honest but might be more easily fooled since Byrnes is smarter but can never give any inspiration" (ER to Elinor Morgenthau, 20 January 1946, quoted in Lash, *World*, 214; "Truman Accepts Resignation of Stettinius from U.N. Post," *WP*, 4 June 1946, 1; Campbell and Herring, eds., *Diaries*, 472–73).

2. The UN General Assembly adopted a Panamanian resolution in February 1946 and a resolution in December, drafted by a special General Assembly subcommittee, that blocked Franco-led Spain's admission to the United Nations and called on member states to cut diplomatic ties with Franco's regime. The United States concurred with these positions, suspending full diplomatic relations with Spain until 1951. Argentina voted against the resolutions, which added to growing tensions with

the United States. For ER's skepticism about Argentina's admission to the United Nations see Document 22 and Document 23.

By 1946, US-Argentinian diplomatic relations showed signs of strain and the election of Juan D. Peron as president in March raised new questions. At that time, however, US War Department officials pursued a less harsh policy toward Argentina while ER's good friend, former undersecretary of state Sumner Welles, argued that "efforts at coercion undertaken by the United States against Argentina" were costing the United States much good will. ER and Welles would correspond extensively on this issue in 1947 (See Document 200 and Document 201). ("UNO Affirms, 45-0, Rebuff to Franco," *NYT*, 10 February 1946, 1; "U.S. Policy Contest Seen in Argentina," *NYT*, 29 May 1946, 7).

3. The US government had not yet settled on a final plan to pursue in Germany, although officials had made several proposals and the US military government had launched a de-Nazification program in its occupation zone. ER did not approve of measures such as completely stripping Germany of industrial capacity. However, she counseled caution on the future of Germany, telling her My Day readers at the end of 1946:

> I do not believe in a "hard peace." I certainly do not believe in taking away hope from the people of any nation. But I believe that, when a nation has brought about two world wars in twenty-five years, we certainly should not consider rebuilding its power in a direction which will make it possible for that nation to bring about another war (*MD*, 31 December 1946; Harold Callender, "Murphy and Clay Report to Byrnes," *NYT*, 1 July 1946, 8; Kathleen McLaughlin, "U.S. to Classify Germans in Zone," *NYT*, 6 March 1946, 18).

4. *MD*, 4 June 1946.

5. Stettinius's notes on his meetings with the president and Secretary of State Byrnes about his resignation suggest that both men attempted to persuade him to remain in the position for at least a time (Campbell and Herring, eds., *Diaries*, 471–75; Harry Truman to Edward Stettinius, Jr., 3 June 1946, trumanlibrary.org/publicpapers/viewpapers.php?pid=1569, accessed 1 August 2005).

ON UNITED STATES POLICY ON PALESTINE

ER wrote Secretary of State Byrnes four times in three weeks. On May 13 she wanted to know about the discrepancy between the number of American and foreign journalists allowed to attend the United States' upcoming atomic tests in the Pacific. On May 21 ER wrote again to ask if her support for a potential plebiscite in the South Tyrol would hamper State Department negotiations. Concerned that British intransigence could deter increased Jewish immigration to Palestine, ER sent this fourth letter to the secretary urging Byrnes to implement the recommendations made by the Anglo-American Committee of Inquiry.[1]

123

Eleanor Roosevelt to James Byrnes
5 June 1946 [New York City]

Dear Mr. Secretary:

I seem to be bombarding you with letters these days but I am wondering what is going to happen about the combined British report on Palestine.[2]

It seems to me that at least 100,000 Jews should be moved and moved quickly. I can not believe that with a little firmness, the Arabs can not be handled.[3] It always seemed to me that this investigation was a work of super-arrogation, since we knew that the Jews were there and that Palestine was there and all that lay in the way was Great Britain's willingness to let them in.[4]

When all is said and done, there are still the others in Europe and I do hope that something definite is being worked out so that they can start their lives anew. It is bad for people to hang doing nothing constructive and being supported even in misery such as the camps provide.

Very sincerely yours,
Eleanor Roosevelt

TLS RG59, NARA II

Undersecretary of State Dean Acheson replied to ER's June 5 letter to Secretary Byrnes.

124

Dean Acheson to Eleanor Roosevelt
12 June 1946 [Washington, DC?]

My dear Mrs. Roosevelt:

I take pleasure in acknowledging your letter of June 5, 1946 regarding Palestine.

You have no doubt seen the President's statement to the press of July 11 announcing the formation of a Cabinet Committee to assist him in formulating and implementing such a policy on Palestine as may be adopted by this Government.[5] I enclose for your convenient reference the President's Executive Order and press release[6] and my statement to the press in this connection.[7]

I wish to thank you for your comments which have been noted by the officers of the Department who are working toward a solution of the Palestine problem.

Sincerely yours,
Dean Acheson

TLcst RG59, NARA II

---

1. Also during this period, ER wrote Byrnes as well as Truman and other senior members of the administration in support of awarding the Medal of Merit to her friend theatrical producer John Golden for his wartime efforts to provide entertainment for the US armed forces (ER to James Byrnes, 13 May 1946, RG59, NARA II; ER to James Byrnes, 21 May 1946, AERP; James Byrnes to ER, 22 May 1946, AERP; Draft of ER to James Byrnes, undated AERP; *MD*, 10 July 1946).

2. See *n*5 Document 82. The April 1946 report of the Anglo-American Committee of Inquiry recommended the immediate admission of 100,000 Jewish refugees then housed in European camps to Palestine and the resumption of land sales there to Jews. The report also recommended that Palestine remain under British authority until the UN could negotiate a new trusteeship agreement. The plan set as its long-term goal an independent government for Palestine composed of equal numbers of Arab and Jewish officials. On April 30, Truman, facing pressure from American Zionists and those opposed to the admittance of refugees to the United States and concerned about the issue's possible impact on the November 1946 congressional elections, endorsed the committee's recommendations regarding immigration and land sales despite British foreign secretary Ernest Bevin's request to Byrnes that the report's publication be delayed. The full report was made public on May 1 (*HSTE*, 95; Cohen, *Palestine*, 96–114; Acheson, 172).

3. On May 20, the Arab states rejected the committee's report and denied the United States' right to intervene. Their rejection prompted the British and the Americans to form a special committee to reassess the situation. In ER's view, the United States' decision to participate in "a joint inquiry" meant the British "would expect us to do our share in carrying out the findings" (Cohen, *Palestine*, 116–20; *MD*, 8 May 1946).

4. For more on the origins of the Anglo-American Committee of Inquiry, see *n*9 Document 79. In an attempt to curb Jewish population growth in Palestine, the British Government in May 1939 issued a White Paper limiting Jewish immigration to 75,000 people for the next five years. After the war the British continued to restrict legal immigration to 1,500 people per month as they had under the White Paper. They did so because they thought it would upset the population balance between the Arabs and Jews in Palestine (the Arabs were then the majority) and lead to more violence and unrest (Seegev, 440, 482; Louis and Stookey, eds., 5).

5. On June 11 (not July 11), 1946, Truman issued Executive Order 9735 creating the Cabinet Committee on Palestine and Related Problems to help him develop and implement US policy on Palestine, negotiate with the British and other foreign governments, and communicate with "private organizations" on matters relating to "the recommendations of the Anglo-American Committee of Inquiry." The committee consisted of the secretaries of state, war, and treasury under the chairmanship of the secretary of state. Truman directed the committee to consider the practical issues (such as transportation and housing) surrounding the admission of 100,000 Jewish refugees to Palestine ("Statement by the President," *Department of State Bulletin*, 23 June 1946, 1089; Acheson, 174; Truman vol. 1, 150; "Cabinet Unit Set Up to Study Palestine," *NYT*, 12 June 1946, 1). See also *n*2 above.

6. The executive order that established the cabinet committee also provided for a Board of Alternates made up of fully deputized representatives of the committee's cabinet-level members.

The secretary of state's alternate chaired this group, which acted as the committee's executive agency. The committee drew its staff from the State, War, and Treasury Departments (Executive Order 9735, "Establishing a Cabinet Committee on Palestine and Related Problems," *Department of State Bulletin*, 23 June 1946, 1089–90).

7. Acheson's press statement announced the appointment of Henry F. Grady (1882–1957) as his representative on the Board of Alternates. A specialist in the economic aspects of foreign relations, Grady led the American Section of the Allied Mission to observe the Greek elections in 1945–46. He had previously served as vice-chairman of the Tariff Commission (1937–39) and assistant secretary of state for reciprocal trade agreement negotiations (1939–41). (When Grady resigned in 1941 to become president of the government-controlled American President Lines, Acheson replaced him at the State Department.) While serving as president of American President Lines, Grady, at FDR's behest, undertook a high-level government mission to Asia to locate and secure strategic materials before the United States entered World War II in December, 1941. After the war began, he returned to India to encourage production of war materials and subsequently headed the economic section of the Allied Control Commission in Italy ("Statement by the Secretary of State," *Department of State Bulletin*, 23 June 1946, 1089; Acheson, 18, 770; "Dr. Henry Grady, Diplomat Is Dead," *NYT*, 15 September 1957, 84).

ON REFUGEES AND DISPLACED PERSONS

Katharine Marjory Ramsay Stewart-Murray, the Duchess of Atholl (1874–1960), chaired the British League for European Freedom, an organization dedicated to the promotion of democracy and the repatriation of displaced persons in Europe.[1] In May 1946, Duchess Atholl cabled ER to express her concerns about the refugee repatriation process.[2] A month later, Duchess Atholl wrote to ER again, this time attaching a memorandum the league distributed to all ECOSOC representatives, criticizing the Report of the Special Committee on Refugees and Displaced Persons. In particular, the league objected to the report's provisions regarding individual repatriation cases:

> We note that if … persecution, or fear, is to be regarded as a valid objection to repatriation, this must be judged based on reasonable grounds, but that it is not stated who is to judge of the reasonableness in a particular case. We venture to suggest that in no case should it be a representative of the government of the country of origin, as that would be to make a party to a case the judge of it. The arbiter should in our opinion, if possible, be someone of legal or judicial experience in possession of full information as to the conditions in the country of origin of the Displaced Person.

The memorandum also suggested that the special committee's exclusions against "assistance given by [the displaced persons] to the enemy in the late war" and "leaders of movements hostile to the government of their country of origin" placed undue responsibility on the refugees to prove innocence and forced them to forego freedom of speech:

> Our information is that in the vast majority of cases, refusal of repatriation is due to political conditions in the country of origin … Why should men who deplore and criticize these conditions be deprived of the help of the proposed international organisation, so long as they do not incite others to violence? Are these not indeed the very men whose courage and initiative should make them valuable citizens in countries needing development?[3]

The memorandum then recommended that "as many as possible of the camp inmates" serve as "liaison officers" and administrative staff in the "future organization" the United Nations would create.[4]

125

Katharine, Duchess of Atholl, to Eleanor Roosevelt

14 June 1946 [London]

Dear Mrs. Roosevelt

Knowing how much your efforts contributed to the passing of that resolution in the UNO Assembly which gave freedom of choice in regard to repatriation to the Displaced Persons,[5] I venture to send you herewith a copy of a memorandum our League has sent this week to the members of the Economic and Social Council in regard to certain findings of the Special Committee which has been sitting here, which we feel would rob the resolution of much of its value. We hope you may be able to find time to read it.

Then I also take this chance to send you the resolution of the Plenary Council of UNRRA to which I referred in a cable I sent you some weeks ago.[6] The official at Polish Headquarters here to whom the Polish liaison officers in the camps report, was so miserable when he heard of this reso-lution,[7] it seemed to me so serious an infraction of the UNO Assembly's resolution—or rather, decision—on this matter, that I felt I must ask you to do what you could. I fear the resolution of the Plenary Council must have been carried by the votes of some of the representatives of countries whose governments want to get the D.P.'s back at any cost. This attitude has been very evident on the Special Committee—hence the memorandum I enclose.

Forgive my troubling you, but this is such a big and urgent human problem.

Yours sincerely,
Katherine Atholl

ALS AERP, FDRL

ER replied five days later.

126

Eleanor Roosevelt to Katharine Atholl
19 June 1946 [Hyde Park]

Dear Dutchess Atholl:

I have received your letter of June 14th. I have written to the President and Mr. Byrnes and spoken to Mr. John Winant[8] but I feel hopeless about accomplishing much.[9]

Very sincerely yours,

TLc AERP, FDRL

---

1. *WH*, 231–34; "League for European Freedom," *The Times* (London), 20 January 1945, 2.

2. A copy of this correspondence no longer remains in ER's files. A letter from Trygve Lie to ER dated June 3, 1946, suggests that ER had forwarded a telegram from Atholl, which concerned "the control of displaced persons camps," to Lie, who in turn forwarded it to Fiorello La Guardia. On May 28, 1946, La Guardia responded to the content of the telegram (which La Guardia said included "a statement that the UNRRA Council at Atlantic City in March agreed to give the con-trol of displaced persons camps to representatives of countries of origin") by insisting that the UNRRA-adopted statement, Resolution 92, "said nothing about turning over to the governments the administration of the camps." La Guardia concluded that "the Duchess of Atholl's fears are groundless." Lie forwarded a copy of La Guardia's response to ER with his June 3 letter (Fiorello La Guardia to Trygve Lie, 28 May 1946, AERP; Trygve Lie to ER, 3 June 1946, AERP; "Resolution No. 92, Resolution Relating to Displaced Persons," AERP).

3. "Memorandum on the Report of the Special Committee on Refugees and Displaced Persons Submitted by the British League for European Freedom to the Delegates of The Economic and Social Council of the United Nations," AERP.

4. Duchess Atholl's hope for an independent organization for refugees would be fulfilled by the establishment of the International Refugee Organization (IRO) in December. On the IRO, see Document 152 and Document 168.

5. On February 12, 1946, the General Assembly adopted Resolution No. 7(I)/8(I), recommending first, that ECOSOC establish a committee to examine the problem of distinguishing between genuine refugees and war criminals; and second, that no displaced person may be forced to return to their native land. See also Document 78 (Glendon, 28–29).

6. Resolution No. 92, "A Resolution Relating to Displaced Persons," prioritized speed and efficiency in the relief administration's repatriation efforts, calling for the administration "to remove any handicaps … to the prompt repatriation of displaced persons" and to "keep in touch" with governments of the countries of origin in administering the refugee camps ("Resolution No. 92, Resolution Relating to Displaced Persons," AERP).

7. Some members of the Polish government-in-exile in London, which had lost its Allied support in July 1945, did not wish to be repatriated to Poland, which had been under Soviet control since liberation in the summer of 1944. The identity of the "official" to whom Duchess Atholl refers is unclear from the available record (Lukowski, 245; "Poles Return Home," *TL*, 21 March 1946, 4).

8. Ambassador John Winant. See *n*10, Document 75.

9. ER also forwarded the information to Dean Acheson. George Warren, the State Department advisor on refugees and displaced persons, responded on July 9, 1946, with a four-page letter rejecting each point the British League memorandum proposed. Furthermore, Warren argued that the league's position on "liaison officers not properly nominated by recognized governments … goes further than the" Soviet proposal which the General Assembly had previously rejected. Warren attributed this to the league's "misunderstanding of the separate and distinct functions of liaison officers and of administrators of the camps." He then summarily dismissed Atholl's argument that change would occur more speedily if the IRO were a specialized agency within the UN rather than "a constituent part." Rather than paraphrase Warren's detailed rebuttals, ER sent the duchess a copy of Warren's letter (George Warren to ER, 9 July 1946, AERP).

REFUTING ANTI-SEMITISM

May 28, Peggie Wingard, an Ohio woman whom ER had never met, wrote ER asserting that "our present programs trying to establish a better understanding between the races" were "doing the very opposite." In a two-page handwritten letter addressed to "Dear Eleanor," Wingard, who "maintained" she was "not anti-Semitic," wrote "particularly" to express her concern that the "class of Jew the U.S. seems to attract ... uses the lectures dished out to the Gentile public in our churches and schools as well as publications to further his interests economically." It was "unscrupulous" for Jews "to group themselves with the negro as a persecuted minority;" they were not "Jim Crowed;" and any call for "racial tolerance" that calls for the acceptance of Jews implies that "the Gentile must accept all the schemes and cunning of ... the Jewish groups" was counterproductive. Concluding "Europe doesn't want them and Britain shuts them out of Palestine—where they belong," she urged ER "to be aware of those motives so they do not injure all of us." She then asked ER "what do you think?"[1]

ER responded two weeks later.

127

Eleanor Roosevelt to Peggie Wingard
14 June 1946 [Hyde Park]

My dear Mrs. Wingard:

Forgive me if I address you somewhat formally, but I was not aware of having made your acquaintance. I have, however, met so many people that I realize I may be wrong in not addressing you by your first name, and if so I ask your forgiveness.

The subject matter of your letter seems to me very odd probably because you are so little aware of certain things that happen.

The Jewish people find themselves oft times "Jim Crowed" as you put it. I am not aware, however, that there is any particular kind of Jew who is attracted to this country. I know as great a variety of Jewish people as I know of Gentiles, or of Negroes. There is no particular type or group, and the sooner we learn that, the better it will be for all of us. There are bad people and good people; people with education and uneducated people in every group. There is a lack of understanding of people which creates racial and religious antagonisms, but I think we are doing better as time goes on. I can remember some of the things that went on at the end of the First World War but there is an improvement, especially among young people since this last War.

Very sincerely yours,

TLc AERP, FDRL

---

1. Peggie Wingard to ER, 28 May 1946, AERP.

ON BERNARD BARUCH AND ATOMIC ENERGY

June 14, Bernard Baruch, the American delegate to the UN's Commission on Atomic Energy (UNAEC), delivered a speech during the commission's first session, in which he made an urgent appeal for international control of atomic energy:[1]

> Behind the black portent of the new atomic age lies a hope which, seized upon with faith, can work our salvation. If we fail, then we have damned every man to be the slave of fear. Let us not deceive ourselves: We must elect world peace or world destruction …

> Now, if ever, is the time to act for the common good. Public opinion supports a world movement toward security. If I read the signs aright, the peoples want a program, not composed merely of pious thoughts, but of enforceable sanctions—an international law with teeth in it.[2]

While widespread agreement on the need for some form of international control existed, the major powers disagreed strongly over the commission's structure and scope.

ER then threw her support behind Baruch. Two days after ER's column appeared, Andrei Gromyko, the Soviet delegate to the UNAEC, formally rejected the American proposal and countered with a draft convention of his own.[3]

128

My Day
17 June 1946

HYDE PARK, Sunday—Bernard M. Baruch's speech on atomic control seems to me a very moving appeal to the governments of the world to listen to the most ardent desire of the peoples of the world. There is no question in my mind that the peoples of the world everywhere want peace, and I think Mr. Baruch made it clear that, as far as he is concerned, the preservation of the peace stood above every other consideration.

It boils down to this: We have temporarily the know-how and the plants where atomic bombs can be made. Temporarily, also, man has not yet found and may never find a preventive which will neutralize the destructive power of the atomic bomb as a war weapon. Eventually, however, more and more great nations will know what we know. Mr. Baruch faces this fact and acknowledges frankly that there is only one thing to do, and that is to wipe out the use of this weapon in war.

To do this, however, we will have to give up some part of our national sovereignty, for we will have to submit to inspection and licensing by an atomic energy authority set up under the United Nations. They will be given all of our secrets. They will license the use of material for industrial and therapeutic purposes throughout the world. On the subject of atomic energy everyone of us, even the big nations, are asked to give up our veto power to insure the safety of every nation. It seems to me that, without question, we can better afford to give up this amount of national sovereignty than we can afford to live in fear of what our neighbor may be doing.

In reading the Baruch report yesterday, I felt it was a document which took into consideration primarily the feelings and hopes of the masses of the people. When one sees the victory of the old type of isolationism in a state like Nebraska,[4] one wonders how much the people of our country really understand what has happened in the world of science in the past few years. I believe, however, that people are isolationists because they think that is the way to obtain peace; and it is only through education and the presentation of the facts that we can hope they will understand the real situation which confronts the world today. I think this report will help to clarify the thinking of the mass of people if they read it carefully, and I hope they will.

The reaction of the USSR to our recent offer of military collaboration with the Central and South American republics was a perfectly natural one, and they, in turn, will increase their efforts for the same type of collaboration wherever their interests lie.[5] Yet increase in power is valueless if it brings war—for all that we do, all that Great Britain does, and all that the USSR does has at its roots the desire for security and peace.

I happen to believe that only the strength of the United Nations can bring us this freedom from fear. I hope all of us will see clearly enough the value of this first move to give the knowledge about this most important weapon only to a United Nations body, and to give them also the power to control for the benefit of mankind the knowledge which the scientists have given us.

TMs AERP, FDRL

---

1. The Baruch Plan provided for the establishment of an international authority, exempt from the veto, to control all aspects of atomic energy. The authority would maintain detailed records and maps of the world's uranium and thorium, control the world's production of fissionable materials, and enjoy unrestricted inspection rights when it deemed a nation's actions in violation of the rules established by the authority. The plan also called for "successive stages" of international control, in which American disclosure of atomic secrets would not occur until after the authority was firmly established and other nations disclosed all information on their own atomic programs ("Baruch's Speech at Opening Session of U.N. Atomic Energy Commission," *NYT*, 15 June 1946, 4; Bernstein and Matusow, 224–32, 238–43).

2. "Baruch's Speech at Opening Session of U.N. Atomic Energy Commission," *NYT*, 15 June 1946, 4; Bernstein and Matusow, 224–32.

3. The Soviets immediately opposed Baruch's proposal to eliminate the veto and grant an international authority the power to inspect and punish nations, even if a permanent member of the Security Council opposed the commission's ruling. June 19, Gromyko, who represented the USSR on both the Security Council and the Atomic Energy Commission, presented a draft convention forbidding the use of atomic weaponry "in any circumstances," outlawing the production and stockpiling of atomic weapons, and committing each nation in possession of stockpiled atomic weapons to destroy their cache within three months after the United Nations ratified the convention (Herken, 164–67; Thomas J. Hamilton, "Soviet Atomic Plan Bans Using or Retaining Bombs and Keeps Big-Power Veto," *NYT*, 20 June 1946, 1). See Document 146 for the debate between Henry Wallace and Baruch on international control of atomic energy.

4. The isolationist incumbent, Senator Hugh Butler (R-NE), repelled a challenge from three-term governor Dwight Griswold, who had Harold Stassen's enthusiastic backing, to win the Republican senatorial primary. Butler had long opposed international aid and financial arrangements, voting against the establishment of UNRRA and the Bretton Woods Accords ("Matter of Fact: Ill Wind from Nebraska," *NYT*, 14 June 1946, 7).

5. May 6, Truman proposed the Inter-American Military Cooperation Act to provide "training, organization, and equipment" to the military forces of the Latin-American countries, a step which he argued not only continued FDR's Good Neighbor policy but also reinforced the Act of Chapultepec. In response, the Soviet Union pursued its own plans for mutual defense with its neighbors. In early June 1946, Yugoslavia's Marshal Tito negotiated an arms agreement with Russia, who also agreed to help rebuild the Yugoslav armaments industry. The USSR had already signed a similar treaty with Poland ("Truman Asks Inter-American Military Tieup," *WP*, 7 May 1946, 1; C. L. Sulzberger, "Blocs in Europe under Formation," *NYT*, 2 June 1946, 23; "New Soviet Pacts

Worry U.S., Britain," *NYT*, 12 June 1946, 14; "Russia to Help Tito Build Arms Plants," *NYT*, 11 June 1946, 1). On the Act of Chapultepec, see also *n*7 Document 23. For more on the inter-American movement, see Documents 201–205.

REBUTTING THE BRITISH POSITION
ON PALESTINE

In an article released earlier that week, Freda Kirchwey, editor of the *Nation*, argued that:

> One country the Arabs are uneasy about is the United States. They believe that if 100,000 Jews come to Palestine it will be because Truman insists they come. They know that an uncompromising stand in Washington, backed by solid promises of material help, would go far to offset the Arab threats and the warnings of Bevin's advisers out here. If our government takes such a stand, it will alter in a most salutary way the balance of forces in the eastern Mediterranean."[1]

ER found this article so "opportune" that immediately after she read it, she devoted her column to it.

129

My Day
22 June 1946

HYDE PARK, Friday—There is an article in The Nation by Freda Kirchwey, editor and publisher, which was written in Cairo about the Palestine question and the attitude of British Foreign Secretary Ernest Bevin. This article appears at a very opportune time. Any one who has been noting what desperate things the Palestinian Jews are doing, in order to hold onto their arms and build up a defense group somewhat akin to underground groups everywhere, must realize the seriousness of the tragedy of the whole situation in Palestine.[2]

I think we should think back over the steps by which we as a nation became involved in this matter. There was a time when we took no responsibility for Palestine. Then Great Britain invited us to take part in a joint commission to study the question.[3]

We knew the conditions in Europe, and so did they. We knew that innumerable Jews in Europe were braving every kind of danger in order to get to Palestine, because it was the only place where they felt they would be at home. We knew the attitude of King Ibn Saud of Saudi-Arabia, and we knew the general Arab position.[4]

There was really no need for a commission of inquiry, but we went along with Great Britain. The obvious reason we went along was that we believed Great Britain would accept the report of such a group and try to implement it. It was only fair to suppose that we both had a clear understanding of what our joint obligations to implement any such report would be.

Now President Truman has appointed a committee to look into this question of implementing the report,[5] but the British Foreign Secretary, Mr. Bevin, has stated that the real reason we are anxious to see 100,000 Jews admitted to Palestine is that we do not want them in New York.[6] He may be right in what he has said, and I am only sorry that we have not made our position so clear that such things could not be said about us.

It might be unwise to bring into New York, which already is larger than any city should be,[7] a great number of any particular group. But certainly throughout this country we could scatter our share of displaced persons without upsetting our economy. We are not yet at the point where an increase in population is a menace. In fact, it would be quite possible to absorb far more than our share of the displaced people in Europe who are seeking homes.

The particular point at issue, however, is that there are 100,000 Jews in Europe who must find homes immediately and they want to go to Palestine. The Arabs threaten dire things. The British talk about the impossibility of increasing the military force. But surely, our allied Chiefs of Staff could work out some form of military defense for Palestine which would not mean an increase in manpower.

The Arabs are intelligent people and so are we. I cannot believe that they are without mercy any more than we are.

TMs AERP, FDRL

---

1. Kirchwey goes on to describe Britain's tactics of press censorship and the ever-present military in public places, as well as the small but increasing Jewish resistance. Strict immigration restrictions and British military control, according to Kirchwey, had driven a small number of Jews "to acts of resistance which are entirely alien to their tradition. Terrorism is still regarded with profound disapproval by official Jewish opinion, but the effort to build and equip a strong defense force and to smuggle refugees through the immigration barriers is universally applauded ... Terrorist acts will increase as long as the present state of suspense continues (Freda Kirchwey, "Palestine and Bevin," *Nation*, vol. 162, 22 June 1946, 738).

2. In response to Great Britain's rejection of the Anglo-American Committee of Inquiry's call for the immediate admission of 100,000 European Jews to Palestine, the military Jewish underground unit in Palestine, Haganah, launched a series of attacks against British installations on the night of June 17, 1946. Eleven bridges connecting Palestine with surrounding nations were destroyed, thereby isolating the country from land communications with its neighbors. Days later the Irgun Z'vai Le'umi, a Jewish militant organization, kidnapped five British officers and held three of them hostage for two Irgun Z'vai Le'umi men who were under sentence of death from a Jerusalem military court (Sachar, *Israel*, 264–67; Julian Lewis Meltzer, "Palestine Terror Mounts as Harbor, Bridges Are Ripped," *NYT*, 18 June 1946, 1; "Tel Aviv Scoured by British Forces," *NYT*, 24 June 1946, 1).

3. The Anglo-American Committee of Inquiry, whose report had recently been issued. See *n*9 Document 79, and *n*2 and *n*3 Document 123.

4. In the spring of 1946, the Arab Higher Committee rejected a proposal from the Anglo-American Committee of Inquiry calling for the admission of 100,000 Jewish refugees to Palestine. The Arabs viewed the plan as a rejection of the British White Paper of 1939, which allowed a maximum of 75,000 Jews to enter Palestine over a five-year period, and the first step toward the creation of a Jewish homeland in Palestine. For more on the Arab position see Document 54 and *n*3 Document 123. For the attitude of Ibn Saud on Jewish immigration see Document 54. On the American perspective on the conditions of Jews in postwar Europe see *n*2, *n*3, *n*8, and *n*9 Document 74 and *n*3 Document 82 (Sachar, *Israel*, 258–60; Cohen, *Palestine*, 97–99).

5. See Document 124.

6. Speaking at the Labour Party meeting at Bournemouth on June 12, Bevin said, "I hope it will not be misunderstood in America if I say, with the purest of motives, that [US policy toward Jewish immigration into Palestine] was because they did not want too many of them in New York" (Acheson, 173).

7. New York City's population was the largest in the United States in 1940 and 1950, with a population of 7,454,995 and 7,891,957, respectively (Campbell Gibson, "Population of the 100 Largest Cities and Other Urban Places in the United States: 1790 to 1990," Population Division Working Paper No. 27, U.S. Census Bureau, http://www.census.gov, accessed 3 August 2005).

CHALLENGING THE COLUMBIA GRAND JURY

Following the February 26 incidents in Columbia, Tennessee, Attorney General Tom Clark sent in FBI agents and federal attorneys to investigate possible civil rights violations. Although these initial reports indicated that no violations had occurred, Clark, whose mailbox overflowed with protests from individuals and organizations committed to civil rights, ordered a grand jury to investigate the Columbia case. On April 8, an all-white grand jury convened, and on June 14, having "exhausted every reasonable venue of inquiry," concluded that it was "wholly impossible to determine the identity" of those responsible for the destruction of African American property, called the Highway Patrol's actions "not unreasonable," and found the jailhouse murders of Johnson and Gordon "justifiable homicide."

The grand jury then turned its attention to "nationwide misrepresentation" of the case, arguing that "Falsehoods and half-truths" abounded. The grand jury saw Communists as the root of the problem: "In disseminating such propaganda the avowed Communist Press of the country has been especially active, having carried a series of inflammatory articles on the racial disturbances at Columbia. This technique is characteristic and dangerous, and manifestly is designed to foster racial hatred and to array class against class."

Enraged by the grand jury's "outrageous whitewash" of events, ER authorized the National Committee for Justice in Columbia, Tennessee to send the following telegram to thirty-seven organizations (including the American Civil Liberties Union, the American Federation of Labor, the American Jewish Congress, the Federal Council of Churches, the National Citizens Political Action Committee, and the YMCA) she hoped would also express similar outrage to the Justice Department.[1]

130

Statement by the National Committee for Justice in Columbia, Tennessee

26 June 1946 [New York City]

THE NATIONAL COMMITTEE FOR JUSTICE IN COLUMBIA TENNESSEE PROTESTED TO PRESIDENT TRUMAN AND ATTORNEY GENERAL TOM CLARK AGAINST THE OUTRAGEOUS WHITEWASH OF MOB LEADERS AND STATE MILITIA WHO DEVASTATED THE NEGRO COMMUNITY IN COLUMBIA TENNESSEE. THE REPORT REFUSING TO FIX RESPONSIBILITY WAS MADE BY A FEDERAL GRAND JURY. THE ATTORNEYS CHARGED WITH THE DUTY OF PRESENTING ALL THE EVIDENCE TO THE GRAND JURY WERE ON THE STAFF OF ATTORNEY GENERAL TOM CLARK.[2] FEDERAL GOVERNMENT IS RESPONSIBLE FOR THIS BREAKDOWN IN FEDERAL LAW ENFORCEMENT. WE ASK THAT YOUR ORGANIZATION PROTEST TO ATTORNEY GENERAL CLARK AND PRESIDENT TRUMAN THE SHAMEFUL GRAND JURY REPORT.[3]

NATIONAL COMMITTEE FOR JUSTICE IN COLUMBIA TENNESSEE

MRS. ELEANOR ROOSEVELT
DR. CHANNING TOBIAS
CO-CHAIRMEN

TStmt FJHH, DLC

1. "Report of Grand Jury in the Matter of the Racial Disturbance at Columbia, Tennessee," AERP, FDRL; O'Brien, 36–39; Mailing list, NAACP Papers, DLC. See Document 105 for background on the Columbia case.

2. John M. Kelley, Jr., Arthur B. Caldwell, and Eleanor Bontecou, lawyers from the Justice Department's Civil Rights Section, joined local assistant district attorneys A. Otis Denning and Z. Thomas "Day" Osborn, Jr., in presenting the case to the grand jury (O'Brien, 36).

3. For Attorney General Clark's response to the NCJCT's protest of the grand jury report, see Document 148 and Document 149.

ON INVOKING FDR'S NAME

June 24, the journalist Steven Feeley wrote ER from the National Press Club in Washington on behalf of his "old friend" Senator James Mead (D-NY), who would soon announce his candidacy to become governor of New York. Feeley relayed a conversation he had with Mead the previous Sunday in which the senator said he "believed President Roosevelt endorsed him as a candidate for this year and that the presidential endorsement came as early as 1942." Feeley, knowing how this endorsement could help his friend's campaign, asked ER, if she was "free to do so," to tell him "whether President Roosevelt told you that he favored Senator Mead for nomination and election this year" and, if so, to give Feeley "permission to publish it in New York State newspapers and radio stations." The journalist then revealed that Senator Robert Wagner (D-NY) and Interior Secretary Harold Ickes recalled FDR's endorsement and that in addition to seeking ER's recollections he had asked Henry Wallace and Frances Perkins if FDR had shared his opinions with them.[1]

ER responded promptly to Feeley; however, she did not offer the assurance he sought.

131

Eleanor Roosevelt to Stephen Feeley
27 June 1946 [Hyde Park]

My dear Mr. Feeley:

I remember very well talking to my husband about his hopes for the candidates and at that time, he told me that he felt if General O'Dwyer could be run for Mayor of New York City, Mr. LaGuardia could be induced to run for the Senate, as running mate for Senator Mead[2] as Governor and that the ticket would be a winning ticket.

I know there has been considerable discussion as to whether consideration might be given to Mr. LaGuardia in view of the fact that at the time of the Mayoralty campaign, no understanding was arrived at and he was not particularly tactful about the Democrats, and there also was a feeling among some of the high Democrats that ex-Governor Lehman[3] should be running with Senator Mead for Senator.

I am in no position to know what anyone is planning to do. I think it is important if Senator Mead decides to run for Governor, the strongest possible candidate for the Senate.

I do not think, however, that my husband should be quoted because when a man is dead, one can not be sure of how he would feel, given new conditions and he might feel quite differently about a situation, so I think you should be careful in any publicity to state the whole background and circumstances of the original feeling. He was always very fond of Senator Mead and I know would have wanted to give him the wisest political advice at any time.

Very sincerely yours,

TLc AERP, FDRL

———————————

1. Stephen V. Feeley to ER, 24 June 1946, AERP. For Ickes's response, see Document 10.

2. For biographical information on James Michael Mead see *n*5 Document 10. Mead ran a losing campaign against Dewey in 1946 on a platform calling for a continuation of New Deal policies and programs (Smith, 459–63).

3. Herbert H. Lehman (1878–1963), FDR's lieutenant governor, succeeded FDR as governor of New York and served until 1942. He then led international relief efforts, becoming the director of the United Nations Relief and Rehabilitation Administration (UNRRA), which he and FDR helped create, in 1943. He ran unsuccessfully for the Senate in 1946 (*FDRE*).

ELEANOR ROOSEVELT AND
CONSCIENTIOUS OBJECTORS, PART 1

ER's attitude toward conscientious objectors (COs) was complex and evolved over time. In her My Day column of September 5, 1945, she wrote:

> I found it very hard during the war to have much patience with the young men who were conscientious objectors. I knew that in those cases where they belonged to religions which did not permit them to take part in war, it often required more courage on their part to live up to their convictions than it would have taken to go into the services and serve with the majority of their friends. In spite of that, it was hard to keep down the feeling that they were exercising this freedom to live up to their religious beliefs at the expense of some other boy's sacrifice.

Now, she wrote, the atomic bomb had made it possible for the human race to commit suicide if it did not give up war. To prevent that danger will "require more thinking on our part and some real convictions—two things that most of us don't find easy." She cited the stories of two people who had lived up to their convictions in the way she felt would now be necessary: one was a conscientious objector who died after contracting polio as a result of his work inoculating monkeys with the polio virus at a Yale School of Medicine lab; the other was a veteran who picketed Mississippi Senator Theodore Bilbo's office because of Bilbo's racist statements. Furthermore, ER had come to admire the conscientious objectors who volunteered to work in mental hospitals during the war as an alternative to military service: "I think it is truthful to say that these volunteers have raised the standards of care for the mentally ill. They did their work with devotion and often with religious fervor such as is rarely contributed by the usual paid attendant." In doing so, these men improved conditions for a segment of the population that ER had long believed was poorly served.[1]

ER had less sympathy for conscientious objectors who refused alternative service. On June 20, 1946, she received an appeal from ten conscientious objectors imprisoned in the Federal Correctional Institution in Sandstone, Minnesota.[2] They said that her position as the chairman of the Commission on Human Rights "prompts us to write you of one of the violations of human rights in the United States."[3] They noted that they were among 2,000 objectors imprisoned for violating the Selective Service Act because "they felt impelled by their consciences or by commands from a Supreme Being to so act." Some were not granted conscientious objector status by their draft boards; others refused to perform noncombatant work in the army, work without pay in labor camps for COs, or endure what they considered unjust conditions in the camps. "The courts," they complained, "with rare exceptions, refused to consider evidence or testimony, offered as a defense by a conscientious objector at his trial, which would show that the conscientious objector was being tried for disobeying an illegal order issued by the draft board." They argued that they could only be released through amnesty or a commutation of their sentences, since the parole system did not work for them:

> Parole released some men from prison under such restrictions as to constitute a modified form of imprisonment. Because we do not feel we should cooperate in the punishment of prisoners of conscience, we would not comply with the conditions of parole if it were offered. Parole does not meet the basic issues nor is parole applicable in a considerable number of cases, including our own, and thus some must serve their entire sentences.

They noted that President Truman had the power to grant amnesty.[4]

132

Eleanor Roosevelt to Malcolm Parker and Friends

27 June 1946 [Hyde Park]

My dear Mr. Parker and Friends:

I am not surprised that the court refused to consider the defense of the conscientious objectors when they alleged that they are disobeying illegal orders, since these orders were government orders and entirely legal.[5] They are only illegal because you choose to consider them so on a conscientious objector basis. When you are in a minority, you are obliged to take the judgement of the majority, even though it makes you suffer what you consider an injustice.

I think not to accept parole is rather stupid on your part. However, I think it will relieve the taxpayers if you are all allowed to be free, and since the war is over, I think you should be free. However, I am not the one to decide so I have referred your letter to the Attorney General.

Very sincerely yours,

TLc AERP, FDRL

ER then forwarded their letter to the attorney general.

133

Eleanor Roosevelt to Tom Clark

27 June 1946 [Hyde Park]

Dear Mr. Attorney General:

Could you tell me what we are still holding conscientious objectors in prison?

It seems to me that the time has come to free these men, no matter how difficult and cantankerous they seem to have been. At least they would no longer be a burden on the taxpayers and can earn their own livings.

Very sincerely yours,

TLc AERP, FDRL

134

Tom Clark to Eleanor Roosevelt

29 July 1946 [Washington, DC]

My dear Mrs. Roosevelt:

In your letter of June 27 you inquired concerning the conscientious objectors in prison and I have delayed my reply in order to obtain the most recent information for you.

There are at present only about 175 persons in prison for violating the Selective Service Act who claim to be conscientious objectors, and not all of these can be described as bona fide conscientious objectors. Many of these were sentenced comparatively recently and most have not been in prison as long as they would have been required to serve in the armed forces or in alternative civilian service if they had complied with the law.[6]

In considering this question, it is very important to know the specific individuals who are involved and the facts in their cases. The factual situations vary widely, thus making it extremely difficult to consider or deal with them as a class. If you have any specific persons in mind we would be very glad to review their cases and advise you regarding them.

In addition to those mentioned above who claim to be conscientious objectors, there are now approximately 1,250 Jehovah's Witnesses in prison for violating the Selective Service Act. As you no doubt know, the Jehovah's Witnesses deny that they are conscientious objectors and refuse classification as such. We have made every effort to get them to accept civilian work assignments, such as work in hospitals, but they refuse civilian work as well as military service.[7]

When I took office a year ago, there were about 3,200 persons in prison who were Jehovah's Witnesses or who claimed to be conscientious objectors. In addition, during the past year there were about 500 new convictions in these categories. However, the number now in prison has been reduced to less than 1,500 and many more will be released in the near future.

Since V-J day I have given careful consideration to the possibility of a general amnesty, but a review of all the factors has indicated that such action would be inappropriate at this time. In the first place, men who complied with the law are still serving in the armed forces and in alternative civilian service. Those who violated the law could hardly expect to return to their homes before the veterans. In the second place, men are still subject to induction. Thus, many of those in prison would be called again for service if they were released. In the third place, it is necessary for the Department of Justice to continue to enforce the Act. A general amnesty for violators would seriously handicap proper future enforcement. In the fourth place, there are a number of old violations pending in various stages of litigation in court. In the fifth place, it is difficult to conceive of just how you would describe the group to be covered by a general amnesty. Lastly, a general amnesty is not necessary to bring about early release from prison in meritorious cases, since such releases can be brought about under the parole provisions.

During hostilities, conscientious objectors and Jehovah's Witnesses were required to perform some type of civilian service, such as work in a hospital, as a condition of parole. In fact, such parole was available after 60 days. This seemed like a reasonable proposition, but it developed that the Jehovah's Witnesses and some of the conscientious objectors would not accept parole under these conditions. I therefore suggested to the Parole Board late last year that those who have served one-third of their sentence, who are not insincere, and who are no longer subject to induction be given parole without any requirement of civilian service. The Parole Board adopted this suggestion and consequently most of those in this category have been released. This accounts in part for the large decrease in the number in prison in recent months.

There is a small group of conscientious objectors in prison who refuse to accept parole. We are working on this problem and may soon be able to find a solution. The largest group remaining in prison is composed of Jehovah's Witnesses who are still subject to service upon their release. This group of young men without children presents the most perplexing problem. Permitting them to return to their homes would likely result in their being called up again and it would also be difficult for their neighbors who are still in service or being inducted to understand the situation. Nevertheless, I am continuing to study the problem presented by this group so that they may be released when such action would not interfere with the future administration and enforcement of the Act. Any suggestions you may have as to this special problem would be deeply appreciated.

I hope that I have been able to give you some insight as to the number of conscientious objectors and Jehovah's Witnesses in prison and what we are doing to bring about their early releases.

The fact that the Committee on Amnesty stated in a letter dated July 6, 1946, to the Editor of the New York Times and published July 14, 1946, that there are 2,100 conscientious objectors in prison discloses that even some of those most interested have failed to keep up with the large number of releases in recent months.[8]

Please let me know if there is any way in which I can be of further assistance to you. I want to assure you that your interest in writing about this matter is appreciated.

With kind personal regards,

Sincerely yours,
Tom C. Clark

TLS AERP, FDRL

––––––––––

1. The CO who died had also worked in a state mental hospital (*MD*, 5 September 1945; "Bilbo to Face More Picketing by Ex-Seaman," *WP*, 1 September 1945, 7).

2. The ten were: Malcolm Parker, Walter Gormly, Charles Worley, David Jensen, Bill Taber, Richard Zumwinkle, Henry Dyer, Glenn Hutchinson, Igal Roodenko, and John E. Hampton.

3. They also quoted a letter dated June 7, 1946, to President Truman from James Loeb, Jr., national director of the Union for Democratic Action, which asked for amnesty for the 2,400 COs still in prison and the 4,000 in Civilian Public Service camps. ER, they pointed out, was an honorary sponsor of the UDA.

4. Malcom Parker, et al., to ER, 20 June 1946, AERP. The COs also suggested that ER raise their case before the UN as part of the larger issue of freeing political prisoners:

> We hope that you will do what you can on this problem of human rights. Perhaps it would be best to bring before the Economic and Social Council the larger problem of the necessity for freeing all political prisoners yet remaining in prisons in this and some other countries. Perhaps you would wish to suggest to some non-governmental organization that it make representations on behalf of political prisoners in this country, principally objectors to war.

5. The Selective Service Act of 1940 included provisions for exemptions from combat for conscientious objectors. COs could apply for exemptions and their local board would, based on consideration of the applicant's beliefs, assign the applicant noncombatant status (1-A-O classification) or conscientious objector status (4-E classification). 1-A-Os served in the military in positions which did not require them to bear arms. Those classified as 4-E were required to perform unpaid "civilian public service." Twelve thousand of these men relocated to Civilian Public Service camps where they worked on agricultural or reforestation projects. A much smaller number of those classified as 4-Es worked in mental hospitals or volunteered to participate as subjects in medical experiments. Although the government hoped that the provisions for COs would alleviate the problem of dealing with those who refused to serve in the military, approximately 15,000 men were in violation of the Selective Service Act. These men either were not granted CO status by their local boards and refused to bear arms after they were drafted into military service, or they were COs who refused to perform their public service or left the camps before completing their required terms of service. Around 6,000 of those who violated the act served prison sentences (*OCAMH*; Brock and Young, 171–203). For ER's continued involvement in the issue of amnesty for COs, see Document 344 and Document 345.

6. For the requirements of the 1940 Selective Service Act applicable to COs, see *n*5 above.

7. Most Jehovah Witnesses refused 4-E (conscientious objector) status outright. They insisted that they be granted ministerial status (4-D) with the unconditional exemption that accompanied such status. In most cases, the local boards refused to grant the Witnesses ministerial status, and approximately 4,300 Witnesses chose to go to prison rather than work in the Civilian Public Service Camps ("Report of the President's Amnesty Board," 7–9, HSTSF, HSTL; Brock and Young, 174).

8. The July 6 letter to the *New York Times* from Dorothy Canfield Fisher, honorary chairman of the Committee for Amnesty, was part of an ongoing campaign to obtain amnesty for conscientious objectors. The letter argued that the recent granting of amnesty to some groups of political prisoners in Germany by American occupying forces should lead to a reexamination of the continued detention of conscientious objectors in the United States, whom the Committee for Amnesty regarded as political prisoners ("Political Prisoners," *NYT*, 14 July 1946, 72).

WOMEN AND THE TRUMAN ADMINISTRATION

Newsweek reported June 17, 1946, that as part of a government reorganization plan, President Truman "has told his advisers to be on the lookout for women who are qualified to take over several top spots," including the posts of assistant secretary of state, secretary of the proposed Department of Welfare, assistant secretary of labor, and special assistant to the president. Despite what appeared as an attempt at diversification, Truman's effort worried a number of women who saw the reorganization "as part of a plot to push them out of high level jobs." The magazine maintained that in "addition to half a dozen top Federal posts lost by women since Truman became President, his organization program would abolish the jobs of Mrs. Jewell W. Swofford and former Sen. Hattie W. Caraway, both members of the Employees Compensation Commission; Mrs. Ellen S. Woodward of the Social Security Board, and Bess Goodykoontz, Assistant Commissioner of Education." Responding to the *Newsweek* article in the following letter, ER applauds Truman for his decision to appoint women to top positions in the administration, but also reminds him to continue promoting the interests of women voters, whose support and involvement were integral to the success of the Democratic Party.[1]

135

Eleanor Roosevelt to Harry Truman
30 June 1946 [Hyde Park]

Dear Mr. President:

I have just received an item from News Week, which states that you have told your advisers to be on the lookout for women qualified to take over several top jobs in the Administration.[2]

This item was sent to a friend of mine, who forwarded it to me, by the chairman of the Women's Congressional Committee, in Washington. This group represents a rather large number of women's organizations[3] and I think among them, there are several people who have been afraid that in the reorganization of the government, women were being eliminated from important jobs and functions, such as the Children's Bureau,[4] which had been of particular interest to women, and in being integrated with other groups, were passing out of control of the women who had headed them and might be completely changed in their aims. This item will, I think, encourage them.

I used to have to remind the gentlemen of the Party rather frequently that we Democrats did not win unless we had the liberals, labor, and women, largely with us. Among our best workers in all campaigns, are the women. They will do the dull detail work and fill the uninteresting speaking engagements which none of the men are willing to undertake.[5] I hope you will impress this fact on those who are now organizing for the Congressional campaigns and in preparation for 1948.[6]

With every good wish, I am,

Very cordially yours,
Eleanor Roosevelt

TLS PPF, HSTL

136

Harry Truman to Eleanor Roosevelt
8 July 1946 [The White House]

Dear Mrs. Roosevelt:

I appreciated very much yours of June thirtieth regarding the item in News Week.

I am hoping we can find some key positions for some of our able Democratic women.

I have been particularly interested in getting Mrs. Perkins placed but I haven't yet had a place I thought was equal to her ability, which I could offer her, and there are several others who ought to be in the Administration set-up.[7] I hope we can work it out.

Sincerely yours,
Harry S. Truman

TLS AERP, FDRL

----

1. *Newsweek*, 17 January 1946, 21.

2. Despite the *Newsweek* report that Truman wished to appoint women to several top government positions, the president had an uncertain commitment to keeping women in the highest posts. See *n*6 Document 2.

3. For the Women's Congressional Committee, see *n*1 Document 99.

4. For information on the Children's Bureau, see *n*12 Document 116.

5. ER's lifelong commitment to women's political involvement is illustrated by her participation in New York organizations such as the bipartisan Women's City Club, the League of Women Voters, and the Women's Division of the Democratic State Committee. She also served as a liaison between women voters and Governor Al Smith and represented women voters in the platform committee at the 1924 Democratic National Convention. For more on ER's concern with women's involvement in the Democratic Party, see Document 16 (Perry, 28; A. Black, *Casting*, 12).

6. When the Democrats suffered stinging defeat the following November, ER wrote:

> Of course, my time for active participation in politics is long gone by. I could not again go barnstorming through the state organizing the women, as Mrs. Daniel O'Day, Mrs. Henry Morgenthau, Jr., Miss Cook, Miss Dickerman and I used to do, after Miss Harriet May Mills had pointed the way. Those, of course, were the days when women's active part in politics was at stake, and it was great fun seeing them learn to participate and seeing the gentlemen learn to consider them as individuals and as voters.
>
> The men haven't learned quite yet how important the women are, but perhaps this election will serve to point up the fact that I have preached for so many years. Women must be enthusiastic for a candidate, and their interests cannot be ignored. Even children should not be ignored. They actually figure in many a candidate's popularity! (*MD*, 8 November 1946).

7. Reflecting on the experience of cabinet reorganization years later in a private, unsent letter to Jonathan Daniels, Truman wrote of Frances Perkins: "a grand lady—but no politician. FDR had removed every bureau power she had." Truman found a position for Perkins in a recently vacated

post on the Civil Service Commission after her resignation as secretary of labor. In this new position, Perkins was the only federal service presidential appointee and the highest-ranking woman in government, although, as the *Washington Post* reported, the Civil Service Commission was actually "a demotion from her former Cabinet rank." Despite the pressure ER and various women's organizations exerted on the president to place more women in top-level government positions, Truman sent to the Senate the names of just three women appointees between 1945 and 1948. His record would improve somewhat during his second term in office (Hamby, *Man*, 306; Jerry Kluttz, "The Federal Diary: Super Job Priority Plan Protested by Agencies," *WP*, 10 October 1946, 7; Jerry Kluttz, "Miss Perkins Is Given Civil Service Post," *WP*, 13 September 1946, 1; *HSTE*).

DECLINING, ONCE AGAIN

With her appointment to the United Nations the previous December and her reemergence into public life, speculation again surfaced about the possibility of ER running for public office. Despite her emphatic denial in her January 3 press conference and her remarks before the New York State Democratic Convention, pundits and supporters continued to urge her to seek elective office. In the article below, published in America's most popular news magazine, ER explained her refusal in more detail and in the process, offered a rare personal glimpse of her private feelings on the sacrifices she made to support candidates and issues she valued.

137

"Why I Do Not Choose To Run"
Look 9 July 1946

There has been some curiosity as to why I am not knocking at the door of the members of my political party, who make up the slates for candidates for office, in order to obtain a nomination for some elective office.[1]

At first I was surprised that anyone should think that I would want to run for office, or that I was fitted to hold office. Then I realized that some people felt that I must have learned something from my husband in all the years that he was in public life! They also knew that I had stressed the fact that women should accept responsibility as citizens.

I heard that I was being offered the nomination for governor or for the United States Senate in my own state, and even for Vice President. And some particularly humorous souls wrote in and suggested that I run as the first woman President of the United States!

The simple truth is that I have had my fill of public life of the more or less stereotyped kind. I do believe that every citizen, as long as he is alive and able to work, has an obligation to work on public questions and that he should choose the kind of work he is best fitted to do.

Therefore, when I was offered an opportunity to serve on the United Nations organization, I accepted it. I did this, not because I really wanted to go to London last January, but because it seemed as though I might be able to use the experiences of a lifetime and make them valuable to my nation and to the people of the world at this particular time. I knew, of course, how much my husband hoped that, out of the war, an organization for peace would really develop.

It was not just to further my husband's hopes, however, that I agreed to serve in this particular way. It was rather that I myself had always believed that women might have a better chance to bring about the understanding necessary to prevent future wars if they could serve in sufficient number in these international bodies. The plain truth, I am afraid, is that in declining to consider running for the various public offices which have been suggested to me, I am influenced by the thought that no woman has, as yet, been able to build up and hold sufficient backing to carry through a program. Men and women both are not yet enough accustomed to following a woman and looking to her for leadership. If I were young enough it might be an interesting challenge, and we have some women in Congress who may carry on this fight.

However, I am already an elderly woman, and I would have to start in whatever office I might run for as a junior with no weight of experience in holding office behind me. It seems to me that fairly young men and women should start holding minor offices and work up to the important ones, developing qualifications for holding these offices as they work.

I have been an onlooker in the field of politics. In some ways I hope I have occasionally been a help, but always by doing things which I was particularly fitted by my own background and experience to do. My husband was skilled in using people and, even though I was his wife, I think he used me in his career as he used other people. I am quite sure that Louis Howe, who was one of the most astute politicians as well as one of the most devoted of friends, trained me and used me for the things which he thought I could do well, but always in connection with my husband's career.[2]

In the last years of his life, Louis Howe used to ask me if I had any ambitions to hold political office myself. I think he finally became convinced that though I understood the worst and the best of politics and statesmanship, I had absolutely no desire to participate in it.

For many years of my life I realized that what my husband was attempting to do was far more important than anything which I could possibly accomplish; and therefore I never said anything, or wrote anything, without first balancing it against the objectives which I thought he was working for at the time. We did not always agree as to methods, but our ultimate objectives were fortunately very much the same.

Never in all the years can I remember his asking me not to say or to write anything, even though we occasionally argued very vehemently and sometimes held diametrically opposite points of view on things of the moment.

I think my husband probably often used me as a sounding board, knowing that my reactions would be the reactions of the average man and woman in the street.

My husband taught me that one cannot follow blindly any line which one lays down in advance, because circumstances will modify one's thinking and one's action. And in the last year since his death I have felt sure that our objectives would remain very much the same. But I have known that I was free and under compulsion to say and to do the things which I, as an individual, believed on the questions of the day. In a way it has lifted a considerable weight from my shoulders, feeling that now, when I speak, no one will attribute my thoughts to someone holding an important office and whose work may be hurt and not helped thereby. If people do not like what I say nowadays, they can blame me, but it will hurt no one else's plans or policies.

There is a freedom in being responsible only to yourself which I would now find it hard to surrender in taking a party office. I believe that the Democratic Party, at least the progressive part of the Democratic Party, represents the only safe way we have of moving forward in this country. I believe that the liberal-minded Democrats hold to the only international policy which can bring us a peaceful world. I will work for the candidates of my party when I think they offer the best there is in the field of public service, and I will even accept mediocre men now and then if I feel that the rank and file of the Party is strong enough in its beliefs to make those inadequate leaders do better than their own ability gives promise of in the way of achievement.

However, if I do not run for office, I am not beholden to my Party. What I give, I give freely and I am too old to want to be curtailed in any way in the expression of my own thinking.

To be entirely honest I will have to confess that I thought at first one of my reasons might be that I did not want to engage in the rough and tumble of a political campaign. This, of course, would be rank self-indulgence and I should be the last one to allow myself to decline to run for public office because of any such reason, since I have urged on other women the need for developing a less sensitive spirit and for learning to give and take as men do.

I do not think that this consideration really enters into my decision. I have lived long in a goldfish bowl, and my husband's death does not seem in any way to have altered the attacks which come upon one from certain quarters. So I do not think that running for office would have brought me any more of the disagreeable things which we must learn to endure. In the long run, the mass of the people are likely to form a fairly truthful estimate of people who are before them in public life.

Had I wanted to run for office, therefore, I imagine in many ways I could have stood up under all types of attack and suffered less than most people. But I would rather help others, younger people, whose careers lie ahead of them and who have years in which to achieve their objectives. What I do may still be important, but it won't last long enough.

In the meantime, I shall be glad to serve wherever my past experiences seem to fit me to do a specific job.

Many people will think that these are all very inadequate answers and that when you are told that you might be useful, you should accept the judgement of others and go to work. All I can say in reply is that during a long life I have always done what, for one reason or another, was the thing which was incumbent upon me to do without any consideration as to whether I wished to do it or not. That no longer seems to be a necessity, and for my few remaining years I hope to be free!

PMag Look, 9 July 1949, DLC

---

1. For examples of those who still lobbied ER to run for office see "For Mrs. Roosevelt as Senator," *NYT*, 17 March 1946, 2; "Mrs. Roosevelt Requests Labor Party Not to Consider Her for Place in Senate," *NYT*, 11 April 1946, 31; and "PAC Will Back 99 For House in Fall," *NYT*, 14 April 1946, 33. For ER's earlier refusals see Document 2, Documents 10 and 11, and Document 74.

2. Louis McHenry Howe (1871–1936), ER's political tutor and friend, was FDR's closest advisor from 1912, when FDR ran for reelection to the New York State Senate, until Howe's death. When ER entered political life in the 1920s, Howe coached her in public speaking and political strategy and encouraged her to write and become a leader. After FDR became president and other advisors achieved greater prominence in FDR's inner circle, ER and Howe became much closer, often working together as a team and acting as FDR's toughest critics. By 1935, Howe told ER that, after FDR's administration ended, she should run for public office or seek an appointed position and even urged her to consider running for president (Cook, vol. 2, 15, 351; *FDRE*).

ON THE EQUAL RIGHTS AMENDMENT

Florence Ledyard Cross Kitchelt (1874–1961), social worker, settlement house worker, and peace activist, directed the Connecticut Branch of the League of Nations Association and chaired the Connecticut Committee for the Equal Rights Amendment (ERA) from 1943 until 1956. On July 9 Kitchelt wrote to ER seeking her support for the ERA, arguing that "after removing the layers of personal opinions about the Equal Rights Amendment, at heart it is nothing more or less than a principle to be written into the Constitution as the accepted guide for governmental action, to wit, that women are to be treated as the peers of men, of equal humanity." Her argument did not sway ER.[1]

138

Eleanor Roosevelt to Florence Kitchelt
23 July 1946 [Hyde Park]

My dear Mrs. Kitchelt:

I think you overemphasize the importance of the Equal Rights Amendment and I can not agree with you that the passage of that Amendment will really help women particularly the groups that need help most in this country.

I have no prejudice about this. I am purely practical.

Very sincerely yours,
Eleanor Roosevelt

TLS FLCKP, MCR-S

---

1. Throughout the 1940s, ER's position on the ERA remained that which she asserted in a May 1945 My Day column: "I feel that if we work to remove from our statute books those laws which discriminate against women today, we might accomplish more and do it in a shorter time than will be possible through the passage of this amendment." See also Document 120 (Florence Kitchelt to ER, 9 July 1946, AERP; "Florence Kitchelt, 1874–1961," Finding Aid, Florence Ledyard Cross Kitchelt Papers, CtY).

ON FAITH AND GOVERNANCE

When the Federal Council of Churches secretary Walter Van Kirk bemoaned the inability of churches to apply spiritual principles to government and social practice, ER, whose *The Moral Basis of Democracy* also called for a political and legal system grounded in the Social Gospel[1], offered the following column calling for churches to develop "greater responsibility for the conditions existing in society."

139

My Day
8 August 1946

HYDE PARK, Wednesday—There is something very interesting in reading about the meeting, in Cambridge, England, of representatives of the World Council of Churches. In one account that I read, Dr. Walter W. Van Kirk of New York said that he found considerable pessimism among the delegates as to the value of the United Nations. He said that the imperfections in that organization were "derived from the paganism of secular society, and that results from the failure of the churches around this table in bringing Christian influence into secular society."[2]

I think many of us would agree that, if we are to have peace, there must be a rise in spiritual leadership. In fact, I think many of us feel that there can be no permanent settlement of the problems that face us nationally and internationally without a real spiritual awakening in the world as a whole.

To have peace, the big powers will really have to want to see the lot of human beings improved. They will have to safeguard the rights of the individual and see to it that justice tempered by mercy is a reality throughout the world. That is a far cry from having your eyes fixed primarily on the economic success of your nation.

One hears so much of power politics.[3] Boiled down, power politics simply means that each great nation is trying to create combinations of power greater than any of the other great nations. We won't get away from that until the people of the big nations say to their leaders, "We want you to do the thing that is right, not for us alone but for humanity as a whole." That will not be said until the people are conscious that spiritual force must rule the world.

Christ's power over men was that of an individual who had great spiritual force. He could inspire those around Him to have the courage to preach and live by a doctrine which was based on unselfishness and the love of humanity. That power has been a moving force down through the ages. But even in so-called Christian countries, it has never quite come into its own and actually been the mainspring in the lives of the majority of people. It will not amount to much unless it affects the individuals in every community.

The churches cannot become just another pressure group.[4] In a country like ours, where church and state are pretty carefully separated, great emphasis will have to be laid on the fundamental principles from which action springs, rather than on the specific actions undertaken by groups of individuals.

The churches will have to take a stand against unthinking and un-Christian prejudices. They will have to develop among the people a greater sense of responsibility for the conditions existing in society. And above all, they will have to watch the sense of values held by the youth of the world, since the world will grow to be material or spiritual exactly in proportion to the aspirations of the rising generation. If their values are spiritual values, the pattern of the world will change.

TMs AERP, FDRL

---

1. See Roosevelt, *Moral.*

2. Walter W. Van Kirk (1891–1956) served as secretary of the Commission on a Just and Durable Peace, an affiliate of the Federal Council of Churches then chaired by John Foster Dulles. Organized in 1908 by thirty Protestant denominations that sought to apply the Social Gospel to government policy, the FCC (reinforced by Dulles's leadership) argued that the churches had a vital transnational role to play in preparing the world for a lasting peace. It had been a strong, early supporter of the UN and Van Kirk had served as an advisor to the American delegation to the San Francisco conference, where he strove to incorporate FCC principles into the UN Charter. Consequently, when Dulles, Van Kirk, and other American church leaders attended the Cambridge conference, they worked to establish a similar international body (the Commission of the Churches on International Affairs) to work among international religious organizations to secure peaceful resolution of international conflicts (Warren, *Theologians*, 78–79, 99–105; "Dr. Van Kirk Dies, Clerical Leader," *NYT*, 8 July 1956, 65; Mallory Browne, "World Body Asked by U.S. Churchmen," *NYT*, 6 August 1946, 1; "Churchmen Differ on New World Unit," *NYT*, 17 August 1946, 15).

3. Van Kirk told the conferees that "power politics is seeking to expand its influence and churches must act to counterbalance that tendency" (Mallory Browne, "World Body Asked by U.S. Churchmen," *NYT*, 6 August 1946, 1).

4. Europeans at the Cambridge conference expressed the fear that the proposed Commission of the Churches on International Affairs would be perceived as one more power bloc (Mallory Browne, "World Body Asked by U.S. Churchmen," *NYT*, 6 August 1946, 1).

ON AMERICAN VALUES AND FOREIGN AID

140

My Day
23 August 1946

NEW YORK, Thursday—None of us can help being worried and indignant over the shooting down of two of our unarmed transport planes which had wandered over the Yugoslav border. Conceding that there may be some hidden reason why our planes are forbidden to fly over a friendly country, it still seems a little difficult for the layman to understand.[1]

It seems, too, a trifle ironic to have American planes shot down, and Americans possibly killed, by planes and ammunition which had probably been acquired through lend-lease from this country! I remember the bitterness we felt when our boys in the Pacific, after some Japanese bombing, picked up bits of material with the imprint of "Made in the United States", and realized they were getting back scrap or manufactured materials which had been bought from us.[2] At least that material was used against us by an enemy in wartime. But what is used against us by Yugoslavia was furnished to them as an ally to help them win the war, in which their interest was even more vital than ours.

I do not want food and medical supplies confused with military supplies, since the former were sent to Yugoslavia to help the people and I hope that we will always distinguish between the people and their governments in countries which are not our type of democracies. In our democracy, we can hold the people responsible for the government. While the people in countries like Yugoslavia, Russia and some other European countries, can still bring pressure in the long run, they cannot act as quickly, and their information is often less complete than ours, so they cannot be held completely responsible.

In spite of indignation and anxiety over what has occurred, I cannot help wondering where we have failed. There was a time during the war when we enjoyed the trust and respect of little and big nations everywhere. What has happened to turn that, in some cases, into suspicion and disdain? We cannot blame our leaders, because we are a democracy. Somehow we the people have failed.

In our haste to get back to the business of normal living, have we forgotten to be the great people that we were expected to be? We were the hope of the world—the people from whom justice and better things were expected. I don't think we were expected to be Santa Claus in a material way, though that is frequently said, but I think we were expected to stand firm for the right as we saw it, and not for the expedient.[3]

Perhaps the trouble has been that, on most of the international questions which have arisen, the people of this country have not bothered to decide what they thought was right. Take, for instance, Trieste, which is probably tied up with some of the things that have recently happened;[4] take the question of Albania[5] and of Italy and her claims.[6] These are three questions on which the people of this country could and should have clear opinions, and they should express them to their leaders. Have they done this? I think not.

We want to avert war. Therefore, we must build up the United Nations. But we do not help them to find a permanent home—our voice is heard only in protest.[7] We seem to have forgotten to weigh our values and to realize that we have to pay for the things we want. The payment which can bring about friendly and peaceful solutions is infinitely less costly than the payments which will have to be made if we are going to be an enemy to all the world.

TMs AERP, FDRL

1. Yugoslav airplanes forced one C-47 airplane down and shot down a second on August 19 in the airspace over Venezia Giulia, which the Yugoslavs contended belonged to them. The Yugoslavs interned the passengers and crew of the first flight and allowed them little or no contact with American embassy officials in Yugoslavia. At the same time they refused to release any information on the deaths of the five people aboard the second flight. Tensions escalated as the Yugoslav government (with Soviet support) accused the United States of violating its airspace on these and other previous occasions in order to spy. The United States denied the charge. On August 21, the United States gave the Yugoslavs an ultimatum: release the survivors of the first incident and let US representatives communicate with the survivors of the second (then thought to be alive) within forty-eight hours or face possible UN Security Council action. On August 22, the Yugoslavs released seven Americans and two Hungarians aboard the first plane. (Another survivor—a Turkish national recovering from wounds sustained during the incident—was released later.) The Yugoslavs also allowed US military representatives to view the remains of those on the second flight to confirm their deaths (Acheson, 195; Lees, 14–16; "Nine Men Released," *NYT*, 23 August 1946, 1; "All Flyers Dead, Survey Indicates," *NYT*, 27 August 1946, 1; "Turk Wounded in Attack on Plane Is Free to Leave, Yugoslavs Say," *NYT*, 28 August 1946, 3).

2. Up until September 26, 1940, when FDR ordered an embargo on sales of scrap metal to Japan, Japan purchased large quantities of scrap iron and steel from the United States, which then were used to make shells, bullets, and other war materiel ("Roosevelt Moves," *NYT*, 27 September 1940, 1; "Silk Cycle," *Time*, 9 March 1942, 9; "Estimate Board Dooms 2D Ave. 'El'," *NYT*, 29 May 1942, 19; "Scrap Made Junk by Our Fighters, Returns from World Battlefields," *NYT*, 17 January 1943, 1).

3. Undersecretary of State Dean Acheson noted this trend in a June 1946 speech when he said, "The slogans, 'Bring the boys home!' and 'Don't be Santa Claus,' are not among our more gifted or thoughtful contributions to the creation of a free and tranquil world" (Acheson, 196).

4. See *n*1 above. The USSR backed the Yugoslavs' claim to Trieste and the surrounding area while Great Britain, France, and United States supported Italy's claim. In June 1945, the area was temporarily divided into two zones with the center zone including Trieste under Allied control and the suburban section under Yugoslav control. However, emotions continued to run high, and riots occurred in the city in March 1946. In April, the foreign ministers of the Four Powers met in Paris to resolve the situation but made little progress. At a second meeting in the summer the Allies reached a compromise that established a Free Territory of Trieste under the authority of the UN Security Council. Both Italy and Yugoslavia continued to contest the settlement that became part of the final treaty signed in 1947 and in 1954, the area was again divided. Italy retained Trieste and the coast zone became part of Yugoslavia (J. Miller, 199–201; Brecher and Wilkenfeld, 250–52; "Trieste Area Agreement," *NYT*, 10 June 1945, 6; "New Fighting in Trieste," *NYT*, 26 March 1946, 6; "Big Four Disagree on Plan for Trieste," *NYT*, 4 August 1946, 19; "Tito to Help Draw Line," *NYT*, 23 June 1947, 6; *OEWH*; *EUN*).

5. Neither the United States nor Great Britain recognized the government of Albanian Communist premier Enver Hoxha, which at this time was purging the elected Albanian assembly of its non-Communist members. Without the support of two of its major members, the UN Security Council delayed Albania's application for membership in the United Nations on August 16 (Zickel and Iwaskiw, eds., 172; "U.N. Group Weighs Membership Bid," *NYT*, 1 August 1946, 7; "Action on Albania Is Delayed in UN," *NYT*, 17 August 1946, 2; *OEWH*).

6. Besides her claim on Trieste and Venezia Giulia, Italy, which argued that its support for the Allies during the last eighteen months of World War II entitled it to be included in peace negotiations with Germany and Japan, wanted a year-long delay on the decision of governance of her African

colonies, Eritrea, Somalia, and Libya. She also wanted the treaty's preamble changed to blame the Fascist government for Italy's alliance with Nazi Germany and to say its overthrow in 1943 resulted from favorable military events rather than "under pressure of military events"—a change the Soviets and Yugoslavs opposed. See also Document 220 (J. Miller, 193–205; *OEWH*; "Italy Sets Terms for Ratifying Pact," *NYT*, 6 August 1946, 5; "Premier Sees Ruin," *NYT*, 11 August 1946, 1; "Yugoslav Rejects De Gasperi's Plea," *NYT*, 12 August 1946, 3; "Italy Asking Role in Treaty Actions on Germany, Japan," *NYT*, 20 August 1946, 1).

7. Some residents of Westchester County, New York, and Fairfield, Connecticut, where the UN proposed building its permanent headquarters and housing for its employees, opposed the plan because of its size, scope, and impact on residents' property and local services. (At the time, the UN wanted to build "a self-contained enclave of up to 40 miles.") Residents were also concerned about the UN's foreign influence. See also *n*11 Document 74 (Lie, 63; "Greenwich Is Cool Pending Hearings," *NYT*, 30 July 1946, 10; "U.N. Lists 15 Sites Picked in Fairfield and Westchester," *NYT*, 30 July 1946, 1).

ON THE IRGUN, BEVIN, AND THE ANGLO-AMERICAN COMMITTEE OF INQUIRY

In August 1946, a British military court tried twenty-two young members of the Stern Gang, a militant Jewish underground organization, for having attacked British railroad workshops at Haifa. The trial ended with eighteen young men condemned to death and four women sentenced to life terms. The court later commuted the death sentences to life terms.[1]

141

Eleanor Roosevelt to Stella Reading
23 August 1946 [Hyde Park]

Dear Lady Reading:

I am writing you this letter which you can pass on if you think wise, to Mr. Attlee[2] and Mr. Bevin. I do not feel I have any right to express my feelings to them officially and yet as a human being, I can not help wanting to tell them how certain actions as regards the situation in Palestine have made me feel.

In the first place, I hope and pray that they will not actually put to death the young terrorists. I do not approve of what any of these people have done in the way of violence. I understand perfectly, however, the fact that this feeling of despair on the part of the Jewish people have been growing for a long time and the show of force by Great Britain has made in Palestine has probably built up this resistance movement, since force always creates a similar attitude in the opposition.

If these young people are killed there will without any question, be a sense of martyrdom and a desire for revenge which will bring more bloodshed. A generous gesture will, I think, change the atmosphere.

In addition, I can not bear to think of the Jews of Europe who have spent so many years in concentration camps, behind wire again on Cypress.[3] Somehow it seems to me that the 100,000 Jews should be let into Palestine and that some real agreement should be reached with the Arabs.[4] Willy-nilly, the feeling grows here that it is [not] just justice which Great Britain is looking for where the Arabs are concerned, but it is that she wishes the friendship in order to get more favorable consideration where oil concessions are concerned.[5] I know this may not be true but no matter what the real reasons are, it is in such a mess that ultimately I feel it should be turned over to the United Nations. In the meantime the gestures should all be on the generous side where Great Britain is concerned.

I think Great Britain is entirely right in stating that if there is a question of military activity, we should assume our share of responsibility and I think we should as a government, have understood that when we accepted a joint commission of inquiry with her.[6] If it was not understood between the two nations, of course, our government can not be held to it and that emphasizes the need for the taking over by the United Nations as soon as possible.

I shall be grateful for whatever you decide to do about this letter.

With every good wish, I am,

Affectionately,

TLc AERP, FDRL

142

Stella Reading to Eleanor Roosevelt

28 August 1946 [London]

My dear Mrs. Roosevelt:

Thank you very much for your letter of the 23rd. I am passing this on as you suggest, in the spirit in which you have written it, and know you would rather the matter be left there.[7]

Of course, there are many wheels within wheels that do not appear to the naked eye, and of which those of us who have been near to this problem for many years are fully aware.[8]

Ever yours affectionately
Stella Reading

TLS AERP, FDRL

---

1. On the night of June 17, 1946, the Stern Gang destroyed Palestine Railway's central workshop in Haifa's harbor with fifteen separate explosions. The Haifa explosions were in connection with a series of attacks by Jewish underground groups against British installations in Palestine on that night in an effort to "demonstrate by force against the alleged intentions of British authorities to liquidate the Palestine Jews' defense organization and cripple its leadership" (Julian Louis Meltzer, "Palestine Terror Mounts as Harbor, Bridges Are Ripped," *NYT*, 18 June 1946, 1; "British Spare 18 Zionists, Bar Mufti at London Talks," *NYT*, 30 August 1946, 1). For more on the attacks against British installations see *n*2 Document 129.

2. See *n*16 Document 87.

3. In response to continued efforts by Jewish refugees to illegally enter Palestine, Prime Minister Clement Attlee launched Operation Igloo, which called for future illegal immigrants to be transferred to camps in Cyprus "and elsewhere" until a decision could be taken as to their future. In announcing this decision, the British government maintained that while they were "deeply sensible" of the sufferings undergone by the Jewish community and "anxious" to bring them to an end as soon as possible, they could not tolerate an attempt by a minority of "Zionist extremists" to exploit the sufferings of unfortunate people in order to "create a situation prejudicial to a just settlement" ("British Halt Palestine Entry, Sidetrack Jews to Cyprus," *NYT*, 13 August 1946, 1; Britain's Statement on Immigration, *NYT*, 13 August 1946, 14).

4. See *n*5 Document 82, *n*2 and *n*3 Document 123, and Document 129.

5. Great Britain's postwar policy in the Middle East was driven in large part by its desire to maintain access to vital oil supplies in the Arab world. Foreign Minister Ernest Bevin, in particular, believed that the best way to defend the Middle East oil fields and pipelines from the designs of the Soviet Union was to foster Arab good will. Accordingly, he opposed large-scale Jewish immigration to Palestine, and tried to further involve the United States in solving the refugee crisis and securing the Middle East for the West (Bickerton and Klausner, 77–78; Shwadran, 532; Cohen and Kolinsky, 23). For more on ER's views on British postwar policies in the Middle East see Document 144 and Document 123.

6. The Anglo-American Committee of Inquiry. See *n*2, *n*3, and *n*4 Document 123.

7. A search of British archives, including the records of the Women's Voluntary Services, and the correspondence of the Reading family, indicates that Stella Reading's correspondence with ER was not preserved.

8. Although Reading herself was not Jewish, her husband, Rufus Isaacs, First Marquess of Reading, who died in 1935, was one of the most prominent Jews in British public life. Lord Reading served as viceroy of India, lord chief justice, special ambassador to the United States and, briefly, as foreign secretary. He was not a Zionist but approved of the Balfour Declaration and, once the work of creating a Jewish national home began, supported Jewish settlement efforts (Hyde, 282–84, 399, 417; Reading, 365–67).

CRITIQUING DEWEY, CHALLENGING THE PARTY

In 1946, Paul E. Fitzpatrick, chair of the New York State Democratic Committee, and other Democratic leaders asked ER to serve as temporary chairman of and deliver the keynote address to the New York State Democratic Convention. Trying to defuse speculation that, despite her earlier denials, she did seek political office, she used My Day to acknowledge that although she was the first woman to serve in this role, she realized:

> of course, that this honor has been given to me in deference to my husband's memory and in recognition of the importance of women in the Democratic Party—that there is nothing personal in the designation. I only hope I will be able to play my part creditably. If possible, I would like not only to express the hopes and purposes of the women in the Democratic Party in this State, but to speak, too, of the things that the party as a whole, men and women together, feel are essential to our success in the State and in the nation as well. New York State has often in the past pioneered in Democratic thinking, and I hope it will again in the future.[1]

143

Keynote Speech, Democratic State Convention
3 September 1946 [Albany, NY]

Mr. Fitzpatrick, delegates to the convention, honored guests:

It is a long time since I have taken part in a New York State Convention, or even in a National Convention.[2] I am glad to be with you today because the Empire State has pioneered before and in this year of 1946, when the war has been over a little more than a year, we must face pioneering again. The war is ended, but there is no peace and good will established yet in the world. We are seeing day by day, that the problems of peace are as complex as the problems of war and require from us qualities of heart and mind which we have only evinced in times past during the stress of war.

We meet here as members of one of the two great national political parties. We believe in this State that the Democratic Party is the party which offers the country an opportunity for growth and progress towards the normal aspirations of man—better living and working conditions, good will and better understanding in the family of nations, and a sense of fulfillment in that "pursuit of happiness" which can only come to the party in our country which gives spiritual as well as economic and political leadership.

In the past several years we have had this sense of satisfaction nationally.

You will pardon me if for a few minutes I look back because while I believe strongly that the past must never govern the future, I also believe that we must have the past in mind to help us shape the future.

On the national scene in 1933, we inherited twelve years of Republican government in Washington. The Democrats can be proud of the record of the following years. First we had to pull the country out of a devastating domestic situation. We managed to do this by giving the people back confidence in themselves and in their ability to win through to success. "Nothing to fear but fear itself" was our slogan and we got rid of fear. As we did this, we also prepared ourselves to meet one of the greatest crises in our history which came with the attack on Pearl Harbor. This preparation was done in spite of the constant opposition of Republicans in Congress and of Republican leadership in the Nation. You will remember that the present Governor of New York State at one time stated that it was ludicrous to imagine that we could reach certain stated goals of production.[3] The Democrats trusted our people and our people made good.

In this State in 1942, after Democratic Governors served the people of the State for 22 years without a break, and Governor Smith's record of social and progressive legislation and administration[4] had been followed by Governor Roosevelt and Governor Lehman,[5] we turned over to the present governor not only a government in good running order, but many plans and programs which made possible the best things which have been done under Republican rule in this State.[6] None of the policies which were initiated by the previous Democratic Governors from Governor Smith through to Governor Lehman, have been changed. The pioneering done by the Democrats in the State in social legislation which was later carried through on a broader front in Washington, is wholly responsible for the laws which have given the people of the State a sense of stability and protection.

Now the Republicans claim as their main achievement the accumulation of a cash surplus in the State. They neglect, however, to point out that some of this surplus has been inherited from the Democratic administration and that the hoarding of this surplus worked great hardship on cities, forcing them to impose excise taxes and to neglect many governmental functions of value to the people.[7]

Just let us take one department of the State Government extremely important to the working people of our State. The Labor Department has been reorganized ostensibly to make it less expensive to run and more efficient. In the past the Labor Department's primary interest was to see that labor's interests were safe guarded but subtly that has changed and today the interests of the employer are paramount in the administration of the Department of Labor. This is shown in the fact that they have decided not to police industrial establishments, as they call it. Take for instance, the enforcement of the Minimum Wage Law. In prior years this law was the most effective instrument that our State had devised to improve sub-standards of living in sweated industries and occupations. A Minimum Wage Order, when promulgated, meant something because a thorough enforcement job was done by the Labor Department. The first thing the current administration did in connection with the Minimum Wage Law was to change the method of enforcement. The Labor Department now employs the system of spot checking. The outstanding virtue of this method is that it saves time and money. Its weakness, of course, is that it affords opportunity for many violations to go undetected.[8]

The present Governor proudly asserts that we have the highest minimum wage rates of any State. He refers of course, to the Retail Trades Minimum Wage Order. He conveniently forgets, however, to mention that this rate applies only to that one trade and that waitresses, laundry workers, hotel workers, dyers and cleaners and beauticians still get the pre-war dolefully low minimums.[9]

One amusing thing in connection with the enforcement of this Order is that instead of dealing directly with employers and workers, the Industrial Commissioner had the Retail Trades posters distributed to the local Chambers of Commerce with the pious hope that they would be redistributed by them to employers. The only time a firm received a Retail Trades poster from the Labor Department was when they specifically wrote in and requested it. These posters in work rooms are the only way the workers know what the rules are under which they work.[10]

In the case of veterans' affairs which is of such vital importance, much has been made of the State Division of Veterans Affairs, set up by the Governor. This group could have been of great assistance if it had consisted of really well qualified people, deeply interested in helping the veterans. Cooperating with the federal government it could have prevented, for instance, the buying by veterans of houses at inflated prices which we are now told will not stand up a few years from now. Their position as counsellors and advisers might have been made of vital help in preventing the exploitation of veterans in job training programs. What is happening to veterans, points to one important fact which all of us should recognize, namely, that the best plans in the world have to be carried out by individuals. If the individuals are good, the plans are well carried out. If they are poor, the plans will go awry and the value of state groups cooperating with the national administration is that they can check on the way people are carrying out the spirit of the law and they can make recommendations which will be listened to at headquarters, where an individual G.I. is powerless.[11]

The Governor's Division of Veterans Affairs could have done much in making the education and the whole employment scene for veterans a better picture. Instead of which it has simply not functioned and therefore the maximum good from the national program is not being achieved and the veterans who gave so much for their country are the victims of poor administration in spite of all the promises which were made to them and which most of us want to see carried out.

In the field of housing the present Governor of the State talks of the difficulties he is under in carrying through the housing program because of the priorities demanded by the National Housing program. He did not have foresight enough to appropriate during the last two years, the money which might have started these programs well on their way, nor had he arranged for close cooperation between the National and State programs so that no difficulties could arise between them.[12] He has been silent and failed to support the bi-partisan Wagner-Ellender-Taft Housing Bill.[13]

In the field of education we, the richest State in the Union, have no state university and rank 23rd in giving educational opportunities to all our children.[14] We are behind every state west of the Mississippi in percentage of youth going to college. New York State stands forty-eighth among the states in money spent for education above the high school level and this is probably a greater hardship to the youth in rural areas than in the cities since some cities provide universities with free tuition for their citizens.

In the field of health, we have made no real progress in plans which would make medical care available to all the people. No plan has been forthcoming under the Republican Administration, even though we have had the results of the draft to remind us of our obligation to the health of our young people. It is true that the Governor set up a commission to study the need for a health program for the State and in this case "special interests" prevented the recommendations which logically should have been made because of the findings of the commission. The result was that after 15 months of deliberation and an expenditure of $100,000 of state funds, the committee majority failed to present any plan at all.[15] Cities again get on better than rural areas when there is no state program, but a coordinated program using all of our facilities would benefit us all.

In the field of agriculture in which I have a special interest because it was one of my husband's greatest interests from his early days in the New York State Legislature, I feel that while the farmers are undoubtedly at present very much better off, it is due to conditions in the world and not to the administration of matters of interest to the farmer in the State of New York. For instance, it would benefit the small farmer in the State if a real investigation could be made in the spread in the price of milk between what farmers receive and what the consumer pays. Certain "interests" have again prevented this investigation and the same old fight which I have watched for years was waged in the Legislature and the "interests" won both in the Legislature and with the Governor.[16]

Much praise has been meted out to the Governor because this State passed a Fair Employment Practices Bill, but passing a Bill, which is good in itself, is not of much use unless something happens under that Bill.[17] I do not think we can boast in this State that discrimination in employment is over. We do not have to pass, thank Heaven, an anti-lynching bill, or an anti-poll-tax bill in our State. It is significant to note that in the Legislature the Republican Gov. had solid Democrat backing for his fair employment practices proposal. The only opposition votes were cast by Rep[ublicans]. Naturally I do not think there has ever been any question of where the representatives in Congress from the State of New York stand on these questions, but we are far from able to sit back and think that because we have a Fair Employment Practices Law we have no discrimination either in opportunities for education or opportunities for employment. I hope that this convention will pledge itself to use this Law to better advantage in the future.

In Washington today the Administration which has adhered to the progressive ideals of the Democratic Party, has been defeated in putting through many of the measures which represent the real spirit of the Democratic Party by a coalition of so-called conservative Democrats and reactionary Republicans. That is why it seems to me extremely important that we have in the Senate of the United States men whom we have known in this State and can count on to stand on domestic and foreign questions for the progressive Democratic point of view. You are here to consider the nominations for the State ticket, and also the nomination of a candidate for the United States Senate and in all of your nominations I hope you will bear this thought in mind. The primaries all over the country have shown that where the victories go to Republicans they always go to conservatives. Never forget that the Republican Party is the party that looks backward. When the Democrats have taken progressive steps, the Republicans as a rule, in time accept what has been done and simply state that they are not going to make changes, but that they will administer better the laws which have been passed under the Democrats.

Administration is a question of choosing good administrators, but it is far more important in times such as these to put in office men who have the creative spirit and can accept unknown conditions and find solutions without always harking back to the security of something they knew in the past which perhaps is entirely inadequate to meet the present. Whomever you choose for United States Senator this year will have great opportunities for service to the State and to the Nation and you must trust him and back him with your interest and your constant support.

Both major parties in this country know quite well that they do not win in elections through the votes cast either by regular Republicans or by regular Democrats. They win because the growing independent vote of the country is with them. This vote is the deciding factor. Victory comes when the candidates and the policies of a party convince these independent voters of their wisdom and sincerity.

The men whom you nominate will, I am sure, have a keen sense of responsibility to you and I hope that every person here will have an equally keen sense of responsibility toward their nominees. I hope that a real fight will be waged in every district not only for the State ticket, but for the local candidates and candidates for the Legislature of the State and the Congress. Unless a Governor has a Legislature with him, he can hardly be blamed if he is not able to put his program into effect and unless a President has a Congress with a clear mandate to put through progressive legislation, the Executive in Washington is powerless.

Democratic government depends for its success on the strength of its smallest unit. If Democratic government is weak in its smallest unit, if the members of the local and county committees are not truly interested in good government, there is failure at the top because there is failure at the bottom. Every individual who believes in democracy must do his job as a citizen to the limit of his ability. Otherwise our form of government is a failure.

Similarly every individual candidate is a link in the line which makes the success of the State and National government possible. You must win because you know and can persuade the voters in your district of what we must do today to meet our great opportunity as leaders in the world. Reconversion must be hurried here to help reconstruction the world over. We are no longer able to think of ourselves only as a small group of people struggling for our own success. We are citizens belonging to a great political party, planning here for the future of the greatest state in the Union, whose influence is powerful today in one of the strongest nations of the world. With strength and power goes responsibility and none of us can shirk it.

The misery of the world cries out to us for leadership. The hunger of the world demands our sympathy and our production. The lack of opportunity staring so many people in the face today in other nations, shames us unless we grasp our great opportunities and use them to the best advantage. That means assuring everyone of our citizens, through their government, of the help and hope which makes individual and group achievement a certainty. We believe in free enterprise and individual initiative but we want it to benefit all and not just a favored few.

To you, the delegates to this State Convention, I give a challenge—make the people of our State conscious of their greatness, make this, your Party, an instrument which will appeal to people who want greater achievements. In that spirit, may we march to victory in November and justify our victory by our performance thereafter.

TSpd AERP, FDRL

1. *MD*, 29 August 1946.

2. In the 1920s, ER became one of the most influential Democrats in New York State. As a leader of the women's division of the state party, she attended the 1922, 1924, 1926, and 1928 state conventions, where, as a delegate, she took an active role in platform and procedural debates. In 1924, she successfully challenged Tammany Hall leader Charles Murray to have the women's division (rather than the party machine) select the women delegates and alternates-at-large. ER stopped attending the state convention once FDR assumed elected office (Lash, *Eleanor*, 278–329).

3. In 1940, Thomas E. Dewey, then district attorney of New York, ridiculed the idea that FDR's administration could work effectively with the private sector to meet its ambitious goals for rearmament. Many, including Dewey, thought these goals unrealistic at the time and the pace of rearmament was slow at first, but American factories more than fulfilled the goals by the end of the war (Smith, *Dewey*, 305; *FDRE*).

4. Alfred E. Smith (1873–1944), governor of New York from 1919 to 1920 and 1923 to 1928, initiated a period of twenty-two years of progressive Democratic reform in New York State politics during a period dominated nationally by the Republican Party. As governor, Smith pushed through social welfare legislation, such as child labor laws and laws protecting women in the workplace, and worked to increase efficiency through government reorganization and by giving the governor the power to initiate the budget (*FDRE*).

5. As governor of New York from 1933 to 1942, Herbert H. Lehman (1878–1963) pursued the policies of the New Deal at the state level, including the regulation of public utilities and labor reform. His fiscal policies wiped out the state's debt and left a surplus for the incoming Republican governor, Thomas Dewey, in 1943 (*FDRE*). See also *n*3 Document 131.

6. When Dewey first ran for governor of New York in 1938, he declared that he was a "New Deal Republican." As governor he built on the progressive policies of his Democratic predecessors by pushing civil rights legislation, the renovation of state mental hospitals, increased pay for state workers, and funds for education (*FDRE*).

7. Under Dewey's administration, New York State accumulated a budget surplus of more than $600 million, largely because wartime restrictions prevented the state from initiating building projects. Dewey placed this surplus in a Postwar Reconstruction Fund to be used to help finance local building projects after the war and help ease the transition to a peacetime economy. During the 1946 campaign Democrats attacked the surplus as a "slush fund," proposed using some of it to aid the poor, and argued that Dewey's plans to build the New York thruway would take funding and scarce building materials away from housing and education (Smith, *Dewey*, 365–66; 460–61).

8. Dewey reorganized the New York State Department of Labor, setting up regional offices and seeking to make it more efficient. He claimed that the state was for the first time "genuinely looking out for the health and safety of its working people" ("Text of Governor Dewey's Review Before State Federation of Advances by Labor," *NYT*, 20 August 1946, 20).

9. On October 3, 1945, Edward Corsi, New York State industrial commissioner, ordered retail merchants to pay a minimum wage of $21 per week, thus making New York's minimum wage for salespeople, elevator operators, office clerks, cleaners, and messengers the highest in the nation. Although this law extended a minimum wage to employees not previously covered, many workers remained uncovered ("Minimum Pay Set for Retail Trade," *NYT*, 4 October 1945, 25; "Sets State Parley on a 55-Cent Wage," *NYT*, 28 February 1946, 17).

10. The 1939 Fair Labor Standards Act mandated that every employer "subject to the Fair Labor Standards Act's minimum wage ... provisions must post and keep posted," in a prominent place visible to all employees, "a notice" explaining what rights the employees have in that particular

workplace. Building upon the FLSA, New York law mandated a poster explaining state laws be posted when the state minimum wage was higher than the federal standard. These posters were (and are) the main way that workers know these rights. As the law required different posters for different industries, these notices are probably what ER meant when she referenced "posters" related to the "Retail trades" ("New York's Minimum Wage Law: The First Twenty Years," Isadore Lubin Papers, FDRL).

11. Dewey signed a bill establishing the New York State Division of Veterans' Affairs on April 17, 1945, and appointed Edward J. Neary, the district attorney of Nassau County and former state commander of the American Legion, as its director. Neary oversaw the agencies set up to provide services to veterans in New York State communities and hired counselors to advise the veterans. The Executive Board of Review, appointed by Dewey, found in 1946 that most of the counselors were doing a satisfactory to excellent job, but that about 15 percent were unqualified or needed further training. "As a whole, this is a very remarkable showing under the conditions of rapid selection," the report concluded. A shortage of housing and building materials, high demand from returning veterans, the availability of loans under the GI Bill, and the eagerness of some realtors and contractors to exploit the situation combined to drive up housing prices after World War II. Unwary GIs sometimes bought poorly constructed homes or homes they could not afford. Employers also sometimes exploited veterans in on-the-job training programs by illegally counting their subsistence pay under the GI Bill as part of their wages ("Neary Will Direct Veterans' Affairs," *NYT*, 27 April 1945, 36; "More Scope Asked for Veterans' Aid," *NYT*, 24 May 1946, 17; "Protect Veteran Loan Group Urged," *NYT*, 15 December 1945, 10; Lee E. Cooper, "New Dangers Seen for Home Building," *NYT*, 9 September 1946, 11; Charles Hurd, "Readjustment," *NYT*, 21 July 1946, 34; "Bradley Condemns Job Training Abuse," *NYT*, 6 August 1946, 16).

12. In her August 29 My Day column, ER wrote: "All of us will agree, I think, that housing not only for veterans but for many other people is most important now. And it is regrettable to find that our Governor feels that our New York State program is impeded by the priorities which have been set to speed the Federal program. It would seem that there must be some lack of coordination when the State and the nation cannot cooperate to build the housing which is most needed, pooling their efforts rather than desiring, apparently, to have the kudos for being "'the' agency to produce some place for the numerous homeless families to lay their heads!" (*MD*, 29 August 1946).

13. The Wagner-Ellender-Taft housing bill would have helped support the construction of 12,500,000 homes over ten years. The Senate passed the bipartisan bill on April 15, 1946, but the House Banking and Currency Committee bottled it up until Congress adjourned in August. The Citizens Housing Council and Democratic politicians criticized Dewey for not speaking out in favor of the bill ("Senate Passes Long-Range Bill on Housing with Wage Clause," *NYT*, 16 April 1946, 1; "Dewey's Silence Scored," *NYT*, 2 August 1946, 15).

14. In 1946 New York was one of only two states lacking a state university. It provided indirect support to private universities (Columbia, Cornell, and New York University) instead. In 1947 Dewey himself would call for the establishment of a state university (Smith, *Dewey*, 472–73).

15. Dewey's Commission on Medical Care, which he appointed on September 5, 1944, could not agree on a set of recommendations. Instead they submitted five separate reports which, as Dewey reported to the state legislature, "reflect the sharp disagreement amongst all people as to the means by which a broad program for medical care can be provided" ("Commission Named on Medical Care," *NYT*, 6 September 1944, 22; "Dewey's Health Message," *NYT*, 5 March 1946, 20).

16. Although the New York State Commission on Agriculture voted on July 13, 1946, to undertake an investigation of the "spread" in price between what farmers received for milk and consumers paid, the Democratic platform, presented to the convention at which ER spoke, called for a thorough investigation of milk prices. Many milk producers and dealers opposed the investiga-

tion ("Veto Milk Price Inquiry," *NYT*, 25 May 1946, 15; "Inquiry on Milk Voted for State," *NYT*, 13 July 1946, 2; "State Democrats Offer Housing Aid," *NYT*, 3 September 1946, 9).

17. March 12, 1945, Dewey signed legislation introduced by New York State Assemblyman Irving M. Ives and Senator Elmer F. Quinn establishing a fair employment practices commission, thus making New York the first state to prohibit employment discrimination on the basis of race, creed, color, or national origin. The Act established the State Commission Against Discrimination to monitor employment practices, authorized "conciliation councils" to investigate claims alleging discrimination, and mandated that all employers delete any discriminatory language when advertising for and soliciting employees (Smith, *Dewey*, 444–47).

ON THE PARTITION OF PALESTINE

On August 28, 1946, Major General George Van Horn Moseley, US Army (Ret.) (1874–1960), wrote ER regarding her August 19 My Day column in which she deplored the recent British policy of forcing illegal Jewish immigrants who attempted to enter Palestine to go to newly opened detention camps on the island of Cyprus. The partition of Palestine into Jewish and Arab areas she wrote presented:

> no answer to the problem, since the main objection originally to Palestine becoming a home for the Jews was the grave doubt entertained by many as to whether the land would be able to support any more people than were already there … To an ordinary citizen like myself, the motives that Britain might have … are very difficult to understand. It looks as though we were forgetting our main objective of peace in this world. It is possible, of course, that what we fear is that the Arabs will go to war with us, but that hardly seems possible. It seems to be a case of deciding what we think is right for people from refugee camps in Europe … In Great Britain and in the United States, if we decided what was right, I don't think we would have much difficulty in getting it done.

Moseley, who testified before the Dies committee in 1939 that a "Jewish-led Communist revolution was about to overwhelm" the United States, asked ER for her solution to the Jewish "problem." He attributed the reluctance of many nations to admit Jewish refugees in the aftermath of World War II to "the low traits of character … which have made them outcasts throughout the ages." He went on to say that "the feeling against the Jew in America is growing, and growing fast … My hope is that the problem of the Jews may be settled on a worldwide basis before the American people become aroused and take drastic action against them."[1]

144

Eleanor Roosevelt to George Van Horn Moseley
5 September 1946 [Hyde Park]

My dear General Moseley:

I think the only possible solution for the Palestine question is to have the nations interested sit down and talk honestly together, and try on the part of Great Britain to recognize that her policies have been influenced by her interest in oil, in the Near East and her interest in the control of the Mediterranean as part of her life-line to other parts of the world.[2]

We have no interests except to see justice to human beings done. Russia has interests because she feels that outlets for her future commerce are necessary and she also is beginning to feel the need for control of oil.[3] We do have, of course, an interest in oil in the Near East but it is not as acute with us.[4]

I think you are unfair to the Jewish people. There are, of course, lower class Jews who because of persecution and difficulties of survival, have developed certain traits of character which are hard for us, who have had easier lives, to accept. However, I know many Jews who are far more disinterested citizens and who take more interest in education and the arts in their communities than many people of other religions and nationalities. They are by far the most responsive to appeals for welfare and civic interests. It is true that you can find Jews in all the bad situations you speak of, but you can also find Gentiles. The division is pretty equal. I disagree with you because I believe our strength in this country has come from the great difference in back grounds which have been assimilated here into a type which is an American type.

Very sincerely yours,

TLc AERP, FDRL

---

1. See *n*3 Document 141 for more information about the detention camps on Cyprus ("General Moseley, 86, Of Army Is Dead," *NYT*, 8 November 1960, 29; *MD*, 19 August 1946; George Van Horn Moseley to ER, 28 August 1946, AERP).

2. For more on British policy in the Middle East, see *n*5 Document 141.

3. For more on the Soviets' desire for an oil concession in Iran, see *n*9 Document 97. In 1944, US corporations controlled 42 percent of the Middle East's proven oil reserves including the oil fields of Saudi Arabia and Bahrain. In addition, American firms had substantial but less extensive interests in Iraq and Kuwait (Paterson et al., 417; Shwadran, 238, 303, 309).

4. Although United States oil companies gained control of 42 percent of the Middle East's oil resources by the end of World War II, the US only imported 8 percent of its domestic oil consumption as late as 1948 (Cohen, *Truman*, 93–94).

OFFERING CAMPAIGN ADVICE

Although ER informed her My Day readers that her "time for active participation in politics is long gone by" and that she "could not again go barnstorming through the state organizing the women, as ... I used to do," she remained politically active behind the scenes.[1]

After conservative challenger Katherine St. George[2] defeated the progressive Republican incumbent, Representative Augustus W. Bennet, in the August primary, Democrats thought they had a chance to capture the seat. As the CIO had endorsed Bennet,[3] the Democrats hoped they could recruit CIO support for their candidate, James K. Walsh. William Schafer, chair of the Sullivan County Democratic Committee, then reached out to influential labor leaders to seek their counsel on how best to secure the CIO endorsement. ER then offered Schafer the following advice to defeat St. George. Schafer embraced the advice and asked ER to "convey" her advice to the Monticello, New York, postmaster Ralph Washington for use in his outreach to veterans. ER agreed and forwarded a copy of her letter to Schafer to Washington the following week.[4]

145

Eleanor Roosevelt to William Schafer
8 September 1946 [Hyde Park]

My dear Mr. Schafer:

I spoke to Miss Rose Schneiderman, president of the New York Women's Trade Union League, 247 Lexington Avenue, New York City, who said she would speak to the local labor representatives in this area.[5]

I feel that the most useful tactics to be employed against Mrs. St. George would be to have her heckled at meetings where she speaks by people who really know the labor and agricultural situations. Start by getting her to make a general statement on her own stand, then attack her on particular bills. I think it will be evident that she is without real knowledge and with many prejudices. If there could be a debate between her and the candidate and the same thing could happen on both of those questions, it would be good. She does know about private charities and has been on the board of trustees of the Tuxedo Hospital and also I think of the infantile paralysis work, but she does not know about labor conditions and I think would be unsympathetic to them and to much of the labor legislation. It should be brought out that she knows very little about the real agricultural situation, and educational conditions in the state and in the nation which affect the agricultural population. She has endorsed Hamilton Fish and his stand, which puts her in a very odd position on international questions.[6]

Very sincerely yours,

TLc AERP, FDRL

---

1. *MD*, 8 November 1946.

2. Katharine Delano Price Collier St. George (1894–1983), a cousin of FDR's, played an active role in the local Republican Party organization, even serving as president of the Tuxedo Republican

Club, prior to FDR's election in 1932 when she decided to refrain from politics out of deference to family. However, when Augustus W. Bennet (then running on the Democratic and American Labor Parties' tickets) defeated her longtime friend Hamilton Fish in the 1944 congressional election, St. George decided to involve herself in Republican politics once again and vowed to run against Bennett in the 1946 primary (*ANBO*).

3. Although the CIO had endorsed Bennet in the primary, the largest local labor organization, the Newburgh Building Trades Council, supported St. George, as did the district's former congressman, Hamilton Fish ("Liberals Back Bryan," *NYT*, 24 October 1946, 22; "Roosevelt Cousin Wins Primary Race," *NYT*, 21 August 1946, 17; "A. H. Raskin, CIO-PAC to Oppose 33 Now in Congress," *NYT*, 10 May 1946, 1; James A. Hagerty, "Trend to the Right Shown in Primary Here and Up-State," *NYT*, 22 August 1946, 1).

4. William Schafer to ER, 11 September 1946, AERP.

5. For ER's relationship with the influential labor leader Rose Schneiderman, see *n*5 Document 31.

6. Hamilton Fish (1888–1991), an outspoken Republican isolationist, represented the Twenty-Ninth Congressional District of New York in the House from 1920 to 1944 when he lost his seat to Augustus W. Bennet. Fish was not an isolationist in the strictest sense of the term: he supported US participation in the World Court and served as the head of the American delegation to the Inter-Parliamentary Union Congress in 1939, where he proposed an armistice "to enable the nations to solve their problems by arbitration and conciliation instead of war." He did, however, oppose American intervention in the war in Europe and founded the National Committee to Keep America Out of Foreign Wars in 1939. Although his stance caused many to label him a Nazi-sympathizer, Fish continued to oppose intervention until the Japanese attack on Pearl Harbor, when he declared that the only proper response was "war to final victory, cost what it may in blood, treasure and tears" (*ANBO*; Freidel, 322–23; "Fish's Peace Project to be Offered Today," *NYT*, 17 August 1939, 10; Hamilton Fish, "Letters to the Times: Mr. Fish States His Position," *NYT*, 26 October 1940, 14; "Fish Is Called 'Dupe of Hitlerism,' Defends His War Stand in Debate," *NYT*, 20 September 1941, 9).

In November, Katharine St. George defeated Walsh and won a seat in the House of Representatives, which she retained until 1964 ("All Republicans Win in Rockland," *NYT*, 6 November 1946, 4).

BARUCH AND WALLACE ON THE ATOMIC BOMB

On September 18 Henry Wallace, pressured by columnist Drew Pearson's imminent revelations, released to the press a letter he had written Harry Truman in which he told the president he felt "increasingly disturbed about the trend of international affairs since the war." The letter revealed Wallace's particular opposition to the "successive stages" and veto plan Bernard Baruch proposed be met before atomic energy was placed under international control. "We are in effect," he wrote, "asking [Russia] to reveal her only two cards immediately—telling her that after we have seen her cards we will decide whether we want to continue to play the game." The only hope for peace, Wallace insisted, lay in "disclosing information and destroying our bombs at a specified time … rather than at our own discretion."[1]

The letter's subsequent publication in the *Washington Post* and the *New York Times* underscored Wallace's disagreement with Truman, which the public first perceived September 12 when Wallace delivered a major address at Madison Square Garden. "During the past year or so," he began:

> the significance of peace has been increased immeasurably by the atomic bomb, guided missiles, and airplanes which soon will travel as fast as sound. Make no mistake about it—another war would hurt the United States many times as much as the last war … He who trusts in the atomic bomb will sooner or later perish by the atomic bomb—or something worse …
>
> We most earnestly want peace with Russia—but we want to be met half way. We want cooperation …
>
> For her part, Russia can retain our respect by cooperating with the United Nations in a spirit of open-minded and flexible give-and-take.
>
> The real peace treaty we need now is between the United States and Russia. On our part, we should recognize that we have no more business in the political affairs of Eastern Europe than Russia has in the political affairs of Latin America, Western Europe and the United States.[2]

The day the letter became public, the secretary of state called the president to complain, Truman met with Wallace,[3] and Baruch called ER and left the following message with "Tommy" Thompson. Later, that evening when ER read the message, she scrawled instructions to her secretary across the bottom of her message: "Send Wallace a wire saying I hope he will talk to Mr. Baruch." Her wire worked. Wallace agreed to meet with Baruch at the end of September.[4]

146

Telephone Message from Bernard Baruch for Eleanor Roosevelt

[18? September] 1946 [New York City]

Mr. Baruch called. He is troubled about Wallace's letter because Mr. B. says Wallace's statements on the atomic bomb are not based on fact. He talked to Wallace and asked him to come up for a discussion. Wallace was not very cooperative. Baruch does not want to make a statement and start a public row with Wallace and thinks Wallace should say he was misinformed.

TNote AERP, FDRL

1. Andrew Russell Pearson (1897–1969) started his journalistic career traveling throughout Europe and Asia as a freelance writer. In 1932, Pearson and fellow journalist, Robert S. Allen, began coauthoring a political column titled the "Washington Merry-Go-Round" after a book of the same name they had anonymously published about the Hoover administration. Allen and Pearson also co-hosted a radio show on station WMAL, but after Allen went on active military duty in 1942, Pearson both wrote the column and hosted the show alone. One of the features of the show was "Predictions of Things to Come," in which he speculated on the future actions of public figures. Pearson had been investigating the private rift between Wallace and Truman (*ANB*; Culver and Hyde, 424–26; "Text of Secretary Wallace's Letter to President Truman on U.S. Foreign Policy," *NYT*, 18 September 1946, 2).

2. Quoted in Culver and Hyde, 421–22.

3. That day, Wallace met privately with Truman and promised to stop his criticism of US foreign policy for the time being. Byrnes did not feel that Wallace's silence was enough. From the Foreign Ministers' Conference in Paris, Byrnes called for Truman to demonstrate American solidarity with either the "appeasement" policies of Wallace or his own firmer stance towards Russia. Truman responded by demanding Wallace's resignation on the morning of September 20 (Hamby, *Beyond*, 126–34; Lewis Wood, "Wallace Reveals He Bade President Treat with Soviet," *NYT*, 18 September 1946, 1; C. L. Sulzberger, "Paris Sees Byrnes' Policy Reinvigorated by Truman," *NYT*, 21 September 1946, 1; "Text of Wallace's Letter to President on Russia," *WP*, 18 September 1946, 1). See also Document 128 for more on the Baruch plan.

4. The two did not reach an agreement, as Wallace did not believe he had misinterpreted any of the facts concerning the Baruch plan. The meeting proved to be their last, and a public row in the major papers followed: Baruch announced at a press conference on October 2 that Wallace's interpretation of the Baruch plan as outlined in his letter was either "misinformation or complete distortion," and Wallace retorted that it was Baruch's "stern and inflexible" stance that "created the impasse" in the UN Atomic Energy Commission (Culver and Hyde, 427n; Schwarz, 502–3; A. M. Rosenthal, "Baruch Rebukes Wallace Groups for Distorting U.S. Atom Plan," *NYT*, 2 October 1946, 1; Lewis Wood, "Wallace Charges Baruch with 'Impasse' over Atom," *NYT*, 4 October 1946, 1).

ON TRUMAN, STALIN, AND CHURCHILL

On September 24, 1946, Arthur Murray wrote ER:

> Heavy weather in Paris; but who, it may be asked, with any real knowledge of the past six and twenty years expected otherwise.[1] The chickens of past blunders are darkening the skies as they scurry home to roost beginning with the catastrophic blunder—as some of us in Parliament pointed out at the time—by Winston Churchill after the First World War in supporting the Russian Generals Denikin and Wrangel in their attempt to overturn the Bolshevist Revolution.[2] Was it likely that Stalin—the ultimate saviour of the Revolution—would ever forget <u>that</u>. Some of us prophesied five and twenty years ago that he would not do so. And he has not.

Murray also told ER that he found Churchill's September 19 speech in Zurich, in which the former prime minister proposed a "United States of Europe," pushed for a strong partnership between France and Germany, and declared that "there can be no revival of Europe without a spiritually great France and a spiritually great Germany,"[3] yet "another ill-judged utterance."

> No Frenchman who has lived through two German aggressions against France, and heard tales from the lips of his grandparents of a third, is going to tolerate Germany as France's partner. Nor in our lifetime will any nation which has endured German rule contemplate the revival, even for the common purpose of European defense, of the Wehrmacht which only last month was declared for ever dissolved. A call for "partnership" with Germany was out of place; was bound to fall on deaf ears; and was fated to arouse mistrust and suspicion, and to throw spanners into the peace-making machine.[4]

As her reply indicates, ER also found the speech "unfortunate."

147

Eleanor Roosevelt to Arthur Murray
10 October 1946 [New York City]

Dear Arthur:

I was much interested to get your letter and I shall be delighted when the book comes and I can sit down and enjoy it.[5]

Just now I am preparing for the Assembly of the United Nations which begins on October 23rd, and I am afraid that we will have some of the repercussions of the heavy weather which has been going on in Paris. I am also afraid that our President is not as well equipped to manage both Mr. Stalin and Mr. Churchill as Franklin was.

I hope your prophecy as to Great Britain coming through the present difficulties stronger than ever before is true, and that we, who are certainly having our difficulties, will be as successful, in working out our troubles.[6]

Mr. Churchill's speech in Fulton, Missouri, I think was unfortunate.[7] I had heard him try out similar ideas on Franklin but Franklin never responded. The Zurich speech, I think, would have been good if he had talked primarily about a break down of trade barriers within Europe and of making travel easier between the different countries. I am just as nervous about building up a strong Germany as France is, but I have a feeling that Mr. Churchill prefers a strong Germany to a strong Russia. Somehow I can not be as much afraid of Russia at the present time. Naturally I am not afraid of Germany now, but I should hate to have some of the people who built up the Second World War left in power in Germany with any chance of building a third world war.

With many thanks and every good wish, I am,

Very cordially yours,
Eleanor Roosevelt

TLS PACM, StEdNL-M

––––––––––

1. In September, negotiations in Paris over the peace treaties to formally conclude the European conflict proceeded slowly. Secretary of State Byrnes, now pursuing a "get tough" policy with the Russians, clashed repeatedly with Soviet Foreign Minister Molotov over issues of reparations, borders between Germany and Poland, and the future of the Adriatic port of Trieste ("The Wallace Case: The Big Three in the Controversy over Foreign Policy," *NYT*, 22 September 1946, E1; Donovan, *Conflict*, 222–28).

2. As the British secretary of war in the aftermath of the Russian Revolution of 1917, Churchill unsuccessfully backed the White Russian, British, and other foreign troops seeking to overthrow the Bolshevik government. General Anton I. Denikin (1872–1947) and Piotr Nikolayevich Wrangel (1878–1928) commanded the White Russian troops (Jenkins, 350–51; *OEWH*).

3. Jenkins, 813–14.

4. Arthur Murray to ER, 24 September 1946, PACM, NLSC.

5. In his letter, Murray told ER that he would soon send her a copy of his forthcoming book, *At Close Quarters*, from which he had read a chapter on FDR to her when she was in London in January. For ER's account of their London evening together, see Document 84.

6. Murray wrote that excessive rain had led to a poor harvest in England, another blow in a long period of hardship that began in 1940 when the nation stood alone against Germany. But, he added, "we are worrying along, and will carry on and through, whatever the rocks that lie in our path" and emerge "better and stronger."

7. For Murray's and ER's views of Churchill's "Iron Curtain" speech of March 5 in Fulton, Missouri, see Document 100 and Document 101.

FOLLOWING UP ON THE COLUMBIA, TENNESSEE, RIOT

In addition to chairing the National Committee for Justice in Columbia, Tennessee, ER served as the committee's contact with the Justice Department. On July 1, 1946, she cabled Attorney General Tom Clark to express her concerns about the federal grand jury's report on the Columbia case. Clark responded on July 9, expressing his appreciation for ER's concern and assuring her that the grand jury had "exhausted every possibility of disclosing a Federal Offense" in their inquiry into the Tennessee Highway Patrol's treatment of African Americans during the "riots" in Columbia. In a handwritten postscript he added:

> The FBI made an exhaustive investigation over a period of some weeks—in addition we have enlisted the assistance of those who happened to be on or near the scene at the time or soon after the riot. No one is able to furnish the names of the perpetrators of the acts of vandalism. The Grand Jury had scores of witnesses before it to no avail. I mention these things so you might know what we have done.[1]

ER forwarded this letter to Walter White, who then sent it to Thurgood Marshall and Robert Carter of the NAACP legal department. Marshall, hospitalized at the time for pneumonia, could not respond to Clark's letter, so White asked Carter to prepare a memo for ER. On August 15, White forwarded Carter's memo to ER, who forwarded it with her own September 23 letter to the attorney general. Clark responded to Carter's memo on October 8 and included a copy of the grand jury's report. He stood by his claim that "the evidence before them [the grand jury] would not justify indictment or presentment for the violation of any Federal statute." After thanking Clark for "giving me the facts about the situation," ER forwarded the correspondence to Thurgood Marshall, whose response to Clark's position follows.[2]

148

Thurgood Marshall to Eleanor Roosevelt

28 October 1946 [New York City]

Dear Mrs. Roosevelt:

I returned to the office a few days ago and have gone over the correspondence between you and Attorney General Tom Clark, concerning the Grand Jury investigation of the Columbia, Tennessee, case.

In the first place, Mr. Clark takes the position throughout the letter that there is no positive identification of any of the state officials responsible for the destruction of property and other items. I have always been surprised at these statements because the United States Department of Justice never seems to have any hesitancy in admitting its inability to perform its functions in regard to Negroes' rights. The F.B.I. has one of the finest records of any investigating organization that we know of. They have been able to ferret out spies and other espionage agents, saboteurs, well-known gangsters such as Dillinger, etc., and I know of no instance where they have been unable to get positive identification of criminals or to build up cases where there has been a violation of federal law except where the victims are Negroes. A huge National Guard Unit was present on the scene when this property was destroyed. There were also a tremendous number of Highway

Patrolmen. There were large numbers of white former mob members standing around, and now the Department of Justice says they cannot get a single person to identify at least one person guilty of what can only be termed as "wholesale destruction of people's property".

Either the Department of Justice, including the F.B.I., fell down on the job of investigating the case or they deliberately closed their eyes. However, I would not be completely frank unless I admitted that I did not expect a whole-hearted attempt by the Department of Justice to bring about any convictions of any state officers in Senator McKellar's home state.[3] I am always aware of at least one other very important case where a sheriff killed at least one Negro without cause and the Department of Justice found itself unable to prosecute because it was, I imagine, too close to Boss Crump's territory. This was, of course, before Attorney General Clark's term of office.

As to the Grand Jury investigation itself, there are several questions which Attorney General Clark has ignored, one of which is that the Negro witnesses who were the victims were placed before the Grand Jury without any consultation whatsoever with any lawyer of the United States Department of Justice. In all of my years of practice, I have never heard of a prosecuting attorney presenting a complaining witness, or witnesses, to a Grand Jury without first talking with him. It has also never been satisfactorily explained to me why it was necessary to hear all of the state officials accused of committing the crimes before hearing from the complaining witnesses. It has never been satisfactorily explained to me why the Negro complaining witnesses before the Grand Jury were required to stand around in the hall waiting day after day to be called in. It likewise has never been satisfactorily explained to me why the Federal Government permitted one of its witnesses, while waiting to testify before the Grand Jury, to be carried away by state officers to be questioned for a long time and otherwise threatened. It is also an anomaly to consider the all-white jury investigating an occurrence between white and colored people where the whole question was as to whether the Negro or the white group was responsible.

Last, but not least, it has never been satisfactorily explained to me why the Attorney General, while conversant with the conditions in Nashville, and especially in view of the fact that the United States District Attorney was a resident of Columbia, Tennessee, who had already issued a statement that no federal rights had been violated, did not proceed by the filing of an information rather than by having a Grand Jury investigation.[4] I do not think there is any doubt that the Grand Jury investigation turned out to be an investigation not of a violation of the civil rights of Negroes, but an investigation of organizations and other matters foreign to the subject.[5]

As to the Grand Jury report, I think we can gather from the admissions of Mr. Bomar at the Columbia trials that there can be no question that federal civil rights were violated.[6] If the Department of Justice would only go after Mr. Bomar as they should, I have no doubt, after observing him at the earlier portions of the Columbia trial, that he would "tell it all".

Sincerely yours,
Thurgood Marshall

TLS AERP, FDRL

"I communicated the contents of your letter about the Columbia, Tennessee case to Mr. Thurgood Marshall of the N.A.A.C.P.," wrote ER in her final letter to Tom Clark on the Columbia case. "Enclosed is a memo of part of his reply and I am sending it to you so you will know how he feels." Clark once again wrote ER to assure her that he and his department did everything within their power to uncover and prosecute any civil rights violations in Columbia.[7]

ER then forwarded a copy of this letter to Thurgood Marshall.[8]

149

Tom Clark to Eleanor Roosevelt
26 November 1946 [Washington, DC]

Dear Mrs. Roosevelt:

I have your letter of November 6, 1946, enclosing a portion of Mr. Thurgood Marshall's memorandum concerning the contents of my letter to you of October 8, 1946. My letter discussed the Columbia, Tennessee, racial disorder and stated, among other things, that the grand jury was unable to return indictments because there was no identification of any person violating Federal laws.

Mr. Marshall expresses surprise at this statement and points out that, at the time the property of the Negro people was destroyed, the National Guard Unit was present, as well as a great number of Highway Patrolmen. The record shows, however, that none of the witnesses appearing before the grand jury could identify any person responsible for the property damage which occurred or for any other act prohibited by Federal laws. As a lawyer, I am sure that Mr. Marshall knows the necessity for such identification and that no indictment could have been returned against the National Guard or Highway Patrolmen as units or organizations without such identification. I might add that the witnesses before the grand jury numbered more than 390 and included those whose names were supplied by the National Association for the Advancement of Colored People and similar organizations.

Mr. Marshall further states that it is to be gathered "from the admissions of Mr. Bomar at the Columbia trials that there can be no question that federal civil rights were violated." In this connection, Mr. Theron L. Caudle, Assistant Attorney General in charge of the Criminal Division, and others of the Department conferred at length on October 23, 1946, with Mr. Leon A. Ransom, one of the NAACP attorneys in the Lawrenceburg trials. At that time, Mr. Ransom expressed an opinion similar to that of Mr. Marshall and promised to furnish the Department with a Transcript of the Testimony containing Mr. Bomar's alleged admissions. The Transcript has not yet been received, but, when it is placed in our hands, it will be given careful study and attention.[9] Should our examination reveal evidence of violation of Federal civil rights statutes, appropriate measures will be quickly taken.

With kindest personal regards,

Sincerely,
Tom C. Clark

TLS AERP, FDRL

---

1. Tom Clark to ER, 9 July 1946, AERP.

2. Memorandum from Walter White to Robert Carter, 29 July 1946, NAACP, DLC; Walter White to ER, 29 July 1946, NAACP, DLC; Memorandum from Robert Carter to Walter White, 14 August 1946, NAACP, DLC; Walter White to ER, 15 August 1946, AERP; ER to Walter White, 22 August 1946, AERP; Walter White to ER, 29 August 1946, AERP; Tom Clark to ER, 8 October 1946, AERP; ER to Tom Clark, 16 October 1946, TCP, HSTL; O'Brien, 42–43. For more on Columbia, see Documents 102 through 106, and Document 130.

3. Kenneth D. McKellar (D-TN), who chaired the Senate Appropriations Committee and had the unquestioned support of the Crump machine, possessed enormous political power both in the

Senate and throughout Tennessee. The grand jury hearing in Columbia caused McKellar anxiety however, because he faced reelection in November 1946. Both McKellar's liberal opposition and conservative support understood the politics that lay behind the proceedings: conservatives saw the grand jury hearing as an attempt by liberals in Washington to displace Crump and McKellar, while liberals argued that Crump and McKellar's domination of the state precluded the possibility of a fair trial (O'Brien, 202).

4. An *information* is an official accusation by a public officer, typically the district attorney, in a criminal case that allows the case to proceed to trial without the state first having to present the merits of the case to a grand jury. It is very similar to an indictment, but it is handed down by a public official rather than a grand jury ("Information," *BLD*, 701).

When Attorney General Clark ordered Judge Elmer Davies to convene a grand jury, Clark sent three attorneys from the Department of Justice's Civil Rights Sector (CRS) to Nashville to work on the case. However, Judge Davies assigned two local assistant district attorneys to try the case, both of whom made it quite clear to the CRS attorneys that they would have little say in the proceedings (O'Brien, 36, 200).

5. See Document 130 for a summary of the grand jury's report.

6. Lynn Bomar, chief of the Tennessee Highway Patrol, testified that while arresting one of the African American men indicted in the Columbia case he put his "foot on the boy's neck." He then defended the actions his command took, declaring that at no time were his men "out of line." Bomar's testimony in the first trial so embarrassed the state (which acquitted the twenty-five defendants in the case), that when the second Columbia-related trial commenced in November, the prosecution chose not to call Chief Bomar to the stand (O'Brien, 45, 265 n107).

7. ER to Tom Clark, 6 November 1946, AERP.

8. Notes written in ER's hand across the bottom of this letter indicate that December 2, she passed a copy of this letter to Marshall. Marshall then wrote Clark directly on December 27 expressing his skepticism regarding the FBI's inability to identify any of the individuals responsible for the violence or destruction of property in the Columbia case. Claiming that even the "inexperienced investigators," whom the NAACP relied on in its previous investigations of mob action, "have usually been able to produce the names of the members of the mobs," Marshall accused the FBI of "one-sided" investigatory practices in civil rights matters:

> The F.B.I. has established for itself an uncomparable record for ferreting out persons violating our federal laws. This great record extends from the prosecution of vicious spies and saboteurs, who are trained in the methods of evading identification and arrest, to nondescript hoodlums who steal cheap automobiles and drive them across the state lines. On the other hand, the F.B.I. has been unable to identify or bring to trial persons charged with violations of federal statutes where Negroes are the victims. Such a record demonstrates the uneven administration of federal criminal statutes, which should not be tolerated.... I believe that you, as Attorney General of the United States, have the clear duty and responsibility of making a complete investigation of one of your departments, namely, the F.B.I., to determine why it is impossible for this department to maintain a record as to crimes in which Negroes are victims comparable to its record as to other crimes (Thurgood Marshall to Tom Clark, 27 December 1946, AERP; Thurgood Marshall to ER, 30 December 1946, AERP).

9. ER wrote "Why not?" in the margin next to this sentence, indicating her interest in why Marshall had not yet received the court transcripts.

ON STRIKES, BIG LABOR, AND WAGE CONTROLS

Strikes that halted production in several of the nation's industries throughout 1946 caused many Americans—even some who had once supported labor's collective bargaining through strikes—to become more and more critical of strikes and the labor leaders who called them. As Hugh Sanford of Knoxville, Tennessee, wrote ER, "In the days when there were only a few labor unions that could effectively force their wage-scales above the amount that could be earned competitively, and when there were only one or two strikes a year,—strikes that did not last very long,—these collective bargainists really got somewhere." He went on to argue that the general strike situation changed everything. In a letter he published in the *Knoxville Journal*, which he included with his letter to ER, he further explained his position:

> Probably automobile workers will have less than six months work this year. They lost only a few weeks on their own strikes, but the steel strikes, the coal strikes, the strikes in the plants of the suppliers of parts, the strikes in the power lines, the strikes in the transportation systems, etc., etc., have shut down the automobile factories to a point that these workers will be lucky if they get half pay this year." Sanford conceded that strikes resulted in a nominal wage increase for the workers, but he pointed out that with strikes so widespread, the price of consumer goods rose much more quickly than wages: the workers were in effect, "cutting their own throats."

Sanford blamed labor leaders, those union officials whose "big salaries" underwrote "their houses, fine clothes, etc., etc." They were not going to tell the workers the "truth"—that strikes were "worse than useless"—because doing so would undermine their lifestyle. Stanford then asked ER to do what labor leaders were not—look out for the workers' best interests. "Will you cooperate? Will you tell the whole story to labor? What better service could you possibly do to this country?"[1]

150

Eleanor Roosevelt to Hugh Sanford
30 October 1946 [New York City]

My dear Mr. Sanford:

I read your letter and the reprint of your letter to the paper.

What are you suggesting as an alternative to strikes? The weapon of the strike should not be used except when collective bargaining, or labor-management committees[2] where they exist, have been unable to find solutions. The strike has always been considered as the last weapon that any man had and the right to strike could not be denied him.

I am entirely in agreement with you that the rift in the ranks of labor which brings about jurisdictional strikes, costs both labor, management and the public much unnecessary loss and I hope that labor will see that it gets together before too long. There are signs that that is happening.

Nobody believes that strikes are the best answer to human relations but we haven't as yet found people who brought out a plan through which real cooperation exists between labor and management. Labor-management committees are the best plan that has been offered so far, but in many cases management has withstood introducing them.

I agree with you that there are some selfish labor leaders, but the vast majority is truly interest in seeing the interests of labor served.

You are right that production is important at the moment and that without production we can not possibly get back on our feet or help the rest of the world, that I think that is as much the responsibility of management as it is of labor. You can not with rising prices expect people to get along without asking for rising wages and wages always lag behind prices.

Very sincerely yours,

TLc AERP, FDRL

---

1. Hugh W. Sanford to ER, 21 October 1946, and enclosed clipping from the *Knoxville Journal*, 9 October 1946, AERP.

2. The National War Labor Board established labor-management committees to arbitrate disputes between labor and management. Many business leaders, labor leaders, and politicians believed that the labor-management committees—composed of representatives of labor, management, and the public—helped avert strikes and contributed to high productivity levels during the war ("Believe Committees Will Stay," *NYT*, 5 September 1945, 28).

ON FAITH AND PREJUDICE

In July 1945, Bishop William Scarlett[1] asked ER to contribute an essay on racial discrimination for inclusion in a report of the Joint Commission on Social Reconstruction to the General Convention of the Protestant Episcopal Church, which was scheduled to convene in September 1946. "There is no one who can do this as you would do it," wrote Scarlett, "No one whom we would rather have speak for the Church on this issue." As a liberal theologian and social activist, Scarlett hoped the commission's report would reflect his conviction that "the solution to our problems is to be found only within a religious view of life and the world." By asking well-known individuals such as ER, Sumner Welles, Frances Perkins, Reinhold Niebuhr, and Arthur H. Compton to contribute essays on American-Soviet relations, the UN, control of atomic energy, treatment of enemy nations, full employment, and racial discrimination, Scarlett hoped the report would demonstrate to both members of the Episcopal Church and the general public that:

> Christianity is not something irrelevant to life, not something that touches only the fringes of life, not something of little importance which we can take or leave as we like … It is either the Rock on which we build our civilization or else it is the Rock against which civilization will continue to pound itself to pieces.

The bishop thought the speech ER had recently delivered before the Southern Educational Foundation was "exactly what we want," and he asked her to forward her text to him. ER replied that she "had no notes and no manuscript when I spoke for the Southern Educational Foundation. It was extemporaneous." However, ER, who appreciated his work, promised to "try to write something for you, but perhaps not as long as you suggest," and hoped that "if it does not appeal to you that you will feel free to criticize it." She completed a draft of her essay in October 1945, revised in the following March, and in 1946, after presenting it as part of the report to the General Convention, Scarlett published her essay, along with the others that comprised the commission's report, as *Toward a Better World*.[2]

151

"The Minorities Question"
Toward a Better World November 1946

I was brought up in a home where learning Bible verses, collects and hymns was a daily and Sunday practice. As children we were often asked if we had read our portion of the Scriptures every morning and every night as we were expected to do, and though I am afraid that those good habits have slid away from me in this busy world of today, when decisive moments come in life it is curious how often the Bible verses that fit the occasion come to mind.[3]

The second commandment, "Love thy neighbor as thyself," has often been before me when I have heard people generalize about groups of their neighbors who, like them, are citizens of the United States of America.[4]

There is no use in shutting our eyes to the fact that racial and religious tensions in this country are becoming more acute. They arise partly from experiences back in the past, experiences very often in other countries where wars were carried on between people of various nationalities. I think they persist in this country largely because of the insecurity of some of our people under our economic system. If times are hard, jobs scarce and food hard to get, we always prefer that someone else be the victim of these difficult situations and we fight to keep ourselves on top. We come to attribute certain characteristics to different races and nationalities. We differentiate too little, and even where religions are concerned, if they are not our own, we are apt to lump people all together as doing certain things because they are Jew or Gentile, Catholic or Protestant.

I have come to think, therefore, that the basic thing we must do is to stop generalizing about people. If we no longer thought of them as groups but as individuals, we would soon find that they varied in their different groups as much as we do in our own. It seems to me quite natural to say: "I do not like John Jones." The reasons may be many. But to say: "I do not like Catholics or Jews" is complete nonsense. Sometimes people go further and say, "All the Irish here are Catholics and all Irish Catholics are politicians, therefore they are corrupt," or, "All Jews engage in sharp business practice." More nonsense and futile generalities. Because the Jews have been oppressed through the ages and have learned in a hard school, since their opportunities are restricted, to work harder when opportunities open up for them is not strange. All disadvantaged people do the same. When opportunities are open to them the Negroes will work hard too.[5]

The Negroes perhaps suffer more from this lumping together of people than any other race. Because the South has created a picture, a charming one of mammies, old fashioned butlers and gardeners and day laborers, we must not believe that that is the whole picture. They have rarely shown us the picture of the intellectual, or of the soldier, or of the inventor. Because of circumstances there are relatively fewer of them in the colored group, but they do exist. I think many people, if they closed their eyes and talked to a mixed racial group, would find it hard to tell the difference, from either the voice or the sentiments expressed, between the cultivated white man and the cultivated Negro.[6]

If we really believe in democracy, we must face the fact that equality of opportunity is basic to any kind of democracy. Equality of opportunity means that all of our people, not just white people, not just people descended from English or Scandinavian ancestors, but all our people, must have decent homes, a decent standard of health, and educational opportunities to develop their abilities as far as they are able. Thus they may be equipped with the tools for the work which they wish to do, and there must be equality of opportunity to obtain that work regardless of race or religion or color.

Where the Negro is concerned, I think he has a legitimate complaint. We have expected Negroes to be good citizens and yet in a large part of our country we haven't given them an opportunity to take part in our government. We have, however, made them subject to our laws and we have drafted them into our Army and Navy. We have done better than ever before, I think, in really integrating some of them with their white brothers in the various services. It has been an uphill fight, however, and the tendency has been to keep them in the menial positions, performing services which are needed, but which do not give an opportunity for glory or for compensation to the same extent that other services might do.[7]

It is true that because of lack of opportunity for education, many of our colored people are not capable of rising to great heights, but we should have differentiated between those who were capable and those who were not. We would not then find so many men with such a deep sense of injustice who, when they return to civilian status and find themselves confronted with discrimination and segregation, may easily become a real menace in our communities.

I am prepared to believe that it will take us some time as a nation to accept the Commandment: "Love thy neighbor as thyself," but I am a little nervous lest the time allowed for readjustment should not be so long as it seemed to be before the war. The day we dropped our atomic bomb we closed an era. Our only real defense in a very insecure world is friendship among peoples. We are the strongest and richest nation today. We are richer in manpower and in national resources than most of the other nations. Our manpower has gained self-confidence as it has rolled up a victory in two distant parts of the world. Our manpower will not lack initiative. They haven't been starved. They haven't been under the heel of a conqueror. Neither has our whole civilian population. Therefore the rest of the world looks to us for leadership.

How much can we give them? If we cannot solve our economic questions, who else in the world has the strength and resources to do so? If we cannot and will not learn to live side by side in peace and unity, how can we expect that the people of the world are going to learn this most difficult lesson? It is much easier to fight about things than to settle them by law. We have come to a rule of law within our borders for most of our citizens. We are ashamed when we hear of a lynching. Most of us hope the day will come when justice is even-handed and the laws operate for all people alike within our borders. The responsibility, therefore, is great. We must find a way to live with our neighbors in peace, in order that we may help the rest of the world with the job of peaceful understanding which must be achieved if we are all of us to remain on this globe and continue to develop our civilization.

What is needed is really not a self-conscious virtue which makes us treat our neighbors as we want to be treated, but an acceptance of the fact that all human beings have dignity and the potentiality of development into the same kind of people we ourselves are. When we look at each individual without thinking of him as a Jew or as a Negro, but only as a person, then we may get to like him or we may dislike him, but he stands on his own feet as an individual and we stand with him on an equal basis. Together we are citizens of a great country. I may have had greater opportunity and greater happiness than he has had, and fewer obstacles to overcome, but basically we build our lives together and what we build today sets the pattern for the future of the world.

Toward a Better World, FDRL

---

1. For more background on William Scarlett, see *n*3 Document 65.

2. Scarlett, 1–3; William Scarlett to ER, 12 July 1945, and ER's response, 26 July 1945, AERP; "For the Joint Commission on Social Reconstruction" draft, October 1945, AERP. Article later published in William Scarlett, ed., *Toward a Better World* (Philadelphia: John C. Winston, 1946), 35–39.

3. In her autobiography ER recalled that each morning during the summer when she was six years old she recited Bible verses to her mother. After her mother died, ER lived with her grandmother, who insisted not only that ER recite verses to her, but also that she spend Sunday mornings with the coachman's daughter, teaching her verses, hymns, collects, and the catechism (*TIR*, 8, 16).

4. This exhortation is the second of Jesus's two Great Commandments as recorded in the Gospels of the New Testament (Matthew 22:39; Mark 12:31; Luke 10:27).

5. The October 1945 and March 19, 1946, drafts included the following paragraph:

> The Irish Catholic can be as scrupulously honest in public office as anyone else. I have known Jews who lived according to the highest ethical standards and were generous not only to people but to causes. It is individuals we must know, not groups! ("For the Joint Commission on Social Reconstruction" draft, October 1945, and "The Minorities Problem," 19 March 1946, AERP).

6. ER's original drafts included a paragraph on miscegenation:

> Many people will tell you they object to breaking down the barriers between the races or to allowing them to associate together without self-consciousness from the time they are children because of their disapproval of inter-marriage between races. They feel that races should stay pure blooded as far as possible. When people say that to me, I sometimes wonder if they have taken a good look at our population. If there ever was a nation where people have mixed blood, it is right here in the United States, and yet we seem to have remained a strong and virile nation. Besides, this particular objection which people

advance is somewhat irrelevant since when people want to marry, they are usually past reasoning with! Reason is swallowed up by emotion and the people involved usually say to all objections: "This is my life and I shall live it as I see fit". It is such a peculiarly personal thing to decide as to whom you will marry that I have a feeling it is a very bad basis on which to decide how people shall live in the year 1945 in a free country under a democratic form of government.

Scarlett, acting upon ER's invitation to "feel free to criticize" her essay, asked her:

…Would you mind greatly if we left out the paragraph … which deals with intermarriage? We have a number of Southerners on the Commission and to them this paragraph seemed to imply approval of intermarriage. As the Commission had adopted a very strong statement against segregation and for complete equality of opportunity, and as any suggestion regarding intermarriage gives rise to such a blind reaction of prejudice, it was felt that our whole position would be stronger if that paragraph were deleted.

This, however, is only a suggestion and if you have any objection to eliminating it the paper will be printed as written.

"Of course leave out the paragraph," ER replied, "I should be very glad to have you delete anything you think might do harm" (For the Joint Commission on Social Reconstruction, draft, October 1945, AERP; William Scarlett to ER, 19 March 1946 and ER's response, AERP).

7. During World War II, ER served as a liaison between civil rights leaders and the Roosevelt administration. She urged FDR, Secretary of War Henry Stimson, General George Marshall, and other members of the administration to integrate African Americans into the armed services, provide black soldiers with better training, and place African American units in combat roles. In 1943 for example, as a result of ER's pressure, the War Department ceased designating recreational facilities as "White" and "Colored only." Also, through her intervention, the first unit of African American combat pilots, the 99th Pursuit Squadron or Tuskegee Airmen, saw action in Europe. The unit won 100 Distinguished Flying Crosses and was the only escort group never to lose a single bomber to enemy fire. Although African Americans made progress during the war, the armed services would not be desegregated until July 1948 when Truman issued Executive Order 9981, ending discrimination in the military (Goodwin, 170–72, 421–24, 626–28).

DEBATING VYSHINSKY AND UNITED NATIONS REFUGEE POLICY, PART 2

On February 12, 1946, the General Assembly passed a resolution that recommended that the Economic and Social Council set up a special committee to study the refugee issue and propose a plan for meeting the situation. This resulted in the drafting of the constitution of the International Refugee Organization (IRO), which was designed to take over the refugee functions of the United Nations Relief and Rehabilitation Administration (UNRRA) when it would cease to exist on June 30, 1947. In November 1946, the Third Committee began debate on the draft constitution of the IRO, which had been submitted to all the member governments for comment. Many governments proposed amendments, which the Third Committee had to assess and debate. The Soviet Union opposed the constitution because it allowed refugees, who did not wish to return to their countries of origin in Eastern Europe where Communist governments had assumed power, to choose resettlement elsewhere. ER debated Vyshinsky on this point in the Third Committee and then debated Gromyko on the same point in the General Assembly.[1]

152

U.S. Position on International Refugee Organization
Statement by Representative of the U.S. Delegation to the United Nations

8 November 1946 [Lake Success, NY]

To begin with, Mr. Chairman, I should like to state very briefly the position of the United States on this International Refugee Organization, which will care for and help to rehabilitate nearly a million people from Europe and the Far East. As long as they are refugees and displaced persons they constitute a threat to peace and good relations among governments.

The maintenance in camps of these persons leads to deterioration among them as human beings and is an economic waste for all the nations of the world. We, in the United States, feel this most keenly, since from practically all the countries where they come from we have received citizens who have built up our nation. Therefore, the United States supports the principles of the General Assembly resolution of February 12, 1946 namely:

(*a*) The problem is international in character.

(*b*) There shall be no compulsory repatriation.

(*c*) Action taken by IRO must not interfere with existing international arrangements for apprehension of war criminals, Quislings, and traitors. This is being done by military occupation forces and is not the responsibility of this new organization.

As a consequence we support the draft constitution of the IRO which reflects the foregoing principles.

The United States has supported the principles advocated by my colleague from the U. S. S. R. which is proved by the numbers of people that have been repatriated from the United States zone. However, it would be foreign to our conception of democracy to force repatriation on any human being. Three and one-half million persons have been repatriated from the United States zone, but our people will always believe in the right of asylum and complete freedom of choice.

The Pilgrims, the Huguenots, and the Germans of 1848[2] came to us in search of political and religious freedom and a wider economic opportunity. They built the United States.

These people now in displaced-persons camps are kin to those early settlers of ours, and many of them might have relatives in the United States.

My Government urges the participation in the IRO as members by all peace-loving nations. There is no question but that this participation will entail financial sacrifices by all participating governments. For a time it will be a heavy burden, but in the long run it will be an economy and well worth the cost.

The finances of our organization will be considered in committee 5, where the financial burden will be allotted to the participating governments, so that the cost will be equitably shared by all, and each government will pay according to the standards laid down by committee 5.[3]

In the interest of brevity I shall comment at this time only on some of the essential points in Mr. Vyshinsky's speech of Wednesday, leaving other points for comment when we discuss the draft constitution article by article.

First of all I should like to say that Mr. Vyshinsky's view that no assistance should be given to those who for valid reasons decide not to return to their countries of origin is inconsistent with the unanimous decision of the General Assembly in the resolution on displaced persons of February 12, 1946.[4] That clearly provides that these persons shall become the concern of the International Refugee Organization.

Mr. Vyshinsky says that this problem is very simple. It can be solved by repatriating all the displaced persons. In fact, those who do not wish to be repatriated must fall into this category. I think this point of view fails to take into consideration the facts of political change in countries of origin which have created fears in the minds of the million persons, who remain, of such a nature that they choose miserable life in camps in preference to the risks of repatriation.

Our colleague from Poland[5] mentioned that since arrangements had been made to give people food allowances after their return home the numbers going home had increased. I think he is quite right that the fear of an economic situation has deterred a number of people from taking the risk of repatriation, but not all of them are actuated by consideration of the economic situation in their country of origin.

Seven million people have already been repatriated; repatriation is still proceeding. One thousand Poles are leaving the U.S. zones of Germany and Austria daily. The military administration which accomplished this result can hardly be held solely responsible for the failure of the last million to return.

It was a new point, I think, which Mr. Vyshinsky raised when he presented his position that those who do not choose to return to their countries of origin shall not be resettled, shall receive no aid towards settling somewhere else. This leaves them with the prospect of spending the rest of their lives in assembly centers as long as the IRO supports them or else of facing starvation. They obviously cannot be left in assembly centers to their own devices. They would continue as an irritant in good relations between friendly governments and contribute to delay in the restoration of peace and order which is the concern of all governments. There is no reason why they should become wanderers if instead they can be given an opportunity for resettlement in some country which has a future to offer them.

By another provision of the General Assembly resolution of February 1946, which, I think, Mr. Vyshinsky must have forgotten, no action taken shall be of such a character as to interfere in any way with the surrender and punishment of war criminals, Quislings, and traitors in conformity with international arrangements or agreements. These arrangements, however, are the responsibility of other government bodies, including the military authorities.

I can tell you very briefly how arrangements for the apprehension of Quislings works out under the U.S. occupational authorities. U.S. officials are continuously engaged in screening the refugee personnel to locate Quislings or those who for other reasons are not entitled to be given asylum. When special complaints are received from other governments they are made by the governments' liaison officers with the United States Forces, European Theater. USFET thereupon makes an investigation through Army channels. If the investigation appears to substantiate the complaint, the case goes before a board of officers, which makes the final determination. This method of procedure has in general been satisfactory; but it must be emphasized that this committee here is not, and should not, be the forum for debate as to its effectiveness. It is not our function here to discuss the adequacy of these arrangements or the performance under them. We are concerned with final decisions on the draft of the constitution of IRO. This draft clearly excludes from the benefits of the organization war criminals, Quislings, and traitors. We can hope that such persons will be entirely eliminated by the time the IRO begins to function.

Mr. Vyshinsky spoke of members of various military groups.[6] The military character of different groups and their members, we think, has been greatly exaggerated. They are the concern of the military authorities, however, and will be handled by them. Those who fought with the Germans and collaborated with them are clearly excluded from assistance from the IRO in the constitution before us. I have asked that the U.S. military authorities supply me with a report on each of the incidents complained of by Mr. Vyshinsky where the U.S. is concerned, and I shall report these findings in writing to the committee, if it so desires, as soon as they are available.

Now we come to the point which Mr. Vyshinsky made that all propaganda should be suppressed in the camps. He challenges us on the point that under the guise of freedom of expression propaganda hostile to the countries of origin is tolerated.[7] On this point I am afraid we hold very different ideas. But this does not preclude cooperation between us. We, in the United States, tolerate opposition provided it does not extend to the point of advocacy of the overthrow of government by force. Unless the right of opposition is conceded, it seems to me that there is very little possibility that countries with differing conceptions of democracy can live together without friction in the same world. Much progress has been made to date in dealing with this problem of propaganda within the framework of these divergent views. With patience and understanding we can achieve still further progress in this direction.

Mr. Vyshinsky objects to the inclusion of certain categories of refugees and displaced persons.[8]

One group consists of those who, as a result of events subsequent to the outbreak of the second World War, are unable or unwilling to avail themselves of the protection of the government of their countries of nationality or of former nationality.

This paragraph covers those who for political reasons, territorial changes, or changes of sovereignty are unable to return to their country. That paragraph is in annex 1, part 1, section A, paragraph 2. I regret that Mr. Vyshinsky cannot confirm the agreement reached at the last session of the Economic and Social Council on this point. We consider it essential that the paragraph be retained. But since he asked who these people are, I should like out of my own experience to mention a few. I visited two camps near Frankfurt, where the majority of people had come from Estonia, Latvia, and Lithuania.[9] I have received innumerable petitions. My mail today carried three from people in different countries, who, because changes had come in the types of government in their countries, felt that they did not wish to return. That does not mean that they do not love their country; it simply means that they prefer the country as it was before they left it. That country they feel no longer belongs to them.[10] I gather that Mr. Vyshinsky felt that anyone who did not wish to return under the present form of government must of necessity be Fascist. I talked to a great many of these people who do not strike me as Fascist, and the assumption that people do not wish to return to the country of their origin because those countries are now under what is called a democratic form of government does not seem to allow for certain differences in the understanding of the word *democracy*. As Mr. Vyshinsky uses it, it would seem that democracy is synonymous with Soviet, or at least a fairly similar conception of political and economic questions. Under that formula I am very sure that he would accept some of the other nations in the world who consider themselves democracies and who are as willing to die for their beliefs as are the people of the Soviet Union.

Mr. Vyshinsky also objected to certain exceptions to the general rule that those who had voluntarily assisted the enemy are excluded from the concern of the IRO.[11] The intent of the exemptions is to cover those who were forced to perform slave labor or who may have rendered humanitarian assistance, such as assistance to wounded civilians. Mr. Vyshinsky proposes to exclude all those who assisted in any manner. Under such language those merely present in any occupied area forced by necessity of survival to perform any form of work or service within the German economy would be considered to have assisted the enemy and would thus be excluded. This would result in cruel hardship on many. We can, however, discuss the point at greater length later.

I sincerely regret having to speak in opposition to some of Mr. Vyshinsky's views. But he will recall that in London there were some things which because of the fundamental beliefs I hold, I had to stand on. I felt strongly about them then and I still do. This does not mean that Mr. Vyshinsky cannot hold to his basic beliefs as well and still achieve with us a solution. This solution can be reached if we are both willing in these fields to try for a spirit of cooperation and a realistic approach to our problems. It is essential to the peace of the world that we wipe out some of our resentments as well as our fears. I hope that as time goes on our two great nations may grow to understand each other and to accept our different viewpoints on certain questions.

DSB, November 24, 1946

---

1. Sydney Gruson, "Russian-Led Move to Gag Refugees Defeated by UNO," *NYT*, 13 February 1946, 1; "Draft Constitution Is Adopted for World Refugee Organization," *NYT*, 21 June 1946, 4; *Department of State Bulletin*, November 24, 1946, 935–38.

2. The English Pilgrims and the French Huguenots were Protestants who fled to America to escape religious persecution in their countries; the Germans of 1848 were political refugees who fled to America during revolutionary upheavals aimed at creating unity and greater democracy in Germany (*OEWH*).

3. Committee Five of the General Assembly had responsibility for the United Nations budget (*EUN*).

4. During the debate with the Soviet Union and its allies on the IRO constitution in the Third Committee, ER had to continually reiterate the point she had won in debate with Vyshinsky in February 1946 and that had been incorporated into the UN resolution of February 12. See Document 90, especially *n*4, for the text of the key paragraphs in the resolution. On November 19, according to the summary report, ER "stressed the necessity of maintaining constant reference to the principle, enunciated in the resolution of the General Assembly of 12 February 1946, to the effect that none was to be repatriated against his will" (Committee Three, Summary Record, 20 November 1946, (A/C.3/85), 97, UNORGA, MWelC).

5. Jozef Winiewicz (1905–1984), the Polish representative on the Third Committee (*HDP*).

6. Vyshinsky claimed that there were military or para-military units in the camps that the Allies had not disbanded and whose purpose was "the liquidation of the USSR as a powerful State" (Third Committee, Seventeenth Meeting, Summary Record, 10 November 1946 (A/C.3/43), 29, UNORGA, MWelC [RM]).

7. Vyshinsky, according to the UN summary record of his remarks at the November 6, 1946 meeting of the Third Committee, said:

> The argument put forward against the position of the Union of Soviet Socialist Republics was that restriction of propaganda discouraging repatriation would be a violation of the

freedom of propaganda, freedom of speech and of the press. But the propaganda carried on by fascists and traitors to prevent persons from returning to their homes and families was a false and fraudulent misrepresentation of facts perpetrated as a screen for those who thought thereby to further their own sinister political aims by coercion, threats, and violence.

The Russians and their Yugoslavian allies continued to complain about the management of the displaced persons camps throughout the debates on the IRO constitution. ER had to repeatedly rebut their charges that war criminals, quislings, traitors, and secret military groups were among the refugees in the camps and that they spread propaganda against repatriation. In early December, she led a successful fight to defeat a Russian proposal calling for the appointment of a UN commission to investigate the camps (Third Committee, Seventeenth Meeting, Summary Record, 10 November 1946 (A/C.3/43), 29, UNORGA, MWelC [RM]; "Russians Beaten in Camp Inquiry," *NYT*, 7 December 1946, 9).

8. The summary reported Vyshinsky as saying:

No support should be given by the International Refugee Organization to quislings, traitors, and war criminals, as laid down in the draft constitution. In addition, however, the delegation of the USSR considered that the International Refugee Organization should not give aid to the similar category of persons who refused to return to their native country, in view of the fact that the States to which these persons, after having freely expressed their views, refused to return, were members of the International Organization (Third Committee, Seventeenth Meeting, Summary Record, 10 November 1946 (A/C.3/43), UNORGA, MWelC [RM]).

9. ER knew the conditions in the camps and their effect on the refugees firsthand. See Document 95.

10. In late October, for example, ER received a handwritten petition from eighteen Estonian refugees asking her to appeal to Attorney General Tom Clark to stay their deportation from the United States until Congress could act. Near the end of the war, these refugees had fled first to Sweden to escape conscription into the German army, then crossed the ocean in "rickety fishing boats" from Sweden to the United States in order to avoid forced repatriation to Estonia, now occupied for a second time by the Soviet Union. When the Soviet Union first occupied Estonia from 1940–41, the petition reported, "thousands of Estonians were murdered, arrested and deported to Siberia. Approximately sixty thousand innocent people got lost in that one year of Soviet rule." They could not go back to Estonia now that it was again in Soviet hands, the refugees concluded. "We are Democrats and honest people and if given a temporary trial we will prove that we will make the best of citizens" (Petition signed by eighteen Estonian refugees, 23 October 1946, AERP).

Such petitions not only provided fuel for ER's efforts to secure the adoption of the IRO constitution, but made urgent the issue of easing US immigration laws, thus making it possible for groups like the Estonians to enter the country. Congress, however, expressed reluctance to expand quotas or even, as Truman proposed, to allow previously unmet monthly quotas to be filled in later months. ER argued in her column of November 20, 1946 in favor of Truman's proposal:

I had been told that women belonging to some of our patriotic organizations such as the DAR were opposed to this humanitarian easing of our immigration rules. One cannot help wondering, however, what makes these women, and other groups that think along the same lines, so fearful of holding out even so mild a helping hand as is suggested.

The years of high immigration in the past were usually prosperous, because at that time we were expanding. At present, we are again in need of labor. And the types of immigrants we could obtain would, in many cases, be of a very high order. We might count on their creating new opportunities for employment, rather than being content simply to hold jobs of their own.

I wonder how many of us would be here today if the founding fathers had been as nervous as we are about the oncoming hordes that threatened to starve them to death when they were not growing much more than they themselves could eat!

I can understand a little better the attitude of the veterans' and the labor groups, because they are in direct competition. But one would expect that women would think of the effect that a shortsighted policy might have on future peace. Unless we show some willingness to absorb our quota of displaced people and refugees, why should other countries make any sacrifices?

When all the repatriation possible has been done in Europe, there will probably remain several hundred thousand people—Jews, Balts, Poles, Yugoslavs, Ukrainians and others—who, for reasons which to them seem valid, do not wish to return to their homes. If they stay where they are in Europe, they delay and impede the return to normal conditions, and they are not able to use their abilities to the best advantage.

We hope, of course, that all people who can possibly go back to their own countries will do so, because those countries need help in rebuilding. It may be hard at first, but it will be rewarding to contribute to the revival of one's native land. But the Jews, for instance, cannot be asked to return to countries where their memories are tragic and bitter, and where, often, they are still not too welcome.

Some other people whose countries have changed their form of government may quite honestly prefer not to live under the new conditions, simply because they would not feel as free as they did before foreign domination wiped out the government that they originally supported. They are not necessarily Fascists, and we of all people should do what we can to help them to start life anew" (*MD*, 20 November 1946).

(*MD*, 14 November 1946; Jay Walz, "Higher DP Quotas Facing Opposition," *NYT*, 8 September 1946; Document 182).

11. Vyshinsky said, according to the summary report, that the USSR objected to the IRO providing aid to "those persons whose voluntary assistance to the enemy was 'purely humanitarian and non-military' ... The idea that one could assist the enemy for 'humanitarian reasons' was absurd" (Third Committee, Seventeenth Meeting, Summary Record, 10 November 1946 (A/C.3/43), 29, MWelC [RM]).

ON THE REPUBLICAN SWEEP IN 1946

On November 7, the Republican Party swept both houses of Congress, 51–45 in the Senate and 246–188 in the House of Representatives. Although the GOP usurped many Democratic strongholds, ER publicly remained optimistic about the outcome of the election. In her November 8 My Day, she declared that "A defeat really is of little importance. The only thing that matters is what you do with your defeat. If you analyze it and learn from it, I think defeat very often can be as valuable for the future as victory." From her "own point of view," she continued, "being out of office has always been a pleasant situation. Having no responsibility, while being able to sit on the sidelines and observe with a critical eye, is one of the most delightful positions I know."

After criticizing the "men [who] haven't quite learned how important the women are," she applauded the reelection of Helen Gahagan Douglas in California, who "never shirked saying what she believed in and certainly ran on her record." [1] Both her campaign and her victory proved "that people like honesty and convictions in their candidates, and that they recognize integrity."

In her private correspondence with Truman the day after the election, ER offered her condolences while speculating that the Eightieth Congress might not inhibit Democratic efforts any more than the Seventy-ninth.

153

Eleanor Roosevelt to Harry Truman
8 November 1946 [New York City]

Dear Mr. President:

I know the election must have been a disappointment to you, as it was to me. I had expected some losses but not quite such sweeping ones. [2]

However, I am not at all sure that you will not get as much out of a straight out Republican Congress, which now has to take the responsibility for whatever happens, as you got out of the type of opposition which the coalition of reactionary Democrats and Republicans created.

With my very best wishes to you and my warm regards to Mrs. Truman and Margaret, I am,

Very cordially yours,
Eleanor Roosevelt

TLS AERP, FDRL

The president replied the following week.

154

Harry Truman to Eleanor Roosevelt
14 November 1946 [The White House]

Dear Mrs. Roosevelt:

I certainly appreciated your note on the election.

You are exactly right about the congressional situation—it couldn't be much worse than it was last winter. In fact, I think we will be in a position to get more things done for the welfare of the country, or at least to make a record of things recommended for the welfare of the country, than we would have been had we been responsible for a Congress which was not loyal to the party.

Mrs. Truman and Margaret want to be remembered.

Sincerely yours,
Harry S. Truman

TLS AERP, FDRL

---

1. *MD*, 8 November 1946.

2. For example, Democrats lost 138 of their nonsouthern seats in the House of Representatives. Liberal and pro-union candidates suffered large defeats in New York, California, Pennsylvania, Michigan, and Illinois, as well as losing ground in the border states. Key Republican victories included Joseph McCarthy's defeat of the Wisconsin progressive Robert La Follette, Jr., and Richard Nixon's defeat of the California Democrat Jerry Voorhis, while Thomas Dewey received the largest margin ever recorded when reelected to the New York governorship (Donovan, 236–37; McCullough, *Truman*, 523).

WOMEN, EQUAL RIGHTS, AND THE UNITED NATIONS

Nora Stanton Barney (1883–1971), Elizabeth Cady Stanton's granddaughter, suffrage organizer, and staunch advocate for the Equal Rights Amendment, wrote ER to express her opposition to a vote she mistakenly believed ER had taken that extended equal rights to men of all races without extending the same protection to women.[1]

155

Nora Stanton Barney to Eleanor Roosevelt
11 November 1946 [Greenwich, CT]

My dear Mrs. Roosevelt:

I was one of those who wrote to congratulate you at the time of your appointment as one of our delegates to the United Nations Assembly in London. I was shocked to hear today that you are taking the same attitude as the legislators of 1864 in standing for equality before the law for the Negro race, while opposing it for women. The American Delegation, as I understand it, has gone on record as favoring the adoption of the principle of Equal Rights regardless of race. What a strange position the American Republic will be placed in if it stands for justice for Negroes and not for women.

If this, by any chance, takes place, the women of the world will turn elsewhere for leaders to champion their cause. Like the sun, hope will set in the West, and rise in the East.

I am mindful that you did not champion the cause of votes for women during the long years of struggle, nor the present fight for equal opportunity and equal economic status.[2] However, I hope that you will, at least, not allow your personal feelings on these matters to influence the stand of the American Delegation. The plea that women are not prepared is equally applicable to men. You cannot learn to use a tool without first having it in your hand.

Yours very truly,
Nora Stanton Barney

TLS AERP, FDRL

A few days after receiving Barney's letter, ER discussed the misunderstanding in My Day and then sent Barney the following reply.

Bodil Begtrup,[3] chair of the Subcommission on the Status of Women, had proposed that the Third Committee adopt a resolution asking the General Assembly "to grant political rights to women where they had not already done so." Although ER believed that the UN Charter had already taken this step and that the committee would pass the resolution "unanimously," "much to [her] amusement," the delegate from India in her speech questioning the resolution, said that ER "felt that women were not 'ready for full political rights.'" When ER asked the delegate where she received that impression, she "discovered afterward that it was from the ladies who back the Equal Rights amendment in this country." This "amused" ER "since these ladies know quite well that I am not opposed to equal political rights for women." She concluded:

> My real feeling about this resolution is that its proponents were misguided in not letting it follow the regular and orderly procedure of reference to the

Economic and Social Council, from which it would have been referred to the Commission on the Status of Women. This commission could than have made concrete suggestions as to how the council might contact the individual nations which have not yet found a way to give their women political rights and urge that initial steps be taken in each particular case. This is the only practical way in which results can be obtained.[4]

A week later she wrote Barney directly.

156

Eleanor Roosevelt to Nora Stanton Barney
25 November 1946 [New York City]

Dear Miss Barney:

I am sorry you have been misinformed on my attitude for equality for women. I do not oppose it and I have never opposed it in the United States.

The confusion arises because I do not support the Equal Rights Amendment. I believe we still need the existing protective laws for women in industry. I know full well of the various state laws which are discriminatory to women. I believe we should work to have such laws repealed in the states. It takes two thirds of the states to ratify an Amendment and that means a lot of work.

Some day the women in industry will not need protective legislation[5] and then they can work with the women in professions for an Equal Rights Amendment. This has nothing to do with the political rights which were under discussion. We have those.

Very sincerely yours,

TLc AERP, FDRL

---

1. Elizabeth Cady Stanton (1815–1902) opposed the Fifteenth Amendment, arguing in 1869 "that not another man should be enfranchised until enough women are admitted to the polls to outweigh those already there" (*NAWMP*; Foner, 256).

2. ER did not immediately embrace women suffrage, later writing that she "had never given the question serious thought" and admitting that she only did so after FDR announced his support for it while campaigning in 1911. "I realized that if my husband were a suffragist I probably must be one too." As she later recalled, she "could not claim to have been a feminist in those early days." As Cook illustrates, however, although ER did not join a specific suffrage organization, "she never uttered a public word in opposition to it. And after 1911 she counted herself a suffragist. Still, her belated and vague support for suffrage set her apart from the ardent activists and so many of her future allies and friends" (Cook, vol. 1, 195).

3. See *n*3 Document 120.

4. *MD*, 18 November, 1946.

5. Historian Alice Kessler-Harris has outlined the divide over "protective" versus "discriminatory" labor legislation. For instance, many labor laws aimed at "providing safe and clean working conditions, minimizing health hazards, putting a floor under wages, [and] shortening hours." These laws usually applied to all laborers. But some legislation that regulated things like seating or ventilation

in the workplace, in effect, barred women from certain types of jobs altogether. These laws can be seen as both protective and discriminatory. In addition, ER is referring to state laws that discriminated specifically against women, such as those regulating income taxes, divorce, domestic violence, and inheritance (Kessler-Harris, *Out to Work*, 180–81 (quote on 180); Kessler-Harris, *In Pursuit of Equity*, 6–7).

ELEANOR ROOSEVELT AND CONSCIENTIOUS OBJECTORS, PART 2

November 27, Albon Mann of the Committee for Amnesty for All Objectors to War and Conscription wrote ER urging her support for their plea to President Truman to grant a Christmas 1946 amnesty to all conscientious objectors still in prison and requesting that she support their efforts in her column. Although she did not discuss their appeal in My Day, she did write the president on their behalf.[1]

157

Eleanor Roosevelt to Harry Truman
2 December 1946 [New York City]

Dear Mr. President:

I am enclosing a letter and release which I received. I have been asked to write you about the conscientious objectors.

I think it might be wise to release these men who are still in prison.[2]

Very sincerely yours,
Eleanor Roosevelt

TLS HSTSF, HSTL

158

Harry Truman to Eleanor Roosevelt
6 December 1946 [The White House]

Dear Mrs. Roosevelt:

I appreciated very much your note enclosing a letter from the Committee for Amnesty for all conscientious objectors. This matter is being worked out in the Justice Department on the basis of individual cases.[3]

I don't think there should be a general release or pardon to those conscientious objectors who shirked their duty as citizens of the United States and profited by the actual risk of the men who were willing to fight.

Some of the conscientious objectors are honestly objectors—a great many just didn't want to fight and I know what I am talking about because I had experience with them in the first World War.[4] We are trying our best to arrange matters so there will be no injustice done to any honest conscientious objector but the malingerers should have all that is coming to them.[5]

Sincerely yours,
Harry S. Truman

P.S. The most sincere conscientious objector I ever have met was one on whom I placed a Congressional Medal of Honor, not long ago.[6] He served in the Medical Corps of the Navy and carried wounded marines and sailors to safety on Okinawia under fire. He was a real conscientious objector who believed the welfare of his country came first. I shall never forget what he said to me when I fastened the medal around his neck. He said he could do the Lord's work under fire as well as anywhere else.

H.S.T.

TLS AERP, FDRL

————————

1. Albon Mann to ER, 27 November 1946, HSTL. See also *n*8 Document 134 for information regarding the publication of the committee's press release in the *New York Times*. See Document 133 and Document 134 for ER's previous discussion of this issue with Attorney General Tom Clark.

2. The Committee for Amnesty for All Objectors to War and Conscription estimated that approximately 1,000 conscientious objectors remained in prison (Committee for Amnesty, "U.S. Groups Renew Pleas for War C.O.'s Amnesty," HSTL).

3. On December 23, 1946, President Truman announced the creation of an Amnesty Board to Review Convictions Under the Selective Service Act (Executive Order 9814).

4. Truman served as an artillery officer and rose to the rank of captain during World War I. During the First World War, only men who belonged to peace churches could be exempted from the draft. Although excused from combat service, the law required COs to act in other capacities, such as medical positions, in the military. During World War I, only 450 individuals were imprisoned for noncompliance with draft laws (*HSTE*; Moskos and Chambers, 5, 12).

5. The government more firmly established the legal parameters of conscientious objection during the Second World War. Those individuals who refused any form of military or civilian service supporting the war effort and who were thus imprisoned totaled approximately 6,000 men. President Truman only pardoned approximately 10 percent of the imprisoned COs after the war, categorizing the remainder as war criminals (*HSTE*; Moskos and Chambers, 35–39).

6. October 12, 1945, Truman conferred the Medal of Honor upon Private First Class Desmond T. Doss, a Seventh-day Adventist conscientious objector who refused a combat position only to serve as a medic in the Pacific Theater. In presenting the medal, the president honored Doss for his service as medical corpsman during the "bloodiest part" of the Pacific Theater, declaring that he "performed so many feats of heroism in aiding his wounded comrades on the battlefields of Guam, Leyte and Okinawa that his name became a symbol throughout the Seventy-seventh Infantry Division" ("Truman Presents Honor Medal to 15," *NYT*, 13 October 1945, 3).

A PROPOSED INTERNATIONAL CONGRESS
OF WOMEN

At the suggestion of Senator Carl A. Hatch (D-NM), Louise Grant Smith, attorney general of Missouri, wrote ER to suggest she call "a congress of women leaders of all nations" to promote world peace. "The women of every country would answer your call," Smith wrote ER, "for they know that your voice is not the voice of a woman of one nation, but that of a woman who desires to know and understand and help all mankind without thought of race or color or nationality." [1]

159

Eleanor Roosevelt to Louise Grant Smith
3 December 1946[2] [New York City]

Dear Mrs. Smith:

I have your letter of October 8th and the delay in answering is because of my work with the United Nations.[3]

I am too old to start leading causes. There have been a number of women's groups meeting of late, among others, the international group which met at South Kortright, New York.[4] I never feel that they get very far and I am beginning to think that men and women have to work together, and it is better for them to work in definite positions within the government and within their parties. Naturally where special interests are involve which are exclusively women's, they will have organizations and meetings to keep their interests, but this question of peace can only come where men and women work together. I doubt if women alone can be very effective.

Very sincerely yours,

TLc AERP, FDRL

---

1. Smith worked with Molly Dewson in FDR's 1932 presidential campaign and thereafter with Dorothy McAllister, May Thompson Evans, and Gladys Tillett. She also knew Lorena Hickock from Hickock's days at the Democratic National Committee. Hickock told ER that Smith was "very smart and a good Democrat." Smith met Hatch, the chairman of the presidential commission to evaluate the 1946 Bikini Atoll atomic bomb tests, following Hatch's speech in Missouri in which he said there was "no defense against atomic warfare" and "the only way to save the world is to eliminate war itself." Hatch allowed Smith to use his name to contact ER. Hatch also authored the Hatch Act of 1939 and 1940, which prohibited federal employees from engaging in political activity (Louise Grant Smith to ER, 8 October 1946, AERP; *NAW*; typewritten secretary's message to ER n.d. AERP; *BDUSC*; Boyer, *Promises*, 47).

2. The original date of this letter, October 30, was crossed out and December 3 written above it.

3. The fall session of the UN General Assembly met in New York from October 23 to December 16 ("Bevin to Miss Opening," *NYT*, 14 October 1946, 3; "World News Summarized," *NYT*, 16 December 1946, 1).

4. ER spoke at two women's peace conferences in 1946. In April she spoke at the conference of Women's Action Committee for Lasting Peace in Louisville, Kentucky. In November she spoke

twice at the International Assembly of Women, which met at the estate of Mrs. Alice T. McLean in South Kortright, New York. (McLean had founded the American version of the wartime Women's Voluntary Services). At the International Assembly of Women, ER urged the delegates to work through the UN and suggested they submit their findings to the General Assembly with the proviso that their suggestions "represent some concrete things that the women want to see done through the United Nations for the people of the world." See also *n*1 Document 183 (*MD*, 27 April, 12 October, and 23 October, 1946; "Mrs. Roosevelt Puts Hope in U.N.," *NYT*, 21 October 1946, 22; "Mrs. McLean Turns Over Up-State Mansion to World Artists and Europe's DP Children," *NYT*, 20 July 1948, 21).

ON RECOGNIZING FRANCO

December 2, the Political and Security Committee of the General Assembly turned its attention to Spain when it considered the Polish resolution demanding all UN member states sever diplomatic ties with Spain.[1] In the midst of the debate, Senator Tom Connally, the American delegate, introduced an alternate resolution demanding that Spain "give proof to the world that they have a Government which derives its authority from the consent of the governed" and recommending Spain be barred from all international agencies and UN-related conferences. The resolution, however, did not recommend that member states take any individual action against Spain.[2]

As the *New York Times* reported, "The new debate on Spain again unites all the members of the United Nations in vigorous condemnation of the Franco regime and in the desire to see it ended as quickly as possible. Unfortunately," the paper continued, "unanimity in the U.N. disappears when it comes to determining what steps, if any, should be taken by outside nations to hasten Franco's end."[3]

Freda Kirchwey, editor of the *Nation* and president of the Nation Associates, could not understand why the United States continued to recognize a government they deemed Fascist when they had just fought a war to end Fascism. A longtime critic of Franco who at a time when most Europeans believed Franco a much lesser danger than Hitler or Mussolini had argued that "the supreme test of an anti-fascist today is not what he says but what he does for Spain,"[4] Kirchwey now hoped that the UN, with United States support, could finally weaken Franco's hold on Spain. She now asked ER to exercise her "enormous" influence once again.

160

Freda Kirchwey to Eleanor Roosevelt
3 December 1946 [New York City]

Dear Mrs. Roosevelt:

I know how busy you are and I assume that this is the reason that there has been no opportunity for you to arrange the appointment which I requested. I had hoped to have a discussion with you on the Spanish situation.

The matter is now before the Political and Security Committee of the General Assembly where a resolution has been introduced by the American representative. Although the resolution does represent an advance by the United States over previous positions, it does not meet the situation. You may have seen how two conservative newspapers, the New York Times and the Herald Tribune, have interpreted that resolution, and interpreted it properly, as an appeal to the military and to the Church.[5]

To us it seems that the conclusions reached in the American resolution are in consonance neither with the actual situation nor our own descriptions of it. If, as we say, Franco does not represent the Spanish people and was put into power by the Axis, why does the United States, which has just concluded a war with the Axis, continue to recognize him? Secondly, the question which asks itself is: Supposing Franco fails to accept our invitation to retire, is not then our declaration an invitation to civil war which we say we want to avoid at any cost? And is not the simplest way of handling the question and the most honest (1) rupture of diplomatic relations; (2) the recognition of the Republic as the legitimate government of the Spanish people; and (3) negotiations for the establishment of a Provisional Republican government consisting of the present government-in-exile and other democratic elements capable of carrying out a free election.[6]

On Friday, Miss Shultz and I had a talk with Senator Austin from which we gathered that Secretary Byrnes is the final arbiter on this matter. For that reason we have taken the liberty of writing to him as per the attached which presents, I believe, another most important reason for destroying Franco now so that we can simultaneously isolate Peron.[7]

Your influence is enormous. I am sure that if you share the views expressed, something can be done to amend the American resolution in accord with decency and justice along the lines suggested.

Cordially yours,
Freda Kirchwey

TLS AERP, FDRL

_____161_____

Eleanor Roosevelt to Freda Kirchwey
4 December 1946 [New York City]

Dear Miss Kirchwey:

The position taken by the United States Delegation on the Spanish issue was checked with one of the members of the Government who is here in New York and who agreed that this kind of resolution from the United States would be the most helpful attitude. Mr. Dulles and I interviewed him and circulated the memorandum containing a summary of the conversations as we understood them.

I, as an individual, would, of course, be willing to recognize the government-in-exile's democratic ties. On the other hand, many people feel that would leave us in the unsatisfactory position of knowing less about what was going on inside Spain than before. If we cut off supplies, we would then create hardship and consolidate the Spanish people behind Franco. At least that is the feeling.

I do not feel actually conversant enough with the whole background to set my opinion up against those of the Department of State. On the other hand, I do recognize that to just tell them to have a free election, and to do nothing about obtaining one, is a futile gesture which has worried me from the beginning.[8] Curiously enough, it worries Senator Vandenberg.[9] I am glad you have written to Secretary Byrnes.

Sincerely yours,

TLc AERP, FDRL

_____162_____

Freda Kirchwey to Eleanor Roosevelt
11 December 1946 [New York City]

Dear Mrs. Roosevelt:

Thank you very much for your letter of December 4. I regret that this has been my first opportunity to answer it in any detail because of preoccupation with many matters, not the least of which has been the Spanish situation.

I am glad that you agree that to call on the Spanish people to hold a free election—ignoring completely the facts of their virtual imprisonment—is a "futile gesture." In fact it is an ironical and even brutal gesture.

I am glad to see in today's papers that the American delegation has finally agreed to support the resolution which passed the Political and Security Committee, which calls for withdrawal of Ambassadors from Madrid and keeping the case within the purview of the United Nations.[10] While this does not meet the situation in its entirety, at least it is an advance.

I may tell you that the most distressing aspect of the whole development has been not simply the American resolution, feeble in itself, but the attitude of Senator Connally, which has been most unworthy of that of the spokesman for a great democracy.[11] And it has been distressing too to hear deputies for the American delegation express their approval in subcommittee of the proposals of the Colombian and Cuban delegations for a negotiated settlement with Franco, the Falange and the Spanish Republicans as co-partners.[12] As one of the delegates put it: "Would Norway have agreed to negotiate with Quisling;[13] or France with Petain;[14] or The Netherlands with De Mussert;[15] or Belgium with Degrelle?"[16]

Since the United States delegation has constantly stated in the present deliberations its belief that Franco is the creature of the Axis, it is totally incomprehensible to me why the same procedures which have been applied to other puppet regimes could not be equally applied to Franco. Surely you agree that if all the United Nations jointly would tell Franco that he must go, there would be no question of his disappearance, without implying at any point—as Senator Connally has—that to oust him would mean the employment by the United Nations of armed force.

I am still afraid that there are those in our State Department who, recognizing that Franco must go, are thinking in terms of replacing him with a regime which differs little in its general purposes from its predecessor. And I am hopeful that you will be on the watchout to prevent such action.

What you say concerning Senator Vandenberg's position is very interesting. I have tried to see him on several occasions, but unfortunately without success. Nor have my letters to Secretary Byrnes been even acknowledged thus far.

With kind regards,

Cordially yours,
Freda Kirchwey

TLS AERP, FDRL

ER responded by dictating the following note to her secretary and instructing her to forward a copy of the fourth paragraph of Kirchwey's December 11 letter to Secretary Byrnes and Durward Sandifer.

163

Eleanor Roosevelt to Freda Kirchwey
[?] December 1946

Kirchwey—

I have your letter of Dec 11 which I read with interest. Of course you know we have no ambassador in Madrid.[17] I am not sure about your statement about telling Franco he must go.

ALd AERP, FDRL

---

1. Unsatisfied with public statements condemning the dictator, the Polish delegate to the Security Council introduced a resolution in April 1946 that demanded all UN member nations sever diplomatic ties with Spain. When the council concluded that Spain had not taken any action that constituted an act of aggression and that the matter therefore remained outside their jurisdiction, the council recommended that the General Assembly consider the resolution (Paul B. Kennedy, "Franco Pushing 'Reform' Program," *NYT*, 22 April 1945, E5; "Franco Condemned," *NYT*, 30 April 1946, 1; "Text of Report on Franco Investigation by the Security Council Subcommittee," *NYT*, 2 June 1946, 32; Liedtke, 5–29; Edwards, 3–100).

2. The American resolution, which employed harsher language than any previous American statement on Franco, referenced "the Franco Fascist Government of Spain, which was imposed by force upon the Spanish people" ("U.S. Resolution on Franco," *NYT*, 3 December 1946, 6).

3. The question of what to do about Franco had divided diplomats since the generalissimo's rise to power, with the aid of Hitler and Mussolini, during the Spanish Civil War (1936–1939). Ten years after the civil war, reports of the arrest and execution of political dissidents continued to fill the pages of newspapers throughout the world. The Soviets and the French called for immediate action, such as severing relations with Spain or imposing sanctions. British and American diplomats, wary of starting another civil war that might allow the Communists to take control of the government, preferred a more moderate approach. At both the Potsdam and San Francisco conferences they declared Spain ineligible for UN membership as long as Franco remained in power ("The U.N. and Spain," *NYT*, 5 December 1946, 28).

4. "Spain Is the Key," *Nation*, 13 February 1937, 172.

5. The *New York Herald Tribune* referred to Connally's resolution as "the first positive American policy on Spain in the U.N." However, given the State Department's fear that any action might prompt a civil war, the paper "failed to see how today's American resolution met that test any better than the proposed diplomatic break which the United States opposes." In effect, the resolution was "an appeal to the militarists and the Roman Catholic Church in Spain, probably the only groups that could possibly persuade Franco to step down." The *New York Times* echoed the *Tribune*'s sentiment that the resolution "marks an advance over the previous attitude of the United States Government," but it too pointed out that getting rid of Franco without outside help might prove "a difficult task, particularly in view of the military equipment received by the Spanish Army, first from Hitler and Mussolini, and more recently by purchase of surplus United States Army supplies at bargain prices" ("U.S. Proposes U.N. Offer Spain Membership if Franco Is Ousted," *New York Herald Tribune*, 3 December 1946, 1; "U.S. Calls on Franco to Quit, Or for Spain to Depose Him," *NYT*, 3 December 1946, 1).

6. In August 1945, Spanish refugees who participated in the short-lived Popular Front government met in Mexico City to establish a Spanish government in exile. Immediately after winning the elections of February 1936, the coalition of left and moderate parties that comprised the Popular Front disintegrated, creating the backdrop of political turmoil against which Franco's Nationalist forces revolted in July 1936. At the Mexico City conference, leftists and moderates once again attempted to unite, chosing leftist Republican José Giral Pereira (1879–1962) over the radical Socialist Juan Negrín Lopez to head their new government. The Communist Party, who endorsed Negrín, refused to support Giral, leaving a coalition comprised of Republicans and Socialists. The Giral government called upon UN nations to sever diplomatic ties with Franco and recognize the government in exile as the rightful government of Spain, a course of action which Giral regarded as the "only … diplomatic means of effecting a pacific solution of the Spanish problem" (William P. Carney, "Spanish Premier Fights Extremists," *NYT*, 22 March 1936, E13; "Republicans Name Premier,"

NYT, 23 August 1945, 8; Camille M. Cianfarra, "Spaniards in Exile Name 10 Ministers," *NYT*, 27 August 1945, 10; Camille M. Cianfarra, "Full Break With Spain Is Needed Premier Says in Paris," *NYT*, 7 March 1946, 13).

7. Kirchwey and Sigrid Lillian Schultz (1893–1980), the director of the Nation Associates, wrote Secretary Byrnes on December 3. As the *Chicago Tribune's* bureau chief in Berlin covering developments in central Europe prior to World War II, the multilingual Schultz made a name for herself among American liberals with her early criticism of European Fascism. In their letter, Schultz and Kirchwey warned the secretary that Perón's Argentina and Franco's Spain constituted "a new Axis." Kirchwey pointed out that both countries provided economic aid to the Axis powers long after the rest of the world condemned Fascism and that, after the war, both nations provided safe haven for Nazi agents. "No liberal American can comprehend the reasons why … we continue to maintain diplomatic relations with [Spain] now that the war is over," Kirchwey continued. "Nor can any American understand that the authority of the United States, coupled with that of the United Nations, should be unequal to finding a peaceful means of disposing of this enemy." In the letter to Byrnes, the *Nation* editor advocated the same actions she suggested in her letter to ER: the United States should sponsor a resolution that explicitly declared Franco the "illegal usurper of authority of the legally elected government of Spain," encouraged UN members to sever diplomatic relations with the Fascist government, and stated the intentions of the UN to work with Giral's government in exile to establish a provisional republican government that all UN nations could recognize (George Goodman, Jr., "Sigrid L. Schultz, Reporter Who Covered Rise of Nazism, Is Dead," *NYT*, 17 May 1980, 28; Freda Kirchwey to James F. Byrnes, 3 December 1946, AERP). For more on the Perón government of Argentina see *n*10 Document 87, *n*2 Document 121, and Document 202.

8. Most observers of developments in Spain doubted that the country would ever enjoy free elections as long as Franco remained in power. Norman Armour, the American ambassador in Madrid, reported in December 1945 that Franco spent more than one-third of the nation's budget on his military and maintained an army of 600,000 to 700,000 soldiers that he did not hesitate to use to consolidate his power. A few months later, C. L. Sulzberger, then correspondent for the *New York Times* in Spain, claimed that Franco held "at least 30,000 political prisoners in jails and an unestimated number in labor camps." Many of these prisoners expressed views akin to "mild liberals by civilized standards," but Franco's police arrested, tortured, and even executed political dissidents whom they deemed subversive "Reds" ("Franco's Changes Toward Democracy Not Yet Satisfactory, Armour Declares," *NYT*, 22 December 1945, 20; "Spain's 70 Per Cent," *NYT*, 27 February 1946, 20; Edwards, 56–57).

9. As Senator Tom Connally (D-TX), not Vandenberg, served on the committee handling the issue, Vandenberg refrained from publicly commenting on the American position. Correspondence between ER and Vandenberg relating to the 1946 UN debates on Franco does not appear in either of their files, suggesting that Vandenberg most likely confided in ER in a face-to-face meeting.

10. On December 11, the *New York Times* reported that the US delegation would vote for the resolution adopted by the Political and Security Committee when it came before the General Assembly. The resolution—a compromise proposed by the Belgian delegate to offer a middle option between the subcommittee's resolution calling upon UN member nations to completely sever diplomatic relations with Spain and the US resolution that refrained from calling upon member nations to take specific actions—recommended "that all members of the United Nations immediately recall from Madrid their Ambassadors and Ministers Plenipotentiary, accredited there." The United States abstained from the vote on this resolution in the Political and Security Committee, but did vote in favor of the resolution on December 12 at the plenary session of the General Assembly ("U.S. to Back U.N. on Spain," *NYT*, 11 November 1946, 20; Thomas J. Hamilton, "U.N. Committee Asks Recall of Mission Heads in Madrid," *NYT*, 10 December 1946, 1; "Text

of U.N. Committee Resolution on Spain," *NYT*, 10 December 1946, 4; "34-to-6 Vote on Spain Urges Recall of Heads of Mission," *NYT*, 13 December 1946, 1).

11. On December 7, during the debates over Spain in the Political and Security Committee, Connally made it clear that the United States would not change its position, stating, "I say very kindly but firmly that you have to adopt some other plan besides the break of diplomatic relations or the imposition of economic sanctions because the United States cannot go along with either one of these plans." Several delegates were taken aback: Justice Wold of Norway described Connally's attitude as "unbecoming" and believed the US delegate to have stated that even if the General Assembly passed a resolution recommending the severing of diplomatic relations, the United States would not break with Spain. Carlos Stolk of Venezuela described Connally's position as a "kind of a veto" which "carr[ied] a lot of weight" and would influence other delegations when the General Assembly considered the resolution. Connally's words provoked such a negative reaction that a spokesman for the American delegation attempted to pacify the situation by explaining that although the United States desired to go on record as opposing a complete diplomatic break with Spain, the government had not yet made a final decision as to their course of action and would do so only after the General Assembly voted on the matter. Two days later, when the committee voted on the various resolutions concerning Spain, Connally exhibited such a flippant attitude that the *New York Times* felt it worthy of comment: "The atmosphere of the committee meeting was the tensest yet encountered at this session of the General Assembly, and Paul-Henri Spaak, the usually urbane president, rebuked Senator Tom Connally when the United States representative jokingly recorded one of his abstentions by pronouncing 'abstention' in what he thought was a French accent" ("U.S. Limits Share in Spanish Break," *NYT*, 8 December 1946, 13; Thomas J. Hamilton, "U.N. Committee Asks Recall of Mission Heads in Madrid," *NYT*, 10 December 1946, 1).

12. The Columbian delegate introduced a resolution that would postpone the vote on taking any action in the Spanish matter until the next session of the General Assembly, declaring that the intervening year would allow the Latin American nations to work with various Spanish groups to establish a new regime in Spain that would include the government in exile. The Cuban delegate supported the idea of postponement, but made it clear that Cuba viewed the government in exile's claims as illegitimate and would not break relations with Spain even if the General Assembly passed a resolution recommending members to do so (Thomas J. Hamilton, "U.N. Committee Asks Recall of Mission Heads in Madrid," *NYT*, 10 December 1946, 1).

13. Vidkun Abraham Lauritz Quisling (1887–1945), who began his career as an Norwegian intelligence officer, represented the Agrarian Party in the Norwegian parliament before becoming minister of defense in 1931. In 1933, after leaving the ministry, he founded Norway's National Party, modeled after Hitler's German National Socialist Party. After traveling to Berlin in 1939, he returned home, pledged to assist in the German invasion of Norway planned for the following year. In reward for his cooperation, Hitler then installed him as governor of Nazi-controlled Norway, a position he used to mirror German social and political practices. After Norway's liberation in 1945, Quisling was convicted of treason and sentenced to death. His surname quickly came to signify a citizen who collaborates with the enemy (*OWWTC*).

14. Henri-Philipe Omer Pétain (1856–1951), the French general who became a national hero after his defense of Verdun, rose rapidly through military ranks before retiring as commander-in-chief of all French forces in 1931. His political career began with his appointment as minister of defense in 1934. In 1940, he replaced Paul Reynaud as prime minister and immediately negotiated a truce with Germany, which required the disarming of French troops and German control of three-fifths of French land. He then governed what was left to France (the Vichy government) in ways that reflected German policy. Arrested by forces loyal to de Gaulle in 1944, Pétain was convicted of treason in 1945 and sentenced to death, only to have his punishment commuted to life-imprisonment due to his old age. He died imprisoned on the Île d'Yeu at the age of ninety-one (*OEWH*, *OWWTC*).

15. In December 1942, Hitler appointed Anton Adriaan Mussert (1894–1946), the Dutch engineer who founded and led the Dutch Nazi Party, "leader of the Netherlands people." Convicted in 1945 of collaboration with the enemy, Mussert was sentenced to death December 12, 1945. His trial drew wide attention when he refused to denounce Hitler and said he had once suggested to Hitler than his homeland become part of a "League of Germanic Peoples" ("Dutch Sentence Mussert to Die as Collaborator," *NYT*, 13 December 1945, 11).

16. Léon Degrelle (1906–1994), head of Belgium's Rexist (Fascist) Party, proved himself so devoted to Hitler's views that Hitler allegedly referred to Degrelle as the man he would like to have for a son. Promoted to major after his service in the campaign against Russia, Degrelle, upon his return home, promoted himself to governor of Belgium. He fled to Germany after Belgium's liberation and, in 1945, commanded an elite Walloon brigade in a futile, last-ditch effort to keep the Allies from reaching Berlin. When Berlin fell, Degrelle fled to Spain, where he remained at the time of this correspondence. Degrelle had been tried (in absentia) and convicted of treason by the Belgian courts, which, December 28, 1944, sentenced him to death ("Degrelle Reported Promoted," *NYT*, 9 April 1944, 9; "Degrelle on Nazis' Coattails," *NYT*, 30 January 1945, 8; "Rexist Reported in Spain," *NYT*, 22 June 1947; Keegan, 518, 525).

17. When Norman Armour, the US ambassador to Spain, announced his plans to retire in November 1945, the State Department did not make public any plans to replace him. Although Armour claimed to retire for "personal reasons," the press speculated that the State Department's failure to immediately replace him was a "diplomatic way of voicing our disapproval of the Franco regime." The State Department refrained from replacing Armour during 1946, so on December 12, when the General Assembly approved the resolution recommending that all UN member nations withdraw their ambassadors from Madrid, the United States did not have to take any action to conform to the resolution. Not until after the UN rescinded this resolution in November 1950 did the United States send another ambassador to Spain ("Armour Expected To Quit Spain Post," *NYT*, 21 November 1945, 10; "U.S. May Not Send New Envoy To Spain," *NYT*, 22 November 1945, 18; "Griffis Appointed Envoy To Madrid," *NYT*, 28 December 1950, 12).

ON MARTIN NIEMÖLLER, PART 2

ER continued to criticize Pastor Martin Niemöller despite the defense noted clergy offered on his behalf.[1] When the clergyman arrived in the United States in early December, she told readers of My Day:

> I see by the papers that Pastor Martin Niemoeller, German Lutheran church-man who was jailed by the Nazis, has arrived in this country and is scheduled to make a lecture tour. I understand that Dr. Niemoeller has stated in the past that he was against the Nazis because of what they did to the church, but that he had no quarrel with them politically. And I think I remember reading a report that, when his country went to war, he offered his services for submarine work in the Navy. One may applaud his bravery and his devotion to his church, but one can hardly applaud his attitude on the Nazi politics, and I cannot quite see why we should be asked to listen to his lectures. I am sure he is a good man according to his lights, but his lights are not those of the people of the United States who did not like the Hitler political doctrines.[2]

The day after the column appeared, ER received the following telegram from Bishop G. Bromley Oxnam, who joined ER the previous year to support the striking GM workers.[3] As president of the Federal Council of the Churches of Christ in America, the organization sponsoring Niemöller's lecture tour, Oxnam objected to ER's position:

> DEEPLY REGRET THE MISINFORMATION ON WHICH YOUR REMARKS ABOUT PAS-TOR NIEMOELLER IN YOUR COLUMN OF DECEMBER 5TH IS BASED. THE RECORD CLEARLY SHOWS THAT HE REPEATEDLY SPOKE AGAINST THE POLITICAL AIMS OF THE NAZIS. AS EARLY AS 1933 HE WAS FORBIDDEN TO PREACH AS A RESULT OF HIS SPEAKING AGAINST HITLER'S RACIALISTIC PROGRAM. WE URGE YOU TO CORRECT ERRONEOUS IMPRESSION CREATED BY YOUR COLUMN AND GIVE RECOGNITION TO THE FACT THAT NIEMOELLER TOOK A COURAGEOUS STAND AGAINST NAZI POLICIES LONG BEFORE OUR OWN COUNTRY WAS ALERT TO THEIR DANGER.[4]

164

Eleanor Roosevelt to G. Bromley Oxnam
6 December 1946 [New York City]

YOUR TELEGRAM ADDRESSED UNITED FEATURE SYNDICATE HAS JUST REACHED ME.[5] MY INFOR-MATION ABOUT PASTOR NEIMOELLER COMES FROM PEOPLE WHO SAW HIM IMMEDIATELY ON LIBERA-TION.[6]

ELEANOR ROOSEVELT

PTel AERP, FDRL

The bishop replied a week later, telling her that

> ... the information you had concerning Pastor Niemoeller was inaccurate. I had the privilege of a long interview with Pastor Niemoeller in Naples imme-diately after his release. I had lengthy conversations with him subsequently in Germany in December of 1945, and of course have discussed the entire matter

here. Pastor Niemoeller has been misrepresented. The people who saw him immediately on liberation whom you quote, I am sure have not quoted him in full. The reports of the press conference held in Naples contradict themselves, and take a single statement without giving the context which gives the real mind of Pastor Niemoeller.

I am sure you are the very first one to desire accurate representation of another's views. When I showed your telegram to Pastor Niemoeller, he said he would very much like to have the privilege of meeting you personally when he reaches New York, so that in a very few minutes he might give to you his views, and then allow you to reach your own judgment. He will be here sometime in January. Would you be willing to allow me to present him?[7] I know your schedule is very crowded; however, Pastor Niemoeller is a significant figure who was brought to this country only after the most careful study upon the part of Protestant leaders.

Oxnam concluded by saying that while ER was correct that the clergyman did volunteer to serve in the German navy, Niemöller only did so because "he wanted to be in a position to join any movement to overthrow Hitler." [8]

Oxnam's argument did not sway ER.[9]

165

Eleanor Roosevelt to G. Bromley Oxnam

21 December 1946 [New York City]

Dear Bishop Oxnam:

I am perfectly willing to meet Pastor Neimoeller[10] though I am not very anxious to see him.

I think you have missed the reason why I do not think the Federal Council of the Churches of Christ in America should have had him come to speak in this country.

After the last war we succeeded as a people in making ourselves believe that the leaders in Germany were to blame and not the people and we brought on a Second World War. This kind of thing which having Pastor Neimoeller come over here and air his view before American audiences repeatedly will lull them to sleep again. I want us to be vividly aware of the fact that the German people are to blame, that they committed horrible crimes.

Therefore, I think you are doing something which is stupid beyond words in bringing this gentleman here and having him touring the country, no matter how much you like him.

Very sincerely yours,
Eleanor Roosevelt

TLS AERP, FDRL

---

1. See Document 27 and Document 29.

2. *MD*, 4 December 1946. (The column appeared in a few newspapers on December 5.)

3. See Document 65.

4. See *DAB*; G. Bromley Oxnam to ER, 5 December 1946, AERP.

5. United Feature Syndicate distributed ER's My Day column.

6. ER did not name her sources. She may have drawn in part on Sam Pope Brewer's column, "Niemoeller Asks Iron Rule of Reich," *NYT*, 6 June 1945, 11. See Document 27 for a full discussion of ER's earlier response to Niemöller.

7. If Niemöller and ER met, they left no written evidence of their encounter.

8. G. Bromley Oxnam to ER, 13 December 1946, AERP.

9. December 27, Oxnam angrily replied to ER's dismissal, saying that while he initially thought ER's objection to Niemöller was based on his volunteering to serve in the navy and "that in so far as he had opposed Hitler, it was merely a matter of objecting to Hitler's coercion of the church," Oxnam realized he was mistaken.

> I now find that it is not because you were mistaken in thinking Pastor Niemoeller a Nazi, but rather because he is a German that you object to his presence here. I hold precisely the same view you do concerning the guilt of the German people … It is because we have wished to make it known in Germany that leadership that admits such guilt and stands for a democratic Germany receives the cooperation of the American churches, that we have brought Pastor Niemoeller here.

Niemöller, Oxnam concluded, "deserves cooperation" because he "is calling the church to repentance. Therefore, he hoped that she would "pardon me when I say that I cannot accept our judgement that what we are doing is stupid beyond words." He found "it very difficult to justify a policy that refuses constructive cooperation with those in Germany who fought the Nazi philosophy before our own country was alerted to its menace" (G. Bromley Oxnam to ER, 27 December 1946, AERP).

10. ER misspelled Niemöller.

INTERCEDING FOR REFUGEES

The publicity ER received as a spokesperson for refugees at the United Nations and as chair of the Human Rights Commission led hundreds of refugees to seek her help in reuniting their families or retrieving lost or stolen property. In most cases, ER could do little to assist them; however, sometimes she forwarded their letters to people whom she knew who were in a position to investigate or intervene on the refugee's behalf.[1]

December 3, ER sent Jan Masaryk, the Czech foreign minister and leader of the Czech delegation to the General Assembly,[2] an appeal she had received with the hope that he might provide assistance. In her cover letter, ER wrote:

> The enclosed letter from Mrs. Ona Ludwig of London tells the story of the detention of her nephew, Hubert Glatzel, by the War Ministry of Czechoslovakia in Prague. She states that he is desperately needed by his family who is without means of support.
>
> It would be appreciated if you would initiate action with a view to uniting Mr. Glatzel with his family.[3]

The following day, ER received a letter from Peter Buschina, a nationalized American citizen of Czech origin then living in Long Island City, New York. Buschina, who had heard ER and Masaryk on a recent radio broadcast wrote, "I can not help in writing to you Mrs. Roosevelt, how a man like Mr. Masaryk can say such nice things and the same time have the devil in him." He then went on to tell ER that the Russians had murdered his father during the Soviet invasion in May 1945, and the Czech government had recently confiscated his mother's property and bank account and sent her to a refugee camp. Attesting that his parents had "never belong[ed] to the Nazis," he asked her to speak with Masaryk to see if he could help Buschina's mother. December 9, ER wrote Masaryk again asking for his advice.[4]

> I receive many letters daily from American citizens appealing to me for justice for their relatives and friends in Europe. I would welcome any factual assistance you can give me relating to the individual case referred to above—and any subsequent inquiries I may have regarding people within the boundaries of your country.[5]

166

Jan Masaryk to Eleanor Roosevelt
13 December 1946 [New York City]

My dear Mrs. Roosevelt:

Thank you for your two letters. I am looking into both cases and will report as soon as I can.[6]

There is a committee, which I am heading, for the specific purpose of ascertaining the properties of our Jews and displaced persons and a decent method of restitution should be forthcoming fairly soon.[7] The legal aspect of these matters is very complicated, hence all these delays and understandable impatience of those concerned.

Please do not hesitate to let me know about any case that comes to your attention.

With best wishes,

Sincerely yours,
Jan Masaryk

TLS AERP, FDRL

————————————

1. See ER to Harry Truman, 1 May 1946, HSTOF, HSTL.

2. See Document 97.

3. ER to Jan Masaryk, 3 December 1946, AERP.

4. Peter Buschina to ER, 4 December 1946, AERP.

5. ER knew that Masaryk was sympathetic to the plight of displaced persons. In her My Day column of February 4, 1946, she wrote: "Masaryk made a very moving address in which he spoke of the innumerable children whom he had seen at the age of six looking like old people of 60 and who, without UNRRA's help, would certainly have died" (ER to Jan Masaryk, 9 December 1946, AERP; *MD*, 4 February 1946).

6. No record of Masaryk's subsequent correspondence with ER on these cases exists.

7. It is unclear as to which committee Masaryk means. Although Masaryk favored restitution, he was outnumbered in a Communist-dominated government that inadequately enforced and often ignored the restitution laws passed in May 1945 and May 1946. As a result, Jews and other displaced Czechoslovakians retrieved little or nothing of their personal property or their businesses. The Czech government's move to nationalize the country's economy which began in October 1945, also discouraged restitution efforts (N. Robinson, 349, 365–66; Institute of Jewish Affairs of the World Jewish Congress, *European Jewry Ten Years After the War*, 96–99; Krejci and Machonin, 79; Myer et al., 92).

ON THE INTERNATIONAL REFUGEE
ORGANIZATION AND UNICEF

On December 11, the General Assembly established the United Nations International Children's Emergency Fund (UNICEF). In the following My Day column, ER explained how the new agency would take over some of the functions and funding of the United Nations Relief and Rehabilitation Administration (UNRRA).

167

My Day
13 December 1946

NEW YORK, Thursday—There is, of course, still going to be a welfare problem when UNRRA comes to an end. Our government has decided we are going to meet that problem, but not by creating an international welfare organization such as UNRRA, since the feeling has been that our Congress would be opposed to entering upon that type of relief again.[1]

We supply the largest percentage of relief, and therefore our government feels that we should have more control over the allocation and distribution of funds than we can have in an international organization. There has also been some criticism of various situations which arose in UNRRA, and this too led to the decision that, in the future, we would be independent in our relief operations, though working on a consultation basis with other nations.[2]

Under UNRRA, there are certain functions such as the special services devoted to children, and other welfare services which are not strictly general relief but encompass special needs. What has been done is to set up a children's international emergency fund. The first money, $550,000, will be for the purchase of special foods for children. It will be presented by UNRRA Director Fiorello H. La Guardia to Sir Carl Berendsen,[3] chairman of Committee 3 of the UN General Assembly, at a special meeting in Washington.

The children's fund will ask for any residue funds which may be allotted to it from UNRRA, for government appropriations and also for contributions from organizations and individuals. This money will supplement any basic relief given and should provide children in need of special foods and medical care with the essentials for recovery.

This special activity will be conducted on an international basis, but also on a voluntary basis which permits governments to stay out if they do not feel able to participate.

If much money is available, a great many children in Europe and Asia may be saved from serious consequences following these years of war. But we must wait until we know how many countries decide to join in this fund and how much they are prepared to contribute, as well as how much appeal this particular part of the welfare picture has for private organizations and individuals, before we can judge the possible accomplishments.

If the administration is efficient and if the sums of money should grow, I can imagine that in four or five years the children of Europe may be well fed again, as the economies of the various countries return to normal. Then there are children in India and China who will need help for a long time. An international fund really well run might eventually do certain things for children all over the world which we have dreamed about, but have not dared to hope might some day materialize.

TMs AERP, FDRL

After almost a year of drafting and often bitter debate about the issues of repatriation and the management of the displaced persons camps, as well as repeated, unsuccessful attempts by the Soviet Union and its allies to amend the draft,[4] the constitution of the International Refugee Organization came up for a vote in the General Assembly.[5] In the following statement ER reviews the constitution's history and presents the case for adoption.

168

Speech to the General Assembly on the International Refugee Organization[6]

15 December 1946 [Lake Success, NY]

MRS. ROOSEVELT (United States of America): I think perhaps that those who are interested in this Organization may have been a little startled, as I was, this morning to read in one of our big papers an article which seemed to take it for granted that we had already set up the International Refugee Organization, and I know that we are going to do so, but if you read that, you must have been as startled as I was.[7] The point of the story, however, was that it mentioned the fact that over a million people would feel much relieved when this Organization was set up, and I want to remind you all that we are dealing, in the work which we are now going to consider, with more than a million people. Some of them will be repatriated; some of them are looking forward to having their rights as human beings assured, and if they, for valid reasons, wish to be resettled, they look to resettlement. They still seek a haven, at home or abroad, a home where they may work in peace and lead useful lives, surrounded by the members of their families. They have suffered cruelly at the hands of the aggressors. As United Nations Members, we owe them a place to live. They shared our fight; they are still seeking their share in victory—a modest share, a place to live under conditions acceptable to them.

We have before us the draft constitution for the establishment of the International Refugee Organization with the provisional budget for the first year of operation and the draft interim arrangement for the establishment of a preparatory commission of the International Refugee Organization. It is now for the Assembly to decide whether these proposals are in order and suitable for presentation to Governments for their signatures.

We are not now voting as representatives of our respective Governments on the question of joining the International Refugee Organization nor of adopting its budget—but rather, as Members of the General Assembly, we are passing expert judgement upon a plan to be submitted to Governments. The Governments will themselves decide at the proper time whether they will participate in the plan by joining the International Refugee Organization.[8]

This plan has been drafted by the Economic and Social Council and its Sub-Committees at the request of the General Assembly which met in London last February. The draft constitution is the product of the continuous labour since that meeting. It is not a casual document. Every word and paragraph has been hammered out through painstaking effort and discussion. No one Government or group of Governments has written the text. All Governments have contributed to it. Opposing concepts have been tested in the democratic process of reaching decisions.

This document was referred to the Governments for comment before the third session of the Economic and Social Council. Their comments are reflected in the final text before us. Fifty-four Governments have participated in its development. Therefore this is a document which merits the approval of the General Assembly. Probably no Government is completely satisfied with it, and that is natural and understandable, but it is a document for which no apologies need be made. It constitutes a rule and a guide for the International Refugee Organization on the basis of which its operations may begin.

I have made clear, I hope, the humanitarian task that we are considering, but that is not the whole story. Each Member Government of the United Nations has a direct, selfish interest in the early disposal of this problem. As long as a million persons remain with refugee status, they delay the restoration of peace and order in the world. They contribute to the impairment of good relations between friendly Governments. They represent, in themselves, political, economic and national conflicts which are symbolic of the work that lies before nations if peace is to be restored. While they remain a solid mass in assembly centres, they deteriorate individually, and collectively they present a sore on the body of mankind which it is not safe for us to ignore.

This situation cannot be ignored. It calls for heroic treatment. It cannot be resolved by indifference or by leaving it to the resources of a few Governments charged by accident of war with immediate responsibility. There is no Government or people so far removed from the source of infection as to feel any sense of security from its effects. Some may argue that they are geographically far removed, or that in their countries there are priorities of need. Many Governments face serious problems of rebuilding and reconstruction and of new development to bring about a better standard of living in their home populations.

All these things are so, but every Government requires peace and order and the restoration of confidence in the world. Peace, order and confidence contribute to the rebirth of economic activity. The labour of a million persons is an asset which cannot be permitted to go to waste. Every day during which it is not utilized adds to the waste.

The Governments of countries of origin clamour for the repatriation of their nationals, as many of them as possible, because they need their work. And the world needs the work of all these people, and those, who for valid reasons decide they cannot go home, must be settled somewhere so that the world may profit by their work as well as by the work of those who can go home.

The budget for this Organization has been estimated at one hundred and sixty million United States dollars. It represents the cost of staff to do the job, of food and supplies for the persons involved, of transport to their homes from their places of displacement, of emigration to friends and relatives overseas and of resettlement for those who have to be colonized in the new areas.

I do not minimize the cost or the sacrifice it represents, but spread among all the nations this is not a large sum in view of the size and importance of the problem. Each nation has been allocated its proportionate share. In comparison with UNRRA budgets and appropriations, the total is not so staggering.[9] The task is one of the unfinished tasks of the war. The results to be gained far outweigh the financial cost.

After the action of the Assembly there will be a period of months during which government administrations will consult their Parliaments and appropriating bodies as to their participation in the IRO. During this period, a preparatory commission consisting of those Governments which initially sign the constitution of the International Refugee Organization will be required.

The resolution before us contains a proposal to the Governments for the setting up of this preparatory commission. Its function will be to consult with Governments, control authorities, UNRRA, and other international bodies with respect to the ways and means by which there can be an orderly transfer of functions and responsibilities for this problem to the IRO.

This preparatory work can be done in the intervening months in full awareness of the resources that will be made available to the IRO by the decisions of Governments to participate in its work. Naturally, the preparatory commission will not assume operating functions until it becomes very clear that the International Refugee Organization is to come into being.

My Government has always supported the concept of the International Refugee Organization. It supports the proposal now. My Government holds strongly to the view that this problem should be handled by international action. We believe that nothing short of international action can deal effectively with the problem. We subscribe to the principles embodied in the constitution before us, and join in the invitation to all Governments to give immediate and serious consideration to this proposal. In the case of my own Government, full powers have been issued to the Chairman of the delegation to sign the constitution of the International Refugee Organization. This will be done immediately and the Constitution will then be submitted to the Congress for its approval.

In making the position of my Government clear as to its intentions with respect to the International Refugee Organization, I wish to say again that our votes on this constitution now have no connexion with the question of whether our respective Governments will join the Organization later. A vote of "yes" now does not represent a commitment by a Government to join the IRO later. As Members of the General Assembly, we are passing judgment on a draft proposal to be submitted to Governments. That judgment we confidently believe will be that this proposal is in order and suitable for presentation to Governments.

I urge all nations here represented to sign and support the constitution in their own interests and in the interest of over a million people who have suffered long enough.

TSptr UNORGA, MWelC

December 16, the General Assembly adopted the resolution authorizing the creation of the International Refugee Organization (IRO), in the process approving a draft constitution and appointing a preparatory commission to guide the organization's work. The draft constitution established two benchmarks which had to be met before a permanent IRO could commence work: fifteen member nations first had to approve the IRO constitution and, second, provide at least 75 percent of the organization's $160,860,500 operating budget.[10] The United States led the campaign to create the organization and committed, pending congressional approval, contributions totaling 45.75 percent of the IRO budget.[11]

Having led the fight to adopt the IRO constitution, ER next turned to the task of persuading a reluctant Congress to approve US participation and to appropriate funds necessary for the United States to meet its obligations to both the IRO and the International Children's Emergency Fund. ER knew from her earlier efforts to secure funding for UNRRA that this would not be a simple task. As the following two letters indicate, ER turned to longtime colleagues for help with particular constituencies.

169

Eleanor Roosevelt to Edward Flynn

17 December 1946 [New York City]

Dear Ed:

I wonder if you would be willing to speak to Cardinal Spellman about enlisting Catholic support for the International Refugee Organization and the Emergency Children's Fund.[12]

I think word will have to come from somebody high up and that we will really have to get busy in the communities so as to get community pressure on the Congress, since I see in the papers that the Republican Congress is going to be against all of these things which seem to me completely essential if Europe is ever to return to a decent standard of living and children are not to be a liability in the next generation.[13]

If The Cardinal would care to talk to me, I should be very happy to meet him at his convenience.[14]

Up to the last, the delegates were talking about the wonderful time they had at your party and I can never tell you how grateful I am.

Very cordially yours,

TLc AERP, FDRL

Just as ER asked Ed Flynn to lobby Cardinal Spellman, ER turned to another good friend, Clarence Pickett, executive secretary of the American Friends Service Committee,[15] for help in securing congressional support for both the IRO and UNICEF. Later that day, ER sent variations of this same letter to Paul Kellogg, editor of *Survey*, the leading journal of social welfare; Professor Joseph D. Chamberlain, chairman, American Council of Voluntary Agencies for Foreign Service, Inc.; and Mrs. LaFell Dickinson, president of the General Federation of Women's Clubs.[16]

170

Eleanor Roosevelt to Clarence Pickett
17 December 1946 [New York City]

Dear Mr. Pickett:

I think it is vitally important that we do all we can to create public support which can be brought to bear on Congress so that the International Refugee Organization and the Emergency Children's Fund will be financially support[ed] and participated in by the United States. I see by the papers that the new Congress is going to be against all of these things.[17] To me it is vitally essential that we actively participate if Europe is to return to a decent standard of living and the children are not to be a liability.

Could I ask you to get in touch with as many groups as possible and ask that some practical work be done and is there any other way in which you think I can reach people to get this sort of thing accomplished?[18]

Very cordially yours,

TLc AERP, FDRL

---

1. Most countries favored replacing UNRRA with a new international organization that would distribute relief supplies. The United States and Great Britain, which together covered 87 percent of UNRRA's costs, preferred, however, to distribute food and other relief supplies under bilateral agreements with individual nations. Under a compromise agreement proposed by Canada, a UN technical committee would determine the amount of aid needed by the recipient countries, leaving the donor nations to determine the actual allocations ("The Record of the Meeting of the United Nations Assembly," *NYT*, 15 December 1946, E5; Frank S. Adams, "IRO Constitution Submitted to Members by 30–5 Vote," *NYT*, 16 December 1946, 1). For UNRRA, see *n7* Document 55 and *n8* and *n9* Document 86.

2. Congress and the press repeatedly criticized UNRRA for its handling of funds and for its sometimes slow delivery of aid, but political issues caused the most controversy. While the United States provided most of the funding and Americans headed up the organization, the countries receiving aid

distributed the supplies provided by UNRRA. Some critics accused Eastern European countries of diverting supplies to the Red Army or other military organizations. Although most of these charges remained unsubstantiated, the accusations, together with rising opposition to assisting Communist countries at all, made Congress demand more control over the allocation of future aid (*HSTE*).

3. Sir Carl Berendsen (1890–1973), New Zealand's ambassador to the United States, headed his nation's delegation to the United Nations from 1946 to 1951 (Dictionary of New Zealand Biography, http://www.dnzb.govt.nz/dnzb/default.asp?Find_Quick.asp?PersonEssay=4B25, accessed 27 October 2005).

4. See Document 91 and Document 152.

5. The United Nations designed the IRO to assume refugee functions handled by the soon to be dismantled UNRRA.

6. General Assembly, Sixty-Sixth Plenary Meeting, 15 December 1948, 1420–24, UNORGA, MWelC.

7. The *New York Herald Tribune* headlined its December 15, 1946, article "I.R.O. Is Set Up, Giving Hope to World Refugees." Despite its title, however, the article explained that unless fifteen nations ratified the IRO constitution and committed sufficient funds, the organization would become nothing more than a small preparatory commission. The *New York Times* presented a more ambiguous account. It reported that "despite Soviet opposition the draft constitution [of the IRO] was approved [by the Third Committee] and an interim commission was created to handle refugee problems between the time UNRRA ends its work and the IRO can take over." It did not say, however, that the General Assembly had not yet voted on the IRO constitution, nor did it report that the IRO would not come into being until a sufficient number of governments had signed the constitution and committed funds to support the organization (Kenyon Kilbon, "I.R.O. Is Set Up, Giving Hope to World Refugees," *New York Herald Tribune*, 15 December 1946, 1; "The Record of the Meeting of the United Nations Assembly: Agreements, Which Will Now Be Carried Out, and Other Important Subjects Where Agreement Failed," *NYT*, 15 December 1946, E5).

8. For the commitments needed from member nations to bring the IRO into being, see the header to Document 169.

9. For UNRRA, see *n*7 Document 55.

10. The IRO budget included $4,800,000 for administrative expenses; $151,060,500 for operating expenses; and $5,000,000 for "large-scale resettlement operations" (Frank S. Adams, "IRO Constitution Submitted to Members by 30–5 Vote," *NYT*, 16 December 1946, 1; "IRO Document Turned Over to U.N. Secretary General," *NYT*, 4 July 1947, 5).

11. Ibid.

12. Francis Joseph Cardinal Spellman (1889–1967), archbishop of New York and vicar of the US Armed Forces, was the most prominent leader of the Catholic Church in America. Spellman, like ER, supported the campaign led by the United Jewish Appeal to raise funds for refugees in Europe. Ed Flynn was Catholic and knew Spellman well (*ANBO*).

13. The Republicans, having won control of Congress in the November 1946 election, would have to approve the IRO appropriation when the new Congress convened in January. They intended to cut taxes and expressed opposition to assuming too much of the burden of overseas refugee and relief efforts. Sen. Vandenberg, the incoming chair of the Senate Foreign Relations Committee, announced the day after the election that he would review United States' contributions to UN specialized agencies alongside the US contribution to the general UN administrative budget and each budgetary decision "will necessarily affect our attitude toward other problems." Furthermore, he announced his intent to revisit the percentage the US currently contributed to the UN's general operating fund ("Vandenberg Vows Biparty Aid to U.N.," *NYT*, 9 November 1946, 1; "After

UNRRA," *NYT*, 16 November 1946, 18; Ernest K. Lindley, "Congress and Relief," *WP*, 11 December 1946, 9).

14. The following month ER told James Hendrick that Catholic and other relief agencies expressed the same reservations about the IRO as they had expressed about UNRRA and UNICEF:

> Mrs. Roosevelt said she had talked with representatives of the Catholic church in regard to the Children's Fund. They are very disturbed over the manner in which it has been handled up to date. What they want to be sure of is that the Children's Fund will make use of voluntary organizations in the field instead of building up a new staff. The Children's Fund would, of course, have the right of inspection.
>
> With regard to contributions, they felt that there should be concentration on securing government contributions rather than individual contributions and that the soliciting of individual contributions should be very carefully handled so as not to conflict with soliciting for private organizations.
>
> Mrs. Roosevelt noted that, while nothing was said on this subject, she felt sure that the Catholic organizations wanted to reserve to themselves the right to continue religious instruction at the same time that they dispensed help; that they feared the Children's Fund might cut down on their possibilities for continuing this work.
>
> If the Children's Fund could be so run that a maximum effort would be directed toward actually feeding children and a minimum used for overhead, and if suitable arrangements could be made with regard to use of voluntary organizations and avoiding conflicts in solicitation, then the Catholic organizations would support the Fund. Otherwise, they would be disposed to take active measures to fight it.
>
> The situation with regard to other voluntary organizations is somewhat similar; and at a meeting of non-governmental organizations held recently a resolution was passed which was derogatory to the Children's Fund (James Hendrick, Memorandum of Conversation, 30 January 1947, RG59, NARA II).

15. For Clarence Pickett, see *n*21 Document 95.

16. ER to Professor Joseph D. Chamberlain, ER to Mr. Paul Kellogg, and ER to Mrs. LaFell Dickinson, 17 December 1946, AERP.

17. On Congressional opposition to overseas refugee and relief efforts, see *n*13. Congress did not appropriate funding to UNICEF until late May 1947, when it voted an allocation of between $15,000,000 and $40,000,000. Congress approved IRO appropriations June 30, the day UNRRA expired and Truman signed the funding bill the following day. The United States did not become an "official and unconditional member" of the IRO until July 4 when ER and UN delegate Warren Austin submitted the papers attesting to congressional support to Secretary-General Lie ("IRO Document Turned Over to U.N. Secretary General," *NYT*, 4 July 1947, 5).

18. Pickett responded:

> I think you know that I have done everything I could to see that the IRO was approved and authorized by Committee 3 and the Assembly of the UN. I know, of course, that what I can do directly with Congress is very limited because I am the secretary of an agency which has tax-exemption on its gifts, but on both the IRO and the Children's Emergency Fund we are arranging to educate our own public to the problems that are to be met by these organizations and the importance of their being met by UN-approved agencies. I am also asking the Friends Committee on National Legislation which is set up to do direct work with Congress and its funds are not tax-exempt to give attention to this matter with Congress itself.
>
> You may be sure that we will do everything we can to muster support for both agencies (Clarence Pickett to ER, 27 December 1946, AERP).

RESPONDING TO A VEHEMENT CRITIC

ER often received stinging criticism from those opposed to her views. For example, December 20, Vincent Burns of Santa Barbara, California, wrote to accuse ER of "pro-pagan propaganda" for the position she took on Niemöller's upcoming visit[1] and the position he thought she took on the trial of twenty-nine individuals indicted under the Smith Act for conspiring with the German government.[2]

ER, he argued, fell "far short of being willing to practice" the principle of free speech:

> You did, as I recall from your speeches, condemn the so-called 28 seditionists, who were imprisoned for more than four years and persecuted unjustly, when in not one single instance was proof adduced which ever established that they advocated overthrow of our government. If the principle above quoted is good now why wasn't it good for those 28 Americans, who were merely exercising their constitutional rights of free speech, even tho their ideas were unpopular?

> Furthermore, every sane person knows that every Communist, every member of that party, not only openly and violently advocates overthrow of our government but actually works with his fellows <u>toward that end</u>. When have you ever said one word against that? Tell me, frankly and honestly, do you not think that the Communist menace, with its millions of spies, its unlimited funds, its diabolically clever propaganda and underhanded methods, is a thousand times more dangerous than the feeble and innocent efforts of 28 uneducated and ineffective so-called seditionists? <u>That being true</u>, why have you failed to point out that menace?

> Still further. The other day you went far out of the way to pour your malice and vicious disapproval upon the head of a visiting Christian clergyman, Niemoeller. You didn't want Americans to listen to him. You called him a Nazi. You were indignant at his presence …

> This to me is a very clear revelation, not of Niemoeller's shortcoming, but of your own. You are constantly attacking intolerance and bigotry. Yet you are in this instance guilty of a very offensive kind of intolerance and bigotry … You were loud in your protestation against the hate Hitler and his friends had for the Jews. Now your hate is proving how shallow and hypocritical was your protest, and that of all Jews.

> But even worse is this point, which you cannot and <u>dare not deny</u>. At the very moment when you were opening your vial of hate on the head of a Christian man Communists and fellow-agitators in Madison Square garden were bitterly attacking our government as "imperialist" and "blocking the peace".[3] Did you raise your voice against these hate-mongers from Moscow? Of course not. Because like your fool son, Elliott, who in Moscow the other day chose to condemn his own flag and his own people to curry favor with the tyrannous clique of the Lenin-Stalin axis,[4] you are at heart disloyal to the two basic foundations of America: number one, its great Christian heritage, and number two, its great principle of equality of justice to all.

After filling the margins of Burns's letter with her rebuttals, ER then asked her secretary to type them as the following reply:

171

Eleanor Roosevelt to Vincent Burns

[? December 1946]

I have your letter of the 20th.

I have condemned the American communists many times both in writing and in speaking. Communism is not a menace to us here in the United States unless we do not make democracy work for all of the people.

I do not remember condemning the 28 seditionists you mention.[5] I have no hate for Pastor Neimoeller or for anyone else for that matter. After the First World War we allowed ourselves to be lulled into a false security by believing that the German people were not to blame, that the Kaiser forced them into war, and I do not want to see us make the same mistake again. The German people were to blame for the Hitler government and a man like Pastor N. speaking to American audiences can possibly make us forget that.

It just so happens that my son, Elliott, did not say any of the things he is alleged to have said.[6]

TLd AERP, FDRL

---

1. See Document 27, Document 29, and Document 164 for ER's position on Niemöller.

2. In the case of *U.S. v. McWilliams* (1944), the government invoked the Smith Act of 1940 and charged twenty-nine individuals with "unlawfully, willfully, feloniously and knowingly" conspiring with "each other and with officials of the government of the German Reich" to cause mutiny in the military. The alleged conspirators—German-American Bundists, German propagandists, and far-right critics of the US government—agreed on little more than the belief that "Communists, international Jews and plutocrats" dominated both of the major political parties in the United States and conspired to involve the nation in World War II against the will of the American people. The government's failed attempt to convict these twenty-nine defendants as Nazi conspirators marked the culmination of state involvement in a public fight against "Fascism" in the 1930s and 1940s ("U.S. Indicts 30, Alleging Nazi Plot to Incite Mutiny and Revolution," *NYT*, 4 January 1944, 1; Ribuffo, 178–224).

3. Burns is probably referencing the September 12 rally at Madison Square Garden where Wallace and others criticized Truman's approach to Soviet-US relations. See Document 146.

4. November 2, 1946, Elliott Roosevelt and his wife Faye flew to Russia for a six-week tour of the country during which he reportedly made statements critical of US foreign policy at a reception held at the US Embassy. Citing an anonymous source, the press reprinted the source's recitation of Elliott Roosevelt's declaration that "the Soviet Union had never broken its word. While the United States and Britain repeatedly violated their pledges at Tehran, Yalta and Potsdam, the Soviets faithfully observed theirs." The source also claimed that Elliott then challenged his audience to "name one instance in which the United States acted to further the cause of peace." When a reporter answered that American support of the UN was an example of the nation's goodwill, Elliott allegedly replied, "You know as well as I do that the United States is supporting the U.N. for purely selfish and imperialistic reasons" ("E. Roosevelt Leaves," *NYT*, 3 November 1946, 27; "Pro-Russian Speech Reported Made by Elliott Roosevelt," *WP*, 27 November 1946, 1).

5. ER did not address the *McWilliams* defendants in My Day or in any public speeches, despite her involvement in the public campaign against Fascism. ER's opposition to loyalty oaths, the Dies committee, and the Smith Act began in the late 1930s. As she told *New York Herald Tribune* pub-

lisher Helen Reid, she had severe misgivings about "the constant battle going on between those who would have us fear the communists and those who would have us fear the fascists." When one is "thrown into the arms of one or the other in order to defeat the opposite trend of ideas" nothing is accomplished. "It is difficult to win a negative battle. Why are we in this country not stressing a constructive campaign for democracy?" June 3, 1940, she told the reporters at her press conference that although the nation did need protection from "Fifth column" activities, she urged "people to keep their feet on the ground," avoid hysteria, and, "emphasized that any steps taken should be under existing law." By the late 1940s, ER would lend her name to the effort to abolish the Smith Act and pardon those convicted under it (Lash, *Eleanor*, 592; "Seeks Air Inquiry on Browder Speech," *NYT*, 4 June 1940, 25; *IYAM*, May 1956).

6. Elliott Roosevelt released a statement admitting he had divulged his private views in a personal ("off the record") conversation and insisting that only when taken out of context could his statements be perceived as anti-American. When asked to clarify his position by providing the proper context, Elliott responded, "I refuse to divulge the conversation of others at a private party just as I expect others to respect my conversation." Public criticism of Elliott reached its pinnacle when Representative Lawrence H. Smith (R-WI) demanded Elliott Roosevelt's passport be revoked for "openly court[ing] Soviet favor at the expense of our standing and prestige abroad."

ER defended her son in her January 17 column:

> I don't think it has ever occurred to any of my sons to be pro-Communist, any more than it has ever occurred to me. And yet, in the course of my career, I have at times been severely criticized for what were called pro-Communist leanings, until I have learned to take what I read in the newspapers with a grain of salt.
>
> For instance, when I read in the papers that my son Elliott was supposed to have said some utterly ridiculous things in Moscow, particularly as regards the United States' activities within the United Nations, I knew without even asking any questions that the whole story was false. I took it for granted that some conversation had occurred, and that someone—not too anxious to avoid trouble for the Roosevelt family—had 'quoted' a few things which were pure imagination and others which were only half-truths. Taken out of the conversation as a whole, these conveyed a wrong impression ("Elliott Charges U.S. Embassy Tricked Him into Statements," *WP*, 30 November 1946, 1; "Demand Inquiries on Moscow Talk," *NYT*, 1 December 1946, 26; *MD*, 17 January 1947).

ON FRANCO AND STALIN

Catherine Gallagher wrote ER a six-page handwritten letter December 11, 1946, to say that after reading "Elliott's book I had to take F.D.R.'s picture down from where it had hung since 1930, in my boys' room," to say that she was "voting Republican for the first time in [her] life," and to object to the My Day she had just finished reading.[1] Gallagher took particular exception to ER's December 10 description of a breakfast conversation she had with servicemen in New York's Central Presbyterian Church.

> One young man asked me about our stand on Franco and how it was possible to expect a nation under Franco to cooperate with the Allies or to increase the chances of peace in the world, since it was obvious that Franco was pro-Fascist and seemed to have had no change of heart. The soldier was all for recognizing the government-in-exile.
>
> I don't wonder that these young soldiers find it hard to understand how we can tolerate and try to work with men who are quite obviously in opposition to the things for which we fought the war. I explained that one finds oneself in difficult positions now and then. The horns of this dilemma are our policy against outside interference in a domestic question and the possibility of making life even harder for the people of Spain![2]

Gallagher strongly disagreed. "Can you honestly say that he is more a threat to World Peace and more a dictator than Stalin and his puppet dictators who have forcibly captured governments and now rule by terror? … At least Franco seems to confine his dictating to his own country—he doesn't foment trouble in the four corners of the World." What would her reaction have been, Gallagher asked, "if American airmen had been shot down over Spain and if Franco had treated out protestations with the indifference and contempt that Tito treated us when that happened in Jugo-slavia?" Labeling the United Nations "the Tower of Babel of our times," Gallagher concluded:

> Why don't you have the courage to lead the American group and to face Molotov squarely and ask him point blank what Franco has done that he isn't equally guilty of?
>
> If our representatives do not ask that they are either downright cowardly or plainly dishonest!
>
> … I do not want to see [my two sons] go to war as my brothers had to do. Their Daddy and I do not want to go through the tortures my parents experienced during the war years … My mother's health has been ruined, I fear she will never be well again.
>
> I look to the U.N. for a chance to convince myself their worry and hardship was not in vain, that the world is now on the road to being a better place, but I cannot honestly see where any major issue has been successfully handled to a peaceful solution … Perhaps if Mothers of the next war's soldiers could be permitted a voice in the future welfare of our country at the U.N. things would be improved …
>
> History teaches us that appeasement never works. A savage, un-trained animal invariably bites the hand that feeds him.
>
> Do something! Time Flies![3]

ER addressed these and other concerns in her dictated reply.

172

Eleanor Roosevelt to Catherine Gallagher

21 December 1946 [New York City]

Dear Mrs. Gallagher:

I understand perfectly why you think Franco is better than Stalin. You seem to have forgotten that the difference is that Franco fought on the side of Germany and Italy, and in fact invited them to help him put down a government of the people. It was only when that government needed help, the Russians were the only power that gave them help and they began to be called communist. They did not start that way and today they are not, as far as I can see, communist, but they are grateful for the help which Russia gave them.[4]

Franco today is the repository of German wealth and of escaped Nazis.[5] The difference between Franco and Stalin is that when Stalin needed more time to prepare, he made a temporary alliance with Germany, but finally fought magnificently against Hitler and we owe him and his people a great deal for their fighting saved thousands of lives which might have been sacrificed on the American side.

Russia is a dictatorship but she is a dictatorship of more than one person. Stalin is the leader but has a group of men with him and the people are gradually learning to take a greater part in their government. They could not be expected to do more after so many years under the Tzar when no education was permitted.[6] I think there is a great deal of difference between Stalin and Franco.

I do not know what Governor Earl is talking about. I happen to know why he was recalled and it had nothing to do with what he saw.[7]

Certainly I am not afraid of the Russians. I have been arguing with them steadily for two months because I believe in certain things and they believe in others, but it is essential that the two nations get on together and I think the arguments have been constructive education.

Of course, you saw Hitler and Molotov shaking hands.[8] You have seen many other people shaking hands when they represented their nations and the nations were not at war. That does not always mean they love each other.

I have never liked what Tito's men did in shooting down our airplanes but I also know that we went where we were not supposed to go because our young men who fly planes are adventurous and saw no reason why they should not take the straightest line to their destination, and they forgot that Yugoslavs shoot before they think. I do not know just what you would have done about it beyond what has been done. I do not think it was taken lightly and I am quite sure the Yugoslavs did not think so.[9]

If the United States decides that communism is better than their own democracy it will be because we do not always make democracy serve the needs of all of the people. If the liberal press which you have been reading is an organ of the Liberal Party which of course, I do not know since I have never seen a copy, then I can assure you that Mr. Dubinsky who is more or less the moving light in the Liberal Party, is very anti-communist. Of course it may represent some other communist controlled union but it certainly would not, if it was communist, represent any large section of labor.[10]

As to your question about formal prayers opening the meetings of the UN, it has nothing to do with the Russians.[11] There are fifty four nations represented and many different religions. I do not question but what a great many delegates open every meeting with a prayer in their hearts, but how would you advise opening a meeting with many different religions?

I never saw anyone cringe or shout in a meeting of the UN, and I am sure it does not happen in the meetings of the Ministers. Your fear of communism is certainly not seen or felt in the UN, or in our own government. I do not have to ask Mr. Molotov what Mr. Franco has done because I know quite well as I told you in the first part of this letter.[12]

If you do not want to see your sons go to war, you had better learn more about the work of the UN and back it with all you have because that is the one hope, and learning to work with the Russians, whether we like their form of government or not, is essential because they are next to our-selves, the strongest nation in the world today and the peace of the future depends on our being able to work together.

Your mother went through what many other mothers went through. I am sorry if she was not able to stand it, and I hope she will be well again if her boys are now at home. I know it can be a terrible strain when they are away.

After three years of war, it will take a long time to come back to normal and a peaceful world. One has to build an atmosphere in which peace can grow and after that it will take patience and understanding and perseverance to keep the peace. It is fortunate for us in the UN that we do not feel it is a "Tower of Babel." Most of us understand at least the two languages which are the work-ing languages.

There are many mothers serving in the UN in one capacity or another from other lands and from our own, whose voices are heard so you need not be fearful that they have no chance to speak.

Very sincerely yours,

TLc AERP, FDRL

––––––––––––

1. Catherine Gallagher to ER, 11 December 1946, AERP.

2. *MD*, 10 December 1946.

3. Catherine Gallagher to ER, 11 December 1946, AERP.

4. For Franco see *n*13, Document 71. For Spain and ER's views on Franco, see Documents 160 through 163.

In 1937, Franco united the disparate nationalist militias with Falange (the Spanish Fascist party) troops into an army dedicated to ousting the working-class focused Republican government. Seeing an opportunity to oust an anti-Fascist government, Germany and Italy promptly violated their noninterventionist agreements with Spain. Hitler dispatched his elite Condor Legion of 100 combat aircraft and Mussolini sent 50,000 infantry troops, tanks, and artillery. The USSR, con-cerned more with stopping Franco and limiting Germany's advance, provided supplies and urged the International Brigade to supply troops (*OEWH*).

5. Both the Spanish Republican government in exile and the US State Department reported that between 9,000 and 15,000 former Nazi agents fled to Spain, where under assumed names and with Franco's strong support, they found sanctuary, reestablished their lives, and protected their wealth. However, US Ambassador Norman Armour reported the Franco government "was helping the Allies dissolve the Nazi establishment in Spain, with German Government and private property and businesses being confiscated in the name of the Allies" ("Franco's Changes Toward Democracy Not Yet Satisfactory, Armour Declares," *NYT*, 22 December 1945, 20; Thomas J. Hamilton, "Spain as Republic Seen in UNO Role," *NYT*, 9 January 1946, 11).

6. Russia experienced a long history of oppression under tsarist rule, beginning with the reign of Ivan the Terrible in 1547. Although some tsars supported more liberal programs than others, the majority of the Russian citizenry remained tied to the land through a system of peasant serfdom, which expanded in the seventeenth century, denying them an education and ensuring a persistent

state of poverty. Russia abolished serfdom in 1861, but many of the people still suffered from the legacy of autocratic rule and the majority remained uneducated (*OEWH*).

7. Gallagher asked ER why George Howard Earle III (1890-1974), who served as US minister to Austria and Bulgaria and as naval attaché to Turkey, left the diplomatic corps the previous September after his recent posting to Samoa. In an April 1946 radio broadcast, Earle claimed "there would have been no World War II if Premier Stalin had not signed his friendship pact with Germany in August, 1939." Stalin, he continued, only entered into the agreement to "bring about war in Europe so that the non-Bolshevist countries should destroy each other, thus bringing world domination to Russia." Convinced of an imminent Russian attack, Earle worked to have Congress appropriate $2 billion per year to develop "great fleets of atomic bombers" in order to prepare for the Soviet onslaught. Why, Gallagher wanted to know, had he "who spent much time in the territory now so firmly gripped by Soviet talons and well behind the iron curtain [who] saw first-hand what happened there" been "exiled to Samoa for trying to warn our government." The reasons for Earle's departure are unclear. However, he had just completed a very public divorce, in which his wife accused him of "desertion by telephone" (Catherine Gallagher to ER, 11 December 1946, AERP; "George H. Earle 3d, 84, Dead; Ex-Governor of Pennsylvania," *NYT*, 31 December 1974, 24; "Stalin-Hitler Pact Called War Cause," *NYT*, 26 April 1946, 2; "Ex-Gov. Earle Divorced," *NYT*, 1 July 1946, 18).

8. Gallagher recalled "seeing pictures of Molotov and Hitler shaking hands—the same Molotov you can shake hands with there at Lake Success. If Franco collaborates with Hitler did not Stalin and Molotov do just the same even more recently?" (Gallagher to ER, 11 December 1946, AERP).

9. For the US-Yugoslav dispute over American planes shot down by Yugoslavia in August 1946, see Document 140, especially *n*1 ("Yugoslavia to Pay $30,000 Each to Dead Fliers' Families," *WP*, 10 October 1946, 8).

10. Gallagher voted Republican "after hearing Earl Browder eulogize F.D.R. and after reading for months previous the 'Liberal Press' sent to my husband by his Union. It was so un-American and so pro Russian editorially that I actually feared all candidates endorsed by them" (Catherine Gallagher to ER, 11 December 1946, AERP).

11. Gallagher asked ER, "Do you United Nations delegates have more respect for Russian atheism than you have respect for God and the religion of most of the delegates that you fail to conduct meetings with a formal prayer for God's blessings on your efforts?" (Catherine Gallagher to ER, 11 December 1946, AERP).

12. Gallagher argued, "If news coming from your meetings wasn't so tragic it would be amusing to see how ... you seem to cringe when they shout, and now the latest is you echo them when they exclaim with sham horror at Franco's dictatorship and his threat to World Peace ... How can you honestly toady to one dictator and go through the elaborate procedure of condemning another, lesser one at the same time?" (Gallagher to ER, 11 December 1946, AERP).

ON THE PROGRESSIVE CITIZENS OF AMERICA

December 17, Morris Cooke, chair of the Philadelphia chapter, Independent Citizens Committee of the Arts, Sciences and Professions (ICCASP),[1] wrote ER, "Something tells me that you realize the importance of emphatically disassociating ourselves from American Communists and American Communism." Convinced that there was "no very gentle way of handling this situation," he concluded, that "unless, we can muster the nerve to really attack the problem, in my opinion we will necessarily pay a heavy price in our future activities." Cooke enclosed a copy of the letter he sent to the national chairs of ICCASP and NCPAC[2] which he thought ER "might be interested in seeing."[3]

"Now that our organizations are planning to unite," Cooke's letter to the chairs began, "it is time to take stock." He then argued that that a direct correlation existed between the "catastrophic defeat … the liberal movement" suffered in the 1946 election and ICCASP and NCPAC's refusal to remove their Communist members:

> [T]he leadership of nearly all our liberal groups was sufficiently tolerant of the affiliation of <u>American</u> Communists or indifferent as to the damage such associations might cause, as to give a malicious opposition with its preponderant and unwavering press support a wide open opportunity to smear us as "fellow travelers." We did not invite the cooperation of these people, but we realize now that in instances they insinuated themselves into our organizations and a certain baneful aroma was thus quite unnecessarily created. This can and must be corrected.
>
> Our own national interest and world interest demand that American policies be formulated within our own borders, without outside dictation of any sort whatever, whether it be from Downing Street, Moscow or Rome. There is nothing in this to suggest that we should not be as cognizant of the problems of other countries as we are of our own or that we should not be fully sympathetic and cooperative in foreign fields. But the initiation and execution of our own American policies must rest with us … Liberals generally emphasize the necessity for learning how to get along with the USSR in spite of all the difficulties—some of our own making.
>
> But an <u>American</u> Communist party, or even an individual <u>American</u> Communist, is inconceivable without USSR ties of one sort or another … <u>American</u> Communism is a political faith quite alien to American thought and American institutions because unlike other political faiths such as Republicanism, Socialism and Democracy, it has its roots in a foreign land. Our Constitution wisely gives a hearing at election time to almost any political group so that in some states Communists have a place on the ballot. But even so, it is clear that American liberalism seeking to regain its dominance in American political affairs can have no traffic of any kind whatsoever with <u>American</u> Communism or <u>American</u> Communists.

Cooke then went on to insist that when the two organizations merged (into what would become the Progressive Citizens of America) that they explicitly denounce any association with American Communism or American Communists, exclude Communists from participation, and disqualify anyone with past Communist affiliations from employment with the organization.[4]

After reading both Cooke's letter to her and his letters to NCPAC chair Jo Davidson and ICCASP chair Frank Kingdon, ER noted in the margin, "I agree completely and it's a fine letter."[5]

December 28, NCPAC and ICCASP merged to form the Progressive Citizens of America, and tapped former NCPAC vice-chair C. B. "Beanie" Baldwin to be PCA's vice-chair and national political director. The following day, ER sent Baldwin, whom she knew from his work with the Roosevelt Agriculture Department, his close ties to Sidney Hillman, and his efforts to keep Wallace on the 1944 ticket, the following letter seconding Cooke's letter to NCPAC.

173

Eleanor Roosevelt to C. B. Baldwin
29 December 1946 [Hyde Park]

Dear Mr. Baldwin:

I have seen the letter which was addressed to you not long ago by Mr. Morris L. Cooke and I have also seen a number of others.[6]

For that reason, I want to tell you personally that I feel it very important that the NCPAC, the CIOPAC, and the ICC[7] make up their minds to remove from their membership all people affiliated with, or supposed to have communist leanings to the American Communist party.[8]

The CIO within its unions is doing a pretty good job of cleaning house. If these political groups do not do the same and continue to be afraid of being called red-baiters, they will not be able to do the thing which is essential, namely, support all those who are liberal and support good understanding with Russia and working with Russia wherever it is possible to do so.

I did not find much sympathy among the Russian delegates to the UN for the American communists.[9]

Very sincerely yours,
Eleanor Roosevelt

TLS CBBP, IaU-LI

174

C. B. Baldwin to Eleanor Roosevelt
13 January 1947 [New York City]

Dear Mrs. Roosevelt:

I was confined to my apartment with a cold at the time your letter of December 29 was received in the office and this is the first opportunity I have had to reply.

A resolution similar to the one passed at the CIO Convention[10] was proposed at the last Steering Committee meeting of the National Citizens PAC which was held several weeks prior to the Joint Convention of the National Citizens PAC and the Independent Citizens Committee of the Arts, Sciences & Professions, at which time the Progressive Citizens of America was formed.[11] The resolution was debated for over two hours and defeated by a vote of 35 to 2. I'm sorry you were not present to hear this discussion. The members of our Committee (which is composed of people who have fought vigorously for progressive government for years and in whom, I think, you have full confidence) rejected this proposal almost unanimously because they felt that to take anything but a positive stand at this time would weaken our organization and because catering to loose charges of interference by the Communist Party in the work of our Committee would be a reflection on the integrity of the members of the Committee.[12] Furthermore, no such charges have been made.

The situation within the CIO which probably occasioned the anti-communist resolution was quite different since charges had been made of political interference by the Communist Party and other groups in their trade union activities.[13]

I regret, too, that you could not have been present to witness the proceedings and listen to the discussion at the Convention. Delegates from 21 states participated and although there were vigorous arguments on how the new organization should function and be governed, not once was any element of factionalism injected. The floor was open for free discussion and any delegate was able to express his opinion or propose any resolution he might care to have considered. (I'm enclosing copies of the Constitutional By-laws and the Program adopted by the new organization.[14])

If I sensed the feeling and the spirit of those who have made possible the formation of the PCA, they are determined to fight vigorously for a progressive program for this country on both foreign and domestic policy, free from the domination of any political party or group. To accept any other position would necessitate resorting to undemocratic snooping and interference with the rights and beliefs of our members.

You have been called a Communist. I have—and hundreds of others who are devoting themselves sincerely to the progressive cause. To weaken under the pressure of the reactionary press, political leaders or big business monopolists would only give these interests the ammunition they need to hopelessly divide and then destroy the liberal movement. The Social Democrats of Germany fell for this type of propaganda and the Republic was destroyed.[15] Can it be possible that this could happen here?

We have worked hard and with considerable success during the past few years to build an effective grass roots organization. This has been done against ever present opposition of some groups who have energetically but without too much success questioned our sincerity and our purposes. I hope the ADA will refrain from using these methods because it might be disastrous. We expect to continue to work and organize in spite of opposition from any source.

I hope that you will let me know when it might be convenient for me to see you and discuss this whole matter at length because I feel that you recognize there are honest differences of opinion among many sincere liberals on this issue.

Sincerely,
C.B. Baldwin

TSL AERP, FDRL

ER replied three days later, citing their "honest differences."

<u>175</u>

Eleanor Roosevelt to C. B. Baldwin

16 January 1947 [New York City]

My dear Mr. Baldwin,

Thank you for your letter of January 13th. There are honest differences. One is the fear of expressing openly the feeling one has about American Communists which I consider essential.

I am sure the A.D.A. will not try to discredit any other group.

Yours very sincerely,
Eleanor Roosevelt

TLS AERP, FDRL

———————

1. Morris Llewellyn Cooke (1872–1960), a staunch New Dealer, had directed FDR's Rural Electrification Administration. He would resign from NCPAC in 1947, citing the organization's failure to rid its ranks of Communist influence ("Morris L. Cooke, Engineer, Dies; First Administrator of R.E.A.," *NYT*, 6 March 1960, 86).

2. For ER's relationship with NCPAC see Document 24 and Document 25.

3. Morris Llewellyn Cooke to ER, 17 December 1946, AERP.

4. Morris Llewellyn Cooke to Jo Davidson and Frank Kingdon, 17 December 1946, AERP.

5. Marginalia in ER's hand on Morris Llewellyn Cooke to ER, 17 December 1946, AERP.

6. ER probably assumed that Baldwin saw the letter Cooke sent NCPAC chair Frank Kingdon.

7. ICCASP (see header).

8. For ER's earlier comments on this, see Document 18.

9. For an elaboration of ER's view that the Russian UN delegates had little sympathy for American Communists, see Document 207.

10. At its 1946 convention the CIO passed a resolution asserting that CIO delegates "resent and reject efforts of the Communist Party … to interfere in the affairs of the CIO" (Lichtenstein, 257).

11. The Progressive Citizens of America formed on December 28, 1946, uniting NCPAC and ICCASP (Hamby, *Beyond*, 159).

12. ADA and PCA leadership mirrored the political divisions dividing their organizations. While the ADA contained more former New Dealers than the PCA, the latter organization included many respected leaders, such as Jo Davidson, Beanie Baldwin, Philip Murray, and Henry Wallace (Hamby, *Beyond*, 160–61).

13. Throughout the 1946 election campaign, the CIO faced heavy public accusation of Communist influence, particularly by red-baiting campaigns in the South. Politicians such as the young Richard Nixon from California and Joseph McCarthy from Wisconsin publicly branded the CIO as Communist (Lichtenstein, 257).

14. The PCA's constitution included a protection of discrimination against Communists, declaring that their political beliefs could not be used to prevent their joining the organization. Its "Program for Political Action" accused the Democratic Party of departing from the Roosevelt tradition and asserting the possible need for a new political party. The rest of the proposal's domestic program represented a standard synopsis of general progressive goals such as repudiating monopoly and discrimination and supporting labor rights (Hamby, *Beyond*, 160).

15. Jo Davidson, co-chairman of the PCA, also made this argument, comparing Hitler's tactics to "confuse the progressives in Germany" to using the scare of Communism to divide the American left (Hamby, *Beyond*, 164).

January–June

1947

"I feel very keenly the importance of this Commission."

Eleanor Roosevelt began 1947 engaged in the debate over how liberals should best

offset the influence American Communists wielded in some reform organizations. In early January, she helped found the Americans for Democratic Action (ADA); however, the establishment of another liberal organization so soon after the founding of the Progressive Citizens of America (PCA) worried those liberals concerned that protracted debate between non-Communist and anti-Communist organizations would undermine the liberal agenda. "American communists seem to have succeeded very well in jeopardizing whatever the liberals work for," ER wrote. "Therefore, to keep them out of the policy making and staff positions," as the ADA planned to do, "seems to be very essential."[1] Rejecting accusations that the PCA was the more progressive body, ER told Helen Bush that the ADA "is really a group to stimulate progressive action in the Democratic Party," and she rejected La Guardia's suggestion that progressives might need to form a third party. When others expressed concern that ER and Henry Wallace, two of the most prominent liberals in American politics, appeared to be in warring camps, she responded that "I am not attacking Mr. Wallace nor other progressives."[2] Nevertheless, while she declared her faith in Wallace's "complete integrity," she found herself "troubled by the fact that he hasn't always gone to the root of questions and got the facts completely straight."[3]

Despite her busy schedule, ER found time to respond to a *Yale Daily News* reporter and the editor of a Wisconsin high school newspaper asking her how students could help secure peace and confront prejudice. ER herself cancelled a speaking engagement at the American Women's Club in Toronto after receiving protests that the club discriminated against Jews.

On the international front, the existence of fascist regimes in Spain and Argentina, and America's apparently growing willingness to accommodate them, continued to bother ER. In the case of Argentina, she turned to her old friend Sumner Welles for insight and asked him to explain why he thought it wise to come to agreement with the government of Juan Perón. She also expressed disappointment to Senator Vandenberg at the proposal to end bi-partisan representation on the US delegation to the UN and asked Truman if something could be done to allow a group of illegal Jewish immigrants to stay in the United States. She urged Undersecretary of State Dean Acheson to consider Lady Stella Reading's proposal to create an organization to train women to defend democratic principles against communist attacks at international meetings. Soon after George Marshall replaced James Byrnes as Secretary of State, ER asked the secretary to meet with representatives from the National Conference on the Problem of Germany to address their concern that the Allied plan to rebuild Germany could redevelop the nation in ways that fostered its economic and military might.

January 27, the permanent UN Human Rights Commission held its first meeting in Lake Success, New York, and unanimously elected ER chairman. She then told her colleagues that while her parliamentary skills might be rusty, "I feel very keenly the importance of this Commission" and "am conscious of that fact that human rights mean something to the people of the world, which is hope for a better opportunity for people in general to enjoy justice and freedom and opportunity."[4] She then guided the HRC through its first two-week session, as it decided how it would approach its work, discussed what its proposed international bill of rights should contain, and aired its philosophical differences that would underlie debates throughout the drafting process. As ER summed up the ideological division in the commission: "Many of us believe that an organized society in the form of a government, exists for the good of the individual; others believe that an organized society in the form of a government, exists for the benefit of a group."[5]

After the HRC sessions ended, ER reflected on the difficulties she had encountered in dealing with the Russians at the UN in an article for *Look* magazine. Calling the Russians "tough," she admitted that "it takes patience and equal firmness and equal conviction to work with" them. However, despite "fundamental differences," she still hoped that "as time goes by … we will find more points of agreement."[6]

As she worked to reach agreement on an international bill of rights and other issues, ER found it "very embarrassing, sometimes" when other UN representatives pointed out how Americans did not live up to their own Bill of Rights. To fulfill its leadership role in the world, ER told a Roosevelt College audience, "each of us who believes that democracy really has the essence of something which can give more to the people than anything else—we who believe that—have to show that it is true."[7]

Several documents in this section record ER's concern over the delivery of humanitarian relief to people abroad. When criticized for lending her name to American Relief for Greek Democracy, an organization her correspondent called "a 'front' for another Communist activity," ER not only rejected his accusation but declared that "I have always felt that women and children should be helped regardless of political ideas."[8] After Truman announced on February 21 that Greece and Turkey would receive economic and military aid directly from the US rather than through the UN, marking a shift in US policy, ER's discomfort intensified to the point where she considered resigning from the US delegation. Dean Acheson twice sent envoys to explain to her the US position on Greece and Turkey. The explanations provided kept her from resigning, but she told Acheson, "I hope never again that this type of action be taken without at least consulting with the Secretary General and with our permanent member on the Security Council beforehand. It all seems to me a most unfortunate way to do things." She then wrote Truman that she did not believe "taking over Mr. Churchill's policies in the Near East, in the name of democracy, is the way to really create a barrier to communism or promote democracy."[9] Despite her disagreement with the administration's policies, ER did not support the attacks Henry Wallace leveled at Truman during his European lecture tour: "I do not believe that it is wise for Mr. Wallace to be making the kind of speeches he is making at the present time in foreign countries."[10]

ER's concern about escalating international tensions increased in May, when the Council of Foreign Ministers ended seven weeks of meetings without reaching agreement on the future of Germany or European peace treaties. After studying John Foster Dulles's report on the results of the meetings, she wrote him to suggest a possible way of reaching agreement with the Soviet Union on economic issues: that the US and Great Britain offer Russia help in building up its industries in exchange for raw materials.

---

1. See Document 190, ER to Max Lerner, 19 January 1947.

2. See Document 195, ER to James Loeb, Jr., January 1947.

3. See Document 178, ER to Helen Bush, 16 January 1947.

4. See Document 200, Excerpt, Verbatim Report of the First Meeting, Commission on Human Rights, 27 January 1947.

5. See Document 206, Excerpt, Verbatim Report of the Fourteenth Meeting, Commission on Human Rights, 4 February 1947.

6. See Document 207, "The Russians Are Tough," 18 February 1947.

7. See Document 226, Speech Before Roosevelt College, 24 May 1947.

8. See Document 187, ER to Harry Boardman, 11 January 1947.

9. See Document 219, ER to Harry Truman, 17 April 1947.

10. See Document 221, ER to Calvin Baldwin, 17 April 1947.

"I have always believed in Mr. Wallace's integrity but that does not mean that you have to agree" in how you "work for your objectives." After he announced he would seek the presidency as a third-party candidate, ER opined "What strange things the desire to be President makes men do!" See Documents 178 and 293. AP/WIDE WORLD PHOTO.

Although ER believed that rebuilding war-torn Germany was central to a "healthy Europe," she opposed permitting the "great business magnates of Germany" to "build up the kind of German economy which would again lead to war." See Documents 198, 223, and 370. AP IMAGES.

Ambassador George Messersmith and Spruille Braden disagreed over how best to deal with the Perón government. ER, like Braden, did not support Perón. Although she conceded that "we must try not to interfere with their internal decisions," she thought the US must disapprove "of anything which encourages the Nazi influence." See Document 203. MARIE HANSEN/TIME LIFE PICTURES/GETTY IMAGES.

"You're Sure You'll Send For Me As So on As Possible?"

ER felt "deeply disturbed" over US aid to Greece and Turkey. She recognized "only" the US could supply the funds, but she urged "consultation with the UN … We had taken a large part in setting up the UN and it now seemed that we are not operating with regard for it." See Document 208. "YOU'RE

"We might have some acrimonious discussions," ER said of Vyshinsky and Molotov. "But I had no personal bitterness ... nevertheless ... one must be alert since if they cannot win success for their point of view in one way, they are still going to try to win in any other way that seems ... possible." See Document 207. © BETTMANN/CORBIS.

Zionist organizations bombed British headquarters at the King David Hotel after the British rejected IM recommendations on Jewish immigration. ER grew "increasingly" troubled about "the Palestine situation." In 1947, she wrote Marshall "our own policy in the UN has been very weak" and seems tacitly "to support a totalitarian government." See Document 227. FOX PHOTOS/GETTY IMAGES.

176

If You Ask Me [excerpt]

Ladies' Home Journal January 1947

I am puzzled about what is going on in [the] U.N. It seems to me that when the Americans or British make a proposal, the Russians ignore it or make a directly opposite one. I get the feeling that we will never be able to work with the Russians. Do you feel that way?

No, I do not feel that way. It seems to me quite possible to get on with the Russians, though I think it is going to take us a long while really to understand each other. There are fundamental differences that exist between us, in our backgrounds and in our points of view, which arise very largely from the fact that Russia is a very young nation—young and virile—but, nevertheless, insecure.[1] We have more than 150 years behind us, and we have attained a good deal of the poise and security which come with maturity.

The desire for security motivates practically every country. They need a sense that they have friends and are safe in the family of nations; that their people and their own strength are adequate to meet the demands which living in the modern world requires.

It is much easier to have confidence in people if you have a sense of security. We have gained it, and I think for that very reason we should perhaps be better able today to be generous about some of the very obvious moves which are made by the Russians, largely because of their lack of security. Only with confidence and trust can peace be a reality.

There is no question, for instance, that ultimately we will all have more security if we have a greater sense of interdependence; put more strength into the United Nations, and count less on our own individual strengths. Even we find that hard to accept, because it is such a new concept of living with other nations, and for the Russians, who have lived on the continent of Europe, where every nation has looked askance at every other nation for years, it is even harder than it is for us.

We are apt to forget the changes that have come over the world, and to judge whatever moves Russia makes to assure her security from the point of view of the world ethics of today, rather than from the point of view which was prevalent years ago when we met our own problems. In many ways, Russia is today where we were a hundred years or more ago. We did not like it when people criticized us. And it was not just because of the criticism; it was because we were a little afraid that some of the things they said were probably true!

One takes criticism better as one grows older; and if we really understood, I think we would face more realistically some of the things which Russia has done, even though we might still oppose them, because we know both the world of today and the world of our youth.

For instance, we proclaimed the Monroe Doctrine[2] for our own security; and many of the other moves which we are reminded of as we go back through the pages of our history were made to give us a sense of security. Many a time in our history we have done highhanded things, but we have done them always with a sense of virtue because they made us more secure! They increased our economic stability, or our defenses; so, as we felt that our motives were good, we justified our self-interests.

That is something we must not forget when we watch another nation, a virile, young nation, in a period when international and national ethics have changed considerably, trying to gain some things which we have already achieved. It is far harder today to live by modern standards and still achieve these things, since the buccaneer days are over. The Atomic Age has wiped out the past in which we grew up.

When all this is considered, however, I think it is essential that the Russians also understand that the nations living around them, who have greater maturity, have set up certain standards, and that to live successfully with them the effort to understand those standards must be made. They will have to stop some of the practices which are relics of the past, and recognize eventually the basic difference between our two beliefs: We think the state must serve the individual; and they think the individual is subservient to the state. Gradually as our conceptions become clearer to each other, and as life becomes more worth while to every individual in his part of the world, we will, I believe, find a happier medium for working together and living together in peace and amity.

TMsex DLC

---

1. ER would make this point again in December 1947 when she wrote:

> There was a time in the United States when the individual was less important than the community as a whole—that grew out of our weakness and our need for expansion. That is probably one of the reasons why the Russians are genuinely surprised that you should be concerned with the fate of smaller nations, since they represent such a small number of people. I am quite sure it has never occurred to the Russian government that the rest of the world might believe that some of the smaller nations they dominate have as much right to consideration as their great nation has.

> The importance of the mass of people as against a small group of individuals will change only as the whole nation reaches a higher standard of living and begins to have time to think of itself on individual lines. The sooner Russia as a nation becomes conscious that there are those of us who have reached the point where individuals and small nations are as important as big nations and masses of people, the sooner we'll begin to understand each other and at least work together in certain fields where we have a community of interest" (*MD*, 22 December 1947; see also *MD*, 1 June 1945 and 7 October 1948).

2. In his annual message to Congress, December 2, 1823, President James Monroe proclaimed that "the American continents ... are henceforth not to be considered as subjects for future colonization by any European powers" and in return, promised that the United States would not interfere with territories then under European control (*RCAH*).

ELEANOR ROOSEVELT AND AMERICANS FOR
DEMOCRATIC ACTION, PART 1

Saturday, January 3, a week after 300 delegates assembled at the Hotel Commodore to form the Progressive Citizens of America, a group of 120 non-Communist, New Deal liberals convened at Washington's Willard Hotel to reorganize and expand the Union for Democratic Action. As covered by Washington's leading newspaper, the *Evening Star*, those who addressed the preconvention banquet focused their remarks on how best to organize against the "forces of reaction." ER, whom UDA executive secretary Loeb hoped would offset the publicity Wallace had brought to the PCA founding meeting, also addressed the activists, calling on liberals to awaken "a sleeping people" to "the sense of responsibility which they have to accept" not only for America but for the rest of the world.[1]

_177_

"Liberals Look Ahead for Gains under Democratic Action"

The Evening Star, Washington, DC
4 January 1947

New Dealers and other liberals of various political faiths rallied today under the banner of the Union for Democratic Action to plan their future, after a dinner last night at the Shoreham Hotel at which leaders called for a stiffened front against triumphant "forces of reaction."

While the question of a third party was unsettled as the delegates were called to a closed session at the Willard Hotel today, Chester Bowles, in a keynote address at the dinner, saw too many obstacles in the way of an effective third party. He said the Democratic Party, "with all its fault, is our most effective instrument for political action."

Mrs. Franklin D. Roosevelt called for a world point of view that encompassed more than the solution of America's domestic problems.

"I have no fear of Communists or Fascists," she said, "if we know what we want, and say it in words simple enough for everybody to understand."

If the people know what they want, they will find leaders to carry out their wishes, Mrs. Roosevelt added, but it must not be for the United States alone, but must take into account the rest of the world.

Wilson Wyatt,[2] former Federal housing expediter, said: "I am convinced that the overwhelming majority of Americans are liberals, the verdict at the polls in November to the contrary notwithstanding. They are looking to leadership and to a rallying point."

All the scientific plans for housing, he told the crowd of more than 400 at the dinner, have not solved the problem of giving the typical American family a typical American home—a decent habitation. In worrying about the two totalitarian extremes of fascism and communism, he said, we are overlooking American democracy, which is the most important issue of the day.

"Will this Nation," asked Leon Henderson,[3] who presided, "find within itself the vision and courage to build a stable and equitable economy, or will it become the powerful center of world reaction and imperialism? Will America be a symbol of hope or fear? This is our challenge."

Mr. Bowles, former head of OPA and director of economic stabilization, made this comment on the radical fringes of liberalism: "We must be prepared to defend the right of American Communists to propagate their views through their own organizations. But we must make it crystal clear that there is no place in the American liberal movement for those who would compromise with the principle of individual liberty.

"There are enormous forces in American life that are both progressive and non-Communist. It is these democrat groups and individuals that must be brought together into the fullest political partnership based on a common conviction that freedom and planning are not only compatible but in the long run inseparable."

Mr. Bowles added: "We should not harbor any illusions about a third party. The legal and organizational obstacles in the way of an effective third party organization are too great. The Democratic party, with all its faults, is our most effective instrument for political action.

"If we expect to regain the ground we shall have lost by 1948, we must elect a liberal President and a liberal Congress. To accomplish this we must work through the Democratic party machinery. In the next two years, we must return the Democratic party to the ideals and objectives of Jefferson, Jackson, Wilson and Roosevelt. This will not be easy."

And Mr. Bowles went on to say "We cannot blink the fact that the party of Roosevelt is also the party of Bilbo and Rankin.[4] But the fact remains that we have no practical alternative. All our efforts, all our ingenuity, must be thrown into the struggle to establish liberal control of the Democratic party in 1948."

He charged extremists of both the Right and Left with saying there are no alternatives to Communism on one hand and narrow capitalism on the other.

"It is the responsibility of American liberals," said Mr. Bowles, "to prove that the extremists are wrong. It is our task to provide a program of democratic action dynamic, politically practical a program designed to provide freedom as well as security for everyday people everywhere. Our success or failure in providing this alternative will determine not only the shape of our own country, but the hope of the world as a whole."

Mrs. Roosevelt wondered how many times in the past such a meeting as the one last night had faced great difficulties and pondered how to solve them. She was sure it happened after the Revolution and again after the Civil War and at other times.

"I am sure," she said, "that what we are facing can be faced. We need to feel that we are able to meet whatever demands are made on us."

The people are disturbed and confused, as she saw it, not only by their own problems, but by the situations in other countries. If Americans confine their efforts to their country alone, she said, "the heart will go out of the rest of the world."

"We are a little nervous about our own spiritual leadership," she added, "though we have always been able to meet our own internal problems when they were serious enough and we faced them. When the people think things through, they usually come up with the answers."

We have, Mrs. Roosevelt said, "the job of awakening a sleeping people to the sense of responsibility which they have to accept."

She warned against the philosophy that troubles are over and people can simply enjoy themselves. They are not over for a majority of the world, she pointed out, and "the world has been telescoped in many ways, so that everybody feels what has happened to everybody else."

Referring to Mr. Wyatt's discussion of housing, Mrs. Roosevelt said: "There are rural slums, too. And we need also to rebuild the thinking in farm homes."

In her work as a delegate to the United Nations, she explained, she has noticed that "you feel the strength of representatives of nations as they identify themselves with their people."

Dr. Reinhold Niebuhr[5] warned that this country cannot solve its problems by production alone, as many have preached.

"We didn't solve housing in that way," he pointed out.

James Wechsler,[6] Washington correspondent, took subscriptions to raise funds to continue the Union for Democratic Action. Mrs. Cornelia Bryce Pinchot[7] and Mrs. J. Wesley Adams[8] were co-chairman of the dinner.

PNews DLC

January 6, ER used My Day to report on the founding meeting of the Americans United for Democratic Action:

> I spent the whole day yesterday from 9:30 in the morning till after five in the afternoon with a group of people, many of whom I have known before, who were trying to set up a liberal and progressive organization. They chose as their name, "Americans United for Democratic Action."[9] If they live up to that name, they will not only lay down certain principles, but they will find ways and means to acquaint the people of the country with their program. In addition, they will organize the action which can be taken in any community in the nation if people are in agreement on specific programs.
>
> Yesterday I received a long screed from someone accusing me of forming a third party. I wish emphatically to deny that I am forming a third party, or in fact that I am forming anything. I am joining with other progressives, many of whom are far younger and more active than I am, and far more influential, in an attempt to carry on the spirit of progress. We do not believe that what has been done in the past is the highest attainment that can be hoped for in a democratic nation. We hope to face new situations and find new answers in line with the needs and best interests of our country and its people, never forgetting our relationship to the family of nations. I am a Democrat because that political party has stood during the last 16 years for this type of work and achievement, and I certainly hope the Democratic party will continue to do so.[10]

ER hoped both her column and the new organization would prod liberal Democrats to act. Helen Bush, associate chairman of the Democratic Committee of Wyoming County, New York, wrote to thank ER on January 8. The new organization "sounded like rock-bottom material and that's what our Women's Democratic Organization here needs for a foundation if I, myself, can continue to be its leader." She then asked ER to send ADA literature that Bush could distribute to a Democratic women's meeting the following week.[11]

She closed the letter asking ER's opinion of Henry Wallace as the new editor of the *New Republic* and whether or not she considered him "a promoter of progressive ideals?"[12]

178

Eleanor Roosevelt to Helen Bush

16 January 1947 [New York City]

My dear Mrs. Bush:

Americans United for Democratic Action is really a group to stimulate progressive action in the Democratic Party, and I have asked Mr. James Loeb, the secretary to send you as soon as the organizing committee has formulated its principles and plans, full information on the projects which they are going to undertake.

A group of twenty-five was named to work on formulating these projects.[13]

At the same time it was suggested to the few remaining progressives in Congress that they get together and start some kind of educational plan for the benefit of all of us working in the state and local party organizations. We should feel that our people have a plan for promoting legislation, and for opposing certain legislation and we should be able to get information from this group and carry it back to our communities.

Mr. Henry Wallace is a fine person and I believe in his complete integrity, but I have been a little troubled by the fact that he hasn't always gone to the root of questions and got the fact completely straight.[14] That is probably the fault of some of the younger people whom he has had around him, and I hope that they have had a lesson.

The New Republic does not reach a very large audience, but it was originally designed to reach leaders and perhaps that is the way in which Mr. Wallace can make his greatest contribution.

Very sincerely yours,

TLc AERP, FDRL

---

1. Gillon, 6, 16.

2. Truman appointed Wilson Wyatt (1905–1996), the former mayor of Louisville, as his national housing administrator in December 1945 and Wyatt developed an ambitious veterans housing program. Wyatt resigned on December 4, 1946, after Truman failed to back his proposals to retain government controls on housing materials and to fully back federal aid to the housing program (Robert McG. Thomas, Jr., "Wilson Wyatt, 90, Politician and Louisville Civic Leader," *NYT*, 13 July 1996, D24; Walter H. Waggoner, "Wyatt Out, Government Policy on Housing Control to be Eased," *NYT*, 5 December 1946, 1).

3. Leon Henderson (1895–1986), an economist who played an influential role in economic policy during the New Deal, headed the Office of Price Administration (OPA) in 1942, but resigned because of public and congressional opposition to his strict imposition of rationing and price controls (*ANB*).

4. Theodore Bilbo (D-MS), the Senate's staunchest segregationist, was the only Senator to vote against ER's appointment to the UN. John Rankin (1882–1960), Democratic congressman from Mississippi from 1920 to 1950, played a leading role on the House Committee on Un-American Activities (HUAC), which he helped create ("John Rankin Dies," *NYT*, 27 November 1960). For more on Rankin, see *n*13 Document 389.

5. Reinhold Niebuhr (1892–1971), who became a socialist and advocate for the labor movement while serving as pastor of the Bethel Evangelical Church in Detroit, Michigan, from 1915 to 1928, emerged as a leading American theologian in the 1930s. As editor of *Christianity and Crisis*, a journal that examined labor, civil rights, and other issues from a religious perspective, and as a founder of ADA he became an influential voice among anti-Communist liberals (*DAB*).

6. James A. Wechsler (1915–1983), one of the nation's leading non-Communist liberal journalists, began his career with Columbia College's the *Spectator*. After graduation he edited the American Student Union's the *Student Advocate* until 1937, when, after becoming disenchanted with American Communists, he joined the *Nation* as assistant editor. In 1940, he joined the staff of *PM* as assistant labor editor, ultimately serving as its national affairs editor and Washington bureau chief. In 1947, protesting that Communists had taken control of *PM*, he left the magazine to edit

the liberal *New York Post* (Wolfgang Saxon, "James Wechsler, a Columnist and Ex-Editor of Post, Dies," *NYT*, 12 September 1983, D13).

7. Cornelia Bryce Pinchot (1881–1960), a long-time Republican political activist and advocate of women's rights who began her career as a suffragist, served as US representative to the International Women's Conference in Paris in 1945 and president of the Americans United for World Organization, Washington chapter. Described as "one of the liveliest and most talked about political women" of the 1930s by the *New York Times*, Pinchot had twice run for elected office and walked picket lines with members of the National Women's Trade Union League. Her husband, the former Pennsylvania governor and noted conservationist Gifford Pinchot, died in 1946 (*NAWMP*).

8. Frances McStay Adams would later direct the Fulbright program in Egypt, review films for the United States Information Agency, and coordinate education programs for Americans in England. Her husband, J. Wesley Adams, a State Department foreign service officer, served in the UN Bureau of United Nations Affairs ("J. Wesley Adams," *WP*, 4 January 1990, D5; Judith Martin, "No Job Shortage for Her," *WP*, 15 July 1962, F8).

9. UDA chair Ethel Epstein, aware of the UDA's limited membership compared to other groups, urged the group not to continue under the UDA mantle. Others rejected "liberal" for its ties to "19th century laissez-faire liberalism" while others rejected "progressivism" for its "connotation of third-partyism." After debating several names, the delegates adopted Americans United for Democratic Action, which the CIO's James Carey had presented on behalf of the labor caucus. The organization would soon go by a shorter version, Americans for Democratic Action (Gillon, 20).

10. The delegates also debated how overtly the group should be tied to the Democratic Party. ER's pronouncement here reflects the argument Franklin, Jr., made to the delegates: "The surest way to make the Democratic Party a liberal party ... is to go into the Democratic Party" (Gillon, 19; *MD*, 6 January 1947).

11. Helen Bush to Eleanor Roosevelt, 8 January 1947, AERP.

12. In his address to the closing session of the PCA meeting, Wallace told the delegates that it was "wrong to divide the progressive movement on minor issues." Progressives "should have no allegiance outside the country of any sort, except to One World, peaceful and prosperous." Arguing that progressives should work with "Russian haters and Russophiles," Wallace urged progressives "not to allow the attacks of the enemy to stampede us into foolish red-baiting nor ... [to] allow those who owe their primary allegiance to some foreign power to determine our course" (quoted in Gillon, 16).

13. The twenty-five individuals named to the organizing committee were Charles G. Bolte; Elmer Davis; George Edwards; Ethel Epstein; Leon Henderson; Hubert Humphrey; Mrs. Clyde Johnson; Reinhold Niebuhr; Edward Prichard, Jr.; Franklin D. Roosevelt, Jr.; Frank W. McCulloch; Mrs. Gifford Pinchot; Bishop William Scarlett; Walter White; Wilson W. Wyatt; Harvey Brow; David Dubinsky; Hugo Ernst; B. F. McLaurin; James Killen; John Green; Walter P. Reuther; Willard Townsend; Samuel Wolchok; and James Loeb, Jr. For a complete list of those attending the meeting, see "130 Liberals Form A Group On Right," *NYT*, 5 January 1947, 5.

14. See also *n*2 Document 194.

BIPARTISANSHIP AND FOREIGN POLICY

> When ER learned that her colleague, Senator Arthur Vandenberg, who had just been elected president pro tempore of the Senate and chair of the Senate Foreign Relations Committee, did not want to return to the United Nations and that he saw no reason for both major political parties to be represented in the American delegation, she urged him to reconsider.

179

Eleanor Roosevelt to Arthur Vandenberg
6 January 1947 [New York City]

Dear Senator Vandenberg:

I have been thinking over your proposal that there should not be on the United States delegation in the future, bi-partisan representation from Congress.

I can quite well see why you and Senator Connolly feel it is not only a burden, but an impossibility to carry out the tasks you have at home as well as abroad. However the only reason we have carried as much weight as we have in the United Nations is because people feel that since we had bi-partisan representation, we really were speaking with some authority. Otherwise the United States delegation would always labor under the difficulty of having other nations feel it might agree to something which would never get through Congress, and the influence and ability to accomplish things would be very small. I do not want to see the United States placed in this position. Now that we have a Republican controlled Congress,[1] I feel it more important than ever that there be bi-partisan representation on the delegations and at the meetings with the Secretary of State or whoever goes to represent him.

The forthcoming meeting in Moscow in March will be important.[2] Would it not be possible for you and Senator Connolly to designate some one on the Foreign Affairs Committee, and the same in the House?[3] These people could keep in close touch with you so that the nations dealing with us will feel that our representatives really speak for the whole government and not for just one branch of the government.

I hate to see you and Senator Connolly not continue your services because I feel very strongly that part of the value of continuous service lies in the fact that personal relationships can be built up between individuals and even if opinions have to differ, they can create a better feeling among the nations especially in these early stages.

I wanted to drop in to see you while I was in Washington but I felt you were too busy to be bothered at the present time. I am deeply grateful to the Senate and its acquiescence in my nomination as a delegate to the General Assembly because I consider it a great privilege to be allowed to work with all of you. I want to thank you personally for your kindness and consideration and I hope that you will allow me to come to see you from time to time since your advice on many things will be much needed.

My congratulations and best wishes on your new responsibilities which you are now undertaking.

Very cordially yours,

TLc AERP, FDRL

Vandenberg replied in detail the day he received ER's letter.

180

Arthur Vandenberg to Eleanor Roosevelt
9 January 1947 [Washington, DC]

My dear Mrs. Roosevelt:

Thanks for your fine letter of January 6th.

I deeply appreciate the spirit in which you have written; and I readily confess that the questions you pose give me much the same concern as they do you. It is possible to canvass the matter adequately within the limits of a letter. But I want to be sure that you have my general point of view on the subject insofar as it can be portrayed in a few brief paragraphs.

Your letter deals with two phases of our representation in the General Assembly and in the Council of Foreign Ministers. One is that the representation should be "bi-partisan". The other is that it should be "Congressional". We can dismiss the former in complete agreement. Whatever our representation is in these international contacts, I cordially and emphatically agree with you that it should be "bi-partisan". I think this theory has paid infinite dividends in the last two years. I think it is one of the major reasons why your distinguished husband succeeded in his peace prospectus where the late President Wilson failed. So long as we can keep partisan politics out of foreign affairs, it is entirely obvious that we shall speak with infinitely greater authority abroad. I am emphasizing this fact in the speech which I am making with Secretary Byrnes at Cleveland next Saturday night.[4] (You may be interested in the enclosed press copy of the speech). Of course "bi-partisanism" is not automatically accomplished by the appointment of bi-partisan spokesmanship. It involves an equal degree of rank and file dedication here at home. Some of our more volatile and violent oracles here at home can jeopardize this result regardless of what our bi-partisan representatives abroad may do. (We have had one or two typical and sinister examples). But I repeat that there is no need to labor this particular point. We are in total agreement.

It is the question of "Congressional" representation which presents the difficulties. I dare to believe that "Congressional" representation in the General Assembly and in the Council of Foreign Ministers has been distinctly useful to the public welfare—as you yourself are good enough to say. I confess that I am very proud of the privilege I have had to participate in these enterprises. I think perhaps it was indispensable in the initial stages of this great adventure. I am not so sure that it is anything like "indispensable" when the new system of international peace and security starts to mature. On the other hand, I am increasingly impressed with the difficulties confronted by "Congressional" representatives because of their dual capacity. Of course it will always be true that a man cannot serve two masters. Yet that is precisely what I undertake to do—for example—when I, as a Senator sit in the General Assembly as a delegate. I am helping to make decisions for the United Nations which must pass in review before the American Congress. Having participated in the United Nations in helping to make the decisions, I am not a "free agent" when I returned to the Senate to function in my "Congressional" capacity. Indeed, it could be a most embarrassing and difficult situation in the event that I did not approve of some decision made by the United Nations. I should dislike to oppose in Congress anything to which I had given my consent (if only by reluctant acquiescence) in the United Nations.

This immediately raises the collateral question that we delegates—for example—in the General Assembly are not "free agents". Indeed, our recent commissions explicitly instructed us that we were to vote as directed by the President. I do not complain of this arrangement. It is contemplated by the basic law under which we are appointed. Nevertheless, it adds to the complications which have me puzzled. I may act under instructions (with which I do not agree) in the

General Assembly; and then I return to Congress under what seems to me to be a moral obligation to support, as a Senator, something which I did not and do not approve. In other words, I think there is a question involved here that goes to the typical "checks and balances" which are the real genius of our American institutions.

Ordinarily the General Assembly of the United Nations will be meeting at a time when Congress will be in recess. Ordinarily, therefore, there will be no conflict. But this has not been true of the Council of Foreign Ministers. Therefore, another question arises as to the extent to which an elected Senator (who has taken an oath of fidelity to his Senatorial function) is entitled to absent himself from the Senate to perform other duties. During the last fifteen months I think I have missed at least six months of Senate sessions. Under the British Parliament system this would be perfectly appropriate. But I think its propriety can be fairly questioned under the American system which deliberately separates and divides the functions of government.

All of these considerations would of course apply not only to Senator Connally and to me, but also to any other members of the Senate whom we might designate to share this "itinerancy". Furthermore, I think continuity of service all important. Indeed, I am not sure but what I shall be ultimately driven to the idea that our delegates to the General Assembly should hold full-time jobs the year round so that we can adequately prepare for the participation of the United States in the work of the General Assembly. I was deeply impressed—particularly at the recent session in New York—with the fact that the United States was not contributing an adequate measure of moral leadership because our program was essentially one of negation (except in one or two important instances with which you were particularly associated).

I suppose my feeling about the matter is accentuated by the fact that I was attempting the impossible at the recent New York meetings. I was trying to sit both in the General Assembly and in the Council of Foreign Ministers and meanwhile I was pursued by my long distance Senatorial responsibilities. Of course that is an accumulation of responsibilities which is more than any man can adequately carry or to which any man would long be physically equal.

Now against all of this argument I agree you can powerfully contend for the viewpoint which you have expressed in your good letter. All I can say is that I am irrevocably committed to the achievement of peace and security and justice. It is my paramount and final interest in life. At best I have only a few more years of service (or of life) and I have no wish other than to dedicate them to this objective. So I am prepared to do whatever circumstances may seem to require; and if they seem to require my continued intimate participation in the work of either the United Nations or the Council of Foreign Ministers, I am quite ready and willing to subordinate all other considerations. But I do not want to take these necessities for granted. I think they must be demonstrated to outweigh the other considerations to which I have heretofore adverted. Meanwhile, of course, we may be discussing a purely academic problem because any such continuing participation on my part is primarily dependent upon Presidential invitations.

Whenever you are in Washington I shall be delighted to see you. I shall always have the most pleasant recollections of our contacts in this great work. I congratulate you again upon the thoroughly fine and constructive and courageous contributions which you have made in connection with these labors.

Happy New Year and good luck!

With warm personal regards and best wishes,

Cordially and faithfully,
Arthur Vandenberg

TLS AERP, FDRL

1. After the 1946 mid-term elections, Republicans controlled the House 246 to 188 and the Senate 51 to 45.

2. The Council on Foreign Ministers was scheduled to reconvene for their fourth session in Moscow from March 10 to April 24, where they were to address the terms to be included in the peace treaties they would propose to Germany and Austria (Chase, 174).

3. The election results forced Connally and Vandenberg to trade positions on the Senate Foreign Relations Committee. Connally now served as its ranking minority member. Rep. Bloom sat on the House Foreign Affairs Committee.

4. In a speech before the Cleveland Foreign Affairs Forum on January 11, 1947, Vandenberg called for a "united American foreign policy so that despite some inevitable dissidence at home, America could enjoy abroad the enhanced authority of a substantially united front." He dared:

> to believe that, despite some distressing domestic interludes, it has borne rich fruit. In any event, partisan politics, for most of us, stopped at the water's edge. I hope they stay stopped—for the sake of America—regardless of what party is in power. That does not mean that we cannot have earnest, honest, even vehement domestic differences of opinion on foreign policy. It is no curb on free opinion or free speech. But it does mean that they should not root themselves in partisanship. We should ever strive to hammer out a permanent American foreign policy, in basic essentials, which serves all America and deserves the approval of all American-minded parties at all times" (Vandenberg, Jr., 334–35).

INTERCEDING FOR ILLEGAL IMMIGRANTS

In late December 1946, Joseph Rosenthal, representing a group of fifteen Jewish detainees on Ellis Island, wrote ER to ask for her "swift intervention" on their behalf. We "young homeless refugees, having suffered through the last years of the catastrophical world conflict in the German concentration camps," decided to "risk the step of coming here illegally." All "the pain and suffering which we endured during these horrible years" made it "very difficult for us to wait for visas." When they arrived in New York, the Immigration and Naturalization Service immediately detained them and "threatened" deportation, despite Rosenthal's insistence that all members of his group had "close relatives and friends who are prepared to take the full responsibility for our settling here."

Rosenthal then made a final plea to ER: "Our only hope remains that with the swift intervention of you, Mrs. Roosevelt and other prominent American personalities, that this edict again[st] us will immediately be annulled."[1]

ER then forwarded his appeal to Truman.

181

Eleanor Roosevelt to Harry Truman
7 January 1947 [New York City]

Dear Mr. President,

I have enclosed an appeal I recently received from a group of interned illegal Jewish homeless immigrants on Ellis Island and wonder if anything can be done to prevent their deportation?

With every good wish, I am,

Yours very sincerely,
Eleanor Roosevelt

TLS HSTOF, HSTL

Truman forwarded ER's January 7 letter to Attorney General Clark who sent the president the draft of a suggested reply on January 15. The president then sent the letter Clark prepared to ER the following day.[2]

182

Harry Truman to Eleanor Roosevelt
16 January 1947

My dear Mrs. Roosevelt:

This is in reply to your letter of January seventh in which you enclosed a letter of appeal sent to you by a group of Jewish stowaways who are now detained on Ellis Island.

I have taken this matter up with the Attorney General and he has carefully gone into the problem with the Immigration and Naturalization Service. These boys are part of a large group of stowaways who arrived in this country during 1946. Under the immigration law, of course, they are required to be returned, at the expense of the steamship company, to the ports of their embarkation.

The Attorney General advises me that because of the increase in the number of stowaways since the end of the war he initiated a survey to ascertain if there was any basis for relief. I am also advised that a Special Committee of the 79th Congress appointed from the House Committee on Immigration and Naturalization conducted an investigation of this situation at the Port of New York where the problem is most acute, and thereafter submitted a bill to the Committee for strengthening the existing immigration law pertaining to the exclusion of stowaways.[3] In view of this it is the Attorney General's opinion that since lawful immigration is so urgently needed by so many displaced persons, the greatest good for the greatest number can only be accommodated by lending all the facilities of our Government to lawful immigration and following a policy of strict exclusion of the illegal or stowaway immigrants.

As you know, in my recent message to the Congress I emphasized the duty of the United States to accept its portion of the world's burden as to displaced persons and urged the Congress to consider appropriate legislation to enable a greater number of displaced persons to lawfully immigrate to the United States.[4] I believe such a measure is of paramount importance and, as much as I am sympathetic with the plight of these particular stowaways, I am, nevertheless, of the opinion that their individual cases must give way to the larger problem of the many thousands of homeless people in Europe who seek to come to the United States as legal immigrants.

I am always grateful to you for your vigilant interest in matters of this kind. I am returning herewith the enclosure with your letter.

Very sincerely yours,
Harry S. Truman

TLc AERP, FDRL

---

1. Joseph Rosenthal to ER, n.d., AERP. For more on ER's attitude towards immigration quotas as they affected Jewish refugees, see Document 244.

2. After receiving this letter, ER wrote Truman again on January 20: "I appreciate your answering my letter about the Jewish stowaways and I can fully understand the situation" (Tom Clark to Harry Truman, 15 January 1947 and attachment; ER to Harry Truman, 20 January 1947, HSTOF, HSTL).

3. Spurred by Justice Department figures detailing 1,909 stowaways had arrived in New York over the past four years, the House Committee on Immigration and Naturalization appointed a subcommittee, headed by Erland Herald Hedrick (D-WV) to conduct an investigation of the Port of New York on June 28 and 29, 1946. Hedrick found this situation "very serious" and argued that "we've got to start clamping down. If not we'll be swamped by stowaways."

Hedrick then submitted a bill to the committee that would have amended Section 3 of the Immigration Act of 1917. The current law denied stowaways entry into the United States, but included the qualification: "except that such stowaway, if otherwise admissible, may be admitted in the discretion of the Attorney General." The senator proposed deleting the clause granting stowaways the right to appeal and fining ship agents $1,000 per stowaway found onboard their vessel. The committee approved Hedrick's bill and submitted it to the full House; however, it never made it to the floor for a vote ("House Group Sets Stowaway Inquiry," *NYT*, 27 June 1946, 14; "House Group Ends Stowaway Inquiry," *NYT*, 30 June 1946, 39; E. H. Hedrick, H.R. 6996 and accompanying report, H. Rep. 2560, 79th Cong., 2nd sess., 1946).

4. In his January 6 State of the Union address, Truman told the nation:

> The United States can be proud of its share in caring for peoples reduced to want by the ravages of war, and in aiding nations to restore their national autonomy. We have shipped more supplies to the hungry peoples of the world since the end of the war than all other countries combined.

> However, insofar as admitting displaced persons is concerned, I do not think that the United States has done its part. Only about 5,000 of them have entered this country since May, 1946. The fact is that the executive agencies are now doing all that is reasonably possible under limitations of the existing law and established quota. And definite assistance in the form of new legislation is needed. I urge the Congress to turn its attention to this world problem in an effort to find ways whereby we can fulfill our responsibilities to these thousands of homeless and suffering refugees of all faiths ("The Text of Truman's Call on Congress to Meet the Country's Grave Problems," *NYT*, 7 January 1947, 16).

ON THE PROPOSED WOMEN'S INTERNATIONAL
INFORMATION SERVICE

Both Lady Stella Reading and ER had attended the International Assembly of Women held the previous October.[1] Lady Reading, disturbed by the well-organized efforts of the assembly's Communist delegates, later proposed to ER that women attending international meetings be trained to defend democratic principles against Communist criticisms and that an independent, voluntary agency be created to provide the world's women with unbiased information on topics of interest to them. ER later conveyed Reading's suggestion to Secretary Byrnes, and sent the following summary of Reading's proposals to Assistant Secretary Acheson.

183

Eleanor Roosevelt to Dean Acheson
8 January 1947 [New York City]

Dear Mr. Secretary:

When I saw Secretary Byrnes the other day I promised to send him a memo on a subject which had been discussed when Lady Reading was here last. I am sending it to you for your advice and final decision as to what should be done.[2]

Lady Reading came over here to attend a meeting called under the auspices of the American Women's Voluntary Services and a number of American women's sponsoring organizations. They met at South Kortright, New York, last autumn and fifty-six countries were represented.[3]

It became evident very soon that from various countries there were delegates with decided communist leanings, and these were often the ablest of people, besides being well disciplined and directed.[4]

This group wants to do something to hold the women together and to be of service to women in different countries and yet they do not want to be entirely in the hands of the communist. Lady Reading agreed she would run, on a voluntary basis for a few years, an information service to be used as "clearing ground for all subjects that the women were interested in, operated until such time as UNESCO could take it over and run it permanently," if they thought it worth while.[5] Lady Reading agreed to do this on a voluntary basis if the United States would send over two volunteers. I think she found these volunteers and they are now at work in London with some British volunteers. She then discussed with Mr. H. M. Phillips and with Sir Alexander Cadogan and Lord Inver-Chapel,[6] the fact that she had found definite anti-British feeling, to a great extent among the Americans, but what was even more important, she had found that the women representing the communist thinking were apt to dominate every meeting. She felt it was important to find a few women with backing from the Foreign Office and the State Department to get together, work in London and talk the whole situation over of how women could be prepared to attend these international meetings and to defend the democratic point of view and not to be bowled over by the communists.

We of the democracies, have not trained women and it may be that it is rather essential at the present time.

Lady Reading talked to Mr. Freeman Matthews of the State Department[7] at some length, and he might be willing to tell you more about it.

Mr. Byrnes seemed to think that this was something which perhaps at once might be taken up by UNESCO though Lady Reading's idea had been that after two or three women had met in

London, talked over the whole situation, a much bigger meeting might be held in this country and plans for education fully defined before UNESCO took over. It may be that UNESCO might like to take over at once and I would be grateful if the proper person could consider this letter and let me know what to say to Lady Reading who is clamoring for something to be done![8]

Very cordially yours,
Eleanor Roosevelt

TLS RG59, NARA II

Acheson finally replied after receiving ER's third letter.

184

Dean Acheson to Eleanor Roosevelt[9]
19 February 1947

My dear Mrs. Roosevelt:

I regret the delay in replying to your letters of January 30, and February 13, 1947, in regard to sending one or two women to England to discuss with Lady Reading the establishment of a women's international information service pending full operation of UNESCO.[10]

The Department has indicated to the British Embassy that it has no objection to this project as long as it is a voluntary one. I do not believe, therefore, that I should indicate individuals who might be asked to meet with Lady Reading in London, but you might find it helpful to discuss this situation with Miss Doris Cochrane of the Department who is thoroughly familiar with the project and has a wide acquaintance among women's groups. She would be glad to see you in New York at your convenience. She can be reached here by telephone on extension 417.[11]

The Women's International Democratic Federation is becoming increasingly active and a voluntary organization of a different type could be of value.[12]

Sincerely yours,

TLcst RG59, NARA II

In April 1947, Lady Stella Reading, founder of the Women's Voluntary Service (WVS)[13] of the United Kingdom, received an offer of the chairmanship of the International Council of Women (ICW).[14] In light of their previous attempts to establish an organization dedicated to preparing British and American women to counteract arguments their Communist counterparts advanced, Lady Reading wrote to ER April 21, explaining her reasons for declining the ICW position.

> … I have so serious a programme here, and so much to do both from the WVS and the BBC angle, that I did not dare take on anything further. It would obviously be mad to take on the International Chairmanship unless one was able to devote a good deal of attention to it and, therefore, very regretfully I have had to refuse it. I am deeply conscious of the fact that I may be making a great mistake in doing this, but as you know, our economic and national sit-

uation here is generally so serious, that I feel I must devote every ounce of my energies to it.[15]

ER responded, offering her support for Reading's decision.

185

Eleanor Roosevelt to Stella Reading
26 May 1947 [Chicago]

Dear Lady Reading:

I quite understand your feeling about taking the chairmanship of the International Council of Women. I think you are doing the right thing to stick to the very important job which you are doing within your own country. Your problems seem to me tremendously difficult to face and I think it will require every bit of brains that can be brought to bear on them for solution.

The great trouble about the project which you and I talked about, is the fact that the State Department is not really interested in doing much about women.[16] It is so upset about its own program and contacts with the USSR,[17] I think it can give very little thought to anything else.

If I get an opportunity to talk to anyone again, I shall do so, but my last conversations with the State Department gentlemen were so discouraging that I decided it was best not to try.

I think of you often with great affection and concern, and admiration for the gallantry which you and the British women are showing.

Affectionately,

TLc AERP, FDRL

---

1. From October 11 to 20, 1946, more than 200 women representing all forms of government and political ideologies (including former Axis powers) met in New York's Catskills Mountains to promote "a road to understanding" and foster approaches to "common problems" in ways that "knock down the walls of prejudice" and "whittle away at their conceptions of national sovereignty in order to create international understanding." ER, who helped sponsor the gathering, addressed its opening assembly, telling the delegates that "this meeting will be effective because it is bringing together women from all parts of the world with a willingness to discuss their differences" ("Women Delegates Arrive for Parley," *NYT*, 11 October 1946, 36; Lucy Greenbaum, "Women of 53 Lands Meet in Catskills," *NYT*, 14 October 1946, 20).

2. Neither ER nor the State Department retained a copy of this memorandum and Lady Reading's papers were not preserved; therefore, its full contents remain unknown.

3. Other sponsors included the National Council for Negro Women, the Greek Red Cross, and the National League of Italian Women.

4. Among the delegates to the assembly were Tsola Dragoycheva, a member of the Bulgarian Communist Party Central Committee and Politburo and the Bulgarian National Assembly, and Madeleine Braun (1907–), a Communist and vice president of the French Constituent Assembly. A Communist Party member since 1919, Dragoycheva organized the Bulgarian Workers' Party before World War II, had been arrested and imprisoned for her party activities, and early in World

War II was condemned to death in absentia. After the war she won election to the posts cited above and, in 1947, appointment as minister of posts, telegraphs, and telephone.

Although Dragoycheva and Braun attended the ten-day meeting, the conference organizers, mindful of the split between the United States and the Soviet Union, did not actively encourage Communist participation or allow any pronouncements that could be construed as having Communist overtones. They did invite Russia to send a delegate, but no one came ("Women Delegates Arrive for Parley," *NYT*, 11 October 1946, 36; Lucy Greenbaum, "French Red Denies Moscow Cash Aid," *NYT*, 16 October 1946, 14; *WWSCE*, vol. 1, 257; Lucy Greenbaum, "Argentine Woman Assails Dictators," *NYT*, 25 October 1946, 5; Lucy Greenbaum, "Women of 53 Lands Meet in Catskills," *NYT*, 14 October 1946, 20; Rupp, 46–47, 244 *n*204).

5. The information service planned to "dispense 'unbiased information and data' to women world-wide to promote global understanding." It selected Mrs. G. H. Dunbar, overseas and special representative for Lady Stella Reading's Women's Voluntary Services, to manage its operations. UNESCO officially began work in November 1946, but was not yet in full operation (Lucy Greenbaum, "Argentine Woman Assails Dictators," *NYT*, 25 October 1946, 5; Lucy Greenbaum, "New World Board Balked by Women," *NYT*, 20 October 1946, 53; *EUN*).

6. The date(s) of Lady Reading's meeting(s) with Herbert M. Phillips, Sir Alexander Cadogan, and Lord Inverchapel are not known. Herbert M. Phillips (1908–1987), formerly an assistant secretary of the British Ministry of Labour and National Service, served as counselor for economic and social affairs to Sir Alexander Cadogan (1884–1968), chief British delegate to the UN. Phillips was also alternate UK delegate to ECOSOC. Cadogan, a career diplomat and war-time advisor to Prime Minister Churchill, also served as permanent representative on the UN Security Council. Lord Inverchapel (1882–1951), a chief British advisor at the Cairo, Tehran, Yalta, and Potsdam conferences and former ambassador to China and the Soviet Union, was British ambassador to the United States from 1946 to 1948 (*Who Was Who, 1981–1990*, 596; "N.Y.U. to Give Lectures," *NYT*, 7 July 1947, 14; "Bill of Rights Tied to World Security," *NYT*, 11 May 1946, 16; "British Name Economic Group," *NYT*, 22 February 1947, 39; "Sir Alexander Cadogan Is Dead; Represented Britain at the U.N.," *NYT*, 10 July 1968, 39; "Lord Inverchapel, Diplomat, Is Dead," *NYT*, 6 July 1951, 18).

7. H. Freeman Matthews (1899–1986), a career Foreign Service officer and a US advisor at the Cairo, Yalta, and Potsdam conferences, was then director of the Office of European Affairs in the State Department. He also spoke with ER about the women's information service sometime between January 8 and January 15, 1947. Matthews supervised the drafting of a reply to this letter for Acheson's signature in which Acheson said that he (Matthews) had notified the British embassy on January 10, 1947, that the State Department agreed with Lady Reading's proposal. Acheson concluded: "I trust Lady Reading has by now been able to go forward with her plans." Lady Reading received a similar response from the British Foreign Office on January 27, 1947 (Acheson to ER, 24 January 1946, RG59, NARA II; "H. Freeman Matthews, Diplomat Since 1920's," *NYT*, 21 October 1986, D31; J. Y. Smith, "H. F. Matthews, Career Envoy, Dies at Age 87," *WP*, 21 October 1986, B7; Florence Kirlin to Mr. Matthews, 15 January 1947, RG59, NARA II; Paul H. Gore Booth to Lady Stella Reading, 27 January 1947, RG59, NARA II).

8. For Reading's persistence in this matter, see *n*10.

9. An internal State Department note suggests that Florence Kirlin drafted this letter for Acheson's signature (T. Wailes to Miss Kirlin, n.d.; Florence Kirlin to Mr. H. Freeman Matthews, 15 January 1947, RG59, NARA II).

10. On January 30, ER wrote Acheson enclosing a letter from Lady Reading "in further reference to sending one or two women whom you trust to London." On February 3, Lady Reading wrote ER asking if it would be "possible for you to 'prod' your end so that somebody comes over? I am very much afraid as things are now, nobody will come before March and it is going to take … all

our time to get anything done quick enough to be of any value. I hate to keep on bothering you but I do feel that the matter is a serious one and I know that you … feel that there is urgency in getting preliminaries looked into, even if nothing further is determined on." On February 13, ER again wrote Acheson and enclosed a letter from Lady Reading. No copy of this second letter could be found in ER's papers (ER to Dean Acheson, 30 January 1947; Lady Stella Reading to ER, 3 February 1947; ER to Dean Acheson, 13 February 1947, RG59, NARA II). See *n*5 for information on the status of UNESCO.

11. See also *n*7 for Acheson's earlier correspondence with ER in which he makes this same point. Doris Cochrane (1903–1954), who worked with several women's organizations, joined the State Department as an informational and liaison officer in March 1945. She served as special assistant to the public liaison officer of the US delegation at the UN's founding conference in San Francisco. In his note to Miss Kirlin (see *n*9 above), Edward Thompson Wailes suggested that "unless Mrs. R knows Miss Cochrane shouldn't we suggest where she can be reached and then perhaps 'prime' Miss Cochrane by phone as to what it is all about?" The notation "done" appears at the end of the note with the initials FK. ER's papers contain no reference to a meeting with Cochrane (*RDS*, 1 December 1946, 180; "Cochrane Rites Set for Monday," *WP*, 6 March 1954, 27; Sonia Kwan to Jan Lambertz, 19 April 2005, ERPGW; T. Wailes to Miss Kirlin, n.d. RG59, NARA II).

12. Founded in late 1945 at an international congress in Paris and initially headquartered there, the Women's International Democratic Federation quickly gained a reputation at the UN for being Communist or Soviet-aligned and ultimately lost its consultative status within ECOSOC altogether in 1954. A US branch of the organization, the Congress of American Women, formed in February of 1946. The American group disbanded in 1950, under pressure from the House Committee on Un-American Activities, which viewed it as subversive, and from the Justice Department, which had ordered CAW's board to register as "foreign agents" (Stienstra, 86–87; Rupp, 47; Alonso, 144–46; Lady Stella Reading to ER, 21 April 1947, AERP; ER to Lady Stella Reading, 26 May 1947, AERP).

13. Reading founded the WVS in 1938 to enlist upper-class British women to help improve national welfare by collecting and distributing food and clothing, organizing fuel-saving drives, and working in hospitals (Hinton, 35, 172–75, 225).

14. Established in 1888 by members of the National Women's Suffrage Association, the ICW sought to address issues of education and workplace equality internationally. Dr. Jeanne Eder of Switzerland became president of the ICW in September, while the outgoing president, Baroness Pol Boel, presided over the Philadelphia convention (Stienstra, 48–49; "Leader in World Group Officially Welcomed Here," *NYT*, 3 September 1947, 32).

15. Lady Reading to ER, 21 April 1947, AERP.

16. On ER and Lady Reading's attempts to secure State Department backing for Reading's proposed information service for women, see Document 183 and Document 184.

17. The typescript in the extant carbon copy reads "USST," but the editors believe ER intended to write "USSR" and thus probably corrected it by hand on the recipient's copy before she mailed the letter.

ANSWERING A COLLEGE STUDENT'S QUESTIONS

Peter R. Lucas, a reporter for the *Yale Daily News*, wrote ER December 27, 1946. Knowing that ER's schedule precluded a face-to-face interview, Lucas hoped ER could take the time to answer the following questions for the Yale student body:

> What do [you] think that a college student, including the veterans, can do to help keep the peace that we have just won?
>
> What can the nation do as individuals to handle the question of the A-Bomb?
>
> Can veterans be of help in forming UN policies? If so, how?
>
> How can both the veteran and non-veteran student be of help in keeping the services from lapsing into the state that they were just previous to Pearl Harbor?
>
> What are your thoughts on College for veterans?[1]

ER answered his letter two weeks later.

186

Eleanor Roosevelt to Peter Lucas
11 January 1947 [New York City]

Dear Mr. Lucas:

In answer to your letter I think probably the best thing that any college students, whether veterans or not, can do is to familiarize themselves with the problems facing their own country and take an active interest in their communities in solving these problems.

I think as individuals they should back up the Baruch report and insist that there be international authority to control atomic energy and that we have inspection and punishment for all areas throughout the world.

I do not think that veterans can be directly helpful in formulating UN policies unless they are working either in the Secretariat or with the delegates or representatives in the various commissions or councils, but since everything that is done in the United Nations must be supported by the countries individually, every veteran can help form public opinion in their own communities and in that way create knowledge among the UN representatives of what the country feels on the various questions which are now coming up.

I have felt that probably a year of service for every man and even for every girl, might tend to make us a more healthy nation and to give us all a sense of responsibility which would extend from military service to our citizen responsibility. This might not prevent another Pearl Harbor but I think it would go a long way toward making us all aware of the duties of a citizen.

College for veterans is a fine thing if the veteran knows just what he wants to do and what he wants to achieve in college.

Very sincerely yours,

TLc AERP, FDRL

———————

1. Peter R. Lucas to ER, 27 December 1946, AERP.

ON AMERICAN RELIEF FOR GREEK DEMOCRACY

> December 24, 1946, Harry N. Boardman of New York City wrote ER objecting to a *New York Times* advertisement in which ER asked readers to contribute to a Christmas fund for Greek children sponsored by the American Relief for Greek Democracy. He could not "understand your permitting the use of your name" in such a manner and asked how she could allow herself to be used "as a 'front' for another Communist activity."[1] She responded two weeks later.

187

Eleanor Roosevelt to Harry Boardman
11 January 1947 [New York City]

My dear Mr. Boardman:

I have never seen a list of supporters of the particular Greek relief organization which Mr. St. John asked me to help.[2] He simply told me that they sent relief impartially, and I know they send their parcels through the Greek War Relief but as it is affiliated strictly with the present government, little or no relief would go to Greek insurgents.[3] I have always felt that women and children should be helped regardless of political ideas, and food and medical supplies should not be used as a political weapon. Hence I have been willing to help any organization obtaining these two things for any portion of the population of the country involved.[4]

I do see, however, that there are a rather large number of fairly well-known communists but I do not know that I feel for that reason that I should resign from a relief organization.[5]

Very sincerely yours,

TLc AERP, FDRL

---

1. The ad, based on a letter written on ARCD letterhead, signed by ER, and mailed to private individuals in New York, was a key part of a fund-raising campaign to provide relief supplies for 5,000 Greek children whose fathers had been "killed, exiled or imprisoned" during the Greek civil war. For more on the Greek civil war see *n*11 Document 87 (Harry N. Boardman to ER, 24 December 1946, AERP; "Mrs. Eleanor Roosevelt Speaks for Greek Orphans," *NYT*, 24 December 1946, 11; Robert St. John to ER, 24 October 1946, 1 November 1946, and 17 December 1946; ER to Robert St. John, 28 October 1946; Draft of Christmas Appeal Letter, n.d., AERP).

2. Broadcast journalist/foreign correspondent Robert St. John (1902–2002) co-chaired the organization along with Dr. Nicholas Cheronis. The sponsors listed in the December 24 ad included novelist Sholem Asch; August Bellanca, founder of the Amalgamated Clothing Workers of America; Pulitzer Prize–winning poet William Rose Benét; former Minnesota governor Elmer A. Benson; writer/critic Van Wyck Brooks; Brooklyn Borough President John Cashmore; Rep. Emanuel Celler (D-NY); American Labor Party candidate Eugene P. Connolly; Rep. Hugh de Lacy (D-WA); Rabbi Mitchel S. Eskolsky; actor José Ferrer; actress (and then spouse of Elmer Rice) Betty Field; Princeton University dean Christian Gauss; Mrs. Louis Gimbel; actress (and then spouse of José Ferrer) Uta Hagen; fashion designer and union activist Elizabeth Hawes; Rep. Ned R. Healy (D-CA); artist and political activist Rockwell Kent; attorney/activist Anna M. Kross; CIO founder Leo Krzycki; athlete/actor Canada Lee; actress Katherine Locke; novelist Albert Maltz;

John T. McManus; Rev. William H. Melish; interior decorator Lady Mendl (Elsie de Wolfe); labor leader Lewis Merrill; playwright Clifford Odets; poet Dorothy Parker; actress Katina Paxinou; Mrs. Lionel Perera, Jr.; Sephardic Jewish leader Dr. David de Sola Pool; archeologist Arthur Upham Pope; Rep. Adam Clayton Powell, Jr. (D-NY); Columbia University professor Walter Rautenstrauch; orchestra conductor Dr. Fritz Reiner; playwright Elmer Rice; New York City Teachers Union legislative representative Rose Russell; Rep. Charles R. Savage (D-WA); Lisa Sergio, a pioneer radio news broadcaster in Fascist Italy who turned against Mussolini; theatrical producer/writer/director Herman Shumlin; arctic explorer Vilhjalmur Stefansson; Oreste Stephano; Mrs. Alice Stephano; artist Arthur Szyk; UAW leader R. J. Thomas; Pulitzer Prize–winning author Carl Van Doren; social worker and director of the Russell Sage Foundation Mary Van Kleeck; journalist/writer Pierre Van Passen; and actress/producer/playwright Margaret Webster ("Mrs. Eleanor Roosevelt Speaks for Greek Orphans," *NYT*, 24 December 1946, 11; Robert St. John to ER, 24 October 1946; Program of the Press-Radio Wing of the American Veterans Committee's All-American Dinner, 24 April 1947, AERP; all biographical information comes from the *New York Times*).

3. The insurgents would receive no aid because the supplies would be shipped under the auspices of an American nonprofit organization with ties to the Greek government ("Mrs. Eleanor Roosevelt Speaks for Greek Orphans," *NYT*, 24 December 1946, 11; "Greek Group Joins Care," *NYT*, 3 August 1946, 6; Offner, 194–96).

4. ER often made this point. For examples, see Document 73, Document 140, and Document 193.

5. On a partial copy of the ad that Boardman enclosed with his letter, he identified Asch, Bellanca, Benét, Benson, Connolly, Gimbel, Hawes, Kent, Krzycki, Maltz, Melish, Merrill, Odets, Parker, Powell, Rice, Russell, Shumlin, Thomas, and Webster as Communists (partial copy of "Mrs. Roosevelt Speaks for Greek Orphans," *NYT*, 24 December 1946, 11, AERP).

ANSWERING A HIGH SCHOOL STUDENT'S
QUESTIONS

The previous June, against the backdrop of the San Francisco conference, ER addressed the Inter-Collegiate Institute, a gathering of high school and college students coordinated by the Collegiate Council for the United Nations.[1] Typifying the way in which young people often sought ER's insight on social and political issues, Beatrice Hauser, a high school student who had attended the conference, wrote ER seeking her advice for how her peers could better confront racial prejudice.

188

Beatrice Hauser to Eleanor Roosevelt
13 January 1947 [Sheboygan, WI]

Dear Mrs. Roosevelt:

Last June, while attending the Inter-collegiate Institute for the United Nations at Finch Junior College, I enjoyed hearing you speak on "Human Rights."

Now, as editor of our high school paper, I'm writing to you in connection with our observance of Brotherhood Week, February 22-29. On February 20 we plan to publish an edition with brotherhood as its theme.

I know that this is a topic in which you are deeply interested, and I feel that the students in our high school would respect your views on it. Would you please give us your opinions on the following questions?

1. What can we as high school students, in a community where there are no colored people, do to promote better race relations?

2. Do you think that prejudices against other races and religions in our own country interfere with the securing of peace in the world?

3. What influence did the war have on American prejudices?

Thank you very much!

> Sincerely,
> Beatrice Hauser

ALS AERP, FDRL

Although ER kept no outgoing copy of her reply, her secretary's notes indicate that ER dictated the following answer.

189

Eleanor Roosevelt to Beatrice Hauser
January 1947

In ans to your questions

1. You can work to make sure that there are no other discriminations because of religion. You can follow state and federal legislation for better opportunities for colored people and thereby build up a good background for the future.

2. Yes I do. It gives other countries definite points where they can attack our democracy. This is especially true of the USSR.

3. I think some of the young men who met colored men during the war, changed their attitude to some extent.

HLd AERP, FDRL

---

1. "Compulsory Study of U.N. Advocated," *NYT,* 30 June 1946, 6; "U.N. Contest Award Made," *NYT,* 19 June 1947, 17.

On Communism, Fascism, and Americans
for Democratic Action

Max Lerner, a Russian Jewish emigre who knew ER from his editorial work at the *Nation*, now edited *PM*, the ad-free, left-liberal New York City newspaper underwritten by ER's friend Marshall Field. January 9, Lerner wrote an editorial for *PM*, criticizing American progressives for failing to establish a unified movement. Admonishing the Progressive Citizens of America for "its lack of clarity and courage on the issue of dissociation from the Communists," Lerner also reproached the Americans for Democratic Action for further weakening the progressive movement by failing to promote "a clear distinction between being *non-Communist* and being *anti-Communist*. The first is essential for independence, the second can become obsessive and destructive." He then criticized the ADA for its "indiscriminate lumping of Communists and Fascists" and its refusal to invite Henry Wallace to the founding meeting.[1]

ER responded to Lerner's criticisms in her column two days later:

> In the last few days, I have seen two individuals express diametrically opposite ideas on Communism and Fascism. In Washington last week-end, Louis Fischer, the writer, said that the two were identical. He said that if you fought Fascism, you fought Communism. And I gathered that he felt that Communism and Democracy could not exist in the same world without one dominating the other.[2]
>
> Yesterday I read with interest Max Lerner's newspaper editorial stating his opinion that there is a world of difference between the Fascism of the right and the Communism of the left.[3] While one may reject American Communist activities, I gather that he feels it is not only possible for us to live in the same world with the USSR, but that it is denying our own belief in Democracy to question the right of people in other countries to hold their own political beliefs.
>
> However, I think that, for most of us, it is not enough to say that there is a difference between the Fascism of the right and the Communism of the left. We would like to have the difference spelled out for us. I, for instance, feel that there are many similarities in these two totalitarian systems. There are also great differences, but I am not yet convinced that I know exactly what these are.
>
> It seems to me that one basic similarity between them is that the individual, as such, is not given supreme importance—and that leads to certain cruelties and to a negation of human rights. On the other hand, the Communism of the left has just fought a war in company with the democracies to do away with the Fascism of the right.[4]

Alfred Baker Lewis, who also attended the founding meeting of the ADA, sent his objections directly to Lerner, calling his criticism of the ADA's lack of distinction between non-Communist and anti-Communist "not quite fair."

> There is only one sense in which genuine liberals should not be anti-Communist, and that is that they should never permit the government, so far as they have the power, to deny to Communists the fundamental civil rights of free speech, press, and assembly. Neither I, nor, so far as they know their records, any of the other persons who joined to form the A.D.A. have ever done that; on the contrary, they have worked to preserve the civil rights of Communists. Of course that stand in support of the rights of Communists is

perfectly consistent with political opposition to Communism and exposure of their attempts to infiltrate liberal organizations under various disguises.[5]

Doubting that *PM* would publish his response, Lewis sent a copy of his letter to ER and urged her to submit a similar reply to *PM*, stating that "the more that are sent in replying to his criticism of us, the more likely they are to publish at least one of them."[6] ER, as the letter below illustrates, did write to Lerner directly; however, as she then wrote Lewis, "I do not think it is very wise for me to appear in *PM*, because I do not want to seem to be forming an organization when I am primarily a member of the Democratic Party, and look to this new organization to needle that party into more effective progressivism."[7]

190

Eleanor Roosevelt to Max Lerner
19 January 1947 [New York City]

Dear Mr. Lerner:

Mr. Alfred Baker Lewis sent me a copy of the letter which he had written you and this gives me an opportunity to write you just a line, but not for publication in PM.

It seems to me that the "Americans for Democratic Action" are trying to do something, which may not succeed, but if it does succeed, it might be of great value to a great many liberals. The American communists seem to have succeeded very well in jeopardizing whatever the liberals work for. Therefore, to keep them out of the policy making and staff positions in an organization, seems to be very essential even at the price of being called red-baiters, which I hope no member of this new group will really be!

Very sincerely yours,
Eleanor Roosevelt

TLS MLP, CtY

191

Max Lerner to Eleanor Roosevelt
22 January 1947

Dear Mrs. Roosevelt:

It is good of you to write me about the Americans for Democratic Action, and I was also interested in reading in one of your recent columns a discussion of my editorial along with Louis Fischer's remarks.

I fear I have not made very clear to you my attitude on the ADA. I agree wholly that a liberal movement in America must be independent, and cannot therefore admit Communists to policy-making and staff positions. It is the failure of the other organization, the PCA, to say this sharply that has led me to criticize it on that score.[8] But I still have a caveat about the ADA, based on its statement lumping Communists and fascists together as equal dangers.[9] And I have some fear, judging from the rather narrow range of opinion among those invited to the Washington meeting, that it may develop a provincialism of its own. To my mind the danger of provincialism in any liberal organization is greater than the danger of Communist infiltration—great as that is. For provincialism means narrowness and leads to sterility. What we need above all else at the present stage of rebuilding the liberal movement in America is a sense of creativeness which can come only from the honest scrutiny of divergent opinions, and cannot come from excluding brands of non-Communist opinion which one may not happen to like.

I am certain that you agree with what I have said. But I have taken this opportunity to spell it out, so that there can be no question about where my emphasis falls.

Sincerely,

TLc MLP, CtY

192

Eleanor Roosevelt to Max Lerner

28 January 1947 [New York City]

My dear Mr. Lerner:

Thank you for your letter of January 22nd. I do hope the ADA will prove itself an organization of which you can approve.

Very sincerely yours,
Eleanor Roosevelt

TLS MLP, CtY

---

1. Max Lerner, "The Long March," *PM*, 9 January 1947, 2–3.

2. Louis Fischer (1896–1970), the *Nation*'s Moscow correspondent from 1924 to 1935, used his column to promote Stalin's early leadership. While covering the Spanish Civil War in 1936, his respect for Stalin cracked when the Soviet leader did not act more aggressively to protect Spaniards from Franco's troops. Yet even his muted criticism proved dangerous—ER had to intervene on his behalf to get Fischer and his family out of Moscow in 1938. He finally broke with Communism when Stalin signed the Nazi-Soviet Pact. Fischer, who had helped found the Union for Democratic Action, attended the founding meeting of the ADA where he argued with ER over how anti-Soviet the organization should become. Fischer, who believed that Communists waged an "ideological war," championed a vehement anti-Soviet declaration. ER disagreed, telling the delegates that "we must work to make peace with the Russians" (*ANBO*; Gillon, 21; "130 Liberals Form a Group on Right," *NYT*, 5 January 1947, 5; "Louis Fischer, A Correspondent in Soviet Union, Is Dead at 73," *NYT*, 17 January 1970, 31).

3. Max Lerner, "The Long March," *PM*, 9 January 1947, 2–3.

4. *MD*, 11 January 1947.

5. Alfred Lewis to Max Lerner, n.d., AERP.

6. Alfred Lewis to ER, 16 January 1947, AERP.

7. ER to Alfred Lewis, 19 January 1947, AERP.

8. For information on the PCA, see the header for Document 173 and *n*14 Document 174.

9. The *New York Times* reported that at its founding meeting, the ADA adopted as one of its tenets the following statement: "We reject any association with Communists or sympathizers with communism in the United States as completely as we reject any association with Fascists or their sympathizers. Both are hostile to the principles of freedom and democracy on which this Republic has grown great." For a list of the organizers, see *n*10 Document 178 ("130 Liberals Form a Group on Right," *NYT*, 5 January 1947, 5).

ON COMMON CAUSE

Natalie Wales Latham (1911–) served as Chairman of Common Cause, Inc., which characterized itself as "a militant citizen movement offering ... a definition of democracy based on the needs of today." In Latham's January 11 letter to ER, she described Common Cause as an organization grounded in the principles envisioned by Thomas Jefferson and Thomas Paine, which proposed "a program of community action to implement these beliefs." Declaring "that America must bring forth—for the world—a great and militant democratic faith that will surpass in its sweep and power the faith of any totalitarian system," Latham told ER that Common Cause would express "the largely unspoken beliefs of the great majority of the American people—not merely an articulate segment or the controversial 'right' and 'left.'" After explaining its "plan to build extensively in towns and communities all through the nation and through existing civic, educational and religious organizations," Latham then attached the group's statement of principles and asked ER "for your help and cooperation in seeing that its message reaches the maximum number of people."[1]

193

Eleanor Roosevelt to Mrs. Wales Latham

19 January 1947 [New York City]

Dear Mrs. Latham:

I was very much interested by the COMMON CAUSE statement of principles which you sent to me.[2]

The one division which I question a little is: "Help Defend America's Freedom by Helping Those Who Defend Freedom Abroad".[3]

There is starvation and deprivation today in many places where Democracy is not practiced and yet I think it is only by showing that Democracy respects all human beings and is inherently humane, regardless of political beliefs, that we will set the example by which people can understand as a contrast[4] to the totalitarian philosophy. I would give priority to those whose need is greatest, but I would never mix need and relief with politics.[5]

Very sincerely yours,

TLc AERP, FDRL

---

1. *IWW*; Latham to ER, 11 January 1947, AERP.

2. The six-page document to which ER refers, "Common Cause: A Call for a New Birth of Freedom," declared that "America is challenged ... both at home and abroad" by a new "Fascism: a second aggressive totalitarian movement which by appealing to the worst in human tradition and by setting religion against religion, nation against nation, and race against race would revive the military state and plunge all mankind again into war." The destruction of the Fascist powers, in sum, did not end "the conditions of insecurity, frustration, and fear out of which Fascism came continue to ride the world." For democracy to triumph, "America must bring forth a great faith" and show the world that democracy means "personal worth, freedom, equality, rule of law, public morality, individual opportunity, [and] individual responsibility."

The attached list of its organizing committee included several liberals with whom ER had longstanding ties: Adolph A. Berle, Jr.; Arthur Schlesinger, Jr.; Constance Sporborg; Dorothy Thompson; and Sumner Welles ("Common Cause," attached to Mrs. Wales Latham to ER, 11 January 1947, AERP).

3. This section of the statement of principles reads:

> The frontiers of freedom today rest in those countries which are struggling to preserve the free way of life and individual, religious, and national freedom under grueling totalitarian pressure. It is to the selfish, as well as to the humanitarian, interest of every American who prizes the free way of life to bring material and moral assistance and comfort to men, women and children who have suffered deprivation, starvation, and persecution because of their devotion to democratic principles.

> The names and addresses of people in France, Italy, Greece, Austria, and other countries, and lists of the simple everyday necessities of life which they need so desperately, will be furnished to any member of Common Cause wishing to participate in the work. Many of these people, both Jews and Gentiles, are in the displaced persons' camps in Europe, unable to return to safety to the lands of their origin and unwelcome in the devastated countries to which they fled or to which they were deported. Many of them have suffered terribly even during the period when they have been under UNRRA, and their fate is now more uncertain than ever. Aid must be given to them, and homes must be found for them. The sacred right of asylum for political refugees must be upheld against totalitarian efforts to force their return ("Common Cause," ibid).

4. Typographical error changed. File copy of document read "contract" rather than "contrast." ER corrected errors in ink on outgoing copies of correspondence only.

5. ER had made this argument previously. For example, see her August 23, 1946, column, in which she stated that she did "not want food and medical supplies confused with military supplies, since the former were sent to Yugoslavia to help the people" and that she hoped "that we will always distinguish between the people and their governments in countries which are not our type of democracies" (*MD*, 23 August 1946).

ELEANOR ROOSEVELT AND AMERICANS FOR DEMOCRATIC ACTION, PART 2

Henry Wallace reacted to his exclusion from the ADA by emphasizing what the ADA and the PCA had in common. He used his new position as editor of the *New Republic* to present his case in a January editorial:

> The point I want to make is that the liberals today in the so-called warring groups are about 90 percent in agreement. Some people who have read about "Mrs. Roosevelt's ADA and Henry Wallace's PCA" have written in, asking, "How does it happen that Henry Wallace and Mrs. Roosevelt are in warring camps?" The answer is, "We are not." I am not a member or an officer of the PCA and Mrs. Roosevelt, to the best of my knowledge, is not a member or an officer of the ADA. I spoke to one organization urging unity in the progressive ranks. Mrs. Roosevelt spoke to the other. We both believe in using the underlying liberal force of the country to make the Democratic Party into a genuine progressive instrument.[1]

Major newspapers covered the dispute with headlines such as "Liberals Attack Wallace's Policy"[2] and the United Press syndicate distributed articles, such as the one below, defining the debate as an ER-Wallace schism to its affiliates.

194

"Mrs. Roosevelt's Position"
23 January 1947

WASHINGTON, Jan. 22 (U.P.)—Americans for Democratic Action, newly formed "liberal independent" group, took Henry A. Wallace to task today for failing to remember that Mrs. Franklin D. Roosevelt helped establish the organization.

James Loeb Jr., secretary-treasurer of the ADA's organizing committee, said:

"It is unfortunate that Mr. Wallace, without consultation with either Mrs. Roosevelt or with responsible officers of the ADA, should have sought to give the impression that Mrs. Roosevelt has severed her connection with the organization.

Mrs. Roosevelt has authorized me to state that she has consented formally to continue to serve as a member of the committee of the whole. Mrs. Roosevelt served as chairman of the nominating committee at the Jan. 4 organizing conference. At that time she made it clear that because of other duties, particularly with the United Nations, and also because of her conviction that the leadership should be taken by younger people, she could not accept office in the ADA."

Pnews New York Times

Despite her displeasure with Loeb's "rather bad" statement, ER continued to discuss her differences with the PCA, writing in My Day that:

> I have always believed in Mr. Wallace's integrity and admired his ability, but that does not mean that you have to agree in the way in which you wish to work for your objectives.
>
> I made it quite clear, when I attended the first meeting of the Americans for Democratic Action, that I was not an active member of any new organization.

I am afraid I am too old and too busy to take on new activities. But all the members who attended that first meeting were asked to consider themselves a "committee of the whole" and, of course, I shall be glad to be helpful whenever it is possible.

I would like to see all progressive groups work together. But since some of us prefer to have our staffs and policy-making groups completely free of any American Communist infiltration if we can possibly prevent it, while others have not quite as strong a feeling on this subject, it is natural that there should be two set-ups. That does not mean that the force of all liberals may not go to some of the same objectives, and I certainly hope this will be the case.[3]

Mrs. Ella Johnson and her son Morse attended the organizing meeting of the ADA and headed the Progressive Citizens of Cincinnati, their local chapter of the ADA. ER's column so disturbed them that on the same day they telegraphed ADA Executive Secretary James Loeb:

> MRS ROOSEVELT'S COLUMN TODAY PRACTICALLY KILLS ANY CHANCE OF LOCAL ADA AFFILIATIONS NOW OR IN THE FUTURE AS IT COMPLETELY JUSTIFIES OPPOSITION ARGUMENT THAT THERE IS NO REAL DIVISION AND ULTIMATE UNITY IS POSSIBLE AND DESIRABLE. WE ARE AT A LOSS TO UNDERSTAND IT AND FRANKLY VERY DISILLUSIONED. GOOD LUCK.[4]

After reading ER's column, Loeb wrote ER that "all of us read your column carefully and were greatly pleased." Loeb, who had included the Johnsons' telegram in this letter, suggested that while "we felt that you had expressed your point of view carefully and diplomatically, but very clearly ... this reaction from Cincinnati indicates that it was not as clear to everyone."[5]

He concluded by asking ER to drop an encouraging and clarifying note to the Johnsons. Although no recipient's copy of ER's response to Loeb exists, her secretary's notes indicate that ER dictated the following answer in response to the Johnsons' telegram and Loeb's announcement in the *New York Times* regarding ER's position in the ADA.

195

Eleanor Roosevelt to James Loeb, Jr.
January 1947

Loeb—

I will write Mrs Johnson as soon as I have time.

I thought your announcement was rather bad as I am not attacking Mr Wallace nor other progressives

HLd AERP, FDRL

---

1. "The Enemy Is Not Each Other," Henry Wallace, *New Republic*, 27 January 1947, 23. Although dated after ER's responding column, the newsstands received the issues prior to the publication dates listed, thus explaining the chronological discrepancy.

2. "Liberals Attack Wallace Policy," *NYT*, 23 January 1947, 14.

3. *MD*, 25 January 1947.

4. Ella and Morse Johnson to James Loeb, 27 January 1947, AERP.

5. James Loeb, Jr., to ER, 27 January 1947, AERP.

REFUSING TO SPEAK IN TORONTO

After ER accepted an invitation to speak at the American Women's Club of Toronto in April, she received protests charging that the club discriminated against Jews. ER then telegraphed Faye McLean, president of the American Women's Club, canceling her appearance.

196

Eleanor Roosevelt to Faye McLean
23 January 1947[1]

I HAVE JUST BEEN INFORMED THAT YOUR CLUB DISCRIMINATES AGAINST JEWISH PEOPLE BOTH IN MEMBERSHIP AND IN AUDIENCES AND WHILE I HAVE NO RIGHT TO QUESTION YOUR POLICIES I CAN NOT GO BACK ON MY OWN PRINCIPLES SO REGRET WILL NOT BE ABLE TO KEEP APRIL ENGAGEMENT

ELEANOR ROOSEVELT

Tel AERP, FDRL

After receiving ER's telegram, McLean tried to reassure her by telephone. However, ER continued to receive protests. One of these came from Rabbi Abraham L. Feinberg of Toronto, who asked Florence Schulkind to convey his concerns to ER. The rabbi reported:

> I have looked into the Club's policy with the utmost caution. The assurances given to Mrs. Roosevelt are absolutely false. First, no Jewish women belong to the American Women's Club in Toronto, for the very simple reason that they were not wanted. I have definite proof that non-Jewish members who wanted to sponsor the applications of Jewish friends were definitely discouraged from doing so, because the Club is a 'social organization and has the right to restrict its membership.' The fact that the Club, which has been in existence for a number of years, does not have any Jewish women on its roster surely is not an accident. There are many Jewesses in Toronto with American citizenship who would have been delighted to join such a group if they had been acceptable.

Moreover, the Club appeared to have deliberately chosen a small auditorium so that the event would have "the nature of a 'posh' party for themselves" and estimated that only 400 of the 1,200 tickets would be available to the general public. The rabbi thus remained convinced that "many hundreds of women who feel themselves entitled to hear one of the most beloved women in the world will resent the 'exclusive' atmosphere which undoubtedly will prevail."[2]

ER then wrote McLean again stating that she wished to cancel her appearance.

197

Eleanor Roosevelt to Faye McLean
23 February 1947 [New York City]

Dear Mrs. McLean:

I am still getting letters of protest about the meeting I am scheduled to attend in Toronto, and in view of the fact that the officers of the Human Rights Commission have been asked to write a

Human Rights Bill with the aid of the secretariat and to have it ready by June 25th, which means holding long and frequent sessions between the time I return from my trip west the latter part of March and the 25th of June, I think I had better cancel my engagement to come to Toronto in April.[3]

Quite frankly any question of discrimination makes me very uncomfortable, I think it would be a much wiser plan for me not to keep this engagement. I am sure you will have plenty of time to find some one to speak in my place.[4]

Very sincerely yours,

TLc AERP, FDRL

––––––––––––

1. In a letter to McLean dated January 23, but not sent (probably because the telegram was sent instead), ER wrote that she had "been surprised to receive protests against my speaking for your club because you are alleged to discriminate against Jewish people in your membership and in your audiences. Of course, I do not know whether this is true, but if it is your policy, I am afraid that I will not be able to keep my engagement. I am against any form of discrimination."

ER drafted a letter expressing the same statements January 23, 1947. Although no recipient's copy of the telegram was preserved and the sender's copy had no date, the editors believe ER sent a telegram on the same day she drafted the unsent letter to guarantee the fastest possible transmission of her concerns (ER to Faye McLean, n.d., AERP).

2. Abraham L. Feinberg to Florence Schulkind, 11 February 1947, AERP.

3. The meetings of the HRC drafting group did not actually begin until June 9, 1947, and the full HRC did not meet until December, but it is possible that the meeting schedule had not been set as of February 23.

4. McLean replied at length on February 27. "Our Club," she wrote:

> like many similar organizations, does reserve the right to accept or reject any application, but to our knowledge no application has been denied by our club on racial or religious principles. It is true, as I told you on the telephone, that we happen not to have any Jewish women in our Club. This, however, is probably due to the fact that new members are sponsored by two members of the Club, and our social activities are different. I doubt if any member of our Club has ever been invited to join Hadassah or the Jewish Council of Women–again because we do not share a common social interest. It would not occur to us, however, to suggest that because we are not members of their societies they are discriminating against us. We all belong to the Local Council of Women and work together through that agency. Thus, we are at a loss to understand what appears to be an organized effort to sabotage your visit to Toronto.

She noted that the club had limited the presale of tickets to members to two so that most of the tickets would be available at the box office without discrimination to whoever wished to attend ER's talk. She also noted that the club had promised to donate $2,500 from the proceeds of ER's lecture to the Save the Children Fund. If the lecture were canceled, the club would be unable to make this contribution. "It was not until after I had talked to you on the telephone," she wrote, "that we advised the Fund of our desire to present the lecture on its behalf. We feel that if we should now have to tell them we could not present you, it would cause a great deal of embarrassment both to our Club and to you." Finally, she enclosed a transcript of a letter from Adeline J. Pearcy, president of the Local Council of Jewish Women, thanking her and the club for extending a warm welcome to her when she attended their 30th Anniversary Luncheon at which Constance Amberg Sporborg (see *n*2 Document 198) spoke. ER replied to McLean on March 6:

> I am sorry I can not reconsider my decision. You need not give the reasons I gave for cancelling this engagement. I am willing, however, to have you use all that I said, but if you prefer you may say that the change in the date of the meeting of the Human Rights Commission, and the drafting of the Bill of Human Rights, make it impossible for me to keep the engagement for April 15th.

On March 14, McLean wrote to say that the club had placed an ad in the Toronto papers saying:

> The American Women's Club of Toronto regrets to announce that, owing to the change in date of the meeting of the Human Rights Commission, and her commitment to assist in drafting the Bill of Human Rights for the United Nations, Mrs. Eleanor Roosevelt has cancelled her engagement to speak in Toronto on April 15th (Faye Gould [Mrs. Charles] McLean to ER, 27 February 1947; ER to Faye Gould [Mrs. Charles] McLean, 6 March 1947; Faye Gould [Mrs. Charles] McLean to ER, 14 March 1947, AERP).

On the Rehabilitation of Germany
and the IRO

> General George Marshall replaced James Byrnes as secretary of state January 21, 1947. In her first letter to Marshall in his new position, ER urged the secretary to meet with representatives planning the National Conference on the Problem of Germany,[1] led by her long-time friend Constance Amberg Sporborg,[2] to address their concerns regarding Germany's rehabilitation.
>
> The following is the first of many letters Eleanor wrote to Marshall during his tenure as secretary of state and one of several she wrote the secretary focusing on the reindustrialization of Germany.[3]

198

Eleanor Roosevelt to George Marshall
27 January 1947 [New York City]

Dear General Marshall:

Mrs. William Dick Sporborg and two or three others from a group in New York City, are going to try to see you in the course of the next few weeks. I hope it will be possible. I would come with them but I find it impossible just now to be away.

They want to talk to you about our policy toward the rebuilding and denazification of Germany. They feel strongly that Germany should not be left hopeless, that her people should be able to carry their own weight, but they also feel strongly that by some economic device in connection with the Ruhr, industries should be built up in other countries of Europe so that Germany should not again be the economic center upon which all of Europe depends for the wherewithal to run its industries.

The fact that the Congressional Committee came out with a report that we agree with Mr. Bevin that we must build up Germany and her industries as a buffer against our former ally, Russia, has deeply disturbed many of us.[4]

We do not know what your policy is going to be. We want to be helpful in every way possible, but we also want you to know what some of our anxieties are.

On a purely personal basis, I am anxious to draw your attention to the fact that Great Britain has not signed up for either the International Refugee Organization nor the Children's Emergency Fund. Her signing would be followed, I think, by the signatures of other countries so we would be able to bring these organizations into being, which we can not do until fifteen countries have signed up and 75 percent of the budget subscribed. Eight countries, I understand, have so far signed and less than half of the budget is represented by those signatories.

Of course, we have to wait until Congress acts on our subscription, but Great Britain's signature would certainly help here as well as in other countries. I do not know if there is any way in which you can make representations to the British Ambassador.

I am afraid that Mr. Bevin's press conference in which he said that Germany should be built up in an industrial way, has made some of us a little suspicious that their willingness to support the Anders army may not be as innocent and as altruistic as it has been announced to be.[5] In addition, there may be in their minds the question of whether it will cost them less to support the camps in their zone on somewhat the same basis that they support the German people by putting the camps directly under the control of the army. This would be a pretty heart rending situation for the displaced people, I am afraid, with very little hope for the future.

I am sorry to add to your burdens because I know your schedule must be a very heavy one so I hope you will not bother to answer this letter but if you can not personally see Mrs. Sporborg and the small group, I hope you will let some one see them who can tell them definitely how you feel about the situation and what you would approve of having done in the way of educating public opinion in this country.

Very cordially yours,
Eleanor Roosevelt

TLS RG59, NARA II

Marshall replied the following week.

199

George Marshall to Eleanor Roosevelt
4 February 1947

Dear Mrs. Roosevelt:

I have your letter of January 27 in which you indicate that Mrs. William D. Sporborg and two or three others from a group in New York City are coming to Washington within the next few weeks to discuss certain aspects of our occupation in Germany. You also told me that they are interested in our policy toward the rebuilding of Germany and of future economic relations of that country.

These, of course, are matters which occupy our attention to a great extent these days and we shall have much discussion of them at the forthcoming Moscow conference.[6]

I have asked Assistant Secretary Hilldring, within whose province these matters directly fall, to meet with Mrs. Sporborg and her group when they come to Washington; therefore I suggest that Mrs. Sporborg communicate directly with Assistant Secretary Hilldring who will be most happy to see and talk with her and her associates.[7]

You will undoubtedly have learned that last week Great Britain signified its intention to adhere to the Constitution of the International Refugee organization and to participate in the Preparatory Commission. Great Britain has served as an active member of the Executive Board of the International Children's Emergency Fund, although no member of the Fund has, as yet, made its contribution.

Cordially,

TLc RG59, NARA II

---

1. Although ER did not accompany the women to Washington, she worked with this "group in New York City" to organize the National Conference on the Problem of Germany (NCPG), held March 6 at the Waldorf-Astoria Hotel in New York. The conference further developed the position ER alludes to here. The press claimed that the NCPG's program was a reiteration of the Morgenthau Plan, but Sporborg and others in the group vehemently denied this characterization. Whereas the Morgenthau Plan called for the complete suppression of German heavy industry, the

NCPG desired a rehabilitated Germany. They argued Germany ought to be self-sufficient, but not so strong as to have the ability to wage another war. In order to ensure that Germany met both of these conditions, the NCPG called for the "expansion of industries for peace" in Germany as well as international control of the Ruhr ("Program Drafted for German Peace," *NYT*, 7 March 1947, 11; Mrs. Wm. Dick Sporborg, Guy Emery Shipler, and Jean Pajus, "Letters to the Times: Program for Germany," *NYT*, 29 March 1947, 14). ER first read the report, authored by committee member Jean Pajus, in 1946 and wrote Wallace that it described "a very dangerous situation" (ER to Henry Wallace, 27 April 1946, AERP).

2. Constance Amberg Sporborg (1879–1961), a long-time associate of ER, served as chairman of the General Federation of Women's Clubs Department on International Relations and was involved in several other women's organizations, including the National Council of Jewish Women and the League of Women Voters. An advocate of women's rights and a believer in the possibility of world peace through international understanding and cooperation, Sporborg represented national women's organizations as a consultant to the US delegation at the San Francisco conference in 1945. She continued her work in fostering international understanding as a member of the American division of the United Nations Educational, Scientific, and Cultural Organization. Sporborg also organized workshops to teach women about international politics and economics in the hopes of raising awareness of international issues among women's groups ("Mrs. William Sporborg, 81, Dies," *NYT*, 3 January 1961, 29; "Foreign Relations Theme of Seminar," *NYT*, 27 March 1946, 21).

3. See also Document 223 and Document 370.

4. On December 29, 1946, a bipartisan House committee endorsed the merging of the American and British zones in Germany in order to create a self-sustaining German economy and to serve as a "bulwark against the westward spread of communism." The plans for the merger originated with Secretary of State Byrnes and British Foreign Secretary Bevin. The two had signed an agreement in early December that called for the complete economic integration of the British and American zones by January 1, 1947. They claimed that the bilateral agreement was a step towards the economic integration of Germany provided for in the Potsdam agreement the United States, Britain, and the USSR signed in August 1945. Despite the State Department's claims, many critics of the Anglo-American merger viewed it as a complete rejection of the goal of Potsdam: cooperation between the Soviet Union and the West (Gaddis, 325–31; "Economic Integration of U.S. and U.K. Zone in Germany," The Record of the Week, *U.S. Department of State Bulletin* 15, no. 389, 15 December 1946, 1102–4; "Bevin Broadcast to Britain on Foreign Policy and Peace," *NYT*, 23 December 1946, 4; Herbert L. Matthews, "Bevin Says Britain Is Not Tied to U.S., Nor Cool to Russia," *NYT*, 23 December 1946, 1; "U.S. Is Urged to Strengthen Reich Economy," *WP*, 30 December 1946, 1).

5. General Wladyslaw Anders (1892–1970) led the 2nd Corps of the Polish government-in-exile in London, which fought in Italy during World War II. In a speech before the House of Commons on March 20, 1946, British Foreign Secretary Ernest Bevin encouraged Polish soldiers to return to their homeland and participate in the "free elections" to be held in January 1947. Declaring, "Our march to a free and independent Poland goes on," Anders refused to return to Poland and publicly spoke out against the "Soviet occupation" of Poland. When, by June 1946, less than 4,000 of Anders's soldiers accepted the chance to return to Poland, the British government established the Polish Resettlement Corps. Approximately 130,000 Polish soldiers were enlisted for two years in the corps, which was under the control of the British Army. The government in Poland reacted by stripping the members of this corps of their Polish citizenship for joining a military arm under the control of a foreign country. Britain argued that the corps was not military in nature, but served the sole purpose of training the men for civilian work so that they might assimilate into British society. Although Bevin denounced Churchill's plan to use these soldiers to monitor the British zone in Germany as provocative to the Polish and Soviet governments, an estimated 10,000 of these

Polish soldiers purportedly served in Germany as late as the summer of 1947 (Sokol, 17–18; Drew Middleton, "Bevin Bids Poles Go Home as Best 'Choice'; Warsaw Promises Land Rights to Soldiers," *NYT*, 21 March 1946, 9; "Anders to Press for 'Free' Poland," *NYT*, 2 June 1946, 25; "Anders Poles Get British Army Plan," *NYT*, 31 August 1946, 7; "British Reply to Poland," *NYT*, 14 September 1946, 3; "2,000,000 on Duty out of Homelands," *NYT*, 12 May 1947, 14).

6. The foreign ministers of the Big Four planned to convene in Moscow on March 10 to discuss the fate of Germany. The *New York Times* captured the hopes and anxieties surrounding the meeting when it declared the Moscow conference "is by all odds the most important international conference since the end of the war. It may well turn out to be the decisive conference which will determine whether the grand coalition that won the war by joint effort can also make a joint peace, or whether that coalition is fated to break apart …" ("The Moscow Conference," *NYT*, 10 March 1947, 20).

7. Major General John H. Hilldring (1895–1974) served as the assistant secretary of state for occupied areas from April 17, 1946, until his retirement in the spring of 1947. When the State Department recruited Hilldring, he headed the War Department's Civil Affairs Division (CAD), a post he had held since 1943. The CAD administered programs to ease the suffering of civilians in the occupied countries. As the State Department began to share responsibility for the occupied zones with the War Department in the spring of 1946, it asked Hilldring to serve as its coordinator with the War and Navy Departments on the forming of US policy towards the occupied zones. Marshall not only requested that Hilldring meet with the New York group, he also had the assistant secretary draft this letter to ER ("Hilldring in New Post," *NYT*, 18 April 1946, 5; U.S. Army Special Operations Command, Memorializations H, "Hilldring Conference Room," http://www.soc.mil/swcs/museum/Hmemo.shtml, accessed March 01, 2006; George C. Marshall to John H. Hilldring, 3 February 1947, RG59, NARA II; John H. Hilldring to George C. Marshall, 4 February 1947, RG59, NARA II).

DETERMINING THE HRC POSITION ON PETITIONS

The Human Rights Commission convened its first full eighteen-member session January 27, 1947.[1] Henri Laugier, the assistant secretary-general for social affairs,[2] opened the session. Laugier, who was recuperating from being struck by a car, left Nassau Hospital to deliver his opening remarks. Speaking from a wheelchair,[3] he told the commissioners that he "insisted upon being present in this first meeting" because he thought it:

> imperative and important to insist upon the fact that the battle for human rights is the very battle of the United Nations in their effort towards a better future. In any action undertaken by the United Nations in order to ensure peace, there is none more powerful or with greater scope than that which consists of ensuring the respect and defense of human rights in the whole world.

After reviewing the positions the UN had submitted to the commission for their review and praising the nuclear commission's work, Laugier then laid out the tasks he hoped the full HRC would complete:

> [You] will have to determine the drafting of an International Bill of Rights and to establish sub-commissions on the freedom of information, on prevention of discrimination, and on the protection of minorities ... I know that you will be equal to these tasks, the importance of which you are aware.

He hoped, however, that the commission would:

> permit me to draw your attention to a matter which I consider essential and by no means an easy one. I am referring to a problem which will be submitted to your debates and which involves the whole future of your action ... This is the problem. On the day when the United Nations proclaimed, in the Charter that binds and commits them, their faith in the fundamental rights of man, their will to ensure that for all, everywhere in the world, these rights shall be respected, on the day when they have entrusted the Economic and Social Council, and on its behalf, your Commission, with the tasks of handling all problems which arise from the defense of human dignity, on that day a great wave of confidence and hope ran through the whole world. Whether we approve of it or not ... what has happened is that for all individuals and for all groups in the world who consider themselves as victims of violations of the rights of man, a sort of right of appeal has emerged from these individuals and these groups to the authority representative of the supreme will of the peoples to the United Nations with its Assembly and its Councils.

> I shall leave it to others more expert than myself on legal matters to decide whether this right actually exists in the texts and whether the texts give an accurate definition of its essence, its scope and its limits. I am personally inclined, slightly, to doubt it, but you will, no doubt, agree with me that it is more important to acknowledge that this right is alive in the hearts and minds of men than merely to find it a dead-letter in an forgotten text.

Laugier then announced that the United Nations had received dozens of appeals asking that it redress violations of human rights and that the number of claims would no doubt grow. He knew this would be hard for the HRC, noting that "nothing could be more moving than this appeal which arises from the most distant parts ... requesting that we ensure everywhere the respect of these rights which make for man's dignity." He, however, had "serious doubts" about the HRC's "competence ... to conduct inquiries or hold hearings with both sides represented." After reviewing the scope of their authority, Laugier concluded that, in this arena, their duty was "to recommend measures … for the establishment of machinery for receiving, screening, investigating and passing judgment on all appeals from all parts of the world" to ECOSOC and the General Assembly. "These appeals, arising from the depths of the conscience of mankind, must find an echo … [and] a pertinent and just reply."[4]

After Laugier concluded his opening statement, Ghasa Meeta,[5] referencing ER's "very good work" on the nuclear commission, proposed ER serve as chair of the full HRC and that "the proposal be accepted unanimously." Carlos Romulo[6] seconded her nomination. Laugier then turned his gavel over to ER, noting that "we have all appreciated the skill, the distinction, and the impartiality with which you presided over" the nuclear commission.

_200_

Verbatim Report of the First Meeting of the Commission on Human Rights [excerpt]
27 January 1947 [Lake Success, NY]

Acting Chairman: Henri Laugier
Secretary: John Humphrey
Rapporteur: Charles Malik

(At this point in the proceeding Mrs. Roosevelt accepted the gavel from Mr. Laugier, and took the Chairman's seat)

CHAIRMAN: Mr. Laugier, I want first of all to thank you very much for coming here this morning, because I know how difficult it was. In addition, I want to say what I know every Member of the Commission who listened to your speech this morning felt, that you had given us a very high standard, one that we will find, I hope, the ability and the courage among us, to live up to.

I think now I must thank the Members of the Commission for having elected me their Chairman. I am deeply conscious of the fact that I am not a very good Chairman. I know no parliamentary procedure, and I will have to proceed as I did in the Nuclear Commission, asking advice when the questions are difficult, and doing the best I can with what common sense I have ordinarily. It is very kind of you to trust me and I will do my best.

I would like to add that I feel very keenly the importance of this Commission. I think appeals have come to me from people and from groups of people that had to do with human rights, not in as great numbers as have come, perhaps, to the Commission, to the Secretary-General, but they have come to me in considerable numbers.[7] I am conscious of that fact that human rights mean something to the people of the world, which is hope for a better opportunity for people in general to enjoy justice and freedom and opportunity.

We in this Commission know that many things will come up. We do not know at all, really, how we can enforce the things we may want to do. That is one of the things that has troubled me from the beginning. We have a mandate to write a Bill of Human Rights, and we really have not as yet any way to enforce our suggestions or our decisions. We have much to do, to first of all accomplish the things which have been laid down for us, and to think out the problems as they arise. I have a feeling that this Commission is so constituted that it will meet the problems and the work which lies before it, and do it adequately.

I ask your cooperation, and I will try to be not only an impartial Chairman, but perhaps at times a harsh driver. For if we are to do the work which lies before us, we will have to stick to the subjects we are discussing, and we will have to do it briefly and as consistently as possible, and we will have to do a great deal of work outside, as well as around this table.

I am not only asking your cooperation, but your forgiveness, if, at times, you think I am a harsh task master. And with that, I hope that we may now proceed to our work.

PVrbmex CHM, DLC

---

1. For the role of the nuclear Human Rights Commission that met in 1946, see header to Document 110.

2. A French doctor and scientist, Henri Laugier (1888–1973) served as the UN's assistant secretary-general for social affairs from 1946 to 1951 ("Henry Laugier, Ex-U.N. Official for Social Affairs, Is Dead at 84," *NYT*, 21 January 1973, 60).

3. Ibid.; "Mrs. Roosevelt Is Elected Chairman of U.N. Human Rights Commission," *NYT*, 28 January 1947, 13.

4. "Verbatim Report of the First Meeting of the Commission on Human Rights, 27 January 1947, 4–7, CHMP, DLC.

5. Mrs. Ghasa Meeta, usually identified as Hansa Mehta.

6. General Carlos Peña Romulo (1899–1995), a Filipino journalist, soldier, diplomat, champion of decolonization, and voice at the United Nations for the newly independent nations established after World War II, served as his nation's permanent representative at the UN from 1945 to 1954 ("Carlos Romulo of Phillippines," *NYT*, 15 December 1985, 1).

7. ER recognized the importance of these appeals too and the difficulty of responding to them but was convinced that they should not divert attention from the main work of the HRC. As she wrote in My Day almost two weeks later:

> I'm afraid that many, many people think that the Human Rights Commission is a tribunal where all people who have complaints can hope that their complaints will be heard. Over and over again in our discussions, it has been brought out that, if we do certain things, we will be raising false hopes among people throughout the world. These people will be disappointed, because they are looking anxiously for some answer to their dilemmas, and the name of our commission misleads them.
>
> The Human Rights Commission is not a court which can deal with individual wrongs. The commission, set up by the Economic and Social Council, is trying to formulate an international bill of rights for acceptance by the member nations of the United Nations. Once this bill is formulated and accepted, it will be a help to people throughout the world because it will be a yardstick for judging appeals made by individuals or groups who desire consideration for their wrongs.
>
> But it must be borne in mind that it would be improper for the Human Rights Commission now even to pass upon such communications received, since many of them would require investigating to ascertain whether the facts are as represented, and the commission has no machinery for investigation. And in many cases, such investigation would be contrary to one of the provisions of the UN Charter, which assures the member nations that there will be no interference in their domestic affairs unless there is a threat to world peace.

Eventually, many of these things will probably come up for consideration. In the meantime, the main objective of the present Commission on Human Rights is to write a bill of rights to be presented to the member nations. However, the communications received from individuals and from groups may serve a useful purpose. They may form a background against which the needs of people will appear more clearly, and in view of these needs, action of various kinds will undoubtedly be recommended in the coming months. Still, it would be unfair to let people continue to feel that any immediate help in their personal problems will be forthcoming through this commission (*MD*, 8 February 1947).

On Braden, Messersmith, Perón, and US Policy toward Argentina

ER continued to be concerned with the administration's growing acceptance of Juan Perón's Argentine government.[1] The public feud between George Messersmith, US ambassador to Argentina, and his predecessor, assistant secretary of state for American republic affairs Spruille Braden, over Perón's compliance with the provisions of the Act of Chapultepec,[2] exacerbated her concerns.

ER sided with Braden. She knew him; he and his family had been guests at Hyde Park during the war when Braden was US ambassador to Cuba and she "admired Braden's courage." Furthermore, she agreed with Braden that the Germans were "the predominating influence" in Argentine politics. She hardly knew Messersmith, a career diplomat, who, at Truman's instructions, worked to normalize US-Argentine relations.[3]

ER then turned to an old and trusted friend, Sumner Welles, for his interpretation. As undersecretary of state, Welles helped draft the Atlantic Charter, plans for the creation of the United Nations, and represented the United States at the 1942 gathering of all foreign ministers of North and South America in Rio de Janeiro.[4]

201

Eleanor Roosevelt to Sumner Welles
2 February 1947 [New York City]

Dear Sumner:

I am very happy that you find Cousin Susie contented and cheerful. I had one letter from her after she reached Palm Beach and she sounded so much better. In fact, she looked better from the time she made up her mind to go, and I am delighted that she could do it. I think she had great courage to rebuild the house in Orange, and I am sure she will be happy to go back to it.[5]

I wonder if you would mind telling me why you think we should come to agreement with the present Argentine government? It seems to me fairly evident that Mr. Braden is right in saying that the Germans are the predominating influence at the present time.[6] One of the leading women who used to be in the Pan American Union from there, complained to me bitterly that we were not sufficiently aware of this influence.[7]

Mr. Messersmith apparently thinks we should cooperate, but I feel somewhat confused, never having been to the southern part of South America and feeling that my knowledge is extremely limited. I have always felt that you had great knowledge on this subject and I know that Franklin counted on your advice, so I would be very grateful if you could tell me what you believe should be done.[8]

Please give my love to Cousin Susie. I shall write to her very soon. I am now serving on the Human Rights Commission and my time is so filled I hardly have a moment in which to breathe and therefore I have been very neglectful. My warm regards to Mathilde.[9]

Cordially yours,
Eleanor Roosevelt

TLS SWP, FDRL

202

Sumner Welles to Eleanor Roosevelt

5 February 1947 [Palm Beach, FL]

Dear Eleanor:

I am glad to have your letter of February 2. Aunt Susie seemed like a new person until last week. She came to have tea with us here at the house one afternoon and when I took her home she told me that it was the first time in some years that she had gone to anyone else's house, that she had enjoyed it very much, and that she had not felt in the least "nervous." After that she saw several friends at her own hotel each afternoon and I suppose got overtired. She subsequently had two or three bad days, but her nurse told me yesterday that she had gone out again and once more felt very much better. I will give her your message the next time I see her.

The question in your letter interests me very much. I will try to answer it as clearly and briefly as I can, given the background and the inherent complexities in the issues which your question raises.

I do not have to tell you that the policy of the United States toward the Latin American Republics until 1933 had been a policy predicated upon the thesis that the Monroe Doctrine established a United States sphere of influence within the Western Hemisphere and that the United States possessed the right to impose its will upon all of the other supposedly sovereign American Republics. At times our policy resulted in open military intervention; at other times in dollar diplomacy of the rankest variety; but at all times in an unconcealed determination to impose our own will upon our neighbors.[10] Nor do I have to tell you that the end of this era only came when the President made the Good Neighbor Policy possible through the participation of the United States Government in an inter-American treaty which specifically provided for the renunciation by every American nation of all attempts to intervene "directly or indirectly" in the internal or external affairs of any other American state. Subsequent inter-American agreements which year by year gradually built up a regional system of the Americas transformed the Monroe Doctrine as a unilateral instrument into a multilateral instrument. The existing body of inter-American agreements in their present form provides both in spirit and in letter for inter-American action, and not for unilateral action, whenever the interests of the Hemisphere are jeopardized.[11]

Notwithstanding the tremendous growth of inter-American solidarity from 1933 to 1944, there is still no nerve in Latin America which is more sensitive than the nerve which responds to the slightest indication that the Government of the United States is reverting to a policy of dictation, of domination, or of unilateral imposition. That is the key point to be borne in mind when we study our present relations with Argentina.

There is no country of the Western Hemisphere more traditionally antagonistic to the United States than the Argentine Republic. The first time that a real change in Argentine popular opinion took place was when the President was in Buenos Aires in 1936. He represented to them a symbol of the democracy for which they themselves hoped.[12]

I will not attempt even to list the chief developments in the Argentine picture since that time. I will only remind you that President Ortiz, whom the President met in Buenos Aires when the former was President-elect, who was determined to advance the cause of true democracy in his own country, and who was a convinced believer in full cooperation between the two countries when the war broke out, died about the time of Pearl Harbor and was replaced by a Vice President who was not only hopelessly isolationist but also a reactionary of the worst type.[13] The corruption of his Government, as well as the unsatisfactory international situation in which Argentina found herself, were in part the cause for the military revolt which took place in June, 1943.[14] I should also remind you that Argentina has been until now a country which has in reality been feudal, where except for very brief periods the Government has been in the exclusive control of a few great land holders, where the conditions of industrial and agricultural labor have been appalling, and where the local and national elections have almost invariably been rigged.[15]

At the same time I should stress the fact that there is no country in the Western Hemisphere which is more exaggeratedly nationalistic and where the reaction of the people as a whole against any attempt on the part of a foreign power to infringe their sovereignty more rapidly becomes a truly national resentment.

During the past three years this Government has lost no opportunity to injure the national susceptibilities of the Argentine people, first, by bringing open pressure to bear in order to bring about a change in their Government's policies and, second, by interfering officially in their internal affairs, particularly at the time of the national elections a year ago.[16] The result has been, as could have been anticipated by anybody who understood Latin American psychology, that Perón is regarded by the rank and file of the Argentine people as a defender of their nation's sovereignty, and has attained a measure of popular support which he would otherwise never have possessed. At the same time the friendship for the United States which the people of Argentina really had during the President's term of office has been transformed into a bitter and sullen hostility.

It is entirely true that German influence has been greater in Argentina than in any other part of South America, except perhaps in southern Brazil, but it is not true to say, as you do in your letter, that "the Germans are the predominating influence at the present time."[17] The influence which is predominating at the present time is Argentine nationalism, and it is only preponderant because of the policies which we ourselves have recently pursued. The last vestiges of German influence would have disappeared long before now if Perón and his leading henchmen had not felt that they would gain "face" by refusing to give in to United States imposition.[18]

What Messersmith is trying to do is the only intelligent policy we can properly follow in view of the recent past. That is to convince the Argentine Government that it is in its own interest to eliminate the last remaining vestiges of Nazi influence, to help the Argentine Government to do this within the framework of Argentina's laws and Constitution and to terminate a long-protracted campaign of public and official insults which are only conducive to an accentuation of the existing antagonism between the two countries. And above all else to operate jointly with the other American Republics, and not unilaterally. He will succeed in achieving every one of these ends if he is given the chance.[19]

Finally, I think I should emphasize the fact that, notwithstanding all of the many disquieting aspects of much of what Perón is doing, his policy is based upon an effort to construct a new social system in Argentina which will bring about decent living standards for labor, social security, and a reasonable division of the vast areas of land now held by a few individuals.[20] That he has real popular support cannot be questioned. Nor can it be questioned that the national elections which brought him to the Presidency were the first really fair elections that had taken place in more than thirty years. He is governing under the existing Constitution with a Congress in which he has a large majority. He is ignorant, a demagogue, and probably wholly unscrupulous, but his Government cannot yet accurately be classified as a dictatorship.

I know Señora de Martinez Guerrero and Señorita Maria Rosa Oliver with whom you may have talked. They are both, I think, wholly sincere in their democratic beliefs and in their feeling that the influence of the United States should be exercised in order to bring about an overthrow of the present freely elected and Constitutional Government of their own country.[21] Leaving aside the question whether any decent international order can ever be created if the more powerful nations, merely because their influence is potent, assume the right to determine what the governments of other independent and sovereign peoples should be—provided the existing governments of such peoples do not jeopardize the security of other nations and the maintenance of world peace—I can assert from the experiences of thirty years that I have never yet seen the United States undertake to interfere in the political concerns of another American Republic without thereby creating bitter feeling against it on the part of the peoples of such Republics. I can equally assert that I have never yet seen any lasting good result from such interference and that the very representatives of the political parties or factions that have been brought into power by such acts of interference on our part have invariably thereafter turned against the United States.

This explanation of my own beliefs is longer than I had intended, but I am very anxious indeed to make you understand why I feel as I do. I believe that every one of the problems we face in Argentina can be solved by resorting to the inter-American machinery which exists and by inter-American rather than unilateral action. I also believe that, if we continue the policies of the past three years, we will utterly destroy the inter-American system and the foundations of the Good Neighbor Policy which the President built up.

I am following with the closest attention and with the deepest interest the work you are doing in the Human Rights Commission. I most earnestly trust that you will have the drafts completed by June.[22]

My best remembrances to you, and believe me, as always,

Yours most sincerely,

TLc SWP, FDRL

Welles did more than express his opinion to ER. He publicly defended Messersmith and obliquely criticized Braden, writing in his February 12 syndicated newspaper column that Messersmith's efforts were being "deliberately sabotaged" by "persons" who "have tried to make American public opinion believe that the Ambassador's endeavor ... represents the 'appeasement' of a 'Fascist dictatorship.'" Welles then called on members of the Senate Foreign Relations Committee and the House Foreign Affairs Committee to investigate "every aspect of this situation in order to ascertain with entire precision who the individuals and influences may be that are responsible for a campaign which jeopardizes the highest interests of this country and of all the Americas."[23]

203

Eleanor Roosevelt to Sumner Welles
12 February 1947 [New York City]

Dear Sumner:

I was very much interested in your letter and grateful to you for going into so much detail. I also read your column today with interest.

What you say about our basic policy of getting on through allowing liberty to the individual governments and not trying to resume our old policy of domination, is absolutely true, but I am wondering whether the suggestion that was made of coordinating our military machines would not lead to legitimate suspicion on the part of governments outside of this Hemisphere and perhaps be considered in some ways as interference by these countries themselves?[24]

The difficulty in the Argentine is a very genuine difficulty because the line our Diplomats must walk is a rather intangible one, namely, we must try not to interfere with their internal decisions and yet we must do nothing which will show approval, in fact we should show disapproval of anything which encourages the Nazi influence.

Isn't it fairly well known that in almost all of Latin America, Germany has carried on a long time policy of infiltration and that there are now Germans who have inter-married to a point where they now have a good basis for spreading their power, and we do have to understand this and combat it in legitimate ways? I know I have been struck by the German relationships in families that I have met and they are not a great many.[25]

I realize that Russia, seeing the rise of German influence, has sent in her people under the guise of trade missions,[26] and I realize also that there are fertile fields in the whole of Latin America for the Russian influence to spread because wherever the middle class is weak and the lower class lives on such a low economic level as is the case in most of South and Central America, communism will make an appeal which, of course, makes the appeal to fascism easier in the monied groups.

I do not happen to know Mr. Messersmith at all well, I know of his record in Germany and in Austria.[27]

I have always felt that at the Chaupultepec Conference and at San Francisco we made a mistake when we insisted on the acceptance of the Argentine before she had really, as I understand it, lived up to her promises. However, like so many other things I felt my information was incomplete and I could not make up my mind.[28]

I have met Mr. Braden several times and I admire his courage, but I realize from your article this morning that you think he is not wise in his approach to the whole question. I would certainly agree with you that the policy we pursued to build up the Good Neighbor Policy was essential to preserving good understanding between our Nation and the nations to the south of us. I wish we had a clearer voice in leadership so that we could say to these countries—"follow our line to real democracy", and not be fighting continuously against fascism and communism without clearly sounding the bugle call for something in which we believe and know is better.[29]

Cousin Susie wrote me that she had had a few bad days, but she sounded very happy and quite well again.[30] I really think being able to see you and a few of her friends now and then, if she does not make too much effort, is doing her a world of good and I look forward to finding her much better when she comes back the latter part of March. I shall be back from my trip to the west coast by then,[31] and I will see her and if possible, meet her if you will be good enough to let me know the time of her arrival.

With many thanks,

Affectionately,
Eleanor Roosevelt

TLS SWP, FDRL

204

Sumner Welles to Eleanor Roosevelt
17 February 1947 [Palm Beach, FL]

Dear Eleanor:

Your letter of February 12 is exceedingly interesting. I would like to touch upon two or three of the points made in your letter.

You are everlastingly right when you say "I wish we had a clearer voice in leadership so that we could say to these countries—'follow our line to real democracy,' and not be fighting continuously against Fascism and Communism without clearly sounding the bugle call for something which we believe and know is better." That in reality is the fundamental issue. What the President represented to the masses of the people in the other American Republics was the personification of that "something better" represented by "real democracy." At the present time there is nothing here in the United States which to them represents such leadership. When you add to that the fact that Latin American public opinion will not tolerate any renewed attempt on the part of this Government to interfere in their internal concerns and bitterly resents insults to their sovereignty and that kind of hectoring and bulldozing approach to the solution of inter-American problems which our own Government has recently undertaken, you can more readily understand why anti-American feeling has been so rapidly growing and why Communism has been able so quickly to grow in many countries where, until recently, "real democracy" was truly the ideal.[32]

I fully agree with what you write me with regard to the San Francisco conference. Nothing could have been more stupid than for us to be maneuvered into fighting for the admission of Argentina into the United Nations until the Argentine Government had carried out the obligations incurred at Mexico City. Had we taken that position at the Chapultepec Conference and had we made it clear that we wanted the cooperation of all of the other American Republics in urging Argentina to comply with the commitments which she had made to all of the other twenty one American states, Argentina would have taken effective action before the end of the San Francisco Conference.[33]

I think you stress the importance of the German influence in Latin America too much. There are powerful German colonies in southern Brazil, in Argentina, in southern Chile, in northern Peru and in Guatemala whose members have for the most part been established there for several generations and the most of whom have married nationals of those countries. Because of their manner of being, they have always a potential influence and their attachment to Germany remains strong. Their local political influence is considerable. I have known of no Latin American country, however, where they proved to have any real determining effect during the Second World War and I am confident that their subservience to the Germany of Hitler was much less than the subservience of these same German colonies to the Germany of William II.[34] Nor do I think that Russia's activities in South America at the present time are in any sense undertaken primarily to counteract what you call the "rise of German influence" in that region. I am convinced that Russian activities have been undertaken primarily as a means of securing some leverage upon the United States and in order to bring pressure to bear with the idea of influencing our own policy should any international emergency arise.[35] It is precisely for that reason that I so thoroughly deplore our failure to perfect our own regional system under the United Nations. The standardization of military equipment in the Western Hemisphere cannot be construed as an act of aggression against the Soviet Union or any other power. It would be fantastic to suppose that any Latin American Republic would ever lend itself to any acts of aggression outside of the Western Hemisphere. The proposed Inter-American Defense Treaty could never envisage anything other than that which its name implies. And I should add that, without exception, every other American Government favors both the conclusion of the Inter-American Defense Treaty and the standardization of military equipment. They are deeply concerned because of the world situation and they sincerely desire full inter-American cooperation and the protection by this means of the Untied States, just as they wanted American protection during the Second World War.[36]

Finally, I have a confession to make which I have never made to anyone else and which, needless to say, I will never publish. I urged the President in 1937 to appoint Spruille Braden as Ambassador to Colombia. I did so because I realized that he had qualities of energy and initiative which had been demonstrated when he was acting as our representative in the Chaco Conference[37] and which I thought would be of value in eradicating the German interests then controlling aviation in Colombia[38] and the Japanese interests which were acquiring large properties dangerously close to the Panama Canal.[39] The President was very reluctant. He did not like him and he referred to him once as a "bull in a china shop."[40] In these more recent years I have often thought how right the President's estimate of Braden was. The President finally agreed to send him as Ambassador to Colombia[41] where on the whole he did an exceedingly good job. He did it, however, in such a way as to offend the susceptibilities of even such a wise and devoted friend of the United States as the then President, Dr. Eduardo Santos, whom you undoubtedly remember.[42] When Braden later went to Cuba he began to run amok[43] and his activities during the short time he was in Argentina were disastrous. The President was wholly right in his estimate and I was altogether wrong.

I shall send you a few lines later on to let you know how Aunt Susie is getting along and, if I am still here, when she returns to New York, I will, of course, send you word of the time of her arrival in New York as you have asked.

Believe me,

Affectionately yours,
Sumner Welles

TLS AERP, FDRL

205

Eleanor Roosevelt to Sumner Welles
23 February 1947 [New York City]

Dear Sumner:

I was very much interested in your letter and rather relieved that you do not think we need fear the German menace as much as I have been led to believe.[44]

I judge you are probably right about Mr. Braden and Franklin who on the whole had a pretty accurate knowledge of people, was right in thinking him a bull in a china shop. I think his intentions are good and his fundamental beliefs, but he just does not know how to handle people and attain his ends without too much friction. I never have known Mr. Messersmith and the few times I have met him, he hasn't seemed very attractive but you seem to trust him so I hope he will be able to handle the Argentine situation.[45]

As I wrote you I shall be away from the 28th of this month to the 23rd of March, but if you should need to get in touch with me, my office staff will be on hand at the above address and will know where I am every day.

Please give my love to Cousin Susie and tell her I will write to her in a day or so.

Affectionately,
Eleanor Roosevelt

TLS SWP, FDRL

---

1. After helping lead a successful coup in 1943, Colonel Juan Perón entered the Argentine government first as head of the Secretariat of Labor and Social Security, rising the following year to become minister of war, and later vice-president and minister of war, only to be deposed and imprisoned in October 1945 by officers jealous of his quick rise to power. Mass popular protest forced his release later that year and in 1946, "in one of the freest elections in Argentine history," he was elected president (*OCPW*). For discussions of his policies, see *n*16 and *n*20.

2. On the Chapultepec conference, see Document 23.

3. Stiller, 228–63; Page, 182–84; *MD*, 14 August 1944.

4. During the 1930s, ER and Welles worked together on several issues. In 1938 she backed his idea for an international conference (that was never held) to deal with fascism in Italy and Germany. In

1939, he supported her efforts to secure passage of a bill that would have admitted 10,000 Jewish children a year for two years beyond the German quota. After the war began in 1941, ER convinced Welles to convert an area reserved for the reception of foreign diplomats in Union Station to a sleeping area for soldiers passing through Washington, DC (Cook vol. 2, 305, 499; Lash, *Eleanor*, 571–72, 576, 656; *FDRE*; Sumner Welles to ER, 17 January 1947, AERP; ER and Edgar Ansel Mowrer to Bernard Baruch, January 1947, BBP, NjP-SC; ER and Edgar Ansel Mowrer to Lewis Mumford, 8 January 1947, LMP, PU-Ar; ER and Edgar Ansel Mowrer to Philip Murray, 14 January 1947, PMP, DCU).

5. In April 1946, an accidental fire destroyed the second and third floors of Susan Parish's house in West Orange, New Jersey. No one was injured, and damage was estimated at $30,000. At this point Parish was a semi-invalid and temporarily staying near Welles in Palm Beach, Florida. She would die in 1950, leaving ER a bequest of $25,000 and the responsibility for cleaning out her house ("$30,000 Fire Sweeps West Orange Home," *NYT*, 23 April 1946, 23; Lash, *Years*, 323; Lash, *World*, 328).

6. An engineer turned diplomat with strong ties to Latin America (his family owned the Braden Copper Company in Chile), Spruille Braden (1894-1978) served as assistant secretary of state for Latin America from 1945 through 1947. He had previously served as US ambassador to Colombia, Cuba, and most recently to Argentina, where he had publicly opposed the election of Argentine president Juan Perón ("Spruille Braden, Former Official of State Department, Is Dead at 83," *NYT*, 11 January 1978, B2; Page, 94–95).

7. Possibly Argentine political activist Ana Rosa de Martinez Guerrero (?–1964), who during World War II headed the pro-Allied organization Junta de la Victoria in Argentina, or Argentine writer/activist Maria Rosa Oliver (1900–1977), vice president of the junta. Both women opposed Perón. Guerrero and ER may have met at the International Assembly of Women in New York State in October 1946 where both spoke (*n*4 Document 159). At that conference, Guerrero discussed the Nazi influences "who are still operating all over the world." The Pan American Union may have been the Pan-American Women's Association (PAWA), a volunteer, nonpolitical educational and cultural organization founded in 1930. Fascism, World War II, and the rise of dictatorships in postwar Latin American countries caused the group to shift its focus to human rights abuses in the 1940s ("Mrs. Ana de Martinez Guerrero of Argentina, Foe of Peron, Dies," *NYT*, 5 September 1964, 19; "Argentine Woman Assails Dictators," *NYT*, 25 October 1946, 5; *ELAACL*; Fernando Perrone, "Biographical Sketch of Frances Grant," Rutgers University Libraries, http://www.2.scc. rutgers.edu/ead/manuscripts/grantf.html, accessed 28 February 2005).

8. George Messersmith (1883–1960), former assistant secretary of state and former US ambassador to Cuba and Mexico, succeeded Braden as US ambassador to Argentina in the spring of 1946. His instructions from Truman and Byrnes were to prepare the way for US military aid to Argentina and other Latin American countries in preparation for a hemispheric defense pact. Braden, Messersmith's supervisor, strongly opposed these instructions, and the two men clashed repeatedly over Messersmith's attempts to work with Argentine president Juan Perón.

By the end of 1946, when Messersmith returned to the United States for medical treatment, the feud between him and Braden was public. The two men met early in January 1947 but were unable to resolve their differences. Events in Washington, notably Byrnes's resignation on January 7, Truman's appointment of General George C. Marshall as secretary of state, and congressional criticism over the postponement of a hemispheric defense conference, postponed the resolution of the disagreement ("George Messersmith Dies at 86; In Diplomatic Service 34 Years," *NYT*, 30 January 1960, 21; Page, 182–84; Stiller, 228–58; "Braden Seen Loser By Shift in Chiefs," *NYT*, 8 January 1947, 11; James Reston, "Argentine Issue to Be Postponed," *NYT*, 14 January 1947, 21; Bertram D. Hulen, "Argentina Is Problem for Marshall," *NYT*, 26 January 1946, E7; "Our Ambassador Returns to Argentina," *NYT*, 6 February 1947, 9; "President Assures Marshall in Tasks," *NYT*, 24 January 1947, 7).

9. Mathilde Townsend Gerry Welles (1885?–1949), Welles's second wife, whom he married in 1925 ("Mrs. Sumner Welles Dies Unexpectedly in Switzerland," *WP*, 9 August 1949, B2).

10. On the Monroe Doctrine, see *n*2 Document 176. President Theodore Roosevelt (1858–1919) added what became known as the Roosevelt Corollary to the Monroe Doctrine in 1904 when several nations threatened to invade the Dominican Republic after that country defaulted on its debts. The Roosevelt Corollary, which provided for US intervention in the internal affairs of any Latin American country whenever "chronic wrongdoing" occurred, allowed the United States to take over the operations of the Dominican Republic's customs service and manage the country's foreign debt.

Subsequent US interventions in Latin America included a military mission to the Dominican Republic (1916–1924) and similar missions to Haiti (1915–1934) and Nicaragua (1912–1925 and 1926–1933) to stabilize the political conditions and allow American civilians to control those countries' economies. The United States also sent troops to Mexico in 1914 and 1916 in an attempt to encourage pro-American government and safeguard American economic interests there. Instances of "dollar diplomacy"—the advancement of American economic interests abroad—included the United Fruit Company's political influence in Guatemala obtained through its large-scale land holdings and ownership of ancillary transportation services (Boyer et al., 650, 652; T. Paterson et al., 230–38, 351–55, 357).

11. While serving as assistant secretary of state, Welles coined the phrase "Good Neighbor" to describe FDR's general attitude toward US diplomacy, but the term soon became associated only with FDR's Latin America policy, replacing the Roosevelt Corollary at the 1933 Pan American conference in Uruguay. As the threat of world conflict grew, US and Latin American representatives held a series of meetings at which they negotiated agreements that expanded the Good Neighbor policy to include regional solidarity in case of an attack from outside the hemisphere. After the United States entered World War II in 1941, all Latin American countries declared war on the Axis Powers except Argentina, which waited until March 1945 to do so. Some, notably Brazil and Mexico, sent military forces to aid the Allies (*FDRE*).

12. FDR went to Argentina in December 1936 to open the Pan-American conference in Buenos Aires. The combination of his speech, which emphasized his desire to unite North and South America through commerce, cultural exchange, and a commitment to world peace, and his public appearances made him the personification of democracy at a time when fascism was making inroads in Argentina. One local journal noted that FDR arrived, "just when he was most needed. When we were being coaxed to believe that democracy [had] failed and we must choose between Fascism and Communism, this great man has communicated to us his optimistic faith in democracy" (Freidel 215–17; Welles, 192–94).

13. Roberto M. Ortiz (1886–1942), an Argentine lawyer and politician, became president of Argentina in a fraudulent election held in 1937. Once in office, Ortiz tried to halt the fraud in the country's provisional elections, but his death in 1942 cut short his reform efforts. Ortiz's successor, Ramón Castillo (1873–1944), used the power of the national government to interfere with local elections and, once the United States entered World War II in December 1941, imposed a state of siege on Argentina that enabled him to suspend constitutional guarantees. For more on the Castillo administration and its relationship with the United States, see *n*4 Document 13 (Page, 42–43).

14. Although Argentina remained nominally neutral in the early part of World War II, Castillo's tolerance for Nazi activity within the country's borders and his government's appeal to Nazi Germany for weapons further increased tensions. At the same time, political, military, and civilian opposition to Castillo began to rise, particularly among Argentines who supported the Allied cause. Castillo's 1943 decision to nominate another conservative as his successor and his attempt to dismiss minister of war Pedro Ramírez (1884–1962), whom Castillo suspected of plotting with the opposition, galvanized the army into revolt in June (Page, 41–53; Whitaker, 111–13, 122–23).

15. The Argentine Constitution institutionalized oligarchic control of the government through a "system of national intervention" that allowed the president to suppress a province's constitution, remove the local legislative, executive, and judicial authorities, and appoint a federal "Interventor" to take over the local government and report directly to the president, without recourse to local or national law (Blanksten, 136–39; Page, 43; Ralph et al., 789).

16. In the aftermath of the 1943 coup, General Edelmiro Farrell became president in March 1944, with Colonel Juan Perón as his vice president. Concerned that Farrell's government was pro-Axis, the US State Department attempted to oust Farrell and Perón by breaking off diplomatic relations and applying economic sanctions (see n4 and n6 Document 13). Diplomatic relations were restored in April 1945 but the two countries continued to spar over Argentina's support of fascism (see n3 Document 23). When Perón declared his candidacy for the Argentine presidency in December 1945, US ambassador Braden publicly opposed him, believing Perón to be a fascist. Many Argentines interpreted Braden's anti-fascist speeches as calls for the overthrow of the Farrell-Perón regime. Braden's overt involvement in the 1945–46 Argentine presidential campaign continued after he returned to the United States, when he authorized the publication of a State Department report discrediting the Castillo, Ramirez, and Farrell-Perón administrations and accusing the Farrell-Perón administration of complicity with the Nazis. Braden's activities antagonized the Argentines and solidified support for Perón (Gaddis, 30–31; Page, 95–105, 145–46, 148–50; Whitaker, 148–49).

17. Though Brazil's German population (more than 2 million in a total population of more than 44 million) outnumbered Argentina's (approximately 300,000 in a population of more than 13 million), German influence was stronger in Argentina where the immigrants were better assimilated. The Argentines also valued German military training, with its emphasis on offensive warfare, and staffed the country's military academy with German military men (Gunther, 386 and chart; Herring, 67; Page, 22–23).

18. Perón exploited this nationalistic feeling, telling a campaign audience at one point, "The choice at this crucial hour is this: Braden or Perón" (Page, 149; Whitaker, 149).

19. On Messersmith in Argentina, see n8 above.

20. Perón continued the purge of the faculty from Argentina's universities begun in 1946 under the Farrell government. He also limited labor union independence and press freedom. In April 1947, the Argentine Chamber of Deputies, which Perón controlled, would impeach the country's Supreme Court Justices, further increasing his power and ensuring that his legislative program would not be declared unconstitutional.

On October 21, 1947, Perón introduced his economic Five Year Plan, consisting of twenty-seven laws to modernize Argentina's society and economy. The plan called for government and private ownership of business and industry. Perón hoped that the plan, which included initiatives for full employment without inflation and public investments of $1.5 billion to develop the country's environmental resources and its industry, would siphon wealth away from the large landowners, improve Argentine living conditions, and ensure a more equitable distribution of income (Stiller, 255–56; Page, 164–69; Blanksten, 254).

21. On Guerrero and Oliver, see n7 above.

22. The first draft of the Universal Declaration of Human Rights was completed on June 25, 1947 (Glendon, 70).

23. Sumner Welles, "Argentine Policy: Clarifying the Issue," *WP*, 2 February 1947, 11.

24. US military planners had suggested that Latin American weapons be standardized on US models as a preliminary step toward a hemispheric conference to hammer out a defensive military alliance against possible Soviet aggression (Newton, 360–64; Stiller, 259).

25. German settlers began arriving in Latin America as early as the sixteenth century but government-sponsored immigration did not begin until the 1830s when the Brazilian government fostered German agricultural settlements in the southern part of that country. Chile did the same in the 1850s and 1860s and German settlers joined these colonies and similar colonies established in Argentina, Uruguay, and Paraguay into the twentieth century. In 1940, all these populations remained small relative to the total populations of their individual countries. After the Nazis came to power in 1933, they attempted to create a Pan-German movement in German communities world-wide including Latin America—an effort that worried US officials fearful of a fifth column in the hemisphere. ER left no record identifying the old families she refers to in this sentence (*ELAHC*, vol. 3; Gunther, 386 and chart; Herring, 67, 232, 251, 254; Blanksten, 40–41; Newton, xvi, 29–30).

26. The visit of a Soviet trade delegation to Argentina in May 1946 and the resumption of diplomatic ties between the two nations in June 1946 worried US military planners and other Latin American countries who feared that an Argentina isolated from the rest of the hemisphere might be tempted to seek arms from the USSR. For more on the Argentine-USSR relationship, see Document 13 and Document 23 (Stiller, 224, 229, 251; "Argentina, Soviet Enter Relations," *NYT*, 7 June 1946, 1).

27. Messersmith, who served as US consul general in Berlin in 1933 and American minister in Austria from 1934 to 1937, was among the earliest American observers to warn of the danger Nazi Germany posed to the rest of the world. While in Berlin, he told Washington that Hitler planned to go to war and while in Austria he reported on the development of the Austrian Nazi organization and its threat to Austrian independence. For more on the rest of Messersmith's career, see *n*8 ("George Messersmith Dies at 76; In Diplomatic Service 34 Years," *NYT*, 30 January 1960, 21).

28. For more on the Chapultepec conference and the San Francisco conference, see Document 13 and Document 23.

29. For ER's previous encounters with Braden and Braden's approach to Argentina, see *n*6 and *n*8.

30. Susan Parish was a semi-invalid. See *n*5 above.

31. Over the course of three weeks (February 28–March 21), ER traveled by train to the West Coast to lecture and see friends and family (her daughter, Anna, and her husband, John Boettiger, then lived in Phoenix, Arizona; her son, James, and his wife, Romelle, were in Los Angeles; and her oldest granddaughter, Anna Eleanor "Sisty" Dall, was a student at Reed College in Portland, Oregon. Her oldest grandson, Curtis, was attending military school in Wisconsin). ER's itinerary for the three-week trip took her to Detroit; Chicago; Portland, Oregon; Chico, California; and San Francisco, Los Angeles, and Phoenix, where she addressed the United Jewish Appeal (Detroit and Phoenix), the Chicago Council on Foreign Relations, the Oakland YWCA, and Chico State College in Chico, California. She also attended the opening convocation of the Pacific Northwest College Congress in Portland, Oregon (*MD*, 3 March, 4 March, 6 March, 7 March, 8 March, 11 March, 13 March, 17 March, 19 March, 20 March, 21 March, 22 March, and 24 March 1947; Lash, *World*, 232–33).

32. Welles's reference to a "hectoring and bulldozing approach" probably meant Braden's efforts to impede Messersmith's negotiations with Perón. See *n*8 above. While Communists did make inroads in Latin America at this time, the number of actual Communists in the region remained relatively small (W. H. Lawrence, "Communism Spreading Fast in Americas, Survey Shows," *NYT*, 29 December 1946, 1; "Communists Claim 18,500,000 in World," *NYT*, 27 February 1947, 8).

33. On Argentina's admission to the United Nations at the San Francisco conference, see Document 13 and Document 23. On the Chapultepec conference, see Document 23.

34. William II (1859–1941), the last king of Prussia and the last emperor of Germany, whose expansionist polices and support for the Austrian-Hungarian Empire led to World War I and cost him his throne. He abdicated in 1918 as World War I was ending (*OEWH*).

35. The "Russian activities" to which Welles referred may have meant the recent rapprochement between the Soviet Union and Argentina, which was viewed by the American press as an effort by the Soviets to make Argentina "one of their key outposts in Latin America." See *n*26 above (Frank L. Kluckhohn, "Argentina to Sign Pact with Soviet," *NYT*, 7 December 1946, 10).

36. US military leaders first proposed the standardization of military equipment in 1943 as a way of allowing the United States to spearhead the defense of the hemisphere, thus heading off arms sales from other countries. Legislation for standardization passed the House of Representatives in 1946, but never went further because of concerted opposition from both sides of the political spectrum. Liberals believed the proposal would siphon off Latin American revenues from social projects and help dictators become more repressive; conservatives worried about treaty commitments such a program would involve, and the costs of such subsidies. Ultimately, its high cost and the priority of American commitments elsewhere—notably Greece, Turkey, Iran, and the Philippines—derailed the legislation, leaving the arms standardization issue in limbo. Nothing more would be done until Secretary of State George Marshall completed a personal review of US policy toward Latin America in the spring of 1947 (Newton, 360–64; Pogue, 381).

37. As chief US negotiator at the Chaco Peace Conference in Buenos Aires from 1935 to 1939, Braden helped negotiate an armistice to end the Chaco War (1932–35), a conflict between Bolivia and Paraguay over control of a large, lowland plain area known as the Gran Chaco, the ownership of which the two countries had contested since the nineteenth century. Paraguay won the war, and in the conference gained most of the territory in question (Page, 95; Murray Illson, "Spruille Braden, Former Official of State Department, Is Dead at 83," *NYT*, 11 January 1978, B2; *OEWH*).

38. Scadta, the first commercial airline in Latin America, operated in Colombia from 1919 until 1939. An Austrian engineer, Paul von Bauer, founded the airline and its staff was German, but its principal shareholder was an American company, Pan American Airways (Gunther, 174).

39. In 1939, some Japanese citizens purchased land in Costa Rica, 250 miles from the Panama Canal, ostensibly to grow cotton. Since the land was purchased at inflated prices and the cotton crop failed, some observers thought the Japanese had actually bought the land for air bases (*ELAHC*, vol. 3, 65, 313; T. R. Ybarra, "Japan, Reich Make Gains in Costa Rica," *NYT*, 13 February 1939, 4).

40. Braden hated both Fascism and Communism and did not hesitate to say so to his colleagues and the government officials of the countries to which he was accredited. Undersecretary of state Dean Acheson, Braden's supervisor when he was assistant secretary of state for Latin America, described him as "a bull of a man physically … with the temperament and tactics of one, dealing with the objects of his prejudices by blind charges, preceded by pawing up a good deal of dust" (Acheson, 160; Stiller, 231).

41. As US ambassador from 1939 to 1942, Braden's assignment was to keep Colombia, located near the Panama Canal, friendly to the United States so that American military resources would not be needed there. To that end, he pressured Pan American Airlines, majority shareholder of the Scadta airline there, to fire its German pilots and technicians and helped Colombia obtain loans from the Import-Export Bank (Gunther, *Latin America*, 174; Bushnell, 57, 119).

42. Eduardo Santos (1888–1974), a leading Latin American journalist and founder of the *El Tiempo* newspaper, served as Colombia's president from 1938 to 1942. An early supporter of collective defense in the hemisphere, he was also one of the most pro-US leaders in Latin America, and his relationship with Braden was close. Although he was quick to sever diplomatic ties with Japan after Pearl Harbor, Santos did not share Braden's concern about the extent of German infiltration into Colombia. Nevertheless he authorized restrictions on the German population there (*ELAHC*, vol. 5; Bushnell, 57–60; "Eduardo Santos, Ex-President of Colombia, a Publisher, Dies," *NYT*, 28 March 1974, 42).

43. Braden often acted in a most undiplomatic fashion. He clashed with Cuban president Fulgencio Batista (1901–1973) over the Cuban theft of lend-lease equipment, supported American business interests in Cuba, and publicly opposed American firms who paid bribes or contributed to Cuban political parties. Braden also became involved indirectly in a duel between a Havana newspaper editor who accused Braden of interfering in his newspaper's campaign to obtain higher prices for Cuba's sugar in America at the expense of US concerns in Cuba and a Cuban politician who defended Braden's actions.

In his memoirs, Braden also claimed to have bypassed Welles's command in the State Department by using a confidante of ER's to get FDR's approval. During World War II, Braden became frustrated by the practice of captured fascist agents bribing their way out of Cuban jails. He had asked Welles for funds to establish a separate, US-run prison for these enemy agents, which Welles refused. Knowing journalist Martha Gellhorn had a link to the White House, he directed her to brief ER and presidential advisor Harry Hopkins on the prisoner situation. ER and Hopkins then spoke to FDR, who authorized the State Department to approve Braden's request ("U.S. Envoy in Cuba Scored," *NYT*, 26 July 1944, 7; "Defender of Braden Challenged to a Duel," *NYT*, 30 July 1944, 12; "Warns Americans in Cuba," *NYT*, 23 September 1943, 11; Braden, 288–89, 300, 307–8).

44. For more on the German influence in Latin America, see *n*17 and *n*25 above.

45. Unable to resolve their differences, Braden and Messersmith left the State Department in June 1947. Accounts vary as to the details of their individual departures. In his memoirs, Dean Acheson says he as undersecretary of state took responsibility "to recall and retire Messersmith and to ask for Braden's resignation." Braden contended that he resigned voluntarily and only on the condition that Messersmith be recalled. As for Messersmith, his biographer, Jesse H. Stiller, writes that his subject learned of his "resignation" from an Argentine newspaper after Truman declared his mission to Argentina complete. For more on the Braden-Messersmith feud, see Document 201 (Stiller, 260–61; Acheson, 190).

PROPOSING GROUND RULES FOR COMMITTEE
DEBATES ON HUMAN RIGHTS

Before it began its point-by-point discussion of which rights should be included in the international bill of rights ECOSOC instructed them to create, the Human Rights Commission first had to establish the procedures it would follow when reviewing material. The morning of February 4, as the HRC prepared to review the draft bills of rights it had requested from various supportive organizations,[1] ER as chair laid out the following guidelines for discussion:

> [W]e come at last to the discussion of the substance of the Bill of Human Rights. This discussion will guide the working group ... We have eighteen Members of this Commission. While all eighteen are not here, I am sure that we have at least eighteen different ideas as to how we should proceed in discussing the Bill of Rights. Judging by our experience to date, I can imagine one Member putting a motion that we should proceed thus and so, and another offering an amendment that we should proceed in a somewhat different way, and so on, until we have a motion with seventeen amendments. After that, I can foresee the possibility of discussion as to which of the seventeen amendments is furthest away from the original motion, and then which amendment comes sixteenth, fifteenth, and so on. If, as seems quite possible, we proceed in this manner, we may get around to actual discussion of the content of the Bill by next summer, by which time we must be prepared for convening our next session.

> I would ask you to cooperate with me to this extent; to make an earnest effort, if your consciences will permit, to allow discussion to be handled in the manner which I am abo[u]t to suggest. If you cannot agree, then I ask your consent to limit speeches on what method we should use, to two minutes each.

> The method I propose is as follows: to base our work on the list of rights contained in the various draft bills—this has been prepared by the Secretariat and is before you, as paper E/CM.4/W18—and to discuss, one after another, the rights which are enumerated with one question only in mind, would this right be included in the first draft of the Bill. We would not be concerned with methods of expression or with questions of duplication, nor would we be deciding irrevocably that any particular right must be included. What we would aim to do would be to eliminate from the first draft any rights which it was generally agreed should not be considered for the present. After we have decided which rights to include and which rights to exclude, I propose that we discuss methods of implementation. I know well that some will feel we should discuss implementation first. Others, we should discuss rights first. Others, that we should discuss both, simultaneously. I urgently ask your consideration of the fact that it does not make much difference. We will have full discussion under any method, and that if you will allow me to lay down, at this time, the method which we should use, it will help us in getting through our work. We only have today, tomorrow, and Thursday. After that, I propose that we discuss the form of the Bill.

> To sum up, my proposal is that we discuss first what rights should or should not be included; second, methods of implementation; third, form of the Bill. If this is not satisfactory, I propose that debate on our method of procedure be limited to speeches of not more than two minutes each.[2]

The commission adopted ER's suggestion. As it debated which rights to include or exclude, the commission then decided that the best guide the drafting committee could receive from it was a verbatim transcript of this discussion, rather than a mere up and down article-by-article vote.[3]

By lunchtime, the commission concurred that the principles of equal rights and the unity of the human race should be included in the bill and had moved on to a discussion of what should be included under the principle of liberty.[4]

When this discussion continued in the fourteenth meeting, sharp philosophical differences emerged. The statements made by Charles Malik of Lebanon and Valentin Tepliakov of the Soviet Union reflect the deep division in the commission between those who believed in the need to protect the rights of the individual from the power of the state and those who believed that the individual should serve the state, or, as ER put it in her response to these statements, between those who "believe that an organized society in the form of a government, exists for the good of the individual" and those who "believe that an organized society in the form of a government, exists for the benefit of a group." This basic difference, which permeated the detailed debates in the HRC about individual articles of the declaration of human rights, made ER's task of steering the commission toward agreement extremely difficult.

206

Commission on Human Rights
Verbatim Record
Fourteenth Meeting [excerpt][5]
4 February 1947 [Lake Success, NY]

CHAIRMAN: Eleanor Roosevelt
RAPPORTEUR: Charles Malik
SECRETARY: John Humphrey

MR. MALIK (Lebanon): Madam Chairman, I would like to make a few general observations about this paper which we have before us and about all three groups taken together, if I may.[6]

What interests me most concerning this question of the Bill of Rights is the whole problem of personal liberty. Now, we are wont usually to use such phrases as personal liberty and freedom of speech and opinion, freedom of information and of the press, and freedom of religious worship, etc.—we are wont to use these phrases, I think, many a time glibly, without full appreciation of the infinite importance of what these phrases really mean. I say this because, I think, if we fail in the formulation of our International Bill of Rights, it is not going to be on the grounds of failing to state explicitly the rights of the individual for food and housing and work and migration, and this, and that, but rather on the grounds of our failing to allow sufficiently for this all-fundamental problem of personal liberty.

My Yugoslav friend and neighbor the other day, in his remarkable speech, said that the social principle today comes first.[7] He defined liberty as the perfect harmony between the individual and the collectivity. Another phrase he used was the identity of interests of society and the individual. Still another phrase was the identity of the rights of individuals with those of society. This is a very well-known doctrine which originally, of course, was taken from Hegel.[8] Then my Yugoslav friend went on to say immediately after that, that the social principle today comes first. So, on the one hand, we have the definition of liberty as the perfect harmony between the individual and society, and on the other the affirmation that society comes first. Now, this means, as I take it, that the

Socialist principle today is dominant throughout the world, or is increasingly becoming so. This is truly a mark of our age, the rise of Social consciousness in its various forms, groups becoming conscious, nations, various types of associations becoming self-conscious.

If I understand the present age correctly, this is our problem; the struggle between the human person and his own personality and freedom on the one hand, and the endless pressure of groups on the other, including, of course, his own nation.

For one must belong to a group today. He must have his identification papers. He must have social loyalties. He must belong to some association.

The claims of groups today—and especially the political group, the nation embodying itself in the institution called the state—are becoming increasingly dominant. These claims have a tendency to dictate to the person what he ought to think, what he ought to do, what even he ought to believe and hope for, concerning himself and the nature of things. The political state is becoming increasingly determinant of the very being of the person, and it does it by its laws, by psychological pressure, by economic pressure, by every possible means of propaganda and social pressure.

In my opinion, there is here involved the deepest danger of the age, namely, the extinction of the human person as such in his own individuality and ultimate inviolability, and therefore, the disappearance of real freedom of choice. Unless our Bill of Rights somehow rejects or embodies a corrective to that danger, I am afraid we will only be expressing in that Bill the dominant forces of the age without sufficient profound reflection on them.

I would like, therefore, Madam Chairman, in order to make my point as clear as possible, to submit the following four propositions which seem to me to cry for recognition by us in this Commission. These are the principles which are in deadly danger today of being forgotten or repudiated by all sorts of systems and philosophies. First, the human person—and I agree with my Belgian friend that we ought to use the word "person" rather than "individual" here,[9] meaning the human being in his real concrete existence in society with all its claims and loyalties—the human person is inherently prior to any group to which he may belong. I repeat, the human being is inherently prior to any group to which he many belong, be that group his class, or his race, or his country, or his nation, or any grouping to which he may belong. He as a human person is in his own essence prior to that group. I do not mean by prior, temporally prior. There never was a Robinson Crusoe. I mean by prior, that in his own being, while belonging necessarily to a manifold of social groups, in his own being, he is prior to any or all of them.

Secondly, therefore, his mind and conscience are the most sacred and inviolable things about him, not his belonging to this or that class, this or that nation, or this or that religion. The most sacred and inviolable thing about him is his mind and conscience which enable him to see the truth and to reject or accept it and freely, therefore, to choose and be.

And in the third place, any social pressure coming from whatever direction which determines his consent automatically is wrong. Any social pressure coming from whatever direction, be that his state, or his religion, or his class, or any direction, which determines his consent automatically is wrong.

And in the fourth place, the group to which he belongs, whatever it be, be it his state, or his nation, or anything, the group can be wrong, just as the individual person can be wrong. In either case, it is only the individual person in his own mind and conscience who is the competent judge of the rightness or wrongness involved.

Madam Chairman, these are ultimate things. I believe they are the most important principles concerning which the present crisis of the world can be interpreted, and unless our proposed International Bill of Rights somehow takes account of them and reflects them, I will regard it as highly deficient.

MR. TEPLIAKOV (USSR)[10]: Madam Chairman, in connection with the remarks just made, may I say that I have to make a short observation in regard to the four principles presented by the representative of Lebanon. I had no time to analyze his remarks to see exactly what he means, but it is quite enough to hear him and to understand that he was warning this Commission not to be wrong when they make a Bill of Rights.

Immediately after, he named four principles. Most of them are quite long. I say it again, I had no time to analyze exactly what he meant, but I would say I oppose such principles or the adoption of such principles for the Bill of Human Rights which would commission rights in the future, or which would be considered at the next session.

First of all, these principles are wrong from the point of view that we are living as individuals in a community and a society, and we are working for the community and the society. The community has provided the material substance for our existence, first of all.

Another one is, if you want to put this human being under a glass cover and let him stay there, it might be possible to say about him, prior to the man or his society.

And one thing I would like you to keep in mind: at least I am right when I speak about the people of the Soviet Union; there are two hundred million people living and enjoying human rights, as they were proclaimed in the Constitution. The Soviet Constitution is not a declaration, but it is a document which fixes what already existed. That is no declaration for the future, but it is just a document which verifies the very existence of these rights. Our principle—you know this principle—is that we cannot divide the individual from the society, from the group, the community. As well, we cannot divide the community from the individual.

As far as the freedom of expression is concerned, it is quite all right, and we have it in the Constitution. We have already discussed it in the previous meeting. But, what does our Lebanon colleague mean when he says the social suppression or oppression, whatever he called it, on an individual? I really do not understand that. What does it mean? And what are the principles which are laid down here? Are you going to create by this Bill, or just proclaim some sort of society without any rule, without any law, without any regulation, for the sake of common people, for the sake of the community?

We already mentioned here, while talking about the right of human beings, the duty and obligation of this human being in regard to the community, the group among which he exists, and which is the main body which provides for his existence, and the enjoyment of the human rights which belong to him.

I repeat again that I will comment later on, after thorough examination of all these principles. But for the time being, I am against such instructions to the Commission and to the group who undertakes this task of formulating the first draft of the Bill of Human Rights.

Mrs. Mehta (India)[11]: Madam Chairman, this question should not be a matter of dispute. The Charter of the United Nations has already said that we are to uphold the dignity and worth of the human person. We are here to reaffirm faith in fundamental human rights, whether the human person comes first or the society. I do not think that we should discuss that problem now. Our object should be to uphold the dignity and worth of the human person. What are the rights which we should recognize, which will carry out this purpose? I think we should not enter into this maze of ideology at this stage …[12]

Chairman: I think perhaps I would like to say a word about what was said by the representative from Lebanon. It seems to me that in much that is before us, the rights of the individual are extremely important. It is not exactly that you set the individual apart from his society, but you recognize that within any society the individual must have rights that are guarded. And while we may, many of us, differ on exact interpretations, I think that is something, in writing a bill of human rights, that you have to think of rather carefully.

Many of us believe that an organized society in the form of a government, exists for the good of the individual; others believe that an organized society in the form of a government, exists for the benefit of a group. We may not have to decide that particular point, but I think we do have to make sure, in writing a bill of human rights, that we safeguard the fundamental freedoms of the individual. If you do not do that, in the long run, it seems to me, that you run the risk of having certain conditions which we have just tried to prevent at great cost in human life, paramount in various groups. So I do think that what the representative from Lebanon said should be very carefully taken into consideration when the drafting committee meets, as well, of course, as every other thing that has been said around this table...[13]

PVrbm CHM, DLC

---

1. John Humphrey and the secretariat staff prepared a memorandum for the commission summarizing in list form all the rights enumerated in the solicited (and unsolicited) proposals major organizations, philosophers, activists, and jurists submitted for the commission's review (Morsink, 4–5).

2. Verbatim Record of the Thirteenth Meeting of the Commission on Human Rights, 4 February 1947, CHMP, DLC.

3. For more on the HRC Drafting Committee, see Document 235.

4. Verbatim Record of the Thirteenth Meeting of the Commission on Human Rights, 4 February 1947, CHMP, DLC.

5. Verbatim Record of the Fourteenth Meeting of the Commission on Human Rights, 4 February 1947, E/24-E/43, CHMP, DLC.

6. Humphrey organized the list of rights into three groups: the status of equality, the status of liberty, and the status of security.

7. Vladislav Ribnikar (1900?–1955), the Yugoslavian delegate on the HRC, expressed his Marxist view of the relationship between the individual and society in a speech in the HRC on January 31, 1947. "We are more and more aware," he said, "that real individual liberty can be reached only in perfect harmony between the individual and the collectivity. It becomes quite obvious, in the common interest, that this common interest is more important than the individual interest, and that man can liberate himself only when the mass of a population is free" ("Verbatim Record of the Eighth Meeting of the Commission on Human Rights," 31 January 1947, E/72, CHMP, DLC).

8. Georg Wilhelm Friedrich Hegel (1770–1831), whose thinking greatly influenced Karl Marx, argued that as long as individuals were in conflict with each other and felt their freedom limited by others, they were not free. Freedom was only possible in a truly rational society in which a person's self-interest and contribution to the welfare of the community as a whole harmonized perfectly (*OCP*).

9. Roland Lebeau, the delegate from Belgium on the HRC, said in the morning session that "section 2 of the document, speaks almost entirely of the human individual and not of the human person as such, the humankind." He then went on to discuss the "rights of the family unit," such as "the right to economic security and a sufficient security to ensure independence and the stability of family life." These rights, he said, "touch the humankind, that is, [the] human individual in his life together with others. I think we ought to keep them in consideration" ("Verbatim Record of the Thirteenth Meeting of the Commission on Human Rights," 4 February 1947, E/81-E/82, CHMP, DLC).

10. Valentin Tepliakov, the Soviet representative on the HRC at the time (Glendon, 40). See header to Document 235.

11. Hansa Mehta.

12. At this point Dr. Ghasseme Ghani, the representative from Iran, argued that in countries where much of the population was still illiterate, freedom of speech and opinion could lead to instability. The UN's first priority, he contended, should be to help such countries provide equal access to education and eliminate illiteracy.

13. ER went on to comment on the ideal of freedom from want and on two specific rights in the third group on Humphrey's list: the freedom to work and the right to medical care and to conditions that promote health. She then suggested that the committee further discuss the rights in this third group.

DIPLOMACY, SOVIET STYLE

> By February 1947 ER had spent many hours negotiating with Soviet delegates to both the Human Rights Commission and the Third Committee. She had debated Andrei Vyshinsky and Andrei Gromyko in both the Third Committee and the General Assembly on the issue of refugees.[1] In the following article, she assesses the character and strength of her opponents, seeks to understand what motivates them, and expresses hope that it will eventually be possible to work more constructively together.

207

"The Russians Are Tough"
Look 18 February 1947

I was leaving in the early morning by Army plane for Berlin.[2] The argument on displaced persons had dragged itself out until a very late hour. When the vote was finally taken and adjournment was finally announced, I made my way over to my opponent, Mr. Vishinsky, the delegate from the U.S.S.R. I did not want to leave with bad feeling between us. I said, "I hope the day will come, sir, when you and I are on the same side of a dispute, for I admire your fighting qualities." His answer shot back: "And I, yours."[3]

That was February, 1946. When I saw Mr. Vishinsky again, it was October, 1946. He came to join his delegation at the second session of the United Nations General Assembly in Flushing, New York. I realized that we might again have some acrimonious discussions. But I had no personal bitterness. I have never had any personal bitterness against any of the people in any of the Eastern European group. I have had, nevertheless, to argue at some length with them because we could not agree on fundamental problems.

I have found that it takes patience and equal firmness and equal conviction to work with the Russians. One must be alert since if they cannot win success for their point of view in one way, they are still going to try to win in any other way that seems to them possible.

For example, the Eastern European group has but one interest in the International Refugee Organization set up to deal with displaced persons in Europe: the repatriation of as many of their nationals as possible.[4] We, on the other hand, while agreeing that repatriation is desirable, feel there will be people who do not wish to return to their home countries. And our belief in the fundamental right of human beings to decide what they want to do must impel us to try to prevent any use of force against displaced persons. We must find the opportunity, if we possibly can, for people to carry out new plans for resettlement somewhere in the world.

I have worked over this and similar questions with the Russians at two meetings of the General Assembly of the United Nations. They are a disciplined group. They take orders and they carry them out. When they have no orders they delay—and they are masterful in finding reasons for delay. They are resourceful and I think they really have an oriental streak—which one finds in many people—which comes to the fore in their enjoyment of bargaining day after day.

When they find themselves outside their own country in international meetings or even in individual relationships, they realize they have been cut off from other nations. They are not familiar with the customs and the thinking of other peoples. This makes them somewhat insecure and, I think, leads them at times to take an exaggerated, self-assertive stand which other people may think somewhat rude. I think it is only an attempt to make the rest of the world see that they are proud of their own ways of doing things.

I always remember that my husband, after one effort to make me useful since I knew a little Italian, relegated me to sight-seeing while he did the buying in old book shops in Italy. He said I had no gift for bargaining! Perhaps that is one of my weaknesses. I am impatient when, once I think the intention of a thing is clear, the details take a long time to work out. Gradually, however, I am coming to realize that the details of words and expressions are important in public documents.

I admire the Russians' tenacity, though it is slightly annoying to start at the very beginning each time you meet and cover the same ground all over again. I have come to accept this as inevitable. It means one hasn't convinced one's opponent that the argument presented was valid. It is perhaps only fair, therefore, that they should go on until they either decide it is useless to continue or one is able to convince them that the opposing stand has truth in it.

I can point to a resolution which was presented after we had finished our discussion on the International Refugee Organization charter and the vote had been taken. Some seventy-odd amendments had been presented and considered. Apparently, it was all over. Then our Yugoslav colleague presented a resolution.

In many ways that resolution tried to do the things which the Eastern European group felt essential regarding displaced persons. Its passage would have nullified many of the things accepted. Our committee voted down the first parts of the resolution, but the third paragraph had in its first line the word "screening", which represented something everybody could agree on.

I think most of our colleagues did not want to show prejudice against the Yugoslav representative. So without reading beyond the first line, they voted "yes" on this paragraph. The last few lines, however, referred back to a former paragraph which we had voted down. It was not until the vote came to the Netherlands that a "no" was heard. He gave no explanation and the "yes" continued to be voted until it came to me. I voted "no" saying, "voting 'yes' on this paragraph makes no sense." I was greeted with laughter. But when they came to read the paragraph, it could only make sense if the preceding paragraph was attached. This paragraph, however, we had voted down!

It was a triumph for our Yugoslav colleague. I hope he realized that the committee desired to show some personal friendliness to him as an individual.[5]

There are many factors which make working with representatives of the U.S.S.R. difficult. Their background and their recent experiences force upon them fears which we do not understand. They are enormously proud to be Russians and are also proud of the advance of their country over the past 25 years.

They also labor under one great disadvantage. Communism started out as a world revolution and undoubtedly supported groups in the other nations of the world which were trying to instill communist beliefs. Leaders of communism today in Russia may or may not believe the whole world should hold the same political and economic ideas. They do realize that for the time being, they have all that they can well do in their own areas. Though they wish to influence the governments of neighboring states to insure safety from aggression, they no longer think it possible to convert the world to communism at present.

It is unlikely that the Russian leaders today would actively encourage groups to work within other non-communist nations. In fact, I think they find it embarrassing to have these groups active. It not only creates in the democracies an active desire to fight back, but extends very often to a general feeling against the U.S.S.R.

I feel sure that the representatives of the U.S.S.R. in this country have little desire to be associated with the American communist groups.[6] One of the difficulties arising here is that among our own citizens we have disagreements about situations in their native lands. For instance, we have Poles who support the present government which is friendly to the U.S.S.R. We have Poles who oppose the Russians and probably would support the old regime in Poland.

There are Russians here who left Russia after the first revolution. There are some who left more recently from Ukraine or from the Baltic states. They all form groups here supporting different groups in Europe.

This makes for us a complex situation. It must make it difficult for representatives of existing governments when they come here.

These differences will eventually be resolved. It is fairly obvious that if existing governments continue to be supported by their people, the rest of the world will have to accept what those people have accepted and learn to work with those governments.

In working with the U.S.S.R., we will have to divorce our fear and dislike of the American communists, as far as possible, from our attitude as regards the representatives of the Soviet government. We will have to insist that the Soviet government give no help or comfort to a communist group within our country. I think when this is clearly established, we can work with Russia as we have with the socialist government in Great Britain. Both differ from our political and economic views, but these views are not static anywhere.

Words alone will never convince the Soviet leaders that democracy is not only as strong, but stronger than communism. I believe, however, that if we maintain as firm an attitude on our convictions as the Russians maintain on theirs, and can prove that democracy can serve the best interests of the people as a whole, we will be giving an effective demonstration to every Soviet representative coming to this country.

We know that democracy in our own country is not perfect. The Russians know that while communism has given them much more than they had under the Czar, it's still not perfect.

The question is, which group will fight more earnestly and successfully for its beliefs? We must come in contact with each other. Therefore, the battle is an individual battle to be fought by every citizen in our respective countries. The language barrier is, of course, one of the things which makes it difficult to work with the Russians. More and more they speak English. I wish I could say that more and more we speak Russian! I have always heard that because the Russian language is so difficult, the Russians learn foreign languages more easily than we do. Perhaps we ought to acknowledge that we are lazier and rely on other people learning the English language.

Talking through an interpreter never encourages friendly relations. I think we feel that it is more difficult to know the representatives of the U.S.S.R. and of the Eastern European group than it is to know someone, for instance, from France, Great Britain, Italy, or any of the South American countries.

It is true, I believe, that official representatives of the U.S.S.R. know that they cannot commit their country without agreement with the Kremlin on some special program of action. It makes them extremely careful in private conversation. We who feel we can express our opinions on every subject find a Soviet representative unsatisfactory on a personal basis. This might not be the case if we met just plain, unofficial Russians who felt they had no responsibility and could converse freely on any subject with a plain American citizen!

We undoubtedly consider the individual more important than the Russians do. Individual liberty seems to us one of the essentials of life in peacetime. We must bear this in mind when we work with the Russians; we cannot accept their proposals without careful scrutiny. We know the fundamental differences which exist between us. But I am hoping that as time goes on, the differences will be less important, that we will find more points of agreement and so think less about our points of disagreement.

On the higher levels, where questions of expansion of territory, trade and influence have to be settled, I think we have to remember our own young days as a new Republic, and that Russia is a young, virile nation. She has to be reminded that world co-operation, international ownership and activity seem more important than any one country's interests. Not an easy lesson for any of us to learn, but one that is essential to the preservation of peace.[7]

PMag AERP, FDRL

1. For ER's debates with Vyshinsky and Gromyko, see Document 90, Document 91, Document 152, and Document 168.

2. ER went to Germany for several days in February 1946 after the UN General Assembly meeting in London. She toured Berlin, Frankfurt am Main, and several Displaced Persons camps (*MD*, 15, 16, and 18 February 1946).

3. See Document 92 for a similar account of this incident, which occurred on February 12, 1946, at the close of the General Assembly meeting. For the text of their exchange, see Documents 91 and 90.

4. The Eastern group of the Communist nations represented in the UN in 1947 included the Soviet Union, Poland, Byelorussia, Ukraine, and Yugoslavia. On the IRO, see the header to Document 152.

5. The Yugoslavian resolution to which ER refers (A/C.3/113) called for the dismantling of military or para-military organizations that Yugoslavia and the Soviet Union repeatedly charged were operating in the refugee camps and the removal of trouble makers that they claimed were discouraging repatriation by intimidating other refugees. The resolution also called for the creation of special bilateral commissions to promote closer cooperation between the countries of origin and the countries operating the camps and to help implement the first two measures. ER, in the words of the summary report of the meeting at which the Third Committee discussed the resolution, "regarded the Yugoslav proposal as a means of reopening a lengthy discussion which had been closed by the Committee's decisions." She reiterated the United States position that no military organizations existed in the camps and that refugees were not being forced by anyone to refuse repatriation (A/C.3/145). The Third Committee voted down paragraphs (a), (b), and (d) of the Yugoslavian resolution, but voted to adopt paragraph (c), although it referred back to paragraph (b), by eighteen to two with thirteen abstentions. Paragraph (c) read: "effect a careful screening of the categories of persons mentioned above and particularly, and with high priority, for those mentioned in paragraph (b) above, in order to identify all war criminals, quislings and traitors who shall be handed over to the authorities of the countries against which they have committed their crimes, regardless of the fact that they may have become stateless or have assumed a new nationality." The summary record notes: "Mrs. Roosevelt pointed out that in its new form paragraph (c) was meaningless." The committee directed Leo Mattes, the Yugoslavian delegate, to revise the paragraph, which he did. Eventually the committee adopted a modified version of that portion of the Yugoslavian resolution (Summary Record, Forty-Sixth Meeting, Third Committee, 9 December 1946, A/C.3/145, 296, 302-310, UNORGA, MWelC; Draft resolution proposed by the delegation of Yugoslavia, A/C.3/113).

6. See MD June 9, 1945 (Document 18), in which she expresses concern that the activities of the American Communist Party will disrupt good relations with the Soviet Union. In December 1946, ER wrote: "I did not find much sympathy among the Russian delegates to the UN for the American communists" (see Document 173).

7. On November 17, 1948, ER wrote to Trude Lash:

> It is sad dear, but I think it will take a long time to get real understanding with the USSR government. It will be the result of long and patient work. Their government and its representatives think differently from the way we do. Even in polite conversation they see things differently. They will have to reach a higher standard of living and not be afraid to let others in and their own out before we can hope for a change (ER to Trude Lash, 17 November 1948, AERP).

QUESTIONING THE ADMINISTRATION'S POLICY
ON GREECE

February 21, 1947, Truman wrote an open letter to Congress recommending that the $350 million appropriation requested by UNRRA as well as all subsequent requests for relief aid to war-ravaged countries be handled in a new manner:

> I recommend that this relief assistance be given directly rather than through an international organization, and that our contribution be administered under United States control. International cooperation in the program and the necessary coordination of our relief activities with those of other contributors can be achieved by informal consultations with all nations concerned through the mechanism of the United Nations and otherwise.[1]

He addressed Congress again March 12, this time offering a proposal for direct US aid specifically to Greece and Turkey:

> I believe that it must be the policy of the United States to support free peoples who are resisting attempted subjugation by armed minorities or by outside pressures.

> I believe that we must assist free peoples to work out their own destinies in their own way.

> I believe that our help should be primarily through economic and financial aid which is essential to economic stability and orderly political processes.

> The world is not static, and the status quo is not sacred. But we cannot allow changes in the status quo in violation of the Charter of the United Nations by such methods of coercion, or by such subterfuges as political infiltration. In helping free and independent nations to maintain their freedom, the United States will be giving effect to the principles of the Charter of the United Nations.[2]

Truman then asked Congress to appropriate $400 million for military and economic aid to Greece and Turkey and "to authorize the detail of American civilian and military personnel to Greece and Turkey, at the request of those countries, to assist in the tasks of reconstruction, and for the purpose of supervising the use of such financial and material assistance as may be furnished."

This new US policy of aiding nations directly—to help them, as Truman put it in his speech, "maintain their free institutions and their national integrity against aggressive movements that seek to impose upon them totalitarian regimes"—became known as the "Truman Doctrine."[3]

As Congress deliberated on the president's proposal the following week, ER reacted to the sudden change in US foreign aid policy by attempting to reach Warren Austin, chief US delegate to the UN, to discuss the matter. Unable to reach Austin, she turned to Dean Acheson, who had testified before the House Foreign Affairs Committee March 20 in favor of the Doctrine.[4] Because ER insisted her questions "were of such immediate importance that she must get in touch with top policy officials at once," Acheson sent Thomas Power to respond to her questions on the US policy toward Greece.[5] Power later told Austin:

> I judge from the telephone call to me from Washington when I was asked to see this arrangement through that Mrs. Roosevelt made plain to Mr. Acheson her intention of resigning from the Commission on Human Rights should she

not be satisfied with the reasons which lie behind the U.S. policy toward Greece … she repeated this statement to me although always speaking in terms of a searcher for knowledge who still had an open mind.[6]

Power detailed his meeting in the memorandum below, addressed to Austin.[7]

208

Memorandum of Conversation between Eleanor Roosevelt and Thomas Power, Jr.

25 March 1947 [New York City]

CONFIDENTIAL

Participants: Eleanor Roosevelt, Thomas F. Power, Jr.

Subject: United States Position on Greece

This morning I delivered to Mrs. Roosevelt a set of papers which Mr. Acheson wished placed in her hands and explained to her as a consequence of her telephone call to him on Monday, March 24. I met Mrs. Roosevelt at 8:00 a.m. at her apartment and talked with her briefly there and then accompanied her to the railroad station.

Mrs. Roosevelt said that she would read the papers carefully and would call Mr. Acheson directly on Wednesday, the 26th, if she had any unanswered questions.

Mrs. Roosevelt then proceeded to explain to me her views on the U.S. policy toward Greece and Turkey. She said that she had called Senator Austin (whom she had been unable to locate because he was in Washington) and then Mr. Acheson because during her recent lecture tour in the West she had been repeatedly questioned regarding the U.S. policy on Greece.[8] She said that she had many questions in her own mind and could only tell her audience that she knew only what she had read in the newspapers. She could add only that she knew that during the GA the U.S. had opposed a continuation of international distribution of relief because it had been mishandled for political advantage. The United States held that there should be no politics in relief. She said that she was unable to explain why the U.S. had changed.

Mrs. Roosevelt continued that she, herself, was deeply disturbed, and that she had found people throughout the country greatly upset as to why the President's statement and the statements from the Department had made no mention of tying aid to Greece and Turkey in with the UN. At least, she asked, why could not the U.S. have said that it would act, as regards Greece and Turkey, in consultation with the UN, using its advice and keeping it informed while recognizing that only the U.S. could supply the necessary funds. She thought that some form of reporting U.S. action to the UN might have been specified. She felt that a considerable number of people were disturbed that the U.S. was once again pulling out of international cooperation. We had taken a large part in setting up the UN and it now seemed that we are not operating with regard for it.

Mrs. Roosevelt stated that she thought the premises for the new Greek policy had not been sufficiently explained to the public, and she had found that the solemn tone with which a major shift in policy had been announced had frightened the people. The change in policy is also of such tremendous importance that she thought it should be thoroughly explained to the American people.

Throughout all of this discussion, Mrs. Roosevelt emphasized that she was asking for information in order to resolve her doubts which she modestly said must come from sheer lack of information. She said she had called Senator Austin and Mr. Acheson because she felt she, personally, wanted to know the answers to these questions, and because she felt that as a U.S. Representative, even in the "humble capacity" as Chairman of the Commission on Human Rights, she should seriously consider whether, upon examination of all the facts in the case, she would be able to continue as a member of the U.S. team at the UN. She thought that the team of Representatives should agree on the basic policies even though those policies might be somewhat outside of there own sphere. Thus, she thought in all honesty that if, after all her questions had been answered, she could not agree with the U.S. policy on Greece, she would feel obliged to resign.

Speaking generally about Greece, Mrs. Roosevelt said that there were several specific questions of fact which bothered her. She understood the need for relief in that war devastated country, and she also considered it a proved fact that Greece was being attacked by her Northern neighbors. Mrs. Roosevelt had difficulty, however, in understanding how it happened that the country was plunged into anarchy if 85 per cent of the people had voted in support of the regime; how, with the British troops there, the terribly small minority had been able to so completely upset the country; what, if anything, the British had done to prevent this deterioration. Mrs. Roosevelt continued that while she very much appreciated all that the British had done on our behalf, and while she had every sympathy with the British people, she also knew that in the past the U.S. had been "used", and she wanted to be certain that U.S. action in that theater was for American interests.

TMemc RG84, NARA II

March 6, ER learned from Nat Einhorn of the American Committee for Yugoslav Relief that despite a January recommendation by the UN "that six of the war devastated nations in Europe be assisted in 1947 to meet their urgent needs for food and other basic essentials," the US State Department had only recommended aid for five countries, "eliminating Yugoslavia." ER forwarded Einhorn's letter to Assistant Secretary of State Acheson with a brief cover note of her own, reading, "In this letter which I am enclosing, Mr. Einhorn says that Congress is being asked to assist five countries and that Yugoslavia needs help. Would you please tell me what the reason is?"[9] Acheson replied two weeks later.

209

Dean Acheson to Eleanor Roosevelt
11 April 1947 [Washington, DC]

Dear Mrs. Roosevelt:

I have received your letter dated March 25, 1947, with which you transmit a letter addressed to you by Mr. Nat. Einhorn, Executive Director of the American Committee for Yugoslav Relief, Incorporated.

We recently communicated to the Yugoslav Ambassador the reasons we did not contemplate extending relief to Yugoslavia from funds which the Congress might appropriate for relief pursuant to the President's recent request for $350,000,000. For the information of Mr. Einhorn I am enclosing a copy of the statement released by the State Department explaining fully the position in this matter.[10] We have completed extensive studies on relief needs based upon information obtained from many sources. On the basis of the studies we believe that Yugoslavia no longer has a need for free relief. Although it is possible that some small food import needs may arise they should not be beyond the ability of Yugoslavia itself to finance. It is clear that in any case our assistance must go where the needs are most urgent.

Sincerely yours,
Dean Acheson

TLS AERP, FDRL

---

1. *SDB*, vol. 16, no. 400, 2 March 1947, 395.

2. "Text of President's Message," *WP*, 13 March 1947, 1.

3. Offner, 200–202; "Text of President's Message," ibid.

4. "Acheson's Statement on Plans to Aid Greece and Turkey," *NYT*, 21 March 1947, 12.

5. Thomas Power, Jr., was a member of the US Delegation at the San Francisco conference and of the Permanent Mission of the US from 1946 until 1949 (*WWUN*, 1975).

6. Thomas Power, Jr., to Warren Austin, 25 March 1947, RG59, NARA II.

7. The memorandum was also distributed to two other members of the US delegation, Leroy Stinebower and Herschel V. Johnson; and to Carlisle Humelsine in the State Department.

8. For more on ER's lecture tour, see *n*31 Document 203.

9. The recommendation by the Committee on Relief Needs After the Termination of the United Nations Relief and Rehabilitation Administration put Yugoslavia's food needs at $68,200,000 (Nat. Einhorn to ER, 6 March 1947, AERP; ER to Dean Acheson, 25 March 1947, RG 59, NARA II; Thomas J. Hamilton, "Europe Relief Cost Put at $583,000,000," *NYT*, 30 January 1947, 8).

10. The State Department issued the press release March 20. It announced that the United States would make no grain available to meet Yugoslavia's food aid requests, having concluded that its needs for free relief were not as urgent as those of certain other devastated countries. The *New York Times* published the statement, along with the commentary, "There was no mention in the announcement of the United States' controversies with Yugoslavia over her shooting down of American planes, of this country's dislike of the Tito regime, or the status of that nation as a Russian puppet state" (Bertram D. Hulen, "U.S. Bars Grain to Yugoslavs; Finds Others in Greater Need," *NYT*, 21 March 1947, 1; "U.S. Statement on Yugoslav Needs," *NYT*, 21 March 1947, 10).

QUESTIONING THE TRUMAN DOCTRINE, PART 1

The morning after ER wrote Acheson regarding aid to Yugoslavia and met with Thomas Power, she met with Francis Russell, director of the State Department Public Affairs Office, to discuss her position on the Truman Doctrine.

Russell then reported to Acheson, who remained concerned that ER might publicly object to the doctrine, that ER thought the president had failed to adequately portray the Greek situation to the American public. Russell then reported that ER also expressed dismay over the executive order Truman signed March 21 describing the procedures the executive branch should use to insure "maximum protection ... against infiltration of disloyal persons into the ranks of its employees."[1]

After assuring Acheson that only a few individuals knew that he and ER met, Russell concluded his report:

> I left with the definite impression that she not only would not take any action to embarrass the Administration in its Greek policy, but on the contrary endorsed it, provided it is regarded as constituting a step toward an effort at thoroughgoing discussions with the Russians as soon as the Secretary may feel that an opportune moment has arrived.[2]

ER then submitted her own report of her meeting with Russell to the secretary.

210

Eleanor Roosevelt to Dean Acheson
26 March 1947 [New York City]

Dear Mr. Secretary

I saw Mr. Russell and I do understand the whole position in the State Department better than I did before.

However, I am wondering what you have decided to do if the USSR were to say: "Since you have acted alone without consulting the United Nations, we are free to do the same. We see no reason why you should send advisers and give them money to arm, obviously against us. We told you we had nothing to do with infiltration of people in the armed bands. We told you we wanted to control the Dardenelles. We are here and have an army and are going to send it in because this is our sphere of interest and not yours."

I do not for a minute think, of course, that the USSR could go to war with us here but she could of course, go into Greece, claiming she is doing exactly what we are doing and we have given her an excuse.

I hope Secretary Marshall will have a talk with Mr. Stalin very soon and that some understanding will be arrived at at the top level between us and Russia, and then that the people of this country will be told exactly what our policy means and what we are really doing and what we intend to do which will strengthen the UN. I hope never again that this type of action be taken without at least consulting with the Secretary General and with our permanent member on the Security Council beforehand. It all seems to me a most unfortunate way to do things.

I hope very much that at least the Foreign Affairs Committee of the House and of the Senate are fully familiar with the whole situation because you will need them to lead this fight. I do not think the people of this country are going to like granting money for military purposes.

As I told you, I found in California the greatest interest in the United Nations. The houses were filled everywhere and that must mean that people are pinning their hopes on the success of this organization.[3]

Very sincerely yours,

TLc AERP, FDRL

211

Dean Acheson to Eleanor Roosevelt
15 April 1947 [Washington, DC]

Dear Mrs. Roosevelt:

I regret the delay in acknowledging your letter of March 26. I hoped for clarification of several points before replying but will not wait any longer.

I believe that most of the questions you ask about the proposal for aid to Greece and Turkey have been answered in my testimony before the House and Senate Committees and in the replies to the questions submitted by Senator Vandenberg. I am enclosing a copy of these questions and answers in the event you have not had an opportunity to read the full text.[4]

I do not believe that any reasonable contention could be made that such aid as we may give to Greece and Turkey could possibly be construed by the Soviet Union as a threat to its security. Neither do I believe that the Soviet Union is apt to send an army into Greece as a consequence of such aid from us. The parallel with German action against small states would be too obvious and too deadly.

I fully agree that the United Nations must be the cornerstone of our foreign policy. We all agree that we must continue to strive for that unity of purpose which is the sole basis upon which our concept of a strong world organization can be built. I do not concur in the thesis that in the meantime we should bind ourselves unalterably and unilaterally.

The Soviet Union has made loans, has given military assistance and has delivered foodstuffs to a number of countries, including Poland, Czechoslovakia and Yugoslavia. They have not reported these matters to the United Nations and they would certainly refuse to permit United Nations supervision of them.

We are, of course, ready and anxious to attempt to reach an understanding with the Russians on all points at issue. I believe that our record from the meeting at Tehran to the present meeting in Moscow is clear proof of our earnest desire to understand the Soviet point of view.[5]

Sincerely yours,
Dean Acheson

TLS AERP, FDRL

---

1. Executive Order 9835.

2. Richard Winslow to Warren Austin, 26 March 1947, RG59, NARA II; Francis Russell to Dean Acheson, 27 March 1947, RG59, NARA II; Donovan, 294.

3. See *n*31 Document 203.

4. Acheson testified before the House Foreign Affairs Committee March 20 to support the administration's position on aid to Greece and Turkey. He warned that the two nations were on the verge of "collapse" unless they received American aid. In the case of Greece, this meant not only economic destitution, but also the threat of "armed bands in the north, under Communist leadership." The undersecretary then argued that "the crisis in Greece and Turkey confronts us with only two alternatives. We can either grant aid to those countries or we can deny that aid." Moreover, "the United Nations and its related organizations are not now in position to extend help of the kind that is required."

When the Senate Foreign Relations Committee convened to deliberate on the Truman Doctrine, it sent the State Department a set of 111 questions about the aid package proposal. Acheson answered in a typewritten document submitted to the committee April 3. The questions ranged in topic from US "self-interest," to the potential of "abandonment of the Monroe Doctrine," to the nature of the proposed military aid to the two countries. Also at issue were implications for US relations with the USSR. For example, one question and answer set read:

Q.—Should the proposed action increase or justify Russia's fear that we are engaged in an encirclement of Russia? Would Russia be justified in viewing our action as a threat now or in the future against Russia's own territorial integrity?

A.—The United States Government does not consider that its proposed action to assist in bringing about stable conditions in Greece and Turkey could in any way be considered as a step in the encirclement of any country. In our view, the establishment of such stable conditions, far from constituting any threat to the territorial integrity of any other country, should on the contrary contribute to the establishment of European peace and tranquility, which is in the best interests of all countries.

The copy of these questions and answers ER received from Acheson, referenced here, was not retained in her records ("Acheson's Statement on Plans to Aid Greece and Turkey," *NYT*, 21 March 1947, 12; "Acheson Answers Aid Bill Questions," *NYT*, 4 April 1947, 8).

5. At the Tehran Conference in December 1943, the Big Three (FDR, Winston Churchill and Joseph Stalin) met to discuss military strategies and attempted to settle questions of postwar Europe. In March of 1947, the Big Four met in Moscow to discuss Germany. See *n*6 Document 199. From 1943 until 1947, then, Acheson claimed that the United States endeavored to cooperate with the Soviet Union.

On the Call for a Third Party

> Upset by the division in the progressive ranks, the lack of unified resistance to the conservative trend, and the Americans for Democratic Action's strongly anti-Communist platform, Fiorello La Guardia wrote ER to express his concerns and to suggest that it may be time to consider the formation of a third party.

212

Fiorello La Guardia to Eleanor Roosevelt
2 April 1947 [New York City]

My dear Mrs. Roosevelt:

I am quite disturbed over the split among progressives in our country. I cannot believe that you can be particularly happy about it.

I do not doubt the good faith and sincerity of all the splendid people who joined with you in the ADA. Nevertheless, it leaves a great many honest, sincere progressives, who have no Communist tinge, who have nothing in common with Communists, entirely out. People like your good self and Wilson Wyatt and Leon Henderson and Chester Bowles and Hubert Humphrey are members of the regular Democratic organizations of your respective states.[1] But a great many of us are not dyed-in-the-wool members of any party.[2] We have, during the past twenty-five years, because of our independent attitude, been able to force good legislation as well as to improved the calibre of candidates. We have never given any party a blanket endorsement in advance.

At the present time, and speaking for myself alone, I note a decided trend on the part of the present Democratic National administration toward ultra-conservatism. I see a shattering and a distortion and a weakening of New Deal principles at every turn. Do not forget that it is but a few weeks that the Republicans have been in control of Congress, so it is hardly fair to blame them for all. They have enough to answer for. But in the last Congress it was with the aid of Democrats in the House and Senate that good laws were weakened and crippled and good bills defeated.

Mention is made in your statement to the Wagner-Ellender-Taft Bill. But the Democrats had the majority in the last Congress. They cannot escape the responsibility for the failure of that bill.[3]

We can discuss legislation at another time. The important thing now is, what can be done to rally all progressive forces into one group, without being the tail of any one of the two major parties. I, for one, will not take in 1947, sight unseen, the candidates and the platform of either party in 1948. I want to see both, examine, scrutinize and compare. It is too early, as we say in New York, "absolutely and positively" to announce that there will be <u>no third party</u>. It may be necessary to have a third party. I don't know now. I hope not.[4] Only machine politicians pledge support so far in advance. Real progressives are not straight party members.

The technique and even the nomenclature of selfish, conservative, money-minded groups seem to have been adopted recently by your group. The brand of Communism is hurled indiscriminately. Do you think that is fair? What is the test of excluding any one from a progressive group? How is a sympathizer or fellow traveler of Fascists and Communists to be identified? In the same breath that reference is made to Communists and sympathizers, objection is raised to the treatment of David E. Lilienthal. Is he not the victim of narrow-minded bigots? Is he not unjustly charged with communistic leaning by the enemies of public ownership of power plants?[5] The same can be true of any citizen or any man or woman interested in public affairs.

Only the other day I was testifying before the Banking and Currency Committee of the House on the Taft-Ellender-Wagner Bill, formerly the Wagner-Ellender-Taft Bill, and a representative from Ohio said that the bill was communistic, that it was inspired and sponsored by Communists, that it was intended to destroy free enterprise in our country, that it was un-American and that only Communists were supporting it.[6] Does that make Senator Taft or even you or me a Communist?

You made reference to Mr. Henry Wallace. Do you consider Henry Wallace a Communist?[7] I do not. Neither would our late President consider him a Communist. I know, for on several occasions he resented the abuse of Mr. Wallace along those lines.

Would you consider the Rev. William Howard Melish, who is interested in maintaining friendly relations with foreign countries, a Communist?[8] Would he be eligible to your group?

Would you consider Joe Davies of Washington, who has on many occasions publicly appeared at rallies and mass meetings of the Friends of Soviet Russia, a Communist?[9] I know he is not.

Elliott has publicly expressed himself in opposition to the Greek-Turkish situation as proposed to Congress.[10] Does that make him a fellow traveler or Communist sympathizer? A great many of us have expressed ourselves. Are we all to be tarred?

Would you consider any group of individuals who are asking for an accounting in their own labor union Communists, just because the group in power does not want to give an accounting?

It has gotten so now that any one who has a difference of opinion or is not in agreement is charged with being a Communist or a friend of a Communist. My dear Mrs. Roosevelt, where will all this end?

Do you not think it possible to have some sort of creed, an American creed, that good, loyal Americans could on their honor subscribe to and accept? Political association cannot be formed on a personal basis. It is formed by agreement on principles and common understanding. Is not the acceptance of a platform and adherence to principle the real test and only qualification?

Should any discrimination be made in feeding hungry children? I know you do not believe that. Some of us have sought to have hungry children fed, regardless of religion or race or politics. Does that prevent us from being good Americans?

It is so easy for one to make a charge against some one he does not like; that fits beautifully into the present picture of those sponsoring a throw-back in our country to the days of 1890.

There is great need in this country for improvement. Our troubles are all economic. Fine talk and pretty platforms are not enough. We are getting away from the New Deal. Much of it has already been destroyed. We certainly will not be able to obtain the objectives of the New Deal—a better, a fuller, a happier life, and economic security—if the progressive forces are divided. The reactionaries see eye to eye. They agree in the House and Senate. Unless there is a strong, independent and progressive movement, there will not be much difference in the platform of the two major parties in 1948. In all likelihood, there will be little difference, other than tonsorial, in the candidates.

On the other hand, if there is a strong progressive movement, and the parties know that we are united and intend to take active part, we would be in a position to render great service to the people of our country. I am quite willing to sit with others and work out a formula under which all honest, sincere progressives could rally.

With kind personal regards, I am

Sincerely yours,
Fiorello La Guardia

TLS AERP, FDRL

ER dictated her reply.[11]

213

Eleanor Roosevelt to Fiorello La Guardia
11 April 1947 [Hyde Park]

My Dear Mr. LaGuardia:

I am afraid I do not agree with you about a third party. It takes so long before a third party wields any power, I can not see much point in trying to build one up at the present time when things need to be done quickly.

It seems to me that all one can hope to do [as][12] liberals is to bring enough influence to bear on questions as they arise, to make the two major parties uncomfortable when they stand for something which is really wrong.

I wish very much that all liberals could work together and if PCA could remove from its leadership the communist element, I do not see any reason why ADA and PCA should not work together.

I do not mean, of course, that I would vote for Democratic candidates regardless of who they were or what they stood for, but I think it is the party to belong to, and we can try to improve the candidates. If we do not succeed, we do not have to vote for them.

In the Democratic party we have always had an element of reaction, just as there is an element of reaction in the Republican party. My husband held a majority together because he started in a crisis and everyone was willing to be told. His leadership toward the end was weakened and of course, President Truman hasn't been able to command as good a following as my husband had.[13]

There really has to be a recognition that the public gets the kind of representation that it wants. If, as it seems, the people want conservatism at present, they will get it, but if they really want better legislation, they can get it, and they can have better candidates if they want them.

Of course, I do not believe in having everyone who is a liberal called communist, or everyone who is conservative called a fascist, but I think it is possible to determine whether one is one or the other and it does not take too long to do so.

I love your illustration about the gentleman from Ohio who called those who supported the Wagner-Ellender-Taft Bill communists, but I am afraid that is not something which we can call real thinking.

I certainly do not consider Mr. Wallace a communist. I do not know Mr. Melish, so I can not say, but I do not consider wanting to preserve friendly relations with Russia makes one a communist. Naturally I know that Elliott is not a communist. Naturally I do not think there should be discrimination in feeding hungry children.

Our troubles are economic, but they are not all economic.

The ADA wrote a platform and tried to express what it believes in. It happens that I do not think it very good on certain points, but nevertheless it was an honest attempt.[14] I am quite willing to sit down with anybody and attempt to do something better, but I do not really feel it is up to me at present to consider myself that important. It would seem to me better if some of you gentlemen, or the younger generation carried through this fight because the younger generation is going to have to live under whatever is decided today. I haven't so very many more years which I need worry about.

Very sincerely yours,

TLc AERP, FDRL

1. Wilson Wyatt (1905–1996), Truman's former housing administrator; Leon Henderson (1895–1986), head of the Office of Price Administration in the early 1940s; Chester Bowles, who served at the time on the American National Committee for UNESCO; and Hubert H. Humphrey (1911–1978), mayor of Minneapolis from 1945 until 1948, were all prominent members of Americans for Democratic Action (ADA). Wyatt served as national chairman of ADA, Henderson served as chairman of the executive committee, and Humphrey served as its vice president. All four were active members of the Democratic Party and three of them had strong ties to the party in their home states: Wyatt in Kentucky, Bowles in Connecticut, and Humphrey in Minnesota (*DAB*; Hamby, *Beyond*, 163; Douglas E. Kneeland, "Hubert H. Humphrey Is Dead at 66 After 32 Years of Public Service," *NYT*, 14 January 1978, 47).

2. As a renegade Republican, Fusion Party candidate, and supporter of the New Deal, La Guardia had never been closely associated with any political party. See Biographical Portraits.

3. The Wagner-Ellender-Taft housing bill would have helped support the construction of 12,500,000 homes over ten years. The Senate passed the bipartisan bill on April 15, 1946, but the House Banking and Currency Committee bottled it up until Congress adjourned in August ("Senate Passes Long-Range Bill on Housing with Wage Clause," *NYT*, 16 April 1946, 1; "Dewey's Silence Scored," *NYT*, 2 August 1946, 15).

4. Liberals frequently debated the idea of forming a third party during this period, but the leaders of the ADA, including Bowles and ER, believed it would be unwise. See Document 177.

5. David E. Lilienthal (1899–1981) directed the development of the Tennessee Valley Authority's controversial public power program from its founding in 1933 and became chairman of TVA in 1941. At the end of 1946, Truman appointed Lilienthal chairman of the newly created Atomic Energy Commission, established to supervise the development of atomic energy both for military and peaceful purposes. Long the subject of criticism by the opponents of public power, Lilienthal now faced further attacks. Senator Kenneth McKellar (D-TN) attempted to block his nomination on the grounds that Lilienthal must have been under Communist influence because his parents had been born in what became Czechoslovakia. After Truman stood by him and nuclear scientists expressed confidence in him, however, the Senate voted in favor of confirmation ("David E. Lilienthal Is Dead at 81: Led U.S. Effort in Atomic Power," *NYT*, 16 January 1981, A1).

6. During questioning of La Guardia by members of the House Committee on Banking and Currency, Frederick C. Smith (1884–1956), Republican congressman from Ohio, said that he concluded from his testimony that La Guardia thought "the answer to the housing problem is communism." He repeatedly characterized rent control and public housing programs as expressions of "socialist philosophy" aimed at "the redistribution of wealth." When La Guardia pointed out that "the Senator from your State" (Republican Senator Robert Taft, one of the sponsors of the Taft-Ellender-Wagner Bill) supported subsidized housing, Smith replied that "he does not speak, in my judgment, for the majority of people of the State of Ohio on that subject" (*BDUSC*; House Committee on Banking and Currency, *Housing and Rent Control*, Hearings on H.R. 2549, 80th Cong., 1st sess., 1947, 370–73, 376).

7. See Document 178.

8. Rev. William Howard Melish (1910–1986), an Episcopal priest in Brooklyn, helped organize Russian war relief chapters and the National Council of American-Soviet Friendship during World War II. He later served as the council's national chairman (Schultz and Schultz).

9. Joseph E. Davies (1876–1958), a successful lawyer and believer in the virtues of capitalism, served as the US ambassador to the Soviet Union from 1936 through 1938. He took a very positive view of the Russians in his memoir, *Mission to Moscow* (1941). In 1945 he served as one of

Truman's advisors during the Potsdam Conference. As a leading advocate of Soviet-American friendship he provoked distrust among hard-line anti-Communists (*DAB*).

10. On March 12, 1947, Truman proposed to Congress that the United States provide direct military and economic assistance to Greece and Turkey, thus bypassing the UN. Elliott Roosevelt opposed the plan, sharing the stage with Henry Wallace as Wallace told those attending the April 1 Madison Square Garden "crisis meeting" that "the President and his Republican backers are less concerned with the need of the Greek people for food than with the need of the American navy for oil. The plan to contain communism is second to that need." At an April 13 rally, Roosevelt again seconded Wallace's position that the UN should administer aid to Greece and Turkey, arguing that "the leaders of our country … are paying lip service to the United Nations on one hand and sounding the drums of war at the same time" (Hamby, *Beyond*, 177, 192; "Wallace Sees U.N. As Sole Peace Hope," *NYT*, 1 April 1947, 9; "Peril in U.S. Policies, Roosevelt Son Says," *NYT*, 13 April 1947, 53).

11. ER scrawled "Dictate" across the bottom of La Guardia's letter to her, indicating to her staff that she wished to dictate her response.

12. The original text in the carbon copy reads "in." As the recipient's copy could not be located, and ER proofread her correspondence and often corrected mistakes in ink on the text before she mailed them, the editors believe that she probably made this correction and then posted the letter.

13. FDR held together a majority in Congress composed of conservative southern Democrats, northern liberals, and some progressive Republicans. During the early years of the New Deal, in response to the crisis of the Depression, this coalition often backed the progressive legislation he proposed. But as the years went by, conservative resistance to New Deal policies grew and FDR became less successful at holding the majority together. Truman, who lacked FDR's political persuasiveness, found it even more difficult to overcome conservative opposition to progressive legislation (*FDRE*; Hamby, *Beyond*, 81–85).

14. At its first national conference in March, the ADA agreed upon a domestic and foreign policy program that included a cautious endorsement of the Truman Doctrine. Since ER had serious reservations about the Truman Doctrine (see Document 208, Document 210, and Document 211), this was probably one of the points on which she thought the ADA platform could be improved (Anthony Leviero, "New Liberal Body Sets Its Program," *NYT*, 31 March 1947, 1; Hamby, *Beyond*, 177–78; Brock, 63–65).

PROGRESSIVE CITIZENS OF AMERICA

Having just completed reading Elliott Roosevelt's book, *As He Saw It*,[1] Nedra Dalmann wrote ER "earnestly" seeking "an answer to confusing questions." She grew "more and more appalled at the present trend away from President Roosevelt's plans and hopes for the post-war world."

In particular, Dalmann could "not understand" ER's "failure to stand beside Wallace when he is fighting to perpetuate the ideals President Roosevelt stood for." Furthermore:

> Here in Minnesota the ADA has attracted the bad elements of the Democratic Party and has concerned itself chiefly with Red-baiting. I am not a Communist, but I work in the office of the Amalgamated Clothing Workers of America, CIO, and it is my firm conviction that all of us have a right to our own beliefs, that all those who are interested in labor must stick together and not be divided by such tactics. We should not ask a person whether he is Catholic, Republican or Communist, but judge them by their actions and their accomplishments. Surely we have good and bad in every walk of life.
>
> Would you be kind enough to take the time and enlighten me in regard to your reasons for being a member of the ADA instead of PCA. My faith in you is such that I feel you must be justified and perhaps my own activity in the PCA is wrong. Perhaps Wallace does not stand for a just peace and the right for everyone to live in that kind of a world and worship and believe as he chooses. Can both of you want the same things and be in different camps—and why can't those camps get together and let us have real unity and real strength?[2]

ER dictated this response the the following week.

214

Eleanor Roosevelt to Nedra Dalmann
11 April 1947 [Hyde Park]

My dear Miss Dalman:

I am sorry to hear that ADA has attracted the worst element of the Democratic party in Minnesota. I thought Mayor Humphrey was a fine young man.[3]

I am sorry too, that you do not think we have a right to ask whether a person is a communist or not. I do not think, however, if we asked them, we would know whether they were or not, but I can not quite understand how you can believe in Democracy and at the same time, think that you can encourage communism in this country. The two aren't compatible.

Naturally anyone who believes in communism has a right to hold their beliefs and admit they are communists in spite of the hardships which that will entail. That is why I belong to ADA instead of PCA. PCA knows that they have communists in their leadership and they are not willing to get rid of them. If they were, we would have no trouble in amalgamating the liberals in the two organizations.

Mr. Wallace is not a member of PCA. He is a very fine person and never wants to be against anyone.[4] I happen to think that one has to be against the communists because I found them untruthful. The religion you belong to has nothing to do with the question of political beliefs. Elliott is not a communist. He is a Democrat, as I am. He does not belong to either the ADA or the PCA, but he would speak for either one, and feels that PCA still has enough good in it not to want to be completely on the outside. I would only be willing to see the two groups amalgamated if I were sure that PCA would be willing to take the communist element out of its leadership.

Very sincerely yours,

TLc AERP, FDRL

---

1. See Document 292 for full discussion of Elliot Roosevelt's book.

2. Nedra Dalmann to ER, 2 April 1947, AERP.

3. Hubert H. Humphrey (1911–1978) then served as mayor of Minneapolis, a position he won in 1945 and would hold until 1949, when he left the mayoralty to represent Minnesota in the US Senate. Humphrey had been a strong supporter of Wallace's renomination as vice president in 1944 and made his political reputation consolidating alliances in the Popular Front tradition. However, by May 1946, state political battles convinced him that James Loeb was correct, "that progressives opposed to Communism had to mobilize or the American left would be lost to the Communists." September 7, 1946, he told the Minnesota AFL that "we must say what we are for and what we are against." Two days later he told a gathering in support of the UN that the Popular Front no longer worked and that its members must now rely on the Four Freedoms as the model for future cooperation. By the time Wallace delivered his Madison Square Garden address September 16, Humphrey could no longer support him: "Mr. Wallace says there are spheres of influence—I say this is one world." When Wallace visited Minnesota soon after their break, Humphrey, who remained convinced that Communists had taken over the Minnesota Farm-Democratic-Labor Party, failed to dissuade him from telling his audience that "his sympathy with the Soviet position was not to be construed as an endorsement of the American Communists" (Solberg, 111–15).

4. See header Document 194 for a similar assessment of Wallace.

ON AID TO YUGOSLAVIA, PART 1

By mid-April the Truman Doctrine dominated discussion of the future objectives of US foreign policy, especially in regard to military aid to Greece and Turkey. At the same time, US-based advocates for aid to postwar Yugoslavia grew increasingly anxious about American relief programs to that country as UNRRA had begun shutting down its operations in the first half of 1947. Michael M. Nisselson, acting president of the American Committee for Yugoslav Relief (ACYR), wrote to Secretary of State Marshall in early March, reminding him that "during discussions which concerned the post-UNRRA relief plans of the United States, the former director-general of UNRRA, Fiorello H. La Guardia, expressed fears that adoption of a unilateral relief policy might result in discrimination against countries such as Yugoslavia. State Department representatives, however, repeatedly emphasized that our Government would take into account hunger and human needs and not politics."

After attacks on US aircraft flying through Yugoslav airspace[1] and lingering questions about free elections and the freedom of religion under Tito's regime, suspicions persisted that any decisions made about US relief to Yugoslavia would henceforth be entangled inexorably with anti-Communist political considerations rather than critical need.[2]

Zlatko Balokovic (1895–1965), a classical violinist from Zagreb who served as the former president of ACYR, knew ER through their joint efforts on behalf of the committee.[3] He and his American wife Joyce defended Tito's government, making a case for its independence from Moscow to anyone they could contact in the State Department. On March 28, 1947, he wrote ER to express his concern about the post-UNRRA food crisis in Yugoslavia, complaining that "Mr. Acheson has absolutely refused to grant any food supplies for Yugoslavia," and asking ER to help by making a "personal and public protest" of her own.[4]

As Marshall was out of the country, ER addressed her concerns to Acting Secretary Dean Acheson.[5]

215

Eleanor Roosevelt to Dean Acheson
11 April 1947 [Hyde Park]

Dear Mr. Secretary:

Mr. Balokovic is a musician, and an American citizen, having come from Yugoslavia. He and his wife went on a trip to Yugoslavia last summer and I quite understand his feeling that the people in Yugoslavia should not be allowed to starve.

I understand also, that there is really not enough wheat to go around, but that UNRRA has enough money to buy and ship potatoes to Yugoslavia at present if it is done quickly. Why should this not be done? Starving people are not friendly to us and will not become less communistic.[6]

Very sincerely yours,
Eleanor Roosevelt

TLS AERP, FDRL

<u>216</u>

Dean Acheson to Eleanor Roosevelt
28 April 1947

Dear Mrs. Roosevelt:

I have your letter of April 11th with reference to the purchase of potatoes by UNRRA for shipment to Yugoslavia.

Approximately 10,000 tons of potatoes were shipped to Yugoslavia on UNRRA account during March and April and another 7,500 tons will move forward early in May. No shipments can be made after that date because of the risk of spoilage.

The price of Maine potatoes is now approximately $3.00 per cwt., which is well above the support price of $2.20 per cwt., and the Department of Agriculture has therefore been unable to acquire enough potatoes under its support price program to fill all orders placed by or on behalf of foreign governments. Priority was given to seed potatoes for shipment to occupied areas during much of April, and other orders have been filled partly on the basis of priority of filing and partly on the basis of need. Since the Department of Agriculture is selling for export at a price of approximately 35 cents per cwt. there is a large element of relief in all sales made and some criterion of need must be applied.

Our latest information from the United States Embassy in Belgrade indicates that if the Yugoslav Government will undertake to ship grain from central stocks within its own borders to the deficit areas, its population can be relatively much better fed than the people of certain other countries which are dependent upon the United States for food supplies.

Sincerely yours,
Dean Acheson

TLcst RG59, NARA II

As she awaited Acheson's reply to her letter of April 11, ER continued to press her point. April 15, ER speculated in My Day that the problem was one of resources rather than political considerations:

> Someone said to me the other day that it is impossible to give wheat to the starving people of Poland and Yugoslavia because not enough wheat could be found in the world. We had again underestimated the world need and therefore we had not processed potatoes last summer when they should have been processed, so we could not supplement wheat with dehydrated potatoes. There is only one alternative in that case. That is to make a plea to people in countries like our own, where they are eating better than ever before, to curtail the amount of wheat products they use and to divert this essential foodstuff to the nations that will starve between now and July if we do not do so. Nobody, as far as I know, is asking the people of the different nations to do this.[7]

The following day, she wrote Acheson for a third time, inserting a handwritten query demanding, "What is the truth?"

217

Eleanor Roosevelt to Dean Acheson

16 April 1947 [New York City]

Dear Mr. Acheson,

I agree that our assistance must go where the needs are most urgent.[8] However, I am told that the United States will not sell to Yugoslavia and that our attitude is part of our "Stop Russia" policy. What is the truth?

Very sincerely,
Eleanor Roosevelt

TLS RG59, NARA II

Even though Acheson received ER's second letter of April 16 prior to drafting his reply to her initial query, he replied to them separately—waiting an additional week before mailing his second response and then referring to material he had sent ER two months before.

218

Dean Acheson to Eleanor Roosevelt

7 May 1947 [Washington, DC]

Dear Mrs. Roosevelt:

I refer to your letter of April 16 in which you mention reports that the United States will not sell to Yugoslavia.

I believe that the enclosed press release will give you the information you desire on this subject.[9] I assure you that immediacy of need [is] the primary consideration in matters of this kind. This country will never sacrifice humanity in order to carry out any policy.

Faithfully yours,
Dean Acheson

TLS AERP, FDRL

---

1. See Document 140.

2. Michael M. Nisselson to George C. Marshall, March 3, 1947, AERP; Lash, *Years*, 96–97; *HSTE.*

3. ER served as ACYR's honorary chair from late 1945 and would continue in that position until the committee disbanded in July 1948. May 30, 1948, after the Justice Department designated ACYR a subversive organization, Balokovic wrote ER defending the organization but offering to let her resign before the committee wound up its affairs in July, lest the affiliation embarrass her.

She responded, "You are so near the closing time I will continue my affiliation until July 1st" (Zlatko Balokovic to ER, 30 May 1948, AERP; ER to Zlatko Balokovic, n.d., AERP).

4. "Yugoslav Aid Unit Plans to Disband," *NYT*, 14 July 1948, 15; finding aid, Zlatko Balokovic Papers, Immigration History Research Center, University of Minnesota; Zlatko Balokovic to ER, 28 March 1947, AERP.

5. Secretary Marshall was in Moscow for a Council of Foreign Ministers meeting in late March and early April 1947. ER also wrote to officials in the Department of Agriculture about wheat shipments to Yugoslavia around this time (Drew Middleton, "Visit by Marshall to Stalin Is Termed No Key to Impasse," *NYT*, 17 April 1947, 1; N. E. Dodd to ER, 6 May 1947[?], AERP).

6. ER's My Day column two days earlier laid out her stance at greater length. Recalling the United States' original policy of unilateral relief on the basis of need, she argued:

> But if you withhold food from a people, you sometimes achieve political results quite as much as if you give them food and allow them to use it for political purposes ... We cannot be of the opinion in our Congress that starving people are going to be better democrats. What we are doing is building up enemies.

She returned to the same theme in a column about Yugoslavia in November:

> ... [R]efusal to render aid to other nations which will keep their people alive and help them reestablish themselves on a healthy economic basis, seems to me a very shortsighted policy. One of the hopes for peace in the future is that we can divorce political beliefs from economic cooperation (*MD*, 9 April 1947; *MD*, 17 November 1947).

7. *MD*, 15 April 1947.

8. March 25, in a letter replying to her questions regarding Yugoslavian relief, Acheson enclosed, without comment or elaboration, State Department press release No. 221, released March 20, 1947, announcing the department's rejection of the Yugoslavian ambassador's request that some of the $350 million congressional relief appropriation be applied to "an immediate allocation of grain" from the United States to Yugoslavia. The release, which the *New York Times* reprinted in toto, stated that the department could not honor the request because, "The United States is in a position to grant free relief only to those countries having the greatest need. After careful consideration of all available information, the United States Government cannot conclude that the needs of Yugoslavia for free relief are in the same category as those of certain of the other devastated countries." Furthermore, the department argued, since current peace treaties require Bulgaria and Hungary to provide "current reparations including agricultural products to Yugoslavia, ... factors indicate that with good administration it would have been possible for the Yugoslav Government within its own resources to have avoided the necessity for now appealing for outside relief" (Press release No. 221, 20 March 1947, attached to Acheson to ER, 25 March 1947, AERP; "U.S. Statement on Yugoslav Needs," *NYT*, 21 March 1947, 10).

9. See *n*8 above.

Undersecretary in the Department of Agriculture N. E. Dodd, to whom ER also wrote, answered much as Acheson had done, arguing that "reliable information available to the United States as well as to the IEFC [International Emergency Food Council] indicates Yugoslavian requests for imports of grain are higher than justified, in the light of the world's short supplies, and the critical needs of many countries. Our information is that grain production was larger than reported by the Yugoslavian Government, collections were inadequate, and distribution has been faulty" (N. E. Dodd to ER, 6 May 1947 [?], AERP).

QUESTIONING THE TRUMAN DOCTRINE, PART 2

ER's correspondence with Secretary Acheson and her meetings with Thomas Power and Francis Russell did not ease her concerns regarding Truman's policy toward Greece and Turkey.[1]

As congressional debate intensified over the president's proposal, ER's worries increased. Senate Democrats split over Claude Pepper's strong rebuke of the Truman Doctrine that after "the United States killed UNRRA by failing to support it," the president now pushed a program that would force the American people to finance "armies in every nation in the world adequate to stamp out a government's opposition and to prevent people with views we don't like from winning the elections in those countries." Pepper offered a joint resolution to provide funds for humanitarian relief only, rather than relief and military assistance, for Greece and have that aid be administered through the United Nations.[2] Four days later Senator Vandenberg countered with an amendment of his own, "designed to meet the objections that the United States has 'by-passed' the United Nations." [3]

April 15, Aubrey Williams, perhaps the New Dealer with whom ER had the closest working relationship, wired ER a three-page telegram he planned to make public, in which he lamented the nation's "confused" leadership, which he thought would "lead only to a new version of the anti-comitern pact." If FDR were still alive, Williams predicted, he would say that a democracy cannot be established "in a nation where a King rules surrounded by Monarchists and Plutocrats"; that while "order and peace must be restored within Greece … [w]e must arm only Greek Republicans and Democrats"; and that the United States "must rebuild the Greek economy" by providing electricity, rebuilding transportation, rehabilitating "private productive enterprises," and establishing "a Greek national bank system similar to our own Federal Reserve system."

He then recommended that this program "be undertaken by American leadership acting under the sponsorship of the United Nations." Williams then closed by arguing, "America's great need today is for a positive program to strengthen democracy rather than a negative program aimed solely at a futile attempt to stop communism without offering anything better than the strengthening of autocracy and dictatorship."[4]

Two days later, ER took her concerns directly to the president.

219

Eleanor Roosevelt to Harry Truman
17 April 1947 [New York City]

Dear Mr. President:

I have carried on a lengthy correspondence with Secretary Acheson and I have seen a State Department representative sent by Secretary Acheson, to explain the Greek-Turkish situation to me.

I went to see Averill[5] Harriman the other day to try to get some enlightenment from him. I know that his appointment was very favorably received. Harry Hopkins thought highly of him but that was largely because he knew he could count on Averill to carry out directions. He is rich and generous and well meaning. I have known him since he was a little boy. I like him very much personally but I came away from talking to him, feeling that there was not sufficient realization of the domestic situation we are facing and its tie up with the foreign situation.

Our domestic and foreign policies are so closely tied together and the various moves made of late are so politically oriented, I feel some very clear sighted thinking is needed.

Between the Pepper Bill and the Vandenberg Amendment to the Administration Bill, I hoped that you might find some middle course. For that reason I am enclosing a copy of a wire which has come to me that expresses anxiety and makes some suggestions similar to those which have been made by other people. I am not sending it because it came from Aubrey Williams, but because it is comprehensive enough to be a good sample of a considerable amount of thinking which seems to be going on throughout the country.[6]

I do not believe that the Democratic party can win by going the Republican party one better in conservatism on the home front. Nor do I believe that taking over Mr. Churchill's policies in the Near East, in the name of democracy, is the way to really create a barrier to communism or promote democracy.

I do not think your advisers have looked far enough ahead. Admiral Leahy as always, will think of this country as moving on its own power.[7]

Both in Commerce and in Agriculture, we have not been far sighted enough to see that:

1. The safe guarding of food supplies for the world, even though it might mean keeping a little more than we need on hand was a wise policy.

2. The getting of business men to work in Europe and Russia is the only way we can really hope to rehabilitate Europe and establish democracy.

Mr. Acheson is rather more sympathetic to the British point of view than I would be and what with Mr. Lewis Douglas, who will certainly be sympathetic to Mr. Churchill's point of view,[8] I am afraid we are apt to lose sight of the fact that if we do not wish to fight Russia, we must be both honest and firm with her. She must understand us, but she must also trust us.

Please give my kind regards to Mrs. Truman and to Margaret. I hope the latter is feeling encouraged about her work. So many people have spoken to me favorably after hearing her on the radio.[9]

Very cordially yours,
Eleanor Roosevelt

TLS HSTOF, HSTL

Dean Acheson drafted Truman's response to ER's letter, to which Truman made only minor changes (indicated below) and then signed.[10] After reading the president's response, ER noted in the margins that she should "Show Elliott and Fjr and Joe."[11]

220

Harry Truman to Eleanor Roosevelt
7 May 1947 [The White House]

Dear Mrs. Roosevelt:

It was thoughtful of you to write me, as you did in your letter of April 17, telling me of your concern over recent world developments and giving me guidance. The Greek-Turkish matter which you mentioned has, I think, caused me more worry and soul-searching than any matter in these past two years. I felt the grave responsibility of the decision and the drawbacks to any course of action suggested. But it has also brought me, when the decision was made and as the issues have developed here and abroad, a growing feeling of certainty in the rightness of our step.

Your own concern and the concern of the sender of the wire you enclosed seem to be mainly, first, that we should not try to stop Communism by throwing our economic weight in at points which are of strategic importance but deficient in democracy, and, second, that we must outsell Communism by offering something better, that is, a constructive and affirmative program which will be recognized as such by the entire world and which can be effected without resort to the totalitarian methods of the Communist police state.

On the first half of this I would argue that if the Greek-Turkish land bridge between the continents is one point at which our democratic forces can stop the advance of Communism that has flowed steadily through the Baltic countries, Poland, Yugoslavia, Rumania, Bulgaria, to some extent Hungary, then this is the place to do it, regardless of whether or not the terrain is good.

The necessity at this point for formulating and carrying out a detailed operation to improve the situation is urged by Mr. Williams in his wire to you. While the details may differ considerably from those outlined by him, I am determined that the instructions to our mission will be worthy of the "support of all democratic nations", and will give no basis for the fear that it may be solely a "futile attempt to stop communism without offering anything better than the strengthening of autocracy and dictatorship."[12] A great deal of study is being carried on in anticipation of the successful passage of the legislation. The FAO Report and the Report of the Porter Mission will be considered and used along with the exceptional knowledge of our two Ambassadors.[13]

In answer to the second part of your concern, I would not disagree that we must have a democratic, constructive and affirmative program of wide scope. But I would argue with deep conviction that we have led in evolving, have helped to build, and have made clear to all who will understand, the most comprehensive machinery for a constructive world peace based on free institutions and ways of life that has ever been proposed and adopted by a body of nations. And I would urge that in evaluating the step we are about to take, we should keep clearly in mind all the efforts this country has engaged in sincerely to make possible a peace economically, ideologically and politically sound.

I know that I do not need to catalogue for you the international organizations to which I refer. Besides this machinery for peace, we have tried to eliminate the sources of war and, by our proposal for a four-power pact for the disarmament of Germany, we have tried to remove from Europe what may be the greatest basic cause of friction: the fear of German aggression or of the use of German territory for purposes of aggression.[14]

To what seems to me nearly the limit, we have made concessions to Russia that she might trust and not fear us. These include: Agreement at Tehran to support Tito's Partisans in Yugoslavia; Agreement at Yalta to give the Kurile Islands and southern Sakhalin to Russia, to recognize the independence of Outer Mongolia and Soviet interests in Dairen, Port Arthur, and the Chinese Eastern Railway; also at Yalta, agreement on the Curzon line as the western border of the Soviet Union, and to the admission of Byelorussia and the Ukraine to the United Nations; at Potsdam, agreement to the annexation by Russia of the northern portion of east Prussia, to the recognition of Soviet claims for preferential reparations from western Germany, to the necessity for modification of the provisions of the Montreaux Convention. In the peace treaty negotiations we have made concessions, particularly in regard to reparations from Italy and in our efforts to meet the Yugoslav and Soviet points of view on boundaries and administration of Venezia Giulia and Trieste.[15]

In addition, we have contributed to the defense of Russia during the war in lend-lease eleven and a quarter billion dollars and provided them with military and technological information. Since the war we have contributed to Russian relief through UNRRA two hundred and fifty million dollars and sold them on thirty-year credit goods totaling another one quarter billion dollars.

We have also protested, so far in vain, against what seemed to us violation of democratic procedures pledged at the Yalta Conference, in Poland, Rumania, Bulgaria and Yugoslavia.

To relieve suffering and to take the first steps toward material rehabilitation we have appropriated nearly four and one-quarter billion dollars and have asked for three hundred and fifty million dollars more in post-UNRRA relief.

Let us think, therefore, of Greek and Turkish aid against the background of these positive measures.

The results of our efforts thus far disappoint and dishearten many in this and other countries. I think we must place the blame not only on the obstructive tactics of elements opposed to our ideas of a democratic peace, but, also, to a certain extent, on our own reticence in stating the democratic purposes we have in mind.

So it seems to me, as it did to 67 senators who voted for the Bill that we must take our stand at this strategic point in a determined effort not to let the advance of Communism continue to overtake countries who choose to maintain a free way of life, who have requested our aid, and who do not wish to submit to subjugation by an armed minority or by outside pressure.

I have emphasized what seems to me to be the inescapable fact that this country has gone to great lengths to develop and carry out a constructive policy in world affairs. I have not discussed specifically the point you make that our domestic policy has a great influence on the manner in which we carry out our foreign policy. I am in complete agreement with you that what happens within this country is perhaps the most decisive factor in the future of world peace and economic well-being. We simply must not fall into political division, economic recession, or social stagnation; there must be social progress at home.[16] I shall continue to point out to the country what seem to me the measures most suited to accomplish this progress. I shall continue to take every action within my own power to see that the United States has a progressive domestic policy that will deserve the confidence of the world and will serve as a sound foundation for our international policy. I shall at all times be grateful for any suggestions and criticisms which you may care to send me.

Nor does it seem to me that we can overlook the fact that as much as the world needs a progressive America, the American way of life cannot survive unless other peoples who want to adopt that pattern of life throughout the world can do so without fear and in the hope of success. If this is to be possible we cannot allow the forces of disintegration to go unchecked.

I certainly appreciate your kind personal message to Mrs. Truman which I was glad to convey to her, and your expressions regarding Margaret's singing are especially gratifying. She too will be greatly pleased.[17]

Very sincerely yours,
Harry Truman

It was necessary to check the facts before I could answer. It took some time—hence the delay. I regret that it took so long. H.S.T.

TLS AERP, FDRL

---

1. See Document 208.

2. "Speech of Senator Claude Pepper Over ABC Network," 27 March 1947, Claude Pepper Library, Florida State University.

3. Vandenberg's amendment required Truman to stop aid to Greece and Turkey if any one of three conditions were met: if a majority of the members of the UN Security Council or the General Assembly requested the program end; if a majority of either of the two nations' governments asked that the program stop; or if Truman thought "the purposes of the program have been accomplished,

or are incapable of being accomplished" ("Mr. Vandenberg's Amendment," *NYT*, 1 April 1947, C26; C. P. Trussell, "Senate Gives U.N. Mid-East Aid Veto," *NYT*, 10 April 1947, 1).

4. Aubrey Williams to ER, 15 April 1947, AERP.

5. ER continuously misspelled Averell Harriman, whom Truman appointed secretary of commerce in September 1946.

6. Social worker, New Dealer, editor, and civil rights activist, Aubrey Williams (1890–1965) worked closely with Harry Hopkins and ER in his positions as deputy director of the Federal Emergency Relief Administration, administrator of the Civil Works Administration, director of the National Youth Administration, and advocate for the FEPC. A close friend of ER, who defended him when Congress attacked him for refusing to denounce Communists and the *New York Times* accused him of working "to introduce socialism through the back door," Williams then served as publisher and editor of the *Southern Farmer* (*ANB*).

7. Admiral William D. Leahy (1877–1959), one of FDR's most trusted aides, first began working with Roosevelt in 1915 when he served as an aide to navy secretary Josephus Daniels. After 1933, Leahy served in a variety of positions in the Roosevelt administration: chief of the Bureau of Navigation, chief of Naval Operations, governor of Puerto Rico, ambassador to the Vichy government, chairman of the Joint Chiefs of Staff, and, finally, chief of staff to FDR himself, a position which allowed him to accompany FDR to Tehran and Yalta, where he questioned British intentions and worried that FDR trusted Stalin too much. As chairman of the Joint Chiefs for both FDR and Truman, Leahy remained strongly anti-Soviet, so much so that Truman once called him one of the "only hard-boiled hard hitting anti-Russians around." Leahy also expressed distrust of those whom he labeled State Department "pinkies" (*ANB*).

8. Lewis W. Douglas (1894–1974), who left Congress after four terms representing Arizona in the House of Representatives to become director of the budget, turned into one of FDR's most vocal critics when FDR abandoned his promise to balance the budget. Accusing FDR of creating "collectivism," Douglas advised Alfred Landon in 1936 and headed Democrats for Wilkie in 1940. In 1947, Truman, who had first tried to nominate Douglas as head of the World Bank only to have him refuse the position, appointed him ambassador to Great Britain. As ambassador, he embraced both the Marshall Plan and the containment doctrine and presided over the secret Canadian-American negotiations that led to the formation of the North American Alliance (*ANB; HSTE*).

9. Margaret Truman, the president's daughter, who aspired to a singing career, made her debut on national radio in March 1947 (Hamby, *Man*, 476).

10. Dean Acheson to Bill Hassett, 6 May 1947, RG59, NARA II.

11. Elliott Roosevelt, Franklin Roosevelt, Jr., and Joe Lash.

12. See *n*4 above.

13. The Food and Agriculture Organization of the United Nations presented its mission's study on the conditions of Greece in a report in March of 1947. UN experts found Greece devastated by war, both in material and economic conditions. They emphasized, however, that Greece would be able to fully redevelop its economy and agriculture with international assistance. The report recommended an international loan in an initial amount of $100 million. American policy regarding Greece and Turkey thus superseded the recommendations of the FAO report, but used their findings to support the argument for immediate and direct aid. In addition to the findings of the FAO report, the Truman administration sent Paul A. Porter (1904–1975) as head of the American Economic Mission to Greece in December 1946 "to do a firsthand evaluation of Greek economic needs." Lincoln MacVeagh (1890–1972), the American ambassador in Greece, and economist Paul R. Porter wired Marshall on February 20, 1947, recommending that the United States immediately implement a policy "not to permit foreign encroachment, either from without or within, on independence and integrity of Greece." On March 28, 1947, Porter reported the results of his two

month study to the House Committee on Foreign Affairs, emphasizing that he found the Greek economy in great peril. He stated, "If this country assumes obligations … I have confidence that Greece will not forfeit what I believe to be her last clear chance for independence" (Richard E. Prince, "Lincoln MacVeagh Dies at 82," *WP*, 17 January 1972, C4; Donovan, 277; Hamby, *Man*, 390; Thomas J. Hamilton, "FAO Greek Project Off Agenda of U.N.," *NYT*, 28 March 1947, 10; Mazuzan, 61; John T. McQuiston, "Paul A. Porter, Capital Lawyer Who Held New Deal Posts, Dies," *NYT*, 27 November 1975, 36; *SDB*, 4 May 1947, 842–47; "What Greece Might Be," *NYT*, 17 March 1947, 22).

14. See *n*4 Document 198.

15. See *n*4 Document 140.

16. Truman deleted the original first clause of this sentence in the Acheson draft, which read, "I believe that the leaders of the Democratic Party and the officials in public office are all aware that …" (Harry Truman to ER, draft, 5 May 1947, attached to Dean Acheson to William Hassett, 6 May 1947, RG59, NARA II).

17. Truman also inserted this paragraph into the final version of his letter (ibid).

On Wallace's European Lecture Tour

Henry Wallace's announcement in January that he would lecture in Europe generated swift reaction. Immediately, seventy prominent self-identified "liberal" Americans telegraphed British foreign minister Bevin that Wallace's sole source of support was "a small minority of Communists, fellow-travelers and what we call here totalitarian liberals." More than a hundred of Wallace's most famous supporters countered the telegram with a scroll of friendship declaring that "the success of the United Nations depends upon the continued cooperation of Great Britain, Russia and the United States." Four days before Wallace's April 7 departure, Secretary of the Navy Forrestal suggested during a cabinet meeting that the president revoke Wallace's passport.[1]

Tensions escalated after Wallace's April 11 speech in London's Central Hall in which he rejected the Truman Doctrine and argued that the "devastated and hungry" world "is crying out, not for American guns and tanks to spread more hunger, but for American plows and machines to fulfill the promise of peace." In a BBC broadcast the following day, Wallace delivered a more ringing criticism:

> A great national awakening has occurred in Asia and in other parts of the world which we used to think of only as colonies. This new nationalism will turn to communism and look to the Soviet Union as their only ally, if the United States declares that this is the American century of power politics rather than the Century of the Common Man.

Churchill, whose "Iron Curtain" speech had also been criticized, labeled Wallace "a crypto-communist." An outraged Congress debated revoking his passport and the French political leaders who supported his appearance in Paris now distanced themselves, announcing that none would be present when he delivered his speech.[2]

ER's April 16 column reflected a calmer viewpoint. She admitted that she had been "troubled" by a question she received during a Connecticut forum as to whether "the Truman policy had hurt the United Nations." She continued:

> That, of course, is basically what troubles Henry Wallace. He feels that we are pulling further and further apart, and that, without realizing it, we may be setting the stage for a two-world catastrophe.

> I am rather sorry that Mr. Wallace had to go to England to make his speeches in order to get them printed in this country, because I do not like criticisms of our country made abroad. I prefer them made at home. But in all fairness we have to recognize that Mr. Wallace's rather dramatic action has brought an amount of attention which probably nothing else would have brought.[3]

After reading her column, C. B. Baldwin wired ER asking her to co-sign the following message from a "group of distinguished progressives" to the leaders of the four major French political parties who had invited Wallace to lecture in France:

> We the undersigned Americans wish to convey our wholehearted support for the sentiments for peace as expressed by Mr. Wallace. Mr. Wallace's trip to Europe is a continuation of his vigilant and constant fight for Franklin Delano Roosevelt's concept of one world. His deep conviction that only through the United Nations can the nations of the world be assured of lasting peace echoes the sentiments of the majority of the American people. We take this opportunity to reaffirm the deep feeling of amity and good will which has long existed between [the] peoples of our nations and to pledge our unflagging energy by

your side in the fight for peace. It is our hope that Mr. Wallace's visit will set a pattern in this one world for the free interchange of opinion between the leaders and the peoples of all nations of good will.[4]

ER refused Baldwin's request.

— 221 —

Eleanor Roosevelt to C. B. Baldwin
17 April 1947 [New York City]

Dear Mr. Baldwin:

I am sorry but I can not sign a message to the people who invited Mr. Henry Wallace to come to France.

I do not believe that it is wise for Mr. Wallace to be making the kind of speeches he is making at the present time in foreign countries.

Naturally I have no idea what my husband's attitude would be if he were alive today, and though I am convinced he would have wanted to strengthen the UN, I doubt if he would want to do it in just the way that Mr. Wallace has found necessary. I have such complete confidence in Mr. Wallace's integrity, I am sure he has taken this course because he felt he had to, but with all my heart I wish for his own sake that he had not done so.

Very sincerely yours,

TLc AERP, FDRL

---

1. The first group included Henry and Clare Booth Luce, *American Mercury* journalist Lawrence Spivak, broadcaster H. V. Kaltenborn, and former Roosevelt aide A. A. Berle; the Wallace supporters included Rexford Tugwell, Helen Keller, Thomas Mann, Dashiell Hammet, and Arthur Miller (Culver, 438).

2. Culver, 438–41; "Wallace Prosecution Asked As Congress Furor Mounts," *NYT*, 15 April 1947, 1; Harold Callender, "French Worried on Wallace Visit," *NYT*, 12 April 1947, 6; Harold Callender, "Paris Politicians 'Disown' Wallace," *NYT*, 22 April 1947, 21.

3. *MD*, 16 April 1947.

4. "Wallace to Visit France," *NYT*, 2 April 1947, 29; C. B. Baldwin to ER, 16 April 1947, AERP.

ON AID TO YUGOSLAVIA, PART 2

The American Committee for Yugoslav Relief (ACYR) sent ER an appeal May 12 to join "a thousand representative Americans from all parts of the country" in a letter-writing campaign to ask Truman to allocate $15 million of "unearmarked" relief appropriation funds to Yugoslavia. Executive director of the ACYR Nat Einhorn ended his entreaty with, "We know of no one whose appeal will get so quick and warm-hearted a response as yourself."

A week later, ER replied, turning down Einhorn's request. "I never send this type of letter to him or to any of the government officials," she explained. "However, I shall write to him on the subject on my own."[1] She then sent the president the following letter.

ER's appeal did not work. Truman forwarded this letter to an aide with a note scrawled across the bottom: "Bill[2]: Think up a good answer. Will talk to you about it. Promise the Jugs <u>nothing</u>. They use help to browbeat their neighbors. H.S.T."

222

Eleanor Roosevelt to Harry Truman
19 May 1947 [Hyde Park]

Dear Mr. President:

I know you are going to receive letters on the food situation in Yugoslavia, and the $15,000,000 in unmarked funds that will be available for distribution by you.

In spite of anything that may have occurred, I feel very strongly that it is important that the Yugoslav people should have relief in the way of food. They did hold the nazis at bay at a time which was crucial in the war.[3]

Many thanks for your long letter in answer to mine. I do appreciate your taking the time to write me so fully.

> Very cordially yours,
> Eleanor Roosevelt

TLS HSTOF, HSTL

---

1. Nat Einhorn to ER, 12 May 1947 and ER to Nat. Einhorn, 19 May 1947, AERP.

2. William D. Hassett (1880–1965), secretary to the president, responded to ER on Truman's behalf June 10, 1947, stating, "The reports which are available to the Government concerning food conditions in Yugoslavia do not indicate that the situation there is as serious as in certain other countries, although food may not be fully adequate in some parts of Yugoslavia." Hassett, a former newspaper reporter, had joined the White House staff in 1935 and served as correspondence secretary since 1944, first for FDR and then for Truman (William D. Hassett to ER, 10 June 1947, HSTOF, HSTL; Edward T. Folliard, "William D. Hassett, Aide to FDR, Truman," *WP*, 31 August 1965, B4; *HSTE*).

3. Partisans in Yugoslavia fought German and Italian occupation forces in irregular, guerrilla actions starting May 1941. Initially, there were two main partisan groups: one, known as the

Chetniks, led by the Serbian monarchist Draza Mihailovic; the other, a group of antimonarchists called simply "the Partisans," led by Marshall Tito (Josip Broz). As the Chetniks began to cooperate with the Axis occupiers, the Partisans gained the confidence and covert support of the Allies. Tito's Partisans led a significant offensive February 1943 in Bosnia that forced the Axis armies into Operation Schwarz, a large, resources-draining counteroffensive. Tito attracted more overt support of the Allies in 1944, acquiring Italian weapons for his approximately 120,000 troops. When the Soviet Red Army entered Yugoslavia, in the autumn, the Partisans assisted them in their final drive to oust the Nazi puppet government from Belgrade October 20, 1944 (Keegan, 492–94).

THE US, GREAT BRITAIN, RUSSIA, AND THE REHABILITATION OF GERMANY

When the Council of Foreign Ministers adjourned their seven-week meeting in Moscow unable to reach agreement either on the economic and political unification of Germany or on treaties to prevent German rearmament and restore Austrian independence, the split between the East and West deepened. The United States and Great Britain (later joined by France) independently pursued plans to unify and economically strengthen their occupation zones in Germany.

When Secretary of State Marshall and John Foster Dulles, who attended the meetings as a special advisor to Marshall, returned home at the end of April, both addressed the nation. Marshall and his colleague agreed that the German government must be weak and decentralized, that the industrial resources of the Ruhr should be shared with the rest of Europe, and that significant reparations would slow the German, and hence the European, recovery. Both men also thought that the main obstacles to agreement remained the Soviet demand for a strong, centralized German government, a German economy crippled by a reduction in German territory, and Russia's insistence that it receive manufactured goods as reparations.

Yet Dulles's remarks offered a more blunt criticism of the Soviets, especially their efforts to penetrate into Western Europe, and a more insistent call for the West to move ahead on its own with the economic and political rehabilitation of the areas of Germany it controlled.

Soviet foreign policy "depends little on getting results by negotiation." Rather,

it depends much on getting results by penetrating into the political parties and labor organizations of other countries … Soviet leaders have such confidence in these methods that they are willing to let Germany again become a great industrial power. They are using those methods now to get the kind of Germany they want.

In the Soviet zone of Germany, the dominant political party and the labor unions are already subject to Soviet will, though they may not know it themselves. It is much the same in the French zone of Germany. In the British and the United States zones, Soviet influence in the political parties and labor unions is growing rapidly. Soviet agitators there, as elsewhere, have ample funds, they are well trained and they are adept at enlisting local zealots and malcontents and getting them into key positions.

The American people should draw some conclusions from that. One conclusion is that we cannot afford to feel complacent merely because, at conferences, we have stopped surrendering our principles. Soviet activity is not suspended merely because the Council of Foreign Ministers disagrees and takes a recess.

Also we must not feel complacent because we have supremacy in certain kinds of military weapons. The challenge we face is not a military one. I am confident that Soviet leaders do not want war. Also, they are too smart to challenge us at a level where, temporarily at least, they are at a grave disadvantage. The present challenge is at a level where they are well equipped and where we are poorly equipped.

Dulles concluded his remarks calling on Americans to "work unceasingly for our ideals … in ways that count."

We should, of course, invoke the aid of the United Nations whenever it can do the job. But we cannot let ourselves be stymied merely because we cannot get agreement or because the United Nations is not yet able to take over the full task of maintaining freedom in the world. It is up to us to show, in every available way, that free institutions are the means whereby men can save themselves from the sea of misery in which they find themselves.[1]

ER listened to the speech over the radio and then "read it over and over again very carefully" when the *New York Times* printed Dulles's remarks the following day.

Three weeks later, she sent Dulles the following suggestion.

223

Eleanor Roosevelt to John Foster Dulles
21 May 1947 [Hyde Park]

Dear Mr. Dulles:

After hearing your report on the Moscow meeting, I have been thinking it over, and I read it over again very carefully on Monday.

I wonder if there is not something which we have not tried. Of course, you may know that what I am about to suggest, has been suggested and rejected. However, it would seem to me that it might possibly solve some of our difficulties with the USSR.

I perfectly see their economic situation, and the reason for their change on Germany.[2] The tactics which you describe are, of course, familiar to me. I know well the Soviet methods of infiltration and effort to control trade unions and other groups. They count on these methods to win peoples to their point of view, just as we count on the freedom we give peoples in our trade unions and the justice and liberty which we enjoy not only to keep, but to win peoples to democracy.

The economic idea which I have seen no where suggested to the Soviet government would be this:

The risk is too great in their plan for Germany. We agree entirely on the international control of the Ruhr, and I am quite sure they would agree too, if they could see some way of getting what they want without requiring German industry to increase so much that they had to have the entire output from the Ruhr.[3]

Great Britain has the capacity to provide a few things. We have the capacity to provide practically everything which is essential to building up the industries of the USSR and countries that depend upon her. We wish, of course, to give proper share to our Allies in Europe which we hope to build up so that they never again depend on Germany in the way they had to depend in the past. A proper distribution of coal from the Ruhr can insure that once they have the set up there, they will not need Germany as they did in the past for their economic life.

The question is how would the USSR pay for the things if we provide them and Great Britain does the same where she can. There is only one way and that is with raw materials. The USSR is rich in raw materials but she has to have the machinery to produce them. She has a shortage of manpower so if she produced the raw materials it would be many years before she could really be in competition with Great Britain or ourselves in manufactured goods. The same thing holds true of many of her neighboring countries.

I am wondering if along this line, something could not be worked out which would actually safeguard us, but at the same time, be of benefit to the other countries and bring about an agreement. I know you realize the need for agreement where it is possible, as well as I do. I think this would help us on the political side because it would help our economic situation at home to straighten itself out and to stay more stable in the next few years. This rehabilitation program from the economic standpoint would, I think, strengthen the belief in democracy on the part of other nations, as nothing else can.

I wanted to write you this letter before I wrote anything about this in my column, because if it has already been tried and rejected, I would treat it in a different way.[4] However, I do not think that having been rejected is any reason for not trying to work for it again and it seems advantageous all around.

Very cordially yours,
Eleanor Roosevelt

TLS JFDP, NjP-SC

224

John Foster Dulles to Eleanor Roosevelt
26 May 1947 [New York City]

Dear Mrs. Roosevelt:

I apologize for not answering more promptly your letter of May 21st. It was because I was in Washington the latter part of last week.

There has been some thinking, principally in private quarters, with reference to the possibility of giving some present relief to Soviet Russia in exchange for their agreement to give us later on some raw material. However, as far as I know, nothing concrete has ever been considered officially, nor, as far as I know, have there been any discussions with the Russians themselves along this line.

There are, I think, some practical difficulties. While the amounts of dollar credits we can vote are theoretically unlimited, there is a limit to the amount of goods we can produce and export. Whether or not we could add large exports to Russia to those we are now making to England, France, etc., is, I think, a question. This point, however, has not been adequately studied. One of the matters with which I was concerned in Washington was that a careful study be made as to relationship between foreign credits voted and available goods. If the credits get out of proportion to the goods, the principal effect is to put up prices. Mr. Bevin complained to me in Moscow that wheat had doubled in price since the British loan was made.[5] That, I suspect, is due to the fact that the French and others were given credits with which to buy wheat and there was not enough to go around.

A political difficulty is the distrust between the two countries and the fear in many quarters here that any economic relief which we give to Russia would be used by them to build up a military establishment which might later be used against us. In talking in Washington with some of the members of Congress, I found that feeling very strong.

Sincerely yours,
John Foster Dulles

TLS AERP, FDRL

225

Eleanor Roosevelt to John Foster Dulles
3 June 1947 [New York City]

Dear Mr. Dulles:

Many thanks for your letter of May 26th. I am very much interested and hope you will let me know the developments.[6]

Very sincerely,
Eleanor Roosevelt

TLS JFDP, NjP-SC

---

1. C. L. Sulzberger, "Allies Seek Unity," *NYT*, 10 March 1947, 1; "Text of Secretary Marshall's Report to Nation on Big 4 Conference," *NYT*, 29 April 1947, 4; "Dulles' Report to the Nation on Moscow Conference of Big 4 Foreign Ministers," *NYT*, 30 April 1947, 12.

2. Under the Potsdam Agreement, the Russians had accepted German reparations in the form of capital assets and had moved machinery and whole factories to Russia. Now the Russians demanded reparations in the form of $10 billion in finished goods. The Russians had also favored a decentralized German government and a weakened German economy. Now they wanted a centralized German government and a reindustrialized Germany capable of delivering finished goods to the Soviet Union (Hoopes, 68–69; "Dulles' Report to the Nation on Moscow Conference of Big 4 Foreign Ministers," *NYT*, 30 April 1947, 12).

3. The Ruhr had long been the most productive industrial complex in Europe and the center of the German armament industry. After World War II, many in the West favored international control of the Ruhr so that its resources would be shared with neighboring countries and Germany could not rearm (*OEWH*). See also Document 198 and notes.

4. ER did not discuss in My Day the proposal to trade manufactured goods to the Soviet Union in exchange for raw materials. But in August, when commenting on an article in the *New York Times* by Lester Markel, she expressed her own ongoing concern about the reindustrialization of Germany. In doing so, she closely echoed the view Dulles had expressed in his report that the Russians were willing to risk the creation of a strong, reindustrialized Germany because they needed what it could produce and felt they could control it through subversion:

> I was interested that Mr. Markel also noted that, because of our concern over Russia, we might find it easy to rebuild an industrial Germany through the Marshall Plan, but that the democratization of the German people was far from easy and far from sure. To rebuild Germany as an industrial empire capable of making war will be opposed, I think, by France and every small Western European nation. It is quite evident that the USSR has decided she needs the things Germany can produce, and that she hopes that, with her usual methods of infiltration, she may control the labor unions and build a strong communist influence in German government. Therefore she is taking a chance on building up German industrial strength. Germany and the USSR together could be a strong combination. But the USSR must realize that this is building two worlds very rapidly (*MD*, 7 August 1947).

5. On British loan, see *n*6 Document 60.

6. On June 16, Dulles sent ER a copy of a commencement speech he was to give at Northwestern University, "which seeks to clarify our national attitude in certain respects where it seems to be unduly aggressive and imperialistic." Dulles thought: "Because our Society is so powerful and because most of us believe in it so completely, it is easy for hostile propaganda to spread fear that we will use our power to coerce others." Therefore, he continued, for the United States to become a moral leader in the world, it "must make it clear, clear beyond a doubt, that it has no thought of using economic or military might to impose on others its particular way of life." ER replied on June 21 that reading the speech "makes me want to talk to you more than ever on certain things" and invited Mr. and Mrs. Dulles to Hyde Park for lunch and, if possible, to bring Ambassador and Mrs. Austin with them. Dulles replied that he and Mrs. Dulles and the Austins would like to come but could not do so in the near future (Dulles to ER, 16 June 1947, AERP; Dulles, Commencement Address, Northwestern University, 18 June 1947, AERP; ER to Dulles, 21 June 1947, JFDP, NjP-SC).

EDUCATION AND THE PERFECTION OF DEMOCRACY

Eighteen months after ER delivered the Roosevelt College Founder's Day address, she returned to Chicago's Hotel Intercontinental to address a ballroom packed with college supporters.[1] The college had made remarkable progress since her last visit, achieving accreditation in only one year, more than doubling its enrollment, and remodeling its new facilities.[2] Furthermore, the national media began to pay close attention to its development. When the college announced a requirement that all students must take a course in "the culture of a non-English speaking people," the *New York Times* noted the announcement in its Education Notes, quoting the faculty who approved the requirement, underscoring the requirement's critical importance by declaring that "this would 'be one world or none.'" The *Washington Post* followed suit, noting the college's "combination of low fees and nondiscriminatory admission" and its "star-studded advisory board" ensured that "Chicago's 'Equality Lab' Thrives." [3]

College president Edward J. Sparling, like his fellow faculty members, recognized the important model the institution offered the nation, telling those assembled that "Roosevelt College offers an important laboratory in democratic education. Not in ivory towers, but in institutions which grapple with real problems in a real way, will the questions of democracy be solved. To prepare ourselves for one world, men of all races must learn to work and play together as they do here in the college."[4]

In the following address, ER seconds Sparling's comments and offers her own explanation why the college's commitment to democratic ideals is so important to America's leadership in the world.

226

Speech on Behalf of Roosevelt College
24 May 1947 [Chicago]

Ladies and Gentlemen of Roosevelt College: I have been enormously interested tonight in all the things that I have heard about Roosevelt College. And in many ways I think one of the things that I have been hoping for is being worked out here.

You know, to me the most important thing in the world today is that we here in this country should consciously work for the perfection of our own democracy, and should understand that it has to come by the improvement of each individual and the individual community. It cannot come from the top down; it has to come from the bottom up.[5]

And the reason that I feel this so keenly is that I have had to work with the representatives of 55 nations, and it is very embarrassing, sometimes, when they come to you and say—because they do read—they come to this country and they read our papers—and they travel around and they meet us—and they come to you and say, "Is this a process of democracy?" You find it a little hard sometimes to just explain what this process is that they have come across.

I have come to feel that when the whole world is looking to a nation because it is the strongest nation in the world, because it is the greatest democracy, then there is a tremendous responsibility on the people of that nation. They—I think most of them—have been living in great comfort, with the Constitution which they like very much but which they didn't feel it incumbent upon them to re-read too often, particularly the Bill of Rights part of it.

And so it was quite possible to go along and say, "O yes—some day we really will live up to all the things that we say we believe in." But when you become the leading nation in the world, you have no longer the comfortable situation of feeling that you can indulge yourself in dreams, about what you really are; you have to come face to face with the facts of how you truly function.

That has brought me to feel that what has to happen here in our country is that we as individuals have to become very conscious of what we mean by democracy; and that democracy must be something you live day by day, and that enters into everything you do. You can't just put it aside and bring it out every now and then when it is convenient; it is something you live by.

That leads you to feel that it has to be strong in every community. If it isn't strong in every community, then the nation will never really be the kind of nation where the people really make the policies; where the people really know that they are represented by their representatives.

And so, to find education going on in a group of young people, which is aimed at making them conscious of their responsibilities in a democracy, is a very heartening thing, because we cannot escape leadership. I think we would like to very much, but we were spared in this war, and merely because of that, leadership must come from us. We must prove that what we believe in really is worth believing in.

Someone said to me the other day that there was no reason at all why we should prove that democracy was better than communism, let us say, since that is the other great force in the world today. Why should we prove anything at all? Why not leave it all to them to prove?

Well, the answer is that at present proof has to be brought about by enthusiasm. Now, there is plenty of enthusiasm in communism; and unless we have as much vitality and as much crusading spirit, we do run a certain danger.

It isn't enough to be <u>against</u> something. You have to be <u>for</u> something with more real feeling, that you have something that is really worth-while for the world as a whole. I do not mean that you have to make everybody else think as you do and live as you do. I simply mean that each of us who believes that democracy really has the essence of something which can give more to the people than anything else—we who believe that—have to show that it is true. We have to make of our nation the kind of a nation that truly can say, "We live up to the things we believe in. We have a unified nation."

It is going to take us a long while to do it, but everything worth-while takes a long while. And it seems to me that if we realize that it is something each of us works at, and that it is something that affects us, of course—it affects how we live; what we do—but it also affects what is going on in the world as a whole.

I am rather glad that attacks come to Roosevelt College from both the right and the left, because that is a pretty sure sign that you are going pretty well down the middle of the road. And you couldn't possibly be a liberal educational force and not be subject to attacks from both sides.[6]

And I am glad that you don't take it too seriously. I am glad that you persist in the processes of democracy, because those processes take time to work out. But they are the processes which really show the difference between our theories and collectivist theories.

I always remember a conversation I heard between a person of considerable importance in his own country and one of our own democratic leaders. There was considerable trouble in this country, and it was causing the government a good deal of worry and anxiety. And I heard the democrat say, "Well, what would you do in your country if you had this situation? And you had certain leaders?"

And the answer was, "O, we deal with that very easily. We would take the leaders and do this (sign of cutting the throat)."

That is a very simple answer, and at times it is much more tempting than going through the process of democracy.

But I think for us the real progress that can be made is if our youth can understand what we are trying to do in this country, and what we hope for in the future. I think if this College can send out people who are trained to a sense of responsibility, personal responsibility, for what happens in their community, in their environment, then I think this College will have done a tremendous work for democracy at home and for a solution to the great world problems that we have to lead in solving today.

Those problems are very difficult problems. Just in the mere small things that happen when you meet with the representatives of 55 nations you come to see how difficult just understanding backgrounds and differences of customs and habits may be.

I will tell you one funny story on myself, which perhaps is not a very good example, but still will show how little we do know about little things, and how easily little things can make for misunderstandings.

When I was elected chairman of our Commission on Human Rights, I thought it was a very bad choice because I know no parliamentary law! So I thought, "What am I going to do? I had better get up and tell them now before I get started and I make terrible mistakes."

So I got up and said I would have to call on the men on the Commission who knew a great deal of parliamentary law to help me out. I said, "I only know two things. One is that when a motion is offered, you have to have a seconder to the motion before you can discuss it." And I saw my Belgian colleague, who is just wonderful at parliamentary law, look at me smilingly.

He said, "Madam, under United Nations' rule, you do not have to have a seconder." So, Rule No. 1 was useless.

I said, "I only know one other rule, and that is that when there is a motion and there are amendments to it, your poor chairman has to try to decide what is the amendment furthest away from the original motion so as to get that voted on first." And I noticed my USSR colleague look at me and shrug his shoulders and look down, and he didn't say anything. I didn't know what it was all about, but I went on.

Several days later we had a little difficulty with our British colleague because he didn't seem to understand a point of view very well, so they suggested that I invite him to lunch, with his advisors. So I invited him to lunch, and we settled the point of view on the question at issue; and then one of his young advisers said, "I spent several years in Russia, Mrs. Roosevelt. I speak Russian. You didn't know it, but you cleared up a point the other day."

I said, "I cleared up a point? What did I clear up? I noticed that my Russian colleague looked sort of queerly at me, but I didn't know I had cleared anything up."

This young man said, "Well, you know in Russia they vote on the motion; they don't vote on the amendment furthest away; and nobody has ever really convinced them here that they weren't being hurt, this wasn't being something that was done to keep them from getting a vote on their motions. And when you just out of a clear blue sky explained that it was a rule, the USSR delegate looked at you, and I'm sure he went and told everybody else, 'Well, Mrs. Roosevelt said it was a rule so it probably is; it probably isn't a game against us.'"

Well, that is a little thing. And I have never known whether it was really true, although I think my young Britisher knew what he was talking about. But it seemed an illustration of how little differences can exist which we know nothing about and how much there is for us to know in so many ways about each other.

And believe me—the amount that needs to be known about us by other nations is considerable, because we take it for granted that all our good intentions are completely understood by everybody else, and that nobody would possibly suspect that we weren't functioning with good will towards the world as a whole. We couldn't have a bad intention of any kind. But you know, everybody doesn't just take that for granted.

And so I think that it really is very important today that we realize that the rest of the world is watching us—watching every community—watching individuals—trying to find out what this is that we call democracy—what it really does in daily living for people. And is it so much better than what they have? And can it do so much more? And do the people have so much more actual strength? And actual ability to control in their hands? And do they use it? And have they the capacity to use it wisely? All those things we are proving day by day; and we must not forget it.

And I think that Roosevelt College is probably doing more towards making a large group of young people understand their responsibility and go out into our country and perhaps through the contacts with many other countries really be able to interpret democracy, to live it, and through that to give us a chance at peace.

Without peace we are never going to succeed in having the benefits that we believe come with democracy. And yet, without democracy, I doubt if we will ever have peace. The two things have to come together. We have to work for them together. And I hope that every student that goes out from Roosevelt College will realize that our objectives today are to achieve understanding and cooperation; that we cannot expect to live in a world which does not have misunderstandings and does not have conflict; but that in the end we hope to achieve a peaceful world; and in that world we hope that people will have greater democracy and that individuals will have greater liberty and justice and freedom for all.

TSptr RUA, ICRC

---

1. Information on the venue of ER's speech received by e-mail from Michael Gabriel, archivist, Center for New Deal Studies, Roosevelt University, 18 November 2005.

2. John F. Sembower, "College for All Races," *NYT*, 16 November 1947, SM28–29; "Education Notes—Roosevelt—Growing," *NYT*, 17 March 1946, E9; and "Chicago's Roosevelt College Grows," *NYT*, 6 April 1947, E9; "Chicago's 'Equality Lab' Thrives," *WP*, 30 March 1947, B3.

3. "Education Notes—Roosevelt—One World," *NYT*, 21 April 1946, 83; "Chicago's Roosevelt College Grows," *NYT*, 6 April 1947, E9.

4. Quoted in "Chicago's Roosevelt College Grows," *NYT*, 6 April 1947, E9. For more on President Sparling and on the admission policies, curriculum, and governance of Roosevelt College, see Document 59 and its header.

5. For ER on making democracy real, see also Document 99 and Document 151.

6. Because of its integrated faculty and student body, ties to the labor movement, and the progressive views of many of its faculty, Roosevelt University became an easy target for critics who chose to label it a hotbed of Communism (Gross, 40–42).

ON THE VIOLENCE IN PALESTINE

Angered by the British refusal to accept the recommendation of the Anglo-American Committee of Inquiry to permit 100,000 European Jews to emigrate to Palestine, Jewish underground military units unleashed a wave of attacks on British authorities in Palestine. On July 22, 1946, the Irgun Z'vai Le'umi bombed the headquarters of the British military at the King David Hotel in Jerusalem, killing more than ninety people; in December, four British soldiers were kidnapped and flogged by the Irgun; and on March 1, 1947, a British officers club in Jerusalem was blown up, and attacks throughout Palestine killed 18 and wounded 25 Englishmen. The British responded with strong measures to control the uprising, imposing a house curfew on populations of the all-Jewish areas of Tel Aviv, Petach Tikvah, and Ramat Gan, and declared martial law for the Jewish quarter of Meash'arim.[1]

Although ER placed much of the blame for the deteriorating situation in Palestine on the "totalitarian" tactics adopted by the British, she indicated in the following letter to Marshall that the failure of the United States to adopt a clear, firm policy within the UN only exacerbated the problem.

227

Eleanor Roosevelt to George Marshall
26 May 1947 [New York City]

Dear Mr. Secretary:

I have been troubled by the Palestine situation and am becoming increasingly so. For some reason, there seems to be established a totalitarian government, or in other words, a police government, with a forgetfulness of all we think of as British principles and justice.

The enclosed from the Palestine Post, I think, is worth reading.[2]

I can not help feeling that our own policy in the UN has been very weak. Either we think it is right to uphold certain things in Palestine, in spite of the Arabs who can not, after all, cause very serious trouble from the military standpoint if we wish to use planes and tanks, or we are going back on something which it seems to me we pledged ourselves to many years ago, tacitly if not in clear words.[3]

I hope you will forgive me for expressing an opinion, but it seemed wrong not to speak out when people are daily losing their lives.

Very sincerely yours,
Eleanor Roosevelt

TLS RG59, NARA II

228

George Marshall to Eleanor Roosevelt
20 June 1947 [Washington, DC]

Dear Mrs. Roosevelt:

I have read your letter of May 26, 1947, with which you enclosed excerpts from the Palestine Post relative to the current situation in Palestine.

Referring to your comment on the present administration of Palestine, Great Britain is responsible for the administration of the Mandate and, acting in this capacity, bears the responsibility for the maintenance of law and order.

I was sorry to read your comment on the policy of our Government during the recent session of the General Assembly of the United Nations. It was our view that this session had been called for the procedural purpose of constituting and instructing a special committee to prepare the Palestine question for consideration at the regular session of the General Assembly in September, and that substantive matters should therefore not be considered by the General Assembly until the Special Committee had completed its work.[4] This opinion was based on the belief that the United Nations would not be in a position to reach conclusions with regard to the substantive issues involved until all of the members had had an opportunity of studying this complicated problem in an objective and impartial manner. Unless the United Nations proceeded in this manner we felt that its conclusions would probably be subject to charges of haste or as having been formulated without sufficient investigation.

You will agree, I am certain, that it is important that the conclusions reached by the United Nations with respect to the Palestine question should command the widest possible support of world opinion. Our position at the special session of the General Assembly was intended to create a feeling of confidence in the work of the United Nations on this problem.

I very much hope my view of this matter will be in accord with you.

Faithfully yours,
G. C. Marshall

TLS AERP, FDRL

———————

1. Sachar, *Israel*, 270–78; Bickerton and Klausner, 81–82; Segev, 476–86; Clifton Daniel, "16 Die in Palestine in Major Upsurge of Terrorist Attacks," *NYT*, 2 March 1947, 1.

2. The *Palestine Post* ran a series of articles in the spring of 1947 on the temporary imposition of martial law and curfews on parts of Palestine and the execution of Jewish insurgents by the British. The particular article that ER sent to Marshall was not retained with correspondence.

3. ER is most likely referring to the Balfour Declaration. In 1917 British foreign secretary Arthur Balfour sent a letter to Lord Rothschild, a leader of the Zionist cause, expressing the support of the British government for the creation of a Jewish "National Home" in Palestine. When the League of Nations granted Great Britain a mandate in Palestine in 1922, under which Great Britain took responsibility for governing the region and preparing it for eventual self-governance, the Balfour Declaration, as it was called, was incorporated into the articles of the mandate. The Balfour Declaration encouraged Jews to found and develop settlements in Palestine with the expectation that the British would redeem the pledge the Zionists believed the British had made. Between 1920 and 1936 the number of Jews living in Palestine increased from 66,000 to more than 400,000. But after 1939, in the wake of rebellion by the Arab population, the British sought to severely curtail the immigration of Jews to Palestine. After World War II, as thousands of Jewish displaced persons from Europe sought refuge in Palestine, pressure grew on the British to create a Jewish state. The British, however, faced with Arab opposition and seeking to maintain their strategic position and access to oil in the Middle East, resisted Zionist demands.

The United States did not officially endorse the Balfour Declaration, but ER felt Americans had given it their indirect approval. In answer to a letter comparing the situation of the Jews in Palestine to the Negroes in the United States, ER wrote:

I think the case of the Jews in Palestine and the American Negro are rather different. We brought the Negroes to this country in bondage and they have been instrumental in developing this country. I think we have an obligation to give them equal opportunity with other citizens, but we never at any time promised them a chance for an independent homeland in this country.

The Jews, on the other hand, went to Palestine and if you will think back to the declaration made by Balfour and the British Government I think you will agree that they practically promised to grant the Jews an opportunity to build a homeland there. Implicitly we have accepted that through the years and have allowed groups of people in our country to contribute in every way possible to the development of Palestine for this purpose. Therefore it seems to me that morally Great Britain and ourselves have accepted the responsibility and it is now too late to go back on it. If we had not thought they had a right to do this, we should long ago have told them that we did not intend to help them here, and if they wanted a homeland we would have to help them find one somewhere else, or they would have to find some corner of the world which was willing to allow them to take it over and develop it.

(Cohen, 3–10; *OEWH*; ER to Warren Austin, 31 May 1947, AERP). ER makes a similar statement in her My Day column of May 14, 1947.

4. At the request of the British, who had decided to give up their mandate, a special session of the General Assembly convened on April 28, 1947, to establish an ad hoc committee to study the problem of Palestine and present a report at the next meeting of the General Assembly in the fall of 1947. The General Assembly agreed that the United Nations Special Committee on Palestine (UNSCOP) would be composed of representatives of eleven smaller nations that had no special stake in the Middle East (Sachar, *Israel*, 280).

229

If You Ask Me (excerpt)
Ladies' Home Journal June 1947

My husband and I decided some years ago that our small contributions to peace would be never to tell or repeat "Eleanor stories," racial-prejudice stories or jokes, but we differ on our reactions to others' telling such stories. My husband says that if other persons make racial jokes, it is like beating your head against a stone wall to argue with them. He just changes the subject. I "light into" them, and tell them if they can't say anything good, not to say anything. Which of us is correct?

I doubt if "lighting into" people ever does much good, but I think the time has come when we ourselves must stand up and be counted for our beliefs. If we can say quietly that we think the attitude that someone is taking is harmful to the co-operation between people of different races and religions and will not help to promote peace in the world, and explain very calmly why we think so, we may plant a seed in even a prejudiced mind, which may of itself bear fruit someday.

TMsex DLC

Preparing to Draft the Declaration

At the end of the first session of the eighteen-member Human Rights Commission, which met from January 27 to February 10, 1947, the commissioners decided that three of its members, "with the assistance of the Secretariat," would prepare a "preliminary draft" of the international bill of rights. This draft would then be revised by the full commission when it met again in December. The commission chose ER, P. C. Chang of China, and Charles Malik of Lebanon, along with John Humphrey, the secretary of the HRC, for this task. After the Soviet and French delegates complained to ECOSOC (the body to which the HRC reported) about the small size of the group and the absence of a European representative, ER expanded the drafting committee to eight members. With the help of his staff and drawing on a wealth of material—including existing and proposed bills of rights sent by governments and non-governmental organizations—Humphrey wrote a first draft of the international bill of rights that became the basis for the version produced by the drafting committee.[1]

During the various stages of the drafting process, the State Department prepared position papers indicating which draft articles it approved of in their current form and suggesting alternatives when it disapproved. The following memorandum of conversation, which was prepared by James P. Hendrick, ER's principal State Department advisor, records a session in which ER met with her State Department advisors to review the department's suggestions. The meeting served to prepare her for the meetings of the drafting committee, which began on June 9, 1947.[2]

230

Memorandum of Conversation with Eleanor Roosevelt

3 June 1947

PARTICIPANTS: Mrs. Roosevelt, James Hendrick, E. N. Thompson, Walter Kotschnig, Mr. Halderman, Marjorie Whiteman[3]

SUBJECT: Human Rights Drafting Committee

I gave Mrs. Roosevelt the position papers on the international bill of rights consisting of ISP D-88/47 and attachments and ISP D-87/47. The document on social and economic rights was not ready since it was being discussed that very afternoon by the ISP Subcommittee.[4] I told Mrs. Roosevelt I would send that to her before the beginning of the Human Rights Drafting Committee session.

Mrs. Roosevelt went over each of the position papers carefully, discussing the various points which might be raised in connection with them, during the three hours that I was there. She said that she would read the papers more carefully on her trip to Los Angeles and return prior to the Committee meeting.[5]

Specific comment on a few of the articles is noted:

In article 9 (Liberty of Movement) Mrs. Roosevelt noted that we would have considerable trouble with the USSR. She cited the example of USSR women who had married foreigners and were not allowed to leave the USSR.[6] In article 11 Mrs. Roosevelt suggested that a limitation be placed on the statement that "the secrecy of correspondence shall be respected" so as to allow censorship during war time.[7] I pointed out that this was intended to be covered by article 2 but Mrs.

Roosevelt was not entirely satisfied that the very general statement of article 2 was satisfactory as making it quite clear in the public mind that the article was limited.[8]

In article 12, Mrs. Roosevelt definitely preferred the U. S. alternative suggestion.[9]

In article 13 (Right to Marriage) Mrs. Roosevelt made a point which had not occurred to the ISP Subcommittee: that by giving women and men the "same" freedoms to marry we were impliedly stating that there was no right to marriage other than that provided for by the local law and that this would be welcomed by the USSR supporting their laws against marriage of foreigners.[10] She felt this must be thought through. Also with reference to article 12,[11] Mrs. Roosevelt recognized there would be considerable difficulty with miscegenation laws. She would support an article which would do away with miscegenation laws; but she recognized that our acceptance of such an article would have to be conditioned by our confession that we could not make the article apply today in certain of our states.[12]

In article 15 she raised a point similar to that made by her with respect to article 11, namely, the adequacy of article 2 to bring the right within reasonable limitations.[13] She pointed out that the right to transmit opinions beyond state borders was necessarily subject to the right of censorship because of obscenity but she was not convinced that article 2 made this sufficiently clear.

With regard to article 16 (Access to all sources of information) she pointed out that there had been a D.C. law preventing teachers from collecting their salaries if they so much as mentioned Russia in their teaching. This in her opinion would be a violation of article 16 and it would be a good thing to force the U. S. to correct such situations.[14]

She was concerned as to whether article 18 (Duty of People Presenting Information) extended to owners and publishers.[15] I told her that in my opinion it did. Article 30 (Right to Take Part in Government) was cited by Mrs. Roosevelt as an example of the type of right which would mean one thing to the USSR and another to us.[16] Mrs. Roosevelt has already gone on record as saying that this is to be expected in the bill and is unavoidable.

INTRODUCTORY STATEMENT BEFORE COMMITTEE

We discussed at some length the methods which might be adopted in connection with the drafting of the bill. It was concluded that Mrs. Roosevelt should make an opening statement to the effect that the task of the Drafting Committee should not be to produce an elegant paper.[17] It would be perfectly satisfactory if the Drafting Committee produced a paper which contained duplications and unpolished language. Attempts at elaborate regrouping or reshifting of the articles could only result in undue prolongation of the present session. If the Committee is to finish within two weeks it cannot expect to do more than obtain some measure of agreement with regard to the rights which should be included.

TMem RG59, NARA II

---

1. The various drafts of the Universal Declaration of Human Rights, beginning with the Humphrey draft, can be found in appendices 1–7 of Mary Ann Glendon, *A World Made New*.

2. Glendon, 35, 45–50.

3. Walter M. Kotschnig (1901–1985) was chief of the Division of International Organizational Affairs at the State Department and Hendrick's supervisor; E. N. Thompson, John Halderman, and Marjorie Whiteman were State Department advisers to the UN delegation (*CB*; Lash, *Years*, 70; "Assignments of Delegates and Advisors by Committees," USSEC/9a, 10 January 1946, AERP).

4. ISP D-88/47 and ISP D-87/47 are detailed position papers prepared by the Subcommittee on Human Rights and the Status of Women of the State Department's Committee on International Social Policy (ISP). They consist of a draft international bill of rights based on the draft Humphrey and his staff in the UN Secretariat had prepared. The subcommittee retained some of the articles in Humphrey's draft without change, amended others, and left out those it felt were unnecessary. In addition, the subcommittee provided comments on the articles in Humphrey's draft explaining its reasons for suggesting inclusion, amendment, or exclusion. The ISP subcommittee's analysis only covered the civil and political rights in Humphrey's draft since the ISP had not finished reviewing the articles on economic and social rights. The ISP consisted of representatives of the Departments of State, Justice, Labor, Interior, and the Federal Security Agency. In addition to human rights and the status of women, its subcommittees dealt with issues related to labor, social welfare, and non-self-governing territories (ISP D-88/47, 29 May 1947, AERP; "Position of the United States for the Third Session of the Human Rights Commission," 2 April 1948, AERP).

5. ER went to Los Angeles to speak at the June 5 Jackson Day Dinner sponsored by the Democratic State Committee of California. See Document 231 and Document 232.

6. In April 1947 the Soviet Union refused, for the fourteenth time in two years, to grant exit visas to fifteen Russian women who had married American citizens. The Russians had also refused to issue visas to the wives of British citizens ("Russian Bar Firm on Visas to Wives," *NYT*, 27 April 1947, 36).

7. The draft of Article 11 ("Liberty and Respect of Private Life") reads: "No one shall be subjected to arbitrary or unauthorized searches and seizures of his person, home, papers and effects, or to unreasonable interference with his person, home, family, relations with others, reputation, privacy, activities or property. The secrecy of correspondence shall be respected" (ISP D-88/47, 29 May 1947, AERP).

8. The draft of Article 2 ("Duty of the Individual Towards Other Individuals") reads: "The state is created by the people for the promotion of their welfare and the protection of their mutual rights. In the exercise of his rights everyone is limited by the rights of others. The state may impose only such limitations on such rights as are compatible with the freedom and welfare of all" (ISP D-88/47, 29 May 1947, AERP).

9. Article 12 concerned the "Right to Possess Legal Personality and Exercise One's Civil Rights." Humphrey's draft reads: "Everyone has the right to a legal personality. No one shall be restricted in the exercise of his civil rights except for reasons based on age or mental condition or as a punishment for a criminal offense." The ISP subcommittee suggested revising the second sentence to read: "No person shall be restricted in the exercise of his civil rights except under general law based on reasons of age or mental incompetence, or as punishment for a criminal offense, or as otherwise permitted in this bill" (Attachment 12 to ISP D-88/47, 29 May 1947, AERP).

10. Article 13 ("Right to Contract Marriage") reads: "Women and men have the same freedoms to marry, to choose their marriage partners, and the same rights to remedies for breach of marriage, and to safeguards for the health and equal status of all their children" (ISP D-88/47, 29 May 1947, AERP). On the Russian prohibition against marrying foreigners, see *n*6 above.

11. 12 appears to be a typo for 13 since the comment regards marriage, the topic of Article 13.

12. Laws against miscegenation existed in many states in 1947. In 1950, thirty states had statutes prohibiting interracial marriage. The US Supreme Court finally invalidated anti-miscegenation laws in *Loving v. Virginia* in 1967. Among the major concerns that vexed ER and the State Department during the drafting of the Universal Declaration of Human Rights was the contradiction between some of the principles being incorporated into the declaration and the denial of civil rights to African Americans (R. Kennedy, *Interracial*, 88, 272–78).

13. Article 15 ("Freedom of Opinion") reads: "Everyone has the right to form and hold opinions and to receive them from, and impart them, within or beyond the borders of the State" (ISP D-88/47, 29 May 1947, AERP).

14. Article 16 ("Freedom of Access to All Sources of Information") reads: "Freedom of everyone to receive, read and listen to all matters of information shall not be impaired, and there shall be free and equal access to all sources of information both within and beyond the border of a State." In 1935 Congress passed an appropriations bill for the District of Columbia containing a "red rider" that required teachers and other employees to certify every time they drew a paycheck that they had not "taught or advocated" Communism in or out of the classroom since they had last been paid. The rider passed without discussion and some congressmen were apparently unaware that it had been attached to the bill. Congress repealed the rider the following year amidst considerable controversy. Opponents of the rider argued successfully that it prevented teachers from teaching "the facts" about Russia (ISP D-88/47, 29 May 1947, AERP; "Congress to Debate Communism Issue," *WP*, 17 May 1936, B1).

15. Article 18 ("Duty of People Presenting Information") reads: "All persons concerned with the dissemination of information shall endeavor to present information in a fair and impartial manner." But a footnote reads: "It is recommended that this article be omitted. The above text is submitted in case it is decided to insert such an article" (ISP D-88/47, 29 May 1947, AERP).

16. Article 30 ("Right to Take Part in the Government of the State–Democracy") reads: "Government derives its just power from the consent of the governed. Everyone has the right to take an effective part in the government of the state or territory of which he is a citizen. The citizens of the state or territory are accordingly entitled to exercise self-government through representatives freely and fairly chosen by them in periodic democratic elections" (ISP D-88/47, 29 May 1947, AERP).

17. According to the summary record of the opening session of the drafting committee:

> Mrs. Roosevelt stated that she was of the opinion that it might be very difficult for the Drafting Committee to complete a perfect draft of an International Bill of Human Rights, either as to substance or as to style, during its two-week session. She reminded the delegates that the draft Bill of Human Rights would have to be considered on six separate occasions, after it was completed by the Drafting Committee, before it could be considered final. She mentioned that her Government had considered submitting a draft Bill but had decided not to do so because it felt that it would be better for the Drafting Committee to work from the documented outline prepared by the Secretariat. She suggested that the first thing to be done was to reach agreement on the rights to be included in the draft Bill, and the definitions of those rights. Because of the preliminary nature of the Drafting Committee's work, she proposed that it be understood that no agreement reached in the Drafting Committee be considered as irrevocably binding the Governments represented there, as these Governments might wish to reconsider various parts of the draft at a later date (HRC, Drafting Committee, Summary Record, 9 June 1947, [E/CN.4/AC/1/SR.1], 2, UNOR ECOSOC, MWelC [RM]).

DRAFT EISENHOWER AND THE
CALIFORNIA JACKSON DAY DINNER

May 27, California State Democratic Committee chair James Roosevelt, who like his brothers hoped that Eisenhower could be convinced to replace Truman as the Democratic nominee, sent his mother an advance copy of the "Statement of Policy of the Democratic Party of California" he planned to present to the state committee. Among other domestic and foreign policy proposals, the statement criticized the "unilateral action" implicit in the Truman Doctrine and expressed the desire to "place responsibility for the execution of the 'Truman Doctrine' upon the United Nations," rather than on the United States alone. Writing his mother that he hoped to "deprive Henry Wallace of the appearance of being the only one who is working for peace," he sent her a copy of his statement to "help you in preparing what you have in mind saying" when she addressed the state party's Jackson Day dinner June 5.[1]

Tensions within the state party, especially the rivalry between James Roosevelt and fellow committeeman Edwin Pauley, escalated throughout the week. ER arrived in Los Angeles June 4. That same day treasury secretary John Snyder suddenly announced that pressing business in Washington forced him to cancel his scheduled address. June 5, Democratic National Committee chairman Gael Sullivan flew in to replace Snyder only to be persuaded by Edwin Pauley to announce his own "eleventh-hour statements of pressure of business in Washington," turn around and fly back to the capital. The cancellations, however, did not dissuade James Roosevelt from criticizing the president's foreign policy.

Dore Schary, the RKO producer scheduled to introduce ER, criticized Sullivan's absence, declaring that "one man who should have been here became worried by the free expression of an idea [and] that by failing to be here, he has insulted a very great lady … and he has insulted a name that he should have always held in great respect and honor." The following day Representative Chet Holifield accused Pauley "of splitting the Democratic Party in California wide open."[2]

As the national media continued to highlight the dispute, ER wrote the president to express, for the second time, her displeasure with Pauley.[3]

231

Eleanor Roosevelt to Harry Truman
7 June 1947 [New York City]

Dear Mr. President:

I was deeply distressed when I got out to Los Angeles to speak at the dinner for the Southern California State Committee group to find that Mr. Pauley and my son, James, had entirely different points of view on a proposed policy plan which had been drawn up by James and the policy committee for submission to the State Committee.

I found that owing to Mr. Pauley's suggestion, this document which was to have been given to the people at the Jackson Day dinner, was not to be distributed but that James told them he would have to have it mailed to members of the State Committee for future action and when that was done, of course it would be in the papers.

Mr. Pauley took the position that he disagreed with certain things in the statement and felt that what was said on foreign policy was an insult to you. I read it through very carefully and it did not seem to me in any way insulting. It voiced simply the questions which are in many people's minds and it seemed to me that it gave to Mr. Gail Sullivan[4] an opportunity, if he wanted to, to clear up some of these questions, and if he disapproved, to ask the State Committee to change the things he thought unwise. He could even have expressed censure of James as state chairman and I think it would have left the feeling better among the people who attended the dinner.

I, of course, had no sense that his presence or absence at the dinner was any insult to me, but I think he did do harm to the position of the Democratic Party in the eyes of one of the largest dinners that they have ever had in Los Angeles.

You know that I have never seen eye to eye with Mr. Pauley. He has always fought Mrs. Helen Gahagen Douglas and I have always believed in the things she has stood for.[5] He did a very good job of raising money for the national committee. He often disagreed with my husband.

As I think back upon the many things which were said about my husband by southern Democrats and others within the Party, I can not see that the language in which this proposed statement is couched, is in any way insulting to you. I think a clever national chairman with a wiser national committeeman could have handled the situation and left the party in better condition instead of in a worse condition.

I understand that Mr. Pauley was much annoyed because in a press conference, I said that I felt ways had to be found to get on with Russia. That does not mean we have to appease Russia. I do not believe the Russians want to go to war. Neither do we but I think the ingenuity to find ways to get what we want rests with us.

I thought General Marshall's speech at Harvard was the beginning of a constructive suggestion,[6] but it seems to me some thing has to happen very soon and some people in the industrial world in this country have got to be brought to the realization that the thing which will strengthen Russia above everything else, is a depression in this country. She is waiting and longing for that and the effect on the rest of the world will be disasterous.[7] I do not attribute high-mindedness to the Politbureau.[8] I think undoubtably they hope that the peoples of the world will turn to communism. There is only one way of answering that and that is by proving to the peoples of the world that Democracy meets their needs better. This isn't a question of Greece and Turkey alone.[9] This is a question of many things which have to be worked simultaneously on a world scale.

There is too much to be done in the world to allow for resentments. The real, honest questioning such as was contained in the California State Committee document might better have been met with real answers. Many people are confronted with these questions and seek wider understanding of government policies.

I hope you will forgive my speaking so frankly, but I have your interests and the interests of the Party at heart.

Very sincerely yours,
Eleanor Roosevelt

TLS HSTOF, HSTL

232

Harry Truman to Eleanor Roosevelt
16 June 1947 [The White House]

Dear Mrs. Roosevelt:

I deeply regret the combination of circumstances which prompted your letter of June seventh which was placed in my hands upon my return from Canada.[10] I am grateful for the assurance that you had no sense of personal insult because of the incident in Los Angeles. That generous expression is characteristic of you.

It would be impossible for me to believe that there was any intent to accord you anything less than the highest measure of courtesy and respect. Any other course is unthinkable.

I want you to know that I have read your thoughtful letter very carefully. I, too, wish some people in the industrial world could be brought to a realization of the consequences which their course will inevitably bring down upon their own heads as well as the Nation.

You have placed the proper emphasis on the paramount issue in our international relations. With what you say on so momentous a problem I am in entire accord. If we are to stem the tide of communism, we must, as you say, prove to the peoples of the world that democracy meets their needs better.

As to the controversy which Mr. Gael Sullivan's action aroused, I can only hope that peace may be made at the meeting which Mr. Sullivan has called for June twenty-sixth, announcement of which has been made in the press.[11]

Very sincerely yours,
Harry S. Truman

TLS AERP, FDRL

ER then told her son what she had written the president.

233

Eleanor Roosevelt to James Roosevelt
26 June 1947 [Hyde Park]

Dearest Jimmy,

I've never written to thank you since I returned, nor to tell you of later developments. You and Rommie were sweet and with the addition of fussing over me when the kids were ill I think you were both wonderful.[12]

I wrote the President after I got home and said I did not feel I could be insulted but I thought it was regrettable for the party and for him.[13] I did not mince words on Pauley.[14] Fjr went in to see Gael Sullivan who told him he hoped I was not annoyed and that he had called Ross at the W.H. from Pauley's house and Ross had told him to come back.[15] Are you going to the meeting Mr. Sullivan has called or is it over?[16] He has not written so I haven't written him. Sunday the President and I speak for the N.A.A.C.P. together and I see him at three and drive over with him at his request. I suppose to disprove all idea of a break!

How are Rommie and the children? Elliott's children are here and a joy to have. Chandler is very pretty, Tony a sturdy, handsome youngster and David altogether charming.[17] We all go to Campo on the 15th and stop to see Faye in her play that night.[18]

Will you send me now the $1200. as I think I'll do some things to the playhouse this coming month?[19]

Much, much love to you dear and I hope you get some rest in spite of political battles.

Devotedly,
Mother

ALS JRP, FDRL

1. James Roosevelt, "Statement of Policy of the Democratic Party of California," 25 May 1947, JRP, FDRL; James Roosevelt to ER, 27 May 1947, AERP.

2. Gladwin Hill, "Democratic Schism Growing in California; Shunning of Dinner Held Insult to Roosevelts," *NYT*, 7 June 1947, 14; United Press notice, 6 June 1947, 14; "James Roosevelt Finds Fault With Greek Aid," *LAT*, 5 June 1947, 1; Lorania K. Francis, "Democratic Rift Laid to Pauley," *LAT*, 7 June 1947, 2; Gladwin Hill, "2 Democrat Chiefs Avoid Coast Dinner," *NYT*, 6 June 1947, 15.

3. For ER's earlier criticisms of Pauley, see Document 97.

4. Gael Sullivan.

5. ER thought highly of Helen Douglas, calling her "one of my favorite members of Congress" (*MD*, 3 April 1946).

6. Secretary of State George Marshall delivered the commencement speech at Harvard University on June 5, 1947, outlining a program of US aid to feed and rebuild postwar Europe that became known as the Marshall Plan. It proposed that Europe draft a plan for economic aid that would become a joint program of the European countries and the United States. The Marshall Plan aspired to achieve "the revival of a working economy in the world so as to permit the emergence of political and social conditions in which free institutions can exist." Although ER thought Marshall's proposal constructive, she had serious reservations about its approach, particularly concerning its apparent circumvention of the UN. For more on ER's views on the Marshall Plan, see Document 239, Document 242, and Document 243. For ER's relationship to Marshall, see header to Document 198 ("The Address of Secretary Marshall at Harvard," *NYT*, 6 June 1947, 2; *OCAMH*; *MD*, 9 June 1947; Lash, *Years*, 99–100).

7. ER made a similar point in her July 5 column, criticizing Molotov's June 30 announcement of Soviet nonparticipation in the Marshall Plan. ER stated, "The Marshall Plan is a bona fide offer to help Europe get back on its feet. Mr. Molotov, in refusing to join the rest of Europe, is creating the very thing he says he fears, which is division instead of cooperation" (Harold Callender, "Molotov Adamant; Bevin and Bidault to Act Alone on Aid," *NYT*, 1 July 1947, 1; *MD*, 5 July 1947).

8. The Politbureau was a committee comprised of the highest-ranking policymakers in the Soviet Union, essentially consisting of Stalin and his most trusted cohorts, including Molotov. The term is a contraction of the Russian words for "political" and "bureau" ("Politbureau," OED; Dziewanowski, 170).

9. On "Greece and Turkey" (i.e., the Truman Doctrine), see Document 208 and Document 210.

10. Truman had spent June 10–12 on a "good will visit" to Canada, during which he met with Governor General Viscount Alexander and Prime Minister W. L. Mackenzie King, and delivered a speech to the Canadian Parliament reiterating the goals of the Truman Doctrine and exhorting Canada to stand by the United States "in the forefront of those who share these objectives and ideals" ("Truman Gets Welcome of Cheering Canadians," *LAT*, 11 June 1947, 1; "Text of President Truman's Address Before the Canadian Parliament," *NYT*, 12 June 1947, 2).

11. Sullivan's announcement of the June 26 Democratic National Committee meeting, to be held in Washington but focusing on the California party, appeared in the June 13 *New York Times*. The "peace" Truman sought did occur. James Roosevelt called for an interim meeting of the Democratic State Central Committee on July 26 in Los Angeles to determine the California party's official platform and to "air differences and re-establish harmony" among California Democrats. On July 27 the state party officially endorsed the Truman campaign, over the objections of the pro-Wallace faction leader Robert W. Kenney, and devised their domestic and international platform, revising

Roosevelt's June 3 policy statement by cutting out his criticisms of the Truman Doctrine. Despite the criticism he received following the Jackson Day Dinner, this revised declaration lauded James Roosevelt's "efforts in promoting the party and laying a solid foundation for its success" (Clayton Knowles, "Democrats Work to Repair Breach," *NYT*, 13 June 1947, 14; "Divided Democrats Meet on Coast," *NYT*, 26 July 1947, 2; "Coast Democrats Endorse Truman," *NYT*, 28 July 1947, 7).

12. James Roosevelt married his nurse and second wife Romelle Theresa Schneider (1916–?, deceased) in 1941. Their children, at this time, were James Roosevelt, Jr., born 1945, and Michael Anthony Roosevelt, born 1946 ("James Roosevelt Weds His Ex-Nurse," *NYT*, 15 April 1941, 46; "Milestones," *Time*, 16 December 1946; "Milestones," *Time*, 19 November 1945; "James Roosevelt," http://www.fdrlibrary.marist.edu/child2.html, accessed 1 March 2006).

13. While polite to ER, Truman remained furious with James Roosevelt, telling him in a brusque face to face exchange later recalled by Secret Service agent Henry Nicholson:

> Your father asked me to take this job. I didn't want it. I was happy in the Senate. But your father asked me to take it, and I took it. And if your father knew what you are doing to me, he would turn over in his grave. But get this straight: whether you like it or not, I am going to be the next President of the United States. That will be all. Good day.

> Truman then turned around and left the room before Roosevelt could respond (Donovan, 401).

14. See ER to Harry Truman, Document 231.

15. "Fjr" is Franklin Delano Roosevelt, Jr., who saw Truman on July 23. Charles "Charlie" Griffith Ross (1885–1950) was Truman's press secretary from 1945 until his death in 1950 ("The Day in Washington," *NYT*, 24 July 1947, 13; "Charles G. Ross Collapses and Dies in White House," *NYT*, 6 December 1950, 1).

16. See *n*11 above.

17. Elliott was married to Ruth Josephine Googins from 1933 through 1944; together they had three children: Ruth Chandler Roosevelt ("Chandler"), born May 1934; Elliott Roosevelt, Jr. ("Tony"), born July 1936; and David Boynton Roosevelt, born January 1942 ("Elliott Roosevelt," http://www.fdrlibrary.marist.edu/child3.html, accessed 20 September 2005).

18. Faye Emerson Roosevelt (1917–1983), an actress and third wife of Elliott Roosevelt. They married in 1944. On July 15, 1947, ER and Elliott's family attended Emerson's performance in *State of the Union* at the Ogunquit Playhouse in Maine while on their way to Campobello Island, New Brunswick, to visit the Roosevelts' cottage there ("Faye Emerson Seen at Ogunquit," *NYT*, 15 July 1947, 26; "Elliot Roosevelt," http://www.fdrlibrary.marist.edu/child3.html, accessed 20 September 2005).

19. James served as executor of FDR's estate and thus held responsibility for dispensing its funds.

CRITICIZING TAFT-HARTLEY AND
JOHN L. LEWIS

In June, Congress passed the Labor-Management Relations Act of 1947, most commonly known as the bill named for its sponsors Rep. Fred Hartley (R-NJ) and Sen. Robert Taft (R-OH). Truman vetoed the bill. June 23, Congress then promptly overrode his veto and the Taft-Hartley Act became law in August.[1]

ER strongly supported the president's decision; however, her staunch opposition to the Taft-Hartley Act did not mean that she remained completely uncritical of labor. She was particularly critical of John L. Lewis, president of the United Mine Workers. Immediately after Congress passed the bill, she wrote:

> In many ways I think labor leaders have themselves to blame for some of their present difficulties—John L. Lewis chief among them, because the people as a whole have come to dread what he can do to our economy. And there are certain union rules which irk the people and which I do not think really help organized labor. These regulations have made the relations between the public and the unions increasingly unsympathetic and should have been studied and corrected long ago.

This critique, and the *Cleveland Press*'s choice of headline for the column,[2] prompted Alexander Fell "A. F." Whitney (1873–1949), president of the Brotherhood of Railroad Trainmen, to write a letter to ER on June 17. He agreed with her criticism of the Taft-Hartley bill but took umbrage at her blaming labor leaders for labor's political troubles—though he did agree that Lewis used "poor judgement" when he broke the UMW contract with the government—and wished that labor's "virtues" were emphasized in ER's column, rather than its "errors." He asked, "Why do so many writers, directly and indirectly, criticize labor and labor leaders and fail to call the public's attention to the iniquities of big business and its leaders?" As ER clarified in this reply to Whitney's June 17 letter, this was not the intention of her article.[3]

234

Eleanor Roosevelt to A. F. Whitney
17 June 1947

In ans. to your letter, I feel that I was being fair in this present labor situation. I have definitely expressed my disapproval of the Taft-Hartley Bill. I am not responsible for the headings on my column and I distinctly said <u>some</u> labor leaders. John Lewis I named specifically.[4]

I have always felt that the railroad unions were above the average. However there are some other unions whose rules and regulations do not make sense—such as for instance, a painter can not use a paint spraying machine on a barn and a man must confine himself to so much work a day, even if it means loafing part of the time. On occasion I am an employer of labor and these rules seem stupid and not conducive to good relations between employer and employee.

I have repeatedly stated my belief in and support of unions and in a man's right to strike. There is, of course, the consumer's rights which must be taken into consideration and we are all consumers.

I am sorry you think I was unfair. Evidently I did not make myself clear enough. I hope the Taft Hartley Bill is killed because it is a bad Bill.[5]

HLd AERP, FDRL

1. See *n*1 Document 253.

2. The headline read, "Labor Leaders Are to Blame for Many of Their Troubles." Neither ER nor her distributor, United Feature Syndicate, titled the My Day columns, but many newspapers that carried the articles titled them as their editors saw fit.

3. *MD*, 10 June 1947; A. F. Whitney to ER, 17 June 1947, AERP; Donovan, 299–303; Patterson, *Grand Expectations*, 46–47, 51–52; William S. White, "Senate Battle On," *NYT*, 21 June 1947, 1; "A.F. Whitney Dies; Head of Rail Union," *NYT*, 17 July 1949, 57. For more on ER's views of organized labor, see Document 64, Document 46, *n*7 Document 87, Document 115, and *n*22 Document 84.

4. On Lewis and the 1946 UMW strike, see Document 115.

5. ER continued to express her disapproval of the Taft-Hartley Bill (the "bad Bill") in My Day in June 1947. On June 14, she called the bill an attack on "the fundamental rights and protections of labor," and said that passage of the bill would "lead to unending agitation and unrest; and it will not achieve the one thing which we need above all else to achieve—namely, increased production … This bill will not help to achieve this essential factor in our return to a normal situation under our present free-enterprise system." As ER predicted, the passage of the Taft-Hartley Act on June 23 did result in worker unrest, with 20,000 New York shipyard workers and 18,000 coal miners in several states staging walkouts the very next day. On June 26, ER observed:

> The papers are full of the news of the number of coal miners who are just calmly walking off their jobs in protest against the Taft-Hartley labor law. Many of us have hoped for unity in this country and for the understanding, on the part of management and labor alike, that the economic salvation of the world lies in our productive capacity. Now we have created groups bitterly divided against each other.
>
> If Congress wanted to hurt democracy and make it difficult for us to show what a united nation can do to give its people the widest distribution of opportunity through a successful, cooperative economic system, they could not have succeeded better (*MD*, 14 June and 26 June 1947; Charles Grutzner, "Miners Walk Out," *NYT*, 24 June 1947, 1; "20,000 Halt Work in Shipyards Here," *NYT*, 24 June 1947, 1).

DEBATING CASSIN'S DRAFT DECLARATION

After its initial discussion of the preliminary draft of the international bill of rights pre-pared by John Humphrey and his staff,[1] the Human Rights Commission delegates assigned to draft the declaration decided to direct a smaller working group consisting of ER, Malik, Cassin, and Wilson to prepare written drafts of the document as the work of the full committee proceeded.[2] The smaller group then asked Cassin to produce a revised and more organized version of the Humphrey draft.[3]

The following excerpt from the thirteenth meeting of the drafting committee records the committee's discussion of an article that at this point in the process was Number 15 and included language drawn from three of the articles in Cassin's draft: Number 15 (right to a legal personality), Number 17 (right to marriage), and Number 20 (right to counsel and a fair trial). As chairman, ER began this portion of the meeting by reading the current text of the article; then, as the US delegate, articulating the American position on the proposed terminology.[4]

235

Verbatim Record of the Thirteenth Meeting of the Drafting Committee of the Commission on Human Rights [excerpt]

20 June 1947 [Lake Success, NY]

Chairman: Eleanor Roosevelt
Secretary: John Humphrey
Rapporteur: Charles Malik

CHAIRMAN: *Article 15*: "Every one has the right to a legal personality everywhere. Every one has the right to contract marriage in accordance with the State. Every one shall have access to inde-pendent and impartial tribunals for the determination of his rights, liabilities and obligations under the law. He shall have the right to consult with and, eventually, be represented by counsel."

The United States delegation desires "eventually" to be omitted because a person should have the right to be represented by counsel from the beginning or from any time he desires representa-tion. I think that is just a drafting change in the translation.

MR CASSIN (France) (Interpretation from French): In regard to the Chair's observations, I am sorry to advise the Chair that there are countries where, in civil proceedings, you could obtain counsel, and where, in criminal trials, you could not obtain counsel.

In France, a man who is brought before a court for a crime cannot send for a lawyer; he must be there himself. That is why we use the word "eventually". This does not have anything to do with the practices in other countries; it is only used in order to allow for the practice in my country.

The entire article is the result of the combination of three other articles because it had been observed, with reason, that the phrase "legal personality" was rather abstract, and that it was better to employ the two most important examples immediately; to wit, the contracting of marriage and the access to impartial tribunals. All human beings should have these elementary rights.

CHAIRMAN: May I just say that the word "eventually" does not literally translate le cas échéant.[5] That is why the United States delegation believes there should be a better translation. That is the only word to which we object.

MR. WILSON (United Kingdom): In the first place, I entirely agree with the Chair concerning the word "eventually". I believe we can work that out easily. However, I think, too, that the whole of that sentence—"He shall have the right to consult with and, eventually, be represented by counsel"—is much more appropriate to a convention than to this document.[6] This is a means and not a principle. It is a means to ensuring a person a fair trial, and the fair trial is embodied in the previous part of that clause. I believe it is sufficiently covered and could be omitted here.

I am also rather worried about the second sentence: "Every one has the right to contract marriage in accordance with the laws of the State." All that in fact says, as it appears here, is that the State may make such laws as it desires to make concerning the subject of marriage. This is certainly not what we want to say. However, that is, in fact, all this wording implies.

I was in some doubt as to the exact abuse at which this clause was aimed until I heard what Professor Cassin said a few days ago concerning aliens being denied the right to marriage through the use of all types of technicalities. If that is in fact the abuse at which this is being aimed, again it appears to me to be much more a case of discrimination and should be dealt with on the basis of discrimination rather than by selecting one subject, however important it may be, for mention in a document of this kind.

The principle that applies to marriage—there should be no discrimination–is one that applies to an entire host of other matters as well: the right to enter into a contract of any kind, fairly and equitably.

I do not see, myself, the reason for singling out one specific instance in a case like this, important though it may be. In the second place, if we do single that out, I think it will have to be reworded in order to have something more definite than appears here.

MR. KORETSKY (USSR) (Interpretation from Russian): I want to dwell on the second paragraph in regard to marriage. I think, as does the representative of the United Kingdom, that this question can only be placed on the plane of non-discrimination. In the present form, if in accordance with the laws of the State, it might prevent marriage. Everybody knows that fascist countries did not permit marriage between aryans and non-aryans, for instance.

I shall not mention certain other laws at this moment which, in one form or another, under certain practices in certain countries, do not permit misogynation, for instance.[7] It is therefore inappropriate to speak about the right to contract marriage as a specific right which must be expressed in the Declaration. I think at this point we can only speak of non-discrimination in the contracting of marriage. I have already called attention to the inappropriateness and even strangeness of a formula such as this in a declaration of human rights. It is natural, of course, that at a certain age human beings are wont to enter into marriage. However, I cannot agree with my colleague from the United Kingdom that marriage is a contract like any other contract. Unfortunately, in certain countries, marriage is still considered a deal. In my country such a view of this particular question has been rejected.

To sum up, it appears to me that this does not have to be mentioned in this form. That is my personal opinion.

CHAIRMAN: Speaking on behalf of the United States, I think we would like to have a little clarification on the phrase "everyone has a right to a legal personality." While that phrase may mean something to lawyers, I am fearful that it will not mean a great deal to the layman. Could you think of a way to change this expression so that it may be a little clearer to the layman?

DR. CHANG: (China): It is a very simple matter to adjust this Article, aside from paragraph 1 which needs clarification. Paragraph 2 may need to be reconsidered. There then remains the beginning of the first sentence and the second sentence may well be combined with part of Article 9. If we are going to re-draft Articles 8, 9, and 10, I should rather think the first sentence of the third paragraph of Article 15 may well be combined with some of the concepts there implied.

RAPPORTEUR:[8] With regard to the second paragraph, it seems to assume that a state has laws regulating marriage. This happens to be the case in many Western countries, but in many Eastern countries the state has absolutely nothing to do with marriage. Marriage is left entirely to the laws regulating religion. A particular phrase like this would be highly ambiguous in those countries and would lead to all sorts of confusion and misunderstanding. It would be highly objectionable in those countries where marriage is not a prerogative of the state or the laws of the state but purely of the religions of that country.

CHAIRMAN: From what has been said, I gather that the second paragraph could be completely omitted. As I understand it, most of us would be willing to omit the second paragraph and perhaps simply submit it to the Sub-Commission on Prevention of Discrimination and Protection of Minorities as a question that they have considered.

I would like to ask Professor Cassin if he could clarify the phrase "legal personality" so that it will be more understandable to the layman.

MR. CASSIN (France) (Interpretation from French): I should like to deal with the two items that have been raised, first of all, with regard to marriage. As a matter of fact, there is a phrase which has persisted in remaining in the text although it was not in the original French text, "the law of the State." In case of foreigners, several laws might apply, the law of the place where the marriage is considered, and the law of the State of origin. Therefore, in any case we should delete the phrase "of the State."

Secondly, in my opinion this is not only a question of discrimination among foreigners or among minorities. There is a very important law existing in many countries to the effect that certain persons do not have the freedom to contract marriage. They are considered as minors during their entire lives. They are obliged either to accept the spouse who is imposed upon them, or else, when they wish to marry, they must always ask for the consent of the chief of the tribe or the clan or the family. For the last quarter of a century, there has been a great social movement to defend the liberty of the person wishing to marry, male or female. It is possible that the place where this is inserted is not quite appropriate. We might have to re-study the problem in the Commission, but I take the liberty to state that we are embarking upon the defense of many rights which are less fundamental than the right of a human being to found a family. I do not think we would give a good impression if, after having raised the question before public opinion, we should simply delete this for technical reasons. I do not believe we can use technical difficulties as a screen. We can admit that our text is imperfect. We can request that the Commission on Human Rights will restudy the problem, but I do not think we should simply ignore the difficulty.

Finally, with regard to the phrase "legal personality", I should like to advise the Chairman that she is quite right in asking to have this clarified. As a matter of fact, the next two paragraphs are intended to make this more specific. However, this is a very important problem. Slavery has two principal aspects. The first aspect is the destruction of the physical liberty of man. This is what we dealt with a few minutes ago in saying that slavery is inconsistent with the dignity of man, and therefore prohibited.

But a very important point remains, namely, that slavery is the negation of the legal personality. For thousands of years it was said that if somebody is a slave, it means he has no right to enter into a contract, he has no right to marry freely, he has no right to inherit or leave inheritances. This is a point which we have not yet examined and I think it is appropriate, since we are studying the fundamental rights of man, to state that not only must everybody be free physically, but to state also that every human being normally possesses rights and obligations, and, therefore, has "legal personality."

If you think we could add to the phrase "legal personality" words to the effect that one may have rights and obligations or responsibilities, some kind of clarifying phrase to that effect, I think public opinion will understand what we are trying to do.

CHAIRMAN: In English, one would say "Everyone has the right to a legal personality." Can you help me translate that?

MR. CASSIN (France) (Interpretation from French): In French, we say "legal personality,"[9] and then we could add the following: "In other words, to be able to be a bearer of rights, obligations, and responsibilities." This is the explanation of that phrase, and I assure you it corresponds to something that is very serious and important.

CHAIRMAN: In other words, he has certain inalienable rights and responsibilities? That is not correct, is it?

What you are aiming at is really not to take away from a man at any time certain legal protection; but the question is: How should that be said? Perhaps, it is better to leave it "legal personality" and it will mean the right thing to the lawyers and perhaps sometimes to the individuals.

MR. KORETSKY (USSR) (Interpretation from Russian): I shall start off with what Mr. Cassin has already mentioned. He gave some examples in connection with marriage. He mentioned certain tribal customs, according to which women and girls are still fully dependent not only on their parents but also on the heads of clans or tribes. Apparently this is not only true in one place; it is true in many places. But I think that what he did use as an example is an example of discrimination against women. Therefore, since we are talking about discrimination, we ought to mention this particular point here. If we are going to mention marriage, we, I am afraid, will have to mention all the other numerous fields with regard to which in many countries women are still dependent and still do not have equal rights.

We are just picking on one phase of discrimination and we are speaking about it particularly. Perhaps, we might have to embark on a listing of all those aspects of social life under which women are still factually and juridically unequal. So much for the question of women.

As regards "legal personality," it seems that this is rather over-legalized, if I may say so, in order to put it into a declaration of the rights of man. Legal personality means the ability to have rights.

According to what we say in Article 1 to the effect that everybody is free and has equal rights and dignity, perhaps this phrase "legal personality" is superfluous, not only because it repeats that same thing, but also because it introduces a rather complicated juridical concept of legal personality. It might be superfluous in view of Article 1.

I sympathize with the Chairman who wanted to have this thing clarified—this expression "legal personality." Perhaps the lawyers who are present might recognize that much midnight oil has been burned by jurists in order to explain this particular juridical phrase. I think it has outlived its utility as a general formula. It was an important point in the battle against feudalism. It was then theoretically necessary in order to give a legal foundation and in order to bring into existence this principle of equality among human beings. But since this very principle is already proclaimed in Article 1 in an extremely broad manner, its repetition here is rather superfluous. I do not think it adds anything to Article 1. However, I agree with the Chairman that it could bring about certain confusion.

Therefore, if I may, I should support the deletion of the first and second sentences of Article 15, because both principles are covered by the Article on non-discrimination. Perhaps, however, the Article on non-discrimination is in need of further development. Perhaps, it might be appropriate not only to repeat the words of the Charter; it might be appropriate to develop those words.

I have already stressed the necessity of developing that non-discrimination problem because discrimination is still extant. It is still an historical phenomenon which is important in many countries. Discrimination will have to be fought against, and a mere repetition of the words of the Charter might be insufficient. However, this expression used in Article 15, sentences one and two, are not necessary.

CHAIRMAN: It has been suggested to me that we might say that everyone has the right to a status in law and the enjoyment of fundamental civil rights.[10] That would perhaps explain to the lay person better than using the words "a legal personality."

There is one other thing. In this question of marriage I really think that that might go to the Sub-Commission on Prevention of Discrimination and Protection of Minorities, for this reason: that the United States of course favours in every way the same freedom for women and men in marriage. But we understand that this matter was considered in the Commission on the Status of Women, and we wonder whether their recommendation should not be reviewed by the Sub-Commission on Prevention of Discrimination and Protection of Minorities in order to get a fully rounded point of view on that—not saying that it shall not appear, but that until we have their review we will not put in a completed text. We will simply say, if you agree with me, that everyone has the right to a status in law and the enjoyment of fundamental civil rights and then a note saying that the question of equal rights and freedom in the contract of marriage was mentioned, but that it was decided to ask the Sub-Commission on Prevention of Discrimination and Protection of Minorities to review what had been said and recommended in the Commission on the Status of Women. Then we could have, I think, the other sentence: "Everyone shall have access to independent and impartial tribunals for the determination of his rights, liability, and obligations under the law."

Dr. Chang suggested that that should better be brought back and be included in the review of Articles 8, 9 and 10, and concerning the sentence that the right to consult with and eventually be represented by Counsel, the word "eventually" we feel strongly should be changed to some other word. If that is included, we should hope that a better translation could be found.

Is that the way this Article should be handled, according to the Committee, or shall we make some other change?

MR. CASSIN (France) (Interpretation from French): It seems to me that the suggestion of the Chairman is very good, and I fully associate myself with what she has said, with the reservation that the words "civil rights" in English should be translated as "droits civils" in French.

As regards the footnote referring the matter to the Sub-Commission on Prevention of Discrimination and Protection of Minorities, I think that is very judicious.

If I have to disagree with anything, it is with what Dr. Chang said when he said that this could be added to Article 8, 9 and 10. I think that Articles 8, 9 and 10 refer to penal law, liberty, and security of man. This Article refers to family rights, the right to patrimony and to a profession, and all such matters which might be brought before certain tribunals. It is not the same thing as the protection of an accused person before a criminal tribunal which is contemplated under Articles 8, 9, and 10.

MR. SANTA CRUZ (Chile) (Interpretation from Spanish): I am in complete agreement with what has just been said by Mr. Cassin with regard to the difference between these rights and the rights mentioned in Articles 8, 9 and 10. I want to make a further observation so that it will be recorded in case there is a need to study this point in the Commission.

Reference is made here to the individual's right of appearing before an impartial and independent court which would determine his rights. Nearly all legislations provide that tribunals should determine civil and political rights, and in general, the civic rights of the person, or the legal rights. There are, however, other rights that arise from the relations between the State and the public administration which is called "administrative law." Some legislations have set up administrative tribunals to determine the rights of individuals in this respect. In other legislations, it is the State itself that determines these rights.

Without expressing an opinion on the convenience of introducing a restriction, I would like this observation to be recorded so that the question I raised will be taken up in the Commission itself.

CHAIRMAN: It will be recorded.

MR. KORETSKY (USSR) (Interpretation from Russian): I only wanted a brief clarification. It seems that no decision has been taken yet with regard to paragraphs 1 and 2 of Article 15. What has been said about civil rights seems to be fully covered by Article 1, and if it is not sufficiently covered in Article 1, we might develop the terms of that Article.

I wonder also whether it is appropriate to leave in the phrase, "in accordance with the laws of the State" because that might mean an approval of polygamy, which still exists in certain States. I do not think that feminist organizations which are interested in the drafting of this Article, would be interested and would approve or support polygamy. Therefore, I should like to know the nature of these two sentences.

CHAIRMAN: I do not think you understood what we have suggested. The suggestion was that Article 15 should read: "Everyone has the right to a status in law and enjoyment of fundamental civil rights," and Mr. Cassin agreed that would explain "legal personality."

The second sentence we decided to leave out and to refer simply a note to the Commission saying that the question of the right to contract marriage had been discussed, but it had been decided that we should wait until we had asked the Sub-Commission on Prevention of Discrimination and Protection of Minorities to review the recommendations made in the Commission on the Status of Women, and then to report back on their own findings.

Dr. Chang had suggested taking out the first part of paragraph 3, and putting it back into Articles 8, 9 and 10, but Mr. Cassin pointed out that it dealt with a different kind of legal right, and therefore, he felt it should be kept in. In view of that, I think we shall have to leave paragraph 3 in, subject to a different translation of the word "eventually" as the United States representative suggested. The word "eventually" does not really interpret the French document properly. Then we would read Article 15 with the first sentence as has been read before; the second sentence with a note for the Commission; and the third as it now stands with the exception of a better interpretation of the word "eventually."

DR. CHANG (China): If the first sentence is to be substituted by the one you just recommended, naturally the third paragraph should go with it. That is a description of what is meant by "civil rights" and "legal status." But I think on the whole, it is still a little too technical for the common man. The common man wants equality, consideration, and he wants to know his relationship with the courts, and if it is not included, then perhaps we may have no third paragraph at all. If it is necessary to mention these rights, perhaps it should stand together with the first paragraph of Article 5. That is only natural. My suggestion at the time was that inasmuch as the first Article may appear too technical and if a clarification of the relation of the individual to the tribunals that is concerned, it may be considered as a part of the consideration of the tribunal relationship with the individual, both civil and criminal.

CHAIRMAN: If I remember rightly, I think that in our former discussion it was held extremely important to have an Article that stressed the right to what was called a "legal personality." We discussed that, and Mr. Cassin pointed out why he thought it was important. He has now accepted the other wording which I suggested simply for the benefit of the layman, not for the benefit of the lawyer. If we accept that, then I understand that we all agree that paragraph 3 should go in. That was what I had suggested to the Committee with the only exception that the word "eventually" be interpreted better.

DR. CHANG (China): Even then, the last sentence may still be a comment instead of being a part of the Article itself, because it does seem to be some sort of a detail instead of a general principle.

In regard to keeping this idea which really has been developed more in countries where legality has been emphasized and defined more clearly, with regard to keeping this Article at all, I would like to reserve my position.

MR. CASSIN (France) (Interpretation from French): Of course each representative is completely free to express his opinion, but taking advantage of the same liberty, I must state that this is one of the most important texts of the Declaration, on a national as well as international level. On the national level, it means that every citizen has the right to have access to justice. He cannot be denied the right of going before a judge if he is going to be tried on a case. For us, this seems to be rather elementary because we live in organized countries. But we have seen so many examples, not so long ago, when people were refused the right to go before judges. I do not think this was only a case of discrimination. There are States who simply do not accept the fact that everyone has the right to be defended or to go before a judge.

On an international plane, it seems to me that we have to improve the foreigners, in my opinion, and this goes for my country as well as for many others. One hundred fifty years were needed after the adoption of the Civil Code or the Napoleonic Code, in order that tribunals should recognize the foreigners living on French soil and should recognize the right of such foreigners to go before a tribunal.

At the beginning, it was said, "Oh, you are a foreigner. Well, French tribunals are made for Frenchmen and you cannot go before them."

I think this should be changed and it was changed in my country.

In the Declaration of Human Rights, we should say that a man, even if he is a foreigner, has the right to go before a tribunal if he has his suitcase stolen or if he is evicted from an apartment.

CHAIRMAN: The position of the United States is that it agrees with this position and the importance of including this Article.

I should like to get the general feeling of the Committee. As I now understand it, the representative of China felt that it might not be necessary to include this Article at all. However, in the general discussion which we have had, the feeling of the majority was that it should be included. It would now read:

"Every one has the right to a status in law and to the enjoyment of fundamental civil rights."[11]

Then we would have the note on the right to contract marriage;[12] then, we would have:

"Every one shall have access to independent and impartial tribunals for the determination of his rights, liabilities, and obligations under the law."[13]

The United States would add the note that they wish to include: "He shall have the right to consult with and be represented by Counsel", changing the translation of the word "eventually".

Now, if that is as the Committee wishes to have it forwarded, that is the way we will agree to.

(No response)

CHAIRMAN: Very well, the Article is adopted.

PVrbmex CHM, DLC

---

1. See header Document 230.

2. The members of the Human Rights Commission drafting committee included: ER (chairman), René Cassin of France, Peng-chun Chang of China, Hernán Santa Cruz of Chile, Colonel William Roy Hodgson of Australia, Vladimir Koretsky of the Soviet Union, Charles Malik of Lebanon (rapporteur), and Geoffrey Wilson of Great Britain. Koretsky (1890–1990), a prominent international lawyer, had replaced Valentin Tepliakov, a junior official, indicating that the Soviets were giving the work of the HRC greater weight (Glendon, 54, 58–64).

3. Cassin's draft drew about 75 percent of its substance from Humphrey's version. His major contribution was to reorganize the articles in a more logical way and to give the bill of rights unity and structure. He added a preamble and placed six general principles at the head of the list of rights. Although the document went through many further revisions over the following year and a half, most of the ideas in Humphrey's draft and the essential structure of Cassin's version survived in the finished Universal Declaration of Human Rights (Morsink, 8).

4. Glendon, 274–80.

5. "Le cas échéant" means "if need be." ER's fluency in French made it possible for her to discuss issues of translation such as this with Cassin (*POFD*).

6. The drafting committee's task was to produce a declaration of principles, not a convention, which is a legally binding document. The HRC would later work on drafting a convention (Glendon, 84).

7. Koretsky is referring to the antimiscegenation laws in the United States. See *n*12 Document 230.

8. Charles Malik.

9. The expression in French is "personnalité juridique."

10. This suggestion may have come from James Hendrick, ER's State Department advisor for the HRC, who sometimes handed her notes during meetings. Some of these notes survive in Hendrick's papers at the Truman Library, but the editors were not able to locate a note on this topic.

11. The wording of this right went through further revision during the drafting process. In the final version of the Universal Declaration of Human Rights (UDHR) the concept appears as Article 6: "Everyone has the right to recognition everywhere as a person before the law."

12. The right to marriage was included in the UDHR as Article 16: "(1) Men and women of full age, without any limitation due to race, nationality or religion, have the right to marry and to found a family. They are entitled to equal rights as to marriage, during marriage, and at its dissolution. (2) Marriage shall be entered into only with the free and full consent of the intending spouses. (3) The family is the natural and fundamental group unit of society and is entitled to protection by society and the State."

13. The right to a fair trial appears in the UDHR as Article 10: "Everyone is entitled in full equality to a fair and public hearing by an independent and impartial tribunal, in the determination of his rights and obligations and of any criminal charge against him." The right to representation by counsel was not included. Instead, the first clause of Article 11 states: "Everyone charged with a penal offense has the right to be presumed innocent until proved guilty according to law in a public trial at which he has had all the guarantees necessary for his defense."

ON NEGOTIATING WITH RUSSIA

ER used her June 23, 1947, My Day column both to critique the Soviet Union's negotiating strategy and encourage American commitment to ongoing dialogue:

> Too often, the USSR announces its position and then, though occasionally it changes the words, it never changes the position. That is not negotiation, nor cooperation. It presupposes that if you stick to your own position, you will wear the other people out and they will finally agree with you merely because they are too weary to go on with discussions. Fortunately, the Americans are not made that way. They wish to negotiate. They will willingly make concessions when they are convinced of the fairness and the wisdom of other suggestions. But they do not make concessions simply because they are being browbeaten.
>
> I think it is not only possible but essential that the United States and the USSR learn to get on together, but I think there must be concessions on both sides.[1]

Chester Bryant of Knoxville, Tennessee, wrote ER the day the column appeared, detailing his disagreements with her position:

> The American people are fed up with making concessions to Russia, that's all we have been doing and where has it gotten us? It is high time we should be getting ready for war with Russia for it is certain to come if we expect to save our democracy from Communism. That is what little we have left. Russia would have all of us slaves as well as all the world for that's her aim.
>
> All your statements concerning our getting along with Russia are doing much harm and no good. That also goes for your remarks about the colored people. You would do your country a great service if you would keep your pen silent.[2]

ER sent Bryant the following brief reply.

236

Eleanor Roosevelt to Chester Bryant
28 June 1947 [Hyde Park]

My dear Mr. Bryant:

In answer to your letter of June 23rd, I doubt if you actually had any one close to you in the recent war, or if you have been in any country where the war actually was fought, or you would not so blithely be considering another war.

If our democracy is not strong enough to assert itself and conquer communism spiritually, economically and politically, then your defeatist attitude might be justified, but I never again want to see any men belonging to any nation, engaged in modern atomic war.

I think you will agree with me that every American has the right to free speech and an obligation when they feel strongly, to say so.

Very sincerely yours,

TLc AERP, FDRL

1. *MD*, 23 June 1947. For more on ER's assessment of Soviet behavior, see Document 207.

2. Charles Bryant to ER, 23 June 1947, AERP.

ER had to be convinced to sit for this, her only portrait. Douglas Chandor strove to capture her energy and her focus. ER was pleased with the result, autographing the painting to Chandor, "a trial made easier by the painter." The portait now hangs in the White House. IMAGE COPYRIGHT 1984. WHITE HOUSE HISTORICAL ASSOCIATION.

Madame Chiang Kai-shek addressed Congress and visited the White House in 1943 to appeal for support for Nationalist China's war against Japan. After the war, ER criticized Madame Chiang, who, she said, "could talk very convincingly about democracy," but "hasn't any idea how to live it." See Document 63. BETTMANN/CORBIS

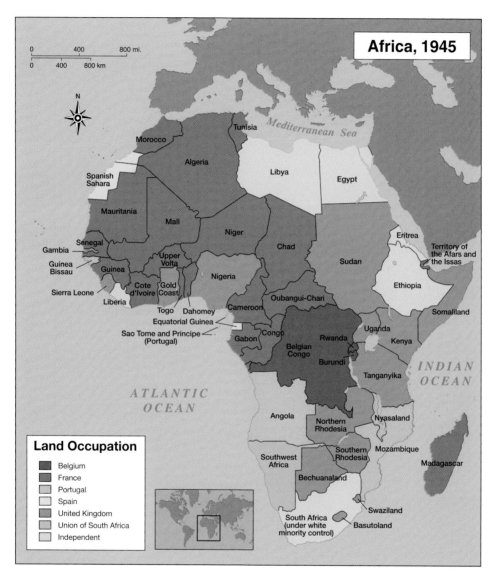

Africa, 1945

0   400   800 mi.
0   400   800 km

N

Morocco
Tunisia
Mediterranean Sea
Algeria
Libya
Egypt
Spanish
Sahara
Mauritania
Mali
Niger
Chad
Eritrea
Senegal
Gambia
Territory of
the Afars and
the Issas
Guinea
Bissau
Upper
Volta
Sudan
Guinea
Nigeria
Ethiopia
Cote
d'Ivoire
Gold
Coast
Sierra Leone
Liberia
Togo Dahomey
Cameroon
Oubangui-Chari
Somaliland
Equatorial Guinea
Sao Tome and Principe
(Portugal)
Gabon
Congo
Rwanda
Uganda
Kenya
Belgian
Congo
Burundi
Tanganyika
INDIAN
OCEAN
ATLANTIC
OCEAN
Angola
Northern
Rhodesia
Nyasaland
Southwest
Africa
Southern
Rhodesia
Mozambique
Madagascar
Bechuanaland
Swaziland
South Africa
(under white
minority control)
Basutoland

Land Occupation

- Belgium
- France
- Portugal
- Spain
- United Kingdom
- Union of South Africa
- Independent

At the end of World War II, most of Africa remained under colonial control. Before ER departed for the 1946 London UN meeting, the NAACP urged her to advocate the preparation of mandated territories for complete independence and the dismantling of "the entire colonial system." See Document 71.

THE GALE GROUP

Date	Friday, April 20
8 A. M.	
8.30	Leave for W. Coor?
9	
9.30	
10	Paul
10.30	
11	
11.30	
12	
12.30 P. M.	
1	
1.30	
2	
2.30	
3	I to of Junas
3.30	Staff for theater fr. Lunon ground
4	
4.30	
5	Office Staff
5.30	
6	Leave Washington
6.30	
7	
7.30	
8	

ER kept her own calendar. Here, in her own hand, is the entry she made detailing her last day in the White House. "It is empty and without purpose to be here now," she told friends and she left Washington "feeling ... melancholy" and somewhat uncertain. See Document 1. COURTESY OF THE FDR LIBRARY.

In May 1945, ER made Val-Kill Cottage her Hyde Park home. She loved to greet guests with flowers cut from her garden. Then the political discussions, such as Jane Ickes's pressing ER on "the possibility of your running for political office," would begin. See Document 10. MARVIN KONER/CORBIS

ER opened Val-Kill Cottage to activists as well as world leaders. Dorothy Tilly thanked ER for her visit, concluding "All the while I was at Hyde Park, I knew that I was seeing more Christianity in action then I could hope to see at the five summer conferences ahead of me." See Document 240. PHOTO © RICHARD CHEEK FOR THE HYDE PARK HISTORICAL ASSOCIATION.

We, the Peoples of the United Nations,

Déclaration
des Droits
de l'Homme

1. - Considering that ignorance and contempt of human rights have
been among the principal causes of the sufferings of humanity and,
inparticular, of the massacres which have polluted the World during
the World Wars; and

Preamble of
Sec. Draft

2. - Whereas there can be no peace unless human rights and freedoms
are respected; and there can be no human freedom or dignity unless
war and the threat of war is abolished; and

Charter and
U.K. Draft

3. - Whereas the institution of conditions wherein human beings,
free to speak and believe, will be protected against fear and want
has been proclaimed as the supreme aim of the recent strife; and

Charter and
U.K Draft

4. - Whereas, in the Charter of June 26th, 1945, we have reaffirmed
our faith in fundamental human rights, in the dignity and worth of
of the human person and in equality of the rights of men and
women; and

U.K. Draft

5. - Whereas it is one of the purposes ofthe United Nations to
achieve international cooperation in promoting and encouraging respect
for human rights and fundamental freedoms for all without distinction
as to race, sex, language or religion; and

U.K. Draft

6. - Whereas the enjoyment of such rights and freedoms by all persons
must be protected by the Commonwealth of Nations and secured by
international as well as national laws;

Now, therefore, we the Peoples of the United Nations have resolved
to define in a solemn Declaration the essential rights and fundamental
freedoms of man, so that this Declaration, being for ever present
to the minds of all members of the human community, may constantly
remind them of their rights and duties and that the United Nations

ER insisted that the preamble to the Declaration be clear and inspirational. The process took months of work. The HRC "finished all the articles for the Declaration ... on Tuesday, but it was by dint of working until ten minutes to one Thursday morning that the committee finished the preamble." See Document 402. COURTESY OF THE FDR LIBRARY.

Organization and the Member States may constantly apply the
principles so declared; and

Have therefore adopted the following Declaration:

CHAPTER I *General Principles*

of all members of the human family ~~free~~ ~~back~~

Article 1 - Human beings ~~belonging to the community of Mankind are free,~~ of
equal dignity and rights and must consider themselves as brothers.

The object of study is

Article 2 - ~~It is the duty of every community to~~ ~~give~~ each of its members
equal opportunity for the full development of ~~his~~ physical, intellectual
and moral personality, without ~~one being sacrificed~~ to others.

Article 3 - As human beings cannot live and develop themselves without the help
and support of the ~~community~~, each one owes to the ~~community~~
fundamental duties which are: obedience to law, exercise of a useful
activity, ~~willful~~ participation in obligations and sacrifices
demanded for the common good.

Article 4 - The rights of ~~each one are~~ limited by the rights of others.

Art. 2 Sec.
Draft and U.S.

Article 5 - Law is equal for all. It ~~commands~~ to public authorities and judges
as well as to individuals. Everything that is not prohibited by law
~~cannot be legally prevented.~~

CHAPTER II

The right to life and physical integrity.

Article 6 - Everyone ~~has the right~~ to life and ~~physical~~ integrity. No one,
even, when guilty, shall be subjected to torture, to cruel
~~punishment or to indignity.~~

Articles 3 & 4
of Sec. Draft

CHAPTER III

Personal Liberties

Article 7 - Everyone has the right to personal liberty.

Art. 5 Sec. Draft.

(Page 2). COURTESY OF THE FDR LIBRARY.

ER surprised her colleagues with her tenacity and debating skills. Dulles confessed that although he first thought her appointment "terrible," he now thought "your work here has been fine." "So—against odds," she told Joe Lash, "the women inch forward, but I'm rather old to be carrying on the fight." See Document 92. COURTESY OF THE FDR LIBRARY.

July–December
1947

*"Either we are strong enough to live as a free people or
we will become a police state."*

Eleanor Roosevelt continued to defend human rights and civil liberties, both at

home and abroad, throughout late 1947. As she and the drafting committee of the Human Rights Commission (HRC) sought to make progress on the Declaration of Human Rights, she turned to Senator Warren Austin to try to secure congressional support for the Declaration and a convention. After Austin conveyed that Congress would sooner approve a declaration than a convention, ER traveled to Geneva in December to ask the HRC to prioritize the drafting of the Declaration. As for a convention, she told her colleagues that "the Commission should not proceed to draw them up until it was sure that such Conventions could be accepted and applied in all good faith by the participating States."[1] Working in close cooperation with French, Soviet, and Filipino colleagues on the drafting committee, ER guided the drafting of a declaration she wanted to be "readily understood by the ordinary man or woman" and a covenant she hoped would "be really binding among nations."[2]

ER also continued to monitor developments in foreign affairs. When foreign ministers of several European countries met in July to begin work on what would become the European Recovery Program (or Marshall Plan), ER wrote Secretary Marshall, urging him to keep the UN involved in the program. That same month, Truman proposed that up to 400,000 Eastern European refugees, especially Jewish orphans, should be allowed to enter the United States. ER supported the proposal in her My Day column: "To do nothing about solving the displaced persons' problem this year means that we leave desperate people with no hope."[3] The plight of the Jewish orphans particularly concerned her, and she urged her friend Charl Williams to mobilize the National Association of Education on behalf of the Stratton bill (the congressional version of Truman's plan), while she sought ways to bring the issue before the HRC.

ER's greatest struggle in her work with the HRC during this period came when, in October, the National Association for the Advancement of Colored People (NAACP) submitted its "Statement on the Denial of Human Rights" to the UN as an entreaty for redress of African American grievances. Walter White asked ER, who then served on the NAACP's Board of Directors, to participate in the petition. ER refused, telling White, "as a member of the delegation I feel that until this subject comes before us in the proper way ... I should not seem to be lining myself up in any particular way on any subject."[4] When ER attempted to reach out to the NAACP in late November, asking the organization for suggestions to bring before the HRC, W. E. B. Du Bois discounted her overture, concluding that the State Department remained "determined that American Negroes shall have no chance to state their grievances before the world."[5] ER could only assure White that "the sub-committee on Implementation is already considering the suggestions" offered by the NAACP.[6]

Outside of her association with the HRC, however, ER freely expressed her sympathy with civil rights struggles and her horror at the persecutions of minorities within the United States. "We can not look down too much on the Nazis or the Communists, when somewhere in our land things like these can happen," she wrote in reply to Dorothy Tilly's news of attempted lynchings in Georgia.[7] In If You Ask Me, ER encouraged friendship and association across color lines, while stopping short of outright endorsement of interracial marriage.[8]

While the HRC worked to secure human rights worldwide, the United States faced infringement of civil liberties at home. The House Un-American Activities Committee (HUAC) launched its investigation of Communist "subversion" in the entertainment industry with the Hanns Eisler case in September. The German film composer, then working in Hollywood, had caught HUAC's attention for his unusual visa application (which had peripherally involved ER) and his suspicious political background. Though she was never called to testify in the Eisler case, ER did express her thoughts on HUAC's ensuing inquest of the "Hollywood Ten" in My Day: "One thing is sure— none of the arts flourishes on censorship and repression."[9] The federal "loyalty test" program, another manifestation of the national "witch hunt," elicited ER's remark to Truman, who supported the government program, "I feel we have capitulated to our fear of Communism."[10] To Marshall, who enforced the loyalty test in the State Department, ER protested, "any Communist would sign to it and the rest of us feel a little besmirched as we sign."[11] As the Taft-Hartley Act went into effect in late August, ER voiced her opposition to its principles, including its provision requiring an anti-Communist loyalty affidavit for union leaders. The increasing distrust of the people by their government that ER perceived led her to declare, "Either we are strong enough to live as a free people or we will become a police state."[12]

In national politics, ER viewed the continuing ascendancy of Henry Wallace with caution. "I think Mr. Henry Wallace is a fine person but I do not think he is very wise as a politician," she wrote in response to an inquiry about Wallace's capabilities, adding that she thought he was "misleading the Russians" in his public stance against the Truman Doctrine.[13] At the end of the year, when Wallace announced his intention to seek the presidency as the nominee of the Progressive Party, ER responded in her column, "as a leader of a third party he will accomplish nothing. He will merely destroy the very things he wishes to achieve"—namely, the progressive ideals on which Wallace, FDR, and ER once stood together.[14]

Other topics that ER addressed in her correspondence, columns, and interviews in the last half of 1947 include support for public schools, the economic hardships of the Navajo tribe, religious freedom, and the importance of women's participation in public life.

---

1. See Document 289, Excerpt, Commission on Human Rights, Summary Record, 2 December 1947.

2. See Document 291, My Day, 18 December 1947.

3. See Document 244, My Day, 23 July 1947.

4. See Document 266, ER to Walter White, 22 October 1947.

5. See Document 285, Walter White to ER, 28 November 1947 (header).

6. See Document 288, ER to Walter White, 12 December 1947.

7. See Document 241, ER to Dorothy Tilly, 31 July 1947.

8. See Document 256, If You Ask Me, September 1947.

9. See Document 271, My Day, 29 October 1947.

10. See Document 277, ER to Harry Truman, 13 November 1947.

11. See Document 279, ER to George Marshall, 13 November 1947.

12. See Document 247, My Day, 13 August 1947.

13. See Document 260, ER to E. Ralph Wiborg, 21 September 1947.

14. See Document 293, My Day, 31 December 1947.

"What Happened To The One We Used To Have?"

U.S. IMMIGRATION POLICY

Like the Herblock cartoon, ER criticized Congress's reluctance to address its immigration policy. "This is simply the kind of delaying tactics which we blame the Russians for using ... Instead of making a gesture which would set an example ... we will do nothing." See Document 244. "WHAT HAPPENED TO THE ONE WE USED TO HAVE?" FROM *THE HERBLOCK BOOK* (BEACON PRESS, 1952).

In 1945, W. E. B. Du Bois opposed the UN Charter for not protecting colonies. In 1947, when ER did not support his petition to the UN, he indicted her for "following orders" from a government "determined that American Negroes shall have no chance to state their grievances before the world." See Document 285. © BETTMANN/CORBIS.

As an NAACP board member, ER worked closely with its senior staff, especially Walter White and Thurgood Marshall. After refusing Du Bois's petition, she asked White for "a memorandum of the items" the NAACP wanted "included in the World Charter of Human Rights" and recommendations for "implementing machinery of those rights." See Document 285. © CORBIS.

"IT'S OKAY --- WE'RE HUNTING COMMUNISTS"

As Congress accelerated its loyalty investigations, ER wrote "I have never liked the idea of an Un-American Activities Committee. I have always thought that a strong democracy should stand by its fundamental beliefs and that a citizen of the United States should be considered innocent until he is proved guilty." See Document 271. "IT'S OKAY, WE'RE HUNTING COMMUNISTS," FROM *THE HERBLOCK BOOK* (BEACON PRESS, 1952).

The Human Rights Commission appointed ER and René Cassin to the committee charged with drafting human rights-related documents. By late 1947, it had produced a draft declaration, a draft covenant, and suggestions for implementation. "I drove them hard," she wrote, "but ... all the men are proud of their accomplishments." See Document 291. © BETTMANN/CORBIS.

Concerned that European economies would collapse before the Marshall Plan could be implemented and that Russia would enter the breach, ER supported Truman's 1947 request for emergency foreign aid. She wrote, "I read your message to Congress and I thought it very courageous and very good in every way." See Document 283. USED BY PERMISSION OF DONALD E. MARCUS. LIBRARY OF CONGRESS, PRINTS & PHOTOGRAPHS DIVISION [LC-USZ62-86602].

ER, like the AFL, encouraged Truman to veto Taft-Hartley. "There are certain things in the bill which, as an American citizen, I resent." Why must labor leaders, and not businessmen, "declare" they are not Communists? Why exclude Fascists? Why declare "things about ourselves" we once "considered nobody's business?" See Document 253. © BETTMANN/CORBIS.

ER thought Henry Wallace "well meaning" and his "reasoning … fuzzy." "As a leader of a third party he will accomplish nothing. He will merely destroy the very things he wishes to achieve. I am sorry that he has listened to people as inept politically as he is himself." See Document 293. © BETTMANN/CORBIS.

ER enjoyed inviting young activists, like this UNESCO committee, to her home for picnics. For example, after a young historian challenged her principles, she replied, "If you come to Hyde Park this summer, let me know ahead of time and if I am here I shall be glad to see you." See Document 292.

COURTESY OF THE FDR LIBRARY.

_237_

If You Ask Me [excerpt]
Ladies' Home Journal July 1947

The overcrowded conditions of our public schools and the low salaries of the teachers present a problem that must be typical of our income group. Do you feel that it is wise to make considerable sacrifice to maintain our children in a good private school in order to get the advantage of individual instruction that the public system cannot give at this time? I hesitate to assume this financial burden unless convinced that it is the wise thing to do.

No, I have always felt that there was only one advantage in private schools and private colleges. That was if they were so conducted that they carried on the experiments in education which public schools and public colleges could not afford to do. Then private institutions of learning serve a good purpose.

On the whole, I think it more important that all of us send our children to public schools and try to make public schools, because of our interest, what they really ought to be. It is true that teachers' salaries should be higher, but only the acceptance of that fact by the taxpayers will ever bring it about. It is true that more money should go into education, but again it is the taxpayers' realization of this fact that will bring it about. I have always felt this way, but my mother-in-law felt very strongly about private schools and we deferred to her wishes where our children were concerned, but I am not at all sure that it was wise in all cases.[1] I am quite convinced that it is not the right and public-spirited thing to do.

Tmsex DLC

---

1. ER deferred to Sara Delano Roosevelt in the upbringing of her children. In addition to nurses and governesses, the Roosevelt children received private education in New York and Washington, DC, and at the Groton School in Massachusetts (Lash, *Eleanor*, 193–99).

ELEANOR ROOSEVELT, WARREN AUSTIN, AND THE PROPOSED COVENANTS ON HUMAN RIGHTS

At its meetings in June, the HRC drafting committee produced a draft human rights declaration, which it forwarded on to the full HRC. It did not have time, however, to draft a convention on human rights. Instead, it sent the draft convention prepared by the British on to the full HRC for its consideration. After the conclusion of the drafting committee session ER and James Hendrick, her State Department advisor, became concerned about whether the US Senate would ratify a convention once the HRC drafted it and the UN approved it.[1]

July 1, Hendrick wrote Dean Rusk, then director of the Office of Special Political Affairs: "It occurred to me (and should have occurred to me yesterday) that a very good approach to Senators Connally and Vandenberg in regard to the desirability of a human rights convention would be through Senator Austin." He suggested that the first step would be for ER to meet with Austin.

The following memorandum records the substance of that meeting.[2]

_____238_____

James Hendrick
Memorandum of Conversation
with Eleanor Roosevelt
3 July 1947

Persons Present: Mrs. Roosevelt, Senator Austin, Mr. Ross, Mr. Winslow and Mr. Hendrick.[3]

Subject: Commission on Human Rights

Relations with Congress—Mrs. Roosevelt explained to Senator Austin that the Human Rights Drafting Committee in its recently concluded session, had produced two documents. One, a declaration on human rights which would have morally binding force, and the other a convention which would have legally binding force. (The declaration was the more carefully prepared document of the two.)

Mrs. Roosevelt explained that the United States position had at all times been that there should be a declaration of human rights and in addition, a convention or conventions to furnish implementation. The United States had not felt that a convention could be achieved at once, but when it was apparent that a strong majority in the Drafting Committee wanted a convention at the same time as a declaration, the United States went along with this view.

Mrs. Roosevelt then asked Senator Austin if he would like to make any comments on two questions which were troubling her: (a) would a convention on human rights be acceptable to the Senate at this time; (b) is it advisable for the Department to sound out Senators Vandenberg and Connolly[4] on the subject.

Senator Austin felt that the first question posed a very difficult problem and he could not undertake to answer it. He agreed with Mrs. Roosevelt that there would be certain elements among the Southern contingent and the reactionaries from other parts of the country where very strong opposition to a convention would be met. With regard to the second question, Senator Austin felt that it would be well to sound out Senators Vandenberg and Connolly on the subject. Senator Austin explained that he was not the person to do this. He had made it a rule to leave Congress alone except on such occasions as he was required to ask them for appropriations. The effect of his silence had, he believed, been beneficial. It was explained that Mr. Lovett might very well be prepared to see the Senators and Senator Austin agreed with this suggested procedure as a very satisfactory method of handling the matter.[5]

Ratification of convention—Mr. Ross suggested that if a convention was adopted on human rights, it might be possible to put it in the form of a joint resolution, in which case both Houses of Congress would participate and a majority vote would be sufficient.

United States policy on Human Rights—Mrs. Roosevelt pointed out that the essential in present day consideration of human rights was to secure publicity. Senator Austin agreed that we should insist at this time upon United Nations provision for human rights which would result in publicity in cases of serious violations. Beyond that Senator Austin felt, and Mrs. Roosevelt agreed, that United States policy should for the time being, be flexible. We should be perfectly willing to enter into a convention as well as a declaration, but we must be reasonably certain that the country will back us up. We should not try for too much. It would be most unfortunate if we were to take the lead in forcing a convention through the General Assembly and then be turned down by the Senate.

U.S.S.R. policy on Human Rights—Mrs. Roosevelt indicated her view that the U.S.S.R. would probably say very little at the second session of the Human Rights Commission and would not start to indicate a definitive position until the first meeting of the Discrimination and Minorities Sub-Commission. She expected that the declaration and the convention would have to be fought out with the U.S.S.R. paragraph by paragraph much in the same manner that the IRO Constitution was fought out. The question of whether the United States should enter into a convention on human rights if the U.S.S.R. and its satellites refuse to do so, was not touched upon with Senator Austin. Mrs. Roosevelt was inclined to feel that the U.S.S.R. position on this matter would not be reached until very late in the proceedings.

Meetings with Non-Governmental Organizations—Mrs. Roosevelt stated that she had informally received excellent reports of the work done by the Department in connection with the education of non-governmental organizations regarding certain U.N. manners. It was indicated that this sort of work might be made extremely effective in connection with problems arising on human rights.

JPH.

TMemI AERP, FDRL

---

1. Glendon, 70–71.

2. James Hendrick to Dean Rusk, 1 July 1947, RG84, NARA II.

3. Warren Austin; John C. Ross (1904–?), senior advisor to Ambassador Austin; Richard S. Winslow (1908–2000), a career State Department official who helped administer the US mission's activities; and James Hendrick. Winslow served in the US Army from 1943 to 1945 and in UNRRA from 1945 to 1946. In June of 1946 he joined the State Department, initially working on the refugee and displaced persons issue. Later that year he became secretary general of the US mission to the UN. John C. Ross joined the State Department as an economic analyst in 1937 and worked in a variety of capacities in the department before being assigned to UN affairs in 1945. Beginning in 1947, he became a member of the US delegation to the UN General Assembly (on Hendrick, see Mazuzan, 42–43; on Winslow, see *RDS* (April 1, 1949), 415; obituary, *Harvard Magazine*, vol. 102 (July–August 2000), http://www.harvardmag.com/classnotes/0304-obituar-

ies.html, accessed 11 November 2005; obituary, *NYT*, 15 February 2000, C27; on Ross, see *BRDS* (1949), 332; "High Aide Leaves U.S. Group in U.N.," *NYT*, 18 August 1954, 5).

4. Senator Tom Connally.

5. The editors could not determine whether Lovett approached Connally and Vandenberg, but Lovett himself opposed the drafting of a covenant. See notes and headers for Document 289 and Document 295.

Assessing the Marshall Plan

June 24, 1947, Mary Ester R. Hill, a former president of the Texas League of Women Voters and a proponent of strengthening the UN, responded to an appeal from the American Association of the United Nations. The letter, distributed over ER's signature, sought support for "the ideal of world organization for peace through the United Nations" and asked readers to endorse the "American policy of aid to Greece and Turkey as amended in the Congress, clearly bringing American policy within the framework of the United Nations."[1]

Hill then wrote ER, saying that "at first" she "intended to sign the form reaffirming faith in the United Nations" but she had changed her mind. She hoped that although ER was "an ambassador to the world ... [she] could afford to throw a re-assuring ray of light upon the path of a trusting but troubled citizen." Although Hill opposed military aid and regretted that action in support of Greece "could not have waited on the slow-moving machinery of the United Nations," she supported Truman's policy of direct assistance to Greece. Hill also leaned toward supporting the Marshall Plan, but she considered Henry Wallace's plan for world reconstruction "bolder and broader" than "the limited plan for economic recovery in Europe as conceived by Secretary Marshall." Yet, she remained conflicted. "While [I am] a long-time and an ardent admirer of Henry Wallace," Hill had "been led to consider that plan best in international intercourse [is that] which can not be misunderstood, circumvented or ignored by the Russians."

Hill, however, did "not enjoy being an advocate of a plan that makes Spain happy and hopeful any more than I presume President Truman and Secretary Marshall do." Moreover, "I regret to seem on the side that hates Russia for I have defended and will continue to defend Russia's rights. But I must believe we have trustworthy leadership now when day to day calls for forthright decisions." She then sought some reassurance from ER about the direction of American foreign policy.[2]

ER dictated the following reply.[3]

239

Eleanor Roosevelt to Mary Ester R. Hill
6 July 1947 [Hyde Park]

My dear Mrs. Hill:

I read your letter with interest and I am very glad to have an opportunity to write you.

Secretary Marshall's plan, I think, is a far bolder and broader plan than Mr. Wallace envisions, or than was the first Truman plan for aid to Greece and Turkey.

If this plan can be put through for the whole of Europe, it will start economic recovery which I think must come about before we can have political peace. It is true that Russia is at present holding aloof. It looks as though she would rather see the people perish than see them succeed under a system which is different from her own. I think it remains to be seen whether the nations of Europe are going to act on economic questions without Russia or with her. If she is wise, I think she will come in. She is afraid, and I think suspects that we will not act entirely altruistically. That suspicion does not surprise me greatly. On the other hand, we have none of the more serious evil intentions which she attributes to us, and that some day she will find it out.[4]

I have great trust in the United Nations and I feel sure that President Truman means to do the right things. His advisers sometimes lead him astray because he has to take their advice, not feeling always secure that he knows more than they do.

By and large, however, as I look at the behavior of the present Congress I think the Democratic Party as a whole, can be trusted to be more liberal and more sane both at home and abroad than the Republican Party and therefore I hope the country will continue to support the Democrats.

Very sincerely yours,

TLc AERP, FDRL

---

1. ER to Dear Friend, 21 May 1947, AAUN, AERP.

2. For the Marshall Plan, see *n*6 Document 231. Wallace called for a ten-year, $50 billion aid program to Europe (including the Soviet Union) under the auspices of the UN (Mary Ester R. Hill to ER, 24 June 1947, AERP; Culver, 440).

3. ER wrote "Dictate" in the upper left margin of Hill's letter.

4. The Soviet Union rejected the financial assistance offered by the Marshall Plan, accusing the United States of seeking to interfere in the internal affairs of other countries and achieve economic domination of Europe under the guise of aiding European recovery. Accepting Marshall's proposal would have required disclosing information about resources and cooperating with the United States and Western Europe in the area of economic planning. On July 5, ER wrote, "the Marshall Plan is a bona fide offer to help Europe get back on its feet. Mr. Molotov, in refusing to join the rest of Europe, is creating the very thing he says he fears, which is division instead of cooperation" (Hogan, 51–53; Patterson, 131; "Statements by Molotov, Bevin and Bidault on European Aid Plan," *NYT*, 3 July 1947, 4; *MD*, 5 July 1947).

ON FAITH, POLITICAL STEWARDSHIP, AND
RACIAL VIOLENCE

> Dorothy Tilly, an Atlanta Methodist whom Truman had appointed to his commission on civil rights, visited ER in Hyde Park in early summer.[1] ER had known Tilly at least since July 1944, when ER spoke at the Missionary Conference of the Methodist Church at Lake Junaluska, North Carolina, where Tilly taught courses. After her visit to Hyde Park, Tilly wrote to thank ER, share some of her impressions of the visit, and report on the efforts she and others were making to combat racism and lynching in Georgia.[2]

240

Dorothy Tilly to Eleanor Roosevelt
14 July 1947 [Lake Junaluska, NC]

Dear Mrs. Roosevelt; –

Thank you so much for a great experience—an experience that will always be with me. All the while I was at Hyde Park, I knew that I was seeing more Christianity in action then I could hope to see at the five summer conferences ahead of me—North Georgia Conference, Lake Junaluska, New Castle Ind., Lincoln Nebr., and Lakeland, Fla.

It was such a privilege to go through the library and the home and to stand near the grave, to be with you and the lovely, lovely children, to have the hours with you and Miss Thompson[3] and get an insight into your mail and your answers.

I am sure that I found the secret of "The Amazing Roosevelts",[4] when I saw the old Dutch Bible open at the 13th chapter of Corinthians, and realized that upon it—faith, hope and charity, a great family had helped a nation in its crisis.[5]

Thank you for all of it.

The North Georgia Conference of The Methodist Church met last week. The Stewardship speaker was Dr. Stidger of Boston University. He told us of his connection with the Roosevelt family and said to us that we of the South needed no one to give us stewardship lessons for we had them.[6] We had them in the Warm Springs Foundation.[7] His story of the Warm Springs Foundation made Westbrook Pegler more and more contemptible. While he did not mention Pegler's name, he certainly answered him.[8]

Dr. Stidger called the TVA, the "greatest political stewardship way of life" of all times, now spreading or that would spread to the Jordan River and to the flood areas of China and Russia. He paid tribute to both Mr. Norris and to President Roosevelt as men who knew how to take God's gifts and give them to men.[9]

After the speech, I told Dr. Stidger I was just back from Hyde Park and he asked about you and the "lovely" grandchildren. He does not know David and Scoopy and I think he has missed something.[10] He spoke of the other children.

Our Conference, made up of ministers and laymen, made some very strong pronouncements against race as an issue in political campaigns and we pledged not to vote for a candidate that dared make it an issue. This is a part of the religious campaign or crusade, I told you we were launching, in which all denominations of the state have promised to promote. It may not be necessary now since the decision on the S.C. white primary. Things are far more serious now in Georgia now.[11] I am accustomed to being called most any time day or night, but the calls are tragically frequent now, due both to the seriousness of the hour and to the fact that I am on the Civil Rights Committee.

In the South, when trouble comes involving Negroes, it immediately takes on a political tinge and we are hopelessly frustrated.

We had a prevented lynching at Carrollton, Ga. some days ago. The would-be lynchers were promised a speedy trial of the Negro who had killed the white man. So far, the judge has paid no attention to the case, the Negro is in Atlanta jail, the grand jury has not drawn an indictment. Some of citizens of the county, frightened by the growing threat of lynching just any Negro, called us and asked us to lay the situation before the governor (they living in the community felt they could not do it themselves). The governor gave an evasive reply. Can you see in this, what Talmadge politics has done to the state. Our Governor is afraid to face issues.[12]

There has been a killing of five Negroes in a convict camp at Brunswick. I am enclosing a clipping. Unless the Federal Government steps in, the investigation will mean nothing.[13]

I talked to you about the situation in Harris County (the county of Warm Springs). In that county the Negroes are living in such fear and in such danger, the leading Negroes of the State requested an interview with Gov. Thompson. He refused the request. The Negroes, frustrated, have appealed to Drew Pearson and asked him to give the story over the radio. Anyone would regret this, yet when the FBI and the governor both fail, you cannot blame the Negroes for trying other methods.

I am enclosing the Harris County stories.[14] All of this has been in the hands of the Atty. General. The FBI has made some investigation as ineffectual as it always is in the South.

I am at Junaluska and I began this letter on Monday—it is Saturday now. The days and nights have been too full to have time to finish the letter. Miss Fleeson has been with us. She took us by storm. I did not agree with all she said. I told her, though, that I was afraid she carried the women with her.[15]

I think I told you, we were having two Negro women and 4 Indian women, living in Mission Inn with us and participating in our school. This, as you know is a great forward step for us. It has worked well and has been so natural that we feel it is the beginning of real fellowship and cooperation in the churches.

I am deeply grateful to you for many things and will be more indebted to you, if you will give us some guidance and help as we try to find our way through these serious situations.

With kindest regards to Miss Thompson and thanks to you, I remain

Yours sincerely,
Dorothy Tilly

TLS AERP, FDRL

241

Eleanor Roosevelt to Dorothy Tilly

31 July 1947 [Campobello Island, Canada]

Dear Mrs. Tilly:

I was very glad to get your letter but horrified by the material which you enclosed. It seems to me dreadful that in our country we should have any people going through such experiences. We can not look down too much on the Nazis or the Communists, when somewhere in our land things like these can happen.

That 13th Chapter of Corinthians you noticed was my husband's favorite Chapter as well as my own.

I am glad that Doris Fleeson was a success. I am very fond of her but I do not always agree with what she says or even believes. I should be glad to know, if you have the time, what it was with which your disagreed.[16]

With every good wish, I am,

Very cordially yours,

TLc AERP, FDRL

---

1. Dorothy Rogers Tilly (1883–1970) became a member of the Commission on Interracial Cooperation and the Association of Southern Women for the Prevention of Lynching in 1931 and went on to play a significant role in the civil rights movement. She investigated lynchings in Georgia and—on behalf of the Southern Regional Council—the race riot in Columbia, Tennessee, that ER also investigated (see Document 102). In 1945, Truman appointed Tilly to the President's Committee on Civil Rights, which would issue its report, *To Secure These Rights*, in October 1947 (*NAWMP*).

2. *NAWMP*, *MD*, 26 July 1944; *MD*, 29 July 1944.

3. Malvina Thompson.

4. Tilly refers to the title of a book by Rev. William L. Stidger. See *n*6.

5. First Corinthians, Chapter 13 reads:

> Though I speak with the tongues of men and of angels, and have not charity, I am become as sounding brass, or a tinkling cymbal. And though I have the gift of prophecy, and understand all mysteries, and all knowledge; and though I have all faith, so that I could remove mountains, and have not charity, I am nothing. And though I bestow all my goods to feed the poor, and though I give my body to be burned, and have not charity, it profiteth me nothing. Charity suffereth long, and is kind; charity envieth not; charity vaunteth not itself, is not puffed up, doth not behave itself unseemly, seeketh not her own, is not easily provoked, thinketh no evil; rejoiceth not in iniquity, but rejoiceth in the truth; beareth all things, believeth all things, hopeth all things, endureth all things. Charity never faileth: but whether there be prophecies, they shall fail; whether there be tongues, they shall cease; whether there be knowledge, it shall vanish away. For we know in part, and we prophesy in part. But when that which is perfect is come, then that which is in part shall be done away. When I was a child, I spake as a child, I understood as a child, I thought as a child: but when I became a man, I put away childish things. For now we see through a glass, darkly; but then face to face: now I know in part; but then shall I know even as also I am known. And now abideth faith, hope, charity, these three; but the greatest of these is charity (1 Cor. 13.1–13 KLV).

6. Rev. William L. Stidger (1885–1949), a Methodist minister and educator, and nationally known radio preacher, led the radio campaign for Roosevelt's reelection in 1936, and often attended informal White House dinners. He also wrote *Those Amazing Roosevelts* (1944) ("Dr. W.L. Stidger, 64, Minister, Author," *NYT*, 8 August 1949, 15; Jack Hyland, "How I Came to Write This Book," www.stidger.com/about.jsp, accessed 10 November 2005).

7. FDR established the Georgia Warm Springs Foundation in 1927 as a nonprofit, rehabilitation center to assist those like himself, to recover from and manage the debilitating effects of polio. He invested a good part of his fortune in the enterprise. After he became governor of New York and, then, president, he continued to visit Warm Springs regularly for rest and relaxation (*FDRE*).

8. James Westbrook Pegler (1894–1969), a nationally syndicated antilabor and anti-Communist columnist, frequently attacked FDR's New Deal programs and members of the Roosevelt family personally. "I want to know more about the whole lot of them," he wrote, "and I want to run up the whole vile record of treachery which I know there to be had and chisel it on a rock as a memorial to Franklin D. Roosevelt." ER refrained from responding publicly to Pegler's attacks, referring to him once as "such a little gnat on the horizon." Neither Pegler nor ER retained a copy of Pegler's column on FDR and the Warm Springs Foundation (*DAB*; *n9* Document 255; Lash, *Years*, 155--56; *IYAM*, *LHJ*, January 1949).

9. George W. Norris (1861–1944), a progressive Republican from Nebraska, supported FDR early in his first campaign for the presidency. The two worked together during the New Deal for the goals they shared, particularly the creation of the Tennessee Valley Authority (TVA). Norris pushed the TVA bill through Congress. The TVA, which developed the Tennessee River Valley for multiple uses under public ownership, became a model for large-scale river development projects elsewhere in the world (*FDRE*).

10. Tilly refers most likely to David Boynton Roosevelt (1942–), son of Elliott and his second wife, Ruth Googins, and Scoop Emerson, the son of Elliott's third wife, Faye Emerson.

11. In April 1944, in *Smith v. Allwright*, the US Supreme Court declared state laws barring African Americans from voting in primaries unconstitutional. In response, legislators in South Carolina quickly organized a new plan to effect the original intent. The state legislature repealed all laws relating to primary elections, leaving the conduct of primary elections up to the political parties. As a "private club" a political party could prohibit whomever they chose from the process. The South Carolina "white primary" plan then inspired white supremacists in other southern states to follow this model. Georgia took the lead. However, in 1947, a federal district invalidated the South Carolina plan in *Elmore v. Rice*. The Supreme Court would uphold the district court decision April 1949 (Klarman, 200–201; "Negro Vote Stands in South Georgia," *NYT*, 20 April 1948, 1; John N. Popham, "White Voting Law Worries Georgia," *NYT*, 25 February 1947, 30).

12. Tilly is referring to Governor M. E. Thompson ("Our Governor") and to the politics of Eugene Talmadge and his son, Herman. Eugene Talmadge (1884–1946) dominated Georgia politics for the better part of three decades, championing white supremacy and rural farmers. Georgians elected him to the state senate five times and the governor's office four times. His stance on race made him a hero for southern Democrats who would eventually make up the Dixiecrats. Talmadge unexpectedly died after his successful gubernatorial bid in 1946, but before he assumed office. Following his death, Talmadge forces managed to install his son, Herman Talmadge (1913–2002) as governor, but after two months, the State Supreme Court declared that under Georgia's Constitution Talmadge's lieutenant governor-elect, M. E. Thompson (1903–1980) must succeed him. The Talmadge forces, however, continued to exercise strong influence in the state. Earlier that year, ER noted the rhetoric of both Talmadges, writing that "neither the late Governor-elect Eugene Talmadge's speeches nor his son's, with their emphasis on white supremacy, sound much like the Constitution of the United States and the Bill of Rights, under which we are supposed to be running our republic" ("Melvin Thompson, 77, Once Georgia Governor," *NYT*, 5 October 1980, 44; *MD*, 18 January 1947; "Talmadge Is Dead at 62 in Georgia," *NYT*, 22 December 1946, 1).

13. ER either did not retain this clipping or passed it on to other interested parties as no copy of it was found in her files.

14. The stories Tilly enclosed to ER cover the case of Mr. Davidson, an African American man from Harris County, Georgia, who disappeared after killing a white man. Law enforcement officers then imprisoned his family members, including small children, who were beaten until they revealed information regarding Davidson's disappearance. The police then jailed Henry Gilbert on the unfounded charge of abetting Davidson's escape. Before a trial could be arranged, Gilbert was killed in jail. The authorities then turned to Gilbert's wife May and charged her with abetting Davidson's

escape. The account Tilly enclosed charged: "This case and all of its ramifications is a glaring example of how local law is impotent to protect the rights of the negro population in the face of rising public feeling." The report then concluded that federal oversight was essential for African Americans to be treated justly by local law enforcement officials ("Negro Children in Jail in Georgia," unsigned TS enclosure with Dorothy Tilly to ER, 14 July 1947, AERP).

15. Doris Fleeson (1901–1970), a Washington-based syndicated columnist and advocate of women's rights, characterized herself as a nonpartisan liberal. A search by the editors did not locate a record of her remarks at the Junaluska conference ("Doris Fleeson, Columnist, Dies; Winner of Journalism Honors," *NYT*, 2 August 1970, 57).

16. If Tilly responded, ER did not preserve the letter.

THE UNITED NATIONS AND
THE MARSHALL PLAN

July 12, 1947, the foreign ministers of fifteen Western European nations,[1] plus Turkey, met in Paris to answer Marshall's call to craft an "agreement among the countries of Europe as to the requirements of the situation and the part those countries themselves will take" in the rebuilding of Europe.[2] As these preliminary discussions to implement the Marshall Plan occurred, ER wrote in My Day that while "it is quite evident to any nation that if the people of Europe are to get together and take stock of what their resources and their needs for rehabilitation are, they must look to the United States and Latin America for help." She still thought it "vital, however, that the U.N. be acquainted with every step that is taken, and that our actions must always be in accord with U.N. interests."[3] Four days later she wrote Secretary Marshall to urge UN involvement in these early discussions.

242

Eleanor Roosevelt to George Marshall
18 July 1947 [Eastport, ME]

Dear Mr. Secretary:

I understand that the United Nations has not been invited to the Paris Economic Conference.[4] I should think it should be.[5]

Very cordially yours,

TLc AERP, FDRL

After reading Marshall's reply, ER scrawled instructions across it to have a copy of it sent to Joe Lash.

243

George Marshall to Eleanor Roosevelt
22 July 1947 [Washington, DC]

Dear Mrs. Roosevelt:

I have your note of July 18 dealing with the absence of the United Nations from the Paris Economic Conference.

This Government was not one of the organizers of this Conference and, therefore, did not participate in extending the invitations to it. The European Governments directly concerned called the Conference on their own initiative and drew up the list of invitations. It was my understanding that the participating countries are keeping the Economic Council for Europe fully informed of the proceedings at Paris.

I would imagine that it will be through this body that the United Nations will be brought into relation with the results of the Paris talks.

Faithfully yours,
G. C. Marshall

TLS AERP, FDRL

---

1. The ministers represented the United Kingdom, Austria, Belgium, Denmark, France, Greece, Iceland, Ireland, Italy, Luxemburg, the Netherlands, Norway, Portugal, Sweden, and Switzerland. None of the Soviet-affiliated nations of Eastern Europe attended this session as Soviet Foreign Minister Vyacheslav Molotov, who had earlier objected to what he claimed were American attempts to violate national sovereignty and walked out of the June 27 planning meeting, boycotted this conference.

2. "The Address of Secretary Marshall at Harvard," *NYT*, 6 June 1947, 2.

3. *MD*, 12 July 1947.

4. Although UN Secretary-General Trygve Lie had more than once offered the UN's assistance in preparing proposals for how the Marshall Plan could best assist Europe, representatives of the UN's Economic Commission for Europe were not invited to the economic conference. British Foreign Minister Ernest Bevin, however, promised Lie that he would keep the secretary-general informed of the ministers' progress (Thomas J. Hamilton, "Bevin Reassures Lie on Aid Plans," *NYT*, 21 June 1947; Hogan, 51–53).

5. Others with whom ER consulted also objected to the UN's exclusion. For example, Clark Eichelberger, whose advice ER sought before she first joined the American delegation, objected to shutting out the UN, arguing that bypassing the assembly unnecessarily exacerbated the division of Europe between East and West ("3-Power Aid Failure Laid to Bypass of U.N.," *NYT*, 4 July 1947, 3).

THE STRATTON BILL AND US REFUGEE POLICY

On July 7, Truman sent a special message to Congress asking for "suitable legislation as speedily as possible" to permit the admission of a "substantial number" of displaced persons from Eastern Europe who refused to return to Communist-controlled countries. The president emphasized that such legislation would apply only to the current situation in postwar Europe and would not mean a general revision of US immigration policy. Truman preferred, however, not to have the White House introduce the bill. Instead, he instructed his aides to tell Representative William G. Stratton (R-IL) privately that the president supported his bill (HR 2910), which called for the admission of 400,000 displaced persons into the United States over the next four years.[1]

Four days before Congress adjourned, ER used her column to urge the bill's adoption.

244

My Day
23 July 1947

CAMPOBELLO ISLAND, N.B. Tuesday—Apparently Congress, in spite of the President's appeal, has decided to do nothing about the Stratton Bill[2] to admit displaced persons to this country. But Sen. Revercomb of West Virginia has managed to get through a resolution to appoint a committee to investigate the whole question of immigration—this at a cost not to exceed $50,000.[3] We hardly need any more investigation, since all the facts are already well known. This is simply the kind of delaying tactics which we blame the Russians for using. The committee does not have to make any recommendations until March, 1948.

Instead of making a gesture which would set an example, by accepting this year 100,000 immigrants from displaced persons' camps on a quota basis, we will do nothing. This means one of two things—either the rest of the world also will do nothing, or the leadership in this matter will shift to some other nation which has the courage to face situations as they are.

To do nothing about solving the displaced persons' problem this year means that we leave desperate people with no hope. I have heard rumors of a death march on the part of the Jews in European camps. Our inaction is the type of thing that would drive refugees to that kind of desperate action. Should it come about, the members of our Congress can have it on their consciences if thousands more of the Jewish people die.[4] If Congress eventually decides that they have investigated sufficiently and that it will not hurt us to take in a few unfortunate people who have been carefully screened, then we will be surprised to find that the people we admit have deteriorated. They will have become so accustomed to having someone look after them, that they will find it hard to return to independence. Here, again, our members of Congress may carry on their consciences the deterioration of these human beings.

I know well that there are people in this country who, for a number of very obvious reasons are afraid to bring anyone in from the displaced persons' camp. I think this fear is far more dangerous than the people whom we might bring in. We are growing so pusillanimous that, in a short time, we will be afraid of our own shadows—and this is no world in which the fearful survive. Good new blood will do us no harm. We are suffering from fear of the unknown. But these people have seen so much that was unknown that they have learned how to accept it and stand up to it.

Here I am, blaming Congress when, after all, the blame really lies with ourselves. It is we who have not been articulate enough and have not educated people as a whole to understand that the displaced persons are just like ourselves. Only, for the moment, they have no country. We have not made people realize to the full what the ruin of Europe will mean in lowering our own standards of living. Again we the people have failed—failed ourselves and failed our brethren overseas.

TMs AERP, FDRL

———————

1. The Stratton bill would have admitted displaced persons using immigration quotas that had gone unfilled during World War II. For more on Truman's efforts to allow European refugees to enter the United States, see *n*7 Document 74. For more on Truman's efforts to modify immigration policy to help Europe's displaced persons, see *n*7 Document 74 (Felix Belair, Jr., "Truman Asks Law for Europe's DP's to Enter the U.S.," *NYT*, 8 July 1947, 1; *HSTE*; Dinnerstein, 132, 135, 148–52; "Refugees' Haven in U.S. Is Sought," *NYT*, 29 October 1946, 15; *MD*, 5 March 1947, "Mrs. Roosevelt's Message," n.d., AERP).

2. ER recognized the difficulty any displaced person legislation would face. Two months after the bill's introduction she wrote her friend and fellow Wiltwyck School supporter "Puss" Boone that preparations were under way to care for the refugees after their arrival because "Congress will not pass the [Stratton] Bill unless we [probably the Citizens Committee on Displaced Persons (CCDP) of which ER was a vice-chair] can present a complete blue print."

ER supported the legislation "because it is essential that the United States makes a gesture" and because she believed such legislation would benefit America in the long run. When the General Federation of Women's Clubs passed a resolution opposing the legislation in June 1947, ER used My Day to point out that the displaced persons would be assets to America. "Under this bill, we would receive people of various nationalities and religion, highly educated people like doctors and lawyers, as well as skilled workers and farm laborers—all of them people who have suffered greatly and who would come with gratitude in their hearts and with a determination to make good in their new homeland." In March she told a crowd of 2,400 in Detroit that some displaced persons might be Fascists or Communists but they would be few in number. She answered concerns about the scarcity of housing for immigrants by saying that many of those admitted would do agricultural work in rural areas where shelter would be easier to find. Moreover, "many of these people are handy with tools … and they might take some pretty bare barracks and make them livable."

Besides her public advocacy and her role as a CCDP vice-chair, ER also labored behind the scenes to build support for the Stratton bill, providing guidance on political strategy to the CCDP and tapping her network of friends and professional contacts to raise funds and build popular support for the measure. Writing to potential contributor "Puss" Boone, she said, "The money you give will not go to office expenses as much as it will go into making people understand … why we should encourage the rest of the world to do likewise and help these people get settled once they arrive." For more on ER's efforts to build public support for the Stratton bill, see Document 252 (Dinnerstein, 126, 136; "Mrs. F. D. Roosevelt Aids Jewish Drive," *NYT*, 20 February 1947, 17; *MD*, 28 June 1947; "For Easing Immigration," *NYT*, 2 March 1947, 54; *IYAM, LHJ*, March 1947, 26; ER to "Puss" Boone, 18 April 1947, 15 June 1947, 5 July 1947, and 12 July 1947, AERP).

3. Congress adjourned on July 27 without passing the Stratton bill or any other immigration legislation. It did, however approve a proposal by Senator William C. Revercomb (R-WV), an opponent of the Truman Doctrine, the Marshall Plan, and immigration, to authorize the Senate Judiciary Committee to investigate the US immigration system and the problems of displaced persons generally. Many observers considered the investigation a delaying tactic to prohibit the admittance of refugees to the United States.

After touring the European refugee camps in the fall of 1947, the members of Revercomb's subcommittee split on the question of immigration for displaced people. In their majority report circulated privately to the full Senate Judiciary Committee in February 1948, Revercomb and

Senators Forrest C. Donnell (R-MO) and Pat McCarran (R-NV) favored the admission of 100,000 displaced persons over a two-year period. In separate minority reports, Senator J. Howard McGrath (D-RI) proposed the admission of 150,000 displaced persons per year while Senator John Sherman Cooper (R-KY) recommended the admission of 150,000 people in two years (C. P. Trussell, "Confirm Perlman," *NYT*, 27 July 1947, 1; Dinnerstein, 151–54, 156; "Senate Group Approves Displaced Persons Entry," *NYT*, 28 February 1948, 15).

4. During the previous six months, refugees in Western Europe protested camp conditions and in some cases rioted because they feared repatriation. In January 1947, some Polish DPs, fearing repatriation to Poland, objected to being transferred to another camp within the US zone; US troops, discounting their protest, forced their relocation. Also in January, another group of refugees in the American zone attacked seven officers from Warsaw, Poland, who attempted to determine the nationalities of a camp's residents for possible repatriation. In March, Jewish refugees in all the camps in the American sector demonstrated on behalf of resolutions that called for private housing, international jurisdiction for displaced persons pending immigration, immigration to Palestine, creation of an international fund for transportation, and restitution from the Germans. In April, 2,000 Jewish displaced persons in Munich ignored US Army regulations to protest British execution of four Jewish terrorists in Palestine causing military authorities to fear that demonstrations would spread to other parts of Germany. Later that same month, American soldiers fired tear gas bombs and submachine gun bullets to disperse Polish refugees who protested the appointment of new administrators in a UNRRA camp. In July, Jewish refugees in Austria barricaded their camp gates rather than move from one camp to another, despite assurances from US Army personnel that the new camp would be "equal or superior" to the first.

ER used the prospect of the refugees' deterioration on several occasions in My Day to buttress her argument for immediate immigration. As early as November 14, 1946, she wrote "we are willing to pay the price to keep these refugees in camps … where they have no future and are constantly deteriorating as human beings, creating a menace to the economy of the whole area where they are." She reiterated this theme in her March 5, 1947, column: "If we leave these people in camps much longer, they will deteriorate to a point where they will be of little value to any nation which they may enter." For more on ER's concern for the welfare of refugees, see *n*8 Document 74. For more on her firsthand impressions of camp conditions and their effect on refugees, see Document 95 ("Poles Resist Transfer," *NYT*, 12 January 1947, 24; Dana Adams Schmidt, "DP's in Camp Riot Mob 'Soviet' Aides," *NYT*, 7 February 1947, 9; "Jews in U.S. Zone Send Plea to Big 4," *NYT*, 25 March 1947, 5; "2,000 DP's Protest Palestine Deaths," *NYT*, 18 April 1947, 15; "Displaced Poles Riot, Lower American Flag," *NYT*, 12 May 1947, 4; "Army to Force Shift of Jews in Austria," *NYT*, 8 July 1947, 20; *MD*, 14 November 1946 and 5 March 1947).

ON JEWISH WAR ORPHANS

Joseph Lash apparently sent ER pamphlets detailing the campaign led by the Commission on the Status of Jewish War Orphans in Europe to have those children resettled in Christian homes transferred to Jewish families who respected their faith. The commission began its campaign June 19, 1947, when commission chair Dr. Isaiah Grunfeld challenged the United Nations Human Rights Commission to return the 40,000 Jewish war orphans estimated to be in Christian homes to Jewish homes or institutions.[1] ER then forwarded the material with the following letter to James Hendrick, her State Department advisor, "to find out State Dept. thinking for I think it will come up in the Gen. Assembly & be assigned to my Committee if I'm still on 3."

The following day she wrote Lash to say she "sent the pamphlets" and that she agreed with him that "in cases of Institutional care the orphans should go back to the Jewish Community." However, "the other cases should be looked into individually, where there is a chance of the child being asked. If the child is happy and the foster parents give him love and care I would feel regardless of religion he was better off I think."[2]

245

Eleanor Roosevelt to James Hendrick

31 July 1947 [Campobello Island, Canada]

Dear Mr. Hendrick:

Do you think this problem of Jewish war orphans should come to our committee and if so, how would it come?

My own feeling is that without any question, these children should be returned to the Jewish community if they are to be under institutional care. If they have been in families, or foster homes where they are wanted, that is a question which requires more serious consideration.[3]

Dr. Grunfeld of the Court of the Chief Rabbi in London, says there are thirty to forty thousand who have been saved during the Nazi occupation by Christian institutions and Christian families, and who have been living since the liberation, in Christian homes and that the Roman Catholic institutions do not want to have them returned to the Jewish community, but the Jewish community is naturally anxious to have them returned.

This is a touchy problem and I do not know whether it has anything to do with the Human Rights Commission, but somewhere it has to be settled and I should like to know where you think it should go for solution, and if it should come to us, how would it come, and what our thinking on it should be?

Very sincerely yours,
Eleanor Roosevelt

TLS RG59, NARA II

August 21, Hendrick and ER discussed the problem of Jewish war orphans living in non-Jewish environments during a phone conversation in which ER said she had discussed the problem with "a number of persons interested in the matter since having written [her] letter." She then reported that "the consensus of opinion was that children who had been adopted by <u>families</u> should not be disturbed as a rule but that children adopted by institutions might very well be moved from Christian <u>institutions</u> to Jewish institutions."[4]

Later that fall Hendrick wrote ER to update her on the State Department's position.

246

James Hendrick to Eleanor Roosevelt
15 October 1947 [Washington, DC]

Dear Mrs. Roosevelt:

You will remember that we had a telephone conversation some time ago on the problem of Jewish war orphans which was discussed in a study of the Commission on the Status of Jewish War Orphans in Europe.

My present letter is by way of an interim report on this matter.

Consideration is being given to broadening the scope of this problem by extending it to include the entire question of legal status of children affected by the war. It may be that this question can be placed on the agenda of the United Nations body best suited to deal with it which would in all probability be the Social Commission.[5]

The matter is receiving study in the interested agencies of the government; a final decision is not expected in the immediate future.

In the meantime it is not believed that any further action can be taken by this country with respect to the particular problem of Jewish war orphans which you raised as it would normally be regarded as a matter of domestic jurisdiction.[6]

Sincerely yours,
James P. Hendrick

TLS AERP, FDRL

---

1. Rabbi Dr. Isaiah Isidore Grunfeld (1900–1975), senior member of the Ecclesiastical Court of the Chief Rabbi of the British Empire, worked for the British Council for Jewish Relief and Rehabilitation after the war. He condemned the "conversionists" who "refuse[d] to part" with the children because they wished to "save the souls of the Jewish war orphans for Christianity." The number of Jewish children who remained with their wartime foster families remains unknown ("Orphans' Return to Judaism Urged," *NYT*, 19 June 1947, 6; Rubin, *Daughters*, 145–46; "Isaiah Isidore Grunfeld," *Who's Who in World Jewry* (1972 ed.), 362; Elaine Sciolino and Jason Horowitz, "Saving Jewish Children, but at What Cost?" *NYT*, 9 January 2005, 6).

2. ER to Joseph Lash, 1 August 1947, JPLP, FDRL. When ER writes "if I am still on 3," she refers to the UN's Third Committee. Neither Lash nor ER retained copies of the correspondence prompting ER's letter to him or his response to her. Nor did Hendrick retain the pamphlet ER included with this letter.

3. ER had long worked to assist refugee children stranded in Europe, agreeing in January of 1940 to head a special advisory committee for the Youth Aliyah movement in the United States, which helped bring Jewish children from Europe to Palestine. Beyond this, ER supported the work of the US Committee for the Care of European Children, which after the war sought to bring war

orphans to the United States for adoption ("To Advise Youth Aliyah," *NYT*, 22 February 1940, 20; *MD*, 15 November 1946).

4. Memorandum of Telephone Conversation, Department of State, 21 August 1947, RG59, NARA II.

5. The Economic and Social Commission (ECOSOC). The Child Search Branch of the International Tracing Service of the IRO tracked down missing children, including children in foster families, but Jewish organizations, such as Rescue Children, Inc., conducted most of the efforts to secure the release of children from Christian families to Jewish families or agencies. These organizations sometimes offered compensation to the Christian families, but most families refused to give up the children whom they now felt were theirs ("Report of the Secretary-General on the Progress and Prospect of Repatriation," 10 June 1948, Economic and Social Council, Official Records, Third Year, Seventh Session, E/816,160–66; "An Inventory of the Rescue Children, Inc. Collection, 1945-1985," Yeshiva University Archives, 1986, 7–9).

6. ER maintained an active interest in the issue of children displaced by the war, visiting the Child Search Branch of the International Tracing Service of the IRO during an October 1948 visit to Stuttgart, Germany, and corresponding with the branch's chief, Herbert H. Meyer; secretary-general of the US Mission to the UN, Richard S. Winslow; and the IRO director-general in Geneva, J. Donald Kingsley in 1949 about the future of the IRO's efforts to trace missing children in Europe (*MD*, 29 October 1948; Herbert Meyer to ER, 12 April 1949; ER to Richard Winslow, 27 May 1949; J. Donald Kingsley to ER, 6 September 1949, AERP).

ON PREJUDICE AND AMERICAN FASCISM

247

My Day

13 August 1947

CAMPOBELLO ISLAND, N.B., Tuesday—This column will deal with a very serious subject—one that I have been thinking about for a long while. It is not to be written about lightly. In fact, I would rather not write about it, but two things which have happened make me feel that perhaps this is the time to speak. Later on may be too late.

In a recently published article entitled "Bystanders Are Not Innocent", Norman Cousins, editor of the Saturday Review of Literature, tells the story of one of these incidents. A Greek scholar, teaching and studying in one of our great mid-Western universities, was attacked one evening in the coffee shop of a well-known hotel by a group of rowdy undergraduates who, after making some loud remarks against the Jews, pointed at him and said: "He looks like a Jew." As a result of this assault, the man spent ten days in a hospital.

The horrible thing to me is that this could happen when other people were about and that no one seems to have tried to prevent it. I feel sure that even one person with courage and conviction could have brought these young people to their senses. We did not fight a war against fascism in order to allow it to develop here.

The closing two paragraphs of Mr. Cousins' article are the ones I want to bring to your attention, so I quote them here.

"In any event, this is no time for bystanders. Those who persist in looking the other way in the presence of evil or necessity exempt themselves from nothing except membership in the human family.

"This week marks the second anniversary of Hiroshima and the Atomic Age. Happy anniversary, everybody."[1]

On top of this incident, I received a sheet from the Congressional Record, into which Rep. Adolph J. Sabath of Illinois had read an article by I.F. Stone on the subject of a man called Marzani.[2] This man, a month after resigning from the State Department, was discharged and then indicted under an act of Congress, passed in 1944, which extended the statute of limitations three years after the cessation of hostilities in case of fraudulent war-contract claims. He is not accused of having tried to defraud the Government, but he is accused of falsely denying certain statements made in 1940 and 1941. He is now in jail, sentenced to from one to three years and denied bail while waiting appeal of the case.[3]

As to his innocence or guilt I know nothing, but on reading the article I feel that our civil liberties are being endangered. Through fear and undisciplined prejudice, we are becoming the very thing which we have condemned other people for being.

It is time we took a look at ourselves and made up our minds that we can no longer joke about questions of race prejudice or religious differences. And even if we do not agree with the political beliefs held by some, we must not reach a state of fear and hysteria which will make us all cowards! Either we are strong enough to live as a free people or we will become a police state. There is no such thing as being a bystander on these questions!

TMs AERP, FDRL

---

1. During his thirty-plus-year editorship, Norman Cousins (1915–1990) saw the *Saturday Review* (as it was later called) circulation increase from 20,000 to more than 600,000. Perhaps best known as a critic of nuclear proliferation, Cousins also used the weekly magazine to voice concerns about social issues such as violence, pollution, and support for the United Nations and a global government. Cousins's opposition to nuclear weapons remained so strong that he helped arrange medical treatment in the United States for Hiroshima residents scarred by the atomic bomb (whom the press quickly dubbed the "Hiroshima Maidens"). The article to which ER refers appeared in the August 2, 1947, issue of the *Saturday Review of Literature* (Eric Pace, "Norman Cousins, 75, Dies; Edited the Saturday Review," *NYT*, 1 December 1990, 31; Norman Cousins, "Bystanders Are Not Innocent," *Saturday Review of Literature*, vol. 30, 2 August 1947, 7–9).

2. Adolph J. Sabath (1866–1952), a Czechoslovakian immigrant, practiced law in Chicago where he held numerous public positions, including serving as Chicago's representative to the US House of Representatives for more than twenty-three sessions (http://bioguide.congress.gov, accessed 1 March 2006).

The article to which Sabath referred is I. F. (Isidor Feinstein) Stone's "New Weapon for Witch Hunters," *The Nation*, vol. 165 (July 12, 1947), 33–35. In its obituary, the *New York Times* described journalist and pamphleteer Stone (1907–1989), as a "short, owlish maverick with dimpled cheeks and major handicaps in hearing and in vision, [who] was a tough-minded but pacifist gadfly, a tireless miner of public records, a persistent attacker of Government distortions and evasions and a pugnacious advocate of civil liberties, peace and truth" (Peter B. Flint, "I.F. Stone, Iconoclast of Journalism, Is Dead at 81," *NYT*, 19 June 1989, D13).

3. On January 17, 1947, Attorney General Tom Clark indicted Carl A. Marzani (1912?–1994) under the "fraud statute" (U.S. Code, Title 18, Section 80), charging eleven counts of false statements made to the US government in order to obtain a position in the State Department. On May 22, 1947, the federal district court found Marzani guilty on all eleven charges. The appeals court, however, only upheld two of the eleven counts in February of 1948. The Supreme Court reviewed the case in June 1948 ruling that Marzani's civil rights had not been violated and upholding the original decision. Surprisingly, the Court agreed to a second review, but in December of 1948 again affirmed the decision. For his failure to disclose Communist Party membership in his original federal loyalty test, the federal district sentenced Marzani to serve a prison sentence of one to three years. He served more than two years. Throughout all of the trials, Marzani maintained his innocence. Upon his death, however, Marzani's son confirmed that his father had been a member of the Communist Party for two years and had resigned in 1941 ("Carl Marzani, 82, 'Loyalty Case' Defendant, Dies," *NYT*, 14 December 1994, B8; "Marzani Guilty of Hiding Red Link; Ex-Government Man Faces Prison," *NYT*, 23 May 1947, 1; "Marzani's Term Upheld," *NYT*, 3 February 1948, 16; "Marzani Wins a Review," *NYT*, 22 June 1948, 12; "Marzani's Conviction Affirmed By Court," *NYT*, 20 December 1948, 20; "Review Is Granted in Marzani's Case," *NYT*, 8 February 1949, 5; "Marzini Conviction Upheld Second Time," *NYT*, 8 March 1949, 22).

ON FEDERAL AID TO PAROCHIAL SCHOOLS

On February 10, 1947, the Supreme Court upheld a lower court ruling in favor of the defendant in *Everson v. Board of Education of Ewing TP*, a case involving the use of public funds for the transportation of schoolchildren attending parochial schools. The majority opinion, written by Justice Hugo Black, equated the busing program in Ewing Township, New Jersey, with "general government services," therefore preventing the school board from singling out anyone "because of their faith, or lack of it, from receiving the benefits of public welfare legislation."[1]

Several groups, particularly Protestant associations, spoke out against the court ruling. ER expressed her concerns about the Court's decision in her My Day column of July 25:

> ... I do not advocate a change in our old-time theory of division between church and state. We have a right to send our children to private schools or to religious schools of any denomination. But such schools should be on an entirely different basis from the public schools, which are free to all children.[2]

Mrs. Philip McMahon of St. Bernard, Ohio, wrote to ER on August 14, 1947, to express her disagreement with ER's criticism of the decision:

> As for the allowance of bus transportation, how can that be interpreted as an aid to religious schools; that means treating the religious school child as any other child, precaution against accident on the public highways, looking after the child's health; isn't it the duty of the government to take care of its citizens, these children are our future citizens, or are they?[3]

ER responded with the following letter, which she instructed McMahon not to make public.

248

Eleanor Roosevelt to Mrs. Philip McMahon
18 August 1947 [Hyde Park]

Personal—not for publication.

My dear Mrs. McMahon:

My great concern is that there shall not arise in this country a deep seated prejudice against any religion and I find a growing fear in many places which comes largely because of economic conditions, against the Roman Catholic Church.[4] Historically, of course, the Catholic Church has done the same kind of thing in other countries. They acquire land and temporal power and pay no taxes. Many communities are beginning to feel that strictly speaking, only the ground occupied by churches or cemeteries should be free of taxes and that only children attending public schools should receive transportation. Naturally public schools would be free of taxation.

If we wish to send our children to private schools, we are of course, entitled to do so but then we do it at our own expense.

In many places now the Roman Catholic Church has acquired a great deal of land on which various types of institutions are built. Other churches to a lesser degree, have done the same thing and as a result I think there is a growing friction which does not differentiate between the right of people to worship as they choose and the right of a church organization to build up temporal power through the acquisition of land. My feeling is that it will create bad feeling and lessen our freedom of religion. That is why I am opposed to public transportation for children attending anything but the public schools. It is really in the interest of preserving a good feeling that I feel this is important at the present time.

Very sincerely yours,

TLc AERP, FDRL

———————————

1. *Everson v. Board of Education of Ewing TP.*, 330 US 1, 16–18 (1947).

2. *MD*, 25 July 1947.

3. Mrs. Philip McMahon to ER, 14 August 1947, AERP.

4. McMahon's August 14 letter did not mention Catholicism or any other denomination. The July 25 My Day column did not single out any denomination either, though ER's editorial centered around her disagreement with "an article answering the criticism which was made by the Northern Baptist Convention" regarding the *Ewing* case. As ER did not retain a copy of the article in her files, the editors could not identify the article in question. However, in March 1947, ER received a copy of a *New Christian Century* editorial that interpreted the *Ewing* decision as a "strategy of the Roman Catholic Church in its determination to secure a privileged position in the common life of this country." The Catholic Church, the editorial stated, "wants the state to provide for the complete support of its parochial schools with money derived from taxes levied on all citizens. Its ultimate purpose is to shift to the public treasury the entire burden of financing its parochial schools, while the church retains control of the educational process in them."

The article was sent to ER by her friend Dr. Charl Ormond Williams (1885–1969), president of the National Education Association. Dr. Williams also sent ER a packet of other editorial excerpts compiled by the Baptist Joint Conference Committee on Public Relations, and commented in her cover letter to ER, "the whole situation has created a storm of protest and it will very probably awaken the nation to the aims and purposes of the Roman Catholic Church" (*MD*, 25 July 1947; Charl Ormond Williams to ER, 28 March 1947, AERP; "Now Will Protestants Awake?," *New Christian Century*, 26 February 1947; "Dr. Charl Williams, Education Crusader," *WP*, 15 January 1969, 47).

LOBBYING FOR THE *EXODUS*

On August 18, Helen Waren, a Broadway actress who had toured western Europe with the USO at the end of the war, sent ER a telegram detailing the situation of 4,500 Jewish refugees who had attempted to immigrate to Palestine on board the *Exodus*. The ship, known as *Exodus 1947*, made an attempt, over British objections, in mid-July 1947 to bring the displaced persons and Holocaust survivors to Palestine. British warships followed the boat and rammed it on July 18 as it neared Palestine. Three passengers were killed and many more injured in the struggle that ensued when British troops attempted to board the ship. The British eventually succeeded in bringing the passengers into the port of Haifa, where they immediately transferred most of the passengers to three prison ships, which headed back to France. The ships containing the displaced passengers now lay off Port de Bouc on the southern coast. The French government offered refuge to the *Exodus* group, but most of the passengers refused to disembark.[1] Waren described conditions on board the ships in her telegram:

> FOR WEEKS NOW THEY HAVE BEEN CRAMPED MEN WOMEN AND CHILDREN IN THE HOLDS OF THESE VESSELS SLEEPING ON BARE BOARDS EXPOSED TO THE HEAT OF THE MEDITERRANEAN SUN IN INTOLERABLE SANITARY CONDITIONS. MY BROTHER, VACATIONING IN FRANCE, WRITES ME FROM PORT DE BOUC WHERE HE MET AN AMERICAN CREW MEMBER OF THE EXODUS WHO DISEMBARKED WITH 35 SERIOUSLY ILL REFUGEES AND MANAGED TO SLIP AWAY FROM THE POLICE, THAT THE BRITISH HAVE BEEN FEEDING THEM A STARVATION DIET OF TEA AND HARD BISCUITS IN THE MORNING, RICE WITH POWDERED MILK IN THE AFTERNOON AND SOUP AT NIGHT. THE SURPLUS BRITISH RATION FOR NURSING MOTHERS HAS BEEN TWO TEASPOONSFUL OF TINNED MILK IN COLD UNBOILED WATER. THIRTY-FIVE BABIES HAVE BEEN BORN ABOARD, MANY PREMATURELY. ONE CHILD OF SEVEN DAYS IN ONE OF THE HOLDS HAS NEVER SEEN THE LIGHT. THE REFUGEES ARE DETERMINED TO CARRY ON THEIR STRUGGLE UNTIL THEIR RIGHTS AS HUMAN BEINGS TO LIFE IN A LAND OF THEIR OWN IS RECOGNIZED AND THEY LOOK TO CIVILIZED HUMANITY TO COME TO THEIR RESCUE.

She urged ER to "raise your courageous voice in their behalf." In reply, ER jotted at the bottom of Waren's telegram: "I think they should stay in France & wld do better to land. Advise."[2] Nevertheless, on August 21, as the deadline neared and the passengers faced the possibility of returning to displaced persons camps, ER sent the following telegram to Truman.

249

Eleanor Roosevelt to Harry Truman
21 August 1947 [New York City]

THE PRESIDENT
THE WHITE HOUSE

I UNDERSTAND THAT THE JEWS ON THE SHIP OF A FRENCH HARBOR HAVE UNTIL SIX OCLOCK TOMOR-ROW AFTERNOON TO LAND IN FRANCE OR BE RETURNED TO CONCENTRATION CAMPS IN GERMANY. IT SEEMS TO ME SINCE THEY WANT TO GO TO CYPRUS SOME PRESSURE MIGHT BE BROUGHT TO BEAR

ON GREAT BRITAIN TO ALLOW THEM TO DO SO. THEIR PLIGHT IS PITIFUL AND I HOPE YOU MAY FEEL THAT YOU CAN EXERT SOME INFLUENCE ON GREAT BRITAIN[3]

ELEANOR ROOSEVELT.

Tel HSTSF, HSTL

250

Harry Truman to Eleanor Roosevelt
23 August 1947 [The White House]

My dear Mrs. Roosevelt:

I read your telegram with regard to the Jews with a lot of interest. This situation is a most embarrassing one all the way around and has been most difficult to approach. I hope it will work out.

I understand that these ships were loaded and started to Palestine with American funds and American backing—they were loaded knowing that they were trying to do an illegal act.

The action of some of our United States Zionists will eventually prejudice everyone against what they are trying to get done. I fear very much that the Jews are like all under dogs—when they get on top they are just as intolerant and as cruel as the people were to them when they were underneath.[4] I regret this situation very much because my sympathy has always been on their side.[5]

Sincerely yours,
Harry S. Truman

TLS AERP, FDRL

Soon after sending her telegram to President Truman about the *Exodus* affair, ER received a letter from Eva Warburg Unger, a German-Jewish refugee then living in the Givat Brenner kibbutz near Rechowot, Palestine.[6] Warburg Unger described the living conditions the Jewish orphans confronted in the Cyprus displacement camps. The children "live on a very little ground with several barbed wires around them, with patrolling soldiers outside, with big flashlights and machine-guns at all corners of the camp. They live in bad barracks and tents with very little water and bad food." Noting that "they are, all of them, survivors from deathcamps or children who were hidden somewhere five long years," Warburg Unger worried that "every day that they stay on Cyprus" would "make it more doubtful" that "we will succeed to reeducate them to 'normal' and happy boys and girls." She then asked ER to intercede on their behalf.

ER responded: "I have your letter of August 17th, and I will try to do what I can. However, I do not know how successful I will be."[7] She then sent a copy of Warburg Unger's letter to Truman with the following note.

251

Eleanor Roosevelt to Harry Truman
30 August 1947 [Hyde Park]

Dear Mr. President:

Many thanks for your reply to my wire.

I have just received the enclosed letter of which I am sending you a copy. The British still seem to be on top and cruelty would seem to be on their side and not on the side of the Jews.[8]

Very sincerely yours,
Eleanor Roosevelt

TLS HSTOF, HSTL

---

1. The British attempted to discourage further illegal immigration to Palestine through a new policy of sending intercepted ships back to their port of embarkation rather than interning their passengers on Cyprus. The British had already forced thousands of people attempting to land in Palestine without valid entry papers into increasingly overcrowded displaced persons camps on that island. The new policy sought to make the *Exodus* into an example. After a long stalemate in which the ships lay anchored off the French coast, in early September British authorities took the group to the British occupation zone of Germany and forcibly moved them into displaced persons camps. Although ER criticized conditions in the British detention camps on Cyprus, she suggested that sending the passengers back to Germany was far worse than sending them to Cyprus (Cohen, *Palestine*, 243–56; Gene Currivan, "Jews Shipped Back to Port in France, Palestine Reports," *NYT*, 21 July 1947, 1; "4,500 Jews Refuse to Land in France," *NYT*, 30 July 1947, 1; "3 Slain on Zionist Vessel as Refugees Fight British," *NYT*, 19 July 1947, 1; Edward A. Morrow, "Jews' Ships Reach Germany; Leaders Reported Isolated," *NYT*, 7 September 1947, 1; "Token Fight Waged as Jews of Exodus Begin Debarkation," *NYT*, 9 September 1947, 1; *MD*, 19 August 1946, 12 September 1947, and 27 March 1948).

2. Helen Waren to ER, 18 August 1947, AERP. As no printed record of Waren's reply could be located, either Waren and ER spoke over the telephone or ER did not preserve Waren's response.

3. Henry Morgenthau, Jr., also lobbied Truman, who recorded in his diary that he would speak with Marshall about it. (See *n*4 below.) When the ships carrying the displaced refugees reached Germany, Secretary of State Marshall announced that the United States had in vain tried to discourage the British government from sending the group to Germany.

ER continued to publicize the plight of the those who had been on the *Exodus* in My Day, writing September 12 that the refugees "have gone through so much hardship and had thought themselves free forever from Germany, the country they associate with concentration camps and crematories. Now they are back there again. Somehow it is too horrible for any of us in this country even to understand" (Bertram D. Hulen, "Futile U.S. Appeal on Exodus Bared," *NYT*, 11 September 1947, 1; *MD*, 12 September 1947).

4. A month earlier, on July 21, 1947, Truman noted in his diary:

> Had ten minutes conversation with Henry Morgenthau about Jewish ship in Palistine [sic]. Told him I would talk to Gen[eral] Marshall about it.

> He'd no business, whatever to call me. The Jews have no sense of proportion nor do they have any judgement on world affairs.

> Henry brought a thousand Jews to New York on a supposedly temporary basis and they stayed. When the country went backward—and Republican in the election of 1946, this incident loomed large on the D[isplaced] P[ersons] program.

> The Jews, I find are very, very selfish. They care not how many Estonians, Latvians, Finns, Poles, Yugoslavs or Greeks get murdered or mistreated as D[isplaced] P[ersons] as long as the Jews get special treatment. Yet when they have power, physical, financial or political neither Hitler nor Stalin has any thing on them for cruelty or mistreatment to

the under dog. Put an underdog on top and it makes no difference whether his name is Russian, Jewish, Negro, Management, Labor, Mormon, Baptist he goes haywire. I've found very, very few who remember their past condition when prosperity comes.

Look at the Congress[ional] attitude on D[isplaced] P[ersons]—and they all come from D[isplaced] P[erson]s.

Henry Morgenthau, Jr., secretary of treasury under FDR, had become chairman of the United Jewish Appeal in early 1947 (Harry S. Truman [July 21] 1947 diary, transcript, HSTL, www.trumanlibrary.org, accessed 1 March 2006; "Morgenthau Gets Jewish Fund Post," *NYT*, 3 January 1947, 44).

5. For Truman's position regarding the immigration of Jewish refugees to Palestine, see *n*2 Document 123 and *n*5 Document 124.

6. Eva Warburg Unger (1912-?) was the daughter of Dr. Fritz Warburg of the banking house M.M. Warburg and Anna Warburg, an educational reformer. Before her emigration to Palestine, Warburg Unger worked in kindergarten education in Hamburg, heading a crèche for Jewish children (Chernow, 425, 607; Warburg-Spinelli, 448).

7. Eva Warburg Unger to ER, 17 August 1947, HSTP; ER to Unger, 30 August 1947, AERP.

8. The editors found no evidence that HST replied to this second note from ER.

MOBILIZING TO SUPPORT THE STRATTON BILL

ER continued to press Congress to pass the Stratton bill. Here she asks her friend, National Association of Education president Charl Williams, to mobilize on its behalf.

252

Eleanor Roosevelt to Charl Williams
24 August 1947 [Hyde Park]

Dear Charl Williams:

A friend of mine is working with the Citizens Committee on Displaced Persons and learned on a recent trip that the Parent-Teachers groups in the various states have done very little to support the legislation which we all want for these Displaced Persons.[1]

The National Executive Committee of the PTA approved it by a resolution passed on June 5th.

I understand there must be ratification by thirty states, and to date Nebraska is the only state to ratify.[2]

Could you urge Mrs. Hughes to exert her influence on the state committees?[3]

Affectionately,

TLc AERP, FDRL

———————

1. Dr. Charl Ormond Williams (1885–1969), a lifelong education lobbyist in Washington, held top positions in the National Education Association (NEA). An active Democrat, Williams worked closely with ER on party and policy issues, twice chairing White House conferences. Founded in December 1946, the Citizens Committee on Displaced Persons (CCDP) lobbied Congress and the public on behalf of legislation allowing European refugees to come to the United States. ER was one of the group's vice-chairs. For more on the CCDP and its efforts to pass the Stratton bill, see *n*2 Document 244. For more on the status of the Stratton bill, see *n*3 Document 244 ("Dr. Charl Williams, Education Crusader," *WP*, 15 January 1969, 47).

2. ER's information on both the national executive committee and the ratification process came from a handwritten note at the bottom of Anna H. Clark's August 18, 1947, letter (written on CCDP letterhead) to Elizabeth Gardiner (CCDP folder, AERP).

3. Mrs. L. S. Hughes was president of the National Congress of Parents and Teachers (NCPT). In a letter dated August 27, 1947, Williams told ER that she had written letters to Hughes and Mrs. Stanley G. Cook, NCPT chairman of legislation. On the same date Williams also wrote a group letter to NCPT staff members Ruth Bottomly, Eva Grant, and Mary Ferre, enclosing ER's letter and asking them to "write me if you think anything can be done to help Mrs. Roosevelt in her desires to help these unfortunate people." She then sent a similar appeal to Elinor Pillsbury, a reporter at the *Oregon Journal* in Portland, Oregon, saying "I do not know whether or not there is anything you can do as a newspaper woman. You might perhaps get in touch with the state president of the Oregon Congress of Parents and Teachers as well as with Mrs. Kletzer [a former NCPT national president] … Anything you can do in any avenue I shall deeply appreciate" (Charl Williams to ER, 27 August 1947; Charl Williams to Ruth Bottomly, Eva Grant, and Mary Ferre, 27 August 1947; Charl Williams to Elinor Pillsbury, 27 August 1947, AERP).

ON TAFT-HARTLEY

Three days after the Taft-Hartley Act went into effect, ER again turned to My Day to voice her opposition to its basic premise.

253

My Day
25 August 1947

HYDE PARK, Sunday—Sometimes it is funny to see how differently people look at the same thing. The Taft-Hartley Act has now come into effect.[1] From now on certain things must be done to comply with that act. One paper headlines an article: "Taft-Hartley Act Reaffirms Employees' Rights."[2] But if you looked at it from the other point of view, you might easily say: "Taft-Hartley Act Begins to Undermine the Rights of Employees." The fact is that, for the first time, we have set apart a group of people in our country—the labor union people.

I think there is no question but what union labor has neglected to assume certain responsibilities which came to it with growing strength, but there are certain things in this act which, as an American citizen, I resent. Why should the head of a union be asked to declare that he is not a Communist? It will shortly become necessary, before we start out to earn a living, to declare all sorts of things about ourselves which we considered nobody's business in the past. If we are going to make labor union leaders register as non-Communists, we had better do the same for the heads of business.

Incidentally, why not have them at the same time assert that they are not Fascists? One is as dangerous as the other, since what we are trying to do is to make sure that, in this country of ours, all people are Americans.

This particular provision in this act of Congress does not seem to me to achieve the desired ends, and I think we the people should look at it with a coldly critical eye.

There was a time when a man was innocent until he was proved guilty, but ten men have recently been dismissed from government service without even being told, I understand, what the charges against them are. It is not going to be easy for these men to get other jobs, and yet they weren't proved guilty.[3] Some of my friends tell me that the average employee of the Government, particularly if he has a wife and child to support, expresses no opinion today on any subject. Is that the way we make good American citizens?

It also seems a bit high-handed to tell unions that members can be expelled only for non-payment of dues. I am sure there have been some abuses in the expelling of members but, on the other hand, there have been some abuses on the part of management in the dismissal of employees because of union membership.[4]

It seems to me that it is an infringement on our liberties to set up for a union, in the matter of health and welfare funds, restrictions for the administration of these funds. Of course, the employer does contribute toward them, but he contributes in order that his employees may be able to accomplish through their organization the things that they desire. The employer is not apt to see things in the same light as the employee. The limitation of the purposes of such funds to medical care, retirement or death benefits, insurance, and compensation for injury or illness resulting from work, might not always meet the ideas of the employees.[5]

Such is the act, however, and we are assured that it is open to amendment. I hope we will watch with interest how it is amended.[6]

TMs AERP, FDRL

ER's opposition to the Taft-Hartley Act caused consternation among her readers, several of whom wrote voicing their criticism. One, Carl Bradt, who met ER during World War II when he worked with the Federal Housing Authority, asked "Who set labor apart—does memory fail you? It was Mr. Roosevelt and his small group. Not until we had the new deal program did we have a class consciousness. Management was pitted against labor on a deliberate program."

After blaming labor leader John L. Lewis for the postwar labor unrest that contributed to the passage of Taft-Hartley, he wrote, "The rank and file of Labor feel that now the individual may get a break and not have it all one-sided—what the Labor Boss wanted."[7]

New York City lawyer Albert Harris also wrote to criticize ER for her lack of sympathy for management.

254

Albert Harris to Eleanor Roosevelt

28 August 1947 [New York City]

Dear Mrs. Roosevelt:

I wish to take issue with you as to some of the statements in your column "Nobody's Business" as reported in the New York World Telegram on August 25, 1947.[8]

You object to labor leaders being compelled to declare themselves communists and state "we had better do the same for the heads of business". Since communists are certainly the enemies of democracy, we certainly ought to list those enemies where those communists are labor union leaders or business leaders. If there were any danger at the present time or if there is any such danger that business leaders are dangerous to democracy either as communists or fascists, they should certainly be listed.[9]

You also object to the Taft-Hartley Act limiting the union's right to expel members to the ground of non-payment of dues and claim that management has dismissed employees because of union membership. Certainly under the Wagner Act and the other government regulations, management has been prevented or punished for dismissing "employees because of union membership". This limitation on management's powers was quite proper because of the abuse of management of its powers. Your illustration is obviously not in point because management does not have the power you claim. You claim in effect that because y wrong is allowed, therefore, x wrong should be allowed, but y wrong is punished. To continue your analogy, x wrong (abuse by unions) should be punished. In addition one would expect you to take the position that all wrong should be punished wherever found and if certain wrongs are not punished, that should be no reason for permitting other wrongs to the unpunished.[10]

You claim that it is an "infringement of our liberties, to set up for a union, in the matter of health and welfare funds, restrictions for the administration of these funds". Then you state "the employer contributes toward them, but he contributes in order that his employees may be able to accomplish through their organization the things that they desire". Your statement just is not so. The contributions made by the employer are made under agreements which provide that the money is to be used for certain specific purposes and the union has agreed to apply the funds for the specific purposes. Employers have always objected being blackjacked into paying funds into union treasuries which may be used for any purpose whatsoever determined by the union membership or by the union officials who have achieved control of union treasuries. The only "infringement of our liberties" is the infringement of violation of contract. If the union membership should contribute its own funds to a union fund and give the union officials complete liberty of disposal of the funds, then the employers and even the union membership might not be privileged to object, but when employers contribute funds for specific purposes, it is certainly an infringement upon the liberties of the employers to be deprived of the right of compelling the unions to abide by their express agreements.[11]

Very truly yours,
Albert Harris

TLS AERP, FDRL

255

Eleanor Roosevelt to Albert Harris

8 September 1947 [Hyde Park]

My dear Mr. Harris:

I think I must have been a little careless or perhaps I took it too much for granted that anyone reading my recent column on the Taft-Hartley Bill would have read my previous columns on this subject. In those I made my position very clear as to the need for labor to clean house—the AFofL to get rid of its racketeers, the CIO to get rid of its communist leaders.[12]

I do not want communists leading our labor unions and the majority of the labor people do not want them either, but that to my mind does not justify setting labor apart as a group that must give certain assurances. From my point of view that is not the American way of doing things. We should all have to do it, or we should not expect any particular group to do it.

I know quite well that it was against the law to dismiss employees for union membership but there were many ways which were used to dismiss people and though that was not the reason given, it was the real reason and you know this as well as I do.[13]

I do not think that two wrongs make a right and I think abuses on the part of unions and on the part of management should both be condemned.

Labor is partly responsible for the passage of the Taft-Hartley Bill because of its failure to clean house, but that does not make the Taft-Hartley Bill perfect nor does it absolve us from stating why we think it is wrong.

I know that contributions made by the employer are made under agreements and I think those agreements should be lived up to and they have been in the past. If agreements are made whereby money will go into certain things, there is no more reason why the trade unions' books should be open for examination than why management's books should not be open to the trade unions for examination. It should be turn and turn about and equal handed justice for all.

Very sincerely yours,

TLc AERP, FDRL

---

1. The Taft-Hartley Act took effect on August 22, sixty days after it was enacted over Truman's veto. For more on the Taft-Hartley Act, see Document 234 (*HSTE*).

2. "Taft-Hartley Act Reaffirms Employees' Rights," *NYWT*, 22 August 1947, 15.

3. Ten State Department employees lost their jobs in August 1947. Two were removed outright; the other eight left before their loyalty investigations ended. State Department officials and the Civil Service Commission gave different reasons for the firings. The State Department said the individuals were fired for security reasons while the Civil Service Commission linked the dismissals to Communism. The firings were the second such incident at the State Department. Two months earlier the department dismissed ten other individuals because "derogatory information" on them "had been developed." Both of these instances were part of the federal government's loyalty program instituted in March 1947 after Congress pressured the Truman administration to increase security and loyalty procedures within the federal government to counter a perceived Communist threat. For more on the federal loyalty program, see *n*6 Document 271 ("U.S. Ousts 10 More in Loyalty Inquiry," *NYT*, 15 August 1947, 8; *HSTE*).

4. For example, in 1941, the Ford Motor Company decided to fire eleven employees who attempted to organize a union at the automaker's largest plant, River Rouge in Dearborn, Michigan. This touched off a major strike that culminated in a union for all Ford workers, higher wages, the abolition of management's spy system, and the reinstatement of all employees dismissed for union activities (Goodwin, 226–30; Lichtenstein, 178–79).

5. Besides these limitations, the Taft-Hartley Act also required that employees and employers be equally represented in the administration of such funds along with neutral people who had the approval of both groups (Hartley, Jr., 227–28).

6. In 1951, Congress amended the Taft-Hartley Act to remove restrictions on the union shop (*HSTE*).

7. "All that was done [during the New Deal] was to equalize the balance which always had been weighted on the side of management," ER replied. "I hope you are right … that the bulk of labor now thinks that under the Taft-Hartley bill they will have a better chance but I feel it will not work that way" (Carl Bradt to ER, [August ?] 1947; ER to Carl Bradt, [August ?] 1947, AERP).

8. "Nobody's Business," *NYWT*, 25 August 1947, 15. For the full text of this My Day column, see Document 253.

9. Another of ER's correspondents, Nard Jones, took her to task on this same point in a letter dated August 27, 1947:

> You say that as a citizen you resent certain things in the Act. Permit me to say that as a citizen I resent your using your considerable influence against the Act now that it has become a law, and particularly with reference to the Communist phase. Should we be so unfortunate as to engage in a war with Russia I will have a boy in the Army. I should like to think of the full weight of the labor unions behind him … You are realistic enough to know that this could not happen in any union that is Communist dominated …"

ER replied:

> I doubt whether it [her influence] will counteract even one of the people like Fulton Lewis or Mr. Pegler, so I do not think you need be concerned. You have one boy … if we have to fight Russia, I would probably have four again, or at least three and probably grandsons, but it is not the individuals that worry me. If we have another war we have begun the annihilation of the whole human race (Nard Jones to ER, 27 August 1947; ER to Nard Jones, 8 September 1947, AERP).

10. For more on management's dismissal of union members, see *n*4 above.

11. For more on the Taft-Hartley Act's regulations regarding union health and welfare funds, see *n*5 above.

12. For example, in a column dated June 10, 1947, ER wrote:

The Congress of Industrial Organizations should have got rid of Communist leaders wherever they existed ... If the Russian government still hopes for world revolution brought about by representatives in other countries guided from Russia, it cannot be honest in trying to work cooperatively with other governments as they now exist. I am more than willing to believe that circumstances may modify the way of life and the forms of existing governments in many countries in the years to come, but the changes must come from the free will of the people, not from infiltration of ideas through the influence of outside governments. That is why union leaders known to be Communists should not have been allowed in our labor movement.

She continued this theme in a September 6 My Day:

I do not believe that unions should be headed by Communists. And I have long stated that the AFL should clean house and remove any racketeers it may have in positions of influence, and the CIO should remove any Communist labor leaders from power. But that is quite a different thing from asking every man who heads a union, and the head officials of these great labor organizations, to sign a declaration that they are not Communists.

That, to me, is taking one group in this country and offering them a kind of treatment which is insulting (*MD*, 10 June 1947; *MD*, 6 September 1947).

13. For more on management's dismissal of labor union members, see *n*4 above.

256

If You Ask Me [excerpt]

Ladies' Home Journal September 1947

My daughter is a student in one of the local high schools. Before the Junior Prom this year a Negro student asked if she expected to attend. When she said "No," he told her he would like to take her if she would go with him. She thanked him, but told him she had made other plans for the evening. What would be your reaction to such a situation? Would you permit your daughter to attend a prom with a colored boy, or would you have felt, as I did, a little bit disconcerted at the idea of his even suggesting such a thing?

Your question is a difficult one to answer because there must be a background to it. If your daughter had known this young boy well, I do not think that it was in any way astonishing that he should ask her to go with him, because if they had been on a purely friendly acquaintanceship basis, there was no more reason why she should not go with him than with any one of the other boys whom she knew equally well.

What lies back of your feeling, of course, is the old fear of intermarriage between races. That is something I feel we have to deal with on an entirely different basis from mere friendly association. There may come a time when it will seem as natural to marry a man from any race, or any part of the world, as it will to marry your next-door neighbor. We haven't reached that time as yet, and there is still considerable feeling when people marry who have different religious backgrounds, and there is, of course, more feeling still about intermarriage between different races. So it seems to me that that question has to be dealt with individually, by families, by individuals and by society. At present intermarriage between races, and even between people of different religions, often brings reprisals from society and from families, which make for great unhappiness. Anyone undertaking such a marriage must have a full realization of what she is actually facing.

However, going to a prom is like any other casual thing which you do; and if we are not going to be able to have ordinary contacts with people who are citizens of our own country, how on earth can we expect that we will be able to have the same kind of contact with people who live in different parts of the world? I think we can have peace in our hearts and real friendship for people even though there may still be some fundamental reason why we would not marry. Therefore, if I were you I would not worry too much about the people with whom your daughter dances. I should hope that she could be unconsciously friendly with all her associates in school, and I would be rather proud that a boy of another race felt that he could ask your daughter to go to a prom—which shows, I think, that her attitude has been kind and mature.[1]

TMsex DLC

---

1. ER's answer provoked intense responses, highlighting both tense race relations as well as the inclination to associate racial equality with Communism. For example, Representative John Rankin (D-MS) labeled ER's column "the most insulting Communist propaganda ever thrown in the face of the white women of America" ("Mrs. FDR Irks Rankin," *PM*, 26 September 1947, AERP).

SELECTING THE PARTY'S CHAIRMAN

When ER learned from Ed Flynn that Truman wanted to replace the ailing Robert Hannegan with Clinton Anderson as chair of the Democratic National Committee, she wrote the president to protest his decision.

257

Eleanor Roosevelt to Harry Truman
3 September 1947 [Hyde Park]

Dear Mr. President:

I have just heard from our National Committeeman, Mr. Flynn, that the probability is, since Mr. Hannegan is going to resign,[1] that Mr. Anderson may be made National Chairman and that his position is going to be opposed to Mr. Anderson.[2]

I thought it only fair that I should tell you that I could never support Mr. Anderson. I consider him a conservative and I consider that the only chance the Democratic Party has for election in 1948, is to be the liberal party. We can not be more conservative than the Republicans so we can not succeed as conservatives. If the country is going conservative, it is not going to vote for any Democratic candidate.

It is very important to the world as well as to the United States that the Democratic Party wins in 1948, but I would feel that the kind of party which was built up and guided by Mr. Anderson would be a conservative party and I would withdraw completely from any activity in connection with it.

Very sincerely yours,
Eleanor Roosevelt

TLS HSTWHCF, HSTL

By the time Truman responded, Anderson was no longer under consideration.

258

Harry Truman to Eleanor Roosevelt
29 September 1947 [The White House]

My dear Mrs. Roosevelt:

Your letter of September third was waiting for me when I returned from Rio de Janeiro.[3] I am glad that you gave me the benefit of your frank opinion about the national chairmanship, even though Mr. Flynn gave you erroneous information.

I sincerely hope that the selection of Senator McGrath, now in process of confirmation, will meet with your approval.[4] Let me assure you once more—if such assurance is necessary—that I shall always welcome an expression of your views on every aspect of party policy. I set a high value on your judgement.

When I see you, if you are interested, I can tell you the reason for Mr. Flynn's pique. He made a recommendation for a judicial appointment which, in all conscience, I could not accept.

With every good wish,

Always sincerely,
Harry S. Truman

TLS AERP, FDRL

---

1. Robert Hannegan, who suffered from advanced cardiovascular disease, resigned when his declining health forced his deputy, DNC vice-chair Oscar Ewing, to assume many of his responsibilities (*ANB*; Hamby, *Beyond*, 295).

2. After serving in the House of Representatives from New Mexico, Clinton P. Anderson (1895–1975) held the position of secretary of agriculture from 1945 until 1948, when he resigned to run for the US Senate. Noted within the administration for his coolness to the Office of Price Supports, Anderson angered many farmers and liberals when he moved away from price controls and toward a lower government parity rate for farm products. Others criticized him for not taking a leading role in the program to combat hunger in postwar Europe. ER thought him much too conservative, pointing to his opposition to full employment and price control policies and his reticence regarding foreign aid (A. Black, *Casting*, 79; Lash, *Years*, 141–42; *HSTE*).

3. Truman had just returned from an inter-American conference on military reorganization in Rio de Janeiro where he delivered the closing address and signed the Inter-American Treaty of Reciprocal Assistance. The Rio Pact, as it soon became known, stipulated that the United States would control Latin American defense policy, help train Latin American military and police, and manage the shipment of arms and military equipment to the region (*HSTE*).

4. Truman nominated Sen. J. Howard McGrath (D-RI) (1903–1966) for national chairman on September 27 after Clinton Anderson, a Protestant, announced (after conversations with Pauley and Hannegan who argued that only an Irish Catholic could lead the party) he would not accept the position. On October 29, the DNC elected McGrath, a Catholic and a liberal Democrat with "a crusading spirit," chair, and thus, helped Truman Democrats increase their appeal to their Wallace-leaning counterparts (Savage, 54–62; Hamby, *Beyond*, 191).

On Humanitarian Aid for Germany

W. D. Kuenzli, minister of the Grove City and Galloway, Ohio, Presbyterian Church, wrote ER August 26, 1947, praising the "sanity, tolerance and understanding" expressed in My Day. He and his wife found fault only in one area: "your consistently vengeful and unforgiving bias against all Germans."[1] He enclosed a letter, which he said "describes the situation being suffered by multiplied millions—many of whom are entirely innocent of guilt for German war-crimes!" The letter, from Elsa von Heydebreck who was then living in the American sector of occupied Berlin, bemoaned the impoverished conditions of daily life, the displacement and expulsion of Germans from eastern Europe, and the difficulty of obtaining basic foodstuffs, fuel, clothing, and linens. Despite these hardships, she complained,"Mrs. Roosevelt thought the Germans still much too well dressed!"[2]

ER replied two weeks later.

_259_

Eleanor Roosevelt to W. D. Kuenzli
8 September 1947 [Hyde Park]

My dear Mr. Kuenzli:

I think you have misunderstood my attitude toward the German people. I have said that relief should come to them after relief[3] to our Allies.[4]

During the war years our Allies suffered more hardships and we have more to make up to the people whose countries were invaded.

Perhaps there are many Germans who were innocent of guilt in the German war crimes, but I can not believe there were many. Too many concentration camps scattered over Germany make one realize how largely the population as a whole have to accept responsibility for Hitler's actions.[5]

Very sincerely yours,

TLc AERP, FDRL

---

1. ER frequently discussed German guilt for the war in her My Day columns and correspondence and she argued for putting limits on the restoration of German industrial capacity so that Germany would not have the ability to wage war again. Her determination that German guilt not be forgotten emerged pointedly in her commentaries on Pastor Martin Niemöller. See Document 165 and Document 171.

2. Elsa von Heydebreck to Mrs. Karn, 30 July 1947, AERP. Both the original letter in German and the English translation cited here were forwarded to Kuenzli by Ilsa Albertz.

3. In the carbon copy of this letter in ER's files the words "after relief" are repeated.

4. For ER's attitude toward treatment of the German population after the war, see, for example, Document 66.

5. ER continued to voice her message about German responsibility after this exchange with Kuenzli and to express wariness about a reconstructed Germany's potential to wage war in the future. "I do not want the Germans to starve," she wrote in her My Day column of June 25, 1948, "but they

have started two wars and I do not want them to be set up again industrially so that they can start a third one." Describing her meeting with German women doctors in Stuttgart in late 1948, she wrote, "I had no intention of letting their coldness prevent me from saying certain things I had in my mind, so I began with a denunciation of the Nazi philosophy and actions. I made it as strong as I could and I expressed the opinion that the German people must bear their share of the blame. I had not expected my audience to be pleased by such remarks and they were not" (*MD*, 25 June 1948; ER, *Autobiography*, 321).

ASSESSING PROTESTANTISM, WALLACE, AND THE TRUMAN DOCTRINE

E. Ralph Wiborg, minister of the Hamden Plains Methodist Church in Hamden, Connecticut, wrote to ER September 11, 1947, to voice his concerns about the potential for another war. "It more and more seems to me," he began:

> that big business and big religion (Roman Catholicism) are about to join forces in a great crusade against Russia and Communism. You know as well as I do what this would mean in terms of death and destruction, probably causing our people more suffering by far than in the recent war. Many families in my parish lost dear ones in that war, and I don't want to have to go through another. But I also believe that in any such coming struggle liberal Protestantism with its emphasis on liberty, tolerance, justice, ethical religion, would find itself crushed between the two totalitarianisms, Russia or Communism and Roman Catholicism, and that would be tragic, even though Protestantism as both of us know has its shortcomings.

He then asked ER to evaluate the Truman Doctrine, the position of Protestantism in America, the legacy of FDR, and the leadership potential of Henry Wallace.[1] The following letter is ER's response to Wiborg's inquiry.

260

Eleanor Roosevelt to E. Ralph Wiborg
21 September 1947 [Hyde Park]

My dear Mr. Wiborg:

I do not think the Truman doctrine is leading us down the path to war. I do not think it was a wise way to do something which obviously had to be done, but that is not going to lead us to war. I think we will get back on the right track very quickly.[2]

No, I do not think there is any danger of democracy and liberal Protestantism being crushed between two totalitarianisms, but I do think that both democracy and liberal Protestantism have got to show good cause as to why they should not be crushed and the way to do it is to really live the Christian doctrine instead of giving lip service, and to really accept the responsibilities as citizens, that democracy to be successful, entails.[3]

I think perhaps that what you forget is that in a democracy the leadership for the most part, comes from the people. Occasionally individuals rise to heights and they point the way, but day by day and year by year, it is the people who have to guide democracy.

I think Mr. Henry Wallace is a fine person but I do not think he is very wise as a politician. He has succeeded in misleading the Russians into believing that the majority of the people of the United States agree with them and that of course, leads them to do things which they would never otherwise do. I think the present times require great patience, great courage and firmness and on the part of each one of us a willingness to work for the things we believe in, day in and day out, and not to be afraid to set our minds so that we keep our country in the right track, and in so doing, keep it an influence for good in the world.

Very sincerely yours,

TLc AERP, FDRL

1. E. Ralph Wiborg to ER, 11 September 1947, AERP.

2. On the Truman Doctrine, see header Document 210.

3. ER did not directly address Wiborg's assertion that Roman Catholicism represented one of the "totalitarianisms." For ER's views of Catholicism as a political power, see *n*3 Document 26, *n*5 Document 151, Document 248, Document 282, and header Document 393.

HUAC AND THE HANNS EISLER CASE

In September 1947, the House Un-American Activities Committee (HUAC) subpoenaed the composer Hanns Eisler (1898–1962), a German Jew who collaborated with Berthold Brecht and whose brother Gerhart was a confessed Communist, to appear before the committee. He and his wife Louise fled from Germany to Cuba in 1933, where they applied for a permanent visa to the United States. In 1939, ER, who had known the Eislers through mutual acquaintances in New York, Donald Stephens of the National Arts Club and Alvin Johnson of the New School of Social Research, interceded on their behalf with two letters to Sumner Welles, who was then the undersecretary of state, expressing her certainty that "the Eislers are not Communists and have no political affiliations of any kind." Though the Eislers' visa application was denied in Cuba, they succeeded a year later, without ER's help, in gaining entry to the United States through Mexico.[1]

In follow-up to Eisler's own testimony, the committee summoned Welles on September 24 to question him about the Eislers' visas. In support of his testimony, Welles submitted ER's two 1939 letters to him, one dated January 11, the second dated February 7. When the *New York Times* reprinted the two letters in their entirety, ER then tried to reach Welles by telephone.[2]

261

Sumner Welles to Eleanor Roosevelt
29 September 1947 [Bar Harbor, ME]

Personal

Dear Eleanor:

I was sorry that I had not reached home when you tried to reach me on the telephone the other evening at Oxon Hill. Owing to Mathilde's illness I was delayed here in Bar Harbor until the last moment, and I was obliged to limit my stay in Washington to the shortest time possible that would enable me to attend the Committee hearings and then return here at once to Bar Harbor.[3]

As I explained to Miss Thompson, there was absolutely nothing in the Department of State file that concerned you except the two notes you had sent me with regard to the Eisler case in the winter of 1939.[4] The Committee had subpoenaed all of this correspondence some months ago and had even made available the text of your two letters to certain favored newspaper correspondents before the hearings. I was given no opportunity to make any statement beyond identifying the notes you had sent me and the replies to them which I had sent to you.

It has, of course, been obvious that the Committee wished to make it appear that the White House was intervening directly in order to facilitate the entrance into this country of notorious communists.

Since the proven facts in the case establish beyond the shadow of a doubt that the entrance of Eisler into this country as a non-quota immigrant had not the slightest connection with the notes you had sent me, nor with the letters which Messersmith and I had subsequently written, but was solely due to the disregard of his standing instructions by the Vice Consul at Mexicali many months later and by the Board of Review of the Immigration Service in Washington subsequent to that, it was arranged that Norman Littell, whom I had retained as counsel, should issue a statement to the press clarifying these facts after the testimony of both Messersmith and myself had been concluded.[5] I am enclosing a copy of this statement for your own files since you may wish to retain it as a matter of record.[6] Except in the Hearst Press and in the McCormick-Patterson Press, this statement seems to have enlightened public opinion as to what the truth really was.[7]

I am, of course, deeply sorry that you should have had this annoyance at a moment when you are confronted with your present problems and burdens in the United Nations.

Believe me,

Affectionately yours,
Sumner Welles

TLS AERP, FDRL

262

Eleanor Roosevelt to Sumner Welles
6 October 1947 [New York City]

Dear Sumner:

Many thanks for your letter of September 29th. I was not bothered at all by the Eisler case. I could not remember anything about it and one of the newspaper women at the United Nations told me I was to be made the "goat" and that is why I called you.[8] I should have been very glad to be called to appear before the committee!

I am sorry Mathilde has been ill and I do hope she is better.

Affectionately,
Eleanor Roosevelt

TLS SWP, FDRL

---

1. William S. White, "Eisler Plea Made by Mrs. Roosevelt to Sumner Welles," *NYT*, 25 September 1947, 1; Mary Spargo, "Eisler's Visa Blamed on Consular Slip," *WP*, 26 September 1947, 1; "Johnson Explains Actions on Eisler," *NYT*, 26 September 1947, 18; Goodman, 204–7; A. Black, *Casting*, 239 *n*46; "Hanns Eisler, 64, Composer, Dead," *NYT*, 7 September 1962, 29.

2. William S. White, "Eisler Plea Made by Mrs. Roosevelt to Sumner Welles," *NYT*, 25 September 1947, 1.

3. Welles and his wife, Mathilde (see *n*9 Document 201), had built a mansion on 250 acres along the Potomac River at Oxon Hill, Maryland. They also owned a thirty-eight-room "summer cottage" near Bar Harbor, Maine (Welles, 126–27, 369–70; Gellman 213).

4. He refers here to Malvina "Tommy" Thompson, ER's secretary. It is unclear from the available written records when and how Welles communicated with Thompson. The "two notes" are the 1939 letters published in the *New York Times*.

5. Messersmith (see *n*8 Document 201), in his capacity as assistant secretary of state, had also interceded on the Eislers' behalf in their 1939 visa applications in Cuba. Norman M. Littell (1899–1994), who had served as an assistant attorney general under FDR and had been active in the National Committee Against Nazi Persecution of Minorities during the war, acted as counselor to Messersmith and Welles in the Eisler case before HUAC. Mexicali is the capital of the state of

Baja California, Mexico. The Eislers finally succeeded in acquiring entry visas from a US consulate there ("Norman Mather Littell," *WW*, vol. 13, 172; Mary Spargo, "Eisler's Visa Blamed on Consular Slip," *WP*, 26 September 1947, 1).

6. Littell's statement began, "the Committee's use of the correspondence between Sumner Welles, as Under Secretary of State, George S. Messersmith, as Assistant Secretary of State, and Mrs. Roosevelt, constitutes a misleading account of the admission of Hanns Eisler for permanent residence in the United States." Littell then asserted that all actions of Messersmith, Welles, and ER on the Eislers' behalf came to "precisely nil for Hanns Eisler," and that the Eislers succeeded in entering the United States only because they "caught a sleepy consular officer in the small town of Mexicali off guard" ("Statement of Norman M. Littell Counsel for Sumner Welles and George S. Messersmith in Hearings Before the Un-American Activities Committee," 25 September 1947, AERP).

7. Colonel Robert R. McCormick (1880–1955) and his cousin Eleanor "Cissy" Patterson controlled a number of newspapers hostile to FDR. These included the *Washington Times-Herald*, whose "Capitol Stuff" column on October 8, 1947, blamed ER for letting "Communist Hanns Eisler slip into this country and join his pinko pals in New York, Washington and Hollywood." On Hearst, see *n*17 Document 74 (Smith, *Colonel*, xx–xxi, 296; John O'Donnell, "Capitol Stuff," *Washington Times-Herald*, 8 October 1947, 16).

8. No written evidence exists identifying the UN reporter ER references. Nevertheless, ER did defend herself in print, telling the *New York Times* that "the note to Sumner Welles simply passed for consideration a name sent to me. When I was in the White House I had hundreds of such requests a month and, depending on the character of the request, the letters were passed on to the correct Government department. I never knew Mr. Eisler and, in fact, I don't remember the note concerning him." When the issue did not disappear as quickly as ER hoped, she told readers of her December If You Ask Me column:

> If you read my letter to Mr. Sumner Welles which was published in the New York papers, you will realize that all I asked was that Mr. Eisler's case be reviewed. A number of papers had been brought to me by a man whom I knew slightly, but I also knew that several other people, such as Miss Dorothy Thompson and Mr. Alvin Johnson, were interested in Mr. Eisler. I had never heard of him before that, and naturally I did not know that he was supposed to be connected with the Communist Party. In any case, at that time one was more concerned as to whether Germans were connected with the Nazi Party, and I was assured that he was not ("Letter Explained by Mrs. Roosevelt," *NYT*, 25 September 1947, 1; *IYAM*, *LHJ*, December 1947, 51).

THE PLIGHT OF THE NAVAJO

While in the White House, ER demonstrated continued interest in Native American issues, especially matters relating to the Navajos.[1] In 1947, the Bureau of Indian Affairs in the Department of the Interior undertook a study of the "Navajo Situation" and found the tribe in dire need of federal assistance for health, education, and employment. After receiving a letter from a reader about the Navajos in August, ER wrote to Interior Secretary Julius "Cap" Krug (1907–1970) inquiring about the "disgrace" of the Navajos' conditions. In reply, he sent her a copy of the BIA report, which provided many of the statistics ER offered in this My Day column.[2]

_263_

My Day
30 September 1947

NEW YORK, Monday—Many times during the years that I spent in Washington the plight of the Indians, who still live on reservations and are, therefore, wards of the United States,[3] was brought to my attention. The other day a letter came to me from a woman who has just discovered some of the facts concerning the Navajo Indian tribes. She was under the impression that no one knew of the conditions as they exist, and I am sure it must have been discouraging to her when I wrote that not only did I think the Indian Bureau knew all about these conditions but, in all probability, Congress had been told about them a number of times.

The Navajo situation primarily is a population problem. In 1868 the tribe numbered about 9,000 people. Today there are more than 60,000, and they are increasing at the rate of 1,000 a year, which is considerably faster than the birth rate in the nation as a whole.

The Navajo country covers about 25,000 square miles but most of it is semi-desert.[4] Part of the land is timbered and limited almost entirely to use as grazing land, and the soil is severely eroded. The range can carry only about 520,000 sheep, which is roughly ten sheep per person, and the variety raised by the Navajos produces less than $7 per animal per year. About half an acre of irrigated land is the average used by a Navajo farmer and this returns him about $13.50.

Therefore, a little over $80 a year is the over-all average income for the Navajo. Only a comparatively few of them are able to earn a little extra income through the sale of minerals, pinon nuts, their arts and crafts and their wood.

Only an Act of Congress can appropriate more land for the Navajos, and for years the appropriation bill for the Department of the Interior has stated that no federal funds appropriated in the bill may be used to buy land for Indian use in the states of Arizona and New Mexico.[5]

The most shocking educational conditions exist among these people. There are 20,000 Navajo children of school age, but the total school facilities, including federal and mission schools, will accommodate only 6,000 children. In view of the fact that in 1868 the United States made a solemn treaty with the tribe, promising a school and a teacher for every 30 children of school age, this puts our government in a decidedly unpleasant light.[6] Also, health conditions are deplorable. Roads through the area are poor, and this adds to the difficulties where health and education are concerned.

The Department of Interior has a program designed to solve some of the problems of these people who once owned this white man's land, and it would seem advisable for Congress to respect the treaty even if it was made with a conquered people who no longer can menace our power.[7]

It is interesting to note that 3,400 Navajos were in World War II and 15,000 were engaged in war work. Their war bond purchases and their contributions to the Red Cross were remarkable, considering their small incomes.[8]

TMs AERP, FDRL

---

1. In 1934, FDR signed the Indian Reorganization Act (IRA, also known as the Wheeler-Howard Act for its congressional sponsors), which emphasized tribal land ownership, encouraged self-government within each tribe, and provided federal funds for education of Native American schoolchildren. The IRA did not address the issue of citizenship—universal suffrage was not guaranteed to Native Americans until passage of the Voting Rights Act of 1965—nor did it markedly raise Native Americans as a whole out of poverty, but its passage represented a milestone in the tribes' struggle for self-determination.

In a 1941 column, ER described a meeting with a Navajo delegation, where she learned that "the government experts have decided that they must raise fewer sheep and they see starvation before them. They have no outside market which is within reach, and they have come to Washington to appeal to the … Indian Affairs Committee in Congress." Shortly after this meeting, ER requested a meeting with Commissioner of Indian Affairs John Collier (1884–1968) so she could learn "something about the Navajo situation." ER subsequently advocated for an irrigation program on the reservation and also worked to increase the sales of Navajo arts, in order to preserve the Indians' culture and generate revenue (*MD*, 12 and 18 June 1941; *FDRE*).

2. ER's August 20 letter to Krug enclosed an August 16 letter from a Gertrude Taber Franklin, referenced in Krug's September 12 reply, that alerted ER to the Navajos' condition. ER did not retain a copy of the Franklin letter, and a copy does not appear in the ER-Krug correspondence (Philleo Nash, "Twentieth-Century United States Government Agencies," *Handbook of North American Indians*, vol. 4, 265–70; Suzanne E. Evans, "Voting," in Hoxie, 658–60; *DAB*; "The Navajo Situation," 8 September 1947, AERP; ER to Julius Krug, 20 August 1947, AERP; Julius Krug to ER, 12 September 1947, AERP).

3. *U.S. v. Nice* (1916) ruled that Indians were in a state of "continued guardianship" and bound by "Congressional regulations adopted for their protection." In 1928, the Arizona Supreme Court ruled in *Porter v. Hall* that Native Americans were under "federal guardianship," a classification synonymous with "persons under disability" (Kelly, 186–88; Suzanne E. Evans, "Voting," in Hoxie, 658–60).

4. The Navajo reservation spans across northern Arizona, northeastern New Mexico, and southern Utah. In 1947 it covered approximately 25,000 square miles ("The Navajo Situation," 8 September 1947, AERP).

5. Appropriations to the Bureau of Indian Affairs were given on the condition that no portion of that money would go toward land acquisition. The land acquisitions of the 1930s and 1940s came under the provisions of the Deficiency Appropriation Act of 1934 and the Wheeler-Howard Act of 1936. Congress extended funds to the Navajos to purchase and lease lands in Arizona until the fiscal year of 1941, whereupon no further funding for the purchase of land was appropriated ("Indian Lands," *Indian Affairs: Laws and Treaties*, vol. 6, Washington: Government Printing Office, 62–63; Taylor, 132–34).

6. The Navajo Treaty of 1868 allowed for the creation of a one-hundred-square-mile reservation for nearly 7,000 Navajos. The treaty also placed responsibility for the "civilization of the Indians" on the national government, which was to provide schools ("Navajo Treaty of 1868," Hoxie, 426–27).

7. The Department of Interior "program" referenced here entailed $2 million for immediate relief and employment assistance. Congress voted to approve the program December 15, 1947 ("Navajo Aid Measure Passed by Congress," *NYT*, 16 December 1947, 30).

8. At least 99 percent of all eligible Indians registered for the draft, and Navajos made up almost 20 percent of Native Americans in the US armed services. More than 300 Navajo were also enlisted to use their language, which was unfamiliar to the Japanese, to encrypt military code. These "code talkers" proved essential to the success of American military operations, particularly the Battle of Iwo Jima in 1945. At home, Native Americans bought over $50 million worth of war bonds and over 40,000 Native Americans left reservations to find jobs in defense industries. In New Mexico, approximately 2,500 Navajos helped construct the Fort Wingate Ordnance Depot. Navajos also gave corn, mutton, silver jewelry, and rugs to the Red Cross in lieu of cash (Adam Jevec and Lee Ann Potter, "The Navajo Code Talkers," *Social Education*, vol. 65 no. 5, 1 September 2001, 262–66; "Navajo Indians Are on Warpath" *NYT*, 10 May 1942, XX2; "11,000 Indians Join Our Armed Forces," *NYT*, 22 December 1942, 17).

ON THE NAACP PETITION TO UNITED NATIONS, PART 1

W. E. B. Du Bois, as director of special research for the NAACP, assembled a team of scholars in 1946 to produce the *Statement on the Denial of Human Rights to Minorities in the Case of Citizens of Negro Descent in the United States of America and an Appeal to the United Nations for Redress*, also known as *An Appeal to the World*. The 155-page document served as an indictment against America's "color caste system," and included statistical analysis of the economic disparity of whites and blacks in America as well as the total number of lynchings perpetrated each year from 1882 to 1946.

Du Bois first contacted Secretary-General Lie the previous November to ask that the UN formally receive the petition. Lie's office replied that the General Assembly would only hear petitions endorsed by member nations. On September 2, 1947, believing that ER's dual role as NAACP board member and American delegate to the UN made her the most likely candidate to help in the matter, Du Bois and White wrote her requesting her support in presenting the petition. One week later, Du Bois's assistant, Hugh Smythe, sent a letter to Warren Austin asking him to add the petition to the General Assembly's agenda. Austin replied that there was an unofficial deadline in the GA to make changes to the agenda and that the deadline had passed the day he received Smythe's letter. Du Bois persisted and wrote to the secretary-general's office again on October 16:

> The case of American Negroes is not going to be kept from knowledge by denial of the right to petition, no more than in the past slavery could bolster itself by silence. We are going to give world-wide publicity to our complaint; but first, we would like to proceed by regular process and lay this petition before the United Nations publicly and in such a manner as their Secretariat suggests.

The evening the secretary-general's office received Du Bois's letter, John Humphrey, head of the secretariat's Human Rights Division, telephoned Du Bois to inform him that the NAACP could formally petition the Human Rights Commission on October 23. Both Humphrey and Henri Laugier, the assistant secretary-general for social affairs, were to receive the petition.

Walter White wrote ER the following letter asking her to attend the NAACP's presentation.

264

Walter White to Eleanor Roosevelt
20 October 1947 [New York City]

Dear Mrs. Roosevelt:

I tried to reach you at the United Nations today but without success. I wanted to ask your advice and, if it would not embarrass you in your official connection, your aid in the matter of arrangements for presentation of our petition to the United Nations on this Thursday at 12 noon in M. Henri Laugier's office. M. Laugier and Mr. John P. Humphrey are to receive the petition.[1]

The ceremony will be brief and simple. I shall make a two-minute preliminary statement and then introduce Dr. Du Bois who will speak for about the same length of time.

We have invited approximately 125 distinguished white and Negro Americans to be present as well as the heads of all delegations to the United Nations. We estimate that between 100 and 150 persons will be present. In addition we have notified the newspapers, newsreel and radio companies.

The fact that such attention is being paid to the petition seems to disturb some of the United Nations personnel and there has been indicated to us a desire to limit the number of persons to not more than five or six including newspaper men. This, I fear, is quite impossible. A dozen or more United Nations delegations have requested copies of the petition including the United Kingdom, Russia, Union of South Africa, India, Argentina, Denmark, Mexico, Poland, Pakistan, Egypt, Haiti and Liberia. Newspapermen from all over the world have requested copies. And even as I dictate this a Norwegian journalist is waiting to see me. The matter cannot be kept secret, so great is the interest.[2] We hope that the matter can be worked out satisfactorily and to this end I ask your advice and assistance.

Mr. Humphrey has informed us that it will not be possible to bring the petition before either the General Assembly or the Economic and Social Council unless the matter is taken up by a member Government and circulation of the petition proposed by it. He adds, however, that there does exist certain machinery for bringing petitions of this kind to the attention of the Commission on Human Rights and that this is what will be done with our petition.

Ever sincerely
Walter White

TLS, AERP, FDRL

October 21, White wired ER, along with several of her fellow NAACP board members, once again requesting her attendance at the NAACP's presentation of *An Appeal to the World* to the UN.[3]

265

Walter White to Eleanor Roosevelt
21 October 1947 [New York City]

MRS. ELEANOR ROOSEVELT

PETITION ON DENIAL OF HUMAN RIGHTS TO CITIZENS OF NEGRO DESCENT IN THE UNITED STATES AND APPEAL TO UNITED NATIONS FOR REDRESS WILL BE PRESENTED TO M. HENRI LAUGIER OF UNITED NATIONS SECRETARIAT AND MR. JOHN P. HUMPHREY DIRECTOR OF THE DIVISION OF HUMAN RIGHTS IN M. LAUGIER'S OFFICE AT LAKE SUCCESS THURSDAY, OCTOBER 23RD AT 12 NOON SHARP BY A DELEGATION REPRESENTING NATIONAL ASSOCIATION FOR THE ADVANCEMENT OF COLORED PEOPLE. WOULD IT BE POSSIBLE FOR YOU TO BE PRESENT AS DEMONSTRATION OF DEEP CONCERN OF RESPONSIBLE AMERICAN OPINION WITH THIS PROBLEM WHICH IS INTERNATIONAL AS WELL AS NATIONAL WE VERY MUCH HOPE YOU WILL ARRANGE TO BE WITH US. PLEASE WIRE OR TELEGRAPH COLLECT IF WE MAY EXPECT YOU. THIS TELEGRAM WILL ADMIT YOU TO M. LAUGIER'S OFFICE.

WALTER WHITE

Tel, AERP, FDRL

ER replied the following day.

266

Eleanor Roosevelt to Walter White

22 October 1947 [New York City]

Dear Mr. Walter White:

I am very sorry that I can not be with you tomorrow morning at twelve o'clock. As an individual I should like to be present, but as a member of the delegation I feel that until this subject comes before us in the proper way, in a report of the Human Rights Commission or otherwise, I should not seem to be lining myself up in any particular way on any subject.

It isn't as though everyone did not know where I stand. It is just a matter of proper procedure.[4]

Very sincerely yours,

TLc AERP, FDRL

---

1. Lewis, 528–29; George Streator, "U.N. Gets Charges of Wide Bias in U.S.," *NYT*, 24 October 1947, 9; "A Summary of the Petition to the UN in Behalf of Negro Americans Presented by the NAACP October 23, 1947," NAACP, DLC; Memorandums from W. E. B. Du Bois to Walter White, 21 November 1946 and 17 October 1947, NAACP, DLC; W. E. B. Du Bois to Warren Austin, 14 October 1947; Warren Austin to W. E. B. Du Bois, 21 October 1947, NAACP, DLC; W. E. B. Du Bois to William H. Stoneman, 16 October 1947, NAACP, DLC. See Document 285 for the outcome of the NAACP's presentation before the UN.

2. The NAACP had trouble fulfilling the large number of requests for *An Appeal to the World*. On October 18, Roy Wilkins informed Walter White that the NAACP would have to publish the *Appeal* in order to meet demand, as copies of the document were spoken for much more quickly than they could be mimeographed. The print version of the *Appeal* appeared in January 1948. The publicity surrounding the document prior to its formal presentation to the United Nations made White anxious. He feared Du Bois, whom he held responsible for publicizing the document, had made "a serious mistake in public relations" through his "violation of protocol and normal courteous procedure." Du Bois resented the charges and told White that he had only offered copies to UN delegations and not the press (Lewis, 529; Memorandum from Roy Wilkins to Walter White, 20 October 1947, NAACP, DLC; Memorandum from Walter White to W. E. B. Du Bois, 11 October 1947; W. E. B. Du Bois to Walter White, 14 October 1947, NAACP, DLC).

3. Although a copy of this final version of the NAACP's invitation was not filed with a list of recipients, there is a handwritten list consisting of seventeen individuals invited to attend the event. Only ten of those invited—including Mr. and Mrs. Walter White, W. E. B. Du Bois, Roy Wilkins, and Arthur Spingarn—indicated they would attend (Draft telegram and attached list of recipients, 20 October 1947; "Invited Delegation to U.N.," 23 October 1947, NAACP, DLC).

4. Although ER did not attend the October 23 presentation of *An Appeal to the World*, she helped White and the NAACP behind the scenes. White and Du Bois wrote to her September 22 and included a copy of the NAACP's petition hoping she would be "interested enough to bring this to the attention of Mr. Lie and to secure for us an opportunity to lay this statement before the Assembly or the Social and Economic Council." On September 24, ER then forwarded the NAACP's letter to Lie.

ER did not decide to decline the NAACP's invitation on her own; Durward Sandifer and Philip M. Burnett, two of her State Department advisors, agreed that "Mrs. R. should not attend."

The State Department did not want to call attention to the racial problems at home, for the Soviet Union would undoubtedly use the existence of such a problem to hurt the United States' prestige abroad (Janken, 307–8; A. Black, *Casting*, 100; Walter White and W. E. B. Du Bois to Eleanor Roosevelt, 22 September 1947; NAACP, DLC; Clyde Nichols to ER, 17 October 1947, AERP; Durward Sandifer's secretary to Philip M. Burnett, n.d., AERP).

Assessing Vyshinsky

In September, the United States sought General Assembly approval of a resolution condemning Greece's three northern neighbors for providing military and economic aid to Greek Communist guerrillas. The resolution also called for an immediate end to such aid and proposed the creation of a UN committee placed along the northern Greek "frontier" to ensure that Yugoslavia, Albania, and Bulgaria no longer interfered in the Greek civil war.[1] The General Assembly then referred the proposal to the Political and Civil Committee. After extensive debate, the committee approved a modified version of the US resolution, endorsing the creation of the UN "frontier" committee, and recommended that the General Assembly approve it at its October 21 session.[2] However, the day before the scheduled vote, Andrei Vyshinsky took the floor to attack the proposal. Rejecting the Security Council's findings that held the Balkan states in violation, the Soviet delegate demanded instead that British troops and American military instructors withdraw from Greece. His argument failed; the General Assembly approved the resolution on the 21st.[3]

Two days later, ER responded to his remarks in her column.

_267_

My Day
23 October 1947

NEW YORK, Wednesday—As I listened the other day to Soviet delegate Andrei Y. Vishinsky's speech in the General Assembly against the United States resolution to set up a permanent Balkan committee, I could not help being impressed first of all with the manner in which this very able prosecuting attorney speaks in the United Nations. Suddenly you feel that you are in a court room and that he is delivering the indictment against the defendant. His use of adjectives and similes is somewhat redundant but decidedly picturesque.[4]

He started his case by discrediting all of the witnesses for the other side—which is, of course, a valuable trick of lawyers. Then he made it appear that any one who did not agree with him must have been "a child born blind."

The only thing Mr. Vishinsky really lacks is a knowledge of the psychology of the people of the United States, who in this case are the judges of their delegates' position. The people of this country are anxious to cooperate with the USSR, as is shown by the fact that our representatives do all they can to bring about cooperation. But this speech of Mr. Vishinsky's destroyed the belief of our people that conciliation is either wise or possible in dealing with the representatives of the Government of the USSR.

We had agreed to certain modifications of our original resolution—not because, as Mr. Vishinsky said, we were convinced that we were wrong, but because other nations felt that the wording was somewhat harsh and that we could achieve the same ends without putting certain nations under outright accusations, as we had originally done. Being more than willing to cooperate, we agreed. But instead of understanding our actions, Mr. Vishinsky attacked us for having taken a position originally which, according to him we really did not believe in.

So our gesture of good will was misunderstood. And we learned a lesson which perhaps Mr. Vishinsky did not mean to teach us—namely, that no modification should ever be made in a position once taken; that no conciliation should ever be attempted; and that, since the USSR is unable ever to modify its position, it looks upon any one else who makes a modification as doing so purely from weakness and a feeling of guilt. We have learned our lesson well, but from my point of view it is unfortunate, because it will mean more votes against the USSR and a greater antagonistic feeling.

I suppose it would not be possible for Moscow to give its representatives sufficient leeway so that wordings and minor positions might sometimes be changed. If this could be done, it might lead occasionally to agreement instead of these constant long-drawn-out battles in which the only solution is to vote your opponent down.[5]

TMs AERP, FDRL

---

1. October 14, the First Committee approved the American proposal accusing Albania, Bulgaria, and Yugoslavia and calling upon these countries "to do nothing which could furnish aid and assistance to the said guerrillas." It then recommended that its special committee be based in Salonika (Thessaloniki) to monitor Greece's northern borders. This border, or "frontier," committee would "observe the compliance" of the Balkan states with the UN recommendations of co-operation and "normal diplomatic and good neighborly relations" (Report of the First Committee: Threats to the political independence and territorial integrity of Greece, 14 October 1947, A/409, Annex 8, 1509-1514, MWelC, ORGAUN; Threats to the political independence and territorial integrity of Greece, Resolution 109 (II), 100th Plenary Meeting, 21 October 1947, 12–14, UNORGA, MWelC).

2. The Political Committee proposed inserting language referencing the Security Council's investigation, which found the three Balkan states guilty of equipping and supporting the Greek guerrillas (Report of the First Committee: Threats to the political independence and territorial integrity of Greece, 14 October 1947, A/409, Annex 8, 1509-1514, UNORGA, MWelC).

3. Threats to the political independence and territorial integrity of Greece, Resolution 109 (II), 100th Plenary Meeting, 21 October 1947, 12–14, UNORGA, MWelC.

4. Vyshinsky's "picturesque" language included a description of the "scheme" to present the Greek issue to the General Assembly and accuse Yugoslavia, Bulgaria, and Albania of violating Greece's independence and territorial integrity as "a puppet show, a piece of crudely concocted political buffoonery, which must bring the blush of shame to the cheek of every unbiased person" (General Assembly, 97th Plenary Meeting, Verbatim Record, 20 October 1947, 368, MwelC, ORGAUN).

5. See "The Russians Are Tough," ER's earlier observations on bargaining with the Russians (Document 207).

DEFENDING SECRETARY MARSHALL AND THE
STATE DEPARTMENT

October 14, 1947, John Marshall Cooper, an attorney from Seattle, Washington, wrote ER a three-page, single-spaced typed letter detailing his concerns regarding the "colossal lack … of the right kind of aggressive, resourceful and arresting leadership in our State Department." Calling the department "disorganized and inept," Cooper noted the department's reliance on press reports for up-to-date information and judged the department's "failure to concentrate this country's full power behind the United Nations … censurable." When the United States tried "to circumvent" the UN with aid to Greece, Cooper continued, that "move cost us a heavy loss in prestige and honor." Moreover, "this same lack of awareness of existing conditions, failure to act in time, and disinclination to keep the citizens of this country currently and fully informed of international developments has characterized the State Department's paternalistic and undemocratic handling of the several phases of the Marshall Plan …"

As evidence of his claim that the press recognized key diplomatic issues before key State Department officials, Cooper emphasized that many reporters berated the department for its leadership failure, and sent ER an article by R. H. Shackford from the *Seattle Times* as an example.[1]

ER dictated the following response.

268

Eleanor Roosevelt to J. Marshall Cooper
24 October 1947 [New York City]

Dear Mr. Cooper:

I do not know what you mean when you say our State Department is not giving leadership and support to the United Nations.

I have been on the delegation for all of the General Assembly meetings and I assure you that no Foreign Office supports its delegation as well as does our State Department.

The Greek situation has two sides. I think perhaps if you would talk to some of the people in the Department you would understand some of the difficulties better and realize that it is not always what lies on the surface that is really the truth.[2]

Naturally this country was aware of the situation in Greece but it was not our responsibility until Great Britain asked us to take it over.

Mr. Shackford's article seems to me one of the stupidest articles I have ever read. I would like our Secretary of State to provide him with good copy by being the person who stands up and argues with Mr. Vishinsky. Russia sent Vishinsky and not Mr. Molotoff to do that. We send Senator Austin, not our Secretary of State.[3]

We have provided all of the issues which are being fought out in the present session. We have brought the Greek question into the UN. We have suggested "The Little Assembly" and it is on our suggestions that other people are working.[4] We do not try to dictate, we bring things to the UN and then let everybody argue them out. We could use our great force and prestige and simply push our suggestions through without discussion, but under Secretary Marshall's wise leadership, we do not even try to push things down the throats of the Latin American countries. It is wise to let people think for themselves—far wiser than to propose something and then give the answers.

[If][5] citizens do not have a little more faith in their own government and back up as good a Secretary as General Marshall with a little more enthusiasm, I do not know how they can expect their public servants to accomplish much for them.

Very sincerely yours,

TLc AERP, FDRL

———————

1. John M. Cooper to ER, 14 October 1947, AERP; R.H. Shackford, "Reds' Revival of Comintern Blow to U.N.," *Seattle Times*, 6 October 1946, 3.

2. Cooper chided the State Department for bypassing the UN in the US intervention in Greece. For additional information on Greece, see Document 87, Document 187, *n*5 Document 194, Document 210, *n*3 and *n*4 Document 219, *n*12 Document 220, Document 221, and Document 231 (John M. Cooper to ER, 14 October 1947, AERP).

3. Roland Herbert "R. H." Shackford (1908–1998), a United Press correspondent, disapproved of the State Department leadership, stating that according to UN representatives, "the United States' promised dynamic U.N. program designed to take the leadership has failed to jell. Secretary of State Marshall, instead of providing the leadership many delegates had hoped for, has remained aloof" (R. H. Shackford, "Reds' Revival of Comintern Blow to U.N.," *Seattle Times*, 6 October 1946, 3; "R.H. Shackford," Biography and Genealogy Master Index. Farmington Hill, Mich.: Thomson Gale, 1980–2005).

4. Secretary of State Marshall proposed a plan for the Little Assembly, to be composed of one delegate from each country, which would serve as an "interim committee" when the General Assembly was out of session. The Soviets disagreed with the creation of the Little Assembly and thwarted efforts to supply a budget for it. Nevertheless, the interim committee convened in 1948. ER supported the creation of the Little Assembly, and described its role in a radio broadcast on November 2, 1947. ER explained that, "some people here said that the establishment of this Interim Committee would infringe on the functions of the Security Council." She therefore clarified the four main responsibilities of the interim committee, which was to meet in between General Assembly sessions:

> 1. It will consider matters in relation to the maintenance of international peace and security and friendly relations between nations which might be submitted for consideration at the next regular session … 2. It can observe what is being done under the recommendations of this present session throughout the world and in cases which deal with peace and security and friendly relations, assigned by the General Assembly to the interim committee, it can be prepared to report on progress made. 3. It can make long range studies for recommendations to the General Assembly on principles of cooperation in the interest of peace and international security and friendly relations among nations. 4. It can advise the General Assembly whether in the light of its own experience a permanent interim committee might [be] of value.

(ER, "For Broadcast, Sunday 2nd, 1947" from "World Security Workshop," AERP; John Foster Dulles, "Challenge of the Little Assembly," *NYT*, 4 January 1948, SM8; A. M. Rosenthal, "'Little Assembly' to Open on Jan. 5," *NYT*, 11 December 1947, 27; "The 'Little Assembly,'" *NYT*, 7 November 1947, 22; "Resolution on U.N. 'Little Assembly,'" *NYT*, 7 November 1947, 8; A. M. Rosenthal, "Russia Will Seek to Block Funds for 'Little Assembly' as Illegal," *NYT*, 8 November 1947, 1).

5. The first word of the sentence is missing from the original document. The typist apparently ran out of room on the carbon paper.

ON MILITARY TRAINING

Mrs. Alma Sue Emrick of Burbank, California, wrote to ER October 10, 1947, to express her concerns about military expansion and the need for peace advocacy.

> Being just a common housewife, I, like many millions of parents sitting "on the sidelines" am taking the opportunity to get off my chest what has heretofore been "taboo" for discussion. I, however, do not understand the reason why we common people cannot glorify peace by talking about it or in our common "horse-sense" manner try to suggest a system for instilling peaceful inclination into every heart in the world.

Emrick also enclosed a document that appeared to be a petition by the California Congress of Parents and Teachers, Inc.,[1] which began:

> We condemn warlike procedure—always have! Military Training will only incite suspicion on us of other nations and will put us in the same category of the Germans who always had military training for youth! How can we be sure that future militarists in power, will not instill glorification of war and hatred for other nations?

The document, which Emrick signed, called for the establishment of an international congress of parents and teachers, uniting PTAs with similar organizations in other nations, as a way to ensure that "every family in the world … be a strong 'peace advocate,' not afraid to 'sit down' on the war radicals."[2]

269

Eleanor Roosevelt to Alma Sue Emrick

24 October 1947 [New York City]

My dear Miss[3] Emrick:

You did not enclose the ballot so I do not know what you received.[4]

I agree with you that the PTA organizations are extremely valuable but I am afraid you will find it hard to unite with women in the same type of organization in Russia. That just does not exist and if it did, you could not possibly get any communication to them.

I think you are unwise not to face the fact military training is not preparation to fight a war, but preparation to prevent war. In two wars we have been saved from being a primary target by the fact that others defended us. We can not always expect to be saved. I hope very much as the UN grows stronger that we may prevent war, but as long as there is force in the world we can only reduce our own as the other nations reduce theirs. We can not do it alone.

I wish you could come and spend six months watching the Russians work. I quite agree with you that the Russian people do not want war any more than we do, but they would have little or nothing to say about it since they only get the news which their government wishes them to have and they probably would believe that we were attacking them.

We all want a government in this country for the people and by the people but that is not the case all over the world and shutting your eyes to facts does not do one any good.

Very sincerely yours,

TLc AERP, FDRL

———————————

1. The California Congress of Parents and Teachers, Inc., was the name of the California State PTA from the 1920s to the 1970s, when it adopted its present name (California State PTA, "A Brief History: Working Together for Children Since 1897," http://www.capta.org/sections/basics/brief-history.cfm, accessed 2 November 2005).

2. Alma Sue Emrick to ER, 10 October 1947, AERP.

3. Though Mrs. Emrick called herself a "common housewife" in her letter to ER, the extant carbon copy of ER's reply in the FDR Library reads as given, "Miss."

4. ER mistakenly calls this document a ballot rather than a petition.

DEFENDING FREEDOM OF THE PRESS

In a speech before the General Assembly, September 18, 1947, Soviet Deputy Foreign Minister Vyshinsky accused the United States, and particularly the American "reactionary" press, of inciting war against the Soviet Union. It was his belief that while the American people, as well as the peoples of other democratic countries, were against a new war, American newspaper magnates were "provoking hatred" towards the Soviet Union and other Eastern European nations. "It cannot be but mentioned as an example that such organs of the press as the *New York Herald Tribune* and a number of similar organs, especially of the Hearst press, publish systematically all possible provocative articles, which promote in the minds of their readers the necessity for 'military action if Europe faces collapse or falls under the control of the Soviet Union,'" he said. Vyshinsky also implied that because the press was "entirely in the hands of the bosses of various newspapers enterprises, and does what is ordered," it was hardly as "free" as it claimed.[1]

Later that same day, Vyshinsky introduced a resolution into the First Committee of the United Nations urging all member governments of the General Assembly to forbid war propaganda within their borders, on pain of criminal punishment.[2]

ER interpreted these attacks on the press as nothing more than propaganda designed to embarrass the United States, and went on a campaign to defend the freedom of the press. In the first of her "The World Security Workshop" broadcasts, October 5, ER made it clear that there was a distinction between "war-mongering" and a "critical attitude:"

The real difference … is that our press is run by individual people or groups, and they are free to say whatever they want to say. It is a very different thing when you have a press that does represent the government and only the government, where everything has to be considered as official.[3]

Three weeks later, in a statement before the Third Committee, ER again defended the right of free speech and the importance of an independent press, but also highlighted the problems of a government-controlled press:

Sometimes what is printed in the controlled press of these countries is not false so far as it goes, but the whole truth is rarely told. A careful selection of items is made to build up the desired general picture, and the rest of the news is frequently omitted or distorted. I think those of us who listened to the debates here must know that by this time, because we have heard cited both here and in Committee One definite quotations, but we have never heard anything on the other side, and there is, of course, more on the other side that could be quoted. I think that that is something that we ought to remember in discussing what happens in a free press.

A recent example of this technique is the treatment by the controlled press of the statements made by Mr. Vyshinsky and Secretary Marshall at the opening session of this Assembly. Mr. Vyshinsky's address was given copious space, frequently being produced verbatim. Secretary Marshall's statement, on the other hand, received no mention whatsoever in many press organs, and where brief mention was given, the account was slanted in the desired direction. In the United States press, on the other hand, Mr. Vyshinsky's statement was reported fully and fairly in all major press organs, despite the fact that it contained an indictment, among other things, of the American press itself. In this way the people of the countries in which the controlled press functions are being sealed off from the outside world, kept in the darkness of governmental and semi-governmental propaganda, and systematically shielded from the light of full truth.

> The threat to international peace and security is indeed grave when behind these walls of contrived ignorance governments persistently slander governments and official propagandists work to poison the wells of international friendship—without possibility of effective reply.[4]

Three days after her statement before the Third Committee, ER continued to stress the importance of the freedom of the press in My Day:

> No one believes in printing untruthful news. Certainly no one wants to see the press or individuals or any organizations incite to war. But I cannot believe that suppression by law or by government edict is going to bring about the desired results.
>
> I found myself in the absurd position of defending the *Chicago Tribune*, since this newspaper was specifically mentioned in the Yugoslav presentation. I defended that paper, certainly not because I either agree with or believe most of the things which it stands for, but because I think we should defend the right of all individuals to their freedom of thought and speech.
>
> And when they began on the columnists and news broadcasters, I could not help smiling again. There are plenty of these gentlemen who have said things that I could deny if I cared to undertake a constant running fight, but even where they are concerned I would have to defend their right to express their points of view. Sometimes, when I hear things or read things which I know quite well are not true, I have almost a wistful feeling about the English libel laws! They would be helpful occasionally if they existed here. Nevertheless, in spite of annoyances and the harm which evil minds can bring about in personal, national and international situations, I still think it would be more serious to curtail, in any way, freedom of thought and expression.[5]

Although ER by this point was firmly on record as opposed to the Soviet and Yugoslav resolutions, she made one last attempt to caution against curtailing the freedom of the press prior to the vote. The following remarks were reproduced by Durward Sandifer's wife in her memoir, *Mrs. Roosevelt As We Knew Her.*[6]

270

Remarks by Eleanor Roosevelt
Meeting of the Third Committee of the General Assembly[7]

28 October 1947

Mr. Chairman,

I am not going to begin by saying that I hope that none of my colleagues here will be offended, because I am going to try not to say anything which will offend them.[8]

Neverless, the longer I listen to this Committee and I hear what happens in other Committees, I think the time has come for some very straight thinking among us all. The ultimate objective that we have is to create better understanding among us, and I will acknowledge that that is going to be difficult. And I will give you the reasons why. I have never yet heard a representative of any of the USSR group acknowledge that in any way their government can be wrong. They may say it at home—I do not know—and they may think it is wrong to do it outside. They are very young and the young rarely acknowledge anything which they may have done that may not be quite right. With maturity we grow much more humble and we know that we have to acknowledge very often that things are not quite perfect. Because we acknowledge it, does not mean that we love our country any less; that we do not basically believe in the rightness of the things that exist in our country. What it does mean is that we know that human nature is not perfect and that we hope that all of us can contribute to something better.

Now, we have been going back and forth on the things which we could produce, that had been said on each side, which were bad. I could now say that the pamphlet from which my USSR colleague cited yesterday is written by a gentleman who belongs to the CIO, American Newspaper Guild[9]—to which I also belong—and I could also say that as you read it, it is quite evident that he is one of our American Communists and we allow American Communists in this country freedom to print what they want to say in criticism of this country.[10] The mere fact that it is printed shows that they have that freedom. Whether that is really very good to base our criticism on, I don't know, but the more we talk—we hear, for instance, the constant repetition of a capitalist press, or a capitalist economy versus a Communist economy.[11] Well, it is true and we have to live in the same world. The point is that somehow or other we have to learn to live together and work together on the bases and places where those economies are going to have to touch—in business, in trade, in the various things.

It is true too that we probably have basically different philosophies. For instance, our Ukrainian colleague said, "The way in which we understand the word freedom," by which he implied that he understood it differently.[12] I am quite sure that we have a different conception of what the meaning is. I think that we will have to grow very gradually over the years to a better understanding. But, in order to do that we must work together. Growing apart is not going to help us. I, for instance, would say, who is going to decide what is truth and what is a lie because some of the things which our colleagues have cited I don't happen to think have absolute truth anymore than they think that some of the things I cite are absolutely true. And it seems to me that if you curtail freedom in any respect, you curtail it sooner or later in every respect.

Now I think there is no such thing as absolute freedom. But I think we have to be careful to curtail as little as possible and I think that at the present time the thing for us to do is to acknowledge that there are basic differences in our economies, in our backgrounds, perhaps in our customs, in the way that we have done things, and that therefore both of us with different points of view have got to try to find some measure of cooperation between us.

I could not vote for the Yugoslav resolution. I did not really feel at first that I could vote for the French as it stood. I am not sure that I like doing anything except turning this over to the people who are experts to discuss it and to recommend what they think is the right thing to do, because I think experts are apt to get away more in the discussion of a subject from the political point of view or any other point of view. Nevertheless, with the amendments which have been introduced by Mexico—and the Luxemburg is very much the same—we will vote for the French resolution[13] because we do not believe that one should incite to war—we would far rather see peaceful things said—and we would hope that as far as possible all responsible writers and speakers and radio commentators and newspapers would try to do the things which will help cooperation. But, believe me, I do not know anything that I can say which will be impressive enough to make this Committee realize that our main objective is to create better understanding, to learn to live together in peace, and to try to make every measure—every act that we undertake—serve the purpose of increasing good will.

Now, I don't expect the millenium immediately, but I do expect and hope and pray that we are going to see the gradual increase in good will rather than a continual backwards and forwards of telling us what dogs we are and how bad we are.[14] I can see no use in that at all. I am weary of it and all I can say to my colleagues is that I hope we can work with good will.

Mrs. Roosevelt As We Knew Her[15]

---

1. "Text of Address by Vishinsky Before United Nations General Assembly Stating Soviet Views," *NYT*, 19 September 1947, 18.

2. The Yugoslav delegation had introduced a similar resolution into the Third Committee, October 4, calling on member states to "take urgent legislative and other measures" to "prevent the publication and dissemination through the channel of governmental or semi-governmental bodies of reports or news which have not been carefully verified," or which "provoke conflicts and incite war … against another State or another nation" (Frank S. Adams, "Russia Urges Gag," *NYT*, 19 September 1947, 1; GA, Request for the Inclusion of an Additional Item in the Agenda of the Second Regular Session, 18 September 1947 [A/BUR/86], AERP; Third Committee, Draft Resolution Submitted by the Delegation of Yugoslavia, 4 October 1947 [A/C.3/162], 256, UNORGA, MWelC).

3. "Air Forum Opened by Mrs. Roosevelt," *NYT*, 6 October 1947, 6.

4. Statement by the U.S. Representative to the General Assembly, 24 October 1947, *DSB*, 2 November 1947, 874–77. For a summary record of these remarks, see Third Committee, Sixty-eighth Meeting, Summary Record, 24 October 1947, 126–34, UNORGA, MWelC.

5. *MD*, 27 October 1947, AERP.

6. Irene Sandifer does not say whether she took down ER's words herself or obtained a transcript in some other way. The *New York Times* quoted briefly from ER's remarks, but did not print them in full in "Amity Plea Made by Mrs. Roosevelt," *NYT*, 29 October 1947, 10.

7. For the summary record of these remarks, see Third Committee, Seventy-first Meeting, Summary Record, 28 October 1947, 144–54, UNORGA, MWelC.

8. ER alludes to the repeated statements by Stephan P. Demchenko, the Ukrainian delegate, asking the American and British delegates not to be offended by the statements he quoted from sources that charged, for example, that wealthy publishers of American, British, and Australian newspapers censored the news (Third Committee, Seventy-first Meeting, Summary Record, 28 October 1947, 150, UNORGA, MWelC).

9. American Newspaper Guild.

10. Valerian A. Zorin, the delegate from the USSR, quoted from a pamphlet later identified by the *New York Times* as "The 'Free Press'" by George Marion and published by New Century Publishers in New York in 1946. The summary report describes Zorin's presentation as follows:

> Replying to the United States representative who had contended that the majority of the United States organs of information were in the hands of private and independent owners, he quoted a book by an American author on the United States Press as showing that the facts completely contradicted the contention of the delegation of the United States. The picture of the American Press as painted by an American journalist, determined, in Mr. Zorin's view, the attitude which the Third Committee should adopt in order to check the malpractices of the Press in relation to certain political problems.
>
> It was no part of the intention to overthrow the systems in force in the United States or elsewhere. He merely sought to demonstrate that if, as the United States claimed, the Press in some countries was a kind of State monopoly, in the United States it was the monopoly of the big financiers (Third Committee, Sixty-Ninth Meeting, Summary Record, 28 October 1947, 138, UNORGA, MWelC).

The *New York Times* reported that Zorin contended that Marion's book exposed the "monopolistic structure of the newspaper business" in the United States.

He added that, according to this source, all the papers in fifteen of the largest cities of the United States belonged to three owners. Where are the "free newspapers" referred to by Mrs. Roosevelt? Mr. Zorin asked. "Apparently there are none," he added.

"All this talk about freedom of the press is simply fog," Mr. Zorin said, "because this freedom does not exist in reality."

Marion, a member of the Communist Party, wrote for the *Daily Worker*. The full title of the pamphlet is "The 'Free Press': Portrait of a Monopoly" ("U.S. Press Scored by 3 States in U.N.," *NYT*, 26 October 1947, 3; "Got Material From Pamphlet," *NYT*, 28 October 1947, 6; "Guide to the Papers of George Marion," Tamiment Library/Robert F. Wagner Archives, http://dlib.nyu.edu:8083/tamwagead/servlet/SaxonServlet?source=/marion.xml&style=/saxon01t2002.xsl&part=body, accessed 15 March 2006).

11. The Communist delegates made many statements like the following one by Demchenko, as summarized by the UN rapporteur: "The people of all countries would reject the idea of freedom to spread malicious slander, but that was not the case with certain monied groups in capitalistic countries" (Third Committee, Seventy-first Meeting, Summary Record, 28 October 1947, [US/A/C.3/116], 149, UNORGA, MWelC).

12. The phrase ER quotes does not appear in the summary report or in the *New York Times*, but the UN rapporteur provides the following summary of Demchenko's remarks on the definition of freedom: "The rights of freedom of speech and of the Press were an important part of the democratic structure, but those freedoms were difficult to define and in certain countries they had no reality" (Third Committee, Seventy-first Meeting, Summary Record, 28 October 1947, [US/A/C.3/116], 149, UNORGA, MWelC).

13. The French resolution stated:

I. *Invites* the Governments of States Members:

1. To study such legislative or other measures as might with advantage be taken on the national plane to combat the diffusion of false or tendentious reports likely to injure friendly relations between States;

2. To submit reports on this subject to the Conference on Freedom of Information so as to provide the Conference with the data it requires to enable it to start its work immediately on a concrete basis.

II. *Recommends* to the Conference on Freedom of Information that it study, with a view to their co-ordination, the measures taken or advocated in this connexion by the various States (Draft Resolution Submitted by the Delegation of France, Annex 11a, 24 October 1947, 257, UNORGA, MWelC).

Luis Quintanilla, the Mexican delegate, rejected the Yugoslavian resolution, but said, according to the summary report, that he could accept the French resolution with certain amendments: "Those amendments would consist first of adding the words 'within the limits of constitutional procedure' to the third paragraph of the preamble and deleting the words 'and tendentious' from that paragraph; secondly, deleting the words 'legislative or other' and 'or tendentious' from the paragraph beginning: 'To study such legislative or other measures …' and adding the words 'within the limits of constitutional procedure' after 'to combat' in that paragraph; and thirdly replacing the words 'with a view to their co-ordination' in part II by the words 'as being relevant to the discussion of item 2 (d) of its provisional agenda,'" (Third Committee, Seventy-first Meeting, Summary Report, 28 October 1947, [US/A/C.3/116], 145–46, UNORGA, MWelC).

The Third Committee voted to reject the Yugoslavian resolution and adopted the French resolution with the proposed amendments by Mexico and Luxemburg.

14. Neither the UN summary reports nor the *New York Times* reports the actual language the Communist delegates used in describing the Americans and British as "dogs."

15. Irene Reiterman Sandifer, *Mrs. Roosevelt As We Knew Her* (Silver Spring, MD: privately printed, 1975), 53–55.

ON HUAC AND THE HOLLYWOOD TEN

May 1947, the House Committee on Un-American Activities began to hold closed hearings in Los Angeles to investigate Communist and "subversive" influence in the Hollywood film industry.[1] Public hearings in Washington, DC, began October 20. The committee asked each witness: "Are you now, or have you ever been, a member of the Communist Party?" Ten directors, producers, and screen writers—dubbed the "Hollywood Ten"—ultimately faced jail sentences for refusing to answer this question. Many others who refused to cooperate with HUAC found themselves banned from further film work in American studios.[2]

ER first referenced HUAC's Hollywood investigations in her October 27 column when she discussed UN debates on freedom of information. After recounting Vyshinsky's "most intemperate attack upon the United States," ER told her readers that she found herself "in the absurd position" of defending the American press which had attacked her most intensely. She "defended" the *Chicago Tribune*, "certainly not because I either agree with or believe most of the things which it stands for, but because I think we should defend the right of all individuals to their freedom of thought and speech." She concluded the column by relating the debate with the Soviets to the HUAC hearings:

> Just this angle, too, is one of the things which worries me a little about the Congressional investigation into the Hollywood movie world. When you begin to let this and that person testify against this or that actor or writer, you take a step toward Nazi and Communist totalitarian attitudes toward the individual. It is so easy to depart from the path of democracy and succumb to the attraction of totalitarian edicts![3]

Two days later, ER revisited the Hollywood hearings, devoting a full column to the subject.

271

My Day
29 October 1947

NEW YORK, Tuesday—I have waited a while before saying anything about the Un-American Activities Committee's current investigation of the Hollywood film industry. I would not be very much surprised if some writers or actors or stage hands, or what not, were found to have Communist leanings, but I <u>was</u> surprised to find that, at the start of the inquiry, some of the big producers were so chicken-hearted about speaking up for the freedom of their industry.[4]

One thing is sure—none of the arts flourishes on censorship and repression. And by this time it should be evident that the American public is capable of doing its own censoring. Certainly, the Thomas Committee is growing more ludicrous daily. The picture of six officers ejecting a writer from the witness stand because he refused to say whether he was a Communist or not is pretty funny, and I think before long we are all going to see how hysterical and foolish we have become.[5]

The film industry is a great industry with infinite possibilities for good and bad. Its primary purpose is to entertain people. On the side, it can do many other things. It can popularize certain ideals, it can make education palatable. But in the long run, the judge who decides whether what it does is good or bad is the man or woman who attends the movies. In a democratic country I do not think the public will tolerate a removal of its right to decide what it thinks of the ideas and performances of those who make the movie industry work.

I have never liked the idea of an Un-American Activities Committee. I have always thought that a strong democracy should stand by its fundamental beliefs and that a citizen of the United States should be considered innocent until he is proved guilty.

If he is employed in a government position where he has access to secret and important papers, then for the sake of security he must undergo some special tests. However, I doubt whether the loyalty test really adds much to our safety, since no Communist would hesitate to sign it and he would be in good standing until he was proved guilty. So it seems to me that we might as well do away with a test which is almost an insult to any loyal American citizen.[6]

What is going on in the Un-American Activities Committee worries me primarily because little people have become frightened and we find ourselves living in the atmosphere of a police state, where people close doors before they state what they think or look over their shoulders apprehensively before they express an opinion.

I have been one of those who have carried the fight for complete freedom of information in the United Nations.[7] And while accepting the fact that some of our press, our radio commentators, our prominent citizens and our movies may at times be blamed legitimately for things they have said and done, still I feel that the fundamental right of freedom of thought and expression is essential. If you curtail what the other fellow says and does, you curtail what you yourself may say and do.

In our country we must trust the people to hear and see both the good and the bad and to choose the good. The Un-American Activities Committee seems to me to be better for a police state than for the USA.[8]

TMs AERP, FDRL

---

1. On HUAC and its earlier incarnation as the Dies Committee, see header Document 144, *n*5 Document 171, *n*20 Document 281, and header Document 261.

2. Goodman, 207–25; *HSTE*; Ceplair and Englund, 254–98, 339–61; "Inquiry Is Started on Reds in Movies," *NYT*, 10 May 1947, 8; "How to Fight Communism," *NYT*, 2 November 1947, E2; Jay Walz, "Ten Film Men Cited for Contempt in Overwhelming Votes by House," *NYT*, 25 November 1947, 1.

3. *MD*, 27 October 1947.

4. Producers Jack Warner, Louis B. Mayer, James K. McGuinness, Walt Disney, Dory Schary, Adrian Scott, and Eric Johnson appeared before the committee in October 1947. The committee deemed all these but Scott "friendly witnesses"—defined by Parnell Thomas as "volunteers of information" who were "cooperating with the Committee" (Ceplair and Englund, 255*n*, 439).

5. ER probably referred to screenwriter John Howard Lawson (1894–1977), who became one of the "Hollywood Ten." In a heated moment of his testimony on October 27, the day before ER wrote this column, Lawson was forcibly ejected from the witness stand and escorted out of the committee room after he verbally skirmished with investigators, who would not allow him to read a statement or register his protests against the proceedings (Samuel A. Tower, "Film Inquiry Seeks Contempt Citation on Defiant Writer," *NYT*, 28 October 1947, 1, 28; C. Gerald Fraser, "John Howard Lawson, 82, Writer Blacklisted by Hollywood in '47," *NYT*, 14 August 1977, 46).

6. Smarting from the Republican victory in the 1946 congressional elections and under pressure from Congress to weed out Communists in government, Truman, who had initially resisted congressional efforts to investigate employee loyalty, created the President's Temporary Commission on Employee Loyalty to study loyalty and security provisions in the federal civil service. In early 1947, the commission proposed installing a federal employee loyalty program, which Truman formally established on March 22 by executive order. Under its provisions, civil service employees perceived

as being disloyal to the US government or allied with subversive causes, organizations, or individuals could be dismissed without full disclosure of the accusations or evidence against them. A program directed against individuals perceived as "security risks" operated at the same time, initially in the War and Navy Departments, and later extended to cover the State Department as well. These federal programs provided the model for future loyalty and security "tests" for employees in both the public and private sectors, empowered the FBI to lead investigations and press charges, and undercut legal procedural protections "in the name of national security." Although no employee was convicted of espionage, the blacklisting of organizations and the imposition of "reasonable grounds" for dismissal led to several hundred employees being fired or denied jobs "all in the name of national security."

ER continued to oppose the program. In her January 5, 1948, My Day she wrote, "I think there is plenty of room in this country for us to fight to improve our democracy. I am frank to say that I was deeply troubled when I read of the machinery to be used by the Loyalty Review Board." Furthermore, in an October column she noted:

> I heard one European statesman whimsically remark that while he disliked the Communists heartily he thought he disliked the anti-Communists more, because almost invariably the latter did the things that increased the Communist influence and power. This amused me because my main objection to the list of subversive organizations, which we got out in the United States, the loyalty tests and the antics of the House Un-American Activities Committee is that instead of effectively fighting the Communist influence they really help toward its development.

See also *n*3 Document 253, *n*1 and *n*2 Document 277, Document 278, Document 280, Document 279, and Document 281 (*HSTE*; *MD*, 5 January and 19 October 1948).

7. The HRC's Subcommission on the Freedom of Information and the Press was created in early 1947, with strong backing from ER and other delegates from the United States, Britain, and France, and held its first meeting on May 19, 1947. Freedom of the press was a vital issue to ER as both a delegate and a working journalist (Glendon, 36; "Free Press Group Meets Tomorrow," *NYT*, 18 May 1947, 28; "Free Information Held Liberty Basis," *NYT*, 29 May 1946, 15; *MD*, 15 May and 5 June 1946 and 12 February 1947).

8. On ER's staunch and often lone opposition to HUAC, see A. Black, *Casting*, 2, 4–5, 147–53, 202. See also Document 261.

On Religious Freedom in Yugoslavia

In the summer of 1947, seven prominent American Protestant clergy accepted an invitation from the Yugoslav government to visit with Yugoslav clergy.[1] The publication of their report, scheduled for November 7, contending that religious freedom existed in Yugoslavia generated intense controversy. American Catholics and others who believed that organized religion was under attack in Communist-dominated Yugoslavia disputed the report's claim and attempted to deny its authors a hearing. Boston's archbishop Richard Cushing labeled the report "a campaign of misrepresentation and of malice" and called on the Knights of Columbus to stop the "poison … now being spread … by men, who—may God forgive them—are introduced as a 'Reverend' and who ask to be heard as the representatives of Christ!" The dean of students for Union Theological Seminary and a leading professor at Yale Divinity School promptly responded to the archbishop, charging that such action infringed on the group's freedom of speech, and circulated a petition to clergymen around the country "calling for a full and free hearing for the forthcoming report."[2]

ER, who continued to support Yugoslav relief efforts and who received additional reports on the Yugoslav situation from Dr. Jean Nussbaum of the International Association for the Defense of Religious Liberty,[3] took a more nuanced view of the report and the reaction to it.[4]

272

My Day
4 November 1947

New York, Monday—One of the basic freedoms that we treasure in this country is freedom of religion—not only the freedom of various churches to hold services and to have ministers of various denominations, but also the freedom to instruct and to converse on religious subjects without interference.

I understand that the complete report of the group of American ministers who visited Yugoslavia is about to be published.[5] In view of the testimony which has come to me from a man who traveled with these ministers, I feel that their report should be read carefully and impartially. I do not believe in shutting one's eyes to the things of which one disapproves, but neither do I believe in passing over without mention the things of which one does approve.

A man who has long traveled throughout Europe and has been primarily interested in the freedom of the small church groups, tells me that he accompanied these ministers in Yugoslavia. He talks the language and has long known many of the people who politically may be in opposition to the present Government. He also knows many of the people in the Government, having interviewed Marshal Tito and a number of others. He is not in any way interested in the political aspects of any country because he is giving his time to the promotion of religious freedom. His knowledge of Yugoslavia stems back to the first World War, when he served as a doctor in that area.[6]

His testimony is that the report of this group of ministers is correct and that complete freedom of religion does exist in that country. He assures me that there has been no interference with religious practice and that the only objection has been to those who have interfered with political situations.[7]

If his testimony can be accepted as authentic, it is encouraging. And it might explain some of the feeling on the part of the Yugoslav representatives on the subject of slander and false representation.[8] It cannot, of course, alter our basic feeling in this country that we do not want the press anywhere controlled, either politically or in any other way. But it should increase our interest in seeing that the Conference on Freedom of Information makes a real study of this subject, with an emphasis on freedom as against repression, from whatever source.[9]

TMs AERP, FDRL

---

1. Rev. Emory Stevens Bucke, editor of *Zion's Herald*; Rev. George Walker Buckner, Jr., editor of the *World Call* of the Disciples of Christ; Dr. Phillips Packer Elliott, minister of the First Presbyterian Church, Brooklyn; Rev. William Howard Melish, assistant rector of the Church of the Holy Trinity, Brooklyn; Dr. Guy Emery Shipler, editor of the *Churchman*; Dr. Samuel Trexler, president of the Lutheran Synod of New York; and Dr. Claude Williams, director of the Peoples' Institute of Applied Religion visited Yugoslavia in the summer of 1947 at the invitation of the Yugoslav government to report on the status of religious freedom there. The Yugoslav government paid the clergymen's expenses. For more on Melish, see *n*8 Document 212. For more on Stepinac, see Document 282 ("Cushing Assails 7 Pastors on Tito," *NYT*, 20 August 1947, 10).

2. "Cushing Assails 7 Pastors on Tito," *NYT*, 20 August, 1947, 10; "Two Groups in Clash Over Melish Speech," *NYT*, 19 October 1947, 2; "Full Hearing Asked for Shipler Group," *NYT*, 21 October 1947, 17; "Survey Report Assailed," *NYT*, 24 October 1947, 8; "Yugoslav Report Endorsed," *NYT*, 31 October 1947, 6; "Shipler Group Scored," *NYT*, 26 October 1947, 5.

3. Dr. Jean Nussbaum, a Swiss national and the general secretary of the European Division of the International Association for the Defense of Religious Liberty, accompanied the Protestant delegation. ER, who served as the group's honorary chairman from 1946 until 1962, noted in a letter to Craddock Goins, editor of the *Mt. Kisco Recorder* and a Catholic, that Nussbaum "happened to be in Yugoslavia" at the same time as the American clergymen. For more on Nussbaum, see *n*28 Document 84 (Craddock Goins to ER, 18 November 1947; ER to Craddock Goins, November 1947, AERP; *Conscience et Liberté*, No. 65, 2004, 1).

4. For more on ER's efforts on behalf of Yugoslavia, see Document 73, Document 209, Document 215, Document 216, Document 217, Document 218, and Document 222.

5. November 7, the clergymen released their report, "Religion in Yugoslavia," at a closed meeting of clergymen in New York City. Based on the authors' talks with Roman Catholic, Orthodox, and Moslem religious leaders, including the imprisoned Roman Catholic archbishop Aloysius Stepinac, the report said that there was "genuine equality of religion before the law and the beginnings of a true tolerance" although the Americans acknowledged that the possibility of sectarian violence existed. They also distinguished between the political and religious activities of Yugoslav clergy noting that the arrests and subsequent trials of individual clergymen or monks (among them Stepinac whose 1946 conviction on charges of wartime collaboration was a cause célèbre in the West) were "individual cases in which collaboration with the enemy, or acts of sabotage against the Government have been involved. They do not in any way represent persecution of religious groups." At the same time the Americans noted that the Yugoslav church was not able to "speak out prophetically" on questions of national interest ("Cushing Assails 7 Pastors on Tito," *NYT*, 20 August 1947, 10; "Clergymen Report on Yugoslav Visit," *NYT*, 7 November 1947, 16; "Report on Yugoslavs Given to Clergymen," *NYT*, 8 November 1947, 9; "Cardinal Stepinac Dead at 61; Was Imprisoned by Yugoslavia," *NYT*, 11 February 1960, 1; Alexander, *Triple*, 186).

6. Nussbaum, who served as a volunteer physician in Serbia at the beginning of World War I, was married to a member of the Serbian nobility and maintained a network of contacts in Yugoslavia. He had already made at least two trips to Yugoslavia in 1947 and he planned to go again in December. ER described Nussbaum to Craddock Goins as "a reputable man ... who has for many years traveled throughout Europe in the interest of seeking freedom of religion of various Protestant

denominations and who knows people from former governments and present day governments" (Bert Beach e-mail to Mary Jo Binker, 30 May 2005; Dr. Jean Nussbaum to ER, 20 January 1947 and 28 July 1947; ER to Craddock Goins, November 1947, AERP).

7. Writing of Nussbaum to Craddock Goins, ER said, he "told me … it was entirely truthful to say there was freedom of religion in practice and in teaching" (ER to Craddock Goins, November 1947, AERP).

8. On October 24, ER called for freedom of the press in Committee Three (Social, Economic and Humanitarian) of the United Nations General Assembly in response to a Yugoslav resolution condemning the "slanderous dissemination" of news. While she acknowledged that "things are said in the United States by irresponsible persons and press organs which might better be left unsaid," ER said the Soviet Union distorted the facts and conducted a "systematic" propaganda campaign against the United States. In her October 27 column, ER noted the similarity between the Yugoslav resolution and the Soviet resolution on freedom of the press then under consideration in Committee One (Political and Security). In September, Soviet Foreign Minister Andrei Vyshinsky had accused the United States, Greece, and Turkey of violating the UN Charter by disseminating "criminal propaganda" against the Soviet Union and called on the UN to condemn such action. He subsequently tried to convince the delegates that the western democracies could punish "warmongers" within their borders "without infringing on freedom of the press"—a position that the United States and Great Britain adamantly opposed.

Committee One defeated the Soviet resolution on October 27 by a vote of 55 to 0. In its place the committee approved a resolution condemning "all forms of propaganda in any country" that could threaten peace or lead to aggression. On October 29, Committee Three voted 49 to 1 to accept a compromise resolution that condemned the spreading of false news and slanderous reports that might disrupt international peace. The vote came after ER asked the Soviet Union to cease its warmongering charges, "acknowledge the basic differences between Eastern and Western countries and seek some means of cooperation." For more on ER's work on freedom of the press as an international issue, see Document 270 (Thomas J. Hamilton, "Broader Freedom of the Press Is Urged By Mrs. Roosevelt," *NYT*, 25 October 1947, 1; *MD*, 27 October 1947; Frank S. Adams, "Russian Urges Gag," *NYT*, 19 September 1947, 1; "Amity Plea Made by Mrs. Roosevelt," *NYT*, 29 October 1947, 10; "U.N. Group, 49 to 1, Hits At False News," *NYT*, 30 October 1947, 19; Thomas J. Hamilton, "U.N. Peace Appeal Adopted, Replacing 'Warmonger' Ban," *NYT*, 28 October 1947, 1).

9. The United Nations International Conference on Freedom of the Press was scheduled to be held in March 1948 in Geneva, Switzerland. The month-long meeting would be marked by continued East-West sparring over the role of the press and result in the approval of three conventions—a US-sponsored convention to facilitate the work of foreign correspondents, a British-sponsored convention to establish principles for freedom of information, and a French-sponsored convention to insure the international right of correction of alleged false reports (Thomas J. Hamilton, "Broader Freedom of the Press Is Urged by Mrs. Roosevelt," *NYT*, 25 October 1947, 1; Kenneth Campbell, "Free Press Drafts Adopted at Geneva," *NYT*, 22 April, 1948, 3).

On the Rights of Displaced Persons

In late 1947, Soviet and US delegates to the United Nations and their allies continued to clash over the future of displaced persons still housed in camps in Western Europe, with the Soviets and their allies continuing to call for repatriation of all nationals from Eastern Europe and the USSR. The conflict had dogged UN debates around the creation of the International Refugee Organization and many camps remained in operation, with the future of their residents unresolved.[1]

November 6, in the midst of a debate on this issue, Ukrainian delegate Stephen P. Demchenko argued:

> The United Kingdom and the United States occupation authorities had placed traitors, nazis and fascists in charge of the displaced persons camps. He cited numerous instances of camps in which the authorities consisted of nazis and traitors. The facts showed that the United States and the United Kingdom had conducted a systematic campaign against repatriation.
>
> The United Kingdom and United States occupation authorities had permitted the establishment of several committees and organizations hostile to his country and to the other popular democracies. Those committees were publishing newspapers and conducting pro-immigration and anti-repatriation propaganda.[2]

ER promptly responded. Later that afternoon, the US Mission released the following unofficial transcript of ER's rebuttal.[3]

_273_

Remarks by Eleanor Roosevelt
Press Release #312
United States Mission to the United Nations
6 November 1947 [New York City]

For immediate release

Mr. Chairman:

I have already spoken and made my position clear on the Soviet resolution.[4] The last speech, however, which was made by the Honorable Delegate from Ukraine was only on the Soviet resolution and I thought that we were discussing the three resolutions that are before us. Therefore, I shall be extremely brief on the subject of the Soviet resolution.

There are only a few remarks that I want to make. Simply, that I have listened with a great deal of interest to the accusations made here. They are very serious accusations. I had thought that where there were found to be quislings and traitors anywhere, if you produced prima facie evidence, they had to be returned. Therefore, if you know that they are in the camps and in responsible positions, produce the evidence. Do not just talk about it here. That I think is the first thing that struck me as you were talking.

The other thing about the newspapers. Of course there are newspapers by what you call anti-repatriation groups. There are particularly anti-repatriation groups. There are groups probably that wish to help people who do not wish to return home. Now _you_ say such people do not exist. You assert one thing, we assert another. I think the only thing that you can do, Sir, is to furnish me with all the names which you mentioned here today and the proof and I will give you my word that I will see that they go to our authorities and that an investigation is made. More than that I cannot do, to show at least that I have good faith. I think it entirely proper since no one is forced to read a paper, that any information on both sides of the question be presented and available in any camp.

Now I am only going to take one point which my colleague from Bylorussia mentioned this morning.[5] There are many things which we can take up, but one point I happen to know about. He spoke of a plan which had the backing of one of our Senators, Senator Brewster from Maine, and he spoke of it as being an accomplished fact, and I happen to know that it was turned down and it was turned down because our authorities found that they did not approve of it.[6] Now, gentlemen, little inaccuracies of that kind are unfortunate because other things might be inaccurate too. That just happens to be one thing which I happen to know intimately from the beginning and therefore I happen to know it was inaccurate, but it is unfortunate to bring up a point of that kind; and then there is one other point that I wish to explain again. In the United States over the past few years we have been constantly passing laws which restrict immigration. I am sorry Sir, but the immigration into this country is very small. The quotas from different countries are set under the law, so that if we want to help, if there really are people who want to come to this country and we want to help, we will have to change those laws; and I assure you it will not be done with ease. So to talk about recruiting for cheap labor to come to this country is utter and complete nonsense. That is all that I am going to take the time to say on these two rather lengthy accusatory speeches which have been delivered.

TPr AERP, FDRL

---

1. Their arguments echoed earlier disputes in the General Assembly: see header Document 86; Document 90, including header; and ER's response, Document 91. On related debates surrounding formation of the IRO, see Document 152, especially *n7*; header Document 168. On developments in 1947 and ER's commentary on repatriation of refugees, see Document 207 and *n4* Document 244.

2. Summary Record of the Third Committee, Seventy-Eighth Meeting, A/C.3/SR-50-82 (1947), 194, RM, MWelC.

3. Mission staff noted on the top of this document: Following is an unofficial transcript of remarks by Mrs. Franklin D. Roosevelt in Committee III (Social, Humanitarian and Cultural). These remarks preceded Mrs. Roosevelt's statement given to the press as press release #309.

4. As recorded in the Summary Record for November 4, ER "reminded the Committee" during the November 4 debate "that the substance of the USSR resolution had already been discussed at length the previous year when the International Refugee Organization had been created. Moreover, a USSR proposal, which had been rejected a fortnight ago by the Sixth Committee at its fifty-third meeting, was drafted in almost identical terms." She then proceeded to counter the Soviet resolution point by point, taking exception to assertions including that Western occupation authorities were preventing or delaying the repatriation of large numbers of displaced persons (DPs) who wished to return to their countries of origin; had restricted access to DP camps; and sought to resettle DPs in new countries where they would be exploited. A summary of ER's statements during the November 4 meeting appears in UND: RM: A/C.3/SR-50-82 (1947), 182–83; a summary of the November 6 debate follows on 195–96.

5. Leonid Ivanovitch Kaminsky (1907-?), a member of the Byelorussian diplomatic service since 1944, served as a representative on a range of early UN bodies (*UN Yearbook 1947-48*, 1069; "Russia Seeks Curb on U.N. News Draft," *NYT*, 22 August 1948, 6).

6. Kaminsky asserted, "Instead of repatriating the displaced persons, the Governments of the United States, the United Kingdom, Belgium, Argentina, Brazil and other countries now planned to agree on a quota system to divide up the cheap labour available in the camps for their own use." He cited "a plan submitted by Senator Ralph Owen Brewster (R-ME) to the United States Congress" as one of the proofs of his assertion. Brewster (1888-1961) had endorsed plans by manufacturer Frank Cohen to turn Passamaquoddy ("Quoddy"), Maine, into a temporary industrial training center for thousands of European DPs from the American zone of Germany, equipping them for future factory work in South America. When a tidal power project sponsored by President Roosevelt in the mid-1930s faltered in the face of political opposition, the village on the northern Maine coastline—not far from Campobello—had become a ghost town. Yet Cohen's proposal provoked the ire of labor unions, which denounced it as a "cruel program for the exploitation of many thousands of displaced persons in Europe." The War Assets Administration, the surplus property agency in charge of evaluating bids on the facilities, eventually rejected the scheme as "essentially industrial rather than educational in character." ER countered Kaminsky by pointing out that Brewster's plan had been rejected and immigration opportunities to the United States remained so low that her country "could hardly be accused of trying to recruit labour in the camps" (On the project touted by Brewster see: "Project at Quoddy Pushed by Cohen," *NYT*, 15 August 1947, 15; Frank L. Kluckhohn," "'Slave Labor' Disclaimed in 'Quoddy' Plan for DP's," *NYT*, 21 August 1947, 1; "Declared 'Cruel' Program," *NYT*, 22 August 1947, 5; Samuel A. Tower, "'Quoddy' DP Training Program Condemned by WAA Labor Group," *NYT*, 24 August 1947, 1; "'Quoddy' Plan Held Ineligible by WAA," *NYT*, 28 August 1947, 11; Finding aid, ROBP, MeB; A/C.3/SR-50-82 (1947), 189–92, 195–96).

"MRS. ROOSEVELT PUTS FUTURE UP TO WOMEN"

274

Eleanor Roberts Interviews Eleanor Roosevelt
Boston Sunday Post 9 November 1947

LAKE SUCCESS, N.Y., Nov. 8—More than anything else in the world today women want peace!

They want it because World war II brought home to them forcefully—through personal loss and privation—the necessity of it.

What they do not know, however, is quite how to go about making that peace.

Yet every woman, from the wealthy young matron with a Radcliffe degree to the scrubwoman who never got beyond the fourth grade, should take an active part in shaping the future.

There is perhaps no greater authority on the role women will assume in the world of tomorrow than Mrs. Eleanor Roosevelt who sits on the United Nations' famous committee number three.

In an exclusive interview with the Sunday Post, Mrs. Roosevelt outlined fearlessly and constructively a workable plan that women everywhere can adopt.

She didn't pull any punches.

And she didn't make it sound easy.

Just very worth while.

When she spoke of the great need women have for self-discipline it was the facing of a fact—not the scoring of a human frailty.

She criticized the present school system for women's lack of ability to concentrate, but she did it gently, just as she remarked that she hoped one day the world would realize that a woman may have as good a brain as a man.

We saw Mrs. Roosevelt first at her Washington sq. apartment, in a comfortably cluttered room where cretonne-covered chairs and exotic Chinese objects of art blended in a happy harmony.[1]

There was about her apartment the same catholicity of taste that characterizes Eleanor Roosevelt herself. It was evident in the Chinese temple bell that sat complacently next to the French period clock on her mantel, and in the companionship of a nicely-bound "Little Iliad" crammed in tightly beside a 25-cent paper covered "Rubaiyat" on her bookshelves.

She wore a violet wool dress and the moment she came forward to take your hand you knew, no matter what your politics or your party, that here was a really great woman.

The only picture of the late President in the room was on the mantel in a wide silver frame, engraved with the personal signatures of such close friends and associates as Marvin McIntyre and Louis McHenry Howe.

It was not the NRA Roosevelt or the tired third-term Roosevelt who led the nation through its greatest crisis.[2] It was the "Happiest Warrior" as Governor of New York and in his own handwriting at the bottom was scrawled, "For E.R., with F.D.R's love."[3]

The former First Lady did not talk about the President or her days in the White House and of the United Nations she spoke only briefly.

She did discuss, with understanding and concern, the tremendous task women of the United States face today in contributing to a sound peace.

That they should have a far greater goal than the acquisition of a mink coat and the presidency of the local bridge club, Mrs. Roosevelt made very clear.

"Not that I object to a mink coat," she smiled. "I think it's perfectly all right to enjoy one if your sense of values is in good order so that owning one doesn't become the most important thing in your life—so that not having one doesn't make you miserable.

"As a country we give too much thought to material things. We can remedy this to a great extent by making both our schools and our churches more dynamic centres in the life of the community, so that they really lead in our thinking.

"I have known communities where teachers cannot say what they think because the school board wouldn't like it. And we only get value out of our teachers if they can think by themselves and have the opportunity to express those thoughts.

"There may be mistakes, but we all make mistakes. It is the only way to grow. If we don't grow we get static and we find ourselves with a community that has little interest."

To Mrs. Roosevelt's mind every woman has definite responsibilities in shaping the world of tomorrow. That they have been lax in shouldering those responsibilities is not strange to her.

Women demanded and received the right to vote; they practice professions and own property. Yet thousands of them have no active voice in the governing of their country, in affairs of the world because of what seems a typically feminine shying away from such things.

"It takes a long time after winning the right to vote to realize that the right itself isn't sufficient, that exercising that franchise doesn't save the peace of the world if it can be saved.

"We are just waking up to the fact that there are other things to do. Most important is making democracy work in our own localities.

"Until the last war most of us didn't know what went on. We ran our homes and were interested in clubs and it was all we needed. We were not concerned about the world because it didn't seem, even if we were, that there was much we could do about it.

"We are gradually realizing, however, that we must do something about it. The crisis that war brings about reaches down into our whole lives. During the war we had to learn self-discipline; we had to go without. We learned how to run our homes better, how to be both mother and father to our children.

"After it was over we thought we'd go back, only to find we couldn't. After four years of struggle and bloodshed the dislocation in people and in things was far too great to go back.

"Some of the boys who went overseas weren't the same when they came home and some of the men who bore the terrific burdens of war can't do it now.

"We objected to rationing but we found we had forces far beyond those we realized. And today we find that while we haven't rationing in the sense of red points and blue points we have rationing of a different sort because we can't afford to pay for the food.

"Women have never before faced the fact that they are a part of the world. It took the lesson of war to show it to us. There was the war of 1917, to be sure, but it seems we have to learn things all over again the hard way."

Emphasizing that participating in world events means that women will have a "quick broadening of their horizons," the former First Lady outlined the steps American women who are better fed and better sheltered than almost any other women in the world, can take.

"If I were a housewife," Mrs. Roosevelt declared, "I would begin by doing things right in my own locality. I would see what people are holding office, what measures have been passed in my town, what the people who are running for office stand for.

"Then I would ask myself, 'Do they really represent the kind of thinking I want?'"

In spite of the great number of women voters in the United States a great majority of them are hard put to tell you who is running for office, let alone investigating the viewpoint of the candidate.

Mrs. Roosevelt attributes this lack of interest in local politics on the part of women, partly to an inertia due to little self-discipline and partly to our present educational system.

"We don't know how to plan our lives," she explained. "It is even harder for the housewife to school herself to be interested in local politics because the pattern of her life requires the least self-discipline. She is not bounded by factory rules. Her time is her own to do with what she wants. And although this involves cooking and cleaning and caring for children, it means she can pretty well arrange the day as she wishes. There is no time clock to punch, no boss to report to.

"It will take an enormous amount of individual adjustment for the average housewife to bring herself to the point where she can and will make time to take an active part in her community affairs.

Ask any housewife why she didn't go to the town meetings, why she hasn't investigated the platforms of the men who run for office, why she isn't working actively in the particular cause her community is pushing and she will inevitably reply, "I haven't the time. I'm all tied up with my children."

To this Mrs. Roosevelt replies, "Make the time. Order your day so that you will have time. It can be done, but it takes effort and it takes self-discipline.

"We must learn that being slaves to our children is not good for them, that being a drudge is not good for our husbands or our friends or our neighbors—or the world!

"If the housewife's world is bounded entirely by the four walls of her home, if she has no outside contacts she is likely to become a drudge. When there are no outside contacts nothing is accomplished, there is no inspiration. She is not taking anything in.

"The unselfish, intelligent mother who gives her children love and care and affection cannot be criticized for her outside interests."

What the average woman hasn't learned to do, Mrs. Roosevelt is convinced, is to plan her leisure time well.

It dribbles away ineffectually, giving her little satisfaction because she has given so little thought to how her leisure can be used most effectively.

"Certainly give some of your leisure time to the things you enjoy doing, to the little pleasures that relax you and make you happy, but don't, for example, give it all to the movies or to idle chatting."

Probably nobody speaks with more authority on this subject than Mrs. Roosevelt whose amazing record in public life has proven beyond any doubt the results of a day carefully planned.

Granted that she has an enormous amount of energy, that because of her early training she can marshal her thoughts and ideas into an orderly procession, it has still taken careful planning and much self-discipline to accomplish what she has.

Throughout the interview the word "self-discipline" wove an intricate thread. This is because "self-discipline" is the foundation-stone of her whole life, and because she believes that it is what women need badly.

Through this medium they can school themselves to take an interest in local politics and community affairs although they have little natural inclination to do so.

"To this day," smiled Mrs. Roosevelt, "I am grateful that I had to learn Latin in school. Not only because of the value it has proven to be to me, but mostly because it trained my powers to do something they didn't like to do.

"I hated Latin," she admitted with frankness, "but I had to learn it. I was fortunate in having a childhood where self-discipline was the law and I have always felt that it enables a child to make adjustments easier and meet disappointment and trial better when he becomes an adult."

Urging women to take an active part in politics because in this manner she can actually help to shape the new peace, Mrs. Roosevelt said, "I think we should join any organization that will bring our collective strength to bear, such as the League of Women Voters' in your locality, the PTA, or take active part in your party headquarters group.

"Certainly if I lived in a rural community where these larger organizations did not exist I would join the home and farm bureau so that I could get more knowledge on the way to live.

"If I were a working girl I would take an active part in whatever my union offers in the way of educational information and activities.

"The political world," she smiled, "is a rough and tumble one. You must be self-disciplined and you must learn to train yourself to become indifferent to criticism that is not constructive, to 'take things.'"

Perhaps few other women know just how rough and tumble the political world is better than Eleanor Roosevelt. Few have been under such withering verbal fire and acquitted themselves as well. During her husband's administration as President for three terms she has been batted around like a shuttlecock by a legion of critics and staunchly defended by an even greater legion of supporters.

Yet she has emerged from bitter controversy unscathed, a gracious, serene woman who today is America's delegate to the United Nations.

It is this tenacity to stick to what she thinks is right regardless of personal criticism that makes the former First Lady such a champion of the right to think and speak freely.

"In a democracy we must watch that what one does is not restricted," she warned. Ever since those earlier days when Roger Williams was driven out of Boston for his religious liberalism there has been a tendency to restrict thought.[4] "At the end of a war this becomes even greater because fears are greater.

"Although there is some reason for taking certain steps," she remarked, "I believe the way in which the State Department has conducted the so-called 'loyalty tests' is quite wrong.[5]

"I think first, that everyone is entitled to a hearing, and second that we must be more careful about whom we employ.

"The care should be exercised in the beginning, before they are employed. The present 'tests' would not seem to achieve the end they desire because a communist would have no scruples about lying.

"We must not, however, go to the other extreme and shut our eyes to all safeguards. Yet we must remember that we live in a democracy where our earliest freedom was the right to think and to express those thoughts.

"If people don't like it," said Mrs. Roosevelt gently, "then it is no concern of theirs."

It is this "freedom of thought" that Mrs. Roosevelt urges the women of America to fight for. She blames, in part, the poor reading tastes of the average woman on the libraries.

"Largely they aren't liberal enough. There is not a wide enough choice and sufficient discussion on both sides of the question.

"While I am not a convinced advocate of the comic books as the sole reading of children neither am I a strong advocate of a strictly classical education. Yet I feel that children miss a lot in having so much to keep them busy today.

"They have so much that they actually don't have anything in the end. Cars, radios, movies!

"Why, I spent five months of the year in the country where there was nothing to do except read books.

"You see very few children today browsing in the library. They come in and get what they want and leave. The days of browsing over the bookshelves are rare and I think they have lost a great deal."

Concerned with the inability of the majority of women to become interested in reading world news and to digest it, Mrs. Roosevelt suggests that women discipline themselves in their reading habits, too.

For the, "Oh, I'm too busy to read the paper" gal, Mrs. Roosevelt proposes the plan she uses herself in reading the papers.

"I read the headlines carefully," she explained, "and then I select what I think I should read first, and then what appeals to me.

"As for the reading of good books, this can be attained best through the medium of discussion groups. Talking about the book means we must read it carefully, for how can we discuss it unless it has been read—not breezily, but carefully?"

The ideal discussion group, to Mrs. Roosevelt's mind, is the one composed of both men and women, but she readily admits that it is usually necessary to start with women first.

As for men, her sisters everywhere will champion her statement that America's home life (where peace and harmony begin) would be better for the participation of men in home tasks.

This does not apply to men with working wives only. If a man gave some of his time at home to helping his wife with the chores, to being with the children it would release her to do some work in the community—enable her to have some contact outside the home, Mrs. Roosevelt declared.

To those who are concerned with the fight against communism, Mrs. Roosevelt has this to say.

"The real way to fight communism is to make democracy work. It's the most successful way of fighting it!

"Communism is an economy of misery. When the people are unable to manage their own affairs, they turn to someone else. It is, however, a very different thing from fascism.

"The Russians have a love of country that is very deep. They have adopted certain methods of doing things because they have come of a depression. We must remember that a country once only 10 per cent literate is now almost 90 per cent literate.

"What they are doing, repressive as it is, indicates that the present methods can't go on because they have an educated people, and it just won't work!

"As for our battle against it, as I said before, the very best weapon we have, is making democracy—here!"

PNews AERP, FDRL

----

1. ER lived at 29 Washington Square West in Greenwich Village.

2. The National Recovery Administration (NRA), a major component of the early New Deal, attempted to stabilize the economy by regulating prices, wages, and production. In his third term (1941–44), FDR led the nation into and through most of World War II (*FDRE*).

3. Although Roberts associates the moniker with him, FDR actually called Al Smith "the Happy Warrior of the political battlefield" when nominating Smith for president at the 1924 Democratic National Convention (*FDRE*).

4. The Puritans banished Roger Williams (1603?-1683) from Massachusetts Bay Colony for his unorthodox religious beliefs and defense of liberty of conscience. He founded the colony of Rhode Island (*RCAH*).

5. For the loyalty tests and the way the State Department handled the firing of employees identified as security risks, see *n*6 Document 271, *n*1 Document 277, and *n*3 Document 253.

Youthful Inquiry into
UN Decision-Making

Middle and high school students often wrote ER, requesting interviews or advice. As the following exchange between a New Jersey high school student and ER illustrates, ER took their requests seriously, often dictating her response to her secretary rather than sending standard, formulaic replies.

275

Louis Darabant to Eleanor Roosevelt
12 November 1947 [Cleveland]

Dear Mrs. Roosevelt:

We the students of Thomas A. Edison School were discussing United Nation Organization problems and we came across this question, "Why doesn't the General Assembly start immediate action for a United Nation's Army?" Why not set aside political problems for the time being because these problems will always arise from time to time. Just how could the U.N. enforce the peace if a war were to break out now?[1]

What about the Dutch and Indonesian Civil War for instance?[2] Shouldn't a U.N. Army be on hand to settle those outbreaks? You don't need an Army when there is peace, why not organize one now to get peace in the world?

Sincerely yours,
Louis J. Darabant

TLS AERP, FDRL

After reading the student's letter, ER then dictated the following response.[3]

276

Eleanor Roosevelt to Louis Darabant
27 November 1947 [New York City]

Dear Mr. Darabant:

In answer to your letter of November 12th, the United Nations could use the armies of any of the present big powers if need arose for the use of force. As a matter of fact it is hoped that even after some form of force has been worked out, it will not be necessary if the UN worked well, to use it.

The Economic and Social Council and the commissions under it, are designed to keep things from reaching the boiling point and to prevent the need of force. If they come to the boiling they go to the Security Council and only the Security can order the use of force.

The Dutch Indonesian situation is one that is being handled now with a good deal of tact. One hopes that other troops will not have to go in.[4]

Very sincerely yours,

TLc AERP, FDRL

---

1. Article 47 of the UN Charter provided for the creation of a "Military Staff Committee to advise and assist the Security Council on all questions relating to the Security Council's military requirements for the maintenance of international peace and security, the employment and command of forces placed at its disposal, the regulation of armaments, and possible disarmament." However, in the late 1940s the Security Council remained unable to reach a unanimous decision regarding the establishment of a UN military force and thus the committee functions were suspended. Article 43 of the charter also held that the UN could retain military volunteers from UN member nations to create a force when necessary to maintain international peace. The first of such operations consisted of a military observer mission to Palestine in May 1948 (*EUN*, 838, 850).

2. See *n*25 Document 71.

3. ER scrawled "dictate" across the bottom of Durabant's letter to her, instructing her secretary that she would dictate her reply.

4. Prior to World War II, Indonesia remained a colony of the Netherlands. Following the removal of the occupying Japanese at the end of the war, Great Britain and the Netherlands kept up a troop presence in Indonesia. In August 1945, the Indonesian People's Movement declared their independence, but the occupying nations refused to acknowledge the declaration. In the summer of 1947, the Security Council created an Information Commission to consider the situation in Indonesia. By November 1949, the UN Commission for Indonesia obtained recognition by the Dutch for the sovereignty of Indonesia except for the territory of West Irian (*EUN*, 381).

ON LOYALTY OATHS

November 2, 1947, the *New York Herald Tribune* published a multipage article by Bert Andrews, its Washington correspondent, describing in great detail the experience of one of the ten men summarily dismissed from the State Department as part of its loyalty program investigations. Entitled "A State Department Security Case: The Story of an Employee Dismissed After an 8-Month F.B.I. Investigation, With the Nature of the Charges Against Him Never Revealed," Andrews's investigation produced "the first such description to be published … a point-by-point story of how the investigation was conducted by the F.B.I. and what the State Department did." Quoting at length from affidavits given by the unnamed man and a transcript of a "hearing" with his State Department superiors, Andrews documented treatment the man received from departmental investigators and recounted how the department repeatedly blocked his attempts to know and respond to the charges against him.

Conceding that "there is no way for any one outside the top echelon to know whether the individual is a victim of a 'witch hunt'" or not, Andrews pressed the State Department for its response to his findings. When confronted by the reporter, the State Department acknowledged "that it was entirely conceivable that an entirely innocent man might be made the victim of a frame-up, granting the unlikely possibility that sufficient enemies ganged up on him" and "that under present procedure, such an innocent man would have no more recourse, no more chance of demanding and getting the charges against him, than would say, an individual guilty of disloyalty and violating security." The department then announced that "it would be very glad if some system of review could be established which would insure any accused individual of the right to have a real review made of his case—a review that would satisfy everyone that no violation of civil liberties had been committed." [1]

Andrews's article and her unhappiness over the actions of the State Department prompted ER to write the following letter to Truman objecting to the loyalty investigations and to his most recent appointments to the Loyalty Review Board.

277

Eleanor Roosevelt to Harry Truman
13 November 1947 [New York City]

Dear Mr. President,

I have wanted to write you for a long time as I have been getting from all of my friends, Republicans and Democratics alike, such violent reactions to the Loyalty Tests. And now, after the dismissal of the ten people from the State Department, and the article in the Herald Tribune, I feel I must write you.

I do not feel that Dr. Meta Glass should be the only woman on the Committee for Review as she is not a strong enough person. I feel more people, not lawyers, should be on and another woman might well be appointed. Perhaps Mrs. Lewis Thompson of Red Bank, New Jersey, who is a strong Republican but also a liberal, might help to interpret the work of this Committee to the public. Certain things need to be interpreted to the public.[2] My own reaction is anything but happy. I feel we have capitulated to our fear of Communism, and instead of fighting to improve Democracy, we are doing what the Soviets would do in trying to repress anything which we are afraid might not command public support, in order to insure acceptance of our own actions.

I am sorry that I cannot see you before I go to Geneva to the Human Rights Commission meetings and since this session of the General Assembly is drawing to an end, I want to thank you for your kindness in appointing me. It has been interesting work and I hope that I have been helpful. When I return from Geneva and the holidays are over, I will try to come to Washington in order to see you again.

With best wishes to Mrs. Truman and Margaret, and congratulations to her on her successes, and wishing you all a Happy Thanksgiving and Christmas season, I am,

Very sincerely yours,
Eleanor Roosevelt

TLS HSTOF, HSTL

Truman waited to respond until Marshall had informed ER of the new procedures the administration implemented in its loyalty investigations.

278

Harry Truman to Eleanor Roosevelt
26 November 1947 [The White House]

Dear Mrs. Roosevelt:

Your letter of November thirteenth was of great personal interest to me, and I have read it with sympathetic reactions to the ideas you express. I can well understand that you may be disturbed by some of the articles and summaries that have been published about the loyalty review of the present incumbents and new employees of the civil service posts.

I have told the Civil Service Commission, the members of the Loyalty Review Board, and the Press that I did not wish this inquiry to become a "witch hunt", but rather to establish what I think is the truth, that the overwhelming number of civil servants in the United States are not only faithful and loyal, but devoted patriots. It is, of course, contrary to American tradition to inquire into the political or philosophical views of anyone, and I think that is why all of us feel a certain repugnance to this program, but I became convinced that it was necessary, not because, as you say, "we were trying to repress anything we were afraid might not command public support", but because there were certain indications of a small infiltration of seriously disloyal people into certain sensitive parts of the Government. The disclosures of the Canadian Government, and in particular the report of the Canadian Civil Service Commission as to the way in which previously quite innocent and simple people had been trapped and led into a situation of securing and revealing information to agents of another government—contrary to all instructions and policies of Government service—were sufficient to convince me that we had to make some positive and constructive inquiry into the state of affairs in our own civil service.[3]

The Civil Service Commission, into whose hands I placed most of the development of the program, is cautious and fully aware of the Constitutional rights of human beings that need to be protected. We all must remind ourselves that no one has a Constitutional right to work for the Government. He has a Constitutional right to express himself and his opinions any way he chooses, and to associate himself with organizations that are quite opposed to the Government, or even to attempt to alter the Constitution, but it is not appropriate that he should carry on such activities while working for the Government of the United States.

The Loyalty Review Board which is made up of distinguished persons outside the Government is, I think, going to prove not only an aid in distinguishing the true from the false and in uncovering actual disloyalty, but it will also serve to protect the civil liberties of individuals in this new and unusual field.

I am interested in your reaction to the Board, and I do want to tell you of a very great difficulty which we experienced in finding enough of the right kind of people to serve.[4] There are a good many lawyers on the Board, I agree. The reason for having so many lawyers is that it is hoped that the Board will sit in panels of three on the cases, and that at least one lawyer will be a member of each panel. A legal mind, while it may be narrow in some instances, is, as I think you know, very strong on the right and proper procedures for the handling of witnesses and the establishing of true evidence as against rumor and slander, before making a conclusion of fact that the individual charged with an offense is guilty. I really believe that a sound, conservative, legal mind will be of great assistance in establishing a proper method of carrying on this inquiry.

However, there are still several posts to be filled on the Loyalty Review Board, and we are attempting to secure a number of other persons of broad public interests who are not lawyers. I have noted with interest your recommendation of Mrs. Lewis Thompson of Red Bank, New Jersey, and I will send her name to the Civil Service Commission with the suggestion that they look into that possibility.[5]

I am grateful for your letter because I am always glad to have your views.

Thank you very much for your good wishes and your congratulations to Margaret on her successes as a singer.

I hope that you will come to see me when you return from Geneva.

Very sincerely yours,
Harry S. Truman

TLS AERP, FDRL

> The same day ER expressed her concerns to the president, she wrote the secretary of state to register her dismay over the department's administration of its loyalty program and to give the secretary notice that she would make her opinion known in My Day "as soon as the Assembly came to an end."

279

Eleanor Roosevelt to George Marshall

13 November 1947 [New York City]

My dear Mr. Secretary,

I had hoped to see you or talk with you over the telephone before you left for Europe, however, I am afraid now you will be off before I have the chance to do so.[6] I wish you well on your trip! It looks to me as though the Russians had reached the point where they wanted to come to terms.[7] I certainly hope so.

There is one thing which has troubled me very greatly. Being on the delegation, I have felt that I could not write about it in my column but I shall do so as soon as the Assembly comes to an end, and before doing so I want to tell you what my feeling is.[8] From every side, from all my Liberal, Democratic and Republican, friends I am getting protests on the State Department's attitude towards the people which it has dismissed. I know it was not a policy initiated by you, but evidently Mr. Lovett felt that he had to go along with it and you felt that you had to back him up. The story in the Herald Tribune has made a deep impression on a lot of people.[9]

There is a rumor in this city that you had to dismiss these people because Mr. Tabor sent you the list and refused any further appropriations unless they were dismissed.[10] I know what pressure Congress can bring to bear. I do not know whether this story is true or not but it seems to me that even Congress would have to recognize that in peacetime, things which might be condoned in wartime, take on a different aspect. People are entitled to a hearing or else resigning without prejudice. The situation will soon be that a person who leaves the State Department unless he is offered a job before leaving, is going to find it hard to get another job as people will think there is something against him. I am not very happy about the President's Loyalty Test because any Communist would sign to it and the rest of us feel a little besmirched as we sign, and not quite sure that our country is a strong enough Democracy not to fear Communism.

I have written the President a letter and I enclose a copy of it.[11] As I go to the Human Rights Commission meetings I am not quite sure that I think our country is preserving its freedoms by strengthening the democratic and refusing the repressive processes.[12]

I hope to leave for home on the 18th of December. I hope that you too will be coming home then from an entirely successful meeting.

Sincerely yours,
Eleanor Roosevelt

TLS RG59, NARA II

> Marshall, who was preparing to leave November 20 for the Council of Foreign Ministers meeting in London, asked Undersecretary of State Robert Lovett to reply to ER's letter and to explain the "reversal" of the department's "earlier position."

280

Robert Lovett to Eleanor Roosevelt
22 November 1947 [Washington, DC]

Personal and Confidential

Dear Mrs. Roosevelt:

The Secretary of State, just prior to his departure,[13] gave me your personal note of November 13 and asked me to reply to it in his behalf.

With respect to the dismissal by the State Department in June of ten employees as "security risks", I believe you will find that the enclosed press release dated November 17 answers one part of your question.[14] It represents a reversal of the State Department's earlier position. In view of the fact that the State Department procedure throughout was based on the assumption that an impartial appeal would be available to these employees, I felt this reversal should be ordered unless appeal was granted. At the first meeting of the newly appointed Loyalty Board, it was decided on technical grounds that this appeal was not available.[15] Accordingly, the only decent thing to do was to let these former employees resign without prejudice since they had not had a fair opportunity to clear themselves because the classified character of the material received by the State Department from other agencies could not be made public except on appeal. And without knowing the charges, obviously the men could not clear themselves. We had been assured that the appeal mechanism would provide such an opportunity.

Now that the Loyalty Board is formally set up, I hope that appeal procedures will be rapidly established, because there is nothing more destructive of morale than this type of uncertainty, even where actual injustice may not result.

My connection with the matter is of relatively recent date, as the action took place before I assumed office.[16] It has, therefore, been necessary for me to question the various personnel and administrative officers in the Department in order to reply to the second part of your inquiry, which relates to a rumor that Mr. Taber imposed these dismissals in connection with appropriations. I can find no evidence of this. There were, of course, general accusations made by several Senators and Congressmen that the Department was a hotbed of fellow travellers. I do not think this is so, although I must say that, among the seven dismissed employees, if the intelligence agencies' reports are to be believed, certain incidents are most disturbing.

I do not believe that the Government has yet found a satisfactory solution to this problem. I am equally sure that the extra-sensitive agencies have similarly not found an adequate answer.[17] None of us who feel strongly about certain of our basic rights are happy about the present procedures but I hope that, as the Loyalty Board gets to work, we will get rulings which should clarify the matter and protect the employees and administrators to a greater degree than has been possible in the past.

I have learned from the Secretary of your very real contribution to the American Delegation and of the superb handling of the Human Rights matters in particular. We are deeply indebted to you and I send you warm thanks for your help and your guidance.

With kindest regards, I am

Very sincerely yours,
Robert A. Lovett

TLS AERP, FDRL

After reading Lovett's letter and other material related to the department's change of policy allowing seven previously discharged employees to "resign without prejudice," ER wrote Marshall again, expressing her gratitude.[18]

281

Eleanor Roosevelt to George Marshall
26 November 1947 [New York City]

Dear Mr. Secretary:

I read in the press of the action taken by the Department and I was very glad. I am grateful to you for your letter and for the sense of security it gives me to know that you are watching out for the preservation of certain fundamental democratic procedures.

One of the other rumors which has come to me is that the accusation primarily urged against one of the people under suspicion was that he was an active member of the P.C.A. It happens that I have given up any activities with P.C.A. because I am convinced that there are people in the top level in that organization that still are closely connected with the Communist Party in this country, or who are too chicken hearted and afraid of being called red-baiters.[19] Therefore, they serve the purposes of the party. Nevertheless, I do know a great many people who are active in P.C.A. who are just straight liberals and are sincerely troubled by the hysteria on Communism which is sweeping the country at the present time as well as by certain government actions which rightly or wrongly they feel tend to create an atmosphere which may bring about war. I do not think that any man can just be condemned because he is a member of P.C.A. unless one finds something on which to question his loyalty.

Of course, I am so familiar with rumors I sometimes discount too much and therefore I had not thought about this very seriously, but when two or three people spoke to me about it I decided it was worth mentioning it. I do not doubt that some of these people have questionable things in their record, but I remember when my husband and I heard about a list the F.B.I. had of organizations that were considered subversive and anyone who had contributed to those organizations was automatically considered by the Dies Committee to be questionable.[20] My husband told me I could ask to see it and we spent an evening going through it and believe it or not, my husband's Mother was one of the first people named because she had contributed to a Chinese Relief organization and both Secretary Stimson and Secretary Knox were listed as having contributed to several organizations.[21] Of course it is evident that they could stand up under those accusations but little people would be condemned for as flimsey a reason.

Forgive me for writing a long letter again, but I have been troubled by what looks like a real chance that some of the methods of the Russians might be coming our way.

Very cordially yours,
Eleanor Roosevelt

TLS AERP, FDRL

---

1. For information on the federal loyalty program, see *n*6 Document 271. For information on the firing of the ten State Department employees and on the federal loyalty program, see Document 253, especially *n*3 (Bert Andrews, "A State Department Security Case," *NYHT*, 2 November 1947, 1).

2. The Civil Service Commission's Loyalty Review Board consisted of nongovernmental employees who heard the cases of employees accused of disloyalty. Dr. Meta Glass (1881?–1967), an educator and president of Sweet Briar College in Virginia for twenty-one years, served on this board. ER's suggestion of Mrs. Geraldine Thompson (1872?–1967) as an appointee to the Loyalty Review Board reflected her close friendship with and confidence in a woman who had been a politically active social worker in New Jersey since 1917. Thompson served on state and county committees and remained a delegate at every Republican National Convention from 1920 to 1952 (Donovan, *Conflict*, 294–95; "Dr. Meta Glass, Educator, Dead," *NYT*, 22 March 1967, 47; "Geraldine M. Thompson Dies; Social Worker and G.O.P. Aide," *NYT*, 10 September 1967, 82; Hamby, *Man*, 428–29).

3. In March 1946, the Canadian government revealed the existence of an organized espionage network directed by agents based in the Soviet embassy in Ottawa who had recruited Canadian government employees to obtain secret information on radar and uranium development, the atomic bomb, and other military matters. The government eventually detained thirteen Canadians, including a Communist member of the Canadian parliament. On July 15, 1946, a report prepared by two Canadian Supreme Court judges appointed to look into the circumstances of the case, stated that "perhaps the most startling single aspect of the entire fifth-column network is the uncanny success with which the Soviet agents were able to find Canadians who were willing to betray their country and to supply to agents of a foreign power secret information to which they had access in the course of their work despite oaths of allegiance, of office and of secrecy which they had taken" (P. J. Philip, "4 Named in Ottawa," *NYT*, 5 March 1946, 1; "Rose Called Spy Ring Key," *NYT*,

29 May 1946, 4; P. J. Philip, "Russian Espionage in Canada Called Highly Organized," *NYT* 16 July 1946, 1).

4. The Loyalty Review Board, chaired by Seth W. Richardson (1880–1953), a well-known Republican corporate lawyer, consisted of twenty representatives. The members of the board were: George W. Alger; John Harlan Amen; Harry A. Bigelow; Aaron J. Brumbaugh; John Kirkland Clark; Harry Colmery; Tom J. Davis; Burton L. French; Meta Glass; Earl Harrison; Garrett Hoag; Wilbur La Roe, Jr.; Arthur W. McMahon; Charles E. Merriam; Henry Parkman, Jr.; Albert M. Sames; Charles Sawyer; Murray Seasongood; and Henry L. Shattuck. Of the twenty, eleven were lawyers, two law professors, and one a judge ("20 Lawyers and Scholars Named to Review Federal Loyalty Cases," *NYT*, 9 November 1947, 1; "Guardians of Civil Rights," *NYT*, 10 November 1947, 28; "Seth Richardson, Attorney, Is Dead," *NYT*, 18 March 1953, 31).

5. Truman never appointed Thompson to the Loyalty Review Board and Dr. Meta Glass remained the only woman who served in that capacity ("Guardians of Civil Rights," *NYT*, 10 November 1947, 28).

6. Marshall left on November 20 for the Big Four conference of foreign ministers in London.

7. The United States and the Soviet Union had just reached an agreement at the UN about Palestine; meanwhile, the Russians were showing signs of wanting to reach a settlement on Germany (George Barrett, "U.S.-Soviet Accord on Palestine Asks British Go by May 1," *NYT*, 11 November 1947, 1; Delbert Clark, "Russians in Germany Show Hope for Accord: Signs Multiply that Soviet May Be Preparing to End the Deadlock," *NYT*, 9 November 1947, E4).

8. ER was an employee of the US State Department only when the United Nations was in session.

9. For background on the federal loyalty program and firing of ten State Department employees, see *n*3 Document 253. Truman initiated the loyalty program by issuing Executive Order 9835 on March 22, 1947. The order authorized the dismissal of federal employees on "reasonable grounds" for either holding disloyal political beliefs or for being actually subversive ("State Department Affirms Dropping 7," *NYT*, 4 October 1947, 7; *HSTE*). For the article in the *Herald Tribune*, see the header to Document 277.

10. Republican Congressman John Taber (R-NY) (1880–1965), chairman of the House Appropriations Committee ("Ex-Rep. John Taber Dies at 85; 'Fiscal Vigilante' Led Committee," *NYT*, 23 November 1965, 45).

11. ER's letter to Truman is Document 277.

12. In the draft of this letter retained in ER's papers at the FDR Library, this sentence reads, "… I am not quite sure that I think our country is preserving its freedoms as carefully as I would like" (Draft Letter from ER to George C. Marshall, 1947, AERP).

13. "Marshall Leaves Today By Air for Big 4 Talks," *NYT*, 20 November 1947, 22.

14. The November 17 press release reported that three of the ten State Department employees who had been dismissed as security risks had been allowed to resign without prejudice after an internal review. The other seven sought to appeal to the newly established Loyalty Review Board in the Civil Service Commission but the board ruled on November 15 that it had no jurisdiction in their cases. Since no other avenues of appeal existed for them, the State Department "has concluded that in order to avoid a possible injustice to them, they should be permitted to resign without prejudice. Furthermore, in view of the great importance which the Department attaches to the right of appeal for its employees, it is taking all steps to insure that its employees will have the right of appeal to the Loyalty Review Board in the future" (For the Press, Department of State, 17 November 1947, No. 909, AERP).

15. President Truman appointed the Loyalty Review Board on November 8 ("20 Lawyers and Scholars Named to Review Federal Loyalty Cases," *NYT*, 9 November 1947, 1). For background

on the loyalty program, see *n3* Document 253 and *n6* Document 271. For the membership of the Loyalty Review Board, see *n4* above.

16. Lovett assumed office as undersecretary of state on July 1, 1947 (Edward B. Lockett, "Robert Lovett—Co-Pilot of 'State,'" *NYT,* 17 August 1947, 112).

17. The "extra-sensitive" agencies included the Department of State and the newly formed Central Intelligence Agency (CIA) ("The Nation," *NYT,* 9 November 1947, E2).

18. The *New York Times,* for example, reported on the shift in State Department policy on November 18 ("7 'Bad Risks' Allowed to Resign in Shift by State Department," *NYT,* 18 November 1947, 1).

19. For background on the PCA and ER's position on Communists within the leadership of the organization, see the header to Document 173, Document 214, and Document 284.

20. The Dies Committee, established in 1938 and named after its chairman, Representative Martin Dies of Texas, was the House Committee for the Investigation of Un-American Activities (HUAC) (*FDRE*).

21. FDR appointed Henry Stimson as secretary of war and William Franklin ("Frank") Knox (1874–1944) as secretary of the navy in 1940; both were Republicans (*FDRE*).

ON RELIGION IN YUGOSLAVIA AND
ALLEGATIONS OF ANTI-CATHOLIC BIAS

Reader reaction to ER's suggestion that "Religion in Yugoslavia" be read "carefully and impartially" ranged from mild rebuke to intense criticism. When referencing ER's source, Edward W. Scully of the Bronx, New York, said, "I gather your friend who advised you … is a Protestant missionary pursuing a work of proselytizing among the Spaniards, Italians and other Europeans. I am sure he is a good man. But can he be accepted as an unbiased reporter on affairs concerning the Catholic Church?"[1] Former FBI agent T. C. Kirkpatrick, managing editor of a new anti-Communist newsletter, "Counterattack," criticized three members of the delegation—the Rev. Claude Williams, the Rev. William Howard Melish, and Dr. Guy Emery Shipler—for their alleged Communist affiliations and asked, "Do you really think that this group of clergymen could possibly issue a 'Fair Report'…?" Francis Griffith, president of the Committee for the Liberation of Archbishop Stepinac, told ER that she was "seriously misinformed about the extent of religious freedom in that unhappy country," and hoped "that in some succeeding column you will find it possible once more to … speak out boldly on behalf of Archbishop Aloysius Stepinac … and persecuted Yugoslav Catholics."

Mrs. H. Kinerk's letter was more pointed. "When I read your column in this morning's paper I at first could hardly believe what I was reading. I have finally come to the conclusion that either you are extremely credulous or are just out and out following the Communist party line."[2]

282

Eleanor Roosevelt to Mrs. H. Kinerk
17 November 1947 [New York City]

Dear Mrs. Kinerk:

I do not think I am anti-Catholic. I am a Protestant but I have always judged religious groups by their individual actions and I have never given a thought to what religion people I know happen to practice, but in the matter of freedom of religious practice in Europe, I think that where there is that freedom, we should acknowledge it.[3]

The gentleman whom I quoted was a man who for many years has traveled over Europe for a great international organization with headquarters in France, which watches over the freedom given to small denominations, mostly Protestant. I have no idea what his own religion is; I never asked him, but he has such a long and wide knowledge, I was glad that he came to this country for a few weeks to talk to some of our leaders of various religious groups. His conclusions were in Yugo here church people, if they adhere to religion only, have complete freedom of teaching and practice.[4]

The trouble with Archbishop Stepinac was that in Yugoslavia there are two racial groups, one of them largely Catholic in religious practice. When Germany attacked, some of them preferred the Germans to the other people within their own country and this led to some very complicated situations. The evidence shows pretty clearly that even such high ranking church officials as Archbishop Stepinac sometimes sat by and watched the murder of groups of which they did not approve, by groups of which they did approve. The result was that when the partisans gained control of the government, there were political accusations made, but all of these things are in the past.

At the present time I think it is important that we encourage as much as possible freedom of religious practice.[5]

Very sincerely yours,

TLc AERP, FDRL

---

1. Dr. Jean Nussbaum, see *n*3 and *n*6 Document 272.

2. For the full text of ER's November 4 column, see Document 272 (Edward W. Scully to ER, 24 November 1947, AERP; T. C. Kirkpatrick to ER, 14 November 1947, AERP; "Ex-FBI Agents Expose Commies," *New York World Telegram*, 12 June 1947, AERP; Francis Griffith to ER, 10 November 1947, AERP; Mrs. H. Kinerk to ER, 5 November 1947, AERP).

3. See Document 272. ER was an Episcopalian.

4. Nussbaum was a Seventh-day Adventist. He spoke at the November 7 closed-door meeting where the delegation's report was presented to an audience of 250 clergymen. For more on this meeting, see *n*3 Document 272. According to one of the Yugoslav interviewees, the American clergymen failed to ask if there were any adverse consequences for those who practiced their religion. The New York meeting was the first of a series of such gatherings planned for other American cities ("Report on Yugoslavs Given to Clergymen," *NYT*, 8 November 1947, 9; Alexander, *Triple*, 186).

5. Stepinac's activities during World War II remain controversial. As a Croatian nationalist, he initially welcomed the Germans' defeat of Yugoslavia in April 1941 and its subsequent dismemberment and the establishment of an independent Fascist Croatian republic free of Serbian domination. However, as the dimensions of the new government's plan to empty Croatia of Serbs (one-third killed, one-third expelled, and one-third converted to Catholicism) became clear, he began to protest publicly, particularly after the government sanctioned the killing of Serbs regardless of whether or not they converted. (Some Catholic priests, among them Croatian army chaplains, were involved in these murders, which further complicated the issue.) Stepinac also began to help those whom the Croatian government persecuted including Jews, Serbs, and Slovenes.

At the same time, he maintained enough of a relationship with the government to conduct religious ceremonies for the government on its behalf and to lead the diplomatic corps in a traditional New Year's greeting to official representatives. These activities plus his willingness to temporarily house the archives of the Croatian government's foreign ministry after World War II made Stepinac vulnerable to charges of collaboration, which the Yugoslav Communist government exploited in his 1946 trial. Stepinac further muddied the question of his collaboration when he denied all the charges, saying, "I do not consider that I have ever betrayed my country." He also refused to speak in his defense and declined to name defense counsel.

Because she viewed Stepinac's situation as primarily a political matter and because of her position as a UN delegate (the US State Department's position on Stepinac was one of "concern and deep worry"), ER declined to help the prelate or speak out in his behalf as several of her correspondents asked. (Her negative reply to one such supplicant, John F. Rapp of the New York State Board of the Ancient Order of Hibernians, appeared in the *Catholic News* under the headline, "Mrs. Roosevelt's Views.") Still, ER did what she could to help the prelate. In 1946, she forwarded a resolution from an unnamed organized group on his behalf to the UN secretary-general for consideration in the appropriate UN committee.

At the same time, ER refused to disassociate herself from the American Committee for Yugoslav Relief (see Document 73). The committee supplied medical aid and extra food then unavailable in Yugoslavia to women and children there even after the Yugoslavian ambassador to the United States suggested at a committee function in his honor that the Catholic Church rather than Tito was responsible for the status of Catholic church-state relations in Yugoslavia.

She defended the committee in My Day writing that

it has ... been suggested to me at various times that one should not be interested in shipments of any kind to Yugoslavia. I do not agree with this ... women and children, who suffer most because of war, are entitled to our help in recognition of the fact that the partisans under Tito did not collaborate with Germans, and did render the Allies a great service ... Moreover, refusal to render aid to other nations which will keep their people alive and help them reestablish themselves on a healthy economic basis seems to me a very short-sighted policy.

For more on ER's relationship with the American Committee for Yugoslav Relief, see Document 73, Document 209, Document 215, Document 216, Document 217, Document 218, and Document 222 (Alexander, *Triple*, 26–40, 107; Kirby, 129; "Stepinatz Denies Guilt at His Trial," *NYT*, 1 October 1946, 15; "Stepinatz Refuses to Defend Himself," *NYT*, 2 October 1946, 13; Gannon, 339; "U.S. Voices Worry at Yugoslav Trial," *NYT*, 12 October 1946, 7; "Envoy Describes Stepinatz 'Plot,'" *NYT*, 23 October 1947, 13; ER to Friedl H. Haas, 5 November 1946, AERP; *MD*, 17 November 1947).

On Truman's Foreign Aid Appropriation

On November 17, Congress, which had been in recess since July, returned to Washington for a special session Truman called to "consider two problems of major concern": the food crisis in Europe and the threat of inflation at home. "The future of the free nations of Europe hangs in the balance," the president began, and "the future of our own economy is in jeopardy … The costly lesson of two world wars" is that "human misery and chaos lead to strife and conquest" and that hunger and poverty tempt the strong to prey upon the weak."

Concerned that the economies of France, Italy, and Austria might collapse before the Marshall Plan could be implemented, Truman then asked Congress to appropriate $597,000,000 in emergency foreign aid. Conceding that "emergency assistance by itself will not solve European problems. Emergency aid is no substitute for a long-range recovery program, but it is a vital prerequisite to such a program. If the Western European nations should collapse this winter, as a result of our failure to bridge the gap between their resources and their needs, there would be no chance for them—or for us—to look forward to their economic recovery." [1]

Turning his attention to the domestic economy, Truman called inflation "an ominous threat" whose "harsh effects … are clear." After proposing that the Federal Reserve monitor consumer spending more closely, the president then called for executive authority to reimplement wage and price controls; the rationing of steel, grain, and other scarce goods; and a stronger rent control law.[2]

ER wrote to the president to offer her congratulations and to request an appointment.

283

Eleanor Roosevelt to Harry Truman

25 November 1947 [New York City]

Dear Mr. President:

I read your message to Congress and I want to tell you that I thought it very courageous and very good in every way. I am sure you have had many favorable comments.

The old Greek Prime Minister came to see me and asked me to tell you how grateful they are for what has been done for Greece. They hope you will back some form of a middle-of-the-road government and try to draw the two extremes together.[3]

I leave on Friday for the Human Rights Commission meeting in Geneva, and I am sorry not to have had the opportunity of seeing you before I go. I hope I shall be able to get to Washington around the 12th of January, and that you will be free to see me. If I may, I shall ask for an appointment when I know just when I will be in Washington.[4]

With my every good wish to you and Mrs. Truman and Margaret, I am,

Very cordially yours,
Eleanor Roosevelt

TLS AERP, FDRL

1. Truman, vol. 2, 117; "Text of President Truman's Appeal for Foreign Aid and Curbs on Inflationary Perils," *NYT*, 18 November 1947, 3.

2. Donovan, 339; "Text of President Truman's Appeal for Foreign Aid and Curbs on Inflationary Perils," *NYT*, 18 November 1947, 3.

3. Constantin Tsaldaris (1884?–1970), who in 1936 succeeded his uncle Panayis Tsaldaris as the leader of the Greek Populist Party, became minister of Greece in 1946 when the party swept the elections. As the civil war escalated, Tsaldaris resigned in January 1947 to facilitate Demetrios Maximos's leadership of a more centrist, anti-Communist coalition. He, however, continued to represent Greece as its deputy premier and foreign minister, successfully lobbying the UN to investigate Communist support of Greek insurgents and persuading the Truman administration to support Greece once the British announced their withdrawal of aid ("Tsaldaris Dead; Greek Minister," *NYT*, 16 November 1970, 40).

4. ER again requested a meeting when she wrote the president on December 23 to praise the report issued by his civil rights commission. "I am coming to Washington on the 12th of January and hope very much you will have some free time on the 13th, as I should like to report to you on the Human Rights Commission session." Truman responded a week later, "of course, I'll be most happy to see you on January thirteenth. I am sure there will be no difficulty about arranging it" (ER to Truman, 23 December 1947, HSTL; Truman to ER, 30 December 1947, AERP).

On the PCA and Taking a Stand
Against Communism

Nina Dexter, a politically active Californian who admired FDR, corresponded with ER several times in 1947 and 1948. However, Truman's loyalty program and staunch anti-Communist rhetoric made Dexter reevaluate her allegiance to the Democratic Party. November 17, 1947, she wrote ER:

> We all believed in the great International understanding and the devotion of all nations, as well as this nation, to your great husband, and it is disgraceful how the Administration, from the White House down to the State Department … are trying in every way to discredit everything which he stood for, and they would like nothing better than to eventually get down to a point so low that he could be connected up after his death … as an "International Communist." The entire plot in Washington is so utterly obvious that those who believe in America as tremendously as I do and in what he stood for, both at home and in the minds of the peoples of the world, feel that we cannot sit back while these "Fascist-minded" persons, as well as militarists and the reactionaries in the State Department are doing everything in their power to tear all of his great work down and discredit him here in America.

Believing that the country was developing a "taint of totalitarianism" under the current hysteria over international Communism, Dexter hoped her November 17 letter to ER and FDR, Jr., to whom she sent a copy, would help them understand why she was breaking with the party to support Wallace.

All political disagreements aside, ER made sure her staff kept Dexter's address so that they could continue to exchange Christmas presents.[1]

284

Eleanor Roosevelt to Nina Dexter
[1 December ?] 1947 [New York City]

Dexter

I agree with you that everybody should have the right to speak. I also agree with you that at the moment we have become somewhat hysterical on the subject of communism.

I do not agree with you in not taking a stand against Communists in our own country because communism today means the spread by force of the doctrine and therefore any group like PCA that is too chicken-hearted to take a stand against Communists within their ranks is a detriment to our heritage of freedom[2]

HLd AERP, FDRL

---

1. Nina Dexter to ER, 17 November 1947, AERP.

2. Dexter and ER continued to correspond on the matter of anti-Communism in the Truman administration through the next year. On February 20, 1948, Dexter wrote:

Millions of people would like to say many, many things they dare not say, but I shall continue to say them to the end of my days whether the Truman Administration likes it or not and whether those who are now serving the Truman Doctrine, which has fully betrayed the great policies of the New Deal, continue to call me a "Communist," "Subversive" or any other name …

…Will you remember some day that I am still an American and that I am still devoted to the great ideal of Franklin Roosevelt and that I do not go out of my way to disseminate anything false either about this country nor would I do it about another country, even though my loyalty is to the United States of America?

ER responded February 27 that, "I have never thought you were not an American or that you were not devoted to the ideal of my husband. I simply think we differ on the way we can best serve our country and the ideals that we hold."

On March 20, Dexter sent ER a telegram that challenged ER's opinions of Henry Wallace, and claimed that "millions" of Americans "have felt that we now understand what it must have been to live under fascist dictatorship in other lands when day after day we are losing all our freedoms and are threatening every nation in the world which does not jump on our side."

To which ER replied, "If you think we are living under Fascism you do not I am afraid, know much of Fascism. Henry Wallace is more menacing than anyone else" (Nina Dexter to ER, 20 February 1948; ER to Nina Dexter, 27 February 1948; Nina Dexter to ER, 20 March 1948; ER to Nina Dexter, n.d., AERP).

On the NAACP Petition to United Nations, Part 2

ER had asked Walter White to have the NAACP prepare "a memorandum of the items we think should be included in the World Charter of Human Rights and implementing machinery of those rights" and "place it in her hands" before she left November 29 to attend the Human Rights Commission meetings in Geneva. Walter White instructed W. E. B. Du Bois, who was to depart on a national lecture tour, to prepare the memorandum. November 17, Du Bois responded, "I have no suggestions for Mrs. Roosevelt."[1] Unsatisfied with Du Bois's response, White instructed his colleague to craft the document he requested:

> The memorandum Mrs. Roosevelt has requested may be one of the most important documents which the Association has ever produced. Even though it is doubtful that all our recommendations will be included, it is imperative that as carefully prepared a statement of our position is presented as is possible. I request therefore that before you leave the city you give me as specific a statement on the points you think the N.A.A.C.P. should recommend as is possible under the circumstances.[2]

November 24, Du Bois again rejected White's request, writing that he saw "no way in which I can be of service in the matter of recommendations to the Human Rights Commission, or the Sub-Commission on Discrimination and Minorities." In a six-point memorandum Du Bois stated he had nothing to offer Mrs. Roosevelt, this time revealing his deep disenchantment with the HRC, the State Department, and ER over their treatment of *An Appeal to the World*. "Mrs. Roosevelt is following orders" from a State Department "determined that American Negroes shall have no chance to state their grievances before the world." Furthermore, Du Bois continued, the biggest obstacle confronting human rights for African Americans was "not a lack of pious statements," but the failure of the UN to stand behind those statements. After recounting the difficulties he faced in presenting the petition, he concluded:

> If Mrs. Roosevelt or the Commission had wished our advice or opinion, they have had a year to ask it. They have, on the contrary, discouraged us from action in every way possible. The present request is, as I understand, from Mrs. Roosevelt to Mr. White for a memorandum for her personal use. It is not a request from the Commission, and there is no promise that it will not reach the wastepaper basket. If we did make a statement, what more could we say than we have said already in 155 pages of carefully documented materials?[3]

Without the detailed memorandum he had hoped Du Bois would prepare, White wired ER with last-minute suggestions for the upcoming session of the HRC.

285

Walter White to Eleanor Roosevelt
28 November 1947 [New York City]

MRS ELEANOR ROOSEVELT

HAD HOPED TO PREPARE DETAILED MEMORANDUM FOR YOU AS REQUESTED BUT PALESTINE AND OTHER ISSUES HAVE PREVENTED DOING SO. MAY I FIRST SAY THAT PROPOSAL MADE NOVEMBER 25TH

AT GENEVA BY JONATHAN DANIELS FOR CREATION OF SMALL COMMITTEE WHOSE AID "ANY GOVERN-
MENT DECLARING A PROBLEM TO BE PURELY INTERNAL WOULD HAVE THE RIGHT TO REFUSE", ITS
TANTAMOUNT TO MAN CHARGED WITH THEFT HAVING RIGHT TO REFUSE INTERFERENCE BY COURT
OF LAW.[4] BELIEVE HUMAN RIGHTS OF UNITED NATIONS CHARTER CAN BE MADE EFFECTIVE ONLY BY
ESTABLISHMENT INTERNATIONAL COURT OF HUMAN RIGHTS WHICH SHALL BE EMPOWERED TO
RECEIVE AND INVESTIGATE COMPLAINTS OF MINORITIES IN ANY COUNTRY AND WHICH EITHER SHALL
HAVE AUTHORITY ITSELF OR OBLIGATION TO REPORT FINDINGS WITH RECOMMENDATIONS OF COR-
RECTIVE ACTION TO SOCIAL AND ECONOMIC COUNCIL WHICH SHALL BE VESTED WITH AUTHORITY
TO ACT. OBTAINING NECESSARY APPROVAL OF SUCH IMPLEMENTING MACHINERY WILL UNDOUBTED-
LY BE DIFFICULT.[5] BUT WE BELIEVE UNITED STATES OCCUPIES UNIQUE POSITION WHICH ENABLES AND
OBLIGATES IT TO TAKE ADVANCED MORAL POSITION ON THIS BASIC QUESTION. HOPE YOU WILL HAVE
SAFE, PLEASANT AND SUCCESSFUL TRIP.

WALTER WHITE

Tel AERP, FDRL

ER replied ten days later, explaining Daniel's position.

286

Eleanor Roosevelt to Walter White

8 December 1947 [Geneva]

My dear Mr. White:

I am enclosing a copy of the proposal of Mr. Jonathan Daniels before the Sub-commission on
the Prevention of Discrimination and the Protection of Minorities, dated November 24th, which is
apparently the proposal to which you referred in your telegram to me of November 28th.[6]

While the proposal was not adopted, I call your attention to the fact that your information
that "any government declaring a problem to be purely internal would have the right to refuse" the
procedure of the proposed small committee, is apparently not entirely accurate. The small committee would have been authorized to request further information and to tender its assistance informally with the state concerned with a view to reaching an agreed settlement, even though the state
concerned advised the small committee that it regarded the matter as essentially within its domestic jurisdiction and the small committee so reported, so long as it did not take any action or make
any recommendation in the nature of "intervention".

Jonathan also proposed that all petitions be received. This proposal was rejected and when the
USSR proposed that petitions be received from the National Association for the Advancement of
Colored People he was forced to vote against it on the ground that one organization should not be
singled out in preference to others.

With the Season's Greetings,

I remain,

TLc AERP, FDRL

After polling his board, White wired ER the following response.

287

Walter White to Eleanor Roosevelt
9 December 1947 [New York City]

MRS ELEANOR ROOSEVELT

NAACP BOARD DIRECTORS UNANIMOUSLY VOTED URGE AMERICAN DELEGATION TO RECOMMEND AND VIGOROUSLY SUPPORT ESTABLISHMENT INTERNATIONAL COURT HUMAN RIGHTS WITH AUTHORITY RECEIVE AND INVESTIGATE COMPLAINTS MISTREATMENT MINORITIES IN ANY MEMBER NATION. SUCH COURT SHOULD EITHER HAVE AUTHORITY ITSELF OR OBLIGATION REPORT FINDINGS AND RECOMMENDATIONS CORRECTIVE ACTION TO GENERAL ASSEMBLY

WALTER WHITE SECRETARY

Tel AERP, FDRL

288

Eleanor Roosevelt to Walter White
12 December 1947 [Geneva]

Dear Mr. White,

The sub-committee on Implementation is already considering the suggestions in your telegram.[7]

Sincerely yours,
Eleanor Roosevelt

TLS NAACP, DLC

---

1. Memorandum from White to Messrs. Chalmers, Lewis, Spingarn, and Tobias, 17 November 1947, WEBDP, UMAWEB.

2. When the President's Committee on Civil Rights released its report, *To Secure These Rights*, October 29, it immediately overshadowed Du Bois's *Appeal*. Upon its release, White hailed the government's report as "the most courageous and specific document of its kind in American history" (Memorandum from Walter White to W. E. B. Du Bois, 18 November 1947, WEBDP, UMAWEB; Anderson, 107).

3. W. E. B. Du Bois to Walter White, 24 November 1947, WEBDP, UMAWEB; Lewis, 529–30; Janken, 309.

4. Jonathan Daniels (1902–1981), son of FDR's ambassador to Mexico, Josephus Daniels, and a former editor of the Raleigh, North Carolina, *News and Observer*, served as the US delegate to the UN's Sub-commission on the Prevention of Discrimination and Protection of Minorities. During his tenure as editor of the *News and Observer*, Daniels criticized discriminatory practices in the South and established himself as a leading southern liberal. Although he personally believed that *To Secure These Rights* and the NAACP's *Appeal* demonstrated that the United States was "unable

or unwilling to ... do anything effective about" its race problem, he refused to allow the USSR to capitalize on the NAACP's interest in publicizing racial tensions in the United States. During the sub-commission meetings held in the last week of November 1947, Daniels repeatedly argued that *To Secure These Rights* revealed the deep commitment of the highest levels of the US government to fighting for racial equality. Using the NAACP's *Appeal*, Alexander Borisov, the Soviet delegate, continually hammered at America's shortcomings and introduced a resolution that would have served as a public rebuke of the United States. Daniels's argument that race relations in the United States were an American problem that the American government was working to improve convinced the sub-commission to reject the Soviet resolution. In his criticism of Daniels's position, White quoted the *New York Times* of November 26, which reported:

> The most concrete proposal of the United States was for the establishment of a 'Small Committee' of three members to offer assistance to the governments against which complaints are lodged with the United Nations for violations of the rights of individuals or minorities.
>
> None of the members of the Small Committee would be nationals of the state affected or of any neighboring state. Any government declaring a problem to be purely internal would have the right to refuse the committee's assistance.

Daniels resented White's criticism and believed that White and Du Bois were "damning me up and down the street in connection with the meeting," in order "to cover ... [their] embarrassment ... that their petition was used as a political weapon by our Russian friends" (Les Ledbetter, "Jonathan Daniels Is Dead at 79," *NYT*, 7 November 1981, 31; Michael L. Hoffman, "U.S. Offers Plans on Human Rights," *NYT*, 26 November 1947, 7; "Intolerance Crime Issue in U.N. Group," *NYT*, 29 November 1947, 2; Anderson, 105–11). See *n*6 below for the actual text of Daniels's proposal.

5. During the HRC's first session in January and February 1946, Colonel William Roy Hodgson, the representative from Australia, proposed that the commission establish an International Court of Human Rights, which could receive petitions from individuals, nongovernmental organizations, and states. Sharing Du Bois's view, he argued that the "Commission should not confine itself to abstractions but was bound to consider immediately effective machinery for implementing Human Rights." As HRC chair, ER voiced the State Department's view that "the establishment of machinery for international supervision of human rights ... cannot be an immediate objective of the Commission on Human Rights." Although Hodgson and Hansa Mehta of India insisted on establishing machinery for implementation immediately, the majority of delegates agreed with ER that the question of implementation should be addressed only after the creation of a bill of rights (Morsink 15–16; Glendon, 38; Anderson, 97; "U.N. Blocks Court for Human Rights," *NYT*, 6 February 1947, 5).

6. The clause in question reads as follows:

> If the state concerned in the alleged discrimination or oppression advises the Small Committee that it regards the matter as one essentially within its domestic jurisdiction, the Committee should report this fact, and, pending further guidance from the Commission [on Human Rights], or the Subcommission [on the Prevention of Discrimination and the Protection of Minorities], should refrain from taking any action or making any recommendation in the nature of "intervention" ("Procedure for Handling 'Urgent Problems,'" Submitted by Jonathan Daniels to the Sub-commission on the Prevention of Discrimination and the Protection of Minorities, 24 November 1947, [E/CN.4/SUB.2/12], UNORGA, MWelC).

7. Although the HRC had voted to move ahead on the drafting of a declaration during its first session, delegates resumed their calls for effective means of implementation at the commission's sec-

ond session in Geneva. The commission agreed to a compromise proposed by Fernand Dehousse of Belgium so the HRC established three working groups to deal with the declaration, the convention, and implementation separately. Chaired by Hansa Mehta of India, the working group on implementation presented its report to the full commission on December 15, 1947. The proposal included provisions for the creation of a standing "Committee of Experts" comprised of at least five individuals who would receive and review petitions, as well as for the establishment of an unspecified international tribunal to hear cases. Colonel William Hodgson of Australia, now backed by Dehousse, still insisted on establishing a new International Court of Human Rights, but other delegates believed a subsidiary of the International Court of Justice might be an adequate body for hearing cases. After a debate over the limits of national sovereignty in which the Soviet bloc (Byelorussia, Ukraine, the USSR, and Yugoslavia) defended state sovereignty as "the oldest democratic principle in the field of State relations," the commission voted 12 to 3 with 1 abstention to send the report to ECOSOC and the governments of UN member nations for review and feedback. ER voted in favor of distributing the report, but she did not participate in the debate on state sovereignty (Glendon, 86–87; Summary Record of the Thirty-Eighth Meeting of the Commission on Human Rights, Second Session, 15 December 1947, E/CN.4/SR.38, UND, MWelC; Summary Record of Thirty-Ninth Meeting of the Commission on Human Rights, Second Session, 15 December 1947, E/CN.4/SR.39, UND, MWelC). For the HRC's decision to continue drafting a declaration and address implementation at a later date, see *n*3 above.

PRESENTING THE US POSITION ON DRAFTING THE DECLARATION AND COVENANTS

When the drafting committee convened in June, the United States, despite its earlier objections, favored the simultaneous preparation of both a declaration and covenant on human rights. At the end of the committee meeting, drafts of both documents had been completed. However, that same month Robert Lovett, who opposed both a declaration and a covenant, became undersecretary of state.

In July, ER asked to meet with Warren Austin, chief of the American delegation, to review the US position on the declaration and the covenant (see Document 238). Concerned that the covenant could not withstand attacks by Senate segregationists and that Lovett could derail both documents, ER then suggested to Austin that he meet with Senators Vandenberg and Connally to determine where they stood on the two issues and then arrange for the senators to meet with Lovett. By the end of their meeting, ER agreed with Austin that priority should be given to drafting the declaration, followed by the preparation of one or more legally binding conventions.

At the Human Rights Commission's first session December 2, ER opened the meeting by asking the HRC if they should focus on drafting a declaration, a convention, or both. After hearing from several of the delegates, she made the following statement on behalf of the United States. Her statement reflects Lovett's reservations about a convention; however, within the State Department, ER continued to argue the case for a convention.[1]

289

Commission on Human Rights
Summary Record[2] Second Session, Twenty-Fifth Meeting [excerpt]
2 December 1947 [Geneva]

The CHAIRMAN said there had been a slight evolution in the United States' position with regard to the form which a Declaration on Human Rights should take. Her delegation thought that priority should be given to the draft Declaration, and that the latter should not be drawn up in such a way as to give the impression that Governments would have a contractual obligation to guarantee human rights. As regards the draft Convention or Conventions, the United States considered that the Commission should not proceed to draw them up until it was sure that such Conventions could be accepted and applied in all good faith by the participating States. Flagrant, prolonged and repeated violations of those Conventions could not fail to harm the United Nations. That did not mean, however, that her delegation would not be willing to examine the draft Convention or Conventions if the Commission so desired. The Commission should, however, take the time factor into account, and, if they had to make a choice, should first tackle the draft Declaration.

She hoped the United Kingdom representative was right in thinking that agreement could readily be reached on the draft Declaration, and that the Commission could then go on to study the draft Convention.[3] Her delegation had proposed a draft Declaration which seemed to it the type of document at which the Commission should arrive.[4] Finally, while emphasizing the primary importance of the Declaration, she was prepared for one or more draft Conventions to be drawn up, which could be adopted as soon as possible.[5]

TSumex RM:UND, MWelC

1. For ER's ongoing discussions with Lovett and other members of the State Department on this subject, see Document 294 and Document 295.

2. HRC, Second Session, Summary Record, Twenty-Fifth Meeting, (E/CN.4/SR.25), 10, MWelC (RM).

3. The British, unlike the Americans, gave first priority to the drafting of a convention and had submitted a draft international bill of rights (E/CN.4/AC.1/4) in the form of a legally binding document rather than a declaration of principles. They hoped that if a declaration were to be drafted at all, it could be done quickly so that there would be time to draft the convention. Lord Dukeston (Charles Dukes), the British representative on the HRC, argued that "A declaration could hardly deal with anything but very general principles, already embodied in the Charter. If the Commission confined itself to producing such a declaration without any means of enforcement it would produce a text too vague to be of real value." He urged that the HRC "proceed immediately to drafting a Convention binding the signatory Governments so that it would be possible to set up machinery for appeal in the event of their not respecting their undertakings." He said the British were only willing to consider a draft declaration if a convention were drafted afterwards. "A Declaration was nothing more than a document of propaganda. He recognized the difficulties involved in drafting conventions, but that was what the world needed today" (Morsink, 8; HRC, Second Session, Summary Record, Twenty-fifth Meeting, [E/CN.4/SR.25], 5–6, 11, MWelC RM).

4. The United States had submitted a draft declaration that paralleled the one prepared by the HRC drafting committee but contained alternative wording and occasionally organized the rights differently (HRC, Parallel Passages in Human Rights Drafting Committee Text and United States Proposal, 26 November 1947 [E/CN.4/36/Add.2], AERP; HRC, Proposal for a Declaration of Human Rights Submitted by the Representative of the United States on the Commission of Human Rights, 26 November 1947 [E/CN.4/36], AERP).

5. In her December 8 My Day column, ER reported on the outcome of the discussions in the HRC regarding the declaration and the convention:

> In several long sessions there was careful discussion of whether the Human Rights Commission was to write a bill which could actually be presented to the General Assembly—but which of course would not have legal weight, since it would not require ratification and implementation from the various nations—or both a bill and a declaration. Our own position as a government has been that on the drafting committee's report we should have sufficient material available to do a fairly finished job as regards a declaration. But many countries like our own would have to consider most carefully the points covered in a convention.
>
> For instance, our government must remember the matter of states rights and decide just how far it can go. Other governments have similar considerations, but we felt it would have a moral value to finish and circulate a declaration even though we might only be able to set down certain principles which we felt could be included in a covenant or a convention.
>
> This was unacceptable, however, to the majority of the other nations present. They felt that the world is expecting a definite commitment which would force the governments to change their laws, if necessary, to conform to an international bill or covenant, and they wished that to be considered first, or at least simultaneously with a declaration. This finally passed, and three working groups have been appointed on each of these subjects. As soon as possible, they will be asked to report to the plenary session (*MD*, 8 December 1947).

At the conclusion of the Human Rights Commission she returned to the subject again, this time stating explicitly that a human rights convention would challenge laws in the United States. See Document 291.

REVIEWING THE COMMISSION'S WORK WITH THE PRESS

> As the full Human Rights Commission prepared to review final drafts of the declaration on human rights, ER held a press conference to discuss its work to date. The *New York Times* covered it.

290

"U.S. Doubts Scored by Mrs. Roosevelt"
Michael L. Hoffman
New York Times 14 December 1947

GENEVA, Dec. 13—The United Nations Commission on Human Rights will complete in its current session a declaration of rights and a convention of human rights, Mrs. Franklin D. Roosevelt, chairman of the group, predicted today.

"We are making progress," she said. "It is slow, but before leaving we will send to the Governments documents which, while imperfect, will mark great progress. They will have there— in the things the Governments should consider and take a position on in this important field."

Mrs. Roosevelt said at a press conference that she doubted that the United States' traditional attitude toward freedom of political expression retained all its force. Asked to explain, she said:

"We don't at present concentrate our forces on a positive development of our democracy and assert our entire confidence in its ability to meet every situation. We tend for a moment to lean toward certain repressive measures which wouldn't be necessary if we were completely secure in our ability to make our own democracy work."[1]

Commenting on differences between the Soviet and American views on rights, she said she thought it was a matter of emphasis. The Russians, Mrs. Roosevelt declared, emphasize economic and social rights, which they want spelled out with extreme care. The American attitude, she explained, emphasizes individual rights and civil and religious liberties. She said she thought a middle ground could be found because, "after all, we have to live in the same world."[2]

The commission approved an important article of its draft convention. The article would guarantee freedom from arbitrary arrest and enumerates cases in which deprivation of liberty is consistent with basic rights. It also provides for prompt trial and for the right to compensation for unlawful arrest.[3]

It was learned that there had been changes in the instructions to the United States delegation on the matter of seeking an immediate convention. Mrs. Roosevelt had opposed trying to draft a convention at this session, arguing that it was enough to draft a declaration of rights. Now, however, it is understood, the United States' position is that the effort to complete both should be supported.[4]

The report of the working party on implementation laid before the commission today contains a suggestion that a commission of five non-governmental individuals should hear petitions against violations of rights and act for the United Nations in the first instance in pressing governments to fulfill obligations they may accept under an international convention.[5]

It was revealed that the Ukrainian delegate, a member of the working party, had announced that he would not take part in the work because he believed implementation should be discussed only after a bill of rights had been completed.[6]

In a night session, the commission, over Russian objections, approved a resolution calling for an end of statelessness and for measures by the United Nations to insure nationality for every person. The commission also approved a Lebanese amendment to the rights declaration placing recognition of the sanctity of the family before protection of marriage as a duty of states.

TNews AERP, FDRL

---

1. Here ER refers to the House Un-American Activities Committee (HUAC). For ER's views on HUAC, see Document 262 and Document 271.

2. In a letter written much later, James Hendrick, ER's State Department advisor, wrote: "With regard to the social and economic rights, Mrs. Roosevelt soon recognized that we would have to have some in our Declaration, although these were rights which we could not as easily, say, technically, be granted [grant?] as socialist and communist countries. Again, this was a situation where she persuaded the United States to adopt a position which the Lovetts and the Marshalls would have preferred we not adopt" (James Hendrick to A. Glenn Mower, Jr., 5 June 1975, JPHP, HSTL). See also *n*1 Document 206 and *n*1 Document 294.

3. Article 5 of the Geneva draft international declaration on human hights reads:

> No one shall be deprived of his personal liberty or kept in custody except in cases prescribed by law and after due process. Every one placed under arrest or detention shall have the right to immediate judicial determination of the legality of any detention to which he may be subject and to trial within a reasonable time or to release (Glendon, Appendix 4, 289).

4. See Document 238, Document 289, and Document 295. The US delegates to the UN had been concerned that a convention, which, like a covenant, would require in the United States a ratification by a two-thirds Senate vote, would be more difficult to implement than a declaration, which did not require such action by the legislative powers of ratifying states. Once the commission voted to draft a convention and a declaration simultaneously, the United States threw its support behind both (Glendon, 84–88).

5. The Human Rights Commission divided itself into three working groups for the Geneva convention: the working group on drafting the declaration, which ER chaired; the group to draft a convention, chaired by Lord Dukeston (Charles Dukes) of the UK; and the working group on implementation, chaired by Hansa Mehta of India. The implementation group's task was to answer essential questions concerning the adoption of the declaration by ratifying states, and to establish the commission's role in addressing violations of the declaration (Glendon, 87; United Nations Report of the Commission on Human Rights, Second Session, UN Doc E/600, 17 December 1947, AERP). See also *n*7 Document 288.

6. The Ukrainian delegate, Michael Klekovkin, felt he could not reconcile the commission's work with his belief that the declaration and convention should be agreed upon before the members began discussions about how to implement them (Glendon, 94).

REVIEWING THE COMMISSION'S WORK WITH THE PUBLIC

The Human Rights Commission had broken up into three subgroups charged with drafting a declaration, a covenant, and strategies for their implementation. The three groups reconvened December 12 to review the initial drafts of both the declaration[1] and the covenant as well as review initial proposals on how they could best be implemented. As chair of the subcommittee charged with drafting a declaration, ER worked closely with French philosopher René Cassin, Filipino general and anticolonialism activist Carlos Romulo, and the Soviet ambassador to France Aleksander Bogolomov to produce a text the commission could agree to distribute among the UN's member nations for review and comment.

When the full committee reassembled, ER, as its chair, pushed her colleagues to complete their assignments, convening sessions that began in the early morning and often lasted after midnight. Although the document still needed a preamble and ER worried that its formal legalese could prevent it being "readily understood by the ordinary man or woman," she left the final session late the night of December 17 pleased with her leadership and her colleagues' work. As she confided to Esther Lape: "We finished last night and I drove them hard but they are glad now it's over and all the men are proud of their accomplishment."[2]

She then dictated this column, published the following day.

291

My Day
18 December 1947

GENEVA, Switzerland—As a result of the work the Human Rights Commission has done here, I feel that the governments in the United Nations will have some very good working papers to consider and comment on—a draft declaration of rights, a draft convention or covenant on rights, and a report on methods of implementation. I hope that these documents will receive close attention in every government.

In the United States, any international convention on rights must be very carefully considered, because it would have the effect of legally binding signatory countries to change their laws to meet its provisions. This would be particularly complicated for us since, under our Constitution, so many rights are reserved by the States. But we have a precedent in the International Labor Organization conventions, and I think some way will be found for working it out.[3]

In both the declaration and the convention, there will be provisions which will entail a change of attitude toward the value of the human being as such, and this may require considerable education among our people—but it's a step forward in the conception of civilization throughout the world.

In order to cover all that we had before us at this session of the commission, every member has had to work under great pressure. And in the latter part of the meeting, we've had to curtail the speeches and discussion in order not to repeat what had already been said in the three working groups.

The commission decided that any amendment proposed could have only one speaker for and one against before a vote was taken. Every one agreed to this until some of the members decided they had something to say, and then there was strenuous objection to the rule which they'd accepted earlier in the day.

Finally, however, the rule was sustained.[4] And that's one of the reasons why a fairly complete bill of rights, covering all three sections under discussion, will now go to the governments.

I think there's more interest in an international bill of human rights over here than in the United States. That's largely because, except for a few minority groups, the people of our country don't feel the need of protection. That's not so for many people in other parts of the world, however. Where there's a need of something which will be really binding among nations, the people await such a bill with eager anticipation.

TMs AERP, FDRL

---

1. When debating the declaration, disagreements quickly emerged over Article I (the nature of humanity and its connection to natural and human rights), how human rights would be protected (how the right to asylum and nationality would effect national sovereignty), and whether women should be mentioned specifically as a separate group or whether they were included in "men" and "brotherhood." When debating the covenant (which covered only civil and political rights), the divisions between East and West became most apparent and Bogolomov quickly objected, as he later reported to Molotov, noting the hypocrisy of "the Anglo-Americans [who] affirm equality without any hint of who is actually responsible for the implementation."

The revised document the HRC approved December 17, and which they planned to distribute to all member states for the review prior to the drafting committee's next meeting in May, is often called "the Geneva draft." The HRC approved the draft, 13 to 0, with the USSR, Byelorussia, Yugoslavia, and the Ukraine abstaining (Glendon, 87–93).

2. Esther Everett Lape (1881–1981), a social scientist, educator, and activist, served as a political mentor to ER beginning in the 1920s, after which the two women became lifelong friends and confidantes. One of the founders of the League of Women Voters, Lape would spend many years campaigning for US entrance into the World Court, which had been established under the League of Nations. Under FDR's presidency, she promoted the recognition of the USSR by the United States, and investigated and publicized the inadequacy of American health care in her position as director of the American Foundation. She co-chaired the Bok Peace Prize Committee with ER in 1924 and her life partner Elizabeth Read served as one of ER's attorneys. See also *n*30 Document 76 (*NAW-CTC*; Josh Barbanel, "Esther Lape, 100, Social Scientist, Favored U.S. Role in World Court," *NYT*, 19 May 1981, B14; Lash, *Love*, 79–82; Glendon, 83–89; Morsink, 9–10; ER to Esther Everett Lape, 18 December 1947, AERP).

3. On the issue of US ratification of international conventions, see *n*4 Document 235, Document 238, Document 289, and Document 290. On ILO conventions, see *n*14 Document 74, and *n*1 and *n*8 Document 294.

4. Paragraph 19 of the December 17 commission report read:

> In discussing the Articles for the Declaration and the Convention, the Commission accepted a ruling of the Chairman (which was challenged and upheld) that in order to save time only one person would be recognized to speak for, and only one to speak against, each Article or proposed amendment (United Nations Report of the Commission on Human Rights, Second Session, [E/600], 17 December 1947, AERP).

"We Are Living in a Transitory Period"

Frank Hawkins, a university student in Bloomington, Indiana, wrote ER December 22 after reading her son Elliott's recent book, *As He Saw It*. He sent the letter "… partly just to get it off my chest, but mostly … because somehow I feel I know you, and that you will understand."

Hawkins then expressed both admiration for the book's insights into "the foreign situation" and his fear that another war was imminent. "If what he says is true, and I believe it with all my heart, what in God's name can be the matter with the educated leaders of the foremost countries of the world? Is it possible that any sane person can desire an atomic war?" Observing that everyone he knew outside of his immediate family seemed to be "either Republicans or Democrats who think like Republicans," Hawkins suggested that some of them would see the book as "a lot of propaganda. In the end I wonder what will happen in a world so mixed up."[1]

292

Eleanor Roosevelt to Frank Hawkins

29 December 1947 [Hyde Park]

Dear Mr. Hawkins:

I do not wonder you find it difficult to understand what is going on today. My son's book is an entirely honest book. He wrote what he knew and saw. I think perhaps he did not understand as much in some ways as he should have understood.[2] For instance, he does not explain what I believe to be true, namely, that my husband was personally very fond of Mr. Churchill and had a real feeling of friendship for him, though he knew that the kind of post-war world which was coming, would be a difficult world for Mr. Churchill. As a war leader he was magnificent and my husband never ceased to be grateful to him for his valiant spirit and his great leadership.[3]

Of course, no one believes in an atom war but your friends think it can be prevented in one way, whereas some of the rest of us think differently.

Favoring big business brought us a great depression. During that period we established the responsibility of the government to see to it that its people at no time starved to death. I think it would be very difficult now for anyone to say that government does not have responsibility for all its citizens.

As to your sister's young man, it is the fashion to call any liberal thinker a communist these days.[4] I can remember when communism was not used in this way, but socialism was the same bugaboo and today some of the socialist theories which once filled us with horror, are being supported by the Republicans.

I can not tell you that you are right in all you believe because I do not know you well enough to know what all your beliefs are, but I can tell you that it is well to remember that from the very beginning we founded a government here to take care of people who believed strongly in the rights and freedoms of the individual, not so much on the economic level. In fact some of our first settlements only survived through economic socialism. Freedom of religion and political belief were fought for from the very beginning.

We are living in a transitory period, perhaps the most difficult period of our history. When I was a child everything seemed settled and easy but people became rather complacent and now after the greatest war that we have ever known, we are trying to build a peace and most of us are surprised that it takes so long and is so difficult.

If you come to Hyde Park this summer, let me know ahead of time and if I am here I shall be glad to see you. The grave at Hyde Park and the grounds are free to anyone, there is a small fee charged by the Park Service for visiting the house and the library. The place is open every day except Monday when it is closed for cleaning.

Very sincerely yours,

TLc AERP, FDRL

----

1. Frank Hawkins to ER, 22 December 1947, AERP.

2. Elliott Roosevelt originally published *As He Saw It* in the autumn of 1946 and it contained a behind-the-scenes account of FDR at the 1941 Atlantic Charter meetings, the January 1943 Casablanca meetings, and the November 1944 Cairo-Tehran conference, to which Elliott and his brother Franklin, Jr., accompanied their father. His account attracted major attention and proved controversial, with reviewers highlighting its critical portrayal of Churchill (as well as British colonial policy) and apparent indulgence toward the Soviets. ER wrote its foreword, in which she stated:

> Naturally every human being reports the things which he sees and hears and lives through from his own point of view. Each personality leaves an impression on any situation and that is one reason why accounts of the same facts are often so varied. I am quite sure that many of the people who heard many of the conversations recorded herein, interpreted them differently, according to their own thoughts and beliefs.

Elliott remained in the public eye in this period, criticizing Truman's domestic and foreign policies, visiting and promoting aid for the Soviet Union, and answering questions before a Senate war investigating subcommittee about his involvement in Howard Hughes's wartime contracts for planes. In 1947 and 1948, Elliott also published editions of his father's correspondence, for which ER also wrote the foreword (ER, "Foreword," *Saw It*, ix; *FDRE*; Sterling North, "'At the Very Least a Potent Relic': FDR's Blueprint Bequeathed Through Elliott," *WP*, 6 October 1946, S7; "FDR Was Sure of 'Showdown' After Munich," *WP*, 18 August 1946, B6; Marquis Childs, "Washington Calling: Battle of Books," *WP*, 26 November 1946, 8; Ernest Lindley, "Elliott's Mission: Misleading Views of FDR's Policy," *WP*, 29 November 1946, 4; "Peril in U.S. Policies, Roosevelt Son Says," *NYT*, 13 April 1947, 53).

3. The relationship between FDR and Churchill became close during the war, but the two men did not see eye to eye on many strategic decisions and they diverged markedly over how best to respond to the Soviet threat at the impending conclusion of the war. Still, at FDR's death, Churchill wrote ER, "I feel so deeply for you all. As for myself, I have lost a dear & cherished friendship which was forged in the fire of war." In her August 24, 1946, My Day column, ER publicly described her husband's relationship with Churchill as one of growing respect and great personal affection. And she added, "No matter how much we may differ with Mr. Churchill in political philosophy—and I personally differ with him on many things—we must never forget what we owe him as a war leader and what he meant to the people of Great Britain when they were all that stood between us and Hitler." In a column just two days later, ER noted the appearance of articles taken from Elliott's book in contemporary magazines such as *Look* and answered some of the reviews that suggested that her son was attacking Churchill. "As a matter of fact, I think that he is trying to report the differences which arise in human relations between any two strong personalities such as Mr. Churchill and my husband. But no matter what anyone says, it must not be forgotten that a deep personal friendship existed between these two men. I think this was a good thing, because it made it possible to argue out differences in a way that one can only do with one's friends."

On ER's opinion of Churchill's speeches in this period, see header Document 100, Document 101, and Document 147 (*FDRE*; Lash, *Eleanor*, 664; Churchill, draft, n.d., Chartwell Trust Papers [Churchill]: 20/199/86; telegram, Winston Churchill to ER, 2 January 1946, AERP; ER, *Autobiography*, 237, 254, 256, 297; Lash, *Years*, 28–29, 84–85; *MD*, 26 August 1946).

4. Hawkins had written ER that his sister, also a student at Indiana University, was dating "a very intelligent likable fellow who hates 'New Dealers.' He thinks I. U.'s Sociology Department is Communistic."

On Wallace, the Progressive Party, and Political Ineptitude

Although Wallace had spent the year criticizing Truman Democrats, he had not made his own political plans public. The Progressive Citizens of America scheduled their nominating convention for January 17 and 18 and most thought it a foregone conclusion that the PCA would nominate Wallace as its presidential candidate. By late December, press reports appeared describing meetings Wallace held in his *New Republic* office with delegations urging his candidacy. Christmas Day, the magazine announced that Wallace would "state his own views" in a nationwide radio broadcast scheduled for the evening of December 29.

After meeting with PCA delegates from the Midwest, Wallace entered a Mutual Broadcasting Studio to tell his radio audience that he would indeed seek the presidency: "If the Democratic Party continues to be a party of war and depression, I will see to it that the people have a chance to vote for prosperity and peace." He continued:

> There is no real fight between a Truman and a Republican. Both stand for a policy which opens the door to war in our lifetime and makes war certain for our children.

> Stop saying, "I don't like it but I am going to vote for the lesser of two evils. Rather than accept either evil, come out boldly, stand upright as men and women and say loudly for all the world to hear—"We are fighting for old-fashioned Americanism at the polls in 1948."

Calling for "a new political alignment in America," one dedicated "to peace and security in America, [and] grounded on a foundation of world peace and security," Wallace rejected both the Marshall Plan and the Truman Doctrine. Declaring that the plans "divide Europe into two warring camps" and thus escalated international tensions, Wallace declared that should the United States continue to circumvent the UN, the nation will follow the trail set by "France and England after the last war and the end result will be the same—confusion, depression and war." He then concluded his address:

> We face the future unfettered by any principle but principle of general welfare. We owe no allegiance to any group which does not serve that welfare. By God's grace, the people's peace will usher in the century of the common man.[1]

Response to Wallace's announcement was fast and intense, even within Wallace's own circles. Several PCA leaders resigned their positions. Prominent journalists such as *PM*'s Albert Deutsch and the *New Yorker*'s A. J. Liebling also withdrew their support.

The next day, ER, whose relationship with Wallace had been quite close,[2] expressed her concerns to David Gurewitsch. Wallace's "reasoning seems to me fuzzy as usual and I am writing some columns about it because people must appraise what he says in the light of the realities of the situation and the stakes that are being played for today. He is so well meaning and will I think defeat the very things he wants to achieve."[3]

She then wrote the following column for publication the next day.

_293_

My Day

31 December 1947

HYDE PARK, Tuesday—So Henry Wallace is really going to head a third party and run for President in 1948! What strange things the desire to be President makes men do!

He has probably forgotten but I remember his coming to see me in the summer of 1945 in Washington. At that time, I felt very strongly that it would be good for the country if Henry Wallace, whom we all believed in and admired, would leave active politics and become the leader of the independents of the country. Their vote had increased greatly in the years between 1929 and 1945, but they needed leadership and organization.[4]

They were neither Republicans nor Democrats. They were primarily interested in getting the kind of leadership which would keep them free of economic depressions. And they wanted to continue what had been a peaceful but steady revolutionary movement which had given us, over the years, a greater number of people in the middle-income brackets and fewer people in the millionaire group or in the substandard-income groups.

This had been accomplished in smaller countries like Norway, Sweden and Denmark, but it was a little more complicated in a country the size of ours and had to come more gradually. It could be done under our capitalistic system with proper regulation and was being done, but the independent vote of the country was very largely responsible for the way our economy and social thinking was developing.

I felt that out of politics Henry Wallace could do a tremendously valuable piece of work to keep both of our political parties on their toes; to make both of them less prone to act for purely political reasons; to make both of them realize that to win any election this independent, liberal vote was essential and must be courted by deeds, not words.

The women of the country belong largely in this group. They are not hidebound and they are very practical. They know that well being spread over a great number of people is a safeguard and the best defense of one of our most important freedoms—freedom from want. The young people of the country needed leadership to be in this group; and to feel that they had with them an older man of complete integrity, would have been a tremendous inspiration.

At that time, Henry Wallace told me he believed it was his duty to stay and work in the Democratic Party. I knew then, as I know now, that he was doing what he thought was right, but he never has been a good politician, he never has been able to gauge public opinion, and he never has picked his advisers wisely.

All of these things might have been less important if he had been a disinterested, non-political leader of liberal thought, but as a leader of a third party he will accomplish nothing. He will merely destroy the very things he wishes to achieve. I am sorry that he has listened to people as inept politically as he is himself.

TMs AERP, FDRL

---

1. "Text of Wallace's Radio Talk Announcing His Candidacy," *NYT*, 30 December 1947, 15; Culver and Hyde, 449–55; Cabell Phillips, "Wallace Boom for '48 is Threat to Truman: Re-emergence of Ex-Vice President Raises Alarm Among Democrats," *NYT*, 21 December 1947, E10.

2. By 1940, ER had grown close to Wallace. She played the critical role in securing his nomination as vice president in 1940 when she flew to Chicago, at FDR's request, to address the delegates—

who were in open revolt against Wallace. She praised his "century of the common man" speech as one of the most important addresses of the century and extolled his other works in her *New Republic* review of *Democracy Reborn*, an anthology of Wallace's speeches and articles. ER wrote, in words that stand in stark contrast to the comments she made to Gurewitsch three years later:

> You will hear people say they are afraid of Mr. Wallace because he is a dreamer, an impractical person, a mystic. No one who reads these speeches attentively would be afraid on any of these accounts. They would recognize a man of curiosity, of deep religious feeling, not bound by any specific doctrine. They would know that he had to be practical because his scientific training was too intense to allow loose thinking … He has traditional American attitudes on so many things that this fear of him which has been implanted in some people's minds, will seem strange to anyone who reads him carefully.

She then tried unsuccessfully to have FDR keep Wallace as his 1944 running mate. Finally, when FDR died, she told Wallace that he was the one "most fitted" to carry out the ideals closest to FDR's heart (A. Black, *Casting*, 44–45; ER, "Henry A. Wallace's *Democracy Reborn*," *The New Republic* 3, 7 August 1944, 165–66; ER to Henry Wallace, 17 April 1945, HAWP, IaU-L).

3. ER to David Gurewitsch, 30 December 1947, GUREW, FDRL.

4. Wallace recorded in his diary that when he met with ER soon after the 1944 election:

> she told me that the liberals looked on me as the outstanding symbol of liberalism in the United States. She said that she was going out to the CIO convention November 20 and she wanted to know whether I would head up a greatly expanded PAC. She felt that Sidney Hillman was not suitable for heading up such a broad liberal organization. She said furthermore that even though I had a position in the government, she thought I could go on in such an organization.

Later that afternoon Wallace phoned ER to decline her suggestion, saying that he "felt the only way any liberalism could express itself on a national basis was through the Democratic Party" and that "it would be damaging to the Democratic Party and the liberalism boys if I should take the position she suggested" (Blum, *Price*, 390).

1 9 4 8

"Needless to say, this whole question is of deep concern to me."

FRANK SHERSHEL/GETTY IMAGES.

Eleanor Roosevelt, as the events of 1948 unfolded, grew increasingly concerned about American commitment to the United Nations, the adoption of a declaration of human rights, the establishment of a Jewish state, and the attack on liberalism, civil rights, and civil liberties at home.

Palestine presented a particular concern in the first months of 1948, as the days counted down toward the birth of the new Jewish state. Although the administration had endorsed General Assembly Resolution 181, which called for partitioning Palestine into separate Arab and Jewish states, senior State Department officials, including Secretary George Marshall, began to distance themselves from the pro-partition platform when it became clear that it would alienate Arab allies, who might restrict American access to oil. ER, however, remained committed to the Resolution. "I feel we have a moral obligation," she wrote Marshall, "due to our acceptance of the Balfour Declaration and our tacit agreement in the forming of a Jewish homeland." Twice, she urged the secretary to protect Palestinian Jews, writing, "Needless to say, this whole question is of deep concern to me."[1]

ER also worried that this sudden shift in policy would undermine the prestige of the United States and the legitimacy of the UN. "We have more or less buried the UN. I can hardly see how it can recover and have the slightest influence, since we were the only ones who could give it any force and we now have been the ones to take it away."[2] She told readers of My Day that in endorsing the trusteeship proposal over the partition plan the United States had "weakened the UN and prevented it from becoming an instrument to keep peace in the world."[3] Indeed, her concerns grew so grave that she offered her resignation to Truman and Marshall so that she might continue to "openly criticize" the policy.

Documents included in this selection also reveal ER's concern over the increasingly tense relationship between the US and the USSR. ER feared that the Communist coup in Czechoslovakia, the Yugoslavian threat to Trieste, the predicted Communist victory in the Italian elections, and the unraveling of the Potsdam agreements indicated that war was imminent. "No one won the last war," she wrote Truman, "and no one will win the next war."[4] Despite assurances from Truman and Marshall and in-depth discussion with Marshall's envoy Chip Bohlen, ER continued to worry that the administration's Russia policies might put the two countries on an inexorable path toward war.

Nevertheless, ER campaigned vigorously on behalf of the Marshall Plan during her month-long trip Europe in April, stressing to audiences in London and the Netherlands the necessity of rebuilding democracies throughout Europe. Evoking her husband's "Four Freedoms" speech, she declared in London, "The Marshall Plan aims to strengthen the United Nations by strengthening the individual member nations. The United Nations can only do its best work if all nations, great and small, are strong and secure and able to make their decisions free from fear."[5] Back home, in My Day and If You Ask Me, ER told her readers that as long as the European Recovery Program succeeded, communism would not sweep over western Europe.

ER also continued to argue that the absence of civil rights policies and the continued discrimination against African Americans undermined America's moral standing as a world leader. "It is the one point which can be attacked and to which the representatives of the United States have no answer," she wrote in My Day, and the one point which actually made the Soviet Union, who repeatedly defined American segregation as American hypocrisy, look most just by comparison.[6]

Despite these pressing crises, ER remained focused on securing US commitment to human rights protocols. ER continued to push the State Department to support the drafting of human rights covenants, lobbying Undersecretary of State Lovett to recognize the effective way the Soviets used US opposition to further its own propaganda campaigns. She then turned to John Foster Dulles for his recommendations on how best to address this potential stalemate. Slowly, the declaration and covenant discussions moved forward. As ER told her readers, "Six weeks of arguing over the weight of each word put down, as well as the legal meaning of every phrase, is not so easy for me, who is somewhat impatient of the things which I do not recognize at first blush as being really important." She then told the press, that despite different national customs and precedents, the commission had "produced a document of very great intrinsic worth. The United States has not always won its points. The Declaration is not exactly as we would have written it … But it is a sure guide. It is not unlikely that it will be of historic importance."[7]

On the domestic front, ER labeled 1948 as "a year of decision" for liberals. As she told a Unitarian assembly in March, "Whether we like it or not … those of us who are liberals find that we are put in the position very often in international meetings of explaining the weaknesses of our democracy. Now you can explain them and excuse them, but you just can't say those weaknesses don't exist, because they do. It is a little trying, because we need very badly a unified country, and at the moment our country is very far from unified. We need that unity because of the position of leadership in which we find ourselves."[8]

Documents included in this section reflect ER's response to the issues she found most "trying": loyalty oaths (which she thought underestimated the American people's own ability to reject Soviet doctrine) and the Mundt-Nixon proposal that Communists register with the Justice Department ("we are not only underlining our fears that democracy cannot stand up against the superficial attraction of Communism, but we are resorting to the very measures which dictatorships—both Fascist and Communist—use to stay in power"[9]). She agreed to forward petitions to the president questioning Truman's legal treatment of those conscientious objectors still incarcerated and his promotion of a Universal Military Training program. Though ER differed with the president on how exactly all Americans—women as well as men—ought to serve their country, she dropped her opposition to Truman's UMT program because "it is a gesture which would be understood by the USSR as having the purpose of keeping us strong" until the United Nations international force could restrain aggressor nations.[10]

By spring, party leaders and political pundits focused their attention on the 1948 elections. The press and the president interpreted Progressive Party candidate Karl Propper's victory over his Democratic rival in a special congressional election as an indicator of Wallace's popularity. ER discounted their pronouncements, telling Truman "in the big, urban centers, even those who are Democrats just do not come out to vote because they are still radical enough to be unhappy about what they feel are certain tendencies they observe in our Administration."[11] Yet she shared Truman's concerns: "You are right when you say that the leadership in the Democratic Party is tired. Perhaps the people are too. Unfortunately, this is a bad time to be tired."[12] She then wrote DNC chair James McGrath suggesting ways to increase and reinvigorate the African American vote. Such behind-the-scenes action and ER's reluctance to campaign led some pundits to report that "Mrs. R will not only oppose Harry for renomination, but may have a friendly talk with him, urging him not to run."[13] Others, like colleagues Chester Bowles and Helen Gahagan Douglas, tried to convince her to support a Draft Eisenhower movement while Adlai Stevenson asked her to kick off his gubernatorial campaign. "I would love to come out to help you," she replied, "but I am in a rather difficult position. I do not know whether I will be renominated for the General Assembly … In any case, in view of the fact that I have disagreed with the policy of the Administration on the Palestine issue and was told by them that they would like me at least, to stay on the Human Rights Commission in spite of my feelings on the Palestine question, I think I had better not take any part in partisan politics as long as I am on the UN. It is a funny, mixed-up world, but for the moment I think the most important thing is to work on the UN as long as I can."[14]

---

1. See Document 300, ER to George Marshall, 28 January 1948.

2. See Document 327, ER to George Marshall, 22 March 1948.

3. See Document 331, My Day, 26 March 1948.

4. See Document 328, ER to Harry Truman, 22 March 1948.

5. See Document 336, Address to the Pilgrim Society, 12 April 1948.

6. See Document 307, My Day, 9 February 1948.

7. See Document 360, Press Statement, 18 June 1948.

8. See Document 355, "Liberals in This Year of Decision," June 1948.

9. See Document 356, My Day, 1 June 1948.

10. See Document 326, ER to John Gurney, 18 March 1948.

11. See Document 311, ER to Harry Truman, 20 February 1948.

12. See Document 313, ER to Harry Truman, 4 March 1948.

13. See header, Document 346, Charl Williams to ER, 13 May 1948.

14. See Document 338, ER to Adlai Stevenson, 28 April 1948.

Twenty-eight British soldiers died after three bombs detonated, derailing the Cairo-to-Jerusalem train. "It is very unfortunate that the delicate situation in Palestine should be made so explosive by the acts of terror and violence," Marshall wrote ER in 1948. See Document 302. AP IMAGES.

The Arab-Israeli war displaced thousands of Arabs. ER thought that US policies contributed to the violence. "I am very unhappy about going back on the Assembly decision on Palestine," she wrote, "and I feel the handling of it up to this time, has brought about much of the Arab arrogance and violence." See Document 338. © BETTMANN/CORBIS.

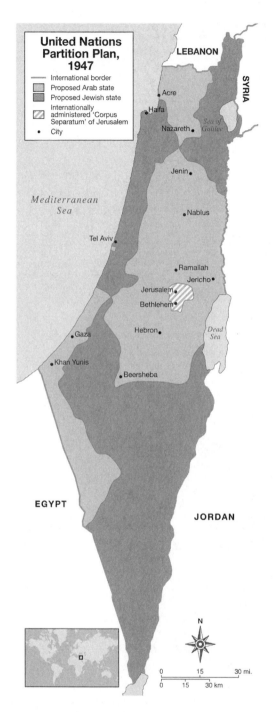

ER supported the UN Partition Plan and criticized Truman and Marshall for their hesitancy to enforce it. "It is though we have taken the weak course of sacrificing the word we pledged and, in so doing, have weakened the UN and prevented it from becoming an instrument to keep peace in the world." See Document 331. MAP BY XNR PRODUCTIONS. THE GALE GROUP.

ER supported Karl Propper and Wallace backed Leo Isacson in a special congressional election. Isacson's victory, she wrote Truman, is not a "good one to hail as a pilot light of what would happen in the national election." Yet, he must recognize how "unenthusiastic" urban Democrats are "at this moment." See Document 311. GEORGE SILK/TIME LIFE PICTURES/GETTY IMAGES.

Journalist Walter Winchell often clashed with ER. In 1945, she protested his report that she had "sharply attacked" Secretary Byrnes. In 1948, she challenged his implication that the US should prepare "for a return to war," writing "People with such influence should use it with great care." See Document 324. © BETTMANN/CORBIS.

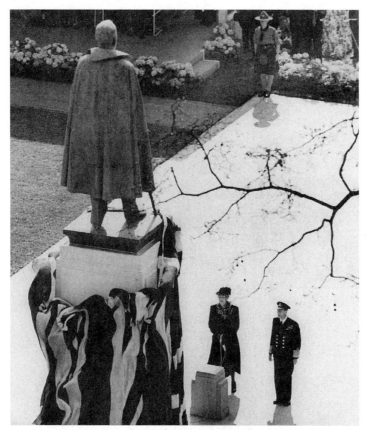

After ER dedicated a statue to FDR in London, she emphasized his conviction that "a careful watchfulness over our own strength and integrity" and an "understanding and sympathy with the points of view of other peoples … could create a lasting bond among men of many nations, in spite of their differences." See Document 336. COURTESY OF THE FDR LIBRARY.

Marshall described early 1948, before the Soviet blockade of Berlin, as "a keg of dynamite." Tensions escalated June 25 when American planes began delivering critical supplies to the city to circumvent the barricaded ground routes. The crisis provided a dramatic backdrop for ER's final work on the Declaration. See n*1 Document 320.* AP IMAGES.

ER, Dulles, Marshall, and Austin often disagreed. "I realize perfectly," she wrote, "that the State Department takes no interest in Human Rights and does not think it very important whether the Commission functions or not." As the Declaration developed, ER secured consistent support from Dulles, Dewey's key advisor. See Documents 358–59 and 366. COURTESY OF THE FDR LIBRARY.

"I know many men are made a little uncomfortable by having women in these [key] positions but the time has come to face facts," ER told party leaders. When she learned Anna Rosenberg "would like to be useful" ER urged Truman to appoint her "head of your consumer food group." See Documents 16 and 296. AP IMAGES.

Reps. Mundt, McDowell, Nixon, and Vail discuss the Mundt-Nixon bill requiring Communists to register with the Justice Department. ER thought the bill "dangerous," arguing "If in a democracy, in order to protect ourselves from Communism, we also surrender our freedom, we are no better off." See Document 356. AP IMAGES.

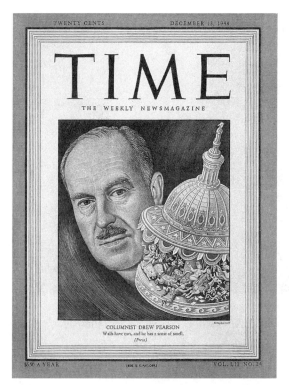

*Columnist Drew Pearson dramatized ER's dissatisfaction with Truman. "Word from Roosevelt circles,"
he wrote, "is that Mrs. R will not only oppose Harry for renomination, but may have a friendly talk
with him, urging him not to run." Later, he will infer she supports Dewey. See Documents 346 and
380.* PHOTO BY TIME LIFE PICTURES/TIME MAGAZINE, COPYRIGHT TIME INC./TIME LIFE PICTURES/GETTY IMAGES.

ER did not join her sons in supporting the Draft Eisenhower movement. Yet when the Republicans nominated Dewey in June she wrote Bowles that although she "knew little" about [Eisenhower], she would "reconsider … in light of the Republican nomination." ER stayed with Truman. See Document 362. © BETTMANN/CORBIS.

LOBBYING FOR A CONVENANT ON
HUMAN RIGHTS

January 13, after returning from Human Rights Commission meetings in Geneva, ER traveled to Washington to review the commission's progress with President Truman. She then gave a similar report to the State Department and the Interdepartmental Committee on International Social Policy (ISP),[1] whose guidance she sought on other pressing commission matters, such as how best to deal with the scores of petitions the HRC received from individuals and groups seeking redress for human rights violations.[2]

As Marjorie Whiteman, a State Department advisor assigned to ER, recorded in the following memorandum to Ernest A. Gross,[3] the department's legal advisor, and Jack B. Tate, his deputy, ER "was most emphatic in expressing the view that the United States must be prepared to go along with the idea of a convention, and the view that something must be worked out in the direction of what to [do] about individual petitions." All involved knew her position contradicted that of Undersecretary of State Robert Lovett.[4]

294

Memorandum of Conversation: Eleanor Roosevelt
Marjorie Whiteman to Ernest Gross and Jack Tate
14 January 1948

Mr. Gross:
Mr. Tate:

At the meeting, at 3:30 yesterday afternoon, between members of the ISP Committee, and others, and Mrs. Roosevelt, which I attended, Mrs. Roosevelt gave a brief summary of the results of the meeting of the Human Rights Commission in Geneva in December, and then invited questions.

She pointed out, in her running statement, that the Commission had in its report submitted three documents to be submitted to members of the United Nations, namely a declaration, a convention, and tentative conclusions with respect to implementation. She indicated that in any new submission of a declaration, the United States, in her opinion, should not limit itself to the submission of its views; rather it should incorporate in a somewhat shorter document than that prepared by the Human Rights Commission the views of the other States, as well as the views of the United States. In this way the United States would not be in the position of telling the other States what they should have in the way of a declaration. She was most emphatic in expressing the view that the United States must be prepared to go along with the idea of a convention, and the view that something must be worked out in the direction of what to [do] about individual petitions.

In answer to Mr. Winslow's[5] question as to why the USSR does not favor the ILO Conventions, though apparently going along with other countries in the matter of social and economic rights so far as the declaration is concerned, Mrs. Roosevelt stated that (a) they did not wish to have anything to do with the League of Nations and (b) desire, instead, to advance the WFTU. She added that they think only in terms of advancing the "mass" not the individual.[6]

In answer to Mrs. Woodward's[7] question as to whether and how it would be possible to speed up Senate action, Mrs. Roosevelt stated that in her mind the way to do it was through the pressure of public opinion, through the "real education of our people" to the proposition "that what was once a domestic question has become an international question".[8]

Mr. Rusk[9] inquired: "Shouldn't we get the backing of the entire Government—including the legislative branch—with respect to the comments of the U.S. on the drafts to be submitted?" Mrs. Roosevelt replied "Yes" but seemed not to have understood the question as she did not discuss the precise question and went on to say at some length that "We should make it clear in our comments that we have difficulties with respect to our domestic problems and be perfectly frank and honest in stating them. We will have to take it to the people of the country and get an understanding of the international problem involved".

Mrs. Miller of the Women's Bureau[10] asked whether a choice had been made between one general convention and several smaller conventions, and Mrs. Roosevelt replied that that question came up at once and it was recognized that on a number of subjects, as for example nationality, there would have to be separate conventions. She added that the first convention "will be a very minimum convention", and that the declaration will "only express aspirations".

Someone tried to make the point that a convention would not be more effective than a declaration "if the States really don't want to carry it out".

Mr. Kotschnig[11] asked "If we say we are willing to accept a convention will that help get a short form declaration". Mrs. Roosevelt replied that "if the US could evolve a short form declaration covering all the points of the longer declaration, that we probably could get that accepted". As to the convention, she stated that we should send in our comments and state that "These are our difficulties on a convention but we are willing to go along and we will try to get it accepted if decided upon. She stressed, with respect to the declaration", that in submitting the new draft we should state that "We have tried to cover all your points—Not, here is our idea of what we think you ought to have".

On the subject of complaints under the convention she stated categorically that it is "obvious that complaints must be limited to states party to the convention". In the matter of complaints under the declaration, she stated that machinery must be devised to do something about the matter.

A person who did not identify himself stated that on reading the declaration he noted that the matter fell into three classes: (1) abstract rights, (2) procedural rights, and (3) obligations of states and governments to enforce these rights by certain social policies, and he suggested that the latter should be taken out of the declaration in order to clarify and simplify it. Mrs. Roosevelt promptly replied that it couldn't be done, as the Eastern bloc of States would then not have anything to do with the Declaration. She thought though that the suggestion might have merit as far as the grouping of articles was concerned.

Someone inquired whether the Secretariat services were adequate in Geneva. To this she replied that they were, but that meeting in Geneva resulted in new people—unfamiliar with what had gone on before—being assigned as representatives.

Mrs. Woodward asked what "protection" meant, in Article 15 of the Declaration, in the sentence reading "All persons who do not enjoy the protection of any government shall be placed under the protection of the United Nations". The answer was not entirely clear, though travel documents of the United Nations were adverted to.

Mrs. Woodward also asked whether the sentence, in Article 25 of the Declaration, "Every one without distinction as to economic and social conditions has the right to the preservation of his health through the highest standard of food, clothing, housing and medical care which the resources of the State or community can provide", indicated or implied "socialization". Mrs. Roosevelt replied "No, it merely sets standards, a flexible one". The question of whether the individual should exert himself to obtain these rights was raised but not answered.

Mrs. Miller asked: "What do the smaller nations want in a convention?" The answer was made that they desire "civil and religious freedoms included; they think that the convention will offer greater protection to the small nations".

Mrs. Roosevelt pointed out that she had taken the position that the drafting of the preamble should be referred by the respective countries to the literary men of their countries, in order that when the preamble is finally drafted they will have most worth while suggestions to consider.[12]

Le/I:MWhiteman

TD RG59, NARA II

Undersecretary of State Robert Lovett thought that the UN's adoption of a declaration on human rights would not be in America's best interests; however, as a declaration did not require Senate approval, the undersecretary limited his objections to disparaging remarks about its content rather than working to derail its adoption. Instead, he focused his attention on preventing the adoption of a covenant. Convinced that the Senate, lead by powerful southern Democrats, would never ratify a covenant on human rights outlawing racial discrimination, Lovett thus opposed drafting such a legally binding human rights instrument. With the hope of winning Lovett's support for a covenant, James Hendrick, ER's State Department advisor, hosted a dinner in Washington in honor of ER to which he invited Lovett, Durward Sandifer, Walter Kotschnig (Hendrick's supervisor), and their wives. The evening's conversation did not convert Lovett and, in the following letter, ER continued to press her case.[13]

In his reply on January 19, Lovett thanked her for the "very sound suggestion" and said he was passing it on to Dean Rusk (then director of the Office of United Nations Affairs) and others working on the issue.[14]

295

Eleanor Roosevelt to Robert Lovett
16 January 1948 [Hyde Park]

Dear Mr. Secretary:

I do not know why I did not think of it the other night, but one of your best arguments to use when the discrimination clause has to be discussed with Congress, is that in this country the people who are the most open to Soviet propaganda are the Negroes because of discrimination. In the international picture this is something we have to consider, in our own world attitude and therefore in our domestic attitude.[15]

It was a great pleasure to me to see you and Mrs. Lovett.

Very cordially yours,

TLc AERP, FDRL

---

1. The Interdepartmental Committee on International Social Policy consisted of representatives of the Departments of State, Justice, Labor, and Interior, and the Federal Security Agency, who met regularly to review UN discussions on their respective areas. Its subcommittees paid particular attention to issues confronting and proposals related to the non-self-governing territories as well as debates regarding human rights, the status of women, workers rights and organized labor, and

social policy, broadly defined (Position of the United States for the Third Session of the Human Rights Commission, 2 April 1948, AERP).

2. From its inception, the HRC received countless petitions from individuals and groups of citizens who sought redress for violations of their human rights. Colonel William Roy Hodgson, the Australian delegate, proposed the creation of an International Court of Human Rights to deal with such complaints, but the United States argued that the HRC should first draft a declaration, then deal with the issue of implementation (Glendon, 38, 84; Lash, *Years*, 66–69).

3. Mazuzan, 39; *RDS, 1946*, 248.

4. See header Document 289 and Document 295.

5. Richard S. Winslow, a career State Department official, coordinated the day to day activities of the American mission to the UN (Mazuzan, 42–43).

6. The International Labour Organization (ILO), which became a specialized agency of the UN in 1946, had been founded as an agency of the League of Nations in 1919 to devise conventions and recommendations for minimum standards of basic labor rights. The World Federation of Trade Unions (WFTU), a leftist labor organization formed in 1945 by the US Congress of Industrial Organizations (CIO), the British Trades Union Congress, and the All-Union Central Congress of Trade Unions, had ties to the Soviet Union. In 1949 the non-Communist faction left the WFTU to form the International Confederation of Free Trade Unions (*NEB*).

7. Either Margaret Rupli Woodward, a foreign affairs specialist assigned to the Office of the Adviser on Refugees and Displaced Persons, or Ellen Woodward (1887–1971), director of the Office of Inter-Agency and International Relations of the Federal Security Agency and advocate of women and children's welfare programs, including the international children's fund (DOS, Office of the Historian; *ANB*).

8. The question of whether the Senate would be willing to ratify a convention on human rights had been discussed by ER and the State Department since June 1947 (see Document 238). Woodward appeared to be asking how the Senate could be persuaded to do so.

9. Dean Rusk.

10. Frieda Miller (1889–1973) was head of the Women's Bureau of the US Department of Labor from 1944 to 1952 (*NAWMP*).

11. Walter M. Kotschnig.

12. ER then sent drafts of the preamble to Archibald MacLeish (1892–1982) for his suggestions. As she reported to him later that spring: "The preamble to the Human Rights Declaration was based on three drafts—French, British, and United States—with a few extra ideas and phrases thrown in. On behalf of the United States, we had withdrawn our previous draft and put in the one you sent me (after a certain amount of editing, relating only to substantive elements). I do not know how pleased or shocked you will be with the compromise result; but I do thank you for a very real contribution." MacLeish responded: "I'm delighted if my draft was of any use to you at all and I'll wait for the final text with the greatest interest." Recalling the drafting of the preamble almost thirty years later, James Hendrick also acknowledged that "the fine preamble is largely the work of the great American poet Archibald MacLeish" who "came across with wording which contributed greatly to the finally approved version" (ER to Archibald MacLeish, 28 June 1948, and Archibald MacLeish to ER, 12 July 1948, RG84, NARA II; James Hendrick to A. Glenn Mower, Jr., 30 June 1975, JPHP, HSTL). For more on MacLeish, see *n*22 Document 3.

13. As Hendrick later recalled:

> Mrs. Roosevelt was fully aware of the difficulties of getting a treaty through the Senate or trying to get an Executive agreement which would dodge the Bricker Amendment, but

she was sympathetic with the idea of pushing for eventually having something "with teeth in it." Her influence in this respect was significant. How far we got with Mr. Lovett on this point is described in the Lash book. The day after the dinner party attended by him and Mrs. Roosevelt, the Geneva draft of the Declaration, which had been on his desk for many days, came back with the comment that he had never read such nonsense. However neither Mr. Lovett nor the immensely powerful General Marshall, then Secretary of State, who I gathered from various indications was no friend of this or any other Declaration, could stand against Mrs. Roosevelt. Without her the whole project could have fallen into bits and pieces (James Hendrick to A. Glenn Mower, Jr., 5 June 1975, JPHP, HSTL).

14. Lash, *Years*, 68, 70, 72–74. See also header Document 289.

15. In a letter written a month later to Bernetta McGuire, an Iowa woman asking for help in preparing a talk on the United Nations, ER expanded on this point:

One of the great causes of war is the lack of Civil Rights for peoples throughout the world. The Human Rights Commission of the United Nations of which I am Chairman has drafted a Bill of Human Rights which is now being considered by every member nation of the United Nations. One major point guarantees no discrimination because of race, creed or color. We must work in our communities to break down prejudice and eliminate discrimination if we are to be an example to the rest of the world. We, as the leading democracy cannot be in the position where other nations can point to our treatment of minority groups (ER to Bernetta McGuire, 11 February 1948, AERP).

ON ANNA ROSENBERG AND TRUMAN'S
CONGRESSIONAL AGENDA

As Truman prepared to battle with the new Congress, ER, who continued to push Truman to appoint more women to important positions in his administration, suggested that he ask Anna Lederer Rosenberg to return to government service.[1]

296

Eleanor Roosevelt to Harry Truman
16 January 1948 [New York City]

Dear Mr. President:

I happened to see Mrs. Anna Rosenberg last evening and I find she is not doing very much in the public field at present and would like to be useful. I do not think she could give full time, but could give several days a week. She is a wonderful organizer and I thought perhaps you would like to consider her as head of your consumer food group.[2]

She would not be interested unless it is really planned this time to do a truly educational job and an honest one all down the line.

I hope that you are going to make a real fight for every one of the social things that you mentioned in your message.[3] Our party people in Congress should truly back you on those. With a little help from the liberal Republicans we ought to get some of them through.

The great trouble is that Mr. Wallace will cut in on us because he can say we have given lip service to these things by having produced very little in the last few years.

Very cordially yours,
Eleanor Roosevelt

TLS AERP, FDRL

297

Harry Truman to Eleanor Roosevelt
19 January 1948 [The White House]

Dear Mrs. Roosevelt:

Replying to yours of the sixteenth in regard to Mrs. Anna Rosenberg, of course, I'd be glad to use Mrs. Rosenberg any time and anywhere—she is a very able person.[4]

I've been making a real fight for all the social things I've advocated ever since I've been here. You will remember, if I hadn't made the fight Henry never would have gotten through the Senate on his last adventure into the Cabinet.[5]

We are faced with a very serious situation in the Congress now, however, because we have more Democrats who are helping the Republicans than we have Republicans who are helping the Democrats in both Houses. There has only been one time in this whole Congress that the Democrats have voted together and that was on an amendment to the Interim Aid Program.[6] We have at least six Senators on the Democratic side who always vote with the Republicans on any forward looking measure and there are only three Republicans on whom we can count in the Senate.[7]

Of course, I intend to continue to make all the fight I am capable of making, just as I always have done. With the help of yourself and forward looking people like you, I think we can make some impression but I am not at all optimistic about the final results. As you can very well remember even when we had a so-called Democratic Congress we had more Democrats who voted with the Republicans than Republicans who voted with the Democrats in both Houses and that situation hasn't improved one bit since the last election.

I think I am as familiar with procedure in the Congress as anybody possibly can be and I use every means at my command to make use of that familiarity. We did succeed in getting an Interim Aid measure through but when it comes to social reforms those people simply are not interested in social reform—in fact they'd like to turn the clock back.

We are making progress on the European Aid Program.[8] We have them extremely worried by our tax proposal.[9] The people are with us on Universal Training.[10] The people are with us on our social program too. We shall keep pounding away and I hope for the right result finally, but I fear that will take an election. I am talking to General Marshall tomorrow about your suggestion.

It was certainly a pleasure to talk with you the other day and I am sincerely sorry that I didn't have a longer period in which to discuss some of the matters that are pending before the Congress.

With kindest regards and best wishes, I am

Sincerely yours,
Harry S. Truman

TLS AERP, FDRL

---

1. A Hungarian immigrant who rose to high-level positions within the Roosevelt and Truman administrations, Anna Lederer Rosenberg (1899-1983) began her political career in New York City Democratic Party politics in the 1920s as a labor and public relations consultant. She followed FDR to Washington where she served in a variety of positions: assistant director of the National Recovery Administration, regional director of the Social Security Board, regional director of the wartime Office of Defense and Health Welfare Services, and FDR's personal envoy on matters relating to military personnel. In the summer of 1945, Truman dispatched her once again to Europe to identify the needs of soon to be demobilized troops. She played an instrumental role in the creation of the GI Bill. She returned to the private sector in August of 1945, with only occasional forays into public service, both for New York City and at the federal level, covering such issues as wage stabilization policy, reconversion, and universal military training. By 1947, she had received the Medal of Freedom, the Congressional Medal of Honor, and the United States Medal for Merit.

ER would send Truman more recommendations for women appointees later in 1948. In July, she sent the president a telegram recommending two women for a position on the newly formed Displaced Persons Commission: Molly Flynn (see *n*11 Document 80) and Anne Laughlin, then an officer at the UNRRA's Ethiopia Mission. Though neither woman received Truman's nomination to the commission, Laughlin later became chief of the Bulgarian Mission of the UN International Children's Emergency Fund. Established by the Displaced Persons Act of 1948, the three-member (all male) commission oversaw federal funding and operations to allow 200,000 displaced persons to immigrate to the United States annually (*NAWMP*; ER to Harry Truman, 30 July 1948, HSTOF; Lash, *Eleanor*, 646; Anne Laughlin to ER, n.d., AERP; "U.N. Names Bulgarian Aid Chief," *NYT*, 2 November 1948, 28; Walter Waggoner, "DP Bill for Entry of 200,000 Is Voted by Senate, 63 to 13," *NYT*, 3 June 1948, 1).

2. In July 1947, Truman established a Food Resources Subcommittee chaired by Chester C. Davis to study the country's available food resources. That September, the president then appointed a twenty-six member Citizens' Food Committee in September of 1947 to strategize about domestic food conservation measures to alleviate ongoing European and world food shortages. Charles Luckman, a soap manufacturer, headed this advisory committee until late November 1947, when he resigned; at this juncture the Cabinet Food Committee took over its administrative responsibilities (Walter H. Waggoner, "U.S. Sets Up 6 Units to Study Economy," *NYT*, 25 July 1947, 5; Bess Furman, "All-Out Conservation Drive Held Cornerstone of Relief," *NYT*, 26 September 1947, 1; Bess Furman, "Food Committee to Lead Campaign from White House," *NYT*, 27 September 1947, 1; "Stillwell Takes Over Food-Saving Effort," *NYT*, 29 November 1947, 6).

3. In his State of the Union address, Truman announced his major aim was "to secure fully the essential human rights of our citizens" and pledged to send Congress a special message on that topic. He then challenged the legislators to pass a comprehensive health care program, extend and increase unemployment benefits, allocate federal funds to education and housing (both public and private), continue rent control policy and the school lunch program, enact price controls and crop insurance for farmers, expand rural electrification, and raise the minimum wage from forty to seventy-five cents an hour. He also proposed raising corporate taxes, while giving a $40 credit to each taxpayer and each of his dependents for a cost-of-living adjustment. Emphasizing that the Marshall Plan would lead "to peace—not war," Truman requested immediate passage of the European Recovery Program and asked Congress to continue proceedings on a Universal Military Training bill (Donovan, 352; Anthony Leviero, "The President Speaks on the State of the Union," *NYT*, 8 January 1948, 1).

4. Truman did not immediately recommend Rosenberg for a government position, but in 1950, George C. Marshall nominated her for assistant secretary of defense. The Senate confirmed her appointment, placing her in the highest-ranking military post then ever held by a woman. She resigned at the end of the Truman administration to return to the private sector (*NAWMP*).

5. When FDR replaced Wallace with Truman as his vice-presidential running mate in 1944, FDR promised Wallace that he could have any job he wanted within the administration except secretary of state. Wallace said that he would like to be secretary of commerce, providing that FDR did want to ask Jesse Jones (whom FDR called "Jesus H. Jones") to leave that position (and his accompanying responsibilities as director of the Reconstruction Finance Corporation and the federal loan board) and accept an ambassadorship or the chairmanship of the Federal Reserve Board. Informing Jones of his decision, FDR then left for Yalta. Jones subsequently started a campaign to remove the RFC from commerce and thus secure his own position while sinking Wallace's confirmation. The Senate Commerce Committee, including its Democratic members, voted 15 to 4 to strip all lending agencies from the Commerce Department, thus providing the ammunition necessary to defeat Wallace's nomination when it came up for a floor vote. FDR refused to intervene and February 1, the Senate voted 42–42 to reconsider Wallace's nomination. Truman, who as vice president presided over the session, voted in favor of reconsidering the nomination "at a later time" and, thus preserved Wallace's nomination until FDR could return from Yalta and sign the congressional measures necessary to insure Wallace's confirmation (Culver and Hyde, 378–84).

6. The Interim Aid bill provided $597 million in aid as a stopgap measure to France, Austria, and Italy until the Marshall Plan went into effect. The Republican-dominated Senate Foreign Relations Committee approved the program in a 13–0 vote and the Senate Democratic Policy Committee offered a unanimous endorsement (*HSTE*; C. P. Trussell, "Interim Aid Called 'Excessive' by Taft," *NYT*, 21 November 1947, 17).

7. It is unclear from available records exactly which senators Truman had in mind with this statement. Judging by senate roll calls on the Taft-Hartley bill and a Republican-introduced tax cut bill in 1947, however, it is possible to guess that the "three Republicans" were Senators William Langer (ND), George Malone (NV), and Wayne Morse (OR). The identity of the "six Democrats" is even

more unclear, as more than six regularly voted against Truman's policies. Most likely, Truman meant a certain group of "Dixiecrats," or southern Democrats, who favored Taft-Hartley and the tax cut: Harry Byrd (VA), Walter George (GA), Kenneth McKellar (TN), Herbert O'Conor (MD), and Bradley Umstead (NC). Other possible candidates include Richard Russell (GA) and James Eastland (MS) (Donovan, 260; "Senate Vote on Labor Bill," *WP*, 7 June 1947, 7; "Senate Vote on Tax Cut," *WP*, 15 July 1947, 6).

8. The Marshall Plan was due to go into effect on April 1, but the Congress had not yet decided on the exact amount of aid to be allocated; the administration had recommended $6.8 billion (James Reston, "Europe Seeks Our Word on How Much to Expect," *NYT*, 15 January 1948, 4).

9. On Truman's tax proposal, see *n3* above.

7. Despite the president's assertion of full public support for Universal Military Training (UMT) in early 1948, the country remained divided over the program as a necessary measure for security. Prominent Americans such as Albert Einstein joined to create the National Council Against Conscription, which viewed the UMT bill as undemocratic and an attempt to spread military influence. The Association of American Colleges also voiced public opposition to UMT. President of Columbia University Dr. Frank Fackenthal, on the other side, organized another group of education executives who believed UMT to be an essential part of national security (Benjamin Fine, "219 College Heads Vote Against UMT," *NYT*, 14 January 1948, 22; "UMT Is Attacked by Einstein Group," *NYT*, 19 January 1948, 5).

THE NAACP PETITION TO THE UN, PART 3

December 28, 1947, ER sent a letter of resignation to the NAACP's Board of Directors to which Walter White replied December 31, promising to present her letter to the NAACP board. However, he remained "absolutely certain that every member of the Board will feel exactly as [he did]—namely that you are one of the most valuable of our members and we would suffer irreparable loss if you were to resign." January 10, White again asked ER to reconsider resigning. The board did not care if she could not "attend as many meetings as you would like, under no circumstances would we want you to resign … Your name means a great deal to us, particularly during this time of reaction when the bigots are trying to undo what" she and FDR "fought for." He also wanted her to know that she had "polled more votes [among local chapters] than any other person" nominated for membership to the board.[1]

ER replied to his two letters, and revisited the dispute over the NAACP's petition, January 20, 1948.

298

Eleanor Roosevelt to Walter White
20 January 1948 [Hyde Park]

Dear Mr. White:

I wrote to the UN about Mr. McClane but I will write again.[2]

I am very much flattered that the Board should want me to remain and of course, I will come to meetings when I can but I am afraid I am going to be a very unsatisfactory member this winter and spring.

I want to tell you that I doubt if you quite understood what happened in the Committee on Minorities and Discrimination in Geneva and in the Human Rights Commission. Jonathan Daniels moved to accept all petitions which would have included accepting the NAACP petition though nothing could as yet be done about it. The Russians refused to include all and promptly suggested that only the NAACP and the International Democratic Women's group, which is communist dominated, should be received because they represented the most people. Naturally it could not consent to that and when it came up in the Human Rights Commission I took the same stand, namely, that we must accept all or none as we could not let the Soviet get away with attacking the United States and not recognize their own shortcomings. I think, however, we did one useful thing which was to recommend to the Economic and Social Council a review of the whole question of petitions and a request that they suggest ways of dealing with the petitions since the present situation is most unsatisfactory.[3]

Very sincerely yours,

TLc AERP, FDRL

---

1. Walter White to ER, 31 December 1947 and 10 January 1948, AERP.

2. Walter White wrote ER on November 18, 1947, and again on January 10, 1948, asking her to use her UN connections to aid G. Warren McClane, who sought employment at the UN's Radio

Liaison Division. ER agreed, and on December 9 forwarded McClane's name to a Mr. Williams, who was probably Chester S. Williams, the public liaison officer for the US delegation to the UN General Assembly. Handwritten marginalia on the recipient's copy of White's January 10 letter suggests that ER also may have sent a letter about McClane to Byron Price, assistant secretary-general of the UN and ranking American in the UN Secretariat; a copy of this correspondence, however, has not been found (Walter White to ER, 10 January 1948, AERP; ER to Mr. Williams, 9 December 1947, AERP; C. Anderson, 139).

3. For White's criticism of Jonathan Daniels's stance in the Sub-Commission on Prevention of Discrimination and Protection of Minorities, see Document 285. ER previously defended Jonathan Daniels in her letter to White of December 8, 1947 (Document 286). The "useful thing" to which ER refers is the decision of the Human Rights Commission to send the Working Group on Implementation's final report to the Economic and Security Council and UN member states for review (see Document 288).

DEFENDING TRUMAN, RESPONDING TO A
YOUNG CRITIC

In his January 27 letter to ER, Larry McEvitt, a history teacher then finishing his degree at Columbia University, wrote to bawl "out Mrs. Roosevelt for not quite doing what I want the future history books to say she did." "Liberalism must remember morals," McEvitt insisted and ER's support of Truman's foreign policy coupled with her criticism of Henry Wallace made "it appear that you are more interested in party than in right." Both FDR, Jr.'s, "terrible" speaking performance and their public support of the ADA made both Roosevelts appear "as apologists and supporters of some things that you can not completely agree with." Moreover, he cautioned her to remember that "if a liberal is one who likes to see the greatest good arrive for the greatest number," then a liberal "must not let the fear of Communism blind him to the right and liberal path." To do so would result in "a policy that could lead to rank militarism and imperialism all in the hypocritical interests of sweet liberty." McEvitt hoped, however, that "as a true and great liberal," ER could "withhold a little of your enthusiasm for the Democracy, as they used to call the party, until it can or does become more worthy of it."[1]

299

Eleanor Roosevelt to Larry McEvitt
30 January 1948 [Hyde Park]

My dear Mr. McEvitt:

I am very grateful to you for taking so much time to write me. I am very much amused, however, at the importance which you seem to attach to my place in history. I assure you I expect no place in history and I do not think it matters in the least historically what I do or what is said about me, since I doubt very much if anything will be said.

As to Franklin, junior, I have no idea what he said which you felt was a terrible performance though you approve of his manner. I imagine he upheld ADA doctrines, most of which I also uphold.[2]

I find plenty of things the matter with the present administration but I think it preferable to a reactionary Republican administration and since you rarely have perfection in this world, I think it is wise to uphold what you think will give you the greatest chance to work for a part, at least, of the things in which you do believe.

I am not in the least afraid of communists but I have worked with the Russians day in and day out and I know exactly what we can expect from them and what we have to guard against and the people who think that by being gentle and kindly and well meaning, that you will impress the Russians favorably, are entirely wrong.

As to Greece, I do not know enough about the present leadership to have a definite opinion.[3] I do know that there is infiltration from outside. I doubt, however, whether the present government is doing what it should do and I think we are probably not being dictatorial enough but I rather think that real signs of recovery from the economic standpoint and food and jobs could buy the present revolutionaries away from those who are buying them with guns. We are not accustomed to this sort of job and we do not do it very well.

The same thing holds good in China. I know nothing about China. I do like what I have heard about Mme. Sun, but China seems to me a pretty difficult problem for outsiders to tackle.[4]

I think the Marshall Plan has some pretty good people back of it. I think it is being sabotaged by the poor ones.

I think President Truman means to do right but he is surrounded by difficulties for which we are partly responsible because we did not elect liberals to Congress in the last election. I agree with you that when we let our fear of communism get the better of us, we probably make more communists just because of the things we do through fear. I do not think it is necessary to be liberal at home and conservative and reactionary abroad. I think you will find that the people administering any program are never all of a piece. Some of them are good and some are not.

I have opposed a good many things and so has the ADA in the present administration so I hardly think we are appeasing or apologizing. We are accepting the fact that at least we can oppose more effectively under a Democratic administration and if we can elect a few more liberals to Congress we may be more successful in our opposition than if we elect a Republican reactionary group for the next four years. I imagine this country could probably stand that period of reaction but I am very much afraid the rest of the world can't.

Of course, anything you do can lead to imperialism and militarism if you do not watch what goes on every day and every minute and how are you going to make the Democratic party any better if you do not work within it? That used to be Mr. Wallace's theory but apparently he has given it up. Do you belong to any political party and do you really work at your citizenship in any particular way?

Very sincerely yours,

TLc AERP, FDRL

———————

1. Larry McEvitt to ER, 27 January 1948, AERP.

2. McEvitt did not specify the ADA pamphlet or reference the remarks for which he criticized FDR, Jr.

3. McEvitt mentioned the leaders of the two main factions in Greece: Markos Vafiades (1906–1992), the leader of the Communist guerrilla forces, and Constantin Tsaldaris, the foreign minister of the legitimate Greek government at the time, and argued, "Honestly, you and I both know, feel is better, that Markos, in spite of all—and I assure you I'm no more of a Communist that I know you to be—is a <u>better</u> Greek than Tsaldaris." On Tsaldaris see *n*3 Document 283 ("Markos Vafiades, 86; Led Greek Communists," *NYT*, 24 February 1992, B10; Larry McEvitt to ER, 27 January 1948, AERP).

4. On the situation in China, McEvitt wrote, "And you and I, I feel sure, could honestly agree, if only privately, that Mao Tse (whatever it is) is a <u>better</u> Chinaman than Chaing, as we both know Mme. Sun Yat-sen is a <u>better</u> woman than Mme. Chaing." See Biographical Portraits for information on Chiang and Madame Chiang (Larry McEvitt to ER, 27 January 1948, AERP).

ELEANOR ROOSEVELT AND THE US POLICY ON PALESTINE

In the January 27 *New York Times*, Pulitzer Prize–winning reporter James "Scotty" Reston wrote that despite the Truman administration's prior endorsement of General Assembly Resolution 181, which partitioned Palestine into separate Jewish and Arab states, unnamed officials inside the State and Defense Departments expressed "strong opposition" to "taking any action that may disturb our relations with the Arab countries of the Near and Middle East." He also cited Secretary of Defense Forrestal's testimony before the House Armed Service Committee, in which the secretary noted "a strategic oil shortage" which threatened to undermine both US "security in times of emergency" and the successful implementation of the Marshall Plan. Reston then noted "service department" concerns that "the Arab states are so disturbed about partition that they will cancel the American oil concession." Lastly, he reported that some state and defense personnel had such "strong opposition to taking any action that may disturb" US relations with Arab nations, that they now urged that the partition plan be enforced by United Nations forces from small "neutral" countries rather than from the US military.[1]

ER, who endorsed the UN partition plan, read Reston's article with alarm, and expressed her concerns separately in the following letters to Secretary of State Marshall and President Truman.

300

Eleanor Roosevelt to George Marshall
28 January 1948 [Hyde Park]

Dear Mr. Secretary:

I read Mr. Reston's article in the New York Times the other day with concern. It seems to me that the decision which was made to support the majority report on Palestine, and our leadership in the UN, places a responsibility on us to see the UN through in actually implementing its policies.[2]

They can probably recruit a volunteer force among the smaller nations but they can not get the necessary modern equipment of war except from us. It would seem to me that the quicker we removed the embargo and see that the Jews and any UN police force are equipped with modern armaments, which is the only thing which will hold the Arabs in check, the better it will be for the whole situation.[3]

I have written to the President but I feel this is a very crucial moment and I think you know that I feel if we fail at the present time, it is more than likely that Russia will step in.[4]

Needless to say this whole question is of deep concern to me. I hope you will forgive my writing you.

> Very sincerely yours,
> Eleanor Roosevelt

TLS RG59, NARA II

January 28, ER's frustrations with Truman's handling of Palestine and his apparent reliance on conservative economic advisors so unsettled ER that she drafted the following blunt missive.

Dear Mr. President:

I have been meaning to write you for the last few days but because the letter is not too pleasant, I have been putting it off.

It is hard for the people around a President to tell him they are troubled and of course, there are many people who tell him only what they think will serve their own interests or what they think he will want to hear.

I spoke to you when I was in Washington of the feelings that I sense that people are worried over the increasing military influence in the government. Now since the photo came out of the Marines going to the Pacific,[5] every young Marine I know has told me that the men went with battle gear and they ask me are we landing in Greece, what are we doing any way, are we getting ready for war?

There is an increasing anxiety everywhere. There is also a fear of the conservative influence that is being exerted on the economic side and I am afraid that this deposition of Mr. Eccles which the New York Times takes as a triumph of "orthodoxy and conservatism in fiscal policy as represented by John W. Snyder, Secretary of the Treasury" is going to emphasize this feeling considerably.[6]

Believe me, Sir, it is going to be impossible to elect a Democrat if it is going to be done by appealing to conservatives. The Republicans are better conservatives than we are. If we are going to vote conservative, it is going to be Taft[7] or Dewey and we might just as well make up our minds to it.

In addition we are going to need Jewish and Negro votes and something must be done about it from that point of view. The present embargo on arms to Palestine and the situation in the UN on that question are very serious. It seems to me that we should be preparing to tell the UN that we, at their request, are removing the embargo on arms and will help them to recruit a police force. It could be done on a voluntary basis but if we do not do it, I am very fearful that the Russians will do it which will move them into that part of the world and make them heroes in the UN.

Now I know very well that the defense people and probably the oil people are saying we must not offend the Arabs, that we need the oil and we will need it particularly if we are going to have trouble with Russia.[8] I feel it absolutely essential that we do not have trouble with Russia but we can prevent it by being cleverer than Russia and keeping her out from the places where we do not wish her to be without offending her. That means we move first and we have a definite policy.

Great Britain has been arming the Arabs and has cooked up much of the trouble in that area for the very simple reason that Gr. Britain knows that only two people will buy Arab oil—the US and the United Kingdom. Russia will walk in and take it when she is ready. We have to out-think Gr. Britain as well as Russia and I am very much afraid that some people in the State Dept. and some people in the defense group are not thinking very far ahead and if the UN becomes a second League and disintegrates as it well may if it gets no support in this situation, then another war is inevitable.[9] On top of that a Republican election is inevitable.

I hate to say these disagreeable things, but I would not feel that I was doing you or the Secy. of State[10] a kindness if I refrained from telling you what I believe at the present time.

I do not know Secy. Forrestal well enough to write him unsolicited, but I am quite willing that you should tell him what I feel.[11] There are two things that I wish to avoid above all else, one, war, two, a republican victory which would I think lead us in time to communism.

However, instead of sending this blunt communique, on January 29, ER sent the following letter, echoing points she made in a letter to Secretary Marshall she mailed January 28.

301

Eleanor Roosevelt to Harry Truman
29 January 1948 [Hyde Park]

Dear Mr. President:

I read Mr. Reston's article in the New York Times the other day and I feel I want to write you on the question of Palestine and the United Nations.[12]

It seems to me that if the UN does not put through and enforce the partition and protection of people in general in Palestine, we are facing a very serious situation in which its position for the future is at stake.[13]

Since we led in the acceptance of the UN majority report on Palestine, and since we feel that the existence of the UN is essential to the preservation of peace, I think we should support a move on their part to create an international police force, perhaps from among the smaller nations.[14] We should stand ready at the request of the UN to remove our embargo on arms and to provide such things as are essential to the control of the Arabs, namely, modern implements of war such as tanks, airplanes, etc.[15]

If we do not take some stand to strengthen the UN organization at the present time, I shall not be surprised if Russia does, which will put us in a difficult position to say the least.[16]

Great Britain's role, of course, is not only to placate the Arabs, but probably to arm them because she knows very well that only the United States and Great Britain are going to buy Arab oil and she wants to be sure to hold her full share.[17]

If the UN is going to be the instrument for peace, now is the crucial time to strengthen it.

With the deepest concern, I am,

Very sincerely yours,
Eleanor Roosevelt

TLS PPF, HSTL

302

George Marshall to Eleanor Roosevelt
16 February 1948 [Washington, DC]

Dear Mrs. Roosevelt:

I have your two letters giving me a frank expression of your views on Palestine.[18]

We are trying hard to formulate and follow policies with regard to Palestine which would seem most likely to promote peace and maintain the prestige and effectiveness of the United Nations.[19] At the same time we must not ignore the humanitarian aspects of the problem.

It is very unfortunate that the delicate situation in Palestine should be made so explosive by the acts of terror and violence committed by both Jewish and Arab elements. Their lack of restraint is not only increasing human misery and suffering but also makes the implementation of the General Assembly's recommendations all the more difficult.[20] The political situation in this country does not help matters.[21]

Since the appropriate organs of the United Nations are now dealing with the Palestine question, we feel that so far as possible we should approach the problem through the United Nations rather than unilaterally.[22]

A decision by the United States, for instance, to permit American arms to go to Palestine and neighboring states would facilitate acts of violence and the further shedding of blood and thus render still more difficult the task of maintaining law and order. We are continuing, therefore, to refuse to license the shipment of arms to that area.

I am told that the United Nations Commission provided for in the November 29 resolution of the General Assembly will shortly make a supplementary report on the question of security in Palestine. It is to be hoped that the report will be of genuine aid to the members of the United Nations in deciding upon a practical course of action which gives some hope for a tranquil solution.[23]

Faithfully yours,
G. C. Marshall

TLS AERP, FDRL

ER continued to lobby Marshall to lift the arms embargo and worked to increase public support for partition and for the UN's role in that process. February 19, she told the 2,500 women attending an event for the United Jewish Appeal:

We must not approach this question as though it were a question of keeping Russia out of the Near East. Our hope for the future is in dealing justly with all nations. I have a feeling that, if the United Nations calls upon the nations of the world to provide them with a force, all nations should answer the call. How they do it within their nations is up to them.

Less than a week later, as the Security Council prepared to consider the security report of the UN Commission on Palestine, bombs exploded in Jerusalem. ER then joined former UNRRA director Herbert H. Lehman, Senator Elbert Thomas (D-UT), and Sumner Welles, then honorary president of the American Association for the United Nations, to propose a four-point program to enforce partition that recommended creating a UN international police force, deploying it immediately to Palestine, invoking Article 41 of the United Nations Charter, and lifting the embargo for those in Palestine who agreed to abide by the partition recommendation.[24]

303

Eleanor Roosevelt to George Marshall
[February] 1948

Dear Mr. Secretary:

Thank you for your letter of Feb. 16th [25]

I am, of course, entirely in accord that we should approach the matter through the UN and not unilaterally, but in placing an embargo on arms we seem not to have interfered with the Arab's ability to get arms and the Jews seem to be getting them sub-rosa, so to speak, which isn't such a good thing. That is why the embargo seemed to me unwise at the present time[26]

I would be in complete accord that we should do whatever the UN asks of us but I am seriously worried that Mr. Forrestal advises the President that even if the UN suggests a UN police force in which all nations have an equal quota, he would feel should Russia go in with the rest of us that he had to mobilize the US fifty percent for war at once.[27] That seems to me utter nonsense and I do not understand it very well It is an explosive situation and I think everyone should try to be as calm about it as they can. This last Jerusalem episode was certainly bad[28]

TLd AERP, FDRL

304

Harry Truman to Eleanor Roosevelt
2 February 1948 [The White House]

Dear Mrs. Roosevelt:

I appreciated very much your letter of January twenty-ninth.

General Marshall and I are attempting to work out a plan for the enforcement of the mandate of the United Nations.[29] I discussed the matter with Franklin, Jr.[30] the other day and I sincerely hope that we can arrive at the right solution.

Your statements on Great Britain are as correct as they can be.[31] Britain's role in the Near East and Britain's policy with regard to Russia has not changed in a hundred years. Disraeli might just as well be Prime Minister these days.[32]

I understand all that and I am trying to meet it as best I can.

Sincerely yours,
Harry Truman

TLS AERP, FDRL

---

1. James Reston, "Bipartisan Policy on Holy Land Seen," *NYT*, 27 January 1948, 8.

2. The United States and the Soviet Union had been instrumental in hammering out the compromise United Nations plan that decided which territory the Arabs and Jews would have, and White House staffers including Administrative Assistant David Niles, Special Counsel Clark Clifford, and possibly Truman himself, lobbied delegates directly during the final forty-eight hours before the vote. In addition, Supreme Court justices Frank Murphy and Felix Frankfurter lobbied the Philippine ambassador to the United States and the Philippine president while former secretary of the treasury Henry Morgenthau sent a telegram to the president of Cuba, and Wall Street financier and sometime presidential advisor Bernard Baruch lobbied the French UN delegation. All this effort convinced many observers that the United States would play a major role in the implementation of partition (Cohen, *Palestine*, 292–98; Cohen, *Truman*, 175).

3. December 5, 1947, the Department of State announced that in view of the current disorders in the Middle East, the United States "is discontinuing … licensing of all shipment of arms to the troubled areas." Because Palestinian Arabs routinely purchased weapons from both the British and neigh-

boring Arab states in defiance of trade restriction, the Jews responded to the American arms embargo by signing an arms contract with Czechoslovakia in December 1947 and received their first arms shipment in April 1948 (*SDB*, 14 December 1947, 1197; "U.S. Embargoes Arms to Mid-East and Bars Passports for Fighters," *NYT*, 6 December 1947, 3; Slonim, 495–514; Lash, *Years*, 125; Barros, 183; Cohen, *Palestine*, 68, 305, 345–48; Cohen, *Truman*, 174; Louis and Stookey, eds., 168).

4. For ER's letter to Truman see header Document 301. For State Department's assessment of Soviet intentions in the Middle East, see *n*16 below.

5. Although ER indicates that the marines left for the Pacific, the photo that ran in the *New York Times* on January 6, 1948, clearly indicates that approximately 1,000 marines from the Second Division at Camp Lejeune boarded two navy transports with full combat equipment "to augment the shipboard training of marines" aboard the carrier *Midway*, and the light cruisers *Little Rock*, *Portsmouth*, and *Providence*, then stationed off the coasts of Italy and Greece ("1,000 Marines Off to Mediterranean," *NYT*, 6 January 1948, 3; Harold B. Hinton, "Marines Going to Mediterranean to Reinforce 4 U.S. Warships," *NYT*, 3 January 1948, 1).

6. On January 27, 1948, President Truman nominated Thomas Bayard McCabe, a Republican banker and paper manufacturer, and a long-time friend of Secretary of the Treasury John W. Snyder, as chairman of the Board of Governors of the Federal Reserve System. In so doing, Truman demoted Marriner S. Eccles, who had headed the Federal Reserve System for twelve years and who had long clashed with Snyder, to the vice-chairmanship. Although Truman maintained that the demotion "reflects no ... disagreement on monetary or debt-management policies, or with official actions taken by the board under [Eccles's] chairmanship," the move was widely seen, as ER noted, as "a triumph for orthodoxy and conservatism" of the fiscal policies promoted by Secretary Snyder (Anthony Leviero, "Eccles Is Demoted in Federal Reserve by Truman's Order," *NYT*, 28 January 1948, 1).

7. Ohio Republicans first elected Robert A. Taft (1889–1953) to the Senate in 1938, where he quickly established himself as one of FDR's most eloquent and persistent critics. Arguing that "the whole history of America reveals a system based on individual opportunity ... individual freedom to earn one's living in one's own way, and to conduct manufacturing, commerce, agriculture or other business" with little government oversight, he criticized the New Deal for making that tradition "so fashionable to deride." As Hitler's military power increased, Taft argued that the United States should respond militarily to Germany only when Germany directly threatened the United States, and thus, voted against the Lend Lease bill. A presidential contender in 1940 and 1944, Taft, in part buoyed by the enactment of his Labor Management Act of 1947 (the Taft-Hartley Act), planned to challenge Dewey again in 1948 (*ANB*).

8. George Marshall, Robert Lovett, Loy Henderson, and James Forrestal, and their supporters within the State and Defense Departments, believed that the loss of Arab support, and access to its oil in case of another war with the Soviet Union, was too steep a cost for the creation of a Jewish state. Forrestal, in particular, saw no domestic political advantage for supporting partition, telling Truman that his Yom Kippur declaration in 1946, did nothing to dampen Dewey's margin of victory in 1946 and telling DNC chair Senator Howard McGrath (D-RI) that "proselytizing for votes and support would add to the already serious alienation of Arabian good will." As Clark Clifford later recalled, Forrestal's argued, "You just don't understand. Forty million Arabs are going to push four hundred thousand Jews into the sea. And that's all there is to it. Oil—that is the side we ought to be on" (Millis, 344–45; Donovan, 371; Hamby, *Man*, 411).

9. For more on British arms sales to the Arabs, see *n*3. For more on Soviet intentions in the Middle East, see *n*16. For more on the breakup of the League of Nations, see Document 74.

10. George C. Marshall.

11. See *n*8 above. Forrestal did not think highly of ER, for example, recalling in his diary January 30, that he "expressed complete agreement with [Oscar] Ewing and ... hoped we would not be burdened with any of the kind of suggestions that Mrs. Roosevelt had tried to promulgate ..." (Millis, ed., 369).

12. For details of Reston's article in the *New York Times*, see header Document 300.

13. The UN resolution of November 29, 1947, which partitioned Palestine into separate Arab and Jewish states, was strictly a recommendation and no machinery or police force existed for its enforcement. In his February 2 reply, Truman told ER, "General Marshall and I are attempting to work out a plan for the enforcement of the mandate … and I sincerely hope we can arrive at the right solution" (Truman to ER, 2 February 1948, AERP; Cohen, *Truman*, 172; Cohen, *Palestine*, 126).

14. ER's call to create an international police force from "smaller nations" was a direct response to the State Department's fierce opposition to sending American forces to Palestine to enforce the UN partition plan. In a memorandum to Secretary Marshall on January 19, 1948, the director of the Policy Planning Staff, George F. Kennan, warned that any assistance the United States might give to the enforcement of partition would result in "deep-seated antagonism for the United States in many sections of the Moslem world," and could lead to the cancellation of valuable US air base rights and US oil pipeline construction in the Middle East, and threaten the overall success of the Marshall Plan (*FRUS 1948*, vol. 5, 545–54).

15. For more on the US arms embargo to Palestine see *n*3 above.

16. The Department of State's Policy Planning Staff determined in a January 19, 1948, memo that the Soviet Union stood to gain by the partition plan if it were to be implemented by force because it gave the Russians the opportunity to assist in "maintaining order" in Palestine. "If Soviet forces should be introduced into Palestine for the purpose of implementing partition," the report concluded, "Communist agents would have an excellent base from which to extend their subversive activities, to disseminate propaganda, and to attempt to replace the present Arab governments by 'democratic peoples' governments." Moreover, the report also declared that the presence of Soviet forces in Palestine would constitute an "outflanking" of the US position in Greece, Turkey, and Iran, and a "potential threat to the stability of the entire Eastern Mediterranean area" (*FRUS 1948*, vol. 5, 551).

17. On January 13, 1948, the *New York Times* reported that the British government had agreed to sell up to $25 million in arms to Egypt, Iraq, and Trans-Jordan under the terms of contracts signed after World War II. The contracts were linked to treaties between each of the three and Great Britain. The British Colonial Office was also secretly arming Arab security forces in Palestine. For more on the British need for Arab oil, see *n*2 Document 310. In his February 2 reply, Truman told ER, "Your statements on Great Britain are as correct as they can be. Britain's role in the Near East … has not changed in a hundred years" ("British Arm Mid-East States; Action Termed Contractual," *NYT*, 13 January 1948, 1; Evensen, 135, 137).

18. In a separate letter to Secretary Marshall written January 28, ER forwarded two letters she had received discussing the British reaction to Arab acts of violence against Palestinian Jews, with the comment that "it does not sound as though Great Britain were behaving wisely" (ER to George Marshall, 28 January 1948; Walter Seligson to ER, 17 January 1948; and Letter from Tel Aviv, Palestine, 27 December 1947, RG59, NARA II).

19. See header Document 300. Four days earlier, February 12, the State Department's Policy Planning Staff had recommended to Marshall three alternative courses of action in Palestine. These included: (1) support the partition plan with "all means at our disposal," including economic assistance to the Jewish authorities and the use of US naval units and military; (2) adopt a passive role, taking no further steps to implement partition and maintaining the embargo on arms to Palestine and neighboring countries; and (3) place Palestine under an international trusteeship or a federal state. The press interpreted this indecision as proof that the administration remained "baffled by the intricacies of the situation and deeply divided about what it can and should do legally and morally" ("U.S. Indecision Growing on Palestine Problem," *NYT*, 15 February 1948, E5; "Memorandum by the Policy Planning Staff, 11 February 1948, *FRUS 1948*, vol. 5, 619–25; Pogue, 357).

20. Violence escalated from sporadic outbursts to systematic attacks. Bombings and sniper attacks proliferated in the towns and cities, while buses were targeted on the roads. At the same time,

groups of Arab irregulars entered Palestine from the east while the Arab countries themselves pre-pared to invade Palestine as soon as the British mandate ended May 15. On February 12, the *New York Times* reported that twenty-five separate attacks occurred in a twenty-four-hour period that resulted in the deaths of three Jews and one Arab (Cohen, *Palestine*, 307; Lie, 166; "4 Die in Palestine in Wide Disorders," *NYT*, 12 February 1948, 16).

21. For more on the relationship of Palestine to the American political situation, see Document 301 and Document 311.

22. At the time the UN General Assembly passed the partition resolution it authorized the creation of a five-member UN Commission for Palestine, which would take over after Britain left Palestine in May and arrange for provisional governments in the two new states. This group, composed of representatives from Bolivia, Czechoslovakia, Denmark, Panama, and the Philippines, began its work in January 1948. The UN Security Council was also discussing the Palestine issue. See also *n*23 below (Pogue, 354; Lie, 163).

23. On February 16, the Palestine Commission (see *n*22 above) issued its security report, which called for "prompt" Security Council action to provide "armed assistance which alone would enable the commission to discharge its responsibilities." The report noted "the existence of a determina-tion to oppose by force the Assembly's plan for partition" and said that without adequate military support the commission would be "unable to establish security and maintain order ..." necessary to carry out the provisions of partition. The report emphasized that failure to provide such a force would adversely affect the UN ("A Challenge Seen," *NYT*, 17 February 1948, 1).

24. "Lehman Asks End of Arms Embargo," *NYT*, 19 February 1948, 6; "U.N. Palestine Force Urged by Mrs. Roosevelt, Welles," *NYT*, 24 February 1948, 1.

25. See Document 302.

26. For more on the Arabs' ability to obtain arms and the United States' arms embargo, see *n*3 above. On January 3 and January 9, New York police discovered multi-ton caches of surplus US military explosives bound for Palestine. The US War Assets Administration embargoed the explosives but as *New York Times* Palestine correspondent Sam Pope Brewer noted, the discovery "raised the question here of what other shipments may have gone through without discovery." Brewer went on to char-acterize Palestine as "undoubtedly one of the world's most heavily armed countries as far as small arms go, but the question of where these arms came from and how they were obtained is ... easy to answer vaguely, though precise details are difficult. [They have] been accumulated through genera-tions by purchase, legal or illegal, by gift and by theft" ("Big TNT Cargo for Tel Aviv Is Found on Freighter Here," *NYT*, 4 January 1948, 1; "WAA Embargo Put on All Explosives; 69 More Tons Held," *NYT*, 10 January 1948, 1; "Plenty of Arms in the Holy Land," *NYT*, 11 January 1948, E5).

27. At a meeting of the National Security Council on February 12, 1948, Forrestal warned the pres-ident that "any serious attempt to implement the General Assembly's recommendation on Palestine would set in train events that must finally result in at least a partial mobilization of US forces, including recourse to Selective Service." Six days later, he again expressed to Truman the "pro-foundly dangerous situation" which would arise for the United States should the United Nations implement its resolution partitioning Palestine into separate Arab and Jewish states, including the "loss of our oil and strategic positions in the Middle East and/or Russian penetration into that area" (Millis, ed., 372–77; Hoopes and Brinkley, 396).

28. On February 22, a bomb exploded on one of Jerusalem's main shopping streets, killing more than fifty people and injuring more than one hundred. Arabs disguised as British soldiers using British military vehicles claimed responsibility for the incident (Sam Pope Brewer, "Jerusalem Blast Kills at Least 33 in Jewish Quarter," *NYT*, 23 February 1948, 1; Sam Pope Brewer, "Blows at Britons Go on in Palestine," *NYT*, 24 February 1948, 1).

29. After weeks of deliberation inside the State Department about how best to enforce the United Nations partition plan for Palestine and bring about an "immediate cessation of violence and ille-

gal acts of all kinds" in that country, February 21, Secretary Marshall recommended to President Truman that Palestine be placed under a temporary UN trusteeship. Such a policy, he stated, "does not represent recession in any way from position taken by us in General Assembly ... Those who may construe trusteeship as a recession hold the incorrect view that Charter authorizes Security Council to impose recommendations by force" (*FRUS 1948*, vol. 5, 637–40, 648–49; Donovan, 370–73).

30. Franklin Delano Roosevelt, Jr.

31. In her January 29, 1948, letter to President Truman, ER stated that Great Britain's role in the Middle East is "not only to placate the Arabs, but probably to arm them because she knows very well that only the United States and Great Britain are going to buy Arab oil and she wants to be sure to hold her full share."

32. Benjamin Disraeli, who as leader of the Conservatives in the House of Commons championed protectionist foreign policy, served as British prime minister from 1874 to 1880, during which time he secured control of the Suez Canal for Great Britain and engineered Queen Victoria's title of empress of India (*OEWH*, 195).

ON WALLACE, THE PCA, AND AMERICAN COMMUNISTS

As ER's criticism of Wallace and the Progressive Citizens of America increased, some "devoted followers" of FDR, such as Curtis MacDougall, wrote to say that they were "shocked and grieved" by her "public statements and writings regarding the candidacy of Henry A. Wallace." MacDougall, who had unsuccessfully run for Congress in 1944 and who now taught journalism at Northwestern University, admitted that although ER brought "some logic to bear against the strategy of establishing a third party now," he found it "extremely difficult to understand … how you have allowed yourself to be persuaded that Mr. Wallace's campaign is Communist-inspired and conducted." He continued:

> … The success of the Goebbels-like red scare propaganda in this country is becoming alarming. I am by no stretch of the imagination a Communist, but I recall how frequently we asked, during the years of Hitler's rise to power: "Why can't the intellectuals of Germany see through it? Why haven't they the courage to speak up?" Today we are learning why.

Concluding, he challenged ER "not only to stop aiding and abetting the dangerous witch hunting but to start opposing it to the fullest extent of your ability."[1]

305

Eleanor Roosevelt to Curtis MacDougall
30 January 1948 [Hyde Park]

My dear Professor MacDougall:

You seem to agree with me that there are some drawbacks to a third party but you do not believe that those backing Mr. Wallace are, in large part, communists. That is something I can not understand if you have followed PAC and the organizations which merged with it and if you have followed the meetings and the general organization back of Mr. Wallace.[2]

Either you do not recognize communist organizations or you are willfully closing your eyes. Too many people are so good that they do not recognize the evil which is before them and that I think, is Mr. Wallace's position, and the position of a few of the people around him.

I do not condone nor agree with the loyalty tests, nor do I agree with many of the other things that are being done both in Congress and in the Administration.[3] Most of us have learned that you do not get one hundred percent perfection and you weigh what is the best that you can get, and with what group you can best fight against the things of which you disapprove.

I can tell the powers-that-be with some chance of being listened to when I disagree on something. If the Republicans were in, I will not be able to tell them anything. The election of a Republican and a reactionary seems to be what Mr. Wallace thinks is the best thing that can happen to us. I think we as a country could stand it, but I doubt if the rest of the world can.

I wish very much that Mr. Wallace had worked with the communists, he would know a great deal more about them. I am not in the least afraid of them, but I know that it is only strength of every kind that they respect.

Very sincerely yours,

TLc AERP, FDRL

1. In addition to a wide variety of press reports, Curtis MacDougall's (1903–1985) publications include *Interpretive Reporting* (1938), a text still used in journalism schools, and the three-volume *Gideon's Army* (1965–66), a history of Henry A. Wallace's 1948 campaign. For an example of ER's criticism of Wallace's decision to run as a third-party candidate, see Document 293 (Curtis MacDougall to ER, 27 January 1948, AERP; "Curtis MacDougall Papers, 1940–1992," Northwestern University Archives).

2. "PAC" is a typographical error referring to the Progressive Citizens of America that ER probably corrected by hand on the copy sent to MacDougall. The Communist Party and the American Labor Party also endorsed Wallace (Schmidt, 35–39).

3. For ER's views on loyalty tests and the House Un-American Activities Committee (HUAC) see Document 271.

ON "THE AMERICAN WAY OF LIFE"

On January 26 Elsa Marcussen, a correspondent for Norwegian and Swedish newspapers, wrote ER that she had "been puzzled by what is frequently referred to as Americanism and also by the frequent labeling of a wide range of attitudes as un-American. I know of no other country that labels her conception of life in quite the same way," she continued, and "I ask you to help me in clarifying for my Scandinavian readers what The American Way of Life is, by stating what Americanism means to you personally and what you regard as un-American."[1]

ER responded with the following letter.

306

Eleanor Roosevelt to Elsa Marcussen

2 February 1948 [Hyde Park]

My dear Miss Marcussen:

I think we are very foolish in the United States in the way we use Americanism and the American way of life without really defining what we mean. In many cases they mean different things to different people in a country as large as ours. I can only tell you what they mean to me.

The American way of life means to me freedom to hear all sides of a question; to state my opinion even where the question concerns my government and its officials.

It means to me the right of association with people I desire to join with for work or for pleasure.

It means belief in civil liberties and an effort to see that they are equal for all people within my country and that opportunity is open to all on an equal basis.

Very sincerely yours,

TLc AERP, FDRL

---

1. At the time Elsa Brita Marcussen wrote for such publications as Oslo's *Arbeiderbladet* and the Stockholm *Morgon-Tidningen* (Elsa Marcussen to ER, 26 January 1948, AERP).

ON CIVIL RIGHTS AND SOCIAL EQUALITY

February 2, 1948, Truman sent Congress a ten-point program based on the report prepared by the President's Committee on Civil Rights, telling members that the report "makes clear that there is a serious gap between our ideals and some of our practices."[1] Declaring that "this gap must be closed," the president urged Congress to adopt anti-lynching and anti-poll-tax legislation; establish a permanent Commission on Civil Rights, a Joint Congressional Committee on Civil Rights, and a Civil Rights Division of the Justice Department; and create a permanent Fair Employment Practices Commission in order to end discrimination in hiring practices.[2]

Southern Congressmen immediately reacted, accusing Truman of "stabbing his best friends in the back" and attacking those members of "both parties [who] get down on their bellies, crawl in the dirt and kiss the feet of minorities." Southern Democrats threatened to stall the European Recovery Program and support a Republican proposal for a drastic income-tax reduction. Louisiana Senator John Overton argued that his constituents should support "a Southern Democratic party of our own" while South Carolina Representative Mendel Rivers declared that "one of these days the so-called leaders are going to find that the so-called Solid South is not as solid as some of the heads of our so-called leaders." As southern governors prepared to convene in Tallahassee, Mississippi Gov. Fielding L. Wright and Alabama Representative Thomas Abernethy called on their colleagues to "revolt," to "formulate plans and adopt a course of action."[3]

In the following column, ER addresses Truman's civil rights proposals and the Southerners' negative reaction to the president's message.

_307_

My Day
9 February 1948

HYDE PARK, Sunday—I went to speak for one of the Y.M.C.A. groups at New York University Medical College late Friday afternoon, and I was interested to see that a good cross section of our New York City population was represented in the audience. There were Protestants, Catholics and Jews, as well as boys of many racial strains, including Negroes. It was easy to talk to them about human rights and the United Nations, for many of them knew, either from personal experience or through affiliations with different people, what the abrogation of human rights means to any group of people.

In this connection I would like to say a word about the reception accorded by a group of Southern Democratic Senators and Representatives to the President's message sent with the report of his Committee on Civil Liberties. Anyone who has worked in the international field knows well that our failure in race relations in this country, and our open discrimination against various groups, injures our leadership in the world. It is the one point which can be attacked and to which the representatives of the United States have no answer.

I wish these Southern gentlemen had a little more faith in the white race and believed that we were capable of associating with and doing justice to another race without of necessity being swallowed up by that race. It seems to me that this hue and cry on the subject of segregation is nothing but an expression of fear. This fear is more understandable in the South, where in certain areas a larger section of the population is colored. Yet if proper conditions existed and there was equal opportunity for education, for economic security and for decent living, there need be no fear. It is because we do not grant civil and economic rights on an equal basis that there is any real reason for fear.

There can be no real democracy where 15,000,000 people feel that they are discriminated against and cannot live on equal terms with their neighbors. Neither will there be real unity in this country until we conquer our prejudices. All of us have them in one form or another, but the time has come when the fight must be made by each one of us to live at home in a way which will make it possible to live peacefully in the world as a whole.

The population of the world is very much greater in the colored areas than in the white areas. For that reason alone, if for no other, I think it behooves us to find a way to live together amicably. It is the white people who really are a minority in the world population, and I sometimes wonder why our arrogance has been tolerated so long. We can be good friends and good neighbors. We do not have to intermarry. That is a personal matter and would not of necessity follow, as some of our Southern friends would have us think, if we had equal opportunity for education in the same schools, or happened to meet on an equal basis in work or even in play.

This is no longer a question which we can regard as a purely domestic issue. It touches the whole world international situation, and it is time we faced it in that way.

TMs AERP, FDRL

L. C. Christian, an attorney from Houston, Texas, took strong objection to the February 9 column. February 11, he wrote to alert ER of the dangerous consequences he thought her politically motivated positions would inspire:

> Because of the unquestioned influence that you are able to wield on the American people—for either RIGHT or WRONG—I warn you that, in advocating social equality between Whites and Negroes, you are "playing with fire," and that there is a dire danger that you, and others like you, shall start a veritable CONFLAGRATION which will utterly devastate the general good will now existing between intelligent Whites and Negroes in the South, and bring upon both races untold trouble, including riots and bloodshed. You should know that an attempt, by New York City Negroes and their Northern and Eastern White associates (not really FRIENDS), to ram down the throats of Southern people SOCIAL EQUALITY by force of arms, will fail. You claim to be a great advocate of "democracy." Democracy means the right to "local self-government." This being true—and it IS true—how can you—a rank outsider—justify yourself in meddling in the affairs of the Southern people? I am convinced that there is, and can be, no justification of your act.[4]

ER replied on February 17.

> I thought I gave the reasons in my column for no longer thinking that segregation and discrimination can continue since we are a member of the United Nations and have signed the Charter. It now becomes a world and not a domestic question any longer. Social equality does not mean you have to invite anyone to be your friend whom you do not wish to have as a friend but it means that in broad ways all are equal.[5]

Christian remained unconvinced.

308

L. C. Christian to Eleanor Roosevelt

21 February 1948 [Houston]

Dear Mrs. Roosevelt:

Your letter, dated February 17, received. I fear that you confuse EXCUSES with REASONS, when you state that you changed your mind, concerning social equality between Whites and Negroes, because "We are a member of the United Nations, and have signed the Charter. It now becomes a world, and not a domestic, question."

There seems to be almost over-whelming evidence that you, and your associates (including President Truman), are actuated solely by political motives. You seek to garner Negro and Jew votes, in politically pivotal States, in the coming November Presidential election. In other words, you people are supinely surrendering to minority political pressure—brazenly ignoring the wishes, and general welfare, of the great majority of American citizens—in an effort to enable "the tail to wag the dog." If this be your purpose—and I charge, and believe, it to be—you will fail. The American people—particularly the Southern people—are not yet willing to submit to political rule by a minority bunch of Negroes and Jews.

You further say: "Social equality does not mean you have to invite anyone to be your friend whom you do not wish to have as a friend; but it means, in a broad ways, all are equal." The forgoing quoted statement is highly disappointing coming, as it does, from a lady whom I have, heretofore, considered highly intelligent. Social equality, between Whites and Negroes, has nothing, whatever, to do with FRIENDSHIP between them. Millions of White Southern men and women have many good Negro friends, but we do not mingle with Negroes on a social equality basis. Intelligent members of both races neither demand, nor desire, such equality, since they well know that it would be bad for all concerned.

As a matter of truth and fact, Mrs. Roosevelt, the attitude of advocates of social equality is priggish, brazenly superior and—in my judgement—outright insulting, to the Negroes. By so magnanimously offering to confer "social equality" upon them, you prove that you actually consider yourself far superior—both personally and racially—to them.

You say you would not compel a White man or woman "to invite a Negro to be his, or her, friend," but you WOULD compel young White girls, by Federal Law, to mix with young Negro "bucks" (many of whom are lecherous-minded) in our schools, churches, railways, buses, theaters, hotels, restaurants, places of business, reside next-door to them, and closely associate with them in all other public places. How long do you think it would be before a young White girl, living under the conditions outlined, and which you would enforce upon her by Federal law, would come to the point where she would WANT to invite some lecherous-minded young Negro "buck" into the privacy of her own home? The inevitable result of social equality would be miscegenation, and the "mongrelization" of the White race. Do you, and your associates, actually DESIRE the destruction of our race? I cannot—as yet—believe that you do. I am still firmly convinced that your stand is taken because of an abysmal lack of understanding of the TRUTH concerning the problem. For this reason, I again warn you to "watch your step." You, and your associates, are playing a very dangerous game—political though it may be—and you promise to bring much trouble to the good people of the South, both White and Negro. You have changed your stand ONCE. I suggest that you change it again.

Sincerely yours,
L.C. Christian

TLS AERP, FDRL

ER dictated the following response to her secretary who then mailed the reply to Christian.[6]

309

Eleanor Roosevelt to L. C. Christian

26 February 1948 [Hyde Park]

I am answering your letter of Feb 21 although I feel there is very little use in doing so.

You know very little about your country I fear. The Negro votes will go almost entirely to Henry Wallace and so will many other minority group votes.[7]

You forget that non-segregation in public places and public conveyances exists in many places without the dire results you picture. The things you say are insulting to both White and Negro people.[8]

HLd AERP, FDRL

———————

1. December 5, 1946, Truman issued Executive Order 9808 establishing the President's Committee on Civil Rights. After telling its fourteen members (including Franklin D. Roosevelt, Jr.) that "I want our Bill of Rights implemented in fact," he asked them to prepare a report on US race relations and propose specific actions which might be taken to improve those relations. The committee presented thirty-five recommendations in its final report, *To Secure These Rights*, to Truman October 29, 1947 (*HSTE*).

2. *HSTE*; "Text of President Truman's Message on Civil Rights," *NYT*, 3 February 1948, 22. For the NAACP's reaction to *To Secure These Rights* and discussion of the report in the UN, see Document 285.

3. Mary Spargo, "Southerners Threaten Bolt on Race Issue," *WP*, 4 February 1948, 1; John Popham, "South's Governors Hear 'Revolt' Talk," *NYT*, 7 February 1948, 19; C. P. Trussell, "South Threatens Anti-Truman Drive Over Civil Rights," *NYT*, 4 February 1948, 1.

4. L. C. Christian to ER, 11 February 1948, AERP.

5. ER to L. C. Christian, 17 February 1948, AERP.

6. ER's staff did not preserve a typed copy of the outgoing correspondence, only the notes recording ER's dictation.

7. By election time, support for Wallace had dwindled among most voters. Truman did especially well among African Americans at the polls, getting over 75 percent of their vote nationally in his 1948 victory (Gardner, 144–46).

8. Christian responded that while

> only ONE Negro was lynched in all the Southern States in 1947, while literally hundreds of White women were brutally raped and beaten by Negro brutes during the same period of time, you devote all your time and attention to the ONE poor Negro lynch-victim, shed tears of shame over his sad fate and his deprivation of his JUST and CONSTITUTIONAL rights, but you have not one word of pity for the hundreds of victims of Negro brutality. On the contrary, you would have enacted Federal Laws which would hang, or

imprison for many years, any White man who DARED defend the honor of his wife or daughter from these lecherous Negro brutes.

If she, he concluded, "could talk to one or both of the victims of the Negro brute" referenced in the two clippings he included with his letter, he was "firmly convinced" that ER "would no longer advocate 'social equality.'" There is no record that ER replied to this last letter (L. C. Christian to ER, 5 March 1948, AERP).

ON ARAB LEADERSHIP AND THE CRISIS IN PALESTINE

Arab nations strongly opposed the UN partition plan for Palestine, which they interpreted as unfairly pro-Zionist. The week before ER wrote the following column, the Arab Higher Committee of Palestine issued a declaration of war against any partition attempt, and, in an open letter to UN Secretary-General Lie, labeled the UN vote for the partition plan illegal and "contrary to the letter and spirit of the United Nations Charter."[1]

As the following column illustrates, ER wondered why "the Arab leaders are so lightly flaunting defiance of the United Nations" and "why some of our own defense officials do not put more emphasis on finding a good substitute for oil."

310

My Day

13 February 1948

HYDE PARK, Thursday—I do not know how other people feel, but I personally am wondering on what theory the Arab leaders are so lightly flaunting defiance of the United Nations. They should know that, in the long run, the existence of the United Nations is of importance to them. If the United Nations is wiped out and we return to the condition of each individual nation looking out for itself, the great nations are the ones that will have the easiest time. The small nations will live in continual uncertainty.

Had the Arabs protested but then accepted the UN majority decision on Palestine—and tried to work it out even though it was not agreeable to them—they would have earned respect and sympathy throughout the world. As it is, they are daily creating a greater sense of irritation among many people who have no special sympathy for the Jews but who do believe that the existence of the UN is important to the world.

To whom will the Arabs sell their oil if not to the great nations, and if they do not sell their oil, how will they live? It seems to me their policies are short-sighted in a world where oil may seem all-important today but where, the day after tomorrow, a new invention may have made it quite immaterial.

I have been wondering for a long time why some of our own defense officials do not put more emphasis on finding a good substitute for oil and worry less about where more oil is to come from. Our people are ingenious. New discoveries are all around us, and when we have to make them, we nearly always do.

For instance, if the war had not made them important, the sulfa drugs and penicillin might still be undeveloped, because it was expensive to do the necessary experimentation. But when these drugs became essential, the expense made no difference.[2] If it is essential to find a substitute for oil or rubber or any other material, I have faith that it can be done, because it has been done in the past.

The Arabs are not using their oil to develop their own countries—to bring water to the desert and make the land support their people in greater comfort. All they do is sell their oil, and only a few people profit. That is short-sighted, for widespread and expanding well-being, which can be brought about by reclaimed land and greater productivity, would be a much surer foundation on which to build future strength.[3]

I do not understand how any people facing an atomic world can want to pull down the United Nations, but for a people who are not on the whole too strong, it seems to me almost suicidal foolishness.

TMs, AERP, FDRL

---

1. December 1947, a political committee of the Arab League met in Cairo to discuss how best to assist the Arab Liberation Army in its efforts to prevent partition. For more information on the UN partition plan, see header Document 300 (Louis and Stookey, 123–26; Mallory Browne, "Palestine Arabs Warn U.N. of War on Partition Army," *NYT,* 7 February 1948, 1).

2. Although sulfa drugs and penicillin were discovered before World War II, neither was produced in large quantities until the military's wartime needs made their availability a necessity. In the case of penicillin, the US government recruited more than twenty chemical companies to produce the drug. By 1945, they were producing 650 billion units a month (Public Broadcasting System, "A Science Odyssey: People and Discoveries: Fleming Discovers Penicillin 1928–1945," http://www.pbs.org/wgbh/aso/databank/entries/dm28pe.html, accessed 3 June 2005).

3. ER expanded on her views of Arab development, or her perceived lack thereof, in her March 1 column:

> Of course, if we were to look upon the question of Palestine from the purely economic standpoint, we might say quite truthfully that the Arabs had never developed Palestine to the extent that the Jews have in the last few years, and that with the irrigation projects possible in the future both Arabs and Jews could probably achieve a better standard of living than they ever had before in that area.

Furthermore, she noted three weeks later, despite "some few people at the top having greatly profited" from the sale of Arab oil to the United States and Great Britain, "there is no notable change in the standard of living of the average, poor Arab citizen" (*MD,* 1 and 26 March 1948).

ON KARL PROPPER, SOUTHERN DEMOCRATS,
AND ELECTORAL POLITICS

February 17, 1948, a special election was held in the Bronx to fill the seat in the House of Representatives vacated by Benjamin J. Rabin, who resigned in December 1947 after being elected to the New York State Supreme Court. Political pundits watched the election with interest, promptly depicting it as the first electoral showdown between Henry A. Wallace's Progressive Party and Democrats who remained loyal to Truman. Despite the predictions of both Bronx Democratic chair Ed Flynn and the *New York Times* that Karl Propper, the Democratic candidate, was "virtually certain" to win, Leo Isacson, the American Labor Party candidate for whom Wallace campaigned, won the election with 22,000 of the 40,000 votes cast. Propper, despite strong support from Flynn's party apparatus and highly publicized campaign appearances by ER and Mayor O'Dwyer, trailed Isacson by 10,000 votes. In his victory speech, Isacson claimed the election signified a "resounding repudiation" of Truman foreign policy and demonstrated the viability of the Progressive Party: "The people have shown that Wallace-endorsed progressive candidates for Congress in the coming national election can win and by their vote they have given the answer to the shaky liberals who have raised the false cry that third-party candidates cannot win."[1]

The day after the election, in a letter telling ER that he had indeed reappointed Judge Marion Harron to the federal tax court, Truman asked, "What do you think of the Bronx and Ed Flynn's control now?"[2]

_____311_____

Eleanor Roosevelt to Harry Truman
20 February 1948 [New York City]

Dear Mr. President:

I was interested in your comment on the defeat of Ed. Flynn's candidate in Bronx County. I think Ed. Flynn has proved the point which he has been trying to make for a long time, namely, that in large urban areas there are great groups of people who are extremely radical and very much opposed to what they feel is Military and Wall Street domination in our present Administration.

These people in the Bronx followed my husband because they felt he understood their needs and they were getting, domestically, protection which they had never had before. There has always been a strong element of communism in this section of the Bronx. I can remember it specifically among the youth groups back in 1933 and 1934. I noticed the night I spoke that every time Mr. Wallace's name was mentioned, it was cheered.[3]

I was not very much surprised by the results of the vote because in the big, urban centers, even those who are Democrats just do not come out to vote because they are still radical enough to be unhappy about what they feel are certain tendencies they observe in our Administration.[4]

Ed. Flynn has told you this, I think, on a number of occasions. It is important because if the Democrats are going to win in a State like New York, they have to carry by a great majority, the big urban centers. I am sure you are well aware of this, but I feel it my duty to re-enforce what already has been said, disagreeable as it is.

I never thought this district was a good one to hail as a pilot light of what would happen in the national election, but naturally it would be one which Mr. Wallace and the American Labor Party would pick to make much of, since they were almost sure of success.

Ed. Flynn, I think, felt that his organization would do much better than it did, but he did not count on the fact that even Democrats in areas such as this are unenthusiastic at the moment.

I wrote in my column the other day, as a result of the indications I find in my mail, that the two things bothering the average man most at present are inflation and the fear of another war.[5] Congress is doing all it can to help us, I think, because certainly they are showing a complete disregard for the high cost of living as it affects the average human being, but you never know how many people realize this.

I know that in order to obtain what we need in the way of Military strength for defense, it would seem almost essential to whip up fear of communism and to do certain things which hurt us with the very element which we need in the election. How we can be firm and strong and yet friendly in our attitude toward Russia, and obtain from Congress what we need to keep us strong, is one of our most difficult problems. I have often thought if you could explain the whole situation over the radio in a series of talks to the people of our country, it might clear up some of our difficulties, because I find great confusion in the minds of the average citizens.

Very sincerely yours,
Eleanor Roosevelt

P.S. James[6] told me of Mr. Forrestal's feeling that no American should be allowed to volunteer in an International Police Force.[7] I think Mr. Forrestal is entirely wrong. I was shocked at the suggestion that any American volunteering to fight in Palestine would lose his citizenship, and I could not understand why that was not invoked when Americans went to Canada and enlisted in the Canadian forces before we were in the war.[8] It seems to me that if the UN calls for an International Police Force, it might very well say that the quotas should be equal from all nations, big and little, and then we should call for volunteers within our nation. To say that just because Russia might have some soldiers in Palestine on an equal basis with us and all other nations involved, we would have to mobilize fifty percent for war, seems to me complete nonsense and I think it would seem so to most of the people of the United States.

E.R.

TLS HSTSF, HSTL

312

Harry Truman to Eleanor Roosevelt
27 February 1948 [Key West]

Dear Mrs. Roosevelt:

I appreciated very much your letter of February 20 in regard to the Bronx election. Naturally, all sorts of conjectures are given as to the reason for that return. It is my honest opinion that people everywhere are in an unsettled frame of mind, that the revolt in 1946 is not yet finished, and that you must also take into consideration the fact that the leaders in the Democratic Party are tired, with the long grind through which we have been, due to the terrible depression and World War Two. I have to do things my own way, but I was a member of the resolutions committee that had a great deal to do with writing the Democratic platform of 1944, and I have been trying religiously to carry it out.[9] We haven't had a Congress since 1944 that had any idea of abiding by that platform.

I can't bring myself to line up with the crackpots who are trying to sell us out to the Russian government, nor can I see anything good in the Harry Byrds and Eugene Coxes.[10] That is the situation with which we are confronted now. I shall continue to do the best I can to meet the problems with which we are faced. The result is probably in the lap of the gods, although sometimes a little help and a little energy will get results in spite of that situation.

I hope you have a most pleasant visit in Great Britain, and that I will have a chance to talk with you when you return as to conditions over there, which you no doubt will observe carefully.[11]

I had a most pleasant visit with Jimmie the other day, and the Secretary of Defense has been informed as to my views on the international police force. Of course, if the United Nations international police force is organized, the citizenship of the members of that force and their native countries should not be disturbed.

Sincerely yours,
Harry S. Truman

TLS AERP, FDRL

ER agreed with the president's assessment of party leadership and then asked Truman if he wanted her to stress any particular points in the speeches she prepared to give in Europe.

_313_

Eleanor Roosevelt to Harry Truman
4 March 1948 [New York City]

Dear Mr. President:

I was very much interested in your letter of February 27th, and I am glad you are not going to line up with those who want to sell us out to the Russian government, or with the Byrds and the Eugene Coxes!

These Southern statesmen seem to be very short-sighted and you are right when you say that the leadership in the Democratic Party is tired. Perhaps the people are too. Unfortunately, this is a bad time to be tired.

Thank you for your good wishes on my trip to Europe. I shall try to observe conditions and I shall try to find out from the Secretary of State before I go whether he has any particular points that he wishes stressed and any he wishes me to avoid in any speeches which I may make.[12] I am going to London as you know, and to Brussels and to Holland. If you have any suggestions I shall be grateful to you if you will send them to me.

I hope your trip to Florida was enjoyable and of great benefit.

Very cordially yours,
Eleanor Roosevelt

TLS HSTSF, HSTL

---

1. "Mayor to Support Bronx Democrat," *NYT*, 4 February 1948, 26; Warren Moscow, "Wallace Man Wins Sweeping Victory in Bronx Election," *NYT*, 18 February 1948, 1.

2. FDR first appointed Judge Marion Harron (1903–1972) to the United States Tax Court in 1936 (*ANB*; Harry Truman to ER, 18 February 1948, AERP).

3. On February 12, 1948, ER and New York mayor William O'Dwyer spoke at a rally for Propper, held at the Hunts Point Palace in the Bronx. O'Dwyer and ER both argued that Wallace was damaging the liberal programs of the Democrats by working outside the party. The *New York Times* reported that ER, likely referring to both the House and presidential races, "declared it was better to elect a regular Democrat who was a liberal than someone 'who would stand by himself' when and if elected" (Warren Moscow, "Wallace Is Urged by Mayor to Drop Third-Party Race," *NYT*, 13 February 1948, 1).

4. Forty-two percent of the eligible voters showed up at the polls for the special election. Whereas 89,000 voters in the district cast a ballot in the 1946 regular election, only 40,597 voted in the special election (Warren Moscow, "Wallace Man Wins Sweeping Victory in Bronx Election," *NYT*, 18 February 1948, 1).

5. In her column of February 20, 1948, ER wrote:

> Two things worry the American people—inflation and the fear of war. Henry Wallace, who supported and spoke for the American Labor Party candidate, tells them that the third party is for a foreign policy which would prevent war, and he excoriates everything that is done by the Democrats even though they have the same objective. It is just a case of two different methods but, being a hopeful soul, Henry Wallace is not afraid to announce authoritatively that his way will keep us out of war. And since that is what the people wanted to hear, they believe him.
>
> He sympathizes with them in the matter of inflation, but the third party does not have responsibility to prevent it—nor will Leo Isacson, the newly elected Congressman from the Bronx, be able to do anything about it. Only two members of the American Labor Party in Congress—Mr. Isacson and Rep. Vito Marcantonio—are not going to accomplish anything on their own. They will vote either with the Republicans or the Democrats, and their votes will count for very little …
>
> I would say that this election points up a very simple thing—namely, that the Republicans and Democrats alike had better bestir themselves to remove the people's two great anxieties, or the course of our government in the next few years may be surprising to both parties! (*MD*, 20 February 1948).

6. ER's eldest son, James, in his capacity as Democratic national committeeman from California, met with Truman at the White House on February 19, 1948 ("In Washington Yesterday," *NYT*, 20 February 1948, 4).

7. James Forrestal's belief relied upon a strict interpretation of existing law. American passports include a statement declaring them void if the individual traveling under the passport does so "for the purpose of entering or serving in armed forces." The US consulate general in Jerusalem reminded Americans in Palestine of this provision on January 30, 1948, when it declared that the United States would not intervene in any situation where an American was captured during the armed conflicts in the region, as any hostage would have forfeited such protection upon fighting for a foreign army. Thus, the question was one of whether or not volunteers to a UN police force would be exempt from this provision (Sam Pope Brewer, "U.S. Warns Citizens in Palestine Fight," *NYT*, 31 January 1948, 1).

8. The *New York Times* reported that more than two thousand American citizens enlisted in Canada's armed forces before the United States entered World War II in 1941 ("2,000 Will Shift to Our Army," *NYT*, 22 May 1942, 18).

9. As a member of the committee charged with drafting the 1944 Democratic platform, Senator Truman pushed his fellow Democrats to place greater emphasis on foreign policy matters, arguing

that "for twelve years the Democratic party's domestic program has been clear and generally accepted. It doesn't need elaboration." He urged the adoption of a strong foreign policy plank clearly articulating "that the United States will take part in world affairs this time and maintain the peace by using the Army and Navy, if necessary." The platform committee concurred. "To speed victory, establish and maintain peace, guarantee full employment and provide prosperity," the platform promised the party would work with the UN to establish peace, support legislation favorable to labor, and protect the rights of minorities ("Urge World View Upon Democrats," *NYT*, 10 July 1944, 16; "Democratic Party Platform of 1944," http://www.presidency.ucsb.edu/showplatforms. php?platindex=D1944, accessed 7 June 2005; Savage, 59).

10. Harry Flood Byrd (D-VA) (1887–1966) criticized New Deal reforms as early as 1933. As chair of the Joint Committee on Reduction of Nonessential Federal Expenditures, Byrd continued to call for the reduction of federal spending in all non-defense-related programs until his resignation in 1965. A vocal critic of Truman's civil rights reforms and staunch advocate of states' rights, Byrd nevertheless remained "silent" during the 1948 election: he neither endorsed Truman nor left the Democratic Party for Strom Thurmond's States' Rights Party.

Eugene Cox (1880–1952), Democratic congressman from Georgia, served as Byrd's counterpart in the House. As a member of the Rules Committee, Cox voted with the conservative Republicans on his committee to kill much progressive legislation before it even reached the floor of the House. Sharing Byrd's states' rights convictions, Cox went a step further than the senator and openly renounced the Democratic Party in the 1948 election in favor of the States' Rights Party of Thurmond (*ANB; DAB; FDRE*; John N. Popham, "Dewey Is Favored to Win in Virginia," *NYT*, 29 October 1948, 7; "Reprisals on Foes of Truman Sought," *NYT*, 12 December 1948, 77).

11. ER left for London on March 27 to attend the Pilgrim Society's unveiling of a statue of FDR ("Politics Shunned by Mrs. Roosevelt," *NYT*, 28 March 1948, 36). For more on ER's European trip, see header Document 336.

12. On March 10, Secretary Marshall responded to ER's inquiry with suggestions, but not without noting, "Events in the world are moving so rapidly that it is difficult to make, even one month in advance, definite suggestions for future speeches." Nevertheless, he thought European audiences would be particularly interested in the European Recovery Plan (the Marshall Plan). Although Congress had not yet approved the plan at the time of Marshall's writing, the secretary was confident it would soon do so. He suggested that ER "stress the fact that its passage is a remarkable manifestation of America's recognition of the urgent necessities of the situation in Europe and of our responsibilities in the world." To explain any apparent reluctance on the part of everyday Americans to help the world, ER should "make clearer to them [Europeans] how difficult it is for farmers in Iowa or Nebraska ... to understand and react promptly to a situation thousands of miles away." Finally, Marshall suggested ER might try to dispel the Communist charges regarding the "imperialist nature" of the ERP. Reminding ER that these were only "tentative suggestions," he concluded his letter with an expression of full confidence in her ability, assuring her, "You will know the right thing to say in any given circumstances." See also *n*9 Document 320 (Marshall to ER, 10 March 1948, AERP).

ON TRAVELING AS A "PRIVATE CITIZEN" AND
THE MARSHALL PLAN

ER first contacted her friend Dutch crown princess Juliana von Nassau as she planned her spring trip to the Netherlands, where she would deliver an address at Utrecht University.[1] As the women discussed logistics that would afford ER the greatest opportunity to meet with the Dutch and assess the problems they faced, ER told Juliana that she hoped to avoid the trappings associated with a state visit, and that she especially did not want a formal state reception. "You must remember that it is Franklin whom the people care about and his work that is appreciated and that I am only a private citizen now." What she really wanted to do was travel as a journalist. "I still write my column and for that reason I think I can be useful in finding out all I can about conditions and telling the people of this country something of what I see in order to make them realize more fully what their responsibilities are."[2] Juliana then invited ER to stay with her family, rather than with her mother, the queen. "For mother it will be easy to meet you at our place. Altho' we don't want to rob mother of her possible hostess ship, if you stay with us it would prove the most practical" as Juliana's home had the "advantage of being near to Utrecht, and generally situated in the centre of the country, at commuting distance from everywhere."[3]

ER responded a short time later, further detailing her plans for the trip.

314

Eleanor Roosevelt to Juliana von Nassau
24 February 1948 [Hyde Park]

Dear Juliana:

I have your letter of February 15th. I can, as you know, stay with Ambassador Baruch if it would be better than staying with you.[4] I simply thought it would be less official and bother your mother less if I were with you. However, you know better than I do what would please everybody most. I do not want anyone to have any more trouble than is necessary.

What I would like to do is to see any thing that I could write about. I am trying to use whatever I do in Europe or see there, to inform people of this country on conditions and if possible, increase their interest in the Marshall Plan, and you will know better than I was is worth seeing and doing.[5]

Of course, I shall be delighted to meet any one you want and to do all that I possibly can in the time that I am in Holland. Miss Thompson is delighted to accept your invitation, and I shall let you know about Major Hooker in a day or two.[6]

It will be a great happiness to see you again and to see the children. I hope the measles are now safely over and that you and the children are well.[7]

Affectionately,

TLc AERP, FDRL

---

1. ER planned to travel to Holland, April 19–22, after she helped dedicate the statue to FDR in London's Grosvenor Square and addressed the Pilgrim Society's annual dinner (Document 336). For ER's address at Utrecht, see Document 337.

2. ER to Juliana, 3 February 1948, AERP. On Princess Juliana and the relationship she developed with ER while the Dutch Royal Family lived in exile during the Second World War, see *n*6 Document 55. Juliana succeeded her mother, Queen Wilhelmina (1880–1962), as queen of the Netherlands on September 6, 1948, when the queen resigned for health reasons (David Anderson, "Wilhelmina Will Abdicate; Juliana to Be Queen in Fall," *NYT*, 13 May 1948, 1; David Anderson, "And Now Enter Queen Juliana," *NYT*, 5 September 1948, SM12).

3. Juliana to ER, 24 January 1948 and 15 February 1948, AERP.

4. Herman Baruch, Bernard Baruch's brother, served as US ambassador to the Netherlands from 1947 to 1949 ("Baruch Sees Dutch Queen," *NYT*, 13 April 1947, 35; "Herman Baruch Sails," *NYT*, 27 August 1949, 5).

5. While in the Netherlands between April 19 and 22, ER spoke at a meeting of Dutch women's organizations at the Ridderzaal, flew over the country surveying war damage, received an honorary Doctor of Laws from the University of Utrecht (see header Document 337), and visited a tuberculosis hospital for students who had taken part in the resistance ("Mrs. Roosevelt in Netherlands" *NYT*, 19 April 1948, 6; *MD*, 22 and 23 April 1948; Lash, *World*, 260–61).

6. Major Harry S. Hooker, a former law partner of FDR and a close friend, accompanied ER as Truman's representative with the rank of ambassador, along with Malvina "Tommy" Thompson; Lash, *Eleanor*, 469; "Politics Shunned by Mrs. Roosevelt," *NYT*, 28 March 1948, 36; Lash, *Love*, 258).

7. Princess Juliana (1909–2004) and her husband Prince Bernhard (1911–2004) had four daughters: Crown Princess Beatrix (1938–), Irene (1939–), Margriet (1943–), and Maria Christina (1947–), the eldest three of whom ER had met in the United States during the war. In her letter of February 15, Juliana explained that her tardy response was "due to measles, absences, etc." (*MD*, 22 April 1948; Juliana to ER, 15 February 1948, AERP).

DEFENDING THE UN PARTITION PLAN FOR PALESTINE

ER's mail often provided material for her column, particularly when her correspondents addressed controversial issues such as the partition of Palestine. One such letter came from Lydia T. Bacon of St. Petersburg, Florida, who wrote February 24, 1948, to criticize ER's stand on partition. Bacon and her family had lived in the Middle East for many years and her husband, Arthur, had taught at the American University in Beirut, where Charles Malik had been his assistant. Bacon's sister still headed a girls' school in Ramallah, a town about ten miles from Jerusalem. "We know these Arabs as a people and love them," she told ER. "They have been there for 1300 years and there is nothing right about the partition … If we feel so badly for the Jews why do we not give them one of our states?"[1]

Although ER recognized the objections to establishing a Jewish homeland in Palestine, she thought the idea that the United States should arbitrarily displace citizens of a certain state, and turn that state over to the Jews, a little far-fetched. In her March 1 column, ER dismissed Bacon's suggestion as "somewhat funny," and insisted that critics who made such proposals had given "very little thought" to the issue. "They seem to take it for granted that the General Assembly voted on this issue without any real thought being given to it—which, of course, is not true," she reported. "Only the General Assembly itself can change its vote, and it seems to me that it would be disastrous to the prestige of the United Nations if a decision once taken were not carried out."[2] She also responded to Bacon with the following letter.

315

Eleanor Roosevelt to Lydia Bacon
27 February 1948 [Hyde Park]

My dear Mrs. Bacon:

You are looking at this question of Palestine from the point of view of giving the land to the Jews. The long and very careful deliberations which the delegation members and the Secretary of State went through in the General Assembly were on a somewhat broader scale.[3]

For thirty years no effort has been made to solve the Palestine question. In the early days when the land was opened up to the Jews, they were given an assurance and an agreement was signed with the Arabs which gave the Jews hope that Palestine would some day be a Jewish homeland.[4] If the peoples concerned had not envisioned that possibility, they should not have allowed hundreds of thousands of Jews to go and sacrifice their lives to reclaim the country.

Since that time there have been efforts made repeatedly to solve this question to the satisfaction of both the Arabs and the Jews. There was even a request on the part of Great Britain for a joint USA-Great Britain commission with the understanding on our part that Great Britain would live up to the decisions of that commission. Nothing happened and finally the appeal was made to the United Nations for a study by that body. Whether their majority report was wise or not, I do not know, but the final decision reached by the whole General Assembly was that that report should be upheld in view of the fact that nothing better was suggested. The Arabs had every opportunity to make constructive suggestions. Both the Arabs and the Jews were heard by our Secretary of State and I am sure by all the representatives before the decision was reached.[5]

Now it seems to me it would be a blow to the prestige of the United Nations from which it would never recover, if they do not implement their decision and if we do not do our share we will be responsible for sabotaging the only machinery we have for having peace today. This is, of course, neither in the interest of the Arabs or the Jews as far as I am concerned as I have never been to Palestine and have no personal feeling on the subject. But as to the preservation of the UN as machinery through which we may work for peace in the future, I have a great deal of conviction and I hope that other people will feel the same way.[6]

                    Very sincerely yours,

TLc AERP, FDRL

———————

1. Lydia T. Bacon to ER, 24 February 1948, AERP.

2. *MD*, 1 March 1948.

3. For more on the UN General Assembly's discussion regarding partition, see header Document 300.

4. The Jews first received an assurance from Great Britain, through a letter from British foreign secretary Lord Arthur Balfour, to the head of the British Zionist Organization, Lord Rothschild, on November 2, 1917, that its government "viewed with favor" the establishment in Palestine of a homeland for the Jewish people. The "Balfour Declaration" also declared that in facilitating this objective nothing should be done that would prejudice the "civil and religious rights of existing non-Jewish communities" in Palestine, or the "rights and political status enjoyed by Jews in any other country." Two years later, Emir Faisal signed an agreement with Chaim Weizmann, president of the World Zionist Organization, stating that the Arabs would work with the Jews to "encourage and stimulate immigration of Jews into Palestine on a large scale," provided that the rights of Arab peasant and tenant farmers would be protected and that they would receive assistance in "forwarding their economic development." For more on the Balfour Declaration see *n*3 Document 82 and *n*3 Document 227 (Bickerton and Klausner, 40–41, 61).

5. On September 23, 1947, Secretary Marshall met Emir Faisal of Saudi Arabia, Faris Bey el-Khouri of Syria, Noury As-Said of Iraq, Dr. Mohamed Hussein Heykal of Egypt, and M. Camille Chamoun of Lebanon to discuss the report of the United Nations Special Committee on Palestine (UNSCOP). Speaking for the group, el-Khouri of Syria noted the disappointment of the Arab states that the secretary had come out in favor of the majority report of the UNSCOP, and emphasized that because of its "biased" position against the Arabs, it was "an unacceptable draft document and not worthy of consideration as a working paper." Marshall also held similar discussions about Palestine with Jewish representatives. On June 19, 1947, he met with the head of the Jewish Agency and Zionist Organization of America, Rabbi Abba Hillel Silver, who pleaded with the secretary to consult with Zionist leaders before making any recommendation with regard to the findings of UNSCOP (*FRUS 1947*, vol. 5, 1159–62, 1105–7).

6. ER made the same point publicly when she described herself as "neither a Zionist nor a non-Zionist" at a United Jewish Appeal dinner in New York. However she remained sympathetic to the plight of Jewish DPs and the situation of Jews in Palestine and concerned about US and British policy in the Middle East. For more on her views, see *n*3 Document 7, Document 249, Document 251, Document 95, Document 82, Document 141 ("Lehman Asks End of Arms Embargo," *NYT*, 19 February 1948, 6).

EXPLAINING HER VOTE, COUNTERING SOVIET
PROPAGANDA, AND CORRECTING THE PRESS

Alice Hussey Balassa, who supported the positions espoused by Henry Wallace and the Progressive Citizens of America, often corresponded with ER. On February 22, Balassa wrote to ER asking her to explain two recent votes she cast at the United Nations. In particular, Balassa wanted know how ER could oppose a clause inserted by the Soviet Union condemning discrimination in the present draft of the declaration of human rights. "I would like to think that we put in the clause on race discrimination," she wrote, "but if [the Soviets] put it in, can we not in this case uphold their hand?" Balassa also questioned ER on her vote to support an amendment to the international conventions in Traffic in Women and Children and Obscene Publications, which permitted colonial powers to declare that their adherence to the convention did not bind all their non-self-governing territories. Balassa believed that this was again a case where ER could have held out the "hand of friendship and support" to the Soviet Union.[1]

After reading her letter, ER believed Balassa had misunderstood the true intentions of her votes, and responded to her with the following letter to clarify her positions.

316

Eleanor Roosevelt to Alice Balassa
27 February 1948 [Hyde Park]

Dear Mrs. Belassa:

I think you did not understand as a great many other people did not, the question on the Traffic in Women and Children and Obscene Publications.

The United States never upheld traffic in women and children, and obscene publications. The question which was being voted on was merely a question of procedure where the United Kingdom was concerned. The United Kingdom has agreements with some of her colonies that they can not as a central government, commit their colonies without consultation first. This was done as a democratic measure many years ago.[2]

The Russians undertook to say that the British were encouraging traffic in women and children because Russia could declare for a colony that their stand would be thus and so. It was explained to them with care that it was a democratic procedure that was at stake and what was more that all of the colonies had ratified Great Britain's own declaration, though Great Britain had not been willing to change the procedure. The USSR could not understand that because their central government declares policies and everybody else jolly well toes the mark, but the United States could understand it and upheld the British position.

The Post report of what I said does not give a correct impression.[3] I said that the clause condemning discrimination in the present draft of the Bill of Human Rights would be the one clause which might make it difficult for our Congress to ratify this first Convention. What I said is amply proved I think, by the attitude of the Southern representatives on the Civil Liberties report of the President. I said that the Russians backed this clause largely because the other things meant nothing to them such as freedom of information and of the press and of assembly, etc., and because they knew that this was the clause which would embarrass us. I did not hide from the Russians that I hoped we would ratify this Convention but that I thought we might have some difficulty and I think you will find that I am correct.

If you worked with the Russians as I have worked with them, you would not blame them as individuals but you would know quite well that the Politbureau had laid down a policy which as government representatives they had to follow whether they wanted to or not, and you would not be in accord with the methods used.

Does the coup in Czechoslovakia change your faith a little?[4]

I happen to believe the best way to deal with Russia is to be very strong in our own Democracy and to remember that they respect military strength, economic strength and political and personal strength.

Do not forget that the infiltration which they have done in Europe goes on here too.

Naturally I do not think the PCA is all communist. There are many groups that have no communists, but the core of the organization is communist controlled. Henry Wallace is either too good or too stupid, I really do not know which, to know that the communists are running him and that what he will do will fit their whole program. He will not help elect liberals. In fact the third party candidates are going to defeat good democratic liberals and they will be in the field for no reason except that those liberals happen to believe in the Marshall Plan and Mr. Wallace has made up his mind that that plan is not good. No plan is perfect but it is the best we have. I do not like the Truman doctrine in Greece either but I think we should elect as many liberal Congressmen as we can. What Mr. Wallace will succeed in doing is to elect reactionary Republicans from a President down the line.

Very sincerely yours,

TLc AERP, FDRL

---

1. Alice Balassa to ER, 22 February 1948, AERP.

2. The Imperial Conference of the British Empire issued the Balfour Declaration of 1926, which announced that all territories considered Dominions of the United Kingdom (Canada, Australia, South Africa, New Zealand, and, for a time, Ireland) "are autonomous Communities within the British Empire, equal in status, in no way subordinate one to another in any aspect of their domestic or external affairs, though united by a common allegiance to the Crown, and freely associated as members of the British Commonwealth." Parliament embraced this recommendation in the December 1931 Statute of Westminister, in which the body renounced any legislative authority over dominion affairs except as specifically provided in dominion law (Bickerton and Klausner, 40–41, 61).

3. On January 25, 1948, the *New York Post* reported that ER believed Russia was backing a clause condemning discrimination in the present draft of the declaration of human rights specifically to embarrass the United States ("Soviet Wants Bias Clause to Hit U.S., Mrs. F.D.R. Says," *New York Post*, 25 January 1948, AERP).

4. In February 1948, communists within the Czechoslovakian government asserted control over the police in anticipation of an electoral defeat in May. The move threw the elected government into chaos, and a new communist government stepped quickly into power. At the end of the coup, March 10, 1948, Foreign Minister Jan Masaryk, the son of the first Czech president and a spokesperson for democracy, fell out of his apartment window in Prague and died. Although many still debate the circumstances surrounding Masaryk's death, the event was widely interpreted at the time as a gesture of defiance to his country's new communist rulers. "It may well be," said Prime Minister Clement Attlee, "that he could not endure to live in the suffocating atmosphere of totalitarianism when all that he had striven for was being ruthlessly destroyed" (Judt, 139; "Europe Is Shocked by Masaryk Death," *NYT*, 11 March 1948, 5).

_317_

If You Ask Me [excerpt]
Ladies' Home Journal March 1948

Is there anything an average American citizen can do about the report of the President's Committee on Civil Rights?

Yes. See that your representatives in Congress are in favor of pushing for the recognition and establishment of the recommendations made by that committee, and in addition see to it that your own community lives up to those recommendations, and live up to them in your own life. That is the best way to make that committee's recommendations become a reality in our nation.[1]

What, in your opinion, will happen to the financial structure of this country if we continue aiding the European countries, who, for the most part, have already taken all but a few remaining steps to communism? Nobody in Washington seems to consider the eventual end to our continually mounting Federal deficit?[2]

There are a great many countries in Europe who have not taken any steps toward communism. Socialism is not communism—in fact, it is very far from it—and if you consider the present government in Great Britain, for instance, is on its way to communism, I think you would find that the British people would vehemently deny your conclusion.

The real value of aid to existing democracies is that they must get on their feet, since chaos and despair are the way to force acceptance of economic communism. If democracies do not make a comeback in the economic field, we will find ourselves facing a constantly increasing area of communism in the world.

I wonder if you have given much thought to what that would mean to our economy. Our only hope of preserving for our people their present standard of living lies in bringing the countries of Western Europe back to economic stability in order that they may be politically stable as well. In Eastern Europe, communism is the answer they have chosen—and perhaps it is the only possible answer to their economic plight—but with our aid it should not be forced on those who have known other standards.

People in Washington are considering very carefully the mounting Federal deficit, but have you considered what would happen if you faced a completely communist Europe? This mounting Federal deficit, as it looks today, would look like a golden age to us.

Incidentally, it would be well for a great many people to realize that even the states which have accepted communism have done so in large part because their economy had reached a point where there seemed to be no other economic solution. I believe, of course, that aid for rehabilitation should go even to the communist countries, since with a better standard of living there is bound to be more insistence on individual rights.

TMsex DLC

---

1. For another example of ER's ideas about citizen responsibility and human rights, see Document 379.

2. The questioner and ER may have meant the national debt, not the deficit. At the end of 1947, the United States had a surplus of over $4 billion, reaching $11.796 billion at the end of 1948. The

national debt, on the other hand, dropped by $5.118 billion between 1947 and 1948. Against these encouraging numbers, however, consumer prices and inflation increased, which threatened to slow economic growth, and led to the perception that the United States would soon face a deficit (Office of Management and Budget, "Historical Tables, Budget of the United States Government, Fiscal Year 2001," 19, 110; "Economic Report," *WP*, 16 January 1948, 20; *HSTE*).

ON LOVETT AND SOCIAL AND ECONOMIC
RIGHTS

ER planned to meet with representatives of fifteen nongovernmental organizations (NGOs) March 4 to solicit their feedback on the drafts of the Declaration and the convention the HRC approved in its December session in Geneva. Prior to conferring with the organizations' representatives, ER met with Durward Sandifer and James Hendrick to discuss how best to address matters associated with social and economic rights, given Undersecretary of State Robert Lovett's objections to these rights in general and the convention in particular. Hendrick wrote the following summary of that conversation for the department's official file.

318

Memorandum of Conversation with
Eleanor Roosevelt
4 March 1948 [New York City]

Present: Mrs. Roosevelt, Mr. Sandifer, Mr. Hendrick[1]

This meeting took place immediately prior to the meeting of the Non-governmental Organizations concerned with human rights.[2]

Mr. Sandifer stated Mr. Lovett had read over a memorandum addressed to him on the subject of human rights by Mr. Sandifer three times and was more confused than ever before. Mr. Lovett was particularly concerned with social and economic rights. He felt that if these were expressed they could far better be expressed in terms of "better standards" rather than a right to a "decent living."[3]

Mrs. Roosevelt said that matters of this sort should in her opinion be viewed from two standpoints: the U.S.S.R. which considers questions only from the view point of the government and the United States which considers the government the employer and the employee.

Mr. Lovett had been worried about any guarantees against unemployment. Mrs. Roosevelt wondered whether this was not covered to some extent by social security.

Mr. Lovett was worried about implementation. On this point Mrs. Roosevelt felt that implementation must be limited to states because she felt individual petitions would not be acceptable to Congress. We must face the fact however that a majority of the Human Rights Commission members are in favor of action on individual petitions.[4]

Mr. Lovett had expressed himself very strongly on the subject of individual petitions. He did not see how we could allow appeals from the United States Supreme Court decisions.

Mrs. Roosevelt felt that we must explain our constitution to the members of the Commission; how it has been interpreted by the U.S. Supreme Court. Right now the Supreme Court allow[s] racial segregation; it may change its opinion later. Mr. Lovett agreed this might very well happen but he was sure we could not get anything through Congress on petitions.[5]

Mrs. Roosevelt agreed we could not get this through Congress and that there was no point in trying to put it through at this time.

The question of discrimination troubled Mr. Lovett a great deal. Our position however looked proper to him on this. He felt we must leave out specific discussion of segregation if possible.[6]

Mr. Lovett stated he did not like the provision on mutilation in the covenant. Mrs. Roosevelt stated this arose out of the war experience—we have never had gas chambers or horrible experimentation on individuals. The war-devastated countries had experience with this.[7] Mr. Lovett admitted that this was a good point.

TMemd JPHP, HSTL

---

1. It is unclear as to whether Lovett also attended the meeting or whether Sandifer merely relayed his concerns.

2. For information on the Geneva drafts, see Document 291. For more on ER's conversations with government officials about the declaration, see Document 294 (Bess Furman, "Human Rights Pact Hailed in Capital," *NYT*, 5 March 1948, 10).

3. Economic and social rights, such as those related to health care, housing, or employment, were and are a frequent topic of controversy. Individual political rights such as those to a fair trial, to be free from torture, or to representation in one's government, were more widely recognized in Western political tradition as rights governments should recognize and defend. In contrast, economic and social rights, most often strongly advocated by those with Socialist and/or Communist ties, are sometimes seen as "standards" to which all nations should aspire, as Lovett argues here, rather than as "rights" which should or could be enforced (Morsink, 158, 191, 217–18).

4. After Lovett discussed the matter of individual petitions with Truman in late April, Lovett sent the president a statement, which ER had already approved, "intended to reflect the position as discussed by Mrs. Roosevelt with you yesterday." The statement read in part:

> It is the position of the United States that implementation should be provided for in the covenant. Complaints under the Covenant should be recognized only when brought by States which have adhered to the Covenant ...

> We have not as yet worked out the international machinery for the consideration of petitions, nor is it believed practicable or desirable in advance of the approval of the proposed Covenant by a substantial number of states to attempt to spell out such machinery.

> Further experience and more thorough study is required. After a substantial number of States have ratified the Covenant, the question of how individual petitions may be handled should be taken up for discussion. If agreement can be reached on an effective procedure, the Covenant can then be amended or a supplemental agreement concluded ...

> The proposed covenant is not expected to cover all possible rights or all possible remedies; and if it were, it would be doomed to failure. The immediate objective of the Commission on Human Rights, should be to produce a workable document which can secure the early adherence of a substantial number of nations (Statement of the Position of the United States on Petitions by Individuals in Relation to a Covenant on Human Rights, attached to Robert Lovett to Harry Truman, 30 April 1948, RG59, NARA II).

On the controversy over whether to allow individual petitions to the HRC on violations of rights, see Document 264, Document 265, Document 266, Document 285, Document 286, Document 287, Document 288, Document 298, and Document 365.

5. Although Hendrick's minutes do not indicate that Lovett attended the meeting, it appears from the notes that Lovett perhaps entered the meeting at this point.

6. For more on Lovett's objections to a binding human rights covenant, see header Document 295. For more on ER's opinion that it would be difficult to get a covenant that accepted individual petitions or discouraged racial discrimination through Congress, see Document 294 and Document 295. Lovett seemed to worry that allowing individual petitions would mean that US citizens could appeal to a world judicial body over the US Supreme Court, one of the many concerns about

national sovereignty raised during the early years of the United Nations. Restrictions on national sovereignty (such as accepting petitions from individuals rather than insisting that a state sponsor each petition) were most often favored by smaller nations, who saw them as protection from the type of aggression towards weaker nations that had been perpetrated by the Axis during World War II (Glendon, 50, 59, 88).

7. A "negotiating" draft of the Covenant on Human Rights contained an article stating that "no one shall be subjected to any form of mutilation or medical or scientific experimentation against his will" ("Covenant on Human Rights, Proposed United States Negotiating Draft," n.d., AERP).

ON AFRICAN AMERICANS AND THE DEMOCRATIC VOTE

> As ER and Charles Campbell, a young radio commentator and Harlem YMCA staffer whom ER had befriended for several years,[1] met the afternoon of March 5, they discussed Leo Isacson's victory in the recent special election and Wallace's special appeal to African American voters in Harlem.[2] After Campbell told ER that he feared a mass exodus of African American Democratic voters, ER relayed his concerns to Democratic National Committee chair Senator Howard McGrath and endorsed Campbell's suggestions as to how the party could best combat the Progressive Party's recruitment drive in Harlem.

_319_

Eleanor Roosevelt to J. Howard McGrath
6 March 1948 [New York City]

Dear Senator McGrath:

This young colored man, Charles Campbell, whom I have known for some time, first as a Y worker in New Jersey and lately here in Harlem, is a very reliable person. He is very much troubled over the fact that many of the younger Negroes are either going to vote for Wallace or for the Republicans.

He says that the regular Democratic organizations are under suspicion, so he started to form an organization, the letterhead of which I enclose, and they use as primary support the Civil Liberties Bill in their efforts to elect liberal Democrats.[3]

Mr. Campbell thinks it would be tremendously helpful if Harlem could have a full time, paid worker who was not apparently employed by the Democratic Committee, either State or National, but who was employed by some independent group.

I wonder whether you would think it worth while to talk this over with the Americans for Democratic Action or whether you could think of some other way in which the State and National Committee might do some apparently independent citizenship work of this kind.

The Y work will end on March 31st, because like many other organizations they haven't raised their budget, and Mr. Campbell will be looking for other work and that is probably part of the reason why he came to see me on this. I think he is an honest, genuine person and I enclose his own publicity in case you want to pass it along to Jim Loeb if you think there would be any value in the next campaign to do so.[4]

He also suggests that when the President comes to New York on the 17th, it might be of great value to have him speak in Harlem, particularly to the younger people. If there is any chance that you would want some thing of that kind organized, you will find his address on the back of the people and his telephone number because it is essential that they organize for that with speed. In any case, will you be kind enough to let him know as soon as possible whether or not you are interested in his suggestions.[5]

Very cordially yours,
Eleanor Roosevelt

TLS ADAR, WHi

---

1. In addition to his YMCA duties, Campbell was completing his doctoral work in sociology at Columbia University (where he also served as a news analyst for the university's radio station). Prior to moving to New York, Campbell served on the faculty of Bethune-Cookman College, and held a variety of positions in the international student movement. A compelling speaker, Campbell addressed the World Christian Youth Conference in 1939; the International Conference on Freedom, Justice and Responsibility at Oxford University in 1946; and the Paris Peace Conference at Luxemburg Palace in August 1946. ER admired his work and recommended that American Youth Hostels, Incorporated, appoint him to a leadership position. When the organization refused to select an African American for a prominent position, he again turned to ER for support and advice (Charles M. Campbell to ER, 30 April 1947, AERP; "Charles M. Campbell: Radio Commentator, Lecturer, Teacher, Student Leader," enclosure attachment, ER to J. Howard McGrath, 8 March 1948, ADAR, WHi).

2. For more on the special election, see Document 311. Campaigning for Isacson, Wallace openly courted the African American vote in Harlem, arguing that Truman's call for action to ensure the rights of minorities was an empty gesture: "Those who perpetuate Jim Crow are criminals ... [who] have no more reason to fear action on Mr. Truman's civil rights message than we have to expect it" (William R. Conklin, "Wallace Rejects Bid to Rejoin Party," *NYT*, 16 February 1948, 1).

3. ER frequently interchanged the term "rights" with "liberties"; she referred here to the Civil Rights bill that Truman advanced in his February 2, 1948, message to Congress.

4. Noting that "the wheels of the Democratic National Committee evidently turn very slowly," James Loeb notified ER on May 24 that the Americans for Democratic Action received this letter dated March 6. Loeb regretted that the ADA could not hire Campbell at the moment. "I do wish that we could afford to hire someone for this special work," he told ER, "We need it badly." Loeb did, however, inform ER that he was talking to representatives of the CIO-PAC who were likely to offer Campbell a position in the near future (James Loeb, Jr., to ER, 24 May 1948, AERP).

5. When Campbell did not hear from McGrath, he wrote ER March 12, asking if she could encourage him to respond. ER replied that she had approached him, that she "fear[ed] he won't do anything" and that she was "so sorry" Campbell's suggestion for a "national committee to back the Civil Rights Program" did not merit DNC support.

McGrath did ask Gael Sullivan to find a position for Campbell, but that did not happen. McGrath himself did not contact Campbell prior to Truman's trip, and ER's hopes that the president might speak in Harlem to discuss his civil rights policy on March 17 went unfulfilled. Truman's two speeches of the day focused solely on foreign policy, especially the adoption of the European Recovery Plan, the implementation of universal military training, and a temporary draft to build up the military until the universal training program could take effect. In his address to the Society of the Sons of St. Patrick, Truman castigated "those who are devoting themselves to sowing the seeds of disunity among our people," singling out "Henry Wallace and his Communists" as the individuals most responsible for divisions among the American people (Charles M. Campbell to ER, 12 March 1948, AERP; M. J. Gilmore to Gael Sullivan, 15 March 1948, ADAR, WHi; Anthony Leviero, "Truman Arrives in Serious Mood, But Crowd's Good Humor Dispels It," *NYT*, 18 March 1948, 32; "The Text of President Truman's Address to the Joint Session of the Congress" and "The Text of the President's Address on Foreign Affairs at the St. Patrick's Day Dinner Here," *NYT*, 18 March 1948, 4).

"THE SITUATION ABROAD SEEMS TO ME TO BE DETERIORATING RAPIDLY"

Secretary of State George Marshall described the world situation in the early months of 1948 as "a keg of dynamite." In addition to the conflict in Palestine, several crises contributed to his apprehension. On February 25, the Communists staged a successful coup in Czechoslovakia, a development that furthered the trend toward separate eastern and western European zones and caused the leaders of the Western European nations to plan a defense alliance they hoped the United States would join. Chinese Communist troops stood poised to defeat the Nationalist forces and take control of China. The future of Trieste, then encircled by Yugoslav forces, remained unresolved. In Italy, a Communist victory seemed likely in the upcoming elections scheduled for April. The Potsdam agreement on Four-Power control of Berlin deteriorated as the Western Allies and the Soviet Union disagreed over the rehabilitation of Germany. Meanwhile, at the UN, the United States and the USSR remained deadlocked over the control of atomic energy.[1]

As ER observed March 10:

There is no doubt that in the past few years the situation between the United States and the USSR has become increasingly dangerous. Some people in this country feel that it is the fault of the U.S. Others feel strongly that it is the fault of Russia. I personally feel that both countries are to blame. We have done a considerable amount of dangerous talking.[2]

Three days later, she addressed her specific concerns about these and other events in the following letters to Marshall and HST, telling both "over-burdened" men that her "conscience" compelled her to do so.

320

Eleanor Roosevelt to George Marshall
13 March 1948 [Hyde Park]

Dear Mr. Secretary:

You will forgive me, I hope, if I write to you at this time, but I am becoming more and more worried. The situation abroad seems to me to be deteriorating rapidly as regards Russia and ourselves.

I think it has almost reached a point where it is essential that you and the President, with a picked group of two industrialists, two labor leaders, two people representing the general public, should really demand that Great Britain, Russia and ourselves, sit down around a table before we actually get to a point where we are in a war.

You say the situation is serious and any one can see that we can not let the USSR go on pulling "coups" in one country after another. It looks as though Sweden and Norway were pretty worried as to whether they will not be treated to the same kind of "invitation" that Finland has had, and certainly it will not be very difficult to pull a coup off in Italy.[3]

Congress should be told in no unmistakable terms that its slowness and lack of imagination have caused much of the difficulty, but they can not remedy that.[4]

I am sure that we have not been blameless and probably the Russians think we have done some things against them. I am sure they believe we are trying to build up Germany again into an industrial state. I some times wonder if behind our backs, that isn't one of the things that our big business people would like to see happen in spite of two World Wars started by Germany.[5]

If war comes and this final effort has not been made, I am afraid the people of this country are not going to feel that we have done all that we should have done to try to find a solution to the deteriorating situation between ourselves and the USSR.

I do not think that Ambassador Austin's speeches on the Palestine question have given much impression that we really know what our policy is and that we are clear and decisive and ready to lead. The result is that I think the Arabs are taking advantage of us and of the situation as a whole.[6]

I think the general public's feeling about the UN is one of increasing fear that it will not get the support from us which will make it a going concern.[7]

Perhaps I am being a pessimist and I pray that I am, but the things that you and the President have been saying, plus the things that have been happening in the world the last few days, give me a sense that we need to do something drastic.[8]

With apologies for troubling an over-burdened man and assuring you that I do not want you to answer this, as I am really saying this so that I will have a clear conscience, I am,

Very sincerely yours,
Eleanor Roosevelt

P.S. Thank you for the suggestions about speeches.[9]

TLS RG59, NARA II

ER then sent a copy of her letter to Marshall to Truman.

321

Eleanor Roosevelt to Harry Truman
13 March 1948 [Hyde Park]

Dear Mr. President:

I am enclosing to you this copy of a letter which I have just sent to the Secretary of State.

I do not think I have been an alarmist before but I have become very worried and since we always have to sit down together when war comes to an end, I think before we have a third World War, we should sit down together.[10]

You and the Secretary must feel the rest of us are a nuisance. Nevertheless, as a citizen I would not have a clear conscience if I did not tell you how I feel at the present time.[11]

Very cordially yours,
Eleanor Roosevelt

TLS AERP, FDRL

322

Harry Truman to Eleanor Roosevelt
16 March 1948 [The White House]

Dear Mrs. Roosevelt:

I appreciated most highly your letter of the thirteenth enclosing copy of the one which you had written to the Secretary of State. I think all of us are in practically the same frame of mind and I, of course, am glad to have your ideas and viewpoint.

I think if you will go over the history of the relationship between Russia and us you will find that every effort was made by President Roosevelt and by me to get along with them. Certain agreements were entered into at Tehran and Yalta and so far as our part of those agreements is concerned we carried them out to the letter.[12]

When I arrived at Potsdam for that conference I found that the Poles at the suggestion of Russia had moved into eastern Germany and that Russia had taken over a section of eastern Poland. The agreement at Yalta provided for free and untrammeled elections in Rumania, Bulgaria, Yugoslavia and Poland. I found a totalitarian Soviet Government set up in Poland, in Rumania, in Yugoslavia and in Bulgaria. Members of our Commissions in Bulgaria and Rumania were treated as if they were stableboys by the Russians in control in those two countries. Russia has not kept faith with us.

I myself discussed the Polish situation with the Polish Government in Potsdam and got no satisfaction whatever from them—yet we made certain agreements in regard to the government of Germany which we have religiously tried to carry out. We have been blocked at every point by the Russians and to some extent by the French. The Russians have not carried out the agreements entered into at Potsdam.[13]

The Russians are of the opinion that Henry Wallace and a depression are facing this country—they honestly believe that Wallace is going to be the next President. Of course, we all know that is absurd—we are much more likely to have the worst reactionary in the country for President than we are to have Wallace.

I shall go to the Congress tomorrow and state the facts.[14] Beginning with my Message to the Congress on September sixth, 1945, I have constantly informed the Congress and the country of our needs in order to make the United Nations work and to arrive at a peace for the welfare and benefit of every country in the World.[15]

The first decision I had to make after being sworn in at 7:09 p.m. April 12, 1945 was whether to have the United Nations Conference at San Francisco on April 25, 1945. The Charter of the United Nations is a document under which we could work and have peace if we could get Russian cooperation. Twenty-two vetoes have been exercised in the last two and one-half years by the Russian Government. As you know, I had to send Harry Hopkins to see Stalin in order to get Molotov to agree to the fundamental principles of the United Nations Charter.[16]

I am still hopeful and still working with everything I have to make the United Nations work.

Our European Recovery Program and the proper strengthening of our Military setup is the only hope we now have for peace in the World. That I am asking from the Congress.[17]

If the people who know the facts and who understand the situation are willing to say that we've done wrong in this matter I don't see how we can expect to come out at all in its solution. It is the most serious situation we have faced since 1939. I shall face it with everything I have.

Of course, I am always glad to hear from you and I appreciate your frankness in writing me as you did.

Sincerely yours,
Harry S. Truman

TLS AERP, FDRL

Marshall, who declared himself "as much concerned as you are," did not reply to ER until he had read Truman's response.

323

George Marshall to Eleanor Roosevelt
17 March 1948 [Washington, DC]

My dear Mrs. Roosevelt:

I received your letter and read it with great care and then immediately referred it to Mr. Armour and the European Section to get their reactions. Also I read the President's reply to the copy you sent him.[18]

I am as much concerned as you are, as much troubled, and I am seeking in every way to find a solution which will avoid the great catastrophe of war. It is evident that we cannot sit quiet in this situation and also that mere words get us nowhere at this time.

I have been terribly disturbed over the rapid growth of a highly emotional feeling in this country which runs to extremes, yet at the same time something must be done.

You are correct in your conjecture regarding Sweden and Norway, particularly Norway whose government now anticipates an immediate pressure from the Soviets and is appealing for support.[19]

The public polls do not confirm your impression of the general public's feeling about the United Nations. They are more favorable apparently than you had thought, but certainly we have a heavy task on our hands to develop an effective operating procedure and build up public confidence.[20]

With regard to your suggestion about a "picked group" I would like to have Bohlen talk this and the entire situation over with you, give you our ideas—particularly in view of his long association with your husband in Russian dealings, and get your ideas at first hand.[21] Unless I hear from you to the contrary, he will call up to make an engagement the early part of the week. He has to be here this weekend because I am leaving in the morning for the West Coast and will not be back until Saturday night and Lovett has been forced to take a rest in Florida—he had been terribly overworked.[22]

Hastily and faithfully yours,
G. C. Marshall

TLS AERP, FDRL

---

1. Donovan, 357, 359; Offner, 236–37, 239, 248; C. L. Sulzberger, "Communist Moves Called Threat to Trieste Status," *NYT*, 5 March 1948, 4; "Partition Powers of U.N. Affirmed," *NYT*, 9 March 1948, 3; "U.N. Fails to Break Impasse on Trieste," *NYT*, 10 March 1948, 2.

2. *MD*, 10 March 1948.

3. In a February 12 speech appealing for congressional action on the Marshall Plan, Marshall said that the world was "in the midst of a great crisis, inflamed by propaganda, misunderstanding, anger, and fear … In the midst of this turmoil, complicated by the distractions of an election campaign, it is important to express one's feelings … in moderate terms. We should … calmly and prayerfully appraise the facts, so nearly as we can judge them to be the facts and then search for a firm conclusion in keeping with our sense of justice."

On February 27, the USSR asked Finland to sign a mutual defense treaty. On March 7 the *New York Times* reported that many Finnish-speaking Karelians were fleeing to Sweden in anticipation of the pact's signing. Formerly Soviet citizens, the Karelians were stateless people who had lived in Finland since 1920. The Soviets also approached Norway for a nonalignment accord, and many observers feared similar approaches would be made to Sweden. In Italy in early March, Western observers feared one of two outcomes: either the Communists and Socialist candidates together would gain enough votes to form a government, or they would win enough votes to force Italian Premier Alcide de Gasperi to include them in a coalition government and thus infiltrate the government, as had happened in Czechoslovakia ("Marshall Urges Calmness to Solve Crisis in World," *NYT*, 12 March 1948, 1; Donovan, 357–58; "Karelians Reported Fleeing," *NYT*, 7 March 1948, 8; James B. Reston, "Basic Decision Facing U.S. in Foreign Policy," *NYT*, 14 March 1948, E3; C. L. Sulzberger, "Communist Moves Called Threat to Trieste Status," *NYT*, 5 March 1948, 4).

4. Two days before ER wrote to Marshall, House Republican leaders decided to lump the European Recovery Program and military aid to China, Greece, and Turkey into one bill. Marshall objected that the resulting delay might help the Italian Communists in the forthcoming elections there ("Interim-Aid Fund Urged by Truman Pending ERP Vote," *NYT*, 12 March 1948, 1; James Reston, "Basic Decision Facing U.S. in Foreign Policy," *NYT*, 14 March 1948, E3).

5. For ER's views on the political and economic restoration of Germany, see Document 198.

6. Warren Austin, the US permanent representative to the United Nations, told the Security Council on February 24, 1948, that the UN Charter did not give the Security Council the power to enforce the partition plan for Palestine, but only to keep the peace among the opposing parties. In the same speech, Austin also suggested the formation of a Security Council committee made up of the five permanent members to investigate the "possible threats to international peace" stemming from the situation in Palestine and consult with all the parties involved. Austin's statement and Truman's subsequent endorsement of it encouraged some Arab political leaders to hope that the United States might move away from partition. On March 9, Austin said that the Soviet Union's demand that the partition of Palestine move forward "prejudged the issues" before the Security Council consultations he formally proposed on February 25 had begun ("Text of Austin Statement Giving U.S. Position on Palestine Plans," *NYT*, 25 February 1948, 2; "Arab Optimism Gains After Talk by Austin," *NYT*, 28 February 1948, 4; Donovan, 372; "U.S. Moves Big Five Report on Outlook in Palestine Strife," *NYT*, 26 February 1948, 1; "U.S. Holds Russia Pre-Judges Parley on Palestine Plan," *NYT*, 10 March 1948, 1). On ER's views of Palestine and the UN, see Document 310.

7. For information on polls taken to ascertain American popular opinion regarding the UN, see *n*20 below.

8. On March 1, Truman evaded reporters' questions on what conditions were necessary before US forces would be sent to Palestine. Ten days later, on the first anniversary of the Truman Doctrine, the president said that recent events had somewhat "shaken" his confidence about the outlook for "ultimate" peace in the world. On March 12, Truman said he was opposed to a Communist government in China "or anywhere else if we can help it" ("Truman Silent on Troops," *NYT*, 2 March 1948, 9; "Interim-Aid Fund Urged by Truman Pending ERP Vote," *NYT*, 11 March 1948, 1; "Truman Opposes Any Red Control," *NYT*, 12 March 1948, 3).

9. ER's letter querying Marshall about suggested topics to address on her forthcoming European trip (see *n*1 Document 314) was not preserved. In his March 10 reply, Marshall suggested she could discuss Congress's passage of the European Recovery Act (the Marshall Plan) and dispel any rumors of its imperialist aims. "Few Europeans ... realize what a complicated business it is under our constitutional structure to pass ... a measure of this magnitude." He also suggested that she could discuss the worldwide threat of Communism and explain "how difficult it is for farmers in Iowa or Nebraska, for example, to understand and react promptly to a situation thousands of miles away." ER could also ease any European doubts that US foreign policy would be "immobilized" because of the upcoming presidential campaign. He concluded: "I make only these general tentative suggestions ... you will know the right thing to say in any given circumstance." ER took Marshall's suggestions and wrote Durward Sandifer March 15 to request "the fullest information on E.R.P. so I can take it with me to Europe" and to solicit his view on "the best answer ... to the accusation of bypassing the UN?" (George Marshall to ER, 10 March 1948, AERP; ER to Durward Sandifer, 15 March 1948, AERP).

This was the second exchange ER had with Marshall regarding upcoming European travel. February 2, three weeks before the coup in Czechoslovakia, she queried him about a prospective trip to Czechoslovakia and the Soviet Union. Marshall's February 10 reply endorsed the idea of a Czechoslovakian trip as being "well worth while" and of "probable assistance." He was more cautious about a visit to the USSR because of "the implication a trip by you to Moscow ... might be given both here and abroad. What I am most uncertain about is the exploitation of anything that you necessarily would have to say regarding the reception which undoubtedly would be given you there. Yalta, Potsdam and the present political battle in this country would inevitably be drawn into the matter, not to mention the European Recovery Program." He promised to "think over and talk over ... the problem and let you hear from me later." Five days later ER wrote, "In view of your doubts, I will decide now not to make this trip ... Please do not take any more of your busy time to think about it "(George Marshall to ER, 10 February 1948 and ER to George Marshall, 15 February 1948, RG59, NARA II).

10. In her public comments, ER took a harder line. "The fate of the world is at stake," she wrote in My Day. "Future men and women ... depend on what the statesmen of today can be made to do by the responsible citizens of the various nations." She blamed both the United States and the USSR for the crisis and called for a meeting between the two superpowers. "I am far from feeling that we are always right in the U.S.A. and that the other fellow is always wrong. I have come to the conclusion that a new start should be made. The heads of the governments of the great European powers and of the U.S.A. should meet again, this time determined to talk truthfully to each other." At the same time, she also urged more consistency in US foreign policy, writing March 11: "We ... must have a clear-cut policy and stick to it—not vacillate ... nor talk belligerently and then act with fear as we have been prone to do on occasion" (*MD*, 28 February, 10 March, and 11 March, 1948).

11. Again, ER used My Day to make the same point. "Statesmen have the right to speak, but it seems to me that individual citizens should carefully consider what is being said by their statesmen and what is being done by their governments" (*MD*, 10 March 1948).

12. On Truman's view of the agreements at Tehran, Yalta, and Potsdam, see Document 220.

13. On decisions at the Potsdam Conference regarding Poland, see *n*26 Document 37 and *n*1 Document 6.

14. In his March 17 congressional address, Truman criticized the Soviet Union as the "one nation" that "has persistently obstructed the work of the United Nations by constant abuse of the veto," and blamed the USSR for "the critical situation in Europe today" (Donovan, 357; "Text of President Truman's Address to the Joint Session of the Congress," *NYT*, 18 March 1948, 4).

15. See header Document 45 for Truman's September 6, 1945, address to Congress.

16. Between May 26 and June 7, 1946, Harry Hopkins met with Josef Stalin and Soviet Foreign Minister V. M. Molotov in Moscow to discuss a number of wartime-related issues and to indicate President Truman's desire to maintain a "working relationship" with the Soviets. While there, Hopkins received a message from Secretary of State Stettinius asking him to take up the "veto issue" directly with Stalin, and to tell him "in no uncertain words" that the United States "could not possibly join an organization based on so unreasonable an interpretation" of the Security Council veto. During his last meeting with Stalin in the Kremlin on June 6, Hopkins explained the American position regarding the veto, and indicated that it was supported by both Britain and China. Stalin, who clearly had not been informed of his own government's position, replied that this was an "insignificant matter" and told Molotov to accept the American position (Truman, vol. 1, 257–65; Hoopes and Brinkley, 200–202). For more on Hopkins's trip to the Soviet Union, see *n*5 Document 13.

17. In his March 17 speech, Truman asked Congress to restore the draft, institute universal military training, and swiftly pass the Economic Cooperation Act of 1948 to address the "rapid changes … in Europe which affect our foreign policy and our national security" (Donovan, 357; "The Text of President Truman's Address to the Joint Session of the Congress," *NYT*, 18 March 1948, 4).

18. Norman Armour (1887–1982) was then assistant secretary of state for political affairs. Armour's diplomatic career included ambassadorships to Chile (1938–39), Argentina (1939–44), and Spain (1944–45). He retired in 1945, but returned to active service in 1947 as assistant secretary (Acheson, 15–16; Albin Krebs, "Norman Armour, 94, Dies," *NYT*, 29 September 1982, D26).

19. For more on Marshall's concerns with Sweden and Norway, and the tenor of public opinion, see *n*3 above. On March 16, the Swedish Defense Staff and the chief of the Swedish army appealed to King Gustaf V for approval to strengthen the country's military training and expenditure in light of the increased threat from the Soviet Union. The next day the Norwegian parliament approved a special appropriation to strengthen its nation's defenses. On March 19, the premiers of Sweden, Norway, and Denmark announced that they would defend their countries "against any outside aggression." Norway's "appealing for support" occurred in February, when the Norwegian defense minister approached US military attachés in Oslo about the possibility of US aid in the event of war ("Stronger Defense Urged on Sweden," *NYT*, 16 March 1948, 15; "Norway Speeds Defense," *NYT*, 17 March 1948, 11; "3 Scandinavian Chiefs Avow Will to Combat Aggression," *NYT*, 19 March 1948, 1; Pogue, 319).

20. In the fall of 1947, George Gallup's American Institute of Public Opinion surveyed the American public in order to gauge attitudes toward and understanding of the United Nations. Among other findings, the poll showed that 85 percent of Americans polled were in favor of the UN, with only 6 percent opposed and 9 percent without an opinion. Despite this overwhelming support, Gallup warned that the American public expressed great concern over the growing rift between the United States and the Soviet Union in terms of the threat to the UN. Fifty-one percent said they were "dissatisfied" with the progress of the organization, with 33 percent "satisfied." When asked, "How important do you think it is that the United States try to [make] the UN a success?" 82 percent answered, "very" (George Gallup, "Nearly 3 out of 4 Voters Feel U.S.-Soviet Split Hurts U.N.," *WP*, 17 September 1947, 13).

21. Charles E. Bohlen (1904–1974), then State Department counselor, was a career diplomat and one of the State Department's top experts on the Soviet Union. Fluent in Russian, Bohlen was among the first American diplomats to serve in the Soviet Union after the United States established diplomatic relations in 1933. As State Department liaison to the White House during World War II, he served as FDR's interpreter at the Tehran and Yalta Conferences. While Bohlen thought the US and Soviet systems were too incompatible to permit a long-term rapprochement, he did not think a conflict between the two superpowers inevitable. ER did not like Bohlen, who served as the State Department's chief advisor on Russian reaction to US policies. "She doesn't know why she

doesn't like him," her friends Betty and John Hight reported to their family, "but every time he speaks she says she has to fight back a terrific prejudice and try to listen objectively to what he says." For more on ER's opinion of Bohlen, see ER to Trude Lash, 17 November 1948, LASH, FDRL (*FDRE, DAB*).

22. Marshall was scheduled to speak at the University of California and the University of Southern California. Robert Lovett was then undersecretary of state and Marshall's closest associate ("Marshall to Speak on Coast," *NYT*, 17 March 1948, 27; Pogue, 150).

PREVENTING WORLD WAR III

Concerned that fears of a possible war with the Soviets would distract Americans from pursuing the goals of "peace and justice," ER challenged her readers to ask themselves if they were "willing to let another nation force us away from our objective and back into the old channels of war, when we still have the strength and power to force events into the channels of peace?"

324

My Day
17 March 1948

NEW YORK, Tuesday—Last Sunday evening, Walter Winchell made a very solemn, serious talk over the air. To the people who listened to him, I think he gave the impression that the time had come actually to prepare ourselves for a return to war conditions. Mr. Winchell has great influence in this country, reaching a wide audience both through his broadcasts and his newspaper column. People with such influence should use it with great care.[1]

I lay awake that night thinking what a return to war would mean, and there must have been many others, young and old, who did the same thing. More production for destruction, less for building up a better economy at home and abroad, restrictions of every kind. Here at home we would have, at the least, great discomforts; abroad there would be starvation and death. Our men mobilized again.

The USA this time would be the first and main target, and a vulnerable one. Desperate preparation, heavy hearts, divided families. A young generation wiped out, and the knowledge in the older generation of what that would mean to the country in the next twenty-five years. The same thing going on in other countries all over the world.

No, Mr. Winchell, this is no light matter that you talked of on Sunday night. This is life or death to the nations of the world.

After every war, the representatives of the countries which survive sit around a table and try to come to some agreements. Before we contemplate war again, let us make every possible effort to sit down around a table now and come to some agreements. Why must men destroy themselves?

I am no advocate of Henry Wallace's mushy policy.[2] I think this world needs strong men with spiritual and moral convictions. But I think it also needs friendly men—men who can try to understand the needs of peoples. Without question there are ruthless men in the Kremlin, and if we are honest with ourselves, we'll admit there are ruthless men right here at home. Without any question, there are ruthless men all over the world. And there are men who put business gains above human gains.

I hoped that the depression and the war had taught us that, above everything else in the world, humanity is important. The rights and well-being of people stand far above the successes of business or of governments. And people are happier in a world which comes to agreements under law.

What did we set up a World Court for?[3] What did we set up a United Nations to achieve? Peace and justice was our objective. Have we so soon forgotten this? And are we willing to let another nation force us away from our objective and back into the old channels of war, when we still have the strength and power to force events into the channels of peace?

This nation of ours has been acting primarily from its fears. We have forgotten that there is nothing to fear except fear itself. But we had better learn that truth again, and act with the confidence that we can obtain the objectives which once we thought were worthwhile for ourselves and the rest of the world.

TMs AERP, FDRL

---

1. In his weekly radio address broadcast March 14, Winchell predicted war with the Soviet Union, a forecast he so often repeated that *Time* and the *Cincinnati Enquirer* editorialized that Winchell had placed the United States "at the very verge of war with Russia almost every Sunday night for the last two years" and lamented his "constant poisoning of the well of public opinion." His broadcasts, however, proved tremendously popular; the FBI even reported that "during the peak radio listening months of January–February 1948, Walter Winchell's broadcasts … placed … in ninth place among all programs in 'popularity' among big city audiences" ("Let the Buyer Beware," *Time*, 1 March 1948, http://www.time.com/time/archive/printout/0,23657,794324,00.html, accessed 8 June 2005; "The Winchell Story," FBI "Walter Winchell File," 30). For more on Winchell, see *n*3 Document 48.

2. In late February, Wallace spoke before the House Committee on Foreign Affairs to outline his "plan for peace." Wallace presented his proposal, which called for the establishment of a UN reconstruction fund free of "political conditions," as an alternative to the Marshall Plan, which he called "the blueprint of the aims of American monopoly." In March, he published a pamphlet titled *The Wallace Plan or the Marshall Plan* that advocated a better paid and racially integrated military and a foreign policy less reliant on military action. For Wallace's views on the Truman Doctrine and the Marshall Plan, see Document 221 and Document 239 (House Committee on Foreign Affairs, *United States Foreign Policy for a Post-War Recovery Program*, 80th Cong., 1st sess., Part 2, 24 February 1948, 1581–85; Culver and Hyde, 472).

3. The "World Court" refers to the international judicial entity, the Permanent Court of International Justice, set up under the League of Nations and replaced in 1945 by the creation of the International Court of Justice by the United Nations. The court is composed of fifteen judges selected by the General Assembly and the Security Council, each of whom serves a nine-year term. Both UN member states and nonmember states that meet set conditions may appeal to the court to arbitrate disputes between states, including interpretations of treaties or any "breach of an international obligation." Once the court issues a ruling, however, the states in dispute have no obligation to comply (*EUN*; Fasulo, 206–7).

GREECE, SPAIN, AND THE PROMOTION OF
DEMOCRACY

After Martha Mathiasen of New York City read an Americans for Democratic Action brochure that reprinted some of ER's statements on the political situation in Greece, she wrote ER March 13 to question why she "believe[d] the Greeks to be at liberty to determine their form of government" when her position "seems at variance with recent reports." Citing recent articles in the *Herald Tribune* that "any democratic elements in the Greek social framework are there only by sufferance of the regime in power and may be withdrawn without apology,"[1] Mathiasen argued:

> It is one thing to term the Greek government one which must be supported as a bulwark against Communism. Sponsoring it as a democracy modeled after our own I'm afraid is losing us many friends in Europe. We are really pushing liberal elements in the various countries into alliance with the Communists by giving them so little help and encouragement.

She went on to suggest that other US foreign alliances were also "seriously weakening the case for democracy" and that "[w]e must develop a positive program of selling democracy if we are to prevent another catastrophe." She then urged the ADA to "recognize that we must keep cool now, that we must not in what James Warburg recently termed 'frantic anxiety' ally ourselves 'with any and all governments'" and challenged it to recognize that "some positive approach must be taken quickly if we are not to fail again in our efforts to establish a framework for peace."[2]

ER responded five days later.

_325_

Eleanor Roosevelt to Martha Mathiasen
18 March 1948 [Hyde Park]

Dear Miss Mathiasen:

In answer to your letter of the 13th, I did not know that anybody thought we were sponsoring Greece as a Democracy modeled after our own.

I personally think we made a mistake to let the British hand over what they had done in Greece to us, by allowing ourselves to be pushed into that position. I now think there is nothing to do but to try to improve the present Greek government and help them to remain free of the communists.[3]

I know nothing about Admiral Hoarthy's invitation, but I should imagine he had been a personal friend of Mr. Wood. It is ridiculous to think that because he was invited as a personal guest to a wedding that it is a sign that the UN would approve of helping the Nazis back into power in order to make them a bulwark against the communists. I hope we are not quite such idiots as that.[4]

We have not shown any friendship for Spain though there are always elements in any country that are working for certain specific things and undoubtedly there are groups in this country that would like to see us friendly with Spain but as far as I know, the Government has not changed its attitude.[5]

I quite agree with you that we must sell Democracy rather than be against communism. Has it ever occurred to you that the communists see to it that in every country they go into, there are native elements that have already been sold to the communists? Where they have been able to create chaotic conditions and hardships, these elements are sure to be there in great numbers.

I think it would be a farce to ask the Russians to supervise a free election since they have no idea what freedom means. I am quite sure if we are clear enough ourselves in what we believe and strong enough that we will be able to convince the Russians that Democracy and communism can live side by side.

Very sincerely yours,

TLc AERP, FDRL

---

1. Mathiasen referred to articles by Homer Bigart, then reporting from Greece for the *Herald Tribune*.

2. Mathiasen trained as an economist, completing an advanced degree at Columbia University in 1949. She did not enclose the pamphlet she mentioned in her letter (Martha Mathiasen to ER, 13 March 1948, AERP; "Martha Mathiasen, R.T. Selden Engaged," *NYT*, 1 February 1953, 82). For background on the relationship between the United States and Greece, see Document 208.

3. ER had made similar points in My Day. In early January, she wrote:

> Rehabilitating the Greek army and providing them with guns and ammunition is not going to answer the Communist menace. There is only one way to answer that. It is to give the young people a vision and a chance to work on the constructive rehabilitation of their country … The chance to work and the hope of future prosperity in their country are the only things that will turn the guerrillas from dissatisfied bandits into loyal and productive citizens.
>
> I have no knowledge whether the present Government of Greece is reactionary or progressive, whether or not it represents fairly accurately the various political factions of the country. However, whatever its politics may be, we are providing the money and presumably the brains for economic rehabilitation (*MD*, 9 January 1948).

See also Document 210.

4. Mathiasen's letter to ER cited a report that "Admiral Hoarthy" had attended the wedding of Consul General Sam Wood in Germany, which "aroused suspicion … that America would not scorn Nazis in the fight against Communists" and would make the case for democracy less palatable. Miklós Horthy (1868–1957), regent of Hungary, established a nationalist dictatorship in Europe following World War I. He allied with the Axis powers during World War II, but attempted to surrender to the Allies in 1944, resulting in his arrest by the Germans. The US Army subsequently took him into custody after the war, but eventually released him without bringing him to trial. He was indeed a guest at the February 1948 wedding of Sam Woods (1892–1953), then US consul general in Munich ("Horthy, Ex-Dictator of Hungary, Dead," *NYT*, 10 February 1957, 1; Martha Mathiasen to ER, 13 March 1948, AERP; "Sam E. Woods Dies; Former U.S. Consul," *NYT*, 23 May 1953, 15; "Wilhelmina Busch Wed," *NYT*, 23 February 1948, 28; "Yugoslavia Gets U.S. Rebuke on Horthy Protest," *WP*, 17 March 1948, 13).

5. In February 1946, the UN refused membership to Spain. For further information on this point, see Document 160.

"MORAL FORCE" AND UNIVERSAL MILITARY
TRAINING

Truman had allowed the draft to expire the previous spring, hoping it could be replaced by his proposal for Universal Military Training. However, the proposal evoked strong reaction from all concerned—insistent support from the military and defense communities and consistent, public opposition from educational, religious, and less militaristic organizations. By 1948, it languished in congressional committees. Truman remained committed to the proposal and once again championed it in his 1948 State of the Union address, telling Congress that he considered Universal Military Training "of even greater importance" than the National Security Act of 1947.[1]

By March 1948, most congressmen agreed that the gap in size between the manpower of Soviet and American military troops posed a threat to the nation's security, although they did not agree as to the most effective way of closing that gap. The Truman administration pushed for a combination of a selective service draft of 19- to 25-year-old men into two years of active service and UMT, which provided 18-year-old men with a year of training before enlisting them in the reserves. Conservative critics of UMT argued that paying young men to serve in the reserves was far more costly than drafting a smaller number of men into active duty. During the spring, the Senate Armed Services Committee held hearings on both the UMT and selective service proposals. Senator John Gurney (R-SD),[2] invited several individuals to testify at these hearings, including Nobel Prize–winning physicist Arthur Compton, Albert Einstein, and ER. Although ER could not attend, Gurney introduced excerpts from the following letter into the record on March 24.[3]

326

Eleanor Roosevelt to John Gurney
18 March 1948 [Hyde Park]

Dear Senator Gurney:

I am sorry I can not appear before your Committee, but as I wired you, I am leaving on the 27th of March for London and I will not be back until April 27th.

In the past I have been opposed to Universal Military Training, but I have always been in favor of one year of Universal Service for girls and boys alike, preferably at the end of the high school period.[4]

The reason I favor this is that I feel it is important that citizens in a Democracy should realize that they have obligations as well as rights and privileges.

Service in war time is a very evident obligation, but if we are to support a United Nations Force,[5] it will I hope, become less and less necessary to have large military installations ourselves. In that case, some kind of service which will draw the attention of the average citizen, in the formative years, to his responsibilities of citizenship in a Democracy, is extremely important.

I would, of course, take into account the type of education that boys and girls wish to acquire and I would try to make that year of service useful to the community and to the individual. A certain amount of basic military training might be included, but I would hope that generally the training would be oriented for peace time service.

At the present time, however, I would not oppose Universal Military Training because I think it is a gesture which would be understood by the USSR as having the purpose of keeping us strong until a force that could control any aggressor has come into being in the United Nations and all nations can disarm gradually and equally.

I would hope that when the United Nations force came into being and was trained and ready for use, we would change our Universal Military Training to Universal Training for Citizenship.

Very sincerely yours,

TLc AERP, FDRL

---

1. Universal Military Training (UMT) would have required all men between the ages of eighteen and twenty to spend one year receiving military training. Rather than serving in a specific branch of the military, these men would remain outside the military and be treated as "trained citizens" who could only be called into active military service by an act of Congress (Donovan, 136–37; *HSTE*; "UMT Is Attacked by Einstein Group," *NYT*, 19 January 1948, 5; "The Text of President Truman's Message to Congress on the State of the Union," *NYT*, 8 January 1948, 4).

2. John Chandler "Chan" Gurney (1896–1985), served two consecutive terms in the Senate, from 1939 to1951 (Biographical Directory of the United States Congress, http://bioguide.congress.gov, accessed 7 June 2005).

3. By May 1948, the Senate Armed Services Committee prepared a defense plan that included both a draft and UMT. The House Armed Services Committee, believing that the House Rules Committee would table any legislation including the costly UMT plan, argued in favor of a defense plan that included only provisions for a draft to call men into active duty. Not until June 1948 did both houses of Congress settle this debate and agree on a compromise bill that omitted all references to UMT. The bill required all men between the ages of 18 and 25 to register with the Selective Service. The Selective Service called about 35,000 men into service prior to February 1949, when the draft's effect of increasing the number of volunteers made further calls unnecessary (*HSTE*; C. P. Trussell, "Senate UMT Ruling Put off to March," *NYT*, 18 February 1948, 12; John G. Norris, "Draft of Men 19-27 Is Part of Defense Plan," *WP*, 25 March 1948, 1; Samuel A. Tower, "Senators Propose Only Youths of 18 Get Year Training," *NYT*, 2 May 1948, 1; C. P. Trussell, "Republicans' Drive for Defense Unity Upset in Congress," *NYT*, 8 May 1948, 1; "Main Points in Compromise Draft Bill," *NYT*, 20 June 1948, 34).

4. As ER wrote in her August 23, 1944, My Day, she believed that young people, young women included, might benefit from a year of service, whether military or civilian:

> It is possible … that a girl might give a year of service in her own community. Such service might well prove of value to the hospitals, or to some of the government agencies—local, state, or national—which happen to be in the vicinity, or to some civic or charitable activity, dealing with child care or recreation, which needed personnel.
>
> In many of these activities, a girl might learn many things which would be a help to her in her future life, either in her home or in work which she may undertake. Quite obviously, it would be useful to any woman to have a knowledge of local conditions, a better knowledge of nutrition or of sanitation, as well as some of the first principles of hygiene or nursing. Some girls might feel that they wanted to see something of their own country beyond their immediate surroundings; but this, after all, could perhaps be offered on a voluntary basis. The essential thing, as I see it, is that we should think out ways to increase our participation in government (*MD*, 23 August 1944).

See also Document 269, for ER's changing views on the necessity of UMT.

5. For more on the creation of a United Nations Force, see *n*1 Document 275.

CRITICIZING THE US POSITION ON THE UN PARTITION PLAN

March 19 Warren Austin announced that the UN partition plan had been met with such violence that the US "government believes that a temporary trusteeship for Palestine should be established under the Trusteeship Council of the United Nations to maintain the peace and to afford the Jews and Arabs of Palestine further opportunity to reach an agreement regarding the future government of that country." Insisting that this shift in policy would not "prejudice … the character of the eventual political settlement, which we hope can be achieved without long delay," he called for a special session of the General Assembly and recommended that the Security Council instruct the United Nations Special Committee on Palestine (UNSCOP) to make no further effort to implement partition until the General Assembly could meet.[1]

Austin's speech caught the world by surprise. The Jewish Agency for Palestine decried this "amazing reversal." Many Democrats, such as Representative Arthur Klein (NY), called the pronouncement "the most terrible sell out of the common people since Munich" while Republicans, such as Senator Homer Ferguson (MI), declared "the Administration cannot seem to get a policy and stand by it." At the UN, members of the Security Council said they would have to ask their governments for instructions and Secretary-General Lie's office "reminded" Austin that while the UNSCOP had reviewed a trusteeship option the previous summer, it decided not to pursue it because "both the Arabs and the Jews would fight it."[2]

Truman, who himself felt caught off-guard by the timing of the speech and the reaction to it, instructed Marshall, then still in California, to make a public statement explaining the new policy. Speaking at a Los Angeles press conference the following day, Marshall announced that the policy appeared "the wisest course to follow," and that he had "recommended it to the President and he approved my recommendation." He then explained why he made that decision:

> The primary and overriding consideration … is the need to maintain the peace and to prevent chaos and the wide-spread disorder upon the termination of the mandate on May 15, 1948. We believe that the United Nations should do everything it can to bring the fighting to an end and save the lives of the men, women, and children which would be lost in the bitter fighting which could otherwise be expected to follow the withdrawal of British troops … The United States supported the partition plan for Palestine in the General Assembly last autumn.
>
> Since that time we have explored every possibility of a peaceful implementation of that recommendation … We then sought to find through consultations among the five principal powers some basis of agreement on which the partition plan might go forward by peaceful means. These consultations were unsuccessful in developing any measure of agreement between the Jews and Arabs of Palestine or any substantial agreement among the permanent members as to how the Security Council might proceed …
>
> We are faced, therefore, with the prospect that the United Kingdom will abandon the mandate … and that no successor government will be in position on that date to maintain law and order.
>
> A truce is essential. A military truce cannot be achieved under existing circumstances without a parallel truce in the political field. A political truce, however, would bring us up to May 15 without elementary arrangements for keeping order in that situation …

... This trusteeship could be ended as soon as a peaceful solution can be found ...

The United States has repeatedly stated that we are seeking a solution for Palestine within the framework of the United Nations and that we are not going to act unilaterally in that matter. The proposal for a temporary United Nations trusteeship, without prejudice to the ultimate solution, made by this Government, is the only suggestion thus far presented which appears to offer any basis for action by the United Nations to meet the existing situation in Palestine.[3]

ER regarded the change in US policy as a grave mistake. She felt so strongly, that immediately upon hearing Austin's remarks she telegraphed Marshall that she was "disturbed by Senator Austin's statement ... and hoped that [Marshall] will have no objection to my stating so publicly."[4] Then, after reading the secretary's speech, she wrote Marshall to say she would have to make her disagreement public, whether he approved or not, even if it meant that she would have to resign from the UN to do so.

_327_

Eleanor Roosevelt to George Marshall
22 March 1948 [Hyde Park]

Dear Mr. Secretary:

Yesterday I read your statement on Palestine twice with great care. I have a deep respect for you, but I feel that what you state is not satisfying from the point of view of achieving the desired results.

You say that we are seeking a peaceful solution of the Palestine problem and you suggest that the new Mandate be set up. The new Mandate will have to enforce peace in just the way that the United Nations Commission would have had to enforce peace. If we have entered into some arrangement by which Great Britain's soldiers remain in Palestine, I do not think we will have peace and certainly if we try to set up a Mandate giving it to several nations and leaving the USSR out, we will offend the USSR deeply and create more tensions between us.[5]

I had heard that Secretary Forrestal was so worried about the possibility that the UN might ask for a force in Palestine to which both the USSR and ourselves would have to contribute, that he felt we would never get the USSR out of Palestine and he would therefore feel that he had to mobilize this country fifty percent for war immediately. I wrote to the President some time ago that this seemed to me ridiculous and that we had to face the fact that joint forces, sometimes of equal strength, were the ultimate objective of the United Nations.[6]

My feeling at the present moment is that in every possible way, the United States is acting to hurt the United Nations and to act on a unilateral basis. Our action on Trieste seems to bear this out[7] and while I am conscious of the fact that we must defend ourselves against the Russians and we must be strong, I think it is unfortunate to do things which bring us legitimate criticism, and in this case, it looks as though the USSR were the only government that was upholding the United Nations Assembly decision.[8]

I can not blame Senator Austin because he never was in agreement with the decision, but since it was taken largely to strengthen the United Nations and since I can not see that we have changed by our present action the possibility of having to use military force, I am deeply unhappy.[9]

As you know, I feel we have a moral obligation, due to our acceptance of the Balfour Declaration and our tacit agreement in the forming of a Jewish homeland by allowing capital to be spent and people to settle in the Palestine area.[10] This new Mandate would have all of the problems such as immigration, and we have added to the Arabs' determination.

My greatest concern is for the UN even though I also have concern for upholding what I think is a moral obligation. I feel at the present time that we have more or less buried the UN. I can hardly see how it can recover and have the slightest influence, since we were the only ones who could give it any force and we now have been the ones to take it away.

I shall have to state my feelings publicly because I have been asked how I feel on this subject, and I do not feel it honest not to say what I believe.

If you wish me to resign from the Human Rights Commission I will, of course, be glad to do so, since I realize it is extremely difficult for you to have some one serve under you who openly criticizes the attitude of the Administration.

Very sincerely yours,

TLc AERP, FDRL

On the day she wrote Marshall, ER also wrote Truman, enclosing a copy of her letter to the secretary. After expressing her reservations about the administration's "increasingly disquieting" foreign policy, especially its "discarding" of the UN, she detailed why she opposed his strategy and, just as she did with Marshall, offered her resignation.

328

Eleanor Roosevelt to Harry Truman
22 March 1948 [Hyde Park]

Dear Mr. President:

The events of the last few days since my last letter to you, have been so increasingly disquieting that I feel I must write you a very frank and unpleasant letter.

I feel that even though the Secretary of State takes the responsibility for the Administration's attitude on Palestine, you can not escape the results of that attitude. I have written the Secretary a letter, a copy of which I enclose, which will explain my feelings on this particular subject.[11]

On Trieste I feel we have also let the UN down.[12] We are evidently discarding the UN and acting unilaterally, or setting up a balance of power by backing the European democracies and preparing for an ultimate war between the two political philosophies. I am opposed to this attitude because I feel that it would be possible, with force and friendliness, to make some arrangements with the Russians, using our economic power as a bribe to obstruct their political advance.[13]

I can not believe that war is the best solution. No one won the last war, and no one will win the next war. While I am in accord that we need force and I am in accord that we need this force to preserve the peace, I do not think that complete preparation for war is the proper approach as yet.

Politically, I know you have acted as you thought was right, regardless of political consequences. Unfortunately, it seems to me that one has to keep one's objectives in view and use timing and circumstances wisely to achieve those objectives.

I am afraid that the Democratic Party is, for the moment, in a very weak position, with the Southern revolt and the big cities and many liberals appalled by our latest moves. The combination of Wall Street objectives and military fears seem so intertwined in our present policies that it is difficult to quite understand what we are really trying to do.[14]

I realize that I am an entirely unimportant cog in the wheel of our work with the United Nations, but I have offered my resignation to the Secretary since I can quite understand the difficulty of having some one so far down the line openly criticize the Administration's policies.

I deeply regret that I must write this letter.

Very sincerely yours,
Eleanor Roosevelt

TLS HSTSF, HSTL

329

George Marshall to Eleanor Roosevelt
24 March 1948 [Washington, DC]

My dear Mrs. Roosevelt:

This can be but a very hasty response to your letter to me of March 22 as I only have a few minutes to devote to my reply.

I was naturally concerned over your feelings in the matter of Palestine and regarding Trieste. I was particularly concerned by your statement that your "feeling at the present moment is that in every possible way, the United States is acting to hurt the United Nations and to act on a unilateral basis". My understanding of our actions and my efforts in the matter have been directed along exactly contrary lines. It has been our endeavor here within the State Department to stay strictly within the Charter and we have been roundly criticized for doing so.[15]

This last proposal for the trusteeship was made after we had exhausted every resource we possessed at Lake Success to get an agreement for partition and other necessary action in the matter. We turned to the sole remaining resource available to us under the Charter to avoid a period of bloodshed after May 15th.

The publicity given the various actions of our Government in the main has been a rather clever propaganda which has twisted the purpose of implication of most of our efforts until there is a nationwide misunderstanding.[16]

Bohlen told me that he was not able to make an appointment with you until Friday next and you are leaving for Europe, I understand, on Saturday.[17] I am sorry there has to be so much delay in this. I am taking the liberty of telling Dean Rusk who is the individual most familiar with all the give-and-take within the Security Council to endeavor to see you for a half hour in order to describe just exactly what has been happening and what has dictated our line of action.[18]

I would be most unwilling to accept your resignation from the Human Rights Commission because I think you can do a great deal of good there, however much it may complicate matters to have you criticizing the attitude of the administration.

Faithfully yours,
G. C. Marshall

TLS AERP, FDRL

Truman waited to reply to ER until he had read Marshall's response, appealing to her "with the utmost sincerity" to remain on the delegation. "There is no one who could, at this time, exercise the influence which you can exert on the side of peace."

330

Harry Truman to Eleanor Roosevelt
25 March 1948 [The White House]

My dear Mrs. Roosevelt:

I have read with deep concern and not without anxiety your letter of March twenty-second together with copy of your letter to the Secretary of State of the same date.

It would be impossible for me to minimize the importance of support of the United Nations with every resource at our command. It is the world's best if not its sole hope for peace. If the United Nations fails all is chaos in a world already beset with suspicion, divisions, enmities and jealousies.

Since you were good enough to let me see the text of your letter to General Marshall I asked him for a copy of his reply, which is before me as I write. I hope sincerely that the conversations which you are scheduled to have with Mr. Bohlen tomorrow will dispel at least some of your doubts and misgivings and that there may be a further clarification if you are able to see Dean Rusk.[19]

I should deplore as calamitous your withdrawal from the work of the United Nations at this critical time. Such a step is unthinkable. The United Nations, our own Nation, indeed the world, needs the counsel and leadership which you can bring to its deliberations.

The United Nations' trusteeship proposed to the Security Council is intended only as a temporary measure, not as a substitute for the partition plan—merely an effort to fill the vacuum which termination of the mandate will create in the middle of May.

I sought to clarify our position in a statement issued today.[20] Although I am sure you have read it, or heard it, I enclose a copy for your convenient reference.

May I appeal to you with the utmost sincerity to abandon any thought of relinquishing the post which you hold and for which you have unique qualifications. There is no one who could, at this time, exercise the influence which you can exert on the side of peace. And peace and the avoidance of further bloodshed in the Holy Land are our sole objectives.

May God bless you and protect you as you set out to fulfill so honored a mission to London.

Very sincerely yours,

TLcst HSTSF, HSTL

ER made her deep opposition to the administration's trusteeship proposal public in the following column.

331

My Day
26 March 1948

HYDE PARK, Thursday—I have read and reread Secretary of State George C. Marshall's recent statement to the press on our change of policy on Palestine.[21] And in my mind I have gone over the history of the years in which the question of Palestine has been before us.

An editorial in the New York World-Telegram stated: "The ideal Palestine solution is a free democratic country in which all enjoy equal rights and live in peace together." Certainly this is the ideal, and this is undoubtedly what the Jews had in mind after the Balfour Declaration, in which we concurred, and after the agreement which Dr. Chaim Weizmann negotiated with the Arab leaders of that day.[22] The British mandate was a bridge to cover the years of settlement and growth of a nation.

At one time the Arabs were not greatly distressed at the idea of not holding sway over Palestine at some future date, any more than they were over the fact that Great Britain held a mandate over the country. I think there has been an evident change in the Arabs' attitude since they have been selling oil to the great companies of Great Britain and the United States and have been living well on the profits. At least some few people at the top have greatly profited, though there is no notable change in the standard of living of the average, poor Arab citizen.[23]

Many reports have been made on the Palestine question, none of them entirely satisfactory to any one. Our country's decision in the United Nations General Assembly to accept the majority report of the commission sent to Palestine by the UN was never based on a belief that it was an ideal solution. But naturally, when the United States decides to take a stand, that stand is influential because many people have to turn to us today to meet their various needs.

It was, of course, the desire of the United States that the Palestine solution should be a peaceful one, and it seemed incredible that the Arabs, in the face of a United Nations decision, would withstand that decision with force.[24] There was every reason to suppose that, since economic unity was envisioned, the partition plan could be carried out, and that the people living in the area, Jew and Arab alike, might gradually find ways of meeting the difficulties of a situation which only they themselves could work out.

I feel that our evident reluctance to accept responsibility and carry out whatever requests the UN might make of us, whether of a military or an economic nature, led to increased resistance by the Arabs. They were sure they could have their own way without any consideration of the wishes of the UN.

The UN would have no force unless it was provided by a call on the great nations. And Great Britain was pulling out. This probably meant that we and Russia would be called upon. And our difficulties in Europe made us feel that added difficulties in the Near East would be inevitable if we and the USSR had soldiers and shared responsibility in that region. It might have created an impossible situation.

It looks to me, therefore, as though we have taken the weak course of sacrificing the word we pledged and, in so doing, have weakened the UN and prevented it from becoming an instrument to keep peace in the world.

TMs AERP, FDRL

The day after ER met with Bohlen, she sent Secretary Marshall the following letter thanking him for arranging the meeting and responding to some of the points his emissary had discussed with her.

_332_

Eleanor Roosevelt to George Marshall
27 March 1948 [New York City]

Dear Mr. Secretary:

I am very grateful to you for sending Mr. Bohlen to see me yesterday. I, of course, understand your problems. I am not quite sure that I think we can rest until six months from now when E.R.P. is rolling even with the move which Mr. Bohlen outlined to me.[25]

On the Palestine question, I still do not see that we are any better off with the present move or have any fewer problems than we had before.

As to the last thing which Mr. Bohlen said to me about the statement which Franklin, junior made,[26] I told him that I never tried in any way to interfere with my children once they were grown. I haven't taken part in partisan politics and I do not intend to as long as I am on the United Nations, but the children must do whatever they think is right. Mr. Bohlen told me that you felt this move would so jeopardize President Truman's standing that it would hurt the position of our foreign policy in the world. I hardly think that is really true. In an election year all countries know that the man who is at the head of the government may not win. I happen to be a Democrat and to believe that it should be the liberal party of the country and I would be distressed to see liberalism in this country such a tremendous defeat that it could never be resuscitated.

I know as you do that Senator Vandenberg is the best educated person on foreign affairs on the Republican side, but we are not sure of his nomination by the Republicans any more than we are of Mr. Truman's or anybody else, by the Democrats.[27]

It is unfortunate that we have to have an election at a crucial time in the nation's history just as it was in 1940 and 1944, but we managed to have elections in both of those years when the rest of the countries gave up holding elections temporarily. I rather think we will weather holding an election this year. The rest of the world, including Russia, is quite conscious of public opinion and feeling that there [is] a movement for any other candidate growing in the country will not I think, be harmful as long as it is clearly understood that the foreign policy which the Administration and you are advocating, has the support of such people as may suggest other individuals for various reasons as possible candidates.

I understand your anxiety not to have anything rock the boat at the present time, but I doubt if the injection of any new Democratic or Republican candidate is going to have any great effect on the actions of the rest of the world.

Very sincerely yours,

TLc AERP, FDRL

ER responded to the president's letter after meeting with Marshall's envoy, Charles Bohlen, and after FDR, Jr., had, over the objections of Secretaries Marshall and Forrestal, announced his support for the Draft Eisenhower movement.

In her two-hour conversation with Bohlen, ER reviewed the state of US-Soviet relations, the Palestine situation, and, albeit briefly, her sons' opposition to Truman's renomination. As Bohlen reported, ER thought the administration, most especially Secretary Forrestal, was "deliberately embarking on an aggressive policy towards Russia leading inevitably to war." She remained concerned that the State Department "might blunder into something with the Russians which could have been avoided if [the department] had been talking to them." If war did break out, she thought it "vitally important" to demonstrate that "no stone was left unturned to avert it, and recommended that Secretary Marshall meet with Stalin to demonstrate "our determination and … our willingness to discuss matters." As for the crisis in Palestine, ER reiterated her criticism—that the administration's current position "represents a step backward involving a loss of prestige to the United States and leaving us with a greater responsibility since they were U.S. proposals with no prospect of a solution." She also stressed that advancing the trusteeship proposal over the partition plan "looked as though we were disregarding a UN recommendation." She thought the Arabs might have been persuaded to accept partition in principle if the United States had taken "a firm line" after the partition vote.[28]

As she wrote the president, "Mr. Bohlen did not give me a feeling of any great decisions on various questions, though … I understand some of the difficulties and intentions better than I did before."

333

Eleanor Roosevelt to Harry Truman
26 March 1948 [New York City]

Dear Mr. President:

Your letter has reached me on the eve of my departure. It is a very fine letter and I am grateful to you.

I had a talk with Mr. Bohlen this afternoon and though I haven't heard from the Secretary he brought me some messages from him. I must say that talking with Mr. Bohlen did not give me a feeling of any great decisions on various questions, though he did make me feel that there was deep concern, and I understand some of the difficulties and intentions better than I did before.

However, I can not say that even now the temporary measures that we have suggested for Palestine really makes anything simpler or safer than it was before, but perhaps it will prove to be a solution and I certainly pray it will.

At the end of his visit Mr. Bohlen asked me about a statement which Franklin, junior had made and I want to tell you that while Franklin told me he intended to make this statement, he did not ask me for my opinion.

There is without any question among the younger Democrats a feeling that the party as at present constituted, is going down to serious defeat and may not be able to survive as the liberal party. Whether they are right or wrong, I do not know. I made up my mind long ago that working in the United Nations meant, as far as possible, putting aside partisan political activity and I would not presume to dictate to my children or to any one else what their actions should be. I have not and I do not intend to have any part in pre-convention activities.[29]

Very sincerely yours,
Eleanor Roosevelt

TLS HSTSF, HSTL

The day ER met with Bohlen, she also submitted the column below for publication the following day. In it, she continued to make her objections known, writing that not only did she "dislike actions … taken from fear" but that she also failed "to see that we have done away with any troubles or problems by our new stand."

334

My Day
27 March 1948

NEW YORK, Friday—I am an outsider, a simple citizen of the United States, and I have no inside knowledge except the knowledge of the way we, as a delegation in the United Nations General Assembly, came to our decision last fall on the question of Palestine. Our responsible officials naturally have knowledge that we ordinary citizens do not have. They may have ample justi-fication for the fears which they spread before Congress in order to get cooperation in what are nec-essary measures for strength and defense. I dislike actions, however, that are taken from fear, since they are very apt to be unwise and unjust.

The United States has now suggested that a special session of the Assembly be called to recon-sider the case of Palestine. I shall be interested to see whether the little nations share our fears or whether they try to give us the courage to stand by a decision once taken, putting more faith than we do in the ultimate value of a strong United Nations.

Under the new suggestion that the UN create a new mandate for Palestine until some peace-ful solution can be worked out between the Jews and Arabs, I cannot help wondering who is going to see to it that an armistice actually is carried out. There are extremists on both sides of this ques-tion. Palestine is accustomed to violence and bloodshed. Announcing an armistice is not going to bring it about.

It seems to me that the UN and we, as a great nation, are going to be faced with exactly the same problem that we had in supporting partition. One of the questions at issue has always been immigration into Palestine by the Jews. If the new mandate government permits any immigration, the Arabs will object; if it permits no immigration, the Jews will object. And in the meantime mis-erable, desperate people will sit in camps in Europe and on Cyprus.[30] With each day, they become less able to be valuable citizens anywhere.

The very group of Jews in this country who consider partition a mistake, and who do not believe in a Jewish homeland, will be demanding vociferously that we take in more displaced per-sons here and that we hasten their establishment in other countries.[31] Both these things, I think, we should do through the International Refugee Organization and through passage of the Stratton Bill or some other similar bill.[32] But we must face the fact that there are many Jews, who have spent months and years being hunted over Europe, who want to go to Palestine and nowhere else. The pressure will be upon the mandate government and there will be another bone of contention to trouble the waters in Palestine.

I fail to see that we have done away with any troubles or problems by our new stand. And if this change in policy was undertaken to lessen the danger of war, I fail to see where it has achieved that end. The USSR stands pat on its previous decision.[33] And I will not be surprised if quite a number of nations refuse to turn about in response to our whim. For they may feel—as I do—that, no solution being perfect, the one already adopted by the UN might as well be implemented since, with all the argument and effort that has been made, no perfect solution has yet been found.

TMs AERP, FDRL

---

1. The *Washington Post* reported an "unofficial tabulation" of 1,877 deaths from November 29, 1947–March 19, 1948 ("Austin Announces Surprise Reversal; Calls on U.N. to Set Up Trusteeship," *WP*, 20 March 1948, 1).

2. "Shift on Palestine a Shock to Capitol," *NYT*, 20 March 1948, 3; Donovan, 375–77; Pogue, 367–68.

3. *FRUS 1948*, vol. 5, 748–49; "Statement by Secretary Marshall," *SDB*, 28 March 1948, 408; "Marshall Upholds Shift on Palestine," *NYT*, 21 March 1948, 10; Pogue, 368.

4. ER to George Marshall, telegram, n.d., AERP.

5. After Austin's March 19 speech, the British announced they would adhere to their original deci-sion to end the mandate on May 15 and withdraw all their troops after August 1, 1948 ("World News Summarized," *NYT*, 21 March 1948, 1).

6. See Document 301.

7. Coming a day after the United States' switch from partition to trusteeship for Palestine, the Western Allies' proposal to give Trieste to Italy was seen as another serious blow to the UN's prestige and ability to function, since the Security Council had agreed to take on the task of assuring Trieste's "integrity and independence" in 1947 ("Issue Up to Soviet," *NYT*, 21 March 1948, 1; "Trieste Proposal Adds to U.N. Gloom," *NYT*, 21 March 1948, 13; "Security Council Votes to Become Trieste Protector," *NYT*, 11 January 1947, 1).

8. The USSR had been pressing for implementation of the UN's partition resolution (Louis and Stookey, 69–71).

9. Although Austin had opposed partition, he initially supported the UN partition plan because he believed that the UN could be effective in situations such as the one Palestine presented. Senator Robert A. Taft (R-OH) agreed with ER's assessment of the need for military force. "If the new plan is accepted, the Security Council will have to send an armed force to Palestine to support the trusteeship. All of the objections raised by the Administration to the use of armed force when it was to enforce partitioning will apply just as strongly to this plan" (Mazuzan, 112; "Shift on Palestine a Shock to Capitol," *NYT*, 20 March 1948, 3).

10. For the Balfour Declaration and the growth of the Jewish population, see *n*3 Document 227.

11. The letter to Marshall to which ER refers is Document 328.

12. For the origins of the conflict over Trieste, see Document 140. On March 20, 1948, the United States, Great Britain, and France, independent of the UN, made a joint proposal to the USSR that the Free Territory of Trieste be returned to Italy ("U.S., Britain, France Urge Trieste Free Territory Be Returned to Italians; Issue Up to Soviet," *NYT*, 21 March 1948, 1).

13. For more on ER's view that the United States should try to work with the Soviet Union, see the header to Document 210 and Document 267.

14. For the Dixiecrats, see *n*7 Document 388. For the Democrats' perceived difficulties with urban liberals and liberal Democrats' attraction to the Wallace candidacy, see Document 311 and Document 312.

15. Press and diplomatic criticism of the Truman administration's policy regarding Palestine centered on its interpretation of the UN Charter, specifically whether or not the situation in Palestine qualified as a threat to international peace and security under Article 42 and thus justified the Security Council's use of force. Austin's speeches of February 24 and March 19 had not clarified this issue, thus leaving the US government open to charges that its Palestine policy was confused and contradictory (see header for Document 328 and *n*9 above) ("U.S. Policy Contradictory, Some UN Delegates Hold," *NYT*, 26 February 1948, 7; Schlesinger, 305; Evensen, 140–44).

16. For examples of press coverage, see Edwin L. James, "The Palestine Tangle Grows Worse Rapidly: United States Backdown on Partition Gives Rise to a Host of Issues Without Quick Answers," *NYT*, 21 March 1948, E3; Thomas J. Hamilton, "Palestine Switch by Austin Sudden: Other Delegates Told Almost to Last that U.S. Would Support Partition Plan," *NYT*, 22 March 1948, 12; "Taylor Demands that Forrestal Be Fired, Charges Policy 'Taint' of Oil Imperialism," *WP*, 22 March 1948, 4; "Shift on Palestine a Shock to Capitol: Some Hold U.S. Plan 'Sellout'" *NYT*, 20 March 1948, 4; "Dr. Silver Scores U.S. on Palestine: Says Trusteeship Plan Would Place America in Position of Fighting Jews There," *NYT*, 22 March 1948, 10; "The Switch on Palestine," *NYT*, 21 March 1948, E8; Dana Adams Schmidt, "Ben-Gurion Spurns a U.N. Trusteeship; Seeks Arab Treaty; He Insists That Jewish State 'Exists' in Palestine and Will Be Defended," *NYT*, 21 March 1948, 1.

17. As Document 332 illustrates, ER did meet with Charles "Chip" Bohlen, special assistant to the secretary of state, two days later.

18. Dean Rusk devised the Palestine trusteeship proposal as a fallback in case partition could not be implemented. He also thought trusteeship would prevent war in the Middle East and forestall Soviet involvement in the area. If they met, neither ER nor Rusk kept a written record of the meeting (*ANB*; Rusk, 146–48, 152).

19. For details of Bohlen's conversation with ER see *n*28 below.

20. In a statement released March 25, Truman announced that the United States had

> "explored every possibility consistent with the basic principles of the Charter" to implement the partition plan and that the United States "could not undertake to impose this solution on the people of Palestine by the use of American troops, both on Charter grounds and as a matter of national policy." He then characterized the trusteeship proposal Austin proposed on March 19 as an "emergency action" designed to "avert tragedy" and "bloodshed" following the termination of the British mandate in mid-May. The trusteeship would not "prejudice the character of the final political settlement," the President explained, but would "establish the conditions of order which are essential to a peaceful solution." He concluded, "The United States is prepared to lend every appropriate assistance to the United Nations in preventing bloodshed and in reaching a peaceful settlement. If the United Nations agrees to a temporary trusteeship, we must take our share of the necessary responsibility. Our regard for the United Nations, for the peace of the world and for our own self-interest does not permit us to do less ("Truman's Palestine Views," *NYT*, 26 March 1948, 11).

21. For Marshall's remarks at his Los Angeles press conference, see header Document 327.

22. Following World War I, Emir Faisal, the son of Sherif Hussein of Mecca, and the leader of the Arab Revolt, met in Aqaba with Dr. Chaim Weizmann, the head of the Zionist Commission to Palestine. Later, at the Paris Peace Conference, the two negotiated and signed a provisional agreement, which declared that the Arabs would work with the Jews in implementing the Balfour Declaration, and would encourage the "immigration of Jews into Palestine on a large scale," provided that the rights of Arab peasant and tenant farmers would be protected (Sachar, *Israel*, 120–21; Bickerton and Klausner, 41–42, 60–62). For more on the Balfour Declaration see *n*3 Document 227.

23. Although Arabs had initially been receptive to a Jewish homeland in Palestine, as evidenced in the Faisal-Weizmann agreement of 1919 (see *n*22), the fear of economic danger posed by massive Jewish immigration to Palestine sparked a wave of violence against the Jews during the 1920s and 1930s. Jewish settlements in Tel Chai, Galilee, and Jaffa were repeatedly attacked by Arabs, and between 1936 and 1939 an "Arab Rebellion" erupted to discourage Jews fleeing anti-Semitic governments in Europe from emigrating to Palestine. "If Jewish immigration continues," one Palestinian journalist wrote in an article for *International Affairs*, "we shall be in a position of being a minority, which is contrary to Article 6 [of the League mandatory award]" (Sachar, *Israel*, 196–201, 210–13).

24. In response to the United Nations recommendation of November 29, 1947, to partition Palestine into Arab and Jewish states, the Arab League formed the "Arab Liberation Army," and quickly began to infiltrate Palestine and attack Jewish communities in the north with thousands of "volunteer" forces. The army concentrated its efforts at isolating the outlying Jewish villages from the main centers of Jewish population in Jerusalem, Haifa, and Tel Aviv, and sought to expand the area under Arab control in cities with mixed Arab-Jewish populations (Bickerton and Klausner, 93–94).

25. The European Recovery Plan (the Marshall Plan). See *n*28 below for the memorandum Bohlen sent to Marshall detailing his conversation with ER.

26. See *n*29 below. In his letter to Marshall, Bohlen said that he did not go into any detail regarding the Draft Eisenhower movement as Franklin, Jr.,'s statement was made before he arrived. "I merely said ... that you felt at this very critical juncture anything which would weaken the hand of the President beyond the normal activities of the Presidential campaign would have a bad effect ... on the conduct of U.S. foreign policy" (Parmet, 13; Lash, *Years*, 145–49; Donovan, 388; Charles Bohlen to George C. Marshall, 30 March 1948, GCMP, ViLxM).

27. The drive to nominate Michigan senator Arthur Vandenberg for president on the Republican ticket began in 1946 after he won reelection by a margin of more than half a million votes. By 1948, Arthur E. Summerfield, one of Michigan's representatives to the Republican National Committee, had secured Michigan support for Vandenberg. Senator Henry Cabot Lodge, Jr. (R-MA), and others worked on Vandenberg's behalf in Washington, and Pennsylvania governor James H. Duff coordinated a nationwide "Stop Dewey" movement. Although Vandenberg continued to deny any interest in the presidency publicly, he privately told friends he would consider running if the party platform hearings seriously considered an isolationist foreign policy plank (Vandenberg, 315–16, 421–28; Donovan, 388–89; "Roosevelt Sons Back Eisenhower," *NYT*, 27 March 1948, 1).

28. Bohlen reported to Marshall:

> In general, Mrs. Roosevelt appeared to be concerned at the growth of war talk and the feeling among people in New York with whom she was in contact that the administration was deliberately embarking on an aggressive policy towards Russia leading inevitably to a war. It was for this reason she told me that she had suggested to you the possibility of a meeting with Stalin. She explained that she felt that if the worst came to the worst and war did break out, it was vitally important that the United States should have demonstrated that no stone was left unturned to avert it. She was very frank and told me that she had not thought through the idea of a meeting or exactly what such a meeting might accomplish but she felt that it was important that the Russians know both of our determination and of our willingness to discuss matters. I explained to Mrs. Roosevelt that we had under constant review the question of direct dealings with the Russians at the appropriate time; that, however, it was our feeling that certain conditions would have to come about before any genuine settlement with the Russians would be possible; that at the present time those conditions did not exist and as long as a state of crisis continued in Europe all of our experience had demonstrated that the Soviets would attempt to exploit it and that there was little prospect for a genuine settlement until some stability had returned to Europe. In the circumstances, a meeting of the type she had in mind could only result in either a complete breakdown which would further accentuate the tension or else a paper agreement which would have no validity. I also told her that it was my personal opinion that in the present circumstances there was only one type of agreement which the Russians could propose which I thought was totally unacceptable to us and that was an agreement to divide the world into spheres of influence. Mrs. Roosevelt was in entire agreement that any such arrangement would be unthinkable for this country.
>
> I also told her that as we saw it in the Department the danger in the situation was twofold: (1) that the Soviet leadership would make a serious miscalculation with regard to our determination and would take some aggressive step in the mistaken belief that this country would do nothing except talk; and (2) the other danger was that the Russians would misjudge on the other side American policy and believe that the United States was determined to destroy them. I said that we were considering continuously the best method of assuring that the Soviet leaders fully and clearly understood our policy and its purposes and not judge our policy only from public statements, debates in Congress and the American press. I told her that we had under constant review both the time and the best method of assuring that the Russians did not either way obtain a wrong impression of our policy and that a diplomatic channel appeared to us to be the most desirable for

any such move at the appropriate time. Mrs. Roosevelt appeared gratified that the Department had this aspect of the question so much in mind as she said her fear had been that we might blunder into something with the Russians which could have been avoided if we had been talking to them. I was careful to explain that we were not crystallized on any course of action but merely wanted her to know that we were fully aware of the dangers (I think this explains her reference to the moves I outlined in her letter to you of March 27th which is going forward to you in the same pouch). I think I convinced her that a highly publicized meeting such as she had suggested (She apparently had in mind a meeting of the principal powers called by the United Nations.) would not accomplish its purpose at this time but might on the contrary have very serious disadvantages.

On Palestine, I delivered the message from you to the effect that our whole effort had been directed towards keeping the Palestine question within the framework of the United Nations and that most of the pressures to which we had been subjected were in the opposite direction, i.e., to have the United States take unilateral action in relation to partition. I explained to her the considerations we had had in mind in deciding to propose the present course; that the prevention of widespread fighting and bloodshed had to be given first place over the execution of any political solution. Mrs. Roosevelt's chief objection to our proposals seemed to be that they did not advance a solution at all. She said she was afraid we had merely gone back to the situation as it existed before the General Assembly last year and that the problem of keeping order in Palestine under trusteeship would be just as difficult as the implementation of partition and that it looked as though we were disregarding a UN recommendation. She seemed to be still of the opinion that the Arabs were engaged in a good deal of bluff and that had a firmer line been taken since last November the Arabs might be induced to accept in principle the partition. I told her that none of our information nor the developments since the General Assembly supported that conclusion but on the contrary the violence of the Arab reaction, particularly among the Arab people, had been considerably stronger than even the most pessimistic had anticipated last fall. On the subject of unilateral action by the United States to implement partition, Mrs. Roosevelt inquired whether or not fear of Russian participation had been a major factor. I told her that that was of course a real consideration but that as a matter of practical fact based on past experience, Russian willingness, as yet undisclosed, to share the responsibility would have meant in practice a Russian zone in Palestine which would not only have been extremely dangerous in giving them a foothold in the Middle East but would not have rendered U.S. participation more palatable to the American people and would probably have resulted in parallel unilateral action in Palestine, with the United States attempting to implement by force of arms the partition recommendation in one part and the Soviet Union in complete control of another.

Mrs. Roosevelt did not bring up Trieste and obviously did not have it very much on her mind but throughout the whole conversation I emphasized how much this Government had attempted to support the United Nations and to make it a workable instrument for the preservation of peace and that it was only when the machinery was obviously stalled or could not take effective action that we had ever gone outside of its framework.

I also did not go into any detail into the question of the "Draft Eisenhower Movement" supported by her sons since they had made their announcement to the press of their intention to start this movement that afternoon before I arrived. I merely said to her that you felt that at this very critical juncture anything which would weaken the hand of the President beyond the normal activities of the Presidential campaign would have a bad effect abroad on the conduct of our foreign policy. I mentioned personally that no matter what happened Mr. Truman would be President of the United States and hence speak for this nation until next January and that between now and then were probably the most critical months that we have ever had to face. Mrs. Roosevelt told me that she never attempted to tell her sons what they should do in matters of this kind as that was entirely up to them. She said that she felt, however, that there was a fear that the democratic party in its present course would suffer such a defeat as to eliminate virtually from the American scene any liberal American party, leaving the field completely free to Mr. Wallace.

In general, Mrs. Roosevelt's fear seemed to be that we were headed straight for war with the Soviet Union and that the administration had not only accepted this fact but was definitely working on that premise. She said that she realized this was not the case but that that impression had been created in large measure she thought because of war-like talk in high places and over-emphasis on military matters. I reminded her that you had on a number of occasions publicly appealed for calm and cool judgment at this critical juncture and had specifically warned against emotional and hysterical talk. Mrs. Roosevelt said she had fully appreciated your efforts in this direction and she had not had anything in mind that you had said or done, it was just the general impression that had been created she felt throughout the country.

Very confidentially, she was extremely critical of Mr. Forrestal in this respect and seemed to think he was the chief offender. She said that visitors from Washington had quoted to her many private statements of Mr. Forrestal which she thought were definitely aggressive and militarist in tone. I told her that I thought these reports were misleading and that I knew that they did not represent Mr. Forrestal's views. I pointed out that as Secretary of National Defense he inevitably had to talk in military terms, particularly before Congress, but that so far as I was aware no one in Washington had accepted the inevitability of war or were basing their actions on that premise, but that in a democracy such as ours even the most elementary steps to restore our military establishment to the minimum safety level required public discussion and explanation which could be seized upon to create the impression she had in mind.

Mrs. Roosevelt was at no time critical of you or of the policies of the Department of State, with the exception of Palestine. I think that she feels deeply that our latest proposal on Palestine represents a step backward involving a loss of prestige to the United States and leaving us with a greater responsibility since they were U.S. proposals with no prospect of a solution. On that subject I do not think I succeeded in convincing her but on our attitude towards the Soviet Union I think she was considerably reassured as to our thinking with the one doubt, however, that matters might get out of hand by shear momentum.

I have written you at this length as I thought you might like to have a rather full account of Mrs. Roosevelt's attitude. I have given a copy of this letter to Mr. Lovett but to no one else in the Department (Charles Bohlen to George C. Marshall, 30 March 1948, GCMP, ViLxM).

29. On March 26, 1948, Franklin D. Roosevelt, Jr., then national vice chairman of Americans for Democratic Action, issued a public statement urging Americans to draft General Dwight D. Eisenhower for the Democratic presidential nomination, despite the fact that Eisenhower had announced in January that he would not be a candidate. In making this announcement, FDR, Jr., also rejected the attempts George Marshall, James Forrestal, and Eisenhower himself made to dissuade him from releasing his statement. His statement declared that because Henry Wallace's candidacy did not reflect "the liberal objectives and principles of my late father" and that no Republican candidate had yet "demonstrated any marked ability to unite the American people," he thought Eisenhower the only person "capable of securing the unity of our country" and dealing with Soviet threat. Roosevelt said that he issued the statement as a private citizen after notifying

Paul E. Fitzpatrick, the New York Democratic state chairman. (He could not reach Ed Flynn, New York State Democratic committeeman.) Later that day, Elliott Roosevelt also announced his support for Eisenhower, in the process rejecting an appeal from Wallace campaign manager Calvin Baldwin. James Roosevelt, then California State Democratic chairman and national committeeman, also supported the draft movement, although in a much less public way. ER herself apparently discussed the possibility of an Eisenhower draft with Hubert Humphrey, then mayor of Minneapolis ("Roosevelt Sons Back Eisenhower," *NYT*, 27 March 1948, 1; Parmet, 13; Lash, *Years*, 145–49; Donovan, 388; Charles Bohlen to George C. Marshall, 30 March 1948, GCMP, ViLxM).

30. See Document 249 and Document 250.

31. The American Council for Judaism, established in 1942 under the leadership of Rabbi Louis Wolsey of Philadelphia, and the American Jewish Committee, founded in 1906 by a small group of American Jews deeply concerned about the pogroms aimed at the Jewish population of Russia, adamantly opposed the establishment of a Jewish state in Palestine. Both groups believed that by supporting the creation of a Jewish state, they would be subjected to charges of dual loyalty. In explaining the philosophy of the American Council of Judaism, Rabbi Wolsey maintained that his group would combat "nationalistic" trends in Jewish life. "We are definitely opposed to a Jewish State, a Jewish flag, or a Jewish army," he said. "We are interested in the development of Palestine as a refuge for persecuted Jews but are opposed to the idea of a political State under Jewish domination in Palestine or anywhere else" ("New Jewish Group Being Formed Here," *NYT*, 12 December 1942, 20; Kolsky, passim).

32. On April 1, 1947, Illinois Representative William G. Stratton introduced a bill into the House of Representatives (HR 2910) to allow 400,000 displaced persons into the country over the next four years. President Truman thought the idea preposterous and wrote to his assistant David Niles: "The idea of getting 400,000 immigrants into this country is, of course, beyond our wildest dreams. If we could get 100,000 we would be doing remarkably well" (Cohen, *Truman*, 115). For further details on and ER's earlier support for the Stratton bill, see Document 244.

33. After Austin announced the US proposal, Andrei Gromyko, the Soviet representative to the UN, announced that the Soviet Union still supported the original partition plan. The following day, Moscow radio alleged that the United States changed its position "to hold oil fields and bases in the Middle East" and that it could prove that whenever the United States "made promises to the Jews," it "simultaneously told various Arab leaders" to ignore those assurances. "In contrast to Britain and the United States," the broadcast concluded, " the Soviet Union continues to work for a solution conforming with the United Nations decision." For more on the IRO, see header Document 152 (Thomas Hamilton, "World Rift Factor," *NYT*, 20 March 1948, 1; "Moscow Lays U.S. Shift About Palestine to Oil," *NYT*, 22 March 1948, 15).

335

If You Ask Me [excerpt]
Ladies' Home Journal April 1948

I am an American and have been living in Belgium for two years. In the opinion of all the Europeans I know, the purpose of the Marshall Plan and other American-aid-to-Europe plans is simply to stabilize American economy.[1] They believe that without European markets the United States would be a bankrupt nation. They are also of the opinion that the United States is going to fight another war for these markets. I have tried to tell them that our reasons for helping Europe are purely humanitarian and to preserve the democratic way of life so that all nations may reap the blessings of freedom. Don't you think it is too bad that while America is spending so much money for aid, it spends so little to publicize its motives?

Yes, I think it is too bad that we do not do a better publicity job; but we must remember that after the last war we built up mutual feelings of distrust—with Europe looking upon us as Uncle Shylock[2] and with us picturing European nations unwilling to pay their debts.[3] Now we have fought another war, far more costly and devastating. Europeans know what that war has cost them on their own doorstep and we do not. Therefore we have allowed in this country a great deal of loose talk about another war, which must be terrifying to the Europeans. It leaves them rather open to believing the U.S.S.R. propaganda which is against the Marshall Plan and against any really orderly return in Europe to democratic procedure and economic recovery.

I think all we can do is to put as much of the burden of planning for recovery on the European nations as we can and to request certain definite things in return for the money given by us. If possible, we should keep our demands reasonable and watch such greedy people at home who might try to get more than a fair return out of whatever plans are made.

Time alone will answer this question for the Europeans. I think we may learn to spend a little more and to do a better publicity job about this country, but it will certainly take time, and during that time actual things should take place which will prove that our intentions are not evil.

I was called a communist by my Republican friends because I espoused the policies of President Roosevelt. Now it appears that I have reached the height of the ridiculous since you have joined the wolf pack screaming "communist." Recently I have seen the finest young people hide their convictions for fear the "loyalty" bill will lose them their jobs. If it is so serious, why hasn't the FBI taken care of it?[4]

I do not happen to like the loyalty tests. I disapprove of them and have said so a number of times, but they will not lose young people their jobs unless their convictions are questionable convictions. You may have been called a communist by your Republican friends because you followed President Roosevelt's policies, but I do not quite know what you mean by "joining the wolf pack screaming 'communist.'" You must know that there are American communists in this country, and unless you are one, you must admit that their beliefs and the beliefs of citizens of a democracy do not coincide.

I hope that the FBI will not do more than it is now doing about communism in this country. In fact, I would prefer to see it do less, and I would prefer to see us, as American citizens, do more.

TMsex DLC

---

1. For background on the Marshall Plan, see *n*6 Document 231.

2. An amalgamation of the term, "Uncle Sam" (an informal name for the United States) and the name of the Jewish merchant in William Shakespeare's comedy, *The Merchant of Venice*, who refuses to forgive a debt and insists upon the debtor's fulfilling the requirements of the loan agreement, which included a pound of the debtor's flesh.

3. At the end of World War I, America's allies, Great Britain and France, owed the United States $11 billion, which the Allies expected to repay from the $30 billion reparation the Treaty of Versailles required Germany to pay them. Inflation and postwar political instability precluded German repayment, further destabilizing the Allied recovery. In 1924 the United States enacted the Dawes Plan, lending money to Germany to finance its mandated reparations to Britain and France. Only a small fraction of that advance was applied to Allied reparations (Brinkley, 709; Turgeon, 114).

4. For information on the loyalty-security program begun with Truman's Executive Order 9835, see *n*6 Document 271.

"OUR DEMOCRATIC IDEALS"

March 27, ER sailed for a month-long visit to Europe.[1] Her trip began in England April 1, after a "stormy" crossing, and centered foremost on the unveiling of a statue honoring FDR in London's Grosvenor Square across from the American Embassy. King George, Queen Elizabeth, Prime Minister Clement Attlee, and Winston Churchill attended the ceremony, scheduled to coincide with the third anniversary of FDR's death, April 12. In remarks following those made by the king and the prime minister, Churchill called FDR "the greatest American friend that Britain ever found, and the foremost champion of freedom and justice who has ever stretched strong hands across the oceans, to rescue Europe or Asia from tyranny or destruction."[2]

In her address that evening before the Pilgrim Society, a group promoting Anglo-American friendship that coordinated the popular subscription drive underwriting the statue's construction, ER expanded on Churchill's proclamation of friendship. As she told the king and queen, Attlee, Churchill, and the other dinner guests, the statue testified to both the affection and esteem the British had for FDR. She then devoted the remainder of her remarks to discussing how "the friendship between the English speaking peoples [should] be used for constructive principles" and strengthening "our democratic ideals."[3]

336

Address by Eleanor Roosevelt at the Pilgrim Society Dinner

12 April 1948 [London]

My Lord Chairman, Your Royal Highnesses, Your Excellencies, Your Grace, My Lords, Ladies and Gentlemen:

I come to this last ceremony of the dinner, given by the Pilgrims, with a heart filled with humility and gratitude. The people of Great Britain have shown me in every way possible since I arrived, great warmth of feeling and I am deeply grateful. It is a sign of greatness when the people of one great country show their gratitude to the citizen of another great country, who was the head of his Nation during a period of great danger to both nations.

Because it was within the power of my husband to be of assistance to Great Britain, the people of Great Britain, from His Majesty the King down to the humblest citizen, have felt an affectionate regard for him. They recognized the way in which he used his opportunities and sustained their great and courageous War Prime Minister, Mr. Churchill, in his valiant efforts to encourage his own people in their darkest hours. No one in the U.S. will ever forget the Battle of Britain and the then Prime Minister's words when he thanked the valiant young fliers to whom so many in my country, as well as here, must be eternally grateful.[4] My husband felt a warm personal regard for Mr. Churchill which facilitated their work together and you will remember that when he turned over to Great Britain the 50 Destroyers and received the bases in the Caribbean, he remarked that Great Britain was our first line of defense.[5] That is true today, Mr. Prime Minister, and in the battle for peace, Great Britain and the European democracies are our first great hope of peace and I hope that our governments of today will co-operate just as successfully.

The memorial which I unveiled today and the very beautiful and moving ceremonies in which Their Majesties were kind enough to take part, will strengthen the tie, I am sure, that has always existed between our two nations. We differ in many ways. We, in the United States, are a nation made up of many peoples and yet the bond of kinship still allows us to quarrel without breaking the bond, so that when we face serious times, the basic tie is still there. We come together in spite of our differences and stand shoulder to shoulder, and together, we and the British people, strengthened by the youth of their Dominions, have great power in the world.

Canada and her people are our closest neighbors and our long time friends, but since modern inventions have drawn the world together more closely, the more distant members of the Commonwealth, which once seemed so far away, are gradually closer neighbors and warmer friends.

Together with our Allies, we won a war nearly three years ago and since then we have been trying, all of us, to make a peace. This peace was close to my husband's heart and he planned the first steps to create the machinery which he hoped might be used to foster and preserve peace on earth.

I would have this friendship among the great English speaking peoples, used for constructive purposes. I would have it strengthen our democratic ideals. The freedom of men throughout the world should be more sure because of our friendship. I would hope that we would guarantee more and more as the years go on, the human rights of the individual man which true democracies hold inalienable. The four freedoms are still our goal:

Freedom of conscience and religion
Freedom from fear of aggression
Freedom from want
Freedom of speech and assembly

These are essential to the achievement of true democracy. These are still the basic freedoms that we hope to spread throughout the world for all people to enjoy.[6]

I should like to see added to these, freedom of movement for men throughout the world so that we could go without red tape of any kind, to see one another and grow to know one another better.

I would have this friendship of ours, however, in no way exclusive. The man whom you so greatly honored today, believed that there could be friendship developed, perhaps slowly, but steadily among all the peoples of the world. He thought that it would require a careful watchfulness over our own strength and integrity. He believed that we must have understanding and sympathy with the points of view of other peoples and in the end, he thought we could create a lasting bond among men of many nations, in spite of their differences. One of your people, Mr. Herbert Parkinson, in a broadcast after his death said, "He has passed from the stress of the doing to the peace of the done."[7] He has gone, but I am sure he fights for the right as he sees it through our strength and striving. We are here to take up the challenge and to do our best.

I, myself, feel that we of the English speaking peoples, have a very great responsibility in the world today, because it is easier for us to understand each other. We speak the same language, in more ways than one. I hope the day will come when all over the world, every child will learn one universal language, which every other child is learning at the same time throughout the world, no matter what their native tongue may be. I am afraid it is too late for those of my generation to hope to communicate easily with the people of the rest of the world, in a common tongue. We are perhaps too lazy or too set in our ways, but there is a language of the spirit which can be translated into action and that we of the older generation must be sure to grasp and to speak.[8]

Between Great Britain and ourselves, it should not be difficult to keep these actions of friendship constantly alive, but we should make them serve the purpose of a shining example. We should prove to other nations that the same thing is possible for us in relation to every nation of the world.

Our very strength which grows with unity, should be the proof that the problems of the world can be solved by greater and wider unity. My country is an amalgamation of various peoples and yet we are one and are strong. We have no feeling that we can not meet whatever problems the future may bring us, because we have faith in each other and in our joint strength and democratic idealism. We know that there will be changes in our way of life but we are ready to meet the changes. You, in the other English speaking nations, have had the strength to meet many changes and yet fundamentally, you also are sure of your ability to weather whatever storms may come. Economic difficulties can be met and mastered by co-operation and that we hope to prove in the carrying out of the Marshall Plan to our mutual advantage. It must first prove of benefit to those who now have faith in it, but with its success we hope to see it benefit all the other nations of Europe and of Asia. In a nutshell, the Marshall Plan aims to strengthen the United Nations by strengthening the individual member nations. The United Nations can only do its best work if all nations, great and small are strong and secure and able to make their decisions free from fear. With persistence in good will and a bridle on self-seeking, great things may be accomplished I feel, in the future.

Our confidence in ourselves should serve as an encouragement to all the peoples of the world who face today the same problems that we do in varying ways. Our strength is the strength of individuals who are free and who come together for joint purposes voluntarily. It should bring encouragement to all men if we use it for the mutual benefit of all those who are willing to try to cast out suspicion and begin to work together wherever a point of agreement can be found.

As I unveiled the statue of my husband today, I could not help remembering a line which was written about President Theodore Roosevelt by his sister, Mrs. Douglas Robinson. She called him "Valiant for Truth". I should like to have my husband thought of as, "Valiant for Friendship".[9]

Not a narrow friendship which extends only to our own people, but for the friendship which is great enough to break down misunderstandings and differences and indefatigably and persistently tries to build the world friendship, which some day may give all the people of the world security in the knowledge that peace is really assured. This can not be done by weaklings. It must be done by strong men and women, strong in their convictions and in the love which casts out fear and makes men free. It must be done by strong nations whose ways are rooted in individual freedom and belief in justice and law. The pure in heart are free of suspicion. The great are humble and can not be humiliated. Pray God, we join together and invite all others to join us in creating a world where justice, truth and good faith rule. May generations to come everywhere live with hope.

We wrote in our Constitution as aspirations, these inherent rights of man—"Life, Liberty and the Pursuit of Happiness". May it be the destiny of the English speaking peoples of the world to begin to make these hopes and aspirations a reality for all men.

TSp AERP, FDRL

---

1. Her schedule also included an April 17 address before an assembly convened by the International Council of Women and an April 20 address to Utrecht University ("Politics Shunned by Mrs. Roosevelt," *NYT*, 28 March 1948, 36).

2. "The Text of Roosevelt Tributes by Churchill and King," *NYT*, 13 April 1948, 13.

3. For her earlier appearance at the Pilgrim Society, see *n*18 Document 84 ("Roosevelt by Mrs. Roosevelt," *Sunday Dispatch*, 11 April 1948; Herbert L. Matthews, "Homage of Britain is Paid Roosevelt," *NYT*, 13 April 1948, 12).

4. In his famous speech to the House of Commons during the Battle of Britain on August 20, 1940, Churchill thanked the fighter pilots, saying:

> The gratitude of every home in our Island, in our Empire, and indeed throughout the world, except in the abodes of the guilty, goes out to the British airmen who, undaunted by odds, unwearied in their constant challenge and mortal danger, are turning the tide of the World War by their prowess and by their devotion. Never in the field of human conflict was so much owed by so many to so few. All hearts go out to the fighter pilots, whose brilliant actions we see with our own eyes day after day; but we must never forget that all the time, night after night, month after month, our bomber squadrons travel far into

Germany, find their targets in the darkness by the highest navigational skill, aim their attacks, often under the heaviest fire, often with serious loss, with deliberate careful discrimination, and inflict shattering blows upon the whole of the technical and war-making structure of the Nazi power. (Churchill, 244-45).

5. As FDR prepared the nation for his bases-for-destroyers plan and Lend-Lease, he sometimes referred to Britain as our "first line of defense" against a foreign invasion. The press adopted that metaphor and used it repeatedly in editorials and coverage of the debates over both plans. For examples, see "Comment by Press on British Accord," *NYT*, 4 September 1940, 13; Frank L. Kluckhorn, "Aid Plan Outlined," *NYT*, 18 December 1940, 1.

6. For more on the Four Freedoms, see *n*1 Document 119.

7. Herbert Parkinson, a British sports journalist, was killed in the invasion of Normandy (http://www.irdp.co.uk/JohnCrook/normandy.htm, accessed April 10, 2006).

8. ER was fluent in French, understood some German and Italian, and was learning Swahili when she died.

9. In addition to the biography, *Theodore Roosevelt: My Brother*, Corrine Roosevelt Robinson wrote two poems praising her brother, of which "Valiant for Truth" was one. She adopted the phrase from the character of the same name in John Bunyan's *Pilgrim's Progress*, about whom Bunyan wrote:

> After this it was noised abroad that Mr. Valiant-for-truth was taken with a summons by the same post as the other, and had this for a token that the summons was true, 'That his pitcher was broken at the fountain.' When he understood it, he called for his friends and told them of it. Then said he, 'I am going to my Fathers, and though with great difficulty I am got hither, yet now I do not repent me of all the trouble I have been at to arrive where I am. My sword I give to him that shall succeed me in my pilgrimage, and my courage and skill to him that can get it. My marks and scars I carry with me, to be a witness for me that I have fought His battles who now will be my rewarder" (Bunyan, 301).

PROMOTING THE MARSHALL PLAN

In preparation for her visit to Europe in April 1948, ER sought Secretary Marshall's advice on what issues she should address in the speeches she planned to make while abroad. Marshall replied March 10, suggesting that since the European Recovery Program will have been passed by Congress by that time, it would be a "very appropriate topic" for any talks ER made during her visit. "Depending upon your audience, you might find it advisable to counteract some of the propaganda charges concerning the allegedly imperialistic nature of the European Recovery Program," the secretary recommended. He also thought it important that she interpret the plan as "a remarkable manifestation of America's recognition of the urgent necessities of the situation in Europe and our responsibilities throughout the world."[1]

April 20, while in the Netherlands to receive an honorary degree of Doctor of Laws from the University of Utrecht,[2] ER heeded Marshall's advice and spoke about the importance of the Marshall Plan in rebuilding democracies throughout Europe as well as the need for "mutual cooperation" between the United States and its European allies.

_337_

Address by Eleanor Roosevelt at Utrecht University
20 April 1948

Your Majesty, Your Highnesses, Mr. President, Ladies and Gentlemen:[3]

It is with a deep sense of gratitude and humility that I accept from this ancient university,[4] a degree which I shall cherish not because of my own achievements, but because I am sure in giving it to me, you have in mind an expression of gratitude to my husband and to the United States of America because of the help which our country was able to give your country during your years of trial.[5]

My husband and I both have a very special tie with Holland. On the Roosevelt side of our families, though we were only fifth cousins, we are both descended from the original Claes Martinson van Roosevelt, who was the first to come to the United States of America and who landed in New York. Since that day our family has come to be known by the name of the place from which our ancestor came, and descendants of that first good Dutchman are now to be found in many different areas throughout the United States. The Roosevelts have played their part in the building of the new world across the Atlantic, and in doing so they have brought closer ties between the so-called new world and the old world of the Netherlands.

During the last war that tie was strengthened by the visits which your Royal Family paid to us on several occasions. Her Majesty Queen Wilhelmina was kind enough to receive us and to visit us on more than one occasion. Princess Juliana and Prince Bernhard came not only to the White House but to our own home on the Hudson River—an area which must have reminded them of home because of the many villages with Dutch names.[6]

A warm personal affection developed and an admiration for the way in which Holland, though overrun, was still resisting and for the constant close interest which the Queen and the rest of your Royal Family took in their people in Holland and in their sufferings.[7] Princess Juliana asked me, long before her return seemed possible, to put her in touch with the best doctors studying tuberculosis so she could learn what should be done, since she knew that the disease would take a particular toll among children.

Today the people of the old world and the people of the new in the United States of America are facing a joint problem of reconstruction of the world after the devastation of a long war. You have suffered greatly. We, in the United States, are fortunate enough to have the means to be of help and assistance. Through the Marshall Plan we hope that all the democracies of Europe will be able to rehabilitate themselves economically over a period of years.[8]

The people of the United States, because of the great territory they occupy, have lived in isolation to a certain extent and it has not been easy to bring them to a realization of the fact that through modern invention the world has become a smaller place in which to live, and therefore if the democracies cease to exist in Europe as a whole, democracy will be menaced in the United States.[9]

The vote on the Marshall Plan, however, in our Congress would indicate that we have finally come to understand the great need for our mutual cooperation and we also recognize the need for a strong United Nations, and the fact that the United Nations can not be strong unless each individual member nation is able to stand on its own feet and feel secure in expressing a free opinion.[10]

There was a time when the whole of Europe dreaded that in passing the Marshall Plan, the United States would attach strings of a supervisory nature that would leave no freedom to the individual nations to plan their own futures. Fortunately the Plan has passed and has no strings attached to it. It is now the responsibility of the Western European democracies to put their plans into action and to use the aid which comes to them for the type of projects which will give the best foundation on which the countries can build again their economic and physical strength.[11]

The return to a sound economic basis will not in itself be sufficient, however, to make the European democracies strong. There must be on their part, a conviction that the type of democracy and the economic system under which they live, can actually give to the majority of people a better existence than they have had in the past. There must be a crusading spirit and a maturity which comes from the love of other human beings, or our best plans will fail. We will rebuild material strength but we will not rebuild the strength of the individual man and woman, and the sense of freedom and the strength of the spirit which is indispensable for participation in the moulding of the world of tomorrow will not develop.

In speaking in London on April 12th, I mentioned the fact that when President Theodore Roosevelt died, his sister, Mrs. Douglas Robinson, called him in a poem she wrote "Valiant for Truth" and that I hope my husband will be remembered as "Valiant for Friendship". That friendship must not be a narrow one, it must extend to the people of every country in the world. My husband believed in human beings and in their ability to choose the right. It was that belief which made it impossible for him at any time to want the power of a dictator. He was sure that if people knew the truth their judgement would eventually be the wisest judgement and their decisions would be the strongest decisions because no one man had taken them. They would be the will of the whole people. This, of course, imposes on citizens who participate in their government, a very great responsibility and I feel sure that this responsibility will be lightened if in the years to come, we grow to know each other better.[12]

Therefore I am anxious to see exchanges between the European Universities and our own increase. I am anxious to see the facilities for travel extended and made easier for people of moderate means. I am anxious to see the exchange of books, of artists, or lecturers, increased to a point where misunderstandings between peoples can be cleared up through contacts between peoples.

I have great respect for the Dutch people as a whole. I have been brought up to consider that we have much to learn and to admire in the traditional characteristics of the Dutch people.

I am greatly honored today and I express my gratitude from a very full heart, and I add to it the hope that I may be able to increase in some small measure, the good-will that must grow between your country and my own to strengthen the bond of good-will that must eventually reach out to all the nations of the world.

TSp AERP, FDRL

1. George C. Marshall to ER, 10 March 1948, AERP.

2. ER described the event in My Day:

> The ceremonies were held in the chapel. As I looked across at the rows of gentlemen opposite me, in their black gowns and white, pleated bibs, I felt as though I were looking at an old painting. I decided that we still have a good deal of Dutch blood in the United States, for many of the faces reminded me of people I have seen in different groups in our country …

> … I received the degree and the brilliant red and white hood that goes with it. After which, my promotor explained in a speech why the senate of the university had decided to confer this honor on a woman for the first time.

> Naturally, the honor bestowed on me is a symbol of Dutch gratitude for the help given by Americans, and particularly, is in recognition of my husband's interest in and concern for Holland, the land of his ancestors …

> When we came out in academic procession, I was handed over to the care of two students, who escorted Miss Thompson and me into a carriage drawn by four horses with plumes in the law-school colors. This, I was told, is traditional procedure when you receive an honorary degree.

> We solemnly drove through crowded streets to one of the clubs of the girl students. As we got out, all the students there sang the song of their organization, while the girls who had ridden ahead of us sat on their horses, waiting for us to go inside. As we had passed one of the boys' clubs, where the boys stood outside and cheered, I had the feeling that the girls were happy for once to have it their day! (*MD*, 23 April 1948).

3. Her Majesty Queen Wilhelmina, the Crown Princess Juliana, and her husband Prince Bernhard (*MD*, 23 April 1948).

4. The University of Utrecht was founded in 1625 (University of Utrecht, "About Utrecht University," http://www.uu.nl/uupublish/homeu/homeenglish/aboututrechtuniv/4469main. html, accessed 7 June 2005).

5. Allied air forces landed at Arnhem and Eindhoven in 1944, liberating Zeeland, North Brabant, and the Limburg provinces (*OCWWII*).

6. For ER's relationship with Princess Juliana, see *n*6 Document 55. The Hudson River valley, colonized by Dutch settlers beginning in 1624, still bears many Dutch names, such as Poughkeepsie, Staatsburg, and Stuyvesant (*CEP*).

7. Germany invaded and conquered the Netherlands in May, 1940. German commissioner of the occupied Netherlands Arthur Seyss-Inquart established a reign of terror, forcing the royal family into exile in Canada, effectively shutting down Dutch universities, and mandating mass deportations and exterminations of Dutch Jews and members of the Dutch Resistance. Numerous students, professors, an underground press, secret organizations, and Dutch Protestant and Catholic churches resisted. During her stay in Holland, ER and Princess Juliana visited a tuberculosis hospital for students involved in the resistance. For more on Princess Juliana's concern over Dutch suffering, see Document 55 ("Nazi Rule in Holland: Growing Strength of Dutch Resistance," *TL*, 2 June 1943, 5; *OCWWII*, 2001; Lash, *World* 260–61).

8. In March 1948, Congress passed one of the first components of the Marshall Plan, the Foreign Assistance Act, which authorized the release of the $5,000,000,000 needed to facilitate the first 12 months of the plan. In August, Congress appropriated $4,835,000,000 in US aid to fourteen European countries, including $506,400,000 to the Netherlands. For more on the Marshall Plan,

see *n*6 Document 231 (Harold Callender, "Figures on Allocation of U.S. Aid Proposed by Europeans Revealed," *NYT*, 20 Aug 1948, 3; Hogan, 89).

9. On March 10, 1948, Marshall responded to ER's request for suggestions on the topics she might cover in her speeches in Europe: "you could possibly make clearer to them how difficult it is for farmers in Iowa or Nebraska, for example, to understand and react promptly to a situation thousands of miles away." See also *n*12 Document 313 and *n*9 Document 320 (George C. Marshall to ER, 10 March 1948, AERP).

10. Congress voted overwhelmingly to approve the conference committee report resolving the allocation differences each proposed for the Marshall Plan. The House voted 318 to 75 within the fifteen minutes of receiving the report and the Senate quickly followed with a similar margin (Felix Belair, Jr., "Aid Voted Swiftly," *NYT*, 3 April 1948, 1).

11. In his letter of March 10, Marshall also suggested ER "counteract some of the propaganda charges concerning the allegedly imperialist nature of the European Recovery Program." See also *n*12 Document 313 and *n*9 Document 320 (George C. Marshall to ER 10 March 1948, AERP).

12. See *n*9 Document 336.

"A RATHER DIFFICULT POSITION"

Adlai Stevenson, whom ER knew from his work with the US delegation to the UN,[1] sought ER's help now that he had secured the Democratic nomination for governor of Illinois. As he wrote March 24, the state committee was "most anxious to persuade you to ... address the State Democratic Convention." As he interpreted the party's strategy, the leaders, hoping to reverse the party's stinging defeat in the 1946 elections,[2] planned "to commence the last lap of the state campaign with a bang-up mass meeting" and hoped that ER would travel to Chicago to lead this meeting because they thought she was "the best 'bang' in the Party." Although Stevenson "suspected" that she would have to be in Paris for the General Assembly and was "most reluctant to even suggest another chore for you," he hoped that she would be able to attend. "I need not add that your presence here would be tonic for all of us—and we have, as of now, a better than even chance of electing the entire state and county tickets, thanks to the support of many Republicans and Independents throughout the State." Concluding that he knew how "unmercifully burdened" she was, he reiterated that she should "not hesitate to decline" this request.[3]

ER did not see this request until she returned from the Human Rights Committee meetings in late April.[4]

338

Eleanor Roosevelt to Adlai Stevenson
28 April 1948 [New York City]

Dear Mr. Stevenson:

I would love to come out to help you but I am in a rather difficult position. I do not know whether I will be renominated for the General Assembly.[5] If I am, I do not know when I would have to leave, but I would probably go a little before the opening as there are two or three things which if I go to Europe, I would like to do.

In any case, in view of the fact that I have disagreed with the policy of the Administration on the Palestine issue and was told by them that they would like me at least, to stay on the Human Rights Commission in spite of my feelings on the Palestine question, I think I had better not take any part in partisan politics as long as I am on the UN. It is a funny, mixed-up world, but for the moment I think the most important thing is to work on the UN as long as I can. I am very unhappy about going back on the Assembly decision on Palestine and I feel the handling of it up to this time, has brought about much of the Arab arrogance and violence. Certainly our proposal for a change does not seem, from my point of view, to have put us in any better position. Somebody will have to implement a truce and somebody will have to implement a trusteeship. Some time the issue of serving on an equal basis with Russia under the UN will have to be faced.

Because I have said all this so firmly to both the President and the Secretary of State, I think it would be unwise for me to take an active part in partisan politics.

With every good wish for the success of your state ticket, I am,

Very cordially yours,
Eleanor Roosevelt

TLS AESP, NjP-SC

1. In 1933 Adlai Stevenson began his involvement with federal government in one of the first New Deal projects, the Agricultural Adjustment Administration (AAA). Stevenson first served as special attorney and assistant to general counsel Jerome Frank and then as chief attorney for the Federal Alcohol Control Administration, a subsidiary of the AAA. After leaving the AAA in 1935 to practice law in Chicago, he returned to work for Roosevelt's administration in 1941 first as an assistant and then special assistant to Secretary of the Navy Frank Knox. As special assistant to Knox, Stevenson "did a little of everything—negotiated the lease of a naval oil reserve, helped settle a defense plant strike, traveled with Knox, and wrote Knox's speeches." After Knox's death in 1944, Stevenson again left the federal government only to return the following year as a special assistant to Secretary of State Edward Stettinius to aid in the creation of the United Nations. Working closely with Assistant Secretary Archibald MacLeish, Stevenson prepared an educational campaign for Americans on the United Nations, and attended the San Francisco Conference, where he served as an unofficial press liaison for Stettinius and the rest of the delegation. His work at the San Francisco Conference led to his appointment to the US delegation to the United Nations as deputy US representative on the Preparatory Commission. After Stevenson completed his work on the Preparatory Commission, President Truman appointed him as an alternate delegate to the UN General Assembly. It was at the second session of the UN in Lake Success, New York, that he met and became friends with ER. At the end of the General Assembly session in late 1947, Stevenson resigned from the US delegation to return to Illinois to run for governor, which he won by the largest plurality in Illinois history by defeating the Republican incumbent Dwight Green. In response to a cable of congratulations from ER, Stevenson wrote "It's all your fault! You told me last fall to go ahead and have a try at it, and I have profited enormously from the experience quite aside from the amazing victory. So I am grateful to you on still another count!" (Martin, 190, 219; McKeever, 126; Adlai Stevenson to ER, 6 November 1948, AERP).

2. The Democrats won only one of the twenty-six Illinois congressional elections in 1946. An extremely effective campaigner, Stevenson won the governorship with 57 percent of the popular vote (*ANB*).

3. Adlai Stevenson to ER, 24 March 1948, AERP.

4. Malvina "Tommy" Thompson to Adlai Stevenson, 30 March 1948, AERP.

5. The State Department, as required under the participation law, nominated a slate of delegates for each session of the United Nations. Thus, although ER had already served on the delegation for two years and had been approved by Congress to be a part of the delegation in 1945, protocol dictated that she be nominated for each session in which she was to serve (C. P. Trussell, "UNO Bill Passed, Mrs. Roosevelt Named A Delegate," *NYT*, 20 December 1945, 1).

CRITICIZING WALLACE, DEFENDING TRUMAN, AND DEFINING FORCE

March 28, Alice Hussey Balassa, who had earlier clashed with ER over her criticism of Wallace, wrote ER to say that ER's recent statements lead her to believe that ER "might be feeling as we do—that Truman is hopeless to control Forrestal et al" and again declaring that "we owe a great debt to Wallace for crystalizing the sentiment against this feverish rush towards war." Balassa then told ER that her husband had heard her speech before the Unitarian Conference, and liked "everything you said except the slaps at Wallace."

ER should be careful when she used the word "force," Balassa continued, because "people will always hear what they want to hear" and "it is dangerous to use the phrase 'force,' unless you say explicitly you mean moral force and examples of democracy." She then criticized ER for "feel[ing] that we need U.M.T. and a military force, as well" and asked if she thought "Forrestal and the present line-up can be trusted with" Universal Military Training.

Despite her criticisms, Balassa concluded, "I can see your kind good face as I write and feel how heavily your position of honor and responsibility must weigh on your shoulders. Thanks from our hearts for speaking out on the Palestine question."[1]

ER responded when she returned from Europe.

339

Eleanor Roosevelt to Alice Balassa
30 April 1948 [Hyde Park]

Dear Mrs. Belassa:

I am just catching up on the mail which accumulated while I was away.

In answer to your letter of March 28th, I am sorry to say I do not think we owe a debt of gratitude to Mr. Wallace. He has done a very dangerous thing and if you could have been in Europe as I have been and have people stop you in the street to tell you how terrified they are at what Mr. Wallace is doing, you would not be grateful to him. They know how little he understands the real situation in Europe.[2]

What I actually said at the Unitarian Conference will be printed so that you and others can read it.[3] What I say everywhere is exactly the same—that we will have to be strong in the military sense. We will have to be wise in the use of our economic strength. Those two combined will not be enough, we should also be strong morally and spiritually.

I have always been against Universal Military Training and I still am in the strict sense of the word, but I would be willing to go along for the next five years until we can build strength in the United Nations which can take care of any aggressor nation—large or small. Then I would be glad to see us have a year of Universal Service which would take into account what a man can do in a democracy in peace time which I think is essential since it is always easier to appeal to patriotism through military service. We must provide that same appeal in peace time service.[4]

I do not like everything that is being done in Washington. There are people with whom I thoroughly disagree. I have on a number of occasions said so. I think President Truman, to the best of his ability, would like to do what is right. I think he has had poor advice, some of it unfortunately from people whom my husband could handle because he understood certain things better than most men in this country, and had many opportunities to understand them.

Just jumping on President Truman, without knowing what the situation is that we face and what we could do about it, seems to me very foolish. We, the people, did not elect liberals to Congress so some of the suggestions the President made have not been accomplished, so it is still on our shoulders what we have in the way of government.

Very sincerely yours,

TLc AERP, FDRL

---

1. Alice Balassa to ER, 28 March 1948, AERP. For more on Balassa, see header Document 316.

2. In 1947, Henry Wallace embarked on a speaking tour in Western Europe, attacking the Truman administration and its policies with respect to Communism. After the tour he continued his vocal opposition to Truman's foreign policy at home (see Document 221).

3. Speaking before the Unitarian Conference in Tarrytown, New York, on March 21, 1948, ER addressed the "role of the liberal" in the post–World War II climate, and in particular challenged the Progressive Party's vision of a "liberal" foreign policy. "I have always been fond of Henry Wallace," ER said of the Progressive Party leader, "but he never has had to work with the Russians and I have. And I don't feel that just 'sweetness and light' by itself is going to win a just peace. I think we need a clear facing of the facts and holding on to our own ideals, and trying to bring the world to a sense of our strength in all ways." The text of ER's remarks were later printed in the *Christian Register* 127, no. 6 (June 1948):26–28, 33. See Document 355.

4. For more on Universal Military Training, see header Document 326. For more on Forrestal, see *n*8 and *n*11 Document 301.

ER periodically highlighted books and plays in My Day that amused her, moved her, or provided special insights into current affairs. In late February 1948 she reviewed an illustrated children's book, *In Henry's Backyard*, which recounted xenophobic Henry's encounters with people of different ethnic backgrounds,[1] calling its publisher "courageous" and the text itself "a most entertaining little book." She continued:

> Both the text and the illustrations are delightful. In popular form, it brings to young and old alike some established scientific facts. They seep into your consciousness with a laugh.

> One hopes that certain pompous Southern gentlemen, now protesting violently that they will never put into effect the recommendations of the President's Civil Rights Commission, may see this book and begin to realize how funny they are.[2]

She again cited the book in her May question and answer column for the *Ladies' Home Journal*.

340

If You Ask Me [excerpt]
Ladies' Home Journal May 1948

Last evening while conversing with some young women I have known for years, the subject of racial equality came up. To my dismay, several girls whom I had always considered fair and unprejudiced made such remarks as: "I don't believe in equal rights for colored and white people." Similar remarks were made regarding Jewish people. Will you kindly tell me how one goes about calmly trying to convince people who consider themselves "nice people" but harbor within their minds such prejudices? Every one of these girls is a member of some church in our community.

I would suggest that the girls you mention be given a copy of In Henry's Back-yard to read as a starter.

Sometimes I think we are a little too calm when we run up against this type of prejudice. However, the best thing to point out is that one is not asking for equal rights to begin with, but equal opportunities, and then when those are obtainable the rights will take care of themselves.

One might suggest that democracy is today at the crossroads, and unless we show some zeal in fighting for fundamental democratic beliefs, we may find other beliefs in the ascendancy.

We have found in a number of instances that states' rights had to be subordinated to the good of the whole people. When we flout the Constitution by an appeal to states' rights, we are, I think, courting disaster. Sooner or later a nation has to make up its mind to be a united nation or fall apart, and the attitude of these young ladies is an attitude which will bring about dissolution, since we cannot remove people who have been here long enough to become citizens.[3]

TMsex DLC

---

1. Written by Columbia University anthropologists Ruth Benedict and Gene Weltfish and based on their best-selling and controversial 1943 pamphlet, "The Races of Mankind," *In Henry's Backyard* aimed to promote racial tolerance in the United States, showing characters who struggle to overcome their "Green Devils" of prejudice toward neighbors from other backgrounds or with

a different outward appearance ("Why We Behave Like Humans," *NYT*, 7 March 1948, BR23; Caffrey, 297–300; Stewart, 11–15).

2. ER also provided an endorsement sentence for the book when its publishers took out an advertisement in the *New York Times*: "I think it is a real contribution to better understanding of the race question" (*MD*, 27 February 1948; Display Ad, *NYT*, 12 March 1948, 21).

3. A number of southern politicians who opposed Truman's February 1948 proposals for federal civil rights measures argued that the proposals represented an unconstitutional invasion of states' rights (Arthur Krock, "The South Is Incensed," *NYT*, 4 February 1948, 6; "Byrd Says 'Rights' Mean Dictatorship," *NYT*, 20 February 1948, 3; "State's Rights Raised in Lynch Bill Hearings," *NYT*, 21 February 1948, 7; "Connally Scores Truman on Rights," *NYT*, 29 February 1948, 1).

DRAFTING A COVENANT
AND RECOGNIZING A JEWISH STATE

While ER chaired the subcommittee charged with drafting both the declaration of human rights and the proposed covenants detailing its enforcement, she received a letter from Secretary Marshall, enclosing a letter from Ambassador Lewis Douglas recounting the "quite extraordinary" reception ER received from British citizens. She used her reply to Marshall to address a number of issues, including her continued dissatisfaction with the State Department's position on Palestine, her recommendation to acknowledge racial discrimination and the legal arguments against Jim Crow, and her assessment of other nations' interest in securing economic and social rights. As she did with her letter to the president, ER closed with a handwritten postscript reaffirming her belief in "the establishment of the Jewish state."[1]

341

Eleanor Roosevelt to George Marshall
11 May 1948 [New York City]

Dear Mr. Secretary:

Thank you for sending me Ambassador Douglas' letter. I am very happy that he told you what I said and that he felt the visit to Great Britain was helpful and created good feeling. I hope the visits to Holland and Belgium did the same.[2]

I have just heard from some of the Jewish organizations that they have heard that Russia will recognize the Jewish State as soon as it is declared which will be midnight on Friday, I imagine.[3] The people who spoke to me are afraid that we will lag behind and again follow instead of lead.

I have no idea what the policy of the Administration and the State Department is going to be on this, and I am only just telling you what you probably already know about the Russian position.[4] I have no feeling that they have any principles or convictions in what they are doing, but wherever they can put us in a hole they certainly are going to do it.

The attitude of the International Law Committee of the Association of the Bar of the City of New York on the draft declaration of Human Rights and the Convention, of course, is going to coincide with the British Government's attitude as expressed by Lord Jowitt in Parliament the other day.[5] Neither country, apparently, is anxious to do anything at the present time. I feel that the Human Rights Commission has an obligation to present the best draft it can to the Economic and Social Council, but if they wish to recommend to the General Assembly that the Assembly consider the present documents and then refer them to governments for further comment, that is up to the Economic and Social Council or even to the Assembly itself.

It would please the Russians to begin all over again as they have suggested in this meeting, and try to find points on which we can all agree and base a Declaration on such points. I doubt very much if they at any time would consider a Convention.[6]

I doubt very much also if the very restricted Convention suggested by the Bar Association will satisfy the European countries or the smaller countries on the Human Rights Commission, but I think we may have to state quite openly that we want a document which the larger number of governments can adhere to, that we hope there will be future conventions and that perhaps even we, ourselves, in view of the fact that Congress would have to ratify such treaties, can not agree to wording which goes beyond our own Constitution.[7] It is an acknowledgment, of course, of the fact that we have discrimination within our own country. As that is well known, I do not see why we should not acknowledge it and bring out the fact that the Supreme Court has just taken a step forward and we feel we are moving forward, but that in international documents it would be a deception to agree to go beyond what we could obtain ratification for in Congress.[8]

I am sorry I did not see you when I was in Washington and I shall be delighted to have a chance to talk with you whenever it is possible. Just now my presence at the UN daily seems to be the most important thing for me.

Very cordially yours,
Eleanor Roosevelt

I failed to say that personally I believe there is right back of the establishment of a Jewish State.[9]

TLS RG59, NARA II

On the same day ER wrote Secretary Marshall, she wrote the president urging the administration to recognize the new Jewish state in Palestine, immediately after the British mandate expired. Emphasizing that it "would be a mistake to lag behind Russia," ER thought the United States needed to set aside its fears of joining the Soviets in an international UN force to help enforce the partition resolution and prevent continued hostilities in the Middle East. As she did in her letter to Marshall, ER then added a handwritten postscript underscoring her personal belief "in the Jewish State."

342

Eleanor Roosevelt to Harry Truman
11 May 1948 [New York City]

Dear Mr. President:

I have just sent a letter to the Secretary of State, a copy of which I enclose for your information.[10]

As I have said, I have no idea what the attitude of the Administration on the recognition of the Jewish State is going to be. If we are going to recognize it, I think it would be a mistake to lag behind Russia. If we are not going to recognize it, I think we should make our position known as quickly as possible and the reasons for whatever position we take.

This action, as far as I am concerned, is interesting to me only from ethical and humanitarian points of view, but of course, it has political implications which I am sure your advisers will take into consideration.[11] I am quite hopeful that whatever our policy is, it will be clear and consistent for I am more convinced every day that had the Arabs been convinced of what we really meant to do, they might have accepted the UN decision and not put us in the rather difficult position which the Security Council, minus any force, finds itself in today. I have heard it said that we were afraid of a UN force which included the Russians because of the difficulties we have had with them in Germany and Korea. Some day or other we have to be willing, if we are going to work out some peaceful solutions, to serve in some kind of a joint force and to agree we will all leave whatever country we may be in when the UN tells us to leave.[12] I was much encouraged by the report of the conversations between Ambassador Smith and Mr. Molotov as it came over the radio this morning. I think that kind of straight forward statement of fact is helpful and leaves the way open for peaceful negotiations in the future.[13]

With my warm regards to Mrs. Truman and Margaret, I am,

Very cordially yours,
Eleanor Roosevelt

I failed to say that I personally believe in the Jewish State.[14]

TLS HSTSF, HSTL

343

George Marshall to Eleanor Roosevelt[15]

19 May 1948

Dear Mrs. Roosevelt:

I much appreciate your letter of May 11, 1948 with regard to problems now before the United Nations Commission on Human Rights and also in respect to Palestine.

I was glad to have your comments on the problems before the Commission on Human Rights, and agree that the United States should do its utmost to obtain the best possible draft both of a Covenant and a Declaration. We will have to wait and see what the Commission does before being able to estimate what our position should be in the Economic and Social Council.[16] This is also the case as to our final position in the Commission itself.

The attitudes now being encountered both within our own country, and in other countries, concerning the Covenant, are about what was to be expected when these negotiations began to near the point of final decisions. The Covenant as a binding legal document must conform fairly closely to the constitutions, laws, and practices of all the countries which ratify it. Either this, or it will be a dead letter treaty. Assuming that states generally do not want the latter, it seems to me that logically the treaty might be expected to be rather more narrow in scope than might originally have been hoped. For these reasons, even though the Covenant has been advanced as the only way of getting "teeth" into United Nations action, I think that its principal value may prove to be in relation to public opinion.

Where our constitution and laws make it impossible for us to agree to an article in the Covenant, we should frankly acknowledge this fact. We are able to show that we are making an effort to deal with these problems through our domestic procedures. It might be a healthy thing to keep before the group the idea that, in addition to concerning itself about what other countries are doing in this field, each country also has an opportunity to improve its own observances through direct action in its own legislature and courts.

Faithfully yours,

TLcst RG59, NARA II

---

1. In a May 3, 1948, letter to Marshall, Lewis William Douglas (1894–1974), reported: "I think that her visit to England improved greatly the general relations between the American people and the people of this island." Douglas also conveyed a message from ER to Marshall, in which she expressed her regret over her disagreement with the State Department's policy in regard to Palestine, but insisted that the disagreement had not deterred her from "vigorously supporting and explain-

ing fully the Marshall Plan" ("U.N. Post Retained by Mrs. Roosevelt," *NYT*, 4 May 1948, 15; Lewis William Douglas to George C. Marshall, 3 May 1948, LWDP, AzU). Neither ER nor Marshall kept a copy of Marshall's cover letter.

2. Harry Hooker conveyed the same impression in his report to Truman, reporting that ER was "greeted with an ovation by the British people when ever she appeared" and that when people realized she was nearby, "crowds in the street were so great the car could scarcely pass through" (Harry S. Hooker to Harry Truman, 13 April 1948, LWDP, AzU).

3. An exhaustive search of ER's papers revealed no correspondence with any Jewish group in the weeks preceding this letter. The communication probably occurred face to face or over the telephone.

4. As ER's later letter to Marshall indicates (Document 351), the United States gave de facto recognition to Israel immediately after the British withdrew in May 1948. However, on May 17, Russia, despite their history of opposition to Zionism dating back to the early 1920s, became the first country to extend full, legal recognition to the new Jewish state. In a letter to Moshe Shertok, the foreign secretary of Israel's provisional government, Soviet foreign minister Molotov expressed his government's desire that "the creation by the Jewish people of its sovereign state will serve the cause of strengthening peace and security in Palestine and the Near East," as well as the "successful development of friendly relations between the U.S.S.R. and the State of Israel." The US ambassador to the Soviet Union, Walter Bedell Smith, expressed the administration's reaction in his letter to Marshall: "Jews and other minority groups provide Kremlin's only immediately useful tool to 'soften up' area for eventual straight communist cultivation" ("Moscow Note to New State Broad in Diplomatic Scope," *NYT*, 18 May 1948, 1; Walter B. Smith to George C. Marshall, 14 November 1947, *FRUS 1947*, vol. 5, 1263–64).

5. On May 5, Viscount Jowitt (1885–1957), Lord Chancellor, announced in the House of Lords that the British government opposed submitting both the declaration and a covenant on human rights to the General Assembly. Jowitt's position coincided with that of the Association of the Bar of the City of New York, whose members voted at their annual meeting on May 11 to recommend that the inclusion of social and economic rights in the draft declaration on human rights be abandoned as neither feasible nor desirable at that time (untitled article, *NYT*, 6 May 1948, 7; "Bar Group Opposes Human Rights Step," *NYT*, 11 May 1948, 19; "City Bar Rejects Report on Rights," *NYT*, 12 May 1948, 12).

6. On the distinction between a UN convention and declaration, see Document 290 and Document 289.

7. In April, the American Bar Association informed ECOSOC of its objections to the inclusion of social and economic rights as human rights. As ECOSOC reported, the ABA declared that

> in principle it is opposed to the establishment of procedure whereby individuals, associations or groups may bring complaints or charges against a State before any Council, Commission or subordinate agency of the United Nations. It urges this right be confined to States parties to any future Convention on Human Rights and that differences of opinion between a State and an organ of the United Nations may be submitted to the International Court of Justice for an advisory opinion the provision for which shall be included in the Convention (U.N. Economic and Social Council, Commission on Human Rights, Third Session, Confidential List of Communications Concerning Human Rights, Received by the United Nations from 24 October 1947 to 15 April 1948, Prepared by the Secretary-General in Accordance with Resolution No. 75(V) of the Economic and Social Council (E/CN.4/CR.2), 30 April 1948, AERP).

8. On May 3, a week before ER wrote this letter, the Supreme Court issued a unanimous decision in *Shelly v. Kraemer*, arguing that the Fourteenth Amendment's prohibitions against "any law which

shall abridge the privileges or the immunities of citizens of the United States" and its endorsement of "the due process of law" invalidated state court support of covenants that discriminated against persons for racial or religious reasons who sought to buy property in certain neighborhoods. ER praised the decision in My Day, calling it "a momentous decision," and declaring that the decision demonstrated "a big step forward in assuring democratic rights in this country" (Arthur Krock, "In the Nation: The Chief Justice Closes a Loophole," *NYT*, 24 May 1948, 24; *MD*, 5 May 1948).

9. ER wrote this handwritten note across the bottom of the letter.

10. See Document 341.

11. In contrast to senior members of the Department of State, who remained adamantly opposed to extending recognition to a Jewish state in Palestine, presidential advisors Clark Clifford and David Niles insisted that recognition would be needed to gain critical Jewish votes in the 1948 presidential election. At a meeting at the White House on May 12, 1948, Clifford urged the president to extend prompt recognition to the Jewish state after the termination of the British mandate on May 15. Secretary of State Marshall, however, countered that such a move would be a "transparent dodge" to win a few votes and would "seriously diminish" the dignity of the office of the president. "The counsel offered by Mr. Clifford was based on domestic political considerations," he charged, "while the problem that confronted us was international" (*FRUS 1948*, vol. 5, 972–76; Hamby, *Man*, 416).

12. The division of the Korean peninsula along the 38th parallel in 1948, and continued problems with Moscow over the joint occupation of Germany, convinced Secretary of Defense James Forrestal that should the Soviets participate in an international force to implement the UN partition resolution for Palestine, he would, in ER's words, have "to mobilize the US fifty percent for war at once." The State Department was also concerned that the introduction of Soviet forces into Palestine for the purpose of implementing partition would constitute an "outflanking" of US positions in Greece, Turkey, and Iran, and would provide Communist agents an "excellent base from which to extend their subversive activities, to disseminate propaganda, and to attempt to replace the present Arab governments by 'democratic peoples' governments.'" For more on ER's views of an international force, see Document 303 (Report by the Policy Planning Staff on Position of the United States With Respect to Palestine, 19 January 1948, *FRUS 1948*, vol. 5, 551–52).

13. In a conversation with Soviet foreign minister Molotov on May 4, 1948, Ambassador Walter Bedell Smith explained that despite disagreements over the future designs of Germany and Moscow's hostility to the Marshall Plan, the United States had "no hostile or aggressive designs whatsoever with respect to the Soviet Union," and emphasized that his government still remained hopeful that their two countries could find "the road to a decent and reasonable relationship … with a fundamental relaxation of those tensions which today exercise so unhappy an influence on international society everywhere." Five days later, Molotov replied that the Soviet Government likewise shared the desire, expressed by Ambassador Smith, "to better these relations, and is in agreement toward a discussion and settlement of the difference existing between us" (*SDB*, 23 May 1948, 679–83).

14. ER added this sentence as a handwritten postscript.

15. Marshall sent carbon copies of this letter to Robert McClintock (1909–1976), an advisor to the US delegation to the UN General Assembly, and John Halderman (see *n*1 Document 230) ("Robert M. McClintock, 67, Retired U.S. Ambassador," *WP*, 3 November 1976, B12).

16. The committee met until the latter half of June before completing its work on the draft declaration of human rights. The inclusion and protection of economic, social, and cultural rights and the rejection of the Soviet position that only nation-states could protect human rights dominated this, the most difficult of all, HRC meetings. Ultimately, the committee agreed with ER's position that "favored the inclusion of economic and social rights in the Declaration, for no personal liberty could exist without economic security and independence. Men in need were not free men." The

committee also concurred with Mehta, Cassin, Loufti, and ER's argument that economic and social rights in question would be implemented "in accordance with the organization of each State" (HRC, Third Session, 17 June 1948 [E/CN.4/SR.64], 5–6, 28–29, UNOR ECOSOC, MWelC; Glendon, 123–42). See also Document 354, Document 357, Document 358, and Document 359.

ON CONSCIENTIOUS OBJECTORS

Truman had addressed the issue of amnesty for conscientious objectors in December 1946 when he issued Executive Order 9814, which provided for the establishment of the President's Amnesty Board. The board, a three-person committee headed by former associate justice of the Supreme Court Owen J. Roberts, reviewed the cases of the roughly 16,000 individuals convicted of violating the Selective Training and Service Act of 1940. In December 1947, the board provided the president with a list of 1,523 individuals they felt Truman should pardon.[1]

In early May 1948, a group of pacifists headed by A. J. Muste, executive secretary of the Fellowship of Reconciliation, visited ER in her Manhattan apartment to argue for the inclusion of the right to refuse military service in the bill of rights then being drafted by the HRC. On May 10, Muste wrote ER to thank her for hearing the group out and to address another issue he had not raised during their meeting: the question of pardon for those conscientious objectors in the US who refused to fight in World War II.[2]

ER sent the following letter—in which she quoted Muste's letter of May 10—to Truman shortly after her meeting with the fellowship.

344

Eleanor Roosevelt to Harry Truman
13 May 1948 [New York City]

Dear Mr. President:

A group of people came to see me the other day about conscientious objection as related to human rights. At the same time they spoke to me about the conscientious objectors of the last war.

The following is an excerpt from their statement to me:

"The second matter has to do with the amnesty or pardon, for conscientious objectors in the United States in World War II. As you undoubtedly know, the commission headed by former Justice Roberts reported to the President in December and on December 23, 1947, the President issued pardons to the persons listed by the Robert's Commission.

"However, only about 1500 of the 15,000 Selective Service violators were included in the pardon. Of the approximately 1100 recognized as conscientious objectors by the Department of Justice only about 150 received pardons. Of the 3,000 or more Jehovah's Witnesses only a couple of hundred were included.[3]

"In a very real sense those who were not included in the Commission's recommendation are now worse off than they were before, since the Department of Justice is taking the position that these persons have all been considered and is therefore declining to consider applications for individual pardons.

"Another extremely serious aspect of the matter is that the Roberts Commission applied a very narrow conception of 'religious belief' in determining which conscientious objectors were entitled to pardon. This appears to open the way for retrogression in dealing with conscientious objectors under any future military training or service act.[4]

"The American Friends Service Committee, the Federal Council of Churches, and the American Civil Liberties Union, as well as the Committee for Amnesty, which is composed mainly of non-pacifist sponsors, have protested and urged a full amnesty, that is restoration of civil rights, for all conscientious objectors and Jehovah's Witnesses. However, at present there appears to be no progress."

I am sending this to you to ask if now full pardon should not be given?

Very cordially yours,
Eleanor Roosevelt

TLS HSTSF, HSTL

Truman took care in crafting his reply. May 17, he reviewed a draft which read:

I read your letter of thirteenth with a great deal of interest. I have thoroughly looked into the conscientious objectors case and, I think, all the honest conscientious objectors have been released.

I'll admit that it is rather difficult for me to look on a conscientious objector with patience[.] While your four sons and my three nephews were risking their lives to save our Government, and the things for which we stand, these people were virtually shooting them in the back.

I ran across one conscientious objector that I really believe is all man—he was a young Naval Pharmacist Mate who served on Okinawa carrying wounded sailors and marines from the battlefield. I decorated him with a Congressional Medal of Honor. I asked him how it came about that he as a conscientious objector was willing to go into the things of the battlefield and he said to me that he could serve the Lord and save lives as well there as anywhere else in the world. He didn't weigh over one hundred and forty pounds and he was about five feet six inches tall. I shall never forget him.

My experience in the first world war with conscientious objectors was not a happy one—the majority of those with whom I came in contact were just plain cowards and shirkers—that is the reason I asked Justice Roberts to make a complete survey of the situation and to release all those that he felt were honestly conscientious objectors and that has been done. My sympathies with the rest of them are not very strong, as you can see. ~~I do appreciate your interest in them and can see now that all danger is passed why they would want to get out of jail.~~

However, two days later, presidential secretary William D. Hassett sent a memo to the attorney general informing Clark that Hassett had "suggested to" Truman "that in the handling of Mrs. Roosevelt's letter the Department of Justice [should] prepare a memorandum covering the situation." Truman would then forward the memo to ER with a brief cover note. Hassett concluded, "I need hardly assure you that the President appreciates your very helpful cooperation."[5]

As Clark prepared the memo, Truman reviewed a second draft of a reply to ER, whose text remained substantively the same as the first.[6]

Truman settled on the brief message to ER reprinted below. An excerpt of Clark's memo follows Truman's letter.[7]

345

Harry Truman to Eleanor Roosevelt
25 May 1948

Dear Mrs. Roosevelt:

I read your letter in regard to the pardon for conscientious objectors with a great deal of interest and I had the Attorney General prepare me a memorandum on the subject.

The memorandum is enclosed for your information—it covers the situation completely.

Sincerely yours,

Memorandum
Tom Clark to Harry Truman
20 May 1948

The questions posed by the representatives of the American Friends Service Committee, the Federal Council of Churches, the American Civil Liberties Union, and the Committee for Amnesty, in their recent interview with Mrs. Franklin D. Roosevelt, relative to a full amnesty for all persons who were convicted of violating the Selective Training and Service Act of 1940, who claimed to be conscientious objectors and Jehovah's Witnesses, have been referred to this Department for appropriate consideration.

There were approximately 1,000 persons who were convicted, who claimed to be conscientious objectors. The President's Amnesty Board in recommending pardons for only about 150, was guided by the factual situation attendant in the individual case. The Board declined to recommend amnesty in those cases where the individual's claim was recognized and he was classified as being opposed to both combatant and non-combatant military service, and was ordered to report for work of national importance in lieu thereof and either failed to so report or violated some phase of the Act while in a civilian public service camp. It appears that the Board adopted the viewpoint that these persons were accorded classification as they had requested but simply set themselves up as being greater than the law. The majority of convictions involving conscientious objectors were for such violations as refusal to transfer from one civilian service camp to another, refusal to carry out work assignments in the camps, desertion, etc., after their claims had been recognized. It therefore follows that the Board declined to recommend many of these persons for amnesty not because they were conscientious objectors whose claims had been denied, but rather because they had committed some violation after their claims were fully accorded them.

Jehovah's Witnesses rarely claimed to be conscientious objectors. Those who did had their claims recognized for the most part. Jehovah's Witnesses claim exemptions from all service under the Act on the basis of being ministers of religion. These "ministers" were invariably engaged in full time secular employment and followed no prescribed course of study that would qualify one to be a minister. The fact that all members of the sect claim to be ministers is indicative that none is a minister in the sense that Congress used the term in the Selective Service Act. Where the facts supported claims to be a minister, Jehovah's Witnesses were generally accorded ministerial classification by local boards. Membership in the sect is hardly the basis per se for ministerial classification.

The criticism that the Board applied a very narrow conception of "Religious belief" does not appear to be warranted. As long as the objection was based on religious training and belief, the Board does not appear to have considered the matter further. In fact some recommendations were submitted in cases where the individual was affiliated with no sect. However, there was little basis for the Board to flaunt the express provisions of the Act and recommend for amnesty those objectors whose grounds were found to be purely political or sociological. To have gone to such lengths at such an early date when the nation continues officially in a state of war would establish a dangerous precedent.

In addition to those who were convicted and who claimed to be conscientious objectors or Jehovah's Witnesses, there were approximately 10,000 who were convicted who made no such claims. These are designated as "wilful violators" or "draft dodgers" for want of a better term.

There is attached hereto a copy of the report submitted by the Board to the President, dated December 23, 1947, which sets forth in detail the basis of its action.[8]

TLcst HSTSF, HSTL

---

1. Although just over six hundred cases the board reviewed involved still-incarcerated men, even those who were no longer imprisoned benefited from a presidential pardon. Without the pardon, an individual convicted under the Selective Service Act retained a criminal record, which restricted his civil rights and hampered his potential employment ("Statement by the President Upon Signing Order Creating an Amnesty Board to Review Convictions Under the Selective Service Act," 23 December 1946, Truman Presidential Museum and Library, http://trumanlibrary.org/publicpapers/viewpapers.php?pid=1840, accessed March 10, 2005; "Report of the President's Amnesty Board," HSTSF). For more on the Selective Service Act of 1940 and ER's attitude toward conscientious objectors, see Document 132.

2. A. J. Muste to ER, 10 May 1948, AERP.

3. The discrepancy between the number of those convicted under the Selective Service Act and those pardoned by the president resulted from the board's classification of cases before it as either draft dodgers or conscientious objectors. The board ruled that many of those who applied for conscientious objector status were motivated by "fear, the desire to evade military service, or the wish to remain as long as possible in highly paid employment," and were therefore not worthy of a pardon. Jehovah's Witnesses posed a particular problem for the board. Whereas most of the violators of the act had originally sought 4-E status but were either denied it or left the Civilian Public Service Camps before completing their service terms, most of the Jehovah's Witnesses refused 4-E status (see *n7* Document 134) and approximately 4,300 of them went to prison. The Roberts Commission did not recommend the Jehovah's Witnesses for pardons, arguing that "to do so would be to sanction an assertion by a citizen that he is above the law; that he makes his own law; and that he refused to yield his opinion to that of organized society on the question of his country's need for service" ("Report of the President's Amnesty Board," HSTSF, HSTL).

4. One of the most important pieces of evidence the Amnesty Board considered in each case was the sincerity of the individual's "religious belief." Some of those who applied for CO status did so based not on religion, but rather on "intellectual, political, or sociological convictions resulting from the individual's reasoning and personal economic or political philosophy." The board refused to pardon these men whom they claimed "set themselves up as wiser and more competent than society to determine their duty to come to the defense of the Nation" ("Report of the President's Amnesty Board," HSTSF, HSTL).

5. Draft Letters from Harry Truman to ER, 17 and 22 May 1948, and Memorandum from William Hassett to Tom Clark, HSTSF, HSTL.

6. The new draft also included two changes in wording. "I admit that I have strong views on the question of dishonest and insincere 'conscience objectors,'" replaced "I'll admit that it is rather difficult for me to look on a conscientious objector with patience." Truman also replaced the sentence

which he struck through in the first draft with, "While I am determined that no honest man shall suffer unfairly, I am equally determined that no imposter shall escape retributive justice."

7. ER forwarded Truman's reply and Clark's memo to A. J. Muste. On June 21, Muste wrote to ER, thanking her for approaching the president on behalf of COs and clarifying his position in regards to the Amnesty Board's decision. As Muste recalled, the board "conceived it to be its duty to enforce the provisions of the Selective Service Act" and in effect retried the COs. He then argued the question before the board was actually, "whether [conscientious objectors'] civil rights, including in many instances entry into the professions, are to remain seriously abridged" so long after the close of the war. Pointing out that "hundreds of thousands, if not millions, of Germans and Japanese who fought against the armed forces of this country have been granted amnesty," Muste asked if ER would be willing to suggest to Truman "that it would be in the public interest to have the question taken up again and dealt with from the point of view which is customarily associated with the idea of amnesty and not from the point of view of enforcing a law." ER forwarded Muste's letter to Truman on June 27. The president did not reply to this letter (ER to Harry Truman, 27 June 1948 and attachment, HSTF, HSTL).

8. ER's papers do not contain a copy of this memorandum, but a memo for the file, dated June 4, 1948, in HSTPF, indicates that Truman mailed this letter and a copy of Clark's memorandum.

ON ER, TRUMAN, AND DREW PEARSON'S PROJECTIONS

ER's disputes with Truman inspired some to suggest she would not support his candidacy in the 1948 presidential election. Drew Pearson reported in his May 4 column that "now, however, word from Roosevelt circles is that Mrs. R will not only oppose Harry for renomination, but may have a friendly talk with him, urging him not to run."[1] At the same time, those frustrated with Truman continued, despite ER's repeated denials, to hope that she would change her mind and run for office. The following letter from National Education Association president Charl Ormond Williams illustrates both the press such speculation received and the hope ER's supporters continued to have that she would indeed become a candidate.[2]

346

Charl Williams to Eleanor Roosevelt

13 May 1948 [Washington, DC]

Dear Mrs. Roosevelt:

I have often wanted to know how Drew Pearson got all the information that he pours out over the radio and through the press that seems to be absolutely accurate.[3] I know that dozens of people have already told you what I am about to write. The Sunday before you landed in New York, Drew said in effect "that when Mrs. Roosevelt returns to this country, she will make a quiet trip to the White House and tell President Truman that he ought to retire and not be a candidate in November, 1948. Further, that he was not the choice of the people but received his nominations largely through the offices of President Roosevelt."[4] It is amazing to me how he could unearth such a story when you had been out of the country almost thirty days!

You will be amused by the following paragraph which came to me in today's mail, written by Paul Strachan, President of the American Federation of the Physically Handicapped. He is a native Georgian and somewhat of a character, though a very fine man.

"I hope you will conserve your strength a bit. No use of being too damned strenuous. Save a bit of steam, so you can enjoy the political suicide party, which, inevitably, will take place Nov. 2, next. I think, as I look over the situation, that I cannot endorse ANY candidate of present note, but, I do not doubt, ere the shades of Conventions have fallen, that we shall see the most vitriolic, lambasting campaign ever held in our lifetimes. You know, privately, I sorter Wish a Ticket could be, Ike, and Eleanor. I fully realize Mrs. R's attitude, and position, but, as sure as God made little green apples, the Democratic Party, for which her husband fought, bled, and died, is falling apart, and she might be persuaded, for that reason alone, to lend her name and her following, to a Ticket. While I have no doubt about Ike's "personality charm", yet, I dunno what he knows about domestic problems, and, I have no doubt about what Eleanor would do, had she the power as an Elected Vice-President, to at least try to do. It's an interesting theory, anyhow."[5]

In the mail last week I received a card from Emily Kneubuhl of Minneapolis, who wrote "wouldn't 'E' make a grand Secretary of State? Also she would make a grand presiding officer of the United States Senate."[6]

Well, my dear, whether or not you ever run for office there are plenty of people in this country who think you could fill almost any one of them with great honor and distinction.

Since you have known Tiffany's all your life and the high standards which are associated with their name, I think you will be amused over the enclosed correspondence concerning the mahogany bases I had made for the two silver trays. I wouldn't have accepted the first trays that they made at any cost, and since I paid a good round sum for them, it was imperative that they do their work over from start to finish. The bases are now ready and I am sending shipping instructions to the firm.[7]

Affectionately,
Charl Ormond Williams

P.S. I thought you would be interested in Mr. Shipman's letter to me of April 18.[8]

TLS, AERP, FDRL

———————

1. Pearson also wrote: "If Mrs. Roosevelt does what her friends say she's going to do about Harry Truman it's going to be one of the hardest political blows the president has ever taken—also a big personal disappointment. Only a few insiders know it, but President Truman has counted on Mrs. Roosevelt to help him swing for his renomination" ("The Washington Merry-Go-Round," *WP*, 4 May 1948, B15).

2. On Charl Ormond Williams, see *n*4 Document 248. For ER's eventual public endorsement of Truman, see Document 383 and Document 384.

3. For Pearson, see *n*1 Document 146.

4. ER returned to the United States from a tour of Europe on April 27, 1948. Drew Pearson's "Washington Merry-Go-Round" column of Sunday, April 25, did not mention ER's feelings about the Truman candidacy. Williams may have referred to Pearson's radio show, which aired in Washington, D.C., on Sundays at 6:00 PM. Pearson's May 4 newspaper column, however, did contain the following item ("Mrs. Roosevelt Reports ERP 'Lift' in Europe," 28 April 1948, *WP*, B1; "Today's Radio Programs," *WP*, 2 May 1948, L4).

5. Paul Ambrose Strachan (1894–1972) both established and served as president of the American Federation of the Physically Handicapped in 1940. He additionally helped develop policies on employment of disabled individuals for the Truman administration in 1945. Strachan suggested, as others had done, that ER consider political office. ER discussed her feelings on this issue in her My Day column of September 13, 1947:

> I have received several letters lately stating how pleased the writers are to hear that I am going to "run for the Senate," and offering me help and support. So far those who would be against me have not written to me in great number. But to all alike I have to reply that I am not going to run for any office! ... Here I am, therefore, forced again to state—as I did when rumors flew about in 1945 and in 1946—that I not only have no political aspirations, but under no circumstances whatsoever would I run for any political office.

> For information about ER's thoughts on running for political office, see Document 137 (*WWWA*, vol. 5; *MD*, 13 September 1947).

6. Emily Kneubuhl (1883–1967) was executive secretary of the National Federation of Business and Professional Women before she served as Minnesota's alternate delegate at the 1948 Democratic National Convention. That same year Kneubuhl wrote to ER encouraging her to consider running for political office.

> To be honest and I mean this—You are my candidate and have been for months—men and women in every poll, I take, agree ... I am knowing you will be led to make only

right decisions. I don't ask you to "save the party" but I could work for a Truman-Roosevelt ticket even tho that is hard to imagine.

("Business Women to Honor Official," *NYT*, 26 January 1936, N6; *WWWA*, vol. 7; "Index to Politicians: Knappe to Kniffin," *Political Graveyard*, http://politicalgraveyard.com/bio/knappen-kniffin.html, accessed 10 January 2005; Emily Kneubuhl to ER, 29 May 1948, AERP).

7. Williams wrote to Tiffany & Company to express her disappointment with the workmanship of two mahogany tray bases she had ordered, which produced a contrite letter of apology from the company (Charl Williams to W. R. Barry, 23 March 1948, AERP; Tiffany & Co. to Charl Williams, 26 March 1948, AERP).

8. Fred Shipman (1903–1978), an archivist, served as director of the Franklin Delano Roosevelt Library in 1940. His letter to Williams discusses his affection for the library and his reluctance to leave (*WWWA*, vol. 7; Fred Shipman to Charl Williams, 18 April 1948, AERP).

RESPONDING TO ARAB CRITICISM

In late spring 1948, as the end of British occupation drew near, Wadad Dabbagh, "an arab wife and citizen of Palestine," wrote ER "to bring to your kind attention some real facts about her poor county." Writing that although she was "sure" that ER "sympathized with the Zionist movement [because of] a bone fide belief on your part that you are helping a suffering portion of the human race," Dabbagh concluded that ER's belief:

> is based upon misrepresentation of the facts. Jews pretend to be persecuted in Europe, and under this pretense try to seek refuge in Palestine. But as soon as they land therein, they become despotic and allow themselves to commit all the unlawful acts of which they were the victims in the countries from which they come. They avenge themselves upon the innocent Arabs who used to live peacefully in their homes for immemorial times.

Dabbagh then asked ER:

> in the name of a suffering and wronged community to stop backing Zionists until you come to Palestine and see with you[r] own eyes what injustice they are causing to us the Arabs. They are driving us [out] of our homes, depriving us of our lands, robbing us of our means of living, and encroaching upon our resources and upon the wealth of our country. They have even committed bloodshed and murder, pulled down buildings and homes upon their inhabitants without any discrimination and even without any pity for helpless men, women, and innocent children.

To augment her argument, Dabbagh sent ER three photographs to document her claims of abuse: pictures of "a child with a broken leg, … a child with a broken backbone, … and an infant girl hit with a bullet in her head." "Do you really, Madam," Dabbagh asked, "tolerate such injustice and wrong doing? Do you wish to defend Zionism, the cause of all these atrocities and unhuman acts?"[1]

ER replied two days before the British Mandate was set to expire.

347

Eleanor Roosevelt to Wadad Dabbagh
13 May 1948 [New York City]

My dear Mrs. Dabbagh:

I read your letter with interest and I realize that once war begins between peoples there is nothing but misery for everyone concerned. Both the Arabs and the Jewish people are suffering as a result of the conflicts between them.

The Arabs, I happen to think, have protested wrongly. They should have agreed to the United Nations report which granted Palestine as an economic unit and which would have made it possible for the two nations to live peacefully side by side even though there was partition and to gradually work out a mutually acceptable plan.[2]

Many years ago when the Balfour Declaration on Palestine was made, the United States agreed to it and Jewish authorities negotiated with Arab authorities an agreement at that time.[3] To turn around now and behave as though no agreement had existed and that something unforeseen is occurring, seems to me unrealistic and stupid and it brings to many people within the Arab areas the horrors of war.

The Arabs are directly defying the decision of the United Nations Assembly and I think, therefore, have incurred the censure of the rest of the world.[4]

My country, because of the war-like attitude of the Arabs, tried to suggest a peaceful change but it hasn't brought peace and I doubt if it will. It is not the Jewish people whom I blame because they are living up to what for a long time now, they have considered were unquestioned agreements. I do not blame the Arab people either, but I do blame the Arab chiefs.

Jerusalem would have been an international area in any case so there was no question of Holy places not being open to all people.

Nothing was ever settled by war and if there had been a willingness on the part of the Arab chiefs to work out a peaceful solution, it could have been done.

I am deeply sorry for the Arab people as I am for the Jewish people who are now suffering but they suffer because of the Arab leaders and their unwillingness to live up to the United Nations decision.

Very sincerely yours,

TLc AERP, FDRL

348

Wadad Dabbagh to Eleanor Roosevelt
30 June 1948 [Beirut]

My dear Mrs. Roosevelt;

I hesitated to bother you again with a reply to your kind letter of May 13th. But having read your excellent speech in Lake Success about the International Charter on Human Rights,[5] I was encouraged to bring to your kind attention some more facts about the tragic story of the poor Arabs of Palestine, so that you may do them some justice in the name of those Human Rights.

During World War I, we, the Arabs, rose against the Ottomans, notwithstanding the relations of kinship and religion which bound us to them. Struggling for our freedom and independence, we fought with the Allies against them. In this way we sustained all kinds of losses in lives and property.[6]

But our hopes were deeply frustrated by the Balfour Declaration, to which we and our leaders never acquiesced. The date of that Declaration was always and still is considered a mourning day every year by all the Arab world. It reminds us of the difference between theory and practice in the matter of the human rights. The Balfour injustice was always the object of Arab protestation. This is illustrated by their constant revolutions and insurrections, esp. those of 1922, 1929, 1933, 1936-39.[7]

The crisis that aroused the present Arab Revolt was caused by the unjust U N O Resolution on the partition of Palestine. This resolution tries to give the Jews the richest part of our land, notwithstanding the fact that they do not own 7% of it, leaving to the Arabs the poorest part. The Arab revolt is utterly justified. The Jews who were only 56000 in 1918 became about 3/4 of a million.[8] These Jews, who are strangers to Palestine, are planning to take it, either by expelling the Arabs out of their homes or by exterminating them. They never accepted to live peacefully among us. Is this permissible by the Law of Nations or by the Laws of Nature?

Moreover, the crimes committed by the Jews are so atrocious and heinous that they remind us of the Dark Middle Ages and of Hitlerian Germans of World War II. Impartial witnesses of such acts of cruelty are the members of the Red Cross.

Wholesale massacres were committed in the village of Deir Yassine, in Haifa, Jaffa, Safad Tiberias and in other Arab cities and Villages of Palestine.[9] The non-combatant population were exposed to shameful indignities. The wombs of pregnant women were bared, children were killed without mercy, nuns were the object of rape, the eyes of the aged were expunged, dwelling houses, churches and mosques were pulled down upon the heads of their inhabitants, houses and properties were robbed. Such barbarities, for example, drove the 70,000 inhabitants of Jaffa out of their city, leaving about 4,000 only, and all their belongings to the plunder of the Jews. This was the fate of this old Arab city, in whose hospitable neighborhood the Jews built their capital Tel-Aviv and established other prosperous colonies.

We are not a savage people who can be colonized or exterminated in such a barbarous way. You know that the Arabs have largely contributed to the cause of civilization, and have propagated to the world the first principles of science, culture and justice. Gustave Le Bon has truly said that the Arabs passed education over to Europe, and Europe passed it over to America.[10] Do we, descendants of those Arabs, deserve after all to be treated by Europe and America, and through their aid and assistance by the Jews, in such a humiliating manner? Does humanity admit of such a state of things in which a whole Arab population must suffer and leave their homes in order to let the Jewish strangers take their place?

Please, Madame, do take these facts into consideration, and be convinced that they are not due to any fault on the part of the Arab leaders. They were caused only by the Zionists, their leaders and by some big States who act under their influence without carefully studying the actual state of things.

I am sure, dear Madame, that you can do something, and you are going to do it in the name of Justice and Human Rights, which you are admirably defending and advocating.

> Your's Very Truly.
> Wadad Mahmassani Dabbagh.

TLS AERP, FDRL

349

Eleanor Roosevelt to Wadad Dabbagh
10 July 1948 [Hyde Park]

I have your letter of June 30 and I regret there is nothing I can do to help in the situation about which you write.

ALd AERP, FDRL

350

Wadad Dabbagh to Eleanor Roosevelt
11 August 1948 [Beirut]

Dear Mrs. Roosevelt,

I was astonished to receive your short reply of july 10; 1948 to my letter of june 30, which I sent to you in the name of human rights which you were defending.

I regret to see that there is a great difference, in the meaning of those human rights, between theory and practice, and I am sorry to feel that I have bothered you in vain with my previous correspondance. I have to thank you any way.

Very sincerely yours,
Wadad Dabbagh

TLS AERP, FDRL

---

1. Wadad M. Dabbagh to ER, n.d., AERP.

2. The United Nations Special Committee on Palestine (UNSCOP) formed in the spring of 1947, was comprised of delegates from eleven neutral states. After holding hearings and meetings in Palestine, Beirut, and Geneva, it issued a summary report August 31, 1947, recommending unanimously that Britain end its mandate and grant independence. A majority of the UNSCOP members recommended partition of Palestine into Jewish and Arab states ("The Recognition of the State of Israel" under www.trumanlibrary.org, accessed March 01, 2006; "Committee Is Split: Minority Urges Federal Status—All Agree on End of Mandate," *NYT*, 1 September 1947, 1; "British Exit," *NYT*, 28 September 1947, E1; Report to the General Assembly by the United Nations Special Committee on Palestine, September 1947 [Doc A/364 3], *SDB*, 21 September 1947, 547–61).

3. In a letter from the British foreign secretary, Lord Arthur Balfour, to the head of the British Zionist Organization, Lord Rothschild, on November 2, 1917, the British government stated that it "viewed with favor" the establishment in Palestine of a homeland for the Jewish people. It also declared that in facilitating this objective nothing should be done that would prejudice the "civil and religious rights of existing non-Jewish communities" in Palestine, or the "rights and political status enjoyed by Jews in any other country." The Balfour Declaration, which was later incorporated into the language of the British Mandate over Palestine, quickly encouraged Jewish immigration to the Holy Land, and became a rallying cry for Arabs, who viewed it as a violation of their sovereignty. For more on the Balfour Declaration see *n*3 Document 82 and *n*3 Document 227 (Bickerton and Klausner, 40–41).

4. See Document 328 for an assessment of violence between Arabs and Jews in the aftermath of the General Assembly's endorsement of UNSCOP's partition plan.

5. In a statement to the press on June 21, 1948, ER called the draft of the International Declaration of Human Rights "a document of very great intrinsic worth" produced "despite variations in attitudes and customs and historic precedent of the nations represented on the commission." She also thought the draft declaration an indispensable step in working to define freedom and determine "what every man and woman have a right to have" ("Rights Plan Hailed by Mrs. Roosevelt," *NYT*, 21 June 1948, 9; "The United States in the United Nations," *SDB*, 7 June 1948, 830–31).

6. The Allies consisted of Great Britain, France, and Russia.

7. In 1922, tensions flared after Britain announced that it would uphold the Balfour Declaration and the proposed constitution for the state of Palestine limiting municipal councils to consultative duty only. The Arab daily, *Palestine*, called on Arabs to follow Egypt's example of resistance and in July, many in the Arab community participated in a general strike, an action that received support from Syria and Transjordan. When the League of Nations announced ratification of the declaration, violence erupted in Hanna, Jaffa, and Ludd. Seven years later, in August 1929, two events occurred that inflamed Arab-Jewish tension: first, Britain allowed the Jewish Agency (originally founded as the Zionist Organization) to expand its membership and recruit Zionist supporters from outside Palestine and, second, as part of preparations for Yom Kippur, a Jewish sexton respon-

sible for the Jewish section of the Wailing Wall placed a screen adjacent to the site (holy to both Arabs and Jews) that would allow Jewish men and women to worship separately. The British agreed with Arab objections that this violated protocol; Jews objected to the ruling; and widespread violence soon erupted, killing 133 Jews and wounding another 399 and killing eighty-seven Arabs and wounding another seventy-eight. Four years later, Arabs attempted an unsuccessful boycott of Zionist- and British-made goods. In April 1936, in retaliation for the robbery and murder of three Jews, two Arabs were killed, an act that sparked a general strike in Jaffa and Nablus. Five Arab groups coalesced to form the Arab High Commission, which, under Haj Amin's direction, organized widespread civil disobedience, tax protests, and the closing of city governments. By the time the rebellion subsided in 1939, 3,764 Arabs, 610 British, and 2,394 Jews had died and millions of dollars of property had been destroyed ("Arabs Are Incited to Rise in Palestine," *NYT*, 15 April 1922, 2; "Palestine Arabs Bitter," *NYT*, 18 May 1922, 3; "Palestine Crisis Believed Near," *NYT*, 3 September 1922, 3; Sachar, *Israel*, 174, 219–22; Mansfield, 203–7).

8. Although the Jews owned only 6 to 8 percent of the total land area in Palestine, and constituted less than half of its population in 1947 (600,000 Jews; 1.3 million Arabs), the UN resolution of November 29, 1947, which partitioned Palestine into separate Jewish and Arab states, allotted the Jews approximately 55 percent of the land, including the agriculturally rich areas of the coastal plain, as well as the Negev Desert. The Arabs, who opposed the partition plan from its inception, were left with the less fertile hill country of central Palestine and northern Galilee (Bickerton and Klausner, 89).

9. On the morning of April 9, 1948, 132 members of the Jewish underground groups Irgun and Stern Gang attacked the small village of Deir Yassin, which lay on the outskirts of Jerusalem, eighteen miles outside the boundaries of the Jewish state outlined in the partition plan. The village was captured and more than 250 men, women, and children were killed, their bodies mutilated and later thrown into a well. Similar attacks also occurred in the towns of Haifa, Jaffa, Tiberias, and Safed in late April and early May, forcing Arabs to flee their homes and their families. It was "a frightening and fantastic sight," the future Israeli prime minister David Ben-Gurion wrote after his tour of the abandoned neighborhoods in Haifa. "A dead city … without a living soul, except for stray cats." The Arabs believed the attacks were part of the Jews' larger "campaign of terrorism" to force the Arab population to leave their villages and homes (Bickerton and Klausner, 99–100; Sachar, *Israel*, 333–34; Segev, 508–9).

10. Gustave Le Bon, *La civilisation des Arabes*, 465–533, 614–32. For an abridged translation, see *The World of Islamic Civilization*, 33–66, 89–94, 137–42. Le Bon (1841–1931), a French social thinker, became renowned in the non-Arab world for his work on crowd psychology ("Dr. Gustave Le Bon, Scientist, Is Dead," *NYT*, 15 December 1931, 27).

The US, the UN, and the Recognition of Israel

When the British Mandate expired at midnight May 14, 1948,[1] David Ben-Gurion, acting as chairman of the Zionist Council of State (the provisional Jewish government in Palestine), declared Israel a state. Truman immediately issued a statement extending de facto recognition to the new nation. The announcement from the White House disturbed members of the US delegation, who were still trying to secure a truce in Palestine between Arabs and Jews, and who had not been given any prior notification of the president's decision. When Dean Rusk, the head of the State Department's UN desk, telephoned chief delegate Warren Austin, and informed him of the president's decision to extend recognition, Austin apparently was so disgusted with the decision that he got in his limousine and went home without informing any of his colleagues about it.

Minutes later, a UN delegate read the news from an Associated Press ticker tape release in front of the General Assembly and demanded an explanation from the US delegation, which was caught completely off guard. Philip Jessup, who, along with Francis B. Sayre, were the only members sitting in the delegation at the moment, quickly left the assembly to find out what was happening. Sayre, also stunned by the news, went to the podium and reportedly said he unfortunately had no additional information to report.

Fearing that pandemonium was breaking loose at the UN, Secretary Marshall immediately sent Rusk up to New York to prevent the entire US delegation from resigning. By the time Rusk arrived, however, cooler heads had prevailed and no resignations ensued. But the episode left the entire delegation, and Eleanor Roosevelt, in particular, bitter at the White House and State Department for keeping them in the dark and undercutting their position.[2]

ER then wrote Marshall to express her "consternation" and "deep concern."

351

Eleanor Roosevelt to George Marshall
16 May 1948 [New York City]

Dear Mr. Secretary:

Having written you before what I had heard on the subject of the recognition of Palestine, I feel I should write you again.[3]

The way in which the recognition of Palestine came about has created complete consternation in the United Nations.

As you know, I never wanted us to change our original stand. When I wrote to the President and to you the other day what I had heard, I thought, of course, that you would weigh it against the reports which you were getting from the United Nations. Much as I wanted the Palestine State recognized, I would not have wanted it done without the knowledge of our representatives in the United Nations who had been fighting for our changed position. I would have felt that they had to know the reason and I would also have felt that there had to be a very clear understanding beforehand with such nations as we expected would follow our lead.

Several of the representatives of other governments have been to talk to me since, and have stated quite frankly that they do not see how they could ever follow the United States' lead because the United States changed so often without any consultation. There seems to be no sense of interlocking information between the United States delegate and the State Department on the policy making level. This is serious because our acts which should strengthen the United Nations only result in weakening our influence within the United Nations and in weakening the United Nations itself.

More and more the other delegates seem to believe that our whole policy is based on antagonism to Russia and that we think in terms of going it alone rather than in terms of building up a leadership within the United Nations.

This seems to me a very serious defect and I do not see how we can expect to have any real leadership if,

1 – We do not consult our people in the United Nations on what we are going to do, and

2 – If we do not line up our following before we do the things, rather than trusting to influencing them afterwards.

I can not imagine that major considerations on policies such as this are taken at such short notice that there is not time to think through every consequence and inform all those who should be informed.

I have seldom seen a more bitter, puzzled, discouraged group of people than some of those whom I saw on Saturday. Some of them I know are favorable to the rights of the Jews in Palestine, but they are just nonplused by the way in which we do things.

I thought I had to tell you this because I had written you before and as you know, I believe that it is the Administration's desire to strengthen the United Nations, but we do not always achieve it because, apparently, there is a lack of contact on the higher levels.

With deep concern, I am,

> Very sincerely yours,
> Eleanor Roosevelt

TLS HSTSF, HSTL

352

George Marshall to Eleanor Roosevelt
18 May 1948 [Washington, DC]

Dear Mrs. Roosevelt:

I have just read your note of May 16 regarding the recognition of Palestine. All I can say in reply is that in relation to the United Nations, Ambassador Austin was advised shortly before the recognition was to be made public, but unfortunately he was not present with the Delegation at the time the public announcement became known, and Mr. Sayre had not been advised of the situation by Mr. Austin.[4]

We were aware here of the unfortunate effect on our situation with the United Nations, which is much to be regretted. More than this, I am not free to say.

With my thanks for your letter,

> Faithfully yours,
> G. C. Marshall

TLS AERP, FDRL

The day after ER wrote Marshall, she forwarded a copy of the letter to Truman, with the caveat that "you will find me such a nuisance you will wish that I could go home and stay there! However," she concluded, "this question of having the foreign policy integrated with the work of the United Nations seems to me of paramount importance."[5]

Truman replied two days later.

353

Harry Truman to Eleanor Roosevelt
20 May 1948 [The White House]

Dear Mrs. Roosevelt:

Thanks very much for yours of the seventeenth enclosing me a copy of a letter you had written to General Marshall about the recognition of Palestine.[6]

I am sorry, of course, that you were disturbed by the procedure but, under the circumstances, there was not much else to be done.[7] Since there was a vacuum in Palestine and since the Russians were anxious to be the first to do the recognizing General Marshall, Secretary Lovett, Dr. Rusk and myself worked the matter out and decided the proper thing to do was to recognize the Jewish Government promptly. Senator Austin was notified of what was taking place but he didn't have a chance to talk with the other members of the delegation until afterward.[8] I am sorry that it caused any disturbance.

Sincerely yours,
Harry S. Truman

TLS AERP, FDRL

---

1. 6:00 PM, Washington, D.C., time.

2. Sachar, *Israel*, 308–11; Donovan, *Conflict*, 384–86; Rusk, 150–51; McCullough, 618; Hamby, *Man*, 416–17; Truman, vol. 1, 164–65.

3. See Document 341.

4. Francis B. Sayre (1885–1972) served as US representative to the United Nations Trusteeship Council (1947–1952).

5. ER to Harry Truman, 17 May 1948, HSTL.

6. For ER's letter to George Marshall, see Document 351.

7. See header Document 351.

8. Dean Rusk thought Warren Austin's decision not to inform the rest of the delegation about President Truman's decision to extend de facto recognition to the new Jewish state of Israel was premeditated. "He had decided that it was better for the American delegation to be caught completely by surprise," he later wrote. "The other delegates had to believe that recognition was a presidential decision and that our delegation had not been hood winking them in recent weeks" (Rusk, 151).

STEERING THE HUMAN RIGHTS COMMISSION

May 26, the third session of the Human Rights Commission convened at the UN's temporary headquarters to review the Geneva drafts of the declaration and covenant the commission prepared the previous December, and to debate the revisions emerging from drafting committee meetings held immediately prior to this full commission meeting.[1] In her capacity as chair, ER "stressed" that the Economic and Social Council (ECOSOC) "had instructed" the commission "to submit to it, in final form, a draft International Declaration, a draft Covenant and provisions for the implementation." To help her colleagues "fulfill this important task imposed upon them by the Council at the present session," ER asked each member to express their views "of the basic objective at which the proposed Declaration should aim," noting that "such an expression of views could only serve to facilitate the actual drafting."[2]

Once ER steered the commission through a number of procedural matters, she, speaking as the US representative to the HRC rather than as its chair, then initiated the discussion she charged her fellow commissioners to undertake.

354

Eleanor Roosevelt's Statement on the Purpose of the Declaration of Human Rights Summary Record, Forty-Eighth Meeting of the Commission on Human Rights Third Session [excerpt]

26 May 1948 [Lake Success, NY]

Speaking as the representative of the United States of America, the Chairman stated that in the opinion of her delegation the Declaration should serve two purposes:[3]

1. To establish basic standards which would guide the United Nations in the realization, within the meaning of the Charter, of international co-operation in promoting and encouraging respect for human rights and fundamental freedoms for all;

2. To serve as a guide and inspiration to individuals and groups throughout the world in their efforts to promote respect for human rights.

The Declaration should not be in any sense a legislative document. The General Assembly was not a legislative body. The manner in which the United Nations could and would wish to undertake the task of promoting and encouraging respect for human rights and fundamental freedoms remained in large measure to be determined. Further, it was clear that the Declaration, as envisaged, did not create legal remedies or procedures to ensure respect for the rights and freedoms it proposed to the world; that ideal would have to be achieved by further steps taken in accordance with international and domestic law. The Declaration would have moral, not mandatory, force.

It was quite otherwise with the Covenant, which bound the parties legally. The Covenant was therefore the document which should contain measures of implementation.

The United States representative stated in conclusion that she could not better express her delegation's view of the nature and purpose of the Declaration than by quoting the words of Abraham Lincoln on the United States Declaration of Independence, and especially the following:

They (the authors of the Declaration) did not mean to assert the obvious untruth that all men were then actually enjoying that equality, or yet that they were about to confer it immediately upon them. In fact, they had no power to confer such a boon. They meant simply to declare the <u>right</u>, so that the enforcement of it might follow as soon as circumstances should permit.[4]

TSumex RM:UND, MWelC

---

1. After the December meeting in Geneva, the governments of the UN member nations reviewed the Geneva drafts of the declaration and covenant and thirteen of the states submitted comments to the HRC. When the HRC drafting committee met from May 3 to May 21, 1948, it set out to prepare a new draft of the declaration, taking the suggestions of the member states into account. Following directions from the Politburo, the new Soviet delegate, Alexei P. Pavlov, first suggested scrapping the Geneva draft and beginning all over again. After the committee rejected that proposal, he argued for changes that would emphasize the individual's duties to the state, strengthen the declaration's antidiscrimination provisions, and fight Fascism. Largely as a result of repeated requests for revisions from the delegates from Eastern Europe, the drafting committee failed to complete its review of the declaration before the full HRC reconvened on May 24, submitting a report only on the progress that it had made. When visa problems delayed the arrival of the delegates from the Ukraine and Byelorussia, the HRC meeting adjourned, at Pavlov's insistence, until May 26 when ER made the statement excerpted here (Glendon, 110–11). For ER on the work of the HRC in Geneva, see Document 291.

2. HRC, Third Session, Forty-Eighth Meeting, Summary Record, 26 May 1948 (E/CN.4/SR.48), 3–6, MWelC (RM).

3. The US State Department's Committee on International Social Policy (ISP), which reviewed the drafts of the declaration and covenant and recommended the positions the US should adopt in the HRC, provided the main ideas and much of the language in ER's statement, including the two purposes of the declaration and the quote from Lincoln.

René Cassin, who spoke immediately after ER, agreed with her interpretation of the purpose of the declaration, arguing that "it was quite clear that the Declaration should bear above all an explanatory character," that it should serve as "a guide," and "have the function of keeping the fullest possible list of human rights in everybody's mind" (Committee on International Social Policy, "Observations, Suggestions and Proposals of the United States Relating to the Draft International Declaration on Human Rights, etc.," 15 April 1948, [E/CN.4/SR.48] RG59, NARA II). For more on the ISP, see *n*4 Document 230.

4. Lincoln delivered these remarks in Springfield, Illinois, June 26, 1857, when discussing the Dred Scott decision (Fornieri, 204–5; Summary Record of the Forty-Eighth Meeting of the Human Rights Commission (E/CN.4/SR.48), UNOR ECOSOC, MWelC).

RESPONDING TO WALLACE

ER did not remain quiet as Wallace asked liberals to leave the Democratic Party. By March, she directly challenged the Progressive Citizens of America's (PCA) notion of "liberal" foreign policy. For example, March 21, she told delegates attending the Middle Atlantic's Unitarian Conference in Tarrytown, New York, that liberals had "a very difficult role" to play and that her experience working with the Soviets at the UN encouraged her to retool her liberal vision:

> … for the liberal, who wants to believe that people are all more or less the same, that they have the same motivations, and that they respond to fair and decent treatment, it is really a very disillusioning thing to work in that fashion with the USSR because you are tempted to come to the conclusion that it isn't important to do what you feel is right. You may have been brought up to believe that if you say you are going to do something, it's important that you do it for your own self-satisfaction. But you wake up to find that you are going to get cooperation only because you are stronger than they are. Now that's a rather awful thing for a liberal to have to face in this world of today, and I think a good many people probably now feel that I am not a liberal in my attitude towards the USSR.

The *Christian Register* published her remarks in its June issue.[1]

355

"Liberals in This Year of Decision"
The Christian Register June 1948

The role of the liberal today is a very difficult role, particularly in this country. We acquired through the fortunes of war the position of being the leading democracy of the world. We didn't like it very much; we have no particular desire to be responsible for what happens in the rest of the world. But because we were left in an economic position which no other country in the world could approximate, because we did not have to rebuild our cities, and our factories; because our civilians, at least, did not suffer as civilians suffered in most of the other countries where war had come to them, we find ourselves as the great democracy on which all other eyes are turned, and it has brought us a searching which I think probably we would far prefer to escape.

But whether we like it or not, that is the position we find ourselves in, and those of us who are liberals find that we are put in the position very often in international meetings of explaining the weaknesses of our democracy. Now you can explain them and excuse them, but you just can't say those weaknesses don't exist, because they do. It is a little trying, because we need very badly a unified country, and at the moment our country is very far from unified. We need that unity because of the position of leadership in which we find ourselves.

We are in a world where force still is the ultimate way of deciding questions. It should be law, but it still isn't law; it still is force. And yet we personally are very adverse to acknowledging that force is still such an important factor. Being less touched than other countries by the war, we wanted as quickly as possible to forget about it and get back to normal. So we reduced our forces; we did away with as many of the restrictions as possible; and we tried to feel that the rest of the world would get back to normal as easily as we would get back to normal.

I think that it has been rather a shock to all of us to find that you cannot fight a war of complete destruction in part of the world for four years, and then settle down as though nothing had happened. Now we have to face the facts, and because we have these conditions and these facts to face, the role of the liberal is twice as difficult.

We feel strongly the desire to think the best of other people—by thinking the best, to draw out the best. It doesn't always work that way. We find that in our own country fears have grown. If they have grown here they probably have grown in other countries just as much, probably more; and we keep wondering what happens from fear and what happens from real malevolence. We watch our own country and we find things happening that we would like to denounce, and, yet, we don't know quite how far to go in denouncing those things.

I'll give you an example. As a liberal, I don't like loyalty tests at all. I have a feeling that it's much more important for us to find out why we believe in democracy and really to know why we believe in it, and to put as much into it as the USSR puts into its Communism, because I have always found that you get a great deal more out of the things you can be positive about. I don't think we should have in the government people whose loyalty we really question handling documents which should be secret documents. I think that would be terrible. But, on the other hand, it doesn't seem to me quite democratic to brand people as disloyal before you give them a chance to bring witnesses and answer their accusers. And so with all the feeling I have that we must not have disloyalty, I am also torn as to whether we really are building up our democracy and doing the positive things that we ought to be doing, or whether we're just tearing our democracy down.[2]

The role of the liberal is hard and decisions are terribly difficult in these days. In the world picture there is no question but that the discrimination in this country hurts our position. It has been up to this time a domestic question. I felt that we could take time about it—time for white people to adjust; time for colored people to become educated, or, referring to other types of racial and religious discrimination, I felt that there was time, and that we needn't move too fast, that we could do it step by step, and gradually. I don't know whether we can now. Never, since I started to work in the United Nations, has there been a meeting where the question of our discrimination has not been brought up, and where we haven't had to answer for our country. It comes up on all kinds of things—it comes up on the question of freedom of information.

I was making what I thought was a perfectly safe speech, explaining why I thought freedom of information was valuable, and why I thought it was far better to have all kinds of opinions printed in the press and have an educated people that would make their decisions on what they read, than it was to have censorship, particularly government censorship. A gentleman whose country does have government censorship, said, "Madam, do you mean that in countries where there is a so-called free press there is no discrimination?" I had to say "touché."[3] Nevertheless, I still believe in a free press because it does allow those of us who would like to fight discrimination to know where it exists, and we can get at the facts.

The very fact that we have discrimination and that we are the leading democracy, brings the whole of democracy into question. It is brought up against us in practically every meeting. I have come to feel that, as a liberal, wanting to defend democracy, we can no longer think of this question purely as a domestic question. We have to think of it in the implication of what it means to our world leadership, and that is very difficult to do at the present time.[4]

I think, too, that probably one of the most difficult things we face is wanting peace, as undoubtedly all the people of the world want it. We still find ourselves in the position where, having set up machinery in the United Nations to create an atmosphere in which peace can grow, the will of the peoples for peace seems to be lacking. We find ourselves increasingly having decisions to make between the USSR and ourselves.

At home, we have certain people who say "we are the only true liberals in the country" and "we will not say that communism is bad. We will work with communism when it agrees with us."[5] That sounds like a good, liberal way to feel. But then your actual experience makes you doubt whether that really is the way that you can feel. I've had quite a long experience with American Communism, because I began with youth groups in '34, and it has been very interesting. My first real disillusionment came when I found they wouldn't tell me the truth, and then, later, when the youth groups, led by the communist element, were picketing the White House. Then suddenly, when Russia was invaded, they had another meeting, and they sent me a telegram saying, "Now we can work together because now we are for preparedness for war," and I had to send the word back to them, "I am sorry but you lied to me and I can't work with anyone who lies." It was one of the most useful things that I ever did, because I learned all the communist tactics.

Many times in our United Nations meetings I have found that if there is a subject up that the USSR wants to get a certain vote on, you won't be able to get a vote easily, and you wonder why the delay. You go on and on until everybody is very tired and they drift out as groups do in these meetings, and if you don't watch, the move will be made for a vote and they will have won the vote while everyone was drifting out. I learned that a long while ago in one of our meetings. Everyone went scurrying to get the people back because the vote was going to be taken and we would have lost.

You learn that dealing with the Russians is not at all a question of "sweetness and light and sense." It is a question of strength. I don't happen to believe that it is a question only of economic and military strength, though I have come to believe that those two are controlling factors. But it's also a question of the strength of individuals and their convictions. You've got to believe in what you stand for just as strongly as they do. Otherwise you're going to be defeated. And that's one of the places where we're not quite as strong as we should be. In a democracy, we allow such latitude for argument on slight differences of opinion, that to get a feeling of a unified backing for certain big things is quite a problem. The lack of such latitude is, of course, the strength of a totalitarian dictatorship.

There isn't a single representative on any of the committees from the USSR, or from any of the satellite states who doesn't know how he's going to vote right straight down the line when he comes into that meeting. Everyone is going to vote just exactly as he was told to vote. He is going to attack just as he was told to attack—and nothing you say is going to make any dent, then. Six months from now, after it has gone back to the Kremlin, to the Politburo, the attitude may be changed. But it's awfully trying, and annoying, and enraging to find yourself answering first, the USSR. Then perhaps the Byelorussians say something and make the same attack and you have to answer them, too. During this last Assembly at one of the committees, I didn't answer the second time. I thought, "Well, I answered it once; I don't have to answer it each time," and the next day the delegate from the USSR got up and said, "Mrs. Roosevelt didn't answer this yesterday, so of course it must have been true!" So I discovered that each time I would have to get up. We had four attacks, exactly the same, and every time I had to say the same thing all over again. That's very enraging, and you wonder why grown people should want to do anything as time-consuming and as stupid. But that's the way it is and you just have to learn.

And, for the liberal, who wants to believe that people are all more or less the same, that they have the same motivations, and that they respond to fair and decent treatment, it is really a very disillusioning thing to work in that fashion with the USSR because you are tempted to come to the conclusion that it isn't important to do what you feel is right. You may have been brought up to believe that if you say you are going to do something, it's important that you do it for your own self-satisfaction. But you wake up to find that you are going to get cooperation only because you are stronger than they are. Now that's a rather awful thing for a liberal to have to face in this world of today, and I think a good many people probably now feel that I am not a liberal in my attitude towards the USSR.

I believe very strongly that while we have to be strong, we also have to be friendly; and that's one of the most difficult things in the world because they are so irritating. However, if you can remember the fact that they are not acting as individuals; that they are acting as government representatives, and they talk as government representatives, then you cannot dislike them as individuals. You keep your sense of liking them as people, even if you dislike their attitude and dislike what they stand for.

I think we might do some things that we haven't done so far. I think our attitude at times has been highly stupid. We do not recognize very often the fact of how sensitive they are because of insecurity. Many times and in many little ways we do not realize their insecurity and we do things that bring about bitterness, very often in little ways that are not important but have important results.

I have discovered often in working with them on committees that they respect the fact that you are not tired, that you can stand up to them, that you will put them through what you had intended to have them do. The Russians respect this. We as liberals need to make our country understand clearly that we feel our sense of security, that we are sure our democracy can be what we want it to be, and that we are going to work to make it what we want it to be. I think that is as important as the economic and military strength.

There is no doubt that we have to have the economic strength. The economic strength is the point from which we should work with Russia because it is the point where she has a tremendous respect for us. But to get that respect depends upon the liberals in this country, those among us whose convictions can make them believe that democracy is going to bring to the greatest number of people the greatest possible opportunity—those who really know that we want justice and opportunity for all the peoples. I think the liberals must accept the fact that force is still here in the world, and yet be strong enough to watch their own country so that force doesn't go to its head, which is always a danger. At the same time we must work to improve what we have and feel about it as the Communists do. They really have a crusading spirit. They really feel. And when you talk to them you understand why they feel the way they do.

In twenty-five years they have taken a people that was ninety per cent illiterate and made it ninety per cent literate. They haven't been able to become experts in a lot of things, and that is the cause of one of their greatest feelings of inferiority. They have been unable to join a lot of the organizations like UNESCO, for instance. They say that they won't join UNESCO because it is too expensive to join all those specialized agencies. But the truth is they haven't got the people to put there. Moreover, they always have two representatives instead of one, because no USSR representative goes alone. And, of course, when you have to have two, always, instead of one, that doubles your expense. You very soon know when you are working with people that are not at all qualified in many fields—they are not prepared for the work they have to do. In twenty-five years you don't create experts in every field. In making their nation literate they have accomplished a lot.

They are still 200 years behind us in many things. But they are a strong and a very young nation. They haven't much more than they ever had before, and when you compare it with what we have, they are awfully afraid of the comparison. I think they were terribly worried about their soldiers who had to go into decadent democracies and see that life was so much easier than they had it at home. I think that worried them very much. On the other hand, they feel they have gained a great deal and in some ways the government has given them a great deal. Far more people, for instance, go to the opera in Russia, probably, than ever go here. Certainly more people go to plays and sit through Shakespeare from beginning to end, uncut. The government has done that with the idea of taking them out of the misery in which most of them still lived. Nonetheless we are dealing with people who are ruthless at times, and we are dealing with people who are hard and who do believe in force—and, yet, who have given their people a sense of crusading. With all our years of civilization in back of us, I think we have got to face the situation as it is and we've got to know that this requires moral and spiritual leadership. It requires a friendly spirit. But it also requires the facing of realities and the knowledge that anything which can be used against us will be used against us. They believe in their way of life and if we believe in ours we've got to fight for it. We've taken it pretty much for granted up to this time.

We liberals, being liberals, are divided. We all like to go off on our own little tangents and just work on the things we are particularly interested in. There is no question in my mind but the things we do at home in a year which is a decisive year are probably very decisive in the international picture, too. There isn't anyone, I think, today—particularly among the young people, who is not really worried whether we are going to be at war in a short time or not. There is no question but what we have people in the government, and certain people outside, who feel that it would probably be much simpler to drop a few bombs on Russia right now than to wait until she is stronger. I have a lot of people say to me, "Really and honestly, now, don't you think it would be a lot better if we wiped up Russia right now?" The trouble with that, from my point of view, is that we would not really settle anything. We could destroy her cities—but she is a whale of a country. And, having once used atom bombs none of us would sleep very peacefully from then on, because somebody someday is going to have atom bombs just as we have them, and if we get into the habit of using them sooner or later we are going to be destroyed. Nobody wins a modern war.

I think that it is the major job of a liberal, if he can get together sufficiently with other liberals to do a job, really to see to it that his community does think through problems, knows what they really are, has a plan and elects people in Congress and then keeps in touch with them. Of course, that is a difficult thing to do. We've taken our rights too loosely, and we haven't thought so much about the fact that we have to preserve them, and now we are facing the need to preserve them. They are at stake. I am much more interested in seeing the liberals achieve a positive program than seeing them just on the defensive. Just being on the defensive is not going to win a peace; I think the other people of the world must feel very strongly about this, too. It's a question of letting government get out of hand.

Now it's very true that the Russians can't control their government, but if we don't control ours it will be because those of us who are liberals don't do the job. Yes, the role of the liberal in this decisive year is a hard one. We've got to do our job at home as we've never done it before in many long years. And we've got to be willing to subordinate these differences among us in order to be able to do it. We've got to be willing to sacrifice. And probably the only thanks we will get is that many people will say that we are not doing the right thing, that we are making many mistakes. They can say so many things. But I think perhaps we had better forget about what people are going to say and try as hard as we are able in the way we think is right to keep the world at peace, to keep ourselves strong in every possible way, and not to be fooled. That is as important as anything else. We can be fooled. I think Henry Wallace is being fooled. I have always been very fond of Henry Wallace, but he never has had to work with the Russians, and I have. And I don't feel that just "sweetness and light" by itself is going to win a just peace. I think we need clear facing of facts and holding on to our own ideals, and trying to bring the world to a sense of our strength in all ways. Without it I don't see any reason why we should win against the other great power that stands out against us today.

PMag NAWSAP, DLC

---

1. *The Christian Register* 127, no. 6 (June 1948): 26–8, 33. See header Document 339 for Alice Balassa's reaction to this speech.

2. For more on Truman's loyalty program, see *n*6 Document 271.

3. This particular exchange occurred at the February 10, 1947, meeting of the Human Rights Commission. When Valentin T. Tepliakov of the USSR asked ER if she believed that "in a country where there is freedom of information and the press, as exists now, there is no violation of human rights," ER retorted, "Certainly not, but at least you know whether there is or not which is a great difference from not knowing" ("U.N. Aims Defined on Human Rights," *NYT*, 11 February 1947, 13; HRC, First Session, Twenty-First Meeting, Summary Record, 10 February 1947 [E/CN.4/SR.21], UNOR ECOSOC, MWelC). For more examples of ER arguing that freedom of information is fundamental to the protection of human rights, see Document 91 or C. Brooks Peters, "Free Information Held Liberty Basis," *NYT*, 29 May 1946, 15.

4. ER often made this point. For example, see Document 307 and Document 308.

5. ER references Wallace's remarks at the founding of the PCA see Document 355.

REFUTING THE MUNDT-NIXON BILL

___356___

My Day
1 June 1948

HYDE PARK, Monday—It is a curious thing that, among those aligned against the Mundt Bill, one finds people belonging to the extreme left and to the extreme right, and also those in the middle—the moderate liberals, like myself, who dislike seeing us fight Communism by extreme measures. I feel that, in using repressive measures, we are not only underlining our fears that democracy cannot stand up against the superficial attraction of Communism, but we are resorting to the very measures which dictatorships—both Fascist and Communist—use to stay in power.[1]

I have always said that I saw a difference between the Communists of Russia and other totalitarian governments, but their methods are strangely similar. The price paid for the results obtained under all forms of totalitarian government is the surrender of individual freedom. If in a democracy, in order to protect ourselves from Communism, we also surrender our freedom, we are no better off. The Mundt Bill is, from my point of view, a dangerous bill.

Our Attorney General has just come to the conclusion, according to the papers, that Communism all over the world stands for the overthrow of existing governments by force, and that therefore no one who declares himself a Communist can be a good citizen of a democracy.[2] I have known a number of theoretical Communists who certainly were not going around with guns.

The only ones that I think have any real justification in being Communists, and who might possibly be tempted to overthrow any government by force, are those for whom democracy has not provided the basic needs of decent living. That is the point on which I wish we would focus our fight against Communism—not on repressive measures which drive Communists underground, but on the development of democracy so that no human being can find any great attraction in the rather drab program of Communism.

Of course, in the USSR everyone is employed by the Government. The interesting thing to know, however, would be the conditions under which many people are obliged to work and live. But that, of course, we cannot know as long as there is no free interchange of visitors between the two countries and no free travel once you are across the borders of Russia.

To obtain one of the four freedoms, Freedom from Want, and not the others, is a poor bargain; and yet, unless one obtains freedom from want, one probably is not much interested in any of the other freedoms. That is why I would like to see us stop all the thought and time given to restrictive measures such as the Mundt Bill, and try to do a little constructive thinking in an effort to advance our democracy and make it stronger and less responsive to fear.

TMs AERP, FDRL

---

1. On May 19, 1948, the House passed the Mundt-Nixon bill, introduced by Congressmen Karl Mundt (R-SD) and Richard Nixon (R-CA), with a vote of 319 to 58. The bill required the Communist Party and "Communist-front" organizations to register with the attorney general and provide membership rolls to the Justice Department. The bill's critics, including Truman who declared his intention to veto the bill if passed by the Senate, argued that the proposed legislation effectively outlawed a political party. Proponents of the bill argued that one of the Communist Party's fundamental objectives was the overthrow of the government. Although the Senate never

voted on the bill, the McCarran Act, based largely on the Mundt-Nixon bill and enacted in 1950 over Truman's veto, required Communist organizations to register with the federal government (John D. Morris, "Bill to Control Communists Passed by House, 319 to 58," *NYT*, 20 May 1948, 1; "Truman Indicates a Mundt Bill Veto," *NYT*, 14 May 1948, 15; Fried, 116–18; Reeves, 329–30).

2. When Seth W. Richardson, chairman of the president's Loyalty Review Board, wrote attorney general Tom Clark asking for clarification on the course of action to be taken if investigations revealed an individual had ties with the Communist Party, Clark instructed him that, under the Hatch Act of 1939, the "board must recognize in its recommendation to the agency that the dismissal of the employee is mandatory." The Hatch Act's Section 9A denied government positions to individuals who belonged to "any political party or organization which advocates the overthrow of our constitutional form of government." Although the act did not specifically mention the Communist Party, Clark argued that the legislative record revealed Congress's intent to include the Communist Party among the groups covered by the act. "It has thus been the intention of the Legislative branch, reinforced by positive action on the part of the Legislative branch, to bar from Government service persons having membership in the Communist party," he wrote Richardson in a letter that both the *New York Times* and *Washington Post* excerpted (Lewis Wood, "U.S. Can Fire Reds, Clark Tells Board," *NYT*, 28 May 1948, 12; Carl Levin, "Hatch Act Bars Reds from Jobs, Clark Says," *WP*, 28 May 1948, 4).

THE CHAIR AS DELEGATE

After a discussion of the objectives of the declaration of human rights, the Human Rights Commission proceeded to an article-by-article review of the draft declaration of human rights prepared at Geneva and modified by the drafting committee earlier in May.[1] The articles on workers' rights (Articles 23 and 24), posed particular problems for the United States, since these articles reflected the relatively new concept of economic and social rights, rather than the principle of civil and political rights long recognized by American law and society, and raised the issue of the role of the state in securing these rights. ER supported the inclusion of economic and social rights in the declaration, but sought to craft the definition of such rights in a broad way that would leave the means of achieving them open.[2] In the case of Articles 23 and 24, the United States supported amendments proposed jointly by India and the United Kingdom that changed "Everyone has the right to work" to "Everyone has the right to work under just and favourable conditions," eliminated references to the role of the state in ensuring that its citizens found employment and to women receiving equal pay for equal work, and replaced the right of a worker "to receive pay commensurate with his ability and skill" with "the right to a standard of living adequate for health and well-being."[3] In the following statement, ER explains the United States' position.

357

Commission on Human Rights Summary Record of the Sixty-Fourth Meeting [excerpt][4]

8 June 1948 [Lake Success, NY]

CHAIRMAN: Mrs. Franklin D. Roosevelt

The CHAIRMAN declared that the United States supported the text presented by India and the United Kingdom (document E/CN.4/99), with the addition of the words: "as well as to form trade unions and to join the trade union of his choice."[5]

The United States delegation favoured the inclusion of economic and social rights in the Declaration, for no personal liberty could exist without economic security and independence. Men in need were not free men. The United States delegation considered that the Declaration should enunciate rights, not try to define the methods by which Governments were to ensure the realization of those rights. Those methods would necessarily vary from one country to another and such variations should be considered not only inevitable but salutary.

As regards article 23, which concerned the right to work, in the opinion of her delegation that right was meaningless unless it was coupled with the mention of "just and favourable working conditions", which would guarantee the worker and his family a decent standard of living.[6] The right to work had to be accompanied by the freedom of choice with respect to work. That was the reason why the United States delegation wished to join the first paragraph of article 23, dealing with the right to work, to article 24, dealing with conditions of work.[7] It should also be borne in mind that the right to work, without qualifications might mean very different things, some of which might be incompatible with other articles of the Declaration. In the opinion of the United States delegation, the right to work, in this Declaration, meant the right of the individual to benefit from conditions under which those who were able and willing to work would have the possibility of doing useful work, including independent work, as well as the right to full employment and to further the development of production and of purchasing power.

The realization of those objectives meant more to individuals in the United States than any state guarantee of full employment. That was why the United States considered the text submitted by India and the United Kingdom to be the best if amended by the addition of the right to set up and join trade unions. It was, moreover, in conformity with the text adopted in the Declaration of Bogota.[8]

TSumex UNOR ECOSOC, MWelC --

––––––––––––––––

1. For more on the process of revision, see *n*1 Document 354.

2. Glendon, 115–17. Glendon notes that René Cassin remembered the debates over economic and social rights in this session of the HRC as among the most heated in the drafting process. For American concerns about the definition of economic and social rights in the declaration, see Document 318. For ER's view of the differences between the American and the Soviet view of the "right to work," see her Sorbonne speech, Document 379.

3. The Geneva draft of Articles 23 and 24, which had not been modified by the drafting committee, read:

Article 23

1. Everyone has the right to work.

2. The State has a duty to take such measures as may be within its power to ensure that all persons ordinarily resident in its territory have an opportunity for useful work.

3. The State is bound to take all necessary steps to prevent unemployment.

Article 24

1. Everyone has the right to receive pay commensurate with his ability and skill, to work under just and favourable conditions and to join trade unions for the protection of his interests in securing a decent standard of living for himself and his family.

2. Women shall work with the same advantages as men and receive equal pay for equal work.

The amended articles proposed by India and the UK read:

Article 23

1. Everyone has the right to work under just and favourable conditions.

Article 24

1. Everyone has the right to a standard of living adequate for health and well-being, including security in the event of unemployment, disability, old age or other lack of livelihood in circumstances beyond his control (HRC, Third Session, India and the United Kingdom: Proposed Amendments to the Draft Declaration of Human Rights, 24 May 1948 (E/CN.4/99), 6, AERP).

4. HRC, Third Session, Sixty-fourth Meeting, Summary Record, 8 June 1948 (E/CN.4/SR.64), 5-6, UNOR ECOSOC, MWelC.

5. In the discussion that followed the next day, ER stated the reasons why the United States wished to add a clause on trade unions:

The CHAIRMAN explained that the United States delegation considered that the right to form and join trade unions was an essential element of freedom. While other associations had long enjoyed recognition, trade unions had met with much opposition and it was only recently that they had become an accepted form of association. The struggle was, in fact, still continuing, and her delegation thought, therefore, that specific mention should be made of trade unions (HRC, Third Session, Sixty-sixth Meeting, Summary Record (E/CN.4/SR.66), 3-4, UNOR ECOSOC, MWelC).

6. In the discussion that ensued the following day, ER:

> expressed her strong support for the principle of equal pay for equal work, which was widely observed in the United States, where many States had equal pay laws on their Statute Books. She felt, however, that there was no need for a specific provision in the Declaration, since the principle was adequately covered by the provision against discrimination in Article 3, and paragraph 1 spoke of "just and favourable conditions of work and pay" (HRC, Third Session, Sixty-sixth Meeting, Summary Record (E/CN.4/SR.66), 5, UNOR ECOSOC, MWelC).

7. In the draft that emerged from the HRC session in Lake Success, the two articles were combined into Article 21, which read:

> 1. Everyone has the right to work, to just and favorable conditions of work and pay and to protection against unemployment.
>
> 2. Everyone has the right to equal pay for equal work.
>
> 3. Everyone is free to form and to join trade unions for the protection of his interests (Glendon, 297).

8. The American Declaration of the Rights and Duties of Man, commonly called the Declaration of Bogotá, was adopted in 1948 at the Ninth International Conference of American States in Bogotá, Colombia. The Organization of American States was also founded at this conference. The Bogotá declaration is divided into two sections, one on rights and one on duties. Article 14 of this declaration states:

> Every person has the right to work, under proper conditions, and to follow his vocation freely, insofar as existing conditions of employment permit. Every person who works has the right to receive such remuneration as will, in proportion to his capacity and skill, assure him a standard of living suitable for himself and for his family.

Article 22 states:

> Every person has the right to associate with others to promote, exercise and protect his legitimate interests of a political, economic, religious, social, cultural, professional, labor union or other nature.

Article 37 states:

> It is the duty of every person to work, as far as his capacity and possibilities permit, in order to obtain the means of livelihood or to benefit his community ("The American Declaration of the Rights and Duties of Man," Inter-American Commission on Human Rights, http://www.cidh.org/Basicos/basic2.htm, accessed 2 February 2006).

STRATEGIZING FOR THE DECLARATION AND A COVENANT

As the third session of the Human Rights Commission drew to a close, ER telephoned John Foster Dulles for advice. In particular, she wanted his opinion as to whether the United States should support the submission of the declaration on human rights to the Economic and Social Council for its review during the summer of 1948 and then to the General Assembly for its consideration in the fall or whether it would be wiser to delay submission of the declaration until the HRC completed the drafting of a covenant on human rights. She then invited Dulles to dinner to discuss the matter in detail. Dulles prepared for their meeting by talking with Durward Sandifer, James Hendrick, and Dr. C. Frederick Nolde.[1] Dulles then sent ER the following letter and memorandum containing his thoughts on the matter.

358

John Foster Dulles to Eleanor Roosevelt
15 June 1948 [New York City]

Dear Mrs. Roosevelt:

In view of your telephone inquiry to me of last Saturday, I have tried to inform myself a little through Mr. Sandifer and Mr. Henrick[2] as to the status of the matter. I have put down some thoughts to which I have come, but which I hope you will consider as very tentative. I do not have your great background of experience with this matter, and I am reluctant out of my relative ignorance to proffer suggestions. If you do not agree with them, I am confident that when we dine together tomorrow you will be able to convince me that you are right and I am wrong.

Sincerely yours,

MEMORANDUM

It is my suggestion that the following course with respect to human rights and fundamental freedoms might be adopted:

1. The Economic and Social Council should submit to the next regular meeting of the Assembly a report which would (a) transmit the draft Declaration on Human Rights as being in form adequate for consideration by the Assembly for adoption; and (b) advise that it has not been practicable as yet to draft a covenant in form suitable for consideration and adoption at this time by the Assembly, and, accordingly, that if the Assembly does not desire to act on the Declaration until there can also be a covenant before it, further time must be given.

2. The General Assembly would receive the above report as a matter for general debate and such action as the Assembly might decide to take.

3. The United States as a Member might consider and exchange views with other like-minded Members as to the feasibility of proposing at the Assembly a resolution along the following lines:

(a) Adopting the Declaration with whatever amendments the Assembly might deem appropriate;

(b) Inviting all Member States to enter into a covenant on such basic human rights as can be unequivocally agreed to by them all;

(c) Inviting Member States which were in substantial agreement with respect to further human rights and fundamental freedoms to enter into covenants on those rights as between themselves;

(d) Calling upon all States to refrain from efforts, and not to tolerate within their territory efforts, to deprive other peoples of rights and freedoms recognized by the Declaration and/or covenants which such States might have made between themselves in accordance with sub-paragraphs (b) or (c) above.

I suggest this program for the reason first that I think it very desirable that there should be a general debate at this next Assembly on the question of human rights so as to emphasize this important aspect of the Charter and take away concentration of attention upon political problems. Also I believe that it is illusory to expect any universal covenant which will really be both adequate and effective. There are such fundamental philosophic and religious differences between the Member States with respect to the nature of man that any covenant that could be universally adopted would be meagre or illusory and probably it would depend on a use of words which had a double meaning. Therefore, I think that the Assembly might as well grapple with the reality of the problem and recognize that just as less than universal pacts may be necessary under Article 51 to develop national security on a less than universal basis, so under Article 56, in order to develop observance of human rights and respect for human freedoms, it may be useful to supplement what can be done universally by what, at the present time, can only be done on a less than universal basis.[3]

This reflects preliminary views, subject to further study.

J.F.D.

TLc JFDP, NjP-SC

ER reviewed Dulles's memorandum before Dulles and Hendrick joined her for dinner. Later that evening Hendrick summarized their discussion in the memorandum below for the State Department.

359

Memorandum of Conversation with Eleanor Roosevelt

16 June 1948 [New York City]

Subject: Human Rights
Participants: Mrs. Roosevelt, Mr. John Foster Dulles, Mr. Hendrick
Copies to: Mr. Gross, Mr. Sandifer, Mr. Kotschnig, Mr. Simsarian[4]

This meeting took place at Mrs. Roosevelt's apartment, 29 Washington Square, New York.

Mrs. Roosevelt expressed sympathy with Mr. Dulles' view that it was important for countries to become fully informed on the subject of human rights. She still questioned whether it was wise to have a declaration approved without at the same time approving a covenant.

The subject was discussed at some length. Finally it was agreed that there should be no objection to the Declaration being sent to the General Assembly this fall. This would be subject to the provision that it be made quite clear that the Declaration by itself was not the whole bill of rights and that further work must be done in connection with a Covenant. It would be up to the General Assembly to decide whether or not to approve the Declaration apart from the Covenant or whether to postpone approval until the Covenant is ready.[5]

Mr. Dulles stated that more should be done in the United Nations with respect to economic and social problems and particularly with respect to human rights. He felt that essentially the human rights program was one for protection of the individual. He referred to the Federalist papers in which there have been lengthy discussions on the necessity for guaranteeing rights to the individual rather than the state.[6] He likened the case of the United Nations to the case of the several states vis-a-vis the Federal Government in the early days of United States history. The decision to allow the individual to go directly to the Federal Government was a crucial one. The state cannot be counted upon to act as advocate for the individual; the state, like a corporation, has no soul.

Mr. Dulles said that he felt very strongly that there should be a covenant or covenants and he did not deny the possibility of implementing measures which would allow the individual to secure protection on his own initiative in a covenant. He was still doubtful as to the feasibility of a covenant between governments which had entirely differing concepts of the worth and nature of the human-being but he did not wish to bar the door to an attempt for a United Nations Covenant. This he felt could be supplemented by further more detailed agreements between like-minded countries.

With regard to the General Assembly session for 1948 Mr. Dulles envisaged the possibility of governments indicating what type of rights they might be willing to include in a covenant with other nations. Mrs. Roosevelt felt that this might be an experiment worth trying. The matter should therefore be given further thought.

TMemc RG59, NARA II

---

1. Dulles grew to admire Nolde, a Lutheran clergyman who represented the Federal Council of Churches at the UN, after he advised the US delegation to the San Francisco Conference, later telling Hendrick "that Dr. Nolde was 'outstanding' among the consultants, his suggestions 'always sound' and many of them 'bore important practical results.'" Nolde had attended the third session of the HRC (James Hendrick, "Memorandum of Conversation," 15 June 1948, RG84, NARA II; "Dr. O. Frederick Nolde Dead," *NYT*, 19 June 1972, 36).

2. Dulles meant Hendrick.

3. Article 51 of the UN Charter states that "Nothing in the present Charter shall impair the inherent right of individual or collective self-defence if an armed attack occurs against a Member of the United Nations, until the Security Council has taken measures necessary to maintain international peace and security." Article 56 states that "All Members pledge themselves to take joint and separate action in co-operation with the Organization for the achievement of the purposes set forth in Article 55," which includes the promotion of "universal respect for, and observance of, human rights and fundamental freedoms for all without distinction as to race, sex, language, or religion" (Avalon Project at Yale Law School, "Charter of the United Nations," http://www.yale.edu/lawweb/avalon/un/unchart.htm, accessed 28 February 2006).

4. Ernest Gross, Durward Sandifer, Walter Kotschnig, James Simsarian. For Gross, see header to Document 294; for Sandifer and Kotschnig, see Biographical Portraits; for Simsarian, see header to Document 375.

5. The General Assembly adopted the Universal Declaration of Human Rights on December 10, 1948. ER and the Commission on Human Rights resumed work on the drafting of a covenant in 1949.

6. See especially James Madison, "Federalist 10" and "Federalist 51."

SUMMARIZING THE DRAFTING PROCESS

June 18, after a series of votes consolidating points and reducing the number of articles to twenty-eight, the Human Rights Commission voted twelve to none in favor of the declaration of human rights and its transmission to the Economic and Social Council, whose support was essential for its adoption by the General Assembly. Although no nation voted against the declaration, the USSR, the Ukraine, Yugoslavia, and Byelorussia abstained from the vote, and, in a minority report, attacked the declaration as "weak and completely unacceptable," noting the commission's failure to include the individual's obligations to the state, and criticizing what they labeled its "rejection of effective measures to combat fascism and nazism." Despite these protests, the commission's endorsement ensured that ECOSOC would consider the declaration at its next session and decide whether or not to forward the draft to the General Assembly for adoption.

As ER replied when an aide expressed concern about the fatigue and strain he thought she exhibited, the session was "a bit fatiguing. But it was worth it!" She told readers of her column that she "was certainly glad to reach the end" of negotiations:

Six weeks of arguing over the weight of each word put down, as well as the legal meaning of every phrase, is not so easy for me, who is somewhat impatient of the things which I do not recognize at first blush as being really important. I have had to learn a great deal in this last session and it has been good discipline, and I am sure my lawyer friends will be pleased to know that I have come to hold a proper respect for their legalistic turn of mind.[1]

ER then went to work generating public interest necessary to shore up support for the declaration. The morning her column appeared, she released, through the US Mission to the UN, a detailed press statement, explaining why she thought the declaration so important and the American legal and political traditions it reflected. Major media, such as the *New York Times*, summarized her remarks with the headline, "Rights Plan Hailed by Mrs. Roosevelt. Declaration Is a Compromise, but Contains Much U.S. Law and Tradition, She Says."[2]

360

Press Statement by Eleanor Roosevelt

United States Mission to the United Nations
18 June 1948 [New York City]

The Human Rights Commission last week finished drafting a <u>Declaration</u> of Human Rights and I suspect that many people are asking: "What good does that do?" The question deserves an answer, and there is an answer, a good and simple answer. But fulfilling the answer is infinitely complex.

The answer is that when this <u>Declaration</u> is adopted by the General Assembly, with the changes that inevitably will be made by the Assembly, we shall have done the equivalent of providing the compass for the ship. In human relations—in the difficult job of living together in international harmony while giving the other fellow his due—we now have an instrument for determining the direction in which we are going.

Every scientist, every economist, every executive, every administrator knows that when he is faced with difficulties, to attack them he must know what he is attacking; to attain a goal he must define the goal. The United Nations knows that the world is far from perfect and that one of its imperfections is the fact that in many areas people are not free. To work toward greater freedom we must first decide what freedom is—what does every man and woman have a RIGHT to have? We have tried to frame an answer in the Declaration of Human Rights. I hope and believe that every country can endorse this Declaration when it is considered in the General Assembly.

Producing a meeting of the minds on what these rights ought to be was most difficult. That which a country or an individual considers a fundamental right depends much upon the history of freedom in that country, on the stage of political, economic and social development, and on the political, economic and social conditions of the moment. The Czarist Government of Russia failed to develop economic prosperity or social equality among the masses of people; it is not unnatural that Communist Russia should emphasize economic and social rights provided by the State. Our own experience was quite different: oppressed American Colonists formed a nation in which the emphasis was on individual rights with a minimum of government.

Customs and political practices change slowly in any country and in no two countries do they advance at the same rate. We in the United States have become so accustomed to women's suffrage that it may seem surprising to us that in some Western European countries women have voted only since the second world war; it is sometimes forgotten that only in this generation have women enjoyed suffrage in this country.[3]

The attitude of a people on the right to employment is deeply influenced by economic conditions at the time—whether they are prosperous or depressed. Attitudes toward free speech and press are influenced, for instance, by conditions of internal security; a country often invaded naturally is more wary of inflammatory speeches and editorials.

Despite these difficulties, despite these variations in attitudes and customs and historic precedent, we have produced a document of very great intrinsic worth. The United States has not always won its points. The Declaration is not exactly as we would have written it; on the other hand, no two Americans would have written it in the same way. But it is a sure guide. It is not unlikely that it will be of historic importance.

Americans will find in the Declaration a good many things with which they are very familiar. A good deal of good, sound American tradition and law are wrapped up in it. For example, the Declaration provides:

> "No one shall be held in slavery or involuntary servitude." (Article 4)

> "Everyone charged with a penal offense is presumed to be innocent until proved guilty … " (Article 9)

> "No one shall be subjected to unreasonable interference with his privacy, family, home, correspondence or reputation." (Article 10)

> "Everyone has the right to own property alone as well as in association with others. No one shall be arbitrarily deprived of his property." (Article 15)

These points are very close to the points made in our own Constitution.

Another article declares, "Everyone has the right to work, to just and favorable conditions of work and pay, and to protection against unemployment." This expression conforms to the declaration of Congress in the Employment Act of 1946 expressing the "continuing policy and responsibility of the Federal Government to use all practicable means … to coordinate and utilize all its plans, functions and resources" to create and maintain "conditions under which there will be afforded useful employment opportunities, including self-employment, for those able, willing, and seeking to work …"[4]

I cite these examples simply to show how the Declaration parallels closely our own traditions in matters of human rights.

The Declaration, upon its approval, will become a document of moral force in the world. But it will not be legally binding upon any government. It does not require ratification by government.

I want to emphasize that the completion of the <u>Declaration</u> on Human Rights is only part of the Commission's work. We must have another meeting of the Commission early next year to draft a <u>Covenant</u> on Human Rights and provisions for the implementation of the rights set forth in the Covenant. The Covenant is the proposed treaty on human rights which, upon final approval by the United Nations, must be ratified by Member States to come into force. It thereupon will become a binding international instrument.

The <u>Covenant</u> and the <u>Declaration</u> are both necessary parts of the Commission's program. Completion of the Declaration is therefore a stepping stone to a higher level of achievement in the peaceful relations of man with his fellow man. All members of the Commission worked with real earnestness to complete the Declaration. I have every reason to believe that they will continue to work with that same earnestness on the Covenant.

TPr AERP, FDRL

---

1. Glendon, 120–21; *MD*, 21 June 1948.

2. Mallory Browne, "Charter of Rights Is Adopted in U.N.," *NYT*, 19 June 1948, 1; "Rights Plan Hailed by Mrs. Roosevelt," *NYT*, 21 June 1948, 9.

3. In 1893, New Zealand became the first nation to recognize woman suffrage. Australia, Finland, and Norway followed shortly thereafter. Not until after World War I did the Soviet Union, Canada, and Britain enact woman suffrage, and many Catholic countries in Europe, including Italy, France, and Belgium, did not do so until after World War II. The first organized call for woman suffrage in the United States came in 1848, when the men and women who met at Seneca Falls, New York, adopted the Declaration of Sentiments. In August 1920, after nearly seventy-five years of political agitation, the three-quarters of states necessary to amend the constitution ratified the Nineteenth Amendment, guaranteeing women the right to vote (*OEWH*).

4. See also *n*5 Document 357 for ER's consideration of the Employment Act of 1946 in the "right to work" debate.

EISENHOWER, TRUMAN, AND PRESIDENTIAL POLITICS

The movement to replace Truman and draft Dwight D. Eisenhower as the Democratic candidate for president continued to gather steam through the spring and early summer of 1948. Many of those close to ER personally and politically joined the effort, including her sons James and Elliott,[1] Helen Gahagan Douglas, and Chester Bowles. In the following letter, Bowles urges ER to lend the movement her support.

361

Chester Bowles to Eleanor Roosevelt
18 June 1948 [Essex, CT]

Dear Mrs. Roosevelt:

Helen Gahagan Douglas called me last night to talk about the political situation. Helen feels, as I do, that we still have a chance—perhaps 1 out of 3—for an open convention at Philadelphia[2] and the nomination of Eisenhower, or possibly even Bill Douglas.[3]

Like many others, I have certain misgivings on General Eisenhower principally because his ideas on domestic issues are so little known. I talked with him about ten days ago and it was my feeling that he was by no means sure exactly where he stands himself on the questions which are so important to all of us. I believe his instincts, however, are good and if he chose liberal advisers there would be every reason to be optimistic. In addition, of course, he would give us a liberal Congress, which would be a tremendous safeguard in the next few years.[4]

Of course, you know a great deal more about him than I.[5]

Helen has prepared a statement which she would like to see published a few days before the Convention signed by eight to twelve liberal Democratic leaders who have some political support. She read it to me over the telephone and it sounded excellent. It was in no sense an anti-Truman statement but simply called for an open convention and the nomination of our strongest candidate.[6]

Helen asked me if I would write to you and urge you to sign this statement. I told her that I was sure that much would depend on whom the Republicans nominate next week at their Convention but that I would be glad to write to you to say that if you were willing to sign it, I am sure we would get some other really top people who would carry real weight with the delegates.

I am going to be away for the next ten days but I will be back in Essex a week before the National Convention, and if there is anything you think I can do I hope that you will call on me.

My best regards.

Sincerely,
Chester Bowles

TLS AERP, FDRL

Republicans had gathered in Philadelphia June 21 to begin selecting their presidential ticket. However, the day ER replied to Bowles's query, the convention had not yet selected its presidential candidate, and Governors Thomas Dewey and Harold Stassen competed with Senators Robert Taft and Arthur Vandenberg for their party's nomination. As the *Washington Post* reported, although Dewey showed "heavy" support, the convention was "still wide open."[7]

362

Eleanor Roosevelt to Chester Bowles

23 June 1948 [Hyde Park]

My dear Mr. Bowles:

Many thanks for your letter of June 18th. I know little about General Eisenhower and hesitate to take any part in politics, but I shall consider again in light of the Republican nomination.[8]

Very sincerely,
Eleanor Roosevelt

TLS AERP, FDRL

---

1. For background on FDR, Jr.'s, draft Eisenhower announcement and ER's correspondence with Truman and Marshall about it, see Document 332 and Document 333.

2. Philadelphia hosted the Democratic Convention from July 12 to 15, 1948 (Hamby, *Man*, 448–50).

3. Liberals within the Democratic Party also looked to Supreme Court Justice William O. Douglas as a possible candidate, if they could not persuade Eisenhower to run. A strong defender of civil liberties who became chair of the Securities and Exchange Commission and worked closely with FDR and ER during the New Deal, Douglas, unlike Eisenhower, possessed solid liberal credentials. In 1944, ER had supported Douglas as a possible replacement for Wallace on the 1944 ballot. On April 11, 1948, the ADA's National Board issued a call for "an open Democratic convention," asserting that "this Nation has the right to call upon men like Dwight D. Eisenhower and William O. Douglas if the people so choose." In June, ADA vice-chairman Hubert Humphrey came out in favor of either Eisenhower or Douglas. Liberals held Douglas in high esteem, but polls showed Eisenhower to be the stronger candidate and Southern Democrats viewed Douglas as too liberal (Hamby, *Beyond*, 224–29, 237–39; Parmet, 75).

4. In his memoirs, Bowles, who in an April 2 radio broadcast called for Truman to step aside, presents his meeting with Eisenhower in a somewhat different light:

> No one knew Eisenhower's political views, and I felt it was quite possible that he did not have any. I decided to find out. I called his office at Columbia University and an appointment was arranged for the following day. After a two-hour discussion I was convinced: (1) that he wanted to become President; (2) that this desire was qualified by his reluctance to participate in the turmoil of political life; (3) that his ideas on domestic policy were almost wholly unformed; and (4) that he was incredibly naive politically. As evidence of this latter point General Eisenhower seriously asked me at the end of our discussion if it might be possible for him to be nominated by both parties. I came away badly shaken (Bowles, 211).

5. ER and Eisenhower did not know each other well, but enjoyed a cordial relationship. He was among those who hosted her trip to England during the war when she visited American troops and she corresponded with him occasionally both during and after the war about issues such as the problems of soldiers waiting for demobilization in 1946. In 1945, after the end of the war, he came to Hyde Park to lay a wreath at FDR's grave.

In June 1948, ER invited Eisenhower and his wife, Mamie, to spend a night in Hyde Park. Eisenhower replied, "I venture to suggest that if you and I should ever, simultaneously, uncover an idle day on our schedules it would be scarcely less than a minor miracle. However, I do hope that the not too distant future will bring us some opportunity to take advantage of your great courtesy and thoughtfulness." The day before Bowles wrote to her about signing the statement Helen Gahagan Douglas had prepared, ER renewed her invitation to Eisenhower, telling him if the Eisenhowers felt like driving up for lunch any weekend after July 3rd, to just call and "say you are coming" (Lash, *Eleanor*, 659, 662; ER, *Autobiography*, 287; ER to Eisenhower, 10 November 194(3?), DDEP, DDEL; ER to Truman, 12 January 1946, HSTSF, HSTL; ER to Eisenhower, 8 June 1948; Eisenhower to ER, 14 June 1948, AERP; ER to Eisenhower, 17 June 1948, DDEP, DDEL).

6. Neither Bowles nor Douglas nor ER retained a copy of the statement Bowles references in this letter. However, on July 3, nineteen party leaders, including Bowles but not Douglas, sent telegrams to all the delegates to the Democratic convention inviting them to participate in a caucus they planned to hold in Philadelphia on July 10, two days before the beginning of the convention. The telegrams called for "an open and free Democratic convention" and urged the delegates to "seek for the leader of our party the ablest and strongest man available" (James A. Hagerty, "19 Party Leaders Make Caucus Call to Block Truman," *NYT*, 4 July 1948, 1).

7. Warren Moscow, "Dewey Desperate, Stassen Declares," *NYT*, 23 June 1945, 12; "Vandenberg to Be 'Available' to End; Statement Indicates," *NYT*, 22 June 1948, 1, 2; Alexander F. Jones, "Convention Still Wide Open As Bands Play," *WP*, 22 June 1948, 1.

8. ER made no public statements of support, before or after the Republican convention, for other presidential candidates or for an open Democratic convention. However, she did hold private conversations about Eisenhower with those she trusted. For example, Joe Lash later recalled that when FDR, Jr., first told ER about his plans to call for the drafting of Eisenhower, his mother wanted to know, "Where did General Eisenhower stand on domestic things? Suppose he reaffirmed his refusal to run? Was he prepared to be cold-shouldered by the president and his friends? Had he consulted people like Bernard Baruch and Ed Flynn?" Hubert Humphrey also recalled that ER discussed the prospect of an Eisenhower draft with him several times in 1948; however, his memoirs do not reveal when they talked or what she said (Lash, *Years*, 146; H. Humphrey, *Education*, 110–11).

1 9 4 8

"I have come this evening to talk with you on one of the greatest issues of our time—that is the preservation of human freedom."

COURTESY OF THE FDR LIBRARY.

Eleanor Roosevelt chafed as 1948 drew to a close. Fearful that the Berlin Blockade,

the Communist victory in China, the re-industrialization of the Ruhr, Soviet entrenchment in the Balkans, the assassinations of Gandhi and Bernadotte, the escalating refugee crisis in Palestine, and the deadlock over atomic energy would hurl the world closer to war, she redoubled her efforts to secure the General Assembly's adoption of the Universal Declaration of Human Rights.

Although the United Nations would ultimately adopt the Declaration without dissent, in early July, that outcome could not be predicted with certainty. Conflicts within the State Department continued, ranging from whether the department should support a legally binding human rights covenant to whether human rights should even be a departmental priority. ER had just finished a contentious meeting with Du Bois regarding the NAACP petition to the Human Rights Commission when she learned that James Hendrick, one of her trusted State Department advisors, had resigned in protest. "Greatly concerned," she wrote Hendrick's supervisor that while "I realize perfectly that the State Department takes no interest in Human Rights and does not think it very important whether the Commission functions or not," she still could not help but "suppose even when the Department is not deeply interested in the subject, it would still want the United States to be properly represented."[1]

By mid-August, a concerned Truman and Marshall summoned ER to Washington to discuss how best to launch a moral offensive toward peace and manage "the coming session of the United Nations." Accepting "the considerable responsibility" the administration placed on her, ER then agreed "to make an opening speech to set this keynote outside the Assembly."[2] Yet, as she told her delegation colleagues the following week, she continued to remain concerned that an early adoption of the Declaration "might prejudice the completion of the draft International Covenant on Human Rights." She then urged that the Declaration's adoption at the upcoming session of the General Assembly be portrayed as the "first step in the Human Rights program" and that the department continue to label "the completion of the Covenant on Human Rights … essential."[3]

ER delivered her keynote immediately upon her arrival in Paris, telling the 2,500 filling the ornate Sorbonne auditorium that "I have come this evening to talk with you on one of the greatest issues of our time—that is the preservation of human freedom." She then addressed the "fundamental difference in the conception of human rights" and argued that those committed to the principles espoused in the Declaration "must not be deluded by the efforts of the forces of reaction to prostitute the great words of our free tradition and thereby to confuse the struggle."[4]

ER's speech set the tone for her work steering the Declaration through the Third Committee and the General Assembly itself. As she chronicled in My Day throughout late November and early December, the drafting process involved eighty-five working sessions (many lasting until well past midnight) in which new delegates revisited each word of the Declaration's thirty articles. As discussions over the right to education, to an adequate standard of living, and to old age pensions (where ER found herself debating a proposal crafted by Eva Perón) continued, ER worried that the committee might not act in time to have the General Assembly approve the Declaration. She became more outspoken about Soviet delaying tactics, telling her readers, "One would admire the Soviet persistence in sticking to their point if it were not for the fact that so often the point is not worth sticking to."[5] When one Soviet delegate used "the presentation of their amendments to expatiate on the perfections of their way of doing things as opposed to the bad customs and ideas of the United Kingdom and the United States," ER reported a colleague's retort, asking if "those in the USSR's forced labor camps enjoyed paid vacations."[6]

She recognized the Declaration's imperfections, but as she told her aunt December 9, "On the whole I think it is good as a declaration of rights to which all men may aspire & which we should try to achieve. It has no legal value but should carry moral weight."[7] Later that evening, she told the General Assembly that although they stood at a great threshold for dignity and rights, it must remember the "basic character" of the Declaration. "It is not a treaty; it is not an international agreement. It is not and does not purport to be a statement of law or of legal obligation." Rather, "it is a declaration of basic principles of human rights and freedoms, to be stamped with the approval of the General Assembly by formal vote of its members, and to serve as a common standard of achievement for all peoples of all nations."[8]

The American home front presented ER with a related, serious set of challenges. The House Un-American Activities Committee's investigations moved into her personal circle when HUAC redirected its attention from the entertainment industry back to government. Lauchlin Currie, a former assistant to FDR well known to ER, and Alger Hiss, who advised the American delegation to the UN, came under scrutiny in August when Elizabeth Bentley, a confessed double agent, testified that both men were Soviet spies and, again, in December after Laurence Duggan's sudden death. "I have begun to wonder what the point of all this is," she wrote in My Day, and "I wonder if all this extra-curricular Congressional activity isn't making it more difficult for the FBI to do its job well."[9] She also thought zealous loyalty investigations (and the Mundt-Nixon bill) would drive qualified, and dedicated, young people from government service. "I would hesitate in these days about accepting a job in the Government … As things are today, there are very few youngsters who have remembered to be wary enough to take a Government job."[10]

The Democrats entered the 1948 election more divided than usual. ER, while continuing to urge liberals to remain with the party, did "not have much enthusiasm for Mr. Truman."[11] Convinced that her UN position dictated that she remain aloof from overt campaign activity, she opted to work behind the scenes, either advising individual congressional candidates or party leaders. Privately, she expressed some doubts as to the President's abilities, telling Frances Perkins that the party's success lay "in electing a very strong group of liberals in Congress." She then turned to her column to rally the party faithful: "No Democrat wants any support from the Progressive Party and I should not think they would want support from the so-called Dixiecrats. Therefore, Democratic voters must concentrate on electing every liberal they possibly can in every state in the Union, and for every office, whether it is for Senator, Representative, Governor, or a member of a state legislature." When Truman sought her overt endorsement to offset press reports of her dissatisfaction, she quickly authorized him to release her endorsement. However, as she celebrated his re-election, she cautioned Democratic leaders to recognize the party's success "puts a responsibility on all of us to see that the promises made during the campaign are carried out."[12]

ER ended the year speaking out on many of the same issues she confronted when the year began: the conflict in Palestine, the need for civil rights legislation and the dangers of racial hatred, the importance of a free press and civil liberties, and the critical role the United Nations and the United States must play as world leaders. December 28, she submitted a report Truman had requested she prepare for their forthcoming meeting. "The thing above all others which I would like to bring to your attention," she wrote, "is that we are now engaged in a situation which is as complicated as fighting the war."[13]

———————————

1. See Document 366, ER to Walter Kotschnig, 2 July 1948.

2. See header to Document 379, Speech Delivered at the Sorbonne, Paris, 28 September 1948.

3. See Document 375, Memorandum of Conversation, 24 August 1948.

4. See Document 379, Speech Delivered at the Sorbonne, Paris, 28 September 1948.

5. See Document 402, My Day, 4 December 1948.

6. See Document 396, My Day, 24 November 1948.

7. ER to Maude Gray, 9 December 1948, DGC, FDRL.

8. See Document 407, Statement by Mrs. Franklin D. Roosevelt, U.S. Representative to the General Assembly, 9 December 1948.

9. See Document 372, My Day, 19 August 1948.

10. See Document 377, My Day, 31 August 1948.

11. See Document 383, ER to Frances Perkins, 4 October 1948.

12. See Document 388, ER to Edward Flynn, 6 November 1948.

13. See Document 410, Memorandum for the President, 28 December 1948.

When Elizabeth Bentley accused Lauchlin Currie and Harry Dexter White of passing information to Communists, ER responded by calling Bentley an "evidently neurotic lady" whom "one can only regard with regret and pity." See Document 371. AP IMAGES.

When HUAC summoned Lauchlin Currie to testify, ER wrote "why should so-called reputable people want to injure entirely innocent individuals? The answer is 'politics,'" a craving "to make the limelight," and the chance for HUAC to "whip up a little more excitement for vigilance in this country." See Document 371. TONY LINCK/TIME LIFE PICTURES/GETTY IMAGES.

Whittaker Chambers's HUAC testimony created a furor. ER, who believed Alger Hiss and Lauchlin Currie innocent, dismissed Chambers's accusations, and wondered "what the point of all this is … I wonder if all this extra-curricular Congressional activity isn't making it more difficult for the FBI to do its job well." See Document 372. © BETTMANN/CORBIS.

Most expected Truman, challenged by Wallace on the left and Thurmond on the right, to lose. To win, ER thought "the state committees" should "make an aggressive campaign, picking up every mistake made by the other side." See Document 373. U.S. SENATE COLLECTION, CENTER FOR LEGISLATIVE ARCHIVES.

Dulles, Austin, and Marshall had put "considerable responsibility" on ER. Shortly after this UN meeting, ER delivered a major address at the Sorbonne where she told the delegates "The issue of human liberty is decisive for the settlement of outstanding political differences and for the future of the United Nations." See Document 379. YALE JOEL/TIME LIFE PICTURES/GETTY IMAGES.

Count Folke Bernadotte, here with Ralph Bunche, thought the Arabs should possess the Negev, in exchange for giving all or part of Western Galilee to Israel. ER, who admired Bernadotte, disagreed, writing "It seems highly unfair to me to turn the whole of the Negev over to the Arabs." See Document 384. AFP/GETTY IMAGES.

During the fall 1948 UN meetings, ER traveled to promote the Declaration and the Marshall Plan. In Stuttgart, she expected "a cold reception ... but to my surprise the restored State Theatre was full ... though my speech was honest they received it warmly. I spoke in German, bad German." See Document 386. © BETTMANN/CORBIS.

FRUITS OF VICTORY

After congratulating Truman, ER admitted to Ed Flynn "the results of the election have left me slightly stunned … This victory," in the face of a deeply divided Democratic Party, "puts a responsibility on all of us to see that the promises made during the campaign are carried out." See Document 388. "FRUITS OF VICTORY," FROM *THE HERBLOCK BOOK* (BEACON PRESS, 1952).

THIS is the OFFICIAL DEMOCRATIC TICKET IN MISSISSIPPI

[1948]

To Vote Democratic on Tuesday, November 2nd You Will Vote This Ticket—

And You Will Vote for These Democratic Presidential Electors

Duly Nominated by the Official Mississippi State Democratic Convention and Pledged to Governors Thurmond and Wright.

TUESDAY, NOVEMBER 2nd
IS THE BIG TEST DAY FOR
ALL MISSISSIPPIANS

—Every Mississippi man and woman should vote — without fail — we must show our full strength to our enemies.

—Every Mississippi man and woman should vote the straight Democratic Ticket as shown on the right. Carry this sample ballot to the polls so you will know who the official Democratic presidential electors are.

—Make it 100 per cent for Governors Thurmond and Wright on November 2nd.

REMEMBER

A vote for Truman electors is a direct order to our Congressmen and Senators from Mississippi to vote for passage of Truman's so-called civil-rights program in the next Congress. This means the vicious FEPC — anti-poll tax — anti-lynching and anti-segregation proposals will become the law of the land and our way of life in the South will be gone forever.

If you FAIL to VOTE you are in fact casting a vote for Truman and his vicious anti-Southern program.

SAMPLE BALLOT

Below are the names of the Official Mississippi Democratic Party candidates that will appear on the official Mississippi ballot on November 2.

DEMOCRATIC PRESIDENTIAL ELECTORS
Pledged to Vote for Thurmond and Wright
(Vote for nine)

THOMAS MURPHY, JR. ....Tupelo
JACK FROST..........Oakland
FRANK EVERETT ....Indianola
HURD HORTON ....Grenada
WALTER DENT MAY ....Mendenhall
JESSE M. BYRD ....Leakesville
JULIUS BRENT ....McComb
EDMUND TAYLOR ....Greenville
CLARENCE MORGAN ....Kosciusko

UNITED STATES SENATOR
(Vote for one)
JAMES O. EASTLAND..........Ruleville

REPRESENTATIVE IN CONGRESS
First District
(Vote for one)
JOHN E. RANKIN ....Tupelo

Second District
(Vote for one)
JAMIE L. WHITTEN ....Charleston

Third District
(Vote for one)
WM. M. WHITTINGTON ....Greenwood

Fourth District
(Vote for one)
THOMAS G. ABERNETHY ....Okolona

Fifth District
(Vote for one)
ARTHUR WINSTEAD ....Philadelphia

Sixth District
(Vote for one)
WM. M. COLMER ....Pascagoula

Seventh District
(Vote for one)
JOHN BELL WILLIAMS..........Raymond

SUPREME COURT JUDGE
First Supreme Court District
(Vote for two)
JULIAN P. ALEXANDER ....Jackson
PERCY M. LEE, SR. ....Forest

Second Supreme Court District
(Vote for one)
LEE D. HALL ....Columbia

Third Supreme Court District
(Vote for one)
WM. G. ROBERDS..........West Point

CHANCELLORS
Third Chancery Court District
(Vote for one)
HERBERT HOLMES ....Senatobia

JUDGE CIRCUIT COURT
Sixteenth District
(Vote for one)
JOHN D. GREEN, JR. ....Starkville

Get in the Fight for **STATES' RIGHTS** — Fight for **THURMOND** and **WRIGHT** — Be Sure to Vote on **NOVEMBER 2nd** — and Vote the **STRAIGHT OFFICIAL DEMOCRATIC TICKET**

Published for your information by the MISSISSIPPI STATE DEMOCRATIC PARTY.

Southern Democrats deserted Truman in 1948 over his "vicious" civil rights proposals. After Truman's reelection, ER asked "what happens now to the Dixiecrats? They certainly no longer are Democrats." The "one [result] I would most like to see is the permanent ousting of the Southern Dixiecrats from the Democratic party." See Documents 388–89. COURTESY OF MISSISSIPPI DEPARTMENT OF ARCHIVES AND HISTORY.

Eva Perón, with President Juan Perón, championed the "Rights of Old Age," a proposal ensuring "old people have the right to decent housing and 'minimum home comforts,'" and pressed for the proposal's inclusion in the Declaration. That "sounds good," ER wrote, but "just what" does "minimum home comforts" mean? See Documents 397 and 402. KEYSTONE/HULTON ARCHIVES/GETTY IMAGES.

[PN: END OF ART]

ER often recorded messages in other languages for organizations she supported. For example, between final committee meetings on the Declaration, she "dashed off a minute-and-a-half speech in German [for the March of Dimes], being sure it was correct and that I could speak it understandably." See Document 405. © BETTMANN/CORBIS.

ABC signed ER and daughter Anna to co-host a radio program. "I don't mind if we don't start till Nov. 1st," ER wrote, "though I was amused at the Republican director not wanting us on the air during the campaign. I wish I thought we could have that much influence." See Document 389.
© CORBIS.

Grand Dragon Samuel Green proclaimed the KKK stood for brotherly love. ER retorted: "Since when … is the smile of friendship hidden behind a mask? The answer of course is that [the Klan] is just what it always has been—a secret, terroristic, organization, hopeful of enforcing the warped ideas of a few hoodlums." See Document 408. AP IMAGES.

363

If You Ask Me [excerpt]
Ladies' Home Journal July 1948

Please explain why it is that the nineteenth-century liberals fought for the liberation of the individual from the control of the state or government, while today's liberals seem to be always on the side of more government controls over the individual.

Because in the nineteenth century the individual had comparatively few liberties. There was no recognition that the government owed an individual certain things as a right. There were charities, but at that time the government was not conceived as doing away with charity. Now it is accepted that the government has an obligation to guard the rights of an individual so carefully that he never reaches a point which needs charity.

Nowadays the government controls which are advocated by the liberals are all to safeguard, in a modern and very complicated world, some of the things which individuals have come to feel they have a right to achieve. For instance, we insist that the government must see that every man who wants to work is able to get work suitable to his ability and at a wage on which he and his family can live. The nineteenth-century liberals did not have to face that problem and therefore no regulation was needed. Regulations have come only as our complicated civilization has made them necessary.

TMsex DLC

On the African Americans' Vote

Negro Digest, a magazine for which ER had written in 1943, solicited her contribution in 1948.[1] For an autumn issue, executive editor Ben Burns (1914?–2000) asked ER in July to assess the political options the 1948 election offered African Americans, suggesting that ER write an essay answering "Can Negroes Afford to Quit the Democrats?" ER submitted the following article, which Negro Digest elected not to publish.[2]

364

Proposed Article for *Negro Digest*
[July?] 1948

The title of your article presupposes that the majority of our Negro citizens have become Democrats. I question very much whether that is so. I think the great majority of our Negro citizens have supported the Democratic Party in the course of the last several years because they felt that Party was offering them, on the whole, a square deal and because it was in power, could actually translate into action the things which it advocated.

In New York State it is true that Governor Dewey, a Republican, put on the statute books an F.E.P.C. law but little was done to make this law show results.[3]

I feel, however, that the natural attitude of our colored citizens who feel that in many ways their rights have been ignored, is not one of hard and fast party affiliation, but that they belong to the big group of independent voters who throw their weight wherever they feel lies the greatest opportunity for achieving the results they desire.

Judged by that standard, it seems to me that the average Negro citizen would probably do as well to remain in the Democratic fold. As I look back over the legislation passed during the last few years, I find that practically all the progressive legislation has been passed during Democratic administrations. The underprivileged groups benefit more from progressive legislation than do the privileged groups. That is one of the first and most obvious reasons for their remaining faithful to the Democratic Party.

No group in this country, of course, votes in a block and there will be, as there always have been, a great many Republicans among this group, a great many Wallace followers, but by and large, the gains of the Negro people in the last sixteen years, have been very great and they have been accomplished under Democratic leadership which believes in progressive measures. The people themselves must decide to keep a liberal party in power and prod them into remaining liberal. It would be wise for our Negro citizens to weigh where their influence can count the most.

Eleanor Roosevelt.

TStmt AERP, FDRL

———————————

1. In 1943, ER submitted an essay to *Negro Digest* that ran under the title, "If I Were a Negro," a recurring guest column in which non-African American writers offered their meditations on this topic. In her submission, ER wrote:

If I were a Negro today, I think I would have moments of great bitterness. It would be hard for me to sustain my faith in democracy and to build up a sense of goodwill toward men of other races …

... I would still feel that I ought to participate to the full in this war. When the United Nations win, certain things will be accepted as a result of principles which have been enunciated by the leaders of the United Nations, which never before have been part of the beliefs and practices of the greater part of the world ("If I Were a Negro: Freedom: Promise or Fact," *Negro Digest*, October 1943, 8–9).

2. The only election-related article the *Negro Digest* published that year was John Temple Graves's October piece entitled "Will the South Ever Go Republican?" Graves's article focused more on the question of whether white Southern voters would switch parties rather than on the party loyalty of African Americans; nothing on that topic appeared in the magazine in the fall of 1948 in lieu of ER's submission (Ben Burns to ER, 8 July 1948, AERP; ER to Ben Burns, 17 July 1948, AERP; Curtis Lawrence, "Ben Burns, First Ebony Editor," *Chicago Sun-Times*, 2 February 2000, 71; John Temple Graves, "Will the South Ever Go Republican?" *Negro Digest*, October 1948, 46–48).

3. In his solicitation to ER, Burns suggested she consider the matter of candidate Thomas Dewey's potential "attractive allure" for black voters because of "his record on the state FEPC in New York." On Dewey's record on the Fair Employment Practices Commission, see *n*7 Document 16 and *n*17 Document 143 (Ben Burns to ER, 8 July 1948, AERP).

Du Bois Meets with ER

With the heightening of international tensions in 1947, Walter White and W. E. B. Du Bois disagreed over how to proceed with publicizing discriminatory practices in the United States. White sympathized with ER and saw in her a valuable ally. When ER told him that she would have publicly endorsed the NAACP's petition had it not been for the propaganda value her support would have provided the Soviets, White accepted her argument. Du Bois, on the other hand, refused to accept that tensions between the United States and USSR should prevent the NAACP from addressing the problem of racial discrimination in the United States.[1] In several letters to Warren Austin in 1947 and 1948, Du Bois urged the delegate to do all within his power to place the NAACP's petition on the General Assembly's agenda. Aware of the reasons for the State Department's reluctance to discuss US race problems in the General Assembly, February 4, 1948, Du Bois wrote in his final letter to Austin:

> It would be a matter of fine and forward-looking statesmanship if the United States would itself voluntarily bring this matter forward to be discussed before the nations, and attest that while our democracy is not perfect, we are perfectly willing to acknowledge our faults and to bring the matter before the world, with the promise and hope that this unfortunate condition will be corrected within the near future.[2]

After the department sat on the Du Bois letter for months, Richard S. Winslow, the Secretary-General of the US Mission to the UN, suggested on May 25 that, rather than write another reply to Du Bois, ER arrange a personal meeting with him. "In view of Ambassador Austin's very great preoccupation with crucial Security Council affairs at this time and because of Mrs. Roosevelt's unexcelled qualifications for handling this particular problem," reasoned Winslow, "it would be deeply appreciated by Ambassador Austin if Mrs. Roosevelt would undertake to handle this matter personally with Dr. DuBois."[3]

Although she expressed concern that the department had taken so long to reply to Du Bois's February 4 letter, ER agreed to meet with the NAACP representative to discuss the State Department's position on the NAACP's petition. Du Bois's recollection of that discussion, which he prepared for White and copied to ER, appears below.

365

W. E. B. Du Bois to Walter White
1 July 1948

Subject: Meeting with Mrs. Eleanor Roosevelt—NAACP Petition

On June 30, I was asked to call on Mrs. Roosevelt at 2 Park Avenue, the offices of the United States Delegation to the United Nations. I talked with her for about one-half hour. She represented Senator Warren Austin, the head of the United States Delegation. What she said was in answer to a letter that I had written to Senator Austin on October 28, 1947. The essence of that letter was as follows:

> Replying to your letter of October 21, I am taking the opportunity of sending you a copy of our petition to the United Nations. I trust that you will do your best to have this matter put on the agenda of the United Nations Assembly, either this year or next. I think it would be an excellent thing if the United States was able to say to the world:

We are perfectly willing to be criticized as to our democracy and to give the public a chance to know what that criticism is.

Senator Austin wrote: "Upon receipt of a copy of your petition, we will be glad to refer it to the Department of State for appropriate consideration."

Mrs. Roosevelt said that the State Department had communicated its decision, and as Mr. Austin was engaged on the Security Council, she was representing him. The Department of State was of the opinion that it would be unwise to put our Petition on the agenda of the next Assembly for discussion, since no good could come from such a discussion. On the other hand, the Declaration of Human Rights, and it was to be hoped also the Covenant, would come up at that session and be discussed and possibly assented to.

I replied that I realized that no international action on our plight was probable nor, indeed, expected; but that I thought that the world ought to know just exactly what the situation was in the United States, so that they would not be depending upon vague references concerning our race problem, but would have factual statements before them; and that if the United States was unwilling itself to put the matter before the Assembly, that one or two other nations had expressed the possibility of their doing this.

Mrs. Roosevelt thought that this would be embarrassing; that it would be seized upon by the Soviet Government and others as an excuse for attacking the United States. Mrs. Roosevelt said that already, several times, she had been compelled to answer attacks upon the United States for its race problem by pointing out the fact that other countries had made similar mistakes. In case, therefore, the matter was discussed in the Assembly, she and her colleagues would be put in the unpleasant position of having to defend the United States. The situation then might be so unpleasant that she would feel it necessary to resign from the United States Delegation to the United Nations.[4]

I expressed the opinion that the placing of facts before an international body need not of necessity be a matter of embarrassment. Naturally, it might be taken up by persons and organizations unfriendly to the United States; but that that was not a reason for suppressing the truth. That in the early days of the National Association for the Advancement of Colored People, when we proposed to expose the facts concerning lynching and discrimination, there many good friends of the Negro race who advised against it and said that it would bring unfavorable criticism upon us. Nevertheless, we insisted and I think that we did right.

Mrs. Roosevelt asked that if any action was taken toward bringing the matter up for discussion before the Assembly of the United Nations, that she be notified as soon as possible, so that she could prepare to act accordingly. I promised that such notification would certainly be given to her.

TMemc AERP, FDRL

———————

1. See header Document 285 for earlier signs of the growing rift between Du Bois and White. See also, A. Black, *Casting*, 100–102; Lewis, 531–34; Janken, 309–13.

2. W. E. B. Du Bois to Warren Austin, 10 and 14 October 1947, and 4 February 1948, NAACP, DLC.

3. Richard Winslow to James Hendrick, 25 May 1948, AERP.

4. In September 1948, Du Bois paraphrased this part of his conversation with ER in a public attack on the NAACP Board of Directors and the Truman administration that ultimately led to his dismissal from the NAACP. According to Du Bois biographer David Levering Lewis, Du Bois hoped to attend the upcoming UN meeting in Paris as a representative of the association; thus, when the board announced its decision to send Walter White as a consultant to the US delegation on

September 7, Du Bois knew that his petition would not be presented to the General Assembly. He then drafted a memo to the board (which he released to the press before submitting it to the board) labeling the decision to send White to Paris, "without a clear, open, public declaration by the board of our position on the Truman foreign policy," an implicit endorsement of the administration's policies which "would, in the long run, align the association with the reactionary, war-mongering colonial imperialism of the present Administration." Finally, he declared that he would never endorse an administration that not only showed a lack of interest in addressing the NAACP's petition, but that also actively "refused … to allow any other nation to bring this matter up." As support for this point of view, Du Bois claimed that "Mrs. Eleanor Roosevelt has declared she would probably resign from the United States delegation" if any other nation raised the issue of US race relations in the General Assembly. September 13, the NAACP Board passed a motion at its regularly scheduled board refusing to renew Du Bois's contract: "That in the view of Dr. Du Bois's written refusal to cooperate with the NAACP executive staff of which he is a member in preparation for representation at the forthcoming meeting at the General Assembly of the UN, in view of his distribution of his memorandum of September 7, addressed to this Board, before its consideration by this Board, it is the conclusion of this Board that it will not be in the best interest of the association to continue the employment of Dr. Du Bois beyond his present contract" ("Racial Unit Scored As Aiding Truman," *NYT*, 9 September 1948, 27; "Negro Group Ousts Its Research Head," *NYT*, 14 September 1948, 25; Lewis, 534, 677; Janken, 309–13, 317; and NAACP Board Minutes, 13 September 1948, NAACP DLC).

ON JAMES HENDRICK'S RESIGNATION FROM THE UNITED NATIONS

ER considered James Hendrick a key and valuable resource in her work with the Human Rights Commission, writing Dean Rusk in mid-June "how deeply" she "appreciated the very remarkable work Jim Hendrick has done during this session." She continued, that without "help such as [he] was able to organize, and which he and other people assigned to me were able to give," she doubted that "the results would have been nearly as satisfactory to the Department." She concluded, thanking Rusk for "having some one as able and as easy and as pleasant to work with … assigned to me." [1]

However, Walter Kotschnig, Hendrick's immediate supervisor at the State Department, did not agree with ER's assessment and on March 31 rated Hendrick's performance as "adequate" rather than "outstanding," taking particular aim at the trait ER praised: "effectiveness in presenting ideas or facts." As the dispute with Kotschnig escalated, Hendrick offered his resignation to the State Department in late June and on July 2, ER sent the following blunt rebuke of Kotschnig's decision and the politics she thought behind it.[2] If Kotschnig replied, neither he nor ER kept a copy of his letter.

366

Eleanor Roosevelt to Walter Kotschnig

2 July 1948 [Hyde Park]

My dear Dr. Kotschnig:

I have just heard of Jim Hendrick's resignation and the reasons for it. I am rather upset about it because I can think of no one with as good a background on Human Rights and whose established relationships and accumulation of knowledge can be as helpful to whomever the United States member may be.

Jim has always organized the complete working force and it has functioned harmoniously, and well, at least as far as I am concerned and I would not want to work with any one else.

I realize perfectly that the State Department takes no interest in Human Rights and does not think it very important whether the Commission functions or not, but without some one as good as Jim, I think whoever you had as a member would be ineffectual, and I suppose even when the Department is not deeply interested in the subject, it would still want the United States to be properly represented.

This situation disturbs me greatly and I wonder if there is a chance that the Department will reconsider it?

Very sincerely yours,
Mrs. Franklin D. Roosevelt

TLd AERP, FDRL

Although ER did not send a copy of her letter to Kotschnig to Rusk, Rusk addressed his response to her letter in the correspondence below.

_367_

Dean Rusk to Eleanor Roosevelt
12 July 1948 [Washington, DC]

Dear Mrs. Roosevelt:

I was very much disturbed upon returning from a month in California to learn that Jim Hendrick had resigned.[3] I was even more disturbed by your letter of July 2 to Mr. Kotschnig which was the first intimation I had that Mr. Hendrick's resignation was connected with difficulties which he had encountered in the Department.

When I first came to the Department of State last year I talked human rights matters over with Mr. Hendrick and his staff and was satisfied that they could be counted upon to keep a strong human rights program moving along as fast as circumstances would permit. I specifically urged them to exercise strong leadership in that field and to press for an adequate program. In addition to that, I know that the Department and the White House wished to leave you yourself maximum freedom of action in the same field.

Both Mr. Sandifer and Mr. Kotschnig made a strong effort to persuade Mr. Hendrick to stay on his assignment. Although promotions are "frozen" by the administrative side of the Department at the present time, it was indicated to Mr. Hendrick that we thought we could get a promotion through for him within a period of two months. Our anxiety to keep him was due not only to his abilities as such but also to the fact that he was carrying responsibilities with you and with the forthcoming session of ECOSOC for which we had no replacement.

I feel certain that there is a misunderstanding somewhere because in a note of June 28 to me Mr. Hendrick said, "In the last analysis it seemed to me that the best thing to do was to be guided principally by Mrs. Roosevelt's advice, and her advice on the subject was so very definite that my decision to leave became inevitable."[4]

If there is any likelihood that Mr. Hendrick wishes to reconsider his resignation, his desk is here waiting for him. Perhaps you know of factors which have escaped me and which you could discuss with Mr. Hendrick and bring about his return. As a matter of fact, his resignation has not been formally tendered and formally accepted; there would be no red tape about his return.

On your general feeling that the Department is not interested in human rights, again I believe that there is some misunderstanding—possibly in the Department. Unfortunately, my own time is completely occupied by the specific disputes before the Security Council and the General Assembly and I have had to rely upon Jim Hendrick and his staff to carry on in the field of human rights. The only instances I know of in which any difference of view had developed between you and the Department resulted, I was assured, in an agreement entirely satisfactory to you.[5]

I shall get in touch with Jim Hendrick immediately to discover what his real wishes are in the matter of his appointment and very much hope that he will return to his work. In his note to me he intimated that he would eventually like to return.[6] Would you be willing to see me at your earliest convenience to go over our work on human rights in order that I might learn more about the differences which you feel have developed between the Department and yourself on this subject? I know that the Department is interested in a vigorous human rights program and any impression to the contrary on your part suggests that something has slipped down here.

Sincerely yours,
Dean Rusk

TLS AERP, FDRL

368

Eleanor Roosevelt to Dean Rusk
13 July 1948 [Hyde Park]

Dear Mr. Rusk:

Thank you for your letter of July 12th. I think, however, your information is slightly erroneous on the subject of Jim Hendrick's resignation and I do hope you will at least ask him to come and tell you his real story.

Mr. Sandifer has always been friendly and absolutely fair.[7] Dr. Kotschnig is the one I think, who made Mr. Hendrick's situation untenable. He told me of the situation and I told him I thought no man had a right to stay in a position where he did not feel he was able to give to the maximum of his ability and that if he felt he could do better work in this new position, he should take it.

I am sure Mr. Hendrick could not return unless there was a very clear understanding not only that he was not demoted, which he told me he had been on his return from the Human Rights Commission meeting in New York, but that the rating given him by Dr. Kotschnig was not completely satisfactory.[8]

I can think of no one with whom I would rather work, and no one whose loss to the Human Rights Commission is greater. I could only conclude that the treatment given him by Dr. Kotschnig had been given because the Human Rights Commission seemed to the Department so unimportant they did not think he was deserving of retaining his same standing.

As far as I am concerned, there has never been anything which Jim Hendrick and I have not worked out with the Department, not always, I fear, to the Department's entire satisfaction, but nearly always so.

I shall be delighted to see you any time you happen to be in New York City. I can come down, or I would be happy to have you come up here for a night.

Very cordially yours,
Eleanor Roosevelt

TLS RG59, NARA II

---

1. ER to Dean Rusk, 19 June 1948, JPHP, HSTL. For examples of the ER-Hendrick collaboration see Document 295. For information on Dean Rusk, see Biographical Portraits.

2. On Walter Kotschnig, see Biographical Portraits. This was not the first time ER had attempted to influence personnel matters in the State Department. In May 1947, she wrote a letter to George Warren, advisor on refugees and displaced persons, concerning the resignation of Arthur J. Altmeyer:

> I am very much troubled about this rumor that Mr. Altmeyer might resign. I have written him an airmail letter, telling him how important I think it is for him to stay on.
>
> If there is anything you can do in the State Department to urge upon him to stay even until September, I hope you will do it … (ER to George Warren, 14 May 1948, RG84, NARA II).

3. Hendrick wrote Rusk June 28 to inform Rusk of his decision to resign. Rusk replied July 7, saying that he was "sorry the circumstances are such that we did not work more closely together," and that "was partly [Hendrick's] fault" as "early in his assignment," Rusk "satisfied [himself] that your attitude on human rights was what we needed in the UNA" and that he could:

> count on [Hendrick] to keep the cause of human rights moving as fast and as strongly as the traffic would bear at any particular time. The great amount of independence with which you were allowed to operate was directly due to that confidence of mine that you would keep pressing for an adequate human rights program until curbed by higher authority.

Rusk concluded by saying that "it will be almost impossible to find a replacement who can do the thing" Hendrick managed and that while he was "not discouraged about the prospects for an adequate human rights program," he "fully recognize[d] that much bitter controversy is ahead of us if we are to mend some of our ways on these matters" (Dean Rusk to James Hendrick, 7 July 1948, JPHP, HSTL).

4. James Hendrick to Dean Rusk, 28 June 1948, JPHP, HSTL.

5. For examples of disagreement between the State Department and ER and the HRC over the drafting of the human rights covenant, see header Document 289 and header Document 295.

6. In a letter to ER dated July 22, Hendrick summarized a discussion he had with Rusk, which probably took place after Rusk wrote to ER:

> I told him there was no use in my trying to work for a person who didn't trust me and whom I didn't trust, and I recited at some length the difficulties I had had. I believe Dean got the point; but he felt it was too late to make readjustments. He did try his best to keep me on—but under unchanged circumstances. So we parted, regretfully, with nothing accomplished. The only spark of hope was that maybe the great work in Human Rights lies ahead of us—not in the next two years, but after that. By this time it may be that circumstances in the State Department will have changed; and if it is humanly possible I shall then be back clamoring at Dean Rusk's and Sandy's [Deputy Assistant Secretary for UN Affairs Durward Sandifer] doors for a job, and hope that the doors will be open.

Hendrick wrote to ER again the next day to add that he felt he had "underestimated the degree of cooperation Dean Rusk offered me," and that Rusk was "doing his best" to keep Hendrick at the Human Rights Commission. He then reported that Rusk had suggested he be transferred to the legal advisor's office, an opportunity Hendrick felt "would be good, perhaps, for a short time but death over a long stretch" because of what Hendrick observed to be a "general atmosphere ... of defeatism" and opposition in the department to the Covenant on Human Rights (Dean Rusk to James Hendrick, 7 July 1948, JPHP, HSTL; James Hendrick to ER, 22 July 1948, AERP; James Hendrick to ER, 23 July 1948, AERP).

7. The same report included Durward Sandifer's review, stating Kotschnig's opinion "that while Mr. Hendrick's individual performance is excellent, his work in directing the work of his subordinates is not outstandingly effective." It is unclear from available documentation to which "subordinates" or events this comment referenced (US Civil Service Commission, "Report of Efficiency Rating," 31 March 1948, JPHP, HSTL).

8. Hendrick did not return to the State Department after his resignation, but instead joined the Economic Cooperation Administration (ECA), the initial implementing agency of the Marshall Plan, in August 1948 (James Hendrick to ER, 18 August 1948, AERP).

ON WALLACE, THE PCA, AND THE MUNDT-NIXON BILL

On June 4, 1948, ER once again used her column to discuss the anti-Communist Mundt bill. Most pundits believed that the bill, which passed the House in May, would die in the Senate Judiciary Committee where members debated the bill's constitutionality. Nevertheless, opponents of the bill converged in Washington by the thousands and staged mass pickets before the White House and the Capitol. Commenting on the spectacle, the *New York Times* reported that the Mundt bill "has stirred divisions so violent as to be without example here in many years."[1] ER, who remained opposed to the bill, questioned the tactics of those who protested the bill in Washington:

> I am afraid that the demonstrations in Washington against the Mundt Bill will have the effect of gaining votes for it rather than reducing them. Why Henry Wallace allows his party to lend itself to this kind of perfectly open Communist manipulation, I will never be able to understand.
>
> If the Mundt Bill passes, it will be one more thing on which the Communists can attack us—another piece of restrictive legislation which all of us who are liberals will deeply regret. It is naive and absurd not to recognize the fact that the Communists will be enchanted if it passes, and that, in inspiring demonstrations such as have occurred in the national capital, they are carrying on the same sort of maneuvers that they have used before. The Communists are using other people, notably Wallace's third party, to accomplish the ends they have in view—their usual tactics.[2]

After reading this column in the *Chicago Sun-Times*, Roy N. Lokken, one of several erstwhile ER supporters to protest her attitude towards Wallace and the Progressives, sent ER a six-page, single-spaced, typewritten letter on June 20. Lokken, a World War II veteran and founding member of Washington State's Progressive Party, argued that "had it not been for the leadership of Henry Wallace and the Progressive Party the Mundt Bill would be the law of the land now." Moreover, he asserted that, in addition to failing to recognize this contribution, ER's columns included "several misrepresentations and falsehoods" concerning Wallace and the Progressives which he would "not like to believe ... were deliberate." He "would rather believe" that ER was "misinformed." Yet he could not help but argue:

> The record shows, however, that since January you have engaged in a number of ill-advised and not altogether truthful attacks on the intellectual integrity of Henry A. Wallace and the intentions of the members of the new party movement. Either you have been much too busy to get the facts, or you have acted out of a desire to protect the party of your husband. The latter reason may be understandable, but I can see no moral foundation for placing party above country, political expediency above the truth. The former reason would constitute intellectual dishonesty which I find it hard to believe of you.

He then disputed the criticisms the Americans for Democratic Action (ADA) launched at his organization, declaring that only the Progressive Party provided the:

> genuine progressive leadership (no generals) and work for the things all progressives profess to believe in, and ADA shoots spitwads at us. I am sorry to say these things, but what else can I say of a group which, for all its high-sounding pretensions, has actually made a record for itself of inaction, defeatism, and ineptness. We are attacked as being barbaric agitators, etc. That is the price

dynamic liberalism has had to pay ever since the days of Jefferson's republicans, when they were called Jacobins and were accused of being inspired by agents of the French government. But it is because we are dynamic, because we are working for progressive principles, that we are attacked. The attacks against us are eloquent testimonies that we are working and that our work is getting results. The ADA is not so attacked, it achieves "respectability," because of its inertia, which suits reaction just fine. The less you do the better you are treated. It is when you get out and work for the things you believe in that you are attacked. Witness the life of your own husband.

Lokken concluded his letter with a challenge to ER: "I hope for better things from you in the future, as there have been better things from you in the past."[3]

ER wrote the following letter in response to this criticism.

_369_

Eleanor Roosevelt to Roy Lokken

10 July 1948 [Hyde Park]

My dear Mr. Lokken:

I would be very much obliged if you would tell me what were the misrepresentations and falsehoods in my column of June 20, 1948. I have never said anything about Mr. Wallace and the third party and its campaign which I did not believe was completely truthful.

If you can prove that I was wrong, I shall be delighted to have you do so.

I am not trying to protect the Democratic Party. I do not consider it necessary where I am concerned. There are other people politically active, who can do that far better than I can. I have never placed either party or political expedience above what I thought was truthful and right.

It was not, in my opinion, the Wallace opposition which helped to defeat the Mundt Bill. It was the opposition of the moderates and liberals in Congress and out of Congress who had no taint of communist affiliation. It was my fear that because of that affiliation, the third party demonstration would do more harm than good.

What you did with your Congressman was excellent but you may be sure it was not the fear of your group alone that changed his mind. I read the Mundt Bill in the press and I imagine it was not carried in your area because your papers haven't the space. After all the effect that you had is a matter of opinion and you may be quite correct in thinking that your party had more affect than I happen to think it had.[4]

You do not seem to understand, or perhaps I was not clear enough in explaining what I meant by saying that the communists would be enchanted if the Mundt Bill passed. Of course, the communists have agitated against the Bill but you should know by now that all communists are glad when bad things come to pass, because one of their objectives is confusion and lack of unity in the democracies.[5]

When you list people who opposed the Bill you show what strength there was against it and minimize the very point you are trying to make, namely, that the third party had such tremendous influence.

I have read the Bill and know just how bad it would have been not for communists alone and I have consistently opposed it.

The support which the communists gave my husband was quite different from the power they have in the third party at present. They are a heart core that does much of the organizing. That does not mean that in your area they have control perhaps, but it does mean that they have control, sometimes without people knowing it, in many important third party organizations.[6]

You sound like a most admirable person and I am so glad you do not entirely brush aside Mr. Marx and that you have decided we can learn from the Soviet Union and they can learn some things from us. That is very broadminded of you.

Some of the things you list as communist, of course, have been planned by the socialists and I think that when you label them all as communist you show a certain lack of understanding of what practical communism is in the USSR today. You are quite right about the Soviet Constitution. It reads very well but it is one thing to give lip service to things and quite another to live by them.[7]

I happen to think the New Deal was democratic and not communist but you have a right to your own opinion. I imagine I have worked more with the communists and understand them better than you do. I believe we will some day be able to live peacefully side by side but it will take a great deal of patience and understanding and force equal to theirs before we will achieve any kind of compromise on their part. If you will look back I think you will find that most of the liberal legislation in this country has been initiated and carried through in democratic administrations, so I would not be quite as pessimistic as you are. If Mr. Wallace's third party is defeated, I would not feel utterly hopeless of having a more liberal democratic party in the future repeat the history of the past.

I am glad you read the article in Foreign Affairs but you evidently do not know that the very things you suggest I should say in my column, I have said a number of times.[8]

I am sure you are entirely honest but you might feel better about other people if you at least believed in their honesty also.

Very sincerely yours,

TLc AERP, FDRL

---

1. "Future of Mundt Bill Clouded in Bitter Fight," *NYT*, 6 June 1948, E7. See Document 356 for background on the Mundt-Nixon bill.

2. *MD*, 4 June 1948.

3. Roy N. Lokken to ER, 20 June 1948, AERP.

4. According to Lokken, Progressives alone were responsible for publicizing the Mundt bill. By not running the full text in the papers, the commercial press was attempting "to fool the people by keeping them in ignorance." He believed that "when people read the bill they protested it," and the Progressive Party distributed free pamphlets including the full text of the bill to solidify opposition to anti-Communist legislation. He also informed ER that his own representative, Henry N. Jackson (D-WA), admitted publicly that he had not read a copy of the bill until the Progressives provided him with one (Roy N. Lokken to ER, 20 June 1948, AERP).

5. Responding to ER's assertion that "it is naive and absurd not to recognize the fact that the Communists will be enchanted if it [the Mundt bill] passes," Lokken wrote:

> The Communists, of course, have agitated considerably against the bill since it does militate against them. It would be 'naive and absurd' to expect them to have remained quiet. Communist Party advertising against the bill was published in the Hearst *Seattle Post-Intelligencer*, probably because that Republican newspaper supposed, as you did, that

such advertising would reduce opposition to the bill. Actually, public sentiment against the bill grew and crystallized so rapidly that passage of the bill so near to election time became politically impractical (Roy N. Lokken to ER, 20 June 1948, AERP).

6. Drawing parallels between the willingness of the Democrats to work with Communists during the Popular Front Era of the 1930s and the Progressives' willingness to do the same in the current political situation, Lokken wrote, "The fact that the Communists supported the New Deal and the progressive legislation of the New Deal era did not provoke me to join the Republicans in attacking the New Deal on the grounds that it was communistic. The fact that the Communists now support Henry A. Wallace and the new party movement does not deter me from joining and working for that movement" (Roy N. Lokken to ER, 20 June 1948, AERP).

7. "My political bible is Jefferson, not Marx," wrote Lokken. However, he viewed capitalism as an economic system that has "always militated against democratic action." Attributing many progressive reforms to the ideas of Marx and Engels as spelled out in *The Communist Manifesto*, Lokken believed that "the graduated income tax, the inheritance tax, the U.S. Post office department, public power, soil reclamation and conservation, reforestation, [and] vocational and industrial education" were examples of "communistic" legislation. He also praised the Soviet Constitution of 1936, arguing that it contained "a civil rights provision unequaled … by any other government in the world" (Roy N. Lokken to ER, 20 June 1948, AERP).

8. Lokken read ER's "The Promise of Human Rights," published in the April 1948 issue of *Foreign Affairs*, and praised her for noting the contribution of the Soviet delegate in fighting for the inclusion of social and economic rights in the declaration of human rights. He noted, however, that *Foreign Affairs* had a relatively small audience compared to My Day and asked her to talk more about cooperating with the Soviets in her column ("The Problem of Human Rights," *Foreign Affairs* 26, April 1948, 470–77, reprinted in A. Black, *What I Hope*, 553–58; Roy N. Lokken to ER, 20 June 1948, AERP).

ON RETURNING THE RUHR TO GERMANY

Throughout 1948, ER remained concerned about the reindustrialization of western Germany's Ruhr Valley and its return to German control. As she noted in a January column, ER particularly worried that the Allied decision to allow former Nazis to participate in the area's rebuilding could reinvigorate tensions capable of starting another war. She criticized Allied reluctance to take "a firm stand, for instance, on the German occupation of the Ruhr," and argued that "we turned our eyes away, partly because our own big business people had an interest in the big business combinations which have branches in almost all of the great countries." Although she conceded that "it is very evident that a healthy Europe must have in the heart of it—in Germany—a self-supporting and contented people," she argued "that does not mean that the great business magnates of Germany, who transferred their wealth to Switzerland, Spain and the Argentine, must be allowed again, in alliance with other big business men, to build up the kind of German economy which would again lead to war."[1]

Throughout April and May she exchanged articles and letters about this issue with her friend Betty Hight, who pointed out to ER that industrial cartels such as I. G. Farben continued to thrive despite US and British control. In anticipation of writing on the subject in her columns or personal letters, ER asked Secretary Marshall for his clarification on the matter.[2]

370

Eleanor Roosevelt to George Marshall
23 July 1948 [Hyde Park]

Dear Mr. Secretary:

I am still getting many rumors to the effect that we are rehabilitating German industry in a way that will benefit the old time German industrialists and that there is still a chance that instead of internationalizing the Ruhr we will turn it back to the German owners. I cannot believe that the people of our country really want to repeat the mistakes that were made before.

Is there anything you can tell me that I can say to people who write me on this subject, to allay their fears?[3]

Very sincerely yours,
Eleanor Roosevelt

TLS RG59, NARA II

---

1. *MD*, 6 January 1948, AERP. On earlier controversies over the reindustrialization and re-Germanification of the Ruhr Valley, see Document 198 and Document 223.

2. ER's friend Betty Hight expressed concern about the reindustrialization of Germany in several letters to ER between May and July. On June 28, Hight wrote:

   I still cannot help but feel that the French are right—the question of ownership of Ruhr industry should be settled now, before Germany is back on her feet. I have not yet heard any honest, forthright statement from U.S. leaders as to why they oppose this policy or what they have in mind for Germany.

In July, Hight sent ER an article by Jean Pajus, a former advisor to the Foreign Economic Administration, that expressed strong disapproval of the presence of Nazi war criminals in positions of power in the US- and British-controlled zones of Germany. The article listed several former members of Hitler's cabinet and Nazi financiers who remained as heads of banks and industrial concerns after the war. Pajus lamented that despite this and the Germans' resistance to cooperating with economic reforms, "the Germans will continue to receive billions from the United States Treasury." Pajus also criticized what he considered the slow effort by the American Bar of Justice at Nuremberg at prosecuting German war criminals, noting that executives at Krupp Munitions and I. G. Farben were being acquitted or receiving amnesty.

July 23, ER wrote Hight that she did not think that:

> my getting hold of Mr. Pajus would do me much good. I have asked Secretary Marshall to tell me honestly what his ideas are on rehabilitation of German industries and what plan they really hold on the Rhur. Whether I will get anything helpful or not, I do not know (Betty Hight to ER, 28 June 1948; Betty Hight to ER, 12 July 1948; and ER to Betty Hight, 23 July 1948, AERP; Jean Pajus, "Have We Learned Our German Lesson? Some Facts Which Raise the Question," The *Churchman*, 1 July 1948, 13–15).

3. August 11, three weeks later, Assistant Secretary of State Charles E. Saltzman replied to ER on Marshall's behalf. Saltzman told ER:

> I think it is fair to say that our progress in the rehabilitation of German industries as a whole, and the Ruhr industries in particular, will inure to the benefit of the European economy rather than of the former German industrialists … This is a problem which is still under consideration between this Government and the other interested countries. It will be resolved in a manner to ensure that the tremendous economic potential of these industries will never again be used to contribute to any future threat to the peace of the world.
>
> The question of the former German owners regaining control of these properties becomes more and more academic as many of these owners, through conviction in denazification proceedings and war crimes trials, are deprived of whatever ownership rights they might have by means of the penalty of confiscation.

Despite these assurances from the State Department, ER continued to lament the possibility of re-nazification of the Ruhr in My Day. In December 1948, she wrote:

> Germany is, of course, destroyed to a far greater extent today. It will take longer to rebuild the country than it did the first time. And, there is no question in my mind that there are people in Germany and forces outside of Germany related to the old Nazi regime who would like nothing better than to repeat the pattern of the old days no matter how long it might take (Charles E. Saltzman to ER, 11 August 1948, AERP; *MD*, 17 December 1948).

ON CURRIE, HISS, AND THE HOUSE UN-AMERICAN ACTIVITIES COMMITTEE

July 31, confessed Soviet agent Elizabeth Bentley named the economist Lauchlin Currie, a former member of the Federal Reserve Board and special economic assistant to FDR,[1] and former assistant secretary of the treasury Harry Dexter White[2] as sources of American military intelligence to the Soviet Union. Bentley, who had never met the men and admitted that she only "suspected" they passed information, singled out Currie, in particular, as the source who allegedly "tipped off" the Soviets that the United States had broken the Russian military code. Currie vigorously denied the accusation, telling the *New York Times* that he "never met Miss Bentley or knew of her existence" and that he had "never known nor associated in any way directly or indirectly with either a Communist or a Communist agent."[3]

Two days after the story broke, ER devoted My Day to attacking the tactics Bentley, "this evidently neurotic lady" whom "one can only regard with regret and pity," leveled against Currie. "It seems to me quite outrageous to use this method of smearing people when you cannot produce proof." She continued:

> … to testify that a reputable person like Lauchlin Currie, whom the lady admits she never saw and has no proof of any kind against him, has furnished her with confidential information can only serve to make those who do not know him wonder if there isn't some tangible proof. The natural question to ask is why should so-called reputable people want to injure entirely innocent individuals? The answer, it seems to me, is "politics" and the chance to make the limelight and whip up a little more excitement for vigilance in this country on the part of the Un-American Activities Committee.
>
> Whether they make people suffer unjustifiably in so doing seems to be of no more importance, except to those among us who believe the Constitution protects us against such goings-on.[4]

She continued this theme three days later, drawing her readers' attention to an editorial in "one of our great metropolitan morning newspapers" which argued that "if there is one thing above all others in our American way of life in which most thoughtful citizens take pride … it is the principles of civil rights enunciated in the first ten amendments to our Constitution." While ER knew that "all of our citizens will not agree with this editorial," she nevertheless wanted their attention drawn to the "precious heritage in this country of protection of the innocent against false accusation, of a fair trial even for the guilty. What price a few headlines if those rights are compromised or violated? A dubious security purchased by those means would be bought far too high."[5]

When Currie appeared before HUAC August 13, he answered all questions presented to him. He told the committee that he had "no knowledge" that the Soviet code was about the be deciphered, that he did not disclose "any inside information," and that his contact with Nathan Gregory Silverman, the economist currently under a loyalty board investigation, was minimal—that he had merely "referred" a request to complete Silverman's appeal to the War Department. As the evidence at the time remained highly ambiguous and after giving his testimony to HUAC, the committee opted not to indict Currie after he testified and shifted its attention to the Alger Hiss case (see next document).

Currie then wrote to thank ER for the support she had given him in her column. However, two years after Currie's death, the National Security Agency began to release its wartime decryptions of Soviet spy communications; among these thousands of documents were KGB messages mentioning contacts with Currie, both via Bentley's spy ring and directly with Soviet officials in the United States.[6]

371

Lauchlin Currie to Eleanor Roosevelt

16 August 1948 [New York City]

Dear Mrs. Roosevelt:

I can't tell you how much I appreciated your mention of me and my case in several of your recent columns. They encouraged me when I needed encouragement badly and many people called my attention to them.

As you perhaps knew, I asked to testify in order that I might deny under oath the Bentley woman's preposterous charge.[7] I really can't complain of the treatment I received at the hands of the Committee during my own actual hearings and Congressman Mundt even went so far as to say that he believed in my Americanism.[8] However, as you pointed out, the Committee had already done the damage by providing a national forum for the airing of Miss Bentley's charges, and I suppose that for the rest of my life and in my obituary my name will be linked with this investigation.

You might be interested in glancing over the prepared statement the Committee permitted me to read.[9]

Again my heartiest thanks.

Sincerely,
Lauchlin Currie

TLS AERP, FDRL

Along with Lauchlin Currie and Harry Dexter White, Elizabeth Bentley also named as a former Communist agent Whittaker Chambers (1901–1961), a senior editor for *Time* magazine. When Chambers appeared before the Thomas committee on August 3 to answer Bentley's charges, he not only admitted to his former membership in the Communist Party, but also offered another name: Alger Hiss, a former clerk to justice Felix Frankfurter and aide to FDR, who then served as president of the Carnegie Endowment for International Peace.[10]

Chambers claimed Hiss was one of the leaders of the "underground" Washington, D.C., group that Chambers managed in the 1930s. Moreover, Chambers told the committee that when he realized he would have to testify against Hiss, he, "at great personal risk," tried to persuade Hiss "to break away from this group." Chambers then concluded his remarks with a dramatic image describing Hiss's tears as they "separated" and Hiss's vague pronouncements about "'the party line' and [how he] wouldn't break with the party."[11]

Two days later, Hiss came before the committee to respond to Chambers's allegations, declaring that not only had he never met Chambers, but that he also "not now and never [had] been a member of the Communist Party," that he "never had been a member of any Communist-front organization," that he had never "followed the Communist Party line directly or indirectly," and that to the best of his "knowledge none of my friends is a Communist." When questioned about Hiss's response to his testimony, Chambers announced that he had "no change whatsoever to make in my testimony concerning him."[12] Committee leaders then asked the two men to confront one another on August 25, which led ER to write the following column.

Although Truman, Byrnes, Acheson, Clark, and Dulles had known that the FBI suspected Hiss of being a Soviet agent, there is no record that they passed their concerns along to ER. Furthermore, Acheson and others in the department held Hiss in high regard. ER had worked with Hiss in his capacity as advisor to the American delegation to the UN General Assembly and spoke well of him in the diary letters she distributed among her friends. As she told readers of My Day August 16:

> Anyone knowing either Mr. Currie or Mr. Hiss, who are the two people whom I happen to know fairly well, would not need any denial on their part to know they are not Communists. Their records prove it. But many people who do not know them would read of the accusations and never know that they were cleared.[13]

Ultimately ER's confidence in Hiss was misplaced. In October, after Hiss was indicted on perjury charges and appealed for a change of venue, ER wrote:

> It seems to me a very wise and sensible move to have the new trial of Alger Hiss in Vermont. Vermonters are not easily stampeded. They are hard-headed, down to earth, conservative and very realistic people. They do not like Communism, but I doubt if they are frightened by it. They are pretty sure of themselves. New York newspapers are apt to be jittery on the subject. … Possibly because New York, much like our other big cities, is the most likely place for Communists to thrive. One finds people more conscious of their fears here than of their confidence in themselves. That doesn't happen in Vermont and I think Alger Hiss will get no soft soap, but complete and fearless consideration of the merits of his case. That is what any American is entitled to and should have, no matter what the accusations are against him.[14]

However, as Hiss and Chambers prepared to confront one another, she threw her very public support behind Hiss.

372

My Day
19 August 1948

HYDE PARK, Wednesday—August 25th will be an interesting day when Mr. Alger Hiss and Mr. Whittaker Chambers meet.[15] Both of them may have changed somewhat since the spy-ring days when Mr. Chambers says he knew Mr. Hiss so well and went to his house so often. It seems to me that the committee must begin to see how funny this whole situation is when they sit in secret sessions for several hours with each man and then have to say that "from the testimony, it is impossible to tell which one is telling the truth".

I have begun to wonder what the point of all this is. The self-confessed people who worked for the Soviet government during the war are now known. They have accused a number of others as being people who worked with them either consciously or unconsciously. It is well, of course, to find out whether people have been spies because they might be spies again, but it would seem that the FBI is the proper agency to find that out. I wonder if all this extra-curricular Congressional activity isn't making it more difficult for the FBI to do its job well.[16] The only thing that really seems important to me at the present time is to know first, whether those who confessed they were once spies for the Russians are trustworthy today or not. Second, if they actually have proof that certain people now in or out of government positions, are untrustworthy. That should be checked, since it is well to know just where they stand. The best people to do this would be the FBI.[17]

The third important thing to know is whether the Soviet government is continuing to try to use Russians in this country, in one capacity or another, for work which is not described in their passports. Next, whether they are still organizing a group of American citizens in or out of the government to keep them informed of things which they want to know.

I am sure that both Mr. Hiss and Mr. Laughlin Currie are about as far from being Communists as is possible—and that they can fight their own battles.[18] I can't help wondering, however, whether the gentlemen on the Congressional investigating committee who sneered at Mr. White because he said he had had a heart attack and asked for a few minutes rest in a private note, are not feeling just a trifle uncomfortable since Mr. White died yesterday of a heart attack.[19]

TMs AERP, FDRL

1. Lauchlin Currie (1902–1993), Canadian born and Harvard trained, became an American citizen in 1934, and then joined the "freshman brain trust" at the US Treasury Department. Working closely with Jacob Viner and Marriner Eccles, Currie outlined an "ideal" monetary system for the nation's weakened banking system and followed Eccles, as his personal assistant, when Eccles joined the Federal Reserve Board. While at the Fed, Currie drafted the Banking Act of 1935 and demonstrated the "strategic role" fiscal policy played in "complementing monetary policy" to revive an acute, depressed economy. In 1937, he convinced FDR, after a four-hour meeting, that the president's budget balancing had hurt rather than restored the economy. Two years later, FDR tapped Currie to serve as White House economist, where he helped direct taxation, social security, and production policy. During wartime, FDR asked Currie to speed up the Flying Tigers program in China, mediate relations between Chiang Kai-Shek and Joseph Stilwell, administer the Foreign Economic Administration, and lead the mission charged with freezing Nazi accounts in Swiss banks. Currie resigned from federal service upon FDR's death. Despite being blamed for "losing" China and his 1948 appearance before HUAC, in 1949 the World Bank selected Currie to conduct its first comprehensive study of a country. After his report on Colombia was released, the Colombian government requested that he return and implement his suggestions. In 1952, he returned to the United States to testify before the grand jury investigating Owen Lattimore's role in releasing state documents to *Amerasia* magazine. However, his 1954 request to renew his passport was denied, in theory, because he now lived abroad. After years of advising Colombian presidents, he received Colombian citizenship and continued to work as the chief economist for Colombia's National Planning Department and the Colombian Institute of Savings and Housing (*ANB*).

2. Harry Dexter White (1892–1948), an economist and international monetary policy expert, worked in FDR's Treasury Department beginning in 1934, rising to the rank of assistant secretary in 1945. White was instrumental in establishing the International Monetary Fund and the World Bank in 1944, and aided Henry Morgenthau in crafting the "Morgenthau Plan" for managing postwar Germany. In November 1945, just as Truman was about to nominate White as executive director of the IMF, FBI director J. Edgar Hoover informed the president that White was under suspicion for Soviet espionage. Nevertheless, Truman went forward with White's nomination, and White served as IMF director for a year before resigning and entering private practice.

The espionage charge did not arise again until Bentley's testimony before HUAC on July 31, 1948. In testimony three days later, Chambers told HUAC that he thought White a "fellow-traveler" but never intimated that he thought White a spy. White, still in frail health from a severe heart attack the previous year, demanded to rebut the charges. August 13, he told the committee that:

> I am not now and never have been a Communist, nor even close to becoming one; that I cannot recollect ever knowing either Miss Bentley or a Mr. Whittaker Chambers, nor juding from the pictures I have seen in the press, have I ever met them.

The Press reported that the witnesses claimed I helped to obtain key posts for persons I knew were engaged in espionage work to help them in that work. That allegation is unqualifiedly false. There is and can be no basis in fact whatsover for such a charge. …

My creed is the American creed. I believe in freedom of religion, freedom of speech, freedom of thought, freedom of the press, freedom of criticism and freedom of movement. I believe in the goal of equality of opportunity, and the right of each individual to an opportunity to develop his or her capacity to the fullest.

I believe in the right and duty of every citizen to work for, to expect and to obtain an increasing measure of political, economic and emotional security for all. I am opposed to discrimination in any form, whether on grounds of race, color, religions, political belief or economic status. I believe in the freedom of choice of one's representatives in Government, untrammeled by machine guns, secret police or a police state. I am opposed to arbitrary and unwarranted use of power or authority from whatever source or against any individual or group.

I believe in a government of law, not of men, where law is above any man and not any man above the law. …

I consider these principles sacred …

… I am ready for any questions you may wish to ask.

The statement, printed verbatim in newspapers across the country, drew strong public support to White.

White left the hearing, after going head-to-head with Representative Richard Nixon (R-CA). Three days after his testimony, White suffered another severe heart attack and died August 18 at his New Hampshire summer home. November 14, almost three months after White's death, Chambers claimed that like Hiss, White had passed along classified information (Rees, 410–18; "Harry Dexter White, Accused in Spy Inquiry, Dies at 56," *WP*, 18 August 1948, 1; Donovan, 173–75).

3. Joseph A. Loftus, "Currie Accused of Helping Spies; A Roosevelt Aide," *NYT*, 1 August 1948, 1.

4. ER repeated this theme in her August 16 column, writing,

I disapprove very much of the way in which these legislative committees work. Smearing good people like Laughlin Currie, Alger Hiss and others is, I think, unforgivable. Though we are told they have every opportunity to clear themselves, the fact that they have been smeared cannot be erased. Anyone knowing either Mr. Currie or Mr. Hiss, who are the two people whom I happen to know fairly well, would not need any denial on their part to know they are not Communists. Their records prove it.

On Alger Hiss, see Document 372 (*MD*, 3 and 16 August 1948).

5. "Due Process in Washington," *NYT*, 4 August 1948, 20; *MD*, 6 August 1948.

6. The National Security Agency's decades-long effort to decipher messages from KGB stations in the United States to Moscow, known as the Venona Project, revealed that many subjects of HUAC interrogation did, in fact, have associations with Soviet agents. The FBI and the congressional committees investigating Communist activity in the United States could not, however, use the Venona decryptions as evidence, lest the KGB discover its code had been cracked. The Venona documents that mention Currie do not specifically corroborate Bentley's testimony, but do indicate that Currie had handed over sensitive US documents directly to KGB agents during World War II, and had had frequent contact with a known spy, Gregory Silvermaster (Joseph A. Loftus, "Currie Accused of Helping Spies; A Roosevelt Aide," *NYT*, 1 August 1948, 1; C. P. Trussell, "Currie and White Deny Under Oath They Aided Spies," *NYT*, 14 August 1948, 1; "Lauchlin Currie, 91; New Deal

Economist Was Roosevelt Aide," *NYT*, 30 December 1993, B6; Reeves, 211; Schrecker, 172–73; Haynes and Klehr, 6, 38, 145–50).

7. Elizabeth T. Bentley (1908–1963), a former member of the American Communist Party, confessed to the FBI in 1945 that she spied for the Soviet Union during World War II. Beginning in August 1948, she testified before HUAC, eventually naming thirty-seven former or current government employees as co-conspirators in her espionage activities. Bentley testified on July 31, 1948, that Lauchlin Currie was part of the "Silvermaster group"—a network of informants centered around the spy Gregory Silvermaster, whom Bentley had recruited. Bentley also stated that Currie had "furnished inside information on this Government's attitude toward China, toward other governments. He once relayed to us the information that the American Government was on the verge of breaking the Soviet code …" ("Elizabeth Bentley Is Dead at 55; Soviet Spy Later Aided US," *NYT*, 4 December 1963, 47; House Committee on Un-American Activities, *Hearings Regarding Communist Espionage in the United States Government*, 80th Cong., 2nd sess., 1948, 519–20; Schrecker, 172; Haynes and Klehr, 129–30).

8. Representative Karl Mundt of South Dakota, a member of the Thomas committee, in questioning Currie about his knowledge of Silvermaster's Communist affiliations, described Currie "as a high Government official, as a man in whose Americanism I believe." Before getting this assurance from Mundt, the two men had the following exchange:

> MR. MUNDT. You would not be able to testify under oath of your own knowledge that you had never unintentionally recommended a man who did have a Communist affiliation because you assumed that if they were in the Government they were loyal?
>
> MR. CURRIE. That is right.
>
> MR. MUNDT. You would not be able to testify under oath that you had never recommended somebody who did turn out to be a Communist or who was a Communist using your good name?
>
> MR. CURRIE. No. All I could testify to under oath is that I never wittingly recommended anybody who was a Communist.
>
> MR. MUNDT. I think a lot of Americans have been under the same illusions that if a person has a job in the Federal Government that he is loyal. We all know now to our chagrin and regret that it is not true, that no test of loyalty, no check on membership in the Communist Party is made of an employee very frequently before he secures his position … (House Committee on Un-American Activities, *Hearings Regarding Communist Espionage in the United States Government*, 80th Cong., 2nd sess., 1948, 863–64).

9. At the start of his August 13, 1948, HUAC testimony, Currie read a statement giving his personal background, his professional history, and his relationship to Gregory Silvermaster and another American spy, Abraham George Silverman. In response to Bentley's accusations, Currie stated:

> … I emphatically deny that I ever knew, believed, or suspected that any statement of mine was repeated to any person acting under cover for the Soviet Government or any foreign government. I have never lent, and would never lend, myself to such disloyal action. I have frequently met and carried on negotiations with accredited representatives of foreign governments, including the Soviet, in the discharge of my official duties, and in all such have been concerned only with the interests of the United States. Among the thousands of loyal Americans who have been my colleagues during my 11 years of Government service, I challenge anyone to find one person who ever doubted my loyalty to this country (House Committee on Un-American Activities, *Hearings Regarding Communist Espionage in the United States Government*, 80th Cong., 2nd sess., 1948, 855).

10. Alger Hiss (1904–1996), a Harvard-educated attorney who would be convicted of perjury relating to this exchange in 1950, joined the Roosevelt administration in 1933, rising quickly with-

in its ranks. By 1936, Hiss left the Justice Department for the State Department, where he served as a key aide to Assistant Secretary of State Sayre and helped develop FDR's Asian and international economics policies. By 1944, as part of the Office of Political Affairs, Hiss worked alongside secretaries Acheson and Stettinius and played a key role in organizing the Dumbarton Oaks Conference. In 1945, he traveled to Yalta with FDR and Stettinius and served as secretary-general of and principal advisor to the American delegation to the UN organizing conference in San Francisco. In November, Attorney General Clark approved the FBI's request to "install technical surveillance." By March 1946, FBI Director Hoover had told Truman, Byrnes, and Clark that he considered Hiss a Soviet operative. Byrnes then ordered that Hiss not be considered for any "responsible duties" and that the department should determine if Hiss could be "dismissed summarily under Civil Service regulations." Hoover cautioned against a hearing, arguing that the evidence was too inconclusive and, with the strong support of Acheson and others within the department, could lead to Hiss's effective rebuttal of the charges against him. In early January 1946, Hiss, who thought he had deflected the suspicions leveled against him by his colleagues in the department, quickly discounted Dulles's offer to place his name before the Carnegie Endowment. When Dulles asked again, Hiss again refused, thinking that it might "look as though I was leaving under fire." However, by November, he wanted to leave the department and asked Acheson to see whether he "would no longer be in the position of resigning under fire." Acheson told him to take the job. Hiss resigned effective January 15, 1947, and two weeks later, he began working for the endowment (Weinstein, 316–29).

11. C. F. Trussell, "Red 'Underground' in Federal Posts Alleged by Editor," *NYT*, 4 August 1948, 1.

12. "Never Saw Him, House Probers Told; Time Editor May Be Called Back," *WP*, 6 August 1948, 1.

13. *MD*, 16 August 1948.

14. *MD*, 8 October 1948.

15. Both Chambers and Hiss were scheduled to testify before the Thomas committee on August 25. But on August 17, the day before ER wrote this column, Hiss met again with members of the committee, this time in New York, to discuss his relationship with Chambers. At this meeting, which was not a formal hearing with sworn testimony, Hiss admitted that he had known Chambers under the pseudonym "George Crosley." According to newspaper reports, Chambers also attended this August 17 meeting, making this, and not the scheduled August 25 hearing as ER suggested here, the two men's first confrontation with each other since Chambers's August 3 accusation (C. P. Trussell, "Alger Hiss Admits Knowing Chambers; Meet Face to Face," *NYT*, 18 August 1948, 1; Edward F. Ryan, "Hiss Confronts Chambers on Stand Today," *WP*, 25 August 1948, 1).

16. After FBI director J. Edgar Hoover reviewed this My Day, which the *Washington Daily News* published under the headline "Isn't Spy Ring Inquiry Really a Job for the FBI?" (the Bureau regularly circulated the column among its directorate), he noted in the margin: "Well, well, I am amazed at her confidence in the FBI!!!" (FBI 62-62-735-26, FOIA, Eleanor Roosevelt).

17. Like Lauchlin Currie, Hiss also had some covert contact with Soviet officials and KGB agents, as revealed in decrypted Soviet spy communications, which were made public in 1995 (see *n*6 above). Code-named "Ales" by the KGB, Hiss was revealed in these messages to have been trying to obtain military and diplomatic information to pass on to the Soviets, and to have been associated with another group of American spies. These messages, like other Venona Project decryptions, were not presented as evidence during the Hiss case before HUAC, though they corroborated some of Chambers's allegations (Weinstein, 319–29, 419–46, 486–513; Haynes and Klehr, 170–73).

18. For ER's defense of Lauchlin Currie, see header Document 371. As the Hiss trial took place outside the time frame of this volume, documents related to it will appear in Volume 2. The case continued to fluster ER. "I have never been able to make up my mind as to what my opinion of Alger Hiss really was," she wrote in 1956.

Therefore, neither time nor events have changed a decision which I have never been able to make. I have always been convinced that he did not tell the complete truth in his testimony during his trial but what was the truth and what the motives that underlay everything he did I have never been able to decide. When I am unable to make up my mind I prefer not to render any judgment. Once the courts have decided one has to accept their verdict, but above all courts there is always the final decision which each man knows he must face alone with his God. Why should we mortals who can't pretend to be all knowing render judgments when we ourselves are in need of mercy, and so from the beginning I have preferred to make no judgment in this case (*IYAM, LHJ* March 1956).

19. Harry Dexter White (see *n*1 Document 371) died on August 16, at his summer home in New Hampshire. He had testified before HUAC on August 13. As with Currie and Hiss, White's name came up in Soviet spy messages as a source of intelligence. During World War II, White had provided the KGB with intelligence on US policy toward Poland and the Baltic states. At the San Francisco Conference in 1945, he again communicated with Soviet agents about American negotiation strategy ("Harry Dexter White, Accused In Spy Inquiry, Dies at 56," *WP*, 18 August 1948, 1; Haynes and Klehr, 140–42).

ADVISING THE DEMOCRATIC NATIONAL COMMITTEE

August 13, Truman called to summon ER to Washington for a two-hour meeting the following Wednesday to discuss the forthcoming General Assembly in Paris. ER, who thought this sudden request burdensome, nevertheless agreed. However, malfunctioning aircraft delayed her arrival, thus truncating her scheduled conversation with the president (see header Document 379).[1] Despite their shortened meeting, however, ER and the president made time to discuss Democratic strategy for the 1948 presidential campaign. The following day, ER sent Truman a note, offering her views on how the Democratic National Committee should seize upon mistakes made by Republican leaders in the campaign.

_373_

Eleanor Roosevelt to Harry Truman
19 August 1948 [Hyde Park]

Dear Mr. President:

I want to thank you for your kindness in seeing me yesterday and to tell you that I appreciate the difficulties under which you have labored. I wish you could have had better assistants.[2]

Above everything else, I hope that the national committee will ask of the state committees that they make an aggressive campaign, picking up every mistake made by the other side, such as this Italian situation[3] and pointing out again and again that they know what you stand for, and therefore it is essential that they give you the kind of men in Congress who will make it possible for you to carry through a program for the benefit of the average man.

I do not feel that the national committee is getting the maximum out of the state committees and while I am a great believer in the necessity for appealing to the independent voter, I also realize that our own machinery must function as well as possible.[4]

I hope your holiday will be a very pleasant one.[5]

Very cordially yours,
Eleanor Roosevelt

TLS HSTOF, HSTL

---

1. She also wrote Joe Lash that in the same conversation, Truman asked ER to "go to Holland for the jubilee and the coronation, but I said I couldn't go" (ER to Joseph Lash, 13 August 1948, JPLP, FDRL).

2. For ER's opinion of Truman's assistants, see Document 383.

3. On August 17, Thomas Dewey told a delegation of Italian Americans that he supported the principle of giving Italy administrative control of its former African colonies—Libya, Somaliland, and Eritrea—under a United Nations trusteeship. "The industrious people of Italy have made great progress toward economic recovery under most difficult conditions," said Dewey. "I strongly believe that this recovery will be assisted, and the Communist menace will receive another setback, if the Italian people are now given an ample opportunity to take part in the future development of the resources of these African areas." Dewey's remark angered Democrats who believed Dewey drew

on information released to him by the State Department as part of a bipartisan approach to world affairs and now used it in a way that could upset negotiations among the United States, Great Britain, Russia, and France over the issue. They also viewed it as a blatant political maneuver to gain Italian votes in the upcoming election. For this very reason, according to the *New York Times*, the Democrats failed to attack Dewey for his statement, fearing that even calling it "ill-advised" might alienate Italian American voters ("Dewey Calls for Italian Rule of Colonies Under the UN," *NYT*, 18 August 1948, 1; "Democrats Roiled By Dewey Proposal on Italian Colonies," *NYT*, 19 August 1948, 1).

4. ER had helped facilitate communications between the national party and state committees in the 1936, 1940, and 1944 presidential elections (Ware, *Partner*, 216; Lash, *Eleanor*, 443–46, 694–712).

5. On August 20, President Truman departed on a nine-day vacation cruise throughout the Chesapeake Bay region on his yacht, the *Williamsburg* ("Truman Off Today on 9-Day Sail," *NYT*, 20 August 1948, 12).

BERNADOTTE AND THE PALESTINIAN
REFUGEE CRISIS

The United Nations General Assembly appointed Count Folke Bernadotte (1895–1948), a member of the Swedish Royal Family and president of the Swedish Red Cross, as mediator for Palestine on May 20, 1948. Bernadotte's charge was to bring about a cease-fire in the first Arab-Israeli war, which began shortly after the state of Israel came into existence on May 14, 1948, and arrange a permanent peace.[1] On August 17, while trying to secure the very tenuous truce in the region, Bernadotte contacted Secretary Marshall with a plea for aid to assist those refugees displaced by the fighting in Palestine. The mediator warned of "sudden human disaster" comparable to an "earthquake or tidal wave" and sent a similar request to the United Nations on the previous day.[2] Marshall may have given a copy of Bernadotte's appeal to ER when they met on August 18 and asked her to help publicize the situation.[3] She responded to the crisis with this column.

_374_

My Day
21 August 1948

HYDE PARK, Friday—I have before me an appeal from the mediator for Palestine, Count Folke Bernadotte to our government. He says: "I am convinced that successful mediation can only continue if solutions can be found for most urgent aspects of great human disaster affecting 330,000 destitute Arab refugees from Jewish-controlled areas and 7,000 Jewish refugees." He does not say where the Jewish refugees come from, but I suppose they come from Arab-controlled areas. The conditions he describes are desperate and he says that thirty percent of these refugees are children under five years of age, and over ten percent are pregnant women and nursing mothers.

They are almost entirely without food and they lack medical care and medicines. They are living alongside roads, under trees, some without shelter and others with just burlap screens. At the moment the weather is warm and dry but by the middle of September the rains will come and it will be cold. Epidemics may start and thousands of children and women, who have no responsibility for the conditions existing in these areas, will die.

The appeal is made to the United States government to help as quickly as possible and the government has made arrangements to help to the best of its ability, but it probably can meet only about half of the immediate needs. Therefore it is asked that private organizations, church groups particularly, cooperate with the government by sending what they can through government channels immediately.[4]

It is not just the refugees who will suffer but the people who are living in the areas where these people have taken temporary refuge. For instance, in one town and sixty villages which under normal conditions have a population of 60,000 people they now have 100,000 refugees. Obviously there is no way locally to care for them. Their present diet is a starvation one and diseases arising from malnutrition among infants and children are becoming more evident daily. The people who live in the area are suffering too, and at any moment their water supply, over-taxed by this influx of people may disappear.

Any mediation between Arabs and Jews can hardly be carried on successfully with conditions such as these at hand, and those of us who hope for less bloodshed and more reasonableness in the settlement of the Palestine question, must, I think, beg all those who can do so to send what supplies they have on hand for the alleviation of this situation.

TMs AERP, FDRL

———————

1. Bernadotte had also been instrumental in saving POWs and German concentration camp prisoners at the end of World War II. Gunmen assassinated the mediator in the Israeli-held area of Jerusalem just a few weeks later, on September 17. For more information on Bernadotte's work see *n*9 Document 380 (Cohen, 387; Lash, *Years*, 134–36; *HSTE*; Julian Louis Meltzer, "Bernadotte Is Slain in Jerusalem; Killers Called 'Jewish Irregulars'; Security Council Will Act Today," *NYT*, 18 September 1948, 1 and 3; "Bernadotte's Life Devoted to Others," *NYT*, 18 September 1948, 3).

2. Thomas J. Hamilton, "Bernadotte Asks Aid for Refugees," *NYT*, 17 August 1948, 6; "Bernadotte Bids U.S. Aid Refugees," *NYT*, 18 August 1948, 10.

3. ER to George Marshall, 19 August 1948, RG59, NARA II.

4. On August 19, 1948, ER sent Marshall a copy of this column and a note saying, "I hope you will get the help you need." Marshall reported back to her on August 27, "Your support of Count Bernadotte's appeal will have a powerful effect. American voluntary relief agencies and American private companies are responding generously. One oil company has come across with $200,000." Truman had authorized the State Department to solicit private donations to alleviate the suffering and by August 28 the *New York Times* reported that "money and goods worth more than $800,000 had been dispatched" (ER to George Marshall, 19 August 1948, RG59, NARA II; George Marshall to ER, 27 August 1948, AERP; "Marshall Notes U.S. Response," *NYT*, 28 August 1948, 3; *HSTE*).

CONFERRING WITH THE STATE DEPARTMENT

As the American representative to the Third Committee of the United Nations General Assembly, ER met regularly with advisors from the State Department to review the department's position on matters that would come before the General Assembly and the Third Committee. Prior to leaving for Paris, where the General Assembly would consider the draft declaration the HRC completed in June, ER met with Durward Sandifer, head of the Office of UN Affairs; James Simsarian, head of the Human Rights Section; and Gilbert "Pete" Stewart, a press officer for the US Mission to the UN. James Simsarian submitted the following report on the conversation for the State Department's records.

375

Memorandum of Conversation

24 August 1948

SECRET

Participants: Mrs. Franklin D. Roosevelt, Mr. D. V. Sandifer, Mr. James Simsarian, Mr. Gilbert Stewart

Subject: Review of General Assembly Position Papers with Mrs. Roosevelt

This is a report of that portion of the conversation with Mrs. Roosevelt relating to the position papers for the third session of the General Assembly. The papers for Committees 2 and 3 were reviewed with her in considerable detail and part of the papers for Committee 1 only briefly.[1] Mrs. Roosevelt had comments of moment with respect to the following:

1. Draft International Declaration of Human Rights

When she was first informed that the Department thinking on this subject is that the draft Declaration should be approved at this session of the General Assembly she expressed her continued concern that such a move might prejudice the completion of the draft International Covenant on Human Rights.[2] Ambassador Austin came into the room to greet Mrs. Roosevelt, and remained for a few minutes to participate in the discussion on this subject. He said that he was not familiar with the question but his offhand judgment would be to press for action at this session. He felt that world opinion demands the approval of the Declaration at this time and that to postpone its approval would be a great disappointment to people throughout the world. Furthermore he felt that there would be considerable misunderstanding if the United States were to take the position that the approval of the Declaration be postponed even though our motives might be commendable ones. Mrs. Roosevelt agreed at the conclusion of this discussion that the United States should support and urge the adoption of the Declaration at the third session of the General Assembly as its first step in the Human Rights program.[3] As pointed out in the Department's position paper it would be made clear in the General Assembly that the Declaration forms only part of the International Bill of Human Rights being prepared by the United Nations Commission on Human Rights and that the completion of the Covenant on Human rights is essential.

2. Chilean Case on the Soviet Wives of Foreign Nationals

Mrs. Roosevelt agreed that the United States should take the initiative in presenting to the attention of the General Assembly relevant data concerning the refusal of the USSR to permit Soviet spouses of American citizens to leave the Soviet Union. She agreed that the Delegation should point out the inhuman character of this treatment of Soviet wives of foreign nationals. She mentioned that she has had some correspondence with Gromyko concerning the Soviet wives of a number of GIs who have asked her to intervene on their behalf; she intends to bring this correspondence with her for possible reading in the General Assembly.[4]

3. Freedom of Information Conventions

Mrs. Roosevelt expressed considerable concern with the inconsistency of the proposed United Kingdom convention on freedom of information with the United States position with respect to the draft International Covenant on Human Rights. She thought that a careful educational job must be done at the General Assembly on this subject delegation by delegation in order that there will be a full appreciation of the undesirability of approving the provisions of the United Kingdom convention which undertakes to list specific limitations to the right to freedom of information.

It was agreed that discussion should be held as soon as possible with the United Kingdom to urge it to withdraw its convention from the General Assembly until after the draft International Covenant has been fully considered at the next session of the Commission on Human Rights. It was recognized that such discussions with the United Kingdom should very likely be held at a high level. If the United Kingdom is unwilling to withdraw the convention the United States Delegation should press for the referral of the United Kingdom convention to the Commission on Human Rights for its consideration in connection with the drafting of the Covenant at its next session in 1949 in order that a preliminary approval of the United Kingdom convention would not prejudice the United States position with respect to the Covenant. Mrs. Roosevelt felt that it might be much too difficult to educate all the delegations at the General Assembly concerning the undesirability of specific limitations without first thoroughly working this matter out in the Commission on Human Rights in connection with the Covenant.[5]

4. Presidency of General Assembly

Mr. Sandifer reported to her that the three persons being considered for the Presidency of the General Assembly are Arce (Argentina), Evatt (Australia) and Bech (Luxembourg). Mrs. Roosevelt said that she would prefer Bech and that her second choice would be Evatt. Mr. Sandifer asked Mrs. Roosevelt if she thought that Madame Pandit (India) would be a satisfactory president of the General Assembly. He said the possibility had been mentioned of the desirability of supporting India for the presidency, if it should be willing to accept this in lieu of a place on the Security Council or the Economic and Social Council. Mrs. Roosevelt thought that Madame Pandit would be a satisfactory president and that the United States might support her for that position if India would be willing to withdraw its candidacy for a seat on the Security Council or the Economic and Social Council.[6]

5. Racial Discrimination

Mrs. Roosevelt said that the NAACP intends to send Walter White to Paris as an observer and that he has asked to see her before leaving for Paris. She agreed to inform the Department of any information she receives from Mr. White relating to the possibility of the question of racial discrimination being raised in the General Assembly.[7]

TMemc RG59, NARA II

---

1. ER most likely examined earlier drafts of the State Department position papers on the Draft Convention on Freedom of Information; Protest by Chile Concerning Refusal of U.S.S.R. to Allow Soviet Daughter-in-Law of Former Chilean Ambassador to Leave Soviet Union and Refusal of U.S.S.R. to Allow Soviet Wives of Foreign Nationals to Leave Soviet Union; Draft International Declaration of Human Rights; and Discrimination Against Negroes in the United States.

In the Draft Convention on Freedom of Information the department argued that it was "highly desirable that agreement be reached with the UK in order to avoid an open split. At the same time, every effort should be made to arrive at a text as satisfactory as possible, especially because of the connection between this convention and the Covenant on Human Rights." Addressing ER's earlier concerns about the "undesirability" of approving the provisions of the UK convention that sought to list specific limitations to the right to freedom of information, the State Department recommended the delegation "substitute a general limitations clause for the list of specific limitations in Article 2."

Concerning the Chilean case on the Soviet wives of foreign nationals the State Department insisted that the US delegation should "take the initiative in presenting to the attention of the General Assembly ... the inhuman character of this treatment," but did not want the delegation to vote for "any resolution which by its language states that the U.S.S.R. violated international law or the provisions of the Charter or any other agreement by refusing to permit the Soviet daughter-in-law of the former Chilean Ambassador to leave the Soviet Union or by refusing to permit the Soviet wives of other foreign nationals to leave the Soviet Union."

With reference to the Draft International Declaration of Human Rights, the department requested that the US delegation secure approval of the draft by the General Assembly "without change." If, however, it proved impossible to secure the approval of the declaration without "substantial" change, the department recommended the delegation "support and vote for the Declaration as amended unless it contains seriously objectionable features."

In case the Soviet Union charged the United States with discrimination against African Americans, the State Department recommended the US delegation respond by pointing out that "while the United States is not perfect, it is undertaking to meet the problem of discrimination in this country and that conditions are decidedly improving year by year." The department also suggested the delegation point out that "basic human rights and freedoms are being increasingly denied in the Soviet Union and that the issue of discrimination naturally is not in as sharp a focus in a country (such as the USSR) where the masses of people are being denied so many of the basic human rights and freedoms such as the freedom of speech, freedom of press, freedom of religion, freedom of assembly, a government subject to the will of the governed, etc." (Draft Convention on Freedom of Information, 8 September 1948, [SD/A/C.3/97], RG84, NARA II; Protest by Chile Concerning Refusal of U.S.S.R. to Allow Soviet Daughter-in-Law of Former Chilean Ambassador to Leave Soviet Union and Refusal of U.S.S.R. to Allow Soviet Wives of Foreign Nationals to Leave Soviet Union, 26 August 1948, [SD/A/C.3/72], RG84, NARA II; Draft International Declaration of Human Rights, 20 August 1948 [SD/A/C.3/65], RG84, NARA II; Discrimination Against Negroes in the United States, 26 August 1948, [SD/A/C.3/69] and 30 August 1948, [SD/A/C.3/76], RG84, NARA II).

2. In a separate memorandum summarizing the discussion at this meeting, Gilbert Stewart explained that ER feared pushing for the adoption of the declaration at the upcoming session of

the General Assembly would result in "a let down when people begin to realize it is not an enforce-able treaty." She also worried that "momentum may be lost in the drive to complete the Covenant" (Gilbert Stewart to Warren Austin, 25 August 1948, RG84, NARA II).

3. Stewart wrote that, by the end of the conversation, ER accepted Sandifer's argument that approving the declaration at this time "might be a stimulus to the drive for a Covenant rather than a retarding factor." He convinced ER that it was "wiser to take advantage of the momentum now generated behind the Declaration lest delay now should cause failure to produce both a Declaration and a Covenant" (Gilbert Stewart to Warren Austin, 25 August 1948, RG84, NARA II).

4. The head of the Chilean delegation to the UN, Hernán Santa Cruz, asked that the General Assembly debate the USSR's practice of prohibiting the emigration of Soviet wives of foreigners at its third session to be held in Paris in the fall of 1948. The State Department had protested the Soviet practice already. In May 1947, the department asked the Soviet embassy to grant exit visas to the 250 Soviet wives of American citizens and they never received a response. Now that the General Assembly considered addressing the issue, Andrei Gromyko wrote a letter to Secretary-General Trygve Lie claiming that discussion of the matter would be "interference … in matters which are within the internal jurisdiction of state," and therefore a violation of the UN Charter. Despite Gromyko's protest, the General Assembly did debate the matter, and ER spoke in favor of censuring the USSR. On April 25, 1949, the General Assembly adopted a resolution that condemned the Soviet policy of refusing to allow the wives of foreigners to leave the country as a violation of "fundamental human rights, traditional diplomatic practices and other principles of the Charter" ("Chile asks U.N. to Study Soviet Ban on Wives' Exit," *NYT*, 29 May 1948, 3; "U.S. Prods Russia on American Wives," *NYT*, 5 December 1947, 1; "Soviet in U.N. Protest on Charge on Wives," *NYT*, 25 June 1948, 14; "U.N. Finds Russians Violating Charter by Curb on Wives," *NYT*, 26 April 1949, 1; "Resolutions Adopted by the General Assembly During Its Third Session," United Nations, http://www.un.org/documents/ga/res/3/ares3.htm, accessed 24 March 2006).

5. From March 23 to April 21, 1948, the UN held an International Conference on Freedom of Information in Geneva, Switzerland. The 600 delegates who represented more than fifty nations approved three draft conventions and several resolutions dealing with freedom of information. Although the United States agreed with the UK on most issues at the conference, the American delegation abstained from the vote approving the UK's Draft Convention on Freedom of Information because it included a clause that allowed governments to take legal action against those responsible for the "systematic diffusion of deliberately false and distorted reports which undermine friendly relations between people and states." By October 1949, when the convention came before the General Assembly, the British abandoned their draft, agreeing with the United States that the convention might actually do more to restrict the free flow of information than to promote it. At that session, ER called for postponement of discussion on the convention, arguing that the UN's efforts would be better directed at finishing a covenant on human rights—a treaty that would include protections for freedom of information—than continuing the debate on the UK's draft convention which had produced "deep disagreement" ("Free Press Parley Opens with Clash," *NYT*, 24 March 1948, 13; "Press Conference Votes More Curbs," *NYT*, 13 April 1948, 10; Kenneth Campbell, "Free Press Drafts Adopted at Geneva," *NYT*, 22 April 1948, 3; "Information Pact Is Shelved By U.N.," *NYT*, 21 October 1949, 2).

6. José Arce (1881–1968) of Argentina served as president of the second special session of the General Assembly, which convened in April and May 1948, to handle the Palestine question. He hoped to retain his position as president during the General Assembly's third regular session. By the time delegates arrived in Paris in September 1948, Arce was no longer eligible for the post as only the ranking member of a delegation may hold the office and Argentina chose to send Arce's superior, foreign minister Juan Atilio Bramuglia (1903–1962) to the third session. On September 21, Australian foreign minister Herbert Vere Evatt (1894–1965) became the new General Assembly president with the votes of thirty-one member nations, including the United States, to Bramuglia's

twenty. Joseph Bech (1887–1975), the chairman of the Political and Security (First) Committee of the General Assembly in 1947, and Vijaya Lakshmi Pandit (1900–1990), the sister of Indian Prime Minister Jawaharlal Nehru and head of India's UN delegation, were not on the General Assembly's presidential ballot in 1948. Pandit was later elected president during the eighth session of the General Assembly, which met in 1953, making her the first female to hold that position ("Dr. Jose Arce, 86, Diplomat, Is Dead," *NYT*, 20 July 1968, 20; "Evatt Leads in U.N. to Head Assembly," *NYT*, 19 September 1948, 54; "Juan Bramuglia, Peron Aide, Dead," *NYT*, 5 September 1962, 38; "Evatt Heads U.N. Assembly," *NYT*, 22 September 1948, 1; "Herbert Evatt of Australia Dies," *NYT*, 2 November 1965, 33; "Joseph Bech, Statesman, Dead," 10 March 1975, 32; "Vijay Lakshmi Pandit, Politician and Nehru's Sister, Is Dead at 90," *NYT*, 2 December 1990, 53).

7. At the invitation of the State Department, White planned to attend the meeting of the General Assembly in Paris as a consultant to the US delegation. ER agreed to meet with White at her apartment in New York City on September 1, 1948. Neither White nor ER kept a written record of their conversation. Chester Williams, public liaison officer for the US Mission to the UN, however, reported in a memorandum of conversation dated September 9 on his recent discussion with White about bringing the issue of racial discrimination before the General Assembly. White, Williams wrote,

> pointed out that this matter was formulated personally by Dr. DuBois; that it is his pet project; that because of his personal prestige and age he is given a good deal of latitude to perform as a lone-wolf; that he takes advantage of this position and fails to consult with committees or boards of directors, knowing that they would be reluctant to criticize him on the substance of the proposal after he had given it public airing.

> Mr. White pointed out, however, that he had no intention of pressing for the matter to be brought up at the General Assembly, although he thought Dr. DuBois might personally try to insinuate it through the Liberian Delegation. He doubted that he would attempt to get any of the Eastern satellites of the Soviet Union to carry the ball. He said that for his part he is much more concerned with the positive work of the Human Rights Commission and the Declaration on the Human Rights. He planned to talk to Mrs. Roosevelt about these matters before sailing.

> He also pointed out that his Board wanted him to go rather than DuBois because of DuBois tendency to act on his own initiative with[out] consultation.

Williams sent a copy of this confidential memorandum to ER. White had further opportunities to discuss issues of importance to the NAACP with ER and other members of the US delegation when he joined them on board the SS *America* for the voyage to Europe. For more on the NAACP petition, Du Bois's efforts to bring it before the UN, and his disagreement with White over the issue, see Document 365 (Walter White to ER, 18 August 1948, AERP; ER to Walter White, 23 August 1948, AERP; Walter White to ER, 27 August 1948, AERP; Chester S. Williams, Memorandum Conversation, 9 September 1948, RG84, NARA II; Lewis, 534; Janken, 309–10).

ON THE KOSENKINA CONTROVERSY AND THE
DEAN OF CANTERBURY

Irving H. Flamm, former president of the Chicago Chapter of the National Lawyers Guild and contributing columnist for the English-language monthly *Soviet Russia Today*, repeatedly wrote ER objecting to her characterization of the Soviet Union as "an aggressor nation."[1] Conceding that "the Russians are sometimes difficult, sullen, oversensitive and occasionally crude," Flamm nevertheless thought their behavior "ought to be charged up to a fear phobia [attributable to] the after-effects of bitter experiences." He then asked if "maybe we deserve some of the blame" and challenged ER to realize that "it is high time to unwind all this before it really leads to a suicidal war neither side can win."[2]

August 25 he drew particular attention to two recent State Department actions that generated sensational press: its refusal to issue a visa to the Very Reverend Hewlett Johnson, the dean of Canterbury, in reaction to his membership in the National Council of American-Soviet Friendship[3] and its response to Soviet teacher Oksana Stepanova Kosenkina's desperate plea for asylum.[4] The American press "puffed up" Kosenkina's resistance to deportation "far beyond its real importance." After all, he wrote:

> To political refugees in displaced person camps, we offer little hope of admission no matter how fine their characters may be. But when a couple of Russian teachers, impressed with our broader freedoms and especially our higher living standards, show a willingness to remain here, immigration barriers are forgotten, our press gives the story daily headlines, ready to push us into a war in defense of our right to keep them here.

He then concluded by asking ER to "use her influence with the State Department to reverse its recent decision barring the Dean of Canterbury," arguing that the department's ruling "is against our tradition of free speech."

ER quickly responded.

376

Eleanor Roosevelt to Irving Flamm
27 August 1948 [Hyde Park]

My dear Mr. Flamm:

I think your analysis of the Kosenkina affair is ridiculous. Our nationals who stay in the USSR do so because they are married to Russians. They haven't denounced our ways, they are there because they want to be there and we have made no effort to remove them.

If you read Mme. Kosenkina's story I think you would realize that she came over here with the intention of getting out of Russia because her husband and son disappeared. That does not happen in our country and it does happen in the USSR.[5]

I quite understand how the cold war started but I can assure you that if war comes it will come because Russia wants it and not because we do. It will come because Russia has decided she has a better chance to win now than later.

As far as the Dean of Canterbury is concerned, he has been known for a long time to be a gentleman who embarrassed the church in Great Britain very much and I think it would be very foolish at this moment to have him traveling around the United States. You say he is a highly respected British citizen which may be true in certain quarters but I assure you the church is none too happy about him. If we were not at present in such a state of jitters I would think there was no reason for not letting him come but at the moment I think it would be unwise.

I do not happen to think that the American-Soviet Friendship report of the news is a very unbiased report.[6]

I hope we can get along with Russia and I certainly hope she will come to her senses it will not be because she thinks we are conciliatory and weak—it will be because she thinks we are strong.

Very sincerely yours,

TLc AERP, FDRL

---

1. Irving Flamm to ER, 5 November 1947, 25 August and 8 September 1948, and Irving Flamm, "The USA and USSR Can and MUST Get Along," *Soviet Russia Today*, n.d., reprint, AERP.

2. Irving Flamm to ER, 25 August 1948, AERP.

3. In August 1948, the Very Reverend Hewlett Johnson (1874–1966) was denied a US entry visa for a six-week lecture tour organized by the National Council of American-Soviet Friendship, which the State Department regarded as "subversive." Popularly known as the "Red Dean," Johnson had written positively about Soviet achievements, served as a member of London's Communist newspaper, the *Daily Worker*, and taken an interest in reconciling Communism and Christianity. After some 300 prominent American citizens campaigned in Johnson's favor, the United States granted him a visa in October 1948 ("The Very Rev. Dr. Hewlett Johnson: Controversial Dean of Canterbury," *TL*, 24 October 1966, 10; Clifton Daniel, "U.S. Refuses Visa to 'Red Dean' as Guest of a 'Subversive' Group," *NYT*, 24 August 1948, 1 and 3; "'Red Dean' of Canterbury Receives Visa from U.S.," *NYT*, 23 October 1948, 5).

4. Employed as a teacher for children of the UN's Soviet delegation, Oksana Stepanova Kosenkina failed to sail back to the USSR in July 1948 and sought refuge at a farm north of New York City run by the anti-Communist Tolstoy Foundation. The farm had hosted many refugees and displaced persons from the Soviet Union who did not wish to be repatriated. On August 7, 1948, Soviet consular officials removed Kosenkina from the farm, claiming that she had been "drugged and kidnapped by 'White Russians.'" They then took her to the Soviet consulate and held her there until August 12, when she leaped from a third-story window of the consulate, sustaining injuries for which she was hospitalized. The House Un-American Activities Committee then subpoenaed her, which allowed her to remain in the United States under US government protection. Kosenkina recovered from her leap, received asylum, and became a US citizen in 1954 (Alexander Feinberg, "Russian Factions Here War Over 'Kidnapping' of Woman," *NYT*, 8 August 1948, 1; "Russian Teacher Gains in Hospital," *NYT*, 20 August 1948, 9; Eric Page, "Peter Hoguet," *NYT*, 28 October 1996, D11).

5. ER made a similar point in her November column for the *Ladies' Home Journal*:

> Her husband and son were evidently suspect and disappeared. Her sorrow and her fear must have been very great, and I think she showed how desperate she was when she determined to jump from the consulate window rather than return to the U.S.S.R. Incidents of this kind point up for us the kind of terror existing in any country which is controlled by secret police (*IYAM, LHJ*, November 1948, 69).

6. Flamm attached "the Simms article" for ER's review. ER did not retain the copy in her files. The National Council did release a State Department statement to the *Times* in which the department announced that it "has nothing against the Dean personally but would not regard his visit under

the auspices of that organization as in the national interest" ("Nothing Against Him Personally," *TL*, 24 August 1948, 4).

ON LOYALTY OATHS AND GOVERNMENT
SERVICE

In an article appearing on the front page of the August 29 *New York Herald Tribune*, reporter Bert Andrews reprinted excerpts from a letter sent to him by a "Troubled Man ... seeking answers to questions which arose because of the wave of loyalty investigations, and which had been given new emphasis by the Hiss-Chambers controversy." Intrigued by the man's concerns, Andrews sought and received permission from him to reprint his letter in its entirety. The letter from the anonymous New Englander reported that although he had received security clearance from the FBI, he wrote Andrews in response to "the apprehensions that have plagued me since I decided to work for the government, apprehensions brought about by the current witch hunts." Disturbed by the "current fit of jitters" dominating government employment, he wondered:

> Is it still possible to think freely and live without fear as an American while serving your country? All I have read recently does not point to this, yet I am not sure as to how bad the situation is. Do you think one can work to improve the existing situation while holding a government job, or are things at such a state that the independent thinking must come from outside the government?

Although Andrews appreciated these concerns, he urged the "Troubled Man" to take the job, insisting that "if a man is sincerely interested in doing a good job and is honestly loyal ... he's sufficiently well armed to bat the ears off of the would-be thought controllers who rise up from time to time." Believing that the "current fit of jitters will pass," the reporter thought a citizen could help his country by going into government because "if he's truly honest and loyal, he isn't going to have much to worry about." [1]

ER thought Andrew's response too optimistic, and used the following column to discuss why she now hesitated "in these days" to advise young people to accept a job in the government.

377

My Day
31 August 1948

HYDE PARK, Monday—I wonder how many people noticed in one of the New York City Sunday newspapers an article in which was quoted a letter from "A Troubled Man," a university professor. The man had accepted a job with the Government, probably on a temporary basis, and was a little bit worried as to what chance he had of serving his country and then leaving the service without having his reputation tarnished and his ability to earn a living impaired for the rest of his life.

There wasn't great prominence given to this article, and yet I think it was one of very great importance. Twenty-five or 50 years ago a young man belonging to certain groups in this country and contemplating going into politics might well have been admonished that he was going to soil his hands. Politics, it was argued at that time put you in touch with a lot of dirty business and with some people who had different standards from those of the well-to-do business men of the early 1900's. It never occurred to the business men of that day that they were responsible for the corrupt politicians. They just felt it was a bad profession and one should not go into it.

Today, however, you have to train a young man who wants to take a government position in the art of considering his every action and his every word very carefully. It might be that he might rent his apartment to some person he had met a few times, and if he did not look into that person's antecedents and into his political beliefs, he might find he had associated himself with a Communist.

He might have thrown in his old jalopy, which he could have sold for $25, but he might have felt a little ashamed to take money for that particular car, so he let this man who was renting his apartment take the car in the bargain. He might have forgotten this transaction in the course of a busy life, but one fine day would wake up to the fact that he had to answer, under cross-examination, for everything that he had done. I think the writer of the article to which I refer above is much too optimistic. I would say to any young man taking a Government position today that he better be a lawyer, trained to weigh every word he utters. Above everything else, he had better keep a diary and write in it every night every detail of his actions and his thoughts. Every week or so his minister might be asked to attest that his diary was a <u>bona-fide</u> document in which only the truth had been put down. In that way he might save himself some embarrassment several years from now.

I used to advise young people to take an interest in their Government. And I think I would still maintain that as far as participation in voting is concerned that interest is still a useful activity. But I would hesitate in these days about accepting a job in the Government. If a young person had been afflicted with liberal tendencies or had been foolish enough to belong to one or two radical organizations in youth then he must expect to lose his job and to find many other jobs closed to him.

As things are today, there are very few youngsters who have remembered to be wary enough to take a Government job.

TMs AERP, FDRL

ER was not the only one who took exception to the view that young people should pursue a career in government in the current political climate. Sabra Holbrook, executive director of Youthbuilders, an organization that sponsored citizenship education programs in public schools, wrote ER September 2 thanking her for the August 31 My Day column.[2] Holbrook reported she had recently attended the August 25 hearing of the Un-American Activities Committee at which Alger Hiss was questioned. "It seemed to me a replica of what Stalin's purges of those who disagreed with him politically, at the Moscow trials, must have been like," she wrote. Holbrook was grateful, therefore, that ER had dropped her usual "gentle and restrained" tone in her August 31 column and spoken in a way that "cannot possibly permit any of your thinking readers to lull themselves into the comforting hope that 'this is just a phase,' and that 'we will muddle through.'" She concluded:

> When a great lady who has come through so many crucial conflicts, and who is therefore in a better position than the rest of us to evaluate the situation from a long-range perspective, can advise youth to stay out of service of their fellow citizens through government,—then it should startle all of us into a compelling realization of our proximity to disaster.[3]

After reading Holbrook's letter, ER dictated the following reply to her secretary, who then forwarded the reply to Holbrook.

378

Eleanor Roosevelt to Sabra Holbrook
[?] September 1948

Holbrook

I wrote the column to which you refer to make people realize what is happening to our liberties. It seems to me we are strangely unaware of the fact that we are acquiring the pattern of the

Soviet. They are succeeding in doing something to us which is quite devastating and I am troubled about it and I think more of us should be aware of it

MnLd AERP, FDRL

---

1. Bert Andrews, "Troubled Man Asks if U.S. Job Invites a Smear," *NYHT*, 29 August 1948, 1 and 2.

2. See Document 377.

3. Sabra Holbrook to ER, 2 September 1948, AERP. For more on the Alger Hiss hearing, see header Document 371 and *n*10 Document 372.

"The Struggle for Human Rights"

August 13, Truman phoned ER to ask her to travel to Washington August 18 for two hours of meetings on how best to handle "the coming session of the United Nations." "A chore," she confided to Joe Lash, "but not too much for him to ask." She was to meet with Marshall at 11:45 AM and the president at 1 PM; however, a malfunctioning aircraft delayed her arrival until 12:40 and she then rushed "horrified" to meet with the secretary. Marshall, she wrote in her column, then spent fifteen minutes and "hurriedly told me of things he wanted to" discuss before ER "rushed" to meet with Truman to hear his expectations "of some of the things that he felt we could do" in Paris.[1]

Tensions with the Soviet Union ran high at the time as the Soviets blockaded Berlin and Communists led strikes and demonstrations in Italy and France. Dulles, then serving as Dewey's foreign policy advisor and who would soon serve also as Marshall's deputy to the General Assembly, believed that the United States should launch a moral offensive against the USSR. Marshall agreed and urged ER "to give a major address in Paris" that might set the tone for the forthcoming deliberations on security and human rights. Truman told ER "the preservation of peace" was paramount. ER concurred, writing two days later:

> If we can't preserve peace, no one in the world whether they be Russian, Polish, German, Italian or French—or from any of the South American continents— will have a chance to make a life of security and happiness in the future.

> What a responsibility the President of the United States carries if he really cares about the well being of the average people throughout our own country and in the world as a whole.[2]

The pressure on ER increased as well. As she admitted to David Gurewitsch, Truman and Marshall:

> … are putting considerable responsibility on me in this session. Dulles has suggested that we point out that all our troubles are rooted in a disregard for the rights and freedoms of the individual and go after the U.S.S.R., not, thank heavens, claiming perfection but saying that under our system we are trying to achieve those rights and succeeding better than most. They want me to make an opening speech to set this keynote outside the Assembly and I am trying to plan it now.[3]

Immediately after leaving Washington, ER wrote René Cassin, the French delegate on the Human Rights Commission, to see if he was "still anxious to have me make an address on Human Rights in Paris. If so, I wonder if it could be arranged for the opening night of the Assembly." She was "fairly sure" she would have no meetings that night and she "would like to make this address before the really hard work" began. She hoped to know "ahead so I can prepare my speech on the way over." She told Sandifer and Simsarian of her overture to Cassin when the two advisors traveled to New York the following week to brief her on "the problems of Committee III and the broad outline of the Assembly agenda." Sandifer then said he would get the US embassy in Paris to contact the French Foreign Office so it might "inform Professor Cassin of the significance of the speech so that all precautions would be taken to prevent any kind of slip up." [4]

The State Department had begun preparing an outline of the speech as soon as ER completed her meetings with Marshall and Truman. As Rusk wrote Marshall, "We shall offer Mrs. Roosevelt all possible help and will have a number of opportunities to comment prior to her final draft." Rusk then prepared a detailed outline of points ER should address for Marshall's review. The secretary approved the proposal, but thought "more prominence should be given [by] more crystal clear wording, to the fact that the denial of certain human liberties is the key to the police state techniques and the heart of our present difficulties." Sandifer and Simsarian then presented ER with the outline during their briefing session in New York; however, ER responded that she "plan[ned] to draft her own speech" and hoped "to have it ready the following week so that it can be released in advance to the press in both English and in French." Two days later, Marshall wrote "to thank you for your willingness to make the Sorbonne speech to the purpose we desire. I cannot think of a better, more potent approach to that particular problem."[5]

ER worked closely with the State Department, but she drafted the speech herself and had the final word on the text. She covered the points in Rusk's outline in her draft and in many cases borrowed or adapted the original wording. However, she fleshed it out considerably and, in doing so, added her own perspective. For example, she expressed more sympathy for the Russian people (see note 17) and referred to the shortcomings of the United States in the area of racial discrimination more candidly (see note 19) than the State Department desired. After ER forwarded her draft to the State Department, Sandifer returned the speech with suggested revisions, which the department hoped she would incorporate. Some of these she adopted; some she did not (see notes 14 and 15). Marshall accepted her edits, instructing Sandifer "to express his satisfaction with the general effect of the speech," his sense that her speech "should accomplish the objectives we have in view," and his thanks for her "patient consideration" of the department's "numerous suggestions."[6]

Twenty-five hundred people packed the ornate, circular Sorbonne auditorium the evening of September 28. Marshall, who would follow the speech from an English transcript, sat on the front row, facing ER. As John Humphrey recorded in his diary, "The great amphitheatre was packed with an enthusiastic audience which gave her a reception the likes of which I have never seen before." ER admitted to feeling "nervous and apprehensive"; "there is," however, "something in the atmosphere of an old building like that and its beautiful hall that has an invigorating effect on speakers. Of course, the French language lends itself to oratory, and long before I spoke I was lost in admiration of the way this language provides words to say things that one would find difficult to say in almost any other language." [7]

Paul Ramadier, the French minister of defense, presided. Cassin delivered an "impassioned introduction." Sandifer reported to his wife that "looking completely unruffled and with her best smile," ER then "rose to a roar of applause" to deliver her remarks in French. "She did a perfect job," Sandifer thought.

> The audience seemed to follow every word and was quite responsive, applauding ten or twelve times. She extemporized at the beginning and Dorothy [Fosdick] said it was just right. Once she got a big laugh when she interpolated that having raised a large family she thought she was a master of patience, but she never knew what patience was until she came into contact with the Russians in the Human Rights Commission.[8]

The State Department published the following text of ER's speech in February 1949. While this published text is an excellent translation of the original French text ER used, the first paragraph differs significantly from the French version (see note 9). The editors chose to publish the English translation as it is the text the State Department elected to preserve as its official record.

_379_

"The Struggle for Human Rights"
Speech at the Sorbonne, Paris

28 September 1948

I have come this evening to talk with you on one of the greatest issues of our time—that is the preservation of human freedom. I have chosen to discuss it here in France, at the Sorbonne, because here in this soil the roots of human freedom have long ago struck deep and here they have been richly nourished. It was here the Declaration of the Rights of Man was proclaimed, and the great slogans of the French Revolution—liberty, equality, fraternity—fired the imagination of men. I have chosen to discuss this issue in Europe because this has been the scene of the greatest historic battles between freedom and tyranny. I have chosen to discuss it in the early days of the General Assembly because the issue of human liberty is decisive for the settlement of outstanding political differences and for the future of the United Nations.[9]

The decisive importance of this issue was fully recognized by the founders of the United Nations at San Francisco. Concern for the preservation and promotion of human rights and fundamental freedoms stands at the heart of the United Nations. Its Charter is distinguished by its preoccupation with the rights and welfare of individual men and women. The United Nations has made it clear that it intends to uphold human rights and to protect the dignity of the human personality. In the preamble to the Charter the keynote is set when it declares: "We the people of the United Nations determined … to reaffirm faith in fundamental human rights, in the dignity and worth of the human person, in the equal rights of men and women and of nations large and small, and … to promote social progress and better standards of life in larger freedom." This reflects the basic premise of the Charter that the peace and security of mankind are dependent on mutual respect for the rights and freedoms of all.

One of the purposes of the United Nations is declared in article 1 to be: "to achieve international cooperation in solving international problems of an economic, social, cultural, or humanitarian character, and in promoting and encouraging respect for human rights and for fundamental freedoms for all without distinction as to race, sex, language, or religion."

This thought is repeated at several points and notably in articles 55 and 56 the Members pledge themselves to take joint and separate action in cooperation with the United Nations for the promotion of "universal respect for, and observance of, human rights and fundamental freedoms for all without distinction as to race, sex, language, or religion."

The Human Rights Commission was given as its first and most important task the preparation of an International Bill of Rights. The General Assembly which opened its third session here in Paris a few days ago will have before it the first fruit of the Commission's labors in this task, that is the International Declaration of Human Rights.

This Declaration was finally completed after much work during the last session of the Human Rights Commission in New York in the spring of 1948. The Economic and Social Council has sent it without recommendation to the General Assembly, together with other documents transmitted by the Human Rights Commission.

It was decided in our Commission that a Bill of Rights should contain two parts:

1. A Declaration which could be approved through action of the Member States of the United Nations in the General Assembly.[10] This Declaration would have great moral force, and would say to the peoples of the world "this is what we hope human rights may mean to all people in the years to come." We have put down here the rights that we consider basic for individual human beings

the world over to have. Without them, we feel that the full development of individual personality is impossible.

2. The second part of the bill, which the Human Rights Commission has not yet completed because of the lack of time, is a covenant which would be in the form of a treaty to be presented to the nations of the world. Each nation, as it is prepared to do so, would ratify this covenant and the covenant would then become binding on the nations which adhere to it. Each nation ratifying would then be obligated to change its laws wherever they did not conform to the points contained in the covenant.[11]

This covenant, of course, would have to be a simpler document. It could not state aspirations, which we feel to be permissible in the Declaration. It could only state rights which could be assured[12] by law and it must contain methods of implementation, and no state ratifying the covenant could be allowed to disregard it. The methods of implementation have not yet been agreed upon, nor have they been given adequate consideration by the Commission at any of its meetings. There certainly should be discussion on the entire question of this world Bill of Human Rights and there may be acceptance by this Assembly of the Declaration if they come to agreement on it. The acceptance of the Declaration, I think, should encourage every nation in the coming months to discuss its meaning with its people so that they will be better prepared to accept the covenant with a deeper understanding of the problems involved when that is presented, we hope, a year from now and, we hope, accepted.[13]

The Declaration has come from the Human Rights Commission with unanimous acceptance except for four abstentions—the U.S.S.R., Yugoslavia, Ukraine, and Byelorussia. The reason for this is a fundamental difference in the conception of human rights as they exist in these states and in certain other Member States in the United Nations.

In the discussion before the Assembly, I think it should be made crystal clear what these differences are and tonight I want to spend a little time making them clear to you. It seems to me there is a valid reason for taking the time today to think carefully and clearly on the subject of human rights, because in the acceptance and observance of these rights lies the root, I believe, of our chance for peace in the future, and for the strengthening of the United Nations organization to the point where it can maintain peace in the future.[14]

We must not be confused about what freedom is. Basic human rights are simple and easily understood: freedom of speech and a free press; freedom of religion and worship; freedom of assembly and the right of petition; the right of men to be secure in their homes and free from unreasonable search and seizure and from arbitrary arrest and punishment.

We must not be deluded by the efforts of the forces of reaction to prostitute the great words of our free tradition and thereby to confuse the struggle. Democracy, freedom, human rights have come to have a definite meaning to the people of the world which we must not allow any nation to so change that they are made synonymous with suppression and dictatorship.

There are basic differences that show up even in the use of words between a democratic and a totalitarian country. For instance "democracy" means one thing to the U.S.S.R. and another to the U.S.A. and, I know, in France. I have served since the first meeting of the nuclear commission on the Human Rights Commission, and I think this point stands out clearly.

The U.S.S.R. Representatives assert that they already have achieved many things which we, in what they call the "bourgeois democracies" cannot achieve because their government controls the accomplishment of these things. Our government seems powerless to them because, in the last analysis, it is controlled by the people. They would not put it that way—they would say that the people in the U.S.S.R. control their government by allowing their government to have certain absolute rights. We, on the other hand, feel that certain rights can never be granted to the government, but must be kept in the hands of the people.

For instance, the U.S.S.R. will assert that their press is free because the state makes it free by providing the machinery, the paper, and even the money for salaries for the people who work on the paper. They state that there is no control over what is printed in the various papers that they subsidize in this manner, such, for instance, as a trade-union paper. But what would happen if a paper were to print ideas which were critical of the basic policies and beliefs of the Communist government? I am sure some good reason would be found for abolishing the paper.

It is true that there have been many cases where newspapers in the U.S.S.R. have criticized officials and their actions and have been responsible for the removal of those officials, but in doing so they did not criticize anything which was fundamental to Communist beliefs. They simply criticized methods of doing things, so one must differentiate between things which are permissible, such as criticism of any individual or of the manner of doing things, and the criticism of a belief which would be considered vital to the acceptance of Communism.[15]

What are the differences, for instance, between trade-unions in the totalitarian states and in the democracies? In the totalitarian state a trade-union is an instrument used by the government to enforce duties, not to assert rights. Propaganda material which the government desires the workers to have is furnished to the trade-unions to be circulated to their members.[16]

Our trade-unions, on the other hand, are solely the instrument of the workers themselves. They represent the workers in their relations with the government and with management and they are free to develop their own opinions without government help or interference. The concepts of our trade-unions and those in totalitarian countries are drastically different. There is little mutual understanding.

I think the best example one can give of this basic difference of the use of terms is "the right to work". The Soviet Union insists that this is a basic right which it alone can guarantee because it alone provides full employment by the government. But the right to work in the Soviet Union means the assignment of workers to do whatever task is given to them by the government without an opportunity for the people to participate in the decision that the government should do this. A society in which everyone works is not necessarily a free society and may indeed be a slave society; on the other hand, a society in which there is widespread economic insecurity can turn freedom into a barren and vapid right for millions of people. We in the United States have come to realize it means freedom to choose one's job, to work or not to work as one desires. We, in the United States, have come to realize, however, that people have a right to demand that their government will not allow them to starve because as individuals they cannot find work of the kind they are accustomed to doing and this is a decision brought about by public opinion which came as a result of the great depression in which many people were out of work, but we would not consider in the United States that we had gained any freedom if we were compelled to follow a dictatorial assignment to work where and when we were told. The right of choice would seem to us an important, fundamental freedom.

I have great sympathy with the Russian people. They love their country and have always defended it valiantly against invaders. They have been through a period of revolution, as a result of which they were for a time cut off from outside contact. They have not lost their resulting suspicion of other countries and the great difficulty is today that their government encourages this suspicion and seems to believe that force alone will bring them respect.[17]

We, in the democracies, believe in a kind of international respect and action which is reciprocal. We do not think others should treat us differently from the way they wish to be treated. It is interference in other countries that especially stirs up antagonism against the Soviet Government. If it wishes to feel secure in developing its economic and political theories within its territory, then it should grant to others that same security. We believe in the freedom of people to make their own mistakes. We do not interfere with them and they should not interfere with others.

The basic problem confronting the world today, as I said in the beginning, is the preservation of human freedom for the individual and consequently for the society of which he is a part. We are fighting this battle again today as it was fought at the time of the French Revolution and at the time of the American Revolution. The issue of human liberty is as decisive now as it was then. I want to give you my conception of what is meant in my country by freedom of the individual.

Long ago in London during a discussion with Mr. Vyshinsky, he told me there was no such thing as freedom for the individual in the world. All freedom of the individual was conditioned by the rights of other individuals. That, of course, I granted. I said: "We approach the question from a different point of view; we here in the United Nations are trying to develop ideals which will be broader in outlook, which will consider first the rights of man, which will consider what makes man more free: not governments, but man."

The totalitarian state typically places the will of the people second to decrees promulgated by a few men at the top.

Naturally there must always be consideration of the rights of others; but in a democracy this is not a restriction. Indeed, in our democracies we make our freedoms secure because each of us is expected to respect the rights of others and we are free to make our own laws.

Freedom for our peoples is not only a right, but also a tool. Freedom of speech, freedom of the press, freedom of information, freedom of assembly—these are not just abstract ideals to us; they are tools with which we create a way of life, a way of life in which we can enjoy freedom.

Sometimes the processes of democracy are slow, and I have known some of our leaders to say that a benevolent dictatorship would accomplish the ends desired in a much shorter time than it takes to go through the democratic processes of discussion and the slow formation of public opinion. But there is no way of insuring that a dictatorship will remain benevolent or that power once in the hands of a few will be returned to the people without struggle or revolution. This we have learned by experience and we accept the slow processes of democracy because we know that shortcuts compromise principles on which no compromise is possible.

The final expression of the opinion of the people with us is through free and honest elections, with valid choices on basic issues and candidates. The secret ballot is an essential to free elections but you must have a choice before you. I have heard my husband say many times that a people need never lose their freedom if they kept their right to a secret ballot and if they used that secret ballot to the full.

Basic decisions of our society are made through the expressed will of the people. That is why when we see these liberties threatened, instead of falling apart, our nation becomes unified and our democracies come together as a unified group in spite of our varied backgrounds and many racial strains.

In the United States we have a capitalistic economy. That is because public opinion favors that type of economy under the conditions in which we live. But we have imposed certain restraints; for instance, we have anti-trust laws. These are the legal evidence of the determination of the American people to maintain an economy of free competition and not to allow monopolies to take away the people's freedom.[18]

Our trade-unions grow stronger because the people come to believe that this is the proper way to guarantee the rights of the workers and that the right to organize and to bargain collectively keeps the balance between the actual producer and the investor of money and the manager in industry who watches over the man who works with his hands and who produces the materials which are our tangible wealth.

In the United States we are old enough not to claim perfection. We recognize that we have some problems of discrimination but we find steady progress being made in the solution of these problems. Through normal democratic processes we are coming to understand our needs and how we can attain full equality for all our people. Free discussion on the subject is permitted. Our Supreme Court has recently rendered decisions to clarify a number of our laws to guarantee the rights of all.[19]

The U.S.S.R. claims it has reached a point where all races within her borders are officially considered equal and have equal rights and they insist they have no discrimination where minorities are concerned.[20]

This is a laudable objective but there are other aspects of the development of freedom for the individual which are essential before the mere absence of discrimination is worth much, and these are lacking in the Soviet Union.[21] Unless they are being denied freedoms which they want and which they see other people have, people do not usually complain of discrimination. It is these other freedoms—the basic freedoms of speech, of the press, of religion and conscience, of assembly, of fair trial and freedom from arbitrary arrest and punishment, which a totalitarian government cannot safely give its people and which give meaning to freedom from discrimination.

It is my belief, and I am sure it is also yours, that the struggle for democracy and freedom is a critical struggle, for their preservation is essential to the great objective of the United Nations to maintain international peace and security.

Among free men the end cannot justify the means. We know the patterns of totalitarianism—the single political party, the control of schools, press, radio, the arts, the sciences, and the church to support autocratic authority; these are the age-old patterns against which men have struggled for three thousand years. These are the signs of reaction, retreat, and retrogression.

The United Nations must hold fast to the heritage of freedom won by the struggle of its peoples; it must help us to pass it on to generations to come.

The development of the ideal of freedom and its translation into the everyday life of the people in great areas of the earth is the product of the efforts of many peoples. It is the fruit of a long tradition of vigorous thinking and courageous action. No one race and no one people can claim to have done all the work to achieve greater dignity for human beings and greater freedom to develop human personality. In each generation and in each country there must be a continuation of the struggle and new steps forward must be taken since this is preeminently a field in which to stand still is to retreat.

The field of human rights is not one in which compromise on fundamental principles are possible. The work of the Commission on Human Rights is illustrative. The Declaration of Human Rights provides: "Everyone has the right to leave any country, including his own." The Soviet Representative said he would agree to this right if a single phrase was added to it—"in accordance with the procedure laid down in the laws of that country." It is obvious that to accept this would be not only to compromise but to nullify the right stated. This case forcefully illustrates the importance of the proposition that we must ever be alert not to compromise fundamental human rights merely for the sake of reaching unanimity and thus lose them.

As I see it, it is not going to be easy to attain unanimity with respect to our different concepts of government and human rights. The struggle is bound to be difficult and one in which we must be firm but patient. If we adhere faithfully to our principles I think it is possible for us to maintain freedom and to do so peacefully and without recourse to force.

The future must see the broadening of human rights throughout the world. People who have glimpsed freedom will never be content until they have secured it for themselves. In a true sense, human rights are a fundamental object of law and government in a just society. Human rights exist to the degree that they are respected by people in relations with each other and by governments in relations with their citizens.

The world at large is aware of the tragic consequences for human beings ruled by totalitarian systems. If we examine Hitler's rise to power, we see how the chains are forged which keep the individual a slave and we can see many similarities in the way things are accomplished in other countries. Politically men must be free to discuss and to arrive at as many facts as possible and there must be at least a two-party system in a country because when there is only one political party, too many things can be subordinated to the interests of that one party and it becomes a tyrant and not an instrument of democratic government.

The propaganda we have witnessed in the recent past, like that we perceive in these days, seeks to impugn, to undermine, and to destroy the liberty and independence of peoples. Such propaganda poses to all peoples the issue whether to doubt their heritage of rights and therefore to compromise the principles by which they live, or try to accept the challenge, redouble their vigilance, and stand steadfast in the struggle to maintain and enlarge human freedoms.

People who continue to be denied the respect to which they are entitled as human beings will not acquiesce forever in such denial.

The Charter of the United Nations is a guiding beacon along the way to the achievement of human rights and fundamental freedoms throughout the world. The immediate test is not only the extent to which human rights and freedoms have already been achieved, but the direction in which the world is moving. Is there a faithful compliance with the objectives of the Charter if some countries continue to curtail human rights and freedoms instead of to promote the universal respect for an observance of human rights and freedoms for all as called for by the Charter?

The place to discuss the issue of human rights is in the forum of the United Nations. The United Nations has been set up as the common meeting ground for nations, where we can consider together our mutual problems and take advantage of our differences in experience. It is inherent in our firm attachment to democracy and freedom that we stand always ready to use the fundamental democratic procedures of honest discussion and negotiation. It is now as always our hope that despite the wide differences in approach we face in the world today, we can with mutual good faith in the principles of the United Nations Charter, arrive at a common basis of understanding. We are here to join the meetings of this great international Assembly which meets in your beautiful capital city of Paris. Freedom for the individual is an inseparable part of the cherished traditions of France. As one of the Delegates from the United States I pray Almighty God that we may win another victory here for the rights and freedoms of all men.

TSp AERP, FDRL

EDITORS' NOTE:

The major newspapers consulted, including the *New York Times, Washington Post, London Times,* and *Le Monde*, did not print transcripts of this speech. The version printed above is that published by the Department of State in February 1949 in publication 3416 (Mrs. Franklin D. Roosevelt, "The Struggle for Human Rights," *Human Rights and Genocide*, Washington, DC: United States Department of State, Office of Public Affairs, February 1949, 1–12). The State Department published the final agreed-upon version of the text, but not a transcript of the speech; ER's files contain two additional pages of extemporaneous remarks made at the Sorbonne that are not included in the State Department publication. These remarks appear below as they do in ER's files, numbered but without any indication of where in the speech they were included.

1. I am indeed happy to be here this evening and I am very grateful for the kind words said in appreciation of my country for the help extended, but whether that help is extended by universities or students or by our government, we, in the United States will always recognize the debt we owe to France not only for the help which she gave us in our time of need, but for the inspiration and stimulus she has given in the fields of arts and letters to the whole world.

When Professor Cassin spoke he was extremely kind to me. You will recognize that such eloquence is of great value in some one who is as passionately devoted to the rights of human beings as is Professor Cassin. I lean upon him and follow him often in the Human Rights Commission.

2. An excellent example is the fact that we give food, clothing and shelter to prisoners who commit criminal offenses but we deprive them of the one thing which gives validity to such security—the freedom of decision and movement.

3. When I was bringing up children I thought I understood well the full significance of patience. Children usually develop that quality in us, but I never knew in the faintest degree what it meant to really have patience until I served on the Human Rights Commission with the delegates from the USSR.

4. This will be accomplished I know, through the close cooperation with you here in France, for you have always fought for the freedom and rights of human beings and will, I know, continue to do so.

Sandifer's remarks to his wife confirm that ER ad-libbed comment number three above and supports the conclusion that she actually included these remarks in her speech ("Extemporaenous Remarks—Sorbonne Speech," 9 November 1948, AERP; Sandifer, 68).

EDITORS' NOTE:

In this and the following notes, ER's original draft is provided where it differs from the published text. The crossed-out text represents text that the State Department asked ER to omit. The department's suggested replacements appear as SMALL CAPS. The original draft from which these paragraphs are taken is attached to Durward Sandifer's September 9 letter to ER, located in ER's papers at the FDR Library.

---

1. ER to Joe Lash, 13 August 1948, JPLP, FDRL; *MD*, 20 August 1948.

2. In a meeting with James Hendrick, in June, "Mr. Dulles emphasized the fact that in his opinion the Human Rights program was one of the most important now facing the United Nations. He pointed out that the U.S.S.R. was basing its expansionist policies, not on the actual taking over of a territory but on the spread of communist ideology. He felt that this was a very important point for the United States to consider" (Hoopes, 71; Divine, 108; James Hendrick, Memorandum of Conversation, 15 June 1948, RG59, NARA II; *MD*, 20 August 1948).

3. ER to Gurewitsch, 26 August 1948, DGC, FDRL.

4. Cassin had invited ER to deliver a speech on human rights before the students of the Sorbonne sometime in April, but she declined his invitation (which she admitted "to treating rather casually") to complete *This I Remember* and to fulfill other speaking engagements (ER to Cassin, 19 August 1948, AERP; Cassin to ER, 23 February and 11 March 1948, AERP; G. W. Stewart, Jr., to Warren Austin, 25 August 1948, RG84, NARA II).

5. Marshall's comment appears as marginalia in an unknown hand on this document under the rubric: "copy of remarks by GCM." Rusk told Marshall that he was also sending the outline to Charles Bohlen and George Kennan (G. W. Stewart, Jr., to Warren Austin, 25 August 1948, RG84, NARA II; Marshall to ER, 27 August 1948, AERP; Rusk to Marshall, 23 August 1948, AERP).

6. Sandifer to ER, 9 September 1948 and attached draft of "The Struggle for Human Rights," AERP.

7. ER also recalled:

The president of the university and Professor Rene Cassin spoke before I did. And when they speak of the Sorbonne one can tell by the feeling and emotion they put into their words that they are not merely talking of an institution of learning. This is a building they love, in which traditions have been built and which mean a great deal in the intellectual life of the French people …

The Sorbonne president also made mention of Benjamin Franklin and how he first came to speak for the United States in this capital city of Paris. And this reminded me of the fact that John Golden, who was here for a few days, made me walk to the end of the block of buildings in which our hotel stands to show me a bronze table that commemorates the fact that in this building Benjamin Franklin and other American statesmen signed the treaty that brought us help from France in the days when we needed it more than France needs our help today.

Our two republics have a long history of friendship and it is good now, when they need a lift to their spirits, that we are able to help them through these arduous years. I was only too glad to be able to thank them not only for what they did for us years ago, but for what they have done in the fields of literature and the fine arts for us and for the world over in all the years of their history (J. Humphrey, *Greatness*, 50; *MD*, 1 October 1948).

8. The foreign service officer covering the speech for the department seconded Sandifer's assessment, reporting that ER "seemed to evoke a response from the audience and to make everyone feel that the fundamental principles of our civilization were still uppermost in the mind of, and being defended by, the United Nations." Others disagreed. Soviet papers dismissed ER as a "hypocritical servant of capitalism" while John Humphrey, writing in his diary on the night of the speech, expressed disappointment:

> … Mrs. R. in spite of her appealing opening failed to seize the opportunity that had been provided for her. The crowd had come to hear the chairman of the Human Rights Commission and the widow of a very great man. It heard a speech that had obviously been written by the State department and ninety per cent of which was devoted to an attack against the U.S.S.R. I do not blame the Americans for talking back; but I do regret that they are using Mrs. R. as their spokesman in these polemics. She had become a symbol that stood above this quarrel around which reasonable men and women could have rallied in a final effort to find a basis not for compromise so much perhaps as for an understanding. That position has been seriously shaken by tonight's speech (Sandifer, 68; Humphrey, 50).

9. ER's original draft:

> I have come this evening to talk with you on one of the greatest issues of our time—that is human freedom. I am happy to do my little speech here in France, at the Sorbonne, because the French soil knows well liberty. Long ago, the roots of the "tree of Liberty" have struck deep and here they have been richly nourished. It was here the Declaration of the Rights of Man was proclaimed, and the noble motto of the French Revolution— liberty, equality, fraternity—fired the imagination of men. I have chosen to discuss this issue in Europe because this has been the scene of the greatest historic battles between freedom and tyranny. I have chosen to discuss it in the early days of the General Assembly because the issue of liberty is decisive for the settlement of outstanding political differences which today divide people and governments and consequently this is a decisive issue that will influence the future of the United Nations.

10. ER's original draft:

> A Declaration which could be ~~accepted by the government representatives in the General Assembly~~ APPROVED THROUGH ACTION OF THE MEMBER STATES OF THE UNITED NATIONS IN THE GENERAL ASSEMBLY

11. ER's original draft:

> The second part of the Bill, which the Human Rights Commission has not yet complet-ed because of the lack of time, is a Covenant which ~~we feel should~~ WOULD BE IN THE FORM OF A TREATY TO be presented to the nations of the world. Each nation, as it is pre-pared to do so, would ratify this Covenant and the Covenant would then ~~have the weight of a treaty between the United Nations and each ratifying nation~~ BECOME BINDING ON THE NATIONS WHICH ADHERE TO IT. Each nation ratifying would then be obligated to change its laws wherever they did not conform to the points contained in the Covenant.

Sandifer argued that these changes were necessary to clarify that the Covenant "will be a treaty among Members of the United Nations and not between the United Nations and Member states."

12. ER's original draft read, "insured." The State Department recommended "assured" as a replace-ment.

13. ER's original draft:

> ~~If it is accepted it will~~, THE ACCEPTANCE OF THE DECLARATION I think, ~~obligate~~ SHOULD ENCOURAGE EVERY nation in the coming months to ~~educate~~ DISCUSS ITS MEANING WITH its people so that they will be better prepared to accept the covenant with a deeper under-standing of the problems involved when that is presented, we hope, a year from now.

14. Although the State Department suggested that "in the future" be deleted from this sentence, ER chose to include it in her final draft.

15. Sandifer asked ER to omit this paragraph in its entirety, but she included it in her final draft.

16. ER's original draft ended this paragraph with, "The representatives of the trade unions are required to sit on the board of management of each enterprise to share responsibility for the oper-ation of that enterprise." Sandifer asked ER to remove this sentence because the State Department had "not been able definitely to verify its accuracy."

17. ER's original draft of the speech included the following paragraphs which Durward Sandifer asked her to omit. This was one of two changes to which Sandifer said in his cover letter "we attach considerable importance."

> I have great sympathy with the Russian people. Through revolution they had to do away with an absolutist government which gave practically no opportunity to the great mass of people. There is no question in my mind but that the greater part of the people in com-munist controlled territories today consider that they have more opportunity for advance-ment and greater security than they ever had in the past. Because I feel that the majority of the Soviet people feel this, I would not countenance the slightest effort to make the peo-ple within the USSR countries believe anything different. I feel confident that if the fun-damental freedoms are accepted for all people, then, as time goes on, the people of the totalitarian states will decide for themselves if certain changes in government practice would be useful to them. In which case they will bring them about by peaceful processes, if laws and not force rule the lands. If the world is allowed to be free, if we believe that the democracies have something better to offer in the democratic form of government and way of life, then we must believe that given freedom of intercourse and of action the peo-ples of the world will be able to know and make up their own minds without any undue effort on our part or on the part of other democracies to convince them.

> [Sandifer accepted: The people of Russia have always loved their country. They are patri-otic and defend it valiantly against invasion.] He then proposed: They have been through a period of revolution where many countries, including the USA, cut them off from out-side contacts. They are still suspicious and the great difficulty today is that their govern-

ment seems to believe that force alone will bring them respect. Neither some of our press nor some of our diplomats, turned authors, contribute to quieting their suspicions.

Sandifer believed that the paragraphs provided "an inaccurate impression of conditions in the Soviet Union":

Taken out of context some of the statements could be cited by the Russians as approving conditions there which we cannot condone. It may be arguable that the Russian people have today more educational and cultural opportunities, but the value of these is doubtful where mind and body are the slave of the police state. The lack of security for the average citizen is the principal indictment of the Soviet system. To say that we would not countenance any efforts to change the views of the Soviet people weakens one of our principal arguments against communism in other countries. This does not mean that we should interfere internally with the Soviet people.

Another point is that the conditions introduced by "ifs" in the latter part of the paragraph are so important as to seem to us to invalidate the propositions to which they are attached. A secondary point is that by revolution the Russians exchanged one absolutist government for another.

We would therefore feel happier if you could see your way clear to dropping this paragraph. The possibility of changes in totalitarian states is discussed elsewhere in the speech.

A related question in the following paragraph is the possible implication that the suspicions mentioned are justified and that Soviet foreign policy rests on suspicion of the United states rather than on its own totalitarian objectives. We query the advisability of reviving reference to United States participation in action against Russia in 1918.

Sandifer suggested that ER replace the omitted paragraphs with the following:

The people of Russia have always loved their country. They are patriotic and defend it valiantly against invasion. They have been through a period of revolution as a result of which they were for a time cut off from outside contacts. They have not lost their resulting suspicion of other countries, and the great difficulty is today that their government seems to believe that force alone will bring them respect.

ER rewrote this suggested paragraph as it appears in the final version of the text printed above.

18. ER originally concluded this paragraph, "Certain government agencies like the post office are examples of socialized methods and many of our welfare laws now accepted by all political parties were once attacked as smacking of socialism." Sandifer wrote a "?" in the margin next to this sentence and asked her to remove it. He explained his apprehension at including this sentence: "It might revive attacks of socialism in the United States (in an election year) and possibly prejudice welfare laws unnecessarily."

19. This is the second paragraph that Sandifer told ER the State Department especially wanted her to change. The State Department asked her to omit her version in its entirety; she in turn crossed out much of their suggested replacement. ER's original paragraph read:

In the United States we are old enough not to claim perfection. We recognize that our minorities have not yet achieved the full rights which this Bill will make the essential rights of every human being. One must remember that in a Republic the people choose their representatives and those representatives respond to public opinion. Discrimination against minorities is caused by bigotry and frequently is the result of ignorance and illiteracy. Economic inequalities also make for discrimination against minorities but in the United States it is safe to say, I think, that as educational levels rise we will definitely see progress in eliminating this evil. The goal is in sight and if the Covenant is agreed upon and our leaders can achieve its ratification throughout the United States then this International Act will have helped to speed the educational fight now being made to achieve human rights for all. In New York State, for instance, discrimination has been made a criminal offense and even in the south in the past few years great changes have come about. However, free discussion on this subject is allowed in the USA and gradually the Supreme Court is rendering decisions which will change many aspects of the rights of minorities within our country.

The State Department attached the following suggested paragraph to ER's draft, and she crossed through those sections which she refused to include in her final speech:

In the United States we are old enough not to claim perfection. We recognize that we have ~~some~~ problems of discrimination but we find steady progress being made in the solution of these problems. ~~In large areas of our country discrimination has already been practically eliminated. In the South in the past few years great changes have also come about. But in the part of the country where slavery was for so long a basic institution, one cannot expect too quickly a complete change in custom and opinion to a new concept of equality.~~ Through normal democratic processes we are coming to understand our needs and how we can attain full equality for all our people. Free discussion on the subject is encouraged. Our Supreme Court has recently rendered decisions to clarify a number of our laws to guarantee the rights of all. ~~We make no apology for our performance to those whose record is one of ruthless suppression. We have as large a measure of freedom, as great we believe, as anywhere else in the world, and we do not propose to surrender or compromise one whit of it.~~

Sandifer explained this suggestion:

We are concerned that a reference to Negroes as a "minority" in the United States would set them apart from Americans in general. Negroes are not a minority in this country in the sense that this word is generally used in international relations, as for example in the Minorities Treaties of World War I. The suggested substitute paragraph endeavors to broaden the scope of the statement, rather than limiting the illustration of progress to a reference to New York State. There is a danger in putting too much emphasis or reliance on the Covenant to bring about the elimination of discrimination in the United States. As you have so often pointed out, we must continue working within our country rather than relying on international agreements to achieve progress with respect to the problem of discrimination in the United States.

20. ER's original draft:

The USSR ~~takes great pride in having~~ CLAIMS IT HAS reached a point where all races within her borders are officially considered equal and have equal rights and they insist they have no discrimination where minorities are concerned.

Sandifer argued that ER's original wording was imprecise; it indicated that the Soviet Union had actually accomplished the task of ending racial discrimination. "It is not clear that this has actually been accomplished," wrote Sandifer, "and if so it is rendered a hollow achievement by other oppressive policies."

21. ER's original text began, "This is a laudable accomplishment …" Acting on Sandifer's suggestion, ER replaced "accomplishment" with "objective."

ON THE RUSSIANS, ATOMIC ENERGY, AND PALESTINE

Prior to her departure for Paris, Bernard Baruch telegraphed ER from Reno, Nevada, sending her his "affectionate good wishes" for success on her upcoming mission to the Third Session of the United Nations General Assembly. As a longtime friend of ER's, Baruch indicated he had "every confidence" in her ability, and advised her that "by not putting forward or agreeing to any proposal that your conscience will not support you can't err."[1] Although ER did not have a chance to reply to Baruch before she sailed, she responded from Paris with the following letter, indicating her continued frustration with the Russian position on atomic energy, and requesting Baruch's assistance with Secretary Marshall on the Palestine problem.

380

Eleanor Roosevelt to Bernard Baruch
4 October 1948 [Paris]

Dear Mr. Baruch:

I have been meaning to write to you ever since I got here.

In my Committee #3, I notice a slight change in the attitude of the Russians. They are less vituperative and in the first item on our agenda which was the control of the new narcotic drugs not covered by previous conventions, they presented their arguments against the Colonial Clause always insisted upon by the British, accepted defeat and accepted the convention and informed the secretariat that when the convention was open for signature, Russia would sign immediately.[2]

This was a great surprise to me and I spoke of it to Mr. Spaak of Belgium and he told me he had noticed exactly the same thing in Committee #1.[3] He feels it might indicate a change of policy in the Kremlin.

Of course, the proposals made by Mr. Vishinsky on atomic energy and arms reduction are utterly and completely dishonest but if people as a whole can be made to see what they really mean so that the Russians are defeated and we can carry better resolutions, I have a feeling they may possibly go along.[4]

For this reason I am going to try to be rather polite to my Russian colleagues. I have also decided that we haven't been wise in not associating more with the Latin-Americans. We have tried very hard to impress them with the fact that we did not intend to dictate to them, but they are murmuring among themselves that supposedly we should be leaders and we indicate in no way what we think should be done. Therefore I had six of them lunch with me last Saturday to discuss the points coming up. I shall continue to do this type of thing with the members of my committee. I have seen General Romulo of the Philippines who has considerable influence with them.[5]

It was fun having John Golden here for a few days but I work such long hours it is very difficult for me to see much of any one outside of the range of one's work.[6]

I often wish that you were here to consult with, but I am glad I have had the opportunities to talk with you fairly often. I think our lines of thought are frequently parallel.

I am enclosing to you a copy of a letter which I sent to the President today.[7] I am sending it to Frances Perkins because she telephoned me last night pointing out that Drew Pearson was saying that I had never come out for the President as the Democratic candidate and was supposedly in favor of Governor Dewey.[8] That, of course, is untrue and I do agree with Frances Perkins that we should try to get as good a Democratic vote as possible. I told her there was no chance of a Democratic victory, but that we might keep some of our liberal Democrats in Congress and even increase the number if we acted wisely. I hope you will approve of this letter even though I was, as you know, loathe to do more than state in general my support of the Democratic Party and its policies.

I hope you are keeping well and are not working too hard. I wish you would do some work in putting pressure on Secretary Marshall so that he will consider his approval of the Bernadotte Plan was not tantamount to complete acceptance of all the recommendations contained in it, but only as being a good basis for negotiation.[9]

It seems highly unfair to me to turn the whole of the Negeb over to the Arabs. The portion of Galilee given to the Jews is not fertile and I do not think it fair compensation because in Jewish hands the Negeb would be developed and may turn out to be the only place where they can receive immigration. I have expressed these thoughts in the delegation meetings but I do not think I carry much weight. I have only one real backer and that is Ben Cohen.[10] Neither of us was consulted before the Secretary made his announcement to the press of the acceptance of the Bernadotte report. We were simply handed a statement to read in the session after he had given it out to the press.

Affectionately always,
Eleanor Roosevelt

TLS BBP, NjP-SC

_381_

Bernard Baruch to Eleanor Roosevelt
15 October 1948 [New York City]

Dear Mrs. Roosevelt:

It was nice to hear from you. As I read the news I think of you often.

I note what you say about the Russians. It had been my hope to go to Russia this year and there talk with the members of the Politburo, spending some time looking over the Russian activities in production on the farms, in factories, mines and transportation. And, perhaps, make some suggestions that would have increased the production of food, clothing and housing. I have been telling those with whom I come in contact that if the Russians could raise their standard of living, it would be very helpful to all concerned.[11]

The impenetrable suspicions that have arisen between the Russians and ourselves are very disheartening; but we must not be moved by fear and permit them to destroy us and in doing so, destroy themselves. I do not know how long it will take, but we should do everything we can to explain to them what our views are. They do not seem to get them, or understand them. Both Gromyko and Skobeltzyn told me that they did not believe we tried to make any arrangement on atomic energy.[12] That of course, I know is untrue, because I tried with all my heart and soul. I never could understand why they did not accept our proposals. If they had accepted them, and they had been acted upon in good faith, the fear of the atom bomb would have been removed and indeed, we would have been well on the road to general disarmament.

There is really no point in getting rid of the atom bomb, if the other terrific instruments of destruction remain. Italy, Germany and Japan were brought to their knees before the atom bomb was used. Japan was helpless when we dropped it there. Russia received terrific punishment without any atom bomb having been dropped. There are plenty of instruments of devastation left after the atom bomb.

I agree with you about the proposals of Mr. Vishinsky on atomic energy and arms reduction.

I also think you are very wise in keeping in close touch with the various commissions.

I was appealed to by General Marshall and Secretary Lovett to say something when the atomic energy matter came up but I would not do so unless asked by them. At the same time, I told them if they asked me, I must make it public because I would not want it to look as if I were tooting my own horn, and if I did it at their request and it became known, it would injure the State Department.

I had known something about the idea of sending a special mission to Russia, which you had in mind many months ago which made good sense then.[13] When I was told about it this time (and it was even suggested that I be on it) I said it was impossible in the present circumstances, and as far as I was concerned, I would not go for it would be by-passing and destroying the usefulness of the UN. The proper person to make the statement, or undertake any discussion now, is either the President, or General Marshall.

You are particularly wise regarding the Latin Americans. We have unnecessarily hurt their feelings and will surely lose their support. They are close to us more because of fear of others than because of respect for us. I think we have been rather cavalier in our treatment of them.

You know of course, how I feel about the Near East and its subservience to oil.

Now as to the letter that you sent to the President. I am sure he will be pleased to get it. I have given my usual support to the House and Senate. I have made no statement on the general election. As you know, I never made one.

I note what you say as regards the Bernadotte plan. I already expressed my views through General Carter[14] to General Marshall regarding Palestine and have not spoken to him since. He called me on the telephone today from Washington but I was unable to get clearly what he had to say because, as usual, they had somebody listening in, which made it very difficult to hear.

I do not see why they ever turned any of the Negeb area over to the Arabs, nor do I yet see why when we lobbied for the Palestine settlement, we turned our back on it. That hurt America's position in the world more than it has been able to recover. In our fears, we are letting England put a lot of things over on us and it is not confined to Palestine. They are doing it in Europe and the Far East.

Drew Pearson and Tucker[15] have been talking about a letter the President wrote me.[16] The President asked me to become a member of the Finance Committee, which I refused to do. He did write me a very cross, stupid and impertinent reply which I have not made public and which I did not answer.

The Vinson incident shook us all up very much.[17] And I do not like the statements being made as to how prepared we are because it is too highly colored and untrue.[18]

It looks to me as if both the Democrats and the Republicans are getting ready to make a statement about de jure recognition of Palestine but if they do it will be entirely political.

That is all, I guess, you will want from me for the moment.

I cannot close without hoping that you had a nice birthday and that you are still holding up under the work. You received a lot of fine notices and pictures here which I presume are being sent you.

My best to Tommy and I hope your grandson is proving not alone useful but is having a good time.[19]

As ever,

Affectionately yours,
B.M.B.

P.S. If I had any sense he might have won, Douglas would have.

TLS AERP, FDRR

382

Eleanor Roosevelt to Bernard Baruch

19 October 1948 [Paris]

Dear Mr. Baruch:

Thank you for your long letter. I wish you could go to Russia. They are behaving in every committee in a purely obstinate manner. With us, in Committee #3, they insist on making attacks and then when any one is foolish enough to answer them by attack in return they insist on answering again, with the result that no work in hand is done. Committee #3 should be discussing questions on its agenda and not questions which come up in Committee #1. We are told by the Russians that the United States is making atom bombs to destroy the other nations of the world. The pretext for that is the discussion of the Article on the right to life. I think you would be interested and amused just following through in the different committees if you were here.

I am going to make a suggestion to the Secretary that in every one of the committees we invite the Russian block to spend an evening with us and tell us all the things they think. We will try to answer them or at least discuss with them. Everyone says they would not come and they would not believe what we said but I can not think of any other way in which we might begin to make a dent in this horrible problem of making people get over their fright and have some kind of confidence in one another.[20]

Of course, they are completely dishonest in their proposals on atomic energy and doing away with armament.

The suggestion made to the President to send Justice Vinson to Russia was a stupid one at this particular time.[21]

I have asked the Secretary on his return from Athens to call a special meeting of the delegation so that we can have a clear understanding of our policy on Palestine and on the Italian colonies.[22] I am much disturbed by what looks to me like British influence which makes us do things which may seem essential to our defense people at the moment, but which do not take into account the long view. I have had a number of talks with various members of the Arab group in which I made it clear that I am not against any people and would be very much interested in having the US help develop the desert, but I have also let it be known fairly widely that we have recognized the State of Isreal and that I think Isreal and should have the Negeb to make it possible for them to develop and to receive emigrants.

On the question of Arab refugees I am refusing to discuss anything about repatriation or removal to some other area until the political question is settled. Of course, they will have to have relief, we can not let four or five hundred thousand people die without doing something for them, but they are a part of the settlement of the political question.

I am sorry the President wrote you as he did. It was both foolish and unjust.[23]

Tommy gave me a birthday party which was attended by many members of the U.S. Delegation staff—no one of the higher eschelons, and in spite of the fact that I was kept an extra hour in committee meeting, we had a very gay time.

So far I haven't been in the least tired but we are beginning to work three nights a week this week, so I imagine the weariness lies ahead.

Buzz has gone with Henry Morgenthau to Palestine which I think will be a very interesting trip for him.[24]

Please take care of yourself. Tommy and I send you our best wishes, and I am as always

Affectionately,
Eleanor Roosevelt

TLS BBP, NjP-SC

---

1. Bernard Baruch to ER, 10 September 1948, AERP.

2. The British delegation contested the second clause of Article 2 of the draft declaration, which stated that the rights set forth in the declaration "also apply to any person belonging to the population of Trust and Non-Self Governing Territories." The British favored a "Colonial Clause," which would make anything signed by colonial powers applicable to their colonial territories. Pressure from the British delegation changed the final draft of Article 2 to read, "No distinction shall be made on the basis of the political status of the country to which this person belongs" (Glendon, 149, 302; *EUN*). As ER later explained:

> Under the constitutions which the United Kingdom has granted to some of its self-governing territories, the government of Great Britain has no right to make certain decisions for those territories. The respective legislatures decide on questions of domestic policy.
>
> Therefore, when the United Kingdom signs a convention it always has to ask to include a clause which says, in brief, that this convention will go into effect immediately within the United Kingdom and its dependencies except where these dependencies have certain constitutional rights of self-government. In the case of these self-governing territories the United Kingdom undertakes to put before them as quickly as possible the undertakings in this convention and to urge them to adhere to the convention.
>
> Always the Soviet Union and its satellites argue that this is pure camouflage, that it is just because the metropolitan territory does not wish to see these colonial territories benefitted and therefore will not adhere for them (*MD*, 29 April 1949).

On the Third Committee of the UN General Assembly, see *n*2 Document 78.

3. Paul-Henri Spaak, the first president of the General Assembly (see *n*32 Document 77). The First Committee, chaired by Dimitri Manuilsky of Ukraine, was responsible for political and security issues (Boyd, 53–54).

4. On September 25, Andrei Vyshinsky introduced a resolution to the General Assembly calling on the five "great powers" to reduce their armed forces by one-third. He then reiterated the Soviet support for a ban on the use of atomic weapons "as intended for aims of aggression and not for those of defense" until an international control agency under Security Council auspices could be established. Vyshinsky's call for an atomic control agency that would be subject to Soviet veto directly challenged the Baruch Plan of 1946 (see *n*1 Document 128). Vyshinsky later criticized the US monopoly on atomic weapons, declaring, "as long as we are looking for a solution not a single state should manufacture the bomb." The next day, however, the Soviet delegation tempered its position, issuing a call for the simultaneous banning of weapons and establishment of a control agency. Still, ER remained wary of the Soviet proposal:

> The US would be glad to start on a program of disarmament if there was a UN inspection force with free access to all nations. The Russian proposal is not an honest one and we would have no way of checking on what they did unless they submitted to inspection which they have refused to do. Until the UN is able to inspect, we can not afford to disarm. I am all in favor of disarmament and the use of atomic energy for peaceful purpos-

es, but I am realistic enough to know that we must be strong militarily and economically to have the USSR respect us (Thomas J. Hamilton, "Russian Spurs U.N.," *NYT*, 26
September 1948, 1; "Excerpt From Statement Made by Vishinsky," *NYT*, 2 October
1948, 2; A. M. Rosenthal, "Vishinsky Changes Atomic Ban Stand; West Is Skeptical,"
NYT, 3 October 1948, 1; ER to Corabelle Burke, 15 November 1948, AERP).

5. Carlos Romulo (1899–1985), a delegate from the Philippines and a member of the Commission
on Human Rights, was present at the UN Charter Conference in San Francisco, where he advocated independence for colonial territories. Also in San Francisco, Romulo, along with representatives
from Latin America and other non-European regions, pushed for language in the charter that
explicitly condemned racial discrimination (William Branigin, "U.N. Signatory Carlos Romulo
Dies," *WP*, 16 December 1985, D8; Glendon, 11–13).

6. John Golden (1874–1955), a theatrical songwriter and producer, and a close friend of ER's, visited ER in Paris ("John Golden Dies at Bayside Home," *NYT*, 18 June 1955, 17; Lash, *Years*, 33;
MD, 1 October 1948).

7. For ER's letter to Truman, see Document 384.

8. For ER's letter to Frances Perkins, see Document 383. On Drew Pearson, see *n*1 Document 146.

9. On Count Folke Bernadotte, see *n*1 Document 374. The Bernadotte Plan, which both Jews and
Arabs opposed, proposed transferring the Negev to the Arabs, in exchange for giving all or part of
Western Galilee to Israel. Bernadotte submitted his report, which he intended as a basis for negotiation, to the General Assembly on September 16. He was assassinated the next day by a Jewish
antipartition underground group (Urquhart, 172–79, 192–93).

10. Cohen wrote to Supreme Court justice Felix Frankfurter November 6 that he felt a "deep sense of
humiliation" over the handling of the Palestine problem. He argued that Secretary Marshall had been
led to believe that any criticism of the department's position was "based on ignorance and political
motives" and felt "only embarrassed and compromised by the piece-meal knowledge that is grudgingly
accorded to us. (By us I mean generally Mrs. R and myself)—the others are generally content to be
relieved of the responsibility and to follow the inside click [*sic*]." Cohen added that he did not believe
that a "public row" would help the situation, as his position "would be ascribed to the fact that I am a
Jew." He concluded: "My thought is therefore to try and find at an early opportunity a colorless excuse
for quietly going home" (Cohen, *Truman*, 249). For more on Benjamin Cohen, see *n*36 Document 84.

11. Baruch did not travel to Russia in 1948.

12. Andrei Gromyko, the Soviet ambassador to the UN, and Dmitri Skobeltsyn, a Soviet atomic scientist and advisor to the Soviet delegation of the Atomic Energy Commission (Holloway, 164–66).

13. In a letter to Secretary Marshall on March 13, 1948, ER suggested that in an effort to ease tensions between the United States and the Soviet Union "you and the President, with a picked group
of two industrialists, two labor leaders, two people representing the general public, should really
demand that Great Britain, Russia and ourselves, sit down around a table before we actually get to
a point where we are in a war" (Document 320). The same day, ER sent a similar letter to Truman:
"I don't think I have been an alarmist before but I have become very worried and since we always
have to sit down together when war comes to an end, I think before we have a third World War we
should sit down together" (Document 321).

14. Brigadier General Marshall S. Carter (1909–1993), assistant to the secretary, Department of
State. (*FRUS 1948*, vol. 1, Part 1, 13; Bruce Lambert, "Marshall Carter, 83, Intelligence Official
and Marshall Aide," *NYT*, 20 February 1993, 48).

15. Baruch is most likely referring to Ray Tucker (1893–1963), a Washington correspondent and
columnist ("Washington Whirlygig") for the McClure Syndicate ("Ray Tucker Dead: Ex-
Columnist, 69," *NYT*, 2 May 1963, 30). On Drew Pearson, see *n*1 Document 146.

16. In response to Baruch's refusal to serve on the Democratic Finance Committee, Truman wrote Baruch August 31 indicating his disappointment with the decision: "A great many honors have been passed your way, both to you and your family, and it seems that when the going is rough it is a one-way street. I am sorry that this is so" (Hillman, 39; Donovan, 418; "Baruch Won't Talk of Truman Letter," *NYT*, 1 November 1948, 18).

17. Sensing that "all traditional avenues of negotiation" with the Russians had been exhausted, on October 5, 1948, President Truman informed Secretary Marshall, who was in Paris for the Third Session of the United Nations General Assembly, that he was sending chief justice Fred M. Vinson on a peace mission to Moscow. Truman later wrote that he hoped Vinson's mission "might expose the Russian dictator to a better understanding of our attitude as a people and our nation's peaceful aspirations for the whole world." Unfortunately for Truman, however, the announcement caused a storm within the State Department and the UN delegation. Marshall, in particular, believed the Vinson mission would appear as a political maneuver right before the presidential election, and would circumvent the efforts of the Security Council. After listening to Marshall's objections, Truman decided not to move forward with the Vinson mission (Donovan, 423–24; *FRUS 1948*, vol. 2, 1157, 1184–86; Truman, vol. 2, 212–17; Vandenberg, 457–58).

18. In an attempt to provide Secretary of State Marshall added leverage at the meeting of the United Nations General Assembly in Paris, on September 21, 1948, the Joint Chiefs of Staff presented to the National Munitions Board a strategic military plan for "total war," which put the United States in its strongest military position since the start of the Cold War. The new military planning program clarified the roles of the army, navy, and air force, and provided the Munitions Board a picture of the weapons and supplies needed in the event of major war (Charles Hurd, "Nation Held Ready in Military Plans," *NYT*, 22 September 1948, 11; "The Machinery of Defense," *NYT*, 22 September 1948, 30).

19. Malvina "Tommy" Thompson and Curtis "Buzz" Roosevelt Dall Boettiger (1930–), ER's grandson, joined ER on this Paris trip (*MD*, 23 September 1948).

20. ER first made this suggestion in letters to Truman and Marshall dated March 13, 1948. See Document 321 and Document 320.

21. See *n*17 above.

22. On the Italian colonies issue, see *n*3 Document 373.

23. See *n*16 above.

24. On October 15, Henry Morgenthau, Jr., general chairman of the United Jewish Appeal, and Curtis Roosevelt Boettiger, serving as ER's personal representative, traveled to Palestine to "make an on-the-spot survey of the way in which the funds contributed by American Jews are supporting large scale immigration into Israel from the DP centers and other parts of Europe." While there, Morgenthau declared that the "overwhelming majority" of Americans were sympathetic to the new Jewish state, and reminded the Israeli people that their current war for independence was reminiscent of the "early critical days of the birth of [the United States], when George Washington faced far superior forces." He also believed that it was "high time" for the Truman administration to clarify its Palestine policy. "The vacillating policy of the United Sates," said Morgenthau, "is most confusing to the people in Israel and must be a great source of satisfaction to Russia. If the Israeli Government is given any kind of a break the Israeli, of all people in the Mediterranean basin, in my opinion, would form a hard core of resistance against the spread of communism." Following their survey in Palestine, ER remarked in her column, "To both of them I think this was a trip of great interest, and I do know that it gave my grandson exactly what I had hoped—a glimpse of a world completely different from any he had ever lived in" ("Morgenthau Goes on Palestine Tour," *NYT*, 16 October 1948, 3; "Morgenthau Says U.S. Backs Israel," *NYT*, 21 October 1948, 8; "Morgenthau Asks a Palestine Policy," *NYT*, 1 November 1948, 3; *MD*, 3 November 1948).

ENDORSING TRUMAN

Other than objecting to Wallace's campaign for the liberal Democratic vote, ER remained uncharacteristically silent about the 1948 election. Indeed, after the national nominating conventions, she devoted only three columns to electoral politics. Written in September, these columns offer generic support to Democrats, singling out only gubernatorial, congressional, and mayoral candidates by name—Chester Bowles and Adlai Stevenson for the state house, Senator Paul Douglas, Representatives Helen Gahagan Douglas and Chet Holifield, and Mayor Hubert Humphrey.[1] As she wrote September 10:

> As a Democrat, I have been giving some serious thought to an important consideration in connection with the national elections in November. No Democrat wants any support from the Progressive Party and I should not think they would want any support from the so-called Dixiecrats.

> Therefore, Democratic voters must concentrate on electing every liberal they possibly can in every state in the Union, and for every office, whether it is for Senator, Representative, Governor, or a member of a state legislature.

> If we are going to elect a Democratic President he deserves to be able to carry out the things he believes in. It has been manifested that he cannot do that unless we elect liberals all the way down the line.

> I have no idea whether the country as a whole has been thinking through the problems facing it and has been deciding what actual policies it wants to support on Election Day. If, however, President Truman in his recommendations to Congress has stood for the things that the average man in this country believes will be of benefit to him, then the duty of the voter in the coming election is clear. He must elect Democrats all the way up and down the board ...

> A Democratic President, if elected, must be able to carry out the things that the people of this country actually believe are the policies that will benefit them in the next four years, both at home and abroad. And he cannot do that alone.[2]

ER did not discuss Truman with readers after that.

"Frances Perkins telephoned me last night from Washington," ER wrote Joe Lash October 4, "asking for a letter endorsing Truman by name. She said Drew Pearson was saying that I was for Dewey. She made the point that we needed as big a Democratic vote as possible even tho' we were defeated, so I've written and sent her a letter to the President. If it ever sees the light of day I hope you will approve."[3]

383

Eleanor Roosevelt to Frances Perkins
4 October 1948 [Paris]

Dear Frances:

I haven't actually endorsed Mr. Truman because he has been such a weak and vacillating person and made such poor appointments in his Cabinet and entourage, such as Snyder and Vaughan, that unless we are successful in electing a very strong group of liberals in Congress, in spite of my feelings about the Republican Party and Governor Dewey, I can not have much enthusiasm for Mr. Truman.[4] Though there are many people in the government that I would hate to feel would not be allowed to continue their work, I still find it very difficult to give any good reasons for being for Mr. Truman.

That is why I told him the last time I saw him, that I was keeping completely inactive in partisan politics, though I would say in my column that I am a Democrat and voting the Democratic ticket, and I would write what I could that would help the Democratic Party.[5]

Nevertheless, since you asked me to send you the enclosed letter, I am doing so because you are quite right, if we are going down to defeat, we probably should go down having done what we could for the candidate and we should try for a good vote. I have addressed my letter to the President as being the most effective way.

Affectionately,

TLc AERP, FDRL

Once Truman received ER's letter, he sought her permission to make it public. She telegraphed "GLAD HAVE YOU USE ANY WAY YOU WISH." Within a week, the letter was prominently incorporated into his print advertising campaign. For example, New York City's Liberal Party made it the focus of its advertisement in the November 1 *New York Times*.[6]

384

Eleanor Roosevelt to Harry Truman
4 October 1948 [Paris]

Dear Mr. President:

I understand that there is some comment in the newspapers in the United States that I have not come out for you as the Democratic candidate and prefer the election of the Republican candidate. I am unqualifiedly for you as the Democratic candidate for the Presidency.

This year I hope every Democrat and independent voter is concentrating on the election of as many liberal Democrats to Congress as possible. I hope for this particularly from the labor and farm groups who have perhaps the greatest stake in the preservation of liberal leadership.

Liberal policies during these next few years are of vast importance on domestic issues. A Democratic administration, backed by a liberal Democratic Congress, could really achieve the policies for which you have stood.

As delegate to the United Nations I have become very much aware of the fact that stability in our own government and in its policies is essential to help the Western Democracies on their road to rehabilitation.

With every good wish, I am,

Very cordially yours,
Eleanor Roosevelt

TLS AERP, FDRL

---

1. See *MD*, 4, 10, and 11 September 1948.

2. *MD*, 10 September 1948.

3. ER to Joe Lash, 4 October 1948, JPLP, FDRL.

4. On ER not publicly supporting Truman, see Document 361. On John W. Snyder, see *n*1 Document 56, header Document 231, and header Document 301. An old friend and war buddy of the president, Harry H. Vaughan (1893–1981) remained closely affiliated with Truman's political career. When Truman assumed the vice presidency, Vaughan became his military aide, a position that he retained when Truman became president (*HSTE*).

5. See Document 333 and Document 361.

6. Harry Truman to ER, 17 October 1948, AERP; ER to Harry Truman, 21 October 1948, HSTSF, HSTL; "A Message from Mrs. Roosevelt," *NYT*, 1 November 1948, 48.

FINALIZING THE UNIVERSAL DECLARATION OF HUMAN RIGHTS, PART 1

The Third Committee convened September 28 to review the draft of the Declaration prepared by the Human Rights Commission (called hereafter the Lake Success draft).[1] After concluding a general discussion of the overall principles the draft presented, the committee began an article by article review, thus providing the nations not represented on the eighteen-member HRC a chance to propose changes by offering amendments to the Lake Success draft. Charles Malik chaired these sessions, which lasted until December 9.

Despite the thoroughness with which the HRC had done its work, the Third Committee spent eighty-five meetings and twenty subcommittee meetings considering almost 170 proposed amendments. From the outset of these discussions ER expressed concern in My Day about the number of amendments submitted, the lengthy speeches of the delegates, the delaying tactics of the Soviet Union and its allies, and the wisdom of a large body attempting to revise a document carefully crafted by a small group: "I am more than ever confirmed in the belief that when a group has worked over something for more than two years, it is very difficult to make any except minor drafting changes without actually beginning again at the beginning and doing the work all over again in the larger group."[2]

The editors opted to include a generous selection of My Day columns from this period to reflect ER's assessment of the issues the Third Committee addressed as it engaged in its final debate over and adoption of the declaration.[3]

385

My Day
9 October 1948

PARIS, Friday—Committee Three, on which I serve, has actually reached the point of discussing the first article of the Bill of Human Rights. Six amendments, I think, are already in, although not all of them have been presented as yet.

When I see how many are coming in for this initial statement, which was designed really to set the tone of the declaration and to emphasize the fact that there is a spiritual feeling back of it and which I thought, therefore, was not a very controversial article, I realize more and more that the original position which the United States took was wrong.[4]

It seems to me it would be better to accept the declaration even though we might see flaws in it than to amend it too much, since amending it might do more harm than good. It is a little like the painter who, having finished a portrait, thinks that a few added touches will make it perfect, and instead of improving it he destroys the personality he had caught in the original painting even though there were some flaws.

One amendment, presented by the delegate for the Union of South Africa, created a great effect upon a number of the members of the committee. I immediately asked to speak, but now I think it was fortunate, since there are many other amendments yet to be presented that the opportunity was not given to me yesterday. I now realize I would have spoken with too much emotion and perhaps not as objectively as the conditions called for.[5]

As far as one can judge, the present government of the Union of South Africa must live under a cloud of fear. I realize I do not know the exact numbers of the white population, and perhaps if I did it might explain to me their basic philosophy as regards all peoples of color and even extends itself to the position of women.[6]

The fundamental human rights and freedoms that the Union of South Africa is willing to accord all peoples do not include, I gather, any social rights and I doubt whether they include equal economic rights.

It was a strange speech, and when you looked around the table where 58 nations are represented you wondered how any nation could live in the world of today and hold such a philosophy.

It was rumored the other day that the Union of South Africa wishes to withdraw from the United Nations because of their difference in point of view. But I think if they make such a decision in the world of today, in which so much of their own population cannot even be drawn into the circle of social acquaintances, they will be standing still while the rest of the world moves forward in a spirit of fraternity and equality.

I lunched yesterday with some members of nongovernmental agencies who are attending these United Nations meetings as observers. A custom has been established whereby at least one member of the United States delegation is on hand at these get-togethers to answer questions that these observers may wish to present.

I was interested to learn that there are representatives here of men's as well as women's organizations, and some of them are in constant touch with branches of their organizations in other countries, which also have sent observers. For instance, it was a representative of the Lions Club, I think, who told me that four other delegates are accompanying him and that a number of South American countries also have sent observers to these sessions.

Among this group many of the men are arranging to make trips to other countries while they are over here to get firsthand information and to observe conditions which should be very valuable to their organizations when they return.

I am constantly amazed at the kindness and hospitality of the French people. Yesterday I was invited to spend next Sunday at a beautiful and historic house outside Paris, and another invitation urged me to go to another lovely house where a cultural center has been established in the memory of the son of the house who was lost in the war. At this latter place a group of young people from many countries gather to visit and to talk, and I am sure that in such historic and beautiful surroundings it must be a great experience for any one who is able to go there.

Unfortunately, I could not accept either invitation, as I never am sure of being free until the last minute.

TMs AERP, FDRL

---

1. The HRC prepared its final draft of the declaration during its meetings at Lake Success, New York.

2. *MD*, 11 October 1948. Although the Third Committee made a few important changes, it left the Lake Success draft more or less intact.

3. See Document 391, Document 392, Document 394, Document 395, Document 396, Document 397, Document 398, Document 399, Document 400, Document 401, Document 402, Document 403, Document 404, and Document 405.

4. It is not clear what ER means by "the original position which the United States took." The context suggests that she is having second thoughts about the United States seeking to amend some of the articles in the Lake Success draft. Yet, she had cautioned against amending the draft in her opening statement to the Third Committee. According to the summary report, ER said that her "delegation was aware that the declaration might be improved upon [but] considered the declaration, as a whole, a good document and was prepared to adopt it in its existing form, without further amendment, if the majority so agreed." She then "warned the Committee of the time which

might be wasted if numerous amendments were to be considered. The declaration had already undergone minute scrutiny. Every Member state had had the opportunity to submit comments, and all comments received had been given careful attention, so that the document as it stood was widely representative of the views of Members of the United Nations" (Third Committee, Third Session, First Part, Eighty-Ninth Meeting, 30 September 1948, 33, UNORGA, MWelC).

5. The Lake Success draft of Article 1 read:

> All human beings are born free and equal in dignity and rights. They are endowed by nature with reason and conscience, and should act towards one another in a spirit of brotherhood (Glendon, 295).

The South African delegate, Charles Theodore Te Water (1887–1964), proposed replacing the phrase "dignity and rights" with "fundamental rights and freedoms," questioning whether equality and dignity were universal concepts. As recorded in the summary report of the meeting, he expressed concern that:

> … the article's reference to equality of rights was an enunciation of the principle of equality in respect of all rights, personal, social, economic and political, whether or not those rights were fundamental. That, enunciated as a general principle, did not and could not correspond with the actual conditions in different countries, with their different legal, social, economic and political systems. Men and women had and always would have different rights. There were, for instance, marked divergences in the property rights as well as in the political rights of women. There was no need to give examples of those differences in the modern world, which was divided between widely divergent economic and social systems. His delegation, therefore, felt that the article should be limited in its language and its scope to *fundamental* human rights.

Vladimir Dedijer, the representative of Yugoslavia, immediately expressed his indignation at Te Water's statement and asked that the secretariat circulate the complete text of the speech. Te Water clarified his position the following day, explaining, according to the summary report, that his delegation believed that "the various articles should be devoted to statements of fundamental rights whereas the dignity of the individual was actually a deeper and broader concept than a right" (*SESA*, 462; Glendon, 144, 146; Third Committee, Third Session, First Part, Ninety-Fifth Meeting, 6 October 1948, 92, 95–96, UNORGA, MWelC; Third Committee, Third Session, First Part, Ninety-Sixth Meeting, 7 October 1948, 96, UNORGA, MWelC).

6. After South Africa's National Party formed a government in 1948, it enforced the racial policy of apartheid through statutes, racial segregation, and the disenfranchisement of black Africans (*OEWH*).

Women and Postwar Germany

October 23, 1948, ER flew to Stuttgart, Germany, to address a public forum organized by the League of Women Physicians of Württember-Baden, taking temporary leave of her Human Rights Commission colleagues in Paris for two days. While there, she met representatives of the International Refugees Organization (IRO) and visited Jewish and Ukrainian displaced persons camps. Once at the forum, the reception ER received from the 1,000 women surprised her. As she reported to David Gurewitsch:

> I was favorably impressed by the women doctors who had invited me. They are conscious of all their needs and conditions are bad but for the first time they do not shy away from all responsibility. I expected a cold reception since Franklin and I were not especially liked during the Hitler regime but to my surprise the restored State Theatre was full with no seats vacant in the three top tiers and though my speech was honest they received it warmly. I spoke in German, bad German, but everyone seemed to understand and I found I could understand them fairly well.[1]

386

Address by Eleanor Roosevelt at Stuttgart, Germany
23 October 1948[2]

This is a very difficult time for the women of Germany, for many women have seen two wars which have required of them great sacrifice and they are now going through a post-war period in many ways probably more difficult than any they have experienced before.

After World War #1 they were not completely occupied. Now part of their country is lost to them and the Germans who lived there, have had to find homes in other parts of Germany, and besides the whole of their country is occupied by foreign troops and foreign civilian officials.[3] In addition, the camps of refugees still complicate their lives.[4]

The nationals of a country naturally always feel that they have not been responsible for bringing about the disasters which have over-taken them. In this last war, however, I think it is well for the people of Germany as a whole, to realize that the people of the rest of the world feel that it was in large part the violation of human rights and a willingness to allow a dictator to make the decisions which should remain with the people themselves, which alienated the peoples of the rest of the world and consolidated public opinion in opposition to the German people.

As far as my own country is concerned, it has always been very easy for us to like the German people. Many of those who came to settle in our country came, of course, to escape political or religious persecution in their own country, or because their ideas of freedom were more advanced than those of their fellow country men. Many have come to us since the days of Carl Schurz.[5] The standards of living in our two countries are more nearly similar than in most of the other countries of Europe, and yet we have found ourselves opposed to one another in two great wars on matters of principle. That is because, in the main, we are a country built from many nations. We evolve into a type which is a very distinct American type, but we keep a sense of divergence of background even in our unity. We can not imagine believing that any one race is superior to any other race and we also believe in the rights of the people to make the final decisions in their government and to hold the reins of power in their own hands. It is true that sometimes we fall short of our ideals, but as a rule, we abide by the will of the majority of our people peacefully expressed in elections held after free and open discussion of the questions at issue in which we have participated by secret ballot.

We elect people to office whose backgrounds as far as heredity goes, may come from any one of the racial strains present in different parts of the European Continent and some times even mixed with strains from other continents. We have prejudices and discriminations but we fight against them and we try constantly to perpetuate the pattern of our free and equal democracy. Sometimes fear or a temporary laziness induces us to permit certain divergences from real ideals, but before long we find ourselves rallying in the majority, to our beliefs.

Now that the German people have been through these years of trial it may be that they will be more anxious to lend their weight to the growth of real democracy in their country. No occupying army is ever a very good example or a very good vehicle through which to teach the ideals of democracy, which are bound up so closely with peace and the obedience to the will of the majority. But I think the analytical and reasonable German people will be able to assess certain differences in the ways of democratic countries and in the ways of totalitarian ones.

It is frequently said that democracies are not as strong as nations under other forms of government, and yet it has been the Democracy of the United States in two European wars which has had to be the final balance, called upon in the hour of need to supply the goods and the men to bring about a final decision. In an economic way, partly because of our resources but also partly because of our freedom, we have become a powerful nation. We glory in our own accomplishments, but we have no desire to control the development and the will of other nations.

The realization that we were to some extent dependent on the well being of certain European nations and that with the development of modern science and economic systems, the world as a whole was more interdependent than ever before, has been in some ways none too easy a fact for our people to assimilate.

The initial move for some joint organization which might maintain peace once it was made, came from our country for the reason that by painful experience we realized that against our will, we were drawn into disturbances which arose in other parts of the world.[6] We want greatly to see the United Nations succeed because we feel that eventually if all the nations of the world are in that organization and stay in it, there will of necessity, grow better understanding and a more cooperative feeling in the various fields where joint action can bring more health and happiness and mutual prosperity to the peoples of the world.

We realize that this will require spiritual growth and leadership as well as material growth, and we hope that the women of the world will be in the forefront of those who exert their influence to these ends.

We were shocked to find that the women in many cases did not stand out as firmly as they should against the encroachment of totalitarian power in Germany, but we hope that the realization will come to all women the world over that they themselves as individuals have a responsibility within every nation to act as citizens to prevent anything which may bring suffering and deprivation again to the people of the world.

There is no longer room in the world for individual self-interest. It leads to nothing but sorrow and suffering and death. The world has become too small for selfishness, too small for purely nationalistic interests.

It is true that the people of Germany exist in the heart of a Continent where a battle is going on between two types of economy and two types of political and spiritual beliefs, but this can be made a peaceful battle. It need not degenerate into an argument carried on by force. It can only remain a peaceful battle if we have firm convictions and beliefs in the freedom of the democratic ideal and if we fight as citizens and refuse to allow again a totalitarian system to engulf us.

I believe that the USSR has a right to develop her own system within her own borders, and I believe she has a right to build up allies along her borders, but not to control those allies through force, in their political ideas and economic and military systems. ~~Germany tried to do it and the communists also see its value.~~[7]

The words nazism and fascism will forever be looked upon with horror by the free peoples of the world and communism[8] must not be allowed to fill the vacuum left by nazism and fascism, and carry on any of the same methods which created the fear and hatred of the other systems.

Democracy believes in the right of people to develop peacefully and in the right of discussion and the rule of the majority. People may change their opinions, but they must do so under the rule of law and through persuasion and not force, if the world is to be freed from the fear of war and the horrors that follow it.

Women can play a role in the development of democracy. They bring children into the world and they are the most influential factor in the early years of the lives of those children. They can build character, they can stand firm for the principles that can lead to the maintenance of peace.

My husband had a deep interest in the well-being of individual people and in their freedom throughout the world. He wanted to broaden the base of security, of freedom from want and freedom from aggression, of free speech, of free action which would allow the individual to grow and develop his fullest powers. He believed that people could make mistakes and through the understanding of those mistakes and a real repentance, could redeem themselves and be again factors in the constant rise to better things that we strive for in this world for the peoples as a whole.

I believe it is easier for women to get together and to work together than it is for men some times. In this matter of developing a basis for democracy in the world, and of supporting the ideas of the United Nations and the gradual development of understanding among the peoples of the world, I believe that women can make and should make a very great contribution.

I am grateful that you have asked me to come and speak to you today and through you, to many of the people of Germany. I have no hatred for any people, but I do have a great desire to see efforts made through deeds so that the people of the world are willing to move forward together to greater confidence in one another and to greater spheres of cooperation. It is the little people who bear the brunt of what the people who are the rulers of their countries decide upon. That is why it is important that the countries be democratic, that they choose their rulers or representatives in government and that they keep in close touch with them so that when their representatives do not respond to the people's wishes, they refuse to keep them in office and put in new people who more rightly represent the longings of the average man and woman. That day, I hope, will come in Germany and in every other nation of Europe.

I offer you my friendship and cooperation if this is the ideal for which you strive. I am sure that the United States will prove to be, not only through the plans it now has made to help in the rebuilding of independent democracies in Europe, but when all the countries have greater strength, a continued help through mutual cooperation for the good of mankind in the world as a whole.

TSpd AERP, FDRL

---

1. ER to David Gurewitsch, 25 October 1948, DGC, FDRL; Irving J. Fasteau to ER, 28 September 1948, AERP; "Mrs. Roosevelt Warns Germans on 'Sovietism,'" *NYT*, 24 October 1948, 12; *MD*, 27 and 28 October 1948.

2. Although the document used for this transcription carries the handwritten date of October 24, accounts given by the Associated Press, and verified by ER's personal correspondence, indicate that the speech occurred October 23 ("Mrs. Roosevelt Speaks to 1000 German Women," *WP*, 24 October 1948, M3; ER to David Gurewitsch, 25 October 1948, DGC, FDRL).

3. See note *n*14 Document 99 for the division of Germany into zones governed by Allied forces. Stuttgart lay in the American zone.

4. Before she delivered her address, "several" German women doctors treated her to a lunch "designed … to give me some ideas of their difficulties in obtaining a variety of foods." After complaining of a diet consisting of "potatoes and vegetables, vegetables and potatoes," the women read ER "a formal report" detailing the conditions they confronted. As ER reported, one section stated that they were:

> … fully aware and regret very much that not only Germany has to suffer from the consequences of the war and National Socialism, but that all European countries are terribly struck and have to fight great difficulties. One problem, however, is characteristic for Germany and seems to be our most difficult and most critical problem, which cannot be solved without foreign assistance. It is the problem of German expellees.

In addition to addressing their concerns in her speech, ER devoted her October 27 column to them as well:

> It is very hard for nationals of any country to face the fact that their present sufferings were brought on by past actions. When I was in Germany in early 1946 the people still seemed to be stunned. Now, after three years of occupation, they have done a great deal of work. There is hope, but the problems loom very large.
>
> In Stuttgart, … after three years, housing facilities are only 65 percent of what they were before the war and very little has been rebuilt in the way of schools and hospitals. The schools are so crowded that children go on a staggered schedule. …
>
> … Overcrowding and a lack of calories and certain vitamins have greatly increased the incidence of tuberculosis …
>
> Also, displaced-persons camps are a burden, and should be removed as soon as possible from the German economy. German expellees from Czechoslovakia and parts of Germany taken over by Poland have meant that a tremendously large number of people are migrating into Germany. From 1945 to 1947 more than fourteen million destitute people came into the British and United States zones, which were already overpopulated and devastated by the war. That's a large migration of people, to say the least, and they are not taken care of by the IRO but are entirely charges on the Germany economy …
>
> I kept thinking to myself that this is what a man like Hitler could bring upon the people of his own nation. And it is no worse, of course, than what he brought on the peoples of many other nations … who are now struggling under similar conditions to rebuild their countries and rehabilitate their people.

For more examples of ER's impressions of displaced persons camps and Germany generally, see *MD*, 28 and 29 October 1948.

5. Carl Schurz (1829–1906) was a German-born American politician, orator, and journalist of much renown. After immigrating to the United States in 1852, Schurz rose to prominence as a vocal Lincoln supporter in 1858 and as commander of a division of German-American troops in the Union army. After the war and a brief career as a reporter, he served as US senator from Missouri (1869–75) and secretary of the interior (1877–81). Upon retirement from public service, he returned to journalism, expressing his opposition to expansionism and war with Spain in editorials for the New York *Evening Post*, the *Nation*, and *Harper's Weekly* (*DAB*).

6. On the origins of the League of Nations, see *n*17 Document 74.

7. This sentence is crossed out in the text ER preserved, thus there is a possibility that ER omitted this sentence when she spoke.

8. Newspaper accounts quoting this section of the speech reported that ER used the term "Sovietism" where "communism" appears in the text ("Mrs. Roosevelt Warns Germans on

'Sovietism,'" *NYT*, 24 October 1948, 12; "Mrs. Roosevelt Speaks to 1000 German Women," *WP*, 24 October 1948, M3).

ON "TRUCE ENFORCEMENT" IN PALESTINE

Approximately 10:00 PM, November 3, ER met with Secretary Marshall, Warren Austin, John Foster Dulles, Philip Jessup, and "Chip" Bohlen to review the American position on the draft UN Security Council Resolution calling on Egypt and Israel to withdraw their forces to positions occupied in the Negev Desert area prior to the outbreak of hostilities there on October 14. Because the Negev had been allocated to the Jews as part of the original United Nations partition plan, ER believed that by endorsing the resolution it would not only appear that the United States was withdrawing its support for partition, but that it was attempting to impose a "final settlement" under guise of "truce enforcement." To resist this charge, Marshall agreed to insert language stipulating that the cease-fire resolution would in no way prejudice the "rights, claims or position with regard to a peaceful adjustment of the future situation of Palestine," but ER remained convinced that the resolution was a change in US position.[1] She expressed her reservations to Marshall in the following letter written shortly after the meeting adjourned.

_387_

Eleanor Roosevelt to George Marshall
3 November 1948 [Paris]

Dear Mr. Secretary:

I felt I must write you this note because I came away rather bewildered from the meeting tonight. I did not understand what you meant by saying that the lawyers told you our change in stand on partition was not really a change, but that it was made to seem so by the papers.[2]

Just what did we intend to do if we did not intend to change our stand? What were we saying? I feel that all this is important because basically there will come a day when we will have to make a decision and I think it is going to come fairly soon. Our weight will have to be thrown back of Isreal if we really mean to sustain partition as it was envisioned in the original majority plan last year.[3] We have been keeping away from making this definite gesture in the hopes of being able to satisfy Great Britain's fears where the Arabs are concerned, and yet I sometimes wonder if we had been a little firmer with the Arabs from the start and with Great Britain, if we might not have solved this question without so much bloodshed a long while ago. That, of course, is problematical and I know it was in the hope of preventing bloodshed that we have taken each step.[4]

As I look into the picture, I realize that Isreal without the Negeb can not possibly be independent and self-supporting in that part of the world. They will undoubtedly fight for it since without it, it means constant fighting in the future.

If our decision is that they should have it under the decision taken last year in the General Assembly, we should make our backing of their claim clear and not permit the situation to become confused by the temporary, truce decisions we support in the Security Council.[5] The whole hope of success in the partitioning negotiations lies in the knowledge on the part of Great Britain and the Arabs that Isreal has our backing. It is one of those situations in which one can not remain neutral though one can be fair.

We accepted the majority report on partition because nothing better had ever been suggested and because it was the only thing that seemed to give the State of Isreal a substantial basis. Since then we have recognized Isreal as a State and have given her to understand that we are ready to give her formal recognition and support her entry into the United Nations and to help her with a loan.

This all seems to me very unrealistic if we are not going to give her the support in the negotiations which will make it possible for her to exist at all.

The Security Council resolution, as it now stands, seems to me fairly satisfactory if we get the modifications we have suggested, but that does not seem to me to settle the real problem which sooner or later we have to face and I have a feeling if we do not settle it soon, it will come upon us suddenly and we will try to act without having thoroughly canvassed the whole situation.

My respect and admiration for you, Sir, is very great and that is why I feel that I have an obligation to tell you what I think. As I told you today, I have at no time communicated with the President on this subject since I left the United States to attend this General Assembly.

Very sincerely yours,
Eleanor Roosevelt

TLS RG59, NARA II

───────────

1. Telegram, United States Delegation to the Acting Secretary of State, 3 November 1948, *FRUS 1948*, vol. 5, 1543–44; "Resolution 61 (1948) Adopted by the Security Council on November 4, 1948," *FRUS 1948*, vol. 5, 1546–47; Sam Pope Brewer, "U.N. Orders a Withdrawal in Negeb, Shelves Sanctions," *NYT*, 5 November 1948, 1.

2. On March 19, 1948, Senator Austin called for a suspension of all efforts aimed at the partition of Palestine and asked for a special meeting of the General Assembly to approve a proposal that would place Palestine under a temporary UN trusteeship. When the media interpreted this as a new policy, Truman responded that this was only an "emergency action" to "fill the vacuum soon to be created by the termination of the [British] mandate on May 15" ("U.S. Abandons Palestine Partition," *NYT*, 20 March 1948, 1; "U.S. Position in the United Nations Regarding Palestine," *SDB*, vol. 18, 4 April 1948, 451).

3. The majority report of the United Nations Special Committee on Palestine (UNSCOP) called for the partition of Palestine into two separate states, one Arab and one Jewish. Of the 10,000 square miles comprising Palestine, the Arabs were to retain 4,300 square miles, while the Jews were allotted 5,700 square miles (Cohen, *Truman and Israel*, 149–55). See also *n*8 Document 250 and Document 300.

4. See Document 302 and header Document 303.

5. In an emergency meeting on October 19, the United Nations Security Council voted unanimously to order an immediate cease-fire in Palestine, where fighting continued between Arabs and Israelis in the Negev area. Because more than 35,000 Egyptian troops still remained in the Negev at the time the United Nations adopted the cease-fire resolution, it was unclear whether Israel would retain control of the majority of the desert as stipulated in UN Resolution 181 of the previous year, or whether they would be forced to concede a portion of that territory to the Arabs (*FRUS 1948*, vol. 5, 1493–94).

ON TRUMAN, WALLACE, AND THE DIXIECRATS

After ER wrote Truman on October 4, 1948, endorsing his reelection as president, Edward Flynn asked her to make a radio broadcast urging Americans to vote for Truman and other Democratic candidates. In her only speech of the campaign, she made the broadcast from Paris on October 31, two days before the election, thus providing last-minute support in a close election. "I still believe in the Democratic party and its leadership," ER told her listeners and she declared that Truman "has shown courage":

> I think that many people may feel an anxiety, as they look at the record of the last Congress, as to what might happen if the people do not go out and vote for progressive liberals, who not only want to keep the steps forward that were made in the social field in the last twelve years, but who want to go forward and to make our country the kind of a country to which people turn as an example of what democracy really means.
>
> Working as I do in an international body, I am quite aware of the fact that communism challenges democracy, and unless we make our democracy meet the needs of the people we do not meet that challenge.[1]

On November 1, Flynn wrote ER to thank her for the broadcast and inform her that "it came over very well." Although he confessed, "It does not seem possible that President Truman can be re-elected," he believed that, at least near the end of his campaign, Truman "came out for the things that we have both stood for and that the late President Roosevelt stood for."[2]

Despite the predictions of a Dewey victory in 1948, the American people voted for Truman at the polls on November 2.[3] Upon hearing news of Truman's victory, ER wired the president to congratulate him: "You deserve to win for the fine campaign you made." Truman in turn wired her, thanking her for her "loyal and invaluable support." In reference to her radio address, he said, "Your contribution was not only timely but was of a character which no one else could make."[4]

She then wrote Joe Lash, "It is rather nice to be an American when the people so evidently take their Democracy seriously and do their own thinking as they did in this election. I did not have enough faith in them! Dewey just wasn't big enough and I think they felt more sincerity if not ability in Truman."[5]

In response to Flynn's expression of thanks for her broadcast, she wrote the following letter.

388

Eleanor Roosevelt to Edward Flynn
6 November 1948 [Paris]

Dear Ed:

I have your letter written on the 1st, and I am glad you feel that my talk came over well. I had to do it in such a rush, I wondered how it would come out.

The results of the election have left me slightly stunned and I shall be interested in your analysis of what turned the tide. I can't tell you how many of the UN delegates have congratulated me. They all seem to have confidence in the Democrats.

This victory puts a responsibility on all of us to see that the promises made during the campaign are carried out.[6]

I was pleased and encouraged that Wallace received such a small vote, and I wonder what happens now to the Dixiecrats? They certainly no longer are Democrats.[7]

My love to Helen.[8]

Very cordially yours,
Eleanor Roosevelt

TLS EJFP, FDRL

Although the American Broadcasting Company contracted with ER and Anna Roosevelt Boettiger to produce a short radio interview program in August, the show did not debut until November 8. The delay amused ER, who wrote her daughter after ABC determined the air date, "As long as you get paid I don't mind if we don't start till Nov. 1ˢᵗ though I was amused at the Republican director not wanting us on the air during the campaign. I wish I thought we could have that much influence." [9]

In introducing the program, Anna explained what she and her mother planned to do:

The program will be a combination of forum and commentary, mixed with recollections and everyday personal happenings. We'll have guests from time to time—some famous, some unknown—chosen just because they're Mr. or Mrs. John Q. Citizen with an interesting story to tell. There will undoubtedly be times when our guests won't agree with us. And for that matter, just because we are Mother and Daughter doesn't mean we will always agree. If we don't— Mother and I will argue out our differences just as though we were at home.

The first broadcast focused on the results of the November 2 election. ER recorded her segment of the show in Paris on November 6; Anna broadcast her part live from Hollywood on November 8, cutting to ER's recorded statement in the middle of the program.[10]

389

Eleanor and Anna Roosevelt Radio Program
[ER's segment]
8 November 1948

MRS. ROOSEVELT: There will probably be several interesting results of President Truman's reelection, and the one I would most like to see is the permanent ousting of the Southern Dixiecrats from the Democratic party.[11]

During the Democratic convention, when it seemed that President Truman had almost no chance of being elected, these reactionary Southerners broke with the Democratic party over the President's Civil Rights program and formed the Dixiecrats. They won four Southern states and 38 electoral votes which might well have defeated Mr. Truman if the voting had been closer.[12]

Now, when to their utter amazement Mr. Truman has been reelected over their strenuous opposition, they are anxious to get back into the Democratic party. Mr. Thurmond, the Dixiecrat candidate for President, says that he and his fellow southerners are still Democrats and that their revolt was just "a family quarrel."

The Southern Dixiecrats are still opposed to the Civil Rights bill and the rest of President Truman's progressive policies which the voters just put their stamp of approval on. However, they have a very good reason to come back now all slicked up as good Democrats and with their explanation that it was "all just a family spat."

The reason is that since the Democrats have now won a majority in both the House and Senate, several of these Southerners are entitled to important committee chairmanships under the seniority system, IF they are considered as Democrats. Among those who would lose committee chairmanships if they are NOT considered Democrats are John Rankin of Mississippi, one of the worst Southern reactionaries,[13] and Senator Olin Johnston of South Carolina who snubbed President Truman, campaigned against him, and then was one of the first on the train at Washington to congratulate Mr. Truman after his election.[14]

As I understand it, the Democratic members of the new Congress will vote on whether Mr. Rankin, Senator Johnston and the rest of the Southerners who walked out and formed the Dixiecrats are now Democrats or Dixiecrats.[15]

It is inconceivable to me how these Southerners who walked out of the Democratic convention, formed their own party, won four states and did their best to beat the Democratic President, can now walk back into the party, explain that "boys will be boys" and then take up several committee chairmanships won by the uphill fight of loyal and progressive democrats. I think the people who voted for President Truman did so out of approval for his Civil Rights bill and other progressive measures, and would not want to see him hampered by having important committee chairmanships in the hands of the very legislators who most bitterly opposed the President.

I have felt for a long time that there are really only two major political factions in the United States—Liberals and Conservatives—and that it would be much more logical if our political parties were divided along those lines. The Democratic party has seemed to me to be predominantly the party of liberalism, although through the sometimes curious evolution of politics it embraced Southerners who number among their ranks some of the most reactionary men in public life. Similarly the Republican party is traditionally the party of conservatism, although it embraces some fine liberals.[16]

Now, for the first time in history the Democrats have won an election without the "Solid South." Some of the more reactionary Southerners have chosen to break with the Democratic party and I think it would be a good idea to make the break final. Possibly the southern conservatives would be welcomed into the Republican party, with whom they have voted so often in recent years. My husband tried to rid the Democratic party of some of the most reactionary Southerners some years ago when he undertook to defeat several legislators whom he felt were sabotaging the liberal measures he felt he had been given a mandate to put into effect. He failed in this, but now that the Dixiecrats have chosen of their own accord to walk out on their party during an election I think the Democrats should insist that they stay out.[17]

TRdstr ARHB, FDRL

---

1. "Mrs. Roosevelt Backs Truman and Party," *NYT*, 1 November 1948, 17.

2. Edward Flynn to ER, 1 November 1948, EJFP, FDRL.

3. The final popular vote was apportioned as follows: Truman (Democrat), 49.5 percent; Thomas E. Dewey (Republican), 45.1 percent; Henry Wallace (Progressive Party), 2.4 percent; and Strom Thurmond (States' Rights), 2.4 percent; *HSTE*.

4. ER to Harry Truman, 3 November 1948, and Harry Truman to ER, 6 November 1948, HSTPF, HSTL.

5. ER to Lash, 5 November 1948, JPLP, FDRL.

6. In his letter of November 1, Flynn quoted the president as saying privately, "Win, lose or draw, we must keep the Democratic Party the liberal party of the country." In her letter to Lash, ER further elaborated on her fears that Truman and other Democrats might forget this commitment, writing, "I do feel however that those among us who want the Democratic party to stay a progressive party will have to try to remind the members of Congress that they were elected on that basis and owe labor groups and liberals some real consideration" (Edward Flynn to ER, 1 November 1948, EJFP, FDRL; ER to Joe Lash, 5 November 1948, JPLP, FDRL).

7. The Democratic Party did not purge the Dixiecrats from its ranks and those Democratic governors, who campaigned for the Dixiecrat ticket, remained in their state parties and worked to shore up coalitions within their state party apparatuses sympathetic to their positions. Strom Thurmond, the States' Rights Party presidential nominee, would remain a Democrat until September 16, 1964, when he announced over a statewide radio broadcast that he had become a "Goldwater Republican." He told his constituents that "if the American people permit the Democratic Party to return to power, freedom in this country as we have known it is doomed." Angry at the party platform and Lyndon Johnson's commitment to enforcing the Civil Rights Act of 1964, Thurmond declared that the party had "turned its back on the spiritual values and political principles which have brought us the blessings of freedom under God and a bountiful prosperity." Moreover, it had "forsaken the people to become the Party of minority groups, power-hungry union leaders, political bosses and big businessmen looking for Government contracts and favors" (Lewis Lord, "Thurmond Switches to Goldwater Party," *WP*, 17 September 1964, A1).

8. Helen Margaret Jones Flynn, whom Flynn married in 1927 (*ANB*).

9. ER agreed to do the show in order to help her daughter Anna out of a large accumulated debt resulting from the failure of Anna's newspaper in Arizona and her separation from her husband, John Boettiger. The show ran as a fifteen-minute, daytime program, three to five days a week, on 200 stations until it went off the air on August 31, 1949, after failing to secure a commercial sponsor. During the show's thirty-nine week run, guests ranged from politicians, notably George C. Marshall and Ralph Bunche, to entertainment figures, such as the actress Tallulah Bankhead (Asbell, 240, 242, 257; Beasely, *Eleanor Roosevelt,* 172).

10. The following excerpt contains the complete transcript of the statement ER recorded for the first program.

11. ER's statement about the Dixiecrats' membership in the Democratic Party made headlines around the country when the Associated Press sent out a wire story on *Eleanor and Anna*, quoting extensively from ER's part of the broadcast. The *Richmond Times-Dispatch* headlined the AP article: "Mrs. Roosevelt Asks Purge of 'Revolters.'" In the weeks leading up to the election, ER criticized the Dixiecrats in My Day, calling their filibustering of the anti-poll-tax legislation "an insult not only to the intelligence of the Senate but to the people of the United States" (*MD*, 5 August 1948). See also, *MD*, 4 and 10 September, and 2 November 1948. For background on the Dixiecrats, see *n*7 above.

12. For the Democratic National Convention of 1948, see *n*3 Document 361. The Dixiecrats won a total of 39 electoral votes in Alabama, Mississippi, Louisiana, and South Carolina.

13. John Rankin (1882–1960), a Democratic congressman from Mississippi from 1920 to 1950, chaired the Committee on World War Veterans' Legislation from 1931 to 1946. On the opening day of Congress in 1945, Rankin's legislative maneuvering created a permanent House Committee on Un-American Activities (HUAC). HUAC provided him with an anti-Communist platform, which he used until he left Congress. Rankin championed rural electrification, TVA, trustbusting, and the GI Bill. He opposed civil rights legislation (including abolition of poll taxes and any law that would weaken segregation), proposed laws to prevent inter-racial marriage, supported Citizens Councils, and vehemently opposed fair employment practices legislation. His 1960 *New York Times*

obituary concludes: "When the Communist issue came to the fore in American politics, the Mississippi legislator seized it as a vehicle for his recurrent anti-Semitism and attacks on Negroes and labor" ("John Rankin Dies," *NYT*, 27 November 1960, 86; Goodman, 167–69, 173–75; Belfrage, 30, 56; Carr, 19–23, 223; Frederickson, 33-34). On HUAC, see *n*1 and header Document 144; *n*11 Document 184, *n*3 Document 223, *n*3 Document 262, and Document 271.

14. Olin Johnston (1896–1965) served as governor of South Carolina from 1935 to 1939 and again from 1943 until elected to the US Senate in 1944. As a senator, Johnston often voted with the Northern liberals on domestic legislation, except on the issue of civil rights. He supported labor legislation and, unlike most of his Southern colleagues, opposed the Taft-Hartley Act. An avowed segregationist, Johnston wanted to "keep white Democratic primaries pure" as well as "maintain white supremacy," and worked to block President Truman's civil rights initiatives (Simon, 251–52; "Senator Olin D. Johnston Dead; South Carolina Democrat, 68," *NYT*, 19 April 1965, 29).

15. Rankin remained a Democrat and became chairman of the House Committee on Veterans' Affairs in 1949 following the Democrats' recapture of the House and Senate. ER is partially mistaken about Sen. Johnston. Johnston "snubbed" Truman by pointedly boycotting the Jefferson-Jackson Day Dinner at the Statler Hotel in Washington, D.C., on February 19, 1948, at which the president was the guest of honor. When the Democratic National Committee chairman, Senator J. Howard McGrath, would not assure Johnston's wife that she would not be seated "next to a Negro," Johnston and a group of his friends cancelled their attendance. Johnston paid a professional boxer to guard their table, located in front of the podium from which Truman spoke, to ensure that it would remain empty. Although Johnston's strong objection to the civil rights plank the Democrats adopted at their 1948 national convention led him to support Eisenhower over Truman for the party's presidential nomination, contrary to what ER says, he never left the party for the Dixiecrats. Once Truman won the nomination, in fact, he campaigned for his election. In 1949, he became chairman of the Post Office and Civil Service Committee (Frederickson, 80–81; "Senator Olin D. Johnston Dead; South Carolina Democrat, 68" *NYT*, 19 April 1965, 29; "Truman Charts Campaign of Progressive Liberalism," *NYT*, 20 February 1948, 1).

16. Liberal Republicans at the time included presidential candidate Harold Stassen of Minnesota, Senators Wayne Morse of Oregon and Irving Ives of New York, Representatives Margaret Chase Smith of Maine and Jacob Javits of New York (Gould, 314; *CDAB*; *NAWCTC*; Savage, 107, 119).

17. FDR tried to carry out a realignment of the Democratic Party during the 1938 mid-term elections by working to defeat Democratic senators and congressmen who, despite his decisive 1936 election victory, had voted with the Republicans to block his more liberal New Deal initiatives. The "Purge" of 1938 proved largely ineffective when Roosevelt's campaigning against conservative Democrats during the primaries did not produce the desired results, especially in the South where most of the candidates he stumped for lost. After the election the split between liberals and conservatives in the Democratic Party became more pronounced and the states' rights segregationists began to coalesce as a political faction (*FDRE*).

ON BEING CALLED A COMMUNIST

While ER struggled in Paris to reach agreement with Soviet and other Communist delegates over the wording of the declaration of human rights, she found herself castigated in the Russian press for making her criticisms public. As the Soviets stepped up their criticism of her, voters in Pennsylvania and Illinois rejected Representatives John McDowell (R-PA) and Richard B. Vail's (R-IL) bids for reelection. Both candidates had used their positions on the House Un-American Activities Committee as a cornerstone of their campaigns, only to have the voters defeat them in great part because of the zealousness with which they participated in committee activity. Moreover, charges of corruption tailed McDowell and HUAC chair J. Parnell Thomas.[1] The juxtaposition of these events inspired the following reflections on the *Eleanor and Anna* radio show.

390

Eleanor and Anna Roosevelt Radio Program[2]
[ER's segment]
17 November 1948

MRS. ROOSEVELT: Thank you, Anna. My experience in working with the delegates of Communist Russia here in the United Nations Assembly has been interesting and sometimes amusing for the reason that I have occasionally been called a Communist myself.

As a matter of fact, it used to be rather a popular pastime in American politics to call anyone with whom you did not agree a Communist, especially if he were at all progressive or interested in liberal causes. This nonsense reached its height a few years ago when Congressman Martin Dies and his House Unamerican Activities Committee was viewing with alarm even such people as Shirley Temple,[3] and a lady named Elizabeth Dilling wrote a book called "The Red Network" which named as Communists almost everyone including, I believe, even Mr. Herbert Hoover. This committee always seemed to me much more interested in making headlines than in finding facts, and my husband used to wait with some amusement for its periodic list of suspects.

We were discussing this one day when I produced the latest list and pointed out among the suspects the name of his mother—Mrs. Sara Delano Roosevelt. At this the President threw back his head and howled, for his mother was nothing if not a staunch American of the old school. She had been listed as a Communist sympathizer because she had donated money to charitable causes which, in the eyes of the House Committee, were Unamerican.[4]

All of this was funny, in a sense, but it could have serious consequences as the charge of Communism could be and was used to harass and defeat people in public office. It also frightened many government employees into a feeling that they could not take part in <u>any</u> outside activity without the threat of being called a Communist.

It always seemed to me that this indiscriminate name-calling was quite unnecessary and that it was relatively easy to tell a Communist. It would seem apparent that anyone who followed the Communist line of criticizing the war as "imperialist" when Germany and Russia were Allies, and then hailed it as a great crusade after Russia was attacked by Germany, must surely be a Communist.[5]

I think that anyone who follows the Moscow line on most issues is certainly suspect, as in the recent election when there was a striking similarity between many of the statements of Henry Wallace and those of Mr. Pavlov, the Russian delegate on my Committee, who became very angry and said I had insulted him when I mentioned this.[6]

I have been interested in many causes—and doubtless there were communists in some of them—but it always used to rather amuse me to be labeled as a Communist because I couldn't resist what the Communists might think of having me wished on them. I, of course, was quite sure that I wasn't a Communist, and now that the Russians know me a little better they are apparently quite sure, not only that I am NOT a Communist, but that they don't want me. Because I have before me a Russian newspaper called the "Literary Gazette" which devotes a column and a half to what it describes as "the unbecoming role of Eleanor Roosevelt." It says in part:

> In her declining years, Eleanor Roosevelt has decided to engage in international politics. This circle which she entered did not fail to exercise influence on her and to employ her popular surname for its very selfish and murky ends. Mrs. Roosevelt is not sparing with her speeches. This senile weakness for loquacity has been combined with a special anti-Soviet tinge which gives no rest to such American peacemakers as Dulles and Austin. The Soviet Delegation gives Eleanor Roosevelt and her friends no peace with its revealing speeches in the General Assembly. In a demagogic article Eleanor Roosevelt openly opposed the Soviet proposal for reduction in armaments and for the prohibition of atomic weapons. It is obvious from her articles and speeches that indeed she does not think too much about what she says and writes.[7]

I think that article in a Communist paper should persuade even the House Unamerican Activities Committee that I am not the close friend of Communism they seemed to suspect. Speaking seriously, though, I do think that the sort of silliness carried on by the Thomas committee is now just about ended.

I see that two members of the Committee were defeated in the election and that the Chairman, J. Parnell Thomas, was indicted for fraud. It seems to me that the defeat of the two members of the committee shows that the American people are tired of this kind of witch-hunting and feel, as I certainly do, that the Justice Department is quite capable and much better equipped to protect the nation from the Communists or anyone else. I think the United States is united in its feeling on Russia and Communism as never before and that because of Russia's recent actions Communism in the United States is now dwindling to its lowest ebb in history.

And now back to my daughter, Anna, in Hollywood.

TRdtr ARHP, FDRL

---

1. A district-wide coalition of Independents, Republicans, and business and religious leaders united against John McDowell (1902–1957), who represented Pennsylvania's 29th District, and denounced him as violating the rights of scientists and citizens by harassing them with "unspecified charges of 'guilty by association,' and by innuendo." McDowell, ironically, refused to testify on his own behalf when subpoenaed to explain why a $5,400 salary intended for his secretary went to the chair of his hometown Republican organization instead.

Richard B. Vail (1895–1955), who represented Illinois' 2nd District, needed a strong Dewey vote to counteract challenges from the left and right. When that vote did not materialize, he lost a race he was heavily expected to win.

J. Parnell Thomas (1895–1970), who as the representative from New Jersey's 2nd District equated "New Dealism" with Fascism, Nazism, and Communism to comprise "the four horsemen of autocracy," became chairman of HUAC in 1947 when party leaders placed their most senior conservatives in leadership positions. In August 1948, Drew Pearson reported that Thomas had billed the government for nonexistent employees and diverted their salaries to his own accounts. Thinking that his ill health would keep him from imprisonment, he plead no contest to the charges. Convicted in November 1949, Thomas served nine months in a federal prison in Danbury, Connecticut, and paid a $10,000 fine (*BDUSC*, William S. White, "House Republicans Put Conservatives in Chairmanships," *NYT*, 14 January 1947, 1; "McDowell of House Un-American Group Fought by Pittsburgh Citizens Committee," *NYT*, 30 October 1948, 8; "'Un-American' Inquiry Is Shelved for 1948," *NYT*, 10 November 1948, 16; *ANB*).

2. For background on the *Eleanor and Anna* radio program, see header and *n*9 Document 389. As in the case of the first show, ER recorded her segment in Paris and Anna cut to ER's statement during the live broadcast from Hollywood.

3. Martin Dies (1901–1972), protégé of vice president John Nance Garner and who later turned against the New Deal out of opposition to its urban and racial policies, held both FDR and ER in contempt. In 1938, the Texas Democrat proposed that a special congressional committee be established to examine "the extent, character and object of un-American propaganda" in the United States. He then used his position as chair of HUAC to attack FDR as the perfect illustration of the incompetence and "creeping totalitarianism" represented by a president dedicated to obliterating the power of Congress. "Stalin," Dies wrote, "baited his hook with a 'progressive' worm and [the] New Deal swallowed bait, hook, line and sinker." At first, FDR ignored Dies but by 1940, the president asked the director of the FBI to investigate the HUAC chair. Dies retired from Congress in 1945 (*ANB*). On HUAC, see Document 262 and Document 271.

   Shirley Temple (1928–), the curly haired, tap-dancing child movie star, was eleven years old when Dies allowed James B. Matthews, past president of the American League Against War and Fascism, to tell HUAC, under sworn testimony, that in sending "hearty greetings" to the Communist-owned "French newspaper Ce Soir," Clark Gable, Robert Taylor, James Cagney, "and even Shirley Temple, ... furthered the cause of communism" ("Red Growth Swift, Matthews Asserts," *NYT*, 23 August 1938, 2).

4. Elizabeth Kirkpatrick Dilling Stokes (1894–1966), whose 1933 *The Red Network: A 'Who's Who' and Handbook of Radicalism for Patriots* argued that FDR, ER, Felix Frankfurter, Charles Evans Hughes, and rabbi Stephen Wise were Communists and created a national sensation, dedicated her career to opposing the Roosevelts. Two more books soon followed: *The Roosevelt Red Record* in 1936 and *The Octopus* in 1940. In 1941, Stokes took the lead in opposing lend lease and two years later, she, with twenty-nine others, was accused "of plotting to set up a Nazi state here ... and to incite mutiny in the Armed Forces." The trial ended four years later when the judge dismissed the indictment ("Mrs. Elizabeth Dilling Stokes, Foe of Communism, Dies at 72," *NYT*, 1 May 1966, 88).

5. For the Nazi-Soviet nonaggression pact of 1939 and the Nazi invasion of the Soviet Union in 1941, see Document 6. ER realized that the Communists had taken control of the American Youth Congress, an organization that she originally supported, when it criticized opponents of Nazi Germany after the Nazi-Soviet pact, then abruptly reversed its position when Hitler invaded the Soviet Union.

6. For more on ER's view of Henry Wallace's ties to the Communists and adoption of Soviet positions on many issues, see Document 305 and Document 355. Alexei Pavlov (1905–?), became the Soviet representative to the Human Rights Commission at the opening of the third session of the HRC at Lake Success in May 1948 (Glendon, 110–11).

7. This excerpt appeared in an undated clipping from the *Literaturnaia gazeta*, a periodical published in Moscow. *Izvestia* launched a similar criticism against ER November 27 after she declared that the Soviet constitution possessed "only pure propaganda significance." Just as a "fly can [not] eclipse the sun," the Soviet correspondent retorted, no "hypocritical servant of capitalism" could darken the "sun" manifested in the Soviet constitution ("Mrs. Roosevelt Assailed, Russian Newspaper Calls Her a 'Fly' on Soviet 'Sun,'" *NYT*, 28 November 1948, 24).

FINALIZING THE UNIVERSAL DECLARATION OF HUMAN RIGHTS, PART 2

October 19, ER told My Day readers that her work on Committee Three "in this General Assembly session is still practically standing still." She continued:

> I feel that if we devoted as much time actually to trying to accomplish something definite on the declaration of human rights as we do to attack and counterattack among the representatives of the big powers, we should be practically finished with this item on our agenda.

> Nevertheless, we are still on Article 3,[1] with any number of articles and amendments before us and a large number of other items on the agenda that have not as yet been touched.

> To some of us it looks almost impossible that the committee will get through any worth-while work at this session. One hopes, however, that the desire actually to pass the Bill of Human Rights and a convention on freedom of information in some form may finally bring about a self-imposed discipline and we will get finished."[2]

By November 18, more than a month into the process of debating each article of the Lake Success draft of the declaration, the Third Committee finally seemed to be making some progress, although it would take several more weeks to complete the process. From here until the conclusion of the meetings, ER used My Day to furnish almost daily reports on the proceedings. These columns are the most detailed accounts she wrote of the drafting process.[3]

_391_

My Day
18 November 1948

PARIS, Wednesday—Upon my return from London early this week, I was delighted to find that good progress was still being made by the Human Rights Commission.[4]

Article 19 of the Declaration of Human Rights, I found, had been argued out and adopted. It reads:

"Everyone has the right to take part in the government of his country directly and through freely chosen representatives.

"Everyone has the right of equal access to public service in his country.

"The will of the people shall be the basis of authority in the government. This will shall be expressed in periodic and genuine elections which shall be universal and equal and which shall be held by secret vote or by the equivalent of free voting procedures."[5]

The first paragraph was passed in its original form without difficulty, but the second was altered as a result of criticisms by Americans who felt it might have given rise to the idea that any government was obliged to employ anyone who wishes to be in government service, regardless of whether or not the government considered them desirable employees.[6] From my point of view, the revised version is clearer and better.

The third paragraph probably caused the greatest difficulty, and a great many people will wonder at the last phrase, "or by the equivalent of free voting procedures."

Most of us think if any election is universal and equal by secret ballot, it is fairly well safe-guarded. But this line was included to protect the rights and customs of people who may be able to manage their own affairs and perhaps have ways of doing so, but who cannot read or write.

All these little peculiarities, which one does not think of at first, always come up for discussion in the final analysis of an article of this kind. Though troublesome, they are of great importance to democracy and the development of democratic procedures throughout the world.

A resolution covering what should be done for Arab refugees was very thoroughly canvassed, and there is a great deal of interest as to who shall be the director of this move.

A number of people have been mentioned, but I am told that the Arabs hoped Mr. Bayard Dodge would be selected. Mr. Dodge, who formerly was head of the Near East College of Beirut, is well known and trusted by the Arabs. In addition, everyone who knows Mr. Dodge is convinced that he will do the right thing for all people concerned. His family long has taken great pleasure in that area of the world and he has the reputation of integrity and unselfish service in the public interest.[7]

The flight back from London was very delightful. The weather was clear and we could see the whole countryside in all its autumnal splendor.

I was very impressed with the experience of one of the pilots on our plane. It was his first visit to France since he was shot down over Paris during the war. He was very anxious to see the French family which had sheltered him from the Germans and aided his escape to Britain.

He was deeply grateful to them and to the others who had helped him. And admired their great courage, for he knew, as they did, that it meant death to them by the firing squad if they were caught.

He said he would like more Americans to visit France in order that they might fully appreciate the great sacrifices made by the French people during the war. He thinks, as I do, that visiting Americans would have a better understanding and appreciation of the Marshall Plan and other aid efforts.

I also had the opportunity to talk with a young enlisted man. He was depressed because his wife and two small children could not be here with him. He lacks one stripe in rating for the privilege.

Even if they were, I doubt if there would be much contentment and happiness for them with the situation as it is here. Europe is too upset right now for settling families.

I feel, however, that men stationed here should be rotated more often, but I realize that this is difficult and that it is just one more of those dislocations created by war. It should make us work even harder to prevent it happening again!

TMs AERP, FDRL

392

My Day
19 November 1948

PARIS, Thursday—We have had many long and irritating sessions this week, discussing the very important Article 12 of the Declaration of Human Rights.[8] It may be that everyone is weary, but as an example of the way grown people should not talk about each other, I think a record of these meetings would be excellent for school rooms of all countries concerned.[9]

Even with all the discussion, we did not finish the article.[10]

Article 12, in its original form, gives everyone the right to work under favorable conditions and at fair wages with protection against unemployment. It also provides that everyone has the right to equal pay for equal work accomplished and everyone is free to form and join trade and labor unions for protection of his rights and interests. It further states every person who works has the right to receive remuneration in proportion to his capacity and remuneration that will assure him a decent standard of living for himself and his family.[11]

The Soviets, as usual, sought to include their regular amendment regarding race, nationality and sex in abbreviated form.[12]

Their persistence in this respect is unwise and unnecessary, for Article 2, which their amendment is really an incomplete modification of, states very completely and without recourse that everyone is entitled to all rights and freedoms without distinctions of any kind, such as race, color, sex, language, religion or social origin.[13]

Thus, it is quite evident that Article 2 covers the subject very much more comprehensively than it could be covered otherwise, unless the entire article were repeated in every instance the subject was referred to. Therefore, if only "race, nationality or sex" are mentioned, it is possible in the future to interpret it in a limiting way.

We have tried over and over to point out to the USSR that Article 2 did a better job of providing for non-discrimination than could possibly be done in their "non-discrimination" clause. But so far we have not been successful in persuading them otherwise.

It is obvious that there are many things yet to be ironed out in these articles and with tempers as short as they are now, I wish it were possible for all of us to relax for a while and begin again refreshed. Some of the bitterly personal frictions which arose in the discussions would have eased when the sessions were resumed.

This is only wishful thinking, though, for we start in again in the morning. It rained almost the whole week; maybe that had a bad effect on everybody.

I had lunch with some of the leaders in the present French government and I confess that despite their lengthy explanations, French politics are still very complicated to me. It seems that because the French are such individualistic people, they must have a great many parties.[14]

It simply is not possible, they told me, to have just two parties, or even three or four. There will always, they believe, be numerous small parties, exerting enormous power sometimes over the bigger ones.

They smilingly told me that one of the government's assistant ministers belonged to a party of just twelve people.

My old friend Tom Campbell and his daughter from Montana dropped in on me earlier this week. They were on their way to North Africa to aid in restoring a great wheat-growing area which was once Europe's breadbasket but now is a desert.[15]

TMs AERP, FDRL

---

1. Article Three read "Everyone shall have the right to life, liberty and the security of person" in both the Lake Success draft and in the draft completed by the Third Committee (Glendon, 295, 302).

2. *MD*, 19 October 1948.

3. See header to Document 385.

4. ER means the Third Committee, not the Human Rights Commission, which had finished its work on the declaration in June. ER had just returned from England where she attended a ceremony in honor of FDR at Westminster Abbey and received an honorary degree from Oxford. During her absence, Durward Sandifer, her State Department advisor, sat in for her at the meetings of the Third Committee (*MD*, 15 and 16 November 1948; Glendon, 155).

5. The article numbers are from the Lake Success draft, not from the final draft of the declaration adopted on December 10, 1948.

6. The Lake Success draft read: "Everyone has the right of access to public employment in his country." The Third Committee dropped "equal" and replaced it with "employment" rather than "service" (Glendon, 297).

7. Bayard Dodge (1888–1972) taught at the American University of Beirut for ten years, then served as its president for twenty-five years before retiring in June 1948. He spoke Arabic fluently. Both Dodge and the university he served thought partition "unwise and unjust to the Arabs." In June 1948, as a member of the executive board of the Committee for Justice and Peace in the Holy Land, Dodge urged American Zionists not to force the issue of a Jewish state "because they were causing danger of disruption of our national unity and encouraging anti-Semitism." After the United Nations established the United Nations Relief for Palestine Refugees in November 1948, Secretary-General Trygve Lie appointed Stanton Griffis, American ambassador to Poland, as its director; Griffis then chose Dodge as his advisor (*CB 1948*; Thomas J. Hamilton, "Palestine Conciliation Body Is Voted by U.N. Committee," *NYT*, 5 December 1948, 1).

8. ER means Article 21, not 12.

9. Alexei Pavlov, the Soviet delegate, and Stephan Demchenko, the Ukrainian delegate, used this discussion to attack capitalist economies and, in particular, the United States, for creating large numbers of unemployed workers and for paying women and minorities lower wages than those paid to white males. The summary reports do not record the actual language used in making these attacks (Third Committee, 139th and 140th Meetings, Summary Record, 16 November, 1948, 517, 524–25, 527–28, UNORGA, MWelC).

10. In a vote taken at this session, the Third Committee deadlocked over Article 21. When the tie vote could not be broken, the committee then referred the article to a drafting subcommittee that reported back to the full committee on November 25. Following further debate, the Third Committee adopted the revised article. See the last few paragraphs of Document 399 (Third Committee, 141st, 142nd, and 143rd Meetings, Summary Record, 16–17 November 1948, 539, 552–54, UNORGA, MWelC).

11. In both the Lake Success draft and the Third Committee draft, Article 21 concerns the right to work. In the Lake Success draft it read: "1. Everyone has the right to work, to just and favorable conditions of work and pay and to protection against unemployment. 2. Everyone has the right to equal pay for equal work. 3. Everyone is free to form and to join trade unions for the protection of his interests" (Glendon, 297).

12. The Soviet amendment to Article 21, which had been previously submitted to and rejected by the HRC, read: "Everyone, without distinction as to race, nationality or sex, has the right to equal pay for equal work." In pressing his attack on discriminatory practices in the United States and the Union of South Africa, Stephan Demchenko said, "There should be no fear of repeating that all discrimination of race, nationality and sex was to be prohibited, so that, when those responsible for such injustices read the declaration, they might perhaps wish to put an end to them" (Appendix, Third Year, Seventh Session, Supplement No. 2, 24 May–18 June 1948, 34, UNOR ECOSOC, MWelC; Third Committee, 140th Meeting, Summary Record, 21 September–8 December 1948, 524, UNORGA, MWelC).

13. Article 2 read in the Third Committee draft: "1. Everyone is entitled to all the rights and freedoms set forth in this Declaration, without distinction of any kind, such as race, colour, sex, language, religion, political or other opinion, property or other status, birth, or national or social origin. 2. The rights proclaimed in this Declaration also apply to any person belonging to the population of Trust and Non-Self-Governing Territories" (Glendon, 302).

14. Although ER told Trude Lash she had lunch "with some French government officials who are upset at our Ruhr policy," she did not identify them (ER to Trude Lash, 17 November 1948, JPLP, FDRL).

15. Thomas D. Campbell (1882–1966), a lifelong Republican who revolutionized large-scale mechanized wheat farming in Montana, shared FDR's commitment to developing North Africa into a productive agricultural resource for Northern Europe. Building on his World War I pioneering efforts to grow wheat on previously untilled land, Campbell traveled to Russia where he helped Stalin develop the first Five-Year Plan, in the process becoming one of the first Americans to meet the Soviet leader. A frequent visitor to the White House, Campbell was dispatched by FDR "as a private citizen" to England to help address the food shortage the bombing of Britain would create. USAF Brigadier General Campbell spent World War II coordinating the reallocation of equipment in China, Burma, India, North Africa, and Italy.

Campbell, convinced that "North Africa could produce a surplus for Europe within three years," had flown to France (accompanied by his daughter Catherine) at the request of the French government to review how best to apply his principles of moisture conservation, erosion control, and summer tillage to the North African desert. He agreed to do so without pay as a contribution to increasing the world food supply (Russell Porter, "U.S. Wheat Expert to Advise Africans," *NYT*, 14 November 1948, 28; "Wheat Expert Plans a Flight to England," *NYT*, 3 March 1941, 3; "Thomas D. Campbell Dies at 84," *NYT*, 19 March 1966, 29; Thomas D. Campbell, "A Land That Could Be Europe's Granary," *NYT*, 23 November 1947, 148).

THE *NATION*, ANTI-CATHOLICISM, AND NEW YORK CITY SCHOOLS

July 23, an "overwhelming majority" of the New York Board of Superintendents voted to remove the *Nation* from public school libraries. Citing a series of "definitely anti-Catholic" articles written by Paul Blanshard, superintendent William Jansen justified the board's action by arguing that the articles "contributed to religious animosity by going into matters of faith and out of the realm of politics and social controversy."

However, not all within the school hierarchy agreed with Jansen's decision. Board of Education vice-chair Maximilian Moss found it "ironical" that the superintendents "take action which would abridge freedoms guaranteed by the Bill of Rights while at the same time demanding that our teachers and children hold them sacred." If the schools "tamper with hard fought American rights in the name of good citizenship," he continued, "we make a sham of the Constitution."[1]

The *Nation* also immediately protested the decision. July 8, Freda Kirchwey, its editor and publisher, announced the formation of the Ad Hoc Committee to Lift the Ban on the *Nation*, chaired by Archibald MacLeish. The committee then released MacLeish's statement calling the ban a threat "not only to the liberal press, but the whole press, and not only the whole press but the educational system of the country and its library system." The controversy escalated throughout July, as education faculty compared the ban to book burning and argued that the banning puts the Catholic Church "in the untenable position of appearing to refuse to tolerate any criticism of the policies of its officials." The American Civil Liberties Union, the American Jewish Congress, the Council Against Intolerance, and the Americans for Democratic Action (ADA) supported the *Nation*'s appeal.[2]

ER quickly lent her support and also lent her name to telegrams. As she explained in My Day:

> It seems to me quite natural that magazine subscriptions and the choice of books to be allowed in school libraries must rest with some group. It is not censorship to make a choice as to the books, for instance, that you allow different age groups to read in school libraries. It is not censorship to subscribe or not to subscribe to certain magazines. The Nation had been subscribed for, however. Therefore, the question at present is whether giving up this subscription was fair under the circumstances.
>
> I joined this committee because it seemed to me unfair to give up a subscription because of these articles. The reason for my feeling is this: within the school system there should be no criticism by teachers or pupils of different religions, but there should be material available to pupils, when they reach the proper age, that will give them an insight into possible criticisms that may be made of different religions as well as different political opinions, or economic theories, or scientific discoveries.
>
> Personally, I believe that the articles under criticism expressed opinions that were derogatory to the Roman Catholic Church and with which I do not agree. But I do not consider that a sufficient reason for giving up a subscription to The Nation.[3]

As the beginning of the school year approached, Jansen defended his actions:

> It is not a question of freedom of speech or the press. We are not raising any question as to the right of a magazine to print any material it wishes to. We maintain that the articles which repeatedly attack the religious beliefs of our

pupils do not belong in public school classrooms or libraries. Freedom of the press has never meant that everything that is printed must necessarily be used in the public schools.

By October, tensions increased. MacLeish accused Jansen of allowing the church hierarchy to dictate school subscription policy and Jansen proclaimed that he was certain that "probably many of" those who signed MacLeish's petition "had not read all of the articles in the series under discussion." In an attempt to change ER's position, Jansen sent her a summary of the actions discussed above, as well as his summaries of the articles he found objectionable.[4] After reviewing the debate once again, ER responded with the following letter.

_393_

Eleanor Roosevelt to William Jansen

21 November 1948 [Paris]

My dear Dr. Jansen:

I received your statement on the banning of the Nation and I have also seen some of the answers which have been sent in.[5]

I was hesitant about joining Mr. MacLeish's group and signing the statement because I felt the article in question had some rather prejudiced statements in it, but on going into it more deeply, I decided that these were things which individuals should be allowed to read and decide on. They could reject them or accept them, and young people of high school age are quite able to do this.

All questions of censorship I dislike very much and I think to remove a magazine from the rolls which has served the public as honestly as has the Nation is a great mistake. I do not always agree with the stands that the magazine takes, but I nevertheless think that the public as a whole has a right to have that point of view before them and I think it is highly unwise for the schools to keep the older children from contacts which they are bound some day to meet.

Very sincerely yours,

TLc AERP, FDRL

---

1. Murray Illson, "Superintendents Ban the Nation from Schools as Anti-Catholic," _NYT_, 24 June 1948, 1.

2. "Ban on The Nation in Schools Fought," _NYT_, 9 July 1948, 17; "School Ban on Nation Reaffirmed; Open Hearing with Mayor Sought," _NYT_, 20 July 1948, 1. For information on MacLeish, see Biographical Portraits.

3. _MD_, 26 July 1948; "School Ban on Nation Reaffirmed; Open Hearing by Mayor Is Sought," _NYT_, 20 July 1948, 1.

4. William Jansen, "Should Religious Beliefs Be Studied and Criticized in an American Public High School?" AERP; "Jansen Stresses The American Way," _NYT_, 11 September 1948, 17; "Ban on the Nation Upheld by Jansen," _NYT_, 12 October 1948, 23.

5. ER reviewed a letter Jansen received from Erwin Griswold, dean of Harvard Law School, and a statement issued by NYU professor George Axtelle, chair of the Departments of History and Education (AERP).

FINALIZING THE UNIVERSAL DECLARATION OF
HUMAN RIGHTS, PART 3

394

My Day
22 November 1948

PARIS, Sunday—Two sessions of our committee Friday were devoted to Article Twenty-two of the draft of the Declaration of Human Rights, but as yet Article Twenty-one, which is being worked on by a subcommittee, has not yet been brought before us. That is because there is a real difficulty which presents itself in Article Twenty-one.

It deals with the right to work and the conditions of work. The Cuban delegate has the conviction that one of the statements in this article, saying that "everyone has the right to equal pay for equal work," should be supplemented by a statement to convey the idea that the needs of a man's family should be taken into consideration in deciding whether he receives adequate pay. This particular question has of course been argued by people for many years. The basis of pay is usually the amount of work you do and the skill or value of that work. If you tie a man's need up with his salary, I think a good many people would feel that one is treading on a somewhat dangerous path, since a man with ten children doubtless may need more than a man with only one or two. If an employer is going to pay more to a man just because he has ten children, then he is going to look for employees who don't have any children.

Long ago a great many of us decided that this question of a man's pay had to be considered in relation to his ability, and that an adequate standard of living would probably have to be achieved in certain circumstances through some kind of social services. For instance, in Great Britain a grant is given to help families with children. The same is done in France. This raises the family resources, and many of us feel that the thought which the Cuban delegate is trying to have embodied in the text should more properly be in Article Twenty-two, which deals with such matters.

After our committee had discussed many amendments, we finally drew up a draft of Article Twenty-two which read as follows:

"1. Everyone has the right to a standard of living adequate to the health and well-being of his family and himself, including food, clothing, housing, medical care and necessary social services, and to security in the event of unemployment, sickness, disability, widowhood, old age or other lack of livelihood in circumstances beyond his control.

"2. Motherhood and childhood have the right to special care and assistance."

This second provision is dear to the heart of the delegate from the Dominican Republic. She has fought for the rights of women for many years in her country, and her main point was that it was a right and not a charity to give special care and assistance to mothers and children. A storm broke loose, however, because the Russian delegate said both the United Kingdom and the United States had noted the fact that while they accepted this paragraph, still motherhood and childhood were really not exactly the right words to use. In Russian, he said, it made no sense, and he would be the laughing-stock of everyone, since any baby would understand that this paragraph was not well worded. Both the United Kingdom delegate and I myself had in fact been originally content to say simply "mother and child," as was stated in the original draft of the article. But for the sake of harmony we had accepted the change and that was the way it was voted in spite of protests.

A third paragraph was added which read: "Children born out of wedlock shall enjoy the same social protection as those born in marriage." This paragraph I had opposed, for it seemed to me entirely obvious that all children, being themselves blameless, were entitled to the same special care and assistance, and I did not feel that special reference to this condition was called for in the

Declaration. Moreover, it seems to me that the provision about childhood already contained in the second paragraph clearly referred to all childhood. But a majority of the committee felt differently, and so the entire article was adopted with this paragraph included.[1]

TMs AERP, FDRL

---

1. In the final draft of the declaration the wording remained essentially the same and became part 2 of Article 25: "Motherhood and childhood are entitled to special care and assistance. All children, whether born in or out of wedlock, shall enjoy the same social protection" (Glendon, 313).

395

My Day
23 November 1948

PARIS, Monday—Last week ended in a rush. I dashed from session to luncheon, back to session and then to dinner and back to session again.

Friday we had a morning, afternoon and evening session scheduled. I tried to sandwich social activities into this jam-packed schedule, but I wasn't too successful, though I did manage to lunch with the Yugoslav delegation on split-second timing. I missed dinner with Mr. James McDonald, our envoy to Israel,[1] and Miss Gertrude Ely, both of whom I wanted to see very much. I had a few words with Miss Ely before the evening session began, but I missed Mr. McDonald entirely.

I was very interested in Miss Ely's trip here for the children's emergency fund, but we had to postpone detailed discussion.[2]

Article 23 of the Declaration of Human Rights was discussed and amended. It reads:

"Firstly, everyone has the right of education which shall be free at least insofar as elementary and fundamental education is concerned. Elementary education shall be compulsory. Technical and professional education shall be made generally available. There shall be equal access to higher education on a merit basis.

"Secondly, parents have the priority right to choose the kind of education that shall be given their children.

"Thirdly, education shall be directed to full development of the human personality and to strengthening the respect for human rights and fundamental freedoms and to the promotion of understanding of tolerance and friendship among nations, religious and racial groups as well as activities of the United Nations for the maintenance of peace."

I must say I do not like the composition of this article as much as that which was originally drafted.[3] The effort to get in everybody's ideas, I think, resulted in so much detail that there is the risk of clouding the entire meaning of educational freedom.

There were many unnecessary improvements to the original article, and I think it is now overloaded and somewhat meaningless.

There are some things in all the paragraphs which I hope the style committee will be permitted to change for the sake of better English, before this draft is finally presented to the General Assembly. For instance, I don't know what "priority right" really means, but I am told it is acceptable.[4]

I particularly liked the simpler wording in the original draft of this article, and was especially impressed with its last paragraph which read, "promotion of understanding tolerance and friendship among all peoples."[5] Instead of the wording we now have which specifies "nations, religious and racial groups" and tacks on activities of the United Nations.

I may be wrong, but I have the feeling that in a document of this kind, which should stand before the world for years to come, at least it is a mistake to emphasize the fact that there are racial and religious groups that are intolerant toward each other. It might be better to simply say all peoples shall strive for understanding, tolerance and friendship.

When you work with an international group, you learn that one person's point of view must be subordinated to the will of the majority and so Article 23 passed as I have given it here.[6]

TMs AERP, FDRL

––––––––––––

1. For James McDonald, see header to Document 109. In June 1948, after the establishment of Israel, Truman appointed McDonald as special US representative to the new nation.

2. Gertrude Ely (1876–1970), ER's good friend and a long-time activist in the Democratic Party from Bryn Mawr, Pennsylvania, began working closely with ER when they volunteered for Red Cross duty during World War I. Throughout the twenties, they collaborated on matters relating to the League of Nations, the Bok Peace Prize, and the American Friends Service Committee. In 1935, Ely joined the New Deal as director of women's programs for the Works Progress Administration and often traveled with ER to visit the Arthurdale Subsistence Homestead Community. During World War II, Ely organized USO clubs in North and South Carolina and began serious involvement with refugee issues, the causes to which she would devote the rest of her life. At war's end, Ely traveled to Europe where for the next three years she worked in refugee camps managed by the Church World Service, the International Refugee Organization, and United Nations Relief and Rehabilitation Administration. In March 1948, after spending three months visiting displaced persons camps in Europe, she deplored the failure of Congress to pass legislation to admit a fair share of these refugees to the United States. By the time she visited ER in November, Ely had become one of the strongest supporters of the children's emergency fund (soon to be named UNICEF). For a discussion of the problems confronting the International Children's Fund and ER's response to them, see Document 395 (Lash, *Eleanor*, 290, 630; "Gertrude S. Ely Dies," *Philadelphia Evening Bulletin*, 27 October 1970, 1; Gertrude Ely, "Failure to Provide for DP's," Letter to the Editor, *NYT*, 4 March 1948, 24; "Gertrude S. Ely Dies," *Philadelphia Inquirer*, 28 October 1970).

3. Article 23 of the Lake Success draft read:

> 1. Everyone has the right to education. Elementary and fundamental education shall be free and compulsory and there shall be equal access on the basis of merit to higher education. 2. Education shall be directed to the full development of the human personality, to strengthening respect for human rights and fundamental freedoms, and to combating the spirit of intolerance and hatred against other nations and against racial and religious groups everywhere (Glendon, 298).

4. The word "priority" became "prior" in the final Third Committee draft.

5. This phrase does not appear in the Lake Success draft, but apparently appeared in an intermediate draft.

6. In the final draft of the declaration adopted by the UN General Assembly, the article on education (now Article 26) reads:

> (1) Everyone has the right to education. Education shall be free, at least in the elementary and fundamental states. Elementary education shall be compulsory. Technical and

professional education shall be made generally available and higher education shall be equally accessible to all on the basis of merit. (2) Education shall be directed to the full development of the human personality and to the strengthening of respect for human rights and fundamental freedoms. It shall promote understanding, tolerance and friendship among all nations, racial or religious groups, and shall further the activities of the United Nations for the maintenance of peace. (3) Parents shall have a prior right to choose the kind of education that shall be given to their children (Glendon, 313).

_396_

My Day
24 November 1948

PARIS, Tuesday—Before launching into another report on the hectic sessions of the Human Rights Commission and the Declaration of Human Rights,[1] I would like to briefly comment on two rather outstanding experiences I enjoyed this week.

I saw the French preview showing of the motion picture "The Roosevelt Story" the other night and enjoyed it very much. The translation was splendid.[2]

I also visited headquarters of the American Friends of France service committee to see the work they were doing. This organization, as you know, has been doing splendid work throughout Europe as well as in France.

A representative told me of their center in Berlin which offered training and nursery facilities for the younger children as well as accommodations for the adolescents who are ready for apprenticeship in some kind of work.[3]

My hope that at least one article for the Declaration of Human Rights would be accepted without any amendments has not yet been realized.

Article 24, the latest, read very simply and broadly! "Every one has the right to rest and leisure."

This simple statement, however, drew so many proposed changes that an unidentified delegate sent a note to the committee chairman which read: "Every one has the right to eternal rest. This rest shall be guaranteed by the state." The latter sentence referred to the many Soviet amendments which invariably stressed state control.

The Soviet amendment to this article read, "Every one shall be guaranteed rest and leisure either by law or by contractual agreements and provision shall be made for limitation of working hours and periodical holidays with pay."

With all these specifications we were again involved in the wearisome argument against spelling out guarantees in limited and inadequate fashion. We simply can not make the Soviets realize that a separate and detailed article—Article 2—in the declaration provides for everything concerning human rights without limitations or recourse, and that it bears directly on every other article in the declaration.[4]

The passion for specification, however, resulted in the acceptance of a text proposed by New Zealand which read, "Every one has the right to rest and leisure and reasonable limitation of working hours with periodic holidays with pay."

I pointed out to the committee that though we had accepted this amendment, I still would have preferred the original and broader declaration, but since this was better than what the Soviets had offered it still seemed to suggest certain possible limitations.

Perhaps they are right, but I am inclined to believe that the original declaration might have been even more valuable. It cannot be considered legally binding and the moral forces may be easier to rally behind its broader statements. To spell out ways in which all rights are to be carried out in the various countries seems unwise to me.[5]

It is a curious thing too, the way in which our Soviet colleagues use the presentation of their amendments to expatiate on the perfections of their way of doing things as opposed to the bad customs and ideas of the United Kingdom and the United States.

Though I mildly protested, the Soviet Union still insisted that they had interest in the worker and that the democracies try to promote discrimination and slave labor.

Finally, an exceptionally long statement levelled at the United Kingdom and the United States drew a heated reply. The Soviet speaker was asked if those in the USSR's forced labor camps enjoyed paid vacations.

The Soviet representative gasped and demanded time to consider this one and to prepare a formal reply. His request for time was refused. He did not reply.

TMs AERP, FDRL

---

1. ER refers here to the work in Committee Three reviewing the draft prepared by the Human Rights Commission.

2. Elliott Roosevelt oversaw the production of *The Roosevelt Story*, a documentary portrait of FDR and the events of his time. It was one of the first films to capture a person's life in newsreel footage and photographs. ER saw the film for the first time in August 1947, when it was released in English, and wrote:

> One could not make such a film which would tell the story as each one of us wants it told, for in this particular case each of us has his own picture in mind. I think perhaps that is why this story is going to be useful. It is going to remind each one of us of that which meant something to us in the years from 1933 to 1945. And perhaps we need that reminder to keep accepting the responsibilities which are ours today (Schatz, 415; *MD*, 23 August 1947).

3. American Friends of France, founded by Anne Tracy Morgan in 1939, fed, sheltered, rescued, and provided medical care for French noncombatants. Its relief centers in France operated continuously throughout World War II, regardless of bombardment or invasion. In 1942, AFF provided the principal monetary support for the care of French soldiers and American soldiers, prisoners, and internees confined in German camps. Constantly pressured to expand their services, by 1944, the area AFF served stretched from the Maginot Line to the beaches of Normandy. By 1947, its postwar work had expanded to include managing day nurseries, vocational schools for boys and girls, circulating libraries, and clinics dedicated to maternal and child health and the prevention of tuberculosis—providing services to 85,000 people in three towns and ninety villages. "The work of the American Friends of France is intensified in importance," ER wrote, "because the American women over here supply the personal touch which is so essential if there's to be a sense of human feeling between peoples of different nations" ("French Send Thanks for American Help," *NYT*, 3 June 1942, 10; Helen Morgan Woods, Letter to the Editor, *NYT*, 5 March 1947, 24; *NAWMP*, *MD*, 20 November 1948).

4. Article 2 of the final draft of the UDHR reads:

> Everyone is entitled to all the rights and freedoms set forth in this Declaration, without distinction of any kind, such as race, colour, sex, language, religion, political or other opinion, national or social origin, property, birth or other status.

Furthermore, no distinction shall be made on the basis of political, jurisdictional or international status of the country or territory to which a person belongs, whether it be independent, trust, non-self-governing or under any other limitation of sovereignty (Glendon, 311).

5. The final version of Article 24 reads: "Everyone has the right to rest and leisure, including reasonable limitation of working hours and periodic holidays with pay" (Glendon, 313).

397

My Day
26 November 1948

PARIS,—The Argentine delegation presented a rather interesting proposal for inclusion in the Declaration of Human Rights today.

They are eager to include a provision for old age rights, which was, I understand, largely inspired by the wife of Argentina's president, Madame Peron.[1]

Though Article 22 of the declaration states that everyone has the right to security in the event of unemployment, sickness, disability, old age, etc.,[2] the Argentine proposal goes into much more detail. It stresses in particular that if families refuse to care for aged members, then the state should force them to do so by law. In any case, the proposal says, old people have the right to decent housing and "minimum home comforts", pointing out that old age is deserving of respect and consideration.

This sounds good, but I can't help wondering just what "minimum home comforts" means.[3] Perhaps it will be detailed later.

I cannot help wondering, too, as I read this document, whether some consideration is not due young people. I have seen a number of young women whose parents have been selfish enough to prevent them from marrying and who, as a result, have been left without support in middle age when their parents died.

I also have seen many young people who could not marry because their elders made such demands on them.

It seems only fair that young people should be allowed to marry and have children when they are still young. Therefore, I believe the Argentine proposal, as good as it is, should be revised to include the rights of youth as well as age. But regardless of what is done, it is clearly essential that aged people who can no longer earn for themselves be taken care of.

I hope we will refer this back to the economic and social councils and perhaps their committees can make favorable recommendations on the whole problem.[4]

Articles 25 and 26 finally were voted on and accepted, with the former article reading:

"Everyone has the right to freely participate in cultural life communally, to share in the arts and to share in scientific advancement and its benefits."

"Everyone has the right to protection of moral and material interests resulting from any scientific, literary or artistic production of which he is the author or producer."

It seemed to most of us that the second paragraph was unnecessary, since any such right would find protection enough through patents, copyrights or specially drawn contracts.

The second article, Article 26, originally read:

"Everyone is entitled to good social and international order wherein rights and freedoms set forth in this declaration can be fully realized."

The Soviets, however, deleted the word "good" and replaced it with "such".

In their elaborate presentation of this amendment, the USSR said capitalist order could not be called "good" social order.[5] To which I pointed out that the article did not specify whether it had been socialist, capitalist or Communist, but only that the rights and freedoms set forth in the declaration should be fully realized therefore, whatever it was had to be good.[6]

Nevertheless, it finally was decided that it might make for better drafting if we accepted their recommendation. It was pleasant to be able to vote for, instead of against, a Soviet amendment.[7]

The Soviets, however, said a lot of unpleasant things in their speech-making which included an accusation that science in the United States was completely dominated by the military and used only for military power. I felt I should answer this one, but I always grieve when I do, for I realize Soviet delegates must say things they are told to say, so most of it isn't worth answering.[8]

TMs AERP, FDRL

---

1. Maria Eva Duarte de Perón (1919–1952), wife of Argentinian president Juan Perón, initially announced "a decalogue for the rights of the aged" at her August 26, 1948, press conference. Her proposal, which would be funded through the Doña María Eva Duarte de Perón Foundation, promised to protect the aged's "unassailable" right to financial aid, housing, food, clothing, physical and mental health, recreation, work, peace of mind, and respect. Those reporters covering "Evita" "understood" that the Argentine government "would seek recognition of the new program" when the General Assembly reconvened in Paris the following month. November 22, Juan Atilio Bramuglia, the Argentine foreign minister, appeared before Committee Three to present the ten-point Argentine resolution while at home, Senora Perón addressed an election rally called to generate support for the referenda on constitutional reforms scheduled for the following day ("Senora Peron Says Aged Will Get Aid," *NYT*, 27 August 1948, 4; "Midas Touch," *NYT*, 10 September 1948, 22; "U.N. Asked to Act On Old-Age Rights," *NYT*, 22 November 1948, 12; "Argentine Work Halt Set," *NYT*, 23 November 1948, 13).

2. Article 22 of the Lake Success draft of the UDHR read:

> 1. Everyone has the right to a standard of living, including food, clothing, housing, and medical care, and to social services, adequate for the health and well-being of himself and his family and to security in the event of unemployment, sickness, disability, old age, or other lack of livelihood in circumstances beyond his control.

> 2. Mother and child have the right to special care and assistance (Glendon, 297–98).

3. Article 2 of the Argentine proposal guaranteed all "who have reached old age … the inherent right to a healthful place of abode, with a minimum of home comfort" (Third Committee, 151st Meeting, Summary Record, 22 November 1948, 626–27, UNORGA, MWelC).

4. ER means the Economic and Social Council (ECOSOC). The Third Committee voted at a later meeting in favor of sending the Argentine proposal to ECOSOC for study (Third Committee, 151st Meeting, Summary Record, 22 November 1948, 626–27, UNORGA, MWelC). See second paragraph of Document 402 (*EUN*).

5. Alexei Pavlov, the Soviet delegate, argued, according to the summary report, that "in the view of the USSR delegation, as long as society was divided into exploiters and the exploited, as long as there was private ownership of the means of production, the social order could not possibly be a good one. The USSR was not asking the Committee to approve its social order. What it did ask was that, since two conflicting views were involved, there should be no moral evaluation in the dec-

laration of either order and that the final verdict should be left to history" (Third Committee, 152nd Meeting, Summary Record, 22 November 1948, 638, UNORGA, MWelC).

6. As recorded in the summary report of the session, ER stated that while she "had no objections to the USSR amendment," she thought it "unnecessary," arguing that "any order which permitted individuals to achieve the rights and freedoms set out in the declaration would obviously be a good one and the adoption of the USSR amendment would not mean the endorsement of any particular political or social system" (Third Committee, 152nd Meeting, Summary Record, 22 November 1948, 640, UNORGA, MWelC).

7. In the final Third Committee draft of the UDHR, Article 26 read:

> Everyone is entitled to a social and international order in which the rights and freedoms set out in this Declaration can be fully realized.

In the UDHR as adopted by the General Assembly, Article 26 became Article 28 and is identically worded except for "set out," which was revised to "set forth" (Glendon, 308, 313).

8. The Ukrainian delegate, Stephan Demchenko, charged that "in many countries, science and education were made to serve the cause of propaganda and to spread racial theories; articles published in the United States showed that science in that country had been placed under military control, whereas it should serve the interest of peace and progress." ER disagreed, replying that "although during the war science in the United States had been placed at the service of the Government, and it might be recalled that all the Allies, including the USSR, had profited therefrom, science was no longer under any control." She then cited a Soviet publication discussing how "all the efforts of the Academy of Sciences should be directed towards the building of Communism" to counteract the Ukrainian's point. "The United States delegation," ER concluded, "did not agree that cultural activities such as literature, music or science should be directed" (Third Committee, 152nd Meeting, Summary Record, 22 November 1948, 632, 636–37, UNORGA, MWelC).

398

My Day
27 November 1948

PARIS, Friday—I managed to get away from the wordy confusion that is the United Nations General Assembly and the Human Rights Commission for a while yesterday. It was my first real break in many days and I was glad to have the opportunity to accomplish a few personal things.

I looked around for Christmas gifts to take home with me, but Paris seems to be only for little girls. I can get all sorts of things for the female species, but it is very difficult to find anything for little boys.

Franklin Junior and his business partner joined me.[1] Their aerial business trip around Europe had been interrupted by bad weather, so they passed the time with me until flights were resumed and they could continue on.

After this brief respite, I plunged back into the session arguing over the very important Article 27 of the Declaration of Human Rights. This is the article in which the duties of individuals to their neighbors and their communities are set forth.

We were, however, permitted to leave before the session's end—mainly because, I think, the chairman was appalled at the number of speeches scheduled for debate on this article.[2] He undoubtedly thought it would be better if all of us retired for a short rest and started over again the next morning.

His judgment, if it was such, paid off, for the next day Article 27 was voted on and passed without incident.

It reads:

"Everyone has duties to the community in which the free and full development of his personality is possible.

"In exercise of his rights and freedoms everyone shall be subject only to such limitations as are prescribed by law solely for purposes of securing due recognition and the respect for the rights of others and just requirements of morality, public order and general welfare in democratic society.

"These rights and freedoms can in no case be exercised contrary to purposes and principles of the United Nations."[3]

The American delegation suggested inclusion of the words "rights and freedoms" in the second paragraph because it has been used so frequently in the declaration it was felt it also should be included in this paragraph for consistency.

Another change, a rather extensive one, also was made in this paragraph by the delegate from Uruguay. He suggested the original words "necessary to secure" be replaced with "prescribed by law solely for the purpose of securing … "[4]

Though this was accepted, it troubled many of the commission members, for they felt that this article should have moral and spiritual force behind it and that to limit it to "prescribed by law" was a mistake.[5]

The article, incidentally, is very important, for it conditions practically every other article in the Declaration of Human Rights.

The USSR, of course, had wanted to say in this article—as well as in every other one—that the law of the individual country must govern rights that were declared or that these rights could only be obtained in measure in which laws of the country permitted them to be obtained.

In this point, the committee as a whole has not agreed. Since this is a declaration of the rights of the individual human being and since we are setting standards toward which all nations of the world shall strive, it does not seem wise to drag in legal points of the many different legal systems as represented in some 58 countries.

In some cases, however, religious differences and customs of the various countries will have to be considered. You can be sure that careful consideration will be given when the declaration is translated into five different languages.

TMs AERP, FDRL

---

1. Franklin Roosevelt, Jr., traveled in Europe in 1948 with Rudolf M. Littauer, FDRJrP, FDRL.

2. Twenty-one delegates spoke during the discussion of Article 27, which took place on November 23 and 24 and which Charles Malik chaired. The summary record does not record Malik's statement permitting delegates to leave before the end of the session on November 23.

3. In the UDHR as adopted by the General Assembly, Article 27 became Article 29 with minor changes in wording (Glendon, 314).

4. Eduardo Jiménez de Aréchaga (1918–1994), the delegate from Uruguay, argued, according to the summary report, that his amendment (A/C.3/268) attempted to introduce two clear ideas into the text of Article 27. The first was that fundamental human rights could only be curtailed by law; and the second that such laws could only be passed when required on the grounds of morality, public order and general welfare in a democratic society.

The amendment would protect personal liberty, in so far as the support of public opinion would be needed to limit human rights. It would always be easier for a Government to close down one newspaper than to have a general law censoring the Press. The latter measure, which the Uruguayan amendment would make necessary, would arouse a much greater reaction among the people of the country concerned" (Third Committee, Summary Record, 153rd Meeting, 23 November 1948, [E/800], 642–43, UNORGA, MWelC).

5. ER argued, according to the summary report, that "the language of the Uruguayan amendment was too restrictive when it was remembered that there was often a difference of opinion regarding what was strictly legal and what was just. She was sure that the Uruguayan representative had not intended to exclude the concept of moral force from article 27, but that actually would be the effect of his amendment." F. Corbet, the British delegate, shared this concern. In the final version adopted by the General Assembly, the word "prescribed" became "determined" (Third Committee, 153rd Meeting, Summary Record, 23 November 1948, [E/800], 644, 647; Morsink, 248; Glendon, 314).

399

My Day
29 November 1948

PARIS, Sunday—Despite a heavy day's work on Thursday, I did a little shopping. On the way to our committee room we have to pass through part of the Marine museum, where large models are on exhibition and where a very attractive stand is set up for the sale of various articles reminiscent of the sea. I stopped to buy a couple of scarfs which I had admired for a long time. They are lovely in color and texture and little sailor boys wigwag their flags in different squares. The profits from these sales are sent to naval charities, so everything one gets there does some little good.[1]

Noone else seemed troubled that we worked all day long on Thanksgiving Day, but when we finally broke up at eleven o'clock it was at the request of the Cuban delegate, who announced it was time the third session of the day came to an end. He did not know how others felt, but as for himself he was exhausted.[2]

The day's labors, however, were fruitful. Article Twenty-eight was passed, and reads: "Nothing in this Declaration shall imply recognition of the right of any state, group or person to engage in any activity or perform any act aimed at the destruction of any of the rights and freedoms described herein."

The discussion brought an attack on the United States from the Ukrainian delegate, who said such organizations as the Ku Klux Klan were helping American fascism to grow stronger at the present time, and from their point of view was a great danger. It is essential in the Declaration, he claimed, to say not only that a state but also groups could not engage in any activity or perform any act which could injure the rights and freedoms proclaimed in this Declaration.[3]

I do not happen to think that the Ku Klux Klan is strong enough to merit all the vehemence with which it is frequently attacked. If those who are members in the United States could see themselves as they are seen internationally, I am sure they would be surprised.[4]

Of course, the notion of political opposition of any kind within a nation is entirely foreign to Soviet political thought. They may be critical of how an individual carries out the job which has been given him to do under the Soviet government, but that he should openly advocate something contrary to the political ideas laid down by the government would be unthinkable. Any group which has left any part of their country because of political differences must of necessity be a criminal group in their eyes, and the words used by one of the delegates in describing those who left their country indicated that he thought of them not simply as civilian citizens preferring some different kind of government but as actual traitors who probably connived with the enemies of their country, for with deep feeling he spoke of them as "scum."[5]

This of course seems very odd to anyone coming from the United States, where we differ heatedly and yet are completely free to do so. How utterly unimportant, however, are these differences when big questions that affect our national or international life come up!

When we finished with Article Twenty-eight, we turned back for consideration of Article Twenty-one, which the hard-working subcommittee had been asked to re-draft.[6] This article now reads:

"1. Everyone has the right to work, to a free choice of employment, to just and favorable conditions of work, and to protection against unemployment.

"2. Everyone, without any discrimination, has the right to equal pay for equal work."[7]

The first paragraph was almost unanimously accepted. In the second paragraph, the Soviet delegate wished to enumerate the different kinds of discrimination, but his amendment was voted down and the second paragraph was agreed on as drafted. We did have one amusing little exchange when the Soviet delegate insisted the word "everyone" customarily meant "every man," and did not include "every woman." The chairman informed him that "everyone" meant men, women, children and, in fact, all human beings, but the Soviet delegate remained unconvinced.

TMs AERP, FDRL

---

1. ER refers to the Musée de la Marine, which is located in the Palais de Chaillot where the UN meetings were being held (Baedeker, 181).

2. Guy Pérez Cisneros (1915–1953) represented Cuba. The summary record does not record his request for adjournment (Third Committee, 156th Meeting, Summary Record, 25 November 1948, [E/800]699-700, UNORGA, MWelC).

3. It was actually Alexei Pavlov, the Russian delegate, who raised the issue of the Ku Klux Klan. He said, as reported in the summary record:

> There was nothing surprising in the attitude of certain occupying Powers, since it was known that in their own countries there were organizations of a fascist character that differed in no respect from those which Nazi Germany had known. The Ku Klux Klan, whose activities were well known in the United States, was one example. Naturally, attempts were made to belittle the importance of those organizations on the ground that their membership was very small and their activity of little consequence. He recalled that the same attitude had formerly prevailed concerning the fascist organizations of Hitler and Mussolini. The disastrous consequences of such indifference were unfortunately all too well known. As the same causes had again arisen, there was every reason to fear the same results (Third Committee, 156th Meeting, Summary Record, 25 November 1948, [E/800], 671, UNORGA, MWelC).

4. ER discussed the activities of the Klan on her radio program soon after she returned to the United States. See Document 408.

5. The summary record of the Soviet delegate's remarks (which furnishes only the substantive points made, not the actual language spoken) uses the words "deserters and traitors" (Third Committee, 156th Meeting, Summary Record, 25 November 1948, [E/800] 671, UNORGA, MWelC).

6. For the initial consideration of Article 21, see Document 392.

7. ER omits the second sentence of paragraph 2 and all of paragraph 3 of Article 21 of the Third Committee Draft. They read:

> Everyone who works has the right to just and favourable remuneration insuring for his family and himself an existence worthy of human dignity and supplemented, if necessary, by other means of social protection. 3. Everyone has the right to form and to join trade unions for the protection of his interests.

The United States was the only nation to vote against Article 21 and did so because it objected to the second sentence of paragraph 2. ER explained, as summarized by the UN rapporteur, that the United States agreed with paragraphs 1 and 3, but voted against the article as a whole because it:

> could not accept the second sentence of paragraph 2. In the first place, it would be a matter for long and difficult discussion to decide exactly what was meant by "a decent existence" [at the time of the vote, the phrase "a decent existence" stood in place of "an existence worthy of human dignity"]. Secondly, the principle of the supplementation of wages would prove extremely difficult of implementation. Different countries had different methods of giving social protection to the worker who needed more than he was able to earn. To assess a worker's wages by his needs rather than by the work he performed was, in her opinion, a false principle. She had therefore voted against article 21, although she fully understood the feelings of the Committee and regretted that she had been unable to support the majority (Glendon, 306; Third Committee, 156th Meeting, Summary Record, 25 November 1948, [E/800], 685, 688, 690, UNORGA, MWelC).

400

My Day
30 November 1948

PARIS, Monday—It is very interesting to find that even in our committee, which has now been working for many weeks on the Declaration of Human Rights, there is a feeling that in one way or another this declaration should be made to carry some legal weight. Every now and again an effort is made by a delegate to inculcate this authority into the document.[1]

The right of petition came up again last Friday. The French delegate[2] from the beginning has felt that no declaration could be complete unless we stated that every human being had the right not only to petition to his own government but to petition to the United Nations.[3]

In the Human Rights Commission the majority of us felt that this particular article should wait until the convention was written in full. In the convention there would have to be a provision made for the carrying out of various rights and freedoms granted to individuals. While everything in the declaration is not to be included in the convention, certain broad provisions for enforcing human rights would have to be decided on.

As most of the petitions that have come before us are about the denial of human rights somewhere in the world, this question will have to be considered. It would naturally follow that some provision would have to be made on ways to handle these petitions. But the Human Rights Commission will have to give this very careful study, and, therefore, the subcommittee on minorities and discrimination has been asked to make some recommendations on the manner of dealing with petitions. It would be wise to wait for its report.

I would not feel that it would be impossible to add another article to the declaration in the future. In fact, I rather think there will be a number of revisions. Or it might well be decided that petitions should be handled in the convention only or even that they would require a convention of their own. In any case, after a long discussion we did decide to ask that the Human Rights Committee give this question of petitions further consideration.

Soviet Russia, for once was vehemently with us on the question. That was because they consider it a violation of the rights of the sovereignty of nations to allow citizens to petition the United Nations. The United Kingdom thought that an article on petitions had no place in the declaration, and we thought that the question should be left entirely without prejudice to the Human Rights Commission, since without its careful study it would be impossible to make any real decision.

We spent last Saturday morning discussing three new articles, proposed by Russia, Yugoslavia and Denmark.[4] All of them had to do with rights of minority groups.

Yugoslavia's proposal seemed to deal chiefly with the situation of whole national groups that are in themselves almost complete nations but that are incorporated within a larger federation or group of nations. Russia, having well over 100 national groups in its domain, spelled out in detail in its amendment the rights of these groups to schools in their own language, to the use of that language in courts, to religious services and many more details that make a federation of nations a possibility without too much friction but which keeps them nevertheless a different people.

Denmark was concerned only about the rights of groups to have the language they preferred used in schools and the right to set up schools of their own if they wished.

So far as I was concerned the point brought most clearly before us was the fact that this was not a subject on which a general article could be written for a universal declaration. All of the Americas' delegates declared that this problem did not exist with them because people who come to our shores do so because they want to become citizens of our countries. They leave behind certain economic, religious and social conditions that they wish to shed and prefer to be assimilated into the new country that they are adopting as their own. They are accepted by us with that understanding, and from our point of view we would like to see the committee recognize the fact that the European problem should be handled differently.

Their situation, it seems to us, is better resolved by individual agreements or treaties among the groups that have federated, each of which desires to preserve its own national identity. It is true that sometimes a group enters a new federation unwillingly, perhaps by conquest, and sometimes it does so willingly, but in any case there are special arrangements that will make such situations more agreeable to all those concerned.

The Russian delegate said that this problem faced us in Puerto Rico. But that is not really the case. Puerto Rico will have a choice as to whether it wishes to become a state.[5] The Polish delegate spoke with feeling of the things that had been done to them under the Nazi occupation in an effort to wipe out their culture,[6] but of course that situation is not applicable in any way to the type of assimilation that goes on in the Americas on a voluntary basis.

TMs AERP, FDRL

---

1. The declaration would not legally bind governments to adhere to it, as a convention, like a treaty, would. For more on this issue, see header to Document 289.

2. René Cassin.

3. For the issue of the right to petition, see *n*4 Document 318 and *n*7 Document 288.

4. The Soviet proposal read:

> All persons, irrespective of whether they belong to the racial, national or religious majority of the population, have the right to their own ethnic or national culture, to establish their own schools and receive teaching in their native tongue, and to use that tongue in the Press, at public meetings, in the courts and in other official premises.

The Yugoslav proposal read:

A. Any person has the right to the recognition and protection of his nationality and to the free development of the nation to which he belongs ...

B. Any national minority, as an ethnical community, has the right to the full development of its ethnical culture and to the free use of its language. It is entitled to have these rights protected by the State.

C. The rights proclaimed in this Declaration also apply to any person belonging to the population of Trust and Non-Self-Governing Territories.

The Danish proposal read:

All persons belonging to a racial, national, religious or linguistic minority have the right to establish their own schools and receive teaching in the language of their own choice (Third Committee, Annexes to the Summary Record, 20 November 1948 [A/C.3/307/Rev.2], 20 November 1948, 45–46, UNORGA, MWelC).

5. The United States occupied Puerto Rico in 1898 at the end of the Spanish-American War and in 1900 established civilian rule there. It granted citizenship to Puerto Ricans in 1917. Puerto Rico remained a territory until 1952 when it became a commonwealth or self-governing territory under its own constitution. ER's response, as summarized by the committee's rapporteur, reiterated that:

... the guarantee of the rights of the individual made any reference to the rights of minorities superfluous. The rights and freedoms enumerated in the declaration fully covered the rights of minorities, with the possible exception of the provisions of the article as drafted by Yugoslavia. That proposal, however, was of a different character since it concerned the rights of ethnic communities and thus alluded to the very special circumstances obtaining in a State composed of a group of States. The question of Porto Rico, where Spanish was the official language and where the governor was a Porto Rican, had been raised in connexion with the United States. Mrs. Roosevelt pointed out that the status of Porto Rico was under discussion and might perhaps be subject to modification and that it would not impede the application of the general principle of voluntary assimilation (*RCAH*; Third Committee, 161st Meeting, Summary Record, 27 November 1948, 726, UNORGA, MWelC).

6. Fryderyka Kalinowska, the Polish delegate, said that "in Poland, the first measures taken by the Nazis had been directed against education, and also against the expression of national cultural life. They had even forbidden the performance of Polish music" (Third Committee, 161st Meeting, Summary Record, 27 November 1948, 718, UNORGA, MWelC).

401

My Day

2 December 1948

PARIS, Wednesday—Yesterday we got our Social Committee[1] meeting started at 10:30 in the morning and rejected all the extra articles for the declaration of human rights except the one presented by the Yugoslavs.[2] This reads:

"The rights proclaimed in this declaration also apply to any person belonging to the population of trust and non-self-governing territories."

This seems like a rather foolish article to me because the whole declaration says "everyone" and "every person" and "every human being," and one would think that that adequately covered even the people in the colonial areas.

The Soviet group, however, lectures the rest of us on our treatment of minorities and contends that they are the only people in the world who give equal rights really without discrimination to all the peoples that form the Soviet Union. Because they have several different peoples within the orbit of their nation, the Yugoslavs also claim that for the first time—since the new government under Marshal Tito came into power—they are able to give real equality to all these peoples.[3]

This new article will, of course, do no harm,[4] and therefore we move on to the preamble with a clear conscience. We hope there will not be many changes in substance in the preamble since it was given such very careful consideration last spring at the Human Rights Commission meeting.

Our work suffered a little break in the middle of the afternoon meeting when the Spanish translation suddenly ceased to come through. We waited five minutes and still nothing could be done. We then moved to another committee room, which happened to be empty, and there also on the first try the Spanish translation again failed. The chairman then announced that if it went off on our next effort, he would consider that there was sabotage being exercised against the Spanish-speaking nations.[5]

However, with the second try it came through perfectly and before the end of our session at 6:30 a number of delegates had presented their amendments. Since we have three meetings today—morning, afternoon and evening—I have hopes that we may finish the preamble.[6] Then the committee on rearrangement and polishing of the text in French and English will go to work and we may be able to present the Bill of Human Rights to the General Assembly before too many days go by.

I had a very interesting lunch yesterday with a group of people representing an organization interested in all subjects that touch upon family life. They have formed an international organization and are trying to keep in touch with the same kind of work being carried on by various organizations in other countries.[7]

One of their representatives attended the National Conference on Family Life held in the White House last May.[8] Miss Jane Hoey of the Federal Security Agency[9] has been in touch with them and they are trying to draw together other organizations in the U.S. to work with them.

The French representative, who has been in the U.S., told me he was much impressed by the fact that in our colleges where there are home economic sections or separate courses given in preparation for marriage these courses are often attended by the men students as well as the women. He had also come into contact with some of our Parent-Teacher organizations and was much impressed by their work.

Many employers in France have worked out a very ingenious scheme by which they supplement a man's wage so that if he has a number of children his family receives so much extra for every child. This keeps the standard of living for a family as a whole on an even keel even if one family has more children than another.

These family grants, as they are called, are given from a fund which is raised by assessing each worker a small percentage of his pay and assessing the employer a much larger amount. The fund is under the direction of representatives of both employers and employees. This group directs the business fund and also decides on allocations. The government has no direction, but it takes cognizance and watches over the effectiveness of this family subsidy.

TMs AERP, FDRL

---

1. The Third Committee.

2. Yugoslavia submitted two other articles, both relating to rights to and recognition of ethnic identity. Other proposed articles the committee voted down included a Soviet article on all persons' rights "to their own ethnic or national culture," including the right to education in their own languages; a Danish proposal similar to the Soviets'; two Cuban proposals, one on judicial procedure

and one stating, "Every person has the right to resist acts of oppression or tyranny"; a proposed article by Lebanon stating that laws within individual states must conform "with the purposes and principles of the United Nations … in so far as they deal with human rights"; and an Egyptian proposal stating that a future document would define "the nature and the extent of the measures to be taken to give effect to the rights laid down in this Declaration" (Third Committee, Annexes to the Summary Record, 20 November 1948, [A/C.3/307/Rev.2], 45–46, UNORGA, MWelC).

3. Both the Soviet Union and Yugoslavia were federations of states with diverse ethnic and religious populations. After Tito came to power, his government encouraged all citizens within Yugoslavia to think of themselves as "Yugoslavs" rather than "Croats," "Serbs," or "Macedonians" and sought to eliminate, not always successfully, any expression of national identity by the groups making up the federation. The textbooks used in Yugoslavian schools said little about the long record of civil and inter-ethnic wars that characterized the history of the states making up the federation, a pattern that resumed during the breakup of Yugoslavia in the 1990s (*OEWH*; Judt, 668–69).

4. The Yugoslav proposal did not survive as a separate article. In the final version of the UDHR, the preamble incorporates the substance of the proposed article into the statement that "every individual and every organ of society" shall promote the principles of the declaration "both among the peoples of Member States themselves and among the peoples of territories under their jurisdiction" (Glendon, 311).

5. The summary record of the meeting does not document this incident.

6. As ER noted in her December 4 column (Document 402), the committee finished the preamble late in the evening of December 2.

7. ER met with representatives of the International Union of Family Organizations (IUFO), an organization established at the World Congress on the Family and Population held in Paris in June 1947. According to Dr. Abraham Stone, an American who served as a vice president of the new organization, the participants in the congress believed that

> The enormous migrations during the war, the increasing participation of women in industrial life, the lack of housing facilities, and numerous other social, physical and psychological factors, are having a disturbing influence on the family, and the number of marital breakdowns is everywhere increasing. Both governmental and private family organizations, it was therefore felt, should strive to ameliorate the social and economic hardships brought to bear upon the family unit and to develop educational and cultural methods for maintaining and strengthening family life.

The purpose of the organization, as stated in its brochure, was "to link up all organizations throughout the world, irrespective of race or creed, who are working for the welfare of the family." The organization, with headquarters in Paris, began holding annual meetings in 1948 in a different city each year that drew representatives of government and private family welfare organizations from around the world. The IUFO planned to work closely with international bodies, especially UNESCO (Jean Delaporte to ER, 27 November 1951, AERP; Stone, "World," 10–11; Stone, "International," 72–75).

8. The National Conference on Family Life, a gathering of 125 voluntary organizations that met in Washington, DC, in May, 1948, sought to strengthen family life, which the organizers, like the leaders of the IUFO, felt had been weakened as a result of the war. The conference developed broad recommendations calling for efforts to provide families with adequate incomes, housing, education, recreational opportunities, home management resources, more effective family courts, and medical, counseling, and social welfare services. Specific suggestions also emerged from the conference, such as asking advertisers not to make American homes appear too clean and free of children in order to encourage more couples to have children and arranging for pregnant women to participate in child-rearing classes. The leaders of the conference urged the establishment of community

councils on family life that would work to implement the recommendations and suggestions made at the conference ("Aid to Family Life Aim of Conference," *NYT*, 5 May 1948, 22; Bess Furman, "Local Aid Urged for Family Life," *NYT*, 9 May 1948, 55).

9. Jane M. Hoey (1892–1968), a social worker whom ER had known since the 1920s, became head of the Bureau of Public Assistance in 1936 and served in that capacity for seventeen years. Her bureau was a division of the Social Security Administration, which, in 1948, was a part of the Federal Security Agency. The Bureau of Public Assistance administered the provisions of the 1935 Social Security Act related to aid to the elderly, the blind, and dependent children. Hoey attended the World Congress on the Family and Population in 1947, whose participants founded the IUFO (*NAWMP*, Stone, "World"; "Social Security Online: History," http://www.ssa.gov/history/orghist.html, accessed 7 March 2006).

402

My Day
4 December 1948

PARIS, Friday—As I told you, we on Committee No. 3 finished all the articles for the Declaration of Human Rights on Tuesday, but it was by dint of working until ten minutes to one Thursday morning that the committee finished the preamble.[1]

The Argentine delegate succeeded in getting his resolution through this late session. He was most anxious that Argentina's proposal for old-age care should be transmitted to the Economic and Social Council for study. This has been done, and I hope that group will refer it to the Social Commission, since this should bear some relation to existing plans for old-age care that have been tried out already in other countries. If it is to be a United Nations proposal it surely should have a universal character and embody the rest of everybody's experience throughout the world and be applicable in all countries even if in a somewhat modified form.

The whole idea had been proposed by the wife of the President of Argentina, Madame Peron, who even made a plea over the radio to the U.N. in favor of her suggestion.[2]

Three meetings of the subcommittee on rearrangement and style were held yesterday with 11 delegates present. Work progressed extremely slowly even though we only were supposed to make changes in style that seemed appropriate.

For some strange reason the Soviet Union changed its delegate, and Mr. Bogomolov,[3] who is the Russian Ambassador to France, has replaced Mr. Pavlov. It is very difficult for a delegate who has not carried on the work on a special subject to take it up near the end of a session in this way, but it also is hard on the committee, since there must of necessity be more delay.

One would admire the Soviet persistence in sticking to their point if it were not for the fact that so often the point is not worth sticking to. I have come to this conclusion often when anything is being translated into Russian. For instance, we spent hours yesterday arguing as to the proper place in a category of subjects to place certain words. The place really had no significance in the English language, but evidently the Soviet delegate felt that in moving those words we were changing the sense and making them less meaningful. He fought to have them kept in the original spot, until he finally was voted down. Even then he threatened to take it up in the whole committee, telling us he would make a speech of eight hours on the particular place those words should be.[4] I repeat, in English it made no difference at all in the meaning—all it did was to make the reading smoother.

Another amusing argument took place over an early article, which said: "Every human being … " Since many articles up to that point began: "Everyone … " or, "No one … " the English-speaking members contended that the declaration would read better if wherever we spoke about "all people" or "every human being" or "every individual" we made it uniform and said "everyone" in each case.

The Cuban delegate[5] contended that it should be "every human being" in this particular article because that implied unborn babies, whereas "everyone" did not have the same meaning. This sudden explanation evidently completely surprised the British delegate, but I was even more amused when the Russian delegate said that we had better maintain "every human being" since we must do no harm to expectant mothers.

We had a small buffet supper last evening for the faithful secretariat staff of Committee No 3, but as most of us had to get back to work by half-past eight we had only about an hour in which to talk to our guests and eat our supper.

I had a pleasant time sitting and talking with Dr. Malik and Mons. Laugier,[6] and was rather surprised to find at our table a young girl who was a stranger to us. I had seen a number of other people come in and go out, on the pretext that they had come to the wrong party by mistake. But this young girl had come in ahead and sat herself with us.

It amused me because it showed that people soon learn where the parties are given which are big enough so that they will not be noticed and no one will know whether they were invited or not. Of course, we let this youngster stay.

TMs AERP, FDRL

---

1. At its meeting on November 30, 1948, the Third Committee set up a subcommittee "to examine the totality of the declaration of human rights, i.e. the twenty-nine articles and the preamble, adopted by the Third Committee, solely from the standpoint of arrangement, consistency, uniformity and style and to submit proposals thereon to the Third Committee." ER served on this committee. The other nations represented were Australia, Belgium, China, Cuba, Ecuador, France, Lebanon, Poland, the USSR, and the United Kingdom (Third Committee, 166th Meeting, Annexes to the Summary Record, 30 November 1948, [A/C.3/400/Rev. 1], 120–21, UNORGA, MWelC).

2. For more on the Argentine proposal and Evita Perón's role in it, see Document 397.

3. Aleksandr Bogomolov (1900–1969) replaced Alexei Pavlov (*BI*, 1967–1970).

4. Bogomolov opposed moving the word "birth" in paragraph 1 of Article 2. The Third Committee text read:

> Everyone is entitled to all the rights and freedoms set forth in this Declaration, without distinction of any kind, such as race, colour, sex, language, religion, political or other opinion, property or other status, birth, or national or social origin.

The subcommittee draft read:

> Everyone is entitled to all the rights and freedoms set forth in this Declaration, without distinction of any kind, such as race, colour, sex, language, religion, birth, national or social origin, political or other opinion, or property or other status.

Bogomolov raised the issue once again after the subcommittee reported back to the Third Committee, arguing that the word "birth" lost its intended meaning if not placed in the list after other "considerations of a social character." René Cassin, according to the summary report, "did not agree that the change in the position of the word 'birth' had robbed it of its meaning. Placed after the word 'religion', it could not lead to ambiguities or acquire biological implications. His country was responsible for the wording of the French text and he urged that the word 'birth' should be retained in the place suggested by the Sub-Committee." The committee finally unanimously accepted a compromise on the order of enumeration proposed by Karim Azkoul of Lebanon, which read: "without distinction of any kind, such as race, colour, sex, language, religion, political or other opinion, national or social origin, property, birth or any other status" (Glendon, 302; Third Committee, Annexes to the Summary Record, 175th Meeting, 4 December 1948, 121–22, UNGA OR; Third Committee, 166th Meeting, Summary Record, [A/C.3/400/Rev. 1] 30 November 1948, 851, 853, UNORGA, MWelC).

5. Guy Pérez Cisneros (1915–1953) (*BI*, 1952–1955; Third Committee, General Information, 7 November 1946 [A/C.3/49], AERP).

6. For Charles Malik and Henri Laugier, see header and *n*1 Document 200.

403

My Day
6 December 1948

PARIS, Sunday—To speed our work, we are now divided into groups, eleven of us working in the subcommittee on the polishing of articles in the draft of the Declaration of Human Rights, while the rest of us try to move on with other items on our regular agenda.[1]

We discussed procedure for a long time on Thursday, hoping we could get a decision on a resolution for the best method of considering three draft conventions on Freedom of Information. It is obvious if we are to close here in a reasonable length of time—say, between December 10 and 15—that these conventions could not be given proper consideration, and so we joined with a number of other delegates in hoping that a conference to consider these conventions could be called at Lake Success next March. The same nations would be invited to attend, and in this way it would be possible to have a comparatively inexpensive conference. Only one delegate versed in this subject and one adviser would be necessary, whereas the cost of reconvening the whole General Assembly in January or February would be a very expensive undertaking. It seemed to me, however, that even if the Assembly had to reconvene, setting up this conference on Freedom of Information would still be the best way of handling these three conventions.[2]

The number of people already on their way home has shown that it is unwise to keep these Assemblies in session for such a long time. People get tired and they have other commitments, and they cannot be held to continuing their work for such a long period as we have been in the present session. As we look at the number of absents that appear in any roll call of our committee, it is enlightening to see the number of nations that have just given up and departed from the scene.[3]

Before closing our meeting, we proceeded to the motion made by New Zealand that we should take up such items on our agenda which have to go to the Fifth Committee, which is the budget committee that goes over every item entailing expenditure of United Nations funds.[4] We met with great opposition from the USSR and others who wished to discuss first the refugee problem on our agenda. There is of course a very real reason for taking up the refugee question. I would hope that under no circumstances would we wish to go home without discussing the Polish item which, the Polish delegate stressed, deals with Polish children deported to Germany.

This horrible practice, which Hitler planned and which is really a dreadful kind of genocide, caused a great many children in Nazi-occupied countries to be sent from their homes into Germany. Frequently they were reduced to a point where they either had forgotten their families and their nationality or were too afraid to say what nationality they might have had. It has now resulted in some very dreadful situations.

A small portion of these children have been found and returned to their families. It is now generally conceded that, although the child's welfare must always be considered, it is better for the children to be returned to their country of origin wherever their nationality is known and their country wishes to look after them. There are exceptional cases of course where the country of origin may no longer be under the same national government or where the parents and relatives have disappeared or where the child is old enough to make his own decision as to what he wishes to do. But, by and large, it is a perfectly natural thing for a country to want to take care of its own children. Of course, when the parents are found, it would be unnatural if the children were not returned to them, even though the children themselves might feel they were being uprooted from the only security they had known over a period of years.[5]

TMs AERP, FDRL

---

1. The United States participated in both groups. Durward Sandifer took ER's place when she could not attend. The other ten members of the declaration subcommittee included representatives from Australia, Belgium, China, Cuba, Ecuador, France, Lebanon, Poland, and the USSR. The other items on the agenda included the draft conventions on freedom of information discussed in this My Day and a resolution on UNICEF (see Document 404).

2. At the meeting of the Third Committee on December 7, ER noted that the American delegation was very disappointed that the General Assembly would not be able to review and adopt the three draft conventions on freedom of information, because:

> while the requisite for peace was international understanding, freedom of information was essential for both objectives, and for that reason the United States believed that there was no more important task before the Organization than that of safeguarding the right of the public to be fully informed.

She then spoke in support of a resolution, jointly sponsored by the United States, and proposing a special conference on freedom of information at Lake Success on March 28, 1949, so that the UN could make progress toward the adoption of these conventions before the next meeting of the General Assembly. The Third Committee voted in favor of this resolution 28 to 8 (Third Committee, Summary Record, [E/800] 21 September–8 December, 1948, 890, UNORGA, MWelC).

3. Representatives of twenty-two of the fifty-eight nations assigned to the Third Committee had already left the session, leaving thirty-six nations out of the fifty-eight on the committee (62 percent) to vote on committee resolutions. The length of the session had increased the average number of absences from seventeen to twenty-two (Third Committee, Summary Record, 21 September–8 December, 1948, [E/800], 893, UNORGA, MWelC).

4. The Summary Record of the Thursday, December 2, meetings of the Third Committee does not record a discussion of the Polish refugee situation. The Soviet representative did object to the New Zealand representative's proposal to delay discussion of refugee matters; Poland, India, and Iran concurred with the USSR objection. Nonetheless, when put to vote, the committee approved the New Zealand proposal, 19 to 9 (Third Committee, 168th Meeting, Summary Record, 2 December 1948, [A/C.3/211], 792–95, UNORGA, MWelC).

5. The afternoon meeting of the Third Committee consisted of a report of the Executive Board of the International Children's Emergency Fund (UNICEF) and a report from the acting director of the UN Appeal for Children (UNAC). These discussions chiefly concerned fundraising for emergency food distribution to children in war-ravaged countries; the only mention of "displaced children" occurred when the Dominican Republic delegate announced her country "was constructing a modern building in one of the healthiest parts of its territory" to "bestow upon 'displaced children' received by the Dominican Republic the special care which they required." For ER's interest in other children displaced by the war, see Document 245 and Document 246 (Third Committee, 169th Meeting, Summary Record, 2 December 1948, [A/646], 795–808, UNORGA, MWelC).

404

My Day

7 December 1948

PARIS, Monday—After a short discussion in our Committee No. 3 we accepted and passed on to the General Assembly the resolution of the Economic and Social Council on the work of the International Children's Emergency Fund. The resolution approves the report of the executive board, expresses its gratification that 25 nations thus far have contributed to the fund—some of them already having made a second contribution—and finally draws the attention of the members to the necessity for prompt contributions in order to carry on the agency's work in 1949.[1]

I think it is interesting to find that while the fund has had to be spread rather thin throughout the world and while at first it gave only such things as milk, cod liver oil and medicines to devastated countries, it is now considering the needs of children who are permanently in need. For instance, it has begun to work in India, Ceylon and other countries of the Pacific and in Latin America. Its work is not being done on a large scale, but at least on projects that can be beneficial permanently.[2]

There is a growing feeling that something in the nature of a children's fund should be continued in the United Nations as a permanent organization to improve conditions of children all over the world.

The next item to come up on our agenda was "The extension during 1949 of the United Nations Appeal for Children[3] and the Amendment of the relevant resolution adopted by the Economic and Social Council. This item is proposed by Australia."

The Economic and Social Council had passed a resolution closing the activities of this fund on December 31 of this year, but the resolution was passed by only one vote. There was opposition on the part of Australia and a number of other countries.

Australia felt that for the first time this United Nations appeal for children had brought the whole U.N. program close to the people. They had conducted a very successful campaign, had given their money entirely to the International Children's Emergency Fund and were very enthusiastic about continuing the appeal.

Our collection in the United States, on the other hand, had a most unfortunate experience. The appeal had been set up as part of the general appeal for overseas agencies and resulted in a very small amount of money being collected. In addition, our Government had real concern about the use of the U.N. name for a charitable appeal.[4]

We wished, however, very much to have appeals go on for the benefit of the Children's Emergency Fund, but we hoped they could be conducted under the names of the countries themselves and clearly state that the people were giving their money to the Children's Emergency Fund of the U.N. or any of the specialized agencies for their programs dealing with children. Even if desired, these funds could be directed to projects at home or to organizations working in this field whom they wished to assist.

However, we found a very great desire here to use the wording, United Nations Appeal, and in an effort to safeguard it and still make a maximum compromise we made the suggestion that such countries that gave their money entirely to the Children's Emergency Fund would be given the privilege of using the name, United Nations Appeal for Children, and such countries that wished to divide their money could use their own name as suggested above.

We also suggested that the headquarters staff be taken out of the Secretary General's office so as to free him of the responsibility and be placed instead with the Children's Emergency Fund group. This agency has its own budget and could pay for a staff. It also has a field staff supervising the distribution of supplies in countries receiving them, and this staff could also supervise any fund-raising appeals in those countries.

The committee agreed finally that the Children's Emergency Fund and the U.N. Appeal for Children should be integrated in one organization, and this is the way it will now carry on.[5]

TMs AERP, FDRL

---

1. The resolution is UN Document A/C.3/392. For background on the establishment and funding of UNICEF, see Document 167.

2. Ludwik Rajchman, chairman for the executive board of UNICEF, reported that out of seventy million people eligible for aid in war-devastated Europe, UNICEF had "only been able to assist 4,130,000 infants and children and 207,000 women, that is to say, one person out of every sixteen." UNICEF had established programs in Southeast Asia, but because of limited funds, these programs focused not so much on "the distribution of foodstuffs as the provision of medical supplies and the development of trained personnel through scholarships, the shipment of scientific equipment, and the organization of campaigns," and, in some countries, an anti-tubercular vaccination campaign. Latin America had been invited to participate in some of the medical programs (Third Committee, 169th Meeting, Summary Record, 2 December 1948, [A/646], 796–97, UNORGA, MWelC).

3. When the General Assembly created the International Children's Emergency Fund in 1946, it also established the United Nations Appeal for Children (UNAC). From 1947 to 1948, with the help of national committees in fifty-six countries and twenty-eight non-self-governing territories, UNAC solicited $30,700,000 in voluntary contributions from private sources. Some of the funds were distributed in the countries in which they were collected, some to nongovernmental organizations working on behalf of children in other countries, and 26 percent went directly to UNICEF (Third Committee, 169th Meeting, Summary Record, 2 December 1948, 807–8, [A/646], UNORGA, MWelC).

4. Whereas Australia made the UN the focus of their child relief efforts, the United States decided at a January 19, 1948, White House conference to collect donations for UNICEF as well as for twenty-six other agencies dedicated to child relief. Organized under the banner "Crusade for Children— Save a Child for the Future," the sixty-member American Overseas Aid subsumed the UN Appeal for Children, and included the International Children's Emergency Fund as one of four programmatic options its donors could support. It then announced a $60,000,000 goal to feed the more than 40 million "physically subnormal children" of Europe and Asia. Although more than one million Americans contributed to the fund, corporations and the government failed to do so; consequently, by June the UN programs (as well a dozen American relief efforts) faced extinction. In mid-July, AOA-UNAC announced that it had only raised 20 percent of its goal. Indeed, by November, the AOA-UNAC efforts raised only $18,848,260, of which $1,235,391 went to UNICEF.

Against the crisis, Rep. Sol Bloom steered a $60,000,000 appropriation through the House only to have the Senate allocate $25,000,000 and insist upon substantive contributions from other nations. The conference committee allocated $35,000,000 and set a requirement that other nations contribute 28 percent of the total goal before the United States would release its complete appropriation. This (which amounted to 1 percent of all funds expended under the European Recovery Program) kept UNICEF afloat for the rest of the year. For a succinct summary of the organizational and turf issues involved, see "U.N. Child Aid Fund Drive Fails," *NYT*, 7 November 1948, M22 ("Group Forms to Aid World's Children," *NYT*, 20 January 1948, 20; "The Appeal for Children," *NYT*, 23 April 1948, 23; "Plea for U.S. Aid to Children Made," *NYT*, 19 July 1948, 3; "Foreign Aid Units Facing Shut-Down," *NYT*, 22 July 1948, 12).

5. Under the plan adopted by the Third Committee (UN document A/C.3/369 as amended), the national committees could continue to raise private funds for UNICEF, but the separate UNAC office at the UN was abolished and UNICEF dealt directly with the national committees (Third Committee, 170th Meeting, Summary Record, 2 December 1948, [A/646], 809–11, UNORGA, MWelC).

405

My Day

9 December 1948

PARIS, Wednesday—Before we left our meeting room at 6:45 last night, our chairman in Committee No. 3 told us that when we returned for the evening session to come prepared to stay until the work on the Declaration of Human Rights was finished. Our job was to arrange the articles in their proper sequence. We were warned the task would run far into the morning.[1]

I dashed for home because I had invited Mr. and Mrs. Charles LaFollette and their daughter to have dinner with us,[2] telling them I would have to leave at 8:15 to go back to work. They accepted that cheerfully, realizing that everyone who works with the General Assembly is now obliged to spend long hours every day and often many nights at meetings.

As I was leaving the committee room, a gentleman stopped me and said, "I am from the Army press and we are going to start a March of Dimes campaign about the fifteenth of January. Would you just do a few minutes on the radio for us before you leave—a minute and a half would do it."[3]

So I dashed off a minute-and-a-half speech in German, being sure it was correct and that I could speak it understandably. Then with unusual firmness I managed to say that from now on until I left I could not do one thing more. He then asked me if, when I got home in America, I would do a short speech for them there, too.

I had visions of accumulated mail, of telephones ringing, of someone asking me every minute to do something, of children arriving for Christmas and all the last-minute Christmas preparations, of a hurried trip to Washington perhaps to report to the President and Secretary of State and of radio shows to be done.

I looked at him for a moment hopelessly and said, "I doubt if, when I get home, up to January 15 I will have time to breathe. But if I have time I will try to do it for you." He was very flattering but instead of feeling flattered I found myself wishing that someone would occasionally realize there are only 24 hours in a day.

It was pleasant to have a few minutes with Mr. and Mrs. LaFollette and their daughter at dinner. I enjoyed being with them in Stuttgart, and I was rather sorry to see them going home, but we will be following them shortly.

And I realize this is a good time for liberals to go home. After being here for the last three months I realize that if we are going to win the battle for democracy, which is, after all, the most important business before us at the moment, we will have to do it largely on the home front.

Everyone of us in Europe or in the international meetings here knows how carefully everything that happens in the United States is watched today. No issue is any longer a completely domestic issue. It reaches the farthest corner of the world and is weighed neither for nor against us as a nation only but for or against democracy and our form of government and way of life.

Just as I thought would happen at our evening session, we had to work until after 3 o'clock this morning.

When I handed my coat to the young check girl at 8:30 last night, I said, "Perhaps you had better show me where you put it in case you will have left when I am ready to go home."

"Oh, no," she replied. "When I know it is Committee No. 3 meeting I plan to stay all night. I sleep right here with the coats. It is the worst committee we have."

However, we did finish our work and, we hope, in time for the General Assembly to consider it and pass it at this session. Even though the declaration is not exactly as the United States delegation would have written it, it nevertheless is the result of 58 countries' work done together over a long period of time, and it represents real and sincere effort and devotion on the part of the members of Committee No. 3 and its chairman, Dr. Charles Malik of Lebanon.[4]

TMs AERP, FDRL

---

1. The summary record does not record Malik's remarks about the need for the delegates to stay the night of December 6 until they completed their work on the UDHR. The meeting concluded at 3:10 AM the morning of December 7 (Third Committee, 178th Meeting, Summary Record, 6 December 1948, 884, UNORGA, MWelC).

2. Charles La Follette (1898–1974), a progressive Republican congressman from Indiana from 1942 to 1946, and a third cousin of Robert La Follette, Jr., of Wisconsin, served as military governor of Baden-Württemberg, Germany, from January 1947 to January 1949. He resigned because he believed American policy in occupied Germany failed to adequately address the needs of workers and the poor and was thus undermining the growth of democracy in the country (*CB*, 1950).

3. FDR founded the March of Dimes to raise money for polio patients and for research on a vaccine to prevent the disease and donated the proceeds from the annual President's Birthday Ball to its campaigns. After FDR's death, ER continued to support the March of Dimes by addressing its fund-raisers and lending her name to its annual development campaigns (*EAI; FDRE*; "Polio Fund Helped by Mrs. Roosevelt," *NYT*, 24 January 1947, 23).

4. The Third Committee voted 29 to 0, with 7 abstentions, to adopt the Universal Declaration of Human Rights (Malik, 11).

After the vote on the Universal Declaration of Human Rights in the early morning hours of Tuesday, December 7, 1948, the Third Committee reconvened in the afternoon to consider further business. ER wrote the following column between the end of that meeting and the submission of the UDHR to the General Assembly on December 9.

406

My Day
10 December 1948

PARIS, Thursday—When we met Tuesday afternoon the Soviet delegation at once made a formal proposal in the form of a resolution to ask the General Assembly to put off consideration of the Declaration of Human Rights bill until next year.[1]

They gave as their reason that there was a whole series of articles that they wished to amend, and they talked at length about the fact that many of us have said the document is not perfect. Therefore, they could not see why we would not continue to work on it, particularly as it seemed such a backward document to a really modern democratic people.

It is, of course, true that any document, wherein 58 nations collaborate, is apt not to seem perfect to any one of them. For instance, at lunch yesterday the delegate from Santa Cruz said I must realize the declaration is based on Anglo-Saxon ideas and in many things it shocked Latin-American ideas. I told him there were many Latin-American ideas I could not accept.[2]

Also, I would have been delighted to see in the preamble a paragraph alluding to the Supreme Power. I knew very well, however, there were many men around the table who would violently be opposed to naming God, and I did not want it put to a vote because I thought for those of us who are Christians it would be rather difficult to have God defeated in a vote.[3]

I preferred greatly to accept the fact that there were people of many religions around the table, among them some who had no religion at all and they had as much right to their conception as what should go into the Declaration of Human Rights as I have.

The position of women, of course, in many Latin-American countries is very different from that which is described in the declaration. For instance, I was told of one country where a woman cannot even cash a check. Her husband has to cash it for her and the idea of her taking part in voting is simply inconceivable.[4]

But when all is said and done, the declaration will set a standard for human rights and freedoms, and if these standards are recognized as good I believe peoples throughout the world, who feel they are not being treated fairly, will gain a knowledge of the declaration. Then that silent pressure of the masses will be felt in the Kremlin in Moscow or any other government abode the world over.

When you think of all the different groups represented at our table in Committee No. 3, it was highly encouraging to find that the Soviet motion to reconsider the bill gathered no outside votes.[5] No one was deceived and no one wanted to put off the day when this declaration would be a part of the world's consciousness.

During the meeting yesterday, Dr. Malik, the chairman, gave us some interesting statistics. He said the declaration had been adopted with no dissenting vote, though the Soviet bloc abstained as usual. He said we held 85 meetings, and the average of absences at these meetings was 17 people. But the aggregate vote was overwhelmingly in favor of almost all the articles.[6]

Very few of the articles were adopted simply because there was no mention of God, and there was a very considerable mention of man's social security in the declaration. Of course, this is so, but I think the spirit of the declaration was inspired by Christianity and it never would have been written if there had not been many people behind it who were motivated by the Christian spirit.

It is true the social and economic rights so much stressed by the Soviet and, for that matter, a great many of the Latin-American countries are discoveries of this century, but I doubt if they show in reality a lack of the Godlike spirit.

I think that spirit is plainly visible by the fact that more and more people accept these facts that men must have a certain degree of security before spiritual ideas can have any real hold on them.

TMs AERP, FDRL

---

1. Aleksandr Bogomolov, the Soviet delegate, introduced this resolution after the Third Committee had voted to adopt the Universal Declaration of Human Rights. He said, according to the summary report, that "The USSR delegation would reserve the right to submit appropriate amendments and proposals to the Assembly when discussion of the declaration took place" (Third Committee, Summary Record, 21 September–8 December, 1948, [E/800] 887, UNORGA, MWelC).

2. ER probably means Hernán Santa Cruz (1906–), the delegate from Chile and a member of the Human Rights Commission. The issue of whether the UDHR is truly universal or reflects a predominantly Anglo-Saxon or Western European bias came up during the drafting and remains a subject of debate. Despite Santa Cruz's remark to ER, however, he spoke in favor of the declaration when it came before the General Assembly on December 9, saying that "both its universal nature

and its juridical significance made the declaration of exceptional importance. All the States which were signatories to it undertook to respect and extend the basic rights proclaimed. It was not of course perfect; but it would constitute a safeguard for all human beings as long as the United Nations existed" (*CB*, 1949; General Assembly, Plenary Meeting, 21 September–12 December, 1948, [E/800] 863, UNORGA, MWelC). For more on the issue of the universality of the UDHR, see Glendon, 221–33.

3. The representatives of several nations tried to introduce a reference to God into the UDHR. The Dutch, for example, proposed that the preamble begin with the sentence: "Whereas recognition of the inherent dignity and of the equal and inalienable rights of all members of the human family, *based on man's divine origin and immortal destiny*, is the foundation of freedom, justice and peace in the world," but the final version omitted any words suggesting that man has a divine origin. Johannes Morsink points out that "There is no presumption in the Declaration that the morality of human rights requires any kind of religious foundation." In the end, the drafters "went out of their way to avoid having the Declaration make a reference to God or to man's divine origin" (Morsink, 285, 263).

4. Most postcolonial Latin American republics based their civil legal systems on the Napoleonic Code, which made women almost completely dependent on their husbands or male relatives in legal matters of property and personal finance. The editors have been unable to determine which specific country ER referred to here; but as of 1948, the following Latin American countries had not extended voting rights to women: Chile, Costa Rica, Haiti, Bolivia, Mexico, Honduras, Nicaragua, Peru, Colombia, and Paraguay (*ELAHC* vol. 3, 49; *ELAHC* vol. 5, 465–66).

5. The Third Committee defeated the Soviet resolution by a vote of 26 to 6 with 1 abstention. Since it was not a roll-call vote, the summary record does not indicate which nations voted for it, but ER apparently means that only the six Soviet bloc countries voted in favor of the resolution. For the fate of the same Soviet resolution when the UDHR came before the General Assembly, see the header to Document 407 (E/800: OR, UNGA, Third Committee, SRs, 21 September–8 December 1948, 890; General Assembly, Plenary Meetings, 21 September–12 December 1948, [A/777], 930–32, UNORGA, MWelC).

6. First, the Third Committee voted on the declaration one article at a time. Eighteen of the articles were adopted without a negative vote. Then the delegates voted on the declaration as a whole, adopting it 29 to 0, with 7 abstentions (the six Soviet bloc nations, plus Canada, which later switched its vote) (Morsink, 11; Glendon, 162).

Once the Third Committee approved the Universal Declaration of Human Rights, it went to the General Assembly for final consideration. In anticipation of the upcoming vote, ER wrote to her aunt, Maude Gray,

> I hope the last lap of my work on the Declaration of Human Rights will end tomorrow & that we get it through the General Assembly Plenary session with the required 2/3 vote. The Arabs & Soviets may balk—the Arabs for religious reasons, the Soviets for political ones. We will have trouble at home for it can't be a U.S. document & get by with 58 nations & at home that is hard to understand. On the whole I think it is good as a declaration of rights to which all men may aspire & which we should try to achieve. It has no legal value but should carry moral weight.[1]

After Emile Saint-Lot of Haiti, the rapporteur for the Third Committee, presented the committee's report on the UDHR to the General Assembly, thirty-three other delegates expressed their opinions about the document. Andrei Vyshinsky spoke first, arguing, as Bogomolov had previously done in the Third Committee, that the General Assembly should postpone consideration of the declaration until its next session because the document remained incomplete and unacceptable in its present form.[2] Then Charles Malik described the long process of drafting and redrafting through which the UDHR came into being, acknowledged the contributions of many individuals both within and without the UN to its composition, and paid tribute to ER's "able leadership" of the Human Rights Commission. He concluded by stating,

> This is the first time the principles of human rights and fundamental freedoms are spelled out authoritatively and in precise detail. I know now what my government pledged itself to promote, achieve and observe when I had the honour to sign the Charter of San Francisco, on its behalf, on 26 June 1945. I can agitate against my government, if it does not fulfil its pledge, and I shall have and feel the moral support of the entire world. In this way, the law and practice of my country, insofar as they do not measure up to the standards proclaimed in this declaration, will be gradually modified.[3]

ER, speaking on behalf of the United States, spoke third. In the following statement, she briefly describes the effort that went into drafting the UDHR, defines the character of the document, and calls for its adoption.[4]

407

Statement by Mrs. Franklin D. Roosevelt
U.S. Representative to the General Assembly
9 December 1948 [Paris]

The long and meticulous study and debate of which this universal Declaration of Human Rights is the product means that it reflects the composite views of the many men and governments who have contributed to its formulation. Not every man nor every government can have what he wants in a document of this kind. There are of course particular provisions in the declaration before us with which we are not fully satisfied. I have no doubt this is true of other delegations, but taken as a whole the Delegation of the United States believes that this is a good document—even a great document—and we propose to give it our full support. The position of the United States on the various parts of the declaration is a matter of record in the Third Committee. I shall not burden the Assembly, and particularly my colleagues of the Third Committee, with a restatement of that position here.

Certain provisions of the declaration are stated in such broad terms as to be acceptable only because of the limitations in article 29 providing for limitation on the exercise of the rights for the purpose of meeting the requirements of morality, public order, and the general welfare.[5] An example of this is the provision that everyone has the right of equal access to the public service in his country.[6] The basic principle of equality and of nondiscrimination as to public employment is sound, but it cannot be accepted without limitations. My Government, for example, would consider that this is unquestionably subject to limitation in the interest of public order and the general welfare. It would not consider that the exclusion from public employment of persons holding subversive political beliefs and not loyal to the basic principles and practices of the constitution and laws of the country would in any way infringe upon this right.

Likewise, my Government has made it clear in the course of the development of the declaration that it does not consider that the economic and social and cultural rights stated in the declaration imply an obligation on governments to assure the enjoyment of these rights by direct governmental action. This was made quite clear in the Human Rights Commission text of article 23 which served as a so-called "umbrella" article to the articles on economic and social rights. We consider that the principle has not been affected by the fact that this article no longer contains a reference to the articles which follow it.[7] This in no way affects our whole-hearted support for the basic principles of economic, social, and cultural rights set forth in these articles.

In giving our approval to the declaration today, it is of primary importance that we keep clearly in mind the basic character of the document. It is not a treaty; it is not an international agreement. It is not and does not purport to be a statement of law or of legal obligation. It is a declaration of basic principles of human rights and freedoms, to be stamped with the approval of the General Assembly by formal vote of its members, and to serve as a common standard of achievement for all peoples of all nations.

We stand today at the threshold of a great event both in the life of the United Nations and in the life of mankind, that is the approval by the General Assembly of the Universal Declaration of Human Rights recommended by the Third Committee. This declaration may well become the international Magna Carta of all men everywhere.[8] We hope its proclamation by the General Assembly will be an event comparable to the proclamation of the Declaration of the Rights of Man by the French people in 1789, the adoption of the Bill of Rights by the people of the United States,[9] and the adoption of comparable declarations at different times in other countries.

At a time when there are so many issues on which we find it difficult to reach a common basis of agreement, it is a significant fact that 58 states have found such a large measure of agreement in the complex field of human rights. This must be taken as testimony of our common aspiration first voiced in the Charter of the United Nations to lift men everywhere to a higher standard of life and to a greater enjoyment of freedom. Man's desire for peace lies behind this declaration. The realization that the flagrant violation of human rights by Nazi and Fascist countries sowed the seeds of the last world war has supplied the impetus for the work which brings us to the moment of achievement here today.[10]

DSB, vol. 19 (19 December 1948), 751.

———————

1. ER to Maude Gray, 9 December 1948, DGC, FDRL.

2. Vyshinsky, as summarized in the official record, found "serious defects" in the UDHR, including "its ultra-legal form," "the absence of provisions for the implementation of the principles laid down," the "abstract form of some articles," "the absence of provisions guaranteeing the rights of national minorities," and its failure to "mention the sovereign rights of States" (General Assembly, 180th Plenary Meeting, Summary Report, [E/777] 9 December 1948, 854, 856–57, UNORGA, MWelC).

3. Malik, 124–25.

4. Durward Sandifer probably prepared an initial draft of this speech, at least of the portions expressing the American position on the articles of the UDHR, as he had been doing for her speeches before the Third Committee. Other State Department advisors probably also contributed. ER then fleshed it out and completed it. The December 8, 1948, US delegation position paper on how the delegation should handle the UDHR, along with the resolutions on its dissemination and the continuing work of the HRC on the covenant and implementation, which the General Assembly was about to consider, states: "A short statement should be made in support, with particular reference to the Declaration." In regard to the discussions of the UDHR in the Third Committee during the fall of 1948, Sandifer later told Joseph Lash that "we drafted statements for her in that debate." A search uncovered no drafts of this speech in ER's papers or in the State Department records, nor did it reveal any vetting of the speech by the State Department in Washington (*FRUS*, 1948, I, 303; Joseph Lash, notes on an interview with Durward Sandifer, 5 May 1970, JPLP, FDRL).

5. Part two of Article 29 reads: "In the exercise of his rights and freedoms, everyone shall be subject only to such limitations as are determined by law solely for the purpose of securing due recog-

nition and respect for the rights and freedoms of others and of meeting the just requirements of morality, public order and the general welfare in a democratic society" (Glendon 314).

6. ER refers to Article 21, paragraph 2, which reads: "Everyone has the right of equal access to public service in his country" (Glendon, 312).

7. The article to which ER refers became Article 22 in the final version of the UDHR and reads:

> Everyone, as a member of society, has the right to social security and is entitled to realization, through national effort and international co-operation and in accordance with the organization and resources of each State, of the economic, social and cultural rights indispensable for his dignity and the free development of his personality.

In the Lake Success draft of this article (Article 20 at that time), the wording was essentially the same, except that the text ended: "of the economic, social and cultural rights set out below" and thus referred specifically to the rights enumerated in the succeeding articles. In both cases, the article serves as a transition from the civil and political rights that precede it and as an introduction to the economic and social rights that follow (Glendon, 313, 297).

8. The Magna Carta, a charter to which King John put his seal in 1215 at the demand of rebellious English barons, restored "due process," limited the king's ability to raise monies for the crown, and formally recognized ancient civil liberties. A feudal, and not democratic, document, the charter protected the property and rights of the elite families who sought to secure their place in a feudal system. Its final clause, however, introduced the concept of "majority rule" and thus set the principle upon which democracy would be built. Yet this application did not occur until 1628, when Sir Edward Coke, as part of Parliament's rebellion against Charles I, "argued that even kings must comply to common law. As he proclaimed to Parliament in 1628, 'Magna Carta ... will have no sovereign'" ("Magna Carta and Its American Legacy," http://www.archives.gov/exhibits/featured_documents/magna_carta/legacy.html, accessed 4 March 2006).

9. The Declaration of the Rights of Man (the Rights of Man and the Citizen), adopted by the Constituent National Assembly of France in 1789, set forth the principles of equality and individual liberty that the French Revolution championed; the American Bill of Rights (1791) is the first ten amendments to the US Constitution (*OEWH*).

10. After ER spoke, the speeches continued through the following day. On the evening of December 10, after the speaking concluded, the General Assembly rejected the Soviet resolution to delay consideration of the UDHR by a vote of 45 to 6 with 3 abstentions. It also voted overwhelmingly to reject four amendments proposed by the Soviet Union, which attempted to substitute new text for three articles and add an additional article, and adopted an amendment offered by the United Kingdom that deleted Article 3 and substituted the following text as paragraph 2 of Article 2:

> Furthermore, no distinction shall be made on the basis of the political, jurisdictional or international status of the country or territory to which a person belongs, whether it be independent, Trust, Non-Self-Governing or under any other limitation of sovereignty (General Assembly, 180th Meeting, Summary Report, 9 December 1948 [E/777], 929–32, UNORGA, MWelC).

At midnight, the General Assembly adopted the UDHR by a vote of 48 to 0. The Soviet bloc (the USSR, Byelorussia, Ukraine, Poland, Czechoslovakia, and Yugoslavia) abstained, as did South Africa and Saudi Arabia. After the vote, Herbert Evatt, president of the General Assembly, praised ER for her leadership in the drafting of the UDHR: "It is particularly fitting that there should be present, on this occasion, the person who, with the assistance of many others, has played a leading role in this work, the person who has raised to greater heights even so great a name: Mrs. Roosevelt, the representative of the United States of America" (General Assembly, 180th Plenary Meeting, Summary Report, [E/777], 9 December 1948, 933–34, UNORGA, MWelC).

REBUTTING THE KU KLUX KLAN

ER returned to the United States on December 16 and she and Anna began broadcasting their radio show together from New York City. While Anna focused her remarks on the criticism women faced for working outside the home, ER used the occasion of her return to rebut the remarks made recently by the imperial wizard of the Ku Klux Klan.

408

Eleanor and Anna Roosevelt Radio Program
22 December 1948

ANNA: Good Morning! And thank you, George Ansbro.[1] Mother is sitting across from me here in the studio, and I know that she has something important to talk about a little later.

But first, I see that the Chief Investigator in the Brooklyn District Attorney's office says that men just simply "can't take it" these day. That they have no sense of responsibility. Let me explain that the D.A's Investigator happens to be a woman! The first woman ever to hold the job by the way. Her name is Florence Quinn Murawski, and she investigates complaints … complaints on everything from big swindles to a bop on the chin from an unidentified assailant. And she says that she has seen eleven men come and go in the office since she's been there. It's too discouraging hearing all the tales of woe, she says … and she adds: "Men simply haven't the patience for this work." She also feels that more and more men are ducking out on their families when the going gets tough and the bills come rolling in. "See what I mean about responsibility," she says sadly. "Too many couples have only a superficial feeling for each other … and," she concludes, "It's an increasingly prevalent mental attitude." Well, I find this extremely interesting, in view of all the drubbings we poor women have had to take lately at the hands of psychologists, sociologists, and assorted experts.

If we stay home and keep house they say we are dissatisfied with our drab existence, unhappy and frustrated. If we try to get out and earn a living for ourselves or our family, they say we're being cheated of our woman's heritage and … again … unhappy and frustrated. Why, there's even a new book entitled: "Modern Woman … The Lost Sex."[2] So now someone comes along and says sweepingly that modern man—poor creature—is unstable and deficient in a sense of responsibility! Well, I can't say I whole-heartedly agree with either school of critics. We have our faults, goodness knows, men and woman alike … but I, for one, have learned to be wary of generalizations of any kind.

It seems to me that the best thing we can do is to be as tolerant as possible of each other's shortcomings and just try to get along together as well as possible … Speaking of getting along well together, I am delighted to learn that bus and trolley car operators here in New York are going to ask their customers to "Step to the Rear" from now on in a pleasant tone of voice. And furthermore, they are going to add a "please".

It's orders. Can this be a sign of the times? Why, I understand that in the Army these days, even formerly fearsome top sergeants are now dealing with tender rookies in a spirit of politeness and courtesy! This is truly amazing, but very welcome.

Mother, I read the other day that a man named Dr. Green, the Grand Dragon of the Ku Klux Klan, had made a speech in which he said that the Klan does not stand for hate, that it stands for love.[3] Paramount Newsreel has asked you to reply to this speech by Dr. Green. Would you tell us what you think of his speech and of the Klan.

MRS. R.: Yes, Anna, I read portions of the speech by Dr. Green[4] and I simply do not believe him when he says the Klan does not hate Jews, Catholics and Negroes, and that Klansmen are sworn to uphold the Constitution and not to take the law into their own hands. He says they are sworn to uphold the Constitution, but the fiery cross of the Klan is still used to intimidate negroes and deny their constitutional right to vote.[5] Dr. Green says that Klansmen are sworn not to take the law into their own hands, but white-robed men are still terrorizing defenseless negroes in the South.[6] The Grand Dragon says that the Klansmen believe in brotherly love, but they still meet secretly and wear masks.[7] Since when, I wonder, is the smile of friendship hidden behind a mask? The answer of course is that the Ku Klux Klan is just what it always has been—a secret, terroristic, organization, hopeful of enforcing the warped ideas of a few hoodlums on a defenseless minority!

However, Dr. Green's speech reveals that there is something new about the Klan. Intolerance now bears a new mask—the mask of brotherhood. Bigotry has been streamlined. In former days, the Klan was more blunt and made no bones about its evil intentions. It boasted of its dislike for Jews and Catholics, and of frightening Negroes with guns and fiery crosses. But now, according to Dr. Green, the Klan no longer hates Jews and Catholics and Negroes. It believes in Christ, he says, and in brotherhood.

One of the strangest things to me is how men can pay lip service to an ideal like love or brotherhood, while at the same time practicing oppression and cruelty. Hitler probably really did not hate the Poles or the Dutch or the Belgians, but he invaded their countries and killed thousands of them. I don't suppose Mr. Stalin actually hates the Lithuanians or the Yugoslavs or the Rumanians, but the fact remains that he holds them in virtual bondage. So, although Dr. Green says that the Klan really doesn't hate Negroes or Jews or Catholics, I'm afraid that I and most Americans will not be able to agree with him until there is some evidence of understanding and good will on the part of the Klan. There is still too great a similarity between a white nightshirt and a Nazi brownshirt.

Only recently the United Nations passed a bill of human rights. For two years a Committee, of which I was a member, worked on this Declaration of Rights to guarantee equal rights to all men. The Russians, like the Klan, apparently do not believe in equal rights, although they—like the Klan—would not admit this. While we worked, slowly and laboriously in committee to formulate these essential rights, there were frequent disagreements and disputes. When these occurred, I usually tried to set forth the American understanding of the rights of men, as outlined in our own Bill of Rights. And almost always the delegates of the U.S.S.R. and her Satellites would ask: "But how about your treatment of Negroes in your country?" "How about your Ku Klux Klan lynchings?" When the Russian delegate asked me those questions, I had no answer.[8] What do you say, standing before a committee of a World Organization, when you are asked about the Ku Klux Klan? You can not excuse it, for there is no excuse for it. You can only say, as I said to the United Nations, that most Americans despise the Ku Klux Klan; that for every hooded Klansman there are thousands of Americans who cherish our traditional freedoms and who desire only to live in peace and brotherhood with their neighbors. I wonder if Dr. Green—who talks of upholding the Constitution—is proud of the fact that his organization was used more than any other weapon by the Russians to attack our country before the countries of the world!

The fight for human understanding and good will is a long and uphill one, but I feel that slowly but surely we make progress. I am not too concerned about the Ku Klux Klan. I think it is gradually dying and that someday it will be only an evil memory like the "Know Nothings", race riots and other blots on our history. But I saw a picture of the meeting in Georgia, which Dr. Green addressed, and something in it distressed me deeply. For in the picture was a little girl, about five years old, dressed in a Klan uniform.[9] I thought to myself, as I saw this picture, that it was a symbol of what is wrong with our world, and why we have Ku Klux Klans. This little girl was not born to hate. She would not hate another little girl because her skin was a different color or because her parents were of another religion. This little girl must instinctively love those around her, but she must be taught to hate. And that is one of the saddest things in the world.

If the Ku Klux Klan does not believe in hate, there is much its members can do. If they sincerely believe in brotherhood I know their help will be welcomed in many places. So many people are needed in slums and pulpits ... in classrooms and in war-devastated cities ... to repair the ravages of old hates and old wars and to build a better world for the future.

ANNA: And that, of course, is the most important job facing us all today … and certainly one which directly concerns us all.

And here's another subject of interest to all Americans … Maybe you know that the Freedom Train, which toured the country last year, is in the midst of another cross-country trip.[10] It's about at the half-way point: for it began Thanksgiving Day … and will wind up in Washington, D.C. on January 22nd. After that, there'll be no more Freedom Train. Several of you probably visited the train when it stopped in your city … and I'm sure you enjoyed seeing its priceless collection of historical documents, all dealing with the birth and heritage of our nation. I know I did. It's truly a stirring experience for any American. That's why I'm so glad to hear that the Heritage Foundation—the organization which sponsors the Freedom Train—now plans to have a motion picture made of the train and its contents … showing also the crowds of visitors thronging to see it, and including dramatic scenes depicting the composition and signing of such history-making documents as the Declaration of Independence. The Heritage Foundation people say that in this way they hope to make a "perpetual record for the advance of patriotism." Well, it's certainly true that the sight of this precious collection aboard the Freedom Train does inspire feelings of patriotism … in the true sense of the word. And I think there was a need for such a movie to be made … I was in Phoenix, Arizona, when the Freedom Train visited that city last year. And since they did such a grand job of advance publicity on it, every school child was a-twitter with excitement, wanting to see the train.

As I mentioned the other day, I have just been named editor of THE WOMAN magazine, and I've been having a busy but grand time getting started on the new job. It's certainly interesting reading stacks of manuscripts and trying to decide which ones you think readers would most enjoy. There's an extremely interesting article in the current issue of THE WOMAN that I think most people would enjoy. It's titled "Diseases You Can Inherit" and it explodes some of the old theories on what diseases can and can not be inherited.

TRdtr AERP, FDRL

---

1. George Ansbro (1915–), a radio announcer for ABC (American Broadcasting Company) introduced the *Eleanor and Anna Roosevelt Radio Program* (Ansbro, 157). For background on the *Eleanor and Anna Roosevelt Radio Program*, see header and *n*9 Document 389.

2. Ferdinand Lundberg and Marynia F. Farnham's *Modern Woman: The Lost Sex* (Harper & Brothers Publishers: New York and London, 1947) found contemporary society "so profoundly disorganized that the disorganization expresses itself in the large number of neurotic personalities among both men and women." However, the neuroses women faced posed the greater danger "because women as mothers transmit the psychological disorientation to the next generation." Trapped between "an empty home and an equally empty life in industry," Lundberg and Farnham's dissatisfied and neurotic women "reject, dominate, overprotect or overstimulate their children in an attempt to right the balance in their own disordered lives" (Margaret Mead, "Dilemmas the Modern Woman Faces," *NYT*, 26 January 1947, BR18).

3. Dr. Samuel Green (1890–1949), an optometrist, became a member of the Ku Klux Klan in the early 1920s. He rose through the ranks of the organization until its temporary ebb during WWII. In 1946 the Klan reorganized under the new name, the Association of Georgia Klans, and Green became its leader. As imperial wizard, Green attempted to revive the Klan by advertising it as an organization that stood for family, church, and brotherhood rather than hate and violence. His approach managed to raise Klan membership, but the political power that Klansmen had enjoyed in the 1920s eluded Green and his followers. National leaders, local politicians, and Americans in all areas of the country were openly hostile to the revived organization. When Green died in 1949, the Klan disintegrated, until its reawakening in the mid-1950s when the federal government began

to enforce public school integration (Chalmers, 325–35; "Green, Klan Chief, Dies at His Home," *NYT*, 19 August 1949, 1).

4. ER did not retain the Green-related briefing materials in her files and the major print media did not cover his remarks. A search of New York and Atlanta papers did not produce a transcript; therefore, the editors relied on ER's interpretation of them in lieu of his text.

5. On the eve of the March 1948 Georgia State Democratic Primary, Dr. Green and the Klan demonstrated against African American voters in Johnson County. In previous elections, voters in the area had supported segregation, but they had begun to show signs of reversing that policy. Addressing a crowd on the courthouse lawn, with a burning cross behind him, Green said that "blood will flow" if the nation continued to move toward racial equality. After the demonstration, not one of the 400 African American men and women who were registered to vote in the county cast a ballot in the election ("No Negroes Vote After Klan Threat," *NYT*, 4 March 1948, 15).

6. November 24, 1948, Robert Mallard, "a prosperous Negro farmer," was shot and killed by five or six men in white robes, after walking from a church to his car with his wife and child. Although Mallard's widow asserted that Klansmen had killed her husband, the police arrested her at his funeral and charged her with his murder. Following her release, Roderick L. Clifton and William L. Howell, two white farmers, were arrested and brought to trial for the murder. In January 1949 a jury acquitted both defendants, despite Mallard's wife's testimony that she had seen the men kill her husband. At the trial itself, two of the jurors were called to the stand by the defense as character witnesses for the accused ("Negro Slaying Spurs Inquiry in Georgia," *NYT*, 25 November 1948, 42; "Widow Held in Killing," *NYT*, 28 November 1948, 23; John Popham, "Georgians Freed in Negro's Killing; Two on Jury Testify for the Defense," *NYT*, 12 January 1949, 1).

7. Green and other Klansmen received a great deal of criticism about their hoods during this period. When asked in March 1948 why the Klan hid their faces during demonstrations, Dr. Green replied "'prejudice by certain minorities—Jews, Catholics, and other foreigners. For example, if a Jew found out an employee of his was a klansmen,' he continued 'that man would be fired'" ("Klan Leader Calls Truman 'Gone Goslin,'" *WP*, 5 March 1948, 15).

8. ER grew increasingly irritated by Pavlov's insistence that the Klan violence and her refusal to accept the NAACP petition meant that American law tolerated Klan violence. As Irene Sandifer recalled, ER responded to a 1947 tirade from Pavlov by saying:

> I would remind my Soviet colleague that since we are dealing with [human rights], we should try not to attack each other or our Governments, but since he has in his speech again chosen to repeat many things which I have heard many times, I would suggest to him that he has used the petition of the NAACP ... that is over a year old, and that lynching in the United States is deplorable but that it is against the law and when it takes place it is a violation of the law and exceptional (Glendon, 150; Sandifer, 71).

9. ER probably refers here to a large induction ceremony held at Stone Mountain, Georgia, on July 23, 1948, at which more than seven hundred new Klansmen joined the order. "Even small children in Klan robes were present," the *New York Times* reported ("Klan Admits 700 in Cross-Lit Rites," *NYT*, 24 July 1948, 28).

10. The Freedom Train transported over a hundred historic documents, including the Magna Carta, Washington's Farewell Address, the Declaration of Independence, the US Constitution, and the Emancipation Proclamation, and displayed them in cities across the country for public view (Gilbert Bailey, "Why They Throng to the Freedom Train," *NYT*, 25 January 1948, SM18).

LAURENCE DUGGAN, KARL MUNDT, AND HUAC

December 20, 1948, Laurence Duggan, Sumner Welles's former deputy who then directed the Institute for International Education,[1] died after falling from a window in his sixteenth-floor Manhattan office.

The next day, Rep. Karl Mundt, acting chairman of the House Committee on Un-American Activities, released the testimony Isaac Don Levine, Whittaker Chambers's nephew and the editor of the anti-Communist magazine *Plain Talk*,[2] gave before the committee's December 8 closed session. The transcript revealed that Levine, who had accompanied Chambers to the 1939 meeting where his uncle gave former assistant secretary of state Adolf A. Berle, Jr., a list of six department employees who "at different times, passed confidential information along," named Duggan as one of the disloyal six. When Mundt was asked to identify the other five people Levine named, he joked, "We will give them out as they jump out of windows." Public records, however, indicated that one of the other five was Alger Hiss, who had recently been indicted by a federal grand jury on two counts of perjury related to his testimony before the committee. That afternoon, the FBI revealed once it learned of Levine's accusations, it had sent agents to question Duggan about his alleged involvement in espionage.[3]

The Duggan case and the way HUAC handled it caused intense controversy. Although initial reports suggested that Duggan committed suicide, several people who knew him, including Sumner Welles, suspected foul play. Calling Duggan "one of the most brilliant, devoted and patriotic public servants I have ever known," Welles wired New York mayor William O'Dwyer calling for an investigation into Duggan's death. December 22, Whittaker Chambers announced he had not named Duggan either in his meeting with Berle or in his HUAC testimony and HUAC member Rep. Richard Nixon announced that Chambers's declaration that he did not name Duggan "clears Duggan of any implication in the espionage ring."[4]

The following day, the *New York Times* editorialized:

> The inference subsequently drawn from Mr. Mundt's transcript was quite obviously what Mr. Mundt had intended, which was to show a connection between the death, under circumstances that still are not clear, of a former State Department official and the Committee's investigation of alleged Communist infiltration of that Department and other departments of the Government. There was probably not a newspaper reader anywhere in whose mind that thought was not planted.
>
> What was this secret testimony which Mr. Mundt released to plant that idea? It was testimony by one witness of his recollection of charges he had heard made … by a self-confessed former Communist spy to a State Department official, who did not take them seriously at that time, or since. The recollections of Isaac Don Levine of this nine-year-old conversation he had overheard between Whittaker Chambers and … Adolf A. Berle Jr. … Mr. Mundt was giving circulation to hearsay evidence. If you count his version, it was hearsay twice removed.[5]

December 24, the day of Duggan's funeral, the following My Day appeared. Later that day, attorney general Tom Clark announced that "the FBI investigation has produced no evidence of Mr. Duggan's connection with the Communist Party or with any other espionage activity. On the contrary, the evidence discloses that Mr. Duggan was a loyal employee of the United States Government."[6] The *New York Times* would print excerpts from this My Day in its front-page coverage of the attorney general's announcement.[7]

409

My Day

24 December 1948

NEW YORK, Thursday—It is hard for me to say exactly how I felt when I read of Laurence Duggan's tragic death.

I met Mr. Duggan only once or twice,[8] but how anyone could suspect him of un-American activities seems inconceivable to me. In any case, without real proof in his hands, the statement issued by Representative Karl E. Mundt strikes me as an irresponsible, cruel piece of publicity. As if it weren't enough on his wife and children to lose a husband and father at such a youthful age, to lose him and then have it darkly hinted that he had once been engaged in or had knowledge of this curious spy ring is indeed a difficult thing for a sorrowing family to bear.

As time progresses I wonder more and more why Whittaker Chambers's word and even Isaac Don Levine's word are accepted without question so much more quickly than is the word of men whose records have been records of helpfulness to their country and their community for years past. I should think that such men as Harry D. White and Laurence Duggan—both dead—might keep some of the members of the House Un-American Activities Committee from sleeping very well at night.[9]

Mr. Duggan's wife says these insinuations against her husband are preposterous, and I think she is right.[10] And, personally, I am going to believe in Alger Hiss' integrity until he is proved guilty.[11] I know only too well how circumstantial evidence can be built up, and it is my conviction that the word of a man, who for many years has had a good record of service to his government, should not be too quickly disbelieved.

Someone took me to task not long ago because I had said I was not sure I would advocate young people going into government service at the present time. This present spy inquiry provides some of the reasons for my hesitation.[12]

The great gift of curiosity, which makes men safe and secure in a really democratic society, is going to be shortly discredited among us. There would be no development, there would be no people who understood what had built the Communist movement in this country unless there were among us some few who were interested enough to find out how other young people think and, in addition, to study opposing regimes and bring us suggestions for better understanding. From the moment that a man is interviewed by the FBI he lives in apprehension nowadays. It is the record of what an individual had done in the mature years of his life that should count in making him a credible witness and one in which the public can put their trust. But that apparently is not the case anymore.

It does not seem to matter how many years one has devoted to doing good work if ever by any chance one has been interested in finding out something about subjects and activities that are today considered taboo or subversive, and this fact comes to light.

I cannot help believing that no matter what the Un-American Activities Committee suspected, Representative Mundt would have done better to withhold his statement until he had some definite proof. I cannot help feeling that we are reaching a point in this country where this type of witch-hunting must come to an end.

If necessary, the FBI must be strengthened and the laws under which they function must be strengthened, but we must preserve the sense of freedom that we have always had. Our greatest protection lies in preserving these freedoms and in holding to the old belief that a man must be presumed innocent until he is proved guilty. Insinuations should not be made unless proof is in hand. A man's job may be jeopardized and his whole life may be wrecked before his innocence is proved.

TMs AERP, FDRL

1. After graduating from Harvard, Laurence Duggan (1905–1948) worked briefly for the Institute and for the publishing firm, Harper and Brothers, before joining the State Department in 1930. Rising quickly, he ultimately became Chief of the Division of American Republics. He worked closely with Sumner Welles on Latin American affairs and served as political advisor to Secretary Cordell Hull. After leaving the department in 1944, Duggan advised the United Nations Relief and Rehabilitation Administration in Latin America before returning to the Institute for International Education ("Fall Kills Duggan, Named with Hiss in Spy Ring Inquiry," *NYT*, 21 December 1948, 1).

2. Isaac Don Levine (1892–1981), a Russian by birth who returned to his native country in the early 1920s to cover the civil war between the Bolsheviks and their opponents for American newspapers, remained an active opponent of the Soviet regime as a journalist and author of books for the remainder of his life ("Isaac Don Levine, 89, Foe of Soviet," *NYT*, 17 February 1981, D15).

3. "FBI Questioned Former Official About 10 Days Prior to Death Plunge," *NYT*, 22 December 1948, 1; "Fall Kills Duggan, Named with Hiss in Spy Ring Inquiry," *NYT*, 21 December 1948, 1.

4. Meyer Berger, "Duggan Is Cleared by Nixon of Spying; No Foul Play Found," *NYT*, 23 December 1948, 1.

5. "The Case of Mr. Duggan," *NYT*, 23 December 1948; Welles, 363.

6. Sandilands, 144–45.

7. C. P. Trussell, "Clark Says Duggan Was Loyal to U.S.," *NYT*, 25 December 1948, 1. Despite HUAC's clearing of Duggan's name, historians John Earl Haynes and Harvey Klehr, citing references to Duggan in the de-classified Venona transcripts, argue that "in fact, he was a KGB agent" (Haynes and Klehr, 201–4).

8. ER lent her strong support to the Institute for International Education, quickly agreeing to Duggan's request that she support its thirtieth anniversary celebration (Laurence Duggan to ER, 21 October 1948, AERP; ER to Duggan, 27 October 1948, AERP).

9. For more on Harry D. White, see Document 371 and Document 372.

10. Mrs. Duggan "completely and totally" denied that her husband knew Chambers and said that she and her husband "just scoffed at" the notion that HUAC could take testimony questioning his loyalty seriously. As she reportedly said to a reporter who phoned her, "This is the biggest lot of hooey I ever heard. It just isn't so—not any part of it. He had no connection with Mr. Chambers. That's all I can say. What more is there to say?" ("Foul Play Hinted by Welles, Mundt in Duggan's Death," *NYT*, 22 December 1948, 1).

11. See also Document 371 and Document 372 for ER's defense of Hiss.

12. For ER's warning that young people should exercise caution before entering public service, see Document 377.

ASSESSING RUSSIA, EUROPE, AND PALESTINE

Upon her return from Paris, ER requested a meeting with Truman to take place in early 1949. December 21, the president replied that he would "be delighted to see you" at noon, January 13, and that he:

> shall look forward with keen anticipation to receiving from you a firsthand account of the deliberations in Paris in which you bore so important a part.
>
> I sincerely hope that you have not overtaxed your strength during the long succession of busy days. I have marveled at the poise and patience that you and the other members of our delegation have maintained in the face of the maddening technique of the Russians. Not only have they been deliberately noncooperative but they have conducted themselves with a boorishness worthy of stable boys. I have observed with great satisfaction that you have put them in their place more than once.

The president concluded: "It would be most helpful to me to receive, in advance of your visit, a memorandum which can be the basis of our discussions." After Christmas, ER prepared the following document for the president's review.[1]

410

Memorandum for the President
28 December 1948 [Hyde Park]

First of all I want to tell you, Mr. President that when the news of your election reached Europe, there was general rejoicing. It gave to many statesmen and even to the people on the street who felt there might have been a change in our foreign policy, a sense of security that that which is now being done would be continued.

Next, I think I should say that generally there is a feeling that Mr. Harriman has done a very good job and a devoted one. As you know, I have not always felt that he had a broad enough point of view and grasp of the world situation, but he struck me as having greatly broadened and having been capable of growing with the opportunity which you have given him, which after all, is the greatest thing that one can ask of any one. He has chosen a good staff and everywhere I heard good things said of these people. People wrote me about the representatives they considered particularly good in a number of cases. I heard also that Mr. Harriman had handled labor very well.[2]

France, as he undoubtedly told you, is the greatest headache still. I think he understands what some of the greatest difficulties are. Many of the young men who fought in the resistance movement, or who were taken to camps and forced labor out of the country returned or finished their period of the war, depleted physically and mentally. The food has not been sufficient in energy giving qualities. You can not, for instance even today, unless you are willing and able to buy in the black market get butter and sugar and only small children can get milk. Until one comes back physically, one can not come back mentally and spiritually. Also the constant change of governments, due in large part to a very complicated situation which I will be glad to explain if you are interested, has made life for the working people in the cities very difficult and creates a lack of confidence in the government.[3]

The hardships are real and the Soviets through their communist party in France have offered both rural and city people certain benefits which they could not well resist. The French are not naturally communists but they find it hard to be staunch in the sense that the British are and so they have accepted many communist things. This does not frighten me for the future but it creates great difficulties for the present.[4]

This question of economic well-being is exploited by the USSR in all nations and they promise much until they gain complete control, then people are worse off than they were before but up to that time they have hopes of being better off and this is what creates one of the dangers for us. Since we are really fighting ideas as well as economic conditions and the Russians do a better propaganda job than we do because it is easier to say that your government is a government of workers for the benefit of workers than it is to say that a democratic government which is capitalistic benefits the workers more in the end. The only way to prove that to them, I think, is gradually to have more of them see conditions in our country, under supervision of course, and with every arrangement made for them to return to their own country, but the USSR is as loathe to let them come over as we have been to allow them to enter which makes this solution very difficult.

Great Britain is going to pull through because it has stood up under incredible drabness of living and I think will know how to use the aid coming to good account. Our relations with the British must, I think, be put on a different basis. We are without question the leading democracy in the world today, but so far Great Britain still takes the attitude that she makes the policies on all world questions and we accept them. That has got to be remedied. We have got to make the policies and they have got to accept them. Mr. Bevin has been unwise in many ways but I will not put on paper what I would be willing to tell you.[5]

I hope very much that the situation between ourselves and the USSR can change in the coming year and that we can accomplish final peace settlements. Germany can not return to any kind of normality until that is done, for at present the heap of ruins and disillusioned people in the center of Europe makes it difficult for all around to recover.

I have a feeling that your attitude on Palestine did a great deal to straighten out our own delegation and help the situation from the world point of view.[6] The Arabs have to be handled with strength. One of the troubles has been that we have been so impressed with the feeling that we must have a united front in Europe that it has affected our stand in the Near East. I personally feel that it is more important for the French and for the British to be united with us than for us to be united with them, and therefore when we make up our minds that something has to be done, we should be the ones to do what we think is right and we should not go through so many anxieties on the subject.

There are all kinds of hidden reasons why nations and their statesmen desire certain things which are not the reasons they usually give. The most truthful of the statesmen that I talked to while in Paris was Robert Schuman[7] of France, but it does require some knowledge of the past and much background to be always on your guard and figure out what are the reasons for certain stands that are taken.

I have great admiration for the Secretary of State and for many of the people in our State Department, but sometimes I think we are a little bit too trusting and forget the past. In giving me as an adviser Mr. Durward Sandifer, a lawyer of great experience and assistant to Mr. Dean Rusk[8] in the Department, I could not have been better served, but I still feel it is hard for the Department to accept policies, without certain individuals trying to inject their own points of view and I do not think all of them have the knowledge and experience to take a world point of view instead of a local one and by local I mean the point of view which is affected by the particular area in which they have special knowledge and experience.

I should like to say a word to you when we meet on the subject of the bi-partisan policy and the representatives of the other party.[9]

I also learned that the Philippine representatives were very much affected by the Equal Benefits Bill which is in Congress and I think if this goes through we will have a remarkable rise in their loyalty.[10]

The thing above all others which I would like to bring to your attention is that we are now engaged in a situation which is as complicated as fighting the war. During the war my husband had a map room and there were experts who daily briefed him on what was happening in every part of the world. It seems to me now we are engaged in the war for peace in which there enter questions of world economy, food, religion, education, health and social conditions, as well as military and power conditions. I have a feeling that it would be helpful if you could build a small group of very eminent non-political experts in all these fields whose duty it would be to watch the world scene and keep you briefed day by day in a map room. No one man can watch this whole world picture or have the background and knowledge to cover it accurately. It must be achieved by wise choice of people in the various fields to do it well and understandingly.

I have a feeling that our situation in Europe will be solved in the next year without too much difficulty. Our real battlefield today is Asia and our real battle is the one between democracy and communism. We can not ruin America and achieve the results that have to be achieved in the world, so whatever we do must be done with the most extraordinary wisdom and foresight in the economic field. At the same time we have to prove to the world and particularly to down trodden areas of the world which are the natural prey to the principles of communist economy that democracy really brings about happier and better conditions for the people as a whole. Never was there an era in history in which the responsibilities were greater for the United States, and never was a President called upon to meet such extraordinary responsibilities for civilization as a whole.

I think you are entitled to the best brains and the best knowledge available in the world today. Congress must understand this picture but it can not be expected to follow it in the way that it has to be followed, for the knowledge must come from a group which you set up and from you to them. You need something far greater than political advice though that is also an essential in the picture at home as well as abroad. The search should be for wise men of great knowledge and devoted to mankind, for mankind is at the cross roads. It can destroy itself or it can enter into a new era of happiness and security. It seems to me that you are the instrument chosen as a guide in this terribly serious situation and if there is anything which any of us can do to help you, you have a right to call upon us all.

TMem HSTSF, HSTL

---

1. Harry Truman to ER, 21 December 1948, AERP.

2. In April 1948, Averell Harriman resigned his post as secretary of commerce and accepted Truman's appointment as the US special representative in Europe for the Economic Cooperation Administration, a position which carried with it the responsibility of coordinating the Marshall Plan. November 19, Harriman flew in from Paris to address the AFL national convention, where he told the delegates that American labor had played "the key role" in "this great enterprise of leading the world to freedom and peace." He then emphasized how critical labor support was to the successful implementation of the Marshall Plan and world peace, telling this audience that while Europe wanted to trust the United States, it found "this unprecedented program of peacetime international cooperation" hard to understand. "No group," Harriman declared, "can speak so convincingly and so effectively as can American labor in building confidence (in Europe) in the American people and their objectives." For an example of ER's prior reservations concerning Harriman's abilities, see Document 219 (Felix Belair, Jr., "Harriman Named Aid Chief Abroad," *NYT*, 22 April 1948, 1; *HSTE*; "Labor World Role Seen By Harriman," *NYT*, 20 November 1948, 7).

3. De Gaulle withdrew from government in 1945 when the French elected a Constituent Assembly October 1945 and then reentered politics in 1947 to challenge the Communist-Socialist Left. The Left, reinvigorated by their work in the resistance, contested among themselves for political supremacy—only to be successfully challenged from the Right in 1947. Like the Third Republic,

instability characterized the Fourth Republic as numerous parties vied for power and no single party received more than roughly a quarter of the vote. Political parties formed temporary coalitions that constantly underwent realignments and resulted in cabinets which lasted on average less than six months (Wright, 396–410).

4. During the early years of the Fourth Republic, the Communist Party consistently received one quarter of the vote in France, making them the most popular political party in France after World War II. Historians have attributed much of their success to the party's effective use of their image as the heroes of resistance: the French government expelled party members in 1939 and therefore the Communists were free from the taint of Nazi collaboration from which the political parties in power in 1940 suffered. By 1947, the French Communists established themselves as champions of the working class, demanding mandatory wage increases and organizing strikes in a variety of industries at a time when their Socialist rivals called for wage freezes and patience to resolve the economic crisis. The failure of the centrist coalition in power to improve the French economy won the Communists a great deal of popular support, but the party's militancy also rendered them politically ineffective, as their erstwhile allies, the Socialists, refused to work with the Communists after 1947 (Wright, 399, 403–4).

5. ER had previously criticized British foreign secretary Ernest Bevin for expecting the United States to follow Britain's lead, particularly in discussions concerning Palestine. When, on February 25, 1947, Bevin criticized Truman before the House of Commons for allowing American politics to come into play in the Palestine issue, ER defended the president from what she considered Bevin's "extraordinary outburst":

> Mr. Bevin will remember that it was at the British Government's request that a commission of inquiry composed of British and Americans restudied the question of Palestine. At the time, it seemed to me an utterly unnecessary commission, since we already knew, as did Great Britain, all there was to know on that subject. Therefore, there could be only one reason for request—namely, that Great Britain desired to have the United States accept some responsibility for any future policy. From later developments it was made clear that we, at least, had not understood that we were assuming any military responsibility, but had thought that the report of the commission would carry some weight …

> It looks strangely like looking for a whipping boy, however, when Great Britain's Foreign Secretary suddenly accuses the President of the United States of having made agreement impossible by restating a stand from which he has never deviated (Charles E. Egan, "Cites Entry Plea: Briton Says He Begged U.S. Not to Press for Opening Holy Land," *NYT*, 26 February 1947, 1; *MD*, 27 February 1947).

For further examples of ER's view of Bevin's policies, see Document 129 and Document 198.

6. In a speech at Madison Square Garden on October 28, Truman recommitted himself to the boundary lines set in the UN Partition Plan for Palestine of November 1947. "Israel," he said, "must be large enough, free enough and strong enough to make its people self-supporting and secure." Truman's remarks were a direct repudiation of his secretary of state, who had come out in favor of the Bernadotte Plan, which called on Israel to return the Negev to the Arabs in exchange for the Galilee. For more on Truman's views on Palestine see Document 330 and Document 353. On the Bernadotte Plan see Document 374 and *n*9 Document 380 (Lash, *Years*, 136; "Truman in Strongest Plea for Israel Backs Boundaries in First U.N. Plan; Crowds in City Street Welcome Him," *NYT*, 29 October 1948, 1; "The Text of Truman's Address at Madison Square Garden," *NYT*, 29 October 1948, 4).

7. Robert Schuman (1886–1963) served as French prime minister from November 1947 to July 1948 and again in September 1948. He resigned less than a week after taking office the second time, when the National Assembly passed a vote of "no confidence" in his cabinet. Shortly thereafter he served as French foreign minister until his resignation in 1952. As foreign minister,

Schuman championed European economic integration and called for the establishment of the European Coal and Steel Community, a precursor to the European Economic Community (Lansing Warren, "Schuman Cabinet Falls, 295 to 289, Accenting Crisis," *NYT*, 8 September 1948, 1; "Schuman Dies at 77; Dies at 77," *NYT*, 5 September 1963, 1).

8. On Dean Rusk, see *n*18 Document 329 and Biographical Portraits.

9. For ER's belief in the importance of a bipartisan approach to foreign policy, see Document 179.

10. On July 26, 1941, President Roosevelt organized the US Armed Forces in the Far East (USAFFE), placing Filipino troops under the direction of US Army General Douglas MacArthur. A provision of the Philippines Independence Act of 1934—the act of Congress that ultimately promised independence to the Philippines on July 4, 1946, but established the archipelago as a commonwealth until that date—granted the president the right to call the Philippine army into service of the US Army during the ten-year transitional period. The regular Filipino troops swore oaths to the United States and were inducted into the US Army, leading them to argue after the war that they were entitled to the same benefits as all US soldiers. In February 1946, Congress passed the Rescission Act, which explicitly excluded Filipinos from the benefits promised under the GI Bill. Truman agreed to sign the bill, but not without declaring that "the passage and approval of this legislation do not release the United States from its moral obligation to provide for the heroic Philippine veterans who sacrificed so much for the common cause during the war." Although individual congressmen have continued to advocate bills extending equal benefits to the Filipino veterans of World War II into the twenty-first century, Congress has yet to pass such a bill (*OCAMH*; John H. Crider, "Command Unified," *NYT*, 27 July 1941, 1; "Truman Hits Curb on Filipino GI Aid," *NYT*, 21 February 1946, 8; Daniel K. Inouye, "Statement Before the House Subcommittee on Health, Committee on Veterans' Affairs," 13 June 2002, http://veterans.house.gov/hearings/schedule107/jun02/6-13-02/dinouye.html, accessed 2 February 2006).

Biographical Portraits

Acheson, Dean Gooderham (1893–1971), lawyer, assistant secretary of treasury, and secretary of state, served in both the Roosevelt and Truman administrations, where he helped solidify America's role as an international power. Although he left the New Deal in 1933, in protest of FDR's gold policy, he returned to the administration as assistant secretary of state for economic affairs in 1941 and became one of the nation's strongest advocates for early intervention against German advances. He wrote the legal brief supporting the bases for destroyers deal and lobbied the US Senate for the acceptance of the UN Charter despite his own conviction that the document was impractical. He also helped establish several other key postwar international organizations including the Food and Agriculture Organization, the United Nations Relief and Rehabilitation Administration (UNRRA), the World Bank, and the International Monetary Fund. Promoted by Truman to undersecretary of state in August 1945, Acheson helped oversee the development of the Cold War policy of containment. Much of US foreign policy developed under Secretaries of State James Byrnes and George Marshall—the Baruch Plan for international control of atomic weapons, aid to Greece and Turkey, the Truman Doctrine and the Marshall Plan—reflects Acheson's belief that only strong alliances with Western nations and large-scale economic, political, and military aid to countries on the perimeter of the Soviet bloc could halt Communism's advance. He left the State Department in 1947 and the following year, helped direct the Citizens Committee for the Marshall Plan congressional lobbying campaign (*ANBO*; *HSTE*).

Austin, Warren Robinson (1877–1962), Republican senator from Vermont, opposed virtually all New Deal domestic measures while, in contrast to the isolationist stance adopted by many of his Republican colleagues, embraced a foreign policy position favoring "limited internationalism." As a member of the Committee of Eight, he supported early plans for the postwar international organization that became the United Nations, a stance which cost him his position as assistant minority leader. Truman, as part of his plan to secure bipartisan support for the United Nations, appointed him US ambassador to the UN in June 1946. Although he served as chief delegate of the US delegation from 1946 to 1953, he had little influence on the policy initiatives emanating from the Truman White House and the State Department. Intense ideological conflict and political standoffs with the Soviets marked Austin's tenure at the UN. Although his faith in the UN's goals remained steadfast, he adopted an increasingly hard-line anti-Communist outlook. Austin asked to leave the post in 1952 for health reasons, but served until January 1953, when former Senator Henry Cabot Lodge, Jr., replaced him (*ANBO*).

Baldwin, Calvin Benham ("Beanie") (1902–1975), a Virginia businessman who became one of the more radical voices in the New Deal, first joined the Department of Agriculture in 1933 as an assistant to agriculture secretary Henry Wallace. Wallace soon tapped Baldwin to help implement the Agriculture Adjustment Act and the Resettlement Administration. In 1940, after assuming the directorship of the Farm Security Administration and encouraging its low-interest loan and farmer cooperative programs, Baldwin increasingly came under attack by conservative congressional critics who accused him of trying to "communize American agriculture." In 1943, he left government service to assist the Congress of Industrial Organizations' Political Action Committee (CIO-PAC) in its effort to secure FDR's reelection. In 1945, after the CIO-PAC reorganized itself into the National Citizens Political Action Committee (NCPAC) to organize nonlabor support for all labor-supported political candidates and reform proposals, Baldwin became the new PAC's executive vice chairman. As head of NCPAC, Baldwin worked closely with pro-Communist CIO leaders Lee Pressman and John Abt and urged other liberals to work with Communists to further progressive causes. When NCPAC and the Independent Citizens Committee of the Arts, Sciences, and Professions (ICCASP) merged in December 1946 to form Progressive Citizens of America (PCA), Baldwin became executive vice chairman of the new organization. In 1947, Baldwin encouraged then Secretary of Commerce Henry Wallace to oppose Truman's "get tough with Russia" policy publicly. Wallace followed Baldwin's advice, prompting the president to demand his resignation. The following year, Wallace accepted the PCA presidential nomination and then turned to Baldwin to manage his 1948 presidential campaign ("Biographical Note," Papers of C.B. Baldwin, University of Iowa Libraries Special Collections Department, http://www.lib.uiowa.edu/spec-coll/MSC/ToMsc350/MsC343/MsC343.htm).

Baruch, Bernard Mannes (1870–1965), wealthy Wall Street financier who made his money in stock speculation, Baruch turned to politics and government service becoming an influential economic policymaker and political kingmaker from the 1920s to the early 1940s. For the most part he eschewed elected or appointive office, preferring to work behind the scenes. Much of his power stemmed from his financial and political support of leading Democratic senators including Alben Barkley of Kentucky and Elmer Thomas of Oklahoma and the Democratic Party in general. His relationship with Franklin Roosevelt was cool but cordial and during the Roosevelt administration he functioned primarily as an outside counselor. However FDR, drawing on Baruch's World War I experience as head of the War Industries Board, turned to him to chair the Rubber Survey Committee during World War II. By 1945, however, the self-described "Park Bench Statesman" had fallen out of favor with Harry S. Truman over Baruch's support for the Morgenthau Plan to de-industrialize Germany and his opposition to the Truman administration's proposed loan to Great Britain. Baruch, however, retained the support of Secretary of State James Byrnes, key Senate conservatives, and the general public for Truman to appoint him US ambassador to the United Nations Atomic Energy Commission in 1946. Although Truman expected Baruch to obtain agreement on the Acheson-Lilienthal plan for the international control of atomic energy, Baruch declared that he would not be "a messenger boy." He then revised the plan, arguing that any nation violating the agreement would receive "immediate and swift punishment" that no member of the Security Council could revoke. The Soviet representatives refused to accept the modified Baruch plan although Soviet leader Josef Stalin later hinted that some accommodation might be possible. Baruch, however, refused to negotiate. Truman blamed Baruch for the failure and their relationship worsened, particularly after Baruch publicly criticized the administration's economic policies. Baruch still remained influential enough for Truman to seek his support for the Truman Doctrine and the Marshall Plan. In 1948, Truman also asked the financier to serve on his election finance committe, an offer Baruch declined. About the same time, when ER, a longtime friend and ally, suggested a diplomatic mission to Moscow to ease East-West tensions, Baruch let it be known that he would like the assignment but Truman refused make the appointment (*FDRE*; Chace, 124–28; *HSTE*; Schwartz, 185–86, 524; *ANB*).

Bethune, Mary McLeod (1875–1955), educator, administrator, civil rights leader, and the fifteenth of seventeen children of two former slaves, devoted her career to improving the lives of African Americans through education and political and economic empowerment. As founder of Bethune-Cookman College and the National Council of Negro Women (NCNW), she joined the Roosevelt administration in 1935 as director of the Office of Minority Affairs for the National Youth Administration (NYA), a position she filled until the NYA closed in 1944. Working closely with ER, Bethune worked to outlaw lynching, abolish the poll tax, and obtain employment and civil and political rights for African Americans. ER also ensured that Bethune saw FDR regularly to brief him on the conditions facing African Americans. Bethune also briefly served as special assistant to the secretary of war for the recruitment of African American women into the Women's Army Corps (WAC) officer training program, and in 1945 she toured military bases as a member of the WAC's National Civilian Advisory Committee. At the same time, she continued her duties as president of both the NCNW and the Association for the Study of Negro Life and History, and as vice president of both the National Association for the Advancement of Colored People (NAACP) and the National Urban League. Along with Walter White and W. E. B. Du Bois, she served as an associate consultant to the American delegation at the UN conference in San Francisco in April 1945. When that conference failed to substantively address issues important to people of color—imperialism, colonialism, human rights, and trusteeship—Bethune noted that the San Francisco meeting pointed to the "common bond" between African Americans and colonial people, and highlighted the fact that African Americans enjoyed "little more than colonial status" in the United States. Yet when other African American leaders wanted to petition the UN on behalf of African Americans in late 1946, Bethune refused to join the effort. She argued that since the plight of African Americans was a US problem, it was inappropriate to ask the international organization to intervene (*ANBO*; "Mary Bethune, 79, Educator, Is Dead," *NYT*, 19 May 1955, 29; C. Anderson, 29, 56–57, 81–84; *DAB*; McCluskey and Smith, 3–16, 17n10, 175–77; *NAWMP*).

Bevin, Ernest (1881–1951), British labor leader, became his nation's foreign secretary in 1945 after serving as minister of labour and national service in Winston Churchill's wartime coalition cabinet. Although he possessed little foreign policy experience, Bevin quickly grasped the Soviet threat to European security in the aftermath of World War II. In response he devised a strategy that sought to oppose Communism, preserve British interests and prestige abroad, and shore up his country's economic weakness. To that end he followed Churchill's policy of enlisting American support. Fortunately, the Truman administration shared Bevin's concern about the political and economic plight of Great Britain and the rest of Europe and developed policies and programs such as the Truman Doctrine and the Marshall Plan that ensured British and European security and helped them recover economically. The United States, however, was less supportive of Great Britain's continued imperial interests in the Middle East, particularly as they applied to Palestine. Truman adamantly disagreed with Bevin's refusal in 1946 to admit Jewish refugees to Palestine, and the following year endorsed the United Nations' plan to partition Palestine into separate Arab and Jewish states rather than support Bevin's call for a binational state. Bevin also opposed Truman's decision to extend *de facto* recognition to the state of Israel upon the termination of the British mandate in May 1948, believing that the US stance undercut British efforts to obtain Arab approval of a truce. Bevin later reflected that the American attitude on Palestine was best described as "let there be an Israel and to hell with the consequences." During the 1948 Arab-Israeli war that ensued, Bevin, lacking the military and economic resources to intervene, encouraged King Abdullah of Jordan to absorb what he called "Arab Palestine" without violating Jewish borders (*HSTE*; Cohen, *Palestine*, 16–20, 388; Raymond Daniell, "Bevin Dies of Heart Attack at 70, Month After Quitting," *NYT*, 15 April 1951, 1; *DPB*; Louis and Stookey, 1–31).

Boettiger, Anna Roosevelt (1906–1975), FDR and ER's oldest child who became one of her father's most trusted confidantes, began her journalism career in 1936 as women's page editor and as, with husband John Boettiger, co-publisher of the *Seattle Post-Intelligencer*. In 1944, her father's loneliness and her husband's overseas deployment encouraged her to accept FDR's invitation to move into the wartime White House. While in Washington, she acted as White House hostess during ER's absences, accompanied FDR to Yalta and, once requested to do so by her father, arranged for Lucy Mercer Rutherford to visit him undetected. After the war, with ER's intercession, the Boettigers bought the *Arizona Times*, a weekly Phoenix newspaper they hoped to develop into a daily. The business faltered, however, and so did the marriage as John, who suffered from depression, became withdrawn. At the end of 1947, the Boettigers separated, and she tried to run the newspaper on her own. When that failed, she moved to Los Angeles, where in November 1948, with ER as co-host, she began a five-day-a-week radio program, "Eleanor and Anna" (*FDRE*; Albin

BIOGRAPHICAL PORTRAITS

Krebs, "Anna Roosevelt Halsted, President's Daughter, Dies," *NYT*, 2 December 1975, 42; Asbell, 158, 232, 240, 242; Lash, *Years*, 181).

Bowles, Chester Bliss (1901–1986), a Connecticut advertising executive, businessman, and civil rights advocate, helped control wartime inflation as administrator of the Office of Price Administration, where he marshaled strong congressional and public support for wage and price controls. When Truman assumed the presidency, he appointed Bowles director of the Office of Economic Stabilization, but Bowles resigned from that position in 1946 after Congress failed to pass a strong extension of price controls. He then returned to Connecticut to seek its governorship. After he lost that election, Truman appointed him a member of the US delegation to the first United Nations Economic and Social Council. In 1947, he accepted a half-time position as special assistant on administrative affairs to UN Secretary General Trygve Lie. While advising Lie on specific administrative and management challenges, Bowles met Aache Ording, who lobbied Bowles to chair the United Nations Appeal for Children's international campaign to raise funds to provide food, clothing, shelter, and health care to children in war-torn areas. Bowles agreed and spent two months traveling Europe for the appeal, an experience that left him convinced that economic aid, literacy education, preventive health care, and local self-government must be the cornerstones upon which the Third World would be built. As he wrote Secretary Marshall, "the danger of positioning ourselves as the great reactionary power in a revolutionary world" is "a far greater threat to American security than the atomic bomb ... The only practical answer lies in an economic and social as well as political offensive designed to identify ourselves in all parts of the world with revolutionary reforms." Elected governor of Connecticut in 1948, Bowles signed into law an end to segregation in the state national guard, and became the first governor to establish a State Commission on Civil Rights (*HSTE*; Schaeffer, 32–33).

Byrnes, James Frances (1879–1972), Democratic representative and senator from South Carolina, Supreme Court justice, director of the Office of War Mobilization, lost the 1944 vice-presidential nomination to Harry Truman only to have Truman appoint him secretary of state the following year. Byrnes, whose support for FDR stretched back to the 1920 Cox-Roosevelt campaign, helped solidify southern, conservative support for FDR's legislative agenda. Known as "the New Deal's ball carrier," Byrnes worked to marshal Senate support for FDR's ill-fated 1937 court reorganization plan, repeal the Neutrality Acts, and implement Lend-Lease. In recognition of his dedication, FDR appointed Byrnes to the US Supreme Court in June 1941. He left the court the following year, when, in the shadow of Pearl Harbor, FDR turned to him to direct the Office of Economic Stabilization. When FDR reconfigured the office to include matters related to wartime mobilization in 1943, Byrnes's authority increased proportionately, covering all matters related to the production and distribution of all war-related material. When conservative Democrats and some party strategists objected to FDR keeping Henry Wallace on the 1944 ticket, many expected that Byrnes would replace the liberal Iowan. However, objections surfaced over Byrnes's segregationist record and support for "hold the line" orders on wages in war industries. Though disappointed, he remained loyal to FDR, who invited Byrnes to Yalta, and Byrnes returned home from the conference determined to secure congressional support for the arrangements FDR made with Stalin and Churchill. As secretary of state in the Truman administration, Byrnes advocated that Truman adopt a tough stance at Potsdam, supported the use of the atomic bomb to end the war with Japan, and pushed for wide latitude in conducting American foreign policy. However, his disregard of advice from experts in the State Department, failure to consult with Senate leaders or keep Truman informed, and criticism of Truman's domestic initiatives eventually alienated the president. The rift between the two men, and Byrnes's concerns about his health, caused Byrnes to offer his resignation in April 1946. He did not leave office, however, until January 1947. Byrnes, embittered, neither endorsed nor opposed Truman for reelection in 1948, thus siding, by his silence, with the Dixiecrats (*ANBO*; *HSTE*; Hamby, *Man*, 341–48).

Cassin, René Samuel (1887–1976), legal scholar and human rights advocate, received his law degree from the University of Aix-en-Provence in 1908. He served in the French infantry in World War I, was wounded in 1916, and founded the French Federation of Disabled War Veterans in 1918. After the war, he represented France at the League of Nations and was professor of law at the Universities of Aix and Lille, and, after 1929, at the University of Paris. When Germany occupied France in 1940, he and his wife fled to London, where Cassin offered his services to General Charles de Gaulle, leader of the Free French. Cassin became de Gaulle's chief legal advisor, conducted sensitive legal negotiations with the British regarding the status of the Free French forces, and held a variety of positions in the French government-in-exile. As vice president of the French Council of State (Conseil d'État) after the war, he oversaw the nation's highest court and managed its approach to administrative law and personnel, thus helping reestablish the legitimacy of the domestic French legal system. As a member of the Constitutional Council, he presided over cases challenging the constitutionality of measures passed by the French assembly. He also served as member (and later president of) the European Court of Human Rights at Strasbourg, and as a delegate to the UN General Assembly, where he helped establish UNESCO. An influential member of the UN Commission on Human Rights, Cassin's legal experience helped bring unity and clarity to the Universal Declaration of Human Rights. He was awarded the Nobel Peace Prize in 1968 (Glendon, 61–63; *CBE*; "René Cassin—Biography," Nobel Foundation, http://nobelprize.org/peace/laureates/1968/cassin-bio.html).

Chiang Kai-shek (1887–1975), Chinese commander-in-chief of the National Revolutionary Army, failed in his attempt to unify China under the Nationalist Government in Nanjing in 1928 and lost much of his territory during the Sino-Japanese War. By 1937, despite his temporary alliance with the Chinese Communists, much of his territory remained under Japanese control and he was forced to relocate to Chongquing. Thanks to his continued resistance and his wife's skill in promoting him abroad, Chiang's prestige remained high enough for him to attend the Cairo Conference, where he helped secure China a permanent seat on the UN Security Council (*ODTCWH*).

Chiang Kai-shek, Madame (Soong Mei-ling) (1898–2003), the American-educated wife of Chiang Kai-shek, ardently promoted the Nationalist Chinese cause abroad while her husband fought imperial Japan in China. During Chiang Kai-shek's rise to power, Madame Chiang advised her husband in matters of domestic and military policy. In 1943, she undertook a lengthy tour of the United States and Canada to speak about her government's struggle against Japan. While in Washington, she met with the Roosevelts at the White House and delivered two speeches before Congress, beseeching the western Allies to make the liberation of China as much a priority as their European goals. After this well-publicized appearance at the Capitol, Madame Chiang became the public face of Nationalist China in the United States. After the war, when civil war broke out in China between the Nationalists and the Communists, she returned to Washington in 1948 to seek US assistance to fight the Communists (W. H. Lawrence, "Mme. Chiang Asks Defeat of Japan, And House Cheers," *NYT*, 19 February 1943, 1; Seth Faison, "Madame Chiang Kai-shek, a Power in Husband's China and Abroad, Dies at 105," *NYT*, 25 October 2003, A15).

Churchill, Sir Winston Leonard Spencer (1874–1965), statesman, orator, and author, served as prime minister of Great Britain from 1940 to 1945. His speeches, particularly those he gave between 1940 and 1941 when Britain stood alone against Nazi Germany, inspired his nation to resist Hitler's advances and helped generate public support for American aid to the British, including Lend-Lease, before the United States entered the war. While Churchill's wartime relationship with FDR was close, the two men disagreed on military strategy, the question of whether Britain should keep its empire in the postwar era, and how best to deal with the Soviet Union in the postwar world. Their positions at the Yalta conference in February 1945 underscored these differences, with Churchill favoring an Anglo-American alliance to check Soviet ambitions and FDR supporting an extension of the wartime alliance. Churchill continued to advocate an Anglo-American alliance and a harder line toward the Soviet Union. Truman, however, wanted to pursue FDR's vision of a cooperative relationship and thus declined to meet with Churchill before they joined Stalin at the Potsdam Conference, lest Stalin think his former allies were conspiring against him. Churchill left Potsdam before the conference ended when he lost the premiership following the Conservative Party's massive defeat in the general election of July 1945. He retained his position as leader of the Conservative Party, began writing a history of World War II, and continued to seek an Anglo-American alliance while opposing the Labour government's plan to dismantle the British empire abroad and nationalize the economy and social services in Great Britain. Although out of power at home, Churchill remained an influential world figure. His March 1946 speech in Fulton, Missouri, describing the "iron curtain" descending across Europe and his call in September in Zurich for a "council of Europe" to defend against Soviet aggression crystalized the heated rhetoric of the early Cold War (*OCPW*; *CBE*; *FDRE*; *HSTE*).

Clark, Tom Campbell (1899–1977), President Truman's attorney general from 1945 to 1949, rose through the ranks of the Department of Justice. Clark became active in politics in the 1920s while practicing law in Dallas, Texas, where he befriended Senator Tom Connally and former House speaker Sam Rayburn. In 1937, he accepted appointment as a special assistant in the Justice Department where he prosecuted war risk insurance and antitrust cases. In that capacity, in February 1942, FDR charged Clark with coordinating the different federal agencies involved in creating and operating the War Relocation Authority program, the relocation of Japanese Americans into internment camps. In 1943, Clark became assistant attorney general in the Criminal Division where he worked alongside the junior senator from Missouri, Harry S. Truman, on the Senate Committee to Investigate the National Defense Program (known as the Truman Committee), which investigated war profiteering during the defense buildup to the Second World War. The following year Clark backed Truman over Henry Wallace as President Roosevelt's vice-presidential candidate after Rayburn withdrew his nomination. Shortly after FDR's death, President Truman replaced Attorney General Francis Biddle with Clark who received a strong endorsement from the Texas delegation, including Connally and Rayburn. As attorney general, Clark served as a major advocate of the administration's anti-Communist campaign, emphasizing national security over civil liberties. His work on national security issues, including expanded use of wiretaps, the creation and execution of a loyalty program for federal employees, the compilation of an official list of "subversive" organizations, and the 1948 prosecution of American Communists under the Smith Act provided a buffer for the administration against charges that it was soft on Communism during the early years of the Cold War. Despite his emphasis on national security, Clark was moderate on civil rights issues. He insisted that the Federal Bureau of Investigation investigate lynchings and called for federal legislation to punish the perpetrators. He also began the Justice Department's support of civil rights cases when he had the department file an amicus brief on behalf of the African American plaintiff in *Shelley v. Kraemer* (1948), successfully arguing that restrictive covenants are unconstitutional. On August 24, 1949, he took the oath of office as associate justice of the US Supreme Court, where he served until he resigned in 1967 (*HSTE*; *ANBO*).

Connally, Thomas Terry ("Tom") (1877–1963), Democratic representative (1917–29) and senator from Texas (1929–52) combined conservatism on domestic issues with internationalism in foreign affairs. Although Connally initially supported New Deal domestic initiatives in the Senate, he opposed the National Industrial Recovery Act of 1933, helped defeat FDR's proposal to reorganize the Supreme Court, and filibustered against antilynching legislation. He also opposed efforts to eliminate the poll tax. During the Truman administration, he opposed the Fair Deal and federal intervention in civil rights matters and supported passage of the Taft-Hartley Act. In international affairs, however, he advocated US membership in the League of Nations and the World Court in the 1920s, led the effort in the Senate to repeal the arms embargo (1939), supported the Selective Service Act (1940), and managed the Senate adoption of the Lend-Lease Act (1941). As chairman of the Senate Foreign Relations Committee from 1941 to 1946, Connally championed collective security abroad and bipartisanship in foreign policy at home. A vocal supporter of the United

Nations, he served as vice chair of the US delegation to the San Francisco conference, and then helped steer the UN Charter through the Senate ratification process. Believing nuclear proliferation the greatest threat to world peace, he pushed in 1946 for the creation of the UN Atomic Energy Commission and urged international acceptance of the Baruch Plan. At the same time, Connally opposed the creation of semiautonomous subsidiary organizations such as UNESCO because he feared their actions would undermine the UN's influence. He also preserved US sovereignty with the 1946 passage of the Connally Amendment, which permitted World Court jurisdiction over the United States only in cases that the government itself deemed nondomestic. Besides his work with the UN and his Senate responsibilities, Connally advised Secretary Byrnes at the 1946 Council of Foreign Ministers meeting. After Senator Arthur Vandenberg (R-MI) became chairman of the Senate Foreign Relations Committee following the Republicans' 1946 victory, Connally worked closely with him to draft the legislation supporting military aid to Greece and Turkey (*HSTE*; *ANBO*).

Dewey, Thomas Edmund (1902–1971), the progressive Republican two-term governor of New York and two-time presidential candidate, rejected the isolationism associated with conservative Taft Republicans and supported a strong role for the United States in world affairs, especially regarding the security of Europe. Although he thought the New Deal excessive, Dewey believed the federal government had a responsibility to promote the public interest. As the Republican presidential nominee in 1944, Dewey campaigned vigorously and, although defeated, garnered 46 percent of the popular vote, the highest Republican total since Herbert Hoover's 1928 victory. Reelected governor of New York in 1946, a fiscally conservative Dewey introduced progressive education, health, civil rights, and transportation policies while insisting upon a balanced budget. In 1948, he defeated Harold Stassen in the Oregon presidential primary by attacking Stassen's proposal to outlaw the Communist Party. He secured the nomination only to lose to Harry Truman, 49 percent to 45 percent, in a four-party race (Smith, *Dewey*).

Douglas, Helen Gahagan (1900–1980), actress, politician, and loyal New Deal Democrat, represented California's racially and economically diverse Fourteenth District in the House of Representatives from 1945 to 1950. After establishing herself as a talented young Broadway actress, Helen Gahagan married actor Melvyn Douglas. The couple soon moved to Hollywood where she starred in one feature-length film, *She*. By the late 1930s, Douglas turned her attention to politics, joining the Hollywood Anti-Nazi League, chairing the John Steinbeck Committee to Aid Migratory Workers, and working with the Farm Security Administration. A 1939 White House dinner with ER solidified her commitment to Democratic politics, and Douglas took a greater interest in the Democratic Party organization. She served as California's Democratic national committeewoman in 1940, and, after contributing to FDR's successful campaign of that year, became the vice chair of the California Democratic Party. As a member of Congress, Representative Douglas championed many progressive causes, including the establishment of a permanent Federal Employment Practices Commission and the continuation of wartime price and rent controls. She co-sponsored the Atomic Energy Act of 1946, which transferred the control of atomic energy from the military to a civilian commission. As a member of the House Committee on Foreign Relations, she called for the United States to play a prominent role in international peace efforts, criticized Truman's plan for military aid to Greece and Turkey, and supported the partition plan for Palestine. A loyal Democrat, she opposed the creation of a third party and attempted to dissuade Henry Wallace from running in the 1948 election (*NAWCTC*).

Dubinsky, David Isaac (1892–1982), political and labor activist, escaped from Russia to New York in 1911 after the czarist government exiled him to Siberia for inciting labor unrest. In New York, he resumed his union involvement, joining the International Ladies' Garment Workers Union (ILGWU). After years of exercising de facto leadership of the union, he became the ILGWU president in 1932, a position he held until 1966. As leader of the ILGWU, Dubinsky worked to increase the political power of labor by founding the American Labor Party (ALP) following the

Supreme Court's 1935 decision to overturn the National Industrial Recovery Act. Formed as the New York division of the National Labor Non-Partisan League, the ALP ran Franklin Roosevelt in 1936, 1940, and 1944 as well as their own candidates at the local level. Believing that Sidney Hillman had ceded control of the ALP to the Communists, Dubinsky, a staunch anti-Communist, and his followers broke away from the ALP in 1944 to form the Liberal Party of New York. When the fear of Communist infiltration divided American liberals between the anti-Communist Americans for Democratic Action (ADA) and the Communist-accommodating Progressive Citizens of America (PCA), Dubinsky and the ILGWU publicly supported the ADA while the other labor leaders followed a program of neutrality. Claiming "reactionaries" in Congress were just as threatening to democracy as the Communists, Dubinsky fought to retain such New Deal reforms as the workers' right to strike, an adequate minimum wage, and moderate price controls. In an attempt to offer international workers an alternative to Communism, Dubinsky called for the formation of the International Labor Relations Department at the American Federation of Labor convention in 1946. This organization provided aid to anti-Communist unions abroad throughout the Cold War. As the most vocal anti-Communist among labor leaders, Dubinsky found an ally in President Truman by 1948. In the 1948 presidential election, the New York liberal vote was split: the Liberal Party endorsed President Truman while the ALP endorsed Henry Wallace. Although Truman lost New York to Thomas Dewey, Dewey's margin of victory was much smaller than expected, and most pundits agreed labor deserved credit for Truman's close finish (Hamby, *Beyond*, 167, 243–44; *ANBO*; James A. Hagerty, "Dewey Plurality in State is 42,777," *NYT*, 4 November 1948, 18; Leo Egan, "ALP Right Wing Secedes, Starts Roosevelt Drive; Chiefs Bitter At Mayor," *NYT*, 30 March 1944, 1; Danish, 16–21; "New York," *NYT*, 28 July 1946, E2).

Du Bois, William Edward Burghardt (W. E. B.) (1868–1963), historian, sociologist, and radical civil rights activist, was the foremost African American intellectual of his day. In 1895, Du Bois earned a Ph.D. from Harvard, the first African American to do so. In 1903 he published *The Souls of Black Folk*, a groundbreaking book that criticized Booker T. Washington, at that time the most influential African American leader, by arguing that Washington's goal of economic opportunity through assimilation for African Americans was meaningless without full political and civil rights. Du Bois helped found the National Association for the Advancement of Colored People (NAACP) in 1910, and edited its journal, *Crisis*, from 1910 until 1934, when his disagreements with NAACP strategy led to his resignation. He then returned to Atlanta, where he joined the faculty of Atlanta University and published his most historically significant work, *Black Reconstruction in America: An Essay Toward a History of the Part Which Black Folk Played in the Attempt to Reconstruct Democracy in America*. Through his world travels and intense examination of Marxism, Du Bois grew increasingly convinced that global capitalism, not simply a lack of political rights, caused the continuing oppression of both Africans and members of the African diaspora. When his key ally, Atlanta University president John Hope, died in 1944, Du Bois lost the protection he needed to remain on the faculty. That same year, however, he accepted an offer from the NAACP as director of special research, where he would soon clash again with NAACP executive secretary Walter White. Du Bois, who remained resolute that the NAACP should not be co-opted by the administration while segregation and lynching continued, quickly clashed with White over his continued insistence upon presenting *An Appeal to the World* to the UN Human Rights Commission and his outspoken support of Henry Wallace and continued criticism of Harry Truman. White dismissed Du Bois in 1948. Du Bois then joined the Council on African Affairs and chaired its committee on African aid (*ANBO*).

Dulles, John Foster (1888–1959), attorney, diplomat, and Republican foreign policy expert, brought bipartisan qualifications to his role as a US delegate to the United Nations. Dulles began his foreign policy career in the Wilson administration as a member of the War Trade Board and was a member of the US delegation to the Paris Peace Conference, where he helped draft a proposed peace treaty that limited German reparations. Disappointed with the Versailles Treaty (he thought it dealt too harshly with Germany), Dulles returned to his international law practice but retained his interest in foreign affairs, publishing *War, Peace and Change* in 1939. With the onset of World War II, Dulles devoted his time and energy to postwar planning, as chairman of the Federal Council of Churches' Commission on a Just and Durable Peace. During the early years of the Cold War, Dulles helped craft a foreign policy that opposed Communism and advocated active US involvement with the world, and he emerged as the foreign policy spokesperson for the eastern wing of the GOP. Seeking bipartisan support, Roosevelt appointed Dulles a delegate to the 1945 United Nations conference in San Francisco. Following suit, Truman named him an alternate to the 1946 General Assembly meeting in London. During this period Dulles also served as a State Department advisor at the Council of Foreign Ministers meetings in Europe. In 1948, Dulles served as Marshall's deputy on the US delegation to the UN General Assembly meeting in Paris. His UN work brought him into contact with ER whose political skill and acumen he came to admire. Dulles served as foreign policy advisor for Republican Thomas E. Dewey in his 1944 and 1948 presidential campaigns. His relationship with Dewey made Dulles the leading candidate for the position of secretary of state in a Republican administration—a situation considered so likely that Marshall actually discussed the transition with Dulles before the election. Dewey's defeat destroyed Dulles's hopes and initially isolated him from the Republican Party. Trying to alleviate Dulles's disappointment, Marshall, who planned to resign as secretary of state, persuaded Truman to name Dulles acting head of the UN delegation in his stead (*HSTE*; *ANBO*).

Eisenhower, Dwight David (1890–1969), general, war hero, and thirty-fourth president of the United States, organized the November 1942 invasion of North Africa and the June 6, 1944, D-Day invasion, which ultimately culminated in the Allied victory in Europe in May 1945. Following World War II, Eisenhower served as head of the occupation forces in the American zone of Germany and later replaced General Douglas MacArthur as chief of staff of the United States Army. Both the Democratic and Republican parties sought to recruit Eisenhower as a presidential candidate in 1948, and Truman even told him he would run as vice president if Eisenhower would accept the presidential nomination. Eisenhower, however, remained ambiguous regarding his party affiliation and said at the time that he did not think a professional soldier should enter politics. In May 1948, he chose instead to accept the presidency of Columbia University where he served until the end of 1950. He also served as the informal chairman of the Joint Chiefs of Staff under Truman when chief of staff Fleet Admiral William D. Leahy became ill in 1948 (*DAB*; Parmet, *Eisenhower,* 12–15).

Flynn, Edward Joseph (1891–1953), Bronx County Democratic Party leader from 1922 until his death, and member of the Tammany Hall political machine, exercised extensive influence in both New York State and national politics. In 1928, Flynn helped elect FDR to the governorship of New York and quickly became one of FDR's key political strategists. As national chairman of the Democratic Party, he organized FDR's 1940 and 1944 campaigns for president and played an instrumental role in making Harry S. Truman the vice-presidential nominee in 1944. Flynn worked closely with ER in the Democratic Party in New York and then in national political campaigns, and they developed a great respect for each other's political skills. After FDR's death, Flynn urged ER to go to Russia to help rescue Soviet-American relations and even thought she should run for governor. ER and Flynn continued to consult with each other about Democratic Party politics, both in New York State and nationally (*FDRE*; *ANBO*; Black, *Casting,* 52).

Gromyko, Andrei Andreyevich (1909–1989), Soviet diplomat and delegate to the UN, joined the Soviet diplomatic service in 1939 and served as counselor at the Soviet Embassy in Washington during the early years of World War II. In 1943, Stalin appointed Gromyko ambassador to the United States and later as head of the Soviet delegation to the Dumbarton Oaks meetings that laid the groundwork for the United Nations, where he urged that a few major nations should be able to veto decisions in the future UN's Security Council. From 1946 to 1948, Gromyko served as permanent Soviet representative to the UN Security Council, where he was known for his austere and gruff demeanor. Gromyko returned to the Soviet Union in 1949, where he became first deputy minister of foreign affairs (*CB*; Bill Keller, "Gromyko, 79, Soviet Voice, Dies of Stroke," *NYT*, 4 July 1989, 1; *CBE*).

Gurewitsch, Arno David (1902–1974), Russian-Jewish physician whose patients included Trude Wenzel Lash, became ER's personal physician after FDR's death in 1945. They became close friends in November 1947 when ER helped Gurewitsch, on his way to Switzerland for treatment of tuberculosis, secure a seat on the plane taking her to Geneva for meetings of the UN Human Rights Commission. During an unexpected layover in Ireland, an intense bond developed between them and, once in Switzerland—ER in Geneva and Gurewitsch in a Davos sanitarium—they kept in touch via letters and phone calls. They also saw each other briefly in the spring of 1948 when ER returned to Europe. By then, she and Gurewitsch were confiding their difficulties to each other, specifically ER's troubled relations with her children and Gurewitsch's unhappiness with his marriage. They were also exchanging political views on such topics as the upcoming presidential election and the situation in Palestine. In July 1948, Gurewitsch left the sanitarium to spend time in England with his estranged wife, Nemone, and their daughter, Grania. In the fall, he visited ER, then in Paris for the UN General Assembly meeting. He then returned to New York to resume his medical career and remained one of ER's closest friends and confidantes for the rest of her life ("Dr. A. David Gurewitsch Dies; Physical-Rehabilitation Teacher," *NYT*, 31 January 1974, 36; Gurewitsch, 21–35; Lash, *Years*, 182–83; Lash, *World*, 238–92).

Hannegan, Robert Emmet (1903–1949), influential St. Louis Democratic Party boss, rescued Harry Truman's political career by breaking with the St. Louis political machine and endorsing Truman's reelection to the Senate in his tight 1940 race against Missouri governor Lloyd Stark. Hannegan's rejection of Stark, the party favorite, alienated him from the rest of the St. Louis political machine, but his loyalty to Truman earned him a federal appointment to revenue commissions for eastern Missouri, despite strong objections from anti-machine Missourians. Impressed by Hannegan's work, FDR promoted him to national commissioner of internal revenue, and three months later to chairman of the Democratic National Committee. In 1944, Hannegan took a lead role in removing Henry Wallace from (and securing for Truman his place on) the 1944 ticket. During that campaign, Hannegan often clashed with ER over the African American vote with ER favoring direct outreach to black voters and Hannegan contending that such action would split the Democratic Party. When Truman assumed the presidency, he made Hannegan his postmaster general and chair of the Democratic National Committee. Hannegan advised the president to be suspicious of labor, discounted women's contribution to the party, and urged a cautious approach to social and economic reform. Failing health forced his resignation in 1948 (*HSTE*; Lash, *Eleanor*, 695, 709).

Harriman, William Averell (1891–1986), businessman, diplomat, and Democratic Party stalwart, spent most of World War II abroad, as FDR's personal Lend-Lease negotiator for England and later as ambassador to the Soviet Union, a position he assumed in 1943. During the war Harriman developed close relationships with FDR, Churchill, and Stalin. Harriman's often-contentious dealings with Stalin convinced him of Soviet intentions to violate the Yalta agreements governing countries on or near the USSR's borders and led him to return to Washington shortly after FDR's death to urge Truman to take a harder line with the Russians. Harriman advocated "a firm but friendly quid pro quo" with the Soviets, telling Truman that "we must have our hand out in friendship but our guard up." At the same time he supported the development of the United Nations noting that if the two superpowers "both adopt the attitude of live and let live as to internal affairs and we both respect the right of all people to choose their own way of life, this barrier needn't be insurmountable." Truman heeded Harriman's advice and stiffened his attitude towards the Kremlin, most notably in his negotiations with the Soviets over the composition of the postwar Polish government. However, Harriman's influence decreased after James Byrnes became secretary of state in July 1945 and refused to allow Harriman to attend the planning sessions for the first postwar Allied Foreign Ministers Conference scheduled for September. Harriman resigned the following February and Truman promptly appointed him US ambassador to Great Britain. After just seven months in London, Truman asked Harriman to lead the Commerce Department. As commerce secretary, Harriman chaired the nonpartisan committee that developed proposals for what became the Economic Corporation Act—the basis of assistance to postwar Europe, also known as the Marshall Plan. In the spring of 1948, Truman named Harriman US special representative in Europe for the Economic Cooperation Administration. As the White House overseer for the Marshall Plan, Harriman traveled widely, coordinating European business and government efforts and overseeing the distribution of American aid (*HSTE*; *DPB*; Isaacson and Thomas, 328–30; Alan S. Oser, "Ex-Gov. Averell Harriman, Adviser to 4 Presidents, Dies," *NYT*, 27 July 1986, 1; *FDRE*).

Hendrick, James P. (1901–1990), a lawyer, entered government service in the War Department in 1941 and became a civilian assistant to Secretary of War Robert P. Patterson. In 1946, Hendrick joined the State Department where he served as ER's principal advisor at the UN during the drafting of the Universal Declaration of Human Rights and the establishment of the International Refugee Organization (IRO) and the United Nations International Children's Emergency Fund (UNICEF). He resigned his position in 1948 to become an administrator for the Marshall Plan ("James P. Hendrick, 88, former Federal Official," *NYT*, 2 July 1990, D10).

Hickok, Lorena Alice (1893–1968), journalist and astute observer of politics, resigned her position with the Associated Press in 1933 when she thought her growing friendship with ER prevented her from remaining objective in her coverage of the First Lady. Hickok then lent her expertise to FDR, ER, and Harry Hopkins as a field reporter for the Federal Emergency Relief Administration and later coordinated public relations for the 1939 World's Fair. One of ER's most trusted and intimate confidantes, "Hick" served as ER's sounding board on politics, family matters, and the various personal crises she confronted and accompanied ER on trips to the West Coast, Puerto Rico, and Gaspé Peninsula. After going to work for the Democratic National Committee (DNC) in 1940, she became executive secretary of its Women's Division for four years and lived in the White House from 1941 until March 1945, when complications from diabetes forced her to retire from her position with the DNC. In June 1945, Representative Mary Norton, a close friend, hired her to do research and political outreach. In 1947, she joined the staff of the Women's Division of the New York State Democratic Committee (*NAWMP*).

Hitler, Adolf (1889–1945), chancellor of Germany from 1933 and Fuhrer from 1934 until his death, led Germany during World War II and was an architect of the Holocaust. As chancellor, he rearmed Germany, discarded the restrictions of the Treaty of Versailles and the League of Nations, and began a program of territorial expansion that culminated in Germany's invasion of Poland in September 1939. Facing opposition from France and Britain abroad, and building upon the Aryan theory of racial and ethnic superiority he first promoted in *Mein Kampf*, Hitler and his followers implemented a genocidal plan to rid central Europe of Jews, Gypsies, homosexuals, Communists, and others they deemed undesirable. By 1942, Hitler, the leader of the National Socialist German Workers' Party (NSDAP, or Nazi) faced defeat by the Soviets in Stalingrad and the British in North Africa. As the Allies and the Soviets stymied the last of the German army's advances, Hitler's attempts to mobilize and rally the people of Germany failed. Allied invasions from the west and Soviet invasions from the east into Germany ended Hitler's hopes for European domination, and without the weapons he had promised, Germany's war effort began to fail. Disillusioned by Nazi defeats, Hitler married his longtime mistress, Eva Braun, on April 28, 1945, and then committed suicide with her on April 30, 1945. On May 7, 1945, the German army issued its first surrender (*OCPW*; *CBE*; *OCAMH*).

Hopkins, Harry Lloyd (1890–1946), social worker, administrator, advisor and diplomat, became a friend and ally of ER's while directing the New York Temporary Relief Agency during FDR's governorship. In 1933, FDR named Hopkins chief relief administrator and then director of the Works Progress Administration (WPA), where he worked closely with ER to ensure that the government met the needs of those out of work. Later, particularly after he moved into the White House in 1940, Hopkins devoted most of his energies to assisting FDR. During World War II, despite chronic ill health, Hopkins played a key role as FDR's personal emissary to Churchill and Stalin and advisor during FDR's negotiations at the wartime conferences with these leaders. After FDR's death, President Truman sent Hopkins back to Moscow to press Stalin about Russia's entry into the war with Japan, coordinate the Allied occupation of Germany, discuss the use of the veto in the UN Security Council, and iron out differences over the future government of Poland. Hopkins returned convinced that if the United States adopted a patient, straightforward approach that recognized Russia's legitimate interests, Russia and the United States could get along. By the fall of 1945, however, Hopkins feared that Truman's aggressive stance toward Moscow would lead needlessly to an end of the wartime alliance, a concern ER shared. Suffering from chronic ill health and in need of more income, Hopkins resigned from government service on July 2, 1945. He accepted a position as mediator between labor and management in the coat and suit industry and planned to write his memoirs. But his health worsened and he died at the age of fifty-five on January 29, 1946 (*DAB*; Lash, *Eleanor*, 388–89, 503–5; McJimsey, 387–97).

Humphrey, John Peters (1905–1995), Canadian diplomat and professor of international law, became the first director of the Human Rights Division in the United Nations Secretariat. Humphrey began practicing law in 1929 and in 1937 took a professorship in the Faculty of Law at McGill University in Montreal. During World War II, he became friends with Henri Laugier, a refugee from occupied France teaching at the Université de Montréal. After the war, when Laugier became assistant secretary-general for social affairs at the UN, he offered Humphrey the directorship of the Human Rights Division. Humphrey brought to his new position a solid background in civil and common law, as well as international law, and a fluency in both English and French. He laid the groundwork for the drafting of the Universal Declaration of Human Rights by assembling a collection of existing and proposed bills of rights and preparing a preliminary draft of the declaration. From 1946 to 1948, he worked closely with ER and the other members of the Human Rights Commission (HRC) on completing the declaration and preparing drafts of the covenant on human rights and proposals for implementation (Glendon, 47–48, 65–66; Humphrey, *On the Edge*, 16–20).

Ibn Saud (King Abd al-Aziz ibn Saʿud Al Saʿud) (1880–1953), monarch of modern Saudi Arabia, re-established the kingdom that his ancestors had ruled from the mid-eighteenth until the latter half of the nineteenth century. Launching his campaign in 1902 from Kuwait, where his family lived in exile, he captured Riyadh in a surprise attack and went on to unite much of the Arabian peninsula under his rule by the late 1920s. The close alliance between the Saudi family and the conservative Wahhabi sect of Islam, which began in the mid-eighteenth century, strengthened his rule, and he made their strict precepts the law of the land. In 1915, Ibn Saud signed a treaty with Great Britain, the major power in the Middle East, that assured British respect for Saudi independence and protected the country against aggression. Ibn Saud remained wary of British influence, however, and, in 1933, partly for that reason, chose to grant an oil concession to Standard Oil of California instead of its British competitor, the Iraq Petroleum Company. Thus began an increasingly important economic and strategic relationship between Saudi Arabia and the United States. During World War II, Ibn Saud favored the Allied cause but remained officially neutral. In a February 1945 meeting with FDR on a US Navy cruiser in Egypt's Great Bitter Lake, Ibn Saud expressed both his desire to continue close relations with the US and his opposition to the creation of a Jewish state in Palestine. Despite his position on Palestine, however, Ibn Saud gave limited support to the Arab cause during the Arab-Israeli war of 1948 because of his enduring rivalry with King Abdullah of Trans-Jordan, one of the major participants in the conflict (*EMME*; "Ibn Saud As Exile Re-Created Realm," *NYT*, 10 November 1953, 14).

Ickes, Harold LeClair (1874–1952), progressive reformer, civil rights activist, and interior secretary, began his career as a progressive Republican associated with the urban reform movement in

Chicago. After Ickes managed the Western Independent Republican Committee for Roosevelt in the 1932 presidential campaign, FDR appointed him secretary of the interior, where he won a reputation as a hard-working, difficult but effective, and incorruptible administrator. He served from 1933 to 1946, longer than any other leading official in the Roosevelt and Truman administrations. As secretary, Ickes administered the education program of the Civilian Conservation Corps (CCC), helped create the Public Works Administration (PWA) and directed its nearly $6 billion construction program, and implemented many conservation initiatives. A strong advocate of civil rights for African Americans, who had served as director of the NAACP in Chicago in 1923, Ickes desegregated the Interior Department, made William Hastie the first African American federal judge (in the Virgin Islands, which came under Interior jurisdiction), and worked with ER to organize a performance by Marion Anderson at the Lincoln Memorial after the Daughters of the American Revolution denied her access to Constitution Hall. After FDR's death Ickes remained in the Truman administration, partly because of his belief in the urgent need to establish a coherent policy to protect domestic oil reserves and ensure access to foreign oil. But Ickes stayed for only ten months, resigning over Truman's nomination of Edwin W. Pauley, a California oil man and Democratic fundraiser, as undersecretary of the navy. In retirement Ickes wrote a syndicated column for the *New York Post*, contributed frequently to the *New Republic*, and supported many liberal causes (*ANBO*).

Kirchwey, Mary Fredrika (Freda) (1893–1976), journalist, began her lifelong career at the *Nation* in 1918 writing for the International Relations Section of the liberal weekly until she became its publisher, editor, and owner in 1937. Kirchwey then established the nonprofit *Nation* Associates and transferred ownership of the *Nation* to the new organization, which included ER among its supporters. During the 1930s, Kirchwey established herself as one of the nation's harshest critics of fascism and slowly moved the *Nation* from its traditionally pacifist position to one of intervention. In the postwar period, she strongly supported the United Nations, emphasized the necessity of peaceful relations between the United States and the Soviet Union, and condemned any escalation in the production of atomic weaponry. Although she had served on the board of the Union for Democratic Action (UDA), Kirchwey refused to side with either the Progressive Citizens of America (PCA) or the Americans for Democratic Action (ADA) when the two liberal organizations opposed each other over the issue of working with Communists. She did, however, oppose Henry Wallace's 1948 third-party campaign for the presidency. ER sat on the board of the *Nation* and regarded Kirchwey as a solid ally until the fall of 1947 when the editor's criticism of the US position on Palestine led ER to resign as co-chair of a *Nation* Associates fundraiser (*ANBO*).

Kotschnig, Walter Maria (1901–1985), administrator, educator, and foreign service officer, Kotschnig spent the early part of his career on the staff of the International Student Service (ISS) in Geneva, Switzerland, becoming general secretary in 1927. In 1934 he left the ISS to work on resettlement issues for the League of Nations High Commissioner for Refugees from Germany. Outspoken in his aversion to the Nazis, Kotschnig and his family came to America in 1936 where he taught comparative education at Smith and Mount Holyoke Colleges and lectured on educational topics around the country. Kotschnig became a US citizen in 1942 and joined the State Department in 1944 as a specialist in international organizations and from 1945 through 1947 led its Division of International Organizational Affairs. In that capacity, Kotschnig represented the department at the Dumbarton Oaks Conference in 1944, as well as the United Nations founding conference in San Francisco, the International Labor Organization conference, and the first preparatory conference for ECOSOC in 1945. The following year he served as acting executive secretary to UNESCO's preparatory commission and subsequently attended its general meetings in Paris (1946) and Mexico City (1947). That same year, he became associate general secretary and consultant to a UN subcommission investigating war damages in Czechoslovakia and Poland (Wolfgang Saxon, "Walter M. Kotschnig Dead; Longtime U.S. Aide to U.N.," *NYT*, 25 June 1985, B6; "Walter Kotschnig, Ex-Official with State Department, Dies," *WP*, 29 June 1985, B6; *RDS* 1946; "Biographical sketch," Walter Maria Kotschnig Papers, University of Albany M.E.

BIOGRAPHICAL PORTRAITS

Grenander Department of Special Collections and Archives, http://library.albany.edu/speccoll/findaids/ger053.htm).

La Guardia, Fiorello Henry (1882–1947), lawyer and New York City mayor from 1934 to 1945, began his career in electoral politics when he won a congressional seat representing Manhattan's Lower East Side as a reform-minded Republican in 1916. The following year, he left Congress to fly fighter planes in Italy. He returned to Congress in 1923 where he called for old-age pensions, workmen's compensation, free speech for socialists, and an end to immigration restrictions. Despite his progressive stance, La Guardia suffered from his membership in the Republican Party and lost his seat in the sweeping Democratic victory of 1932. He won the mayoralty of New York City in 1933 as the candidate of the Fusion Party—a group of Republicans, Socialists, and anti-Tammany Democrats. Using federal funds made available under New Deal recovery programs, La Guardia built bridges, roads, sanitation systems, schools, public housing, hospitals, and parks in the city, making New York a symbol of New Deal success. Despite their different political affiliations, La Guardia and FDR had an excellent working relationship. La Guardia campaigned for FDR's reelection in 1940 and 1944, calling for a renewal of the prewar New Deal programs, and when FDR established the Office of Civilian Defense in 1941, he appointed La Guardia as director. After months of struggling to manage his time between duties in Washington and his office in New York, La Guardia asked ER to serve as his assistant director, and she accepted the offer. La Guardia retired after the completion of his third term as mayor in 1945. Although ER hoped that the Democratic Party would run him as their candidate for senator in the 1946 election, La Guardia never returned to electoral politics. He accepted an appointment as director general of the United Nations Relief and Rehabilitation Administration (UNRRA) in the spring of 1946, but resigned by the end of the year when the United States and Britain announced they would not contribute to the organization in the future (*ANBO*; Lash, *Years*, 139; "La Guardia is Dead," *NYT*, 21 September 1947, 1).

Lash, Joseph P. (1909–1987), journalist, biographer, and political organizer, became a close personal friend to ER during the Depression when he emerged as one of the most important student leaders of the era. When the House Un-American Activities Committee called Lash, the head of the American Student Union (ASU), to testify about Communist infiltration into student organizations, ER sat in the caucus room to lend Lash and ASU her moral support. During World War II Lash spent two years in the Pacific with the US Army, and married Trude Wenzel in 1944; their son Jonathan was born in 1945. Upon Lash's discharge in 1945 he resumed his political activities, taking a job with the Union for Democratic Action. In 1947, he and ER, along with other liberal Democrats, helped found Americans for Democratic Action (ADA) and he served for a time as the ADA's New York secretary. During this period Lash also worked closely with Franklin Roosevelt Jr., helping him evaluate his chances of winning election to Congress from New York. Lash and his wife, Trude, both remained important and influential members of ER's inner circle, spending weekends with her in Hyde Park and communicating regularly about issues of common concern. Later, Lash became ER's biographer (Lash, *World*, 204, 216, 223, 234, 228–30, 271–72).

Lash, Trude Wenzel Pratt (1908–2004), teacher and children's advocate, emigrated from her native Germany shortly after Hitler came to power, and married ER's longtime friend and confidante Joseph P. Lash in 1944. The couple's son, Jonathan, was born the next year with ER in attendance. ER tried to stay close to the couple but by 1946 the pressures of their respective careers and families strained the relationship. Sensitive to ER's difficulties with her children, the Lashes were reluctant to intrude even though ER often asked them to stay at Val-Kill on weekends and during the summer. The couple also had their own career and personal concerns. Trude, in particular, was juggling the demands of work and family (in addition to Jonathan, she had three children from a previous marriage). ER sympathized and helped when she could. She obtained a short-term job for Trude as secretary of the Nuclear Human Rights Commission in 1946. Later that year, Trude began what became a long career as a children's advocate and expert on child welfare programs when she joined the Citizens Commission for Children of New York, an organization that ER had helped found in 1944. Despite the pressures of their respective lives the Lashes maintained a warm relationship with ER (she and Trude spoke every morning by phone), and the couple remained among ER's closest friends and advisors. (Lash, *World*, 145–46, 204, 216, 223, 228–30; Lash, *Love*, 343–44, Adam Fifield, "A Living Primer of 20th-Century Causes: For Trude Lash, A Lifetime on the Barricades," *NYT*, 3 June 2001, CY3).

Lehman, Herbert Henry (1878–1963), FDR's lieutenant governor, became governor of New York in 1933 and served until 1942. Lehman pursued the policies of the New Deal at the state level, including the regulation of public utilities and labor reform. His fiscal policies eliminated the state's debt and left a surplus for his Republican successor, Thomas Dewey, who took office in 1943. In December 1942, Lehman accepted FDR's request to head the Office of Foreign Relief and Rehabilitation Operations in the State Department. The following year he helped the Roosevelt administration create the United Nations Relief and Rehabilitation Administration (UNRRA) and the UNRRA council elected Lehman its first director general, a position for which he refused salary and held until March 1946 when he resigned to campaign for the US Senate. After losing that election, he devoted himself to philanthropic and public campaigns, including numerous child welfare organizations and the campaign for a Jewish state. He would win a special senatorial election in 1949 and serve in the US Senate until 1957 (*FDRE*; "Lehman Embraced the Fields of Politics, Banking and Philanthropy in Long Career," *NYT*, 6 December 1963, 23).

Lerner, Max Albert (1902–1992), scholar, educator, and journalist, became one of the most prominent liberal political writers and activists in the post–World War II period. Trained as an economist, he wrote books and essays on political theory, taught at Sarah Lawrence and Williams Colleges, and served on the editorial board of the *Nation* during the 1930s. From 1943 until it collapsed in 1948, Lerner served as editorial director of the left-liberal New York newspaper *PM*. A member of the National Citizens Political Action Committee (NCPAC), he advocated creating a unified liberal movement. When the Republicans won the 1946 elections, Lerner attributed the victory to the use of "the Red scare" and challenged liberals and labor to form a coalition in which "a militant non-Communist leadership" would replace "Communist influence." He regarded fascism as a far more dangerous enemy than Communism, however, and feared that liberals would weaken their cause if they diverted their energies into Red-baiting. Although he recognized the need to exclude Communists from leadership positions in liberal organizations, when ER and other liberals founded Americans for Democratic Action (ADA) in January 1947, he feared it would become narrow and sterile by excluding a broad range of non-Communist opinion. On the other hand, he faulted the Progressive Citizens of America (PCA) for failing to clearly state its independence from Communism. Like Freda Kirchwey, he hoped that the two organizations would overcome their differences and work together. Lerner opposed a third party, which he also felt would divide the liberal movement, and tried to persuade Henry Wallace not to run as the candidate of the Progressive Party in 1948 (Richard Severo, "Max Lerner, Writer, 89, is Dead; Humanist in Political Barricades," *NYT*, 6 June 1992, 11; Hamby, *Beyond*, 157, 166–67, 207; Max Lerner to ER, 22 January 1947, AERP).

Lewis, John Llewellyn (1880–1969), labor leader, began his rise to power in 1901 as a coal miner in Panama, Illinois. By 1911, the American Federation of Labor recognized his arbitration skills and appointed him its national field representative. He quickly allied with AFL president Samuel Gompers and United Mine Workers president John White. By 1920, Lewis assumed de facto control of the UMW, a subsidiary union of the AFL and the organization he would lead for the next forty years. As the Great Depression assailed the coal industry, Lewis consolidated his control over the union by centralizing its decision-making apparatus and filling the organization with his allies. A Republican, Lewis appealed to Hoover for government assistance, urging the imposition of fair wage, price, and production costs and rules governing worker safety. This departure from voluntary unionism coupled with his insistence upon organizing relatively unskilled industrial workers led him to challenge AFL leaders to focus more on industrial, rather than trade, workers. The day following the 1935 AFL convention, Lewis and supportive AFL leaders established the Committee on Industrial Organizations to lead the AFL's industrial worker campaign. Lewis and the CIO would dominate American labor politics until the outbreak of the Second World War. He created political action committees supporting FDR and other pro-labor candidates, supported the dramatic, successful sit-down strike against General Motors, and helped negotiate a settlement with US Steel. However, in 1937, a series of defeats with the "Little Steel" companies undercut Lewis's prominence with the AFL. In November 1938, his CIO left the AFL federation and began operations as an independent federation, the Congress of Industrial Organizations. Lewis, who thought FDR had abandoned reform, turned against him in 1938, campaigned for Willkie, and promised to resign from the CIO if FDR won reelection in 1940. Lewis and the UMW left the CIO and remained unaffiliated until they rejoined the AFL in 1946. During the war, Lewis called a major coal strike in 1943 and, as Truman grappled with wage and price control politics, called additional strikes in 1946, 1948, and 1949. Truman viewed the 1946 strike as a direct threat to the nation and seized the mines. In November after Lewis called a second strike, Truman instructed the Justice Department to prosecute him under the Smith-Connally Act, a 1943 law prohibiting strikes in plants or mines necessary for war production and imposing criminal penalties on those found guilty of leading strikes. The judge ruled in the administration's favor, finding that because the country was still under a wartime economy, the antistrike law still applied. He fined the UMW $3.5 million and Lewis $10,000. After the UAW struck in 1948, Truman issued a back-to-work order under the Taft-Hartley Act and when Lewis resisted it, the union again had to pay substantial fines (*HSTE*; Dulles and Dubofsky, 308–11; *DAB*).

Lie, Trygve Halvdan (1896–1968), lawyer, politician, and the first secretary general of the UN, joined the Norwegian Labour Party in 1919, after receiving his law degree from Oslo University, and became the party's national secretary in 1926. When the Labour Party won control of the Norwegian government in 1935, Lie became the minister of justice, a post he held until 1939. Serving as minister of supply and shipping from 1939 to 1940, Lie ordered all Norwegian ships to sail for Allied ports, saving the nation's fleet from the invading Germans. The following year, Lie served as the foreign minister of the exiled Norwegian government in London and continued on in that post until 1946. As head of the Norwegian delegation to the San Francisco conference and chair of the commission responsible for drafting the Security Council provisions of the UN Charter, Lie won the confidence of both the US and Soviet diplomats. Both nations voted for him to serve as the first president of the General Assembly at the London Conference of 1946. However, Lie lost the election to Belgian foreign minister Paul-Henri Spaak by a vote of 28 to 23. The Big Five nations then met privately and agreed on Lie, a statesman with ties to neither the Western nor Soviet spheres, as the Security Council's recommendation for secretary-general. Lie assumed office in February 1946 and spent the next seven years attempting to build the Secretariat—the administrative backbone of the UN—into an effective, independent office for mediating world affairs. In addition to negotiating the establishment of the UN's permanent headquarters in New York City, Lie coordinated the UN's handling of several international crises, including Palestine, Berlin, and Korea. Lie also proved himself a strong advocate of human rights and women's rights in particular, declaring in November 1946, "We will not rest until women everywhere enjoy equal rights and equal opportunities with men." In 1952, Lie resigned and Dag Hammarskjöld succeeded him the following year ("Trygve Halvdan Lie," United Nations Organization, http://www.un.org/Overview/SG/sg1bio.html; James B. Reston, "UNO Opened: Attlee Asks World Unity," 11 January 1946, 1; "Norwegian Leads as UNO Secretary," *NYT*, 29 January 1946, 4; Lauren, 216).

Loeb, James Isaac, Jr. (1908–1992), liberal organizer and strategist, co-founded the Union for Democratic Action (UDA) in 1941 and served as its executive director. An able administrator, Loeb devoted himself to organizing a unified and effective liberal movement, a goal made more difficult by the question of whether or not Communists would be allowed to participate. Unlike its larger, more dynamic rivals, the Independent Citizens Committee of the Arts, Sciences, and Professions (ICCASP) and the National Citizens Political Action Committee (NCPAC), the UDA excluded

Communists. In a 1946 letter to the *New Republic*, Loeb criticized the infiltration of Communists into liberal organizations. Many liberals took issue with Loeb's position, arguing that liberals and Communists could work together, and that attacking Communists would divide and weaken liberals. ER supported Loeb's efforts and personally argued the UDA's position to Philip Murray, president of the CIO, whose participation was crucial to any effort at liberal unity. Loeb blamed the defeat of liberal candidates in the 1946 congressional elections on many liberals' refusal to denounce Communism. That December, when NCPAC and ICCASP merged to form the Progressive Citizens of America (PCA), with Murray as one of its vice presidents, the organization's constitution forbade excluding anyone from membership or leadership on the basis of political belief. In response, Loeb joined ER and other liberals who felt the need for a strong, new, anti-Communist liberal organization, to found Americans for Democratic Action in January 1947. Loeb served as its executive secretary until 1953 when he purchased and co-published the *Adirondack Daily Enterprise* (Eric Pace, "James I. Loeb, 83, Former Envoy and Organizer of Liberal Group," *NYT*, 14 January 1992, B6; Hamby, *Beyond*, 35, 152–64).

Lovett, Robert Abercrombie (1895–1986), Republican investment banker, World War I naval aviator, and business associate of Averell Harriman, served as assistant secretary of war for air during World War II. In that capacity he worked closely with General George C. Marshall, then army chief of staff. When Truman appointed Marshall secretary of state in 1947, Marshall tapped Lovett, who had returned to his banking career, as undersecretary of state. In that capacity, Lovett took a skeptical view of the benefits of an international declaration of human rights to the United States and opposed a human rights covenant because he feared it could never pass muster with the segregationists in Congress if it contained strong anti-discrimination provisions. On the question of Palestine, Lovett initially opposed partition and US recognition of the state of Israel on the grounds that such action would alienate the Arabs, push them toward the Soviets, and jeopardize US access to Middle Eastern oil. Lovett also feared that recognition would lead to American military involvement since it was widely assumed the Jews were too weak to withstand Arab attack without outside military help. However, once Truman decided to recognize Israel in May 1948, Lovett supported the decision and persuaded Marshall to do so as well. During the Berlin crisis of June 1948, Lovett, in Marshall's absence, first refused to allow American dependents to leave the beleaguered city, which the United States, Great Britain, France and the USSR jointly administered. Then, drawing on his previous aviation experience, he devised the plan to provision Berlin via air. Initially begun as a "temporary expedient," the Berlin airlift ultimately caused the Soviets to back down and reopen land access to Berlin. Given Lovett's views, his relationship with ER during this period was difficult. They worked together but did not often agree. Labeling Lovett "dangerous," ER hoped that he would resign from the department, which Lovett did early in 1949 (Cohen, *Palestine*, 283; *HSTE*; Issacson and Thomas, 451–53; Alben Krebs, "R.A. Lovett, Ex-Chief of Defense Who Pressed Buildup in 50's, Dies," *NYT*, 8 May 1986, B24; Lash, *Years*, 73–74, 154; Lash, *World*, 290–91).

MacLeish, Archibald (1892–1982), poet, worked with both Roosevelts during the New Deal and World War II. His work with ER began with his strong support of the Federal Writers' Project and the American Youth Congress. FDR appointed him librarian of Congress in 1939. During World War II, he served as director of the Office of Facts and Figures and then as assistant director of the Office of War Information. After resigning as librarian of Congress in 1944, he accepted the post of assistant secretary of state for cultural affairs, where he coordinated American support for the nascent UN. MacLeish's use of radio and film to promote the conference encouraged FDR to appoint MacLeish to the US delegation to San Francisco and to ask that he draft FDR's opening speech to the delegates. Once in San Francisco, MacLeish applied his literary skills to the UN Charter, arguing successfully that the preamble should "move men's minds" and "be *written*—not constructed like a cross word puzzle out of political and academic odds and ends." He then wrote the preamble and edited a significant portion of the document. Although he left the State Department after San Francisco, he accepted Truman's request to lead the American delegation to the conference charged with organizing UNESCO, a position he held until late 1946 (*ANBO*; "Dinner will Honor First Lady Tonight," *NYT*, 21 February 1939, 16; "Roosevelt Dedicating Library, Asks World Peace," *WP*, 20 November 1939, 1; Schlesinger, 54–55, 67, 69; and Donaldson, 388).

Marshall, George Catlett (1880–1959), Army chief of staff during World War II and presidential envoy who would become Truman's secretary of state, presided over the creation of an 8.5 million-man army, supervised its supply lines, and devised its strategy, including the June 6, 1944, D-Day invasion. Within weeks after his November 1945 retirement from the army, Truman asked the general to serve as his personal representative to Chiang Kai-shek and negotiate an end to the Chinese civil war. In January 1947, Marshall replaced Byrnes as secretary of state, where he sought to contain Communism, rebuild a war-shattered Europe, and prevent the outbreak of another military conflict. Among his principal accomplishments was securing popular support for an active US presence in the international arena, most notably the Truman Doctrine and the Marshall Plan. Despite his earlier outreach to China, Marshall refused to extend US involvement in China because he believed no amount of military or economic aid would alter the outcome. He did, however, support limited aid to the Nationalist Chinese government, mostly to mollify the US supporters of Nationalist Chinese leader Chiang Kai-shek and to ensure congressional support for the Marshall Plan. Marshall's *realpolitik* extended to Palestine and led to the only serious disagreement he had with Truman. Like most of his senior colleagues at the State Department, Marshall opposed US recognition of a Jewish state in Palestine. Such a step, he believed, would embroil the United States in a Mideast conflict, deny it access to oil needed to implement the Marshall Plan, and allow the Soviet Union to become influential in the area. Marshall resigned as secretary of state in January 1949 for health reasons, but returned to public office the following year when President Truman appointed him secretary of defense (Cray, 654–64; *DPB*; *HSTE*; Stoler, 170–73).

Marshall, Thurgood (1908–1993), NAACP staff attorney whose landmark legal victories led to a position on the US Supreme Court, began his career in Baltimore in 1933 after graduating first in his class from Howard University Law School. The following year, he became counsel for the Baltimore chapter of the NAACP, only to move to New York City in 1936 to join his Howard mentor Charles Houston as a member of the national NAACP legal team. When Houston returned to Howard two years later, Marshall replaced his mentor as the association's chief counsel, a position he held until 1961 when he left for a seat on the US Court of Appeals for the Second Circuit. In 1938, Marshall argued *Missouri ex rel Gaines v. Canada*, the first of a series of cases challenging segregation in higher education, which led to the historic 1950 ruling that the separate law school Texas opened for African Americans was not "equal" to its white counterpart. In 1940, the NAACP established its Legal Defense and Education Fund and appointed Marshall its executive director. In that capacity, he successfully argued *Smith v. Allwright* (the 1944 decision overturning the white primary) and *Shelley v. Kraemer* (the 1948 decision declaring racially "restrictive covenants" in housing unconstitutional). In 1954, he successfully argued the landmark case *Brown v. Board of Education* in which the US Supreme Court found segregation in public schools unconstitutional, and in 1967 became the first African American appointed to the Supreme Court (*ANBO*; "Thurgood Marshall Bibliography," Thurgood Marshall Law Library, http://www.law.umaryland.edu/marshall/researchguides).

Masaryk, Jan Garrigue (1886–1948), Czechoslovakian ambassador and foreign minister, joined the diplomatic corps in 1918 and quickly rose through its ranks. In 1925, five years after serving as key aide to President Eduard Beneš at the Paris Peace Conference, Beneš appointed him ambassador to Great Britain, a position he held until 1938 when he resigned to protest the British-supported Munich Accords and its abandonment of Czechoslovakia. In 1941, Masaryk joined the Czechoslovak government in exile in London as foreign minister and deputy prime minister. After Allied forces liberated his homeland in 1945, Masaryk returned to Czechoslovakia as foreign minister and, in that capacity, served as head of the Czech delegation at the first session of the UN General Assembly in 1946. In February 1947, he criticized those non-Communist officials who resigned from Beneš's government, arguing their departure paved the way for the Soviet coup. Later that year, when he failed in his attempts to secure Soviet approval for Czechoslovakia to accept American aid under the Marshall Plan, Masaryk protested the Soviet position. After the Communist coup of 1948, Masaryk retained his position as foreign minister, only to be found dead three weeks later, his body lying on the ground underneath an open window at the Foreign Ministry. Although officially ruled a suicide, the circumstances surrounding his death remain a mystery (*DCWH*; *DPB*).

Mehta, Hansa (1897–1995) represented India on the UN Human Rights Commission, playing an active role in the drafting of the Universal Declaration of Human Rights and chairing the working group on implementation of the human rights convention. In the 1930s and 1940s Mehta emerged as a leader in the struggle for Indian independence and strongly criticized the British policy of detaining opponents of British rule without trial, censoring news, and confiscating property. Beginning in 1945 she served as Vice-President and President of the All India Women's Conference and in the Indian Constituent Assembly (Simpson, 88, 366, 478; Glendon, 35).

Molotov, Vyacheslav Mikhailovich (1890–1986), Soviet diplomat and a Stalin loyalist throughout his life, held the posts of first deputy prime minister from 1941 to 1957 and Soviet foreign minister from 1939 to 1949 and 1953 to 1956. Molotov negotiated and signed the non-aggression treaty between Nazi Germany and the USSR in 1939, which opened the way for the Soviet occupation of the Baltic states and part of Romania and led many people around the world to abandon the Communist movement. After Hitler invaded the Soviet Union and Japan attacked the United States in 1941, Molotov became the chief negotiator with Great Britain and the United States in forging an alliance against Germany and Japan. Once the Allies won the war, Molotov turned his attention to creating a bloc of states subservient to the Soviet Union in Eastern Europe. He served as Stalin's chief advisor at both the Yalta and Potsdam conferences in 1945. Known to some as "iron pants" for his endurance during negotiations, Molotov resisted compromise and repeatedly attacked the West during the early years of the Cold War (Raymond H. Anderson, "A Lifetime in History," *NYT*, 11 November 1986, A1, B7).

Mundt, Karl Earl (1900–1974), conservative Republican congressman and senator from South Dakota, gained a national reputation as a militant anti-Communist. After entering Congress in 1939, Mundt adhered to an isolationist foreign policy, voting against the Selective Service Act and Lend-Lease; however, after the attack on Pearl Harbor, he became a strong supporter of the war effort and of international cooperation after the war. In 1942, as a member of the special subcommittee charged with investigating the internment of Japanese-Americans, Mundt supported the conclusion that the "pampered" internees "were the best fed civilians in the country." In 1943, he joined another special committee, chaired by Texas congressman Martin Dies, charged with investigating "unAmerican activities." When the war ended, Mundt secured a seat on the House Un-American Activities Committee, the permanent committee charged with continuing the work the Dies Committee began. May 17, 1946, he told his colleagues that the committee would not be deterred by the "the extreme privilege of free press and free speech" from investigating anyone "engaged in actions which are un-American even though their activities are legal." At the same time, Mundt continued to support strong international aid, supporting the United Nations Relief and Rehabilitation Administration and calling for the United States to join the United Nations Educational, Scientific and Cultural Organization (UNESCO), an agency he would later criticize. In 1948, when he had become acting chairman of the House Committee on Un-American Activities (HUAC), Mundt and California congressman Richard Nixon conducted controversial hearings on accusations that Communists had infiltrated the State Department and other government agencies. Mundt and Nixon also introduced a bill in 1948 aimed at restricting Communist Party activity in the United States that would have required members of the Communist Party USA to register with the government. The bill passed the House, then died in the Senate, but the McCarran Internal Security Act of 1950 incorporated some of its provisions (though not mandatory registration of party members) (*ANBO*; "Karl E. Mundt Dead at 74; Ex-South Dakota Senator," *NYT*, 17 August 1974, 26; http://dosfan.lib.uic.edu/usia/usiahome/overview.pdf).

Niemöller (Niemoeller), Martin Friedrich Gustav Emil (1892–1984), Protestant theologian and German nationalist, originally supported the National Socialist German Workers' (Nazi) Party and its criticism of Communism and the Weimar Republic. In early 1934, however, after Hitler and Bishop Ludwig Müller of the German National Church attempted to merge church and state, Niemöller helped organize the Pastor's Emergency League, assumed leadership of the Confessional Church, and spoke out against Nazi encroachment on church sovereignty. Although Niemöller limited his criticism of the Nazi regime to its interference with the church, his insistence that the Confessional Church—not the German National Church—constituted the legitimate German Protestant church represented a rare instance of German opposition to Hitler, and as such, attracted international attention. Coverage of his defiance in the foreign press and Niemöller's own friendships with Nazi officials temporarily protected him, but by 1937 Hitler ordered Niemöller's arrest. Upon Niemöller's release from prison in 1938, Hitler again ordered his arrest and officials placed him in "protective custody" in the Sachsenhausen concentration camp where he remained in custody until the Allied liberation in the spring of 1945. Between December 1946 and May 1947, Niemöller embarked on a speaking tour of the United States sponsored by the Federal Council of Churches of Christ in America. In his lectures, he declared the guilt of all Germans for Nazi crimes but urged American forgiveness (*WWNG*; Eric Pace, "Martin Niemöller, Resolute Foe of Hitler," *NYT*, 8 March 1984, D22).

Noel-Baker, Philip John (1889–1982), British Labour politician, Quaker, and disarmament proponent, and the recipient of the 1959 Nobel Peace Prize, played significant roles in the founding of both the League of Nations and the United Nations. As special assistant to Lord Robert Cecil, he helped draft the covenant establishing the League of Nations in 1920 and served as a member for the first League Secretariat from 1920 to 1922. In 1929 he began a two-year term as a member of the British delegation to the League, where he chaired its conference on disarmament. After securing reelection to the House of Commons in 1936, he won election to the Labour Party's National Executive Committee, becoming its chair in 1946. He served in Churchill's war cabinet as joint parliamentary secretary to the Minister of War Transport, represented his government at both the San Francisco conference, where he helped draft the UN Charter, and the Food and Agriculture Organization in Quebec. Attlee then appointed him in his capacity as minister of state to head the British delegation to the UN, where he served as the British delegate to the Economic and Social Council, a position he used to call for the eradication of poverty, financial aid for refugees, regulation of weapons sales, and the unification of Allied economic interests in their respective German zones ("Phillip Noel-Baker—Biography," http:www.nobelprize.org/nobel_prizes/peace/laureates/1959/index.html).

Norton, Mary Teresa (1875–1959), Democratic congresswoman from the working-class Twelfth District of New Jersey and the first woman elected to Congress in her own right, Norton defended labor and argued for equal treatment for women workers. As chair of the House Labor Committee she waged a long, successful struggle to pass the Fair Labor Standards Act of 1938, which established a minimum wage and maximum hours for nonunion workers and did away with differential pay scales based on sex. An opponent of racial discrimination, Norton introduced legislation in every session of Congress from 1944 until 1951 to create a permanent Fair Employment Practices Commission, only to see all of the bills die in committee. During World War II she backed federal support for day care centers and argued after the war for continued government support. Although a strong proponent of equal pay for equal work, she opposed the Equal Rights Amendment because she felt it would eliminate protective legislation for women workers. A stalwart ally of labor, she worked unsuccessfully in 1947 to defeat the antilabor Taft-Hartley Act. In 1945, she had asked FDR to appoint her to the delegation attending the United Nations organizing conference in San Francisco; however, Truman refused to appoint her, opting instead to make her an alternate delegate to the International Labor Organization Conference in Paris. An active Democratic Party leader, Norton became chair of the New Jersey Democratic Committee in 1932, the first woman to head a state party organization. In 1944 she joined the Democratic National Committee and in 1948 served as chair of the Credentials Committee at the Democratic National Convention (*NAWMP*).

O'Dwyer, William (1890–1964), Irish immigrant, policeman, and attorney, began his political career when he opened his legal practice in 1925 and began promoting the Irish national soccer team's American tour. "Bill-O" quickly made a name for himself, thus securing a series of politically appointed positions: New York City magistrate (1932), the first judge of the Brooklyn Adolescent Court (1935), and a seat on the Kings County Court (1937). Less than three months after the 1939 race for Brooklyn district attorney, O'Dwyer made his major mark when he prosecuted members of the organized crime syndicate known as Murder, Inc. The following year, he challenged La Guardia in the New York City mayoral race, charging that the mayor's appointment to the Office of Civilian Defense made him neglect the city. Despite critics' contention that his prosecution of Murder, Inc., was filled with irregularities and suspicious conduct, he lost the election by only 130,000 votes, the smallest margin in thirty years. After Japan attacked Pearl Harbor, O'Dwyer enlisted in the US Army, where he served as an army lawyer, chief of the Economic Section of the Allied Commission, FDR's personal representative to the Foreign Economic Administration, and head of the War Refugee Board. After leaving the army in 1945, he ran for mayor of New York City again, and this time, with La Guardia out of the race, won. Although some alleged that Tammany Hall had helped secure his nomination, O'Dwyer worked during his first term to try to distance city government from Tammany influence. As mayor, O'Dwyer established the Office of City Construction Coordinator to undertake capital projects delayed by the Depression and war, created the Division of Labor Relations to deal with growing labor unrest, and, in 1948, led a successful effort to bring the United Nations headquarters to New York (*ANBO*).

Parish, Susan Ludlow ("Cousin Susie") (1865–1950), first cousin to ER's mother, Anna Hall Roosevelt, became ER's godmother and remained one of ER's strongest links to the New York society in which she grew up. As a child, ER stayed with Cousin Susie often, particularly after ER's parents separated, and lived with Cousin Susie and her husband, New York banker Henry Parish Jr., off and on before her marriage in 1905 (the couple had no children of their own). As ER's surrogate mother, Cousin Susie took an active part in ER's wedding plans, helping ER buy her trousseau and linens and hosting the wedding in her home. After the marriage, Cousin Susie, like ER's mother-in-law Sara Delano Roosevelt, scrutinized every aspect of ER's life and criticized many of her decisions. ER never completely broke with Cousin Susie, however, and remained closer to Susie than she became to Sara. As she aged Susie became increasingly reliant on prescription drugs to combat a variety of psychological illnesses. Her self-centeredness combined with her rigid social views made ER's time with her difficult, but the two women continued to see each other annually, usually at one of Susie's homes (Cook, vol.1, 115–16, 136, 162, 178–79, 187, 299; Cook, vol. 2, 121; Lash, *Eleanor*, 99, 137–39, 155, 245; Lash, *Years*, 237, 323).

Pauley, Edwin Wendell, Sr. (1903–1981), oil tycoon, real estate and commodity speculator, and conservative California Democrat, joined the Democratic National Committee in 1941, becoming its treasurer in 1944. A prodigious fundraiser, Pauley retired the party's debt and as chair of the 1944 Democratic National Convention worked with DNC chairman Robert Hannegan, to secure Truman's vice-presidential nomination. FDR, who had appointed Pauley special representative to Britain and the Soviet Union in charge of tanker exchange under the Lend-Lease program and a member of the Petroleum Administration for War, flirted with awarding Pauley with a more prestigious naval appointment. ER objected, highlighting Pauley's strong ties to the oil community. A member of Truman's "kitchen cabinet," Pauley joined the administration officially in 1945 when Truman appointed him US representative to the Allied Reparations Commission. The following year, Truman nominated Pauley for undersecretary of the navy but strong opposition to the appointment from Secretary of the Interior Harold Ickes, based on questionable efforts Pauley had made in the past to secure government concessions for the oil industry, killed the appointment. Later, in 1947, Truman named Pauley special assistant to the secretary of the army, but Pauley resigned in January 1948 when his role as a major speculator on the commodity exchange became public. Although he returned to his business career, Pauley continued to be an important Truman ally, championing the interests of real estate, commodities, oil, and big business in California (*HSTE*).

Perkins, Frances Coralie (1880–1965), economist and social worker, served as industrial commissioner of the state of New York during FDR's governorship. In 1933, she became the first woman cabinet member when FDR appointed her secretary of labor, a position she held throughout FDR's presidency. As a key labor advisor to FDR, Perkins helped shape and implement key pieces of New Deal legislation, such as the Civilian Conservation Corps Act, the Federal Emergency Relief Act, the National Labor Relations Act, the Social Security Act, and the Fair Labor Standards Act. She also shepherded US entry into the International Labor Organization in 1934 and remained an active supporter of the ILO throughout her life. A moderate on labor issues related to women, she, like ER, opposed the Equal Rights Amendment because she believed it would eliminate protective legislation for women workers. She resigned July 1, 1945, as secretary of labor and Truman appointed Lewis Schwellenbach to succeed her. Later that fall, Truman denied her request for an appointment to the Social Security Board, naming her instead to the Civil Service Commission, a position she held until 1953. Devoted to FDR, she defended his record in her 1946 memoir, *The Roosevelt I Knew* (*NAWMP*; *HSTE*).

Reading, Lady Stella (Charnaud Isaacs), Marchioness of Reading (1894–1971), British philanthropist, was a close friend of ER. Born in Constantinople to a British Foreign Service officer, she met her husband, the Marquess of Reading, when she served as his secretary in India. Lord Reading (Rufus Isaacs), was one of the most prominent Jews in British public life, serving in such posts as special ambassador to the United States, lord chief justice, viceroy of India, and foreign secretary. She began her career in voluntary relief work in the United Kingdom with her chairmanship of the Personal Service League, which assisted the needy during the Depression, in the early 1930s. After her husband died in 1935, Lady Reading took an extensive automobile tour across the United States. Traveling under assumed names, she struck up acquaintances with people from all walks of life and familiarized herself with American relief work. While traveling incognito, Lady Reading still attracted the attention of the President and First Lady, who invited her to the White House, initiating a deep friendship between ER and Lady Reading. Back in Britain, Lady Reading helped found the Women's Voluntary Service (WVS) at the request of the home secretary in 1938. She served as longtime head of the organization, which otherwise was nonhierarchical, and enlisted over a half million women from across the class spectrum for welfare work such as food and clothing distribution, fuel-saving drives, and hospital work. During ER's wartime visit to England, Lady Reading served as her tour guide, taking her to see WVS women at work on community service projects. ER studied Lady Reading's work closely, and considered WVS a model for American civil defense efforts. After the war, Lady Reading continued her work with WVS, and worked with ER to address the housing and nutrition crises confronting postwar Britain. She also became governor of the British Broadcasting Corporation (BBC) and, in 1947, founded Women's Home Industries, Ltd., a nonprofit organization promoting the employment of British women in handicrafts manufacture (*CB*, 1948; *DNB*; Hinton, 19, 24, 31, 34, 90, 172–75, 209–11, 215–17, 232; Lash, *Eleanor*, 637–39; "Lady Reading, the First Woman In House of Lords, Is Dead at 77," *NYT*, 23 May 1971, 60).

Reuther, Walter Philip (1907–1970), the United Auto Workers (UAW) leader the automobile industry dubbed "the most dangerous man in Detroit" because of his skill "in bringing about the revolution without seeming to disturb the existing forms of society," revolutionized organized labor's political clout. Although Reuther supported Norman Thomas in the 1932 presidential election, by 1936 he had become an avid New Deal Democrat and campaigned actively for FDR in 1940 and 1944. His UAW career began when, in the immediate aftermath of the passage of the Wagner Act, he accepted a position with the union as a full-time field organizer. In 1936, in a precursor to his role in the 1945–1946 strike against General Motors, he organized a successful sit-in strike against Kelsey-Hayes—which helped set the stage for the 1937 sit-in in Flint, Michigan, and the organizing of the GM and Ford workforces. His unrivaled success as an organizer and contract negotiator, combined with Reuther's abandonment of the socialism he had embraced in his twenties, helped him secure widespread support among labor's rank and file. In 1940, he submitted a plan to FDR for the reorganization of aircraft manufacturing, arguing that if implemented, the US could produce "500 planes a day" for the war effort. Throughout World War II, Reuther served as vice-president of the UAW's GM division and in 1946, the union elected him president. An outspoken anti-Communist, Reuther helped found the Americans for Democratic Action, one of the many political and labor actions he shared with ER. In 1948, a would-be assassin shot Reuther, who had been hospitalized in 1937 for beatings sustained while leading a strike, permanently crippling his right hand (*ANBO*, Lichtenstein).

Roosevelt, Elliott (1910–1990), the Roosevelts' second son and the child closest to ER, refused to attend college after completing his Groton School education, opting instead to explore business opportunities in a variety of industries—advertising, publishing, and aviation—before settling into radio broadcasting in the late 1930s. In 1940, he enlisted in the Army Air Corps, the precursor of the modern air force. Once the United States declared war on Germany and Japan, Captain Roosevelt declined to use his father's influence to keep himself out of the war, and flew several dangerous reconnaissance missions in the Atlantic theater. He was wounded twice in combat, received several decorations, and was ultimately promoted to brigadier general. He also attended several diplomatic conferences with FDR during the war, including Casablanca (1943) and Cairo-Tehran (1944) and published a controversial eyewitness account of those conferences, *As He Saw It* (1946). ER defended her son's book and allowed him to publish a four-volume set of FDR's letters in the late 1940s. From 1946 to 1952 Elliott lived in FDR's Top Cottage near ER's Val-Kill residence and with ER as his business partner managed an ill-fated farming operation on the land ER had purchased from FDR's estate (*ANBO*; *TER*).

Roosevelt, Franklin Delano (1882–1945), thirty-second president of the United States, led the United States through the Great Depression and World War II. Assuming the presidency in 1933 at a time of economic collapse, FDR asserted an active role for the federal government in stimulating the economy, creating jobs, regulating economic institutions such as banks, conserving natural resources, engaging in regional economic development, protecting the right of workers to form unions and participate in collective bargaining, and providing security for the aged, infirm, and unemployed. The key legislation and programs of the New Deal, such as the Social Security Act (1935), the National Labor Relations Act (1935), the Civilian Conservation Corps (CCC), and the Tennessee Valley Authority (TVA), embodied these initiatives. At the outset of World War II, and before America entered the conflict, FDR articulated an idealistic vision of freedom "everywhere in the world" in the Four Freedoms and the Atlantic Charter. While leading the Allies to victory over the course of the war, he also constructed an internationalist framework for a postwar world order through the establishment of the International Monetary Fund, the World Bank, and the United Nations. Although he did not live to see the UN Charter adopted, he was the chief architect of the new organization. When he died, people throughout the world mourned his passing, and he remained especially revered in the liberated countries of Europe. The agreements he had reached with Stalin at Yalta, however, quickly came under attack and the liberal-left coalition he had held together during the war unraveled over the issues of Communism and how best to pursue a liberal agenda (*FDRE*; *HSTE*; *RCAH*).

BIOGRAPHICAL PORTRAITS

Roosevelt, Franklin Delano, Jr. (1914–1988), lawyer, businessman, politician, and fifth child of Franklin and Eleanor Roosevelt, enlisted in the navy in 1941. By the time of his 1945 discharge, Lieutenant Commander Roosevelt had received the Purple Heart, the Silver Star, the Navy Cross, and other awards for valor in combat. He returned to New York in 1945 where he joined the New York law firm of Poletti, Diamond, Rabin, Freiden, and MacKay. He also planned a career in politics, chairing the American Veterans Committee housing activities task force from 1945 to 1947, co-chairing the President's Commission on Civil Rights in 1946–47, serving as national vice chairman for Americans for Democratic Action in 1947, and holding a variety of local political appointments. In 1948, now a rising star in the Democratic Party, FDR, Jr., led an unsuccessful effort to draft Dwight D. Eisenhower as the Democratic nominee for president in place of Truman. In 1949, after Representative Sol Bloom's death, the Liberal Party appointed FDR, Jr., to fill Bloom's congressional seat and he represented the Twentieth District of New York until 1955 (*ERE; FDRE*).

Roosevelt, James (1907–1991), businessman, party leader, and the oldest son of Franklin and Eleanor Roosevelt, took an active part in his father's political career. After managing the Massachusetts wing of the 1932 presidential campaign, "Jimmy" worked at times alongside his father in the White House during the 1930s as an unofficial, and sometimes official, aide, despite ER's fears that his involvement in FDR's administration would raise suspicions of nepotism. He left the White House in 1938 when internal and congressional objections arose regarding James's increased responsibilities and he moved to California to work as a motion picture executive. He joined the Marines in 1940, volunteering for combat duty after the attack on Pearl Harbor and received the Navy Cross and the Silver Star for distinguished service. After leaving the Marines in 1945, he returned to California where he opened the West Coast branch of his insurance company, Roosevelt and Sargent, and began his own career in politics. He joined the California State Democratic Central Committee, served as its chair in 1946, and as one of its Democratic national committeemen from 1948 until 1952. In 1950 he sought the governorship but lost to Earl Warren (*FDRE*).

Rusk, Dean David (1909–1994), Rhodes Scholar, professor of government, and diplomat, served as deputy chief of staff for war plans for General Joseph Stillwell in the China-Burma-India theater, and then in Washington as assistant chief of the Operations Division of the War Department General Staff. Rusk's experience as a student at Oxford of watching Hitler's unchecked rise to power, and his observations of the war against Japan in the Far East, led him to believe "that if aggression is allowed to gather momentum, it can continue to build and lead to general war." After Rusk left the army, the new secretary of state, George Marshall, who knew of Rusk's service in the Far East and Washington, offered him a position in the State Department. Rusk served first as assistant chief of the Division of International Security Affairs, as director of the Office of Special Political Affairs (renamed the Office of United Nations Affairs in January 1948), a position he held until 1949. In that capacity he directed the formulation of US policy on UN affairs, including human rights and refugees, and supervised the work of the State Department advisors who provided advice to ER and the other members of the US delegation to the United Nations (*ANBO*).

Sandifer, Durward Vladimir (1900–1981) served as one of the leading US State Department specialists on the United Nations from its inception. Originally in the department's Legal Adviser's Office, he began working with the team assigned to planning a postwar international organization in 1942. In 1944, he participated in the Dumbarton Oaks Conference, which laid the groundwork for the United Nations and, in 1945, served as secretary general and chief technical expert of the American delegation to the San Francisco conference at which the founding nations adopted the UN Charter. He held the position of division chief for international organizations from 1945 to 1947 and of deputy director of the Office of UN Affairs from 1947 to 1948. As executive officer and principal advisor to the US delegation to the United Nations, he worked closely with ER, with whom he developed a relationship of great mutual respect. He also became a delegate to UNESCO and the World Health Organization ("Dr. Durward Sandifer Dies; Retired U.S. Official, Professor," *WP*, 3 June 1981, C9; Glendon, 27, 105, 134, 138; Sandifer, 1).

Stalin, Josef Vissarionovich (1879–1953), general secretary of the Communist Party of the Soviet Union from 1929 to 1953, first rose to power when he drew Lenin's attention by robbing banks to finance party activities. By 1912, Lenin had appointed him to the Central Committee and asked him to edit *Pravda*. After the Bolshevik Revolution, he became commissar of the nationalities and a member of the first Politburo. In 1922, Lenin arranged his promotion to general secretary, despite reservations about his behavior. After Lenin's death, Stalin sided against the Trotsky wing of the party, joined forces with Bukharin's New Economic Policy, and consolidated his power within the party and government bureaucracy. In 1927, he purged Bukharin's supporters from the party and launched the Stalin Revolution—collectivizing peasants, increasing the labor camp system, and expanding the use of heavy machinery necessary to implement his Five Year Plans. Rejecting Marxist tenets regarding the decline of the state, he regulated expression, championed Russian nationalism and "soviet realism,"and, until the outbreak of World War II, persecuted all religions. In the late 1930s, concerned about collective security, he instructed party followers to engage in Popular Front coalitions, only to renounce them with the German-Soviet Nonaggression Pact of 1939. Stalin had purged the military leadership during his rise to power, thus, when Germany suddenly reversed course and invaded the Soviet Union, his military did not have the leadership or the equipment to repel the invasion. Nevertheless, Stalin's USSR held the Eastern Front against the German advance and used military supplies provided by Lend-Lease to help turn the tide against the Germans. The successful alliance of the Soviet Union, the United States, and Great Britain fell apart, even as all three joined the nascent United Nations. Stalin pressed for broader control in the countries the USSR occupied and insisted on large reparations payments from Germany. Truman's decision to keep the secret of the atomic bomb from him made Stalin increasingly suspicious of American motives. Tensions between the two only heightened after 1946 (*OCPW*; *HSTE*).

Stettinius, Edward Reilly, Jr. (1900–1949), businessman, social reformer, and diplomat, was General Motors vice president for industrial and public relations and an active volunteer in various unemployment-related projects when FDR recruited him to serve as the liaison between the National Industrial Recovery Administration and the Industrial Advisory Board in 1933. In 1939, FDR again turned to Stettinius to chair the War Resources Board. Stettinius, who then served as chairman of US Steel, accepted and placed all his assets in a blind trust. Three years later, FDR tapped Stettinius to oversee the administration of Lend-Lease aid to the Allies, a position he held until he replaced Sumner Welles as undersecretary of state in September 1943. As undersecretary, he reorganized the department by integrating its policy and foreign relations departments, launching an effective public relations campaign, and helping craft the plans for the United Nations at the Dumbarton Oaks conference. When Cordell Hull's health declined, FDR asked Stettinius to take the secretary's position in November 1944. As secretary of state, he attended the Yalta conference with FDR in February 1945 and helped prepare the way for the creation of the Organization of American States; however, he served more as an effective mediator and efficient implementor of policy than as a policy advisor. When Truman became president in April 1945 he retained Stettinius through the San Francisco conference in June, so that he could complete the negotiations that culminated in the adoption of the United Nations Charter. At San Francisco, Stettinius strove to achieve consensus among all the delegates and worked closely with Harry Hopkins to resolve Stalin's objections to Security Council procedures. After the conference, Truman appointed Byrnes secretary of state and Stettinius chair of the American delegation to the United Nations Preparatory Commission and, then, head of the US delegation to the first meeting of the UN General Assembly. He resigned in June 1946, frustrated by the administration's circumventing of the United Nations (*FDRE*; *ANBO*).

Stimson, Henry Lewis (1867–1950), attorney, cabinet official, progressive Republican, and statesman, began his political career under the tutelage of Elihu Root and Theodore Roosevelt. In 1911,

William Howard Taft named him secretary of war, a position Stimson used to enhance the power of the secretary and his staff, increase departmental efficiency, and promote military preparedness. He volunteered for artillery duty once the First World War began and after leaving the army in 1919, returned to his legal career on Wall Street. In 1927, he accepted Herbert Hoover's request to mediate the political crisis in Nicaragua, in the process drafting the agreement calling for US supervision of the 1928 election and training of a national police force. That same year, Hoover appointed him governor general of the Philippines where Stimson implemented policies based on the prevailing notion of "the white man's burden." A year later, Hoover summoned Stimson back to Washington as secretary of state to help manage the crisis in Manchuria. In 1932, he announced the policy soon to be called the Stimson Doctrine: the US would not "recognize any situation, treaty or agreement" induced by aggression, threat, or war. Stimson returned to his legal practice when FDR defeated Hoover in 1932. However, in 1940, FDR brought Stimson out of retirement to oversee the buildup of the country's army as secretary of war. In that capacity, Stimson urged the implementation of the draft, became a leading advocate for Lend-Lease, and oversaw the secret Manhattan Project. After FDR's sudden death, Stimson informed Truman of the project, and his influence led Truman to authorize the use of the bomb on Japan. Stimson also played a key role in planning the future of postwar Germany. He convinced FDR to oppose the Morgenthau Plan to divide Germany into several agrarian states, and persuaded Truman to assist Germany's reindustrialization. Opposed to hardline anti-Soviet sentiments, Stimson encouraged mutual trust with the Soviet Union, telling Truman that "the chief lesson I have learned in a long life is that the only way you can make a man trustworthy is to trust him; and the surest way to make him untrustworthy is to distrust him and show your distrust." Yet throughout his long career, Stimson's racial and socioeconomic prejudices shaped his views on foreign and domestic policy. When ER offered her public support for the equal rights of African Americans, Stimson protested her advocacy of people he believed were "second-class citizens." In 1948, two years before his death, Stimson published his memoirs, entitled *On Active Service in Peace and War* (*ANBO*; *ERE*).

Sullivan, Gael (1904–1956), Democratic Party activist, worked his way up through Mayor Edward J. Kelly's political machine in Chicago, where he served as the Illinois director of the Federal Housing Administration. He served as assistant postmaster general under Robert Hannegan until February 12, 1947, when Truman appointed him executive director of the Democratic National Committee (DNC). Hannegan, who served as both the chairman of the DNC and postmaster general, found little time to steer the committee and allowed Sullivan to exercise virtual control of the DNC. Sullivan's determination to use the president's opposition to the Taft-Hartley Act to strengthen labor's ties to the party succeeded; however, his actions illuminated the growing schism in the party as those Democrats who supported Taft-Hartley found themselves increasingly alienated from the national organization. In his first months as executive director, Sullivan found himself involved in two party controversies. First, he prepared and published a petition calling for bipartisan support of Truman's foreign policy, which he hoped Republican National Committee head Carroll Reece would sign, an overture that generated stark criticism from Republicans and the administration who thought Sullivan had overstepped boundaries. The second controversy arose when Edwin Pauley convinced Sullivan to return to Washington rather than appear at the California Jackson Day Dinner honoring ER at which he had been scheduled to speak. Despite these early mistakes, Sullivan succeeded in allying labor with the Democrats, even convincing A. F. Whitney, leader of the Brotherhood of Railroad Trainmen, to support Truman in the 1948 election after Whitney had publicly disavowed Truman for his attempt to draft rail workers in 1946. Frustrated by the administration's inability to implement its liberal promises, Sullivan resigned from the DNC in April 1948. He nevertheless continued to advise the administration during the campaign and suggested that Truman embark on a "whistle-stop" tour to cultivate his image as a "man of the people" ("Gael E. Sullivan Is Dead at 51; Started Helicopter Mail Service," *NYT*, 28 October 1956, 88; Hamby, *Beyond*, 81, 179–80, 199–201, 226, 233–34; Savage, 63–64, 118).

Thompson, Dorothy (1893–1961), syndicated journalist and political commentator, headed the Berlin bureau of the *New York Evening Post* and the *Philadelphia Public Ledger* in the 1930s. An early opponent of Hitler and fascism, her negative reporting on the rise of Adolf Hitler and the Nazis led to her expulsion from Germany in 1934. She returned to the United States, where, beginning in 1936 her thrice-weekly column, "On the Record," ran in the *New York Herald Tribune* and more than 170 other newspapers. That column—together with a monthly column she wrote for the *Ladies' Home Journal* and her work as a lecturer and NBC radio commentator—made her one of the most influential women in pre–World War II America. She devoted considerable energy to publicizing the plight of European refugees on the eve of the war, promoting a broad, multinational approach to resettlement, and suggesting in *Refugees, Anarchy, and Organization?* that Palestine's history might not make it a suitable haven for Jews seeking a new home. Although she had supported Zionism since 1920, in 1946, after the bombing of the King David Hotel, she became a pronounced critic of the Zionist movement and continued to urge a broad, multinational resettlement plan for all refugees. By 1948, she had become increasingly pro-Arab and began to view the Cold War as primarily a cultural and ideological battle (*NAWMP*).

Thompson, Malvina ("Tommy") Schneider (1893–1953), nicknamed "Tommy" by ER's daughter Anna, worked beside ER for almost forty years as her personal secretary, gatekeeper, editor, confidant, and travel companion. "In almost everything I did," ER recalled, "she was a help but she was also a stern critic." The women first met in 1922 when Thompson left the Red Cross to work part-time for the women's division of the New York State Democratic Committee, where ER coordinated campaign activities for Governor Al Smith. When the Roosevelts moved to the White House in 1933, Thompson left her husband and moved to the capital to continue working with ER. Working eighteen-hour days, she helped ER manage her mail and her calendar, monitored her press conferences, fended off the "unscrupulous" who tried to manipulate her boss, and reviewed ER's draft manuscripts. Although Thompson accompanied ER on three trips around the world, she did not go with her to United Nations meetings. Instead, she remained in New York to handle whatever work ER needed done at home. When ER relocated to Val-Kill, she had a wing of the cottage turned into an apartment suite for Thompson. ER said of her, "she wanted to be useful and in many, many ways she not only made my life easier but gave me a reason for living" (*TERE*).

Tito (Josip Broz) (1892–1980), metalworker, Communist activist, guerrilla fighter, and prime minister and defense minister of Yugoslavia, joined the Communist Party when, after fighting in the Russian Revolution, he returned home to the newly created Croatia. Arrested and tried for his political beliefs in 1928, Broz's outspoken defense of Communism, and five-year incarceration increased his fame and stature within the party. Upon his release, the Comintern (Third International) in Moscow instructed him to return to Yugoslavia as an organizer for the Yugoslav Communist Party. He then adopted the underground name "Tito." When the Germans attacked the Soviet Union in 1941, Tito hid in Belgrade, coordinating guerilla campaigns against German and Italian occupation forces and their collaborators. With little outside help for their struggle, Tito formed a national liberation committee in 1942, appointed himself a marshal, and positioned himself to assume leadership of the country after the war. When the war ended, the November 1945 elections abolished the monarchy and established a solidified Communist government with Tito as both prime minister and foreign minister. Tito then instituted a Stalinist purge of his detractors; however, because he had secured power without Soviet aid, he refused to accept all Soviet dictates and a dramatic break between Tito and Stalin occurred in 1948 when Tito refused to accede to Stalin's expectations. As a result, the Tito clique was ousted from the Cominform. Tito would rule his country with a tight fist for 35 years, steering it on a path of independence from both East and West in foreign affairs and adhering to a partial market economic system. Intrigued by the leader who was a symbol of Yugoslavia's independence, ER visited Tito with David Gurewitsch in the summer of 1953, where they spent several days talking about Communism, the Soviets, and dictatorship. Yugoslav relations with Moscow would also thaw for a time after Stalin's death in early 1953 and a conciliatory Khrushchev visited the country (*DPB*; Roosevelt, *Autobiography*, 346–52).

BIOGRAPHICAL PORTRAITS

Tobias, Channing Heggie (1882–1961), civil rights leader, minister, and reformer, served as one of three African American international secretaries of the YMCA's Colored Work Department from 1924 to 1946, and as the first African American director of the Phelps-Stokes Fund, a foundation devoted to the educational improvement of African Americans. In the midst of the battle to establish the Fair Employment Practices Committee, Tobias joined the Committee on Negroes and the Defense Industries and co-wrote its manifesto. Two years later he was elected to the national NAACP board of directors. In 1946, Truman then selected him as one of the two African Americans to serve on the fifteen-member President's Committee on Civil Rights. Selected chairman of the board of the NAACP in 1953, Tobias called for an end to racial segregation by January 1, 1963, the centennial of President Lincoln's Emancipation Proclamation (*ANBO*).

Townsend, John Gillis, Jr. (1871–1964), banker, manufacturer, strawberry farmer, and noted Delaware Republican, served as his state's governor from 1917 to 1921. As governor, Townsend secured the adoption of measures some deemed "dangerously liberal"—workers' compensation, vocational education, graduated income and inheritance taxes, and protective legislation for women workers. However, when he entered the US Senate in 1929, he allied himself with the conservative Taft wing of the party. He served on the agriculture and forestry and became the ranking minority member of the Senate Banking and Currency Committee, a position he used to urge the United States not to sell gold to the USSR. He also chaired the Republican Senate Campaign Committee in 1936. His constituents' support for FDR's 1940 reelection cost him reelection and he returned to his agriculture business in 1941. In 1946, Truman appointed him alternate delegate to the first meeting of the UN General Assembly, where he served with ER on the Third Committee. Later that year, Truman appointed Adlai Stevenson to replace him ("John G. Townsend, Jr., 92, Is Dead," *NYT*, 11 April 1964, 25).

Truman, Harry S. (1884–1972) became the thirty-third president of the United States following FDR's death on April 12, 1945. In July 1945, Truman met with Stalin and Churchill at Potsdam and the three demanded Japan's unconditional surrender. When Japan refused, Truman approved the use of the atomic bombs on Hiroshima and Nagasaki. After Japan surrendered on September 2, a series of domestic crises undermined public confidence in his leadership. Of particular concern was his seeming inability to manage the reconversion to a peacetime economy. The debate over full employment legislation and continuing price and wage controls escalated into a series of wildcat strikes and presidential threats to force arbitration. Truman forced Henry Wallace out of the cabinet after Wallace differed with administration policy toward the Soviet Union. Truman's approval ratings plummeted from a high of 82 percent (June 1945) to a low of 32 percent (September 1946). Republicans seized control of Congress in the 1946 mid-term elections, and Democrats, divided over how best to lead the country, remained united in their conviction that Truman would not be reelected. In 1947, Truman regained the initiative with a series of bold foreign policy decisions: financial aid to Greece and Turkey, the Truman Doctrine, and the Marshall Plan. He vetoed the Taft-Hartley Act only to have Congress override his veto, and he imposed loyalty oaths on federal workers. In 1948, Truman targeted the eightieth as the "do nothing" Congress, calling a special summer session to debate civil rights legislation, federal aid to education, tax relief for low-income workers, federally financed housing, and national health insurance. When Congress refused his package, Truman attacked it for ineptitude and issued an executive order desegregating the military. Facing challenges from Democrats Strom Thurmond and Henry Wallace, he campaigned unceasingly, crisscrossing the country by train. Truman defeated Republican Thomas Dewey by a 4 percent margin in 1948 to win reelection (*HSTE*).

Vandenberg, Arthur Hendrick (1884–1951), Republican senator from Michigan and diplomat, entered the Senate in 1928 and became a pivotal figure in postwar American foreign policy. Through his efforts, the Truman administration achieved bipartisan consensus on a number of landmark issues that shaped the course of the Cold War. Anti–New Deal and an isolationist until World War II, Vandenberg emerged in the postwar era as a leading advocate of international cooperation through the United Nations. He helped formulate the Connally Resolution for US membership in the United Nations and, in return, FDR appointed him to the US delegation to the San Francisco conference, where he drafted Articles 51–54 of the UN Charter, dealing with regional collective security. As ranking minority member of the Senate Foreign Relations Committee, Vandenberg worked to solidify Republican support for the UN Charter, an effort which encouraged Truman to appoint Vandenberg a delegate to the first two General Assemblies of the United Nations. When Republicans took back the Senate in 1946, Vandenberg resigned his UN position so that he could devote his full attention to his duties as Foreign Relations Committee chairman. He then advised Truman in 1947 and 1948 that if Congress were to support the Truman Doctrine the President must "scare the hell out of the country" in order to rally popular support of expanded congressional allocations. In 1948 Vandenberg supported the Marshall Plan and drafted the Vandenberg Resolution, the basis of the North Atlantic Treaty Organization (NATO). Originally opposed to ER's appointment to the UN, Vandenberg quickly recognized her dedication and success on the Third Committee and publicly praised her work (*ANBO*; *HSTE*; Boyer, 48).

Vyshinsky, Andrei Yanuaryevich (1883–1954), Soviet jurist, professor of law, and diplomat, served as deputy foreign minister and leader of the Soviet delegation to the United Nations. Vyshinsky took part in the Russian Revolution of 1917 and the creation of the Soviet state that followed. He became state prosecutor of the USSR in 1923, winning renown for his oratorical skill, and then professor of law at Moscow University. From 1928 onward he expended part of his energy on academic work, the rest in the courtroom. One of the architects of the Soviet judicial system, Vyshinsky wrote over 100 books, including *The Organization of the Soviet State* (1937) and *Marx on the Problem of Law and State* (1938). He gained world-wide notoriety and earned Stalin's trust as the chief prosecutor during the Moscow "show trials" of 1936 through 1938, when he sent Bukharin, Zinoviev, and other close comrades of Lenin to their deaths for alleged counterrevolutionary activities. When World War II broke out, Vyshinsky began his diplomatic career as deputy people's commissar for foreign affairs, working under Vyacheslav M. Molotov. After the war, as the Soviet delegate to the UN, Vyshinsky often engaged in vitriolic rhetoric against the West and participated in debates with ER on the issues of freedom of the press, the management of displaced person camps, and the repatriation of refugees. In 1949, Vyshinsky replaced Molotov as Soviet foreign minister, a position he held until 1953 (*CB*; *DPB*; Lash, *Years*, 53–54, 102–3; "Death of Spokesman at the U.N. Deprives Moscow of One of Its Ablest Envoys," *NYT*, 23 November 1954, 14).

Welles, Benjamin Sumner (1892–1961), assistant secretary and then undersecretary of state in the Roosevelt administration, was the architect of FDR's Good Neighbor policy. A classmate of ER's younger brother Hall, Welles and ER lived a block apart as children in New York City and remained lifelong friends. Beginning in the early 1920s, when he emerged as a leading expert on the Western Hemisphere, Welles became an important source of knowledge and advice on foreign policy for both FDR and ER. He accompanied FDR to his secret rendezvous with Churchill aboard the *Prince of Wales* and helped draft the Atlantic Charter. In 1942, he traveled to Rio de Janeiro as US representative to a meeting of the hemisphere's foreign ministers. As chairman of the State Department committee charged during World War II with planning international cooperation after the war, he helped draft the initial plans for the United Nations. He left the State Department in 1943 when J. Edgar Hoover, armed with rumors of homosexual conduct and reckless behavior, allied with Cordell Hull, who had clashed with Welles in Rio, to urge FDR to remove Welles. FDR then offered Welles the position of roving ambassador to Latin America if he would resign. Welles resigned, but did not accept FDR's offer. He then dedicated his career to writing about foreign affairs, including two inside appraisals of FDR's diplomacy, *Time for Decision* (1944) and *Where Are We Now?* (1946) (*ANBO*).

White, Walter Francis (1893–1955), executive secretary for the National Association for the Advancement of Colored People from 1931 until his death in 1955, defined the NAACP's organizational structure, forged its political alliances, and helped implement the legal strategy it would adopt for most of the twentieth century. Capitalizing on his Caucasian-like features to blend into riotous white crowds, White investigated more than forty lynchings and dozens of race riots, often placing himself at risk in the process and drawing national attention to the anti-lynching campaign. By the time FDR entered the White House, White had capitalized on the successful coalition he built to block Judge John J. Parker's nomination to the US Supreme Court to bring the NAACP before a wide array of groups committed to social justice issues. A close friend and ally of ER, the two worked together to lobby for anti-lynching legislation, to abolish the poll tax, to improve access to education, to support Marion Anderson's 1939 Lincoln Memorial concert, and to challenge seg-regation in the defense industries. During World War II, he used his weekly *Chicago Defender* col-umn to argue that the power of fascism and the lure of communism underscored the need for a color-blind society at home. Following FDR's death in 1945, White asked ER to join the NAACP Board of Directors, and she accepted. White remained a staunch supporter of President Truman, helping to influence the president's positions on desegregation of the military and fair employment practices. Long realizing the importance of expanding the civil rights movement to the internation-al arena, White became an advisor to the US delegation both at the San Francisco conference, where he left disappointed with the US position on decolonization, and again at the 1948 General Assembly at Paris (*ANBO*).

Wilson, Woodrow Thomas (1856–1924), twenty-eighth president of the United States, won the 1919 Nobel Peace Prize. From 1913 to 1916, Wilson championed the "New Freedom," govern-mental regulatory policy designed to attack privilege and restore competition. As World War I threatened American maritime and economic interests, Wilson strove to maintain the appearance of neutrality. When the war began, he sent a close aide to broker a truce between Great Britain and Germany, and when that failed, he appeared before the League to Enforce Peace to call for a glob-al organization of nations dedicated to collective security and "peace without victory." When he asked Congress to declare war on Germany in 1917, he presented a postwar vision of a world defined by the Fourteen Points, among them national self-determination; "open covenants of peace, openly arrived at;" effective disarmament; free trade; and the League of Nations. In January 1919 he led the American delegation to the Paris Peace Conference to work for inclusion of the Fourteen Points in the treaty. While in France, Wilson's commitment to the concept of an organi-zation dedicated to global governance only increased, and he insisted that the creation of the League of Nations be included in the treaty. The League, he declared, was "not merely an instru-ment to adjust and remedy old wrongs under a new treaty of peace," but humanity's "only hope" which had "come about ... by the hand of God." But with the League included in the treaty, secur-ing the support of the US Senate proved difficult, and Wilson refused any attempt at compromise. When an October 1919 stroke left him paralyzed, the campaign for the League lost its most effec-tive advocate. The Senate twice rejected the treaty, and with it, American membership in the League. In March 1921, a recuperating Wilson retired to his Washington home and continued to promote his view that democracy and capitalism, self-determination for nations, and an organiza-tion promoting collective security would "make the world safe" (*ANBO*).

Winant, John Gilbert (1889–1947), a progressive Republican and friend of FDR's, served as ambassador to Great Britain from 1941 to 1945. After teaching history at St. Paul's School in Concord, New Hampshire, and serving in the state house and senate, Winant won the New Hampshire governorship in 1924. Defeated for reelection in 1926, he won again in 1930 and served two terms during the Great Depression. He adopted an activist, experimental approach to the situation, promoting, for example, a four-day week so that employers could use the hours of the fifth day to hire the unemployed. When FDR instituted the New Deal in 1933, Winant strong-ly supported it, making New Hampshire the first state to fill the Civilian Conservation Corps enrollment quota and becoming the first governor to work with the National Planning Board. In 1935, FDR appointed Winant assistant director of the International Labor Organization (ILO) in Geneva. Winant described the purpose of the ILO as working with governments, employers asso-ciations, and organized labor toward "the realization of social justice." In 1936, FDR called him to

Washington to direct the Social Security Board, established by the Social Security Act of 1935. He soon resigned, however, in order to rebut attacks on the Social Security Act by Alfred M. Landon, the Republican candidate for president. In 1939 he resumed his work with the ILO, this time as director, and served until FDR appointed him ambassador to Great Britain in 1941. As wartime ambassador, he walked the streets during air raids, limited his household to the same rations allowed to British civilians, and spoke at gatherings throughout the country, winning the affection of the British people. He signed the Lend-Lease agreement in 1941, which furnished Britain with its first American aid. In 1942, he helped arrange ER's wartime visit to Great Britain. He assisted in organizing the conference of foreign ministers in Moscow in 1943 and, as a member of the European Advisory Commission (EAC), participated in planning for postwar Germany. Following the war, President Truman appointed Winant US representative to UNESCO. He held that post until December 1946 when he retired to his home in Concord, New Hampshire, to write his memoirs. Financial difficulties plagued Winant throughout his career. Poorly managed investments in Texas oil fields in the 1920s, ill-advised stock purchases before the 1929 stock market crash, unwillingness to cut household staff and expenses during the Depression, and unrestrained philanthropic giving left him bankrupt by 1935. By 1946, he owed creditors about three-quarters of a million dollars, and despair over his indebtedness contributed to his suicide in 1947 (*ANBO*; Bellush, 81–85, 92, 121, 134, 227).

Wise, Stephen Samuel (1874–1949), Jewish reform rabbi, American Zionist leader, and social activist, helped to found the National Association for the Advancement of Colored People (NAACP), the American Civil Liberties Union (ACLU), and the Free Synagogue in New York City. He was also an active supporter of labor. However, as the acknowledged leader of America's Zionists for many years, Wise lobbied at the highest levels nationally and internationally for a Jewish state in Palestine. Many younger, more militant Jewish leaders considered his approach too cautious, particularly after the Holocaust, and internal divisions in the Zionist movement at home and abroad led to a decline in his influence after World War II. As president of the American Jewish Congress, he did, however, continue to pressure President Harry S. Truman to establish a Jewish homeland in Palestine. In March 1948 he denounced the administration for its failure to support the United Nations partition plan for Palestine, and he continued to criticize American policy toward Israel even after the United States's *de facto* recognition of the infant state (*ANBO*; "Dr. S.S. Wise Dead; Leader in Zionism," *NYT*, 20 April 1949, 1).

Credits

The publisher wishes to thank the copyright holders in this volume and the permissions managers of many book and magazine publishing companies for assisting us in securing reproduction rights. Following is a list of the copyright holders who have granted us permission to reproduce material in this volume of the Eleanor Roosevelt Papers, Vol. 1. Every effort has been made to trace copyright; if omissions have been made, please contact the publisher.

COPYRIGHTED EXCERPTS WERE REPRODUCED FROM THE FOLLOWING PERIODICALS:

Atlantic Monthly, v. 215, March, 1965, for "Churchill at the White House" by Eleanor Roosevelt. Reproduced by permission of the Literary Estate of the author.

Look Magazine, July 9, 1946, for "Why I Do Not Choose To Run" by Eleanor Roosevelt. Copyright © 1946 by Cowles Magazine Inc. Renewed 1974 by Cowles Communications, Inc. Reproduced by permission of the Literary Estate of the author.

Look Magazine, February 18, 1947, for "The Russians Are Tough" by Eleanor Roosevelt. Copyright © 1947 by Cowles Magazines, Inc. Renewed 1974 by Cowles Communications, Inc. Reproduced by permission of the Literary Estate of the author.

United Nations, January 9, 1946; January 28, 1946; February 12, 1946; May 6, 1946; November 8, 1946; November 20, 1946; December 15, 1946; December 16, 1946; January 27, 1947; January 31, 1947; February 4, 1947; May 29, 1947; June 20, 1947; November 4, 1947; November 6, 1947; December 17, 1947. © 1946, 1947 United Nations. All reproduced by permission.

PHOTOGRAPHS AND ILLUSTRATIONS WERE RECEIVED FROM THE FOLLOWING SOURCES:

A. F. of L.–sponsored rally in Madison Square Garden, photograph. © Bettmann/Corbis.

African American woman almost overcome with grief as the Franklin D. Roosevelt funeral passes in Washington, D.C., April 14, 1945, photograph by Raoul Fornezza. AP Images.

American Youth for Democracy members deliver food to strikers at the General Motors Linden plant, photograph. © Bettmann/Corbis.

Arab refugee camp tents for refugees from the war zones of Palestine, 1948, photograph. © Bettmann/Corbis.

Attlee, Clement, addressing the first meeting of the U.N. Organizations General Assembly in the Methodist Church's Central Hall, London, England, photograph. David E. Scherman/Time Life Pictures/Getty Images.

Baruch, Bernard, at the Atomic Energy Committee meeting in the Bronx, photograph. Keystone/Hulton Archives/Getty Images.

CREDITS

Bentley, Elizabeth T., testifying before the House Committee on Un-American Activities, August 11, 1948, photograph. AP Images.

Bernadotte, Count Folke, of Sweden, with the U.S. diplomat Dr. Ralph Bunche, 1948, photograph. AFP/Getty Images.

Bevin, Ernest, of Great Britain, Vyacheslav M. Molotov of the Soviet Union, and James F. Byrnes of the United States, at the Spiridonovka Palace in Moscow, December 29, 1945, photograph. AP Images.

Braden, Spruille, talking with George S. Messersmith, photograph. Marie Hansen/Time Life Pictures/Getty Images.

Chambers, Whittaker, with John Slater, March 2, 1949, photograph. © UPI/Corbis-Bettmann.

Churchill, Winston, at Westminster College in Fulton, Missouri, March 5, 1946, photograph. AP Images.

Color map of Africa, ca. 1945. Reproduced by permission of Thomson Gale.

Currie, Lauchlin, testifying at the hearing on Communist spy activities in the United States, photograph. Tony Linck/Time Life Pictures/Getty Images.

Demonstration in Philadelphia for Progressive Party presidential nominee Henry Wallace, photograph. © Bettmann/Corbis.

Displaced European Jews talk to reporters from behind a barbed wire fence on the island of Cyprus, November 29, 1946, photograph. AP Images.

Displaced German war victims waiting in Berlin, photograph by Press Association Incorporated. © Corbis.

Du Bois, W. E. B., Mary McLeod Bethune, and Walter White, photograph. National Park Service, Mary McLeod Bethune Council House National Historic Site, National Council of Negro Women Records. Catalog number: MAMC 000073, image number MAMC-073-0474. Reproduced by permission.

Du Bois, W. E. B., at a hearing before the Senate Foreign Relations Committee, photograph. © Bettmann/Corbis.

Eisenhower, Dwight D., and Eleanor Roosevelt, July 8, 1948, photograph. © Bettmann/Corbis.

Female SS guard at Bergen-Belsen concentration camp putting a body in a mass grave, April 1945, photograph. AP Images.

Flynn, Edward J., David E. Lawrence, Edward J. Kelly, and James A. Farley, seated on a platform during the Democratic National Convention, photograph. Lisa Larsen/Time Life Pictures/Getty Images.

"Fruits of Victory," cartoon by Herb Block. From *The Herblock Book*. Beacon Press, 1952. Reproduced by permission.

German women cleaning up rubble and debris on Berlin's Tauentzienstrasse, 1945, photograph. AP Images.

Green, Dr. Samuel, the Georgia Green Dragon of the Ku Klux Klan, Wrightsville, Georgia, March 2, 1948, photograph by Horace W. Cort. AP Images.

"Hard for Him to Plow a Straight Furrow," cartoon by Clifford Berryman. U.S. Senate Collection, Center for Legislative Archives. Reproduced by permission.

Hiroshima one month after atomic bombing, photograph. © Bettmann/Corbis.

Illegal immigration ship *Exodus*, carrying Jewish refugees from war-torn Europe at the Haifa port, July 18, 1947, photograph. Frank Shershel/Getty Images.

"It's Okay, We're Hunting Communists," cartoon by Herb Block. From *The Herblock Book*. Beacon Press, 1952. Reproduced by permission.

Jewish deportees in Berlin receive their food ration, 1945, photograph. Keystone/Hulton Archives/Getty Images.

Kennedy, John F., talking with Eleanor Roosevelt in Washington, D.C., photograph. AP Images.

King David Hotel, Jerusalem, Israel, after bombing by Zionist terrorists, photograph. Getty Images.

Map of 1947 United Nations General Assembly partition plan for Israel and Palestine, illustration. Map by XNR Productions, Inc. Reproduced by permission of Thomson Gale.

Marcus, Donald E. Political cartoon from *The New York Times*, March 14, 1948. Used by permission of Donald E. Marcus.

Mundt, Karl (R-SD), John McDowell (R-PA), Richard Nixon (R-CA), and Richard Vail (R-IL) discuss the House passage of the Mundt-Nixon anti-Communism bill, May 19, 1948, photograph. AP Images.

NAACP members protest at the Coronado Hotel in Washington, D.C., October 16, 1945, photograph. AP Images.

Niemöller, Pastor Martin, addressing a Presbyterian church in Seattle, December 12, 1946, photograph. © Bettman/Corbis.

Page 1 of a letter from President Harry Truman to Eleanor Roosevelt appointing her one of the U.S. representatives to the first session of the General Assembly of the United Nations. Courtesy of the FDR Library.

Page 1 of the draft of the preamble of the Declaration of Human Rights by the United Nations, edited by Eleanor Roosevelt. Courtesy of the FDR Library.

Page 2 of a letter from President Harry Truman to Eleanor Roosevelt appointing her one of the U. S. representatives to the first session of the General Assembly of the United Nations. Courtesy of the FDR Library.

Page 2 of the draft of the preamble of the Declaration of Human Rights by the United Nations, edited by Eleanor Roosevelt. Courtesy of the FDR Library.

Page from Eleanor Roosevelt's desk calendar. Courtesy of the FDR Library.

Pearson, Drew, photograph. © Time Inc./Time Life Pictures/Getty Images.

Perón, Juan, photograph. Thomas D. McAvoy/Time Life Pictures/Getty Images.

Perón, Maria Eva, handing over Rights of Old Age to her husband, President Juan Perón, Buenos Aires, Argentina, photograph. Keystone/Hulton Archives/Getty Images.

Police search rioters during the Black Riots, Columbia, Tennessee, February 27, 1946, photograph. Fox Photos/Getty Images.

Polish slave laborers, liberated from German concentration camps, receiving food and blankets supplied by the UNRRA at the Weimar Station, photograph. Hacker/Hulton Archives/Getty Images.

Religious leaders picket for the freedom of Conscientious Objectors, photograph. Marie Hansen/Time Life Pictures/Getty Images.

Roosevelt, Eleanor, and Fiorello H. La Guardia, with Sidney Hillman, at a testimonial dinner for the First Lady given by New York labor leaders, photograph. © Bettmann/Corbis.

CREDITS

Roosevelt, Eleanor, and James F. Byrnes leaving Central Hall, photograph. © Bettman/Corbis.

Roosevelt, Eleanor, and Mayor William O'Dwyer addressing a meeting, photograph. George Silk/Time Life Pictures/Getty Images.

Roosevelt, Eleanor, and President Harry S. Truman at Franklin D. Roosevelt's gravesite on the first anniversary of his death, photograph. © Corbis.

Roosevelt, Eleanor, at an Americans for Democratic Action (ADA) meeting, photograph. Americans for Democratic Action (ADA). Reproduced by permission.

Roosevelt, Eleanor, broadcasts in the Soviet Union, photograph. © Bettmann/Corbis.

Roosevelt, Eleanor, carrying her suitcase as she leaves the Hotel Crillon, photograph. © Bettmann/Corbis.

Roosevelt, Eleanor, holding a Spanish translation of the Universal Declaration of Human Rights, photograph. Courtesy of the FDR Library.

Roosevelt, Eleanor, hosting members of UNESCO outdoors, photograph. Courtesy of the FDR Library.

Roosevelt, Eleanor, in a garden at her home in New York, photograph. © Marvin Koner/Corbis.

Roosevelt, Eleanor, John Foster Dulles, Warren R. Austin, George C. Marshall, Francis B. Sayre, and Dean Rusk, attending the United Nations General Assembly Meeting, photograph. Yale Joel/Time Life Pictures/Getty Images.

Roosevelt, Eleanor, painting by Douglas Chandor. Image copyright 1984 White House Historical Association. Reproduced by permission.

Roosevelt, Eleanor, photograph. Courtesy of the FDR Library.

Roosevelt, Eleanor, portrait, ca. 1950–1962, photograph. © Bettmann/Corbis.

Roosevelt, Eleanor, riding in a coal car with miners at the Willow Grove Mine in Bellaire, Ohio, May 22, 1935, photograph. © Bettmann/Corbis.

Roosevelt, Eleanor, shaking hands with Vyacheslav M. Molotov, photograph. © Bettmann/Corbis.

Roosevelt, Eleanor, sitting outside with Madame Chiang Kai-shek, photograph. AP Images.

Roosevelt, Eleanor, speaking at the club Rainbow Corner in London, photograph. Miles/Express/Hulton Archives/Getty Images.

Roosevelt, Eleanor, speaking at the first meeting of the United Nations General Assembly, photograph. Courtesy of the FDR Library.

Roosevelt, Eleanor, speaking to René Cassin, UN Commission on Human Rights, December 1947, photograph. © Bettmann/Corbis.

Roosevelt, Eleanor, Thurgood Marshall, Dr. James McClendon, Walter White, and Roy Wilkins go over the 1947 NAACP program, photograph. © Corbis.

Roosevelt, Eleanor, visits the memorial to Holocaust victims at the Zeilsheim displaced persons camp, photograph by E. M. Robinson. United States Holocaust Memorial Museum. The views or opinions expressed in this book, and the context in which the images are used, do not necessarily reflect the views or policy of, nor imply approval or endorsement by, the United States Holocaust Memorial Museum.

Roosevelt, Eleanor, visits Zeilsheim Jewish displaced persons camp, near Wiesbaden, West Germany, photo by Maxine Rude. Collection of Center for Holocaust and Genocide Studies, University of Minnesota. Reproduced by permission.

Roosevelt, Eleanor, with Fiorella H. La Guardia and A. Philip Randolph at a rally to save the FEPC from extinction, photograph. © Bettmann/Corbis.

Roosevelt, Eleanor, with headphones on, listening to a speech at the United Nations, photograph. © Bettmann/Corbis.

Roosevelt, Eleanor, with her daughter Anna Roosevelt Boettiger, photograph. © Corbis.

Roosevelt, Eleanor, with John F. Dulles, George Marshall, and Warren Austin, photograph. Courtesy of the FDR Library.

Roosevelt, Eleanor, with King George VI (of England) at the unveiling of a statue of Franklin D. Roosevelt, London, photograph. Courtesy of the FDR Library.

Roosevelt, Eleanor, with Malvina Thompson at the National Democratic Headquarters, photograph. © Corbis.

Roosevelt, Eleanor, with Senator Arthur H. Vandenberg, Edward Stettinius, and Senator Tom Connally, January, 1946, photograph. © Bettmann/Corbis.

Roosevelt, Eleanor, with Walter P. Reuther at a CIO Convention Assembly, Los Angeles, December 8, 1945, photograph. © Bettmann/Corbis.

Roosevelt, Franklin D., with Saudi King Abdul Aziz Ibn Saud, photograph. Fox Photos/Hulton Archives/Getty Images.

Rosenberg, Anna, receiving the first Medal of Freedom from Secretary of War Robert P. Patterson, October 29, 1945, photograph. AP Images.

Sample of the official 1948 Mississippi Democratic ballot. Courtesy of Mississippi Department of Archives and History.

Taft, Senator Robert, leaving the Yale Club in New York, surrounded by picketers denouncing the Taft-Hartley labor act, photograph. © Bettmann/Corbis.

Truman, Harry S., addressing Congress on the railroad strike crisis, May 25, 1946, photograph. AP Images.

Truman, Harry S., and Eleanor Roosevelt in the Oval Office, photograph. © Bettmann/Corbis.

Truman, Harry S., attending the San Francisco Conference to witness the signing ceremony, photograph. George Skadding/Time Life Pictures/Getty Images.

Val-Kill Cottage, Eleanor Roosevelt's home, Hyde Park, New York, photograph. Courtesy of Roosevelt-Vanderbilt National Historic Sites.

Wallace, Henry, Progressive Party presidential candidate, Knoxville, Tennessee, 1948, photograph. AP Images.

West Berlin children perched on a fence, 1948, photograph. AP Images.

"What Happened to the One We Used to Have?" cartoon by Herb Block. From *The Herblock Book*. Beacon Press, 1952. Reproduced by permission.

Winchell, Walter, photograph. © Bettmann/Corbis.

Wooden coach car of the Cairo-to-Jerusalem train hangs down an embankment at Rehovot, Palestine, February 29, 1948, photograph. AP Images.

"You're Sure You'll Send for Me as Soon as Possible," cartoon by Herb Block. Copyright 1947 by Herblock in *The Washington Post*. Reproduced by permission.

CREDITS

From a petition from the California Congress of Parent and Teachers, Inc. FDR Presidential Library, 1947. Reproduced by permission.

From the minutes of a meeting of the National Committee for Defense of Columbia, Tennessee "Riot" Victims. Library of Congress, NAACP Collection, April 4, 1946. Reproduced by permission of The National Association for the Advancement of Colored People.

Moseley, George Van Horn. From a letter to Eleanor Roosevelt. Library of Congress, Papers of George Van Horn Moseley, August 28, 1946. The Library of Congress.

Hopkins, Harry L. From a letter to Eleanor Roosevelt. FDR Presidential Library, Anna Eleanor Roosevelt Papers, June 26, 1945. Reproduced by permission.

Johnson, Ella and Morse. From a telegram to James Loeb, Jr. FDR Presidential Library, Anna Eleanor Roosevelt Papers, January 25, 1947. Reproduced by permission.

Jones, Nard. From a letter to Eleanor Roosevelt. FDR Presidential Library, Anna Eleanor Roosevelt Papers, August 27, 1947. Reproduced by permission.

Kirchwey, Freda. From a letter to Eleanor Roosevelt. Radcliffe Institute, December 11, 1946. Reprinted with permission of *The Nation* and Nation Associates.

Kirchwey, Freda. From a letter to Eleanor Roosevelt. Radcliffe Institute, December 3, 1946. Reproduced by permission.

Kneubuhl, Emily. From a letter to Eleanor Roosevelt. FDR Presidential Library, Anna Eleanor Roosevelt Papers, May 29, 1948. Reproduced by permission.

Lerner, Max. From a letter to Eleanor Roosevelt. Manuscripts and Archives, Yale University Library, January 22, 1947. Reproduced by permission.

Lewis, Alfred Baker. From a letter to Eleanor Roosevelt. FDR Presidential Library, Anna Eleanor Roosevelt Papers, January 16, 1947. Reproduced by permission.

Lewis, Alfred Baker. From a letter to the editor of *PM*. FDR Presidential Library, Anna Eleanor Roosevelt Papers. Reproduced by permission.

Loeb, James, Jr. From a letter to Eleanor Roosevelt. Rauner Special Collections Library, Papers of James I. Loeb, Dartmouth College, 1947. Reproduced by permission.

Lucas, Peter R. From a letter to Eleanor Roosevelt. Yale News, December 27, 1946. Reproduced by permission.

McLean, Faye Gould. From a letter to Eleanor Roosevelt. American Women's Club of Toronto, February 27, 1947. Reproduced by permission.

Murray, Arthur. From a letter to Eleanor Roosevelt. National Library of Scotland, March 19, 1946. Reproduced by permission of The Trustees of the National Library of Scotland.

Murray, Arthur. From a letter to Eleanor Roosevelt. National Library of Scotland, September 24, 1946. Reproduced by permission of The Trustees of the National Library of Scotland.

Oxnam, G. Bromley. From a letter to Eleanor Roosevelt. Office of the Bishop, United Methodist Church, New York Episcopal Area, December 13, 1946. Reproduced by permission.

Oxnam, G. Bromley. From a telegram to Eleanor Roosevelt. Office of the Bishop, United Methodist Church, New York Episcopal Area, December 5, 1946. Reproduced by permission.

Pickett, Clarence E. From a letter to Eleanor Roosevelt. American Friends Service Committee, December 27, 1946. Reproduced by permission.

CREDITS

Randolph, A. Philip. From a letter to Eleanor Roosevelt. Library of Congress, A. Philip Randolph Papers, Brotherhood of Sleeping Car Porters, January 28, 1946. A. Philip Randolph Institute. Reproduced by permission.

Reading, Stella. From a letter to Eleanor Roosevelt. FDR Presidential Library, Anna Eleanor Roosevelt Papers, August 28, 1946. Reproduced by permission.

Reading, Stella. From a letter to Eleanor Roosevelt. FDR Presidential Library, Anna Eleanor Roosevelt Papers, April 21, 1947. Reproduced by permission.

Reuther, Walter P. From a letter to Eleanor Roosevelt. Walter P. Reuther Library, October 15, 1945. Reproduced by permission.

Reuther, Walter P. From a telegram to Eleanor Roosevelt. Walter P. Reuther Library, December 14, 1945. Reproduced by permission.

Rose, Ben L. From an interview with Pastor Martin Niemöller. FDR Presidential Library, Anna Eleanor Roosevelt Papers, September 3, 1945. Used by permission of the Southern Historical Collection, Wilson Library, The University of North Carolina at Chapel Hill.

Rose, Ben Lacy. From a letter to Eleanor Roosevelt. General Manuscripts, Wilson Library, University of North Carolina at Chapel Hill, September 4, 1945. Used by permission of the publisher.

Tilly, Dorothy. From a letter to Eleanor Roosevelt. Robert W. Woodward Library, MARBL, Emory University, July 14, 1947. Reproduced by permission.

Welles, Sumner. From a letter to Eleanor Roosevelt. FDR Presidential Library, Sumner Welles Papers, February 5, 1947. Reproduced by permission.

White, Walter. From a letter to Dr. Allen Knight Chalmers, Alfred Baker Lewis, Arthur E. Spingarn, and Dr. Channing Tobias. University of Massachusetts Library, W. E. B. Du Bois Papers, November 17, 1947. Reproduced by permission.

White, Walter. From a letter to Eleanor Roosevelt. Library of Congress, NAACP Collection, December 28, 1945. Reproduced by permission.

White, Walter. From a letter to Eleanor Roosevelt. Library of Congress, NAACP Collection, March 25, 1946. Reproduced by permission.

White, Walter. From a letter to Eleanor Roosevelt. Library of Congress, NAACP Collection, October 20, 1947. Reproduced by permission.

White, Walter. From a letter to W. E. B. Du Bois. University of Massachusetts Library, W. E. B. Du Bois Papers, November 18, 1947. Reproduced by permission.

White, Walter. From a telegram to Eleanor Roosevelt. Library of Congress, NAACP Collection, December 9, 1947. Reproduced by permission.

White, Walter. From a telegram to Eleanor Roosevelt. Library of Congress, NAACP Collection, March 19, 1946. Reproduced by permission.

White, Walter. From a telegram to Eleanor Roosevelt. Library of Congress, NAACP Collection, November 28, 1947. Reproduced by permission.

White, Walter. From a telegram to Eleanor Roosevelt. Library of Congress, NAACP Collection, October 21, 1947. Reproduced by permission.

Williams, Charl Ormond. From a letter to Eleanor Roosevelt. Library of Congress, Charl Ormond Williams Papers, May 13, 1948. Reproduced by permission.

Bibliography

Acheson, Dean. *Present at the Creation: My Years in the State Department.* New York: W. W. Norton, 1969.

Alexander, Stella. *Church and State in Yugoslavia Since 1945.* New York: Cambridge University Press, 1979.

———. *The Triple Myth: A Life of Archbishop Alojzije Stepinac.* Boulder, CO: East European Monographs, 1987. Distributed by Columbia University Press.

Alinsky, Saul. *John L. Lewis: An Unauthorized Biography.* New York: G. P. Putnam's Sons, 1949.

Allen, Oliver E. *The Tiger: The Rise and Fall of Tammany Hall.* Reading, MA: Addison-Wesley, 1993.

Alonso, Harriet Hyman. "Mayhem and Moderation: Women Peace Activists during the McCarthy Era." In *Not June Cleaver: Women and Gender in Postwar America, 1945–1960.* Ed. Joanne Meyerowitz. Philadelphia: Temple University Press, 1994. 128–50.

Alpern, Sara. *Freda Kirchwey, A Woman of the Nation.* Cambridge, MA: Harvard University Press, 1987.

Anderson, Carol. *Eyes Off the Prize: The United Nations and the African American Struggle for Human Rights, 1944–1955.* New York: Cambridge University Press, 2003.

Anderson, Jervis. *A. Philip Randolph: A Biographical Portrait.* New York: Harcourt Brace Jovanovich, 1973.

Andrews, George Reid. *Afro-Latin America, 1800–2000.* New York: Oxford University Press, 2004.

Ansbro, George. *I Have a Lady in the Balcony: Memoirs of a Broadcaster in Radio and Television.* Jefferson, NC: McFarland, 2000.

Asbell, Bernard, ed. *Mother and Daughter: The Letters of Eleanor and Anna Roosevelt.* New York: Fromm International, 1988.

Bailey, Stephen Kemp. *Congress Makes a Law: The Story Behind the Employment Act of 1946.* New York: Columbia University Press, 1950.

Barros, James. *Trygve Lie and the Cold War: The UN Secretary-General Pursues Peace, 1946–1953.* DeKalb, IL: Northern Illinois University Press, 1989.

Beasley, Maurine H. *Eleanor Roosevelt and the Media: A Public Quest for Self-Fulfillment.* Urbana: University of Illinois, 1987.

———, ed. *The White House Press Conferences of Eleanor Roosevelt.* New York: Garland, 1983.

Belfrage, Cedric. *The American Inquisition, 1945–1960: A Profile of the "McCarthy Era."* New York: Thunder's Mouth, 1989.

Bellush, Bernard. *He Walked Alone: A Biography of John Gilbert Winant.* The Hague: Mouton, 1968.

BIBLIOGRAPHY

Bendiner, Elmer. *A Time for Angels: The Tragicomic History of the League of Nations.* New York: Alfred A. Knopf, 1975.

Benedict, Ruth, and Gene Weltfish. *In Henry's Backyard: The Races of Mankind.* New York: H. Schuman, 1948.

Bernstein, Barton J., and Allen J. Matusow, eds. *The Truman Administration: A Documentary History.* New York: Harper and Row, 1968.

Beyer, Barry K. *Thomas E. Dewey, 1937–1947: A Study in Political Leadership.* New York: Garland Publishing, Inc., 1979.

Bickerton, Ian J., and Carla L. Klausner. *A Concise History of the Arab-Israeli Conflict.* 3rd ed. Upper Saddle River, NJ: Prentice-Hall, 1998.

Bishop, Jim. *FDR's Last Year, April 1944–April 1945.* New York: William Morrow, 1974.

Black, Allida M. *Casting Her Own Shadow: Eleanor Roosevelt and the Shaping of Postwar Liberalism.* New York: Columbia University Press, 1996.

———. "Championing a Champion: Eleanor Roosevelt and the Marian Anderson Freedom Concert." *Presidential Studies Quarterly* (Fall 1990), 719–36.

———, ed. *Courage in a Dangerous World: The Political Writings of Eleanor Roosevelt.* New York: Columbia University Press, 1999.

———, ed. *What I Hope to Leave Behind: The Essential Essays of Eleanor Roosevelt.* Brooklyn, NY: Carlson, 1995.

Black, Conrad. *Franklin Delano Roosevelt: Champion of Freedom.* New York: Public Affairs, 2003.

Blanksten, George I. *Peron's Argentina.* Chicago: University of Chicago Press, 1953.

Blum, John Morton. *From the Morgenthau Diaries.* Vol. 3. Boston: Houghton Mifflin, 1967.

———, ed. *The Price of Vision: The Diary of Henry A. Wallace, 1942–1946.* Boston: Houghton Mifflin, 1973.

Blutstein, Howard I., J. David Edwards, Kathryn Therese Johnston, David S. McMorris, and James D. Rudolph. *Area Handbook for Colombia.* 3rd ed. Washington, DC: US Government Printing Office, 1977.

Bone, Hugh A. "Political Parties in New York City." *The American Political Science Review,* 40, no. 2 (April 1946), 272–282.

Bowles, Chester. *Promises to Keep: My Years in Public Life, 1941–1969.* New York: Harper and Row, 1971.

Boyd, Andrew. *The United Nations Organization Handbook.* London: Pilot Press, 1946.

Boyer, Paul S. *Promises to Keep: The United States Since World War II.* Lexington, MA: D. C. Heath, 1995.

Boyer, Paul S., Clark E. Clifford, Jr., Joseph F. Kett, Neal Salisbury, Harvard Sitkoff, and Nancy Woloch. *The Enduring Vision: A History of the American People.* 4th ed. Boston: Houghton Mifflin, 2000.

Braden, Spruille. *Diplomats and Demagogues: The Memoirs of Spruille Braden.* New Rochelle, NY: Arlington House, 1971.

Bramsted, Ernest K. *Goebbels and National Socialist Propaganda, 1925–1945.* East Lansing: Michigan State University Press, 1965.

Brands, H. W. *Inside the Cold War: Loy Henderson and the Rise of the American Empire, 1918–1961.* New York: Oxford University Press, 1991.

Brecher, Michael, and Jonathan Wilkenfeld. *Study of a Crisis.* Ann Arbor: University of Michigan Press, 1997.

Brinkley, Alan. *The Unfinished Nation: A Concise History of the American People.* New York: McGraw-Hill, 1993.

Brock, Clifton. *Americans for Democratic Action: Its Role in National Politics.* Washington, DC: Public Affairs Press, 1962.

Brock, Peter, and Nigel Young. *Pacifism in the Twentieth Century.* Syracuse, NY: Syracuse University Press, 1999.

Brown, David, and W. Richard Bruner. *How I Got That Story.* New York: Dutton, 1967.

Bunyan, John. *The Pilgrim's Progress.* New York: Dodd, Mead and Co., 1979.

Burgwyn, H. James. *Italian Foreign Policy in the Interwar Period, 1918–1940.* Westport, CT: Praeger, 1997.

Bushnell, David. *Eduardo Santos and the Good Neighbor, 1938–1942.* Gainesville, FL: University of Florida Press, 1967.

Byrnes, James F. *All in One Lifetime.* New York: Harper, 1958.

Caffrey, Margaret M. *Ruth Benedict: Stranger in this Land.* Austin: University of Texas Press, 1989.

Campbell, Thomas M., and George C. Herring. *The Diaries of Edward R. Stettinius, Jr., 1943–1946.* New York: New Viewpoints, 1975.

Carr, Robert K. *The House Committee on Un-American Activities, 1945–1950.* Ithaca, NY: Cornell University Press, 1952.

Ceplair, Larry, and Steven Englund. *The Inquisition in Hollywood: Politics in the Film Community, 1930–1960.* Garden City, NY: Anchor Press/Doubleday, 1980.

Chace, James. *Acheson: The Secretary of State Who Created the American World.* New York: Simon and Schuster, 1998.

Chalmers, David M. *Hooded Americanism: The History of the Ku Klux Klan.* 3rd ed. Durham, NC: Duke University Press, 1987.

Chamberlin, Waldo, Thomas Hovet, Jr., and Erica Hovet. *A Chronology and Fact Book of the United Nations, 1941–1969.* Dobbs Ferry, NY: Oceana Publications, 1970.

Chernow, Ron. *The Warburgs: The Twentieth-Century Odyssey of a Remarkable Jewish Family.* New York: Random House, 1993.

Cherny, Robert W., William Issel, and Kieran Walsh Taylor, eds. *American Labor and the Cold War: Grassroots Politics and Postwar Political Culture.* New Brunswick, NJ: Rutgers University Press, 2004.

Churchill, Winston. *Never Give In! The Best of Winston Churchill's Speeches.* Ed. Winston S. Churchill. New York: Hyperion, 2003.

Cohen, Michael J. *Palestine and the Great Powers, 1945–1948.* Princeton, NJ: Princeton University Press, 1982.

———. *Truman and Israel.* Berkeley and Los Angeles: University of California Press, 1990.

Cohen, Michael J., and Martin Kolinsky, eds. *Demise of the British Empire in the Middle East: Britain's Responses to Nationalist Movements, 1943–55.* London: Frank Cass, 1998.

BIBLIOGRAPHY

Connally, Tom. *My Name Is Tom Connally.* As told to Alfred Steinberg. New York: Thomas Y. Crowell, 1954.

Cook, Blanche Wiesen. *Eleanor Roosevelt.* 2 vols. New York: Viking, 1992, 1999.

Cooney, John. *The American Pope: The Life and Times of Francis Cardinal Spellman.* New York: Times Books, 1984.

Cooper, John Milton, Jr. *The Warrior and the Priest: Woodrow Wilson and Theodore Roosevelt.* Cambridge, MA: Belknap Press of Harvard University Press, 1983.

Cott, Nancy F. *The Grounding of Modern Feminism.* New Haven: Yale University Press, 1987.

Craig, R. Bruce. *Treasonable Doubt: The Harry Dexter White Spy Case.* Lawrence, KS: University Press of Kansas, 2004.

Cray, Ed. *General of the Army: George C. Marshall, Soldier and Statesman.* New York: W. W. Norton, 1990.

Culver, John C., and John Hyde. *American Dreamer: The Life and Times of Henry A. Wallace.* New York: W. W. Norton, 2000.

Dailey, Jane, Glenda Elizabeth Gilmore, and Bryant Simon, eds. *Jumpin' Jim Crow: Southern Politics from Civil War to Civil Rights.* Princeton, NJ: Princeton University Press, 2000.

Dallek, Robert. *Franklin D. Roosevelt and American Foreign Policy, 1932–1945.* New York: Oxford University Press, 1979.

Daniel, Robert L. *American Women in the 20th Century: The Festival of Life.* San Diego: Harcourt Brace Jovanovich, 1987.

Danish, Max D. *The World of David Dubinsky.* Cleveland: World Publishing Co., 1957.

Davis, Kenneth S. *Invincible Summer: An Intimate Portrait of the Roosevelts, Based on the Recollections of Marion Dickerman.* New York: Atheneum, 1974.

Daws, Gavan. *Holy Man: Father Damien of Molokai.* New York: Harper and Row, 1973.

Dinnerstein, Leonard. *America and the Survivors of the Holocaust.* New York: Columbia University Press, 1982.

Divine, Robert A. "The Cold War and the Election of 1948." *Journal of American History* 59, no. 1 (June 1972): 90–110.

Donaldson, Scott. *Archibald MacLeish: An American Life.* In collaboration with R. H. Winnick. Boston: Houghton Mifflin, 1992.

Donovan, Robert J. *Conflict and Crisis: The Presidency of Harry S. Truman, 1945–48.* New York: W. W. Norton, 1977.

Duggan, John P. *Neutral Ireland and the Third Reich.* Totowa, NJ: Barnes and Noble, 1985.

Dulles, Foster Rhea, and Melvyn Dubofsky. *Labor in America: A History.* 4th ed. Arlington Heights, IL: Harlan Davidson, 1984.

Dwyer, T. Ryle. *Irish Neutrality and the USA, 1939–1947.* Totowa, NJ: Rowman and Littlefield, 1977.

Dziewanowski, M. K. *A History of Soviet Russia.* 4th ed. Englewood Cliffs, NJ: Prentice-Hall, 1993.

Edens, John A. *Eleanor Roosevelt: A Comprehensive Bibliography.* Westport, CT: Greenwood, 1994.

Edwards, Jill. *Anglo-American Relations and the Franco Question, 1945–1955.* New York: Oxford University Press, 1999.

Egerton, John. *Speak Now Against the Day: The Generation Before the Civil Rights Movement in the South.* New York: Alfred A. Knopf, 1994.

Elliott, Lawrence. *Little Flower: The Life and Times of Fiorello La Guardia.* New York: William Morrow, 1983.

Evensen, Bruce J. *Truman, Palestine, and the Press: Shaping Conventional Wisdom at the Beginning of the Cold War.* New York: Greenwood, 1992.

Fasulo, Linda. *An Insider's Guide to the UN.* New Haven, CT: Yale University Press, 2004.

Fornieri, Joseph R. *The Language of Liberty: The Political Speeches and Writings of Abraham Lincoln.* Washington, DC: Regnery, 2003.

Fox, James. *Five Sisters: The Langhornes of Virginia.* New York: Simon and Schuster, 2000.

Fraser, Steven. *Labor Will Rule: Sidney Hillman and the Rise of American Labor.* New York: Free Press, 1991.

Frederickson, Kari. *The Dixiecrat Revolt and the End of the Solid South, 1932–1968.* Chapel Hill: University of North Carolina Press, 2001.

Freeze, Gregory L., ed. *Russia; A History.* 2nd ed. New York: Oxford University Press, 2002.

Freidel, Frank. *Franklin D. Roosevelt: A Rendezvous with Destiny.* New York: Little, Brown, 1990.

Fried, Richard M. *Nightmare in Red: The McCarthy Era in Perspective.* New York: Oxford University Press, 1990.

Gabler, Neal. *Winchell: Gossip, Power, and the Culture of Celebrity.* New York: Alfred A. Knopf, 1994.

Gaddis, John Lewis. *The United States and the Origins of the Cold War, 1941–1947.* New York: Columbia University Press, 1972.

Gannon, Robert I. *The Cardinal Spellman Story.* Garden City, NY: Doubleday, 1962.

Gardner, Michael R. *Harry Truman and Civil Rights: Moral Courage and Political Risks.* Carbondale, IL: Southern Illinois University Press, 2002.

Gati, Charles. *Hungary and the Soviet Bloc.* Durham, NC: Duke University Press, 1986.

Gellman, Irwin F. *Secret Affairs: Franklin Roosevelt, Cordell Hull, and Sumner Welles.* Baltimore: Johns Hopkins University Press, 1995.

Gilbert, Martin. *History of the Twentieth Century: A Concise Edition of the Acclaimed World History.* New York: Harper Collins, 2002.

Glendon, Mary Ann. *A World Made New: Eleanor Roosevelt and the Universal Declaration of Human Rights.* New York: Random House, 2001.

Goodman, Walter. *The Committee: The Extraordinary Career of the House Committee on Un-American Activities.* New York: Farrar, Straus and Giroux, 1968.

Goodwin, Doris Kearns. *No Ordinary Time: Franklin and Eleanor Roosevelt: The Home Front in World War II.* New York: Simon and Schuster, 1994.

Gordon, Linda. *The Moral Property of Women: A History of Birth Control Politics in America.* 3rd ed. Urbana: University of Illinois Press, 2002.

———. *Pitied But Not Entitled: Single Mothers and the History of Welfare, 1890–1935.* New York: Free Press, 1994.

Gould, Lewis L. *Grand Old Party: A History of the Republicans.* New York: Random House, 2003.

BIBLIOGRAPHY

Graff, Henry F., ed. *The Presidents: A Reference History.* 2nd ed. New York: Charles Scribner's Sons, 1997.

Greely, Andrew M. *An Ugly Little Secret: Anti-Catholicism in North America.* Kansas City: Sheed Andrews and McMeel, 1977.

Gross, Theodore L. *The Rise of Roosevelt University: Presidential Reflections.* Carbondale, IL: Southern Illinois University Press, 2005.

———. *Roosevelt University: From Vision to Reality, 1945–2002.* Chicago: Roosevelt University, 2002.

Grunberger, Richard. *The 12-Year Reich: A Social History of Nazi Germany, 1933–1945.* New York: Holt, Rinehart and Winston, 1971.

Gunther, John. *Inside Latin America.* New York: Harper and Brothers, 1941.

Gurewitsch, Edna P. *Kindred Souls: The Friendship of Eleanor Roosevelt and David Gurewitsch.* New York: St. Martin's, 2002.

Hahn, Peter L. *Caught in the Middle East: U.S. Policy toward the Arab-Israeli Conflict, 1945–1961.* Chapel Hill: University of North Carolina Press, 2004.

Halecki, O. *A History of Poland.* 9th ed. New York: David McKay, 1976.

Hamby, Alonzo. *Beyond the New Deal: Harry S. Truman and American Liberalism.* New York: Columbia University Press, 1973.

———. *Man of the People: A Life of Harry S. Truman.* New York: Oxford University Press, 1995.

Hartley, Fred A., Jr. *Our New National Labor Policy: The Taft-Hartley Act and the Next Steps.* New York: Funk and Wagnalls, 1948.

Hartmann Susan M. *The Home Front and Beyond: American Women in the 1940s.* Boston: Twayne Publishers, 1982.

Haynes, John Earl, and Harvey Klehr. *Venona: Decoding Soviet Espionage in America.* New Haven, CT: Yale University Press, 1999.

Heckscher, August. *When LaGuardia Was Mayor: New York's Legendary Years.* New York: W. W. Norton, 1978.

Hennessy, James Pope. *Robert Louis Stevenson.* New York: Simon and Schuster, 1975.

Herken, Gregg. *Brotherhood of the Bomb: The Tangled Lives and Loyalties of Robert Oppenheimer, Ernest Lawrence, and Edward Teller.* New York: Henry Holt, 2002.

Herring, Hubert C. *Good Neighbors: Argentina, Brazil, Chile and Seventeen Other Countries.* New Haven, CT: Yale University Press, 1941.

Hewlett, Richard G., and Oscar R. Anderson, Jr. *A History of the United States Atomic Energy Commission.* Vol. 1, *The New World, 1939–1946.* University Park: Pennsylvania State University Press, 1962.

Higham, Charles. *Orson Welles: The Rise and Fall of an American Genius.* New York: St. Martin's, 1985.

Hill, Herbert. *Black Labor and the American Legal System: Race, Work and the Law.* Washington, DC: Bureau of National Affairs, 1977.

Hillman, William. *Harry S. Truman in His Own Words.* New York: Bonanza Books, 1980.

Hinton, James. *Women, Social Leadership, and the Second World War: Continuities of Class.* Oxford: Oxford University Press, 2002.

Hodges, Donald C. *Argentina, 1943–1987: The National Revolution and Resistance.* Rev. ed. Albuquerque: University of New Mexico Press, 1988.

Hoff-Wilson, Joan, and Marjorie Lightman, eds. *Without Precedent: The Life and Career of Eleanor Roosevelt.* Bloomington: Indiana University Press, 1984.

Hogan, Michael J. *The Marshall Plan: America, Britain, and the Reconstruction of Western Europe, 1947–1952.* New York: Cambridge University Press, 1987.

Holborn, Louise W. *The International Refugee Organization, A Specialized Agency of the United Nations: Its History and Work, 1946–1952.* London: Oxford University Press, 1956.

Hollis, Daniel Webster, III. *The History of Ireland.* Westport, CT: Greenwood, 2001.

Holloway, David. *Stalin and the Bomb: The Soviet Union and Atomic Energy, 1939–1956.* New Haven, CT: Yale University Press, 1994.

Holly, David C. *Exodus 1947.* Annapolis: Naval Institute Press, 1995.

Hoopes, Townsend. *The Devil and John Foster Dulles.* Boston: Little, Brown, 1973.

Hoopes, Townsend, and Douglas Brinkley. *FDR and the Creation of the U.N.* New Haven, CT: Yale University Press, 1997.

Hudson, Winthrop S. *Religion in America: An Historical Account of the Development of American Religious Life.* 3rd ed. New York: Charles Scribner's Sons, 1981.

Humphrey, Hubert H. *The Education of a Public Man: My Life and Politics.* Garden City, NY: Doubleday, 1976.

Humphrey, John P. *Human Rights and the United Nations: A Great Adventure.* Dobbs Ferry, NY: Transnational Publishers, 1984.

————. *On the Edge of Greatness: The Diaries of John Humphrey, First Director of the United Nations Division of Human Rights.* Vol. 1, *1948–1949.* Ed. A. J. Hobbins. Montreal: McGill University Libraries, 1994.

Hunt, John Gabriel, ed. *The Essential Franklin Delano Roosevelt.* New York: Gramercy Books, 1995.

Hutten, Kurt. *Iron Curtain Christians: The Church in Communist Countries Today.* Minneapolis: Augsburg Publishing House, 1967.

Hyde, H. Montgomery. *Lord Reading: The Life of Rufus Isaacs, First Marquess of Reading.* New York: Farrar, Straus and Giroux, 1967.

Institute of Jewish Affairs. *European Jewry Ten Years After The War: An Account of the Development and Present Status of the Decimated Jewish Communities of Europe.* New York: Institute of Jewish Affairs of the World Jewish Congress, 1956.

International Council of Women. *Women in a Changing World: The Dynamic Story of the International Council of Women.* London: Routledge and Kegan Paul, 1966.

Iriye, Akira. *The Cold War in Asia: A Historical Introduction.* Englewood Cliffs, NJ: Prentice-Hall, 1974.

Isaacson, Walter, and Evan Thomas. *The Wise Men: Six Friends and the World They Made.* New York: Simon and Schuster, 1986.

Isserman, Maurice. *Which Side Were You On? The American Communist Party During the Second World War.* Middletown, CT: Wesleyan University Press, 1982.

Janken, Robert Kenneth. *White: The Biography of Walter White, Mr. NAACP.* New York: New Press, 2003.

Jenkins, Roy. *Churchill: A Biography*. New York: Farrar, Straus and Giroux, 2001.

Jevec, Adam, and Lee Ann Potter. "The Navajo Code Talkers." *Social Education* 65, no. 5 (1 September 2001): 262–66.

Judt, Tony. *Postwar: A History of Europe Since 1945*. New York: Penguin, 2005.

Karabell, Zachary. *The Last Campaign: How Harry Truman Won the 1948 Election*. New York: Alfred A. Knopf, 2000.

Kaufman, Natalie Hevener. *Human Rights Treaties and the Senate: A History of Opposition*. Chapel Hill: University of North Carolina Press, 1990.

Keegan, John. *The Second World War*. New York: Viking, 1990.

Kelly, Lawerence. *The Navajo Indians and Federal Indian Policy*. Tucson: University of Arizona Press, 1968.

Kennedy, David M. *Freedom from Fear: The American People in Depression and War, 1929–1945*. New York: Oxford University Press, 1999.

Kennedy, Randall. *Interracial Intimacies: Sex, Marriage, Identity, and Adoption*. New York: Pantheon, 2003.

Kershaw, Ian. *Hitler*. New York: Longman, 1991.

Kessler-Harris, Alice. *In Pursuit of Equity: Women, Men, and the Quest for Economic Citizenship in 20th Century America*. New York: Oxford University Press, 2001.

———. *Out to Work: A History of Wage-Earning Women in the United States*. New York: Oxford University Press, 1982.

Kessner, Thomas. *Fiorello H. La Guardia and the Making of Modern New York*. New York: McGraw-Hill, 1989.

Key, V. O. *Southern Politics in State and Nation*. New York: Alfred A. Knopf, 1949.

Kirby, Dianne, ed. *Religion and the Cold War*. New York: Palgrave, 2003.

Klehr, Harvey. *The Heyday of American Communism: The Depression Decade*. New York: Basic Books, 1984.

Kolsky, Thomas A. *Jews Against Zionism: The American Council for Judaism, 1942–1948*. Philadelphia: Temple University Press, 1990.

Krejci, Jarosalv, and Pavel Machonin. *Czechoslovakia, 1918–92: A Laboratory for Social Change*. New York: St. Martin's Press, 1996.

Lash, Joseph P. *Eleanor and Franklin: The Story of Their Relationship, Based on Eleanor Roosevelt's Private Papers*. New York: W. W. Norton, 1971.

———. *Eleanor: The Years Alone*. New York: W. W. Norton, 1972.

———. *Roosevelt and Churchill, 1939–1941: The Partnership that Saved the West*. New York: W. W. Norton, 1976.

———. *A World of Love: Eleanor Roosevelt and Her Friends, 1943–1962*. Garden City, NY: Doubleday, 1984.

Lauren, Paul Gordon. *The Evolution of International Human Rights: Visions Seen*. Philadelphia: University of Pennsylvania Press, 1998.

Laville, Helen. *Cold War Women: The International Activities of American Women's Organisations*. Manchester, UK: Manchester University Press, 2002.

———. "The Memorial Day Statement: Women's Organizations in the 'Peace Offensive.'" *Intelligence and National Security* 18, no. 2 (June 2003): 192–210.

Leaming, Barbara. *Orson Welles: A Biography.* New York: Viking, 1985.

Le Bon, Gustave. *La civilisation des Arabes.* Paris: Firmin–Didot, 1884.

———. *The World of Islamic Civilization.* New York: Tudor Publishing, 1974.

Leckie, Robert. *Delivered from Evil: The Saga of World War II.* New York: Harper and Row, 1987.

Lees, Lorraine M. *Keeping Tito Afloat: The United States, Yugoslavia, and the Cold War.* University Park: Pennsylvania State University Press, 1997.

Lerner, Natan. *The U.N. Convention on the Elimination of all Forms of Racial Discrimination: A Commentary.* Rockville, MD: Sijthoff and Noordhoff, 1980.

Leuchtenburg, William E. *The FDR Years: On Roosevelt and His Legacy.* New York: Columbia University Press, 1995.

———. *Franklin D. Roosevelt and the New Deal, 1932–1940.* New York: Harper and Row Publishers, 1963.

Lewis, David Levering. *W.E.B. Du Bois: The Fight for Equality and the American Century, 1919–1963.* New York: Henry Holt, 2000.

Lichtenstein, Nelson. *The Most Dangerous Man in Detroit: Walter Reuther and the Fate of American Labor.* New York: Basic Books, 1995.

Lie, Trygve. *In the Cause of Peace: Seven Years with the United Nations.* New York: MacMillan, 1954.

Liedtke, Boris N. *Embracing a Dictatorship: US Relations with Spain, 1945–53.* New York: St. Martin's Press, 1998.

Louis, William Roger. *Imperialism at Bay: The United States and the Decolonization of the British Empire, 1941–1945.* New York: Oxford University Press, 1978.

Louis, William Roger, and Robert W. Stookey, eds. *The End of the Palestine Mandate.* Austin: University of Texas Press, 1986.

Lounsbury, Thomas R., ed. *Yale Book of American Verse.* New Haven, CT: Yale University Press, 1912.

Lukowski, Jerzy, and Hubert Zawadzki. *A Concise History of Poland.* New York: Cambridge University Press, 2001.

Lundberg, Ferdinand, and Marynia F. Farnham. *Modern Woman: The Lost Sex.* New York: Harper and Brothers, 1947.

MacDougall, Curtis D. *Gideon's Army.* Vol. 1, *The Components of the Decision.* New York: Marzani and Munsell, 1965.

MacMillan, Margaret. *Paris 1919: Six Months That Changed the World.* New York: Random House, 2001.

Mansfield, Peter. *A History of the Middle East.* New York: Penguin, 1992.

Malik, Habib C., ed. *The Challenge of Human Rights: Charles Malik and the Universal Declaration.* Oxford: Charles Malik Foundation; Center for Lebanese Studies, 2000.

Marett, Sir Robert. *Peru.* New York: Praeger, 1969.

Martin, George Whitney. *Madam Secretary, Frances Perkins.* Boston: Houghton Mifflin, 1976.

BIBLIOGRAPHY

Martin, John Bartlow. *Adlai Stevenson of Illinois: The Life of Adlai Stevenson.* Garden City, NY: Doubleday, 1976.

Mazuzan, George T. *Warren R. Austin at the U.N., 1946–1953.* Kent, OH: Kent State University Press, 1977.

McCluskey, Audrey Thomas, and Elaine M. Smith, eds. *Mary McLeod Bethune: Building a Better World, Essays and Selected Documents.* Bloomington: Indiana University Press, 1999.

McCullough, David. *Mornings on Horseback.* New York: Simon and Schuster, 1981.

———. *Truman.* New York: Simon and Schuster, 1992.

McGuire, Phillip. *He, Too, Spoke for Democracy: Judge Hastie, World War II, and the Black Soldier.* New York: Greenwood Press, 1988.

McJimsey, George. *Harry Hopkins: Ally of the Poor and Defender of Democracy.* Cambridge, MA: Harvard University Press, 1987.

McKeever, Porter. *Adlai Stevenson: His Life and Legacy.* New York: William Morrow, 1989.

Meacham, Jon. *Franklin and Winston: An Intimate Portrait of an Epic Friendship.* New York: Random House, 2003.

Meisler, Stanley. *United Nations: The First Fifty Years.* New York: Atlantic Monthly Press, 1995.

Meron, Theodor, ed. *Human Rights Law-Making in the United Nations: A Critique of Instruments and Process.* Oxford: Clarendon Press, 1986.

Meyer, Peter, Bernard D. Weinryb, Eugene Duschinsky, and Nicolas Sylvain. *The Jews in the Soviet Satellites.* Syracuse, NY: Syracuse University Press, 1953.

Miller, Carol. "Geneva—the Key to Equality: Inter-war Feminists and the League of Nations." *Women's History Review* 3 (1994): 219–45

Miller, James Edward. *The United States and Italy, 1945–1950: The Politics and Diplomacy of Stabilization.* Chapel Hill: University of North Carolina Press, 1986.

Millis, Walter, ed. *The Forrestal Diaries.* With the collaboration of E. S. Duffield. New York: Viking, 1951.

Morgan, Thomas. "Native Americans in World War II." *Army History: The Professional Bulletin of Army History* 35 (Fall 1995): 22–27.

Morgenthau, Henry, III. *Mostly Morgenthaus: A Family History.* New York: Ticknor and Fields, 1991.

Morsink, Johannes. *The Universal Declaration of Human Rights: Origins, Drafting, and Intent.* Philadelphia: University of Pennsylvania Press, 1999.

Mower, A. Glenn, Jr. *The United States, the United Nations, and Human Rights: The Eleanor Roosevelt and Jimmy Carter Eras.* Westport, CT: Greenwood Press, 1979.

Murray, Stuart, and James McCabe. *Norman Rockwell's Four Freedoms.* New York: Gramercy, 1998.

Myles, Bruce. *Night Witches: The Untold Story of Soviet Women in Combat.* Novato, CA: Presidio Press, 1981.

Newton, Ronald C. *The "Nazi Menace" in Argentina, 1931–1947.* Stanford, CA: Stanford University Press, 1992.

Nyrop, Richard F., ed. *Guatemala: A Country Study.* Washington, DC: Foreign Area Studies, The American University, 1983.

O'Brien, Gail Williams. *The Color of the Law: Race, Violence, and Justice in the Post–World War II South.* Chapel Hill: University of North Carolina Press, 1999.

O'Connor, Kevin. *The History of the Baltic States.* Westport, CT: Greenwood Press, 2003.

Offner, Arnold A. *Another Such Victory: President Truman and the Cold War, 1945–1953.* Stanford, CA: Stanford University Press, 2002.

Page, Joseph A. *Perón: A Biography.* New York: Random House, 1983.

Parmet, Herbert S. *The Democrats: The Years After FDR.* New York: Macmillan, 1976.

———. *Eisenhower and the American Crusades.* New York: Macmillan, 1972.

Paterson, Thomas G., J. Garry Clifford, and Kenneth J. Hagan. *American Foreign Policy: A History, 1900 to Present.* 3rd ed., rev. Lexington, MA: D. C. Heath, 1991.

Patterson, James T. *Congressional Conservatism and the New Deal.* Lexington: University of Kentucky Press, 1967.

———. *Grand Expectations: The United States, 1945–1974.* New York: Oxford University Press, 1996.

Penkower, Monty Noam. *Decision on Palestine Deferred: America, Britain and Wartime Diplomacy, 1939–1945.* London: Frank Cass, 2002.

Perica, Vjekoslav. *Balkan Idols: Religion and Nationalism in Yugoslav States.* Oxford: Oxford University Press, 2002.

Perry, Elisabeth Israels. "Training for Public Life: ER and Women's Political Networks in the 1920s." In *Without Precedent: The Life and Career of Eleanor Roosevelt.* Edited by Marjorie Lightman and Joan Hoff-Wilson. Bloomington: Indiana University Press, 1984.

Pidgeon, Mary Elizabeth. *International Documents on the Status of Women.* United States Department of Labor, Women's Bureau, Bulletin No. 217. Washington, DC: US Government Printing Office, 1947.

Pogue, Forrest C. *George Marshall: Statesman, 1945–1959.* New York: Penguin, 1989.

President's Committee on Civil Rights. *To Secure These Rights: The Report of the President's Committee on Civil Rights.* Washington, DC: US Government Printing Office, 1947.

Radi, Heather, ed. *Jessie Street: Documents and Essays.* Broadway, NSW: Women's Redress Press, 1990.

Ralph, Philip Lee, Robert E. Lerner, Standish Meacham, and Edward McNall Burns. *World Civilizations.* Vol. 2, 8th ed. New York: W. W. Norton, 1991.

Ramet, Sabrina P. *Nihil Obstat: Religion, Politics, and Social Change in East-Central Europe and Russia.* Durham, NC: Duke University Press, 1998.

Ramsden, John. *Man of the Century: Winston Churchill and His Legend Since 1945.* New York: Columbia University Press, 2002.

Reading, Gerald Rufus Isaacs, Marquess of. *Rufus Isaacs: First Marquess of Reading, 1914–1935.* London: Hutchinson and Co., 1945.

Rector, John L. *The History of Chile.* Wesport, CT: Greenwood Press, 2003.

Redding, John M. *Inside the Democratic Party.* Indianapolis: Bobbs-Merrill, 1958.

Reed, Merl E. *Seedtime for the Modern Civil Rights Movement: The President's Committee on Fair Employment Practice, 1941–1946.* Baton Rouge: Louisiana State University Press, 1991.

Rees, David. *Harry Dexter White: A Study in Paradox.* New York: Coward, McCann, and Geoghegan, 1973.

Reeves, Thomas C. *The Life and Times of Joe McCarthy: A Biography.* New York: Stein and Day, 1982.

Ressler, Everett, Neil Boothby, and Daniel J. Steinbock. *Unaccompanied Children: Care and Protection in Wars, Natural Disasters, and Refugee Movements.* New York: Oxford University Press, 1988.

Reynolds, David. *One World Divisible: A Global History Since 1945.* New York: W. W. Norton, 2000.

Ribuffo, Leo P. *The Old Christian Right: The Protestant Far Right from the Great Depression to the Cold War.* Philadelphia: Temple University Press, 1983.

Robinson, Greg. *By Order of the President: FDR and the Internment of Japanese Americans.* Cambridge, MA: Harvard University Press, 2001.

Robinson, Nehemiah. "War Damage Compensation and Restitution in Foreign Countries." *Law and Contemporary Problems* 16, no. 3 (Summer 1951): 347–76.

Rodman, Bella. *Fiorello La Guardia: A Biography.* In collaboration with Philip Sterling. New York: Hill and Wang, 1962.

Roman, Eric. *Hungary and the Victor Powers, 1945–1950.* New York: St. Martin's Press, 1996.

Romero, Luis Alberto. *A History of Argentina in the Twentieth Century.* Translated by James P. Brennan. University Park: Pennsylvania State University Press, 2002.

Roosevelt, Eleanor. *The Autobiography of Eleanor Roosevelt.* New York: Harper and Brothers, 1961.

———. "Churchill at the White House." *Atlantic Monthly,* March 1965, 77–79.

———. *On My Own.* New York: Harper and Brothers, 1958.

———. *This I Remember.* New York: Harper and Brothers, 1949.

Roosevelt, Elliott. *As He Saw It.* New York: Duell, Sloan and Pearce, 1946.

Rowbotham, Sheila. *A Century of Women: The History of Women in Britain and the United States in the Twentieth Century.* New York: Penguin Books, 1999.

Rubin, Devora, ed. *Daughters of Destiny: Women Who Revolutionized Jewish Life and Torah Education.* Brooklyn, NY: Mesorah, 1988.

Rupp, Leila J. *Worlds of Women: The Making of an International Women's Movement.* Princeton, NJ: Princeton University Press, 1997.

Rupp, Leila J., and Verta Taylor. *Survival in the Doldrums: The American Women's Rights Movement, 1945 to the 1960s.* New York: Oxford University Press, 1987.

Rusk, Dean. *As I Saw It.* As told to Richard Rusk. Edited by Daniel S. Papp. New York: W. W. Norton, 1990.

Sachar, Howard. *A History of Israel: From Zionism to Our Time.* 2nd ed. New York: Alfred A. Knopf, 1998.

———. *A History of Jews in America.* New York: Knopf, 1992.

Sadie, Stanley, ed. *The New Grove Dictionary of Music and Musicians.* 2nd ed. New York: Grove, 2001.

Sandifer, Irene Reiterman. *Mrs. Roosevelt: As We Knew Her.* Silver Spring, MD: n.p., 1975.

Sandilands, Roger J. *The Life and Political Economy of Lauchlin Currie: New Dealer, Presidential Adviser, and Development Economist.* Durham, NC: Duke University Press, 1990.

Savage, Sean J. *Truman and the Democratic Party.* Lexington: University of Kentucky Press, 1997.

Scarlett, William, ed. *Toward a Better World.* Philadelphia: The John C. Winston Co., 1946.

Schatz, Thomas. *Boom and Bust: The American Cinema in the 1940s.* New York: Charles Scribner's Sons, 1997.

Schlesinger, Stephen. *Act of Creation: The Founding of the United Nations.* Boulder, CO: Westview Press, 2003.

Schmidt, Karl M. *Henry A. Wallace: Quixotic Crusade 1948.* Syracuse, NY: Syracuse University Press, 1960.

Schopen, Lynn, Hanna Newcombe, Chris Young, and James Wert. *Nations on Record: United Nations General Assembly Roll Call Votes (1946–1973).* Oakville-Dundas, ON: Canadian Peace Research Institute, 1975.

Schrecker, Ellen. *Many Are the Crimes: McCarthyism in America.* Princeton, NJ: Princeton University Press, 1999.

Schultz, Bud, and Ruth Schultz. *It Did Happen Here: Recollections of Political Repression in America.* Berkeley: University of California Press, 1989.

Schwarz, Jordan A. *The Speculator: Bernard M. Baruch in Washington, 1917–1965.* Chapel Hill: University of North Carolina, 1981.

Scobie, Ingrid Winther. *Center Stage: Helen Gahagan Douglas, A Life.* New York: Oxford University Press, 1992.

Seeber, Frances M. "'I Want You to Write to Me': The Papers of Anna Eleanor Roosevelt." *Prologue* 2 (Summer 1987), 95–105.

Segev, Tom. *One Palestine Complete: Jews and Arabs Under the British Mandate.* New York: Metropolitan Books, 2000.

Sharp, Ian G. *Industrial Conciliation and Arbitration in Great Britain.* London: Allen and Unwin, 1950.

Simon, Bryant. "Race Reactions: African American Organizing, Liberalism, and White Working-Class Politics in Postwar South Carolina." In *Jumpin' Jim Crow: Southern Politics from Civil War to Civil Rights.* Edited by Jane Dailey, Glenda Elizabeth Gilmore, and Bryant Simon. Princeton, NJ: University of Princeton, 2000.

Sklar, Kathryn Kish, ed. *Women's Rights Emerges within the Anti-Slavery Movement, 1830–1870: A Brief History with Documents.* Boston: Bedford/St. Martin's, 2000.

Slonim, Shlomo. "The 1948 American Embargo on Arms to Palestine." *Political Science Quarterly* 94, no. 3 (Autumn 1979): 495–514.

Smith, Gaddis. *American Diplomacy During the Second World War, 1941–1945.* New York: John Wiley and Sons, 1965.

Smith, Jean Edward. *Lucius D. Clay: An American Life.* New York: Henry Holt and Co., 1990.

Smith, Page. *America Enters the World: A People's History of the Progressive Era and World War I.* New York: McGraw-Hill, 1985.

Smith, Richard Norton. *The Colonel: The Life and Legend of Robert R. McCormick, 1880–1955.* Boston: Houghton Mifflin, 1997.

———. *Thomas E. Dewey and His Times.* New York: Simon and Schuster, 1982.

BIBLIOGRAPHY

———. *An Uncommon Man: The Triumph of Herbert Hoover.* New York: Simon and Schuster, 1984.

Solberg, Carl. *Hubert Humphrey: A Biography.* New York: W. W. Norton, 1984.

Stargardt, Nicholas. *Witnesses of War: Children's Lives under the Nazis.* London: Jonathan Cape, 2005.

Starr, Paul. *The Social Transformation of American Medicine.* New York: Basic Books, Inc., 1982.

Steel, Ronald. *Walter Lippmann and the American Century.* Boston: Little, Brown, 1980.

Sterett, Susan M. *Public Pensions: Gender and Civic Service in the States, 1850–1937.* Ithaca, NY: Cornell University Press, 2003.

Stewart, Maxwell S. *20th Century Pamphleteering: The History of the Public Affairs Committee.* New York: Public Affairs Committee, 1976.

Stienstra, Deborah. *Women's Movements and International Organizations.* New York: St. Martin's, 1994.

Stiller, Jesse H. *George S. Messersmith: Diplomat of Democracy.* Chapel Hill: University of North Carolina Press, 1987.

Stoler, Mark A. *George C. Marshall: Soldier-Statesman of the American Century.* Boston: Twayne Publishers, 1989.

Stone, Abraham. "The International Union of Family Organizations Lisbon Conference." *Marriage and Family Living* 16, no. 1 (February 1954): 72–75.

———. "World Congress on the Family." *Marriage and Family Living* 10, no. 1 (February 1948): 10–11.

Stone, Geoffrey R. *Perilous Times: Free Speech in Wartime from the Sedition Act to the War on Terrorism.* New York: W. W. Norton, 2004.

Street, Jessie M. G. *Truth or Repose?* Sydney: Australasian Book Society, 1966.

Takaki, Ronald. *Double Victory: A Multiracial History of World War II.* Boston: Little, Brown, 2000.

Tanenhaus, Sam. *Whittaker Chambers: A Biography.* New York: Random House, 1997.

Taylor, Graham. *The New Deal and American Indian Tribalism: The Administration of the Indian Reorganization Act, 1934–1945.* Lincoln: University of Nebraska Press, 1980.

Tobin, James. *Ernie Pyle's War: America's Eyewitness to World War II.* New York: Free Press, 1997.

Townshend, Charles. *Ireland: The 20th Century.* London: Arnold, 1999.

Treadwell, Mattie E. *The Women's Army Corps.* United States Army in World War II, Special Studies. Washington, DC: Office of the Chief Military Historian, Dept. of the Army, 1954.

Truman, Harry S. *Memoirs.* 2 vols. Garden City, NY: Doubleday, 1956–1957.

Turgeon, Lynn. "The Political Economy of Reparations." *The New German Critique* 1, no. 1 (Winter 1973): 111–125.

United Nations Relief and Rehabilitation Administration. *UNRRA: The History of the United Nations Relief and Rehabilitation Administration.* Prepared by a special staff under direction of George Woodbridge, Chief Historian of UNRRA. New York: Columbia University Press, 1950.

United States Congress, House Committee on Foreign Affairs. *United States Foreign Policy for a Post-War Recovery Program: Hearings before the Committee on Foreign Affairs, House of Representatives, Eightieth Congress, Second Session. Part 2.* Washington, DC: US Government Printing Office, 1948.

United States Congress, House Committee on Un-American Activities. *Hearings Regarding Communist Espionage in the United States Government: Hearings Before the Committee on Un-American Activities, House of Representatives, Eightieth Congress, Second Session.* Washington, DC: US Government Printing Office, 1948.

United States Department of the Interior. *Indian Affairs: Laws and Treaties.* Vol. 6. Charles J. Kappler, ed. Washington, DC: US Government Printing Office, 1972.

United States Office of Management and Budget. *Historical Tables, Budget of the United States Government, Fiscal Year 2001.* Washington, DC: US Government Printing Office, 2000.

Urofsky, Melvin I. *A Voice That Spoke for Justice: The Life and Times of Stephen S. Wise.* Albany: State University of New York Press, 1982.

Urquhart, Brian. *Ralph Bunche: An American Life.* New York: W. W. Norton, 1993.

Vandenberg, Arthur, Jr., ed. *The Private Papers of Senator Vandenberg.* With the collaboration of Joe Alex Morris. Boston: Houghton Mifflin, 1952.

Vernant, Jacques. *The Refugee in the Post-War World.* New Haven, CT: Yale University Press, 1953.

Warburg-Spinelli, Ingrid. *Dringlichkeit des Mitleids und die Einsamkeit, Nein zu Sagen.* Hamburg: Dölling und Galitz Verlag, 1990.

Ware, Susan. *Beyond Suffrage: Women in the New Deal.* Cambridge, MA: Harvard University Press, 1981.

———. *Partner and I: Molly Dewson, Feminism, and New Deal Politics.* New Haven, CT: Yale University Press, 1987.

Warren, Heather. *Theologians of a New World Order: Reinhold Niebuhr and the Christian Realists, 1920–1948.* New York: Oxford University Press, 1997.

Watkins, T. H. *Righteous Pilgrim: The Life and Times of Harold L. Ickes, 1874–1952.* New York: Henry Holt and Company, 1990.

Weil, Thomas E., Jan Knippers Black, Howard I. Blutstein, Kathryn Therese Johnston, and David S. McMorris. *Area Handbook for Brazil.* 3rd ed. Washington, DC: US Government Printing Office, 1975.

Welch, Robert. *The Politician.* Belmont, MA: Belmont Publishing Co., 1964.

Welles, Benjamin. *Sumner Welles, FDR's Global Strategist: A Biography.* New York: St. Martin's Press, 1997.

Whitaker, Arthur P. *The United States and Argentina.* Cambridge, MA: Harvard University Press, 1954.

Whittaker, D. J. *Fighter for Peace: Philip Noel-Baker, 1889–1982.* York, England: William Sessions Limited, 1989.

Wilson, James Q. *The Amateur Democrat: Club Politics in Three Cities.* Chicago: University of Chicago Press, 1962.

Winnick, R. H., ed. *Letters of Archibald MacLeish, 1907–1982.* Boston: Houghton Mifflin, 1983.

Winslow, Anne, ed. *Women, Politics, and the United Nations.* Westport, CT: Greenwood Press, 1995.

Woldman, Albert A. *Lincoln and the Russians.* Cleveland: World Publishing Co., 1952.

Woloch, Nancy. *Women and the American Experience.* 3rd ed. Boston: McGraw-Hill, 2000.

BIBLIOGRAPHY

Woolner, David B., ed. *The Second Quebec Conference Revisited: Waging War, Formulating Peace: Canada, Great Britain, and the United States in 1944–1945.* New York: St. Martin's Press, 1998.

Wright, Gordon. *France in Modern Times: From the Enlightenment to the Present.* 5th ed. New York: W. W. Norton, 1995.

Zevin, B. D., ed. *Nothing to Fear: The Selected Addresses of Franklin D. Roosevelt, 1932–1945.* Boston: Houghton Mifflin, 1946.

Zickel, Raymond, and Walter R. Iwaskiw, eds. *Albania: A Country Study.* Washington, DC: Library of Congress Federal Research Division, 1994.

Zieger, Robert H. *The CIO, 1935–1955.* Chapel Hill: University of North Carolina Press, 1995.

Zweiniger-Bargielowska, Ina. *Austerity in Britain: Rationing, Controls, and Consumption, 1939–1955.* Oxford: Oxford University Press, 2000.

Index

US immigration policy, 346*n*6; US Palestine policy criticized by, 323, 345–346, 346*n*6; Wallace's European lecture tour, 539; wartime labor policy of, 315*n*4

Bey, Abdel Rehman Azzam: on FDR and Ibn Saud, 122; Truman's discounting of, 122

Bible: ER's study of, 392; I Corinthians:13, 592–593, 594*n*5; Luke 10:27, 394*n*4; Mark 12:31, 394*n*4; Matthew 22:39, 394*n*4

Bigart, Homer, 770*n*1

Bigelow, Harry A., 671*n*4

bigotry. *See* discrimination, racial; prejudice

Bilbo, Theodore: career of, 453*n*4; opposes ER's appointment to UN, 163*n*6, 453*n*4; picketing of, 351

Bill of Rights (US Constitution), 973, 974*n*9; apathy toward, 548; Four Freedoms and, 328; on living up to, 275

bipartisanship, 455–458; ER on importance of in foreign policy, 455

Black, Hugo: on federal aid to parochial schools, 607

Blaisdell, Mrs., 199*n*26

Blanshard, Paul, 944

Bloom, Sol: career of, 458*n*3; ER meets with, 249; as UN delegate, 20*n*6, 163*n*3, 225*n*23; UNICEF appropriation, 967*n*4

Boardman, Harry N.: ER's aid stance criticized by, 468

Boettiger (Halstead), Anna Roosevelt, 36, 502*n*31, 858*p*; biographical portrait, 989–990; correspondence with ER, 222*n*2; as editor of *The Woman*, 977; ER and, 13; FDR's death and, 13; financial problems of, 934*n*9; *letter to*, 222*n*2; new radio show of, 932; as publisher, 38*n*11. *See also Eleanor and Anna* radio show

Boettiger, Curtis Roosevelt: visit to Palestine (Oct., *1948*), 914, 917*n*24; visit to Paris (Oct., *1948*), 917*n*19

Boettiger, John, 36, 502*n*31, 934*n*9

Boettiger, Johnny (grandson), 36

Bogomolov, Aleksandr: *Article 2* amendments proposed by, 962, 963*n*4; move to postpone consideration of UDHR, 970*n*1; as Soviet delegate, 962, 963*n*3; UDHR, 689, 690*n*1

Bohlen, Charles E. "Chip": diplomatic career of, 765*n*21; dispatched to ER by Marshall, 762; ER on, 765–766*n*21; ER rejects "truce enforcement" proposal of, 969; FDR, USSR, and, 762; Palestine trusteeship proposal (meeting with ER on), 776–780, 784*n*26, 784*n*28; Soviet threat to Europe, 762; on US-USSR relations, 698, 765*n*21, 784*n*28

Bok Peace Prize: ER collaboration with G. Ely on, 948*n*2

Bolivia, 503*n*37, 729*n*22

Bolte, Charles G., 454*n*13

Bomar, Lynn, 387–388, 389*n*6

Bontecou, Eleanor: Columbia, TN, grand jury and, 348*n*2

Boone, "Puss", 600*n*2

Borgward Goliath, 259*n*10

Borisov, Alexander, 683*n*4

Boston Globe: on ER as UN delegate, 128*n*9

Boston Post: ER's speech reprinted in, 125–127

Bottomly, Ruth, 613*n*3

Bowles, Chester: Anderson, food aid to Europe, and, 151*n*2; biographical portrait, 990; on Democratic Party, 450–451; Draft Eisenhower movement, 699, 708, 844–845, 846*n*6; ER's support of, 149, 918; La Guardia on, 522; *letter from*, 844; *letters to*, 708, 845; as non-communist, 450–451; as OPA administrator, 151*n*2; political career of, 525*n*1; on price controls, 149; Snyder clashed with, 139; third party opposed by, 450–451, 525*n*4; as Truman advisor, 139; UDA addressed by, 450–451; Vinson's disagreement with, 151*n*2

Bowman, Isaiah: career of, 94*n*20; ER's criticism of, 91

Braden, Spruille: Argentine presidential campaign and, 501*n*16; Batista and, 504*n*43; career of, 492, 499*n*6, 503*n*37, 503*n*40; Chaco War and, 503*n*37; on Communism, 503*n*40; ER's relationship with, 492; on fascism, 503*n*40; FDR on, 497–498, 504*n*3; on German influence in Argentina, 492; Messersmith and, 445*p*, 492, 499*n*8, 502*n*32, 504*n*45; Pan American Airlines pressured by, 503*n*41; Perón and, 499*n*6, 501*n*16, 501*n*18; resignation of, 504*n*45; Santos and,

fears of, 147; invites ER to China, 96, 98; wartime activities of, 98*n*3; *color insert*

Chicago Civil Liberties Committee: ER and, 287*n*3, 288

Chicago Council on Foreign Relations: ER speaks to, 502*n*31

Chicago Sun-Times, 869

Chicago Tribune, 644, 649

Chico State College: ER speaks to, 502*n*31

Child Search Branch of the International Tracing Service of the IRO: ER's visit to, 604*n*6

children: British aid to, 275; as casualties of war, 236*n*5; civic education of, 240*n*8; deported by Hitler, 964; diet of, 275; in displaced persons camps, 256–258, 259*n*4; education of, 264, 274; grants to families with, 946, 960; needs of, 264, 275; orphaned by war, 236*n*5; right to special care and assistance, 946; as soldiers, 274; of unmarried mothers, 946–947. *See also* United Nations International Children's Emergency Fund (UNICEF)

Children's Bureau: activities of, 316*n*12; ER's concerns re Truman and, 356; reorganization of, 313–314, 316*n*9

Childs, Marquis, 92*n*7; on trusteeship, 89

Chile: elected to first ECOSOC sessions, 291*n*3; Soviet wives of nationals of, 888, 889*n*1

China: civil war, 147, 148*n*4, 759; on committee for final edit of UDHR, 963*n*1; elected to first ECOSOC session, 291*n*3; ER visit proposed, 58*n*6, 96–97; ER on, 140, 147, 720; Flying Tigers program, 878*n*1; Japanese occupation of, 141, 143*n*13, 165*n*20; NAACP on, 161; UNCIO trusteeship debates and, 93*n*19; US military aid to, 763*n*4

Chinese Americans: discrimination against, 309

Chinese Eastern Railway, 535

Christian, L. C.: *letters from*, 735, 736, 737*n*8; *letters to*, 735, 737

Christian Century: Niemöller interviewed for, 71

Christian Register, 828–832

Christianity: ER's view of, 624; forgiveness, Germany, and, 75*n*11; Jewish orphans raised under, 602–604

Christmas: as amalgamation of customs, 68; irony of, 154; refugees during, 154

church: combating prejudice and, 363; ER on role of, 363; separation of state and, 363

Church World Service, 948*n*2

Churchill, Winston: Battle of Britain speech, 729*n*4; biographical portrait, 991–992; ER lunches with, 194; ER on FDR and, 32*n*12; ER on Truman and, 2; ER's criticism of, 28, 281*n*2; ER's praise of, 790; ER's relationship with, 226*n*29; FDR compared with, 29; FDR, trusteeship, and, 90; FDR's relationship with, 691, 692*n*2–3, 790; founding of UN and, 20*n*5; German surrender and, 30*n*4; on humor and, 29; "Iron Curtain" speech of, 173, 178, 279, 281*n*7, 384; *letter from*, 692*n*3; *letter to*, 24*n*3; Murray on, 280, 384; Near East policy of, 534; New York speech of, 281*n*7; Palestine immigration and, 143*n*8; poetry and, 29, 32*n*12; redrawing Poland's boundaries and, 25*n*1; *Pravda's* criticism of, 32*n*11; as proposed UN Secretary, 207; remarks at FDR statue dedication, 790; responds to critics, 281*n*7; Soviets criticized by, 31*n*11; speeches quoted, 31*n*11; at Tehran Conference, 521*n*5; telegrams quoted, 30*n*4; Truman on, 30*n*4; Truman's reassurance of, 45*n*9; "United States of Europe" concept of, 384; on US-British alliance, 279; US-USSR relations and, 45*n*9; USSR, German surrender, and, 28, 30*n*4; on Wallace as crypto-Communist, 539; as war leader, 274; White Russia backed by, 385*n*2. *See also* Cairo Conference; Casablanca Conference; Potsdam Conference; Tehran Conference; Yalta Conference

Cisneros, Guy Pérez, 955, 956*n*2

Citizens Committee on Displaced Persons (CCDP), 134*n*1, 600, 613

Citizens' Food Committee, 716*n*2

Citizens' Non-Partisan Committee, 78*n*3

Citizens' Union, 78*n*3, 83*n*24

citizenship: ER on "narrow vision" and, 271; international responsibilities of, 18, 271, 548; political responsibilities of, 114, 125, 137, 328, 359, 365, 374, 524, 549; social responsibilities of, 137, 470, 471; Universal Service, 467, 771, 772*n*4

Citrine, Sir Walter, 216, 218*n*2

Four Freedoms: democracy and, 791; ER on, 112, 328, 791, 833; Hubert Humphrey on, 528*n*3; Marshall Plan and, 698; origins of, 278*n*19, 328*n*1. *See also* freedom from fear; freedom from want; freedom of religion; freedom of speech

four horsemen of autocracy, 937*n*1

Fowler, William: on British refugee proposal, 204*n*8; career of, 204*n*8; on ECOSOC and refugees, 203–204; refugee study of, 202

Framingham, MA, 125

France: anti-Semitism in, 187*n*2; colonial possessions of, 92*n*11, 166*n*28; on committee for final edit of UDHR, 963*n*1; debt to US, 789*n*3; as delegate to first ECOSOC sessions, 291*n*3; ER on, 900, 906*n*7, 907*n*10, 922, 982–983; ER's visits to, 277*n*8, 848, 911, 917*n*19, 953, 954*n*1; *Exodus 1947* (vessel) and, 609; food shortages in, 982; Franco policy of, 414*n*3; German policy and, 543; grants to families with children, 946, 960; Jewish refugees, 611*n*1, 613; occupation of Germany, 543; petitioning as right, 957; political conditions, 125; political parties in, 941; refugee policy and, 232*n*8; strikes and demonstrations in, 898; tuberculosis in, 125; UN war propaganda resolutions, 645, 647*n*13; UNCIO trusteeship debates, 93*n*19, 166*n*21; US aid to, 142*n*6, 268*n*5, 676, 716*n*6; wartime tours of FDR and, 277*n*9; women's suffrage, 843*n*3

Franco, Francisco: Allied stance re, 414*n*3; career of, 435*n*4; compared to Hitler and Molotov, 436*n*12; Dunn's support of, 93; ER on, 433–436; General Assembly debates re, 411; Kirchwey's opposition to, 411–413; NAACP on, 161; Potsdam decision re, 31; refugees and, 250*n*11; Spanish Civil War and, 148*n*4, 250*n*11; UN admission of, 433; US delegation resolution re, 414*n*3; US policy toward, 415

Frank, Jerome, 799*n*1

Frankfurt, Germany: ER's visit to, 252

Frankfurter, Felix: Communist charges against, 938*n*4; Palestine policy of the US, 726, 916*n*10

Franklin, Benjamin, 907*n*7

Franklin, Gertrude Taber, 630*n*2

Franklin D. Roosevelt National Historic Site. *See* Springwood

Fraser, Peter: career of, 211*n*8; as chair of Third Committee, 208, 238; ER on, 213; Yugoslavia and Soviet opposition to, 239*n*6

free trade: anti-colonialism and, 45*n*11; Atlantic Charter and, 45*n*11

Freedman's Bureau, 167*n*35

freedom, 252, 925, 926, 980, 984; Churchill on FDR and, 790; Common Cause declaration re, 477*n*3; from discrimination, 293, 950*n*4; equality and, 923*n*5; ER on preservation of, 848, 900; ER's definitions of, 901–905; on hope, the human heart and, 252; HRC discussions re, 489, 507, 971*n*3, 973; of the individual, 360, 902–903; La Guardia on anti-communism and, 523; of movement, 791; NAACP on trusteeships and, 161; of opinion, 559*n*13; of thought, 661; postwar planning and, 451; UN Charter on, 515; as tool, 903; war aim, 68*n*1, 70, 92*n*12

freedom from fear: African Americans and, 734; Communism and, 720–721, 833; ER on, 112, 720–721, 734, 767; UN's role in securing, 343. *See also* Four Freedoms

freedom from want: ER on, 112, 278*n*19, 510*n*13, 695, 833, 926. *See also* Four Freedoms

freedom of association: ER on CPUSA and, 54, 527

freedom of conscience, 507

freedom of information: 488, 559*n*14, 829, 832*n*3, 888, 889*n*1, 890*n*5, 964

freedom of religion: conscientious objectors and, 351; ER on 68, 397, 529, 652–654, 691, 901; federal aid to parochial schools and, 608; HRC debates re, 506; Navajos and, 579; Nussbaum's interest in, 222, 226*nn*28; Soviets and, 889*n*1; UDHR and, 971*n*3; H. D. White and, 879*n*2; in Yugoslavia and, 529, 673–675. *See also* Four Freedoms

freedom of speech, 245, 248; displaced persons and, 333, 400*n*7; ER on, 182, 248, 733; HRC debates re, 506, 508, 647*n*12, 661, 687; HUAC and, 649–650; Iran's concerns re IBR and, 510*n*12; La Guardia on anti-Communism and, 523; MacLeish, UN Charter, and, 164*n*14; partisanship and, 458*n*4; propaganda and, 400*n*7, 901;

Hornaday, Mary: ER and career of, 198*n*16; ER's visit with, 193; on Yugoslavia and Greece, 195

Horthy, Miklós, 769, 770*n*4

Hot Springs, AR: Allied Conference in, 19*n*4

Hot Springs Food Declaration: FAO established by, 19*n*4

House Armed Services Committee: Forrestal testifies before, 722

House Banking and Currency Committee: housing bill, 376*n*13; La Guardia's testimony before, 525*n*6; red-baiting in, 522–523

House Expenditures Committee: full employment and, 132*n*4, *n*10

House Foreign Affairs Committee, 242, 519; Acheson testifies before, 515, 520, 521*n*4; and Council of Foreign Ministers, 455; US aid to Greece, 538*n*13

House Immigration and Naturalization Committee: investigates Port of New York, 460*n*3; legislative proposals of, 460*n*3; recommendations of, 460

House of Commons, 218*n*2, 238

House of Representatives, US: drafting of strikers, 316*n*13; standardization of, 503*n*36

House Un-American Activities Committee (HUAC): Hanns Eisler case, 578, 626–628; FBI list of subversive organizations, 670; Hollywood Ten case, 649–651; investigation of ER's acquaintances, 849; Kosenkina subpoena, 893*n*4; Rankin's creation of, 934*n*13. *See also* Currie, Lauchlin; Hiss, Alger

House Ways and Means Committee: unemployment insurance and, 128*n*10, 130

housing: Dewey and, 373; Foreman, ER, and Detroit, 287*n*6; in Palestine, 220*n*5; on postwar London, 225*n*25; rising cost of, 139; shortage of, 190*n*19; Truman on, 106

Howe, Louis McHenry: ER's political ambition and, 360; ER's relationship with, 360, 361*n*2, 658

Hoxha, Enver: US opposition to, 366*n*5

Hsia, C. L.: on composition of HRC, 300, 301; ER nominated nuclear HRC chair by, 297

Hsu Mo, 291*n*4

Hughes, Charles Evans: Communist charges against, 938*n*4

Hughes, Howard, 692*n*2

Hughes, Mrs. L. S., 613*n*3

Huguenots, 397, 399*n*2

Hull, Cordell: Argentina as Chapultepec topic, 43*n*4; Army's criticism of, 104; Chapultepec plans of, 43*n*4; ER's defense of, 105; ER's wartime trips to Europe, 38*n*13; free trade and, 34*n*2; gold standard and, 34*n*2; on independence, 93*n*19; Pearl Harbor and, 105; Stettinius replaces, 93*n*14

human nature, ER on, 85, 217

human rights: and censorship, 557; as central to UN, 488; as component of peace, 43*n*3; CPUSA and, 53; in the cultural field, 951; democratic government, 559*n*16; Democrats as party of, 48; discrimination as counter to, 119, 734; due process, 688; Dulles's advice re, 838–840; ER on need for broadening of, 904; ER's Sorbonne speech (draft changes), 906–910; ER's Sorbonne speech on differing conceptions of, 848, 853, 898–910; ER's Sorbonne speech (text), 900–905; fair trial as, 574*n*13; of foreigners, 569, 573; as freedom, justice and opportunity, 442; freedom from discrimination as, 950*n*4; having a legal personality as, 558*n*9, 567–570, 572; holding opinions and, 559*n*13; and the ICJ, 684*n*7; information access, 557, 559*n*14; labor union membership and, 836, 857*n*7; Laguier on defining, 297; League of Nations and, 299; liberty of movement, 556; as lure to democracy, 544; marriage contracting, 557, 567–572, 574*n*12, 668*n*10; minority language use, 958; of mothers and children, 946–947; need for education on, 947, 948*n*6; for old age, 951, 952*n*1–4, 962; on personal dignity and, 508; petitioning as individuals, 957–958; privacy, 558*n*7; on propaganda and, 248; as protection for the individual, 840; religion and, 971*n*3; representation by counsel, 567–568, 571, 573, 574*n*5; on rest and leisure, 949–950; social and economic order and, 951–952; Soviet policy, 508, 588; on State Department disinterest in, 848, 865–866; states may not abrogate, 955; Stettinius on importance of, 43*n*3; UN Charter and,

Soviet taking of Polish land, 25; Soviet-US relations, 448–449; value to ER of, 2. *See also My Day*; Roosevelt, Anna Eleanor: viewpoint

immigration: assimilation and, 67–68; ER's actions re, 459; Immigration Act (*1924*), 188*n*7; importance of, 66; INS policy re, 459; Latin American policies re, 167*n*33; statistics re, 66, 188*n*6; Truman's policy re, 188, 189*n*7, 461*n*4; Truman's use of refugees and, 188*n*7; US policy on, 69*n*2, 580; US quotas re, 67

Immigration Act (*1924*): Truman's actions under, 188*n*7

Immigration and Naturalization Service (INS), 459

Imperial Conference of the British Empire, 751*n*2

Import-Export Bank: USSR and, 143*n*6, 268

independence: Arabs and, 819; Bowman on trusteeships and, 94*n*20; Bunche's efforts for colonial, 166*n*21; communism as threat to, 472, 905; displaced persons and personal, 599; ER's support of colonial, 89–91, 94*n*24; for European colonies, 89–95, 166*n*21; FDR and the Philippines, 45, 978*n*10; FDR on importance of, 90; Greece, 537*n*13, 637*n*4; India and, 166*n*26; Indonesia and, 664; as prerequisite for UDHR, 808*n*16, 835; Puerto Rico and, 250*n*12; role of economic and political security in ensuring, 509*n*9; Romulo as advocate for, 916*n*5; Taussig on FDR and, 89–90, 92*n*11, 93*n*19; Trieste and, 782*n*7; of trusteeships, 90; UN charter and, 93*n*19, 164*n*13; UNSCOP, Palestine, and, 821*n*2; US Declaration of, 826, 977, 978*n*8; US delegation to UNICO and, 93*n*18; USSR and Yugoslavia's, 529; White on colonial, 161–162. *See also* Greece

Independent Citizens Committee of the Arts, Sciences and Professions (ICCASP): Cooke on Communist presence in, 437; ER on CPUSA and, 322, 438; PCA and, 438

independent voters: La Guardia on, 522; on party appeals to, 374

India: customs of, 56; independence movement in, 166*n*26; as member of first ECOSOC sessions, 291*n*3; NAACP on, 161; Pandit UNGA presidency, 888;

potential famine in, 265, 268*n*6; refugees, 965*n*4

Indian Reorganization Act (*1934*): as increase in self-determination, 630*n*1; land acquisition under, 630*n*5

indifference, 328

individuals: duties of, 558*n*8; importance of, 449; responsibilities of, 112, 258, 363, 451; Soviet state and, 449

Indo-China: FDR on France and, 92*n*11; occupation of, 166*n*28

Indonesia: British troops in, 292*n*7–8; NAACP on, 161; occupation of, 166*n*25; UN role in civil war, 663–664

Institute for International Education, 981*n*8

Inter-American Conference on Problems of War and Peace. *See* Mexico City Conference

Inter American Defense Treaty: Welles's support of, 497

Inter-American Military Cooperation Act, 343*n*5

Inter-American Treaty of Reciprocal Assistance, 621*n*3

Inter-Collegiate Institute: ER and, 470

Interdepartmental Committee on International Social Policy (ISP), 709, 711*n*1

interdependence, 925; ER on, 448

Intergovernmental Committee on Refugees, 232*n*6, *n*8; appeals to ECOSOC, 233*n*9; British role in, 232*n*8; establishment of, 231; founding of, 232*n*8; insufficient resources of, 231; US role in, 232*n*8

Interim Aid Bill (*1948*): as predecessor to Marshall Plan, 716*n*6

International Agricultural Institute: founding of, 19*n*4

International Assembly of Women: Communist delegates to, 464*n*4; ER addresses, 464*n*1, 499*n*7; ER, Reading, and Communist presence in, 462; ER's advice to, 410*n*4; ER's assessment of, 409

International Bill of Rights (IBR): British version of, 686*n*2; debated in HRC, 505; drafting committee debate on, 567–574; drafting committee for, 556; ECOSOC instructions re, 505; enforcement of, 489; equal rights and, 506; ER on, 489, 508–509, 510*n*13; ER's Sorbonne speech and, 900–901; ER's work on, 442–443,

825; US recognition of, 805, 913; US, UN, and recognition of, 823–825. *See also* Galilee; Jewish immigration to Palestine; Jews; Negev; Palestine; Zionism

Italy: as colonial power, 365, 366*n*6; Communist electoral prospects (*1948*), 759, 763*n*3; Dewey proposal for UN trusteeships by, 883*n*3, 914; draft treaties with, 304*n*1; ER's visits to, 277*n*8; 1948 elections, 759, 763*n*3; postwar demands of, 365, 366*n*6; strikes and demonstrations in, 898; US emergency aid to, 676, 716*n*6; US Marines stationed off the coast of, 727*n*5; women's suffrage, 843*n*3

Ives, Irving M.: fair employment practices commission, 377*n*17; as liberal Republican, 935

Izvestia, 938*n*7

Jackson, Henry N., 871*n*4

Jansen, William: *letter to*, 945; *Nation's* banning from NYC schools, 944–945

Japan: China occupied by, 141, 143*n*13, 165*n*20; FDR's plans for, 90–91; Indonesia and, 166*n*25; mandated territories of, 210*n*2; Stimson on colonies of, 92*n*12; surrender of, 85, 87, 107*n*3; trusteeship policies re, 89–90

Japanese Americans: discrimination against, 66, 156–157; ER's defense of, 156; Truman's support of, 156

Javits, Jacob: as liberal Republican, 935

Jehovah's Witnesses, 810–813; conscientious objector status of, 353, 355*n*7

Jensen, David, 354*n*2

Jerusalem: violence in, 726, 729*n*28

Jessup, Philip: truce enforcement in Palestine, 929; US recognition of Israel, 823

Jesus Christ: ER on leadership of, 363; quoted in ER's Albert Hall speech, 218*n*8

Jewish Agency for Palestine, 749*n*5, 773, 821*n*7

Jewish Council of Women, 482*n*4

Jewish immigration to Palestine: Anglo-American Committee of Inquiry on, 143*n*8, 220*n*7, 295, 296*n*4, 336*n*2; Arab views on, 220*n*3, 336*n*3, 346*n*4; Bevin on, 323, 346*n*6, 369*n*5; British interception of ships of, 611*n*1; British White Paper (*1939*) on limits to, 220*n*5, 336*n*4, 346*n*4; displaced persons desire for, 256, 259*n*3;

ER on UK and, 140, 345–346, 368, 552, 554; ER's views on, 219, 326, 335; *Exodus 1947*, 609–611, 697*p*; FDR on, 123; history of, 553*n*3, 749*n*4; housing availability for, 220*n*5, 336*n*5; Operation Igloo, 369*n*3; transportation for, 336*n*5; US policy in UN, 552–553; US public support of, 917*n*24; US troops in support of, 296*n*5; Youth Aliyah movement, 603*n*3. *See also* Anglo-American Committee of Inquiry; Balfour Declaration (*1917*); Israel; Palestine; Truman, Harry S.; United Nations Special Committee on Palestine (UNSCOP); Zionism

Jews: against Zionism, 781, 787*n*31; aid to, 219; attacks by Arabs against, 783*n*23–24; Balfour Declaration and, 748; British protection of, 219; Dutch, 796*n*7; emigration to the US, 341, 345, 442, 599–600, 613, 781; ER on discrimination against, 442; FDR, Ibn Saud, and, 122; Holocaust monument at displaced persons camp, 177*p*, 256; KKK view of, 975–976; in Nazi concentration camps, 135*n*4; Nazi persecution of, 188*n*5; plight of, 609–610; refugees and, 609; stereotyping of, 322, 341, 610–611; Truman on, 610–611, 612*n*4; US protection of, 219; violence and prejudice against, 187*n*2, 605, 736; war orphans, 578, 602–604, 604*n*5. *See also* Israel; Jewish immigration to Palestine; Palestine

Jim Crow, 23, 293–294

Jiménez de Aréchaga, Eduardo, 954, 954*n*4, 955*n*5

Jodl, Alfred: German surrender and, 31*n*9

Johnson, Alvaney, 315*n*3, 316*n*6

Johnson, Alvin, 626, 628*n*8

Johnson, Edwin: German famine relief and, 155*n*5

Johnson, Ella, 479

Johnson, Eric, 650*n*4

Johnson, Herschel V., 518*n*7; German surrender and, 27, 30*n*4

Johnson, Hewlett: US visa refused to, 892, 893*n*3

Johnson, Hugh, 143*n*7

Johnson, Lyndon B., 934*n*7

Johnson, Morse: on ER on the ADA and PCA, 479

Johnson, Mrs. Clyde, 454*n*13

Odets, Clifford, 468*n*2

O'Dwyer, William, 49, 250*n*16; biographical portrait, 1007; as district attorney, 84*n*40; Dubinsky's criticism of, 78; ER on, 51*n*18, 349; ER's endorsement of, 77, 80; FDR's support of, 35, 349; FEPC and, 229*n*4; Ickes on, 35; *New York Post* on, 78; NYC mayoral race and, 77; Propper's candidacy and, 741, 744*n*2; on Truman's health care proposal, 146*n*2

Office of Civilian Defense (OCD): ER as assistant director of, 214*n*11; La Guardia and, 37*n*7; Volunteer Participation Division of, 214*n*11

Office of Price Administration (OPA): Bowles as director of, 149, 151*n*2; ER on postwar policies of, 88*n*3

Office of War Mobilization and Reconversion (OWMR), 133*n*11; ER's concerns re, 130

oil: Arab states and, 739–740; British foreign policy and, 369*n*5, 533*n*3; British need for, 723; ER calls for, 739; ER on Iran and, 290; ER on Pauley and, 286–287, 270*n*16; ER on substitutes for, 739; ER on UK and, 368, 378; impact on Palestine policy, 140; Middle East dependence on, 913; Palestine and, 143*n*9; Soviet fields, 292*n*11; US corporate investment in, 143, 379*n*4; US need for, 378, 722–724, 727*n*8, 728*n*4; US pipelines, 143; USSR desire for, 269*n*9, 290, 292*n*11; Wallace on Truman Doctrine and, 526*n*10

Okinawa, 147; Ernie Pyle's death in, 16

old age care, 951, 952*n*1–4, 962

old age pensions: ER, Eva Perón, and, 848, 857*p*

Oliver, Maria Rosa: opposes Perón, 499*n*7; Welles on, 494

O'Mahoney, Joseph: German famine relief and, 155*n*5

One World: ER on, 249; ER quotes Willkie on, 159; goals of, 251*n*17; Humphrey on, 528*n*3; peace and, 159; Wallace's support of, 539

Operation Schwarz, 542*n*3

Operation Igloo, 369*n*3

opinions, 559*n*13

opportunity: lack of, 276

Organization of American States (OAS), 837*n*8

Ortiz, Roberto M.: career of, 500*n*13; democratic views of, 493; FDR meets with, 493

Osborn, Z. Thomas, Jr.: Columbia, TN, grand jury and, 348*n*2

Ottoman Empire, 165*n*20

Overton, John: filibusters FEPC, 229*n*4; Truman's 10-point civil rights proposal, 734

Owen, David K., 291*n*6

Owens, Chester D., 290

Oxnam, G. Bromley: career of, 152*n*16; Dulles and, 152*n*16; ER, Niemöller, and, 322, 418–420; ER, UAW's GM strike, and, 150; refugee work of, 152*n*16

Pacific Northwest College Congress: ER attends, 502*n*31

Pajus, Jean, 874*n*2

Palestine: ad hoc UN Committee established on, 554*n*4; Arab rebellion in, 553*n*3, 701, 783*n*23, 798; Arab view of, 819–820; Arabs in, 219, 220*n*5, 725; arming of factions in, 727*n*3, 729*n*26; Austin and, 763*n*6; Austin, partition, and, 782*n*9; Austin, trusteeship, and, 773–774, 782*n*15, 783*n*20, 787*n*33, 930*n*2; Bacon on partition of, 748; bombing of Cairo-Jerusalem train, 701*p*; British censorship in, 346*n*1; British Mandate over, 220*n*3, 553, 553*n*3, 554*n*4, 729*n*20; British Mandate termination of, 729*n*20, 773, 781*n*5, 783*n*20, 808*n*11, 823, 930*n*2; British policy in, 368, 723; British tactics in UN and, 552; deteriorating situation in, 759; ER, Bohlen and 777–780, 784–786; ER, Marshall, and, 722, 724–726, 759–760, 774–776, 778–779, 929–930; ER on arms embargo for 722–726; ER on development of, 740*n*3; ER on Jewish immigration to, 219, 220*n*3, 326, 335; ER on military defense of, 346; ER on partition plan for, 702, 722, 725, 748–749, 773–779, 781, 853, 912, 914; ER on truce enforcement in, 929–930; ER on trusteeship proposal, 774–781; ER on UK position on immigration to, 140, 345–346, 368, 552, 554; ER on UK troops in, 219; ER on US troops in, 219; ER, Truman, and, 722–724, 726, 730*n*1, 775–777, 780, 805–806; FDR and, 220*n*3; FDR on, 122;

FDR policy re, 122–123; Forrestal and, 722–723; four-point program proposal, 725; Henderson and, 220*n*5, 723, 727*n*8; housing shortage in, 220*n*5; international police force for, 296*n*5, 368; international trusteeship for, 728*n*19; Irgun Z'vai Le'umi's actions in, 346*n*2, 552, 822*n*9; Jewish industry in, 220*n*5; Jewish state in, 219, 220*n*3–*n*4, 748; Jewish violence in, 368, 369*n*1; Jews and, 219; Jews on, 259*n*3; Kennan on, 728*n*14; King David Hotel bombing and, 447*p*, 552; Kirchwey on, 345, 346*n*1; Marshall on arms embargo over, 725; Marshall on Jewish state in, 727*n*8; Marshall on partition of, 724–725, 749*n*5; Marshall on trusteeship proposal for, 773–774, 776; Marshall on violence in, 725; oil and, 143*n*9, 368, 369*n*5; partition of, 698, 722, 724–725, 728*n*13, 728*n*19, 729*n*22, 739, 763*n*6; Peel Commission and, 220*n*5; as possible UN trusteeship, 166*n*20; Ibn Saud and, 122–123, 345; security in, 725; Soviet military role in, 742–743, 774, 778; Stern Gang's activities in, 368; symbolism of, 256; territorial disputes in, 219; terrorism in, 725–726, 728*n*20, 729*n*28, 820, 822*n*9; truce enforcement in, 929–930; Truman on Jewish immigration to, 122, 141; Truman on partition of, 702, 726, 728*n*13, 985*n*6; Truman on trusteeship proposal for, 773, 777, 783*n*20, 930*n*2; Truman on US forces of, 763*n*8; UJA and, 260–261*n*17; UN as impacted by US policy toward, 723; UN Charter and, 725, 763*n*6; UN Charter and partition of, 739; UN deliberations on, 748; UN police force proposed for, 722, 725, 742–743; UN role in partitioning of, 763*n*6; UN Security Council and, 725, 763*n*6, 773, 930*n*5; UN trusteeship proposal, 773–787; US arms embargo over, 722–726, 728*n*19, 729*n*26, 727*n*3; US military intervention in, 296*n*5, 763*n*8, 808*n*12; US on immigration to, 296*n*5; US policy re, 701, 722–730; US politics and, 727*n*8; US-Soviet agreement on, 671*n*7; USSR and, 722, 726; violence in, 552, 725–726, 728–729*n*20, 729*n*28, 820, 822*n*9; Wailing Wall riots in, 822*n*7; Youth Aliyah movement, 603*n*3. *See also* Anglo-American Committee of Inquiry; Balfour Declaration (*1917*); Cabinet Committee on

Palestine; Irgun Z'vai Le'umi; Israel; Jerusalem; Jewish immigration to Palestine; King David Hotel; Negev; Stern Gang; United Nations Special Committee on Palestine (UNSCOP)
Palestine Post, 552, 553*n*2
Pan American Conference (*1933*), 500*n*11
Pan American Conference (*1936*), 499*n*12; FDR's address to, 500*n*12
Pan American Union, 492
Pan-Germanism: defined, 74*n*8; in Latin America, 502*n*25; Niemöller and, 72–73
Panama, 167*n*33; Spain's UN membership opposed by, 333*n*2; UN Commission for Palestine role of, 729*n*22
Pandit, Vijaya Lakshmi: as UNGA presidential candidate, 888, 891*n*6
Pankhurst, Christabel, 223*n*11
Paraguay, 503*n*37
Parent-Teacher Associations (PTAs): ER on women as actors in, 661; French view of, 960; military training, 641; Stratton bill, 613
Paris Economic Conference, 597
Paris Peace Conference (*1919*), 94*n*20, 214*n*7, 783*n*22
Parish, Susan, 502*n*30; bequest to ER, 499*n*5; biographical portrait, 1007; ER, Welles, and, 492–493, 496; house fire and, 499*n*5
Parker, Dorothy, 468*n*2
Parker, Malcolm: imprisonment of, 352; *letters from*, 351, 354*n*4; *letter to*, 352; parole rejected by, 351–352; on petitioning ECOSOC, 354*n*4
Parkinson, Herbert: on FDR, 791
Parkman, Henry, Jr., 671*n*4
Parnell, Thomas: Perkins attacked by, 51*n*14
parochial schools, 607–609
partisans, 542*n*3. *See also* Tito, Josip Broz
Pastor Hall (film): Roosevelts and, 70, 73*n*5
Pasvolsky, Leo: career of, 92*n*13; ER meets with, 189*n*12; Taussig's criticism of, 90
patience: importance of to peace, 274
patriotism, 159
Patterson, Eleanor "Cissy", 628*n*7; Ickes on Dewey and, 37*n*3
Patterson, Robert: ER on, 236*n*9
Paul, Alice: ERA and, 331*n*7
Pauley, Edwin: biographical portrait, 1007–1008; ER disagrees with, 560–561;